ECONOMICS

MICHAEL PARKIN MELANIE POWELL
KENT MATTHEWS

FOURTH EDITION

An imprint of Pearson Education

Harlow, England · London · New York · Reading, Massachusetts · San Francisco
Toronto · Don Mills, Ontario · Sydney · Tokyo · Singapore · Hong Kong · Seoul
Taipei · Cape Town · Madrid · Mexico City · Amsterdam · Munich · Paris · Milan

Pearson Education Limited
Edinburgh Gate
Harlow
Essex CM20 2JE
England

and Associated Companies around the World.

Visit us on the World Wide Web at:
www.pearsoneduc.com

Original 4th edition entitled Economics published by Addison-Wesley
Publishing Company, Inc.
A Pearson Education company

This edition published by Pearson Education Limited 2000

ISBN 0201-59608-3

British Library Cataloguing-in-Publication Data
A catalogue record for this book can be obtained from the British Library.

10 9 8 7 6 5 4 3 2 1
04 03 02 01 00

Typeset in 10/12pt Century by 35
Printed and bound by Grafos S.A., Arte sobre papel, Barcelona, Spain

ABOUT THE AUTHORS

Michael Parkin received his training as an economist at the Universities of Leicester and Essex in England. Currently in the Department of Economics at the University of Western Ontario, Canada, Professor Parkin has held faculty appointments at Brown University, the University of Manchester, the University of Essex and Bond University. He is a past president of the Canadian Economics Association and has served on the editorial boards of the *American Economic Review* and the *Journal of Monetary Economics* and as managing editor of the *Canadian Journal of Economics*. Professor Parkin's research on macroeconomics, monetary economics and international economics has resulted in over 160 publications in journals and edited volumes, including the *American Economic Review*, the *Journal of Political Economy*, the *Review of Economic Studies*, the *Journal of Monetary Economics* and the *Journal of Money, Credit and Banking*. He became most visible to the public with his work on inflation that discredited the use of wage and price controls. Michael Parkin also spearheaded the movement toward European monetary union. Professor Parkin is an experienced and dedicated teacher of introductory economics.

Melanie Powell took her first degree at Kingston University and her MSc in economics at Birbeck College, London University. She spent three years as a research fellow in health economics at York University before moving on to become a principal lecturer heading the economics division of the business school at Leeds Metropolitan University. Melanie Powell then moved to Leeds University where she was director of economic studies and part-time MBAs at the Leeds University Business School. She is now a Principal Lecturer at Derby University Business School. Her main interests as a micro economist are in applied welfare economics and health economics. Her publications include papers on economic aspects of alcohol and tobacco consumption, health policy and risk in decision making. Her research into economic decision making under uncertainty uses experimental techniques and explores the interface of economic theory and psychology.

Kent Matthews received his training as an economist at the London School of Economics, Birbeck College University of London and the University of Liverpool. He is currently the Sir Julian Hodge Professor of Banking and Finance at the University of Wales, Cardiff. He has held research appointments at the London School of Economics, the National Institute of Economic and Social Research, the Bank of England and Lombard Street Research Ltd and faculty positions at the Universities of Liverpool, Western Ontario, Leuven, and Liverpool John Moores. He is the author (co-author) of 6 books and over 40 articles in scholarly journals and edited volumes.

Brief Contents

CONTENTS

To change the way students see the world: this is our purpose in teaching economics and it has remained our goal in preparing the fourth edition of this text. There is no greater satisfaction for a teacher than to share the joy of students who have begun to understand the powerful lessons of the economic approach. But these lessons are hard to learn. Every day in the classroom we relive the challenges of gaining the insights that are called the economist's way of thinking and recall our own early struggles to master this discipline. In preparing this edition, we have been privileged to draw on our experiences not only of our students but also of the many teachers who have used the previous three editions.

The principles of economics course is constantly evolving, and the past few years have seen some major shifts of emphasis, especially in macroeconomics. Today's principles course springs from today's issues: the slowdown in productivity growth; the information revolution; the emerging market economies of Central Europe and Asia; the expansion of global trade and investment. More and more, we recognize the value of teaching long-run fundamentals as a basis for understanding these issues and as a springboard to understanding short-run economic fluctuations. This book allows you to place an early emphasis on long-run fundamentals and, for the first time, to reach the theory of long-run economic growth, using nothing more than the familiar tools of supply and demand.

The Fourth Edition Approach

This book has been crafted to meet five overriding goals:

- Focus on the core principles
- Use the core principles to explain the issues and problems of our times
- Create a flexible teaching and learning tool
- Make modern economics accessible
- Make use of new information technologies

Focus on the Core Principles

The core principles of choice and opportunity cost, marginal analysis substitution and incentives, and the power of the competitive process are the focus of the micro chapters. The core tools of demand and supply are thoroughly explained and repeatedly used throughout both the micro and the macro chapters. New ideas – such as dynamic comparative advantage, game theory and its applications, the modern theory of the firm, information, public choice, new growth theory and real business cycle theory – also appear in this book. But they are described and explained by using the core principles; that is, new ideas are explained by using familiar ideas and tools.

Explain the Issues and Problems of Our Times

The core principles and tools are also used to help students understand the issues that confront them in today's world. Among the issues that are explored, some at length, are the environment, health care, widening income gaps, the productivity growth slowdown, restraining inflation, watching for the next recession and understanding the consequences of the emerging markets of Central Europe and Asia. These issues are studied repeatedly by using the same core principles within economic models.

Flexible Teaching and Learning Tool

One of the most exciting facts about economics is that its teachers hold strong views about what to teach and how to teach, yet they do not hold the same view. This poses a special challenge to a textbook author, especially in the macro part of our subject. To be useful in a wide range of situations and to a diversity of teachers, a book must be flexible.

This book can be used to teach a range of microeconomic courses, including business and management economics and microeconomic policy. It can be used to teach all traditional macro courses, which emphasize short-term fluctuations in output, prices and unemployment, with either a Keynesian or monetarist emphasis. This book can also be used to teach a macroeconomics course that places an early emphasis on long-term growth.

However, the order in which the chapters appear is only one of several orders in which they can be used. The tables on pp. xxxii–xxxiii show how the focus of the chapters can be grouped into core theory, policy analysis and optional developments to suit different needs. The tables on pp. xxx–xxxi show some of the alternative sequences for mixing chapters for different types of micro and the macro courses.

Make Modern Economics Accessible

This book presents economics as a serious, lively and evolving science. It presents new ideas – dynamic comparative advantage, game theory and its applications, public choice, new growth theory and real business cycle theory – all using the familiar core ideas and tools. Our emphasis on core economic models creates a high degree of rigour which does not require a high level or mathematical bias.

In some areas economic theory is unchanging, but in others controversy persists. Where matters are settled, we present what we know; where controversy persists, we present the alternative viewpoints. This positive approach to economics is, we believe, especially valuable for students as they prepare to function in a world in which simple ideologies have become irrelevant and the economic landscape is changing rapidly.

Always recalling our own early struggles with economics, we place the student at centre stage and write for the student foremost. We are conscious that many students find economics hard. As a result, our goal has been to make the material as accessible as possible. We use a style that makes for an easy read and that doesn't intimidate. Our approach reinforces core models to encourage confidence. Each chapter opens with a clear list of learning objectives, a vignette that connects with the student's world and seeks to grab attention, and a statement of where we are heading. Once in the chapter, we don't reduce economics to a set of recipes to be memorized. Instead, we encourage students to try to understand each concept. To accomplish this goal, the book illustrates every principle with examples that have been selected both to hold the student's interest and to bring the subject to life. To encourage a sense of enthusiasm and confidence, when the book has explained a new principle, it puts it to work and uses it to illuminate a current real-world problem or issue.

Make Use of New Information Technologies

The supplements that accompany this text, and the text itself, make carefully thought out use of new information technologies. We have worked hard to avoid the hype that often surrounds software and Web-based supplements and create true value for students and teachers. Our *Economics in Action* tutorial and quizzing software has been redesigned and revised and has been thoroughly tested by students. It provides a superb quality tutorial system directly linked to the text. Students can buy the CD Rom separately or in a package with the book. We also encourage teachers to apply for a site licence for the software. *Economics in Action* is an ideal way of creating a student self-study guide, with integral feedback, that involves no additional work for teachers. In addition, we now have a new World Wide Web site (http://www.econ100.com) which has been an outstanding success. This site provides features and content that is timely and constantly updated. Students can talk to other students around the world, ask questions and get fast answers to their queries. This text has problems which link to the Web site and encourage students to explore Web based information sources as well as some questions which link to *Economics in Action*. Students do not need to have access to *Economics in Action* to use this book – it is a supplementary learning tool.

Revisions in the Fourth Edition

The structure of the Fourth Edition has been revised to:

- Place a stronger focus on the use of core concepts and related economic models
- To explain current issues and recent economic developments
- To shorten the content and make it even more accessible
- To strengthen pedagogical features
- To strengthen the European focus

To achieve this throughout the book, we have added and cut some chapters, we have reorganized material and changed the order of chapters, as well as updating material. A new innovation is the additional problems which link to the Web site. These questions are designed to encourage students to use new information sources and to develop critical thinking. These questions are identified thus ❶. We have also added additional questions which encourage debate and discussion and can be answered in short essay format. We are also developing a new European data supplement to allow teachers and students to focus analysis on particular countries or to undertake cross country analysis.

Changes in the Microeconomics Section

Chapter 1, 'What is Economics?' uses a magazine format with colour pictures to lay out the key questions and big ideas of economics. The photos and pictures have been picked to motivate students and show them that economics is part of their lives. We have brought the core concept of efficiency forward, introducing it in Chapter 3, and cut the content of Chapter 3 to tighten the focus. Efficiency is then developed in the new Chapter 6, which links efficiency to the model of demand and supply and to the concept of surplus. This approach creates a new unity to the micro chapters and provides a stronger framework and preparation for the applied analysis in Chapter 7, 'Markets in Action'. Chapter 7 now includes a discussion of the potential inefficiency of rent ceilings, minimum wages and taxes as well as potential benefits.

The chapters have been separated into six new parts which focus on developing ideas. Part 1 introduces economic ideas and Part 2 explains how markets work. Part 3 examines competition and monopoly and Part 4 introduces factor markets. The chapter on Inequality and Redistribution has been brought forward to Part 4 so that household income is addressed immediately after the chapter on labour markets, wages and discrimination. Finally, Part 5 examines market failure and Government.

Chapter 15 is new chapter which combines components of separate chapters in the 3rd edition to introduce demand and supply in all factor markets in one chapter. The applied materials in Chapters 17 to 20 have been updated and revised. The chapter on uncertainty and information has been cut to maintain the focus on core ideas. All mathematical boxes have been removed but are available on the Web site for students who wish to develop a mathematical approach.

Changes in the Macroeconomics Section

The macroeconomics chapters have been restructured, updated and reworked in certain places to provide a structure that is more in keeping with the European teaching tradition. As with the 3rd edition, Chapter 21 shows the entire macro landscape, its origins and rebirth in the depression of the 1930s, the short-term and long-term issues, business cycles, unemployment, inflation and the current account deficit. The chapter seeks to discuss facts both current and historical that relate to the UK and touches on the Asian crisis and its implications for the world economy. Chapter 22 is similar to the 3rd edition in its treatment of the circular flow and the measurement of GDP and it touches on the revision of the national accounts in 1998 in keeping with the European System of Accounts.

Chapter 23 describes the measurement of employment, unemployment, real wages and trends in the labour market. It also has a discussion of the effects of the minimum wage leg in Chapter 23, the discussion of short-run fluctuations in aggregate demand and supply is brought forward in Chapter 24. It brings out the distinction between sticky prices and flexible prices which itself follow naturally from the discussion of sticky wages in Chapter 23.

The Keynesian aggregate expenditure multiplier is brought in earlier and discussed in Chapter 25. The treatment of the multiplier has been simplified and is distinguished between fixed and flexible aggregate price effects.

Fiscal policy is introduced in Chapter 26 and its structure is similar to the 3rd edition. It describes the components of the UK budget and recent fiscal history, examines the fiscal multiplier and discusses fiscal policy in the context of the supply-side. Chapters 27 and 28 cover, money, credit, the banking system and monetary policy. The coverage is similar to the 3rd edition but a new section on the responsiveness of the economy to changes in the rate of interest has been added. More emphasis is placed on the flow of funds approach use of funding policy in controlling the money supply. A new section on the monetary policy in the 1990s, the operational independence of the Bank of England and the Monetary Policy Committee has been included.

Chapter 29 is substantially new. It describes the Keynesian-monetarist controversy and how it was settles and examines the problem of fiscal and monetary policy interaction and co-ordination. It examines how the mix of fiscal and monetary policy influences the level and composition of aggregate expenditure and the price level. An appendix derives the IS–LM model and links it to the AS–AD approach taken in the book. Keynesian and monetarist special cases are examined in the IS–LM framework. Additional IS–LM material can be found on the Parkin, Powell and Matthews Web site.

Chapter 30 is more streamlined and has a clearer explanation of modern theories of inflation. Long-term issues of capital accumulation, savings and growth are examined in Chapters 32 and 33 and is similar in content to the 3rd edition but the section on growth accounting is substantially simplified. Chapter 34 is another big picture chapter similar in intent to the 3rd edition but has been updated to deal with topical issues relating to UK and EU policy.

The book ends with chapters that focus on global issues. Chapter 35 has simplified. It describes recent trends in UK trade and uses core theory to debunk the arguments for protection. Chapter 36 has been revised and updated to examine exchange rate determination, the Exchange Rate Mechanism of the European Monetary System, European Monetary Union and the far eastern crisis financial crisis.

Features that Enhance the Learning Process

The fourth edition, like its predecessors, is packed with special features designed to enhance the learning process.

The Art Programme: Showing the Economic Action

Previous editions of this book set new standards with their highly successful and innovative art programmes. Our goal has always been to show clearly 'where the economic action is'. The figures and diagrams in this book continue to generate enormously positive feedback, confirming our view that graphical analysis is the most important tool for teaching and learning economics. But it is a tool that gives many students much difficulty. Because many students find graphs hard to work with, the art has been designed both to be visually attractive and engaging and to communicate economic principles unambiguously and clearly. In the fourth edition the clear style of the data-based art that reveals the data and trends has been retained. In addition, diagrams that illustrate economic processes now consistently distinguish among key economic players (firms, households, governments and markets).

Our consistent protocol in style, notation and use of colour, includes:

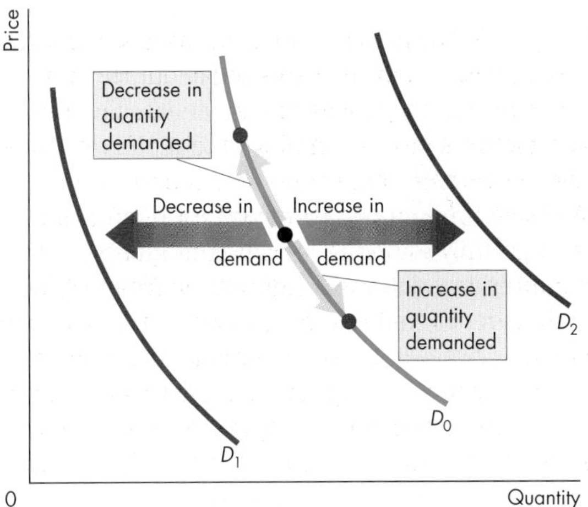

- Highlighting shifted curves, points of equilibrium and the most important features in red.
- Using arrows in conjunction with colour to lend directional movement to what are usually static presentations.
- Pairing graphs with data tables from which the curves have been plotted.
- Using colour consistently to underscore the content, and referring to such use of colour in the text and captions.
- Labelling key pieces of information in graphs with boxed notes.

The art programme has been developed with the study and review needs of students in mind. It has retained the following features:

- Marking the most important figures and tables with a red icon ◆ and listing them at the end of the chapter as Key Figures and Tables.
- Using complete, informative captions that encapsulate the major points in the graph, so that students can preview or review the chapter by skimming through the art.

Interviews: Leading Economists Lend a Hand

Substantive interviews with famous economists were another popular feature in previous editions. We are continuing the tradition and have included many new interviews with economists who have contributed significantly to advancing the thinking and practice in our discipline. We have interviews with UK and continental European economists, including two female economists. Our opening interview in this edition is with one of the most famous working economic journalists, Will Hutton. We hope that this interview will encourage students to appreciate the wider importance of economics, beyond the academic, and into the realm of everyday news and life.

The interviews open parts and each interview has been carefully edited to be self-contained. Because each interview discusses topics that are introduced formally in the subsequent chapters, students can use it as a preview to some of the terminology and theory they are about to encounter. A more careful reading afterwards will give the students a fuller appreciation of the discussion. Lastly, the whole series of interviews can be approached as an informal symposium on the subject matter of economics as it is practised today.

Reading Between the Lines: News Articles for Critical Thinking

Another feature of the previous editions that is always well received is *Reading Between the Lines*. This feature is designed to help students build critical thinking skills and use economic principles to interpret daily news events (and their coverage in the media). We have updated the news articles in this edition and have deliberately selected topics that appeal to students, such as graduate salaries, football markets and food scares, or have a European focus. The *Reading Between the Lines* spread contains three passes at a story. It begins with a facsimile (usually abbreviated) of an actual newspaper or magazine article. These news stories come from major newspapers and magazines, including *The Economist, The Financial Times, The Sunday Times, The Guardian* and *The Independent*. The second pass presents a digest of the article's essential points. The third pass provides an economic analysis of the article. In order not to disrupt the flow of the material, these features are placed at the end of each chapter.

Economics in History: Path-breaking Ideas

The *Economics in History* feature helps students trace the evolution of path-breaking economic ideas and recognize the universality of their application, not only to the past but also to the present. For example, Adam Smith's powerful ideas about the division of labour apply to the creation of the computer chip as well as to the pin factory of the eighteenth century. In order not to disrupt the flow of the material, these features are located at the end of chapters. We have revised the existing features and introduced one new feature on Understanding Market Power.

Learning Aids: Pedagogy that Leads to Active Learning

The careful pedagogical plan has been refined to ensure that this book complements and reinforces classroom learning. Each chapter contains the following pedagogical elements.

Objectives Each chapter opens with a list of objectives that enable students to see exactly where they are going and to set their goals before starting the chapter. The goals are linked to the chapter's major headings.

Chapter Openers Intriguing puzzles, paradoxes or metaphors frame the important questions that are unravelled as the chapter progresses.

Highlighted In-text Reviews Succinct summaries for review are interspersed through the chapter. In this edition, these in-text reviews have a list format that is designed to give students a more easily digested statement of the key points.

Key Terms Highlighted within the text, these concepts form the first part of a three-tiered review of economic vocabulary. These terms are repeated with page references at the end of the chapter and they are compiled in the end-of-book glossary.

Key Figures and Tables The most important figures and tables are identified with a red icon ◆ and are listed at the end of each chapter.

End-of-chapter Study Material Chapters close with a summary that includes lists of key terms, figures and tables; short review questions and more searching problems. New to this edition is the end-of-chapter summaries in a concise list form.

End of chapter problems have been revised to include new problems and some that use diagrams. Problems identified with a 2 number are designed to encourage students to use a computer spread sheet to answer the question. In some cases, these questions may link to the *Economics in Action* software package or the Parkin, Powell and Matthews Web site. We have continued to develop questions related to the *Reading Between the Lines* feature to encourage students to study the feature more closely. Where we use a 3 number, students are sent to Internet sites.

The Teaching and Learning Package

Pearson Education's editors, the supplement author and ourselves have worked closely together to ensure that our integrated text and supplements package provides students and teachers with a seamless learning and teaching experience. The author of the supplements is an outstanding economist and teacher who has brought his own human capital (and that of his students) to the job of ensuring that the supplements are of the highest quality and value. The package contains three broad components:

- Tools to enhance learning
- Tools to enhance teaching
- Tools for the electronic classroom

Tools to Enhance Learning

Study Guide The fourth edition Study Guide has been prepared by Brian Atkinson formerly of the University of Central Lancashire. Carefully coordinated with the main text, each chapter of the *Study Guide* contains:

- Chapter in perspective
- Helpful hints
- An explanation of key figures and tables
- Answers to self-test questions

The Self-test section includes:

- Concept review questions
- True/false questions that ask students to explain their answers
- Multiple-choice questions
- Short-answer questions
- Problems
- Discussion questions
- Data questions

In each chapter of the *Study Guide*, students can test their cumulative understanding of the subject in a number of ways. A data question exercise asks them to apply what they've learned by analysing a news article and answering short-answer questions. Each multiple-choice test presents a selection of questions to test the student's knowledge. The self-test exercises allow students to practise exam-style questions.

Several elements of the *Study Guide* are geared to building critical thinking, such as the true/false questions, multiple-choice answers that include explanations of why the answer is correct, *Reading Between the Lines* exercises, problems, and discussion and data questions. Other elements are geared to making the study of economics a bit easier. The chapter in perspective provides a brief summary of key definitions, concepts and material in the textbook chapter; the helpful hints focus on ways to better understand the principles of economics and to help students understand the most important graphs, equations and techniques for problem-solving; and an explanation of selected key figures and tables reviews students' understanding and helps with exam revision.

Economics in Action Interactive Software
Students around the world have used the path-breaking *Economics in Action*, a widely acclaimed computer learning tool, to increase their success in the principle course.

With the European version of *Economics in Action*, students will have fun working with the tutorials, answering questions that give instant explanations and testing themselves ahead of their exams. The new release of the software has the following features:

- Step-by-step, graph-based tutorials
- A graph-making tool with data for the United States, Canada, twelve European countries, Japan and Australia
- A quiz tool that generates drag-and-drop, true/false, multiple-choice and numeric questions
- A self-testing tool that simulates tests and gathers results
- A problem-solving tool that allows students to solve homework problems from the text
- A figure gallery that builds text figures and captions.

This superb quality tutorial and quizzing software links directly with the text. The Economics in Action CD-ROM is available seperately or in a package with the book. The software is also available in the form of a site licence to adopters of the book.

The Parkin, Powell and Matthews Web site
The Parkin, Powell and Matthews Web site provides a rich array of learning tools that are carefully integrated with the text and other components of the package. A weekly electronic *Reading Between the Lines* provides an effective way of motivating students and keeping them up to date on economics in the news. A periodic electronic Point-Counterpoint feature encourages students to participate in the contemporary policy debate. A weekly quiz that uses completely new questions (not found in the study guide, test bank or *Economics in Action*) provides students with frequent review and testing material. On-line office hours enable students to consult Michael Parkin directly with their learning problems. And carefully selected links provide students with a guide to economic resources on the Internet.

The Parkin, Powell and Matthews Web site will become a must-visit site for all teachers and students of the principles of economics. Whether you are a teacher or a student, you can reach all our Internet services at http://www.econ100.com.

Updates in Economics This is a yearly supplement edited by Brian Atkinson. It contains topical articles linking important news items with the theory in the textbook. It is copyright free to allow instructors to copy and circulate the articles to students for private study or seminar use. It is available to qualified adopters of the textbook by contacting Pearson Education.

Tools to Enhance Teaching

Test Bank To reflect the content and terminology of the fourth edition, these paper and computerised versions of the test bank include 5,000 multiple-choice, true/false and short answer questions.

Lecturer's Handbook A revised lecturer's handbook has been prepared by Brian Atkinson. The *Lecturer's Handbook* is designed to integrate the teaching and learning package. Each chapter includes a chapter outline, teaching suggestions, cross-references to the overheads, software units, additional discussion questions, answers to the review questions and answer to the problems.

Tools for the Electronic Classroom

PowerPoint Figures Key figures and tables from the text are rendered in full colour. The figures are enlarged and simplified to be more legible in large classrooms. The figures and tables can be printed out and copied on to acetates. They can also be modified to suit the needs of your course.

Economics in Action Software Instructors can use *Economics in Action* interactive software in the classroom. Its full-screen display option makes it possible to use its many analytical graphs as "electronic transparencies" and to do live graph manipulation and curve-shifting in lectures. Its figure gallery of animated slides from the text provides high quality graphics for the classroom. Its real-world data sets and graphing utility enable time-series graphs and scatter diagrams to be made and displayed in the classroom. Additionally, *Economics in Action* is a helpful review tool for instructors to use with their students to help reinforce economic principles before tests or exams. A site licence will be available to adopters of the book and CD package. Contact your Pearson Education sales representative for details.

Parkin, Powell and Matthews on the World Wide Web Instructors can use the web site in a suitable equipped classroom. The weekly electronic *Reading Between the Lines* provides an effective way of motivating and organizing a lecture. The electronic Point-Counterpoint feature provides a handy way of organizing a classroom debate. The weekly quiz can also be used for in-class review. The web site can be found at http://www.econ100.com.

Acknowledgements

One of the problems with writing an introductory text, particularly in a new edition, is that there are so many people who provide help and encouragement, either directly or indirectly, that it becomes impossible to name them all. We would like to extend our gratitude and thanks to the many people who have made a contribution to this new edition, and to all those who made such important contributions to the previous editions on which this edition is based.

In particular, the authors would like to thank their colleagues, past and present, who have helped to shape their understanding of economics and provided information and assistance in the creation of this new edition. We would also like to thank our families for their input and patience.

Melanie Powell and Kent Matthews would like to Michael Parkin and Robin Bade for their innovative work on the *Economics in Action* software and the new Web site. They would also thank colleagues at the Leeds University Business School and Leeds Metropolitan University, and many colleagues at the Cardiff Business School particularly Sally-Anne Jones. We would also like to thank Paul De Grauwe of Katholieke Universiteit Leuven, Nick Crafts of the London School of Economics and Patrick Minford of Liverpool University for their work on the earlier edition. They extend a particular thanks to the many reviewers who have provided invaluable information for changes to this edition.

Michael Parkin has acknowledged many people in the Preface to the US edition of *Economics*, including friends and colleagues and the particular input of Robin Bade, to whom the US edition is dedicated, and Richard Parkin for graphics work. The authors of this edition would extend similar tributes to these individuals for their work.

We would like to acknowledge our debt to students past and present who have used previous editions and given us invaluable feedback in the form of comments, criticisms and praise. It would not be possible to write a textbook primarily in the interests of such students without their help and input.

Last, we would like to thank the editorial and production team at Pearson Education Limited. Yet again, this edition was created under very tight schedule, and as a result everyone has had to work at speed to meet the deadlines. In addition, this was all achieved in the middle of the new company merger and internal restructuring. The consistent good humour, vigilance and patience of the team was, as ever, outstanding. Without underestimating the input of other members of the team, we extend special thanks to Paula Harris, Anita Bennett, Geraldine Lyons and Julie Knight, whose patience was most tested because they had the most personal contact with the authors.

As always, the proof of the pudding is in the eating! The impact and value of this book will be decided by its users and we would like to encourage all instructors and students who use this new edition to feel free to send us comments and suggestions for future developments.

Michael Parkin
Department of Economics
University of Western Ontario
London, Ontario N6A 5C2, Canada

Melanie Powell
Derbyshire Business School
University of Derby
Keddleston Road
Derby, DE22 1GB, United Kingdom

Kent Matthews
Cardiff Business School
University of Wales
Cardiff, CF1 3EU, United Kingdom

REVIEWERS

Pearson Education would like to express appreciation for the invaluable advice and encouragement they have received from many educators in the United Kingdom and elsewhere in Europe for this edition.

Steve Bradley, Lancaster University

Alan Carruth, University of Kent

Sarah Connolly, University of East Anglia

Dr Lynne Evans, University of Dundee

Klas Fregert, Lund University

Gianluigi Giorgini, University of Abertay Dundee

Paul Herrington, University of Leicester

Hilary Ingham, Lancaster University

Dr Ernie Jowsey, Sheffield Hallam University

Roy Murphy, Bolton Institute of Higher Education

Brendan O'Rourke, Dublin Institute of Technology

Ebbe Rasmussen, Herning Institute of Business Administration & Technology, Denmark

Amanda Roberts, University of Wolverhampton

Dr Schuller, University of Skovde

Leslie Simpson, Heriot-Watt University

Gillian Waters, University of Reading

The publisher would like to thank the following for permission to use material in this book.

Chapter 1: Cartoon © **The New Yorker Collection** 1985 (Modell) from cartoonbank.com. All Rights Reserved. Grape harvesting machinery, **George Rose © Gamma Liaison**. Grape field, **Owen Franken © Tony Stone Images**. Kellogg's, **Charles Gupton © The Stock Market**. Lecture theatre, **Patrick Ward © Corbis**. MacDonald's, **David Young-Wolff © PhotoEdit**. Intel chip, **courtesy of the Intel Corporation**. Electric and gas company, **Joseph Sohm © Corbis**. Cartoon **© The Independent** 1993 Chris Riddell. Café scene, **Tony Stone Images**. Stadium flags (close-up), **Scott Foresman/Addison Wesley Longman**. Stadium flags (small), **Focus on Sports**. European weather map **The Guardian**.

Chapter 3: Cartoon © John Appleton, The News Chronicle Adam Smith, **Corbis-Bettman**. Pin factory, **Culver Pictures**. Woman with silicon wafer, **Tony Stone Images/Bruce Ando**.

Chapter 6: Cartoon **© The New Yorker Collection** 1988 (Mike Twohy) from cartoonbank.com. All Rights Reserved.

Chapter 7: Alfred Marshall, **Stock Montage, Inc**. Railway suspension bridge, **Corbis-Bettmann**. Concorde and other craft, **The Royal Aeronautical Society**.

Chapter 9: Jeremy Bentham, **Mary Evans Picture Library**. Women on production line, **Corbis-Bettmann**. Woman executive, **Davina Arkwell, Addison Wesley Longman**.

Chapter 14: John von Neuman, **Corbis Bettman**. Female executive/mobile phone, **Robert Harding**. Workers on sugar plantation, **Corbis-Bettmann**.

Chapter 15: Cartoon **© Hector Breeze**, The Guardian.

Chapter 16: Cartoon, **© Jeremy Banks**, The Financial Times.

Chapter 17: Robert Malthus, **Mary Evans Picture Library**. Cartoon **© Robert Hunt, The Economist** Traffic congestion in Manchester, **Manchester Central Library, Local Studies Unit**.

Chapter 19: Cartoon, **© Nick Baker**, The Financial Times.

Chapter 20: Ronald Coase, **David Joel Photography**. Lake pollution, **Corbis-Bettmann**. Fishing on the River Thames, **Angling Times**.

Chapter 21: John Maynard Keynes, **Corbis-Bettmann**. Spinning Jenny, **Hutton Getty Picture Collection**. BT Control Centre, **Robert Harding**.

Chapter 24: Cartoon **© Stephen Jeffery,** The Economist.

Chapter 27: Milton Freidman, **© Marshall Heinrichsa and Addison Wesley Longman. Taken from the book ECONOMICS 4th edn (p. 610) by Parkin, © Addison Wesley Publishing Company, Inc. Reprinted by permission of Addison Wesley Longman**. German housewife burning Reichmarks, **Corbis-Bettemann**. Brazil – inflation in South America, **Carlos Humberto (Contact Colorifics)**.

Chapter 32: Joseph Schumpter, **Corbis Bettemann**. McCormick Reaper, **Hutton Getty Picture Collection**. Fibre optics, **Robert Harding**.

Chapter 33: Irving Fisher, **Corbis-Bettmann**. Cartoon © **David Austen**, The Guardian. Gathering outside bank, **Corbis-Bettmann**. Boarded-up shop, **Davina Arkell, AWL**. Irving Fisher, **Corbis-Bettmann**.

Chapter 35: David Ricardo, **Mary Evans Picture Library**. Clipper Ship, **Corbis-Bettmann**. Containership, **Sealand Services**.

The publisher would like to acknowledge: **The Guardian, London** for permission to reproduce articles in *Reading Between the Lines* in Chapters 4, 5, 6, 7, 8, 9, 12, 13, 17, 18, 19 and 20; **The Times Newspapers Limited** for permission to reproduce articles in *Reading Between the Lines* in Chapters 10, 23, 30 and 33; **The Observer, London** for permission to reproduce articles in *Reading Between the Lines* in Chapter 15; **The Independent** for permission to reproduce article in *Reading Between the Lines* in Chapter 16; **The Economist** for permission to reproduce articles in *Reading Between the Lines* in Chapters 24 and 29; **The Financial Times** for permission to reproduce articles in *Reading Between the Line* in Chapters 3, 11, 14, 21, 22, 28, 31, 32, 34 and 35; **Business Week** for permission to reproduce articles in *Reading Between the Lines* in Chapters 25 and 26; **The New York Times** for permission to reproduce articles in *Reading Between the Lines* in Chapter 27; and **The Evening Standard** for permission to reproduce articles in *Reading Between the Lines* in Chapter 36.

Four Alternative Sequences for a Micro Principles Course

MICROECONOMIC THEORY	BUSINESS ECONOMICS	MICROECONOMIC POLICY	MANAGEMENT ECONOMICS
3 Production, Growth and Trade	3 Production, Growth and Trade	3 Production, Growth and Trade	3 Production, Growth and Trade
4 Demand and Supply	4 Demand and Supply	4 Demand and Supply	4 Demand and Supply
5 Elasticity	5 Elasticity	5 Elasticity	5 Elasticity
6 Efficiency and Equity	6 Efficiency and Equity	6 Efficiency and Equity	6 Efficiency and Equity
8 Utility and Demand	10 Organizing Production	7 Markets in Action	10 Organizing Production
9 Possibilities, Preferences and Choices	11 Output and Costs	8 Utility and Demand	11 Output and Costs
11 Output and Costs	12 Competition	11 Output and Costs	12 Competition
12 Competition	13 Monopoly	12 Competition	13 Monopoly
13 Monopoly	14 Monopolistic Competition and Oligopoly	13 Monopoly	
14 Monopolistic Competition and Oligopoly	15 Demand and Supply in Factor Markets	15 Demand and Supply in Factor Markets	15 Demand and Supply in Factor Markets
15 Demand and Supply in Factor Markets	16 Labour Markets	16 Labour Markets	16 Labour Markets
16 Labour Markets	18 Market Failure and Public Choice	17 Inequality, Redistribution and Welfare	18 Market Failure and Public Choice
18 Market Failure and Public Choice	19 Regulation and Privatization	18 Market Failure and Public Choice	19 Regulation and Privatization
19 Regulation and Privatization	20 Externalities, The Environment and Knowledge	19 Regulation and Privatization	20 Externalities, The Environment and Knowledge
20 Externalities, The Environment and Knowledge	35 Trading with the World	20 Externalities, The Environment and Knowledge	35 Trading with the World

Four Alternative Sequences for a Macro Principles Course

KEYNESIAN PERSPECTIVE	MONETARIST PERSPECTIVE	EARLY LONG-TERM GROWTH	LATE LONG-TERM GROWTH
21 A First Look at Macroeconomics	21 A First Look at Macroeconomics	21 A First Look at Macroeconomics	21 A First Look at Macroeconomics
22 Measuring GDP, Inflation, and Economic Growth	22 Measuring GDP, Inflation, and Economic Growth	22 Measuring GDP, Inflation, and Economic Growth	22 Measuring GDP, Inflation, and Economic Growth
23 Employment and Unemployment	23 Employment and Unemployment	23 Employment and Unemployment	23 Employment and Unemployment
25 Expenditure Multipliers	24 Aggregate Demand and Aggregate Supply	31 Capital, Investment, and Saving	27 Aggregate Demand and Aggregate Supply
24 Aggregate Demand and Aggregate Supply	27 Money	32 Long-term Economic Growth	25 Expenditure Multipliers
26 Fiscal Policy	28 Monetary Policy	33 The Business Cycle	26 Fiscal Policy
27 Money	30 Inflation	24 Aggregate Supply and Aggregate Demand	27 Money
28 Monetary Policy	25 Expenditure Multipliers	25 Expenditure Multipliers	28 Monetary Policy
29 Fiscal and Monetary Interactions	26 Fiscal Policy	26 Fiscal Policy	29 Fiscal and Monetary Interactions
30 Inflation	29 Fiscal and Monetary Interactions	27 Money	30 Inflation
33 The Business Cycle (omit real business cycle)	33 The Business Cycle (omit real business cycle)	28 Monetary Policy	33 The Business Cycle
34 Macroeconomic Policy Challenges	34 Macroeconomic Policy Challenges	29 Fiscal and Monetary Interactions	34 Macroeconomic Policy Challenges
31 Capital, Investment, and Saving (optional)	31 Capital, Investment, and Saving (optional)	30 Inflation	31 Capital, Investment, and Saving (optional)
32 Long-term Economic Growth	32 Long-term Economic Growth	34 Macroeconomic Policy Challenges	32 Long-term Economic Growth
36 The Balance of Payments, The Pound and The Euro	36 The Balance of Payments, The Pound and The Euro	36 The Balance of Payments, The Pound and The Euro (optional)	36 The Balance of Payments, The Pound and The Euro (optional)

Microeconomic Focus

CORE	POLICY	OPTIONAL
1. What is Economics?		2. Making and Using Graphs Good chapter for students with fear of graphs.
3. Production, Growth and Trade		
4. Demand and Supply		
5. Elasticity		
6. Efficiency A new chapter that unifies the entire coverage of micro.	7. Markets in Action A unique chapter that gives extensive applications of demand and supply.	
8. Utility and Demand Some teachers like to cover this material before Chapter 4. Some like to skip it. Both are possible.		9. Possibilities, Preferences, and Choices Easy to teach coverage of indifference curves. Strictly optional.
10. Organizing Production This chapter may be skipped.		
11. Output and Cost		
12. Competition		
13. Monopoly		
14. Monopolistic Competition and Oligopoly		
15. Demand and Supply in Factor Markets This chapter gives an overview of all factor markets–labour, capital, and natural resources.		16. Labour Markets
	17. Inequality, Redistribution and Welfare	
	18. Market Failure and Public Choice A general introduction to the role of government in the economy and the positive theory of government.	
	19. Regulation and Privatization	
	20. Externalities, the Environment and Knowledge	

Macroeconomic Focus

CORE	POLICY	OPTIONAL
21. A First Look at Macroeconomics		
22. Measuring GDP, Inflation and Economic Growth		
Chapter 23, Employment, Wages, and Unemployment may be studied immediately following Chapter 22.		
24. Aggregate Supply and Aggregate Demand		
Chapter 24 may be delayed and studied after Chapter 25		
23. Employment, Wages, and Unemployment 31. Capital, Investment, and Saving 32. Long-term Economic Growth This section on growth theory is optional		
25. Expenditure Multipliers 27. Money	26. Fiscal Policy 28. The Central Bank and Monetary Policy	
30. Inflation		33. The Business Cycle
	34. Macroeconomic Policy Challenges	
		35. Trading with the World 36. The Balance of Payments, The Pound and The Euro

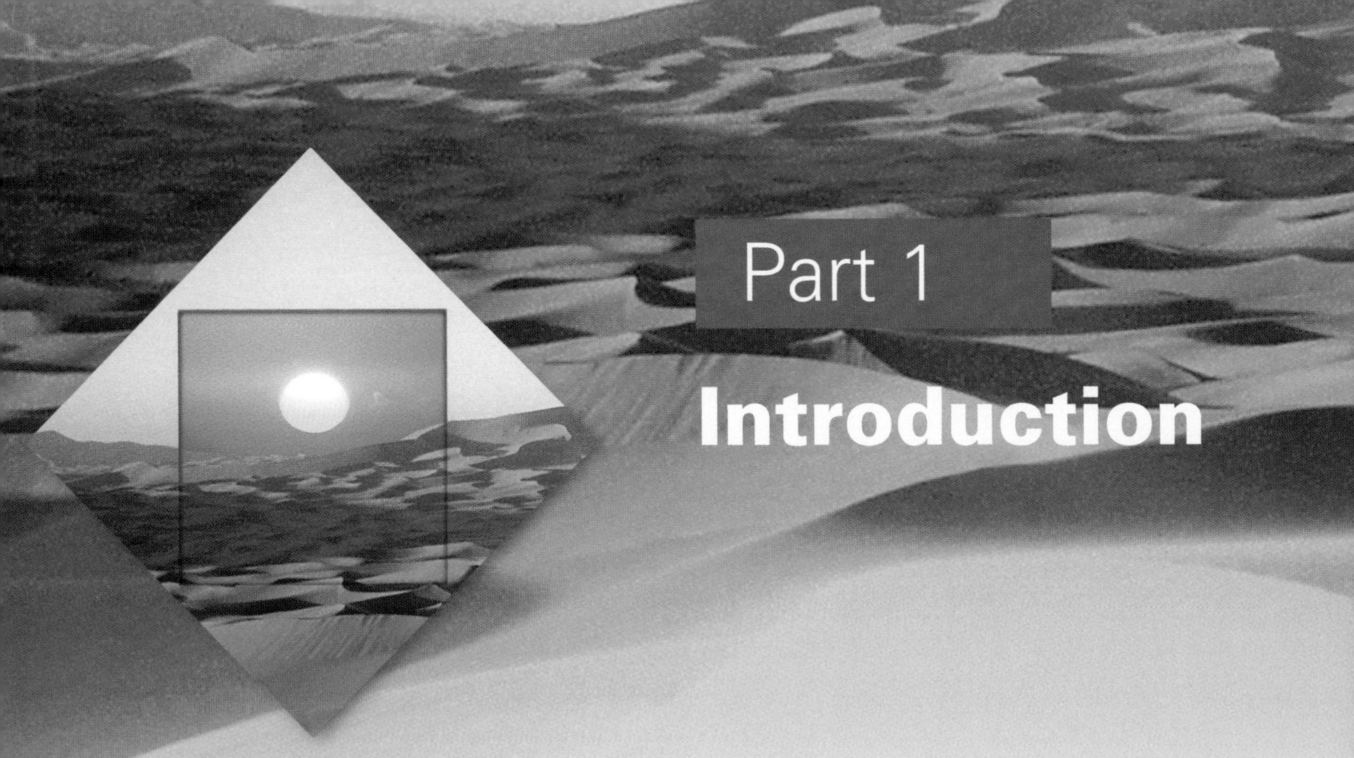

Part 1 Introduction

Your Economics Course

You are living at a time that future historians will call the *Information Revolution*. We reserve the word "Revolution" for big events that influence all future generations.

◆ During the *Agricultural Revolution*, which occurred 10,000 years ago, people learned to domesticate animals and plant crops. They stopped roaming in search of food and settled in villages and eventually towns and cities, where they developed markets in which to exchange their products.

◆ During the *Industrial Revolution*, which began 240 years ago, people used science to create new technologies. This revolution brought extraordinary wealth for most, but created conditions in which some were left behind. It brought social and political tensions that we still face today.

◆ During today's *Information Revolution*, people who have the ability and opportunity to embrace the new technologies are prospering on an unimagined scale. But the incomes and living standards of the less educated are falling behind, and social and political tensions are increasing. Today's revolution has a global dimension. Some of the winners live in previously poor countries in Asia, and some of the losers live in the European Union.

◆ So you are studying economics at an interesting time. Whatever *your* motivation is for studying economics, *our* objective is to help you do well in your course, to enjoy it, and to develop a deeper understanding of the economic world around you.

◆ There are three reasons why we hope that you succeed. First, a decent understanding of economics will help you become a full participant in the Information Revolution. Second, an understanding of economics will help you play a more effective role as a citizen and voter and enable you to add your voice to those who are looking for solutions to our social and political problems. Third, you will enjoy the sheer fun of *understanding* the forces at play and how they are shaping our world.

◆ Studying economics gives the best training available in problem solving, offers lots of opportunities to develop conceptual skills, and opens doors to a wide range of graduate courses, including the MBA, and to a wide range of jobs.

◆ Economics was born during the Industrial Revolution. We'll look at its birth and meet its founder, Adam Smith. In the next three chapters, we'll begin to study the science that Adam Smith began. You will encounter the questions, methods, and ideas of economics in Chapter 1. And in Chapter 3, you will learn about Adam Smith's key insight: specialization and exchange bring economic wealth. In optional Chapter 2, you have an opportunity to learn about the graph tools that we use in economics.

What is economics?

After studying this chapter you will be able to:

- Define economics
- Explain the five big questions that economists seek to answer
- Explain eight ideas that define the economic way of thinking
- Describe how economists go about their work

A Day in the Life

From the moment you wake up each morning to the moment you fall asleep again each night, your life is filled with choices. When the alarm goes off, will you linger for a few minutes and listen to the radio? What will you wear today? You check the weather forecast and make that decision. Then, what will you have for breakfast? Will you drive to university or take the bus? Which classes will you attend? Which assignments will you complete? What will you do for lunch? Will you play tennis, swim or run today? How will you spend your evening? Will you study, relax at home with a video, or go to see a film? ◆ You face decisions like these every day. But on some days, you face choices that can change the entire direction of your life. What will you study? Will you specialize in economics, business, law or English? ◆ While you are making your own decisions, other people are making theirs. And some of the decisions that other people make will have an impact on your own subsequent decisions. Your university decides what courses it will offer next year. Stephen Spielberg decides what his next film will be. A team of eye doctors decides on a new experiment that will lead them to a cure for short sightedness. The government decides to reduce poverty. The European Bank decides to cut interest rates. ◆ All these choices and decisions by you and everyone else are all examples of economics in your life.

◆ ◆ ◆ ◆ This chapter takes a first look at the subject you are about to study. It defines economics. Then it expands on that definition with five big questions that economists try to answer and eight big ideas that define the economic way of thinking. These questions and ideas are the foundation on which your course is built. The chapter concludes with a description of how economists go about their work, the scientific method they use, and the pitfalls they try to avoid. When you have completed your study of this chapter, you will have a good sense of what economics is about and you'll be ready to start learning economics and using it to gain a new view of the world. We are going to answer these questions in this chapter.

A Definition of Economics

All economic questions and problems arise from **scarcity**. They arise because our wants exceed the resources available to satisfy them. We want good health and long life, material comfort, security, physical and mental recreation and knowledge. None of these wants is completely satisfied for everyone, and everyone has some unsatisfied wants. While many people have all the material comfort they want, many others do not. No one feels entirely satisfied with her or his state of health and expected length of life. No one feels entirely secure, even in the post-Cold War era, and no one has enough time for sport, travel, holidays, films, theatre, reading and other leisure pursuits.

The poor and the rich alike, face scarcity. A child wants a can of soft drink and a pack of biscuits but has only £1.00 in her pocket. She experiences scarcity. A student wants to go to a party on Saturday night but also wants to spend that same night catching up on late assignments. He experiences scarcity. A millionaire wants to spend the weekend playing golf and attending a business strategy meeting and cannot do both. She experiences scarcity. Even parrots face scarcity – there just aren't enough crackers to go around as the cartoon shows.

Faced with scarcity, we must choose among the available alternatives.

Economics is the science of choice – the science that explains the choices that we make and how those choices change as we cope with scarcity.

All economic choices can be summarized in five big questions about the goods and services we produce. These questions are: What? How? When? Where? Who?

'Not only do I *want a cracker-we* all *want a cracker!'*

Drawing by Modell; © 1985 The New Yorker Collection.

The Five Big Economic Questions: What? How? When? Where? Who?

1. What Goods and Services are Produced and in What Quantity?

Goods and services are all the things that we value and are willing to pay for. We produce a dazzling array of goods and services that range from necessities such as houses to leisure items such as sports clothing and equipment. We build more than a million new homes every year. These homes are more spacious and better equipped than they were twenty years ago. We make millions of new items of sports equipment, walking boots, sports shoes, footballs, tennis rackets, mountain bikes and racing bikes, all of which make our sports and leisure time more comfortable and challenging.

What determines whether we build more homes or develop more sporting facilities? How do these choices change over time? And how are they affected by the ongoing changes in technology that make an ever-wider array of goods and services available to us?

2. How are Goods and Services Produced?

In a vineyard in France, basket-carrying workers pick the annual grape crop by hand. In a vineyard in California, a huge machine and a few workers do the same job that a hundred French grape harvesters do. Look around you and you will see many

examples of this phenomenon. The same job being done in different ways. In some supermarkets checkout staff key in prices, in others they use a laser scanner. One farmer keeps track of his livestock feeding schedules and inventories by using paper and pencil records, while another uses a personal computer. Volkswagen hires workers to weld auto bodies in some of its plants and uses robots to do the job in others.

Why do we use machines in some cases and people in others? Does mechanization and technological change destroy more jobs than it creates? Do people working with new technology earn more than those working with traditional methods? If so, why? Does introducing new technology make us better off or worse off?

3. When are Goods and Services Produced?

On a building site, there is a surge of production activity and people must work overtime to keep production flowing fast enough. A car factory closes for two weeks and temporarily lays off its workers and its production dries up.

Sometimes, economy-wide production slackens off and even shrinks in what is called a recession. At other times, economy-wide production expands rapidly. We call these ebbs and flows of production the business cycle. When production falls, jobs are lost and unemployment climbs. Once, during the Great Depression of the 1930s, production fell so much that one quarter of the workforce was jobless.

During the past few years, production has decreased in Russia and its Central and Eastern Europe neighbours as these countries try to change the way they organize their economies. What makes production rise and fall? When will production rise and when will it fall again in the European Union member states? Can government action prevent production from falling? Would the member governments of the European Union be better able to control recessions individually, or would government action at the European Union level be more effective?

4. Where are Goods and Services Produced?

The Kellogg Company, of Battle Creek, Michigan, makes breakfast cereals in 20 countries and sells them in 160 countries. Kellogg's business in Japan is so huge that it has a Japanese language Website to promote its products! Honda, the Japanese car producer, makes cars and motor cycles on most continents. 'Globalization through localization' is its slogan. But it produces some cars in one country and ships them for sale in another. In today's global economy, people who are separated by thousands of miles, cooperate to produce many goods and services. For example, software engineers work via the Internet with programmers in India. But there is a lot of local concentration of production as well.

A large proportion of UK furniture is made in Wales. There is a strong concentration of car manufacturers in the North East in England and in Wales. Financial services are concentrated in the major capital cities of Europe. Why is this? A large proportion of Europe's oranges are grown in Spain. What determines where goods and services are produced? How do changing patterns of production location change the types of jobs we do and the wages we earn?

5. Who Consumes the Goods and Services that are Produced?

Who consumes the goods and services produced depends on the incomes that people earn. Doctors earn much higher incomes than nurses and physiotherapists. So, doctors get more of the goods and services produced than nurses and physiotherapists.

You probably know about many other persistent differences in incomes. University graduates, on average, earn more than school leavers without degrees and school leavers with school certificates earn more than those who leave school without qualifications. You can see the rates of return from education in Table 1.1. Women gain more, on average, than men from being qualified, but men, on average, still earn more than women. It is also the case that whites, on average, earn more than ethnic minorities. Europeans, earn more on average than Asians and Africans. But there are some significant exceptions. The people of Japan and Hong Kong now earn a similar amount to Europeans. But there is still a huge gap between incomes in rich countries and those in poor countries. A typical income in the poorest counties of the world is just a few hundred pounds, less than the equivalent of a typical weekly wage in the richest countries of the world.

What determines the incomes we earn? Why do doctors earn larger incomes than nurses? Why do women and minorities earn less than white

Table 1.1 Return from Education

	Qualification		
	Degree	A Levels	5+ O Levels
Men	17.5%	13%	21%
Women	35%	11%	26%

The percentage rates of return measure the average increase in your earnings resulting from education.

Source: Blundell, R. *et al.* (1999) Human Capital Investment: the returns from education and training to the individual, the firm and the economy. *Fiscal studies*, **20**.

males? These five big economic questions give you a sense of what economics is about. They tell you about the scope of economics. But they don't tell you what economics is. They don't tell you how economists think about these questions and seek answers to them. Let's find out how economists approach economic questions by looking at some big ideas that define the economic way of thinking.

Eight Big Ideas of Economics

The economic way of thinking can be summarized in eight big ideas.

1. Every Choice is a Trade-off

When we make a choice we must give up one thing to get something else? Every choice is a **trade-off**. The highest valued alternative we give up is the opportunity cost of the activity chosen. Whatever we choose to do, we could have done something else instead. We trade-off one thing for another. 'There's no such thing as a free lunch' is not just a clever throwaway line. It expresses the central idea of economics – that every choice involves a cost.

We use the term opportunity cost to emphasize that when we make a choice in the face of scarcity, we give up an opportunity to do something else. The opportunity cost of any action is the highest valued alternative foregone. The action that you choose not to do – the highest valued alternative foregone – is the cost of the action that you choose to do. You can quit college or university right now or you can stay in education. If you quit and take a job at McDonald's, you might earn enough to buy some CDs, go to see a film and spend lots of free time with your friends. If you remain in education, you can't afford these things. You will be able to buy these things later and that is one of the payoffs from being in school. But for now, when you've bought your books, you have nothing left for CDs and films. Doing assignments means that you've got less time for hanging around with your friends. The opportunity cost of being in school is the alternative things that you would have done if you had quit school. Opportunity cost is the highest valued alternative foregone. It is not all the possible alternatives foregone. For example, your economics lecture is at 8:30 on a Monday morning. You contemplate two alternatives to attending the lecture: staying in bed for an hour or jogging for an hour. You can't stay in bed and jog for that same hour. The opportunity cost of attending the lecture is not the cost of an hour in bed and the cost of jogging for an hour. If these are the only alternatives you contemplate, then you have to decide which one you would do if you did not go to the lecture. The opportunity cost of attending a lecture for a jogger is a foregone hour of exercise; the opportunity cost of attending a lecture for a late sleeper is a foregone hour in bed.

2. Choice at the Margin

We make choices in small steps, or choices at the margin. Choices are influenced by incentives. Everything that we do involves a decision to do a little bit more or a little bit less of an activity. You can allocate the next hour between studying and e-mailing your friends. But the choice is not 'all-or-nothing'. You must decide how many minutes to allocate to each activity. To make this decision, you compare the benefit of a little bit more study time with its cost.

The mother of a young child must decide how to allocate her time between being with her child and working for an income. Like your decision about study time, this decision too involves comparing the benefit of a little bit more income with the cost of a little bit less time with her child. The benefit that arises from an increase in an activity is called marginal benefit. For example, suppose that a mother is working 2 days a week and is thinking about increasing her work to 3 days. Her marginal benefit is the benefit she will get from the additional day of work. It is not the benefit she gets from all 3 days. The reason is that she already has the benefit from 2 days work, so she doesn't count this benefit as resulting from the decision she is now making.

The cost of an increase in an activity is called marginal cost. For the mother of the young child, the marginal cost of increasing her work to 3 days a week is the cost of the additional day not spent with her child. It does not include the cost of the two days she is already working. To make her decision, the mother compares the marginal benefit from an extra day of work with its marginal cost. If the marginal benefit exceeds the marginal cost, she works the extra day. If the marginal cost exceeds the marginal benefit, she does not work the extra day.

By evaluating marginal benefits and marginal costs and choosing only those actions that bring greater benefit than cost, we use our scarce resources in the way that makes us as well off as possible. Our choices respond to incentives. An incentive is an inducement to take a particular action. The inducement can be a benefit – a carrot, or a cost – a stick. A change in opportunity cost – in marginal cost – and a change in marginal benefit changes the incentives that we face and leads to changes in our actions.

For example, suppose the daily wage rate rises and nothing else changes. With a higher daily wage rate, the marginal benefit of working increases. For the young mother, the opportunity cost of spending a day with her child has increased. She now has a bigger incentive to work an extra day a week. Whether or not she does so depends on how she evaluates the marginal benefit of the additional income and marginal cost of spending less time with her child.

Similarly, suppose the cost of day care rises and nothing else changes. The higher cost of day care increases the marginal cost of working. For the young mother, the opportunity cost of spending a day with her child has decreased. She now has a smaller incentive to work an extra day a week. Again, whether or not she changes her actions in response to a change in incentives depends on how she evaluates the marginal benefit and marginal cost. The central idea of economics is that by looking for changes in marginal cost and marginal benefit, we can predict the way choices will change in response to changes in incentives

3. Voluntary Exchange

Voluntary exchange makes both buyers and sellers better off, and markets are an efficient way to organize exchange. When you shop for food, you give up some money in exchange for a basket of vegetables. But the food is worth the price you have to pay. You are better off having exchanged some of your money for the vegetables. The food shop receives a payment that makes its operator happy too. Both you and the food shop owner gain from your purchase. Similarly, when you work at a summer job, you receive a wage that you've decided is sufficient to compensate you for the leisure time you must give up. But the value of your work to the firm that hires you is at least as great as the wage it pays you. So again, both you and your employer gain from a voluntary exchange.

Drawings by Chris Riddell, 1993, *The Independent.*

You are better off when you buy your food. And you are better off when you sell your labour during the summer holidays. Whether you are a buyer or a seller, you gain from voluntary exchange with others.

What is true for you is true for everyone else. Everyone gains from voluntary exchange. In our organized economy, exchanges take place in markets and for money. We sell our labour in exchange for an income in the labour market. And we buy the goods and services we've chosen to consume in a wide variety of markets, markets for vegetables, coffee, films, videos, pizzas, haircuts, and so on. At the other side of these transactions, firms buy our labour and sell us the hundreds of different consumer goods and services we buy.

Markets are efficient in the sense that they send resources to the place where they are valued most highly. For example, a frost kills the orange crop and sends the price of orange juice through the roof. This increase in price, with all other prices remaining unchanged, increases the opportunity cost of drinking orange juice. The people who place the highest value on orange juice are the ones who keep drinking it. People who place a lower value on orange juice now have an incentive to substitute other fruit juices.

Markets are not the only way to organize the economy. An alternative is called a command system. In a command system, some people give orders (commands) and other people obey those orders. A command system is used in the military and in many firms. A command system was used in the former Soviet Union to organize the entire economy. You can see from the cartoon comparing towns in Russia and the United Kingdom that the allocation method in the old command systems was quite different from the allocation method in market systems.

4. Market Failure and Government Action

The market does not always work efficiently and sometimes government action is necessary to overcome market problems and lead to a more efficient use of resources. **Market failure** is a state in which the market does not use resources efficiently. If you pay attention to the news media, you might get the impression that the market almost never does a good job. It makes credit

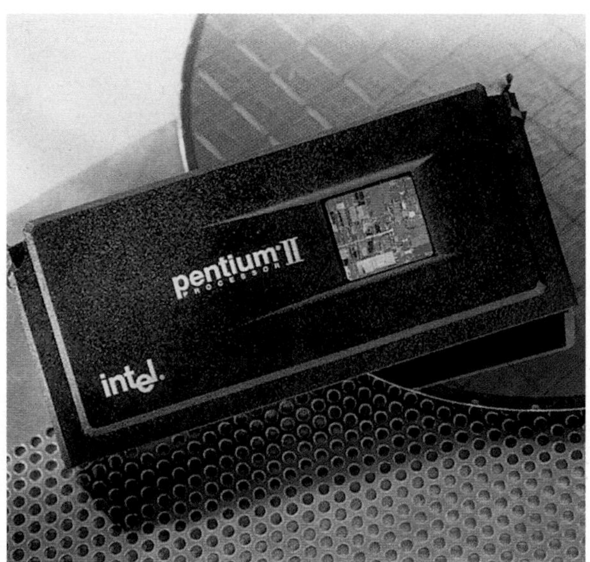

card interest rates too high. It makes the wages of fast-food workers too low. It causes the price of coffee to go through the roof every time Brazil has a serious frost. It increases the world price of oil when political instability threatens the Middle East. These examples are not cases of market failure. They are examples of the market doing its job of helping us to allocate our scarce resources and ensure that they are used in the activities in which they are most highly valued.

Because a high price brings a bigger gain to the seller, there is an incentive for sellers to try to control a market. When a single producer controls an entire market, it can restrict production and raise the price. This action brings market failure. The quantity of the good available is too small. Some people believe that Intel restricts the quantity of computer chips when it introduces a new design in order to get a high price for it. Eventually, the price falls, but at first, Intel sells its new design for a high price and makes a bigger profit.

Market failure can also arise when producers don't take into account the costs they impose on other people. For example, electricity utilities create pollution such as acid rain that destroys plants and forests and lowers farm production. If these costs were taken into account, we would produce less electricity. Market failure can also arise because some goods, such as the air traffic control system, must be consumed by everyone equally. None of us has an incentive voluntarily to pay our share of the cost of such a service.

Instead, we try to free ride on everyone else. But if everyone tries to free ride, no one gets a ride!

To overcome market failure, governments regulate markets with antitrust laws and environmental protection laws. And the government discourages the production and consumption of some goods and services (tobacco and alcohol for example) by taxing them and encourages the production and consumption of some other items (health care and schooling for example) by subsidizing them.

5. Expenditure Equals Income

For the economy as a whole, expenditure equals income equals the value of production. When you buy a coffee you spend £2. But what happens to that money? The server gets some of it in wages, the owner of the building gets some of it as rent, and the owner of the café gets some of it as profit. The suppliers of the milk and coffee also get some of your £2. But these suppliers spend part of what they receive on wages and rent. And they keep part of it as profit. Your £2 of expenditure creates exactly £2 of income for all the people who have contributed to making the cup of coffee, going all the way back to the farmer in Brazil who grew the coffee beans. Your expenditure generates incomes of an equal amount. The same is true for everyone else's expenditure. So, for the economy as a whole, total expenditure on goods and services equals total income.

One way to value the things you buy is to use the prices you pay for them. So the value of all the goods and services bought equals total expenditure. Another way to value the items you buy is to use the cost of production. This cost is the total amount paid to the people who produced the items – the total income generated by your expenditure. But we've just seen that total expenditure and total income are equal, so they also equal the value of production.

6. Living Standards and Productivity

Living standards improve when **productivity**, production per person, increases. By automating a car production line, one worker can produce a greater output. But if one worker can produce more cars, then more people can enjoy owning a car. The same is true for all goods and services. By increasing output per person, we enjoy a higher standard of living and buy more goods and services. The value of production can increase for any of three reasons: because prices rise, because production per person increases or because the population increases.

But only an increase in productivity brings an improvement in living standards. A rise in prices brings higher incomes, but only in pounds. The extra income is just enough to pay the higher prices, not enough to buy more goods and services. An increase in population brings an increase in total production, but not an increase in production per person.

7. Rising Prices

We find rising prices when the quantity of money increases faster than production. Prices rise in a process called inflation when the quantity of money in circulation increases faster than production. This leads to a situation of 'too much money chasing too few goods'. As people bring more money to market, sellers see that they can raise their prices. But when these sellers go to buy their supplies, they find that the prices they face increase. With too much money around, money starts to lose value.

In some countries, inflation has been rapid. One such country is Poland. Since 1990, prices in Poland have risen more than sevenfold. In most European countries, we have moderate inflation of about 3–5 per cent a year. Some people say that by increasing the quantity of money, we can create jobs. The idea is that if more money is put into the economy, when it is spent, businesses sell more and so hire more labour to produce more goods. Initially, an increase in money might increase production and create jobs. But eventually, it only increases prices and leaves production and jobs unchanged.

8. Unemployment

Unemployment can result from market failure but some unemployment is productive. Unemployment is ever present. Sometimes its rate is low and sometimes it is high. Also, unemployment fluctuates over the business cycle. Some unemployment is normal and efficient. We choose to take our time finding a suitable job rather than rushing to accept the first one that comes along. Similarly, businesses take their time in filling vacancies. The unemployment that results from these careful searches for jobs and workers improves productivity because it helps to assign people to their most productive jobs. Some unemployment results from fluctuations in expenditure and can be wasteful.

These eight ideas lie at the heart of economics and you will repeatedly return to them at every point in your study of the subject. To complete your introduction to economics, we next describe how economists go about their work. We're going to describe what economists do.

What Economists Do

Economists work on the wide array of problems that arise from the five big questions that you reviewed at the start of this chapter. And they use the big ideas that you've just studied to search for answers. How do they go about their work? What special problems and pitfalls do they encounter?

Microeconomics and Macroeconomics

You can take either a micro or a macro view of the spectacular display of national flags in a Korean sports stadium. The micro view is of a single participant and the actions he or she is taking. The macro view is the patterns formed by the joint actions of all the individuals participating in the entire display.

You can look at the economy with either a micro or a macro view. These two views define the two major branches of the subject: microeconomics and macroeconomics.

Microeconomics is the study of the decisions of individual people and businesses and the interaction of those decisions in markets. It seeks to explain the prices and quantities of individual goods and services. Microeconomics also studies the effects of government regulation and taxes on the prices and quantities of individual goods and services. For example, microeconomics studies the forces that determine the prices of cars and the quantities of cars produced and sold. It also studies the effects of regulations and taxes on the prices and quantities of cars.

Macroeconomics is the study of the national economy and the global economy as a whole. It seeks to explain average prices and the total employment, income and production. Macroeconomics also studies the effects of taxes, government spending and the government budget deficit on total jobs and incomes. It also studies the effects of money and interest rates.

Economic Science

Economics is a social science (along with political science, psychology and sociology). A major task of economists is to discover how the economic world works. In pursuit of this goal, economists (like all scientists) distinguish between two types of statement:

1 What is.

2 What ought to be.

Statements about what is are called positive statements. They say what is currently believed about the way the world operates. A positive statement might be right or wrong. And a positive statement can be tested by checking it against the facts. When a chemist does an experiment in her laboratory, she is attempting to check a positive statement against the facts.

Statements about what ought to be are called normative statements. These statements depend on values and cannot be tested. When the European Parliament debates a motion, it is ultimately trying to decide what ought to be. It is making a normative statement.

To see the distinction between positive and normative statements, consider the controversy

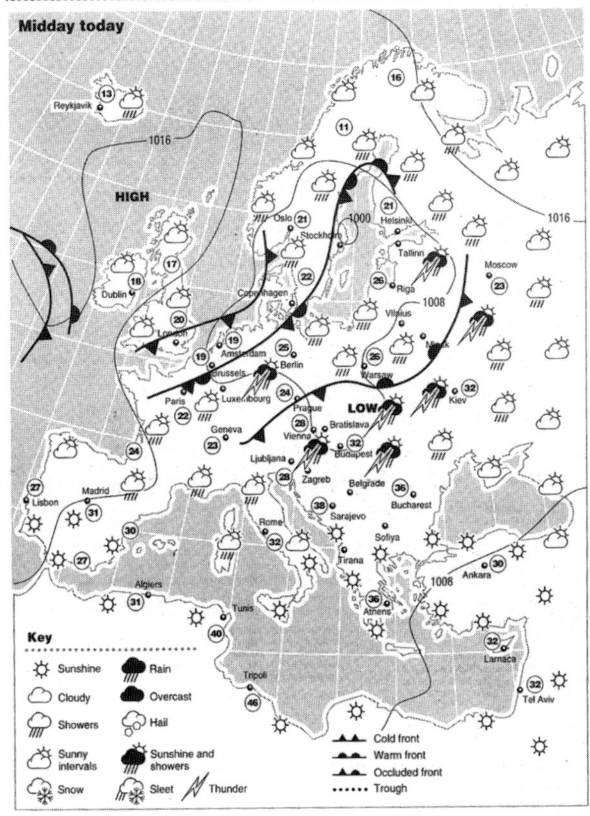

over global warming. Some scientists believe that centuries of the burning of coal and oil are increasing the carbon dioxide content of the earth's atmosphere and leading to higher temperatures that eventually will have devastating consequences for life on this planet. 'Our planet is warming because of an increased carbon dioxide build-up in the atmosphere' is a positive statement. It can (in principle and with sufficient data) be tested. 'We ought to cut back on our use of carbon-based fuels such as coal and oil' is a normative statement. You may agree with or disagree with this statement, but you can't test it. It is based on values.

Health care reform provides an economic example of the distinction. 'Universal health care will cut the amount of work time lost to illness' is a positive statement. 'Every European should have equal access to health care' is a normative statement. The task of economic science is to discover and catalogue positive statements that are consistent with what we observe in the world and that enable us to understand how the economic world works. This task is a large one that can be broken into three steps:

1 Observation and measurement.
2 Model building.
3 Testing models.

Observation and Measurement First, economists keep track of the amounts and locations of natural and human resources, of wages and work hours, of the prices and quantities of the different goods and services produced, of taxes and government spending, and of the quantities of goods and services bought from and sold to other countries. This list gives a flavour of the array of things that economists can observe and measure.

Model Building Model building is the second step toward understanding how the economic world works. An economic model is a description of some aspect of the economic world that includes only those features of the world that are needed for the purpose at hand. A model is simpler than the reality it describes. What a model includes and what it leaves out result from assumptions about what is essential and what are inessential details.

You can see how ignoring details is useful – even essential – to our understanding by thinking about a model that you see every day, the TV weather map. The weather map is a model that helps to predict the temperature, wind speed and direction, and precipitation over a future period. The weather map shows lines called isobars – lines of equal barometric pressure. It doesn't show the motorways. The reason is that our theory of the weather tells us that the pattern of air pressure, not the location of the motorways, determines the weather.

An economic model is similar to a weather map. It tells us how a number of variables are determined by a number of other variables. For example, an economic model of inflation would show which variables determined inflation and how a change in each variable affected inflation.

Testing Models The third step is testing the model. A model's predictions may correspond, or be in conflict, with the facts. By comparing the model's predictions with the facts, we are able to test a model and develop an economic

Figure 1.1 How Economic Theories are Developed

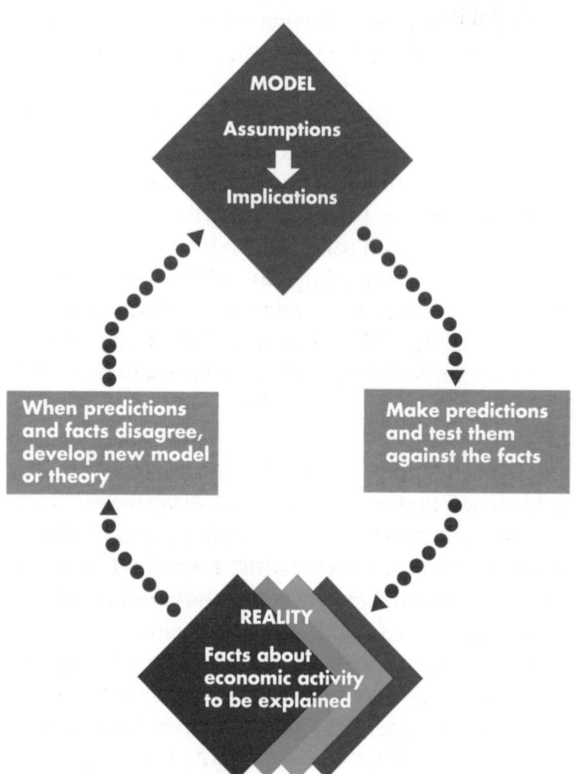

Economists develop economic theories by building and testing economic models. An economic model is based on *assumptions* about what is essential and what can be ignored and the *implications* of these assumptions. The implications of a model form the basis of *predictions* about the world. Economists test those predictions by checking them against the facts. If the predictions are in conflict with the facts, the model-building process begins again with new assumptions. Only when the predictions agree with the facts has a useful theory been developed.

theory. An economic theory is a generalization that summarizes what we think we understand about the economic choices that people make and the performance of industries and entire economies. It is a bridge between an economic model and the real economy.

A theory is created by a process of building and testing models. For example, meteorologists have a theory that if the isobars form a particular pattern at a particular time of the year (a model), then it will snow (reality). They have developed this theory by repeated observation and by carefully recording the weather that follows specific pressure patterns.

Figure 1.1 shows the logical structure of the search for new economic knowledge. Economists build a model to create predictions about the way the world works. Theories are developed from generating and testing the model. When the model's predictions conflict with the facts, the theory is discarded or the model modified.

Economics is a young science. It was born in 1776 with the publication of Adam Smith's *The Wealth of Nations* (see pp. 64–65). Over the past 220 years, economics has discovered many useful theories. But in many areas, economists are still looking for answers. The gradual accumulation of economic knowledge gives most economists some faith that their methods will, eventually, provide usable answers to the big economic questions. But progress in economics comes slowly. Let's look at some of the obstacles to progress in economics.

Obstacles and Pitfalls in Economics

Economic experiments are difficult to do. Also, economic behaviour has many simultaneous causes. For these two reasons, it is difficult to unscramble cause and effect in economics.

Scientists try to unscramble cause and effect by changing one factor at a time and holding all the other relevant factors constant. In this way, scientists isolate the factor of interest and are able to investigate its effects in the clearest possible way. This logical device, that all scientists use to identify cause and effect, is called ***ceteris paribus***. *Ceteris paribus* is a Latin term that means 'other things being equal' or 'if all other relevant things remain the same'. Ensuring that other things are equal is crucial in many activities, including athletic events, and all successful attempts to make scientific progress use this device.

Economic models (like the models in all other sciences) enable the influence of one factor at a time to be isolated in the imaginary world of the model. When we use a model, we are able to imagine what would happen if only one factor changed. But ceteris paribus can be a problem in economics when we try to test a model.

Laboratory scientists, such as chemists and physicists, perform experiments by actually holding all the relevant factors constant except for the one under investigation. This method is called using a 'control'. In the non-experimental sciences such as economics (and astronomy), we usually observe the outcomes of the simultaneous operation of many factors. Consequently, it is difficult to set up a control. It is hard to sort out the effects of each individual factor and to compare the effects with what a model predicts.

To cope with this problem, economists take three complementary approaches.

First, they look for pairs of events in which other things were equal (or similar). An example might be to study the effects of unemployment benefit on the unemployment rate by comparing different European countries on the presumption that the people in the two economies are sufficiently similar. Second, economists use statistical tools called econometrics. And third, when they can, they perform experiments. This relatively new approach puts real subjects (usually students) in a decision-making situation and varies their incentives in some way to discover how they respond to one factor at a time.

Economists try to avoid fallacy – errors of reasoning that lead to a wrong conclusion. But two fallacies are common, and you need to be on your guard to avoid them. They are:

1 The fallacy of composition.

2 The *post hoc* fallacy.

Fallacy of Composition The fallacy of composition is the (false) statement that what is true of the parts is true of the whole or that what is true of the whole is true of the parts. Think of the true statement, 'Speed kills', and its implication, going more slowly saves lives. If an entire freeway moves at a lower speed, everyone on the highway has a safer ride.

But suppose that one driver only slows down and all the other drivers try to maintain their original speed. In this situation, there will probably be more accidents because more cars will change lanes to overtake the slower vehicle. So, in this example, what is true for the whole is not true for a part.

The fallacy of composition arises mainly in macroeconomics, and it stems from the fact that the parts interact with each other to produce an outcome for the whole that might differ from the intent of the parts. For example, a firm lays off some workers to cut costs and improve its profits. If all firms take similar actions, incomes fall and so does spending. The firm sells less, and its profits don't improve.

***Post Hoc* Fallacy** Another Latin phrase – *post hoc ergo propter hoc* – means 'after this, therefore because of this'. The *post hoc* fallacy is the error of reasoning that a first event causes a second event because the first occurred before the second. Suppose you are a visitor from a far off world. You observe lots of people shopping in early December and then you see them opening gifts and partying on Christmas Day. Does the shopping cause Christmas, you wonder. After a deeper study, you discover that Christmas causes the shopping. A later event causes an earlier event.

Unravelling cause and effect is difficult in economics. And just looking at the timing of events often doesn't help. For example, the stock market booms, and some months later the economy expands – jobs and incomes grow. Did the stock market boom cause the economy to expand? Possibly, but perhaps businesses started to plan the expansion of production because a new technology that lowered costs had become available. As knowledge of the plans spread, the stock market reacted to anticipate the economic expansion. To disentangle cause and effect, economists use economic models and data and, to the extent that they can, perform experiments.

Economics is a challenging science. Does the difficulty of getting answers in economics mean that anything goes and that economists disagree on most questions? No, but disagreement and debate are part of the way in which science develops new answers to current problems. Disagreement is a healthy sign in science.

Agreement and Disagreement

Economists have a reputation for not agreeing. Perhaps you've heard the joke: 'If you laid all the economists in the world end to end, they still

wouldn't reach agreement'. But actually, whilst economists like to argue about theory, there is a remarkable amount of agreement. Here is a sample of the degree of concensus on a range of issues[1]. Seventy per cent of economists agree that:

- Rent ceilings cut the availability of housing.
- Import restrictions have larger costs than benefits.
- Wage and price controls do not help slow inflation.
- Wage contracts are not a primary cause of unemployment.

Sixty per cent of economists agree that:

- Monopoly power of big oil companies was not the cause of a rise in the price of petrol during the Kuwait crisis.
- Curtailing the power of environmental agencies would not make the economy more efficient.
- If the budget is to be balanced, it should be balanced over a business cycle, not every year.

But economists are divided on these issues:

- Anti-monopoly laws should be enforced more vigourously to curtail monopoly power.
- Effluent taxes are better than pollution limits.
- The government should try to make the distribution of income more equal.

Which are positive and which are normative? Notice that economists are willing to offer their opinions on normative issues as well as their professional views on positive questions. Be on the lookout for normative propositions dressed up as positive propositions.

You are now ready to start doing economics. As you get into the subject, you will see that we rely heavily on graphs. You must be comfortable with this method of reasoning. If you need some help with it, take your time in working carefully through Chapter 2. If you are already comfortable with graphs, then you are ready to jump right into Chapter 3.

1 The views of economists are taken from Richard M. Alston, J.R. Kearl and Michael B. Vaughan, Is there a Concensus Among Economists, *American Economic Review*, May 1992, **82**, 203–209.

Summary

Key Points

A Definition of Economics (p. 5)

- Economics is the science of choice – the science that explains the choices that we make to cope with scarcity.

The Five Big Economic Questions (pp. 5–8)

- Economists try to answer five big questions about goods and services:

  1. What? 2. How? 3. When? 4. Where? 5. Who?

- What are the goods and services produced, how, when, and where are they produced, and who consumes them?
- Answers to these questions interact to determine the standards of living and the distribution of well-being around the world.

Eight Big Ideas of Economics (pp. 8–13)

- A choice is a trade-off and the highest value alternative foregone is the opportunity cost of what is chosen.
- Choices are made at the margin and are influenced by incentives.

- Markets enable both buyers and sellers to gain from voluntary exchange.
- Sometimes government actions are needed to overcome market failure.
- For the economy as a whole, expenditure equals income, and equals the value of production.
- Living standards rise when production per person increases.
- Prices rise when the quantity of money increases faster than production.
- Unemployment can result from market failure but can also be productive.

What Economists Do (pp. 13–18)

- Microeconomics is the study of individual decisions and macroeconomics is the study of the economy as a whole.
- Positive statements are about what is and normative statements are about what ought to be.
- To explain the economic world, economists build and test economic models.
- Economists use the *ceteris paribus* assumption to try to disentangle cause and effect, and they are careful to avoid the fallacy of composition and the *post hoc* fallacy.
- Economists agree on a wide range of questions about how the economy works.

Key Terms

Ceteris paribus, 16
Command, 11
Economics, 5
Economic model, 16
Economic theory, 16
Efficient, 11
Expenditure, 12
Goods and services, 5
Incentive, 11
Income, 7
Inflation, 13
Macroeconomics, 14
Margin, 9
Marginal benefit, 9
Marginal cost, 10
Market, 11
Market failure, 11
Microeconomics, 14
Opportunity cost, 8
Productivity, 13
Scarcity, 5
Trade-off, 8
Unemployment, 13
Value of production, 13
Voluntary exchange, 10

Review Questions

1 Give a definition of economics.

2 What is scarcity? Give some examples of rich people and poor people facing scarcity.

3 Why does scarcity force us to make choices?

4 Give some examples, different from those in the chapter, of each of the five big economic questions.

5 Why do you care about what goods and services are produced? Give some examples of goods that you value highly and goods on which you place a low value.

6 Why do you care about how goods and services are produced? [Hint: Think about cost.]

7 Why do you care about when or where goods and services are produced?

8 Why do you care about who gets the goods and services that are produced?

9 What do we mean by the related ideas of trade-off and opportunity cost? Give some examples of trade-offs that you have made today and of opportunity costs that you have incurred.

10 What is marginal cost and marginal benefit and why are they relevant for making a decision? Give some examples.

11 What is a market and why does it enable both buyers and sellers to gain from exchange?

12 Give some examples for market failure.

13 Explain why for the economy as a whole, expenditure equals income and the value of production.

14 What makes living standards rise?

15 What makes prices rise?

16 Why does unemployment occur? Is all unemployment a problem?

Problems

1 You plan to go to university summer school. If you do, you won't be able to take a contract job that pays £6,000 for the summer and you won't be able to live at home for free. The cost of your tuition will be £2,000, textbooks £200, and living expenses £1,400. What is the opportunity cost of going to the university summer school?

2 On Valentine's Day, Stephen and Trudy exchanged gifts: Stephen sent Trudy red roses and Trudy bought Stephen a box of chocolates. Each spent £10. They also spent £30 on dinner and split the cost evenly. Did either Stephen or Trudy incur any opportunity costs? If so, what were they? Explain your answer.

3 The local shopping centre has free parking, but the centre is always very busy and it usually takes 30 minutes to find a parking space. Today when you found a vacant spot, your friend Donald also wanted it. Is parking really free at this mall? If not, what did it cost you to park today? When you parked your car today, did you impose any costs on Donald? Explain your answers.

4 Which of the following statements are positive and which are normative?

a A cut in wages will reduce the number of people willing to work.
b High interest rates prohibit many young people from buying their first home.
c No family ought to pay more than 25 per cent of its income in taxes.
d The government should reduce its expenditure on roads and increase its expenditure on railways.
e Privatizing the public health services will make health provision more efficient.
f The government ought to behave in such a way as to ensure that resources are used efficiently.

5 You have been hired by Soundtrend, a company that makes and markets tapes, records and compact discs (CDs). Your employer is going to start selling these products in a new region that has a population of 100 million people. A survey has indicated that 40 per cent of people in this region buy only popular music, 5 per cent buy only classical music, and no one buys both types of music. Another survey suggests that the average income of a pop music fan in the region is £10,000 a year and that of a classical music fan is £20,000 a year. Based on a third survey, it appears that, on the average, people with low incomes spend one-quarter of one per cent of their incomes on tapes, records and CDs, while people with high incomes spend two per cent of their income on these products.

Build a model to enable Soundtrend to predict how much will be spent on pop music and classical music in this new region in one year. In doing so:

a List any assumptions you make.
b Work out any implications of your assumptions.
c High light any potential sources of errors in your predictions.

6 Imagine a homeless man on the street. All this man's possessions are contained in two carrier bags. Use the five big questions and the eight big ideas of economics to identify the main characteristics of the economic life of this homeless man. Does he face scarcity? Does he make choices? Can you interpret his choices as being in his own best interest? Can either his own choices or the choices of others make this man better off? If so, how?

7 Go back and look at the picture of the weather map on page 15, which represents a model of the weather system. Then answer the following:

a What do the isobars represent?
b When the isobars are close together, what prediction would you make about the weather?
c When the isobars are further apart, what prediction would you make about the weather?
d Suppose you make a prediction about tomorrow's weather from today's weather map and it turns out to be wrong, does this mean that weather maps are poor models of weather systems? Explain your answer.

8 Find a copy of an Underground Train or Metro Train system in a city that you know and then answer the following:

a In what ways does the Underground or Metro map differ from a City street map?
b What is the purpose of these differences?
c In what way does the Underground or Metro map serve as a 'model' of the real Underground or Metro system?
d Choose two different points on the map and identify a route between them. How would you test whether the predicted route derived from your model is correct?
e What conclusions would you draw about your model if you followed the predicted route and ended up at the wrong destination?
f What conclusion would you draw about the real world Underground or Metro system if you followed the predicted route and ended up at the wrong destination?
g How would you change your model, if at all, if you followed the predicted route and ended up at the wrong destination?

CHAPTER 2

Making and Using Graphs

After studying this chapter you will be able to:

- Make and interpret a scatter diagram, a time-series graph and a cross-section graph
- Distinguish between linear and non-linear relationships and between relationships that have a maximum and a minimum
- Define and calculate the slope of a line
- Graph relationships among more than two variables

Three Kinds of Lie

Benjamin Disraeli, a British prime minister in the late nineteenth century, is reputed to have said that there are three kinds of lie: lies, damned lies and statistics. One of the most powerful ways of conveying statistical information is in the form of a graph. Like statistics, graphs can lie. But the right graph does not lie. It reveals a relationship that would otherwise be obscure. ◆ Graphs were invented in the eighteenth century, but with the development of the mass media and personal computers, graphs have become as important as words and numbers. What do graphs reveal and what can they hide? How and why do economists use graphs? How are graphs used to present economic information? ◆ It is often said that in economics, everything depends on everything else. Changes in the quantity of wheat for world consumption are caused by changes in the world price of wheat, the temperature, unusual weather conditions and many other factors. Graphs can help us interpret relationships among all these factors because a picture tells a thousand stories.

◆ ◆ ◆ ◆ In this chapter, you are going to look at the kinds of graph that are used in economics. You are going to learn how to make them and read them. You are also going to learn how to calculate the strength of the effect of one variable on another. If you are already familiar with graphs, you may want to skip (or skim) this chapter. But before you do, try the last few problems at the end of the chapter to check your understanding. It may not be as good as you think.

Graphing Data

Graphs represent a quantity as a distance on a line. Figure 2.1 shows two different quantities on one graph. Temperature is shown on the horizontal line. The quantity is measured as the distance on a scale, in degrees centigrade. Movements from left to right show increases in temperature. Movements from right to left show decreases in temperature. The point marked 0 represents 0 degrees or freezing point. To the right of zero, the temperatures are positive. To the left of zero, the temperatures are negative (as indicated by the minus sign in front of the numbers). Height is measured on the vertical line in thousands of metres from sea level. The point marked 0 represents sea level. Points above zero represent height above sea level. Points below zero (indicated by a minus sign) represent depth below sea level. There are no rigid rules about the scale for a graph. The scale is determined by the range of the variable being graphed and the space available for the graph.

Figure 2.1 Graphing Two Variables

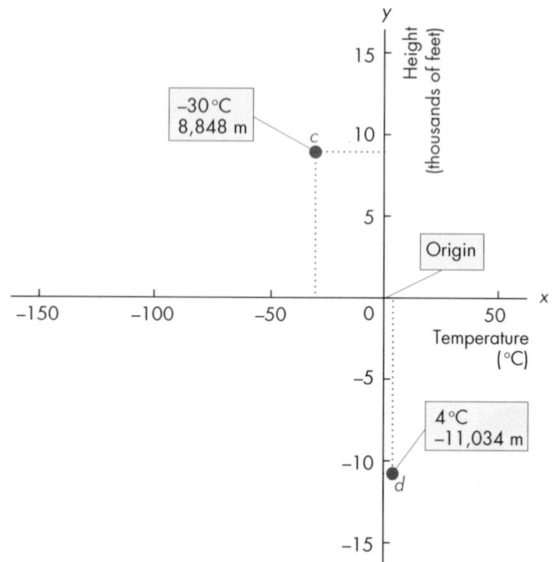

The relationship between two variables is graphed by drawing two axes perpendicular to each other. Height is measured here on the *y*-axis. Point *c* represents the top of Mount Everest, 8,848 metres above sea level (measured on the *y*-axis) with a temperature of –30 °C (measured on the *x*-axis). Point *d* represents the depth of the Mariana Trench in the Pacific Ocean, 11,034 metres below sea level with a temperature of 4 °C.

Two-variable Graphs

The two scale lines in Figure 2.1 are called *axes*. The vertical line is called the y-axis and the horizontal line is called the x-axis. The letters x and y appear as labels on the axes of Figure 2.1. Each axis has a zero point shared by the two axes. The zero point, common to both axes, is called the *origin*.

To show something in a two-variable graph, we need two pieces of information. For example, Mount Everest, the world's highest mountain, is 8,848 metres high and, on a particular day, the temperature at its peak is –30 °C. We show this information in Figure 2.1 by marking the height of the mountain on the y-axis at 8,848 metres and the temperature on the x-axis at –30 °C. The values of the two variables that appear on the axes are marked by point c. The values which represent the depth and temperature of the world's deepest oceanic trench are marked by point d.

Two lines, called *coordinates*, can be drawn from points c and d. The line running from c to the horizontal axis is the y-coordinate, because its length is the same as the value marked off on the y-axis. Similarly, the line running from d to the vertical axis is the x-coordinate, because its length is the same as the value marked off on the x-axis.

Economists use graphs like the one in Figure 2.1 to reveal and describe the relationships among economic variables because one picture can tell many stories. The main types of graph used in economics are:

- Scatter diagrams.
- Time-series graphs.
- Cross-section graphs.

Let's look at each of these types of graph and the stories they can tell.

Scatter Diagrams

A **scatter diagram** plots the value of one economic variable against the value of another variable. Such a graph is used to reveal whether a relationship

Figure 2.2 A Scatter Diagram

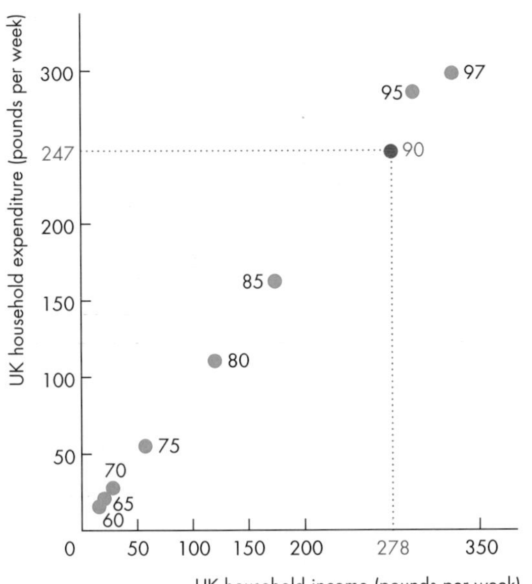

A scatter diagram shows the relationship between two variables. This scatter diagram shows the relationship between average weekly household expenditure and average weekly household income during the years 1960 to 1997. Each point shows the values of the two variables in a specific year; the year is identified by the two-digit number. For example, in 1990 average household expenditure was £247 per week and average income was £278 per week. The pattern formed by the points shows that as UK household income increases, so does household expenditure.

exists between two economic variables. It is also used to describe a relationship.

The Relationship Between Expenditure and Income Figure 2.2 shows a scatter diagram of the relationship between consumer expenditure and income. The x-axis measures household income and the y-axis measures household expenditure. Each point shows average household expenditure and income in the United Kingdom in a given year between 1960 and 1997. The points for all seven years are 'scattered' within the graph. Each point is labelled with a two-digit number that shows us its year. For example, the point marked 90 shows us that in 1990, each household spent £247 a week on average and had an income of £278 a week.

This graph shows us that a relationship exists between household income and expenditure. The dots form a pattern which shows us that when income increases, expenditure also increases on average.

Other Relationships Figure 2.3 shows two other scatter diagrams. Part (a) shows the relationship between the price of cigarettes and the percentage of the population over 15 years old who smoke. The pattern formed by the points shows us that as the price of cigarettes has risen, the proportion of the population who smoke has fallen.

Part (b) looks at inflation and unemployment in the European Union. The pattern formed by the points in this graph does not reveal a clear relationship between the two variables. The graph shows us, by its lack of a distinct pattern, that there is no clear relationship between inflation and unemployment.

Correlation and Causation A scatter diagram that shows a clear relationship between two variables, such as Figure 2.2 or Figure 2.3(a), tells us that the two variables are highly correlated. When a high correlation is present, we can predict the value of one variable from the value of the other. But correlation does not imply causation. Of course, it is likely that high income causes high spending, and rising cigarette prices cause a reduction in the percentage of people who smoke, but sometimes a high correlation arises by coincidence or the effect of a third variable.

Breaks in the Axes Three of the axes in Figure 2.3 have breaks in them, as shown by the small gaps. The breaks indicate that there are jumps from the origin, 0, to the first values recorded. For example, the break is used on the x axis in part (a) because in the period covered by the graph, the proportion who smoke never falls below 30 per cent. With no break, there would be a lot of empty space. All the points would be crowded into the right-hand side, and we would not be able to see clearly whether a relationship existed between these two variables. By breaking the axes we are able to bring the relationship into view. In effect, we use a zoom lens to bring the relationship into the centre of the graph and magnify it so that it fills the graph.

A scatter diagram enables us to see the relationship between two economic variables. But it

Figure 2.3 More Scatter Diagrams

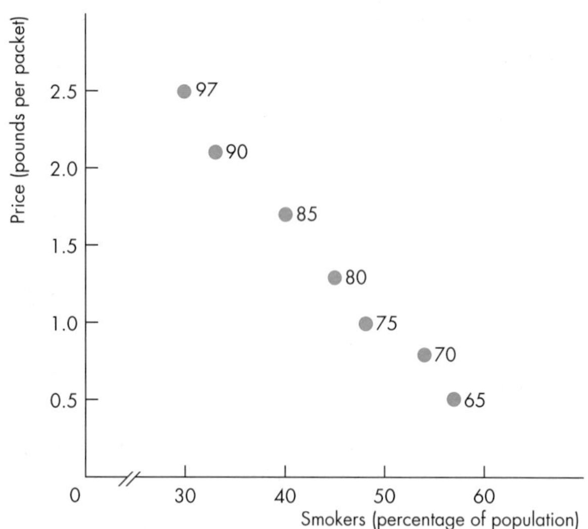

(a) Price and smoking in the United Kingdom

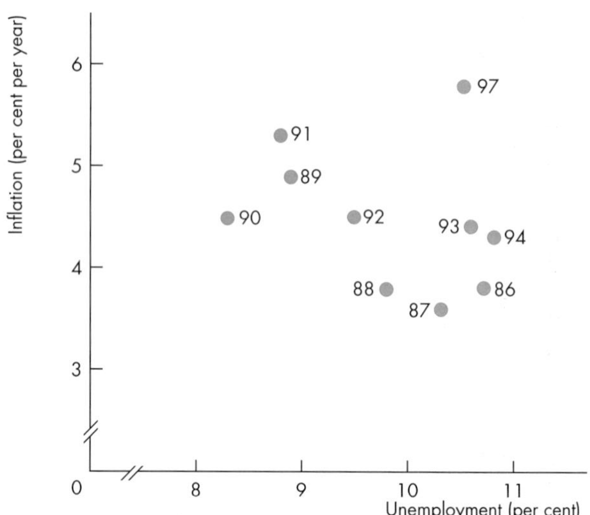

(b) EU unemployment and inflation

Part (a) is a scatter diagram that plots the price of a packet of cigarettes against the percentage of the population who are smokers for years between 1965 and 1997. This graph shows that as the price of cigarettes has risen, the percentage of people who smoke has decreased. Part (b) is a scatter diagram that plots the inflation rate against the unemployment rate for the European Union as a whole. This graph shows that inflation and unemployment are not closely related.

does not give us a clear picture of how these variables evolve over time. To see the evolution of economic variables, we use a time-series graph.

Time-series Graphs

A **time-series graph** is used to show how economic variables change over time (for example, months or years). Figure 2.4 is an example of a time-series graph. Time is measured in years on the x-axis. The economic variable that we are interested in – the UK inflation rate (the percentage change in retail prices) – is measured on the y-axis. This time-series graph tells many stories quickly and easily:

1 It shows us the level of the inflation rate. When the line is a long way from the x-axis, the inflation rate is high. When the line is close to the x-axis, the inflation rate is low.

2 It shows us how the inflation rate changes, whether it rises or falls. When the line slopes upward, as in the early 1970s, the inflation rate is rising. When the line slopes downward, as in the early 1980s, the inflation rate is falling.

3 It shows us the speed with which the inflation rate is changing. If the line rises or falls steeply, then the inflation rate is changing quickly. If the line is shallow, the inflation rate is rising or falling slowly. For example, inflation increased quickly from 1971 to 1974 but increased more slowly in the late 1980s. Similarly, inflation was generally decreasing rapidly between 1975 and 1978, but fell more slowly after 1990.

A time-series graph also reveals trends. A **trend** is a general tendency for a variable to rise or fall. You can see that inflation had a general tendency to increase from 1967 to 1975, and then a general tendency to fall towards 1997. There is also a regular tendency for smaller fluctuations within the trend periods.

A time-series graph also lets us compare different periods quickly. Figure 2.4 shows that the 1950s

Figure 2.4 A Time-series Graph

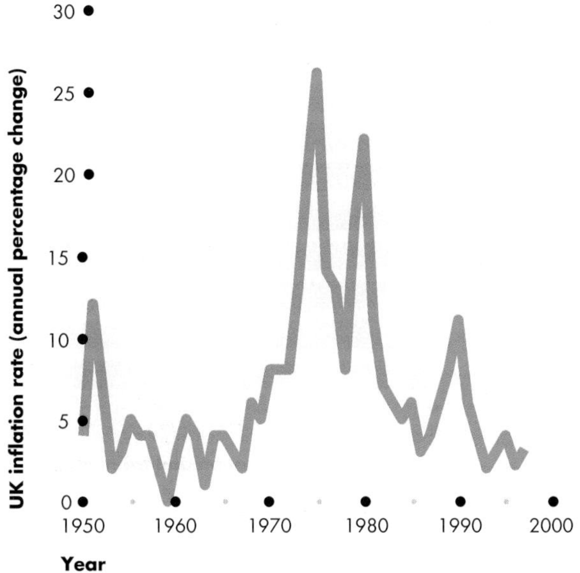

A time-series graph plots the level of a variable on the y-axis against time (day, week, month or year) on the x-axis. This graph shows the UK inflation rate each year from 1950 to 1997.

and 1960s were different from later periods because the trend in inflation was constant, neither rising nor falling.

Comparing Two Time-series Sometimes we want to use a time-series graph to compare two different variables. For example, suppose you wanted to know how the unemployment rate fluctuates with the balance of the government's budget in the United Kingdom. You can examine the unemployment and budget balance by drawing a graph of each of them on the same time scale. We can measure the government's budget balance either as a deficit or as a surplus. Figure 2.5(a) plots the unemployment rate as the orange line and the budget balance as a surplus – the blue line. The unemployment scale is on the left side of the figure and the surplus scale is on the right side of the figure. It is not easy to see the relationship between inflation and the budget balance in Figure 2.5(a). In these situations it is often revealing to flip the scale of one of the variables over and graph it upside

Figure 2.5 Seeing Relationships in Time-series Graphs

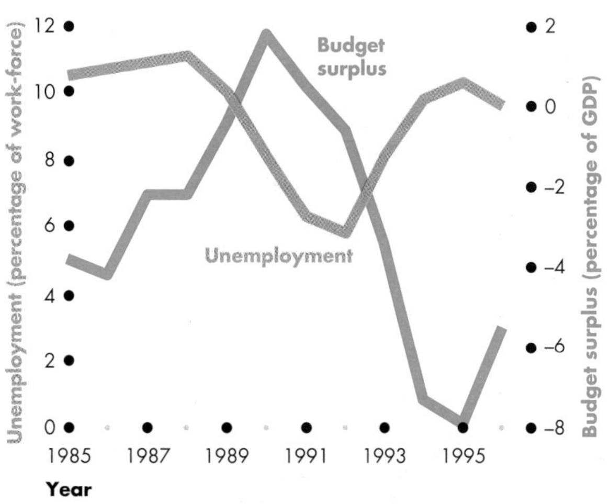

(a) Unemployment and budget surplus

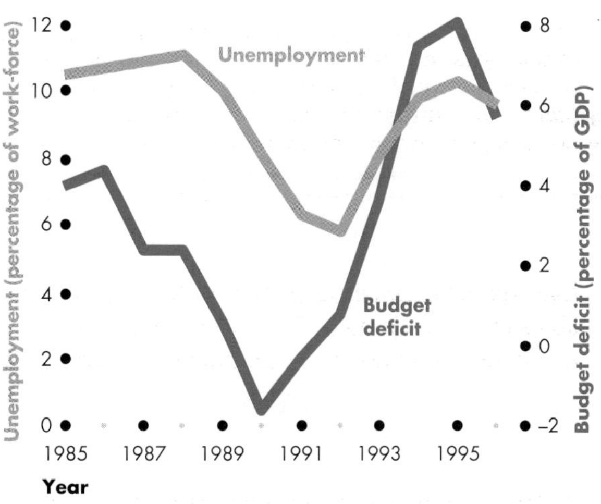

(b) Unemployment and budget deficit

These two graphs show UK unemployment and the UK government's budget balance between 1985 and 1996. The unemployment line is identical in the two parts. Part (a) shows unemployment on the left-hand scale and the budget balance as a surplus – measured on the right-hand scale. It is hard to see a relationship between inflation and unemployment. Part (b) shows unemployment again, but the government budget is measured as a deficit on the right-hand side – the scale has been inverted. The graph now reveals a tendency for unemployment and the budget deficit to move together.

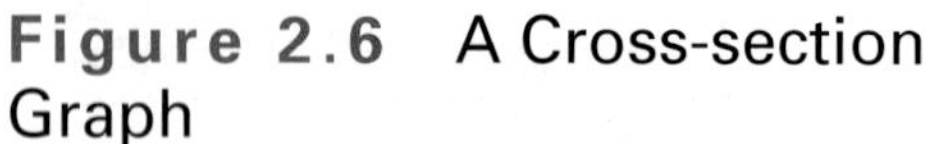

Figure 2.6 A Cross-section Graph

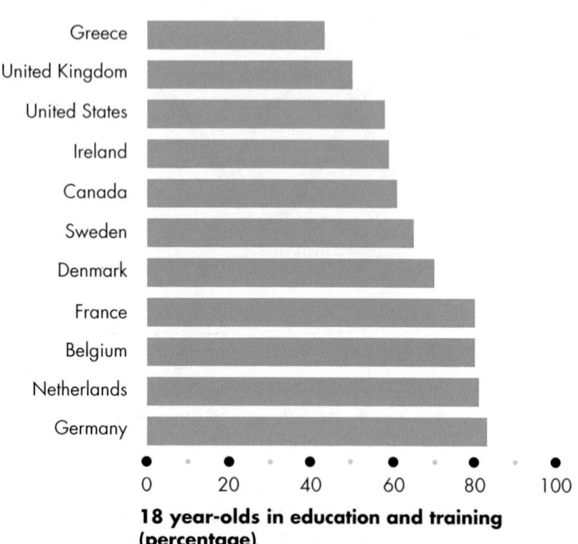

A cross-section graph shows the level of a variable across the members of a population. This graph shows the percentage of 18 year-olds in education and training in different developed countries.

Figure 2.7 A Misleading Graph

A graph can mislead when it distorts the scale on one of its axes. Here, the scale measuring the percentage of 18 year-olds in education and training has been stretched by chopping off values below 40 per cent. The result is that the comparison of percentages across the different countries is distorted. The percentage of 18 year-olds who are in education and training looks much lower in Greece and the United Kingdom when compared with countries with the highest rate.

down. In Figure 2.5(b) the budget balance has been inverted and plotted as a deficit. You can now see the tendency for unemployment and the budget deficit to move together.

Cross-section Graphs

A **cross-section graph** shows the values of an economic variable for different groups in a population at a point in time. Figure 2.6 is an example of a cross-section graph. It shows the percentage of 18 year-olds in education and training across different developed countries in 1996. This graph uses bars rather than dots and lines, and the length of each bar indicates the percentage. Figure 2.6 enables you to compare the level of education and training for 18 year-olds in these 11 countries much more quickly and clearly than by looking at a table of numbers.

Misleading Graphs

All types of graph – time-series graphs, scatter diagrams and cross-section graphs – can mislead. A cross-section graph gives a good example. Figure 2.7 dramatizes a point of view rather than revealing the facts. A quick glance at this graph gives the impression that the level of education and training for 18 year-olds is extremely low in Greece and the United Kingdom compared with France, Belgium, Netherlands and Germany. But a closer look reveals that the scale on the axis has been stretched and percentages between zero and 40 have been chopped off the graph. Breaks in axes, like those in Figure 2.3, are a common way of stretching and compressing axes to make a graph tell a misleading story. You should always look at the numbers on the axes before looking at the main graph to avoid being misled, even if the intention of the graph is not to mislead you. Try this with graphs in newspapers and magazines to see if you can spot a misleading graph.

We have seen how graphs are used to describe economic data and relationships between variables.

Figure 2.8 Positive (Direct) Relationships

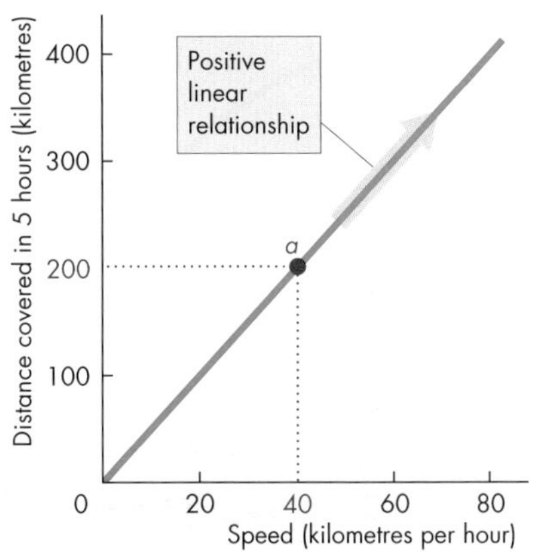

(a) Positive linear relationship

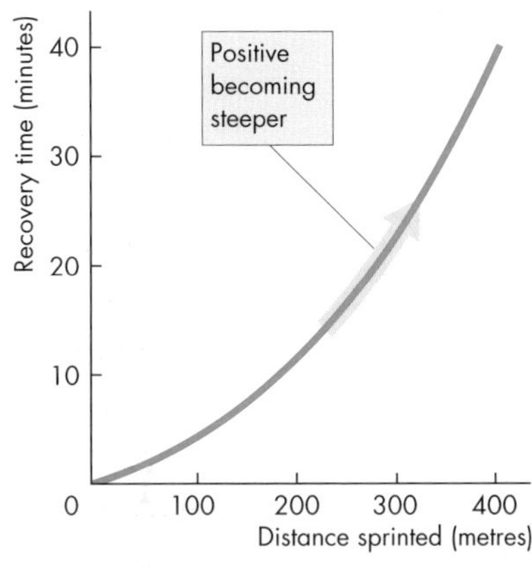

(b) Positive becoming steeper

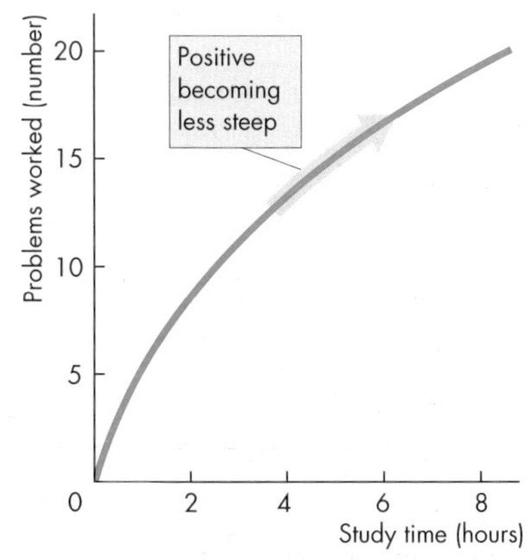

(c) Positive becoming less steep

Each part of this figure shows a positive relationship between two variables. That is, as the value of the variable measured on the *x*-axis increases, so does the value of the variable measured on the *y*-axis. Part (a) shows a linear relationship – a relationship whose slope is constant as we move along the curve. Part (b) shows a positive relationship whose slope becomes steeper as we move along the curve away from the origin. It is a positive relationship with an increasing slope. Part (c) shows a positive relationship whose slope becomes flatter as we move away from the origin. It is a positive relationship with a decreasing slope.

Now we are going to see how economists use graphs in a more abstract way. Diagrams and graphs are often used by economists to explain economic models.

Graphs Used in Economic Models

The graphs used in economics are not always designed to show data. Graphs are often used to show the relationships among the variables in an economic model. Economic models are simplified descriptions of how economies, markets, firms and individuals behave. You will be learning about some of these models in the chapters that follow. Although you will encounter many different kinds of graph in economic models, there are many similarities in their pattern. Once you have learned to recognize these patterns, they will instantly convey to you the meaning of a graph. The patterns to look for are:

- Variables that move in the same direction.
- Variables that move in the opposite direction.
- Variables that are unrelated.
- Variables that have a maximum or a minimum.

Let's look at these four cases.

Variables That Move in the Same Direction

Figure 2.8 shows graphs of the relationships between two variables that move in the same direction. This is called a **positive** or a **direct relationship**. Such a relationship is shown by a line that slopes upward. In the figure, there are three types of positive relationships, one shown by a straight line and two by curved lines. A relationship shown by a straight line is called a **linear relationship**. But all the lines in these three graphs are called curves. Any line on a graph – no matter whether it is straight or curved – is called a curve.

Figure 2.8(a) shows a linear relationship between the number of kilometres travelled in 5 hours and speed. A linear relationship has a constant slope. For example, point *a* shows us that we will travel 200 kilometres in 5 hours if our speed is 40 kilometres

Figure 2.9 Negative (Inverse) Relationships

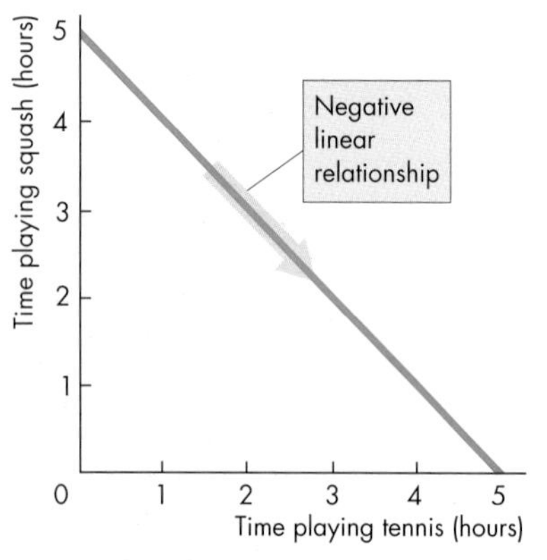

(a) Negative linear relationship

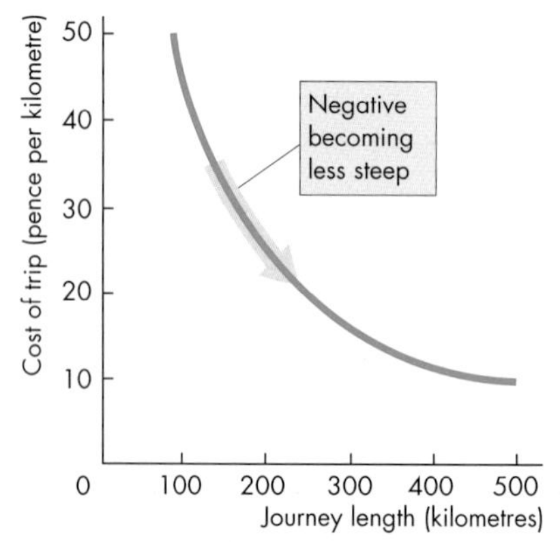

(b) Negative becoming less steep

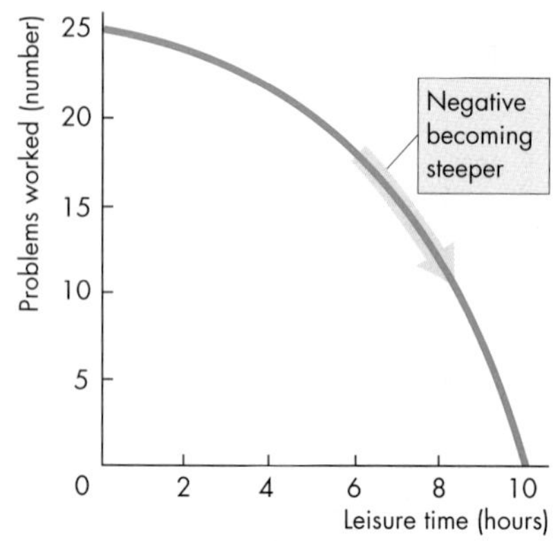

(c) Negative becoming steeper

Each part of this figure shows a negative relationship between two variables. Part (a) shows a linear relationship – a relationship whose slope is constant as we travel along the curve. Part (b) shows a negative relationship with a slope that becomes flatter as the journey length increases. Part (c) shows a negative relationship with a slope that becomes steeper as the leisure time increases.

an hour. If we double our speed to 80 kilometres an hour, we will travel 400 kilometres in 5 hours.

Part (b) shows the relationship between distance sprinted and recovery time (recovery time being measured as the time it takes the heart rate to return to normal). This relationship is upward-sloping but the slope changes. The curved line starts out with a gentle slope but then becomes steeper as we move along the curve away from the origin.

Part (c) shows the relationship between the number of problems worked by a student and the amount of study time. This relationship is also upward-sloping and the slope changes. This time the curved line starts out with a steep slope but then becomes more gentle as we move away from the origin.

Variables That Move in the Opposite Direction

Figure 2.9 shows relationships between variables that move in opposite directions. This relationship is called a **negative** or an **inverse relationship**.

Part (a) shows the relationship between the number of hours available for playing squash and the number of hours for playing tennis. One extra hour spent playing tennis means one hour less playing squash and vice versa. This relationship is negative and linear.

Part (b) shows the relationship between the cost per kilometre travelled and the length of a journey. The longer the journey, the lower is the cost per kilometre. But as the journey length increases, the cost per kilometre decreases and the fall in the cost is smaller, the longer the journey. This feature of the relationship is shown by the fact that the curve slopes downward, starting out steep at a short journey length and then becoming flatter as the journey length increases.

Part (c) shows the relationship between the amount of leisure time and the number of problems worked by a student. Increasing leisure time produces an increasingly large reduction in the number of problems worked. This relationship is a negative one that starts out with a gentle slope at a small number of leisure hours and becomes steeper as the number of leisure hours increases.

Variables That are Unrelated

There are many situations in which one variable is unrelated to another. No matter what happens to the value of one variable, the other variable remains

Figure 2.10 Variables that are Unrelated

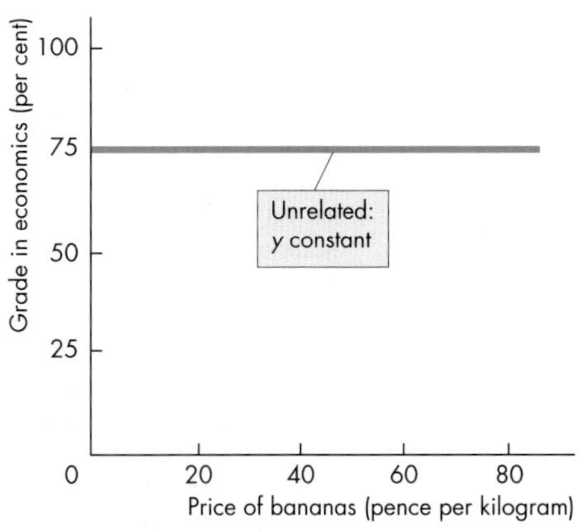

(a) Unrelated: *y* constant

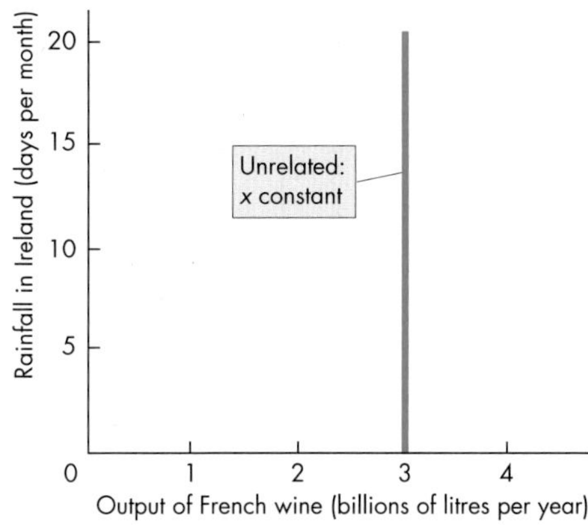

(b) Unrelated: *x* constant

This figure shows how we can graph two variables that are unrelated to each other. In part (a), a student's grade in economics is plotted at 75 per cent regardless of the price of bananas on the *x*-axis. The curve is horizontal. In part (b), the output of the vineyards of France does not vary with the rainfall in Ireland. The curve is vertical.

constant. Sometimes we want to show the independence between two variables in a graph. Figure 2.10 shows two ways of achieving this. In Figure 2.10(a), your grade in economics is shown on the y-axis against the price of bananas on the x-axis. Your grade (75 per cent in this example) is unrelated to the price of bananas. The relationship between these two variables is shown by a horizontal straight line. This line slopes neither upward nor downward. In part (b), the output of French wine is shown on the x-axis and the number of rainy days a month in Ireland is shown on the y-axis. Again, the output of French wine (3 billion litres a year in this example) is unrelated to the number of rainy days in Ireland. The relationship between these two variables is shown by a vertical straight line.

Variables That Have a Maximum and a Minimum

Many relationships in economic models have a maximum or a minimum. For example, firms try to make the maximum possible profit and to produce at the lowest possible cost. Figure 2.11 shows relationships that have a maximum or a minimum.

Part (a) shows the relationship between rainfall and wheat yield. When there is no rainfall, wheat will not grow, so the yield is zero. As the rainfall increases up to 10 days a month, the wheat yield also increases. With 10 rainy days each month, the wheat yield reaches its maximum at 40 tonnes a hectare (point a). Rain in excess of 10 days a month starts to lower the yield of wheat. If every day is rainy, the wheat suffers from a lack of sunshine and the yield falls back almost to zero. This relationship is one that starts out with a positive slope, reaches a maximum at which its slope is zero, and then moves into a range in which its slope is negative.

Part (b) shows the reverse case – a relationship that begins with a negative slope, falls to a minimum, and then becomes positive. An example of such a relationship is the petrol cost per kilometre as the speed of travel varies. At low speeds, the car is creeping along in a traffic jam. The number of kilometres per litre is low so the petrol cost per kilometre is high. At high speeds the car is travelling faster than its most efficient speed and, again, the number of kilometres per litre is low and the petrol cost per kilometre is high. At a speed of 55 kilometres per hour, the petrol cost per kilometre travelled is at its minimum (point b). This relationship is one that starts out with a negative slope, reaches a minimum at which its slope is zero, and then moves into a range in which its slope is positive.

Figures 2.8 through to 2.12 show 10 different shapes of graphs that we will encounter in economic models. In describing these graphs, we

Figure 2.11 Maximum and Minimum Points

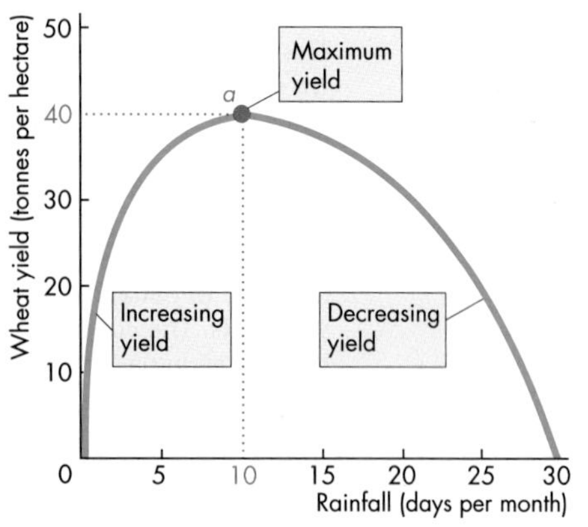

(a) Relationship with a maximum

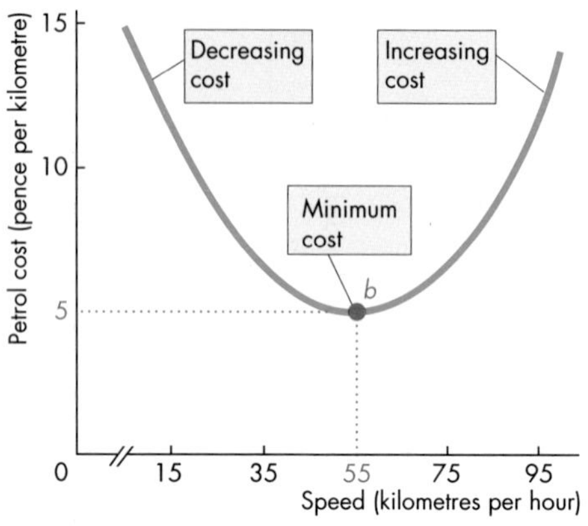

(b) Relationship with a minimum

Part (a) shows a relationship that has a maximum point, *a*. The curve has a positive slope as it rises to its maximum point, is flat at its maximum, and then has a negative slope. Part (b) shows a relationship with a minimum point, *b*. The curve has a negative slope as it falls to its minimum, is flat at its minimum, and then has a positive slope.

have talked about the slopes of curves. The concept of a slope is an intuitive one. But it is also a precise technical concept. Let's look more closely at the concept of slope.

The Slope of a Relationship

The **slope** of a relationship is the change in the value of the variable measured on the y-axis divided by the change in the value of the variable measured on the x-axis. We use the Greek letter Δ to represent 'change in'. Thus Δy means the change in the value of the variable measured on the y-axis, and Δx means the change in the value of the variable measured on the x-axis. Therefore, the slope of the relationship is:

$$\frac{\Delta y}{\Delta x}$$

If a large change in the variable measured on the y-axis (Δy) is associated with a small change in the variable measured on the x-axis (Δx), the slope is large and the curve is steep. If a small change in the variable measured on the y-axis (Δy) is associated with a large change in the variable measured on the x-axis (Δx), the slope is small and the curve is flat.

We can make the idea of slope sharper by doing some calculations.

The Slope of a Straight Line

The slope of a straight line is the same regardless of where on the line you calculate it. Thus the slope of a straight line is constant. Let's calculate the slopes of the lines in Figure 2.12. In part (a), when x increases from 2 to 6, y increases from 3 to 6. The change in x is plus 4, that is, Δx is 4. The change in y is plus 3, that is, Δy is 3. The slope of that line is:

$$\frac{\Delta y}{\Delta x} = \frac{3}{4}$$

In part (b), when x increases from 2 to 6, y decreases from 6 to 3. The change in y is minus 3, that is, Δy is –3. The change in x is plus 4, that is, Δx is 4. The slope of the curve is:

$$\frac{\Delta y}{\Delta x} = \frac{-3}{4}$$

Notice that the two slopes have the same magnitude (3/4), but the slope of the line in part (a) is positive (+3/+4) = 3/4), while that in part (b) is negative (–3/+4 = –3/4). The slope of a positive relationship is positive; the slope of a negative relationship is negative.

The Slope of a Curved Line

The slope of a curved line is not constant. It depends on where on the line we calculate it. There are two ways to calculate the slope of a curved line:

Figure 2.12 The Slope of a Straight Line

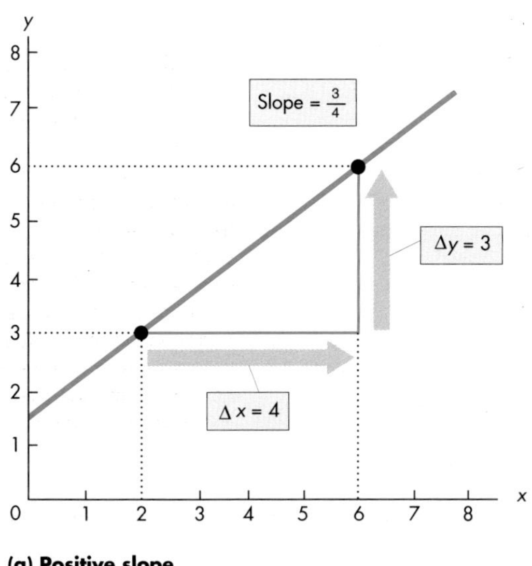

(a) Positive slope

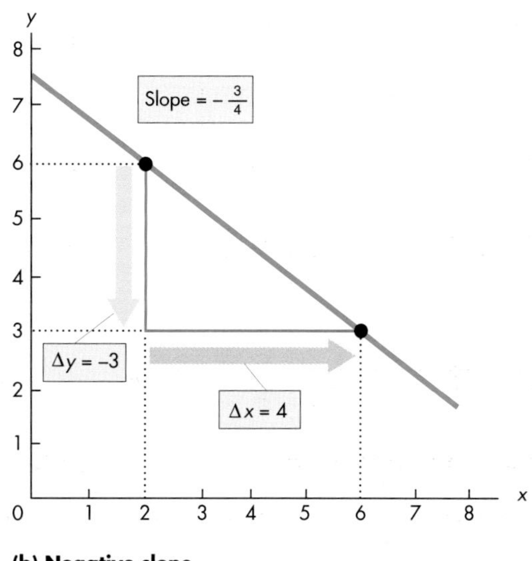

(b) Negative slope

To calculate the slope of a straight line, we divide the change in the value of the variable measured on the *y*-axis (Δy) by the change in the value of the variable measured on the *x*-axis (Δx). Part (a) shows the calculation of a positive slope. When *x* increases from 2 to 6, Δx equals 4. That change in *x* brings about an increase in *y* from 3 to 6, so Δy equals 3. The slope ($\Delta y/\Delta x$) equals 3/4. Part (b) shows the calculation of a negative slope. When *x* increases from 2 to 6, Δx equals 4. That increase in *x* brings about a decrease in *y* from 6 to 3, so Δy equals −3. The slope ($\Delta y/\Delta x$) equals −3/4.

at a point on the curve or across an arc of the curve. Let's look at them.

Slope at a Point To calculate the slope at a point on a curve, you need to construct a straight line that has the same slope as the curve at the point in question. Figure 2.13 shows how this is done. Suppose you want to calculate the slope of the curve at point a. Place a ruler on the graph so that it touches point a and no other point on the curve, then draw a straight line along the edge of the ruler. The straight red line in part (a) is this line and it is the tangent to the curve at point a. If the ruler touches the curve only at point a, then the slope of the curve at point a must be the same as the slope of the edge of the ruler. If the curve and the ruler do not have the same slope, the line along the edge of the ruler will cut the curve instead of just touching it.

Having found a straight line with the same slope as the curve at point a, you can calculate the slope of the curve at point a by calculating the slope of the straight line. Along the straight line, as x increases from 0 to 4 ($\Delta x = 4$) y increases from 2 to 5 ($\Delta y = 3$). Therefore, the slope of the line is:

$$\frac{\Delta y}{\Delta x} = \frac{-3}{4}$$

Thus the slope of the curve at point a is 3/4.

Slope Across an Arc Calculating a slope across an arc is similar to calculating an average slope. An arc of a curve is a piece of a curve. In Figure 2.14(b), we are looking at the same curve as in part (a), but instead of calculating the slope at point a, we calculate the slope across the arc from b to c. Moving along the arc from b to c, x increases from 3 to 5 and y increases from 4 to 5.5. The change in x is 2 ($\Delta x = 2$) and the change in y is 1.5 ($\Delta y = 1.5$). Therefore, the slope of the line is:

$$\frac{\Delta y}{\Delta x} = \frac{1.5}{2} = \frac{3}{4}$$

Thus the slope of the curve across the arc bc is 3/4.

Figure 2.13 The Slope of a Curve

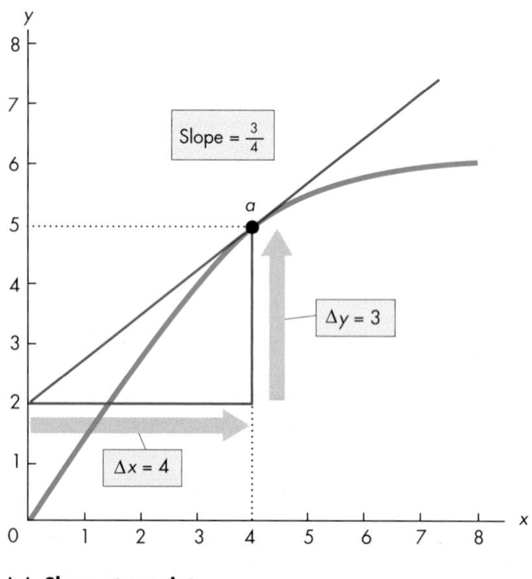

(a) Slope at a point

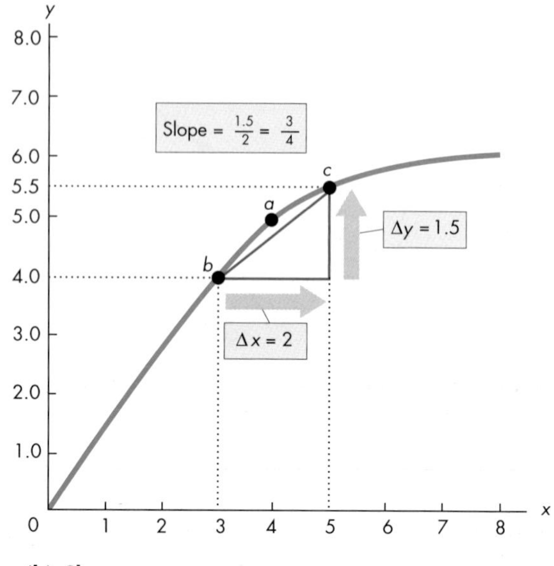

(b) Slope across an arc

To calculate the slope of the curve at point *a*, draw the red line that just touches the curve at *a* – the tangent. The slope of this straight line is calculated by dividing the change in *y* by the change in *x* along the line. When *x* increases from 0 to 4, Δ*x* equals 4. That change in *x* is associated with an increase in *y* from 2 to 5, so Δ*y* equals 3. The slope of the red line is 3/4. So the slope of the curve at point *a* is 3/4.

To calculate the average slope of the curve along the arc *bc*, draw a straight line from *b* to *c* in part (b). The slope of the line *bc* is calculated by dividing the change in *y* by the change in *x*. In moving from *b* to *c*, Δ*x* equals 2, and Δ*y* equals 1.5. The slope of the line *bc* is 1.5 divided by 2, or 3/4. So the slope of the curve across the arc *bc* is 3/4.

In this particular example, the slope of the arc *bc* is identical to the slope of the curve at point *a* in part (a). But the calculation of the slope of a curve does not always work out so neatly. You might have some fun constructing counter-examples. If you visit the Parkin, Powell and Matthews Web site you can find out how calculus is used to measure the slope of an arc in an algebraic example.

Graphing Relationships Among More Than Two Variables

We have seen that we can graph a single variable as a point on a straight line and we can graph the relationship between two variables as a point formed by the x and y coordinates in a two-dimensional graph. You may be thinking that although a two-dimensional graph is informative, most of the things in which you are likely to be interested involve relationships among many variables, not just two.

For example, the amount of cola consumed depends on the price of a can of cola and the temperature. If a can of cola is expensive and the temperature is low, people drink much less cola than when a can of cola is inexpensive and the temperature is high. For any given price of a can of cola, the quantity consumed varies with the temperature, and for any given temperature, the quantity of cola consumed varies with its price.

The graph in Figure 2.14 tells this more complicated story. Figure 2.14 shows the relationship among three variables. The table shows the number of cans of cola consumed each day at various temperatures and prices for cans of cola.

Figure 2.14 Graphing a Relationship Among Three Variables

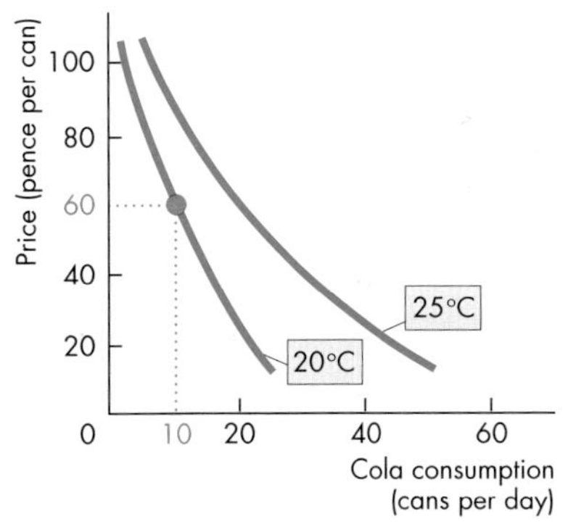

(a) Price and consumption at a given temperature

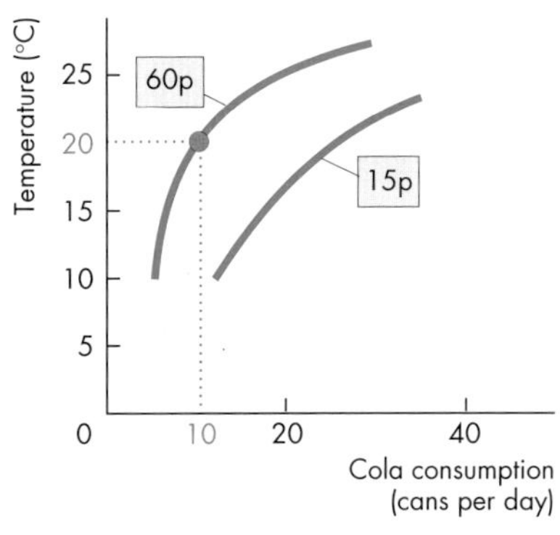

(b) Temperature and consumption at a given price

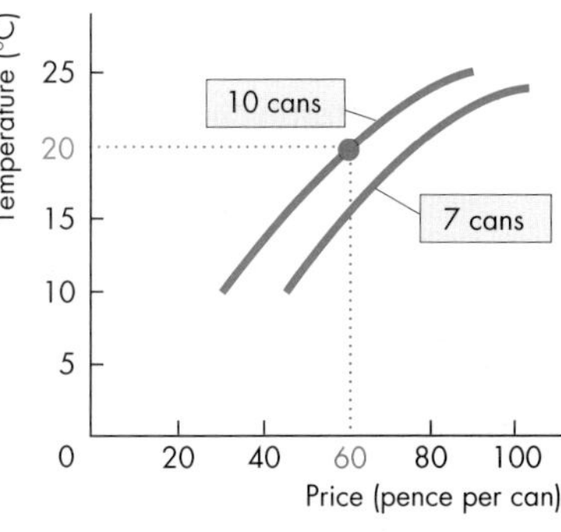

(c) Temperature and price at a given consumption

Price (pence per can)	Cola consumption (cans per day)			
	10 °C	15 °C	20 °C	25 °C
15	12	18	25	50
30	10	12	18	37
45	7	10	13	27
60	5	7	10	20
75	3	5	7	14
90	2	3	5	10
105	1	2	3	6

The quantity of cola consumed depends on its price and the temperature. The table gives some hypothetical numbers that tell us how many cans of cola are consumed each day at different prices and different temperatures. For example, if the price is 30 pence per can and the temperature is 10 °C, 10 cans of cola are consumed. In order to graph a relationship among three variables, the value of one variable is held constant. Part (a) shows the relationship between price and consumption, holding temperature constant. One curve holds temperature at 25 °C and the other at 20 °C. Part (b) shows the relationship between temperature and consumption, holding price constant. One curve holds the price at 60 pence and the other at 15 pence. Part (c) shows the relationship between temperature and price, holding consumption constant. One curve holds consumption at 10 cans and the other at 7 cans.

To graph a relationship that involves more than two variables, we consider what happens if all but two of the variables are held constant. When we hold other things constant, we are using the *ceteris paribus* assumption that is described in Chapter 1, p. 14. An example is shown in Figure 2.14(a). There, you can see what happens to the quantity of cola consumed when the price of a can varies while the temperature is held constant. The line labelled 20 °C shows the relationship between cola consumption and the price of a can of cola when the temperature stays at 20 °C. The numbers used to plot this line are those in the third column of the table in Figure 2.14. For example, when the temperature is 20 °C, 10 cans are consumed when the price is 60 pence and 18 cans are consumed when the price is 30 pence. The curve labelled 25 °C shows the consumption of cola when the price varies and the temperature is 25 °C.

We can also show the relationship between cola consumption and temperature while holding the price of cola constant, as shown in Figure 2.14(b). The curve labelled 60 pence shows how the consumption of cola varies with the temperature when cola costs 60 pence, and a second curve shows the relationship when cola costs 15 pence. For example, at 60 pence a can, 10 cans are consumed when the temperature is 20 °C and 20 cans when the temperature is 25 °C.

Figure 2.14(c) shows the combinations of temperature and price that result in a constant consumption of cola. One curve shows the combination that results in 10 cans a day being consumed, and the other shows the combination that results in 7 cans a day being consumed. A high price and a high temperature lead to the same consumption as a lower price and a lower temperature. For example, 10 cans are consumed at 20 °C and 60 pence per can and at 25 °C and 90 pence per can.

The three graphs in Figure 2.14 tell a story which has taken us more than 500 words to explain. Once you have learned to read graphs, you too will be able to see this much information at a glance.

With what you have learned about graphs, you can move forward with your study of economics. There are no graphs in this book that are more complicated than those that have been explained here.

Summary

Key Points

Graphing Data (pp. 24–28)

- A scatter diagram plots the value of one economic variable against the value of another and reveals whether or not there is a relationship between the two variables. If there is a relationship, the graph reveals its nature.
- A time-series graph shows the trend of economic variables over time, and the level, direction of change and speed of change of each variable.
- A cross-section graph shows how a variable changes across the members of a population.
- A graph can mislead if its scale is stretched (or squeezed) to exaggerate (or understate) a variation.

Graphs Used in Economic Models (pp. 29–32)

- Graphs are used to show relationships among variables in economic models.
- Relationships can be positive (an upward-sloping curve), negative (a downward-sloping curve), unrelated (a horizontal or vertical curve), positive and then negative (a maximum), and negative and then positive (a minimum).

The Slope of a Relationship (pp. 32–34)

- The slope of a relationship is calculated as the change in the value of the variable measured on the y-axis divided by the change in the value of the variable measured on the x-axis – $\Delta y/\Delta x$.
- A straight line has a constant slope, but a curved line has a varying slope.
- To calculate the slope of a curved line, we calculate the slope at a point or across an arc.

Graphing Relationships Among More Than Two Variables (pp. 34–36)

- To graph a relationship among more than two variables, we hold constant the values of all the variables except two.
- We then plot the value of one of the variables against the value of another.

Key Figures

Key Terms

Cross-section graph, 28
Direct relationship, 29
Inverse relationship, 30
Linear relationship, 29
Negative relationship, 30
Positive relationship, 29
Scatter diagram, 24
Slope, 32
Time-series graph, 26
Trend, 26

Review Questions

1 What are the three types of graph used to show economic data?

2 Give an example of a scatter diagram.

3 Give an example of a time-series graph.

4 Give an example of a cross-section graph.

5 List three things that a time-series graph shows quickly and easily.

6 What do we mean by trend?

7 How can a graph mislead?

8 Draw some graphs to show the relationships between two variables:

a That move in the same direction.
b That move in opposite directions.
c That have a maximum.
d That have a minimum.

9 Which of the relationships in Question 8 is a positive relationship and which is a negative relationship?

10 What is the definition of the slope of a curve?

11 What are the two ways of calculating the slope of a curved line?

12 How do we graph relationships among more than two variables?

Problems

1 The unemployment rate in the United Kingdom between 1986 and 1996 was as follows:

Year	Unemployment rate (per cent per year)
1986	11.1
1987	10.0
1988	8.1
1989	6.3
1990	5.8
1991	8.1
1992	9.8
1993	10.3
1994	9.4
1995	8.1
1996	7.4

Draw a time-series graph of these data and use your graph to answer the following questions:

a In which year was unemployment highest?
b In which year was unemployment lowest?
c In which years did unemployment increase?
d In which years did unemployment decrease?
e In which year did unemployment increase most?
f In which year did unemployment decrease most?
g What have been the main trends in unemployment?

2 The UK government's budget deficit as a percentage of GDP between 1986 and 1996 was as follows:

Year	budget deficit (percentage of GDP)
1986	2.2
1987	0.4
1988	–1.8
1989	–0.5
1990	0.6
1991	3.4
1992	7.3
1993	7.9
1994	5.5
1995	5.5
1996	5.9

Use these data together with those in Problem 1 to draw a scatter diagram showing the relationship between unemployment and the deficit. Then use your graph to determine whether a relationship exists between unemployment and the deficit and whether it is positive or negative.

3 Use the following information on the relationship between two variables x and y.

x	0	1	2	3	4	5	6	7	8
y	0	1	4	9	16	25	36	49	64

a Draw a scatter diagram of the relationship between variables x and y.
a Is the relationship between x and y positive or negative?
b Does the slope of the relationship rise or fall as the value of x rises?

4 Using the data in Problem 3:

a Calculate the slope of the relationship between x and y when x equals 4.
b Calculate the slope of the arc when x rises from 3 to 4.
c Calculate the slope of the arc when x rises from 4 to 5.
d Calculate the slope of the arc when x rises from 3 to 5.
e What do you notice that is interesting about your answers to (b), (c) and (d), compared with your answer to (a)?

5 Calculate the slopes of the following two relationships between two variables x and y:

a

x	0	2	4	6	8	10
y	20	16	12	8	4	0

b

x	0	2	4	6	8	10
y	0	8	16	24	32	40

6 Draw a graph showing the following relationship between two variables x and y:

x	0	1	2	3	4	5	6	7	8	9
y	0	2	4	6	8	10	8	6	4	2

a Is the slope positive or negative when x is less than 5?
b Is the slope positive or negative when x is greater than 5?
c What is the slope of this relationship when x equals 5?
d Is y at a maximum or at a minimum when x equals 5?

7 Draw a graph showing the following relationship between two variables x and y:

x	0	1	2	3	4	5	6	7	8	9
y	10	8	6	4	2	0	2	4	6	8

a Is the slope positive or negative when x is less than 5?
b Is the slope positive or negative when x is greater than 5?
c What is the slope of this relationship when x equals 5?
d Is y at a maximum or at a minimum when x equals 5?

8 Plot the two variables y_1 and y_2 against variable x on one graph. The scale for variable x should be on the x axis. The scales for variables y_1 and y_2 should be on the left and right hands of the y axis as in the example of Figure 2.5.

x	y_1	y_2
1	5	45
2	10	40
3	15	35
4	20	30
5	25	25
6	30	20
7	35	15
8	40	10
9	45	5
10	50	0

a What is the slope of variable y_1?
b What is the slope of variable y_2?
c What is the value of x where the two lines representing y_1 and y_2 cross?
d What is the value of y_1 and y_2 at the point where the two lines cross?

9 At each value of x, add 5 to the corresponding value of y_2, and call this new variable y_3.

a Add your new variable y_3 to the graph you have drawn for Problem 7.
b What is the slope of your new variable y_3?
c What is the value of x where the lines representing y_3 and y_1 cross?

d What is the value of y_2 and y_3 at the point where the two lines cross?

e What is the value of x where the lines representing y_3 and y_1 cross?

f Look at your graph and describe in words the effect of adding 5 to each value of y_2?

10 The following table gives data on the price of a balloon ride, the temperature, and the number of rides taken per day.

Price (£ per person per ride)	Balloon rides (number per day at different temperatures)		
	18 °C	21 °C	25 °C
5.00	32	40	50
10.00	27	32	40
15.00	18	27	32
20.00	10	18	27

Draw graphs that show the relationship among

a The price and the number of rides taken.

b The number of rides taken and temperature, holding price constant.

c The temperature and price, holding the number of rides taken constant.

11 Use the link on the Parkin, Powell and Matthews Web site and find the Retail Price Index (RPI) for the latest 12 months.

a Make a graph of the RPI over the lastest 12 months.

b During the most recent month, is the RPI rising or falling?

c During the most recent month, is the rate of rise or fall increasing or decreasing?

12 Use the link on the Parkin, Powell and Matthews Web site and find the monthly unemployment rate for the latest 12 months.

a Graph the unemployment rate over the lastest 12 months.

b During the most recent month, is unemployment rising or falling?

c Is the rate of rise or fall increasing or decreasing?

W http://www.econ100.com

Production, Growth and Trade

After studying this chapter you will be able to:

- Explain the fundamental economic problem
- Define the production possibility frontier
- Define production efficiency
- Calculate opportunity cost
- Explain how economic growth expands production possibilities
- Explain how and why specialization and trade expand production possibilities

Making the Most of It

We live in a style that surprises our grandparents and would have astonished our great grandparents. We live in bigger homes, eat more, grow taller and are even born larger than they were. Video games, mobile phones, genetic engineering, personal computers and microwave ovens did not exist 20 years ago. But today it is hard to imagine life without them. Economic growth has made us richer than our grandparents. But it has not liberated us from scarcity. Why not? Why, despite our immense wealth, must we still make choices and face costs? Why are there no 'free lunches'? ◆ We see an incredible amount of specialization and exchange in the world. Each one of us specializes in a particular job – as a lawyer, a factory worker, a parent. We have become so specialized that one farm worker can feed 100 people. Less than one in four of the EU workforce is employed in manufacturing. More than half of the workforce is employed in agriculture, wholesale and retail trade, banking and finance, government and other services. Why do we specialize? How do we benefit from specialization and trade? ◆ Over many centuries, institutions and social arrangements have evolved that we take for granted. One of them is markets. Another is property rights and a political and legal system that protects them. Yet another is money. Why have these arrangements evolved? How do they extend our ability to specialize and increase production?

◆ ◆ ◆ ◆ These are the questions that we tackle in this chapter. We begin with the core problems of scarcity and choice and the concept of the production possibility frontier. We use these to measure opportunity cost and describe production efficiency. We then discover how production is increased by specialization, trade and social institutions in market economies.

Resources and Wants

We begin our study of economics by looking at the problem of choice when we have limited resources but unlimited wants. The combination of limited resources and unlimited wants create **scarcity** because the resources available cannot meet all our wants. *Scarcity* is everywhere. Most of us face scarcity because we cannot afford what we would like. But even the fabulously rich face scarcity when they cannot buy the happiness and health they seek.

'Well dear, if the extra cost of food is offset by the income tax relief and what we save in petrol by not having a car pays the extra on the house, what's become of the money we were going to save by not smoking?'

Drawing by Arthur Horner, 1952 *News Chronicle*.

Economics is the study of the choices people make when facing scarcity. Choosing more of one thing always means having less of something else. There is no such thing as a free lunch as the couple in the cartoon are finding out. The cartoon vividly shows the central idea in economics: that every choice involves giving up something. The **fundamental economic problem** is how to use our limited resources to produce and consume the things that we value the most. So let's take a closer look at our limited resources and unlimited wants.

Limited Resources

The **limited resources** which are used to produce goods and services are called **factors of production**. There are four types of limited resources:

1. Land.
2. Labour.
3. Capital.
4. Entrepreneurship.

Land is all the gifts of nature. The term includes the air, the water, the land surface, as well as the minerals that lie beneath the surface.

Labour is the time and effort that people devote to producing goods and services. It includes the physical and mental activities of the many thousands of people who make cars and cola, biscuits and glue, wallpaper and watering cans.

Capital is all the resources which have been produced for use in the production of other goods and services. *Physical capital* includes the motorway system, ancient buildings and modern homes, dams and power stations, airports and jumbo jets, car and shirt factories, cinemas and shopping centres. *Human capital* is the skill and knowledge of people, which arise from their education and on-the-job training. *Environmental capital* includes elements of land which are destroyed in the production process, the biodiversity among species and the ability of the environment to absorb waste from production.

Entrepreneurship is the resource that organizes land, labour and capital. Entrepreneurs are people who think up ideas about what, how, when and where to produce. They are the people who develop businesses and bear the risks of business failure. We have separated entrepreneurship from human capital because it is special. Everyone has some human capital, but only a few people are willing or able to be entrepreneurs.

Unlimited Wants

Our wants are limited only by our imagination and desires. They are unlimited because as soon as we have satisified our wants, we imagine or desire new things. Some of our wants are quite basic. Most of us want food and drink, decent clothing and housing, good education and health care, good careers and a stable income. When these wants affect our ability to survive or our basic well-being, we call them necessities. But let's face it, many of our wants are luxuries even though we think of them as needs.

Perhaps you want the latest mobile phone, internet technology or digital television. Perhaps you want the latest Tomb Raider video game or the latest fashion fabric in your clothes. We cannot even imagine some of the things we will want in the future. We were satisfied with a two second response delay on our 486 megahertz PC five years ago, but now it would drive us mad. Did anyone think that space travel was a realistic possibility one hundred years ago. Now you may hope to go to the moon as a retirement holiday. Who can say what your grandchildren will want when you have retired?

Our wants will always exceed our limited resource. This scarcity forces us to make choices. We must rank our wants and decide which ones to satisfy first. When we choose to satisfy one want, we leave another unsatisfied.

Review

- Economics is the study of the choices people make to cope with scarcity.
- The economic problem is how to use our limited resources to produce the things we want most.
- Our limited resources are land, labour, capital and entrepreneurship.
- We must choose to use our limited resources to satisfy those wants that we rank most highly.

We can now begin our study of the choices people make by looking at production possibilities and the fundamental implication of the economic problem – unsatisfied wants or opportunity cost.

Resources, Production Possibilities and Opportunity Cost

Every day, a huge variety of goods and services are produced by 235 million people across the European Union. *Production* is the process of converting our limited resources into the goods and services we want, using available technologies. These technologies are limited only by our knowledge – our human capital and entrepreneurship – and by our other resources. The limit of our production potential is described by the production possibility frontier.

The **production possibility frontier** (*PPF*) is the boundary between those combinations of goods and services that can be produced and those combinations that cannot be produced. To study the production possibility frontier, we will consider just two goods at a time. In focusing on two goods, we use the *ceteris paribus* assumption. This means we hold the quantities produced of all the other goods constant. We use this assumption to create a *model* in which everything remains the same except the production of the two goods that we are (currently) considering. Let's begin by looking at the production possibility frontier for two goods that you probably buy, textbooks and video games like Tomb Raider.

Production Possibility Frontier

The production possibility frontier for books and video games shows the limits to the production of these two goods, given the total resources available to produce them. Figure 3.1 shows this production possibility curve. The table lists some combinations of the quantities of books and video games in units of one thousand that can be produced given the resources available. Figure 3.1 graphs these combinations. The quantity of video games produced is shown on the x-axis and the quantity of books produced is shown on the y-axis.

Because the *PPF* shows the *limits* to production, our economy cannot produce the combination of points outside the frontier. These are points that describe what we want but cannot have. We can only produce those combinations of books and video games shown *on* or *inside* the PPF.

Suppose that in a year, 4,000 new games and 2,000 new books are produced – point *e* in Figure 3.1

Figure 3.1 The Production Possibility Frontier for Books and Video Games

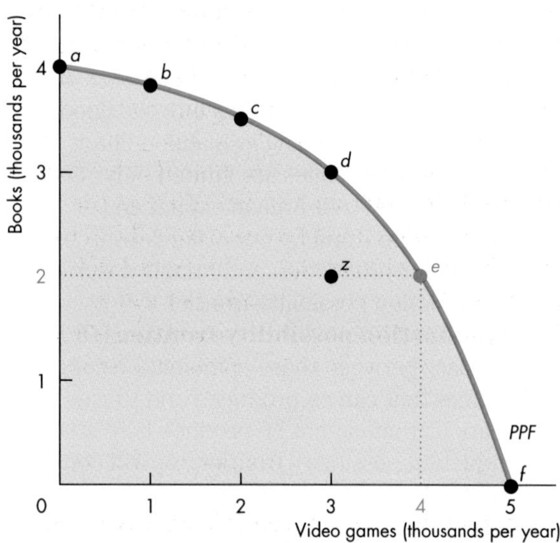

The figure shows six points on the production possibility frontier for books and video games. Point *a* tells us that if we produce no games, the maximum quantity of books we can produce is four thousand a year. The line passing through points *a, b, c, d, e,* and *f* is the production possibility frontier (*PPF*). It separates the attainable from the unattainable. We can produce at any point inside the orange area or on the frontier. Points outside the frontier are unattainable. Points inside the frontier such as point *z* are inefficient because it is possible to use the available resources to produce more of either or both goods.

and possibility *e* in the table. The figure shows other production possibilities. For example, if we want a better educated population we might stop producing games and put all the creative people who devise them and all the programmers, production and marketing staff, computers, buildings and other resources used to produce games into the publishing industry to produce books. This case is shown as point *a* in the figure. The quantity of books produced increases to 4,000 a year and games' production dries up. Alternatively, we might close down the publishing industry and switch the resources into producing games. This case is shown as possibility *f*. The quantity of books produced decreases to zero, and the quantity of games produced increases to 5,000 a year.

Production Efficiency

Production efficiency is achieved when it is not possible to produce more of one good without producing less of some other good. Efficiency occurs only at points on the production possibility frontier. Possible production points *inside* the frontier, such as point *z*, are *inefficient*. They are points at which resources are being either wasted or misallocated.

Resources are wasted when they are idle but could be working. For example, a printing system is wasteful if it is running just 8 hours a day when it could be running for 24 hours a day. Resources are misallocated when they are assigned to inappropriate tasks. For example, a print worker might be assigned to designing video games, and a video game designer might be assigned to printing books. We could get more books and more video games if we reassigned these same workers to the jobs which most closely match their skills.

If we produce at an inefficient point such as *z*, our resources could be more efficiently used to produce both more books and more video games. But if we are producing at a point like *e* on the *PPF*, we can only produce more of one good if we produce less of the other. We face a trade-off.

Trade-offs

At all points along the *PPF*, there is a trade-off – we must give up something to get something else. On the *PPF* in Figure 3.1, we must give up books to get more video games, or give up video games to get more books.

The lesson we've learned from this example is a fundamental one that applies to every imaginable real-world situation. At any given point in time, the world has a fixed amount of labour, land and capital. By using the available technologies, these resources can be employed to produce goods and services. But there is a limit to what they can produce that defines a boundary between what is attainable and what is not attainable. This boundary is the real-world economy's production possiblity frontier which defines the trade-offs we must make. On the real world *PPF*, producing more of any one good or service requires producing less of some other goods or services.

A prime minister who promises better welfare and better education must at the same time, to be credible, promise either cuts in budget spending or tax increases. Higher taxes mean less money left over for holidays and other consumption goods and services. The trade-off is between better welfare and educational services and less of other goods and services. On a smaller scale but equally important, each time you decide to rent a video you decide not to use your limited income to buy cola, or pizzas, or some other good. The trade-off is renting one more video or having less pizza and cola. All trade-offs involve a cost – an opportunity cost. Let's explore this idea of opportunity costs more closely.

Opportunity Cost

The **opportunity cost** of an action is the best alternative foregone. Of all the things you choose not to do – the alternatives foregone – the best one is the opportunity cost of the action you choose. The concept of opportunity cost can be made more precise by using the production possibility frontier. Along the *PPF* in Figure 3.1, there are only two goods. If we want more of one good there is only one alternative foregone, the other good. Given the current resources and technology, we can produce more books and less video games. Thus the opportunity cost of producing an additional book is the quantity of video games foregone. Similarly, the opportunity cost of producing additional video games is the quantity of books foregone.

For example, at point *c* in Figure 3.1, we produce more books and fewer video games that we do at point *d*. If we choose point *d* over point *c*, the additional 1 unit of video games (measured in thousands) *costs* 0.5 books (measured in thousands). The opportunity cost of 1 video game is half a book.

We can also work out the opportunity cost of choosing point *e* over point *d* in Figure 3.1. If we move from point *d* to point *e*, the quantity of video games increases by one unit and the quantity of books falls by one unit. The additional 1 unit of video games costs 1 unit of books. The opportunity cost of 1 video game is 1 book.

Opportunity Cost is a Ratio

The opportunity cost of producing one additional unit of a good is a ratio. It is the decrease in the quantity produced of one good divided by the increase in the quantity produced of another good as we move along the production possibility frontier.

Because opportunity cost is a ratio, the opportunity cost of producing good *X* (the quantity of units of good *Y* foregone) is always equal to the inverse of the opportunity cost of producing good *Y* (the number of units of good *X* foregone). Let's check this proposition by returning once more to Figure 3.1 and the movement from point *e* to point *f*. To increase the production of video games from 4,000 to 5,000, an increase of 1,000, the quantity of books must decrease from 2,000 to zero. The opportunity cost of the extra 1,000 games is 2,000 books, or 2 books per game. So, the opportunity cost of 1 book is 0.5 games and the opportunity cost of 1 game is 2 books ($1/0.5 = 2$).

Increasing Opportunity Cost

The opportunity cost of a book increases as the quanity of video games produced increases. Also the opportunity cost of video games increases as the number of books produced increases. This is reflected in the shape of the *PPF* in Figure 3.1, which is bowed outward.

When a large quantity of books and a small quantity of video games are produced – between points *a* and *d* – the *PPF* has a gentle slope. When a large quantity of games and a small quantity of books are produced – between points *e* and *f* – the *PPF* is steep. So the whole frontier bows outward.

The shape of the *PPF* in Figure 3.1 is a reflection of the fact that we assume that not all resources are equally productive in all activities. Game inventors and programmers can work on books, so if they switch from making games to producing books – moving along the frontier from *f* to *a* – the production of books increases. But these people are not as good at producing books as the original publishing industry workers. So for a small increase in the quantity of books produced, the production of games falls a lot.

Similarly, publishing industry workers can produce video games, but they are not as good at this activity as the people currently making games. So when publishing industry workers switch to producing games, the quantity of games produced increases by only a small amount and the quantity of books produced falls a lot. The more we try to produce either good, the less productive are the additional resources we use to produce that good and the larger is the opportunity cost of producing a unit of that good.

Increasing Costs are Everywhere

Increasing opportunity cost and the bowed-out production possibility frontier are two different ways of expressing the same idea: resources are not equally productive in all activities. Most production activities that you could think of will involve increasing opportunity costs. Almost all the available labour, land and capital is relatively more productive in some activities than in others.

For example, some people are creative and good at making entertaining movies while others are well-coordinated and good at performing challenging physical tasks. Some land is fertile and good for farming while other land is rocky and good for building shopping centres. Most capital (tools, machines and buildings) are custom-designed to do a small range of jobs. For example, doctors and nurses, CT scanners and operating theatres in hospitals, are not much use if we want to produce more food. If we shift our resources away from health care and into farming, we must use more doctors and nurses as farmers and more hospitals and hospital equipment as dairy farms. The decrease in health care services is large but the increase in dairy production is relatively small. So the opportunity cost of dairy produce rises.

Whilst there may be a few occasions when land, labour and capital are equally productive in different uses, it is usually the case that limited resources must be assigned to tasks for which they are an increasingly poor match. Increasing opportunity costs are a fact of life, they are everywhere. *Reading Between the Lines* on pp. 62–63 explores the opportunity costs of a university degree in terms of foregone consumption and earnings.

Review

- The production possibility frontier (*PPF*) is the boundary between attainable and unattainable levels of production.
- Points on the *PPF* are efficient, and points inside it are inefficient.
- Choosing between points on the *PPF* involves a trade-off of one good for another.
- Every trade-off involves an opportunity cost – the highest valued alternative foregone.
- As we move along the *PPF* and produce more of one good, the opportunity cost of a unit of that good increases.

We have seen that production possibilities are limited by the production possibility frontier and that production at that point on the *PPF* is efficient. There are lots of efficient combinations of production along the *PPF*, so which one is best? How can we choose between them? We can use our idea of rising opportunity cost to show that there is one point on the *PPF* that is better than all the rest – the one we value most highly.

Efficient Choice

We now know that all production of goods and services involves choice and opportunity cost. So what is the best combination to choose? What is the most **efficient choice**? How do we know if we should spend more on health care and less on building roads? How do we know whether we should expand production of digital television services or terrestrial cable television services? These are very important questions. We can illustrate the answer by using a much simpler example.

Let's use our example of books and video games again. How do we decide how many books and how many video games to produce? We know that all the combinations along the *PPF* are produced efficiently, so which combination along the *PPF* should we choose? We decide by calculating and comparing two numbers:

1 Marginal cost.

2 Marginal benefit.

Marginal Cost

Marginal cost is the opportunity cost of producing one more unit of a good or service. We already know how to calculate opportunity cost as we move along the production possibility frontier. The marginal cost of an additional unit of video games is just of the opportunity cost of the additional game. As we move along the *PPF*, the opportunity cost of the additional game is the quantity of books that we must give up to get one more unit of video games.

Figure 3.2 illustrates the opportunity cost and the marginal cost of video games. If all the available resources are used to produce books, 4 units of books (measured in thousands) and no video games are produced each year. If we now produce 1 unit of video games (measured in thousands) we move from *a* to *b* in Figure 3.2(a) and the quantity of books decreases by 0.2 units. The opportunity cost of the first unit of video games is 0.2 units of books.

If we now decide to produce another unit of video games we move from *b* to *c*, and the quantity of books decreases by 0.3 units of books a year. The second unit of video games costs 0.3 units of books. You can carry on and calculate the opportunity cost of increasing video game production to 3, 4 and finally 5 units. Figure 3.2(a) shows these opportunity costs as a series of steps. The steps – the opportunity costs – get bigger as we produce each additional unit of video games each year.

In Figure 3.2(b), the line labelled *MC* shows the marginal cost of producing video games in terms of the number of books foregone. The marginal cost of each unit of video games (in thousands) is just the opportunity cost of producing that unit. So we plot the marginal cost of each unit of video games in Figure 3.2(b) from the height of the steps in Figure 3.2(a). The marginal cost of each unit of video games increases so the marginal cost of video games slopes upward.

To work out our most efficient choice, we need to compare the marginal cost with the marginal benefit of producing video games. Let's look at marginal benefit.

Marginal Benefit

The **marginal benefit** is the benefit that people receive from consuming one more unit of a good or service. The marginal benefit from a good or service is measured by the maximum amount that a person is willing to pay for that extra unit. In general, the more we get of any good or service, the smaller is the marginal benefit that we get from it – so marginal benefit decreases.

To understand why marginal benefit decreases think about your own consumption of video games. When video games were first available, they were

Figure 3.2 Opportunity Cost and Marginal Cost

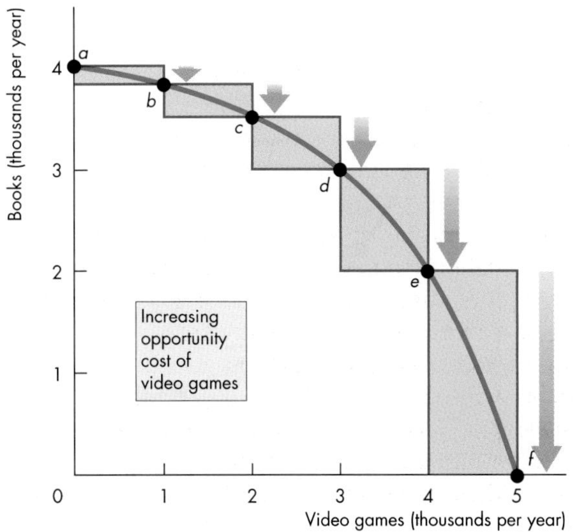

(a) Opportunity cost of video games

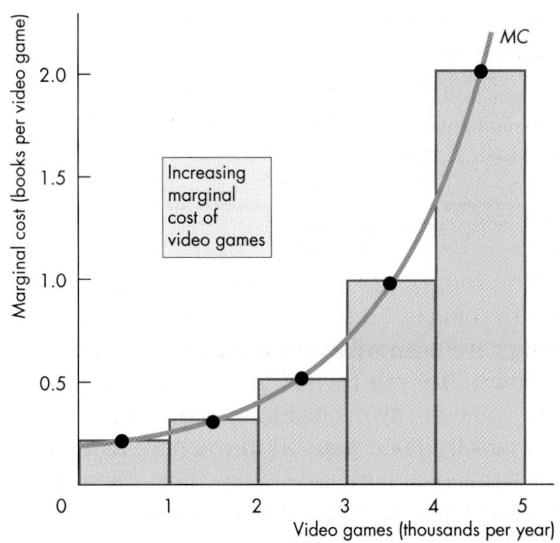

(b) Marginal cost

Opportunity cost is measured along the *PPF* in part (a). If the production of games increases from zero to one thousand, the opportunity cost of the first one thousand games is 200 books. If the production of games increases from one thousand to two thousand, the opportunity cost of the second one thousand games is 200 books. The opportunity cost of video games increases as the production of video games increases. Marginal cost is the opportunity cost of producing one more unit. Part (b) shows the marginal cost of video games as the *MC* curve.

Figure 3.3 Marginal Benefit

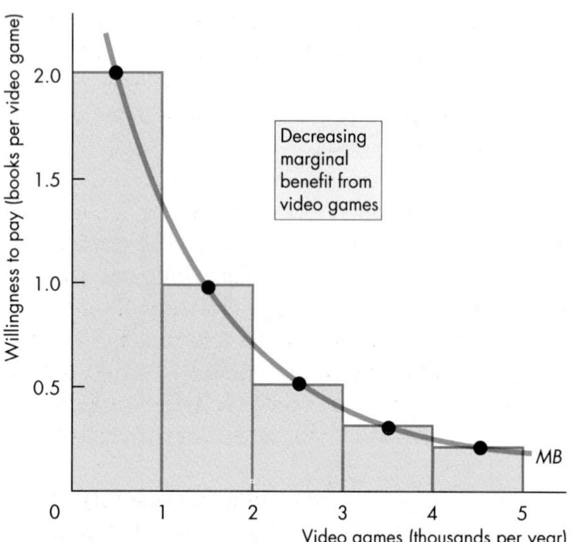

The fewer the number of video games available, the more books people are willing to give up to get an additional game. If only one unit of games (in thousands) is available a year, people are willing to pay two units of books for an additional game. But if four units of games are available, people will only pay 0.2 books for an additional game. Marginal benefit decreases as the quantity available increases.

hard to come by and everyone wanted them. You would have been willing to pay a high price for one to show off to your friends. As video games became more common, everyone began collecting them and their novelty value wore off. If you have more video games than you have time to use them, then you would be willing to pay very little for another one.

Usually we think of how much we are willing to pay in terms of prices. But you have just been learning about cost as an opportunity cost – an alternative foregone. You can also think about prices or willingness to pay in this way. The price you are willing to pay is not measured as money but in terms of the goods and services you could have bought with that money.

We can see how this works by continuing with our example of video games and books. The marginal benefit of a video game is measured by the number of books people are willing to give up to get the video game. This amount decreases as the quantity of video games that is available increases. The line labelled *MB* in Figure 3.3 shows the marginal benefit of video games. People are willing to pay 2 units of books for the first unit of video games, but only 1 unit of books for the second unit of video games. As the quantity of video games increases, the amount people are willing to pay falls. People are only willing to pay 0.2 units of books for the fifth unit of video games.

The marginal benefit and the marginal cost of a unit of video games are both measured in terms of books, but they are not the same. The marginal cost is the opportunity cost of an additional unit of video games – or the amount of books people *must give up* to get that unit. The marginal benefit is the value people place on an additional unit of video games – is the amount of books people are *willing to give* up to get that unit.

You now know how to calculate marginal cost and marginal benefit. Let's now use these concepts to find out how many video games to produce, and the most efficient choice of video games and books.

Efficient Choice

Efficient choice is when we produce the goods and services that we value most highly – when we are using our resources efficiently. We use our resources most efficiently when we cannot produce more of anything without giving up something that we value even more highly. It's easy to see where the most efficient choice is if we choose at the *margin*. Choosing at the margin means comparing marginal cost and marginal benefit for each unit we produce.

There is a simple set of rules to help us find the most efficient choice when we choose at the margin. At any level of production, if the marginal benefit is higher than the marginal cost, we increase production of that good or service. If the marginal benefit is lower than the marginal cost, we decrease production of that good or service. If the marginal benefit equals the marginal cost, we stay at the current level of production of that good or service.

You would use the same kind of concept when you are out shopping. Suppose you have £15 to spend on either a CD or a T-shirt. You are choosing at the margin. You will buy the CD if the you think you will get more benefit from having that CD than it costs. The opportunity cost or the marginal cost is

Figure 3.4 Efficient Choices

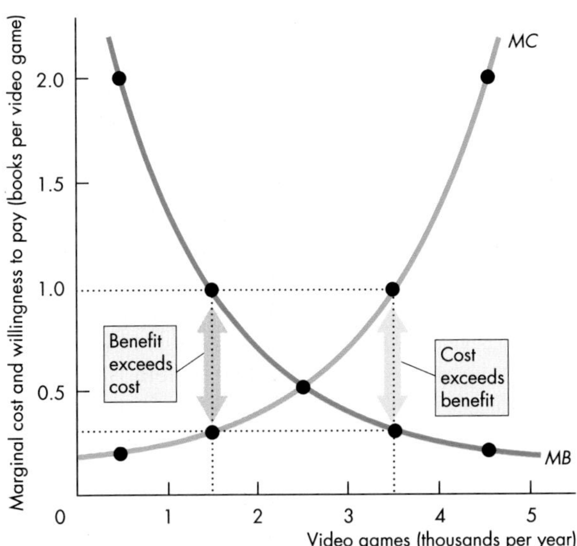

The greater the quantity of video games produced, the smaller is the marginal benefit (*MB*) from a game – the fewer books people are willing to give up to get an additional game. But the greater the quantity of games produced, the greater is the marginal cost (*MC*) of a game – the more books people must give up to get an additional game. When marginal benefit equals marginal cost, resources are being used efficiently.

the foregone benefit of having the T-shirt. You will always buy something if you can afford it and you think the benefit is greater than the cost. Otherwise, you will keep your money or buy something else.

We can illustrate efficient choice using our example of video games. Figure 3.4 shows the marginal cost and marginal benefit curves for video games. Should we produce the first unit of video games? To answer this question, we compare marginal cost and marginal benefit. When production is one unit, marginal cost is 0.2 units of books. But the marginal benefit is 2 units of books. So people value the first unit of video games more highly than the cost to produce that unit. This means we can get more out of our resources by switching some resources into producing video games and out of producing books.

Suppose we were producing 4 units of video games. The marginal cost of the fourth unit of video games is 1 unit of books but the marginal benefit is only 0.3 units of books. Because the marginal cost is greater than the marginal benefit, we know that people value the fourth unit of video games less highly than the cost of producing it. We can get more from our resources if we switch some resources out of video game production and into book production.

Now suppose that we produce the third unit of video games. Marginal cost and marginal benefit are now equal at 0.5 units of books. This choice between video games and books is efficient. Our resources are allocated most efficiently. If more video games are produced, the foregone books are worth more than the additional unit of video games. If fewer video games are produced, the foregone books are worth less than the additional unit of video games.

In our example, the most efficient quantity of video games to produce is 3 units. So what is the most efficient combination of video games and books? Look back at the *PPF* in Figure 3.1 to find out. The efficient combination is at the point on the PPF which shows 3 units of video games and 2 units of books.

Review

- The marginal cost of a good or service is the opportunity cost of increasing its production by one unit.
- The marginal benefit from a good or service is the maximum amount we are willing to pay for an additional unit.
- Efficient choice is where resources are used most efficiently – where they cannot be reallocated to increase the value of production.
- The efficient choice can be found where marginal benefit equals marginal cost.

You now understand the limits to production and how to make efficient choices about what to produce. Now we are going to look at how production possibilities can be expanded through economic growth.

Economic Growth

Over the past 30 years, production in the European Union has expanded by 4 per cent per annum. This expansion in production is called **economic growth**. By the year 2010, if the same pace of growth continues, our production possibilities will be even greater. Does growth mean that we can avoid the constraints imposed on us by our limited resources? Can we avoid opportunity costs? The answer is no. As you will see, the faster production grows, the greater is the opportunity cost of economic growth.

The Cost of Economic Growth

The two key factors that influence economic growth are technological progress and capital accumulation. **Technological progress** is the development of new and better ways of producing goods and services and the development of new goods. **Capital accumulation** is the growth of capital resources. As a consequence of technological progress and capital accumulation, we have an enormous quantity of cars and aircraft that enable us to transport more than when we had only horses and carriages; we have satellites that make transcontinental communications possible on a scale much larger than that produced by the earlier cable technology. But developing new technologies and accumulating capital involves a new opportunity cost. That opportunity cost is a decrease in the quantity of consumption goods and services because resources are used in research and development as well as to make new machines and other forms of capital. Let's look at this opportunity cost.

Instead of studying the *PPF* for books and video games, we'll hold the quantity of books constant and look at the *PPF* for video game cassettes and machines for making video game cassettes. Figure 3.5 shows this *PPF* as the blue curve *abc*. If we devote no resources to producing machines, we can produce 5,000 cassettes a week at point *a*. If we devote one-fifth of our capacity to producing machines, we can produce 4,000 cassettes a week and 1 machine at point *b*. If we produce no cassettes, we can produce 2 machines at point *c*.

The amount by which our production possibilities expand depends on how much of our resources we devote to technological change and capital accumulation. If we devote no resources to this activity, the *PPF* remains at *abc* – the original blue curve. If we cut current production of cassettes and produce 1 video game cassette making machine (point *b*), then the *PPF* moves out in the future to the position shown by the red curve in Figure 3.5. The fewer resources we devote to current production and the more resources we devote to producing machines, the greater is the expansion of our production possibilities.

But economic growth is not free. There are no free lunches. To achieve growth, we must devote more resources to producing new machines and

Figure 3.5 Economic Growth in a Video Cassette Factory

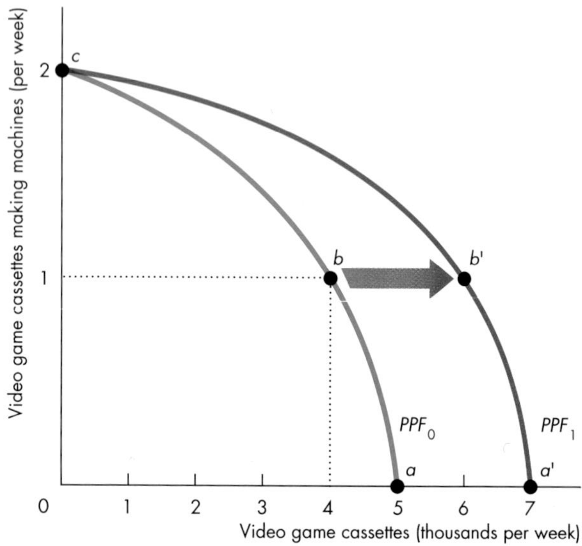

PPF_0 shows the limits to the production of video game cassettes and video game cassette making equipment, with the production of all other goods and services remaining constant. If we devote no resources to producing video game cassette making machines and produce five million cassettes a week, we remain stuck at point *a*. But if we decrease cassette production to four thousand a week and produce 1 cassette making machine a week, at point *b*, our production possibilities will expand. After a week, the production possibility frontier shifts outward to PPF_1 and we can produce at point *b'*, a point outside the original *PPF*. We can shift the *PPF* outward, but we cannot avoid opportunity cost. The opportunity cost of producing more cassettes in the future is fewer cassettes today.

Figure 3.6 Economic Growth in the European Union and Hong Kong

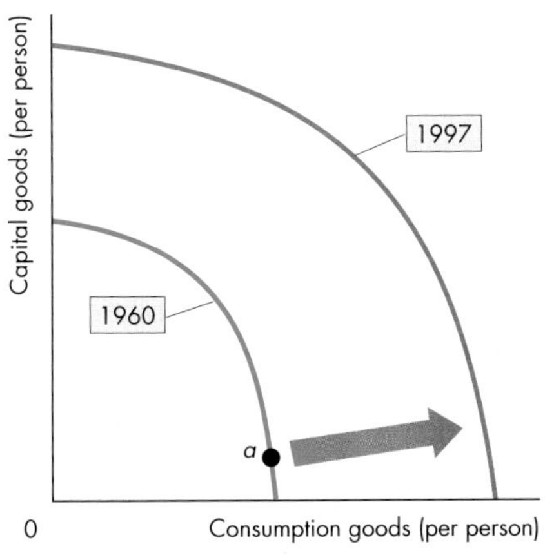

(a) European Union

Capital goods (per person)
1997
b
1960
c
a
0
Consumption goods (per person)

(b) Hong Kong

In 1960, the production possibilities per person in the European Union, the blue line in part (a), were much larger than those in Hong Kong, the blue line in part (b). But Hong Kong devoted a larger share of its resources to accumulating capital, than the European Union – point *a* in each part of the figure. By 1997, the two production possibilities per person had become similar. If Hong Kong can continue to produce at point *b* on its 1997 frontier, it might overtake the European Union.

less to current production. Economic growth is no magic formula for abolishing scarcity. Also, on the new production possibility frontier, we continue to face opportunity costs.

The ideas about economic growth that we have explored in this example also apply to nations. Let's see why.

The Economic Growth of Nations

If as a nation we devote all our resources to producing food, clothing, housing, vacations and other consumer goods and none to research, development and the accumulation of capital, we will have no more capital and no better technologies in the future than we have at present. Our production possibilities in the future will be the same as today. To expand our production possibilities in the future, we must produce fewer consumption goods today. The resources that we free up today enable us to accumulate capital and to develop better technologies for producing consumption goods in the future. The decrease in the output of consumption goods today is the opportunity cost of economic growth and the attainment of more consumption goods in the future.

The experiences of the European Union and some East Asian economies, such as Hong Kong, provide a striking example of the effects of our choices on the rate of economic growth. In 1960, the production possibilities per person in the European Union (then the European Economic Community) were much larger than those in Hong Kong (see Figure 3.6). The European Union devoted one-fifth of its resources to accumulating capital and the other four-fifths to consumption, as illustrated by point *a* in Figure 3.6(a). But Hong Kong devoted more than one-third of its resources to accumulating capital and less than two-thirds to consumption, as illustrated by point *a* in Figure 3.6(b). Both areas experienced economic growth, but growth in Hong Kong since 1960 has been much more rapid than in the European Union because Hong Kong devoted a bigger fraction of its resources to accumulating capital.

If Hong Kong continues to devote such a large proportion of its resources to accumulating capital (point b on its 1997 production possibility frontier), its economy may continue to grow more rapidly than the economies of the European Union. Its production possibility frontier could move out beyond that of the European Union. If Hong Kong increases its consumption and decreases its capital accumulation (moving to point c on its 1997 production possibility frontier), then its rate of economic expansion could slow down to a rate similar to that in Europe.

Hong Kong has been the fastest-growing East Asian economy, but others, such as Singapore, Taiwan, South Korea and recently China, have performed similarly to Hong Kong. These economies were closing the gap on the European Union until the collapse of East Asian currencies in 1998.

Review

- Economic growth results from technological change and capital accumulation.
- The opportunity cost of faster economic growth is a decrease in current consumption.
- By decreasing current consumption, we can devote more resources to developing new technologies and accumulating capital and can speed up the rate of economic growth.

Now we are going to look at how specialization and trade can help us expand the production possibilities of our economies.

Gains from Trade

People can produce for themselves all the goods that they consume or they can concentrate on producing one good (or perhaps a few goods) and then trade with others – exchange some of their own products for the products of others. Concentrating on the production of only one good or a few goods is called *specialization*. We are going to discover how people gain by specializing in the production of the good in which they have a *comparative advantage* and by trading with each other.

Comparative Advantage

A person has a **comparative advantage** in an activity if that person can perform the activity at a lower opportunity cost than anyone else. Differences in opportunity costs arise from differences in individual abilities and from differences in the characteristics of other resources.

No one excels at everything. One person is an outstanding sales person but a poor investor; another person is a brilliant lawyer but a poor teacher. In almost all human endeavours, what one person does easily, someone else finds difficult. The same applies to land and capital. One plot of land is fertile but has no mineral deposits; another plot of land has outstanding views but is infertile. One machine has great precision but is difficult to operate; another machine is fast but often breaks down.

Although no one excels at everything, some people excel and can outperform others in many activities. But such a person does not have a comparative advantage in every activity. For example, a UK chat show presenter, Clive Anderson, is a better lawyer than most people. But he is an even better humourous chat show host. His comparative advantage is in television. Differences in individual abilities and differences in the quality of other resources mean that there are differences in individual opportunity costs of producing various goods. Such differences give rise to comparative advantage. Let's use a production possibility frontier model of two video cassette factories to look at the idea of comparative advantage. One factory is owned by Galactic Games and the other is owned by Ace Videos. Both factories can allocate their employees' time between producing video cassettes or installing more video cassette making machines. However, another choice would be to modify existing machines to produce other goods. Suppose that the technology exists to modify the video game cassette making machine to make video film cassettes and vice versa.

Galactic Games' *PPF* for game and film cassettes is shown in Figure 3.7(a). If all the resources are used to make game cassettes, output will

Figure 3.7 The Gains from Specialization and Trade

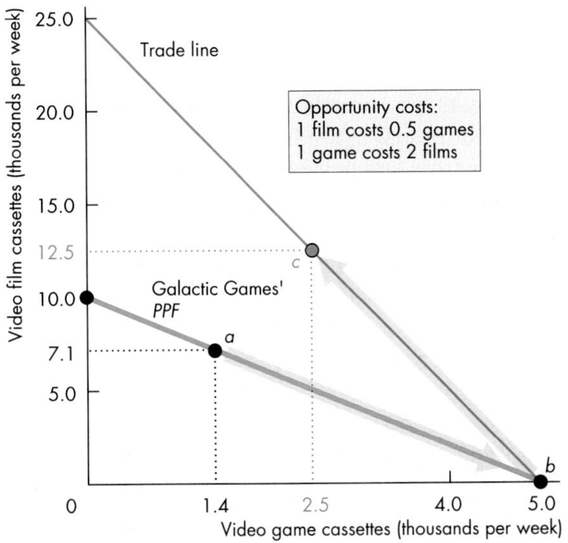

(a) Galactic Games' factory

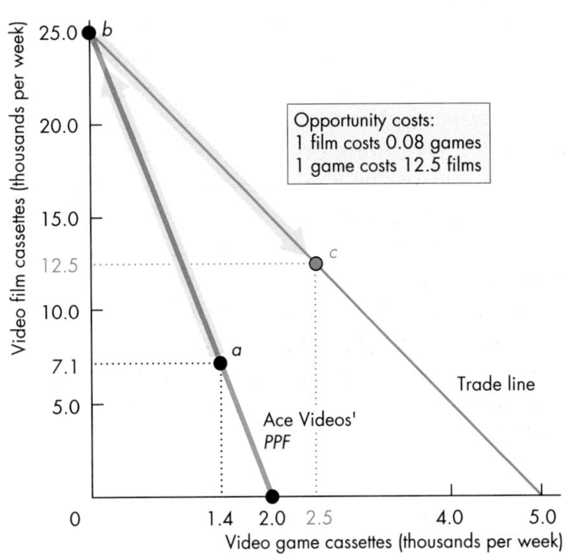

(b) Ace Videos' factory

Galactic Games (part a) and Ace Videos (part b) each produce at point *a* on their respective *PPF*. For Galactic Games, the opportunity cost of one game is two films and the opportunity cost of one film is 0.5 games. For Ace Videos the opportunity cost of one game is 12.5 films – higher than Galactic Games and the opportunity cost of one film is 0.08 games – lower than Galactic Games. Ace Videos has a comparative advantage in films and Galactic Games has a comparative advantage in games.

If Ace Videos specializes in films and Galactic Games specializes in games, they each produce at point *b* on their respective *PPF*. They then exchange films for games along the red 'Trade line'. Ace Videos buys games from Galactic Games for less than its opportunity cost of producing them, and Galactic Games buys films from Ace Videos for less than its opportunity cost of producing them. They each go to point *c* – a point outside their *PPF* – where a total of 2,500 games and 12,500 films are produced per week.

be 5,000 game cassettes a week. The blue *PPF* curve in Figure 3.7(a) tells us that if all the resources are used to make film cassettes, factory production will be 10,000 film cassettes a week. But to produce film cassettes, production of game cassettes must decrease. For each 1,000 film cassettes produced, production of game cassettes must fall by 500.

The opportunity cost of producing 1 film cassette at Galactic Games is 0.5 game cassettes.

Similarly, if the owner of Galactic Games wants to increase production of game cassettes, production of film cassettes must fall. For each 1,000 game cassettes produced, production of film cassettes must fall by 2,000.

The opportunity cost of producing 1 game cassette at Galactic Games is 2 film cassettes.

Ace Videos' *PPF* for game and film cassettes is shown in Figure 3.7(b). If Ace Videos uses all its resources to make films, the factory produces 25,000 film cassettes a week. If all the resources are used to make games, the factory produces 2,000 game cassettes a week. To produce games, of course, Ace Videos must decrease production of films. For each 1,000 additional games produced, Ace Videos must reduce production of films by 12,500.

The opportunity cost of producing 1 game cassette at Ace Videos is 12.5 film cassettes.

Similarly, if Ace Videos want to increase production of films, production of game cassettes must fall. For each 1,000 additional film cassettes produced, production of game cassettes must fall by 80.

The opportunity cost of producing 1 film cassette at Ace Videos is 0.08 game cassettes.

Suppose that both factories decide to produce the same quantities of game and film cassettes. That is, they each produce at point *a* on their respective *PPF*s. At this point each produces 1,400 game cassettes and 7,100 film cassettes each week. Their total production is 2,800 game cassettes and 14,200 film cassettes.

In which of the two goods does Ace Videos have a comparative advantage? Recall that comparative advantage is a situation in which one person's opportunity cost of producing a good is less than another person's opportunity cost of producing the same good. You can see the comparative advantage by looking at the production possibility frontiers for Ace Videos and Galactic Games in Figure 3.7. Ace Videos' *PPF* is steeper than Galactic Games' *PPF*. To produce one more film cassette, Ace Games gives up fewer film cassettes than Galactic Games. Hence Ace Videos' opportunity cost of a film cassette is less than Galactic Games'. This means that Ace Videos has a comparative advantage in producing film cassettes.

Notice the PPF for Galactic Games is flatter than Ace Videos'. This means that Galactic Games gives up fewer film cassettes to produce one more game cassette than Ace Videos does. Galactic Games' opportunity cost of producing game cassettes is less than Ace Videos', so Galactic Games has a comparative advantage in producing game cassettes.

Achieving the Gains from Trade

If Galactic Games, who have a comparative advantage in game cassette production, put all available resources into game production, the factory can produce 5,000 game cassettes a week – point *b* on its *PPF*. If Ace Videos, who have a comparative advantage in film cassette production, puts all available resources into film production, the factory can produce 25,000 film cassettes a week – point *b* on its *PPF*. By specializing, Galactic Games and Ace Videos together can produce a total of 5,000 game and 25,000 film cassettes a week.

To achieve the gains from specialization, both factories must trade with each other. Suppose they agree to the following deal. Each week, Ace Videos produces 25,000 film cassettes and Galactic Games produces 5,000 game cassettes. Ace Videos supplies Galactic Games with 12,500 film cassettes in exchange for 2,500 game cassettes. With this deal in place, Galactic Games and Ace Videos move along the red 'Trade line' to point *c* in Figure 3.7. At this point, each has 12,500 film cassettes and 2,500 game cassettes – an additional 1,100 game cassettes and an additional 5,400 film cassettes. These are the gains from specialization and trade, and both the parties to the trade share the gains. By specialization and trade, both factories get quantities of game and film cassettes that are *outside* their individual *PPF*s.

Absolute Advantage

We've seen that Galactic Games has a comparative advantage in producing game cassettes and Ace Videos has a comparative advantage in producing film cassettes. We've also seen that Galactic Games can produce a larger quantity of game cassettes than Ace Videos, and Ace Videos can produce a larger quantity of film cassettes than Galactic Games. Neither factory can produce more of both goods than the other.

If one person can produce more of both goods than another person that person is said to have an **absolute advantage** in the production of both goods. In our example, neither factory has an absolute advantage.

It is tempting to suppose that when a person (factory or country) has an absolute advantage, it is not possible to benefit from specialization and trade. But this line of reasoning is wrong. To see why, let's look again at the model of the two factories. Suppose that Ace Videos invent and patent a production process that makes the factory four times as productive as before. With the new technology, Ace Videos can produce 100,000 film cassettes a week (four times the original 25,000), if all available resources go into that activity. Alternatively, the factory can produce 8,000 game cassettes (four times the original 2,000), if all the resources go into that activity. Notice that Ace Vidoes now has an absolute advantage in producing both goods.

We have already worked out that the gains from specialization arise when each person specializes in producing the good in which he or she has a *comparative advantage*. Recall that a person has a comparative advantage in producing a particular good if that person can produce the good at a *lower opportunity* cost than anyone else. Galactic Games' opportunity costs remain exactly the same as they were before. What has happened to Ace Videos' opportunity costs now that the factory has become four times as productive?

You can work out Ace Vidoes' opportunity costs by doing exactly the same calculation as before. You can see that the opportunity costs have not changed. Ace Videos can produce four times as much of both goods as before. But to increase the production of game cassettes by 1,000 along the new production possibility frontier, production of film videos must fall by 12,500, so the opportunity cost of 1 game cassette is still 12.5 film cassettes. To increase the production of film cassettes by 1,000, production of game cassettes must fall by 80, so the opportunity cost of 1 film cassette is still 0.08 game cassettes.

When Ace Videos becomes four times as productive as before, each unit of resources produces more output, but the opportunity costs remain the same. Since neither factory's opportunity costs have changed, Ace Videos continues to have a comparative advantage in producing film cassettes and Galactic Games continues to have a comparative advantage in producing game cassettes. So both factories continue to gain by specialization and trade.

The key point to recognize is that it is not possible for anyone, even someone who has an absolute advantage, to have a comparative advantage in everything. So gains from specialization and trade are always available.

Dynamic Comparative Advantage

Comparative advantage is not a static concept. At any given point in time, the resources available and the technologies in use determine the comparative advantages that individuals and countries have. But as technological change and capital accumulation shift the production possibility frontiers outward, so comparative advantages change. Also, people get better at doing what they do repeatedly. Just by repeatedly producing a particular good or service, people can become more productive in that activity, a phenomenon called learning-by-doing. Learning-by-doing is the basis of dynamic comparative advantage. **Dynamic comparative advantage** is a comparative advantage that an individual (factory or country) possesses as a result of having specialized in a particular activity and, through learning-by-doing, gained the lowest opportunity cost.

Dynamic comparative advantage applies to individuals, firms and countries. Some people have a steep 'learning curve' – initially they do not seem to be much different from anyone else but through practice and hard work they become outstanding in some activity. Boeing, the world's largest maker of wide-bodied jet aircraft, has pursued dynamic comparative advantage. As Boeing's workforce and management have gained experience in building wide-bodied aircraft, they have successively lowered costs and strengthened their comparative advantage. Singapore, South Korea, Hong Kong and Taiwan are examples of countries that have pursued dynamic comparative advantage vigorously. They have developed industries in which initially they might not have had a comparative advantage and, through learning-by-doing, have become low opportunity cost producers of high-technology products. A recent example is the decision of Singapore to develop a genetic engineering industry. It is not clear that Singapore has a comparative advantage in this activity at present, but it might acquire one as its scientists and production workers become more skilled in this area.

Review

- A person has a comparative advantage in producing a good if that person's opportunity cost of producing the good is lower than everyone else's.
- Production increases if people specialize in the activity in which they have a comparative advantage.
- By specializing in the activities in which they have a comparative advantage and trading, everyone can gain.
- Dynamic comparative advantage can result from specialization and learning-by-doing.

The Market Economy

Individuals and countries can gain by specializing in the production of those goods and services in which they have a comparative advantage. But to reap the gains from trade from billions of people specializing in millions of different activities, trade must be organized. Buyers and sellers need information and they face opportunity costs for the time taken in the trading activity. Trade could be organized and managed through a central authority as it has been in the past in Russia and China. But most countries have now adopted a market economy for organizing trade. Let's see why.

Transactions Costs

The costs of trading and negotiating are called **transactions costs**. These include the costs of finding the buyers and sellers you want to trade with, finding information about the quantity and quality of goods and services for trade, organizing production and distribution, and negotiating prices, amongst many other things. Organizing trade through social institutions is the main way of reducing transactions costs. The most important of these social institutions are:

- Markets.
- Property rights.
- Payment systems.

Markets A *market* is any arrangement that enables buyers and sellers to get information and to do business with each other. **Markets** can be physical locations, such as a wholesale meat or fish market. But most markets are networks in which people trade by telephone, fax or computer link. For example, modern stock exchanges are computerized markets for company shares. All markets share a common feature. They bring producers and consumers of goods and services together to buy and sell.

Markets are helpful because they reduce the transactions costs of buying and selling. Markets pool an enormous amount of information about the plans of buyers and sellers in just one number, a *price*. The price moves in response to the sum of the decisions of the buyers and sellers. It rises when there is a shortage and it falls when there is a relative abundance. Markets coordinate the decisions of buyers and sellers. To see how, think about the market for hamburgers at a major football match.

Suppose that some people who want to buy hamburgers are not able to do so. To make the choices of buyers and sellers compatible, buyers must scale down their appetites and/or more hamburgers must be offered for sale. A rise in the price of hamburgers produces this outcome. The higher price encourages sellers to offer more hamburgers. It also curbs the appetite for hamburgers and changes some lunch plans. Fewer people buy hamburgers and more buy, say, sandwiches.

Alternatively, suppose more hamburgers are available than people want to buy. In this case, to make the choices of buyers and sellers compatible, more hamburgers must be bought and fewer must be offered for sale. A fall in the price of hamburgers achieves this outcome. The lower price discourages sellers from producing more hamburgers. It also encourages consumption.

Market prices send signals to buyers and sellers. All potential buyers or sellers know their own opportunity cost of producing or consuming a good or service. By comparing their own opportunity cost with the market price, each person can decide whether to become a buyer or a seller without needing to know the plans or every other trader. So markets help people to specialize and gain from trade by reducing the transactions costs of trade. The transactions costs to trading in a managed economy would be much higher than in a market economy. The central planner would need to know all the plans of all the potential buyers and sellers. This is why most trade now takes place in market, rather than managed, economies.

Property Rights **Property rights** are social arrangements that govern the ownership, use and disposal of property – our resources, goods and services. Property rights are protected by laws. *Real property* includes land and buildings, and durable goods such as plant and equipment. *Financial property* includes stocks and bonds and money in the bank. *Intellectual property* is the intangible product of creative effort. This type of property includes books, music, computer programs and inventions of all kinds, and it is protected by copyright and patent laws.

Figure 3.8 Circular Flows in the Market Economy

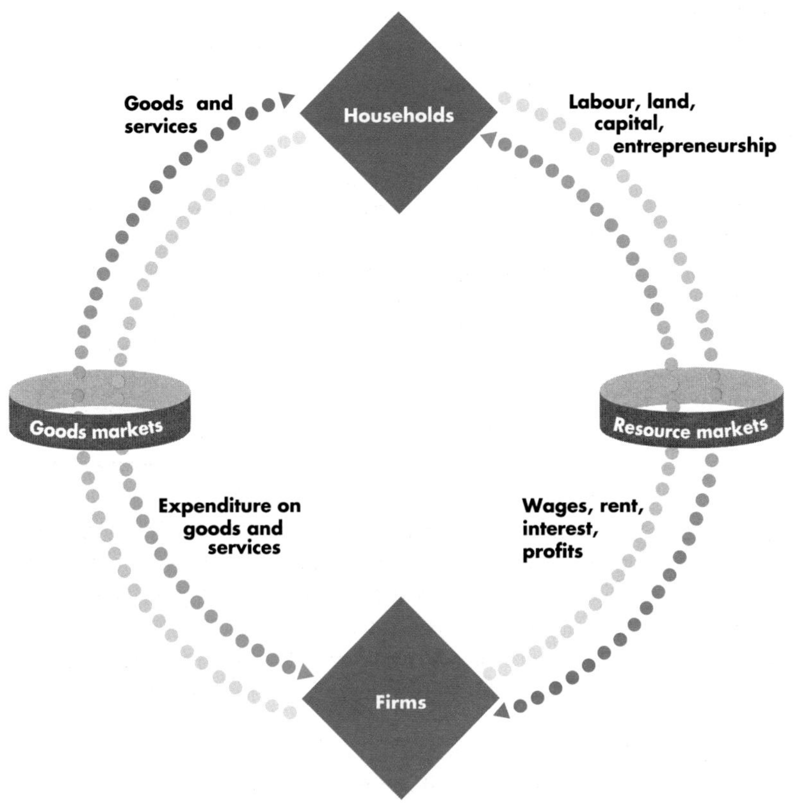

Households and firms make economic choices. Households choose the quantities of labour, land, capital and entrepreneurship to sell or rent to firms in exchange for wages, rent, interest and profits. Households also choose how to spend their incomes on the various types of goods and services available. Firms choose the quantities of resources to hire and the quantities of the various goods and services to produce. Goods markets and resource markets coordinate these choices of households and firms. Resources and goods flow clockwise (red), and money payments flow counterclockwise (green).

If property rights are not enforced, the incentive to specialize and produce the goods in which each person has a comparative advantage is weakened. Some of the gains from specialization and trade are lost. If people can easily steal other people's property, then time and resources which could be used for production will be wasted on protecting property. Production will not be efficient. Worse still, the transactions costs to trading may be so high that buyers and sellers decide not to trade at all.

Establishing property rights is one of the greatest challenges facing Russia and other Central European countries as they seek to develop market economies. Even in European Union countries, where property rights are well established in law, upholding intellectual property rights is still proving a challenge. Modern technologies make it relatively easy to pirate copy audio and video material, computer programs and books.

Payment Systems A payment system defines the accepted method of payment in trade. There are two main **payment systems**:

1 Barter.
2 Money.

Barter is the direct trade of one good or service for another. This method of trading severely limits the amount of trade that takes place. If one person wants to sell meat and buy fruit they must find another person who wants to sell fruit and buy meat. Because it may take a long time to find this perfect match, the transactions costs to trade are high in a barter system.

But quite a lot of barter still takes place. For example, before the recent changes in Eastern Europe, hairdressers in Poland obtained their hairdressing equipment from England in exchange for hair clippings that they supplied to London wigmakers. Even today, Australian meat processors swap cans of meat for Russian salmon, crab-meat and scallops; Australian wool growers swap wool for Russian electrical motors.

Money is a commodity, or token, that serves as the means of payment in trade. Money reduces transactions costs and makes millions of transactions possible that otherwise would not be worth undertaking. Imagine the chain of barter transactions you would have to go through every day to get your coffee, cola, textbooks, lunch and all the other goods and services you consume. In a monetary system, you exchange your time and effort for money and use that money to buy the goods and services you consume. Money cuts out most of the transactions costs you would face each day in a world of barter.

We normally think of money as coins and paper notes. But money can be any commodity which is durable, divisible and widely accepted. For example, prisoners often use cigarettes as money. Increasingly, electronic banking and sales will mean that money is nothing more than an electronic adjustment to our bank accounts.

Circular Flow in the Market Economy

Figure 3.8 illustrates how money and property rights are combined with markets to coordinate decisions in a market economy. Two types of market are shown in Figure 3.8: goods and resource markets. *Goods markets* are those in which goods and services are bought and sold. *Resource markets* are those in which resources for production – factors of production – are bought and sold. Households decide how much of their resources – labour, land and capital – to sell in resource markets. They receive incomes in the form of wages, rent, interest and profit. Households also decide how to spend their incomes on goods and services produced by firms.

Firms decide the quantities of resources to hire, how to use them to produce goods and services, what goods and services to produce, and in what quantities. They sell their output in goods markets.

The flows resulting from these decisions by households and firms are shown in Figure 3.8. The red flows are the factors of production that go from households to firms and the goods and services that go from firms to households. The green flows in the opposite direction are the money payments made in exchange for these items.

Government sets the laws which protect property rights in both goods and resource markets.

You have now begun to see how economists go about the job of trying to answer economic questions. Scarcity, choice and opportunity costs explain why we specialize and trade and why markets, property rights and money develop.

Summary

Key Points

Resources and Wants (pp. 42–43)

- Economic activity arises from scarcity because of limited resources and unlimited wants.
- Our limited resources are labour, land, capital (inlcuding human capital) and entrepreneurship.
- The economic problem is how to use our limited resources to produce the best combination of resources.

Resources, Production Possibilities and Opportunity Cost (pp. 43–46)

- The production possibility frontier, *PPF*, is the boundary between attainable and unattainable production.
- Production is efficient at all points on the *PPF* as no resources are wasted or misallocated.
- The opportunity cost of producting more of one good is the amount of the other good that must be given up to produce it.
- The opportunity cost of a good increases along the *PPF* as production of the good increases.

Efficient Choice (pp. 46–49)

- The marginal cost of a good is the opportunity cost of producing one more unit.
- Marginal cost increases as the amount of the good available increases.
- The marginal benefit of a good is the maximum someone is willing to pay to get one more unit, measured in terms of the quantity of another good foregone.
- Marginal benefit decreases as the amount of the good available increases.
- Efficient choice occurs where resources are used to produce the best combination of goods – where marginal benefit equals marginal cost.

Economic Growth (pp. 50–52)

- Economic growth is the expansion of production possibilities.
- Economic growth results from capital accumulation and technological change.
- The opportunity cost of economic growth is foregone current consumption.

Gains from Trade (pp. 52–55)

- A person has a comparative advantage in producing a good if that person can produce the good at a lower opportunity cost than everyone else.
- People gain by specializing in the activity at which they have a comparative advantage and by trading with others.
- Comparative advantage changes over time and dynamic comparative advantage arises from learning-by-doing.

The Market Economy (pp. 56–58)

- Property rights, markets and money reduce transactions costs and enable people to gain from specialization and trade.
- Markets coordinate decisions and help to allocate resources efficiently – to their most valued use.

Key Figures

Key Terms

Review Questions

1 How does the production possibility frontier illustrate scarcity?

2 How does the production possibility frontier illustrate efficiency?

3 How does the production possibility frontier illustrate opportunity cost?

4 Why does the production possibility frontier bow outward for most goods?

5 Why does opportunity cost generally increase as the quantity produced of a good increases?

6 What shifts the production possibility frontier outward and what shifts it inward?

7 What is marginal cost and how is it measured?

8 What is marginal benefit and how is it measured?

9 Why is choice and resource use efficient when marginal benefit equals marginal cost?

10 Explain how our choices influence the pace of economic growth.

11 What is the opportunity cost of economic growth?

12 Why does it pay people to specialize and trade with each other?

13 What are the gains from specialization and trade? How do they arise?

14 Why do social arrangements such as markets, property rights and money become necessary?

15 What is money? Give some examples of money. In the late 1980s, people in Romania used Kent cigarettes to buy almost everything. Was this monetary exchange or barter? Explain your answer.

16 What are the advantages of monetary exchange over barter?

Problems

1 Suppose that Leisureland produces only two goods – food and sunscreen. The table lists its production possibilities:

a Draw a graph of Leisureland's production possibility frontier.
b What are the opportunity costs of producing food and sunscreen in Leisureland? List them at each output given in the table.
c Why are the opportunity costs the same at each output level?

Food (kilograms per month)		Sunscreen (litres per month)
300	and	0
200	and	50
100	and	100
0	and	150

2 Workland also produces only food and sunscreen, and its production possibilities are:

Food (kilograms per month)		Sunscreen (litres per month)
150	and	0
100	and	100
50	and	200
0	and	300

a Draw a graph of Workland's production possibility frontier.
b What are the opportunity costs of producing food and sunscreen in Workland? List them at each output given in the table.
c Why are the opportunity costs the same at each output level?

3 Suppose that in Problems 1 and 2, Leisureland and Workland do not specialize and trade with each other. Leisureland produces and consumes 50 kilograms of food and 125 litres of sunscreen a month. Workland produces and consumes 150 pounds of food a month and no sunscreen. Then the countries begin to trade with each other.

a What good does Leisureland export, and what good does it import?
b What good does Workland export, and what good does it import?
c What is the maximum quantity of food and sunscreen that the two countries can produce if each country specializes in the activity at which it has the lower opportunity cost?

4 Suppose that Workland becomes three times as productive as in Problem 3.

a Show, on a graph, the effect of the increased productivity on Workland's production possibility frontier.
b Does Workland now have an absolute advantage in producing both goods?
c Can Workland gain from specialization and trade with Leisureland now that it is three times as productive? If so, what will it produce?
d What are the total gains from trade? What do these gains depend on?

5 Peter enjoys playing tennis but the more time he spends on tennis, the lower is his grade in economics. The figure shows the trade-off he faces.

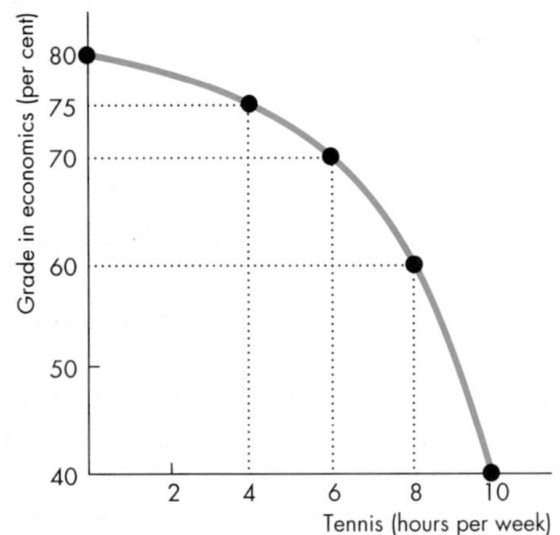

Calculate the opportunity cost of two hours of tennis if Peter increases the time he plays tennis from:

a 4 to 6 hours a week.
b 6 to 8 hours a week.

6 By using the figure in Problem 5, describe the relationship between the time Peter spends on playing tennis and the opportunity cost of an hour of tennis.

7 Study the story about the cost of studying for a full-time degree in *Reading Between the Lines* on pp. 62–63 then:

a Identify the opportunity costs of studying full-time for a university degree.
b Explain why the production possibilities for graduates expand beyond those of non-graduates.
c Give your opinion on whether students should pay tuition fees. Explain your opinion using the ideas of production possibilities and opportunity costs.

8 Turn to p. 64 and read the *Economics in History* material about Adam Smith. Then:

a Explain how the division of labour creates economic wealth.
b Describe the effect of automation and robotics on the division of labour in modern car manufacture. What is the link between this effect and the growth of global car markets?

9 Use the links on the Parkin, Powell and Matthews Web site and obtain data on the cost of enrolling on an MBA program of a school that interests you. Then answer the following questions:

a If an MBA graduate can earn up to 20 per cent more than a university graduate without an MBA, does the marginal benefit of an MBA exceed its marginal cost?
b Why doesn't everyone do an MBA?

Opportunity Cost: The Cost of a University Degree

The Essence of the Story

- Since September 1998, UK students have started to pay tuition fees and no longer receive a grant. Students must now borrow money to pay for books and tuition.
- Whilst the number of new graduates owing money increased by only 4% between 1994 and 1998, the amount owed more than doubled.
- The average amount owed in 1998 was £4,500, but nearly half of graduates feel comfortable with this level of borrowing. Some students are worried about their level of debt.
- Graduates are applying for fewer jobs and gaining higher paid jobs more quickly. Since 1994, graduate salaries have increased by 17 per cent to an average of £13,388 a year.

Financial Times, 17 April 1999 

Degrees become more expensive but also more valuable

Graduates are another year older and deeper in debt, but the gains from getting a degree remain significant.

Barclays Bank's fifth annual graduate survey shows graduate borrowing to finance their education has risen by 103 per cent since 1994. This figure is soon likely to rise even more sharply: since last September students have had to pay tuition fees and the maintenance grant has been replaced by state-backed loans.

Graduates now owe a total of £814m. But since 1994, graduate salaries have increased 17 per cent, and improvements in the labour market mean their jobs outlook remains positive.

The survey found that the number of students owing money when they graduated rose only 4 per cent between 1994–98. But the gradual reduction in student grants in recent years meant the amount they borrowed rose 103 per cent.

Eighty-five per cent of new graduates now had some debt, averaging close to £4,500. Almost 80 per cent owed the student loan company an average of £2,865. Just under 60 per cent owed their bank an average of £1,112.

Forty-four per cent of graduates now felt comfortable about their level of borrowing against 30 per cent in 1994 – even though the 1998 graduates had borrowed much more. However, 37 per cent remained worried or angry about the amount owed.

Graduates on average applied for only 17 jobs in 1998, against 27 in 1994, and 89 per cent had found employment within six months. Average salary was £13,388 a year, a £1,900 increase since 1994.

Economic Analysis

■ The opportunity cost of a university degree is foregone consumption. The payoff is an increase in lifetime production possibility.

■ Figure 1 shows choices facing school (or college) leavers considering full-time university education. They can consume university educational goods such as books, study time, and tuition measured on the *y* axis, or non-educational goods and services measured on the *x* axis.

■ All points along the blue *PPF* are attainable. Becoming a full-time student is shown by moving from point *a* to point *b*. Increasing consumption of university educational goods and services means decreasing consumption of non-educational goods and services.

■ With a university degree, consumption possibilities expand to the red *PPF* in Figure 1. At point *c*, the level of non-educational goods and services associated with level *B* of university education has increased.

■ The opportunity cost of full-time university education can be measured by the full-time salary foregone, which provides the income for buying non-educational consumption.

■ Figure 2 shows that for each year of study, the full-time student gives up £7,000, replacing a typical school leaver's full-time salary of £10,000 with a part-time student job worth £3,000. On graduating, the student earns a typical salary of £13,338.

■ The opportunity cost of a three-year degree is £21,000 (£7,000 times three years). The payoff is a permanent increase in annual salary of £3,388 minus the graduate debt. If salaries and prices never changed, and no interest is paid on the debt, a student would be better off in seven and a half years. As graduates have a greater chance of earning higher salaries than non-graduates, the payback time will usually be a lot less.

■ Nearly half of all graduates feel comfortable with their level of debt, suggesting they anticipate an early payoff for studying. Cutting student grants and introducing tuition fees does not raise the opportunity cost (consumption foregone), but lengthens the payback period. Net gains are still positive for most students.

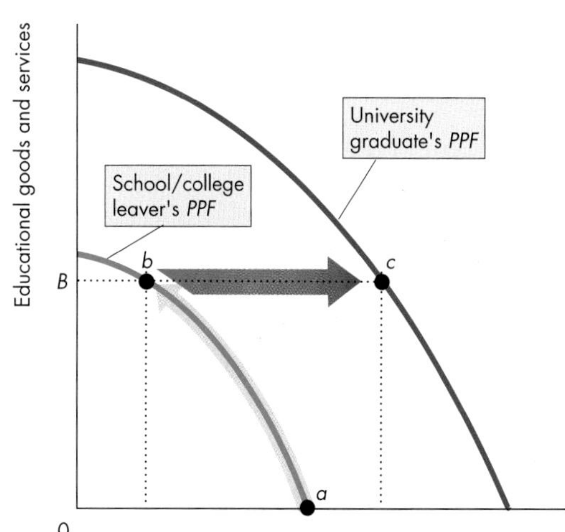

Figure 1 School leaver's choice

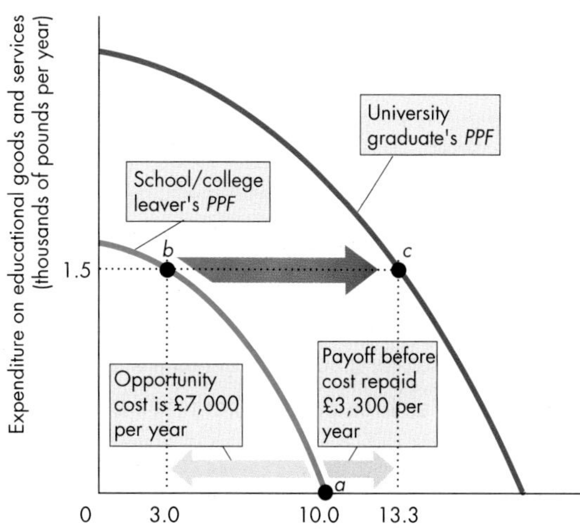

Figure 2 Opportunity cost

Understanding the Sources of Economic Wealth

"It is not from the benevolence of the butcher, the brewer, or the baker that we expect our dinner, but from their regard to their own interest."

Adam Smith, *The Wealth of Nations*

The Father of Economics: Adam Smith

Adam Smith was a giant of a scholar who contributed to ethics and jurisprudence as well as economics. Born in 1723 in Kirkcaldy, a small fishing town near Edinburgh, Scotland, Smith was the only child of the town's customs officer (who died before Adam was born).

His first academic appointment, at age 28, was as Professor of Logic at the University of Glasgow. He subsequently became tutor to a wealthy Scottish duke, whom he accompanied on a two-year grand European tour, following which he received a pension of £300 a year – ten times the average income at that time.

With the financial security of his pension, Smith devoted ten years to writing *An Inquiry into the Nature and Causes of the Wealth of Nations*, which was published in 1776. Many people had written on economic issues before Adam Smith, but he made economics a science. Smith's account was so broad and authoritative that no subsequent writer on economics could advance ideas without tracing their connections to those of Adam Smith.

The Issues and Ideas

Why are some nations wealthy while others are poor? This question lies at the heart of economics. And it leads directly to a second question: what can poor nations do to become wealthy?

Adam Smith, who is regarded by many scholars as the founder of economics, attempted to answer these questions in his book *The Wealth of Nations*, published in 1776. Smith was pondering these questions at the height of the Industrial Revolution. During these years, new technologies were invented and applied to the manufacture of cotton and wool cloth, iron, transportation and agriculture.

Smith wanted to understand the sources of economic wealth and he brought his acute powers of observation and abstraction to bear on the question. His answer was:

- The division of labour.
- Free markets.

The division of labour – breaking work down into simple tasks and becoming skilled in those tasks – is the source of "the greatest improvement in the productive powers of labour", said Smith. The division of labour became even more productive when it was applied to creating new technologies. Scientists and engineers, trained in extremely narrow fields, became specialists at inventing. Their powerful skills accelerated the advance of technology, so by the 1820s, machines could make consumer goods faster and more accurately than any craftsman could. By the 1850s, machines could make other machines that labour alone could never have made.

But, said Smith, the fruits of the division of labour are limited by the extent of the market. To make the market as large as possible, there must be no impediments to free trade both within a country and among countries. Smith argued that when each person makes the best possible economic choice, that choice leads as if by "an invisible hand" to the best outcome for society as a whole. The butcher, the brewer and the baker each pursue their own interests but, in doing so, also serve the interests of everyone else.

Then . . .

Adam Smith speculated that one person, working hard, using the hand tools available in the 1770s, might possibly make 20 pins a day. Yet, he observed, by using those same hand tools but breaking the process into a number of individually small operations in which people specialize – by the division of labour – ten people could make a staggering 48,000 pins a day. One draws out the wire, another straightens it, a third cuts it, a fourth points it, a fifth grinds it. Three specialists make the head, and a fourth attaches it. Finally, the pin is polished and packaged. But a large market is needed to support the division of labour: one factory employing ten workers would need to sell more than 15 million pins a year to stay in business.

. . . And Now

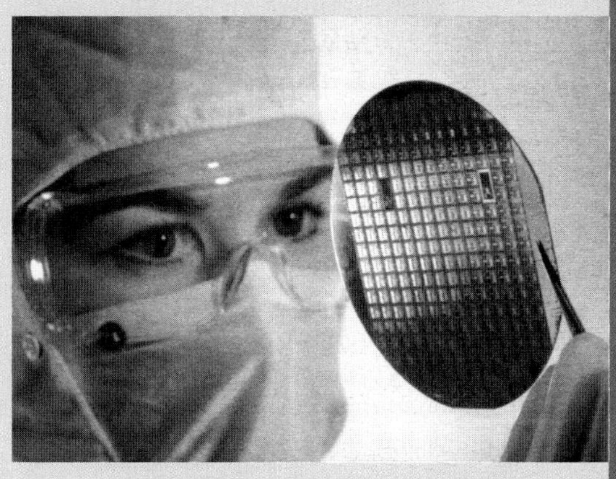

If Adam Smith were here today, he would be fascinated by the computer chip. He would see it as an extraordinary example of the productivity of the division of labour and of the use of machines to make machines that make other machines. From a design of a chip's intricate circuits, cameras transfer an image to glass plates that work like stencils. Workers prepare silicon wafers on which the circuits are printed. Some slice the wafers, others polish them, others bake them, and yet others coat them with a light-sensitive chemical. Machines transfer a copy of the circuit onto the wafer. Chemicals then etch the design onto the wafer. Further processes deposit atom-sized transistors and aluminium connectors. Finally, a laser separates the hundreds of chips on the wafer. Every stage in the process of creating a computer chip uses other computer chips. And like the pin of the 1770s, the computer chip of the 1990s benefits from a large market – a global market – to buy chips in the huge quantities in which they are produced efficiently.

Testing These Ideas Today

Using what you have learned in Chapter 3 about growth and trade, and what you know about Adam Smith's ideas, you should be able to answer the following questions:

- How does automation and robotics affect the division of labour in a modern car factory?
- How will the introduction of automation and robotics affect the growth of global car markets today?

Part 2

What is Economics?

Talking with **Will Hutton**

Will Hutton is Editor-in-Chief of *The Observer* newspaper and Director of Guardian National Newspapers. He joined *The Guardian* as Economics Editor in 1990 after a successful career in television and radio journalism and production. He has been the Editor in Chief of the European Business Channel, Economics Editor for BBC2's Newsnight programme, and has produced and appeared in many programmes on radio and television. He is currently a Governor of the London School of Economics and Chairman of the Employment Policy Institute. He is a visiting Professor at both Manchester University Business School and the Institute of Public Policy, University College London, and also a visiting Fellow at Nuffield College, Oxford. As well as writing many articles and reports on the economy, Will Hutton has written three influential books outlining the problems of modern capitalism. He is currently the Chairman of the Commission on NHS Accountability.

Why did you become an economist?

I became an economist because I found it an extraordinarily useful tool kit for explaining the world. From doing A level economics, I found I could explain a lot that a 17-year-old boy wanted to explain, such as why my father wasn't paid as much as he wanted to be paid, my own career choices, and why there was inflation and trade unions. I have found economics as useful all through my life, briefly as a professional economist working in stock broking in the early 1970s, but also as an investment analyst, and now as a journalist. I always find myself looking for the incentive pattern in any context and I guess I share that with other economists. I believe, like all economists, that economic agents respond to an array of incentives. But of course, I may come to rather different conclusions than many economists.

What do you think are the most important and useful concepts in economics?

There are so many important and interesting concepts such as trading and game theory, equilibrium, disequilibrium and general equilibrium, let alone interest rates and exchange rates, monopoly and market power, and diminishing returns. I could go on. But if I had to single some out, well I think incentives, opportunity costs and trade-offs at the margin are the central concepts. They really define the economic way of thinking. When I think about real life problems, I am steered by opportunity costs and trade-offs initially. Economics is my compass when writing, but also a compass in my professional and personal life.

As a journalist, you have done a great deal to promote general understanding of economics. Do you think it is important for people to understand basic economics?

Absolutely, yes it is. Let me give you an example. I was writing about Manchester United in the summer of 1999 because I was interested in why the team was becoming the Harlem Globetrotter of football. The answers are not cultural or sociological, but economic. I first started to look at the pattern of incentives for players, the manager, and the board, by being quoted on the stock exchange. The market incentive is profit maximization, but it needn't be if the ownership structure were different. I think a grounding in economics, such as a year of economics at University, is essential if you want to understand such things. You are living in the country of the blind without economics.

Which areas of the economy do you think require most regulation and why?

With regulation we are trying to iron out irregularities in markets. The markets which you can afford to regulate less are those which are nearer the description of a perfect market. These are markets with few barriers to entry, where consumers have a lot of counter-veiling power and where information is easy to get. The trouble is that there are very few of them and almost every market requires regulation. Banking, for example, needs regulating because entry into the industry is hard and there are huge asymmetries of information. The consumer is largely ignorant and the banker knows far more, hence the misselling of pensions and poor loan deals. Almost all markets in Britain are franchise markets where the companies have control over entry to the market and can extract economic rent. So most markets should be regulated. Capitalism may be the least bad way of producing goods, but it doesn't mean that it should not be regulated.

To what extent should government policy aim to reduce inequality?

It was Plato who said there is no friendship amongst the unequal. Any society which gives up on the value of equality is making a big mistake. If you give up on equality, you give up on equality before the law, on equality of voting, on equality of health, and on friendship. This is a big one for economists. There are some economists who say there is nothing that can be done about the unequal outcomes of market processes and that we should not attempt to regulate them or close the inequality gaps. I believe we have to say that inequality should be reduced for the reasons I said before. But how do we constrain the growth of inequality? Inequality is partly a by-product of excessive private power, monopoly and excessive economic rent. It is also partly a by-product of lack of counter-veiling power by underprivileged workers, who are weak in relation to capital. In all these areas we have reason to intervene.

What are the most important policy decisions facing Western European governments in the next few years?

The big issue facing the British Government is whether to join the euro or not, and the big issue facing other European Union economies is whether they can sustain membership of the euro. I think the arrangements for international finance are poor. I do not think that floating exchange rates have actually worked as an optimal system for organizing international finance. We have had systematic over and under valuation of exchange rates and huge misallocations of resources as a result. We know that as financial markets get more and more instruments, the effect is to drive up exchange rate volatility. This is one of the reasons why unemployment is so high in Europe and so low in the US. The dollar over the past 25 years has been generally falling, whereas the European exchange rate has been rising. Europe has had low inflation but less growth and slower take-up of new technologies.

If we want a new regime, we can either have an exchange regime like the old exchange rate mechanism, or a single currency. The old regime was not very good at riding shocks. So the single currency is a better option but is it optimal? The institutional systems and the cyclical and structural conjuncture in the European economies are broadly similar, so I think the euro will work. The real argument against the single currency is political. It really comes down to do we want to be part of the European project or be under the control of the Americans. We live in an American empire and we need counter-veiling power, and that power can be provided by the European Union.

Demand and Supply

After studying this chapter you will be able to:

- Distinguish between a money price and a real price
- Explain the main influences on demand
- Explain the main influences on supply
- Explain how prices are determined by demand and supply
- Explain how quantities bought and sold are determined
- Explain why some prices fall, some rise and some fluctuate
- Make predictions about price changes using demand and supply

Slide, Rocket and Roller-coaster

Slide, rocket and roller-coaster – are these EuroDisney rides? No. They're commonly used descriptions of the behaviour of prices. CD players have taken a price slide. In 1983, when they first became available, their price tag was around £1,000. Now you can buy one for less than £100, and during the time that CD players have been with us, the quantity bought has increased steadily. Why has there been a slide in the price of CD players? Why hasn't the increase in the quantity bought kept their price high? ◆ The prices of houses and theatre tickets were rocketing in the 1980s. Despite rising prices, why did people continue to buy these increasingly expensive goods? ◆ The prices of apples, corn, coffee, wheat and other agricultural commodities are examples of roller-coasters. Why does the price of apples roller-coaster even when people's taste for them hardly changes at all? ◆ The prices of many of the things we buy have remained remarkably steady. The price of cassette tapes is an example. But despite their steady price, the number of tapes bought has increased each year. Why do firms sell more tapes even though they're unable to get higher prices for them, and why do people buy more tapes even though their price is no lower than it was a decade ago? ◆ The model that explains how markets work is demand and supply. When you have studied demand and supply, you will be able to answer all these questions. You will be able to explain how prices reflect opportunity cost, and how prices help people to cope with scarcity. You will understand how markets determine prices and quantities.

◆ ◆ ◆ ◆ You should study this chapter very carefully. The model of demand and supply is central to the whole of economics. It is used to study issues as diverse as wages and jobs, housing and health care, money and interest rates, as well as markets for goods and services. When you understand demand and supply you will see the world through new eyes. You will be able to make predictions about price rockets, slides and roller coasters. But first, we must take a closer look at the concept of price. What is a price?

Opportunity Cost and Price

Economic actions arise from *scarcity* – wants exceed the resources available to satisfy them. Faced with scarcity, people confront *opportunity cost* and must make choices. Choices are influenced by opportunity costs. If the opportunity cost of a good or service increases, people look for cheaper substitutes and decrease their purchases of the more expensive item.

We are going to build on these fundamental ideas and create a model to help us study both the way people respond to *prices* and the forces that determine prices. To do this, we need to understand the relationship between opportunity cost and price.

In every day life, the *price* of a good is the number of pounds or euros that we must give up to buy the good. This is called the *money price*.

The opportunity cost of an action is the best alternative foregone. When you buy a cup of coffee, you forego something. If the best thing foregone is some biscuits, then the opportunity cost of buying a cup of coffee is a quantity of biscuits foregone. We can calculate this quantity, from the money prices of coffee and biscuits.

If the money price of coffee is 50 pence a cup and the money price of biscuits is 25 pence a packet, then the opportunity cost of one cup of coffee is two packets of biscuits. To calculate this opportunity cost, we divide the price of a cup of coffee by the price of a packet of biscuits and find the *ratio* of one price to the other. The ratio of one price to another is called a **relative price** and a relative price is an opportunity cost. It is the price of good *X* divided by the price of good *Y* and it tells us how many units of good *Y* must be given up to get one more unit of good *X*.

There are trillions of relative prices – coffee to biscuits, coffee to cola, coffee to everything else, biscuits to cola, biscuits to everything else, cola to everything else – and we need a convenient way of expressing relative prices.

The normal way of expressing a relative price is in terms of a 'basket' of representative goods and services rather than in terms of one particular good or service. That is, we divide the money price of a good by the price of a basket of all goods (called a *price index*). The resulting relative price is called a **real price**. A real price tells us the opportunity cost of an item in terms of how much of the basket of all goods must be given up to buy it. A real price is expressed in units of money but based on the average prices prevailing in a given year.

Figure 4.1 gives an example of the distinction between a money price and a real price. The green curve shows the money price of wheat and tells us that the money price has been rising. But this line does not tell us what has happened to the real price of wheat and hence does not tell us about its opportunity cost. The red line shows the real price of wheat measured in 1994 pounds. This line tells us what the price would have been each year if prices *on the average* had been the same as they were in 1994. The real price of wheat has followed a falling trend since 1976, rising only for short peiods.

The theory of demand and supply that we are about to study determines real prices, and the word

Figure 4.1 The Money Price and the Real Price of Wheat

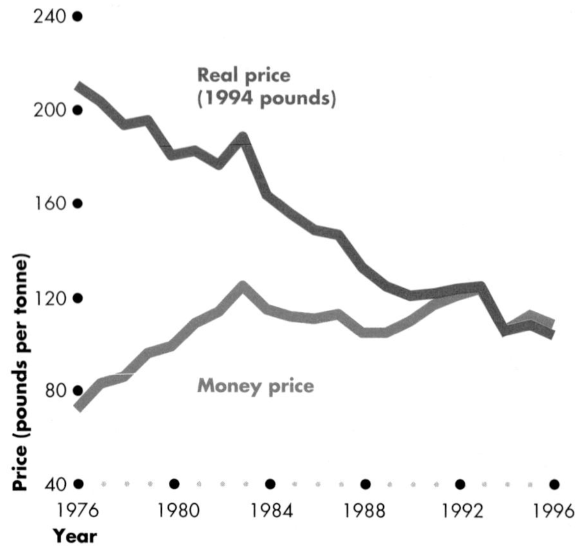

The money price of wheat in the United Kingdom – the number of pounds that must be given up for a tonne of wheat – has fluctuated between £59.80 pounds a tonne and £124.70 a tonne. But the real price or opportunity cost of wheat, expressed in 1994 pounds, has fluctuated between £106.40 and £218.58. The money price of wheat has tended to rise, but the real price of wheat has tended to fall, a fact obscured by the behaviour of its money price.

Source: Central Statistical Office, *Annual Abstract of Statistics*, London, HMSO.

'price' means real (relative) price. When we predict that a price will fall, we do not mean that its money price will fall – although it might. We mean that its real price will fall. That is, its price will fall *relative* to the average price of other goods and services.

Let's now begin our study of demand and supply by creating a model of demand.

Demand

To demand something, you must:

- Want it.
- Be able to afford it.
- Plan to buy it.

Wants are the unlimited desires or wishes that people have for goods and services. How many times have you thought that you would like something 'if only you could afford it' or 'if it weren't so expensive'? When we make choices, scarcity guarantees that many – perhaps most – of our wants will never be satisfied. Demand reflects our plans about which wants to satisfy.

The **quantity demanded** is not necessarily the same amount as the quantity actually bought. Sometimes the quantity demanded is greater than the amount of goods available, so the quantity bought is less than the quantity demanded.

The quantity demanded is measured as an amount per unit of time. For example, suppose a person consumes one cup of coffee a day. The quantity of coffee demanded by that person can be expressed as 1 cup per day or 7 cups per week or 365 cups per year. Without a time dimension, we cannot tell whether a particular quantity demanded is large or small.

What Determines Buying Plans?

The amount of any particular good or service that consumers plan to buy depends on many factors. The main ones are:

- The price of the good.
- The prices of related goods.
- Income.
- Expected future prices.
- Population.
- Preferences.

Let's start our model by looking at the relationship between the quantity demanded and the price of a good. To study this relationship, we hold constant all other influences on consumers' planned purchases. We can then ask: how does the quantity demanded of the good vary as its price varies?

The Law of Demand

The law of demand states:

> Other things remaining the same, the higher the price of a good, the smaller is the quantity demanded.

Why does a higher price reduce the quantity demanded? There are two reasons;

1 Substitution effect.

2 Income effect.

Substitution Effect When the price of a good rises, other things remaining the same, its price rises relative to the prices of all other goods. Equivalently, its opportunity cost increases. Although each good is unique, it has substitutes – other goods that serve almost as well. As the opportunity cost of a good increases, relative to the opportunity costs of its substitutes, people buy less of that good and more of its substitutes.

Income Effect When the price of a good rises, other things remaining the same, the price rises relative to people's incomes. Faced with a higher price and an unchanged income, the quantities demanded of at least some goods and services must decrease. Normally the good whose price has increased will be one of the goods bought in a smaller quantity.

To see the substitution effect and the income effect at work, think about blank cassette tapes, which we'll refer to as tapes. Many different goods provide a similar service to a tape; for example, a compact disc (CD), a prerecorded tape, a radio or television broadcast and a live concert. Tapes sell for about 90 pence each. If the price of a tape doubles to £1.80 while the prices of all the other goods remain constant, the quantity of tapes demanded decreases. People substitute CDs and prerecorded tapes for blank tapes – the substitution effect. Faced with a tighter budget, buy fewer tapes as well as less of other goods and services. If the price of a tape falls to 60 pence while the prices of all the other goods remain constant, the quantity of tapes demanded increases. People now substitute blank tapes for CDs and prerecorded tapes – the income effect. With a budget that has some slack from the lower price of tapes, people buy more tapes as well as more of other goods and services.

Demand Schedule and Demand Curve

You are now going to study one part of the most important model in economics. The model of demand and supply. When economists talk about the demand for a good, they are talking about people's plans to buy. These plans are influenced by the price of a good, but also by other things such as people's incomes. Our model of these plans is called a demand curve. Before we look at a demand curve, we must understand the demand schedule.

The table in Figure 4.2 sets the demand schedule for tapes. A *demand schedule* lists the *quantities demanded* at each different price, when all the other influences on consumers' planned purchases – such as the prices of related goods, income, expected future prices, population and preferences – are held constant. For example, if the price of a tape is 30 pence, the quantity demanded is 9 million tapes a week. If the price of a tape is £1.50, the quantity demanded is 2 million tapes a week. The other rows of the table show us the quantities demanded at prices between 60 pence and £1.20.

Figure 4.2 shows the demand curve for tapes. A **demand curve** shows the relationship between the quantity demanded of a good and its price, all other influences on consumers' planned purchases remaining the same. It is a graph of a demand schedule. By convention, the quantity demanded is measured on the horizontal axis and the price is measured on the vertical axis. The points on the demand curve labelled *a* to *e* represent the rows of the demand schedule. For example, point *a* on the graph represents a quantity demanded of 9 million tapes a week at a price of 30 pence a tape.

Figure 4.2 The Demand Curve

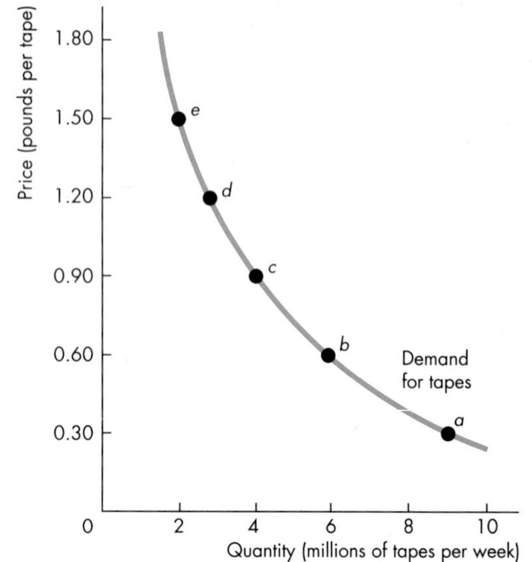

	Price (pounds per tape)	Quantity (millions of tapes per week)
a	0.30	9
b	0.60	6
c	0.90	4
d	1.20	3
e	1.50	2

The table shows a demand schedule listing the quantity of tapes demanded at each price if all other influences on buyers' plans remain the same. At a price of 30 pence a tape, 9 million tapes a week are demanded; at a price of 90 pence a tape, 4 million tapes a week are demanded. The demand curve shows the relationship between quantity demanded and price, everything else remaining the same. The demand curve slopes downward: as price decreases, the quantity demanded increases. The demand curve can be read in two ways. For a given price it tells us the quantity that people plan to buy. For example, at a price of 90 pence a tape, the quantity demanded is 4 million tapes a week. For a given quantity, the demand curve tells us the maximum price that consumers are willing to pay for the last tape bought. For example, the maximum price that consumers will pay for the 6 millionth tape is 60 pence.

Willingness and Ability to Pay Another way of looking at the demand curve is as a willingness-and-ability-to-pay curve. It tells us the highest price that someone is willing and able to pay for the last unit bought. If a large quantity is bought, that price is low; if a small quantity is bought, that price is high.

In Figure 4.2, if 9 million tapes are bought each week, the highest price that someone is willing to pay for the 9 millionth tape is 30 pence. But if only 2 million tapes are bought each week, someone is willing to pay £1.50 for the last tape bought.

A Change in Demand

The term **demand** refers to the entire relationship between the quantity demanded and the price of a good, other things remaining the same. The model of demand for tapes is described by both the demand schedule and the demand curve in Figure 4.2. To construct a demand schedule and demand curve, we hold constant all the other influences on consumers' buying plans. This part of the model allowed us to see how demand changes with price alone.

But we already know that demand changes with other factors like the price of related goods, people's incomes and preferences. So let's expand the model to look at how these other factors influence demand.

1. Prices of Related Goods The quantity of any goods and services that consumers plan to buy depends in part on the price of related goods and services. There are two types: substitutes and complements.

A **substitute** is a good that can be used in place of another good. For example, a bus ride substitutes for a train ride; a hamburger substitutes for a hot dog; a pear substitutes for an apple. As we have noted, tapes have many substitutes – mini disks, CDs, radio and television broadcasts and live concerts. If the price of one of these substitutes increases, people economize on its use and buy more tapes. For example, if the price of a CD rises, more tapes are bought and there is more taping of other people's CDs – the demand for tapes increases.

A **complement** is a good used in conjunction with another good. Some examples of complements are hamburgers and chips, party snacks and drinks, cars and petrol, PCs and software. Tapes also have complements: Walkmans, tape recorders and stereo tape decks. If the price of one of these complements increases, people buy fewer tapes. For example, if the price of a Walkman rises, fewer Walkmans are bought and, as a consequence, fewer tapes are bought – the demand for tapes decreases.

2. Income Another influence on demand is consumer income. Other things remaining the same, when income increases, consumers buy more of most goods, and when income decreases, they buy less of most goods. Although an increase in income leads to an increase in the demand for most goods, it does not lead to an increase in the demand for all goods. Goods for which demand increases as income increases are called **normal goods**. Goods for which demand decreases when income increases are called **inferior goods**. Examples of inferior goods are cheap cuts of meat and tinned foods. These two goods are a major part of the diet of people with low incomes. As incomes increase, the demand for these goods usually declines as more expensive meat and fresh products are substituted for them.

3. Expected Future Prices If the price of a good is expected to rise in the future, and if the good can be stored, the opportunity cost of obtaining the good for future use is lower now than it will be when the price has increased. So people substitute over time. They buy more of the good before the expected price rise and the demand for the good increases. Similarly, if the price of a good is expected to fall in the future, the opportunity cost of the good in the present is high relative to what is expected. So again, people substitute over time. They buy less of the good before its price is expected to fall, so the demand for the good now decreases.

4. Population Demand also depends on the size and the age structure of the population. Other things remaining the same, the larger the population, the greater is the demand for all goods and services, and the smaller the population, the smaller is the demand for all goods and services. Also, other things remaining the same, the larger the proportion of the population in a given age group, the greater is the demand for the types of goods and services used by that age group.

5. Preferences Finally, demand depends on consumer preferences. *Preferences* are an individual's attitudes towards and tastes for goods and services. For example, a music fanatic has a much greater taste for tapes than a music-hating workaholic. As a consequence, even if they have the same incomes, their demands for tapes will be different. Preferences are shaped by past experience, genetic factors, advertising information, religious beliefs, and other cultural and social factors.

Table 4.1 The Demand for Tapes

THE LAW OF DEMAND

The quantity of tapes demanded

Decreases if:	*Increases if:*
◆ The price of a tape rises	◆ The price of a tape falls

CHANGES IN DEMAND

The demand for tapes

Decreases if:	*Increases if:*
◆ The price of a substitute falls	◆ The price of a substitute rises
◆ The price of a complement rises	◆ The price of a complement falls
◆ Income falls*	◆ Income rises*
◆ The price of a tape is expected to fall in the future	◆ The price of a tape is expected to rise in the future
◆ The population decreases	◆ The population increases

*A tape is a normal good.

Table 4.1 summarizes the influences on demand and the direction of these influences.

Movement Along Versus a Shift of the Demand Curve

Changes in the factors that influence buyers' plans cause either a movement along the demand curve or a shift of the demand curve.

Movement Along the Demand Curve If the price of a good changes but everything else remains the same, there is a movement along the demand curve. For example, if the price of a tape changes from 90 pence to £1.50, the result is a movement along the demand curve, from point *c* to point *e* in Figure 4.2. The negative slope of the demand curve reveals that a decrease in the price of a good or service increases the quantity demanded – the law of demand.

A Shift of the Demand Curve If the price of a good remains constant but some other influence on buyers' plans changes, there is a change in demand for that good. We illustrate a change in demand as a shift of the demand curve. For example, a fall in the price of a Walkman – a complement of tapes – increases the demand for tapes. We illustrate this increase in demand for tapes with a new demand schedule and a new demand curve. Whether the price of tapes is high or low, if the price of a Walkman falls, consumers buy more tapes. This is what a shift of the demand curve shows. It shows that more tapes are bought at each and every price.

Figure 4.3 An Increase in Demand

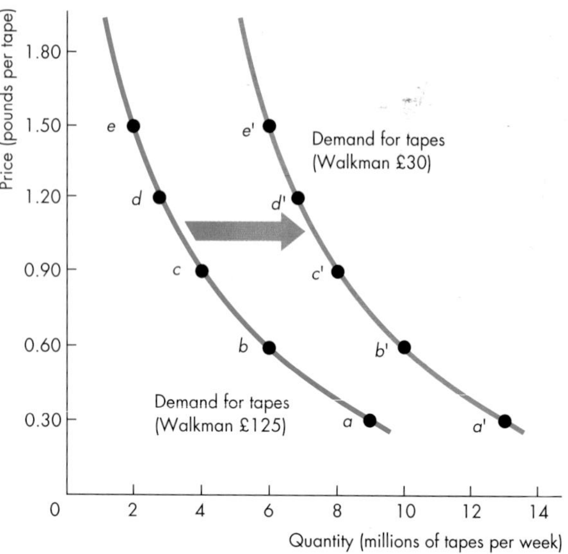

	Original demand schedule (Walkman £125)			New demand schedule (Walkman £30)	
	Price (pounds per tape)	Quantity (millions of tapes per week)		Price (pounds per tape)	Quantity (millions of tapes per week)
a	0.30	9	*a'*	0.30	13
b	0.60	6	*b'*	0.60	10
c	0.90	4	*c'*	0.90	8
d	1.20	3	*d'*	1.20	7
e	1.50	2	*e'*	1.50	6

A change in any influence on buyers other than the price of the good itself results in a new demand schedule and a shift of the demand curve. A change in the price of a Walkman changes the demand for tapes. At a price of 90 pence a tape (row *c* of the table), 4 million tapes a week are demanded when a Walkman costs £125 and 8 million tapes a week are demanded when a Walkman costs only £30. A fall in the price of a Walkman increases the demand for tapes because it is a complement of tapes. When demand *increases*, the demand curve shifts rightward, as shown by the shift arrow and the resulting red curve.

Figure 4.4 A Change in Demand Versus a Change in Quantity Demanded

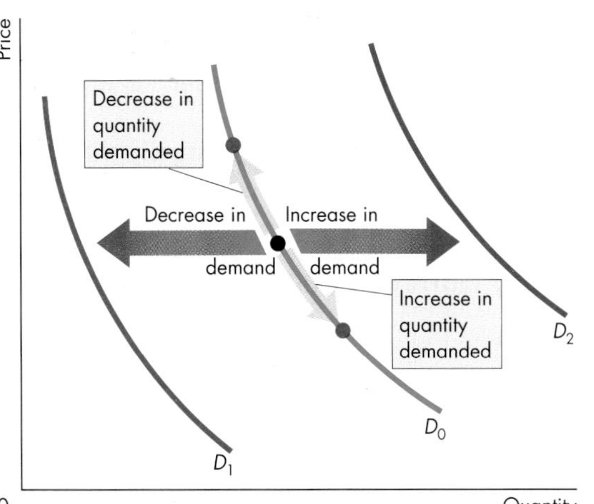

The blue arrow shows a *change in the quantity demanded* when the demand curve is D_0. A rise (fall) in the price of the good leads to a decrease (increase) in the quantity demanded and a movement along the demand curve as shown by the arrow. A change in any factor other than the price of the good, leads to a *change in demand* by shifting the demand curve – to D_2, an increase in demand and D_1, a *decrease in demand.*

Figure 4.3 illustrates such a shift. The table sets out the original demand schedule when the price of a Walkman is £125 and the new demand schedule when the price of a Walkman is £30. These numbers record the change in demand. The graph in Figure 4.3 illustrates the corresponding shift of the demand curve. When the price of the Walkman falls, the demand curve for tapes shifts rightward.

A Change in Demand Versus a Change in Quantity Demanded A point on the demand curve shows the quantity demanded at a given price. A movement along the demand curve shows a **change in the quantity demanded**. The entire demand curve shows demand. A shift of the demand curve shows a **change in demand**.

Figure 4.4 illustrates and summarizes these distinctions. If the price of a good falls but nothing else changes, then there is an increase in the quantity demanded of that good (a movement down the demand curve D_0). If the price rises, but nothing else changes, then there is a decrease in the quantity demanded (a movement up the demand curve D_0). When any other influence on buyers' planned purchases changes, the demand curve shifts and there is a *change* (an increase or a decrease) *in demand*. A rise in income (for a normal good), in population, in the price of a substitute or in the expected future price of the good, or a fall in the price of a complement, shifts the demand curve rightward (to the red demand curve D_2). This represents an *increase in demand*. A fall in income (for a normal good), in population, in the price of a substitute or in the expected future price of the good, or a rise in the price of a complement, shifts the demand curve leftward (to the red demand curve D_1). This represents a *decrease in demand*. (For an inferior good, the effects of changes in income are in the opposite direction to those described above.)

Review

- The quantity demanded is the amount of a good that consumers plan to buy during a given period of time.
- The model of demand shows the relationship between quantity demanded and price, other things remaining the same.
- When the price of the good changes, other things remaining the same, we can predict a change in the quantity demanded and a movement along the demand curve.
- When any other influences on buying plans change, we can predict a change in demand and a shift of the demand curve.

Supply

If a firm supplies a good or service, the firm must:

- Have the resources and technology to produce it.
- Be able to profit from producing it.
- Plan to produce and sell it.

Supply is more than just having the resources and technology to produce something. Resources and technology are the constraints that limit what is possible.

Many useful things can be produced, but they are not produced unless it is profitable to do so. Supply reflects a decision about which technologically feasible goods and services to produce.

The **quantity supplied** of a good is the amount that producers plan to sell during a given time period. The quantity supplied is not the amount producers would like to sell but the amount they definitely plan to sell. But the quantity supplied is not necessarily the same as the quantity actually sold. If consumers do not want to buy the quantity producers plan to sell, the sales plans will be frustrated. Like quantity demanded, the quantity supplied is expressed as an amount per unit of time.

What Determines Selling Plans?

The amount that producers plan to sell of any particular good or service depends on many factors. The main ones are:

- The price of the good.
- The prices of factors of production.
- The prices of related goods.
- Expected future prices.
- The number of suppliers.
- Technology.

Let's start to build a model of supply by looking at the relationship between the price of a good and the quantity supplied. In order to study this relationship, we hold constant all the other influences on the quantity supplied. We want to know how the quantity supplied of a good varies as its price varies.

The Law of Supply

The law of supply states:

> Other things remaining the same, the higher the price of a good, the greater is the quantity supplied.

Why does a higher price increase the quantity supplied? It is because of increasing marginal cost. As the quantity produced of any good increases, the marginal cost of producing that good increases. (You can refresh your memory of increasing marginal cost and opportunity cost in Chapter 3, p. 46).

It would never be worth producing a good if the price you sold it for did not cover the marginal cost of producing it. So producers are only willing to incur the higher marginal cost of increased supply, other things remaining the same, when the price of a good rises. The higher price results in an increase in the quantity supplied.

Let's now illustrate the law of supply with a supply schedule and supply curve.

Supply Schedule and Supply Curve

The table in Figure 4.5 sets out the supply schedule for tapes. A *supply schedule* lists the quantities supplied at each different price, when all other influences on the amount producers plan to sell remain the same. For example, if the price of a tape is 30 pence, no tapes are supplied. If the price of a tape is £1.20, 5 million tapes are supplied each week.

Figure 4.5 illustrates the supply curve for tapes. A **supply curve** shows the relationship between the quantity supplied and the price of a good, everything else remaining the same. It is a graph of a supply schedule. The points on the supply curve labelled *a* to *e* represent the rows of the supply schedule. For example, point *d* represents a quantity supplied of 5 million tapes a week at a price of £1.20 a tape.

Minimum Supply Price Just as the demand curve has two interpretations, so too does the supply curve. It shows the quantity that producers plan to sell at each possible price. It also shows the minimum price at which the last unit will be supplied. For producers to be willing to supply the 3 millionth tape each week, the price must be at least 60 pence a tape. For producers to be willing to supply the 5 millionth tape each week, they must get at least £1.20 a tape.

A Change in Supply

The term **supply** refers to the relationship between the quantity supplied of a good and its price, other things remaining the same. The supply of tapes is described by both the supply schedule and the supply curve in Figure 4.5. To construct a supply schedule and supply curve, we hold constant all the other influences on suppliers' plans. This part of the

Figure 4.5 The Supply Curve 

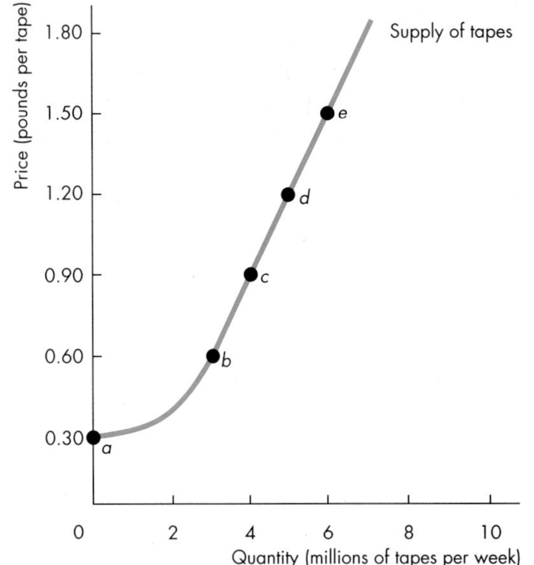

	Price (pounds per tape)	Quantity (millions of tapes per week)
a	0.30	0
b	0.60	3
c	0.90	4
d	1.20	5
e	1.50	6

The table shows the supply schedule of tapes. For example, at 60 pence a tape, 3 million tapes a week are supplied; at £1.50 a tape, 6 million tapes a week are supplied. The supply curve shows the relationship between the quantity supplied and the price, everything else remaining the same. The supply curve usually slopes upward: as the price of a good increases, so does the quantity supplied. A supply curve can be read in two ways. For a given price, it tells us the quantity that producers plan to sell. For example, at a price of 90 pence a tape, producers plan to sell 4 million tapes a week. The supply curve also tells us the minimum acceptable price at which a given quantity will be offered for sale. For example, the minimum acceptable price that will bring forth a supply of 5 million tapes a week is £1.20 a tape.

model allowed us to see how supply changes with price alone.

But we already know that supply changes with other factors like the price of factors of production and related goods, expected future prices and technology. So let's expand the model to look at how these other factors influence supply.

1. Prices of Factors of Production The prices of the factors of production used to produce a good influence its supply. For example, an increase in the prices of the labour and the capital equipment used to produce tapes increases the cost of producing tapes. So for a given market price, the supplier is willing to supply fewer tapes.

2. Prices of Related Goods The supply of a good can be influenced by the prices of related goods. For example, if a car assembly line can produce either sports cars or saloons, the quantity of saloons produced will depend on the price of sports cars and the quantity of sports cars produced will depend on the price of saloons. These two goods are *substitutes in production*. An increase in the price of a substitute in production lowers the supply of the good. Goods can also be complements in production. *Complements in production* arise when two things are, of necessity, produced together. For example, extracting chemicals from coal produces coke, coal tar and nylon. An increase in the price of any one of these by-products of coal increases the supply of the other by-products.

Blank tapes have no obvious complements in production, but they do have substitutes in production: prerecorded tapes. Suppliers of tapes can produce blank tapes and prerecorded tapes. An increase in the price of prerecorded tapes encourages producers to use their equipment to produce more prerecorded tapes and so the supply of blank tapes decreases.

3. Expected Future Prices If the price of a good is expected to rise in the future, and if the good can be stored, the return from selling the good in the future is higher than it is in the present. So producers substitute over time. They offer a smaller quantity for sale before the expected price rise and the supply of the good decreases. Similarly, if the price of a good is expected to fall in the future, the return from selling it in the present is high relative to what is expected. So again, producers substitute over time. They offer to sell more of the good before its price is expected to fall, so the supply of the good increases.

Table 4.2 The Supply of Tapes

THE LAW OF SUPPLY

The quantity of tapes supplied

Decreases if:	*Increases if:*
◆ The price of a tape falls	◆ The price of a tape rises

CHANGES IN SUPPLY

The supply of tapes

Decreases if:	*Increases if:*
◆ The price of a factor of production used to produce tapes increases	◆ The price of a factor of production used to produce tapes decreases
◆ The price of a substitute in production rises	◆ The price of a substitute in production falls
◆ The price of a complement in production falls	◆ The price of a complement in production rises
◆ The price of a tape is expected to rise in the future	◆ The price of a tape is expected to fall in the future
◆ The number of firms supplying tapes decreases	◆ The number of firms supplying tapes increases
	◆ More efficient technologies for producing tapes emerge

4. The Number of Suppliers When new firms enter a market and no firms leave a market, the quantity of the good supplied will increase. Other things remaining the same, the larger the number of firms supplying a good, the larger is the supply of the good.

5. Technology New technologies that enable producers to use less of each factor of production or cheaper factors of production lower the cost of production and increase supply. For example, the development of a new technology for tape production by BASF, Sony and Minnesota Mining and Manufacturing (3M) has lowered the cost of producing tapes and increased their supply. Over the long term, changes in technology are the most important influence on supply.

Table 4.2 summarizes the influences on supply and the directions of those influences.

Movement Along Versus a Shift of the Supply Curve

Changes in the factors that influence producers' planned sales cause either a movement along the supply curve or a shift of the supply curve.

Movement Along the Supply Curve If the price of a good changes but everything else influencing suppliers' planned sales remains constant, there is a movement along the supply curve. For example, if the price of tapes increases from 90 pence to £1.50 a tape, there will be a movement along the supply curve from point *c* (4 million tapes a week) to point *e* (6 million tapes a week) in Figure 4.5. The positive slope of the supply curve reveals that an increase in the price of a good or service increases the quantity supplied – the law of supply.

A Shift of the Supply Curve If the price of a good remains the same but another influence on suppliers' planned sales changes, then there is a change in supply and a shift of the supply curve. For example, as we have already noted, technological advances lower the cost of producing tapes and increase their supply. As a result, the supply schedule changes. The table in Figure 4.6 provides some hypothetical numbers that illustrate such a change. The table contains two supply schedules: the original, based on 'old' technology, and one based on 'new' technology. With the new technology, more tapes are supplied at each price. The graph in Figure 4.6 illustrates the resulting shift of the supply curve. When tape-producing technology improves, the supply curve of tapes shifts rightward, as shown by the shift arrow and the red supply curve.

A Change in Supply Versus a Change in Quantity Supplied A point on the supply curve shows the quantity supplied at a given price. A movement along the supply curve shows a **change in the quantity supplied**. The entire supply curve shows supply. A shift of the supply curve shows a **change in supply**.

Figure 4.7 illustrates and summarizes these distinctions. If the price of a good falls but nothing else changes, then there is a decrease in the quantity supplied of that good (a movement down the supply curve S_0). If the price of a good rises but nothing else changes, there is an increase in the quantity supplied (a movement up the supply curve S_0). When any other influence on sellers changes, the supply curve shifts and there is a *change in supply*. If the supply curve is S_0 and there is, say, a technological change that reduces the amounts of the factors of production needed to produce the good,

Figure 4.6 An Increase in Supply

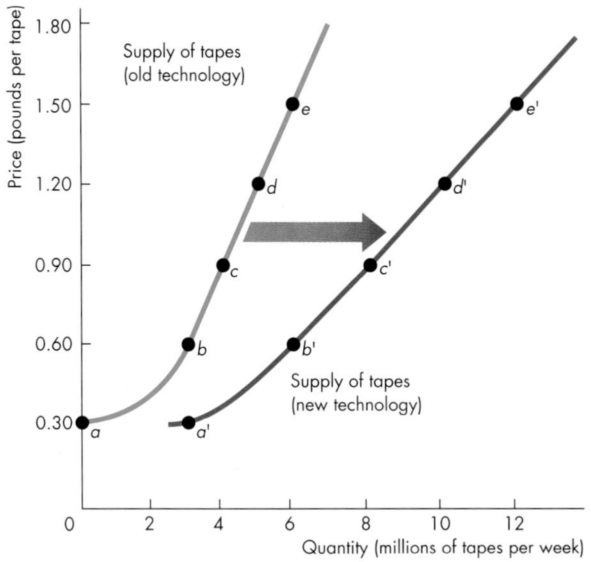

	Original supply schedule (original technology)			New supply schedule (new technology)	
	Price (pounds per tape)	**Quantity (millions of tapes per week)**		**Price (pounds per tape)**	**Quantity (millions of tapes per week)**
a	0.30	0	*a'*	0.30	3
b	0.60	3	*b'*	0.60	6
c	0.90	4	*c'*	0.90	8
d	1.20	5	*d'*	1.20	10
e	1.50	6	*e'*	1.50	12

A change in any influence on sellers other than the price of the good itself results in a new supply schedule and a shift of the supply curve. For example, if BASF, Sony and 3M invent a new, cost-saving technology for producing tapes, the supply of tapes changes. At a price of 60 pence a tape (row *b* of the table), 3 million tapes a week are supplied when the producers use the old technology, and 6 million tapes a week are supplied with the new technology. An advance in technology increases the supply of tapes and the supply curve shifts rightward, as shown by the shift arrow and the resulting red curve.

then supply increases and the supply curve shifts to the red supply curve S_2. If production costs rise, supply decreases and the supply curve shifts to the red supply curve S_1.

Figure 4.7 A Change in Supply Versus a Change in the Quantity Supplied

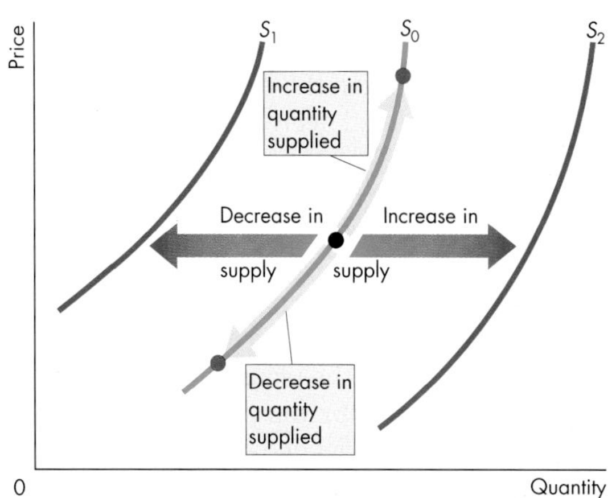

The blue arrow shows a *change in the quantity supplied* when the supply curve is S_0. A rise (fall) in the price of the good leads to a decrease (increase) in the quantity supplied and a movement along the supply curve as shown by the arrow. A change in any factor other than the price of the good, leads to a *change in supply* by shifting the supply curve – to S_2, an *increase in supply* and S_1, a *decrease in supply.*

Review

- The quantity supplied is the amount of a good that producers plan to sell during a given period of time.
- The model of supply shows the relationship between quantity supplied and price, other things remaining the same.
- When the price of the good changes, other things remaining the same, we can predict a change in the quantity supplied and a movement along the supply curve.
- When any other influences on selling plans change, we can predict a change in supply and a shift of the supply curve.

Let's now bring the two concepts of demand and supply together to create a model which will show how prices and quantities are determined.

Market Equilibrium

We have seen that when the price of a good rises, the quantity demanded decreases and the quantity supplied increases. We are now going to see how prices coordinate the choices of buyers and sellers and achieve equilibrium.

An equilibrium is a situation in which opposing forces balance each other, so there is no tendency for change. Market equilibrium occurs when the market price balances the plans of both buyers and sellers. The **equilibrium price** is the price at which the quantity demanded equals the quantity supplied. The **equilibrium quantity** is the quantity bought and sold at the equilibrium price. A market moves towards its equilibrium because:

- Price regulates buying and selling plans.
- Price adjusts when plans don't match.

Price as a Regulator

The price of a good regulates the quantities demanded and supplied. If the price is too high, the quantity supplied exceeds the quantity demanded. If the price is too low, the quantity demanded exceeds the quantity supplied. There is one price, and only one price, at which the quantity demanded equals the quantity supplied. Let's work out what that price is.

Figure 4.8 shows the market for tapes. The table shows the demand schedule (from Figure 4.2) and the supply schedule (from Figure 4.5). If the price of a tape is 30 pence, the quantity demanded is 9 million tapes a week, but no tapes are supplied. The quantity demanded exceeds the quantity supplied by 9 million tapes a week. In other words, at a price of 30 pence a tape, there is a shortage of 9 million tapes a week. This shortage is shown in the final column of the table. At a price of 60 pence a tape, there is still a shortage but only of 3 million tapes a week. If the price of a tape is £1.20, the quantity supplied exceeds the quantity demanded. The quantity supplied is 5 million tapes a week, but the quantity demanded is only 3 million. There is a surplus of 2 million tapes a week. There is one price and only one price at which there is neither a shortage nor a surplus. The equilibrium price is 90 pence a tape. At that price the equilibrium quantity demanded is equal to the quantity supplied – 4 million tapes a week.

Figure 4.8 shows that the demand curve and the supply curve intersect at the equilibrium price of

Figure 4.8 Equilibrium

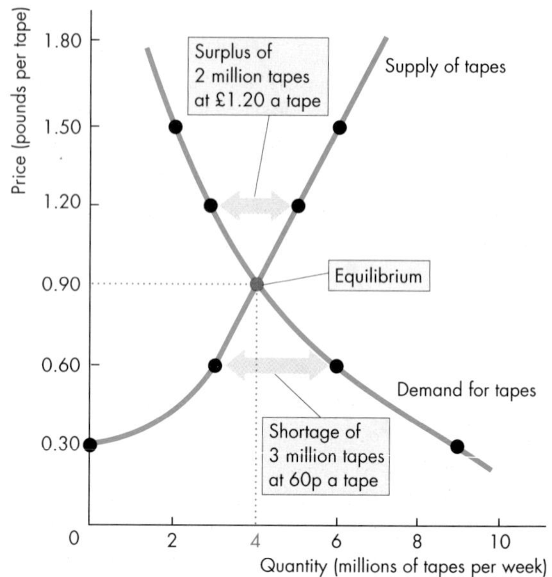

Price (pounds per tape)	Quantity demanded	Quantity supplied	Shortage (–) or surplus (+)
	(millions of tapes per week)		
0.30	9	0	–9
0.60	6	3	–3
0.90	4	4	0
1.20	3	5	+2
1.50	2	6	+4

The table lists the quantities demanded and quantities supplied as well as the shortage or surplus of tapes at each price. If the price of a tape is 60 pence, 6 million tapes a week are demanded and 3 million are supplied. There is a shortage of 3 million tapes a week, and the price rises. If the price of a tape is £1.20, 3 million tapes a week are demanded but 5 million are supplied. There is a surplus of 2 million tapes a week, and the price falls. If the price of a tape is 90 pence, 4 million tapes a week are demanded and 4 million are supplied. There is neither a shortage nor a surplus. Neither buyers nor sellers have any incentive to change the price. The price at which the quantity demanded equals the quantity supplied is the equilibrium price.

90 pence a tape. At that price, the equilibrium quantity demanded and supplied is 4 million tapes a week. At each price *above* 90 pence a tape, the quantity supplied exceeds the quantity demanded. There is a surplus of tapes. For example, at £1.20 a tape the surplus is 2 million tapes a week, as shown by the blue arrow in the figure. At each price *below* 90 pence a tape, the quantity demanded exceeds the quantity supplied. There is a shortage of tapes. For example, at 60 pence a tape, the shortage is 3 million tapes a week, as shown by the red arrow in the figure.

Price Adjustments

You have seen that shortages arise if price is below the equilibrium price, and surpluses arise if price is above the equilibrium price. But why should price change to eliminate a shortage or a surplus? Price will adjust when there is a shortage or a surplus because it is beneficial to both buyers and sellers. Let's see why?

A Shortage Forces the Price Up Suppose the price of a tape is 60 pence. Consumers plan to buy 6 million tapes a week and producers plan to sell 3 million tapes a week. Consumers can't force producers to sell, so the quantity actually offered for sale is 3 million tapes a week. In this situation, powerful forces operate to increase the price and move it towards the equilibrium price. Some people, unable to find the tapes they planned to buy, offer to pay more. Some producers, noticing lines of unsatisfied consumers, move their prices up. As buyers try to outbid one another, and as producers push their prices up, the price rises towards its equilibrium. The rising price reduces the shortage because it decreases the quantity demanded and increases the quantity supplied. When the price has increased to the point at which there is no longer a shortage, the forces moving the price stop operating and the price comes to rest at its equilibrium.

A Surplus Forces the Price Down Suppose the price of a tape is £1.20. Producers plan to sell 5 million tapes a week and consumers plan to buy 3 million tapes a week. Producers cannot force consumers to buy, so the quantity actually bought is 3 million tapes a week. In this situation, powerful forces operate to lower the price and move it towards the equilibrium price. Some producers, unable to sell the quantities of tapes they planned to sell, cut their prices. Some buyers, noticing shelves of unsold tapes, offer to buy for a lower price. As producers try to undercut one another, and as buyers make lower price offers, the price falls towards its equilibrium. The falling price reduces the surplus because it increases the quantity demanded and decreases the quantity supplied. When the price has decreased to the point at which there is no longer a surplus, the forces moving the price stop operating and the price comes to rest at its equilibrium.

The Best Deal Available for Buyers and Sellers
Both shortages and surpluses lead to price changes. In the tape market example, prices were forced up or down until they hit 90 pence a tape. So why don't buyers refuse to pay as price increases? Buyers pay higher prices because they value the good more highly than its current price. So why don't sellers refuse to sell at lower prices? Sellers continue to sell as the price falls because their minimum supply price is below the current price.

At the equilibrium price, the quantity demanded and the quantity supplied are equal and neither buyers nor sellers can do business at a better price. Consumers pay the highest price they are willing to pay for the last unit bought, and producers receive the lowest price at which they are willing to supply the last unit sold.

When people freely make bids and offers and when buyers seek the lowest price and sellers seek the highest price, the price at which trade takes place is the equilibrium price. At this price, the quantity demanded equals the quantity supplied. Price has coordinated the plans of buyers and sellers.

Review

- The equilibrium price is the price at which buyers' and sellers' plans match each other – the price at which the quantity demanded equals the quantity supplied.
- At prices below the equilibrium, there is a shortage and the price rises.
- At prices above the equilibrium, there is a surplus and the price falls.

- Only at the equilibrium price are there no forces acting on the price to make it change.

The theory of demand and supply is now a central part of economics. But this was not always the case. Only 100 years ago, the best economists of the day were quite confused about matters that today even students in introductory courses can get right (see *Economics in History* on pp. 94–95). You'll discover in the rest of this chapter that the theory of demand and supply helps us to understand and make predictions about changes in prices – including the price slides, rockets and roller-coasters described in the chapter opener.

Predicting Changes in Price and Quantity

The theory we have just studied provides us with a powerful way of analysing influences on prices and the quantities bought and sold. According to the theory, a change in price stems from either a change in demand or a change in supply or a change in both. First, let's use our model to discover the effects of a change in demand.

A Change in Demand

What happens to the price and quantity of tapes if demand for tapes increases? We can answer this question with a specific example. If the price of a Walkman falls from £125 to £30, the demand for tapes increases as is shown in the table in Figure 4.9. (Recall that tapes and Walkmans are complements and that when the price of a complement falls the demand for the good increases.) The original demand schedule and the new one are set out in the first three columns of the table. The table also shows the supply schedule for tapes.

The original equilibrium price is 90 pence a tape. At that price, 4 million tapes a week are demanded and supplied. When demand increases, the price that makes the quantity demanded equal the quantity supplied is £1.50 a tape. At this price, 6 million tapes are bought and sold each week. When demand increases, both the price and the quantity increase.

Figure 4.9 shows these changes. The figure shows the original demand for and supply of tapes. The original equilibrium price is 90 pence a tape and the quantity is 4 million tapes a week. When demand increases, the demand curve shifts rightward. The equilibrium price rises to £1.50 a tape and the quantity supplied increases to 6 million tapes a week, as is highlighted in the figure. There is an

Figure 4.9 The Effects of a Change in Demand

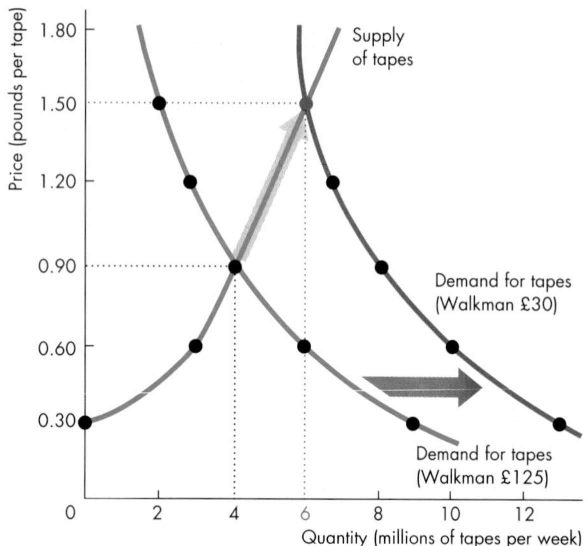

Price (pounds per tape)	Quantity demanded (millions of tapes per week)		Quantity supplied (millions of tapes per week)
	Walkman £125	Walkman £30	
0.30	9	13	0
0.60	6	10	3
0.90	4	8	4
1.20	3	7	5
1.50	2	6	6

With the price of a Walkman at £125, the demand for tapes is the blue curve. The equilibrium price is 90 pence a tape and the equilibrium quantity is 4 million tapes a week. When the price of a Walkman falls from £125 to £30, there is an increase in the demand for tapes and the demand curve shifts right – the red curve. At 90 pence a tape, there is now a shortage of 4 million tapes a week. The quantities of tapes demanded and supplied are equal at a price of £1.50 a tape. The price rises to this level and the quantity supplied increases. But there is no change in supply. The supply curve does not shift. The increase in demand increases the equilibrium price to £1.50 and increases the equilibrium quantity to 6 million tapes a week.

increase in the quantity supplied but *no change in supply*. That is, the supply curve does not shift.

The exercise that we've just conducted can easily be reversed. If we start at a price of £1.50 a tape, trading 6 million tapes a week, we can work out what happens if demand decreases to its original level. You can see that the decrease in demand lowers the equilibrium price to 90 pence a tape and decreases the equilibrium quantity to 4 million tapes a week. Such a decrease in demand might arise from a decrease in the price of CDs or of CD players. (CDs and CD players are substitutes for tapes.)

We can now make our two clear market predictions. Holding everything else constant:

1 When demand increases, both the price and the quantity traded in the market increase.

2 When demand decreases, both the price and the quantity traded in the market decrease.

A Change in Supply

Suppose that BASF, Sony and 3M introduce a new cost-saving technology in their tape-production plants. The new technology changes the supply. The new supply schedule (the one that was shown in Figure 4.6) is presented in the table in Figure 4.10. What is the new equilibrium price and quantity? The answer is highlighted in the table: the price falls to 60 pence a tape and the quantity increases to 6 million a week. You can see why by looking at the quantities demanded and supplied at the old price of a tape. The quantity supplied at that price is 8 million tapes a week and there is a surplus of tapes. The price falls. Only when the price is 60 pence a tape does the quantity supplied equal the quantity demanded.

Figure 4.10 illustrates the effect of an increase in supply. It shows the demand curve for tapes and the original and new supply curves. The initial equilibrium price is 90 pence a tape and the original quantity is 4 million tapes a week. When the supply increases, the supply curve shifts rightward. The equilibrium price falls to 60 pence a tape and the quantity demanded increases to 6 million tapes a week, highlighted in the figure. There is an increase in the quantity demanded but *no change in demand*. That is, the demand curve does not shift.

The exercise that we've just conducted can be reversed. If we start at a price of 60 pence a tape with 6 million tapes a week being bought and sold, we can work out what happens if supply decreases to its original level. You can see that the decrease in supply increases the equilibrium price to 90 pence a tape and decreases the equilibrium quantity to

Figure 4.10 The Effects of a Change in Supply

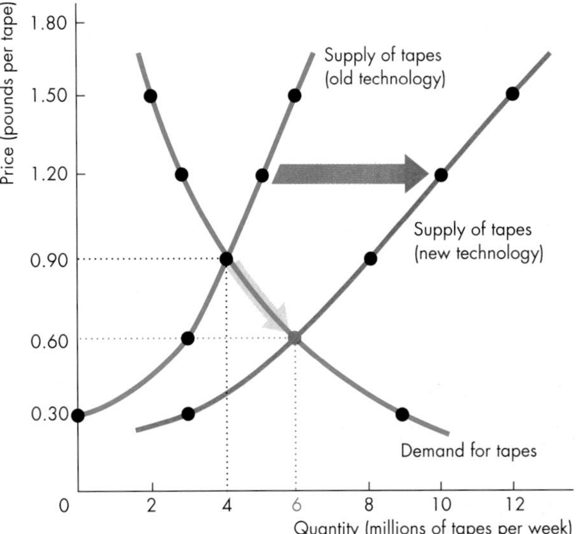

Price (pounds per tape)	Quantity demanded (millions of tapes per week	Quantity supplied (millions of tapes per week)	
		Original technology	New technology
0.30	9	0	3
0.60	6	3	6
0.90	4	4	8
1.20	3	5	10
1.50	2	6	12

With the original technology, the supply of tapes is shown by the blue curve. The equilibrium price is 90 pence a tape and the equilibrium quantity is 4 million tapes a week. When the new technology is adopted, there is an increase in the supply of tapes. The supply curve shifts right – the red curve. At 90 pence a tape there is now a surplus of 4 million tapes a week. The quantities of tapes demanded and supplied are equal at a price of 60 pence a tape. The price falls to this level and the quantity demanded increases – there is a movement along the demand curve. But there is no change in demand. The demand curve does not shift. The increase in supply lowers the price of tapes to 60p and increases the quantity to 6 million tapes a week.

4 million tapes a week. Such a decrease in supply might arise from an increase in the cost of labour or raw materials.

We can now make two more predictions. Holding everything else constant:

1 When supply increases, the quantity traded increases and the price falls.

2 When supply decreases, the quantity traded *decreases and the price rises.*

A Change in Both Supply and Demand You can now predict the effects of a change in either demand or supply on price and quantity. *Reading Between the Lines* on pp. 92–93 shows how the surplus of student accommodation could have been predicted when student numbers applying to Hull University fell sharply. But what happens if both demand and supply change together? To answer this question, we will look first at the case when demand and supply both change in the same direction – both increase or decrease together. Then we'll look at the case in which they move in opposite directions – demand decreases and supply increases or demand increases and supply decreases.

Demand and Supply Change in the Same Direction We've seen that an increase in the demand for tapes increases the price of tapes and increases the quantity bought and sold. We've also seen that an increase in the supply of tapes lowers the price of tapes and increases the quantity bought and sold. Let's now examine what happens in our model when both of these changes happen to occur together.

The table in Figure 4.11 brings together the numbers that describe the original quantities demanded and supplied and the new quantities demanded and supplied after the fall in the price of a Walkman and the improved tape production technology. These same numbers are illustrated in the graph. The original (blue) demand and supply curves intersect at a price of 90 pence a tape and a quantity of 4 million tapes a week. The new (red) supply and demand curves also intersect at a price of 90 pence a tape but at a quantity of 8 million tapes a week.

An increase in either demand or supply increases the quantity. Therefore when both demand and supply increase, so does quantity. But an increase in demand increases the price and an increase in

Figure 4.11 The Effects of an Increase in both Demand and Supply

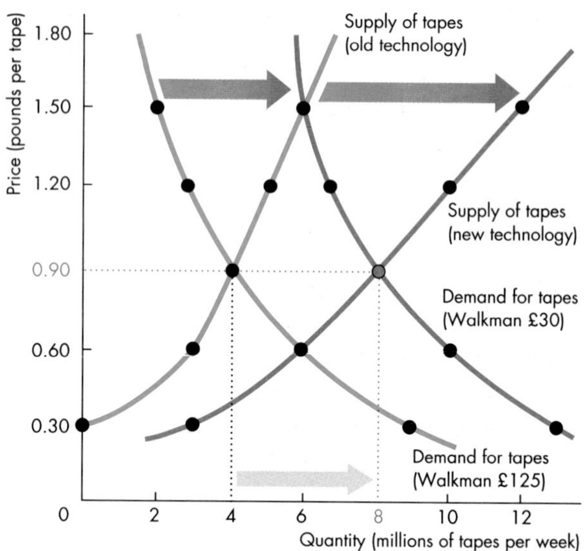

Price (pounds per tape)	Original quantities (millions of tapes per week)		New quantities (millions of tapes per week)	
	Quantity demanded (Walkman £125)	Quantity supplied (original technology)	Quantity demanded (Walkman £30)	Quantity supplied (new technology)
0.30	9	0	13	3
0.60	6	3	10	6
0.90	4	4	8	8
1.20	3	5	7	10
1.50	2	6	6	12

When a Walkman costs £125, and the old technology is used to produce tapes, the price of a tape is 90 pence and the quantity is 4 million tapes a week. A fall in the price of a Walkman increases the demand for tapes, and improved technology increases the supply of tapes. The new technology supply curve intersects the higher demand curve at 90 pence, the same price as before, but the quantity increases to 8 million tapes a week. These increases in demand and supply increase the quantity but leave the price unchanged.

supply lowers the price, so we can't say for sure which way the price will change when demand and supply increase together. In this example, the increases in demand and supply are such that the rise in price brought about by an increase in demand is offset by the fall in price brought about by an increase in supply – so the price does not change. But notice that if demand had increased slightly more than shown in the figure, the price would have risen. If supply had increased by slightly more than shown in the figure, the price would have fallen.

We can now make two more market predictions:

1 When *both* demand and supply increase, the market quantity increases and the price increases, decreases or remains constant.
2 When *both* demand and supply decrease, the market quantity decreases and the price increases, decreases or remains constant.

Demand and Supply Change in Opposite Directions Let's now see what happens when demand and supply change together but move in *opposite* directions. We'll look yet again at the market for tapes, but this time supply increases and demand decreases. An improved production technology increases the supply of tapes as before. But now the price of CD players falls. A CD player is a *substitute* for tapes. With less costly CD players, more people buy them and switch from buying tapes to buying CDs and the demand for tapes decreases.

The table in Figure 4.12 describes the original and new demand and supply schedules and these schedules are shown as the original (blue) and new (red) demand and supply curves in the graph. The original demand and supply curves intersect at a price of £1.50 a tape and a quantity of 6 million tapes a week. The new supply and demand curves intersect at a price of 60 pence a tape and at the original quantity of 6 million tapes a week. In this example, the decrease in demand and the increase in supply are such that the decrease in the quantity brought about by a decrease in demand is offset by the increase in quantity brought about by an increase in supply – so the quantity does not change.

A decrease in demand or an increase in supply lower the price. Therefore when both a decrease in demand and an increase in supply occur together, the price falls.

Figure 4.12 The Effects of a Decrease in Demand and an Increase in Supply

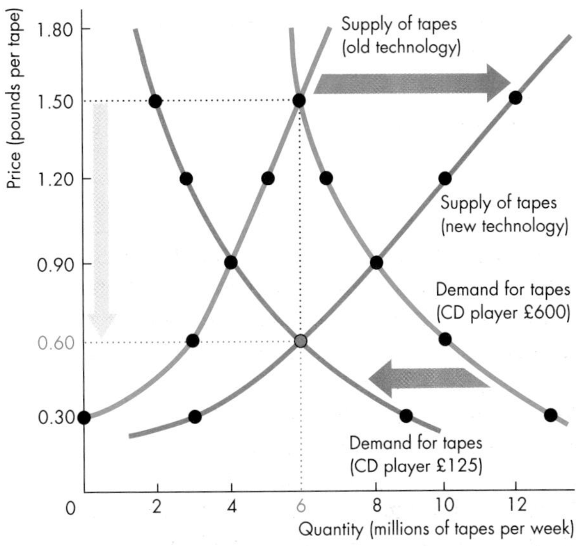

Price (pounds per tape)	Original quantities (millions of tapes per week)		New quantities (millions of tapes per week)	
	Quantity demanded (CD player £600)	Quantity supplied (original technology)	Quantity demanded (CD player £125)	Quantity supplied (new technology)
0.30	13	0	9	3
0.60	10	3	6	6
0.90	8	4	4	8
1.20	7	5	3	10
1.50	6	6	2	123

When CD players cost £600 and the old technology is used to produce tapes, the price of a tape is £1.50 and the quantity is 6 million tapes a week. A fall in the price of CD players decreases the demand for tapes, and improved technology increases the supply of tapes. The new technology supply curve intersects the lower demand curve at 60 pence, a lower price, but in this case the quantity remains constant at 6 million tapes a week. The decrease in demand and increase in supply lower the price but leave the quantity unchanged.

Figure 4.13 Price Slide, Rocket and Roller-coaster

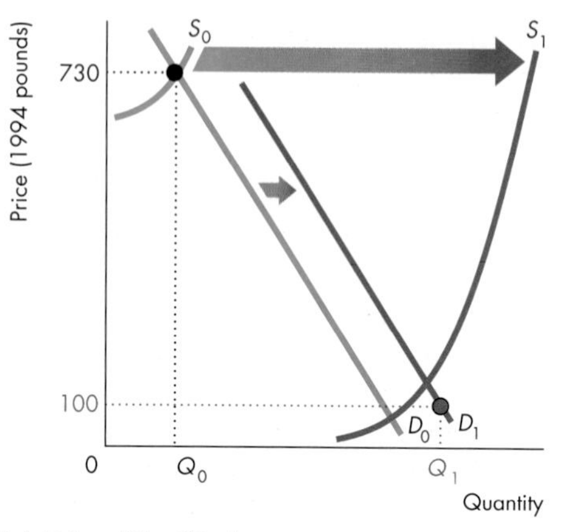

(a) Price slide: CD players

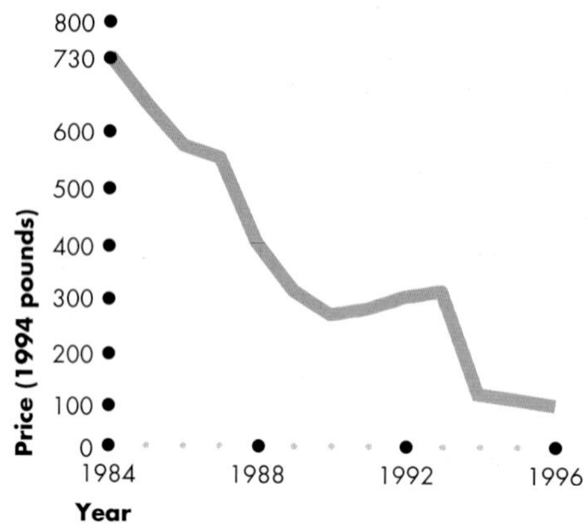

A large increase in the supply of CD players, from S_0 to S_1, between 1984 and 1996, combined with a small increase in demand, from D_0 to D_1, over the same period, resulted in a fall in the average (real) price of CD players from £1,000 in 1984 to £100 in 1996. The quantity of CD players bought and sold increases from Q_0 to Q_1 (part a). Part (b) shows this price slide.

Source: Author's calculations from retail data.

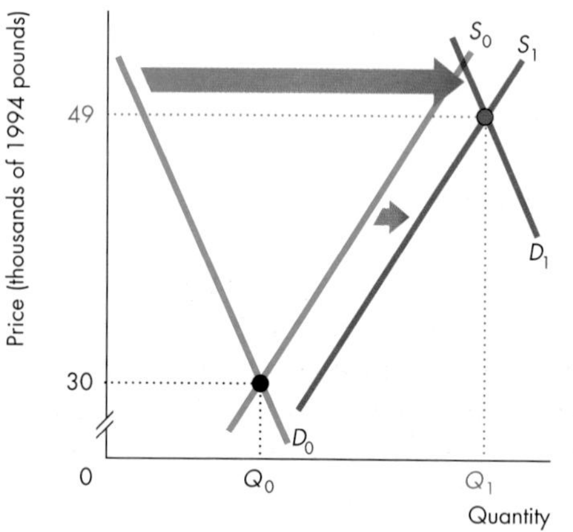

(b) Price rocket: housing

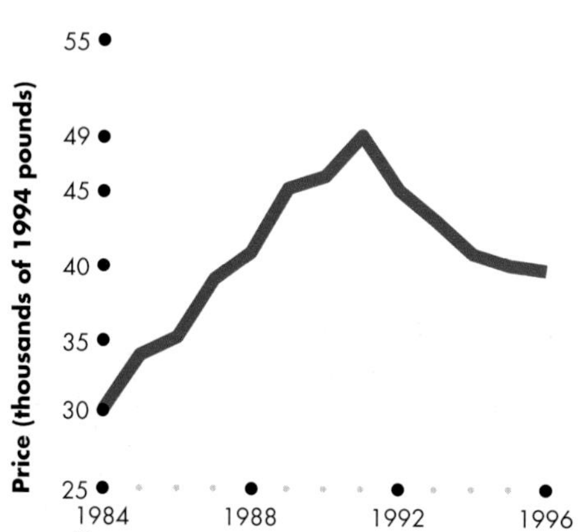

A large increase in demand for housing, from D_0 to D_1, combined with a smaller increase in the supply, resulted in a rise in the (real) average price of a house from £30,000 in 1984 to £48,695 in 1991 and an increase in the quantity, from Q_0 to Q_1 (part a). Part (b) shows this price rocket.

Source: Department of Environment, *House Price Series*, 1997, London, HMSO.

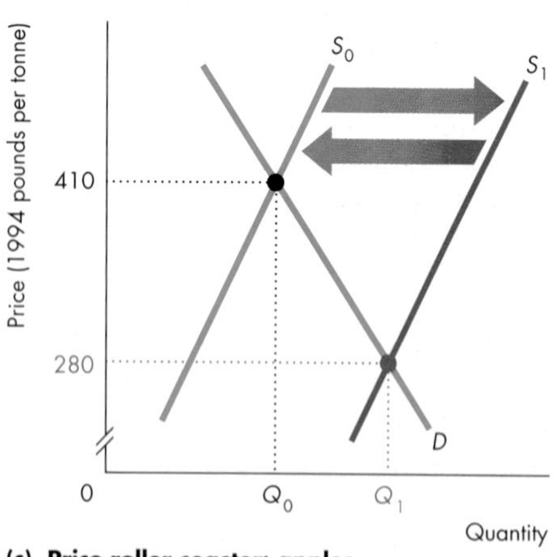

(c) Price roller coaster: apples

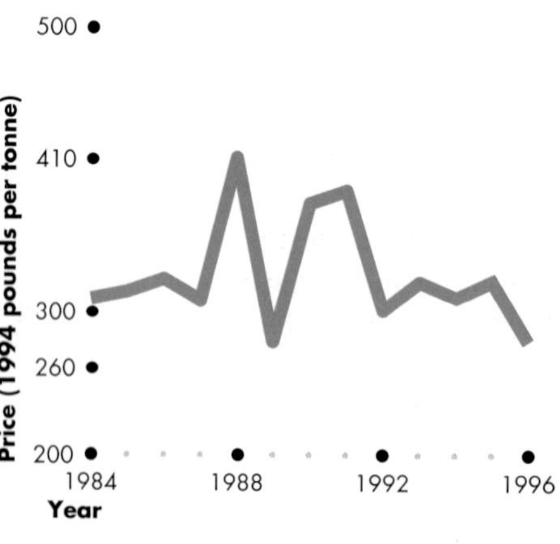

The demand for apples remains constant at *D*. But supply fluctuates between S_0 and S_1. As a result, the (real) price of apples has fluctuated between £260 per tonne and £408 per tonne – a roller-coaster. Part (c) shows this price roller-coaster.

Source: Central Statistical Office, *Annual Abstract of Statistics*, London, HMSO.

A decrease in demand decreases the quantity and an increase in supply increases the quantity, so we can't say for sure which way the quantity will change when demand decreases and at the same time, supply increases. In this example, the decrease in demand and the increase in supply are such that the increase in quantity brought about by an increase in supply is offset by the decrease in quantity brought about by a decrease in demand – so the quantity does not change. But notice that if demand had decreased slightly more than shown in the figure, the quantity would have decreased. And if supply had increased by slightly more than shown in the figure, the quantity would have increased.

We can now make two more predictions:

1 When demand decreases and supply increases, the price falls and the quantity increases, decreases, or remains constant.

2 When demand increases and supply decreases, the price rises and the quantity increases, decreases, or remains constant.

CD Players, Houses and Apples

At the beginning of this chapter, we looked at some facts about prices and quantities of CD players, house prices and apples. Let's use the theory of demand and supply that we have just studied to explain the movements in the prices and the quantities of these goods.

A Price Slide: CD Players Figure 4.13 (a) shows the market for CD players. In 1984, few firms made CD players and supply was limited. The supply curve was S_0. In 1984, the demand curve was D_0. The quantities supplied and demanded in 1984 were equal at Q_0, and the real price was £730 (1994 pounds). As the technology for making portable CD players improved and as more and more factories began to produce CD players, the supply increased by a large amount and the supply curve shifted rightward from S_0 to S_1. At the same time, increases in incomes and a decrease in the price of CDs increased the demand for CD players. But the increase in demand was much smaller than the increase in supply. The demand curve shifted to the right from D_0 to D_1. With the new demand curve D_1 and supply curve S_1, the equilibrium price fell to £100 and the quantity increased to Q_1. The large increase in supply combined with a smaller increase in demand resulted in an increase in the quantity of CD players sold and a dramatic fall in the real price. Figure 4.13(a) shows the CD player price slide.

A Price Rocket: Houses Figure 4.13(b) shows the market for owner-occupied houses. In 1984, the supply curve for housing in the United Kingdom was S_0. The supply of housing increased between 1984 and 1989 to S_1, following new house building and more people wanting to sell existing houses. However, the increase in demand was much higher. Demand increased rapidly because of rising incomes, expectations of rising house prices, expectations of capital gains and more people wanting to set up new households – the growth in demand outstripped the growth in supply. The demand curve shifted from D_0 to D_1 between 1984 and 1989. The combined effect of a large increase in demand and a smaller increase in supply was a rapid rise in average real house prices in that period. Part (b) shows the price rocket. The quantity increased from Q_0 to Q_1. After 1990, the pressure of demand reduced and house prices fell on average.

A Price Roller-Coaster: Apples Figure 4.13(c) shows the market for apples. The demand for apples does not change much over the years. It is described by curve D. But the supply of apples depends mainly on the weather and changes a great deal. The supply of apples fluctuates between S_0 and S_1. With good growing conditions, the supply curve is S_1. With bad growing conditions, supply decreases and the supply curve is S_0. As a consequence of fluctuations in supply, the real price of apples fluctuates between £408 per tonne (1994 prices), the maximum price, and £260 per tonne, the minimum price. The quantity fluctuates between Q_0 and Q_1. Figure 4.13(c) shows the apples price roller-coaster.

By using the theory of demand and supply, you can explain past fluctuations in prices and quantities and also make predictions about future fluctuations. But you will want to do more than predict whether prices are going to rise or fall. In Chapter 5, you will examine a method of predicting *by how much* they will change. In your study of macroeconomics you will learn to explain fluctuations in the economy as a whole. In fact, the theory of demand and supply can help answer almost every economic question.

Summary

Key Points

Opportunity Cost and Price (pp. 70–71)

- Opportunity cost is measured by a relative price or real price.
- Real prices are measured by dividing the money price of a good divided by a price (index) of a basket of all goods.
- Demand and supply determines real (relative) prices.

Demand (pp. 71–75)

- The quantity demanded of a good or service is the amount that consumers plan to buy during a given time period at a particular price.
- The quantity that consumers plan to buy of any good depends on: the price of the good; the prices of related goods – substitutes and complements; income; expected future prices; population; preferences.
- Other things remaining the same, the higher the price of a good, the smaller is the quantity demanded of that good.
- The relationship between quantity demanded and the price of a good can be modelled with a demand curve.
- The demand curve shifts when factors other than the price of a good change.

Supply (pp. 75–80)

- The quantity supplied of a good or service is the amount that producers plan to sell during a given time period.
- The quantity that producers plan to sell of any good or service depends on: the price of the good; the prices of factors of production; the prices of related goods; expected future prices; the number of suppliers; technology.
- Other things remaining the same, the higher the price of a good, the larger is the quantity supplied of that good.
- The relationship between quantity supplied and the price of a good can be modelled with a supply curve.
- The supply curve shifts when factors other than the price of a good change.

Market Equilibrium (pp. 80–82)

- At the equilibrium price, the quantity demanded equals the quantity supplied.
- At prices above the equilibrium, there is a surplus and the price falls.
- At prices below the equilibrium, there is a shortage and the price rises.

Predicting Changes in Price and Quantity (pp. 82–87)

- An increase in demand leads to a rise in price and to an increase in the quantity traded.
- A decrease in demand leads to a fall in price and to a decrease in the quantity traded.
- An increase in supply leads to an increase in the quantity traded and a fall in price.
- A decrease in supply leads to a decrease in the quantity traded and a rise in price.
- An increase in both demand and supply, brings an increase in quantity but the change in price cannot be predicted.
- An increase in demand and a decrease in supply, brings an increase in price, but the change in quantity change cannot be predicted.

Key Figures and Tables 

Key Terms

Review Questions

1 Distinguish between a money price and a real or relative price. Which is an opportunity cost and why?

2 Define the quantity demanded of a good or service.

3 Define the quantity supplied of a good or service.

4 List the main factors that influence the amount that consumers plan to buy and say whether an increase in the factor increases or decreases consumers' planned purchases.

5 List the main factors that influence the quantity that producers plan to sell and say whether an increase in that factor increases or decreases firms' planned sales.

6 State the law of demand and the law of supply.

7 If a fixed amount of a good is available, what does the demand curve tell us about the price that consumers are willing to pay for that fixed quantity?

8 If consumers are only willing to buy a certain fixed quantity, what does the supply curve tell us about the price at which firms will supply that quantity?

9 Distinguish between:

a A change in demand and a change in the quantity demanded.
b A change in supply and a change in the quantity supplied.

10 Why is the price at which the quantity demanded equals the quantity supplied the equilibrium price?

11 What is the effect on the price of a tape and the quantity of tapes sold if:

a The price of CDs increases?
b The price of a Walkman increases?
c The supply of CD players increases?
d Consumers' incomes increase and firms producing tapes switch to new cost-saving technology?
e The prices of the factors of production used to make tapes increase?

Problems

1 Consider each of the following *events* labelled *a* to *n*:

- a The price of petrol rises.
- b The price of petrol falls.
- c All speed limits on motorways are abolished.
- d A new fuel-effective engine that runs on cheap alcohol is invented.
- e The population doubles.
- f Robotic production plants lower the cost of producing cars.
- g A law banning all car imports from outside the European Union is passed.
- h The rates for car insurance double.
- i The minimum age for drivers is increased to 25 years.
- j A massive and high-grade oil supply is discovered in Norway.
- k The environmental lobby succeeds in closing down all nuclear power stations.
- l The price of cars rises.
- m The price of cars falls.
- n The summer temperature is 10 degrees lower than normal.

Now take each of the above events in turn and decide which of the following *effects* could result from each *event*. For example, event *a* could result in a movement along the demand curve for petrol, (effect 1) and a movement along the supply curve for petrol, (effect 4), as well as other effects.

1 A movement along the demand curve for petrol.
2 A shift of the demand curve for petrol rightward.
3 A shift of the demand curve for petrol leftward.
4 A movement along the supply curve of petrol.
5 A shift of the supply curve of petrol rightward.
6 A shift of the supply curve of petrol leftward.
7 A movement along the demand curve for cars.
8 A movement along the supply curve of cars.
9 A shift of the demand curve for cars rightward.
10 A shift of the demand curve for cars leftward.
11 A shift of the supply curve of cars rightward.
12 A shift of the supply curve of cars leftward.
13 An increase in the price of petrol.
14 A decrease in the equilibrium quantity of oil.

2 The demand and supply schedules for bags of crisps are as follows:

Price (pence per week)	Quantity demanded	Quantity supplied
	(millions of bags a week)	
10	200	0
20	180	30
30	160	60
40	140	90
50	120	120
60	100	140
70	80	160
80	60	180
90	40	200

- a What is the equilibrium price of a bag of crisps?
- b What is the equilibrium quantity of bags of crisps?

3 Suppose that a huge fire destroys one-half of the crisp-producing factories. Supply decreases to one-half of the amount shown in the above supply schedule.

- a What is the new equilibrium price of crisps?
- b What is the new equilibrium quantity of crisps?
- c Has there been a shift in or a movement along the supply curve of crisps?
- d Has there been a shift in or a movement along the demand curve for crisps?
- e As the crisp factories destroyed by fire are rebuilt and gradually resume crisp production what will happen to:

  1 The price of crisps?
  2 The quantity of crisps bought?
  3 The demand curve for crisps?
  4 The supply curve of crisps?

4 Suppose the demand and supply schedules for crisps are those in Problem 2. An increase in

the teenage population increases the demand for crisps by 40 million bags a week.

a Write out the new demand schedule for crisps.
b What is the new equilibrium quantity of crisps?
c What is the new equilibrium price of crisps?
d Has there been a shift in or a movement along the demand curve for crisps?
e Has there been a shift in or a movement along the supply curve of crisps?

5 Suppose the demand and supply schedules for crisps are those in Problem 2. An increase in the teenage population increases the demand for crisps by 40 million bags a week, and simultaneously the fire described in Problem 2 occurs, wiping out one-half of the crisp-producing factories.

a Draw a graph of the original and new demand and supply curves.
b What is the new equilibrium quantity of crisps?
c What is the new equilibrium price of crisps?

6 Read the *Reading Between the Lines* article on pp. 92–93 and then answer the following questions:

a Why might landlords prefer to offer 'free extras' rather than reduce the price of rented accommodation for students?
b Use demand and supply diagrams to show what you think might happen to the market for student accommodation in Hull in the next few years.

7 Turn to p. 94 and read the Economics in History material. Then:

a Explain why there was so much interest in trying to understand the principles of demand and suppy during the period of the industrial revolution.
b Explain why Alfred Marshall is considered to be the 'father' of modern economics.

8 Use the links on the Parkin, Powell and Matthews Web site and obtain data on the prices and quantities of wheat.

a Use a demand and supply diagram to illustrate the market for wheat in 1998.
b Show the changes in demand and supply and the changes in the quantity demanded and the quantity supplied that are consistent with the price and quantity data.

9 Use the link on the Parkin, Powell and Matthews Web site and read the story about the prices of millennium cruises.

a Describe how the millennium changes the price of a cruise.
b Draw a demand–supply diagram to explain what happens to the price when there is an increase in demand and no change in supply.
c What do you predict would happen to the price of a cruise if air fares to Australia and the South Pacific decreased?
d What do you predict would happen to the price of a cruise if the price of oil increased?

W http://www.econ100.com

Demand and Supply: Student Housing in Hull

The Guardian, 16 December 1998

Students in a buyers' market for digs

Martin Wainwright

The student slum of college legend and parental nightmare has been replaced in one of Britain's university cities by dream homes with satellite TV, pre-stocked fridges and cashback vouchers for beer.

A sudden slump in the number of students in Hull has wrong-footed both landlords and the two local universities, after several years of room shortages and emergency "tent cities" on the floors of gyms and libraries.

Flat-letting company, APS Services, now offers satellite TV and microwave ovens as standard.

"The numbers have gone down by something like 1,500 to 2,000 students, and everyone's trying to snap them up for next year," said one estate agent.

Beer money, free computer accessories, and draws to win portable CD-players have also been rushed on to the market, while housing adverts are flooding Hullfire, the student union newspaper.

Mike Kirby, president of the union at the University of Humberside and Lincolnshire, said: "Because there's so much competition, Hull is now one of the cheapest places for students to live in the country."

It follows a glut in provision by landlords after university problems fixing up students with rooms in previous years. The expansion then coincided with a shortfall of places at Humberside and Lincolnshire and the move of up to 1,000 students to a new campus across the Humber at Lincoln.

"A few years ago, students had to sleep on the floors of gyms, halls and libraries when they first arrived because there was so little housing," said landlord Hanif Jivani. "This meant a lot of people bought properties in the city to house students in the hope of making a lot of money. But the shoe's on the other foot now, and landlords are taking pretty desperate steps to get tenants."

The battle is focusing on contracts for the next academic year, with students sorted out for 1998/9 but starting to think about where to live after the end of next summer.

Sinead Graf, vice-president for welfare support at Hull university union, said: "We're telling everyone to take it easy and not rush, because the market's completely in their favour. But they're facing offers like free Sky TV if they sign a contract before Easter, or cashback to buy beer or fill the fridge."

The battle has spread with a counter-attack by "no gimmick" agencies, which are offering security improvements or rent reductions from the average £38 a week. The two universities, whose own accommodation is pricier but more accountable, have joined in with the pledge of shorter contracts than the private sector's standard one year.

The Essence of the Story

- The number of students going to Hull to study at one of its two universities has slumped by 2,000 after several years of expansion. Now there is a surplus of high quality student accommodation after several years of serious accommodation shortages.
- The shortfall in students has coincided with the move of 1,000 students to a new campus at Lincoln. Hull's landlords must now compete to attract the smaller number of students in Hull.
- The competition has made Hull one of the cheapest places in the country for student accommodation.
- Landlords are trying to attract students into signing contracts for accommodation by offering free extras such as free satellite television or a free fridge full of beer.
- Some landlords are also offering better security, shorter contracts and cheaper rents.

Economic Analysis

■ Figure 1 shows the demand and supply for student accommodation in Hull between 1994 and 1995. In 1994, demand for student accommodation was D_{94} when 4,000 rooms were available for rent at a price of £45 per week.

■ Student numbers expanded rapidly over the next few years. In 1995, demand increased to D_{95} as shown in Figure 1 creating a shortage of 1,500 rooms. Students were forced to sleep on the floor of University gyms and libraries initially.

■ The pressure of excess demand led to an increase in rent to £55 which encouraged existing landlords to let out spare rooms to students, leading to the movement up the supply schedule, S_{94}. In the final equilibrium in 1995, there were 5,000 rooms available for rent at £55 per week.

■ Higher rents encourage existing and new landlords to buy properties and refurbish them for student accommodation. This new supply is shown as the shift in the supply shedule from S_{95} to S_{97} in Figure 2. Rents decrease to £40 a week and more students demand accommodation at lower rents shown as a movement down the demand schedule, D_{97}.

■ Then in 1998, the number of students applying to Hull's universities fell and the demand for student accommodation decreased. Figure 3 shows the fall in demand from D_{97}. to D_{98}. The fall in demand is the result of student decisions about which university to attend, not the price of accommodation, which would cause a movement along the demand schedule. In 1998, when the rent was still £40 a week, the fall in demand created a surplus of 2,000 rooms and forced landlords to compete for the limited number of students wanting accommodation.

■ Some landlords have tried to maintain the rental price and attract students with free extras such as free satellite TV, and well-stocked kitchens. If they can get students to sign a year-long contract before the students realize other cheaper accommodation is available, they will gain more rental revenue.

■ Other landlords have cut prices and are offering shorter contracts. As students get wise and learn about the market, they realize that cheaper rents are better than free extras. The rental prices have fallen to £38 pounds a week but will need to fall to £30 per week to remove the surplus.

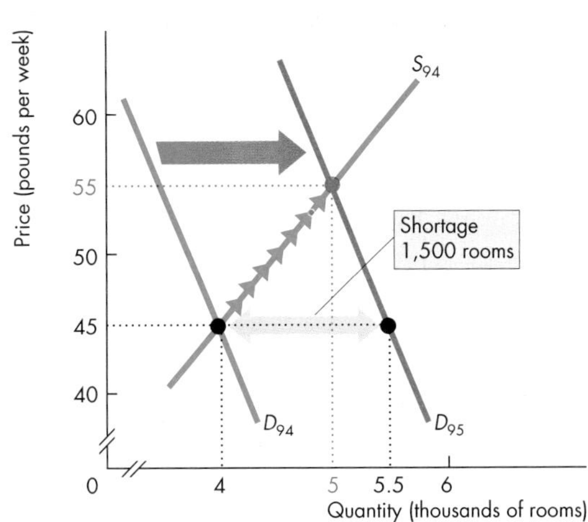

Figure 1 Market in 1994 and 1995

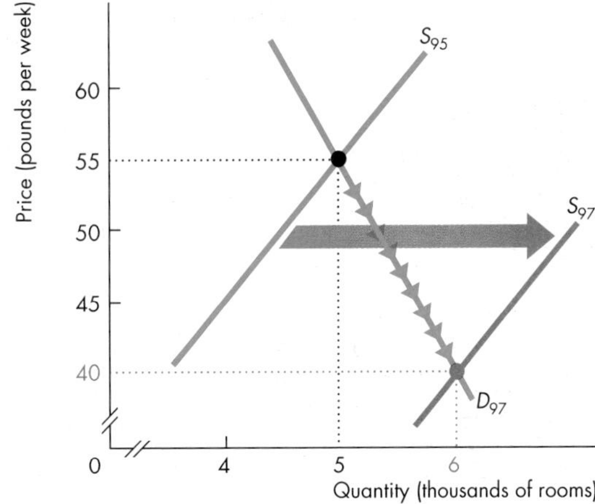

Figure 2 Market in 1995 and 1997

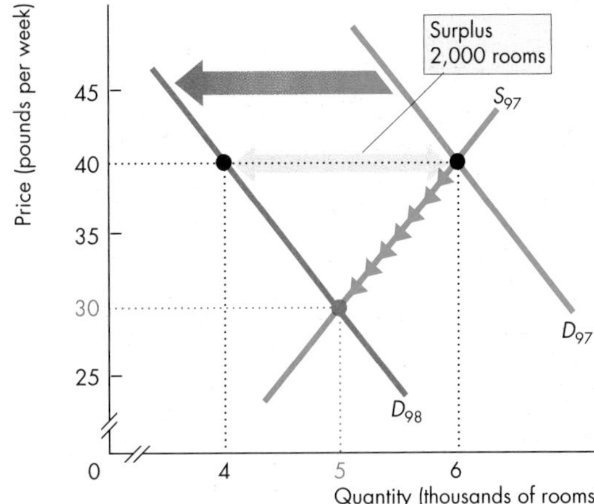

Figure 3 Market in 1997 and 1998

Discovering the Laws of Demand and Supply

"The forces to be dealt with are . . . so numerous, that it is best to take a few at a time. . . . Thus we begin by isolating the primary relations of supply, demand, and price."

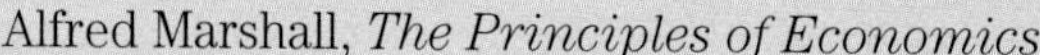

Alfred Marshall, *The Principles of Economics*

The Economist: Alfred Marshall

Alfred Marshall (1842–1924) grew up in an England that was being transformed by the railway and by the expansion of manufacturing. Mary Paley Marshall was one of Marshall's students at Cambridge, and when Alfred and Mary married, in 1877, celibacy rules barred Marshall from continuing to teach at Cambridge. By 1884, with more liberal rules, the Marshalls returned to Cambridge, where Alfred became Professor of Political Economy.

Many others had a hand in refining the theory of demand and supply, but the first thorough and complete statement of the theory as we know it today was set out by Alfred Marshall, with the acknowledged help of Mary. Published in 1890, the monumental treatise *Principles of Economics*, became the textbook on economics on both sides of the Atlantic for almost half a century. Marshall was an outstanding mathematician, but he kept mathematics and even diagrams in the background. His supply and demand diagram appears only in a footnote.

The Issues and Ideas

The laws of demand and supply that you studied in Chapter 4 were discovered during the 1830s by Antoine-Augustin Cournot (1801–1877), a professor of mathematics at the University of Lyon, France. Although Cournot was the first to use demand and supply, it was the development and expansion of the railways during the 1850s that gave the newly emerging theory its first practical applications. Railways then were at the cutting edge of technology just as airlines are today. And as in the airline industry today, competition among the railways was fierce.

Dionysius Lardner (1793–1859), an Irish professor of philosophy at the University of London, used demand and supply to show railway companies how they could increase their profits by cutting rates on long-distance business on which competition was fiercest and by raising rates on short-haul business on which they had less to fear from other transport suppliers. Today, economists use the principles that Lardner worked out during the 1850s to calculate the freight rates and passenger fares that will give airlines the largest possible profit. The rates calculated have a lot in common with the railway rates of the nineteenth century. On local routes on which there is little competition, fares per kilometre are highest, and on long-distance routes on which the airlines compete fiercely, fares per kilometre are lowest.

Known satirically among scientists of the day as "Dionysius Diddler", Lardner worked on an amazing range of problems from astronomy to railway engineering to economics. A colourful character, he would have been a regular guest of Clive Anderson if talk shows had been around in the 1850s. Lardner visited the École des Ponts et Chaussées (School of Bridges and Roads) in Paris and must have learned a great deal from Jules Dupuit.

In France, Jules Dupuit (1804–1866), a French engineer/economist, used demand to calculate the benefits from building a bridge and, once the bridge was built, for calculating the toll to charge for its use. His work was the forerunner of what is today called *cost–benefit analysis*. Working with the principles invented by Dupuit, economists today calculate the costs and benefits of motorways and airports, dams and power stations.

Then . . .

Dupuit used the law of demand to determine whether a bridge or canal would be valued enough by its users to justify the cost of building it. Lardner first worked out the relationship between the cost of production and supply and used demand and supply theory to explain the costs, prices and profits of railway operations. He also used the theory to discover ways of increasing revenue by raising rates on short-haul business and lowering them on long-distance freight.

. . . And Now

Today, using the same principles devised by Dupuit, economists calculate whether the benefits of expanding airports and air-traffic control facilities are sufficient to cover their costs, and airline companies use the principles developed by Lardner to set their prices and to decide when to offer "seat sales". Like the railways before them, the airlines charge a high price per kilometre on short flights, for which they face little competition, and a low price per kilometre on long flights, for which competition is fierce.

Trying These Ideas Today

Using what you know about demand and supply from Chapter 4, and what you have learned about the ideas of Jules Dupuit, you should be able to answer the following questions:

- What types of transport compete with the big national coach companies for long distance intercity travel?
- Why is it cheaper to travel the 300 kilometres from Leeds to London by coach than it is to travel just 60 kilometres from Leeds to Manchester by coach?

After studying this chapter you will be able to:

- Define and calculate the price elasticity of demand
- Explain what determines the elasticity of demand
- Use elasticity to determine whether a price change will increase or decrease total revenue
- Define and calculate other elasticities of demand
- Define and calculate the elasticity of supply

OPEC's Dilemma

You are the chief economic strategist for the Organization of Petroleum Exporting Countries (OPEC) and you want to increase OPEC's revenue. But you have a dilemma. You know that to increase the price of oil, you must restrict its supply. You also know that to sell more oil, you must lower its price. What will you recommend: restrict supply or lower the price? Which action will increase OPEC's revenue? ◆ As OPEC's economic strategist, you need to know a lot about the demand for oil. For example, as the world economy grows, how will that growth translate into an increase in demand for oil? What about substitutes for oil? Will we discover inexpensive methods to convert coal and tar sands into usable fuel? Will nuclear energy become safe and cheap enough to compete with oil? ◆ OPEC is not the only organization with a dilemma. A bumper grape crop is good news for wine consumers. It lowers the price of wine. But is it good news for grape growers? Do they get more revenue? Or does the lower price more than wipe out their gains from larger quantities sold? ◆ The government also faces a dilemma. Looking for greater tax revenue to balance its budget, it decides to increase the tax rates on tobacco and alcohol. Do the higher tax rates bring in more tax revenue? Or do people switch to substitutes for tobacco and alcohol on such a large scale that the higher tax rate brings in less tax revenue?

◆ ◆ ◆ ◆ In this chapter you will learn how to tackle questions such as the ones just posed. You will learn how we can measure in a precise way the responsiveness of the quantities bought and sold to changes in prices and other influences on buyers or sellers.

Elasticity of Demand

As OPEC's economic strategist, you are trying to decided whether to advise a cut in production that decreases supply and shifts the supply curve leftward. To make this decision, you need to know how the quantity of oil demanded responds to a change in price. You also need some way to measure that response.

You are going to discover that the concept of **price elasticity of demand** can help you to make your decision. The price elasticity of demand is a measure of the responsiveness of the quantity demanded of a good to a change in its price, when all other influences on buyers' plans remain the same. Before we find out how to calculate this number, let's look more closely at your problem at OPEC.

The Responsiveness of the Quantity Demanded to Price

To understand the importance of the responsiveness of the quantity of oil demanded to a change in its price, let's compare two possible scenarios in the oil industry, shown in Figure 5.1. International oil prices are always quoted in dollars. In the two parts of the figure, the supply curves are identical, but the demand curves differ.

The supply curve S_0 in each part of the figure shows the initial supply. It intersects the demand curve, in both cases, at a price of $10 a barrel and a quantity of 40 million barrels a day. Suppose that you contemplate a decrease in supply that shifts the supply curve from S_0 to S_1. In part (a), the new supply curve S_1 intersects the demand curve D_a at a price of $30 a barrel and a quantity of 23 million barrels a day. In part (b), with demand curve D_b, the same supply curve shift increases the price to $15 a barrel and decreases the quantity to 15 million barrels a day. You can see that in part (a) the price increases by more and the quantity decreases by less than it does in part (b). What happens to the total revenue of the oil producers in these two cases?

The **total revenue** from the sale of a good equals the price of the good multiplied by the quantity sold. An increase in price has two opposing effects on total revenue. It increases the revenue on each unit sold (blue area). But it also leads to a decrease in the quantity sold, which decreases

Figure 5.1 Demand, Supply and Total Revenue

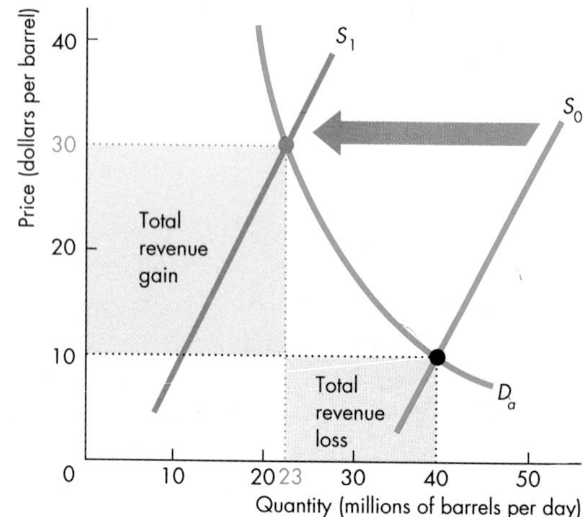

(a) More total revenue

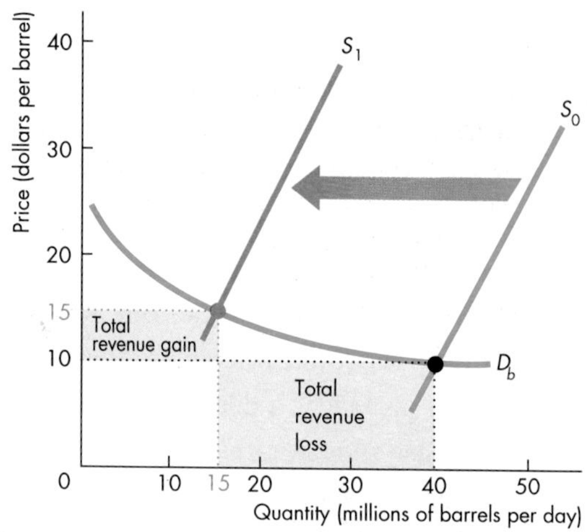

(b) Less total revenue

If supply is cut from S_0 to S_1, the price rises and the quantity decreases. In part (a), total revenue – the quantity multiplied by the price – increases from $400 million to $690 million a day. The increase in total revenue from a higher price (blue area) exceeds the decrease in total revenue from lower sales (red area). In part (b), total revenue decreases from $400 million to $225 million a day. The increase in total revenue from a higher price (blue area) is less than the decrease in total revenue from lower sales (red area). These two different responses of total revenue arise from different responses of the quantity demanded to a change in price.

revenue (red area). Either of these two opposing effects could be the larger. In case (a) the first effect is larger (blue area exceeds red area), so total revenue increases. In case (b) the second effect is larger (red area exceeds blue area), so total revenue decreases.

Slope Depends on Units of Measurement

The difference between these two cases is the responsiveness of the quantity demanded to a change in price. Demand curve D_a is steeper than demand curve D_b. But we can't compare two demand curves simply by their slopes, because the slope of a demand curve depends on the units in which we measure the price and quantity. Also, we often need to compare the demand curves for different goods and services. For example, when deciding by how much to change tax rates, the government needs to compare the demand for oil and the demand for tobacco. Which is more responsive to price? Which can be taxed at an even higher rate without decreasing the tax revenue? Comparing the slope of the demand curve for oil with the slope of the demand curve for tobacco has no meaning since oil is measured in litres and tobacco in grams – completely unrelated units.

To overcome these problems, we need a measure of responsiveness that is independent of the units of measurement of prices and quantities. Elasticity is that measure.

Elasticity: A Units-free Measure

The *price elasticity of demand* is a units-free measure of the responsiveness of quantity demanded of a good to a change in its price, other things remaining the same. It is calculated by using the formula:

$$\text{Price elasticity of demand} = \frac{\text{Percentage change in quantity demanded}}{\text{Percentage change in price}}$$

Elasticity is a units-free measure because the percentage change in a variable is independent of the units in which the variable is measured. For example, if we measure a price in pounds, an increase from £1.00 to £1.50 is a 50 pence increase. If we measure a price in pence, an increase from 100 pence to 150 pence is also a 50 pence increase. The first increase is 0.5 of a unit and the second increase is 50 units, but they are both 50 per cent increases.

Minus Sign and Elasticity When the price of a good *increases* along a demand curve, the quantity demanded *decreases*. Because a *positive* price change results in a *negative* change in the quantity demanded, the price elasticity of demand is a negative number. But it is the magnitude, or *absolute value*, of the price elasticity of demand that tells us how responsive – how elastic – demand is. To compare elasticities, we use the magnitude of the price elasticity of demand and ignore the minus sign.

Calculating Elasticity

To calculate the elasticity of demand, we need to know the quantities demanded at different prices, all the other influences on consumers' buying plans remaining the same. Let's assume that we have the relevant data on prices and quantities demanded of oil and calculate the elasticity of demand for oil.

Figure 5.2 enlarges one section on the demand curve for oil and shows how the quantity demanded responds to a small change in price. Initially the price is $9.50 a barrel and 41 million barrels a day are sold – the original point in the figure. Then the price increases to $10.50 a barrel and the quantity demanded decreases to 39 million barrels a day – the new point in the figure. When the price increases by $1 a barrel, the quantity demanded decreases by 2 million barrels a day.

This calculation measures the elasticity at an average price of $10 a barrel and an average quantity of 40 million barrels.

To calculate the elasticity of demand, we express the changes in price and quantity demanded as percentages of the *average price* and the *average quantity*. By using the average price and average quantity, we calculate the elasticity at a point on the demand curve midway between the original point and the new point. The original price is $9.50 and the new price is $10.50, so the average price is $10. The $1 price increase is 10 per cent of the average price. The original quantity demanded is 41 million barrels and the new quantity demanded is 39 million barrels, so the average quantity demanded is 40 million barrels. The 2 million barrel decrease in the quantity demanded is 5 per cent of the average quantity. So the price elasticity of demand, which is the percentage change in the quantity demanded

Figure 5.2 Calculating the Elasticity of Demand

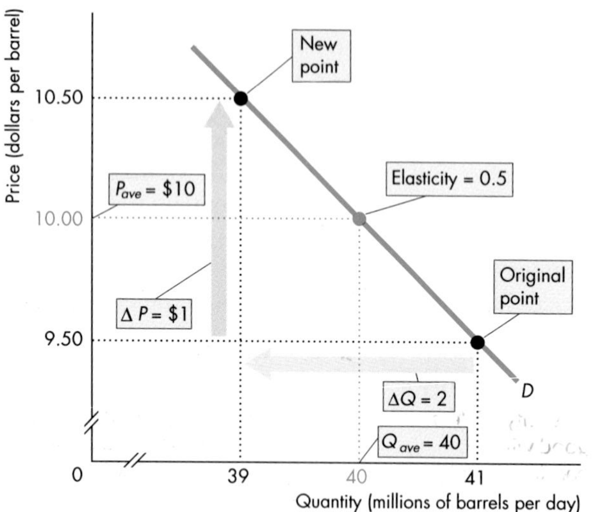

The elasticity of demand is calculated by using the formula[1]:

$$\text{Price elasticity of demand} = \frac{\text{Percentage change in quantity demanded}}{\text{Percentage change in price}}$$

$$= \frac{\%\Delta Q/Q_{ave}}{\%\Delta P/P_{ave}}$$

$$= \frac{2/40}{1/10}$$

$$= 0.5$$

1 In the formula the Greek letter delta (Δ) stands for 'change in' and % Δ stands for 'percentage change in'.

(5 per cent) divided by the percentage change in price (10 per cent), is 0.5. That is:

$$\text{Price elasticity of demand} = \frac{\%\Delta Q}{\%\Delta P}$$

$$= \frac{5\%}{10\%} = 0.5$$

Average Price, Average Quantity and Arc Elasticity We use the average price and average quantity to avoid having two values for the elasticity of demand, depending on whether the price increases or decreases. A price increase of \$1 is 10.5 per cent of \$9.50, and 2 million barrels is 4.9 per cent of 41 million barrels. If we use these numbers to calculate the elasticity, we get 0.47. A price decrease of \$1 is 9.5 per cent of \$10.50, and 2 million barrels is 5.1 per cent of 39 million barrels. Using these numbers to calculate the elasticity, we get 0.54. Using the average price and average quantity demanded, the elasticity is 0.5 regardless of whether the price increases or decreases. The average price method gives an estimate of the price elasticity of demand between two points on the demand curve – between the prices \$9.50 and \$10.50 in this case. This is called the **arc elasticity of demand**. You can find examples of how to find the price elasticity value at one specific point – point elasticity – on the Parkin Web site as well as examples using differential calculus.

Percentages and Proportions Elasticity is the ratio of the percentage change in the quantity demanded to the percentage change in the price. It is also, equivalently, the proportionate change in the quantity demanded divided by the proportionate change in the price. The proportionate change in price is $\Delta P/P_{ave}$ and the proportionate change in quantity demanded is $\Delta Q/Q_{ave}$. The percentage changes are the proportionate changes multiplied by 100. So when we divide one percentage change by another, the 100s cancel and the result is the same as we get by using the proportionate changes.

Inelastic and Elastic Demand

Figure 5.3 shows three demand curves that cover the entire range of possible elasticities of demand. In Figure 5.3(a), the quantity demanded is constant regardless of the price. If the quantity demanded remains constant when the price changes, then the elasticity of demand is zero and demand is said to be **perfectly inelastic**. One good that has a low elasticity of demand is insulin. Insulin is of such importance to some diabetics that they will buy the quantity that keeps them healthy at almost any price. Even at low prices, they have no reason to buy a larger quantity.

If the percentage change in the quantity demanded is less than the percentage change in price, then the magnitude of the elasticity of demand is between zero and 1 and demand is said to be **inelastic**. The demand curve in Figure 5.3a is an example of inelastic demand. If the percentage change in the quantity demanded exceeds the percentage change in price, then the magnitude of the elasticity is greater than 1 and demand is said to be **elastic**. The dividing line between inelastic and elastic demand is the case in which the percentage change

Figure 5.3 Inelastic and Elastic Demand

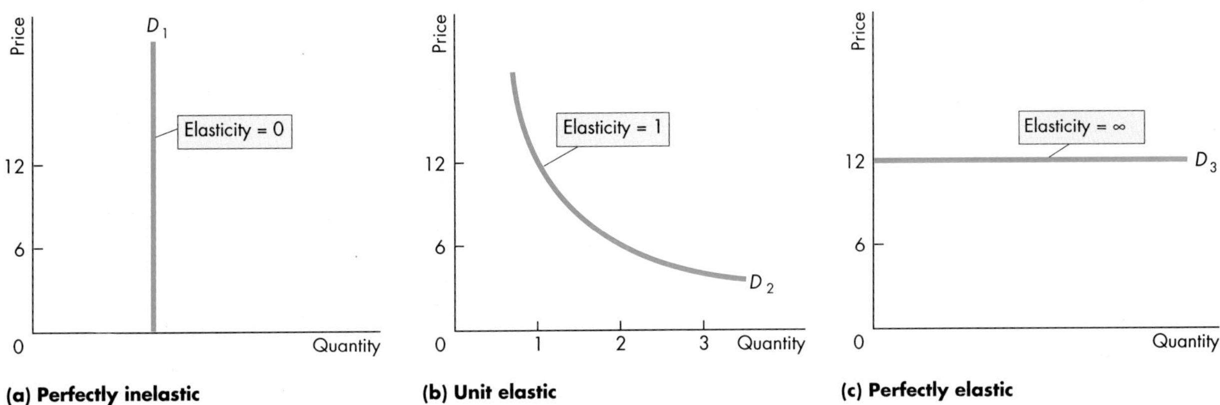

Elasticity usually varies along the demand curve, but each demand curve illustrated here has a constant elasticity. The demand curve in part (a) is for a good that has a zero price elasticity of demand. The demand curve in part (b) is for a good with a unit elasticity of demand. The demand curve in part (c) is for a good with an infinite elasticity of demand.

in the quantity demanded equals the percentage change in price. In this case, the elasticity of demand is 1 and demand is said to be **unit elastic.** The demand curve in Figure 5.3(b) is an example of unit elastic demand.

If the quantity demanded is infinitely responsive to a price change, then the magnitude of the elasticity of demand is infinity and demand is said to be **perfectly elastic**. The demand curve in Figure 5.3(c) is an example of perfectly elastic demand. An example of a good that has a high elasticity of demand (almost infinite) is ballpoint pens from the university bookshop and from the newsagent's shop close by. If the two shops offer pens for the same price, some people buy from one and some from the other. But if the bookshop increases the price of pens, even by a small amount, while the shop close by maintains the lower price, the quantity of pens demanded from the bookshop will fall to zero. Ballpoint pens from the two shops are perfect substitutes for each other.

Elasticity Along a Straight-line Demand Curve

Elasticity is not the same as slope, but the two are related. To understand how they are related, let's look at elasticity along a straight-line demand curve – a demand curve that has a constant slope.

Figure 5.4 illustrates the calculation of elasticity along a straight-line demand curve for oil. Let's calculate the elasticity of demand for oil at an average price of $40 a barrel and an average quantity of 4 million barrels a day. To do so, imagine that the price rises from $30 a barrel to $50 a barrel. The change in the price is $20 and the average price is $40 (average of $30 and $50), which means that the proportionate change in price is:

$$\frac{\Delta P}{P_{ave}} = \frac{20}{40}$$

At a price of $30 a barrel, the quantity demanded is 8 million barrels a day. At a price of $50 a barrel, the quantity demanded is zero. So the change in the quantity demanded is 8 million barrels a day and the average quantity is 4 million barrels a day (the average of 8 million and zero), so the proportionate change in the quantity demanded is:

$$\frac{\Delta Q}{Q_{ave}} = \frac{8}{4}$$

Dividing the proportionate change in the quantity demanded by the proportionate change in the price gives:

$$\frac{\Delta Q / Q_{ave}}{\Delta P / P_{ave}} = \frac{8/4}{20/40} = 4$$

Figure 5.4 Elasticity Along a Straight-line Demand Curve

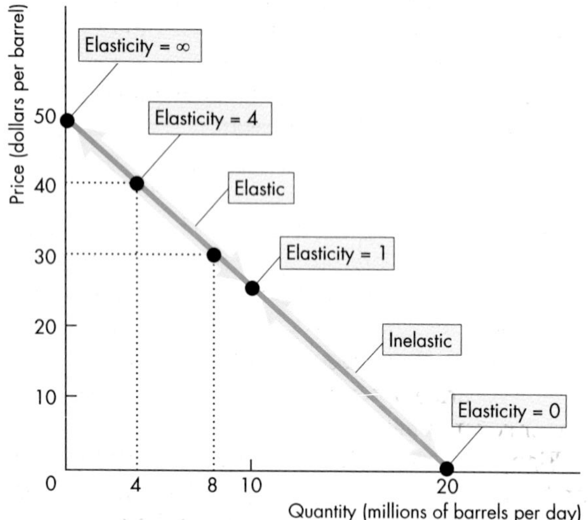

On a straight-line demand curve, elasticity decreases as the price falls and the quantity demanded increases. Demand is unit elastic at the midpoint of the demand curve (elasticity is 1). Above the midpoint demand is elastic, and below the midpoint demand is inelastic. Demand is perfectly elastic (elasticity = infinity) where quantity demanded is zero, and demand is perfectly inelastic (elasticity = zero) where the price is zero.

Table 5.1 Some Real-world Price Elasticities of Demand

Good or Service	Elasticity
ELASTIC DEMAND	
Fresh meat	1.4
Spirits	1.3
Wine	1.2
UNIT ELASTICITY	
Services	1.0
Cereals	1.0
INELASTIC DEMAND	
Durable goods	0.9
Fruit juice	0.8
Green vegetables	0.6
Tobacco	0.5
Beer	0.5
Bread	0.0

Sources: Ministry of Agriculture, Food and Fisheries, *Household Food Consumption and Expenditure*, 1992, London, HMSO. C. Godfrey, Modelling Demand. In *Preventing Alcohol and Tobacco Problems*, Vol. 1, (A. Maynard and P. Tether, eds), Avebury, 1990. J. Muellbauer, 'Testing the Barten Model of Household Composition Effects and the Cost of Children', *Economic Journal*, (September 1977).

By using this same method, we can calculate the elasticity of demand at any price and quantity along the demand curve. Because the demand curve for oil in this example is a straight line, a \$20 price change brings an 8 million barrel quantity change at every average price. So in the elasticity formula, $\Delta Q = 8$ and $\Delta P = 20$ regardless of average quantity and average price. But the lower the average price, the greater is the average quantity demanded. So the lower the average price, the less elastic is demand.

Check this proposition by calculating the elasticity of demand for oil at the midpoint of the demand curve, where the price is \$25 a barrel and the quantity demanded is 10 million barrels a day. The proportionate change in price is $\$20/\$25 = 0.8$, and the proportionate change in the quantity demanded is $8/10 = 0.8$, so the elasticity of demand is 1. On a straight-line demand curve, the price elasticity is always 1 at the midpoint. Above the midpoint demand is elastic, and below the midpoint demand is inelastic. Demand is perfectly elastic (infinity) where the quantity demanded is zero and perfectly inelastic (zero) where the price is zero.

The Factors that Influence the Elasticity of Demand

Actual values of elasticities of demand have been estimated and some examples for the United Kingdom are set out in Table 5.1. You can see that these real-world elasticities of demand range from 1.4 for fresh meat, the most elastic in the table, to zero for bread, the least elastic in the table. What makes the demand for some goods elastic and the demand for others inelastic? Elasticity depends on three main factors:

1 The closeness of substitutes.
2 The proportion of income spent on the good.
3 The time elapsed since a price change.

Closeness of Substitutes The closer the substitutes for a good or service, the more elastic is the demand for it. For example, housing has few real substitutes (sleeping on a friend's floor, in a hostel, or on the street). As a result, the demand for housing is inelastic. In contrast, metals have good substitutes such as plastics and car travel has substitutes in public transport, so the demand for these goods is elastic.

In everyday language we call some goods, such as food and housing, *necessities* and other goods, such as exotic vacations, *luxuries*. Necessities are goods that have poor substitutes and that are crucial for our well-being, so generally they have inelastic demands. Luxuries are goods that usually have many substitutes and so have elastic demands.

The degree of substitutability between two goods also depends on how narrowly (or broadly) we define them. For example, even though oil does not have a close substitute, different types of oil are close substitutes for each other. Saudi Arabian Light, a particular type of oil, is a close substitute for Alaskan North Slope, another particular type of oil. If you happen to be the economic adviser to Saudi Arabia (as well as the OPEC economic strategist!), you will not contemplate a unilateral price increase. Even though Saudi Arabian Light has some unique characteristics, other oils can easily substitute for it, and most buyers will be sensitive to its price relative to the prices of other types of oil. So the demand for Saudi Arabian Light is highly elastic.

This example, which distinguishes between oil in general and different types of oil, applies to many other goods and services. The elasticity of demand for meat in general is low but the elasticity of demand for beef, lamb, or chicken is high. The elasticity of demand for personal computers is low, but the elasticity of demand for an Elonex, Dell, or IBM is high.

The closeness of the substitutes for a good also depends on some other factors discussed below.

Proportion of Income Spent on the Good Other things remaining the same, the higher the proportion of income spent on a good, the more elastic is the demand for it. If only a small fraction of income is spent on a good, then a change in its price has little impact on the consumer's overall budget. In contrast, even a small rise in the price of a good that commands a large part of a consumer's budget induces the consumer to make a radical reappraisal of expenditures.

To appreciate the importance of the proportion of income spent on a good, consider your own elasticity of demand for textbooks and crisps. If the price of textbooks doubles (increases 100 per cent), there will be a big decrease in the quantity of textbooks bought. There will be an increase in sharing and in illegal photocopying. If the price of a packet of crisps doubles, also a 100 per cent increase, there will be almost no change in the quantity of crisps demanded. Why the difference? Textbooks take a large proportion of your budget while crisps take only a tiny portion. You don't like either price increase, but you hardly notice the effects of the increased price of crisps, while the increased price of textbooks puts your budget under severe strain.

Figure 5.5 shows the proportion of income spent on food and the price elasticity of demand for food in 20 countries. This figure confirms the general tendency we have just described. The larger the proportion of income spent on food, the more price elastic is the demand for food. The general pattern is strong but there are a few exceptions in the figure. For example, Tanzania, a poor African country where average incomes are just a few per cent of incomes in the United Kingdom, and where 62 per cent of income is spent on food, the price elasticity of demand for food is 0.77. In contrast, in the United Kingdom where 15 per cent of income is spent on food, the elasticity of demand for food is 0.3. These numbers make sense. In a country that spends a large proportion of income on food, an increase in the price of food forces people to make a bigger adjustment to the quantity of food bought than in a country in which a small proportion of income is spent on food.

Time Elapsed Since Price Change The greater the time lapse since a price change, the more elastic is demand. When a price changes, consumers often continue to buy similar quantities of a good for a while. But given enough time, they find acceptable and less costly substitutes. As this process of substitution occurs, the quantity purchased of an item that has become more expensive gradually declines. That is, given more time, it is possible to find more effective substitutes for a good or service whose price has increased. It is also possible to find more uses for a good whose price has decreased.

Figure 5.5 The Price Elasticity of Demand for Food in 20 Countries

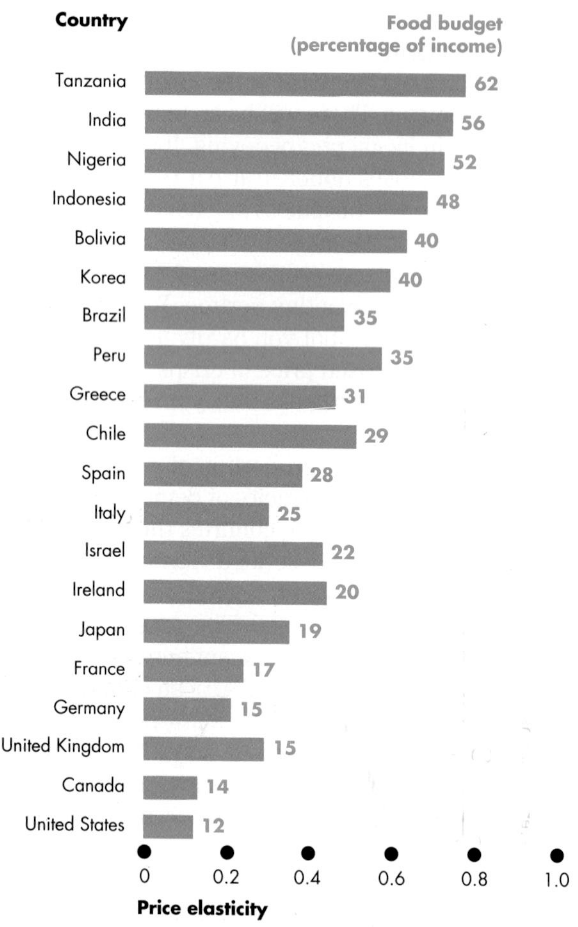

As income increases and the proportion of income spent on food decreases, the demand for food becomes less elastic.

Source: Henri Theil, Ching-Fan Chung and James L. Seale Jr, *Advances in Econometrics, Supplement 1*, 1989, *International Evidence on Consumption Patterns*. Greenwich, Connecticut JAI Press Inc.

To describe the effect of time on demand, we distinguish between two time-frames:

1 Short-run demand.

2 Long-run demand.

Short-run demand describes the response of buyers to a change in the price of a good *before* sufficient time has elapsed for all the possible substitutions to be made. Long-run demand describes the response of buyers to a change in price *after* sufficient time has elapsed for all the possible substitutions to be made.

An example of a long-lasting price increase was the four-fold rise in the price of oil that occurred during 1973 and 1974. The higher price of oil led to sharp increases in the costs of home heating and petrol. Initially, consumers maintained consumption at more or less their original levels. Then, gradually, buyers responded to higher oil and petrol prices by using their existing capital – boilers and gas guzzlers – in a way that economized on the more expensive fuel. But there were severe limits in the extent to which people felt it worthwhile to cut back on their consumption of the now much more costly fuel. Thermostats could be turned down but that imposed costs – costs of discomfort. Drivers could lower their average speed and economize on petrol. But that also imposed costs – costs of increases in travel time. So the short-run buyer response in the face of this sharp price increase was inelastic. With a longer time to respond, people bought more energy-efficient capital. Boilers and electric power generators became more fuel-efficient. Cars became smaller, on the average, and car and aircraft engines became more fuel-efficient.

The short-run and long-run demand curves for oil in 1974 looked like those in Figure 5.1. Look back at that figure and refresh your memory about the demand curves in parts (a) and (b). The short-run demand curve is D_a and the long-run demand curve is D_b. The price of oil in 1974 was \$10 a barrel and 40 million barrels a day were bought and sold. At that price and quantity, long-run demand, D_b, is much more elastic than short-run demand, D_a.

Elasticity, Total Revenue and Expenditure

This chapter began with a dilemma. How can a producer of oil (or anything else) increase total revenue: by decreasing production to increase price, or by lowering price to sell a larger quantity? We can now answer this question by using the concept of the price elasticity of demand.

The change in a producer's total revenue (and in the total expenditure of the buyers) depends on the extent to which the quantity sold changes as the price changes. But the responsiveness of the quantity sold to a price change depends on the elasticity of demand. If demand is elastic, a 1 per cent price cut increases the quantity sold by more than 1 per cent and total revenue increases. If demand is unit elastic, a 1 per cent price cut increases the quantity sold by 1 per cent and the price decrease and the quantity increase offset each other so total revenue does not change. If demand is inelastic, a 1 per cent price cut increases the quantity sold by less than 1 per cent and total revenue decreases.

Total Revenue Test We can use this relationship between elasticity and total revenue to estimate elasticity using a total revenue test. The total-revenue test is a method of estimating the price elasticity of demand by observing the change in total revenue that results from a price change (with all other influences on the quantity sold remaining unchanged). If a price cut increases total revenue, demand is elastic; if a price cut decreases total revenue, demand is inelastic; and if a price cut leaves total revenue unchanged, demand is unit elastic.

Figure 5.6 shows the connection between the elasticity of demand and total revenue for oil. Part (a) shows the same demand curve that you studied in Figure 5.4. Over the price range from $50 to $25, demand is elastic. Over the price range from $25 to zero, demand is inelastic. At a price of $25, demand is unit elastic.

Figure 5.6(b) shows total revenue. At a price of $50, the quantity sold is zero so total revenue is also zero. At a price of zero, the quantity demanded is 20 million barrels a day, but at a zero price, total revenue is again zero. A price cut in the elastic range brings an increase in total revenue – the percentage increase in the quantity demanded is greater than the percentage decrease in price. A price cut in the inelastic range brings a decrease in total revenue – the percentage increase in the quantity demanded is less than the percentage decrease in price. At the point of unit elasticity, total revenue is at a maximum. A small price change either side of $25 keeps total revenue constant. The loss in total revenue from a lower price is offset by a gain in total revenue from a greater quantity sold. You can read about the elasticity of demand for the block-buster Monet art exhibition, and the effect of elasticity on revenue for the Royal Academy of Art, in *Reading Between the Lines* on pp. 116–117.

We have seen that long-run demand is more elastic than short-run demand. It is possible,

Figure 5.6 Elasticity and Total Revenue

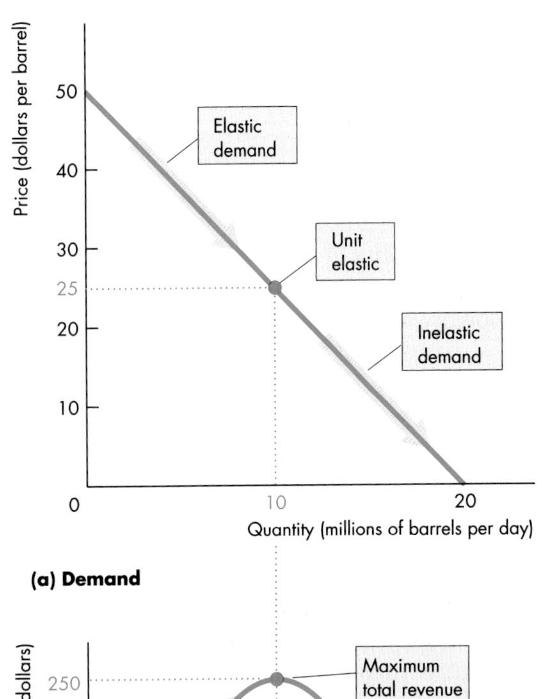

(a) Demand

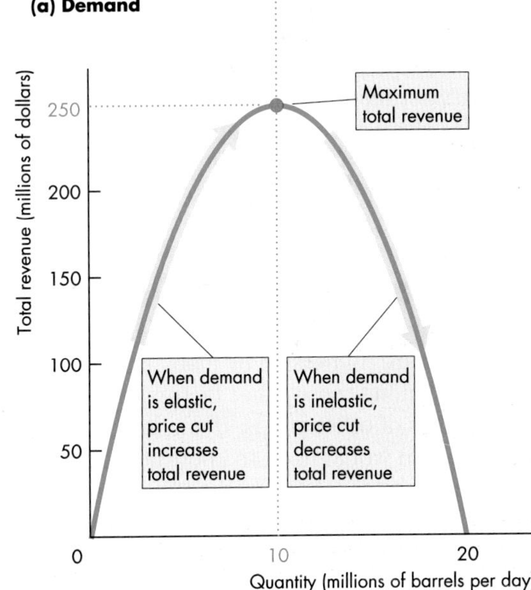

(b) Total revenue

When demand for oil is elastic, in the price range from $50 to $25, a decrease in price (in part a) brings an increase in total revenue (in part b). When demand for oil is inelastic, in the price range from $25 to zero, a decrease in price (in part a) brings a decrease in total revenue (in part b). When demand is unit elastic, at a price of $25 (in part a), total revenue is at a maximum (in part b).

therefore, that a price cut will decrease total revenue in the short run but increase total revenue in the long run. This outcome occurs if short-run demand is inelastic but long-run demand is elastic.

Review

- Price elasticity of demand measures the responsiveness of the quantity demanded of a good or service to a change in its price.
- The price elasticity of demand is the percentage change in the quantity demanded of a good divided by the percentage change in its price.
- The price elasticity of demand for a good is determined by the closeness of substitutes for it, the proportion of income spent on it, and the time lapse since its price changed.

So far, we've studied the most widely used elasticity – the *price* elasticity of demand. But there are some other useful elasticity of demand concepts. Let's look at them.

Figure 5.7 Cross Elasticity of Demand

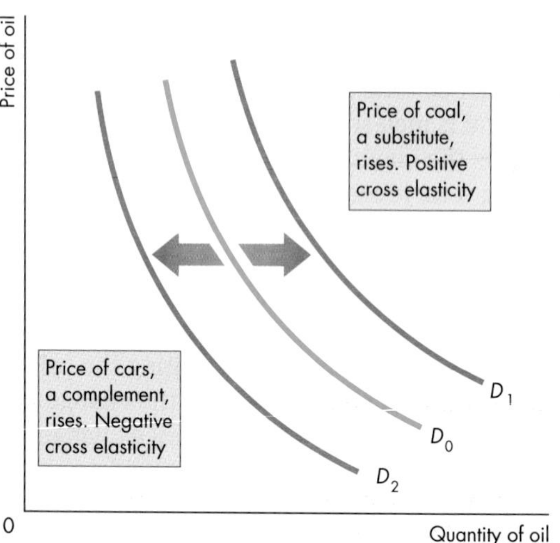

When the price of coal increases, the demand for oil, a *substitute* for coal, increases and the demand curve for oil shifts rightward from D_0 to D_1. The cross elasticity of the demand for oil with respect to the price of coal is *positive.* When the price of a car increases, the demand for oil, a *complement of cars,* decreases and the demand curve for oil shifts leftward from D_0 to D_2. The cross elasticity of the demand for oil with respect to the price of a car is *negative.*

More Elasticities of Demand

Buying plans are influenced by many factors other than price. Among these other factors are incomes and the prices of other goods. If you were OPEC's economist, you would need to know how the development of alternative fuels might affect the demand for oil. How would a slump in the world economy and countries' incomes reduce the demand for oil? You can answer these questions by calculating two other types of elasticities. Let's look at these other elasticities.

Cross Elasticity of Demand

The quantity of any good that consumers plan to buy depends on the prices of its substitutes and complements. We measure these influences by using the concept of the cross elasticity of demand. The **cross elasticity of demand** is a measure of the responsiveness of the demand for a good to a change in the price of a substitute or complement, other things remaining the same. It is calculated by using the formula:

$$\text{Cross elasticity of demand} = \frac{\text{Percentage change in quantity demanded}}{\text{Percentage change in the price of a substitute or complement}}$$

The cross elasticity of demand is positive for a substitute and negative for a complement. Figure 5.7 makes it clear why. When the price of coal – a substitute for oil – rises, the demand for oil increases and the demand curve for oil shifts rightward from D_0 to D_1. Because an increase in the price of coal brings an increase in the demand for oil, the cross elasticity of demand for oil with respect to the price of coal is positive. When the price of a car – a complement of oil – rises, the demand for oil decreases and the demand curve for oil shifts leftward from D_0 to D_2. Because an increase in the price of a car brings a decrease in

Figure 5.8 Income Elasticity of Demand

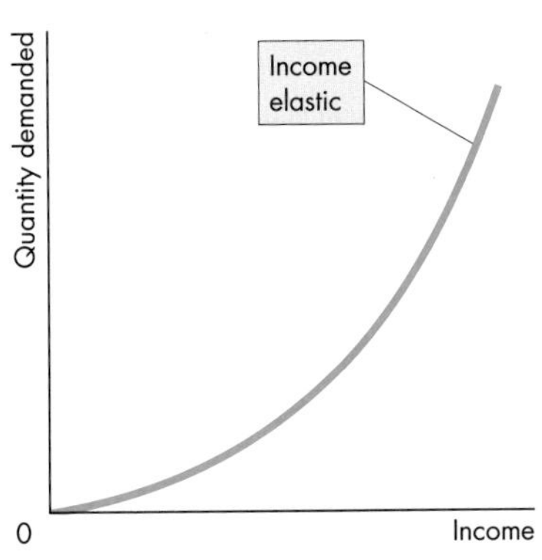

(a) Elasticity greater than 1

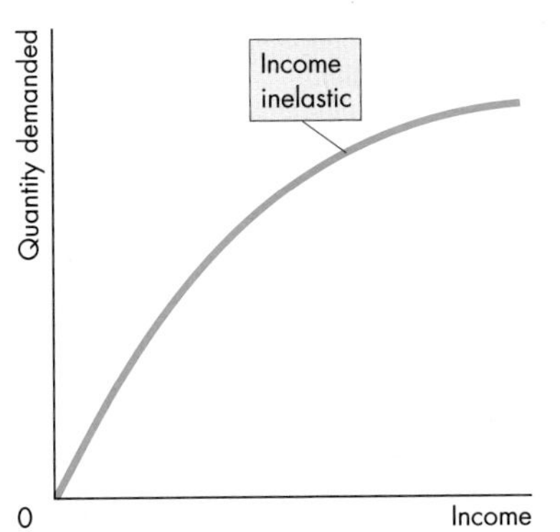

(b) Elasticity between zero and 1

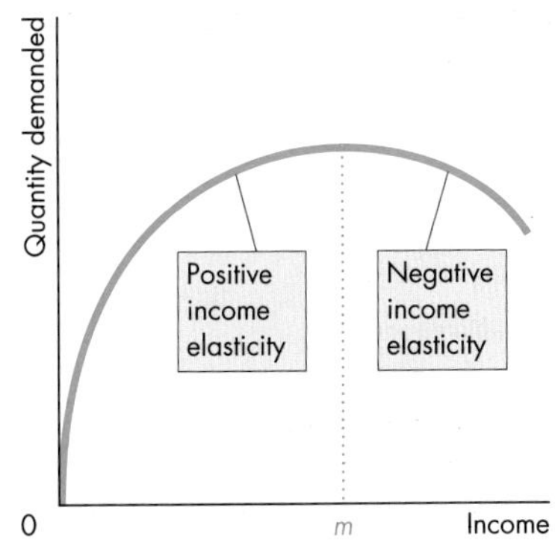

(c) Elasticity less than 1 and becomes negative

Income elasticity of demand has three ranges of values. In part (a), income elasticity of demand is greater than 1. In this case, as income increases, the quantity demanded increases but by a bigger percentage than the increase in income. In part (b), income elasticity of demand is between zero and 1. In this case, as income increases, the quantity demanded increases but by a smaller percentage than the increase in income. In part (c), the income elasticity of demand is positive at low incomes but becomes negative as income increases above level *m*. Maximum consumption of this good occurs at the income *m*.

the demand for oil, the cross elasticity of demand for oil with respect to the price of a car is negative. So positive values identify substitutes and negative values identify complements.

Income Elasticity of Demand

As income grows, how does the demand for a particular good change? The answer depends on the income elasticity of demand for the good. The **income elasticity of demand** is a measure of the responsiveness of demand to a change in income, other things remaining the same. It is calculated by using the formula:

$$\text{Income elasticity of demand} = \frac{\text{Percentage change in quantity demanded}}{\text{Percentage change in income}}$$

Income elasticities of demand can be positive or negative and fall into three interesting ranges:

1 Greater than 1 (normal good, income elastic).
2 Between zero and 1 (normal good, income inelastic).
3 Less than zero (inferior good).

Figure 5.8 illustrates these three cases. Part (a) shows an income elasticity of demand that is greater than 1. As income increases, the quantity demanded increases, but the quantity demanded increases faster than income. Some examples of income elastic goods are extreme luxuries such as ocean cruises, international travel, jewellery and works of art. But many other non-necessity goods are income elastic, such as the services of hair-dressers and accountants.

Part (b) shows an income elasticity of demand that is between zero and 1. In this case, the quantity demanded increases as income increases, but income increases faster than the quantity demanded. Examples of goods in this category are food, clothing, furniture, newspapers and magazines.

Part (c) shows an income elasticity of demand that eventually becomes negative. In this case, the quantity demanded increases as income increases until it reaches a maximum at income m. Beyond that point, as income continues to increase, the quantity demanded declines. The elasticity of demand is positive but less than 1 up to income m. Beyond income m, the income elasticity of demand is negative. Examples of goods in this category are small motorcycles, potatoes, rice and bread. Low income consumers buy most of these goods. At low

Table 5.2 Some Real-world Income Elasticities of Demand

Good or Service	Elasticity
NORMAL ELASTIC DEMAND	
Wine	2.6
Services	1.8
Spirits	1.7
Durable goods	1.5
NORMAL INELASTIC DEMAND	
Fruit juice	0.9
Beer	0.6
Green vegetables	0.1
Fresh meat	0.0
Cereals	0.0
INFERIOR	
Tobacco	–0.1
Bread	–0.3

Sources: Ministry of Agriculture, Food and Fisheries, *Household Food Consumption and Expenditure*, 1992, London, HMSO. C. Godfrey, Modelling Demand. In *Preventing Alcohol and Tobacco Problems*, Vol. 1, (A. Maynard and P. Tether, eds), Avebury, 1990. J. Muellbauer 'Testing the Barten Model of Household Composition Effects and the Cost of Children', *Economic Journal*, (September 1977).

income levels, the demand for such goods increases as income increases. But as income increases above point m, consumers replace these goods with superior alternatives. For example, a small car replaces the motorcycle; fruit, vegetables and meat begin to appear in a diet that was heavy in bread, rice or potatoes.

Real-world Income Elasticities of Demand

Table 5.2 shows estimates of some income elasticities of demand in the United Kingdom. The income elasticities in the table range from 2.6 for wine to – 0.3 for bread. Most basic necessities such as food and clothing are income inelastic, while luxury goods such as wines and spirits, services and durable goods – cars, electrical goods and furniture – are income elastic. Some goods such as tobacco and bread are inferior goods but their income elasticity values are close to zero.

Figure 5.9 Income Elasticity of Demand for Food in 20 Countries

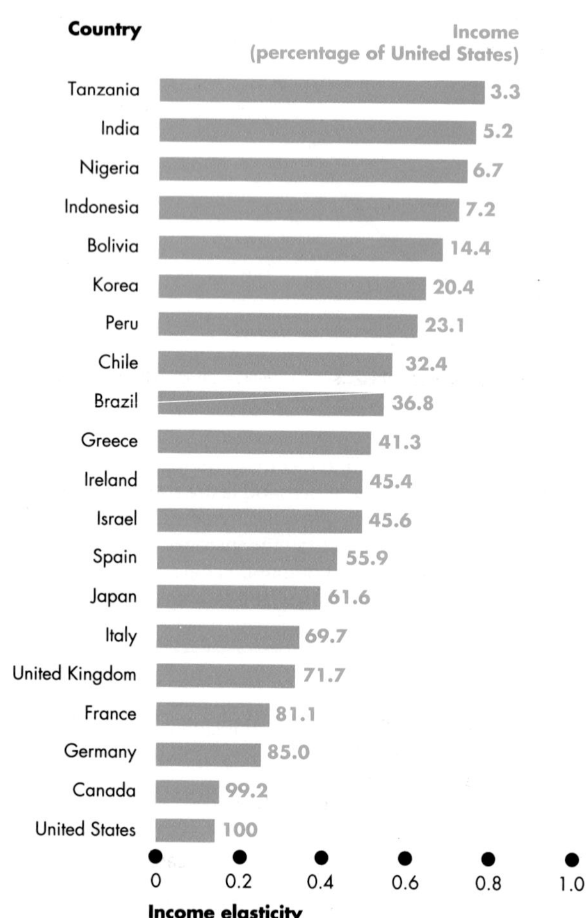

As income increases, the income elasticity of demand for food decreases. For low-income consumers, a larger percentage of any increase in income is spent on food than for high-income consumers.

Source: Henri Theil, Ching-Fan Chung and James L. Seale Jr, *Advances in Econometrics, Supplement 1*, 1989, *International Evidence on Consumption Patterns* 1989, Greenwich, Connecticut JAI Press Inc.

What is a necessity and what is a luxury depend on the level of income. For people with a low income, food and clothing can be luxuries. So the *level* of income has a big effect on income elasticities of demand. Figure 5.9 shows this effect on the income elasticity of demand for food in 20 countries. In

Table 5.3 A Compact Glossary of Elasticities of Demand

PRICE ELASTICITIES

A relationship is described as	When the elasticity value is	Which means that
Perfectly elastic or infinitely elastic	Infinity	The smallest possible increase (decrease) in price causes an infinitely elastic large decrease (increase) in the quantity demanded
Elastic	Less than infinity but greater than 1	The percentage decrease (increase) in the quantity demanded exceeds the percentage increase (decrease) in price
Unit elastic	1	The percentage decrease (increase) in the quantity demanded equals the percentage increase (decrease) in price
Inelastic	Greater than zero but less than 1	The percentage decrease (increase) in the quantity demanded is less than the percentage increase (decrease) in price
Perfectly inelastic or completely inelastic	Zero	The quantity demanded is the same at all prices

CROSS ELASTICITIES

A relationship is described as	When the elasticity value is	Which means that
Perfect substitutes	Infinity	The smallest possible increase (decrease) in the price of one good causes an infinitely large increase (decrease) in the quantity demanded of the other good
Substitutes	Positive, less than infinity	If the price of one good increases (decreases) the quantity demanded of the other good also increases (decreases)
Independent	Zero	The quantity demanded of one good remains constant regardless of the price of the other good
Complements	Less than zero	The quantity demanded of one good decreases (increases) when the price of the other good increases (decreases)

INCOME ELASTICITIES

A relationship is described as	When the elasticity value is	Which means that
Income elastic (normal good)	Greater than 1	The percentage increase (decrease) in the quantity demanded is greater than the percentage increase (decrease) in income
Income inelastic (normal good)	Less than 1 but greater than zero	The percentage increase (decrease) in the quantity demanded is less than the percentage increase (decrease) in income
Negative income elastic (inferior good)	Less than zero	When income increases (decreases), quantity demanded decreases (increases)

countries with low incomes, such as Tanzania and India, the income elasticity of demand for food is around 0.75, while in countries with high incomes, such as the United Kingdom, France, Germany, Canada and the United States, the income elasticity of demand for food is low. These numbers tell us that a 10 per cent increase in income leads to an increase in the demand for food of 7.5 per cent in India and less than 4 per cent in North America and Northern Europe. These numbers make sense and confirm the idea that necessities have a lower income elasticity of demand than luxuries. What for a high-income European is a basic necessity remains beyond the reach of a low-income Indian.

Table 5.3 gives a compact summary of all the different kinds of demand elasticities you've just studied.

Elasticity of Supply

If Germany's machine tool industry expands, it will increase its demand for steel. There will be a *change in demand* for steel. Both Germany's machine tool producers and European steel producers will want to know the likely changes in the price of steel that this increase in demand could bring. A change in demand shifts the demand curve and leads to a *movement along the supply curve*.

To predict the changes in price and quantity, we need to know how responsive the quantity supplied is to the price of a good. That is, we need to know the elasticity of supply.

The **elasticity of supply** measures the responsiveness of the quantity supplied of a good to a change in its price. It is calculated by using the formula:

$$\text{Elasticity of supply} = \frac{\text{Percentage change in quantity supplied}}{\text{Percentage change in price}}$$

There are two interesting cases of the elasticity of supply. If the quantity supplied is fixed regardless of the price, the supply curve is vertical. In this case, the elasticity of supply is zero. An increase in price leads to no change in the quantity supplied. Supply is perfectly inelastic. If there is a price below which nothing will be supplied and at which suppliers are willing to sell any quantity demanded, the supply curve is horizontal. In this case, the elasticity of supply is infinite. The small fall in price reduces the quantity supplied from an indefinitely large amount to zero. Supply is perfectly elastic.

The magnitude of the elasticity of supply depends on:

- Resource substitution possibilities.
- The time-frame for the supply decision.

Resource Substitution Possibilities

Some goods and services are produced by using unique or rare resources of production. These items have a low, and perhaps zero, elasticity of supply. Other goods and services are produced by using more common resources that can be allocated to a wide variety of alternative tasks. Such items have a high elasticity of supply.

A Van Gogh painting has been produced by a unique type of labour – Van Gogh's. No other resource can be substituted for this labour. There is just one of each painting, so its supply curve is vertical and its elasticity of supply is zero. At the other extreme, wheat can be grown on land that is almost equally good for growing barley. So it is just as easy to grow wheat or barley, and the opportunity cost of wheat in terms of foregone barley is almost constant. As a result, the supply curve of wheat is almost horizontal and its elasticity of supply is large. Similarly, when a good is produced in many different countries (for example, sugar and beef), the supply of the good is a highly elastic supply.

The supply of most goods and services lies between the two extremes. The quantity produced can be increased but only by incurring higher cost. If a higher price is offered, the quantity supplied increases. Such goods and services have an elasticity of supply between zero and infinity.

Elasticity of Supply and the Time-frame for Supply Decisions

To study the influence of the length of time elapsed since a price change, we distinguish three time-frames of supply:

1. Momentary supply.
2. Short-run supply.
3. Long-run supply.

Momentary Supply When the price of a good rises or falls, the *momentary supply curve* describes the initial change in the quantity supplied. The momentary supply curve shows the response of the quantity supplied immediately following a price change.

Some goods, such as fruits and vegetables, have a perfectly inelastic momentary supply – a vertical supply curve. The quantities supplied depend on crop planting decisions made earlier. In the case of grapes, for example, planting decisions have to be made many years in advance of the crop being available.

Other goods, such as long-distance phone calls, have an elastic momentary supply. When many people simultaneously make a call, there is a big surge in the demand for cable, computer switching and satellite time and the quantity bought increases (up to the physical limits of the telephone system) but the price remains constant. Long-distance carriers monitor fluctuations in demand and re-route calls to ensure that the quantity supplied equals the quantity demanded without raising the price.

Long-run Supply The *long-run supply* curve shows the response of the quantity supplied to a change in price after all the technologically possible ways of adjusting supply have been exploited. In the case of wine, the long run is the time it takes a new vineyard to grow to full maturity – about 15 years.

In some cases, the long-run adjustment occurs only after a completely new production plant has been built and workers have been trained to operate it – typically a process that might take several years.

Short-run Supply The *short-run supply curve* shows how the quantity supplied responds to a price change when only some of the technologically possible adjustments to production have been made. The first adjustment usually made is in the amount of labour employed. To increase output in the short run, firms make their employees work overtime and perhaps hire additional workers. To decrease their output in the short run, firms lay off workers or reduce their hours of work. With the passage of time, firms can make additional adjustments, perhaps training additional workers or buying additional tools and other equipment. The short-run response to a price change, unlike the momentary and long-run responses, is not a unique response but a sequence of adjustments.

Three Supply Curves Figure 5.10 shows three supply curves that correspond to the three time-frames. They are the supply curves in the world market for grapes on a given day in which the price is £2 a kilogram and the quantity of grapes grown is 3 million kilograms. Each supply curve passes through that point. Momentary supply is perfectly inelastic, as shown by the blue curve *MS*. As time passes, the quantity supplied becomes more responsive to price and is shown by the short-run supply curve, *SS*. As yet more time passes, the supply curve becomes the red long-run curve *LS*, the most elastic of the three supplies.

The momentary supply curve, *MS*, shows how quantity supplied responds to a price change the moment that it occurs. The blue momentary supply curve shown here is perfectly inelastic. The purple short-run supply curve, *SS*, shows how the quantity supplied responds to a price change after some adjustments to production have been made. The red long-run supply curve, *LS*, shows how the quantity supplied responds to a price change when all the technologically possible adjustments to the production process have been made.

The momentary supply curve is vertical because, on a given day, no matter what the price of grapes, producers cannot change their output. They have picked, packed and shipped their crop to market and the quantity available for that day is fixed. The short-run supply curve slopes upward because producers can take actions quite quickly to change the quantity supplied in response to a price change. They can, for example, stop picking and leave grapes to rot on the vine if the price falls by a large amount. Or they can use more fertilizers and improved irrigation and increase the yields of their existing vines if the price rises. In the long run, they can plant more vines and increase the quantity supplied even more in response to a given price rise.

You have now studied the theory of demand and supply, and you have learned how to measure the responsiveness of the quantity demanded to changes in prices and income. You have also learned how to measure the responsiveness of the quantity supplied to a change in the price. In the next chapter, we are going to use what we have learned to study some real world markets – markets in action.

Figure 5.10 Supply: Momentary, Short-run and Long-run

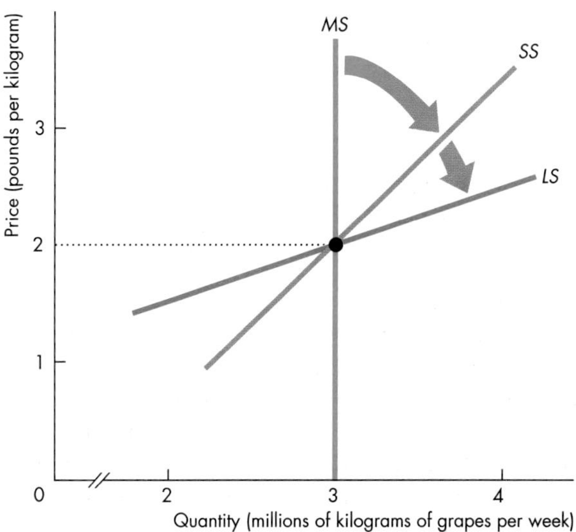

The momentary supply curve, *MS*, is perfectly inelastic. The short-run supply curve, *SS*, is more elastic as quantity supplied responds to a price change after some adjustments to production have been made. The long-run supply curve, *LS*, is even more elastic as quantity supplied responds to a price change when all the technologically possible adjustments to the production process have been made.

Summary

Key Points

Elasticity of Demand (pp. 98–106)

- Price elasticity of demand is a measure of the responsiveness of the quantity demanded of a good to a change in its price. It is calculated as the percentage change in the quantity demanded divided by the percentage change in price.
- The larger the magnitude of the elasticity of demand, the greater is the responsiveness of the quantity demanded to a given change in price.
- Price elasticity depends on how easily one good serves as a substitute for another, the proportion of income spent on the good and the length of time that has elapsed since the price change.
- If demand is elastic, a decrease in price leads to an increase in total revenue.
- If demand is unit elastic, a decrease in price leaves total revenue unchanged.
- If demand is inelastic, a decrease in price leads to a decrease in total revenue.

More Elasticities of Demand (pp. 106–109)

- Cross elasticity of demand measures the responsiveness of demand for one good to a change in the price of another good (a substitute or a complement).
- Cross elasticity of demand is calculated as the percentage change in the quantity demanded of one good divided by the percentage change in the price of another good.
- The cross elasticity of demand with respect to the price of a substitute is positive.
- The cross elasticity of demand with respect to the price of a complement is negative.
- Income elasticity of demand measures the responsiveness of demand to a change in income.
- Income elasticity of demand is calculated as the percentage change in the quantity demanded divided by the percentage change in income.
- For normal goods, the income elasticity of demand is positive.
- For inferior goods, the income elasticity of demand is negative. Inferior goods are consumed only at low incomes.
- When income elasticity is greater than 1, as income increases, the percentage of income spent on the good increases.
- When income elasticity is less than 1 but greater than zero, as income increases, the percentage of income spent on the good decreases.

Elasticity of Supply (pp. 109–111)

- The elasticity of supply measures the responsiveness of the quantity supplied of a good to a change in its price.
- Elasticity of supply is calculated as the percentage change in the quantity supplied of a good divided by the percentage change in its price.
- Supply elasticities are usually positive and range between zero (vertical supply curve) and infinity (horizontal supply curve).
- Supply decisions have three time-frames: momentary, long run and short run.
- Momentary supply refers to the response of suppliers to a price change at the instant that the price changes.
- Long-run supply refers to the response of suppliers to a price change when all the technologically feasible adjustments in production have been made.
- Short-run supply refers to the response of suppliers to a price change after some adjustments in production have been made.

Key Figures and Table 

Key Terms

Review Questions

1 Define the price elasticity of demand.

2 Why is elasticity a more useful measure of responsiveness than slope?

3 Draw a graph, or describe the shape of a demand curve that represents a good that has an elasticity of demand equal to:

a Infinity.
b Zero.
c Unity.

4 What three factors determine the size of the elasticity of demand?

5 What do we mean by short-run demand and long-run demand?

6 Explain why the short-run demand curve is usually less elastic than the long-run demand curve.

7 What is the connection between elasticity and total revenue? If the elasticity of demand for books is 1, by how much does a 10 per cent increase in the price of books change total revenue?

8 Define the income elasticity of demand.

9 Give an example of a good whose income elasticity of demand is:

a Greater than 1.
b Positive but less than 1.
c Less than zero.

10 Define the cross elasticity of demand. Is the cross elasticity of demand positive or negative?

11 Define the elasticity of supply. Is the elasticity of supply positive or negative?

12 Give an example of a good whose elasticity of supply is:

a Zero.
b Greater than zero but less than infinity.
c Infinity.

13 What do we mean by momentary, short-run, and long-run supply?

14 Why is momentary supply perfectly inelastic for many goods?

15 Why is long-run supply more elastic than short-run supply?

Problems

1 The demand schedule for video camera rental per day is:

Price (pounds)	Quantity demanded (number per day)
0	150
1	125
2	100
3	75
4	50
5	25
6	0

a At what price is the elasticity of demand equal to:

1 1?
2 Infinity?
3 Zero?

b At what price is total revenue maximized?
c Calculate the elasticity of demand for a rise in the rental price from £4 to £5.

2 Assume that the demand for video camera rentals in Problem 1 increases by 10 per cent at each price.

a Draw the old and new demand curves.
b Calculate the elasticity of demand for a rise in the rental price from £4 to £5.

Compare your answer with that to Problem 1(c).

3 Which item in each of the following pairs has the larger elasticity of demand:

a *The Economist* newspaper or newspapers in general?
b Vacations or vacations in Africa?
c Broccoli or vegetables?

4 You have been hired as an economic consultant by OPEC and given the following schedule showing the world demand for oil:

Price (dollars per barrel)	Quantity demanded (millions of barrels per day)
10	60,000
20	50,000
30	40,000
40	30,000
50	20,000

Your advice is needed on the following questions:

a If the supply of oil is decreased so that the price rises from \$20 to \$30 a barrel, will the total revenue from oil sales increase or decrease?
b What will happen to total revenue if the supply of oil is decreased further and the price rises to \$40 a barrel?
c What is the price that will achieve the highest total revenue?
d What quantity of oil will be sold at the price that answers Problem 4(c)?
e What are the values of the price elasticity of demand for price changes of \$10 a barrel at average prices of \$15, \$25, \$35 and \$45 a barrel?
f What is the elasticity of demand at the price that maximizes total revenue?
g Over what price range is the demand for oil inelastic?

5 State the sign (positive or negative) and, where possible, the range (less than 1, 1, greater than 1) of the following elasticities:

a The price elasticity of demand for ice cream at the point of maximum total revenue.
b The cross elasticity of demand for ice cream with respect to the price of frozen yoghurt.
c The income elasticity of demand for Caribbean cruises.
d The income elasticity of demand for toothpaste.
e The elasticity of supply of Irish salmon.

f The cross elasticity of demand for corn ready to be popped with respect to the price of popcorn machines.

6 The following table gives some data on the demand for long-distance telephone calls:

Price (pence per minute)	Quantity demanded (millions of minutes per day)	
	Short-run	Long-run
10	700	1,000
20	500	500
30	300	0

At a price of 20 pence a minute:

a Calculate the elasticity of short-run demand.
b Calculate the elasticity of long-run demand.
c Is the demand for calls more elastic in the short run or the long run?

7 In Problem 6, does total expenditure on calls increase or decrease as the price of a call decreases from 20 pence a minute to 10 pence a minute?

8 The following table gives some data on the supply of long-distance phone calls:

Price (pence per minute)	Quantity supplied (thousands per day)	
	Short-run	Long-run
10	300	0
20	500	500
30	700	10,000

At a price of 20 pence a minute, calculate the elasticity of:

a Short-run supply.
b Long-run supply.

9 In Problem 8, which supply is more elastic and why? Compare the elasticities of supply when the price of a call is 15 pence a minute and when it is 25 pence a minute.

10 Read the article in *Reading Between the Lines* on p. 116 about the Monet exhibition and then:

a Calculate the elasticity value for the demand for the Monet exhibition when price rises from £2.00 to £9.00.
b Calculate the elasticity value for the demand for typical classic art exhibitions when price rises from £2.00 to £9.00.

11 Use the link on the Parkin, Powell and Matthews Web site to:

a Find the price of petrol in the summer of 1999.
b Use the tools of demand and supply and the concept of elasticity to explain the recent changes in the price of petrol.
c Find the latest price of crude oil.
d Use the tools of demand and supply and the concept of elasticity to explain the recent changes in the price of crude oil.

12 Use the link on the Parkin, Powell and Matthews Web site to answer the following:

a Find the number of gallons in a barrel.
b What is the cost of the crude oil in one gallon of petrol?
c What are the other costs that make up the total cost of a gallon of petrol?
d If the price of crude oil falls by 10 per cent, by what percentage would you expect the price of petrol to change, other things remaining the same?
e In light of your answer to part (d), do you think the elasticity of demand for crude oil is greater than, less than, or equal to the elasticity of demand for petrol?

W http://www.econ100.com

Elasticity: Making the Most from Monet

The Guardian, 15 January 1999

Academy Offers £1.8m look at Monet

Report by Amelia Gentleman

Next week the Royal Academy gallery's turnstiles will start spinning as visitors arrive to view what promises to be the blockbuster exhibition of the year, Monet in the 20th Century.

Over the next three months, staff expect at least 500,000 people to visit the show, despite the £9 entrance fee, the highest the academy has charged. The exhibition brings together for the first time 80 works painted in the years from 1900, when Monet was 60, until his death in 1926, all of which build on the Impressionist style he pioneered in the 19th century.

The high ticket price has not dissuaded many art lovers. About 111,000 people have bought tickets already, with bookings made from Hawaii, Hong Kong and New Zealand.

Nick Blackburn, director of the Ticketmaster agency which is handling advance sales, said demand had been phenomenal and matched those for Premier League football matches and hit West End musicals.

"We have never sold so many tickets for an art exhibition.These are very, very hot tickets," he said.

Monet is an infallible money-spinner and the RA is looking forward to paying off a large chunk of its £500,000 overdraft with profits from the show.

But exhibition organisers stress that — even with the help of their sponsors Ernst and Young — mounting such a large show is extremely expensive.

The overall budget stands at £1.8 million.

The gallery has been forced to build a marquee in the forecourt to accommodate the extra visitors; the cost of insuring and providing security for the paintings quickly mounts up.

The RA has to pay not only for the shipping of the paintings from public and private galleries — in Paris, Honolulu, Kyoto and elsewhere — but also for air fares and accommodation for the couriers who accompany each work.

But souvenir sales may also prove profitable. A wide variety of associated knickknacks is to be plied in the gallery shop and staff expect Philippe the Frog — a cuddly toy which lives in Monet's lily pond — to be a big seller. Seeds which will grow into a Monet-esque landscape are also tipped for strong sales.

Curator MaryAnne Stevens was unsurprised by Monet's pulling power.

"His paintings are very accessible. They are everybody's vision of a typical landscape in summer, they appeal to a certain nostalgia for a golden age.

The Essence of the Story

- The Royal Academy's Monet exhibition in London will be a blockbuster at which 80 pictures by the popular impressionist artist will be exhibited together for the first time.
- More than 500,000 visitors are expected even though the ticket price of £9.00 is the highest ever set for entry to a Royal Academy art exhibition.
- The ticket price of £9.00 has not put art lovers off as 111,000 advance tickets have already been sold.
- The Royal Academy have just £1.8 million from sponsors to set up the Monet exhibition, but the profits (ticket sales minus the cost of setting up the exhibition) should be enough to pay off the Royal Academy's £500,000 overdraft.
- Merchandizing will help to raise revenue and add to the profit from the exhibition.

Economic Analysis

■ Figure 1 shows two exhibition demand curves. D_M is the demand curve for the Monet exhibition and D_C is the typical demand curve for classic art exhibitions.

■ At a ticket price of £2.00, both the Monet and typical classic art exhibitions attract 600,000 visitors. The elasticity values along the two demand curves are compared in Figure 1 by the relative slope of the two demand curves above and below a price of £2.00 a ticket.

■ The Monet exhibition demand curve, D_M, has a steeper slope than the typical demand curve, D_C. A rise in the ticket price from £2.00 to £9.00 cuts the number of visitors to the Monet exhibition by just 100,000, compared to a cut of 500,000 for typical classic art exhibitions.

■ This shows that demand for the Monet exhibition, D_M, is relatively inelastic, compared to the demand for typical classic art exhibitions, D_C. Raising the price of the tickets for the Monet exhibition should raise revenue compared to typical exhibitions.

■ If tickets cost £2.00, both types of exhibition generate £1.2 million in revenue (£2.00 times 600,000 tickets), shown by the pink, red and blue areas in Figure 2. Raising the ticket price to £9.00, raises revenue to £4.5 million for the Monet exhibition (the orange, green, pink and red areas), but reduces revenue to £0.9 million for typical classic art exhibitions (the orange and pink areas).

■ Only £500,000 profit will be made from ticket sales revenue of £4.5 million, implying the exhibition will cost over £5.8 million to set up (£4 million from the ticket sales and £1.8 from sponsors). The costs are high because of the extra security, insurance, shipping and accommodation required for such a large number of highly valued pictures. Profits may rise if merchandizing boosts revenue.

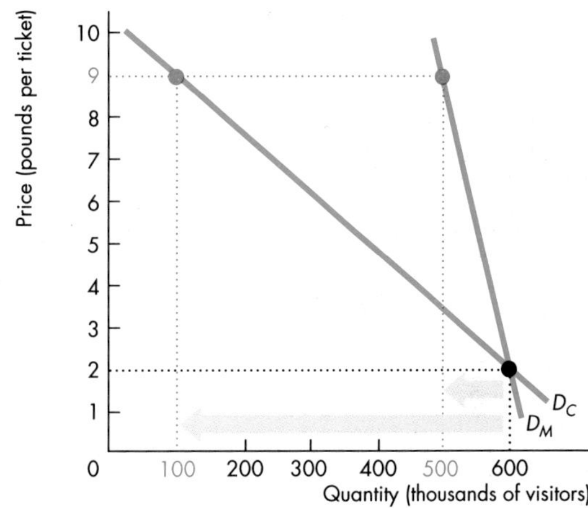

Figure 1 Two exhibition demand curves

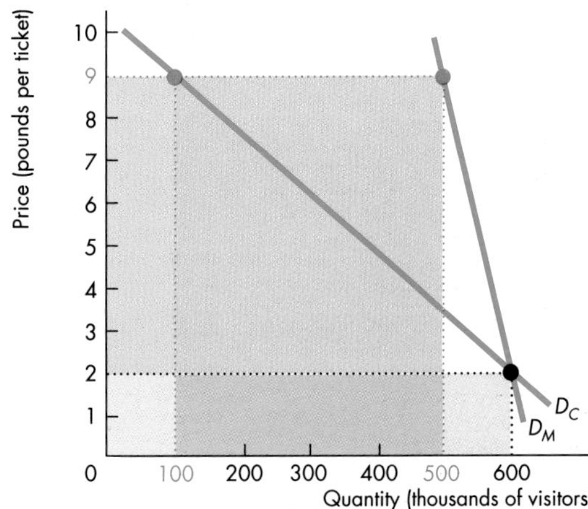

Figure 2 Total revenues

CHAPTER 6

Efficiency and Equity

After studying this chapter you will be able to:

- Define efficiency
- Distinguish between value and price and define consumer surplus
- Distinguish between cost and price and define producer surplus
- Explain when and why competitive markets move resources to their highest value
- Explain the sources of inefficiency in market economies
- Explain notions of fairness and assess whether competitive markets result in unfair outcomes

More for Less

People constantly strive to get more for less. As consumers, we love to get a bargain. We enjoy telling our friends about the great deal we got on CDs or some other item we bought at a good price. When we buy something, we express our view about how scarce resources should be used. We try to spend our incomes in ways that get the most out of our scarce resources. For example, we balance the pleasure we get from our expenditure on leisure against the value we get from textbooks and other educational resources. ◆ Is the allocation of our resources between leisure and education, pizza and sandwiches, sports wear and designer jeans, and all the other things we buy the right one? Could we get more out of our resources if we spent more on some goods and less on others? ◆ Scientists and engineers devote enormous effort to find technological innovations that will make more productive use of our scarce land, labour and capital resources. Workers in factories often make suggestions that increase productivity. Is our economy an efficient mechanism for producing goods and services? Do we get the most out of our scarce resources in factories, offices and shops? ◆ Some firms make huge profits year after year. Microsoft, for example, has generated enough profit over the past ten years to make one of its founders, Bill Gates, one of the richest men in the world. Is that kind of business success a sign of efficiency?

◆ ◆ ◆ ◆ These are the kinds of question that you will explore in this chapter. You will learn some concepts that will help you to think about efficiency more broadly than the everyday use of the word. You will discover that competitive markets can be efficient. You will also discover that markets can be inefficient and that government action can improve market efficiency. Finally, you will learn that firms that make huge profits may be efficient in one sense, but inefficient in a broader sense.

Efficiency: A Refresher

It's hard to talk about efficiency in an ordinary conversation without generating disagreement. To an engineer, an entrepreneur, a politician, a working mother, or an economist, getting more for less seems like a sensible thing to aim for. But some people think that the pursuit of efficiency conflicts with other more worthy goals. Environmentalists worry about contamination from 'efficient' nuclear power plants. Car producers worry about competition from 'efficient' foreign producers.

Economists use the idea of efficiency in a special way that avoids these disagreements. An efficient allocation of resource occurs when we produce the goods and services that people value most highly (see Chapter 3, pp. 48–49). Equivalently, resource use is efficient when we cannot produce more of a good or service without giving up some other good or service that we value more highly.

If people value a nuclear-free environment more highly than they value cheap electric power, it is efficient to use higher-cost, non-nuclear technologies to produce electricity. Efficiency is not a cold, mechanical concept. It is a concept based on value and value is based on people's feelings.

Think about the efficient quantity of pizza. To produce more pizza, we must give up some other goods and services. For example, we might give up some sandwiches. To get more pizzas, we forego sandwiches. If we have fewer pizzas, we can have more sandwiches. What is the efficient quantity of pizza to produce? The answer depends on marginal benefit and marginal cost.

Figure 6.1 The Efficient Quantity of Pizza

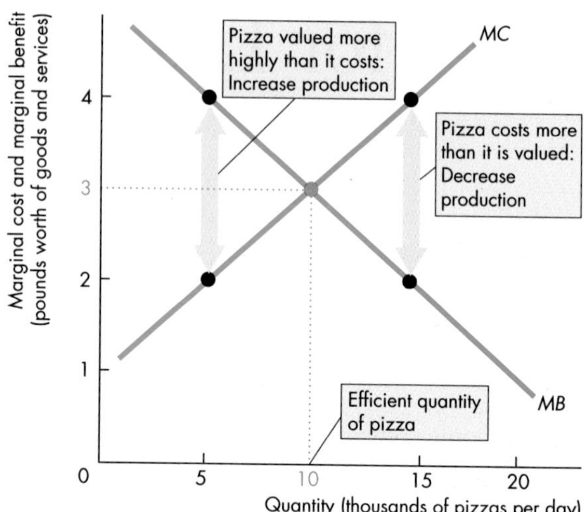

The marginal benefit curve (*MB*) shows what people *are willing to* forego to get one more pizza. The marginal cost curve (*MC*) shows what people *must* forego to get one more pizza. If fewer than 10,000 pizzas a day are produced, marginal benefit exceeds marginal cost. Greater value can be obtained by producing more pizzas. If more than 10,000 pizzas a day are produced, marginal cost exceeds marginal benefit. Greater value can be obtained by producing fewer pizzas. If 10,000 pizzas a day are produced, marginal benefit equals marginal cost and the efficient quantity of pizza is available.

Marginal Benefit

If we consume one more pizza, we receive a marginal benefit. Marginal benefit is the benefit that a person receives from consuming one more unit of a good or service. The marginal benefit from a good or service is measured as the maximum amount that a person is willing to pay for one more unit of it. So the marginal benefit from a pizza is the maximum amount of other goods and services that people are willing to give up in order to get one more pizza. The marginal benefit from pizza decreases as the quantity of pizza consumed increases – the principle of *decreasing marginal benefit*.

We can express the marginal benefit from a pizza as the number of sandwiches that people are willing to forego to get one more pizza. But we can also express marginal benefit as the pound value of other goods and services that people are willing to forego. Figure 6.1 shows the marginal benefit from pizza expressed in this way. As the quantity of pizza increases, the value of other items that people are willing to forego to get yet one more pizza decreases.

Marginal Cost

If we produce one more pizza, we incur a marginal cost. Marginal cost is the opportunity cost of producing *one more unit* of a good or service. The marginal cost of a good or service is measured as the value of the best alternative foregone. So the marginal cost of a pizza is the value of the best alternative foregone to get one more pizza. The marginal cost of a pizza increases as the quantity of pizza produced increases – the principle of *increasing marginal cost*.

We can express marginal cost as the number of sandwiches we must forego to get one more pizza. But we can also express marginal cost as the pound value of other goods and services we must forego. Figure 6.1 shows the marginal cost of pizza expressed in this way. As the quantity of pizza produced increases, the value of other items we must forego to get yet one more pizza increases.

Efficiency and Inefficiency

To determine the efficient quantity of pizza, we compare the marginal cost of a pizza with the marginal benefit from a pizza. There are three possible cases:

1 Marginal benefit exceeds marginal cost.

2 Marginal cost exceeds marginal benefit.

3 Marginal benefit equals marginal cost.

Marginal Benefit Exceeds Marginal Cost

Suppose the quantity of pizza produced is 5,000 a day. Figure 6.1 shows that at this quantity, the marginal benefit of a pizza is £4. That is, when the quantity of pizza available is 5,000 a day, people are willing to pay £4 for the 5,000th pizza.

Figure 6.1 also shows that the marginal cost of the 5,000th pizza is £2. That is, to produce one more pizza, the value of other goods and services that we must forego is £2. If pizza production increases from 4,999 to 5,000, the value of the additional pizza is £4 and its marginal cost is £2. By producing this pizza, the value of the pizza produced exceeds the value of the goods and services foregone by £2. Resources are used more efficiently – they create more value – if we produce an extra pizza and fewer other goods and services. This same reasoning applies all the way up to the 9,999th pizza. Only when we get to the 10,000th pizza does marginal benefit not exceed marginal cost.

Marginal Cost Exceeds Marginal Benefit

Suppose the quantity of pizza produced is 15,000 a day. Figure 6.1 shows that at this quantity, the marginal benefit of a pizza is £2. That is, when the quantity of pizza available is 15,000 a day, people are willing to pay £2 for the 15,000th pizza.

Figure 6.1 also shows that the marginal cost of the 15,000th pizza is £4. That is, to produce one more pizza, the value of the other goods and services that we must forego is £4.

If pizza production decreases from 15,000 to 14,999, the value of the one pizza foregone is £2 and its marginal cost is £4. So by not producing this pizza, the value of the other goods and services produced exceeds the value of the pizza foregone by £2. Resources are used more efficiently – they create more value – if we produce one fewer pizza and more other goods and services. This same reasoning applies all the way down to the 10,001st pizza. Only when we get to the 10,000th pizza does marginal cost not exceed marginal benefit.

Marginal Cost Equals Marginal Benefit

Suppose the quantity of pizza produced is 10,000 a day. Figure 6.1 shows that at this quantity, the marginal benefit of a pizza is £3. That is, when the quantity of pizza available is 10,000 a day, people are willing to pay £3 for the 10,000th pizza.

Figure 6.1 also shows that the marginal cost of the 10,000th pizza is £3. That is, to produce one more pizza, the value of other goods and services that we must forego is £3.

In this situation, we cannot increase the value of the goods and services produced by either increasing or decreasing the quantity of pizza. If we increase the quantity of pizza, the 10,001st pizza costs more to produce than it is worth. And if we decrease the quantity of pizza produced, the 9,999th pizza is worth more than it costs to produce. So when marginal benefit equals marginal cost, resource use is efficient.

Review

- If the marginal benefit exceeds marginal cost, we can use resources more efficiently by increasing the production of pizza and decreasing the production of other goods. The value of the extra pizza exceeds the value of the other goods foregone.

- If marginal cost exceeds marginal benefit, we can use our resources more efficiently by decreasing the production of pizza and increasing the production of other goods.

The value of the other goods exceeds the value of the pizza foregone.

- If marginal benefit equals its marginal cost, we are producing the efficient quantity of pizza.

So does a competitive pizza market produce the efficient quantity of pizza? Let's answer this question now.

Value, Price and Consumer Surplus

To investigate whether a competitive market is efficient, we need to look at the connection between demand and marginal benefit, and supply and marginal cost.

Value, Willingness to Pay and Demand

In everyday life we talk about 'getting value for money'. When we use this expression we are distinguishing between *value* and *price*. Value is what we get, and the price is what we pay.

The value of one more unit of a good or service is its *marginal benefit*. Marginal benefit can be expressed as the maximum price that people are willing to pay for another unit of the good or service. The willingness to pay for a good or service determines the demand for it.

In Figure 6.2(a) the demand curve shows the quantity demanded at each price. For example, when the price of a pizza is £3, the quantity demanded is 10,000 pizzas a day. In Figure 6.2(b), the demand curve shows the maximum price that people are willing to pay when there is a given quantity. For example, when 10,000 pizzas a day are available, the most that people are willing to pay for a pizza is £3. This second interpretation of the demand curve means that the marginal benefit from the 10,000th pizza is £3.

When we draw a demand curve, we use a *relative price*, not a *money* price. A relative price is expressed in pound units, but it measures the number of pounds-worth of other goods and services foregone to obtain one more unit of the good in question (see Chapter 4, p. 72). So a demand curve tells us the quantity of other goods and services that people are willing forego to get an

Figure 6.2 Demand, Willingness to Pay, and Marginal Benefit

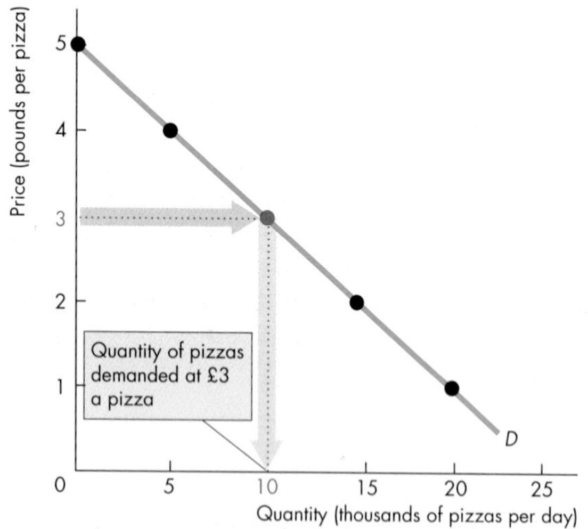

(a) Price determines quantity demanded

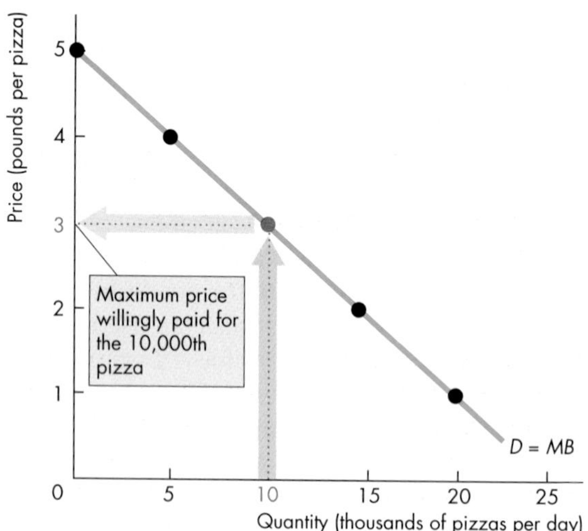

(b) Quantity determines willingness to pay

The demand curve for pizza, *D*, shows the quantity of pizza demanded at each price, other things remaining the same. It also shows the maximum price that consumers are willing to pay if a given quantity of pizza is available. At a price of £3, the quantity demanded is 10,000 pizzas a day (part a). If 10,000 pizzas a day are available, the maximum price that consumers are willing to pay for the 10,000th pizza is £3 (part b).

additional unit of a good. But this is what a marginal benefit curve tells us too. So, *a demand curve is a marginal benefit curve*.

We don't always have to pay the maximum price that we are willing to pay. When we buy something, we often get a bargain. Let's see how.

Consumer Surplus

When people buy something for less than it is worth to them, they receive a consumer surplus. A consumer surplus is the value of a good minus the price paid for it.

To understand consumer surplus, let's look at Lisa's demand for pizza, which is shown in Figure 6.3. Lisa likes pizza, but the marginal benefit she gets from it decreases quickly as her consumption increases.

If a pizza costs £5, Lisa spends her monthly lunch budget on items that she values more highly than pizza. At £4 a pizza, she buys 1 pizza a month. At £3 a pizza, she buys 2 pizzas a month; at £2 a pizza, she buys 3 pizzas a month, and at £1 a pizza, she buys 4 pizzas a month.

Lisa's demand curve for pizza in Figure 6.3 is also her *willingness-to-pay* or marginal benefit curve. It tells us that if Lisa can have only 1 pizza a month, she is willing to pay £4. Her marginal benefit from the first pizza is £4. If she can have 2 pizzas a month, she is willing to pay £3 for the second pizza. Her marginal benefit from the second pizza is £3.

Figure 6.3 also shows Lisa's consumer surplus from pizza when the price of a pizza is £3. At this price, she buys 2 pizzas a month. A price of £3 a pizza is the most she is willing to pay for the second pizza, so its marginal benefit is exactly the price she pays for it.

But Lisa is willing to pay almost £5 just to get a slice of the first pizza. So the marginal benefit from a slice of this first pizza could be close to £2 more than she pays for it. She receives a *consumer surplus* of almost £2 from just a slice of the first pizza. At a quantity of 1 pizza a month, Lisa's marginal benefit is £4 a pizza. So on this pizza, she receives a consumer surplus of £1. To calculate Lisa's consumer surplus, we must find the consumer surplus on each pizza and add these surpluses together. This sum is the area of the green triangle in Figure 6.3. This area is equal to the base of the triangle (2 pizzas per month) multiplied by the height of the triangle (£2) divided by 2, which is £2 a month.

The blue rectangle in Figure 6.3 is the amount that Lisa pays for pizza, which is £6 a month – 2 pizzas at £3 each. All goods and services are like the pizza example you've just studied. Because of decreasing marginal benefit, people receive more benefit from their consumption than the amount they pay.

Figure 6.3 A Consumer's Demand and Consumer Surplus

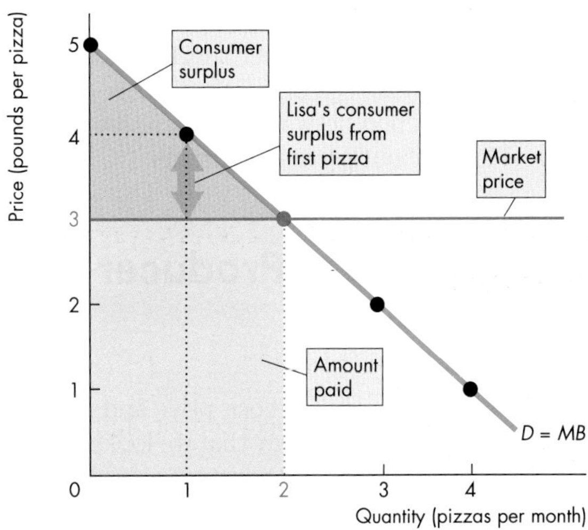

Lisa's demand curve for pizza tells us that at £5 a pizza, she does not buy pizza. At £4 a pizza, she buys one pizza a month; at £3 a pizza, she buys two pizzas a month. Lisa's demand curve also tells us that she is willing to pay £4 for the first pizza and £3 for the second. She actually pays £3 a pizza – the market price – and buys two pizzas a month. Her consumer surplus from pizza is £2 – the area of the green triangle.

Review

- The value or marginal benefit from a good or service is the maximum amount that someone is willing to pay for it.
- The demand curve shows marginal benefit.

- Consumer surplus is the marginal benefit minus the price of each item consumed.

You've seen how we distinguish between value – marginal benefit – and price. And you've seen that buyers receive a consumer surplus because marginal benefit exceeds price. Next, we're going to study the connection between supply and marginal cost, and learn about producer surplus.

Cost, Price and Producer Surplus

We are now going to look at cost, price and producer surplus in the same way that we looked at the ideas about value, price and consumer surplus in the previous section.

Firms are in business to make a profit. To do so, they must sell their output for a price that exceeds the cost of production. Let's investigate the relationship between cost and price.

Cost, Minimum Supply-price and Supply

Earning a profit means receiving more (or at least receiving no less) for the sale of a good or service than the cost of producing it. Just as consumers distinguish between *value* and *price*, so producers distinguish between *cost* and *price*. Cost is what a producer gives up, and price is what a producer receives.

The cost of producing one more unit of a good or service is its *marginal cost*. And the marginal cost is the minimum price that producers must receive to induce them to produce another unit of the good or service. This minimum acceptable price determines supply.

In Figure 6.4(a), the supply curve shows the quantity supplied at each price. For example, when the price of a pizza is £3, the quantity supplied is 10,000 pizzas a day. In Figure 6.4(b), the supply curve shows the minimum price that producers must be offered to produce a given quantity of pizza. For example, the minimum price that producers must be offered to get them to produce

Figure 6.4 Supply, Price and Producer Surplus

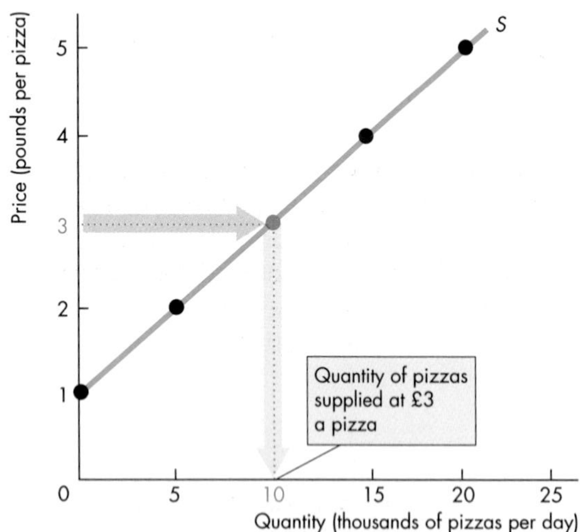

(a) Price determines quantity supplied

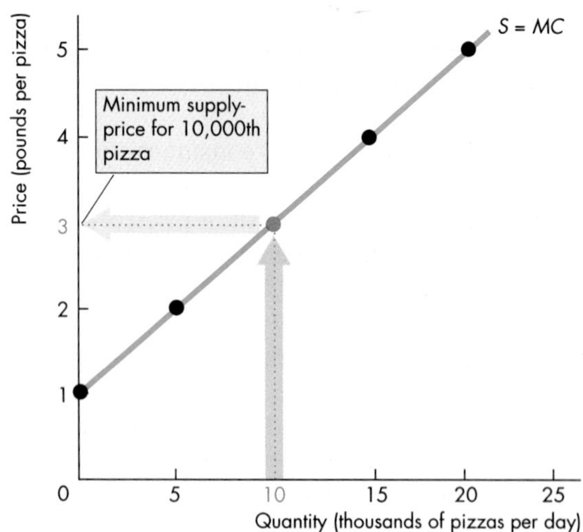

(b) Quantity determines minimum supply-price

The supply curve of pizza, *S*, shows the quantity of pizza supplied at each price, other things remaining the same. It also shows the minimum price that producers must be offered if a given quantity of pizza is to be produced. At a price of £3, the quantity supplied is 10,000 pizzas a day (part a). If 10,000 pizzas a day are produced, the minimum price that producers must be offered for the 10,000th pizza is £3 (part b).

10,000 pizzas a day is £3 a pizza. This second view of the supply curve means that the marginal cost of the 10,000th pizza is £3.

Because the price is a relative price, a supply curve tells us the quantity of other goods and services that *sellers must forego* to produce one more unit of the good. But a marginal cost curve also tells us the quantity of other goods and services that we must forego to get one more unit of the good. So, *a supply curve is a marginal cost curve*.

If the price producers receive exceeds the cost they incur, they earn a producer surplus. This producer surplus is the mirror image of the idea of consumer surplus.

Producer Surplus

When price exceeds marginal costs the firm obtains a producer surplus. A producer surplus is the price of a good minus the opportunity cost of producing it. To understand producer surplus, let's look at Mario's supply of pizza in Figure 6.5.

Mario can produce pizza or bake bread that people like a lot. The more pizza he bakes, the less bread he can bake. His opportunity cost of pizza is the value of the bread he must forego. This opportunity cost increases as Mario increases his production of pizza. If a pizza sells for only £1, Mario produces no pizzas. He uses his kitchen to bake bread. Pizza just isn't worth producing. But at £2 a pizza, Mario produces 50 pizzas a day, and at £3 a pizza, he produces 100 a day.

Mario's supply curve of pizza is also his *minimum supply-price* curve. It tells us that if Mario can sell only one pizza a day, the minimum that he must be paid for it is £1. If he can sell 50 pizzas a day, the minimum that he must be paid for the 50th pizza is £2, and so on.

Figure 6.5 also shows Mario's producer surplus. If the price of a pizza is £3, Mario plans to sell 100 pizzas a day. The minimum that he must be paid for the 100th pizza is £3. So its opportunity cost is exactly the price he receives for it. But his opportunity cost of the first pizza is only £1. So this first pizza costs £2 less to produce than he receives for it. Mario receives a *producer surplus* from his first pizza of £2. He receives a slightly smaller producer surplus on the second pizza, less on the third, and so on until he receives no producer surplus on the 100th pizza.

Figure 6.5 shows Mario's producer surplus as the blue triangle formed by the area above the supply curve and beneath the price line. This area is equal to the base of the triangle (100 pizzas a day) multiplied by the height (£2 a pizza) divided by 2, which equals £100 a day. Figure 6.5 also shows Mario's opportunity costs of production as the red area beneath the supply curve.

Figure 6.5 A Producer's Supply and Producer Surplus

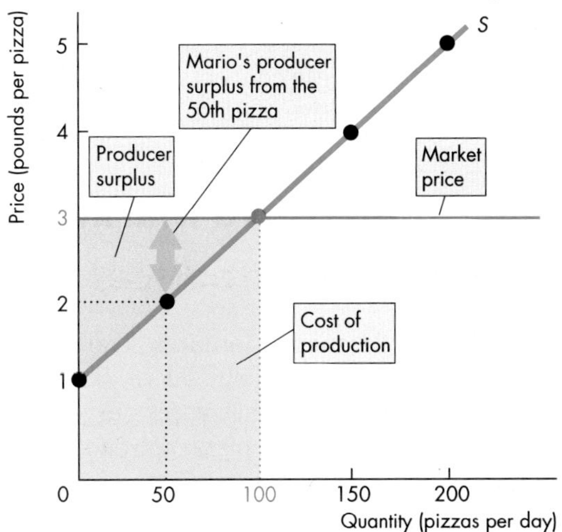

Mario's supply curve of pizza tells us that at a price of £1, Mario plans to sell no pizza. At a price of £2, he plans to sell 50 pizzas a day; and at a price of £3, he plans to sell 100 pizzas a day. Mario's supply curve also tells us that the minimum he must be offered is £2 for the 50th pizza a day and £3 for the 100th pizza a day. If the market price is £3 a pizza, he sells 100 pizzas a day and receives £300. The red area shows Mario's cost of producing pizza, which is £200 a day, and the blue area shows his producer surplus, which is £100 a day.

Review

- The marginal cost or opportunity cost of producing a good or service is the minimum supply price – the minimum price that producers must be offered.
- The marginal cost is shown by the supply curve.

- Producer surplus is the price received from the sale of a good minus the opportunity cost of producing it.

Consumer surplus and producer surplus can be used to measure the efficiency of a market. Let's see how we can use these concepts to study the efficiency of a competitive market.

Is the Competitive Market Efficient?

Figure 6.6 shows the market for pizza. The demand for pizza is shown by the demand curve, *D*. The supply of pizza is shown by the supply curve, *S*. The equilibrium price is £3 a pizza, and the equilibrium quantity is 10,000 pizzas a day.

The market forces that you studied in Chapter 4, pp. 80–82, will pull the pizza market to this equilibrium. If the price is greater than £3 a pizza, a surplus will force the price down. If the price is 124less than £3 a pizza, a shortage will force the price up. Only if the price is £3 a pizza is there neither a surplus nor a shortage and no forces operating to change the price.

So the market price and quantity are pulled towards their equilibrium values. But is this competitive equilibrium efficient? Does it produce the efficient quantity of pizza?

Figure 6.6 An Efficient Market for Pizza 

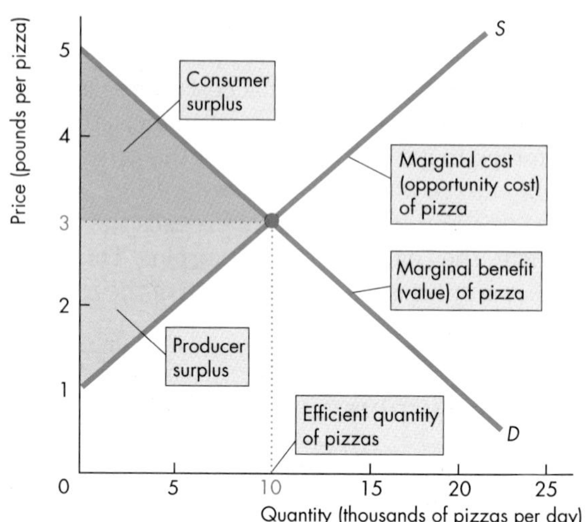

Resources are used efficiently when the sum of consumer surplus and producer suplus is maximized. Consumer surplus is the area below the demand curve and above the market price line – the green triangle. Producer surplus is the area below the price line and above the supply curve – the blue triangle. Here consumer surplus is £10,000, and producer surplus is also £10,000. The total surplus is £20,000. This surplus is maximized when the willingness to pay equals the opportunity cost. The *efficient quantity* of pizza is 10,000 pizzas per day.

Efficiency of a Competitive Market

The equilibrium in Figure 6.6 is efficient. Resources are being used to produce the quantity of pizza that people value most highly. It is not possible to produce more pizza without giving up some other good or service that is valued more highly. And if a smaller quantity of pizza is produced, resources are used to produce some other good that is not valued as highly as the pizza foregone.

To see why the equilibrium in Figure 6.6 is efficient, think about the interpretation of the demand curve as a marginal benefit curve and the supply curve as a marginal cost curve. The demand curve tells us the marginal benefit from pizza. The supply curve tells us the marginal cost of pizza. So where the demand curve and the supply curve intersect, marginal benefit equals marginal cost.

But this condition – marginal benefit equals marginal cost – is the condition that delivers an efficient use of resources. It puts resources to work in the activities that create the greatest possible value. So a competitive equilibrium is efficient.

If production is less than 10,000 pizzas a day, the marginal pizza is valued more highly than its opportunity cost. If production exceeds 10,000 pizzas a day, the marginal pizza costs more to produce than the value that consumers place on it. Only when 10,000 pizzas a day are produced is the marginal pizza worth exactly what it costs. The competitive market pushes the quantity of pizza produced to its efficient level of 10,000 a day. If production is less than 10,000 a day, a shortage raises the price, which stimulates an increase in production. If production exceeds 10,000 a day, a surplus lowers the price, which decreases production.

In a competitive equilibrium, resources are used efficiently to produce the goods and services that people value most highly. And when the competitive market uses resources efficiently, the sum of consumer surplus and producer surplus is maximized.

Buyers and sellers each attempt to do the best they can for themselves and no one plans for an efficient outcome for society as a whole. Buyers seek the lowest possible price and sellers seek the highest possible price.

The Invisible Hand

Writing in his *The Wealth of Nations* in 1776, Adam Smith was the first to suggest that competitive markets send resources to the uses in which they have the highest value. Smith believed that each participant in a competitive market is 'led by an invisible hand to promote an end [the efficient use of resources] which was no part of his intention'.

You can see the invisible hand at work in the cartoon. The cold drinks seller has both cold drinks and shade. He has an opportunity cost of each and a minimum supply-price of each. The park-bench reader has a marginal benefit from a cold drink and from shade. You can see that the marginal benefit from shade exceeds the marginal cost, but the marginal cost of a cold drink exceeds its marginal benefit. The transaction that occurs creates producer surplus and consumer surplus. The seller obtains a producer surplus from selling the shade for more than its opportunity cost and the reader obtains a consumer surplus from buying the shade for less than its marginal benefit. In the third frame of the cartoon both the consumer and the producer are better off than they were in the first frame. The umbrella has moved to its highest value use.

Drawing by M. Twohy; © 1885 The New Yorker Collection.

The Invisible Hand at Work Today

The market economy relentlessly performs the activity illustrated in the cartoon and in Figure 6.6 to achieve an efficient allocation of resources. And rarely has the market been working as hard as it is today. Think about a few of the changes taking place in our economy that the market is guiding towards an efficient use of resources.

New technologies have cut the cost of producing computers. As these advances have occurred, supply has increased and the price has fallen. Lower prices that have encouraged an increase in the quantity demanded of this now less costly tool. The marginal benefit from computers is brought into equality with their marginal cost.

An early frost cuts the supply of grapes. With fewer grapes available, the marginal benefit from grapes increases. A shortage of grapes raises their price so that the market allocates the smaller quantity available to the people who value them most highly.

Market forces persistently bring marginal cost and marginal benefit to equality and maximize the sum of consumer surplus and producer surplus.

Sources of Inefficiency

Although markets generally do a good job at sending resources to where they are most highly valued, they do not always get it right. Sometimes, markets produce too much of a good or service, and sometimes they produce too little. The most significant obstacles to achieving an efficient allocation of resources in a market economy are:

- Price ceilings and floors.
- Taxes, subsidies and quotas.
- Monopoly.
- Public goods.
- External costs and external benefits.

Price Ceilings and Floors A price ceiling is a regulation that makes it illegal to charge a price higher than a specified level. An example is a price ceiling on housing rents, which some local and regional authorities impose. A price floor is a regulation that makes it illegal to pay a lower price than a specified level. An example is the minimum wage. (We study both of these restrictions on buyers and sellers in Chapter 7.)

The presence of a price ceiling or a price floor blocks the forces of demand and supply and results in a quantity produced that might exceed or fall short of the quantity determined in an unregulated market.

Taxes, Subsidies and Quotas Taxes increase the prices paid by buyers and lower the prices received by sellers. Taxes decrease the quantity produced (for reasons that are explained in Chapter 7, on pp. 148–153). All kinds of goods and services are taxed, but the highest taxes are on petrol, alcohol and tobacco.

Subsidies, which are payments by the government to producers, decrease the prices paid by buyers and increase the prices received by sellers. Subsidies increase the quantity produced.

Quotas, which are limits to the quantity that a firm is permitted to produce, restrict output below the quantity that a competitive market produces. Farms are sometimes subject to quotas.

Monopoly A monopoly is a firm that has sole control of a market. For example, Microsoft has a near monopoly on operating systems for personal computers. Although monopolies earn large profits, they prevent markets from achieving an efficient use of resources. The goal of a monopoly is to maximize profit. To achieve this goal, it restricts production and raises price. (We study monopoly in Chapter 13.)

Public Goods A public good is a good or service where one person's consumption has no effect on the quantity available for everyone else, even if they don't pay for it. Examples are national defence and the enforcement of law and order. Competitive markets would produce too small a quantity of public goods because few people are willing to buy the good. Each person wants to free-ride on the consumption of someone else. It is not in each person's interest to buy her or his share of a public good. So a competitive market produces less than the efficient quantity. (We study public goods in Chapter 18.)

External Costs and Benefits An external cost is a cost not borne by the producer (or consumer) but borne by other people. The cost of pollution is an example of an external cost. When an electric power utility burns coal to generate electricity, it puts sulphur dioxide into the atmosphere. This pollutant falls as acid rain and damages vegetation and crops. The producer does not consider the cost of pollution when it decides what quantity of electric power to supply. Its supply curve is based on its own costs, not on the costs that they inflict on others. As a result, the utility produces more power than the efficient quantity.

An external benefit is a benefit that accrues to people other than the buyer of a good. An example is when someone in a neighbourhood paints their home or landscapes their garden. The homeowner does not consider her neighbour's marginal benefit when she decides whether to do this type of work. So the demand curve for house painting and garden improvement does not include all the benefits that accrue. In this case, the quantity falls short of the efficient quantity. (We study externalities in Chapter 20.)

The impediments to efficiency that we've just reviewed and those which you will study in greater detail in later chapters are called market failures. They result in two possible outcomes:

1. Underproduction.
2. Overproduction.

Figure 6.7 Underproduction and Overproduction

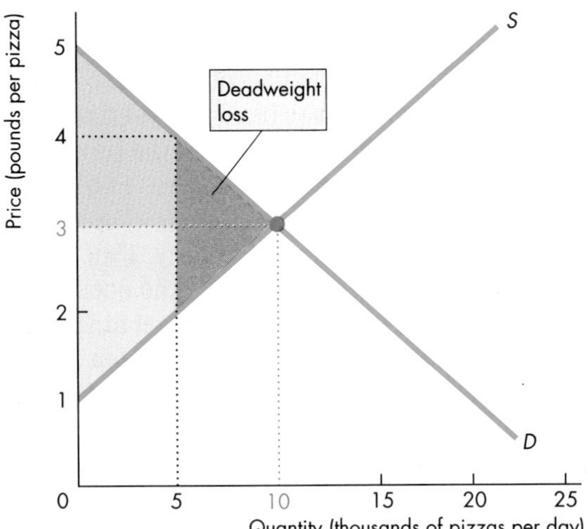

(a) Underproduction

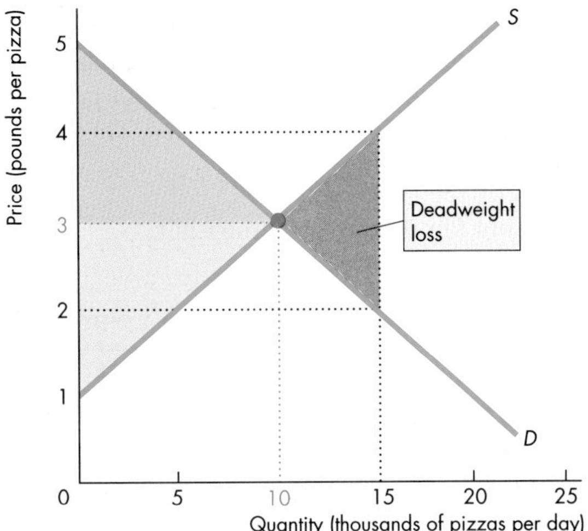

(b) Overproduction

If production is restricted to 5,000 a day, a deadweight loss (the grey triangle) arises. Consumer surplus and producer surplus is reduced to the green area. At 5,000 pizzas, the benefit of one more pizza exceeds its cost. The same is true for all levels of production up to 10,000 pizzas a day. If production increases to 15,000, a deadweight loss arises. At 15,000 pizzas a day, the cost of the 15,000th pizza exceeds its benefit. The cost of each pizza above 10,000 exceeds its benefit. Consumer surplus plus producer surplus equals the greeen triangle minus the deadweight loss.

Underproduction

Suppose that one firm owned all the pizza outlets in a city and that it restricted the quantity of pizza produced to 5,000 a day. Figure 6.7(a) shows that at this quantity, consumers are willing to pay £4 for the marginal pizza – marginal benefit is £4. The marginal cost of a pizza is only £2. So there is a gap between what people are willing to pay and what producers must be offered – between marginal benefit and marginal cost.

The sum of consumer surplus and producer surplus is decreased by the amount of the grey triangle in Figure 6.7(a). This triangle is called deadweight loss. Deadweight loss is the decrease in consumer surplus and producer surplus that results from an inefficient level of production.

The 5,000th pizza brings a benefit of £4 and costs only £2 to produce. If we don't produce this pizza, we are wasting almost £2. Similar reasoning applies all the way up to the 9,999th pizza. By producing more pizza and less of other goods and services, we get more value from our resources.

The deadweight loss is borne by the entire society. It is not a loss for the consumers and a gain for the producer. It is a *social* loss. You can read about inefficiency and the deadweight loss caused by UK Retail Price Maintenance for over-the-counter medicines in *Reading Between the Lines* on pp. 138–139.

Overproduction

Suppose the pizza lobby gets the government to pay the pizza producers a fat subsidy and that production increases to 15,000 a day. Figure 6.7(b) shows that at this quantity, consumers are willing to pay only £2 for that marginal pizza but the opportunity cost of that pizza is £4. It now costs more to produce the marginal pizza than consumers are willing to pay for it. The gap gets smaller as production approaches 10,000 pizzas a day, but it is present at all quantities greater than 10,000 a day.

Again, deadweight loss is shown by the grey triangle. The sum of consumer surplus and producer surplus is smaller than its maximum by the amount of deadweight loss. The 15,000th pizza brings a benefit of only £2 but costs £4 to produce. If we produce this pizza, we are wasting almost £2. Similar reasoning applies all the way down to the 10,001st pizza. By producing less pizza and more of other goods and services, we get more value from our resources.

Review

- Competitive markets make marginal benefit equal marginal cost and use resources efficiently.
- Price ceilings and floors; taxes, subsidies, and quotas; monopoly; public goods and externalities all result in markets producing an inefficient quantity.
- Only if production is at the competitive equilibrium level is deadweight loss zero and resource use efficient.

You now know the conditions under which the resource allocation is efficient. You've seen how a competitive market can be efficient and you've seen some impediments to efficiency.

But is an efficient allocation of resources fair? Does the competitive market provide people with fair incomes for their work? And do people always pay a fair price for the things they buy? Don't we need the government to step into some competitive markets to prevent the price from rising too high or falling too low? Let's now study these questions.

Is the Competitive Market Fair?

When a natural disaster strikes, such as a major flood, the price of many essential items jumps. The reason for the price jump is that some people have a greater demand and greater willingness to pay while the items are in limited supply. So the higher prices achieve an efficient allocation of scarce resources. News reports of these price hikes almost never talk about efficiency. Instead, they talk about fairness, or more particularly, unfairness. The claim is that it is unfair for profit-seeking dealers to cheat the victims of natural disaster.

Similarly, when low-skilled people work for a wage that is below what most would regard as a 'living wage', the media and politicians talk of employers taking unfair advantage of their workers.

How do we decide if something is fair or unfair? You know when *you* think something is unfair. But how do you know? What are the *principles* of fairness?

Philosophers have tried for centuries to answer this question. Economists have offered their answers too. But before we look at the proposed answers, you should know that there is no universally agreed answer.

Economists agree about efficiency. That is, they agree that it makes sense to make the economic cake as large as possible and to bake it at the lowest possible cost. But they do not agree about fairness. That is, they do not agree about what are fair shares of the economic cake for all the people who make it. The reason is that ideas about fairness are not exclusively economic ideas. They touch on politics, ethics and religion. Nevertheless, economists have thought about these issues and have a contribution to make. So let's examine the views of economists on this topic.

To think about fairness, think of economic life as a game – a serious game. All ideas about fairness can be divided into two broad groups. They are:

1 It's not fair if the *result* isn't fair.

2 It's not fair if the *rules* aren't fair.

It's not Fair if the *Result* Isn't Fair

The earliest efforts to establish a principle of fairness were based on the view that the result is what matters. And the general idea was that it is unfair if people's incomes are too unequal. It is unfair that bank directors earn millions of pounds a year, while bank tellers earn only thousands of pounds a year. It is unfair that a shop owner enjoys a larger profit and her customers pay higher prices in the aftermath of a winter storm.

There was a lot of excitement during the nineteenth century when economists thought they had made the incredible discovery that efficiency requires equality of incomes. To make the economic pie as large as possible, it must be cut into equal pieces, one for each person. This idea turns out to be wrong, but there is a lesson in the reason that it is wrong. So this nineteenth century idea is worth a closer look.

The nineteenth century idea that only equality brings efficiency is called utilitarianism.

Utilitarianism is a principle that states that we should strive to achieve 'the greatest happiness for the greatest number'. The people who developed this idea were known as utilitarians. They included the most eminent minds such as David Hume, Adam Smith, Jeremy Bentham and John Stuart Mill.

Utilitarianism Utilitarians argued that to achieve 'the greatest happiness for the greatest number', income must be transferred from the rich to the poor up to the point of complete equality – to the point that there are no rich and no poor.

They reasoned in the following way: first, everyone has the same basic wants and are similar in their capacity to enjoy life. Second, the greater a person's income, the smaller is the marginal benefit of a pound. The millionth pound spent by a rich person brings a smaller marginal benefit to that person than the marginal benefit of the thousandth pound spent by a poorer person. So by transferring a pound from the millionaire to the poorer person, more is gained than is lost and the two people added together are better off.

Figure 6.8 illustrates this utilitarian idea. Tom and Paul each have the same marginal benefit curve, *MB*. (Marginal benefit is measured on the same scale of 1 to 3 for both Tom and Paul.) Tom is at point *a*. He earns £5,000 a year and his marginal benefit of a pound of income is 3. Paul is at point *b*. He earns £45,000 a year and his marginal benefit of a pound of income is 1. If a pound is transferred from Paul to Tom, Paul loses 1 unit of marginal benefit and Tom gains 3 units. So, adding Tom and Paul together, they are better off. They are sharing the economic pie more efficiently. If a second pound is transferred, the same thing happens: Tom gains more than Paul loses. And the same is true for every pound transferred until they each reach point *c*. At point *c*, Tom and Paul each have £25,000 and each have a marginal benefit of 2 units. Now they are sharing the economic pie in the most efficient way. It is bringing the greatest attainable happiness to Tom and Paul.

The big trade-off One big problem with the utilitarian ideal of complete equality is that it ignores the costs of making income transfers. The economist, Arthur Okun, in his book *Equality and Efficiency: The Big Tradeoff*, described the process of redistributing income as like trying to transfer water from one barrel to another with a leaky bucket. The more we try to increase equity by redistributing income, the more we reduce efficiency. Recognizing the cost of making income transfers leads to what is called 'the big trade-off', – a trade-off between efficiency and fairness.

Figure 6.8 Utilitarian Fairness

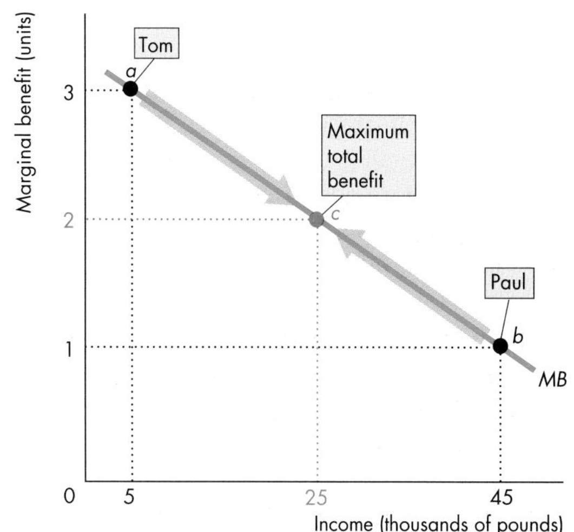

Tom earns £5,000 and has 3 units of marginal benefit of point *a*. Paul earns £45,000 and has 1 unit of marginal benefit of point *b*. If income is transferred from Paul to Tom, Paul's loss is less than Tom's gain. Only when each of them has £25,000 and 2 units of marginal benefit (at point *c*) can the sum of their total benefit increase further.

The big trade-off is based on the following facts. Income can be transferred from people with high incomes to people with low incomes only by taxing incomes. Taxing peoples' income from employment makes them work less. It results in the quantity of labour being less than the efficient quantity. Taxing peoples' income from capital makes them save less. It results in the quantity of capital being less than the efficient quantity. With smaller quantities of both labour and capital the quantity of goods and services produced is less than the efficient quantity. The economic cake shrinks.

The trade-off is between the size of the economic cake and the degree of equality with which it is shared. The greater the amount of income redistribution through income taxes, the greater is the inefficiency – the smaller is the economic cake.

There is a second source of inefficiency. A pound taken from a rich person does not end up as a pound in the hands of a poorer person. Some of it is spent on administration of the tax and transfer system. The cost of tax-collecting agencies, such as the European Community, and welfare-administering agencies, such as the British Child Benefit Agency, as well as regional government welfare departments, must be paid with some of the taxes collected. Also, taxpayers hire accountants, tax specialists and legal experts to help them ensure that they pay the correct amount of tax. These activities use skilled labour and capital resources that could otherwise be used to produce goods and services that people value.

You can see that when all these costs are taken into account, transferring a pound from a rich person does not give a pound to a poor person. It is even possible that with high taxes, those with low incomes end up being worse off. Suppose, for example, that highly taxed entrepreneurs decide to work less hard and shut down some of their businesses. Low-income workers get fired and must seek other, perhaps even lower-paid work.

Because of the big trade-off, those who say that fairness is equality propose a modified version of utilitarianism.

Rawlsianism A Harvard philosopher, John Rawls, proposed a modified version of utilitarianism in a classic book entitled *A Theory of Justice*, published in 1971. Rawls says that, taking all the costs of income transfers into account, the fair distribution of the economic pie is the one that makes the poorest person as well off as possible. The incomes of rich people should be taxed and, after paying the costs of administering the tax and transfer system, what is left should be transferred to the poor. But the taxes must not be so high that they make the economic pie shrink to the point that the poorest person ends up with a smaller piece. A bigger share of a smaller cake can be a smaller piece than a smaller share of a bigger cake. The goal is to make the piece enjoyed by the poorest person as big as possible. Most likely this piece will not be an equal share.

The 'fair results' ideas require a change in the results after the game is over. Some economists say these changes are themselves unfair and propose a different way of thinking about fairness.

It's not Fair if the *Rules* Aren't Fair

The idea that it's not fair if the rules aren't fair is based on a fundamental principle that seems to be hard wired into the human brain. It is the symmetry principle. The symmetry principle is the requirement that people in similar situations be treated similarly. It is the moral principle that lies at the centre of all the big religions. It says, in some form or other, 'behave towards other people in the way you expect them to behave towards you'.

In economic life, this principle translates into *equality of opportunity*. But equality of opportunity to do what? This question is answered by another Harvard philosopher, Robert Nozick, in a book entitled *Anarchy, State, and Utopia*, published in 1974.

Nozick argues that the idea of fairness as an outcome or result cannot work and that fairness must be based on the fairness of the rules. He suggests that fairness obeys two rules. They are:

1 The state must enforce laws that establish and protect private property.
2 Private property may be transferred from one person to another only by voluntary exchange.

The first rule says that everything that is valuable must be owned by individuals and that the state must ensure that theft is prevented. The second rule says that the only legitimate way a person can acquire property is to buy it in exchange for something else that the person owns. If these rules, which are the only fair rules, are followed the result is fair. It doesn't matter how unequally the economic pie is shared provided it is baked by people each one of whom voluntarily provides services in exchange for the share of the pie offered in compensation.

These rules satisfy the symmetry principle. And if these rules are not followed, the symmetry principle is broken. You can see these facts by imagining a world in which the laws are not followed.

First, suppose that some resources or goods are not owned. They are common property. Then everyone is free to participate in a grab to use these resources or goods. The strongest will prevail. But when the strongest prevails, the strongest effectively *owns* the resources or goods in question and prevents others from enjoying them.

Second, suppose that we do not insist on voluntary exchange for transferring ownership of resources from one person to another. The alternative is *involuntary* transfer. In simple language, the alternative is theft.

Both of these situations violate the symmetry principle. Only the strong get to acquire what they want. The weak end up with only the resources and goods that the strong don't want.

In contrast, if the two rules of fairness are followed, everyone, strong and weak, is treated in a similar way. Everyone is free to use their resources and human skills to create things that are valued by themselves and others and to exchange the fruits of their efforts with each other. This is the only set of arrangements that obeys the symmetry principle.

Fairness and Efficiency Resources will be allocated efficiently if private property rights are enforced and if voluntary exchange takes place in a competitive market, and if there are no market or government failures such as:

- Price ceilings and price floors.
- Taxes, subsidies, and quotas.
- Monopolies.
- Public goods.
- External costs and external benefits.

According to the Nozick rules, the resulting distribution of income and wealth will be fair. Let's study a concrete example to examine the claim that if resources are allocated efficiently they are also allocated fairly.

A Price Hike in a Natural Disaster An earthquake has broken the pipes that deliver drinking water to a city. The price of bottled water jumps from £1 to £8 a bottle in the thirty or so shops that have water for sale.

First, let's agree that the water is being used *efficiently*. There is a fixed amount of bottled water in the city and given the quantity available, some people are willing to pay £8 to get a bottle. The water goes to the people who value it most highly. Consumer surplus and producer surplus are maximized.

So, the water resources are being used efficiently. But are they being used fairly? Shouldn't people who can't afford to pay £8 a bottle get some of the available water for a lower price that they can afford? Isn't the fair solution for the shops to sell water for a lower price that people can afford? Or perhaps it might be fairer if the government bought the water and then made it available to people through a government store at a 'reasonable' price. Let's think about these alternative solutions to the water problem of this city.

The first answer that jumps into your mind is that the water should somehow be made available at a more reasonable price. But is this the correct answer?

Shop Offers Water for £4 Suppose that a shop owner, offers water at £4 a bottle. Who will buy it? There are two types of buyer. Jane is an example of one type. She values water at £8 – is willing to pay £8 a bottle. Recall that given the quantity of water available, the equilibrium price is £8 a bottle. If Jane buys the water, she consumes it. Jane ends up with a consumer surplus of £4 on the bottle and the shop owner receives £4 *less* in producer surplus than would have been created at the market price of £8.

Mary is an example of the second type of buyer. Mary would not pay £8 for a bottle. In fact, she wouldn't even pay £4 to consume a bottle of water. However, she buys a bottle for £4. Why? Because she plans to sell the water to someone who is willing to pay £8 to consume it. When Mary buys the water, the shop owner again receives a producer surplus of £4 *less*. Mary now becomes a water dealer. She sells the water for the going price of £8 and earns a producer surplus of £4.

So, by being public spirited and offering water for less than the market price, the shop owner ends up £4 a bottle worse off and the buyers end up £4 a bottle better off. The same people consume the water in both situations. They are the people who value the water at £8 a bottle. But the distribution of consumer surplus and producer surplus is different in the two cases. The shop owner ends up with a smaller producer surplus if the water is sold for £4 and Jane and Mary end up with a larger consumer surplus and producer surplus.

So, which is the fair arrangement? The one that favours the shop owner or the one that favours the buyers? The fair-rules view is that both arrangements are fair. If the shop owner voluntarily sells the water for £4, this will help the community to cope with its water problem. But the choice is for the shop owner who owns the water. It is not fair to compel the shop owner to help. The final distribution will depend on shop owner's attitude towards charitable behaviour and ability of Jane and Mary to pay for water.

Government Buys Water Now suppose instead that the government buys all the water. The going price is £8 a bottle, so that's what the government pays. Now they offer the water for sale for £1 a bottle, its 'normal' price.

The quantity of water supplied is exactly the same as before. But now, at £1 a bottle, the quantity demanded is much larger than the quantity supplied. There is a shortage of water.

Because there is a large water shortage, the government decides to ration the amount that anyone may buy. Everyone is allocated one bottle. So, everyone lines up to collect his or her bottle. Two of these people are Jane and Mary. Jane, you'll recall, is willing to pay £8 a bottle. Mary is willing to pay less than £4. But they both get a bargain. Jane drinks her £1 bottle and enjoys a £7 consumer surplus. Mary sells her bottle to another person who values the water at £8, and enjoys a £7 producer surplus from her temporary water trading business.

So, the people who value the water most highly consume it. But the consumer and producer surpluses are distributed in a different way than free market outcome. Again, the question arises, which arrangement is fair?

The main difference between the government scheme and shop owner's private charitable contributions lies in the fact that to buy the water for £8 and sell it for £1, the government must tax someone £7 for each bottle sold. So, whether this arrangement is fair depends on whether the taxes are fair.

Taxes are an involuntary transfer of private property so, according to the fair-rules view, they are unfair. But most economists, and most people, think that there is such a thing as a fair tax. In this case a fair tax might redistribute income so that everyone can afford the basic minimum. So it seems that the fair-rules view is too strong. Agreeing that there is such a thing as a fair tax is the easy part. Agreeing on what is a fair tax brings endless disagreement and debate.

Review

- Economists generally agree about what is efficient, but there is no agreement about what is fair.
- The two main ideas about fairness are that an allocation is unfair if: the *results* are not fair, or if the *rules* are not fair.
- Fair-results ideas generally result in income transfers from the rich to the poor, but income transfer may result in a big trade-off between fairness and efficiency.
- Fair-rules ideas require property rights and voluntary exchange, but fair outcome depends upon the initial distribution of attitudes and resources.

You've now studied the two biggest issues that run right through the whole of economics: efficiency and equity, or fairness. In the next chapter, we study some sources of inefficiency and unfairness. And at many points throughout this book – and in your life – you will return to and use the ideas about efficiency and equity that you've learned in this chapter.

Summary

Key Points

Efficiency: A Refresher (pp. 120–122)

- The marginal benefit received from a good or service – the benefit of consuming one additional unit – is the *value* of the good or service to its consumers.
- The marginal cost of a good or service – the cost of producing one additional unit – is the *opportunity cost* of one more unit to its producers.
- Resources allocation is efficient when marginal benefit equals marginal cost.
- If marginal benefit exceeds marginal cost, an increase in production increases the value of production.
- If marginal cost exceeds marginal benefit, a decrease in production increases the value of production.

Value, Price and Consumer Surplus (pp. 122–124)

- Marginal benefit is measured by the maximum price that consumers are willing to pay for a good or service.
- Marginal benefit determines demand, and a demand curve is a marginal benefit curve.
- Value is what people are *willing to* pay; price is what people *must* pay.
- Consumer surplus equals value minus price, summed over the quantity consumed.

Cost, Price and Producer Surplus (pp. 124–126)

- Marginal cost is measured by the minimum price producers must be offered to increase production by one unit.
- Marginal cost determines supply, and a supply curve is a marginal cost curve.
- Opportunity cost is what producers pay; price is what producers receive.
- Producer surplus equals price minus opportunity cost, summed over the quantity produced.

Is the Competitive Market Efficient? (pp. 126–130)

- In a competitive equilibrium, marginal benefit equals marginal cost and resource allocation is efficient.
- Monopoly restricts production and creates deadweight loss.
- A competitive market provides too small a quantity of public goods because of the free-rider problem.
- A competitive market provides too large a quantity of goods and services that have external costs and too small a quantity of goods and services that have external benefits.

Is the Competitive Market Fair? (pp. 130–134)

- Ideas about fairness divide into two groups: those based on the notion that the *results* are not fair, and those based on the notion that the *rules* are not fair.
- Fair-results ideas require income transfers from the rich to the poor.
- Fair-rules ideas require property rights and voluntary exchange.

Key Figures

Key Terms

Review Questions

1 What is the distinction between *price* and *value*? How do economists define the value of a good or service?

2 Explain the connection between the demand curve and the concept of the willingness to pay for a good or service.

3 How does the willingness to pay for a good or service change as the quantity available of that good or service changes? Why does willingness to pay change in the way you describe?

4 What is consumer surplus? How do we measure consumer surplus?

5 What is the distinction between *price* and *cost*? How do economists define cost?

6 Explain the connection between the supply curve and the concept of the minimum supply-price of a good or service.

7 How does the minimum supply-price of a good or service change as the quantity bought of that good or service changes? Why does the minimum supply-price change in the way you describe?

8 What is producer surplus? How do we measure producer surplus?

9 What conditions must be satisfied if resources are to be used efficiently?

10 When does a competitive market achieve an efficient use of resources?

11 What is a deadweight loss?

12 Does a deadweight loss occur only if production is less than the efficient level?

13 List the main impediments to achieving an efficient use of resources.

14 Give an example of each of the impediments to achieving an efficient use of resources.

15 How does monopoly prevent a market from achieving an efficient use of resources?

16 How do public goods prevent a market from achieving an efficient use of resources?

17 How do external costs prevent a market from achieving an efficient use of resources?

Problems

1 The figure shows the demand for and supply of floppy disks.

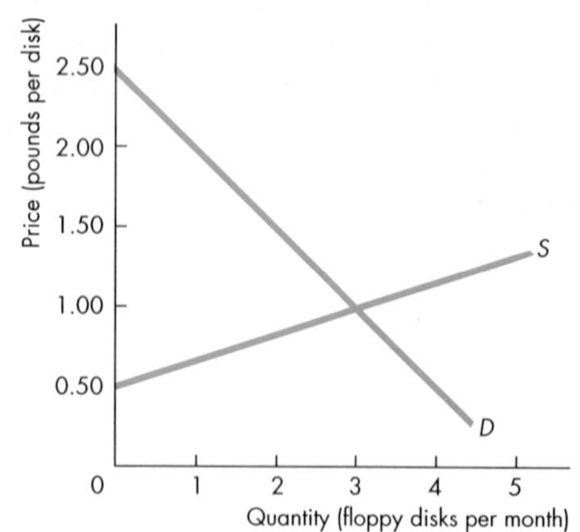

a What are the equilibrium price and equilibrium quantity of floppy disks?
b What is the consumer surplus?
c What is the producer surplus?
d What is the efficient quantity of floppy disks?

2 The table gives the demand and supply schedules for sandwiches.

a What is the maximum price that consumers are willing to pay for the 250th sandwich?
b What is the minimum price that producers are willing to accept for the 250th sandwich?
c Are 250 sandwiches a day less than or greater than the efficient quantity?

d What is the consumer surplus if the efficient quantity of sandwiches is produced?

e What is the producer surplus if the efficient quantity of sandwiches is produced?

f What is the deadweight loss if 250 sandwiches are produced?

Price (pounds per sandwich)	Quantity demanded (sandwiches per hour)	Quantity supplied (sandwiches per hour)
0	400	0
1	350	50
2	300	100
3	250	150
4	200	200
5	150	250
6	100	300
7	50	350
8	0	400

3 The table gives the demand and supply schedules for spring water.

Price (pounds per bottles)	Quantity demanded (bottles per day)	Quantity supplied (bottles per day)
0	80	0
0.50	70	10
1.00	60	20
1.50	50	30
2.00	40	40
2.50	30	50
3.00	20	60
3.50	10	70
4.00	0	80

a What is the maximum price that consumers are willing to pay for the 30th bottle?

b What is the minimum price that producers are willing to accept for the 30th bottle?

c Are 30 bottles a day less than or greater than the efficient quantity?

d What is the consumer surplus if the efficient quantity of spring water is produced?

e What is the producer surplus if the efficient quantity of spring water is produced?

f What is the deadweight loss if 30 bottles are produced?

4 The table gives the demand schedules for train travel for Ben, Beth and Bill.

Price (pence per passenger kilometer)	Quantity demanded (passenger miles)		
	Ben	Beth	Bill
10	500	300	60
20	450	250	50
30	400	200	40
40	350	150	30
50	300	100	20
60	250	50	10
70	200	0	0

a If the price of train travel is 40 pence a passenger kilometre, what is the consumer surplus of each consumer?

b Which consumer has the largest consumer surplus? Explain why.

c If the price of train travel rises to 50 pence a passenger kilometer, what is the change in consumer surplus of each consumer?

d If the price of train travel is 50 pence a passenger kilometer, what is the consumer surplus of each consumer?

e Which consumer has the largest consumer surplus? Explain why.

f If the price of train travel falls to 30 pence a passenger kilometer, what is the change in consumer surplus of each consumer?

5 Write a short description of how you would calculate your own consumer surplus on some item that you buy regularly.

6 Write a short description of how you would determine whether the allocation of your time between studying different subjects is efficient? In what units would you measure marginal benefit and marginal cost? Explain your answer by using the concepts of marginal benefit, marginal cost, price, consumer surplus, and producer surplus.

Inefficiency: Retail Price Maintenance and Medicines

The Guardian, 8 May 1999

Asda cuts price of medicines

The Asda supermarket chain yesterday cut the cost of over-the-counter medicines in the latest round of its battle to lower the price of drugs, claiming the elderly and families with children were victims of a £300m "health tax".

Asda said it had urged the manufacturer of Setlers indigestion remedy against taking legal action and seeking an injunction against the cost-cutting.

The move comes after three years of campaigning by Asda to break resale price maintenance (RPM) on over-the-counter medicines such as cold remedies and painkillers.

Asda claims RPM targets vulnerable sections of society who buy more painkillers and branded medicines, such as the elderly.

Yesterday's price cuts of 25% cover seven Setler's products, including Wind-eze which is down from £3.29 to £2.46.

In the past, such moves have been met by injunctions from pharmaceutical companies.

But Asda is hoping that recent government moves to scrap RPM will persuade brand owners to voluntarily stop the practice.

The office of fair trading recently won the right to legally challenge RPM later this year.

Asda won another victory against price maintenance controls in 1995 when it succeeded in smashing the net book agreement.

Asda's health and beauty director, James Wilson, said "If drug companies, like publishers before them, voluntarily withdraw from price-fixing, shoppers would save £300m a year."

He added: "It is time that everyday healthcare items such as Setler's were available at fair prices and it is time to put an end to this health tax."

The Essence of the Story

- Asda, one of the top three UK supermarket chains, has cut the price of some of its over-the-counter drugs. Only a very limited number of drugs, such as painkillers, indigestion remedies and cough mixtures, can be sold over-the-counter, or without a prescription, in the United Kingdom. Government allows the manufacturer to set the retail price of these drugs – a form of monopoly pricing.

- The supermarket is challenging the Retail Price Maintenance practice for over-the-counter drugs. Asda claims that because it is not allowed to set a competitive price for these drugs, customers have to pay a higher price than is necessary. Shoppers pay £300 million a year more than they would do if the retail market was allowed to price competitively.

- Asda claims many of the customers who have to pay the £300 million 'health tax' are amongst the most vulnerable and poor.

- The supermarket broke the Retail Price Maintenance agreement by slashing the price of an indigestion remedy called Setlers by 25 per cent. It expects the manufacturers will take out a legal injunction against Asda, forcing it to raise the price again.

■ Asda has already successfully campaigned against Retail Price Maintenance in the book markets and the Office of Fair Trading, which investigates monopoly, will also challenge Retail Price Maintenance of drugs.

Economic Analysis

■ Figure 1 shows the demand curve for Setlers, the indigestion remedy, labelled *D*. The demand curve is also the marginal benefit curve and is also labelled *MB*. It tells us the value to consumers of one more packet of Setlers.

■ The marginal cost of producing Setlers, *MC*, is also shown in Figure 1. The slope is relatively shallow as the marginal cost of producing more indigestion remedy tablets is quite low because they are low technology products with low research and development costs.

■ If Setlers were manufactured and sold in competitive markets, the marginal cost curve would also be the supply curve. In this case, equilibrium would occur at point *a*, where the demand and supply curves intersect, and the price is £2.46 per packet.

■ Production and retail are efficient at point *a* – marginal benefit equals marginal cost. The consumer surplus created by Setlers is the green area and the producer surplus is the blue area in Figure 1. But the Setlers market is not at point *a*.

■ Retail Price Maintenance means that the price is set at £3.29 per packet and the market is at point *b* in Figure 2. The manufacturer can make extra profit by raising the price and restricting quantity. But point *b* is inefficient because marginal benefit exceeds marginal cost, creating a deadweight loss shown by the grey area.

■ The blue rectangle in Figure 2 is the 'health tax' from this product, consumer surplus transferred to the producer. The deadweight loss is a social loss because many people who need indigestion remedies cannot afford to buy them at the higher price.

■ The manufacturers argue that Retail Price Maintenance is needed to support the revenue of small local pharmacies which would otherwise go out of business. Local pharmacies provide health advice which the manufacturers argue is a benefit which outweighs the deadweight loss.

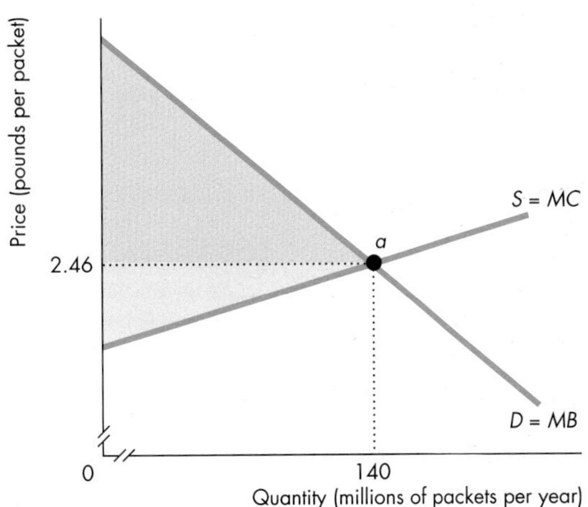

Figure 1 Efficient quantity

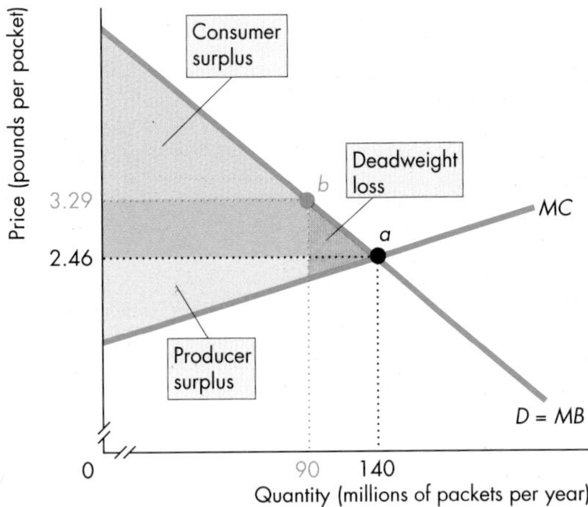

Figure 2 Inefficient quantity

Markets in Action

After studying this chapter you will be able to:

- Show that government regulation can affect market prices and quantities
- Explain how price ceilings affect markets and efficiency
- Explain how price floors affect markets and efficiency
- Explain how sales taxes affect markets and efficiency
- Explain how prices and quantities are determined for illegal goods
- Explain why farm prices and revenues fluctuate
- Explain how stores and farm policies limit price and revenue fluctuations

Turbulent Times

In January 1995, the Netherlands suffered a devastating flood that destroyed many homes but killed few people. How did the housing market cope with this enormous shock? What happened to rents and to the quantity of housing services available in the flooded regions? Would rent controls have helped to keep housing affordable? ◆ Almost every day, new machines are invented that save labour and increase productivity. How do labour markets react to labour-saving technology? Will the fall in the demand for labour drive wages lower and lower? Can minimum wage laws stop wages from falling and help us to use labour more efficiently? ◆ Almost everything we buy is taxed. How do taxes affect the prices and quantities of the things we buy? Is it the buyers or the sellers who have to bear the tax? ◆ Trading in items such as automatic firearms, certain drugs and enriched uranium is illegal. Does prohibiting trade in these goods actually restrict the amount of these goods consumed? And how does it affect the prices paid by those who trade illegally? ◆ In 1996, droughts reduced grain yields everywhere. How do farm prices and revenues react to such output fluctuations? How do the actions of speculators and agricultural policy influence farm revenues?

◆ ◆ ◆ ◆ In this chapter, we use the theory of demand and supply (from Chapter 4), the concept of elasticity (from Chapter 5), and the concept of efficiency (from Chapter 6) to answer the questions we have just asked. We start by looking at how a housing market responds to a severe and sudden supply shock.

Housing Markets and Rent Ceilings

To see how unregulated markets cope with supply shocks, let's consider the consequences of the flood in the Gelderland province of the Netherlands in January 1995. How did the region cope with such a vast reduction in the supply of housing? Almost overnight, 70,000 people left the area and their devastated homes behind them. The floods wrecked homes and businesses causing more than £700 million worth of damage.

The Market Response to a Decrease in Supply

The market for housing in the worst affected area in the Gelderland province is shown in Figure 7.1. The demand curve for housing before the flood is *D* in part (a). There are two supply curves: the short-run supply curve, labelled *SS*, and the long-run supply curve, labelled *LS*. The short-run supply curve shows how the quantity of housing supplied varies as the price (rent) varies, while the number of houses and blocks of flats remains constant. Supply varies with the intensity with which existing buildings are used. The quantity of housing supplied increases if families decide to rent out rooms that they previously used themselves, and decreases if families decide to use rooms they previously rented out to others.

The *long-run* supply curve shows how the quantity supplied varies over the period of renovation and rebuilding. We will assume that the long-run supply curve is perfectly elastic, as shown. This is reasonable as the cost of building is much the same regardless of whether there are 5,000 or 15,000 flats and houses in existence.

The equilibrium price (rent) and quantity are determined at the point of intersection of the *short-run* supply curve and the demand curve. Before the flood, the equilibrium rent is 400 guilders a month and the quantity is 10,000 units of housing. In addition (for simplicity), the housing market is assumed to be on its long-run supply curve, *LS*. Let's now look at the situation immediately after the flood.

Figure 7.1(a) shows the new situation. The damage to buildings decreases the supply of housing and shifts the short-run supply curve *SS* leftward to SS_A. If people use the remaining housing

Figure 7.1 The Gelderland Housing Market in 1995

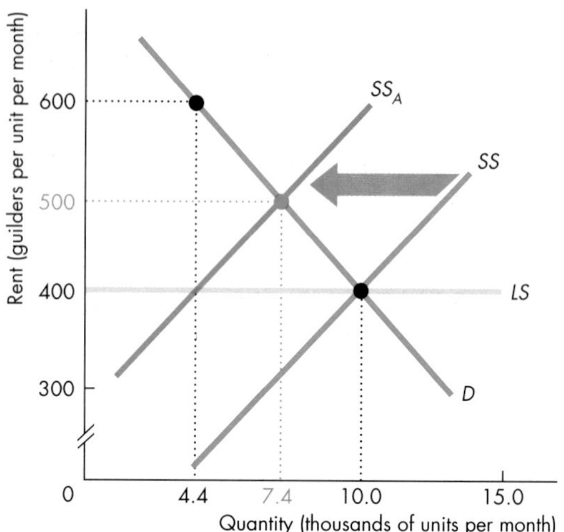

(a) After flood

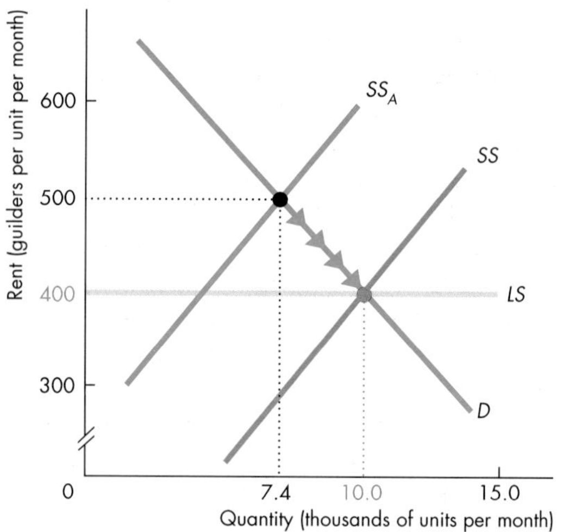

(b) Long-run adjustment

Before the flood, the local housing market in the worst affected area is in equilibrium with 10,000 housing units being rented each month at 400 guilders a month (part a). After the flood, the short-run supply curve shifts from *SS* to SS_A. The rent rises to 500 guilders a month, and the quantity of housing falls to 7,400 units.

With rents at 500 guilders a month, it is profitable to renovate or rebuild flats and houses quickly. As the renovation and rebuilding programme proceeds, the short-run supply curve shifts rightward (part b). Rents gradually fall to 400 guilders a month and the quantity of housing gradually increases to 10,000 units.

units with the same intensity as before the flood and if the rent remains at 400 guilders a month, only 4,400 units of housing are available. But rents do not remain at 400 guilders a month. With only 4,400 units of housing available, the maximum rent that someone is willing to pay for the last available apartment is 600 guilders a month. So, to get a flat, a higher rent than 400 guilders is offered. Rents rise as people try to outbid each other for the available housing. In Figure 7.1(a), they rise to 500 guilders a month. At this rent, the quantity of housing supplied is 7,400 units. People economize on their use of space and make spare rooms, attics and basements available to others.

The response we've just seen takes place in the short run. What happens in the long run?

Long-run Adjustments

With sufficient time for renovation and building, supply will increase. The long-run supply curve tells us that in the long run, housing will be supplied at a rent of 400 guilders a month. Because the current rent of 500 guilders a month is higher than the long-run supply price of housing, there will be a rush to supply new housing. As time passes, more housing is renovated or rebuilt, and the short-run supply curve gradually shifts rightward.

Figure 7.1(b) illustrates the long-run adjustment. As more housing is available, the short-run supply curve shifts rightward and intersects the demand curve at lower rents and higher quantities. The market equilibrium follows the arrows down the demand curve. The process ends when there is no further profit in renovating or building housing units. Such a situation occurs at the original rent of 400 guilders a month and the original quantity of 10,000 units of housing.

The analysis of the short-run and long-run response of a housing market that we've just studied applies to a wide range of other markets. It applies regardless of whether the initial shock is to supply (as it is here) or demand.

A Regulated Housing Market

We've just seen how a housing market responds to a decrease in supply. We've also seen that a key part of the adjustment process is a rise in rents. Suppose the government passes a law to stop rents from rising – it imposes a price ceiling. A **price ceiling** is a regulation making it illegal to charge a price higher than a specified level. When a price ceiling is applied to rents in housing markets it is called a **rent ceiling**. How does a rent ceiling affect the way the housing market works?

The effect of a price (rent) ceiling depends on whether it is imposed at a level that is above or below the equilibrium price (rent). A price ceiling set above the equilibrium price has no effect. The reason is that the market forces are not constrained by the price ceiling. The force of the law and the market forces are not in conflict. But a price ceiling below the equilibrium price has powerful effects on a market. The reason is that it prevents the price from acting as the regulator of the quantities demanded and supplied. The force of the law and the market forces are in conflict, and one (or both) of these forces must yield to some degree. Let's study the effects of a price ceiling set below the equilibrium price by returning to the flood region.

What would have happened after the flood if a rent ceiling of 400 guilders a month – the rent before the flood – had been imposed by the government? This question and some answers are illustrated in Figure 7.2. If a rent ceiling holds the rent at 400 guilders a month, then the quantity of housing supplied is 4,400 units and the quantity demanded is 10,000 units. So there is a shortage of 5,600 units of housing – the quantity demanded exceeds the quantity supplied by 5,600 units.

When the quantity demanded exceeds the quantity supplied, the smaller quantity – the quantity supplied – determines the actual quantity bought and sold. The reason is that suppliers cannot be forced to offer housing for rent, and at a monthly rent of 400 guilders, they are willing to offer only 4,400 units.

So the immediate effect of a rent ceiling of 400 guilders a month is that only 4,400 units of housing are available and a demand for a further 5,600 units is unsatisfied. But the story does not end here. Somehow the 4,400 units of available housing must be allocated among the people demanding 10,000 units. How is this allocation achieved?

In an unregulated market, the shortage would drive the rent up (as shown in Figure 7.1(a)) and the price mechanism would regulate the quantities demanded and supplied and allocate the scarce housing resources. As long as one person was willing to pay a higher price than another person's minimum supply price, the price would rise and the quantity of housing available would increase.

Figure 7.2 A Rent Ceiling

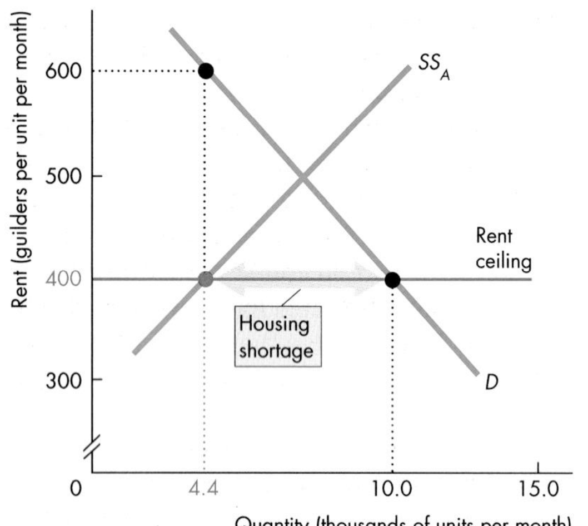

If there had been a rent ceiling of 400 guilders a month after the flood, the quantity of housing supplied would have been stuck at 4,400 units. People would willingly have paid 600 guilders a month for the 4.4 thousandth unit. Because the last unit of housing available is worth more than the regulated rent, frustrated buyers will spend time searching for housing and frustrated buyers and sellers will make deals in a black market.

When a rent ceiling blocks the market mechanism by making rent increases illegal, two developments occur. They are:

1 Search activity.

2 Black markets.

Search Activity

When the quantity demanded exceeds the quantity supplied, many suppliers have nothing to sell and many demanders have nothing to buy. So unsatisfied demanders devote time and other resources to searching for a supplier. The time spent looking for someone with whom to do business is called **search activity**. Of course, without full information, some search activity occurs in markets even if prices adjust freely, but search activity increases when markets are regulated.

Search activity is costly. It uses time and other resources – telephones, cars, petrol – that could be used in other productive ways. People look for any kind of information about newly available housing to try to avoid the queues. The *total cost* of housing is equal to the rent – the regulated price, plus the cost of search activity – an unregulated price. So rent ceilings might control the rent portion of the cost of housing, but they do not control the total cost. The total cost may well be *higher* than the unregulated market price.

Black Markets

A **black market** is an illegal trading arrangement in which buyers and sellers do business at a price higher or lower than the legally imposed price. There are many markets that are regulated or taxed and in which economic forces result in black market trading. In countries like Italy and the United Kingdom, the black market is estimated to be worth more than 10 per cent of national output.

In regulated housing markets, a black market usually takes the form of a buyer and a seller colluding to avoid the rent ceiling. They have a written agreement that uses the regulated rent, but agree informally to raise the actual rent. The level of the black market rent depends mainly on how tightly the government polices its rent ceiling regulations, the chances of being caught violating them and the scale of the penalties imposed for violations.

At one extreme, the chance of being caught violating a rent ceiling is small. In this case, the black market will function similarly to an unregulated market, and the black market rent and quantity traded will be close to the unregulated equilibrium. At the other extreme, where policing is highly effective and where large penalties are imposed on violators, the rent ceiling will restrict the quantity traded. In the flood example, strict enforcement of the rent ceiling would restrict the quantity of housing available to 4,400 units. A small number of people would offer housing for sale at 600 guilders a month – the highest price that a buyer is willing to pay – and the government would detect and punish some of the black market traders.

Rent Ceilings and Efficiency

In an efficient housing market, rents are determined by the interaction of demand and supply. The scarce housing resources are allocated efficiently

Figure 7.3 The Inefficiency of a Rent Ceiling 

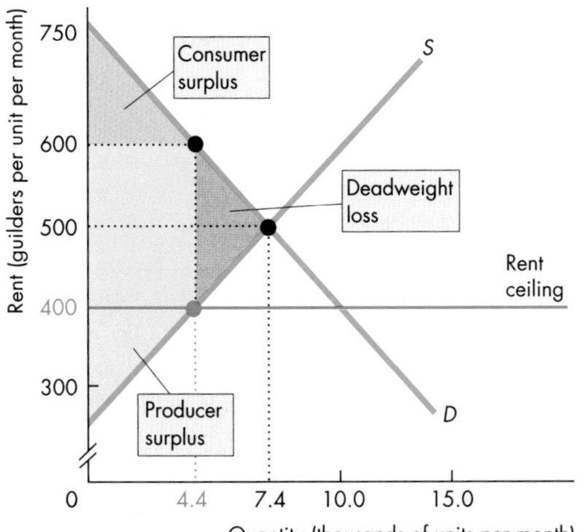

A rent ceiling of 400 guilders a month decreases the quantity of housing supplied to 44,000 units. People are willing to pay 600 guilders a month for 44,000th unit, so there is a large consumer surplus. Producer surplus shrinks to the blue triangle. A deadweight loss (the grey triangle) arises. If people use no resources in search activity, consumer surplus is shown by the green triangle plus the pink rectangle. But people might use resources in search activity equal to the amount they are willing to pay for the available housing, the pink rectangle.

and the sum of producer and consumer surplus is maximized (see Chapter 6).

Figure 7.3 shows how a rent ceiling can cause inefficiency. If the Gelderland government sets the maximum rent at 400 guilders a month, then only 4,400 units are supplied. The producer surplus is shown by the blue triangle above the supply curve and below the rent ceiling line. There is a deadweight loss because the quantity of housing supplied is below the competitive quantity. This loss is borne by consumers and producers. Some consumers would have found housing at the higher rent of 500 guilders but now face a housing shortage. Some suppliers, who would have supplied housing when rents were 500 guilders a month, now find they can't cover their costs. If there are no search costs, consumers who find housing at the regulated rent will gain more consumer surplus, the area shaded green and pink. But search costs might eat up part of that gain, possibly by as much as the entire amount that consumers are willing to pay – the pink rectangle. So rent ceilings can prevent resources from flowing to their highest-valued use. They can generate inefficiency shown as the deadweight loss.

Rent controls have been widely used throughout Europe. When rent ceilings are in force, factors other than rent must allocate the scarce housing. One common method is for landlords to increase the effective rent by charging new tenants a high price to replace locks and keys – a device called 'key money'. But another way is simply for landlords to discriminate on the basis of race, age, family size, or sex.

The effects of rent ceilings in cities such as London, Paris and New York have led Assar Lindbeck, chairman of the economic science Nobel Prize, to suggest that rent ceilings are the most effective means yet invented for destroying cities, even more effective than the hydrogen bomb. By the time the UK government decided to remove rent controls in 1989, the size of the private rented sector had fallen from more than 60 per cent to less than 10 per cent of the housing market.

Review

- A decrease in the supply of housing increases equilibrium rents.
- In the short run, higher rents result in a decrease in the quantity of housing demanded and an increase in the quantity supplied as existing houses and blocks of flats are used more intensively.
- In the long run, higher rents stimulate building. The supply of housing increases and rents fall.
- Rent ceilings limit the ability of the housing market to respond to change and can result in a permanent housing shortage. They can create inefficiency.

We've studied the effects of a change in supply in the housing market. Let's now look at the effects of a change in demand in the labour market.

The Labour Market and Minimum Wages

For most of us, the labour market is the most important market in which we participate. It is the interaction of demand and supply in the labour market that influences the jobs we get and the wages we earn. Firms make decisions about the quantity of labour to demand and households make decisions about the quantity of labour to supply. The wage rate balances the quantities demanded and the quantities supplied and determines the level of employment. But the labour market is constantly being bombarded by shocks, particularly from technological advances. This means that wages and employment prospects are constantly changing.

Labour-saving technology is constantly being invented. As a result, the demand for certain types of labour, usually the least skilled types, is constantly decreasing. How does the labour market cope with this continuous decrease in the demand for unskilled labour? Does it mean that the wages of unskilled workers are constantly falling? Let's find out.

Figure 7.4 shows the market for unskilled labour. Labour is demanded by firms and, other things remaining the same, the lower the wage rate, the greater is the quantity of labour demanded. The demand curve for labour, *D* in part (a), shows this relationship between the wage rate and the quantity of labour demanded. Labour is supplied by households and, other things remaining the same, the higher the wage rate, the greater is the quantity of labour supplied. But the longer the period of adjustment, the greater is the elasticity of supply of labour. Thus there are two supply curves, a short-run supply curve *SS* and a long-run supply curve *LS*.

The short-run supply curve shows how the hours of labour supplied by a given number of workers changes as the wage rate changes. To get employees to work longer hours, firms must offer higher wages, so the short-run supply curve is upward sloping.

The long-run supply curve shows the relationship between the quantity of labour supplied and the wage rate after enough time has passed for people to acquire new skills and move to new locations and new types of job. The number of people in the unskilled labour market depends on the opportunity

Figure 7.4 A Market for Unskilled Labour

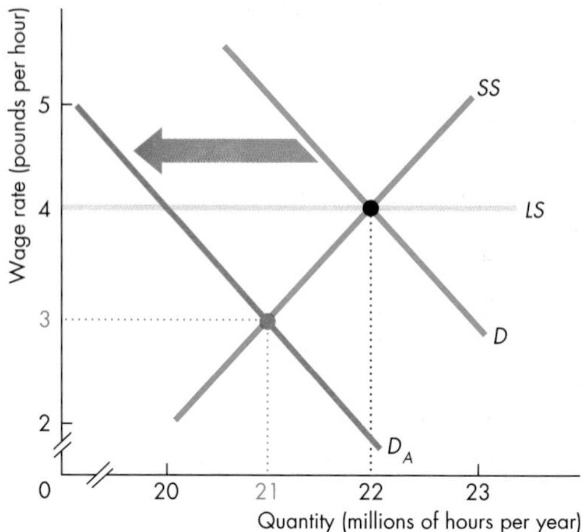

(a) After invention

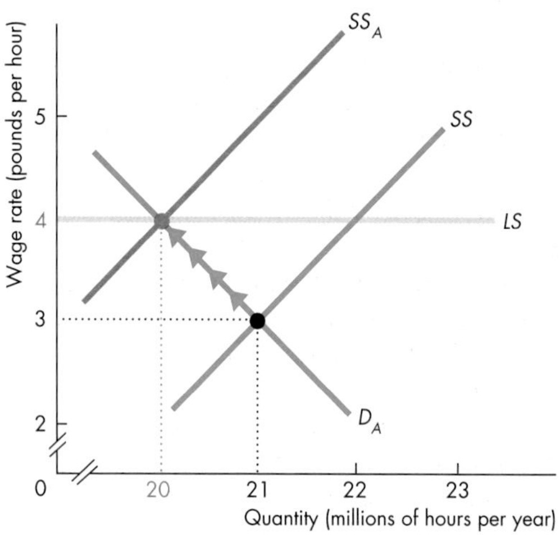

(b) Long-run adjustment

A market for unskilled labour is in equilibrium (part a) at a wage rate of £5 an hour with 22 million hours of labour a year being employed. A labour-saving invention shifts the demand curve from *D* to D_A. The wage rate falls to £4 an hour and employment decreases to 21 million hours a year. With the lower wage, some workers leave this market and the short-run supply curve starts to shift to SS_A (part b). The wage rate gradually increases, and the employment level decreases. Ultimately, wages return to £5 an hour and employment falls to 20 million hours a year.

cost – the unskilled wage rate compared with skilled wages and the value of leisure time. If the wage rate is high enough, people will enter this market. When it is too low, people leave the labour market – to seek training to enter the skilled labour market, to retire, or to work at home.

Because people are free to enter and leave the unskilled labour market, the long-run supply curve is highly elastic. In Figure 7.4, for simplicity, the long-run supply curve is assumed to be perfectly elastic (horizontal). The unskilled labour market is in equilibrium at a wage rate of £4 an hour and 22 million hours of labour are employed.

What happens if a labour-saving technology decreases the demand for unskilled labour? Figure 7.4(a) shows the short-run effects of such a change. The demand curve before the new technology is introduced is D. After the introduction of the new technology, the demand curve shifts leftward, to D_A. The wage rate falls to £3 an hour, and the quantity of labour employed decreases to 21 million hours. But this is not the end of the story.

People who are now earning only £3 an hour look around for other opportunities. They see that there are many other jobs for workers with more skills that pay wages above £3 an hour. One by one, workers decide to quit the market for unskilled labour. Some may retire, but many go to college to get new qualifications, or take jobs that pay less initially but offer on-the-job training. As a result, the short-run supply curve begins to shift leftward.

Figure 7.4(b) shows the long-run adjustment. As the short-run supply curve shifts leftward, it intersects the demand curve D_A at higher wage rates and lower levels of employment. In the long run, the short-run supply curve must shift all the way to SS_A. At this point, the wage has returned to £4 an hour, and employment has decreased to 20 million hours a year.

If the adjustment process we've just described is long and drawn out, wages remain low for a long period. In such a situation, the government is tempted to intervene in the labour market by legislating a minimum wage to protect the lowest-paid workers.

The Minimum Wage

A **minimum wage law** is a regulation that makes hiring labour below a specified wage illegal. If the minimum wage is set *below* the equilibrium wage, it has no effect. The law and the market forces are not in conflict. But if a minimum wage is set *above* the equilibrium wage, the minimum wage is in conflict with the market forces and does have some effects on the labour market. Let's study these effects by returning to the market for unskilled labour.

Suppose that when the wage rate falls to £3 an hour (in Figure 7.4(a)) the government imposes a minimum wage of £4 an hour. What are the effects of this law? The answer can be found by studying Figure 7.5. The minimum wage is shown as the horizontal red line labelled 'Minimum wage'. At the minimum wage, only 20 million hours of labour are demanded (point a) but 22 million hours of labour are supplied (point b). Because the number of hours demanded is less than the number of hours

Figure 7.5 Minimum Wages and Unemployment

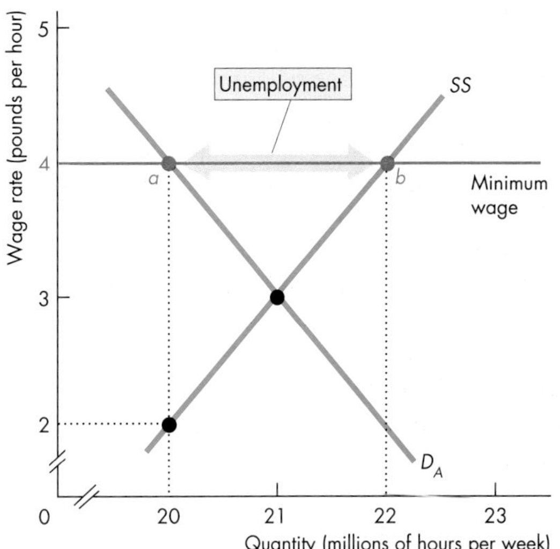

The demand curve for labour is D_A and the supply curve is *SS*. In an unregulated market, the wage rate is £4 an hour and 21 million hours of labour a year are employed. If a minimum wage of £5 an hour is imposed, only 20 million hours are hired but 22 million hours are available. This results in unemployment – *ab* – of two million hours a year. With only 20 million hours being demanded, some workers will willingly supply that 20 millionth hour for £3. These frustrated unemployed workers will spend time and other resources looking for a job.

supplied, 2 million hours of available labour are unemployed.

Inefficiency and the Minimum Wage

A labour market without a minimum wage can be allocated scarce labour resources to the jobs in which they are valued most highly. The minimum wage blocks the market mechanism and results in unemployment – wasted labour – and an inefficient amount of job search.

Look again at Figure 7.5. When only 20 million hours of work are available, you can read off from the supply curve that the lowest wage at which workers are willing to supply that 20 millionth hour is £2. Someone who manages to find a job will earn £4 an hour – £2 an hour more than the lowest wage rate at which someone is willing to work. Therefore it pays the unemployed workers to engage in search activity. Even though only 20 million hours of labour actually get employed, each person spends time and effort searching for one of the scarce jobs.

The Minimum Wage in Reality

Minimum wage laws are used by most governments in Europe and North America. Many European countries have a statutory national minimum wage across all industries, adjusted at regular intervals for changes in the price level or average earnings. In Belgium and Greece, the national minimum wage is set by a process of collective bargaining with trade unions, and a similar process determines industry minimum wages in Denmark, Germany and Italy. A minimum wage law was introduced in the UK in April 1999. The minimum wage was set at £3.60 an hour for workers aged over 22 years, and at £3 an hour for workers aged between 18 and 21 years. It is estimated that 2 million workers will be affected by the new minimum wage.

There is now a hot debate about whether to introduce a Europe-wide minimum wage as part of the European Union's new labour market strategy. Some economists believe that bringing down the barriers to trade in the new single European market will increase competition and create an increasingly low-wage workforce – a process called *social dumping*. Firms will be attracted to low-wage countries and governments will start to compete for this investment by cutting back welfare provision, training and employer costs. Growth will be limited to the low-skill, low-wage sector. Minimum wages are needed to halt the downward pressure on wages.

Other economists believe that minimum wages will fuel inflation as higher paid workers try to raise their wages to keep the same differentials with the lowest paid workers. Minimum wages also stop the market reaching equilibrium and low paid workers only gain higher wages at the opportunity cost of fewer jobs. As low wages are more common among young people, existing minimum wage laws may explain why the highest rates of unemployment in Europe are among such people.

In Chapter 15, we will look at some examples of when minimum wages do not lead to unemployment.

Review

- A decrease in the demand for unskilled labour lowers the equilibrium wage.
- In the short run, lower wages result in a decrease in the quantity of unskilled labour supplied and an increase in the quantity demanded.
- In the long run, lower wages encourage some people to leave the workforce and others to train and obtain skills. The supply of unskilled labour decreases and wages rise.
- Minimum wage laws can block the market mechanism and create unemployment.

Let's look at the effects of another set of government actions on markets – taxes.

Taxes

In 1996, the UK government raised more than £7.8 billion – an average of £1,180 per person – from indirect tax, that is taxes on the goods and services we buy. These taxes include Value Added Tax (VAT), sales taxes on goods and services like insurance and housing, and excise taxes on petrol, alcoholic beverages and tobacco. VAT is an *ad valorem* tax – a tax set as a percentage of the selling price on all

Figure 7.6 The Sales Tax

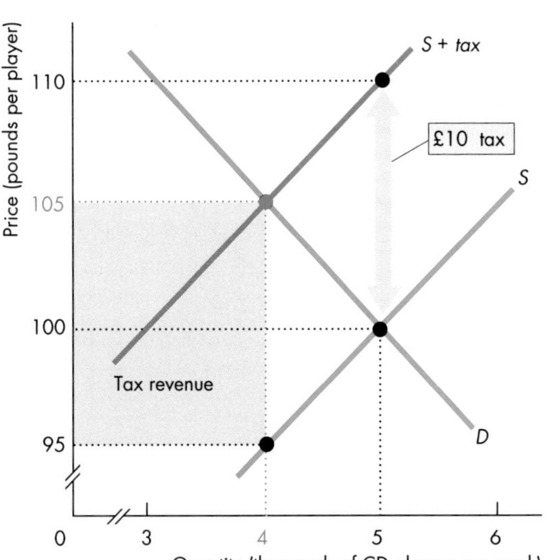

The demand curve for CD players is *D* and the supply curve is *S*. With no tax, the price is £100 a player and 5,000 players a week are bought and sold. Then a sales tax of £10 a player is imposed. The price on the vertical axis is the price *including* the tax. The demand curve does not change, but supply decreases and the supply curve shifts leftward. The curve *S* + *tax* shows the terms on which sellers will make CD players available. The vertical distance between the supply curve *S* and the new supply curve *S* + *tax* equals the tax – £10 a player.

The new equilibrium is at a price of £105 with 4,000 CD players a week bought and sold. The tax increases the price by less than the tax, decreases the price received by the supplier, and decreases the quantity bought and sold. It brings in revenue to the government equal to the blue shaded area.

transactions. All countries in the European Union levy this tax, but different countries impose different rates. Excise taxes are usually specific taxes – a specific amount of tax per unit, say 5 pence per cigarette levied on the manufacturer. Sales taxes may be *ad valorem* or specific taxes but are levied at the final point of sale.

If a good or service is taxed, you pay the retail price *plus* an additional amount, the *tax*. What are the effects of taxes on the prices and quantities of goods bought and sold? Do the prices of the goods and services you buy increase by the full amount of the tax? Isn't it always you – the consumer – who pays the entire tax? It can be, but usually it isn't. It is even possible that you actually pay none of the tax, forcing the seller to pay it for you. Let's see how we can make sense of these apparently absurd statements.

Who Pays a Sales Tax?

To study the effect of a tax, we start by looking at a market in which there is no tax. We'll then introduce a tax – a specific sales tax – and see what changes arise. The results for other forms of tax are not examined here but they are similar.

Figure 7.6 shows the market for CD players. The demand curve is *D* and the supply curve is *S*. The equilibrium price of a CD player is £100, and the quantity traded is 5,000 players a week.

Suppose the government puts a £10 sales tax on CD players. What are the effects of this tax on the price and quantity in the market for CD players? To answer this question, we need to work out what happens to demand and supply in this market.

When a good is taxed it has two prices – a price that excludes the tax and a price that includes it. Consumers respond only to the price that includes the tax. Producers respond only to the price they receive – the price that excludes the tax. The tax is like a wedge between these two prices.

Let's think of the price on the vertical axis of Figure 7.6 as the price paid by the consumer that includes the tax. When a tax is imposed, there is no shift in demand. The demand curve shows quantities demanded at different levels of the total price, with or without a tax.

But the supply curve *does* shift. When a sales tax is imposed on a good, it is offered for sale at a higher price than in a no-tax situation. The supply curve shifts leftward to *S* + *tax*. The new supply curve is found by adding the tax to the minimum price that suppliers are willing to accept for each quantity sold. For example, with no tax, suppliers are willing to sell 4,000 players a week for £95 a player. So with a £10 tax, they will supply 4,000 players a week for £105 – a price that includes the tax. The new supply curve *S* + *tax* lies to the left of the original curve – supply has decreased – and the vertical distance between the original supply curve *S* and the new supply curve *S* + *tax* equals the tax. The curve *S* + *tax* describes the price at which the good is available to buyers.

A new equilibrium is determined where the new supply curve intersects the demand curve – at a

Figure 7.7 Sales Tax and the Elasticity of Demand

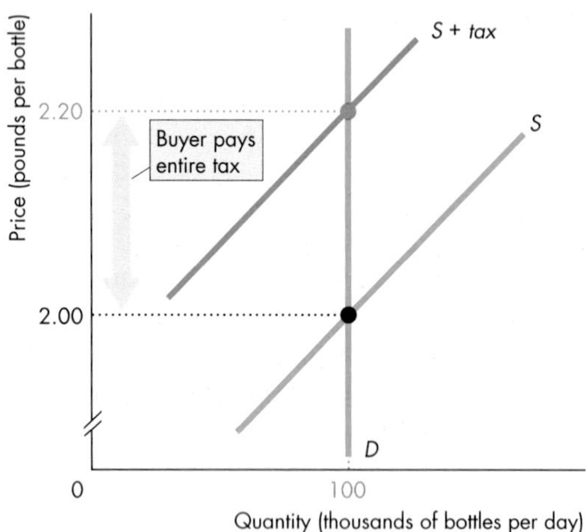

(a) Inelastic demand

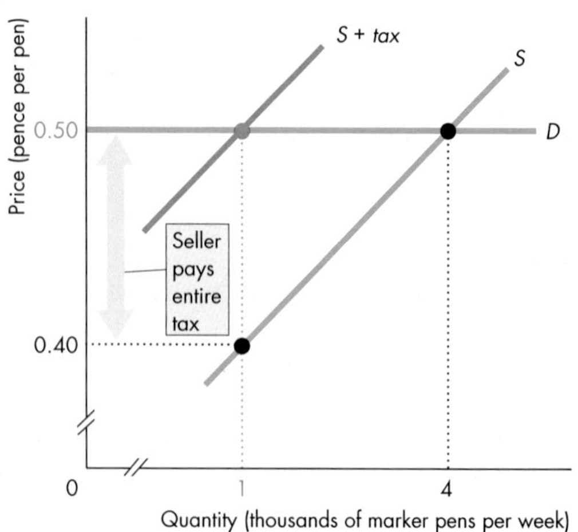

(b) Elastic demand

Part (a) shows the market for insulin. The demand for insulin is perfectly inelastic, as shown by the curve *D*. The supply curve of insulin is *S*. With no tax the price is £2 a bottle and 100,000 bottles a day are bought. A sales tax of 20 pence a bottle increases the price at which sellers are willing to make insulin available, and shifts the supply curve to *S + tax*. The price rises to £2.20 a bottle, but the quantity bought does not change and buyers pay the entire tax.

Part (b) shows the market for pink marker pens. The demand for pink marker pens is perfectly elastic at the price of other coloured marker pens – 50 pence a pen. The demand curve is *D*, the supply curve is *S*, and with no tax the price of a pink marker pen is 50 pence and 4,000 a week are bought. A sales tax of 10 pence a pink pen decreases the supply of pink marker pens, shifting the supply curve to *S + tax*. The price remains at 50 pence a pen, and the quantity of pink markers sold decreases to 1,000 a week. Suppliers pay the entire tax.

price of £105 and a quantity of 4,000 CD players a week. The £10 sales tax has increased the price paid by the consumer by only £5 (£105 versus £100), which is less than the £10 tax. And it has decreased the price received by the supplier by £5 (£95 versus £100). The £10 tax paid is made up of the higher price to the buyer and the lower price to the seller.

The tax brings in tax revenue to the government equal to the tax per item multiplied by the items sold. It is illustrated by the blue area in Figure 7.6. The £10 tax on CD players brings in a tax revenue of £40,000 a week.

In this example, the buyer and the seller split the tax equally; the buyer pays £5 a player and so does the seller. The proportion of the tax paid by the buyer and the seller is determined by the elasticity of demand and supply. In extreme cases, the buyer or the seller might have to pay the entire tax. Let's look at these cases.

Tax Division and Elasticity of Demand

The division of the total tax between buyers and sellers also depends on the elasticity of demand. Again, there are two extreme cases:

1 Perfectly inelastic demand – buyer pays.

2 Perfectly elastic demand – seller pays.

Perfectly Inelastic Demand Figure 7.7(a) shows the market for insulin, a life-saving daily medication for diabetics. The quantity demanded is 100,000 bottles a day, regardless of the price. Each one of the 100,000 diabetics in the population would sacrifice all other goods and services for their daily insulin dose. In the absence of a national health service, demand for insulin would reflect this fact and would be perfectly inelastic. It is shown by the vertical curve *D*. The supply curve of insulin is *S*. With no tax, the price is £2 a bottle, and the quantity is 100,000 bottles a day.

If insulin is taxed at 20 pence a bottle, we must add the tax to the minimum price at which the drug companies are willing to sell insulin to determine the post-tax supply to consumers. The result is a new supply curve $S + tax$. The price rises to £2.20 a bottle, but the quantity does not change. The buyer pays the entire sales tax of 20 pence a bottle.

Perfectly Elastic Demand Figure 7.7(b) shows the market for pink marker pens. Demand is perfectly elastic at 50 pence a pen as shown by the horizontal curve D. If pink markers are less expensive than the others, everyone will use pink. If pink markers are more expensive than the others, no one will use them. The supply curve is S. With no tax, the price of a pink marker is 50 pence and 4,000 a week are bought at that price.

If the sales tax of 10 pence a pen is levied on pink, and only pink, marker pens, we must add the tax to the minimum price at which suppliers are willing to sell them. The new supply curve is $S + tax$. The price remains at 50 pence a pen, and the quantity of pink markers decreases to 1,000 a week. The 10 pence tax has left the price paid by the consumer unchanged, but decreased the amount received by the supplier by the full amount of the tax – 10 pence a pen. As a result, sellers decrease the quantity offered for sale.

In most markets, demand is neither perfectly inelastic nor perfectly elastic, so the tax is split between the buyer and the seller. But the division depends on the elasticity of demand and will rarely be equal. The more inelastic the demand and the more elastic the supply, the larger is the portion of the tax paid by the buyer.

Tax Division and Elasticity of Supply

The division of the total tax between buyers and sellers depends, in part, on the elasticity of supply. There are two extreme cases:

1 Perfectly inelastic supply – seller pays.

2 Perfectly elastic supply – buyer pays.

Perfectly Inelastic Supply Figure 7.8(a) shows the market for water from a mineral spring which flows at a constant rate that can't be controlled. The quantity supplied is 100,000 bottles a week, regardless of the price. The supply is perfectly inelastic and the supply curve is S_I. The demand curve for the water from this spring is D. With no tax, the price is 50 pence a bottle and the 100,000 bottles that flow from the spring are bought at that price.

If the spring water is taxed at 5 pence a bottle. The supply curve does not change because the spring owners still produce 100,000 bottles a week – even though the price has fallen. Consumers, on the other hand, are willing to buy the 100,000 bottles available each week only if the price is 50 pence a bottle. So the price remains at 50 pence a bottle, and the suppliers pay the entire tax. The tax of 5 pence a bottle reduces the price received by suppliers to 45 pence a bottle.

Perfectly Elastic Supply Figure 7.8(b) shows the market for sand from which computer-chip makers extract silicon. There is a virtually unlimited quantity of sand available, and its owners are willing to supply any quantity at a price of 10 pence a kilogram. So supply is perfectly elastic – the supply curve S_E. The demand curve for sand is D. With no tax, the price is 10 pence a kilogram, and 5,000 kilograms a week are bought at that price.

If sand is taxed at 1 penny a kilogram, we add the tax to the minimum supply price. Suppliers are willing to supply any quantity at 11 pence a kilogram along the curve $S_E + tax$. A new equilibrium is determined where the new supply curve intersects the demand curve – at a price of 11 pence a kilogram and a quantity of 3,000 kilograms a week. The sales tax has increased the price paid by consumers by the full amount of the tax – 1 penny a kilogram – and has decreased the quantity sold.

We've seen that when supply is perfectly inelastic, the seller pays the entire tax and when supply is perfectly elastic, the buyer pays it. In the usual case, where supply is neither perfectly inelastic nor perfectly elastic, the tax is split between the seller and the buyer. But the division depends on the elasticity of supply. The more elastic the supply, the larger is the portion of the tax paid by the buyer.

Indirect Taxes in Practice

We've looked at the range of possible effects of a sales tax by studying extreme cases. In practice, supply and demand are rarely perfectly elastic or

Figure 7.8 Sales Tax and the Elasticity of Supply

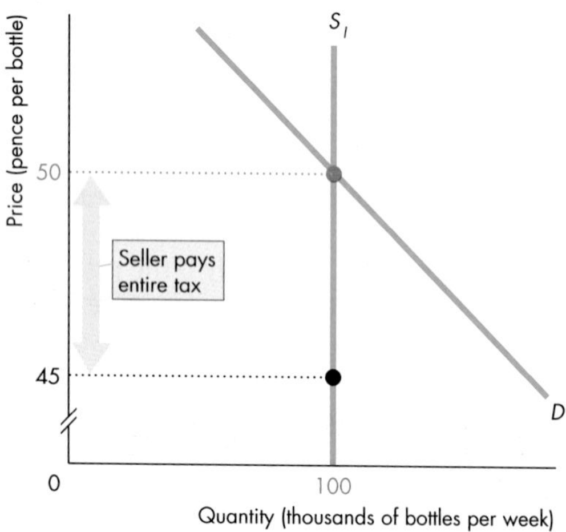

(a) Inelastic supply

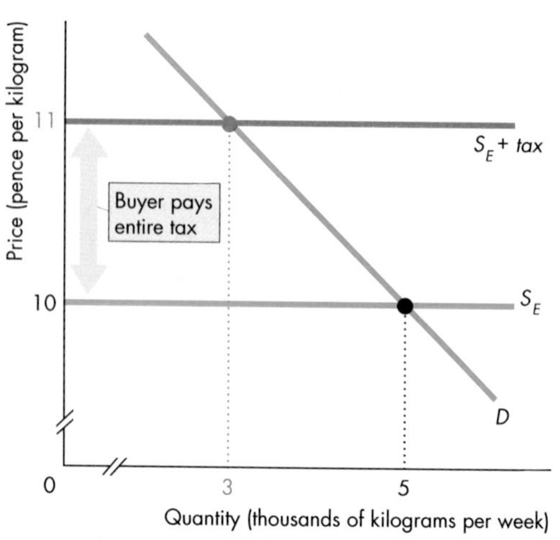

(b) Elastic supply

Part (a) shows the market for water from a mineral spring. Supply is perfectly inelastic and the supply curve is S_I. The demand curve is *D*, and with no tax the price is 50 pence a bottle. A sales tax of five pence decreases the price received by sellers, but the price remains at 50 pence a bottle and the number of bottles bought remains the same. Suppliers pay the entire tax.

Part (b) shows the market for sand from which silicon is extracted. Supply is perfectly elastic at a price of 10 pence a kilogram. The supply curve is S_E, the demand curve is *D*, and with no tax the price is 10 pence a kilogram and 5,000 kilograms a week are bought. A sales tax of one penny a kilogram increases the minimum price at which sellers are willing to supply to 11 pence a kilogram. The supply curve shifts to S_E + *tax*. The price increases to 11 pence a kilogram, the quantity bought decreases to 3,000 kilograms a week, and buyers pay the entire tax.

inelastic. So does our model of tax help us to understand government tax policy? Let's see. We know that governments tend to choose goods such as alcohol, tobacco and petrol for excise taxes. Why? Because they have a low elasticity of demand. Although the tax raises the price and the quantity bought falls, it does not fall by much. Tax revenue will rise even if the tax is increased. Of course, governments must raise the specific tax on goods every year to keep the real value of the tax constant. Otherwise revenue will start to fall, other things remaining the same. Alternative reasons for taxing these goods are examined in Chapter 20, and in the next section.

Taxes and Efficiency

We've seen that a tax can place a wedge between the price paid by buyers and the price received by sellers. The price paid by buyers is also the buyers' willingness to pay or marginal benefit. The price received by sellers is the sellers' minimum supply price or marginal cost. If a tax puts a wedge between the buyers' price and the sellers' price, it also puts a wedge between marginal benefit and marginal cost. This creates inefficiency.

Figure 7.9 shows the inefficiency of a sales tax on CD players. The tax results in a shift of the supply curve to $S + tax$. Price increases to 105 pence and quantity falls to four thousand players a week. But both consumer and producer surplus shrink. Part of consumer and producer surplus is transferred to government as tax revenue (the purple area) and so is not lost. But the grey area of consumer and producer surplus becomes a deadweight loss.

The size of the deadweight loss depends on elasticity of demand and supply. In the extreme cases where demand and supply are perfectly inelastic, there will be no deadweight loss as

Figure 7.9 Taxes and Efficiency

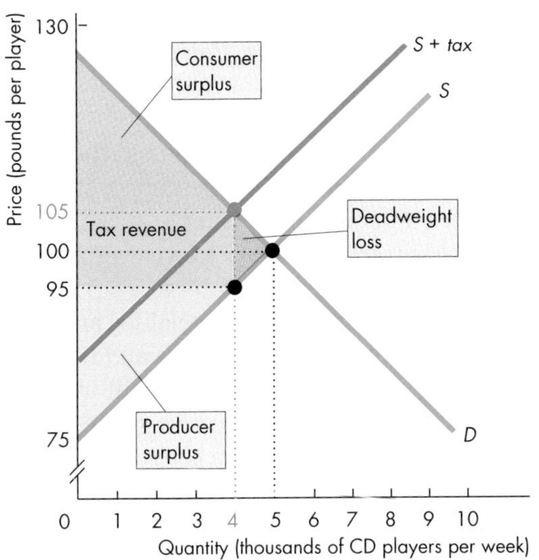

With no sales tax, 5,000 players a week are bought and sold at £100 each. With a sales tax of £10 a player, the buyers' price rises to £105 a player, the sellers' price falls to £95, and the quantity decreases to 4,000 CD players a week. Consumer surplus shrinks to the green area, and producer surplus shrinks to the blue area. Part of the loss of consumer surplus and producer surplus goes to the government as tax revenue, which is shown as the purple area. A deadweight loss also arises, which is shown by the grey area.

quantity does not change with a price change. The more inelastic either demand or supply, the smaller is the deadweight loss. Most indirect excise duties are put on goods which are inelastic in demand and these taxes may not create much inefficiency. There are also other cases when a tax may create an increase in efficiency and we will look at these in Chapter 20.

Review

- For a given demand curve, the more elastic the supply, the larger is the price increase, the larger is the quantity decrease, and the larger is the portion of the tax paid by the buyer.
- For a given supply curve, the less elastic the demand, the larger is the price increase, the smaller is the quantity decrease, and the larger is the portion of the tax paid by the buyer.
- Taxes can create a deadweight loss and inefficiency.

Taxes are just one method of changing prices and quantities. Let's look at another: prohibiting trade in a good.

Markets for Prohibited Goods

The markets for many goods and services are regulated, and buying and selling some goods is prohibited – the goods and services are illegal. The best known examples are drugs. Alcohol and tobacco are currently legally available drugs, but their supply and consumption is regulated in most European countries. Other drugs such as cannabis, ecstasy, cocaine and heroin are more commonly illegal.

Despite the fact that some drugs are illegal, trade in them is a multi-billion pound global business. This trade can be understood by using the same economic models and principles that explain trade in legal goods and services. There are also occasions when legal drugs are prohibited and illegal drugs are legalized. For example, alcohol has been prohibited during wartime and cannabis is legally available in the Netherlands. We can use our models to look at the economic impact of different regulation and control systems.

To study the market for prohibited goods, we're first going to examine the prices and quantities that would prevail if these goods were not prohibited. Next, we'll see how prohibition works. Then we'll see how a tax might be used to limit the consumption of these goods.

A Free Market for Drugs

Figure 7.10 shows a market for a drug. The demand curve, *D*, shows that, other things remaining the same, the lower the price of the drug, the larger is the quantity demanded. The supply curve, *S*, shows

Figure 7.10 The Market for a Prohibited Good

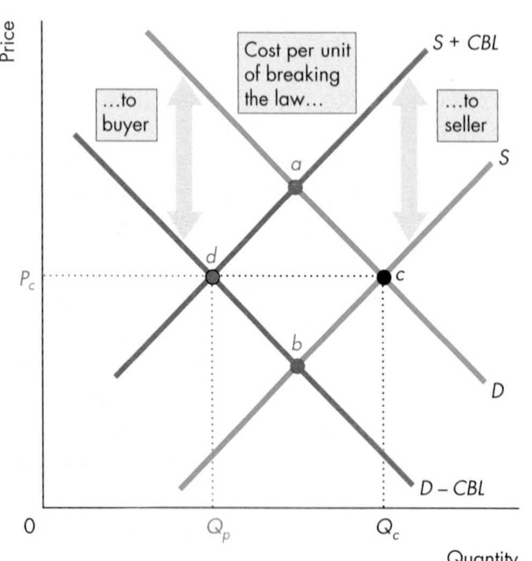

The demand curve for the drug is *D* and the supply curve is *S*. With no prohibition or regulation, the quantity consumed is Q_c at a price of P_c – point *c*. If selling the drug is illegal, the cost of breaking the law (*CBL*) is added to the other costs and supply decreases to *S* + *CBL*. The price rises and the quantity consumed decreases – point *a*. If buying the drug is illegal, the cost of breaking the law is subtracted from the maximum price that buyers are willing to pay, and demand decreases to *D* – *CBL*. The price falls and the quantity consumed decreases – point *b*.

If both buying and selling are illegal both the supply curve and the demand curve shift – the quantity consumed decreases even more, but (in this example) the price remains at its unregulated level – point *d*.

that, other things remaining the same, the lower the price of the drug, the smaller is the quantity supplied. If the drug were not prohibited or regulated, the quantity bought and sold would be Q_c and the price would be P_c.

Prohibiting a Drug

When a good is prohibited, the cost of trading in the good increases. By how much the cost increases and on whom the cost falls depend on the penalties for breaking the law and the effectiveness with which the law is enforced. The larger the penalties and the more effective the policing, the higher are the costs to traders. Fines impose a direct cost but prison sentences involve the opportunity cost of lost earnings and discomfort. Penalties may be imposed on sellers, buyers, or both.

Penalties on Sellers Drug dealers in the United Kingdom face fines and prison sentences if their activities are detected. For example, a cannabis dealer would probably serve a 1.5 year prison term, whereas a heroin dealer would serve a 2.5 year prison term on average. These penalties are part of the cost of supplying illegal drugs and they lead to a decrease in supply – a leftward shift in the supply curve. To determine the new supply curve, we add the cost of breaking the law to the minimum price that drug dealers are willing to accept. In Figure 7.10, the cost of breaking the law by selling drugs (*CBL*) is added to the minimum price that dealers will accept and the supply curve shifts leftward to *S* + *CBL*. If penalties are imposed only on sellers, the market moves from point *c* to point *a*. The price increases and the quantity bought decreases.

Penalties on Buyers In the United Kingdom, it is also illegal to possess drugs such as cannabis, cocaine and heroin for personal consumption. The penalty for illegal possession of cannabis is usually a fine and prison sentences are rarely more than three months, whereas the penalty for illegal possession of heroin is usually a nine-month prison sentence. Penalties for possession fall on buyers and the cost of breaking the law must be subtracted from the value of the good to determine the maximum price buyers are willing to pay. Demand decreases and the demand curve shifts leftward. In Figure 7.10, the demand curve shifts to *D* – *CBL*. If penalties are imposed only on buyers, the market moves from point *c* to point *b*. The price and the quantity bought decrease.

Penalties on Both Sellers and Buyers If penalties are imposed on sellers *and* buyers, both supply and demand decrease and both the supply curve and demand curve shift. In Figure 7.10, the costs of breaking the law are the same for both buyers and sellers, so both curves shift leftward by the same amounts. The market moves to point *d*. The price remains at the competitive market price but the quantity bought decreases to Q_p.

The larger the penalty and the greater the degree of law enforcement, the larger is the decrease in demand and/or supply and the greater is the shift of the demand and/or supply curve. If the penalties are heavier on sellers, the price will rise above P_c, and if the penalties are heavier on buyers, the price will fall below P_c. In the United Kingdom, the penalties on sellers are larger than those on buyers. As a result, the decrease in supply is much larger than the decrease in demand. The quantity of drugs traded decreases and the price increases, compared with an unregulated market.

With high enough penalties and effective law enforcement, it is possible to decrease demand and/or supply to the point at which the quantity bought is zero. But in reality, such an outcome is unusual. It does not happen in the case of illegal drugs. The key reason is the high cost of law enforcement and insufficient resources for the police and customs officers to achieve effective enforcement. Because of this, some people suggest that drugs (and other illegal goods) should be legalized but regulated. In particular, legalized drugs could be taxed at a high rate in the same way that legal drugs such as alcohol are taxed. You can read about the loss of tax in illegal bootleg markets for alcohol and tobacco in *Reading Between the Lines* in this Chapter on pp. 164–165.

Legalizing and Taxing Drugs

From your study of the effects of taxes, it should now be clear that government could also reduce the quantity of drugs bought and sold if drugs were legalized and taxed. A high tax rate would probably be needed to keep drug consumption at the level in the market before legalization. High taxes would lead many drug dealers and consumers to evade the tax. This problem can be reduced by requiring sellers to have a licence, as in the case of alcohol and tobacco. Tax evaders would also face the cost of breaking the tax law. If the penalty for tax law violation is severe and the law is as effectively policed as drug dealing laws, then a regulated market could achieve a similar result to prohibition. The quantity of drugs consumed in a regulated market would depend on the penalties for law breaking and on the way in which the penalties are assigned to buyers and sellers.

Some Pros and Cons of Taxes versus Prohibition So which works more effectively, prohibition or taxing? The comparison we've just made suggests that the two methods can be made to be equivalent if the taxes and penalties are set at the appropriate levels. But there are some other differences.

In favour of taxes and against prohibition is the fact that the tax revenue can be used to make law enforcement more effective. Some economists argue that a great deal of inner city crime is caused by the prohibition of drugs – burglaries, muggings, shootings and money laundering. Legalization would reduce the social and policing costs associated with this crime. Tax revenue can also be used to run a more effective education campaign against drugs. In favour of prohibition and against taxes is the fact that prohibition sends a strong signal that may influence preferences, decreasing the demand for drugs. Also, some people intensely dislike the idea of the government profiting from trade in harmful substances.

Review

- Penalizing sellers of an illegal good increases the cost of selling the good and decreases supply and market quantity.
- Penalizing buyers of an illegal good decreases the willingness to pay for the good and decreases demand and market quantity.
- Taxing a good at a sufficiently high rate can achieve the same consumption level as prohibition plus a tax revenue.

Stabilizing Farm Revenue

Freak gale force storms in 1993 wiped out many crops. Farm output fluctuates a great deal because of fluctuations in the weather. How do changes in farm output affect farm prices and farm revenues? And how might farm revenues be stabilized? The answers to these questions depend on how the markets for agricultural goods are organized. We'll begin by looking at an unregulated agricultural market.

Figure 7.11 Harvests, Farm Prices and Farm Revenue

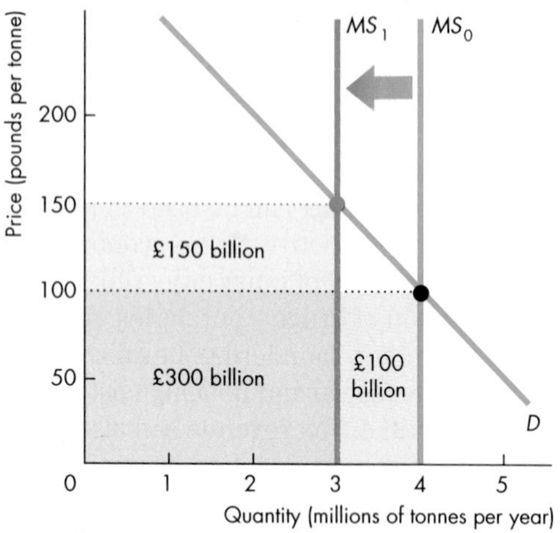

(a) Poor harvest: revenue increases

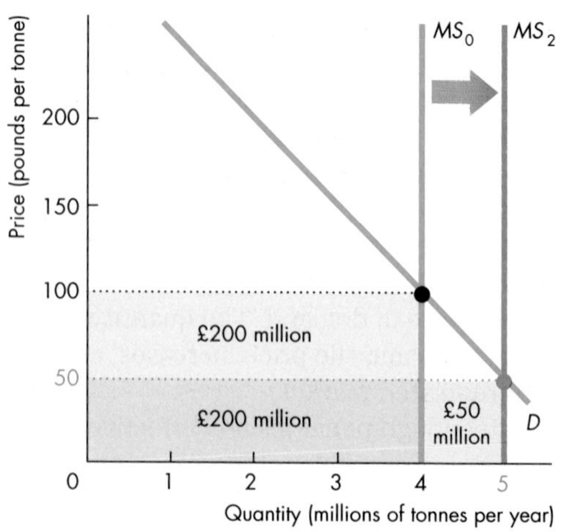

(b) Bumper harvest: revenue decreases

In both parts, the demand curve for wheat is *D*. In normal times, the momentary supply curve is MS_0, and four million tonnes are sold for £100 a tonne. In part (a), a poor growing season decreases supply, shifting the momentary supply curve to MS_1. The price increases to £150 a tonne and farm revenue *increases* from £400 million to £450 million – the increase in revenue from the higher price (£150 million light blue area) exceeds the decrease in revenue from the smaller quantity (£100 million red area). In part (b), a bumper harvest increases supply, shifting the momentary supply curve to MS_2. The price decreases to £50 a tonne and farm revenue *decreases* to £250 million – the decrease in revenue from the lower price (£200 million light blue area) exceeds the increase in revenue from the increase in the quantity sold (£50 million red area).

An Unregulated Agricultural Market

Figure 7.11 illustrates the unregulated European market for wheat. In both parts the demand curve for wheat is *D*. Once farmers have harvested their crop, they have no control over the quantity supplied and supply is inelastic along a *momentary supply curve*. In normal climate conditions, the momentary supply curve is MS_0 (in both parts of the figure) – the price is £100 a tonne, the quantity produced is four million tonnes, and farm revenue is £400 million (dark blue and red areas).

Suppose the opportunity cost to farmers of producing wheat is also £400 million. Then in normal conditions, farmers just cover their opportunity cost.

Poor Harvest What happens to the price of wheat and the revenue of farmers when there is a poor harvest? These questions are answered in Figure 7.11(a). Supply decreases and the momentary supply curve shifts leftward to MS_1 where three million tonnes of wheat are produced. With a decrease in supply, the price increases to £150 a tonne. But notice farm revenue *increases* to £450 million (light and dark blue areas). On average, farmers are now making a profit in excess of their opportunity cost.

A decrease in supply will increase the price and farm revenues because the demand for wheat is *inelastic*. The percentage decrease in the quantity demanded is less than the percentage increase in price. You can verify this fact by noticing in Figure 7.11(a) that the increase in revenue from the higher price (£150 million light blue area) exceeds the decrease in revenue from the smaller quantity (£100 million red area).

Although total farm revenue increases when there is a poor harvest, some farmers, whose entire crop is wiped out, suffer a fall in revenue. Others, whose crop is unaffected, make an enormous gain.

Bumper harvest Figure 7.11(b) shows what happens when there is a bumper harvest. Now, supply increases to five million tonnes and the momentary supply curve shifts rightward to MS_2. With the increased quantity supplied, the price falls to £50 a tonne. Farm revenues also decline – to £250 million because the demand for wheat is inelastic. To see this, notice that the decrease in revenue from the lower price (£200 million light blue area) exceeds the increase in revenue from the increase in the quantity sold (£50 million red area).

Elasticity of Demand What happens if the demand for wheat is elastic? The price fluctuations go in the same directions as when demand is inelastic, but revenues fluctuate in the opposite directions. Bumper harvests increase revenue and poor harvests decrease it. In fact, the demand for most agricultural goods is inelastic, and our inelastic example is the relevant one.

Because farm prices fluctuate, institutions have evolved to stabilize them. There are two types of institution:

1 Speculative markets in stocks.
2 Price support policy.

Speculative Markets in Stocks

Many goods, including a wide variety of agricultural goods, can be stored. These **stocks** of goods – or stores – provide a cushion between production and consumption. If production decreases, goods can be sold from stocks; if production increases, goods can be put into stocks.

In a market that has stocks, the quantity produced is not the same as the quantity supplied. The quantity supplied exceeds the quantity produced when goods are sold from stocks. The quantity supplied is less than the quantity produced when goods are put into stocks. The supply curve, therefore, depends on the behaviour of stock holders who keep stocks. Let's see how they behave.

The Behaviour of Stock Holders Stock holders speculate. They hope to buy goods and put them into stores when the price is low, and sell them from stores when the price is high. They make a profit or incur a loss equal to their selling price minus their buying price and minus the cost of storage.[1]

1 We will suppose that the cost of storage is so small that we can ignore it. This assumption, though not essential, helps us to see the effects of stock holders' decisions on prices.

Figure 7.12 How Stocks Limit Price Changes

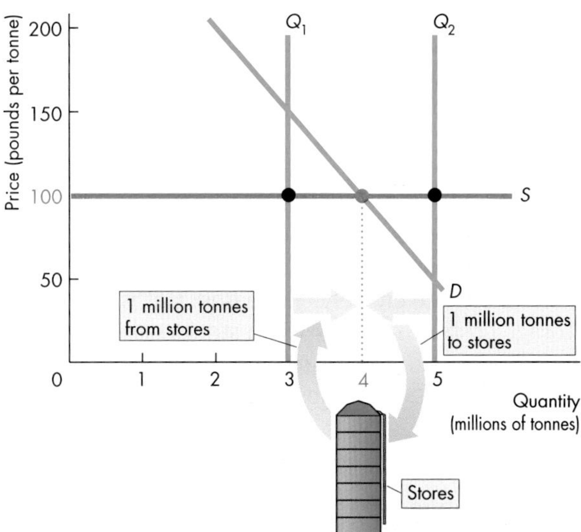

Stock holders supply goods from stores if the price rises above £100 per tonne and take wheat into stores if the price falls below £100 per tonne, making supply perfectly elastic along the supply curve *S*. When production decreases to Q_1, one million tonnes are supplied from store; when production increases to Q_2, one million tonnes are added to store. The price remains constant at £100 per tonne.

But how do stock holders know if the price is high or low? First, stock holders must make their best forecast of future prices. If the current price is above the forecast future price, they sell goods from stores. If the current price is below the forecast future price, they buy goods to put into stores. This activity makes the supply curve perfectly elastic at the future price forecast by stock holders.

Let's work out what happens to price and quantity in a market in which stocks are held when production fluctuates. Let's look again at the wheat market.

Fluctuations in Production In Figure 7.12 the demand curve for wheat is *D*. Stock holders forecast the future price to be £100 a tonne. The supply curve is *S* – supply is perfectly elastic at the forecast price. Production fluctuates between Q_1 and Q_2.

When production fluctuates and there are no stocks, the price and the quantity fluctuate. We saw this result in Figure 7.11. But if there are stocks, the price does not fluctuate. When production is low, at Q_1 or three million tonnes, stock holders sell one million tonnes from stores and the quantity bought by consumers is four million tonnes. The price remains at £100 a tonne. When production is high, at Q_2 or five million tonnes, stock holders buy one million tonnes and consumers continue to buy four million tonnes. Again, the price remains at £100 a tonne. Stocks reduce price fluctuations. In Figure 7.12, the price fluctuations are entirely eliminated. But when storage costs are high or when stocks become almost depleted, price fluctuations do occur, but they are smaller than those occurring in a market without stocks.

Farm Revenue Even if stock speculation succeeds in stabilizing prices, it does not stabilize farm revenue. With the price stabilized, farm revenue fluctuates as production fluctuates. Let's look at how farm revenues can be stabilized by an agricultural price support policy.

Price Support Policy

In every country, the government intervenes in agricultural markets. The most extensive example is the **Common Agricultural Policy** (CAP) of the European Union. The CAP was set up in 1957 to make sure the bad experiences of wartime shortages and low farm incomes would not be repeated.

The CAP takes the form of price floors set above the equilibrium price – similar to the minimum wage that we studied earlier – and above the production cost of efficient farms. Each year the European Union sets a target price for each agricultural product. The price floor is above the equilibrium price which would have occured in the European market and the world market. A levy is charged on all imported agricultural products to make sure their price is the same as the target price and to stop a flood of cheap imports. Just as the minimum wage was shown to create unemployment – excess supply of labour – the agricultural price floor creates excess supply of farm products. These surpluses have to be bought up each year by the European Union and stored in the hope of selling the produce in times of shortage.

Unfortunately, the target price has been consistently above the equilibrium price, so the European Union buys more than it sells and ends up with mountains of wheat, beef and butter and lakes of wine! The cost of buying and storing agricultural goods falls on tax payers and the main gainers are the large, efficient farms. As a result, the European Union has begun to reform the CAP – reducing target prices and levies, and introducing direct income support payments to farmers. EU agricultural markets are now more open to world competition and the mountains of butter and lakes of wine are smaller.

Review

- The demand for most farm goods is inelastic.
- With no stores, a poor harvest (a decrease in supply) increases price and increases farm revenue and a bumper harvest (an increase in supply) decreases price and decreases farm revenue.
- Stock holders speculate by trying to buy at a low price and sell at a high price. Successful speculation reduces price fluctuations.
- Farm price support policies limit price fluctuations but usually create surpluses which are costly to store.

We've now completed our study of demand and supply and its applications. You've seen how this model enables us to make predictions about prices and quantities bought and sold and also how it enables us to understand a wide variety of markets and situations. We're now going to start digging a bit more deeply into people's economic choices, and in the next section we'll study the economic choices of households.

Summary

Key Points

Housing Markets and Rent Ceilings (pp. 142–145)

- A decrease in the supply of housing decreases short-run supply and increases equilibrium rents.
- Higher rents increase the quantity of housing supplied in the short run and stimulate building activity, which increases supply in the long run. Rents decrease and the quantity of housing increases.
- If a rent ceiling prevents rents from increasing, the quantity supplied remains constant and there is a housing shortage, which creates wasteful search and black markets.

The Labour Market and Minimum Wages (pp. 146–148)

- A decrease in the demand for unskilled labour lowers the wage and reduces employment.
- The lower wage encourages people to quit the unskilled market and to acquire skills, decreasing the supply of unskilled labour. The wage rises gradually to its original level and employment decreases.
- Imposing a minimum wage above the equilibrium wage, decreases the demand for labour, creates unemployment and increases the amount of time spent searching for a job.
- Minimum wages bite hardest on people having the fewest skills.

Taxes (pp. 148–153)

- When a good or service is taxed, it is usually offered for sale at a higher price than if it is not taxed. Usually, the quantity bought decreases and the price increases but by less than the amount of the tax. The tax is paid partly by the buyer and partly by the seller.
- The portion of the tax paid by the buyer and by the seller depends on the elasticity of supply and the elasticity of demand.
- The more elastic the supply and the less elastic the demand, the greater is the price increase, the smaller is the quantity decrease, and the larger is the portion of the tax paid by the buyer.
- If supply is perfectly inelastic or demand is perfectly elastic, the seller pays the entire tax. If supply is perfectly elastic or demand is perfectly inelastic, the buyer pays the entire tax.

Markets for Prohibited Goods (pp. 153–155)

- Penalties on sellers of an illegal good increase the cost of selling the good and decrease its supply. Penalties on buyers decrease their willingness to pay and decrease demand for the good.
- The higher the penalties and the more effective the law enforcement, the smaller is the quantity bought. The price is higher or lower than the unregulated price, depending on whether penalties on sellers or buyers are higher.
- A tax set at a sufficiently high rate will also decrease the quantity of a drug consumed, but there will be a tendency for the tax to be evaded.

Stabilizing Farm Revenue (pp. 155–158)

- Farm revenues fluctuate because supply fluctuates.
- The demand for most farm goods is inelastic, so a decrease in supply increases the price and increases farm revenue while an increase in supply decreases the price and decreases farm revenue.
- Stock holders and government agencies act to stabilize farm prices and revenues.

Key Figures

Key Terms

Review Questions

1 Describe what happens to the rent and to the quantity of housing available if a disaster such as a flood suddenly and unexpectedly reduces the supply of housing. Trace the evolution of the rent and the quantity of housing rented over time.

2 In the situation described in Question 1, how will things be different if a rent ceiling is imposed?

3 Describe what happens to the price and quantity in a market in which there is an increase in supply. Trace the evolution of the price and quantity in the market over time.

4 Describe what happens to the price and quantity in a market in which there is an increase in demand. Trace the evolution of the price and quantity in the market over time.

5 Describe what happens to the wage rate and quantity of labour employed when there is an increase in demand for labour. Trace the evolution of the wage rate and employment over time.

6 In the situation described in Question 5, what would happen if a minimum wage was introduced?

7 Why might a minimum wage create unemployment?

8 When government regulation prevents a price from changing, what forces come into operation to achieve an equilibrium?

9 How does the imposition of a sales tax on a good influence the supply of and demand for that good? How does it influence the price of the good and the quantity bought?

10 How does prohibiting the sale of a good affect the demand for and supply of the good? How does it affect the price of the good and the quantity bought?

11 How does prohibiting the consumption of a good affect the demand for and supply of the good? How does it affect the price of the good and the quantity bought?

12 Explain the alternative ways in which the consumption of harmful drugs can be controlled. What are the arguments for and against each method?

13 Why do farm revenues fluctuate?

14 Do farm revenues increase or decrease when there is a bumper crop? Why?

15 Explain why speculation can stabilize the price of a storable commodity, but not the revenues of the producers.

16 How does the European Union support agricultural prices? What is the effect of this type of price support?

Problems

1 You have been given the following information about the market for rented one-bedroom flats in your town:

Rent (pound per month)	Quantity demanded	Quantity supplied
100	20,000	0
150	15,000	5,000
200	10,000	10,000
250	5,000	15,000
300	2,500	20,000
350	1,500	25,000

a What is the equilibrium rent?
b What is the equilibrium quantity of rented housing?

2 Now suppose that a rent ceiling of £150 a month is imposed in the housing market described in Problem 1.

a What is the quantity of housing demanded?
b What is the quantity of housing supplied?
c What is the excess quantity of housing demanded?
d What is the maximum price that demanders will be willing to pay for the last unit available?
e Suppose that the average wage rate is £10 an hour. How many hours a month will a person spend looking for housing?

3 The demand for and supply of teenage labour are as follows:

Wage rate (pounds per hour)	Hours demanded	Hours supplied
2	3,000	1,000
3	2,500	1,500
4	2,000	2,000
5	1,500	2,500
6	1,000	3,000

a What is the equilibrium wage rate?
b What is the level of employment?
c What is the level of unemployment?
d If the government imposes a minimum wage of £3 an hour for teenagers, how many hours do teenagers work?
e If the government imposes a minimum wage of £5 an hour for teenagers, what are the employment and unemployment levels?
f If there is a minimum wage of £5 an hour and demand increases by 500 hours, what is the level of unemployment?

4 The following table illustrates three supply curves for train travel:

Price (pence per passenger mile)	Quantity supplied (billions of passenger miles)		
	Momentary	Short-run	Long-run
10	500	300	100
20	500	350	200
30	500	400	300
40	500	450	400
50	500	500	500
60	500	550	600
70	500	600	700
80	500	650	800
90	500	700	900
100	500	750	1,000

a If the price is 50 pence a passenger mile, what is the quantity supplied in:
   1 The long run?
   2 The short run?
b Suppose that the price is initially 50 pence, but that it then rises to 70 pence. What will be the quantity supplied:
   1 Immediately following the price rise?
   2 In the short run?
   3 In the long run?

5 Suppose that the supply of train travel is the same as in Problem 4. The following table gives two demand schedules – original and new:

Price (pence per passenger mile)	Quantity demanded (billions of passenger miles)	
	Original	New
10	10,000	10,300
20	5,000	5,300
30	2,000	2,300
40	1,000	1,300
50	500	800
60	400	700
70	300	600
80	200	500
90	100	400
100	0	300

a What is the original equilibrium price and quantity?

b After the increase in demand has occurred, what is:

1 The momentary equilibrium price and quantity?

2 The short-run equilibrium price and quantity?

3 The long-run equilibrium price and quantity?

6 The short-run and long-run demand for train travel is as follows:

Price (pence per passenger mile)	Quantity demanded (billions of passenger miles)	
	Short-run	Long-run
10	700	10,000
20	650	5,000
30	600	2,000
40	550	1,000
50	500	500
60	450	400
70	400	300
80	350	200
90	300	100
100	250	0

The supply of train travel is the same as in Problem 4.

a What is the long-run equilibrium price and quantity of train travel?

b Serious floods destroy one-fifth of the trains and train tracks. Supply falls by 100 billion passenger miles. What happens to the price and the quantity of train travel in:

1 The short run?

2 The long run?

7 The following are the demand and supply schedules for chocolate cakes:

Price (pence per cakes)	Quantity demanded (millions per day)	Quantity supplied
90	1	7
80	2	6
70	3	5
60	4	4
50	5	3
40	6	2

a If there is no tax on cakes, what is their price and how many are produced and consumed?

b If a tax of 20 pence a cake is introduced, what happens to the price of a cake and the quantity produced and consumed?

c How much tax does the government collect and who pays it?

8 Calculate the elasticity of demand in Figure 7.10 when the price of wheat is £300 a tonne. Does its magnitude imply that farm revenues fluctuate in the same direction as price fluctuations or in the opposite direction?

9 The demand and supply schedules for coffee are:

Price (£ per pot)	Quantity demanded (pots per hour)	Quantity supplied (pots per hour)
1.50	90	30
1.75	70	40
2.00	50	50
2.25	30	60
2.75	10	70

a If there is no tax on coffee, what is the market price of coffee and quantity consumed?

b If a tax of £0.75 per pot of coffee is introduced, what would be the price of a pot of coffee and how many pots of coffee would be consumed?

c Who would pay the tax?

10 On Turtle Island, the government is considering ways of stabilizing farm prices and farm

revenues. Currently the egg market is competitive, and the demand and supply of eggs are as follows:

Price (pounds per dozen)	Quantity demanded (dozens per week)	Quantity supplied
1.20	3,000	500
1.30	2,750	1,500
1.40	2,500	2,500
1.50	2,250	3,500
1.60	2,000	4,500

a Calculate the competitive equilibrium price and quantity bought and sold.
b The government introduces a floor price of £1.50 a dozen. Calculate the market price, the quantity of eggs bought and sold, and farm revenues. Calculate the surplus of eggs.
c Calculate the amount the government must spend on eggs to maintain the floor price.

11 The demand and supply schedules for rice is:

Price (pounds per box)	Quantity demanded (boxes per week)	Quantity supplied (boxes per week)
1.20	3,000	500
1.30	2,750	1,500
1.40	2,500	2,500
1.50	2,250	3,500
1.60	2,000	4,500

A storm destroys part of the crop and decreases supply by 500 boxes a week.

a What do holders of rice stocks do?
b What is the market price and farm revenue after the now?

12 Suppose that in Problem 11, instead of a storm, perfect weather increases supply by 500 boxes a week.

a What do holders of rice stocks do?
b What is market price and farm revenue now?

13 Read the article in *Reading Between the Lines* on pp. 164–165 again and then answer the following questions:

a What is the opportunity cost of the European Single Market to the United Kingdom in terms of tax revenue?
b What other policies could the United Kingdom adopt to reduce smuggling?

14 Use the links on the Parkin, Powell and Matthews Web site to obtain information about cigarette tax rates, tax revenues, purchases, population and incomes. Then answer the following questions about the relationship between the number of packs of cigarettes purchased and the price of a pack of cigarettes.

a How would you describe the relationship?
b What does the relationship tell you about the demand for cigarettes?
c What does the relationship tell you about the amount of cigarette smuggling?

W http://www.econ100.com

A Taxing Problem

The Guardian, 8 December 1998

Bootleg is booming

Dan Atkinson

Down in the Channel ports, just about every third person is either a Customs officer, a policeman, a Benefits Agency investigator or a member of the overloaded-van hit-squad. Christmas is coming and this is the front line of Operation Mistletoe, the latest round in a centuries-old cat and mouse game between smugglers and Crown officers.

The driving force behind the current tidal wave of smuggling against which Operation Mistletoe is battling is a free-trade agreement, the Single European Act of 1986.

Members of the free-market Adam Smith Institute, believe smuggling to be "the crime that nature never meant to be so"**(1)**. Chancellor Gordon Brown, regards smuggling as primarily an enforcement problem and would be more likely to announce a 100 per cent penal tax on high earners than he would be to slash alcohol and tobacco duties to something approaching French and Belgian levels.

Smuggling is a venerable British tradition, with the combination of a very long coastline and a cultural propensity to regard foreign produce as desirable luxury goods adding up to an on-again off-again battle of wits between the smugglers and the "preventive men" of the Customs & Excise. Whatever the state has sought to nail down and tax, the smuggler has cheerfully brought in at dead of night, whether cognac in the 18th Century or Swiss watches in the 1950s.

The Single act came into force on January 1 1993, since when British consumers could shop, duty paid, to their heart's content south of the Channel, provided the goods bought were for their own consumption. Given the wide disparities in duty in Britain compared to the Continent – French beer duty, for example, is one-sixth the British level – it did not take a BSc in economics to predict what would happen. Pouring through the yawning gap between British and Continental duties came millions of litres of beer and wine and

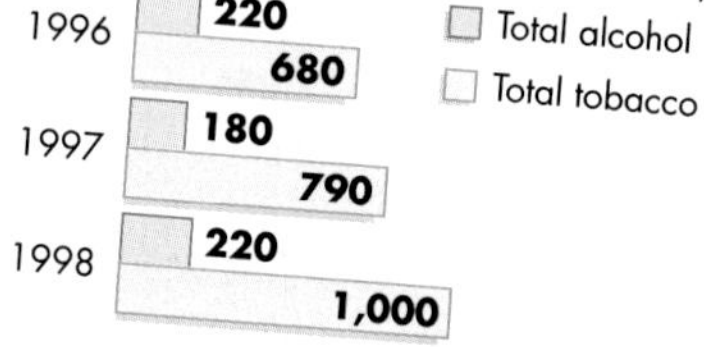

hundreds of tonnes of tobacco. To take one example, three quarters of all hand-rolled cigarettes smoked in Britain are imported across the Channel, legitim- ately and (mostly) illegitimately. Drum, Britain's third-favourite handrolling brand, is not officially on sale in this country.

Five years into the single market, the bootlegging figures are spectacular. Bootleg beer accounts for about 5 per cent of all British sales, and 13 per cent of beer brewed in France is destined for British consumption**(2)**. One million smokers routinely buy their smokes on the black market, with three out of four handrolled cigarettes originating across the Channel.

But if there is some compensation for domestic drink and tobacco manufacturers, there is none for the two biggest losers: the legitimate domestic trade (pubs, tobacconists and offlicences) and the Treasury, thought to be down by between £800 million and £1 billion in lost revenues. By the time Labour took power in May 1997, there was ill-concealed panic in Whitehall at the prospect of virtually uncontrollable bootlegging. Mr Brown promptly set up a review into the problem, the conclusion of which, unsurprisingly, was that tougher enforcement rather than lower duties would stem the flood of smuggled goods. Cranking up the enforcement machine since the March Budget led to Mistletoe, launched in October and now reaching peak activity as Christmas approaches.

Sources: (1) Adam Smith, The Wealth of Nations, 1776.
(2) Campaign for Real Ale, March 18 1998.

The Essence of the Story

- The UK government has introduced a new crackdown on smuggling to stop the growing trade in bootleg alcohol and tobacco.
- Bootleg traffic in alcohol and tobacco has grown because the tax levels in the United Kingdom are higher than in other countries, and the Single European Market now allows virtually unlimited imports of duty paid goods from other countries if these goods are for personal consumption.
- More people are buying their cigarettes and alcohol legally in France as the total price (supply price plus tax plus travel cost) is less than the cost of the equivalent goods in the United Kingdom.
- More people are also buying cigarettes and alcohol illegally in France for resale in the United Kingdom.
- The UK government estimates that between £800 million and £1 billion of revenue is lost each year as a result of the growing legal and bootleg trade in alcohol and tobacco abroad.

Economic Analysis

■ Figure 1 shows the UK demand and supply for cigarettes before the Single Market in 1993. High UK tax levels raise the price of cigarettes by £2.50 a packet and the quantity sold is 2 billion packets. The UK government gains tax revenue from cigarettes of £5 billion as shown by the blue area in Figure 1 (£2.50 times 2 billion packets).

■ Before 1993, UK smokers had to pay UK duty levels on any cigarettes brought into the country above the small duty-free allowance. The European Single Market has opened up free trade between member countries so that UK smokers can now import cheaper cigarettes bought in France without paying extra duty, providing they are for personal consumption.

■ Figure 2 shows UK smokers' demand for cigarettes in France, *D*, and the supply curve shows the fixed price that UK travellers face for cigarettes sold in France, S_F. French cigarette tax raises prices by just 50 pence per packet, but the real cost to UK smokers also includes the cost of travel to France, which adds another 20 pence to the price. Given the exchange rate, Figure 2 shows that the total cost of a packet of cigarettes in France to UK smokers is just £2.20 and that they buy 0.4 billion packets each year.

■ The price difference of at least 80 pence a packet is sufficient to make some UK smokers travel to France to buy cigarettes, but also for smugglers to buy cigarettes illegally in France to bring home to resell in the United Kingdom.

■ The change in duty-paid rules allowed UK smokers to buy cheaper substitutes for UK cigarettes, making the demand for UK cigarettes more elastic after 1993. Figure 3 shows the demand curve D_{UK} (1998) is shallower than the demand curve D_{UK}(1993). UK sales fell by 400 million packets and the UK government has lost £1 billion of revenue from cigarette tax, as revenue has decreased from £5 billion to £4 billion.

■ Tougher enforcement by Customs and Excise will help to cut revenue loss from smuggling by £80 million but the cost of 'Operation Mistletoe' will be £35 million.

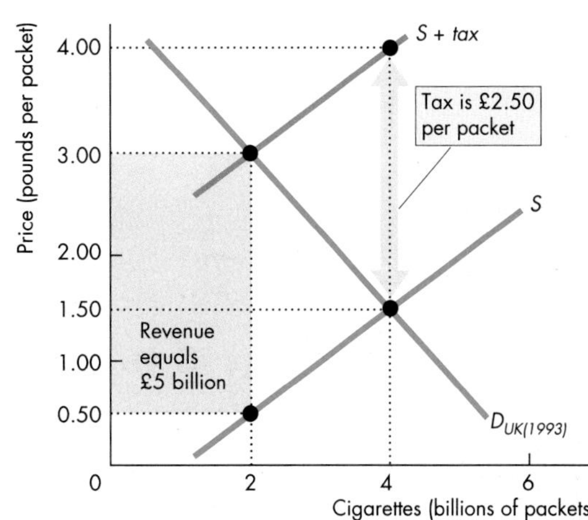

Figure 1 UK cigarette market in 1993

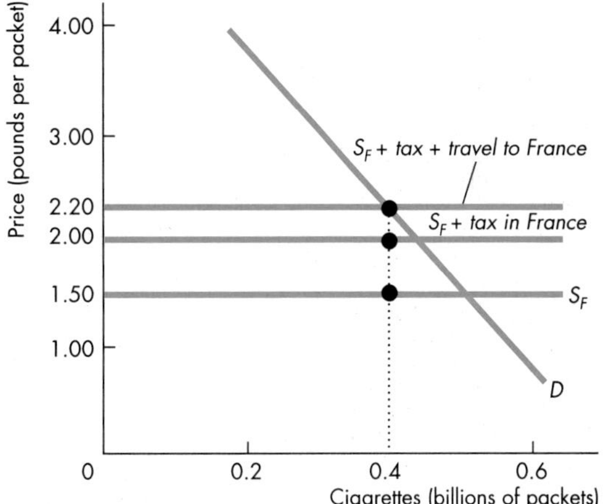

Figure 2 UK buyers in France

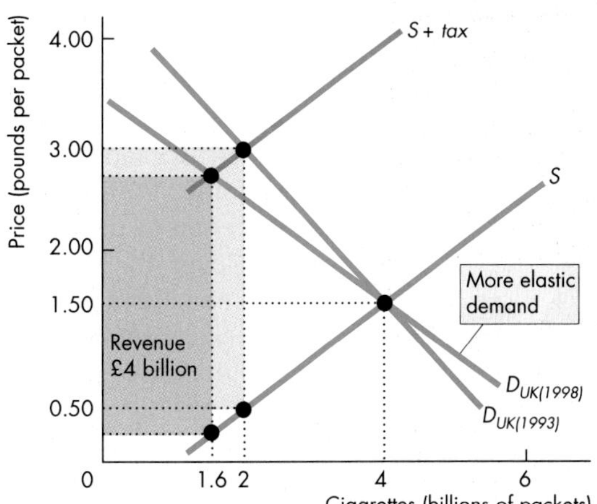

Figure 3 UK cigarette market in 1998

Part 3

How Markets Work

Talking with **Sheila Dow**

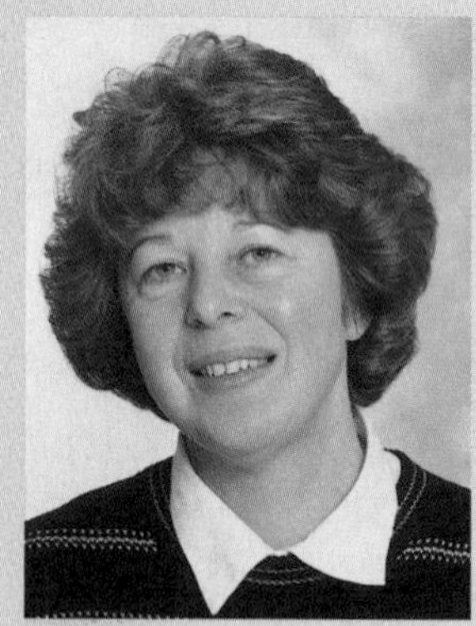

Sheila Dow holds a Personal Chair in Economics at the University of Stirling, where she has taught since 1979. She previously worked as an economist for the Bank of England and for the Government of Manitoba, Canada, and has had visiting posts with the Universities of Cambridge and Toronto. Her research interests lie in money and banking theory, methodology, history of thought, regional finance and post-Keynesian economics.

Why did you specialize in economics?

Mainly because I found economics interesting. It appealed to me to try to understand how economic systems work, at different times in history and in different types of economies. And it is interesting to try to understand why particular theories emerge and others disappear. It will reveal how long ago I started to learn economics when I say that I found it a nice contrast to my other subject, pure mathematics.

I then worked for several years as a non-academic economist in the public sector. It became obvious that there are many important policy areas to which economists can make important contributions, like the design of the international financial system, or innovations in taxation. Regardless of how economists approach issues, they can contribute important insights which make policy-making more effective. It is amazing how much mileage can be made with basic concepts.

One such concept is opportunity cost, which is useful for government departments, for example, in allocating their budgets between alternative expenditures. But the concept is subject to limitations. Where there are unemployed resources, increasing one economic activity does not necessarily mean having to reduce another. The margin is another useful concept, which allows important distinctions to be drawn, such as between marginal and average tax rates. The concept is a central one for mainstream economic theory, but has limitations in its applicability to policy questions. Changes in a firm's capital stock, for example, are generally discrete (irreversible) shifts from a limited range of possibilities, rather than marginal (reversible) movements along a continuous, infinite array of possibilities.

What are the main principles which distinguish different perspectives on the role of markets and how they work?

In mainstream economics, markets are the centrepiece of economic analysis. They are the vehicle through which individual preferences are satisfied, given factor endowments and technology. In the process they allocate resources and determine the distribution of income. The participants in markets are isolated, rational individuals. The benchmark of analysis is the position of equilibrium in which markets clear. The norm is to assume perfect competition, but there is an expanding area of work in which the implications of imperfect competition are explored.

Other (neo-Austrian) economists share the focus on market activity, but analyse markets as a process, where flux rather than equilibrium is the norm. Others, such as post-Keynesian and Institutionalist economists, prefer to put the emphasis more on production and distribution than exchange, and to see markets in terms of social interaction rather than isolated individuals, with imperfectly competitive markets the norm. One consequence is that supply and demand are seen as interdependent, with production conditions influencing marketing effort and thereby demand, for example. The emphasis then is put more on how supply and demand conditions evolve over time, as a process, rather than on equilibrium outcomes of market clearing.

Within each of these approaches there are different views as to how far markets are socially beneficial, and therefore whether government intervention is required. But as a generalization, it is probably more common for mainstream and neo-Austrian economists to support *laissez-faire* policies, and for post-Keynesian and Institutionalist economists to support intervention.

Are there any basic principles on which most economists agree?

This is a hard question. Whenever I think of a possible shared principle I immediately picture some particular economist raising objections. What precludes shared principles is the absence of a shared theoretical framework.

This is not something to regret; it is inevitable when abstracting from a complex reality that some will choose one form of abstraction and some another. I don't mean just that different economists make different assumptions, but that different groups of economists use terms and concepts quite differently, so that a principle expressed by one economist might convey something quite different to another economist. 'Equilibrium', for example, means something quite different in a model where everything happens at once, compared with a model analysing a process which occurs over time, and which cannot be reversed.

What is the link between microeconomics and macroeconomics?

The link is an obvious one, that the macroeconomy is made up of individual markets, firms and households. There has been an increasing tendency to make sure that theory encapsulates that link by requiring that macroeconomics be built on explicit micro foundations. But economic systems are extraordinarily complex. There is therefore a trade-off between choosing to separate macroeconomics and microeconomics, and accepting the limitations of a theory which extends from assumptions about individuals to the economy as a whole. The main problem to grapple with is that, traditionally, microeconomics dealt with market clearing whereas macroeconomics dealt with markets (particularly the labour market) not clearing. The link is much easier for those whose microeconomics does not require market clearing.

Are there any lessons from the history and development of Western European economies from which Eastern Europe can learn?

The main lesson is that, whether or not market processes are preferable to state planning, institutions and conventions are the glue which holds market economies together in an uncertain world. These are not easy to generate quickly. Nor are there universal truths about which institutions and which conventions will work; so much depends on the economy's prior history.

What do you think are the most important economic problems facing the world today?

The most important problems are undoubtedly distributional, from the problems of the impoverished, unemployed underclass in Western economies to the plight of persistent low-income countries.

Utility and Demand

After studying this chapter you will be able to:

- Explain the connection between individual demand and market demand
- Define total utility and marginal utility
- Explain the marginal utility theory of consumer choice
- Use the marginal utility theory to predict the effects of changing prices and incomes
- Explain the paradox of value

Water, Water, Everywhere

We need water to live, but we use diamonds mainly for decoration. If the benefits of water far outweigh the benefits of diamonds, why, then, does water cost practically nothing while diamonds are very expensive? ◆ When OPEC restricted its sale of oil in 1973, it created a dramatic rise in price, but people continued to use almost as much oil as they had before. Our demand for oil was price inelastic. But why? ◆ When the CD player was introduced in 1983, it was sold at a relatively high price and consumers didn't buy many. Since then the price has decreased dramatically, and many households have bought one. Our demand for CD players is price elastic. What makes the demand for some things price elastic while the demand for others is price inelastic? ◆ Over the past 40 years, the real value of incomes in the UK has risen. Over the same period, expenditure on cars has increased from less than 1 per cent of total spending to 15 per cent, while expenditure on food has fallen from 25 per cent of total expenditure to just 14 per cent today. Thus the proportion of income spent on cars has increased and the proportion spent on food has decreased. Why, as incomes rise, does the proportion of income spent on some goods rise and on others fall?

◆ ◆ ◆ ◆ In the last three chapters, we've seen that demand in any market has an important effect on the price of a good. But what shapes market demand? This chapter examines market demand by looking at individual behaviour and its influence on demand. It explains why demand is elastic for some goods and inelastic for others. It also explains why the prices of some things, such as diamonds and water, are so out of proportion to their total benefits.

Individual Demand and Market Demand

The relationship between the total quantity demanded in a market and the price of a good is called **market demand**. And the relationship between the quantity demanded of a good by an individual and its price is called **individual demand**. The market demand is simply the sum of all the individual demands.

The table in Figure 8.1 illustrates the relationship between individual demand and market demand. In this example we will assume that Lisa and John are the only people. The market demand is the total demand of Lisa and John. At £3 a cinema ticket, Lisa demands 5 films a month and John demands 2 films, so that the total quantity demanded in the market is 7 films a month. Figure 8.1 illustrates the relationship between individual and market demand curves. Lisa's and John's demand curves for films, shown in parts (a) and (b), sum *horizontally* to give the market demand curve in part (c).

> The market demand curve is the horizontal sum of the individual demand curves formed by adding the quantities demanded by each individual at each price.

We're going to investigate what shapes market demand by looking at what shapes individual demand. We will do this by studying how an individual makes consumption choices.

Individual Consumption Choices

An individual's consumption choices are determined by many factors, and we can model the impact of these factors using two new concepts:

Figure 8.1 Individual Demand and Market Demand Curves

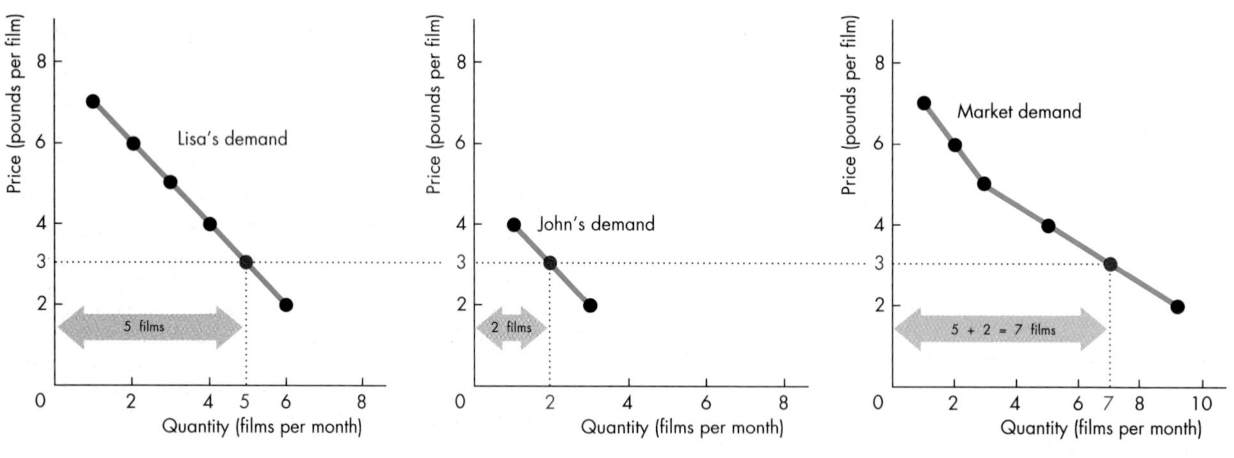

(a) Lisa's demand **(b) John's demand** **(c) Market demand**

Price of a cinema ticket (pounds)	Quantity of films demanded		
	Lisa	John	Market
7	1	0	1
6	2	0	2
5	3	0	3
4	4	1	5
3	5	2	7
2	6	3	9

The table and the figure illustrate how the quantity of films demanded varies as the price of a cinema ticket varies. In the table, the market demand in the final column is the sum of the individual demands. For example, at a price of £3, Lisa demands 5 films and John demands 2 films, so the total quantity demanded in the market is 7 films per month. In the figure, the market demand curve is the horizontal sum of the individual demand curves. Thus when the price is £3, the market demand curve shows the quantity demanded as the sum of Lisa and John's demands – 7 films.

1 Budget line.
2 Preferences.

Budget Line

In this model of individual consumption, choices are constrained by income and by the prices of goods and services. We will assume that each individual has a given amount of income to spend, that everyone consumes all the goods they purchase within the relevant time period, and that individuals cannot influence the prices of the goods and services they buy.

The limits to individual consumption choices are described by a *budget line*. To make the concept of the individual's budget line as clear as possible, we'll consider a simplified example of one individual – Lisa – and her choice. Lisa has an income of £30 a month to spend. She spends her income on two goods – cinema films and cola. Cinema tickets cost £6 each; cola costs £3 for a six-pack. If Lisa spends all of her income, she will reach the limits to her consumption of films and cola.

In Figure 8.2, each row of the table shows affordable ways for Lisa to see cinema films and buy cola packs. Row *a* indicates that she can buy 10 six-packs of cola and see no films. You can see that this combination exhausts her monthly income of £30. Row *f* says that Lisa can see 5 films and drink no cola – another combination that exhausts the £30 available. Each of the other rows in the table also exhausts Lisa's income. (Check that each of the other rows costs exactly £30.) The numbers in the table define Lisa's maximum consumption possibilities of films and cola. These consumption possibilities are graphed as points *a* to *f* in Figure 8.2.

Lisa's budget line is a constraint on her choices. It marks the boundary between what is affordable and what is unaffordable. She can afford all the points on the line and inside it. She cannot afford points outside the line. The constraint on her consumption depends on prices and on her income, and the constraint changes when prices and her income change.

Figure 8.2 Consumption Possibilities

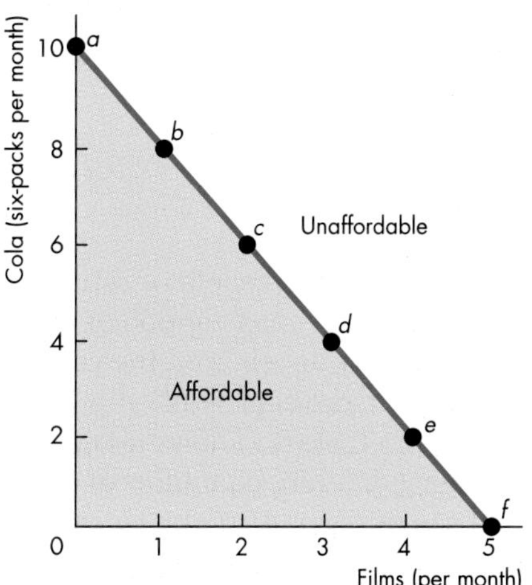

Possibility	Films		Cola	
	Quantity	Expenditure (pounds)	Quantity (six-packs)	Expenditure (pounds)
a	0	0	10	30
b	1	6	8	24
c	2	12	6	18
d	3	18	4	12
e	4	24	2	6
f	5	30	0	0

Six possible ways of allocating £30 to films and cola are shown as the rows *a* to *f* in the table. For example, Lisa can see 2 cinema films and buy 6 six-packs (row *c*). Each row shows the combinations of film and cola that cost £30. These possibilities are points *a* to *f* in the figure. The line through those points is a boundary between what Lisa can afford and cannot afford. Her choices must lie inside the orange area or along the line *af*.

Preferences and Utility

How does Lisa divide her £30 between these two goods? The answer depends on her likes and dislikes – or her **preferences**. Economists use the concept of utility to describe preferences. The benefit or satisfaction that a person gets from the consumption of a good or service is called **utility**. But what exactly is utility and in what units can we measure it? Utility is an abstract concept and its units are arbitrary. The concept of utility helps us make predictions about consumption choices in much the same way that the concept of temperature helps us make predictions about physical phenomena. It has to be admitted, though, that the marginal utility theory is not as precise as the theory that enables us to predict when water will turn to ice or steam.

Let's now see how we can use the concept of utility to describe preferences.

Total Utility

Total utility is the total benefit or satisfaction that a person gets from the consumption of goods and services. Total utility depends on the person's level of consumption – more consumption generally gives more total utility. Table 8.1 shows Lisa's total utility from consuming different quantities of cinema films and cola. If she does not go to the cinema, she gets no utility from seeing films. If she goes once a month, she gets 50 units of utility. As the number of visits in a month increases, her total utility increases so that if she sees 10 films a month, she gets 250 units of total utility. The other part of the table shows Lisa's total utility from cola. If she drinks no cola, she gets no utility from cola.

Table 8.1 Lisa's Total Utility from Films and Cola

Films		Cola	
Quantity per month	Total utility	Quantity (six-packs per month)	Total utility
0	0	0	0
1	50	1	75
2	88	2	117
3	121	3	153
4	150	4	181
5	175	5	206
6	196	6	225
7	214	7	243
8	229	8	260
9	241	9	276
10	250	10	291
11	256	11	305
12	259	12	318
13	261	13	330
14	262	14	341

As the amount of cola she drinks rises, her total utility increases.

Marginal Utility

Marginal utility is the change in total utility resulting from a one-unit increase in the quantity of a good consumed. The table in Figure 8.3 shows the calculation of Lisa's marginal utility from seeing films. When her consumption of films increases from 4 to 5 a month, her total utility from films increases from 150 units to 175 units. Thus for Lisa, the marginal utility of seeing a fifth film each month is 25 units. Notice that marginal utility appears midway between the quantities of consumption. It does so because it is the *change* in consumption from 4 to 5 films that produces the marginal utility of 25 units. The table displays calculations of marginal utility for each level of film consumption.

Figure 8.3(a) illustrates the total utility that Lisa gets from seeing films. As you can see, the more films Lisa sees in a month, the more total utility she gets. Part (b) illustrates her marginal utility. This graph tells us that as Lisa sees more films, the marginal utility that Lisa gets from seeing films decreases. For example, her marginal utility from the first film is 50 units, from the second 38 units, and from the third 33 units. We call this decrease in marginal utility as the consumption of a good increases the principle of **diminishing marginal utility**.

Marginal utility is positive but diminishes as the consumption of a good increases. Why does marginal utility have these two features? In Lisa's case, she likes films, and the more she sees the better. That's why marginal utility is positive. The benefit that Lisa gets from the last film seen is its marginal utility. To see why marginal utility diminishes, think about how you'd feel in the following two situations. In one, you've just been studying for 15 evenings in a row. An opportunity arises to see a new film. The utility you get from that film is the marginal utility from seeing one film in a month. In the second situation, you've been on a cinema binge. For the past 15 nights, you have not even seen an assignment or test. You are up to your eyeballs in films. You are happy enough to go to a film on yet one more night. But the thrill that you get out of that sixteenth film in 16 days is not very large. It is the marginal utility of the sixteenth film in a month.

Figure 8.3 Total Utility and Marginal Utility

Quantity	Total utility	Marginal utility
0	0	50
1	50	38
2	88	33
3	121	29
4	150	25
5	175	

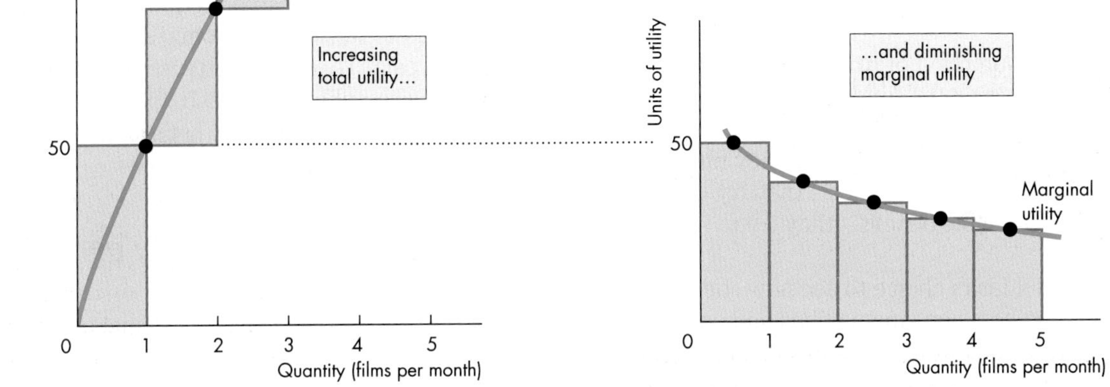

(a) Total utility

(b) Marginal utility

The table shows that as Lisa's consumption of films increases, so does the total utility she derives from films. The table also shows her marginal utility – the change in utility resulting from the last film seen. Marginal utility declines as consumption increases. The figure graphs Lisa's total utility and marginal utility from films. Part (a) shows her total utility. It also shows the extra utility she gains from each additional film – her marginal utility. Part (b) shows how Lisa's marginal utility from films diminishes by placing the bars shown in part (a) side by side as a series of declining steps.

Review

- Consumption possibilities are limited by the consumer's income and the prices of goods.
- Consumers' preferences can be described by using the concept of utility.
- Marginal utility theory assumes that as more of a good consumed, the total utility from consuming that good increases, but the marginal utility of it decreases.

Maximizing Utility

Individual income and prices limit the utility an individual can obtain from consumption. The key assumption of marginal utility theory is that, taking into consideration the income available for spending and the prices people face, individuals consume the quantities of goods and services that maximize total

Table 8.2 Lisa's Utility-maximizing Combinations of Films and Cola

Films		Total utility from films and cola	Cola	
Quantity	Total utility		Total utility	Quantity
0	0	291	291	10
1	50	310	260	8
2	88	313	225	6
3	121	302	181	4
4	150	267	117	2
5	175	175	0	0

utility. The assumption of **utility maximization** is a way of expressing the fundamental economic problem. People's wants exceed the resources available to satisfy these wants, so they must make hard choices. In making choices, they try to get the maximum attainable benefit – they try to maximize total utility.

Let's model Lisa's choice to see how she allocates her spending between cinema films and cola to maximize her total utility. Lisa makes her choice knowing cinema tickets cost £6 each, cola costs £3 a six-pack, and she has £30 a month to spend.

The Utility-maximizing Choice

The most direct way of calculating how Lisa spends her money if she maximizes her total utility is by making a table like the one shown in Table 8.2. This table shows the same affordable combinations of films and cola that you can find on her budget line in Figure 8.2. The table records three things: first, the number of cinema films seen and the total utility derived from them (the left side of the table); second, the number of six-packs of cola consumed and the total utility derived from them (the right side of the table); and third, the total utility derived from both films and cola (the centre column of the table).

The first row of Table 8.2 records the situation if Lisa does not go to the cinema but buys 10 six-packs. In this case, she gets no utility from films and 291 units of total utility from cola. Her total utility from films and cola (the centre column) is 291 units. The rest of the table is constructed in the same way.

The consumption of films and cola that maximizes Lisa's total utility is highlighted in the table. When Lisa consumes 2 films and 6 six-packs of cola, she gets 313 units of total utility. This is the best Lisa can do given that she has only £30 to spend and given the prices of cinema tickets and six-packs. If she buys 8 six-packs of cola, she can see only 1 film and gets 310 units of total utility, 3 fewer than the maximum attainable. If she sees 3 films and drinks only 4 six-packs, she gets 302 units of total utility, 11 fewer than the maximum attainable.

We've just described a consumer equilibrium. A **consumer equilibrium** is a situation in which a consumer has allocated his or her income in the way that maximizes total utility.

In finding Lisa's consumer equilibrium, we measured her *total* utility from the consumption of films and cola. There is a better way of determining a consumer equilibrium, which does not involve measuring total utility at all. Let's look at this alternative.

Equalizing Marginal Utility per Pound Spent

Another way to find out the allocation that maximizes a consumer's total utility is to make the marginal utility per pound spent on each good equal for all goods. The marginal utility per pound spent is the marginal utility obtained from the last unit of a good consumed divided by the price of the good. For example, Lisa's marginal utility from consuming the first film is 50 units of utility. The price of a cinema ticket is £6, which means that the marginal utility per pound spent on films is 50 units divided by £6, or 8.33 units of utility per pound.

Total utility is maximized when all the consumer's income is spent and when the marginal utility per dollar spent is equal for all goods.

Lisa maximizes total utility when she spends all her income and consumes films and cola such that

$$\frac{\text{Marginal utility of seeing a film}}{\text{Price of a cinema ticket}} = \frac{\text{Marginal utility of a six-pack of cola}}{\text{Price of a six-pack of cola}}$$

Call the marginal utility from films MU_f, the marginal utility from cola MU_c, the price of a

Table 8.3 Maximizing Utility by Equalizing Marginal Utilities per Pound Spent

	Films (£6 per ticket)			Cola (£3 per six-pack)		
	Quantity	Marginal utility per pound spent	Marginal utility	Quantity (six-packs)	Marginal utility	Marginal utility per pound spent
a	0	0		10	15	5.00
b	1	50	8.33	8	17	5.67
c	2	38	6.33	6	19	6.33
d	3	33	5.50	4	28	9.33
e	4	29	4.83	2	42	14.00
f	5	25	4.17	0	0	

cinema ticket P_f, and the price of cola P_c. Then Lisa's utility is maximized when she spends all her income and when

$$\frac{MU_f}{P_f} = \frac{MU_c}{P_c}$$

Let's use this formula to find Lisa's utility-maximizing allocation of her income.

Table 8.3 sets out Lisa's marginal utilities per pound spent for both films and cola. For example, in row *b* Lisa's marginal utility from films is 50 units and, since cinema tickets cost £6 each, her marginal utility per pound spent on films is 8.33 units per pound (50 units divided by £6). Each row contains an allocation of Lisa's income that uses up her £30. You can see that Lisa's marginal utility per pound spent on each good, like marginal utility itself, decreases as consumption of the good increases.

Total utility is maximized when the marginal utility per pound spent on films is equal to the marginal utility per pound spent on cola, possibility *c*, where Lisa consumes 2 films and 6 six-packs – the same allocation as we calculated in Table 8.2.

Figure 8.4 shows why the rule 'equalize marginal utility per pound spent on all goods' works. Suppose that instead of consuming 2 films and 6 six-packs (possibility *c*), Lisa consumes 1 film and 8 six-packs (possibility *b*). She then gets 8.33 units of utility from the last pound spent on films and 5.67 units from the last pound spent on cola. In this situation

Figure 8.4 Equalizing Marginal Utility per Pound Spent

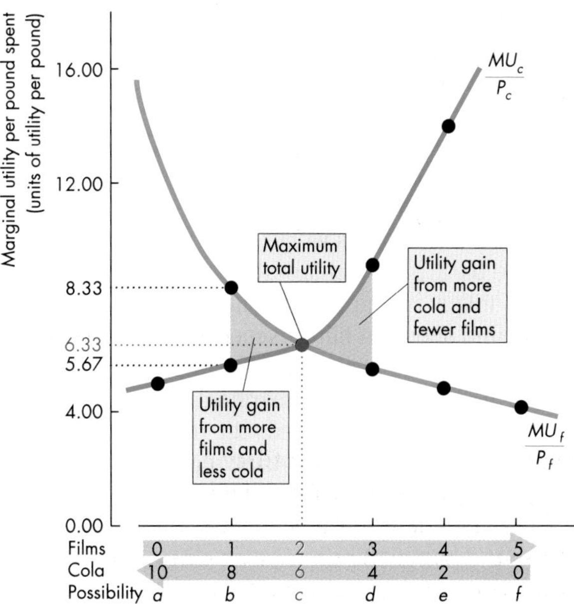

If Lisa consumes 1 cinema film and 8 six-packs of cola (possibility *b*) she gets 8.33 units of utility from the last pound spent on films and 5.67 units of utility from the last pound spent on cola. She can get more total utility if she sees one more film. If she consumes 4 six-packs and sees 3 films (possibility *d*) she gets 5.50 units of utility from the last pound spent on films and 9.33 units of utility from the last dollar spent on cola. She can get more total utility by seeing one film fewer. When Lisa's marginal utility per pound spent on both goods is equal, her total utility is maximized.

Lisa can increase her total utility by spending less on cola and more on films. If she spends a pound less on cola and a pound more on films, her total utility from cola decreases by 5.67 units and her total utility from films increases by 8.33 units. Lisa's total utility increases by 2.66 units (a gain of 8.33 minus a loss of 5.67) if she spends less on cola and more on films.

Or, suppose that Lisa consumes 3 films and 4 six-packs (possibility *d*). In this situation, her marginal utility from the last pound spent on films is less than her marginal utility from the last pound spent on cola. Lisa can now increase her total utility by spending less on films and more on cola.

The Power of Marginal Analysis The method we've just used to maximize Lisa's utility is an example of the power of *marginal analysis*. By comparing the marginal gain from having more of one good with the marginal loss from having less of another good, Lisa is able to ensure that she gets the maximum attainable utility.

In the example, Lisa consumes at the point at which the marginal utility per pound spent on films and cola are equal. Because we buy goods and services in indivisible lumps, the numbers don't always work out so precisely. But the basic approach always applies. The rule to follow is simple: if the marginal utility per pound spent on films exceeds the marginal utility per pound spent on cola, see more films and drink less cola; if the marginal utility per pound spent on cola exceeds the marginal utility per pound spent on films, drink more cola and see fewer films.

More generally, our model of behaviour says that if the marginal gain from an action exceeds the marginal loss, take the action. You will meet this principle time and again in your study of economics. And you will find yourself applying this model every time you make your own economic choices. You will find an example of how marginal analysis can be used to explain one particular consumers' choice between Dr Pepper and Coca-cola in *Reading Between the Lines* on pp. 186–187.

Units of Utility In calculating the utility-maximizing allocation of income in Table 8.3 and Figure 8.4 we have not used the concept of total utility at all. All the calculations have used marginal utility and price. By making the marginal utility per pound spent equal for both goods, we know that Lisa has maximized her total utility.

This way of viewing maximum utility is important; it means that the units in which utility is measured do not matter. We could double or halve all the numbers measuring utility, or multiply or divide them by any other positive number. None of these transformations of the units used to measure utility makes any difference to the outcome. It is in this respect that utility is analogous to temperature. Our prediction about the freezing of water depends on the model or concept of temperature, not on the temperature scale; our prediction about maximizing utility depends on our model of choice, not on the units of utility.

Review

- Consumers make consumption choices that maximize total utility.
- Consumers maximize total utility by spending all their available income and by making the marginal utility per pound spent on each good equal.
- When marginal utilities per pound spent are equal for all goods, a consumer cannot reallocate spending to get more total utility.

Predictions of Marginal Utility Theory

Let's now use marginal utility theory and our model of choice to make some predictions. What happens to Lisa's consumption of films and cola when their prices change and when her income changes?

A Fall in the Price of Cinema Tickets

To determine the effect of a change in price on consumption requires three steps. First, determine the combinations of films and cola that can be bought at the new prices. Second, calculate the new marginal utilities per pound spent. Third, determine the consumption of each good that makes the marginal utility per pound spent on each good equal and that just exhausts the money available for spending.

Table 8.4 shows the combinations of films and cola that exactly exhaust Lisa's £30 of income when cinema tickets cost £3 each and cola costs £3 a six-pack. Her preferences do not change when prices change, so her marginal utility schedule remains the same as that in Table 8.3. But now we divide her marginal utility from films by £3, the new price of a cinema ticket, to get the marginal utility per pound spent on films.

What is the effect of the fall in the price of a cinema ticket on Lisa's consumption? You can find the answer by comparing her new utility-maximizing allocation (Table 8.4) with her original allocation (Table 8.3). Lisa responds to a fall in the price of a cinema ticket by seeing more films (up from 2 to 5 a month) and drinking less cola

Table 8.4 How a Change in Price of Films Affects Lisa's Choices

Films (£3 per ticket)		Cola (£3 per six-pack)	
Quantity	Marginal utility per pound spent	Quantity (six-packs)	Marginal utility per pound spent
0		10	5.00
1	16.67	9	5.33
2	12.67	8	5.67
3	11.00	7	6.00
4	9.67	6	6.33
5	8.33	5	8.33
6	8.00	4	9.33
7	6.00	3	12.00
8	5.00	2	14.00
9	4.00	1	25.00
10	3.00	0	

(down from 6 to 5 six-packs a month). That is, Lisa substitutes films for cola when the price of a cinema ticket falls. Figure 8.5 illustrates these effects. In part (a) a fall in the price of cinema tickets produces a movement along Lisa's demand curve for films and in part (b) it shifts her demand curve for cola.

A Rise in the Price of Cola

Table 8.5 shows the combinations of films and cola that exactly exhaust Lisa's £30 of income when cinema tickets cost £3 each and cola costs £6 a six-pack. Now we divide her marginal utility from cola by £6, the new price of a six-pack, to get the marginal utility per pound spent on cola.

The effect of the rise in the price of cola on Lisa's consumption is seen by comparing her new utility-maximizing allocation (Table 8.5) with her previous allocation (Table 8.4). Lisa responds to a rise in the price of cola by drinking less cola (down from 5 to 2 six-packs a month) and seeing more films (up from 5 to 6 a month). That is, Lisa substitutes films for cola when the price of cola rises. Figure 8.6 illustrates these effects. In part (a) a rise in the price of cola produces a movement along Lisa's demand curve for cola and in part (b) it shifts her demand curve for films.

Figure 8.5 A Fall in the Price of Cinema Tickets

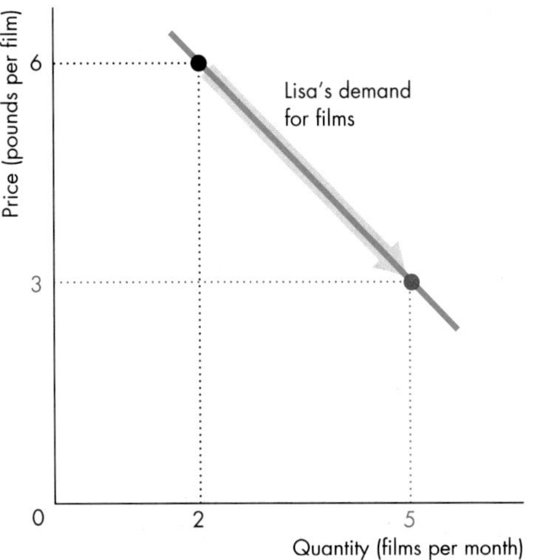

(a) Films

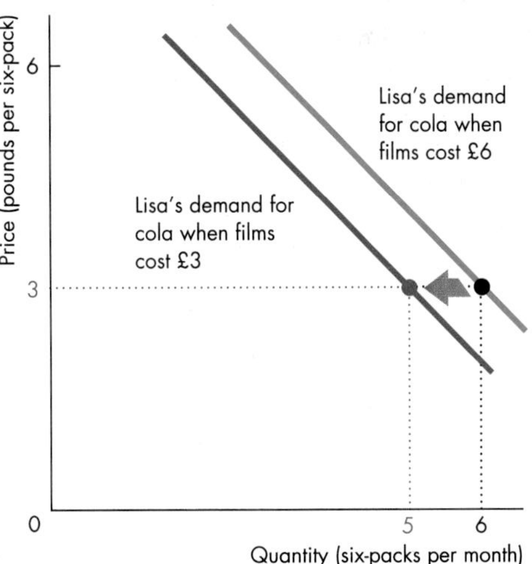

(b) Cola

When the price of cinema tickets falls and the price of cola remains constant, the quantity of films demanded by Lisa increases and in part (a), Lisa moves along her demand curve for films. Also, Lisa's demand for cola decreases and in part (b), her demand curve for cola shifts leftward.

Table 8.5 How a Change in the Price of Cola Affects Lisa's Choices

Films (£3 per ticket)		Cola (£6 per six-pack)	
Quantity	Marginal utility per pound spent	Quantity (six-packs)	Marginal utility per pound spent
0		5	4.17
2	12.67	4	4.67
4	9.67	3	6.00
6	8.00	2	8.00
8	5.00	1	12.50
10	3.00	0	

Marginal utility theory predicts these two results: when the price of a good rises, the quantity demanded of that good decreases; if the price of one good rises, the demand for another good that can serve as a substitute increases. Does this sound familiar? It should. These predictions of marginal utility theory correspond to the assumptions that we made about consumer demand in Chapter 4. There we *assumed* that the demand curve for a good sloped downward, and we *assumed* that a rise in the price of a substitute increased demand.

We have now seen that marginal utility theory predicts how the quantities of goods and services that people demand respond to price changes. The theory helps us to understand both the shape and the position of the demand curve. It also helps us to understand how the demand curve for one good shifts when the price of another good changes. Marginal utility theory also helps us to understand one further thing about demand – how it changes when income changes.

Let's study the effects of a change in income on consumption.

A Rise in Income

Let's suppose that Lisa's income increases to £42 a month and that cinema tickets cost £3 each and a six-pack costs £3 (as in Table 8.4). In Table 8.4,

Figure 8.6 A Rise in the Price of Cola

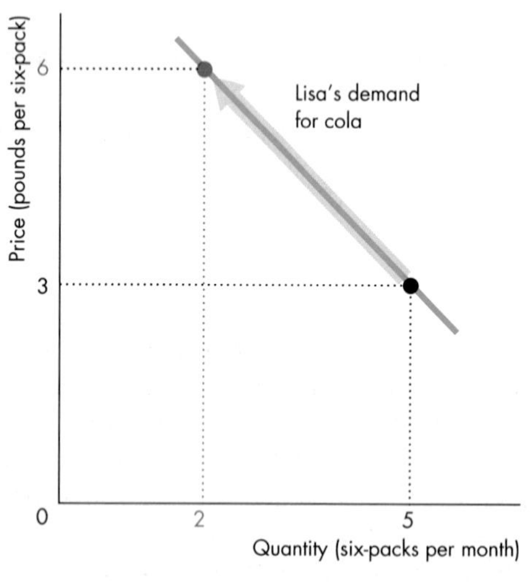

(a) Cola

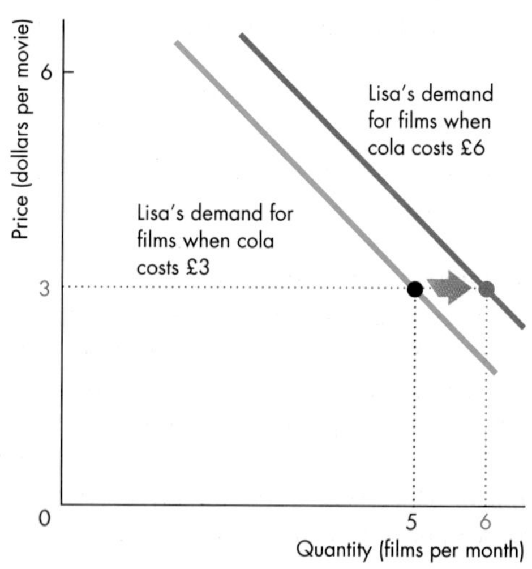

(b) Films

When the price of cola rises and the price of cinema tickets remains constant, the quantity of cola demanded by Lisa decreases and in part (a), Lisa moves along her demand curve for films. Also, Lisa's demand for films increases and in part (b), her demand curve for films shifts to the right.

Table 8.6 Lisa's Choices with an Income of £42 a Month

Films (£3 per ticket)		Cola (£6 per six-pack)	
Quantity	Marginal utility per pound spent	Quantity (six-packs)	Marginal utility per pound spent
0		14	3.67
1	16.67	13	4.00
2	12.67	12	4.33
3	11.00	11	4.67
4	9.67	10	5.00
5	8.33	9	5.33
6	8.00	8	5.67
7	6.00	7	6.00
8	5.00	6	6.33
9	4.00	5	8.33
10	3.00	4	9.33
11	2.00	3	12.00
12	1.00	2	14.00
13	0.67	1	25.00
14	0.33	0	

Table 8.7 Marginal Utility Theory

ASSUMPTIONS

- A consumer derives utility from the goods consumed.
- Each additional unit of consumption yields additional utility; marginal utility is positive.
- As the quantity of a good consumed increases, marginal utility decreases.
- A consumer's aim is to maximize total utility.

IMPLICATION

Utility is maximized when all the available income is spent and when the marginal utility per pound spent is equal for all goods.

PREDICTIONS

- Other things remaining the same, the higher the price of a good, the lower is the quantity bought (the law of demand).
- The higher the price of a good, the higher is the consumption of substitutes for that good.
- The higher the consumer's income, the greater is the quantity demanded of normal goods.

we saw that with these prices and with an income of £30 a month, Lisa sees 5 films and consumes 5 six-packs a month. We want to compare this consumption of films and cola with Lisa's consumption at an income of £42. The calculations for the comparison are shown in Table 8.6. With £42, Lisa can see 14 films a month and drink no cola or drink 14 six-packs a month and see no films or any combination of the two goods as shown in the rows of the table. We calculate the marginal utility per pound spent in exactly the same way as we did before and find the quantities at which the marginal utilities per pound spent on films and on cola are equal. With an income of £42, the marginal utility per pound spent on each good is equal when Lisa sees 7 films and drinks 7 six-packs of cola a month.

By comparing this situation with that in Table 8.4, we see that with an additional £12 a month, Lisa drinks 2 more six-packs and sees 2 more films. This response arises from Lisa's preferences, as described by her marginal utilities. Different preferences produce different quantitative responses. But for normal goods, a higher income always brings a larger consumption of all goods. For Lisa, cola and films are normal goods. When her income increases, Lisa buys more of both goods.

You have now completed your study of marginal utility theory and Table 8.7 summarizes the key assumptions, implications and predictions of the theory.

Marginal Utility and the Real World

Marginal utility theory can be used to answer a wide range of questions about the real world. The theory can also be used to interpret some of the facts set out at the beginning of this chapter – for example, why the demand for CD players is price elastic and the demand for oil is price inelastic. Elasticities of demand are determined by preferences – by how rapidly marginal utility diminishes.

The marginal utility of CD players diminishes more rapidly than the marginal utility of oil. One CD player yields much more marginal utility than a second CD player. In contrast, the marginal utility of a second and third and fourth litre of oil (or of petrol derived from oil) is almost as large as the marginal utility of the first litre. If marginal utility diminishes rapidly, a small change in the quantity bought brings a big change in the marginal utility per pound spent. So it takes a big price change to bring a small quantity change – demand is inelastic. Conversely, if marginal utility diminishes slowly, even a large change in the quantity bought brings a small change in the marginal utility per pound spent. So it takes only a small price change to bring a large quantity change – demand is elastic.

But the marginal utility theory can do much more than explain *consumption* choices. It can be used to explain *all* individual choices. One of these choices, the allocation of time between work in the home, office, or factory and leisure is the theme of *Economics in History* on pp. 210–211.

Review

- When the price of a good falls and the prices of other goods remain the same, consumers increase their consumption of the good whose price has fallen and decrease their demands for other goods.
- These changes result in a movement along the demand curve for the good whose price has changed and a shift in the demand curves for other goods whose prices have remained constant.
- When a consumer's income increases, the consumer can afford to buy more of all goods and the quantity bought increases for all normal goods.

Efficiency, Price and Value

Marginal utility theory helps us to deepen our understanding of the concept of efficiency that we developed in Chapter 6. It helps us to see more clearly the distinction between value and price. Let's see how.

Consumer Efficiency and Consumer Surplus

When Lisa allocates her limited budget to maximize utility, he is using her resources efficiently. Any other allocation of her budget would waste some resources.

We know that if Lisa allocates her limited budget to maximize utility, she will be on her demand curve for each good. A demand curve is a description of the planned quantity demanded at each price when utility is maximized. We also know from Chapter 6, that the demand curve shows Lisa's willingness to pay. It tells us her marginal benefit – the benefit from consuming an extra unit of a good. You can now see a deeper meaning in the concept of marginal benefit.

Marginal benefit is the maximum price that a consumer is willing to pay for an extra unit of a good or service when utility is maximized.

The Paradox of Value

More than 200 years ago, Adam Smith posed a paradox that we also raised at the start of this chapter. Water, which is essential to life itself, costs little, but diamonds, which are useless compared with water, are expensive. Why? Adam Smith could not solve the paradox. Not until the theory of marginal utility had been developed could anyone give a satisfactory answer.

You can solve Adam Smith's puzzle by distinguishing between *total* utility and *marginal* utility. The total utility that we get from water is enormous. But remember, the more we consume of something, the smaller is its marginal utility. We use so much water that the marginal utility – the benefit we get from one more glass of water – diminishes to a tiny value. Diamonds, on the other hand, have a small total utility relative to water, but because we buy few diamonds, they have a high marginal utility.

When an individual has maximized total utility, he or she has allocated his or her budget in the way that makes the marginal utility per pound spent equal for all goods. That is, the marginal utility from a good divided by the price of the good is equal for all goods. This equality of marginal utilities per pound spent holds true for diamonds and water. Diamonds have a high price and a high marginal utility. Water has a low price and a low marginal utility. When the high marginal utility of diamonds

Figure 8.7 The Paradox of Value

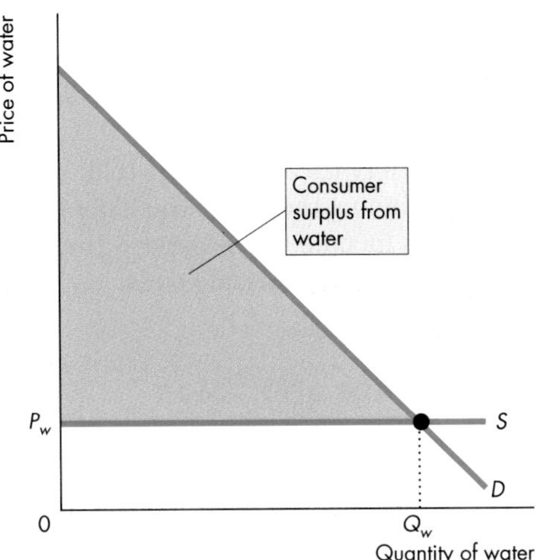

(a) Water

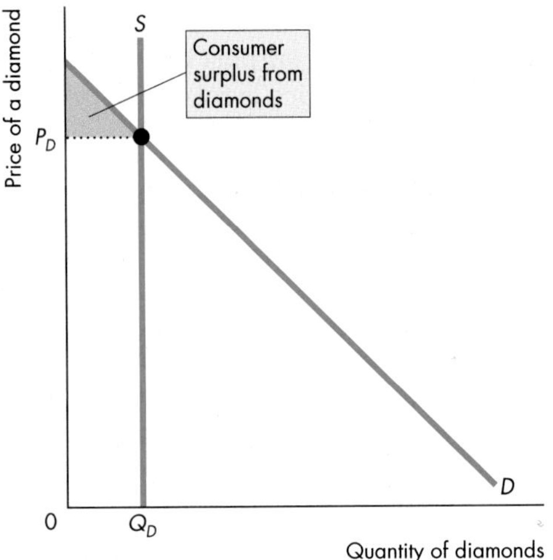

(b) Diamonds

Part (a) shows the demand for water, *D*, and the supply of water, *S*. The supply is (assumed to be) perfectly elastic at the price P_W. At this price, the quantity of water consumed is Q_W and the consumer surplus from water is the large green triangle. Part (b) shows the demand for diamonds, *D*, and the supply of diamonds, *S*. The supply is (assumed to be) perfectly inelastic at the quantity Q_D. At this quantity, the price of a diamond is P_D and the consumer surplus from diamonds is the small green triangle. Water is valuable – has a large consumer surplus – but is cheap. Diamonds are less valuable than water – have a smaller consumer surplus – but are expensive.

is divided by the high price of diamonds, the result is a number that equals the low marginal utility of water divided by the low price of water. The marginal utility per pound spent is the same for diamonds as for water.

Another way to think about the paradox of value is through the concept of *consumer surplus*. Figure 8.7 explains the paradox of value using this concept. The supply of water (part a) is perfectly elastic at price P_W, so the quantity of water consumed is Q_W and the consumer surplus from water is the green area. The supply of diamonds (part b) is perfectly inelastic at price Q_D, so the price of diamonds is P_D and consumer surplus is the smaller green area. Water is cheap but brings a large consumer surplus, while diamonds are expensive but bring only a small consumer surplus.

Review

- Consumer choices are efficient along a demand curve.
- A low-priced good, such as water, has a small marginal utility but a large total utility and a large consumer surplus.
- A high-priced good, such as diamonds, has a large marginal utility but a small total utility and a small consumer surplus.

We've now completed our study of the marginal utility theory of consumption. We've used that theory to examine how one individual – Lisa – allocates her income between the two goods that she consumes – films and cola. We've also seen how the theory can be used to resolve the paradox of value. Furthermore, we've seen how the theory can be used to explain our real-world consumption choices. In the next chapter, we're going to study an alternative theory of individual behaviour. To help you see the connection between the marginal utility theory of this chapter and the more modern theory of consumer behaviour of the next chapter, we'll continue with the same example. We'll meet Lisa again and discover another way of understanding how she gets the most out of her £30 a month.

Summary

Key Points

Individual Demand and Market Demand (p. 17)

- Individual demand is the relationship between the price of a good and the quantity demanded by a single individual.
- Market demand is the sum of all individual demands and the market demand curve is found by summing horizontally all the individual demand curves.

Individual Consumption Choices (pp. 170–173)

- Consumer choices are determined by consumption possibilities and preferences.
- Consumer consumption possibilities are constrained by income and prices. Some combinations of goods are affordable, and some are not affordable.
- Consumer preferences can be described by marginal utility.
- The key assumption of the marginal utility model is that the marginal utility of a good decreases as consumption of it increases.
- Another assumption is that people buy the affordable combination of goods that maximizes total utility.

Maximizing Utility (pp. 173–176)

- Total utility is maximized when all the available income is spent and when the marginal utility per dollar spent on each good is equal.
- If the marginal utility per dollar spent on good A exceeds that on good B, the consumer can increase total utility by buying more of good A and less of good B.

Predictions of Marginal Utility Theory (pp. 176–180)

- Marginal utility theory predicts how prices and income affect the amounts of each good consumed. First, it predicts the law of demand. That is, other things remaining the same, the higher the price of a good, the lower is the quantity demanded of that good.
- Marginal utility theory predicts that, other things remaining the same, the higher the consumer's income, the greater is the consumption of all normal goods.

Efficiency, Price and Value (pp. 180–181)

- When a consumer maximizes utility, they use resources efficiently.
- Marginal utility theory resolves the paradox of value.
- In common speech, we are thinking about *total* utility or consumer surplus when we speak about value. But price is related to *marginal* utility.
- Water, which we consume in large amounts, has a high total utility and a large consumer surplus, but a low price and low marginal utility.
- Diamonds, which we consume in small amounts, has a low total utility and a low consumer surplus, but a high price and high marginal utility.

Key Figures and Table 

Key Terms

Consumer equilibrium, 174
Consumer surplus, 180
Diminishing marginal utility, 172
Individual demand, 170
Marginal utility, 172
Marginal utility per pound spent, 174
Market demand, 170
Maximize total utility, 175
Preferences, 171
Total utility, 172
Utility, 171
Utility maximization, 174
Value, 180

Review Questions

1 What is the relationship between individual demand and market demand?

2 How do we construct a market demand curve from individual demand curves?

3 What do we mean by utility?

4 Distinguish between total utility and marginal utility.

5 How does marginal utility change as the level of consumption of a good changes?

6 Susan is a consumer. When is Susan's utility maximized?

a When she has spent all her income?
b When she has spent all her income and marginal utility is equal for all goods?
c When she has spent all her income and the marginal utility per pound spent is equal for all goods?

Explain your answers.

7 What does the marginal utility theory predict about the effect of a change in price on the quantity of a good consumed?

8 What does the marginal utility theory predict about the effect of a change in the price of one good on the consumption of another good?

9 What does the marginal utility theory predict about the effect of a change in income on consumption of a good?

10 How would you answer someone who says that the marginal utility theory is useless because utility cannot be observed?

11 How would you respond to someone who tells you that the marginal utility theory is useless because people are not smart enough to compute a consumer equilibrium in which the marginal utility per pound spent is equal for all goods?

12 What is consumer surplus? How is consumer surplus calculated?

13 What is the paradox of value? How does the marginal utility theory resolve it?

Problems

1 Shirley's demand for books is given by the following:

Price (pounds per book)	Quantity (books per month)
1	12
2	9
3	6
4	3
5	1

a Draw a graph of Shirley's demand for books.

Daniel also likes books. His demand for books is given by the following:

Price (pounds per book)	Quantity (books per month)
1	6
2	5
3	4
4	3
5	2

b Draw a graph of Daniel's demand curve.
c If Shirley and Daniel are the only two individuals, construct the market demand curve for books.
d Draw a graph of the market demand for books.
e Draw a graph to show that the market demand curve is the horizontal sum of Shirley's demand curve and Daniel's demand curve.

2 Calculate Lisa's marginal utility from cola from the numbers given in Table 8.1. Draw two graphs, one of her total utility and the other of her marginal utility from cola. Make your graphs look similar to those in Figure 8.3.

3 Max enjoys windsurfing and snorkelling. He obtains the following utility from each of these sports:

Half-hours per month	Utility from windsurfing	Utility from snorkelling
1	60	20
2	110	38
3	150	53
4	180	64
5	200	70
6	206	75
7	211	79
8	215	82
9	218	84

a Draw graphs showing Max's utility from windsurfing and from snorkelling.
b Compare the two utility graphs. Can you say anything about Max's preferences?
c Draw graphs showing Max's marginal utility from windsurfing and from snorkelling.
d Compare the two marginal utility graphs. Can you say anything about Max's preferences?

4 Max has £35 to spend. Equipment for windsurfing rents for £10 a half-hour while snorkelling equipment rents for £5 a half-hour. Use this information together with that given in Problem 3 to answer the following questions:

a What is the marginal utility per pound spent on snorkelling if Max snorkels for:
  1 Half-an-hour?
  2 One-and-a-half hours?

b What is the marginal utility per pound spent on windsurfing if Max windsurfs for:
  1 Half-an-hour?
  2 One hour?

c How long can Max afford to snorkel if he windsurfs for:
  1 Half-an-hour?
  2 One hour?
  3 One-and-a-half hours?

d Will Max choose to snorkel for one hour and windsurf for one-and-a-half hours?
e How long will Max choose to windsurf and to snorkel?

5 Max's sister gives him £20 to spend on his leisure pursuits, so he now has £55 to spend. How long will Max now windsurf and snorkel?

6 If Max has only £55 to spend and the rent on windsurfing equipment decreases to £5 a

half-hour, how will Max now spend his time windsurfing and snorkelling?

7 Does Max's demand curve for windsurfing slope downward or upward?

8 Max takes a Club Med holiday, the cost of which includes unlimited sports activities – including windsurfing, snorkelling and tennis. There is no extra charge for any equipment. Max decides to spend a total of three hours each day on windsurfing and snorkelling.

a What is Max's opportunity cost of windsurfing?
b What is Max's opportunity cost of snorkelling?
c How does Max allocate his three hours between windsurfing and snorkelling?

9 Sara's demand for windsurfing is given by:

Price (pounds per half-hour)	Time windsurfing (half-hours per month)
12.50	8
15.00	6
18.50	4
20.00	2

a If windsurfing costs £18.50 a half-hour, what is Sara's consumer surplus?
b If windsurfing costs £12.50 a half-hour, what is Sara's consumer surplus?

10 Read the article in *Reading Between the Lines* on pp. 186–187 again then:

a Use a diagram similar to Figure 2 to show what would happen if Coca-Cola now cut the price of its 2-litre bottles to \$0.80.
b Show the impact of the fall in the price of a bottle of Dr Pepper on the market for bottles of fizzy drinks using a demand and supply diagram.

11 Use the links on the Parkin, Powell and Matthews Web site and read what Henry Schimberg, CEO of Coca-Cola Enterprises, says about the market for bottled water. Use the marginal utility theory you have learned in this chapter to interpret and explain Mr Schimberg's remarks about the bottled-water market.

12 Why do you think the percentage of income spent on food has decreased while the percentage of income spent on cars has increased during the past 50 years? Use the marginal utility theory to explain these trends.

13 Smoking is banned on all airline flights in the European Community and on most international flights. Use marginal utility theory to explain your answers to the following questions:

a What effect does this ban have on the utility of (i) smokers and (ii) non-smokers?
b How do you expect the ban to influence the decisions of (i) smokers and (ii) non-smokers? In your answer to this question, consider decisions about smoking, flying, and the willingness to pay for a flight.

W http://www.econ100.com

Reading between the lines

Utility Theory: Party Drinks Preferences

The Guardian, 14 November 1998

Pepper adds spice to drink war

Roger Cowe finds a British firm with the bottle to challenge Pepsi and Coke

Cadbury owns Dr Pepper Seven-Up (DPSU), the third placed player in the US City drink business. It is trying to compete with Coke and Pepsi, and aims to do that more effectively by building its own bottling network, just like the two big drinks groups. Karin Bledsoe is having a party tomorrow at her home in Dallas, Texas.

Ms Bledsoe knows nothing of all this. All she knows is that she loves Dr Pepper, and for her party she has been able to buy it at an unprecedentedly low price — 88 cents (about 50p) for a two litre bottle, then 50 cents off that with a special coupon.

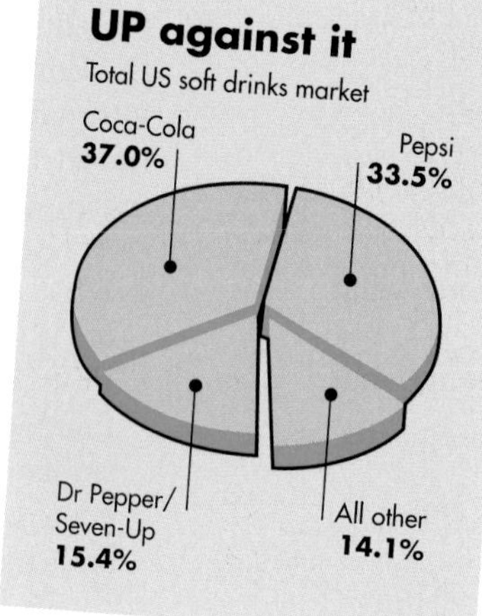

"We all love Dr Pepper. I can drink Coke but I hate Pepsi," she said. "Normally for these parties I get five 24-can packs, but when I saw the price of 88 cents I thought I might as well get the bottles."

Not that the cans were expensive, at just $1.97 for 12 of the standard size — about 10p per can. But when you are buying so many soft drinks, you may as well take advantage of the bargains — something Cadbury has in mind for its bottling build-up.

Standard price for a two-litre cola bottle in most US cities is just 99 cents (about 58p), more or less the same as it has been for the last 8 or 10 years.

This low price is partly explained by Americans' astonishing capacity for fizzy drinks. They drink about 900 cans a year each, more than three times as much as in the UK and a higher per capita consumption than anywhere in the world.

Those volumes mean it is a good business to be in, and every slither of market share is fiercely fought over, especially between the two cola giants. Between them Pepsi and Coke sell $30 billion worth of the sticky brown liquid around the world each year.

The Essence of the Story

- Dr Pepper is owned by the British company Cadbury Schweppes, which is trying to increase the popularity of the drink by expanding its bottling plant. Dr Pepper has 15.4 per cent of the US fizzy drinks market. Its main rivals are Coca-Cola, which has 37 per cent of the market, and Pepsi, which has 33.5 per cent of the market.

- Karin Bledsoe lives in Texas and loves Dr Pepper. She likes Coca-Cola but hates Pepsi. She buys fizzy drinks for her parties and has to choose between the drinks she likes, and whether she buys in cans or bottles. Her choice is affected by her budget, her preferences and the price of the drinks.

- The Cadbury Schweppes bottling strategy has lowered the price of Dr Pepper. Karin normally buys 5 24-can packs for her parties at $1.97 a pack (about 10 pence a can), but she has now decided to buy bottles because they are cheaper.

- A two-litre bottle of Dr Pepper now costs $0.80 (about 50 pence) compared to a similar bottle of Coca-Cola which costs $0.88 (about 58 pence). Even a small increase in the share of the $30 billion market is worth having.

■ About three times more fizzy drinks are consumed each year in the United States than in the United Kingdom. High levels of consumption are determined by tastes, high per capita income and the low price which can be maintained in such a huge market.

Economic Analysis

■ Karin allocates her drinks budget between Dr Pepper and Coca-Cola when shopping for her party. Normally she buys 5 24-can packs. Assuming 24-can packs are twice the price of 12-can packs at $1.97, Karin's budget is $19.70.

■ Karin will maximize her utility by making the marginal utility per dollar spent on can packs equal to the marginal utility per dollar spent on bottles. That is:

$$\frac{MU_{cp}}{P_{cp}} = \frac{MU_b}{P_b}$$

■ Figure 1 shows Karin's marginal utility of can packs as MU_{cp}/P_{cp} and Karin's marginal utility of bottles as MU_b/P_b. Karin maximizes her utility, given her party drinks budget, by setting MU_{cp}/P_{cp} to MU_b/P_b and buys 5 24-can packs and no bottles.

■ When the price of a two-litre bottle of Dr Pepper is cut from the 88 cents to 80 cents, the marginal utililty per dollar spent increases to MU_b/P'_b (providing Karin's budget and preferences do not change) as shown in Figure 1. Karin now maximizes utility by buying no can packs and 24 bottles (her expenditure is $19.20).

■ The price cut also affects Karin's choice between Dr Pepper and Cola as shown in Figure 2. Before the price cut, Karin maximizes her utility by setting the marginal utility of a dollar spent on Dr Pepper, MU_{dp}/P_{dp}, equal to the marginal utility of a dollar spent on Coca-Cola, MU_{cc}/P_{cc}. She buys 14 bottles of Dr Pepper and 10 bottles of Coca-Cola.

■ The price cut raises the marginal utility of a dollar spent on Dr Pepper to MU_{dp}/P'_{dp} as shown in Figure 2. Karin maximizes utility by buying 18 bottles of Dr Pepper and 6 bottles of Coca-Cola. If Karin is a typical consumer, the market demand for Dr Pepper will increase.

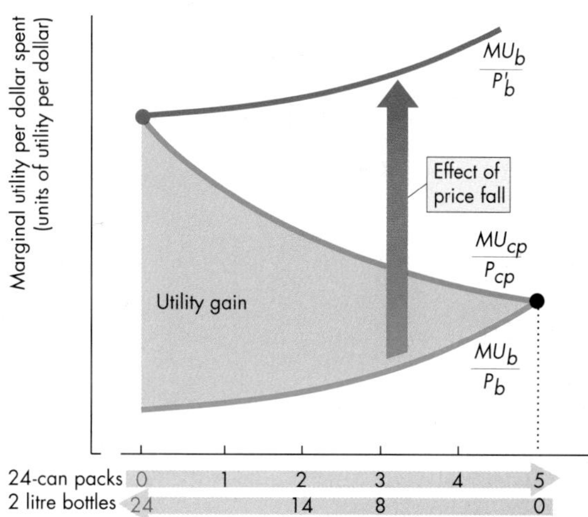

Figure 1 Party drinks: cans and bottles

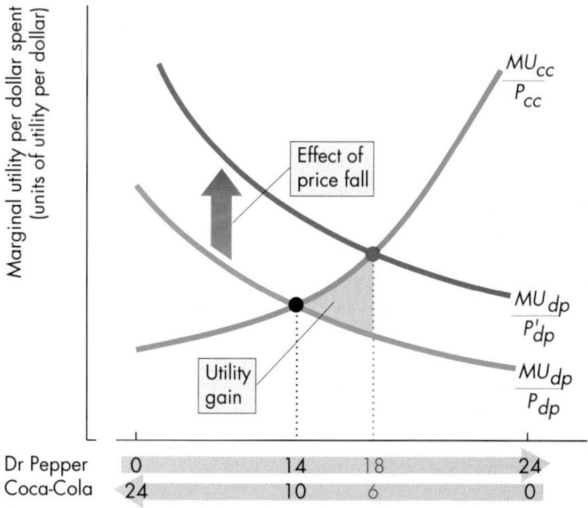

Figure 2 Dr Pepper and Coca-Cola in bottles

CHAPTER 9

Possibilities, Preferences and Choices

After studying this chapter you will be able to:

- Calculate and graph a household's budget line
- Work out how the budget line changes when prices or income change
- Make a map of preferences by using indifference curves
- Explain the choices that households make
- Predict the effects of price and income changes on consumption choices

Subterranean Movements

Like the continents floating on the earth's mantle, our spending patterns change steadily over time. Goods such as home videos and microwave chips now appear on our shopping lists while 78 rpm gramophone records and horse-drawn carriages have disappeared. ◆ But these surface disruptions obscure deeper and slower changes in our spending. We spend a smaller percentage of our income today on food and clothing than we did in 1950. At the same time, the percentage of our income spent on fuel, housing and cars has grown steadily. Why does consumer spending change over the years? How do people react to changes in income and changes in the prices of the things they buy? ◆ Similar subterranean movements govern the way we spend our time. For example, the average working week has fallen steadily from 70 hours a week in the nineteenth century to 38 hours a week today. Although the average working week is now much shorter than it once was, far more people now have jobs. This change has been especially dramatic for women. Why has the average working week declined? And why do more women work?

◆ ◆ ◆ ◆ In this chapter we are going to study a model of household choice that predicts the effects of changes in prices and incomes on what households buy and how much work they do. As a household is just a group of individuals living together as a single decision-making unit, we will assume our household acts as if it were an individual. In this way we can use our model of individual choice from Chapter 8.

Consumption Possibilities

Consumption choices are limited by income and by prices. A household has a given amount of income to spend and cannot influence the prices of the goods and services it buys. It takes prices as given. The limits to a household's consumption choices are described by its **budget line**.

Let's look at Lisa's[1] budget line. Lisa is the only person in her household and she has an income of £30 a month to spend. She consumes two goods – cinema films and cola. Cinema tickets cost £6 each; cola costs £3 for a six-pack. If Lisa spends all of her income, she will reach the limit of her consumption of films and cola.

Figure 9.1 shows the affordable ways for Lisa to consume films and cola. Each row shows an affordable way to consume films and cola which just use up Lisa's monthly income of £30. The numbers in the table define Lisa's household consumption possibilities. We can graph these consumption possibilities as points *a* to *f* in Figure 9.1.

Divisible and Indivisible Goods Some goods – called divisible goods – can be bought in any quantity desired. Examples are petrol and electricity. We can best understand the model of household choice we're about to study if we assume that all goods and services are divisible. For example, Lisa can consume half a film a month *on average* by seeing one film every two months. When we think of goods as being divisible, the consumption possibilities are not just the points *a* to *f* shown in Figure 9.1, but these points plus all the intermediate points that form the line running from *a* to *f*. Such a line is a budget line.

Lisa's budget line is a constraint on her choices. She can afford all the points on the line and inside it. She cannot afford points outside the line. The constraint on her consumption depends on prices and her income, and the constraint changes when prices or her income change. Let's see how by studying an equation that describes her consumption possibilities.

1 If you have read the preceding chapter on marginal utility theory, you have already met Lisa. This tale of her thirst for cola and zeal for films will sound familiar to you – up to a point. But in this chapter we're going to use a different method for representing preferences – one that does not require us to resort to the idea of utility.

Figure 9.1 The Budget Line 

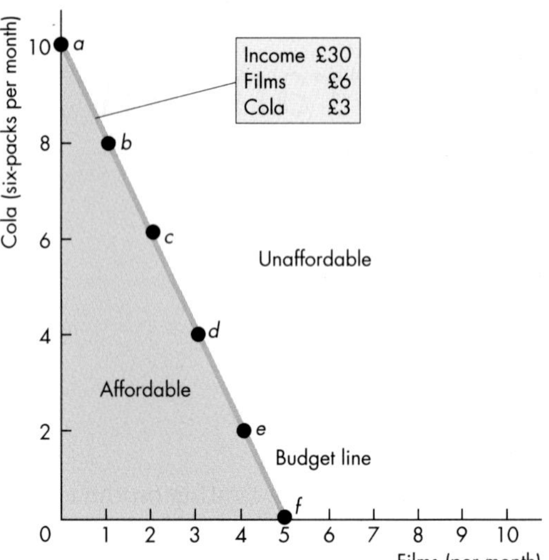

Consumption possibility	Films (per month)	Cola (six-packs per month)
a	0	10
b	1	8
c	2	6
d	3	4
e	4	2
f	5	0

Lisa's budget line shows the boundary between what she can and cannot afford. Each row of the table lists Lisa's affordable combinations of cinema tickets and cola when her income is £30, the price of cola is £3 a six-pack, and the price of a ticket is £6. For example, row *a* tells us that Lisa exhausts her £30 income when she buys 10 six-packs and sees no films. The figure graphs Lisa's budget line. Points *a* to *f* on the graph represent the rows of the table. For divisible goods, the budget line is the continuous line *af*. To calculate the equation for Lisa's budget line, start from the fact that expenditure equals income. That is:

$$(£3 \times Q_c + £6 \times Q_f) = £30$$

Divide by £3 to obtain:

$$Q_c + 2Q_f = 10$$

Subtract $2Q_f$ from both sides to obtain:

$$Q_c = 10 - 2Q_f$$

The Budget Equation

We can describe the budget line by using a *budget equation*. The budget equation starts with the fact that:

$$\text{Expenditure} = \text{Income}$$

In Lisa's case, expenditure and income equal £30 a week. Expenditure is equal to the sum of the price of each good multiplied by the quantity bought. For Lisa:

$$\begin{aligned}\text{Expenditure} = {} & \text{Price of cola} \times \text{Quantity of cola} \\ & + \text{Price of a cinema ticket} \\ & \times \text{quantity of films}\end{aligned}$$

Call the price of cola P_c, the quantity of cola Q_c, the price of a cinema ticket P_f, the quantity of films Q_f, and income Y. Using these symbols, Lisa's budget equation is:

$$P_c \times Q_c + P_f \times Q_f = Y$$

Using the prices Lisa faces, £3 for a six-pack and £6 for a cinema ticket, and Lisa's income, £30, we get:

$$£3 \times Q_c + £6 \times Q_f = £30$$

Lisa can choose any quantities of cola (Q_c) and films (Q_f) that satisfy this equation. To express the relationship between these quantities, we rearrange the equation so that it describes Lisa's budget line. To do so, divide both sides of the equation by the price of cola (P_c) to get:

$$Q_c + \frac{P_f}{P_c} \times Q_f = \frac{Y}{P_c}$$

Now subtract the term $P_f/P_c \times Q_f$ from both sides of this equation to give:

$$Q_c = Y - \frac{P_f}{P_c} \times \frac{Q_f}{P_c}$$

For Lisa, income (Y) is £30, the price of a cinema ticket (P_f) is £6 and the price of a six-pack (P_c) is £3. So Lisa must choose the quantities of films and cola to satisfy the equation:

$$Q_c = \frac{£30}{£3} - \frac{£6}{£3} \times Q_f$$

or

$$Q_c = 10 - 2 \times Q_f$$

This equation tells us how Lisa's consumption of cola (Q_c) varies as her consumption of films (Q_f) varies. To interpret the equation, go back to the budget line of Figure 9.1 and check that the equation you've just derived gives you the results of that budget line. Begin by setting Q_f, the quantity of films, equal to zero. In this case, the budget equation tells us that Q_c, the quantity of cola, is Y/P_c, which is £30/£3, or 10 six-packs. This combination of Q_f and Q_c is the same as that shown in row *a* of the table in Figure 9.1. Setting Q_f equal to 5 makes Q_c equal to 0 (row *f* of the table in Figure 9.1). Check that you can derive the other rows.

The budget equation contains two variables chosen by the household (Q_f and Q_c) and two variables (Y/P_c and P_f/P_c) that the household takes as given. Let's look more closely at these variables.

Real Income A household's **real income** is the maximum quantity of a good that the household can afford to buy. In the budget equation, real income is Y/P_c. This quantity is the maximum number of six-packs that Lisa can buy and is Lisa's real income in terms of cola. It is equal to her money income divided by the price of cola. Lisa's income is £30 and the price of cola is £3 a six-pack, so her real income in terms of cola is 10 six-packs. In Figure 9.1, real income is the point at which the budget line intersects the y-axis.

Relative Price A **relative price** is the price of one good divided by the price of another good. In Lisa's budget equation, the variable (P_f/P_c) is the relative price of a film in terms of cola. For Lisa, P_f is £6 a film and P_c is £3 a six-pack, so P_f/P_c is equal to 2 six-packs per film. That is, to see one more film, Lisa must give up 2 six-packs.

You've just calculated Lisa's opportunity cost of a film. Recall that the opportunity cost of an action is the best alternative foregone. For Lisa to see 1 more film a month, she must forego 2 six-packs. You've also calculated Lisa's opportunity cost of cola. For Lisa to consume 2 more six-packs a month, she must give up seeing 1 film. So her opportunity cost of 2 six-packs is 1 film.

The relative price of a film in terms of cola is the magnitude of the slope of Lisa's budget line. To calculate the slope of the budget line, recall the formula for slope (introduced in Chapter 2): slope equals the change in the variable measured on the y-axis divided by the change in the variable measured on the x-axis as we move along the line. In Lisa's case (Figure 9.1), the variable measured on the y-axis is the quantity of cola and the variable measured on the x-axis is the quantity of films. Along Lisa's budget

Figure 9.2 Changes in Prices and Income

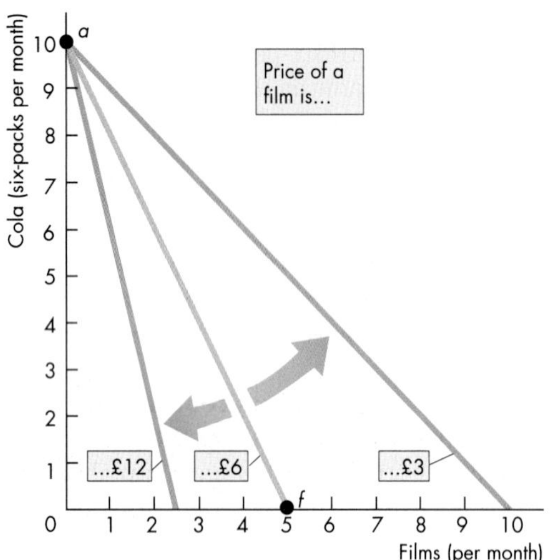

(a) A change in price

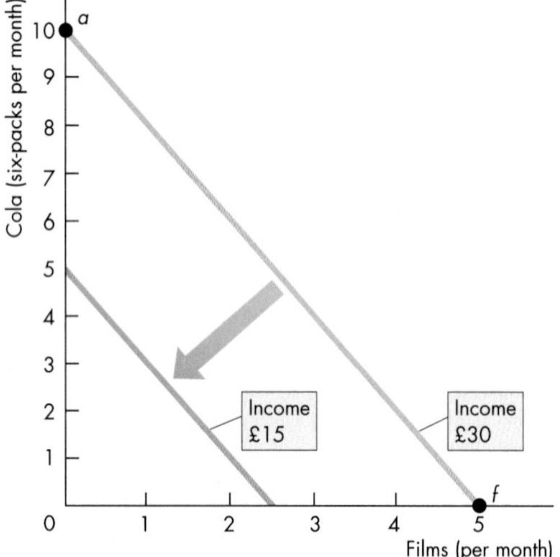

(b) A change in income

In part (a), the price of a cinema ticket changes. A fall in the price from £6 to £3 rotates the budget line outward and makes it flatter. A rise in the price from £6 to £12 rotates the budget line inward and makes it steeper. In part (b), income falls from £30 to £15 while prices remain constant. The budget line shifts leftward but its slope does not change.

line, as cola decreases from 10 to 0 six-packs, films increase from 0 to 5. Therefore the slope of the budget line is 10 six-packs divided by 5 films, or 2 six-packs per film. The magnitude of this slope is exactly the same as the relative price we've just calculated. It is also the opportunity cost of a film.

A Change in Prices When prices change, so does the budget line. The lower the price of the good measured on the horizontal axis, other things remaining the same, the flatter is the budget line. For example, if the price of a cinema ticket falls to £3, real income in terms of cola does not change but the relative price of seeing a film falls. The budget line rotates outward and becomes flatter as shown in Figure 9.2(a). The higher the price of the good measured on the horizontal axis, other things remaining the same, the steeper is the budget line. For example, if the price of a cinema ticket rises to £12, the relative price of seeing a film increases. The budget line rotates inward and becomes steeper as shown in Figure 9.2(a).

A Change in Income A change in *money* income changes real income but does not change relative prices. The budget line shifts, but its slope does not change. The bigger a consumer's money income, the bigger is real income and the farther to the right is the budget line. The smaller a consumer's money income, the smaller is real income and the farther to the left is the budget line. The effect of a change in income on Lisa's budget line is shown in Figure 9.2(b). The initial budget line is the same one that we began with in Figure 9.1 when Lisa's income is £30. A new budget line shows how much Lisa can consume if her income falls to £15 a month. The new budget line is parallel to the old one but closer to the origin. The two budget lines are parallel – have the same slope – because the relative price is the same in both cases. The new budget line is closer to the origin than the initial one because Lisa's real income has decreased.

Review

- The budget line describes the limits to a household's consumption, which depends on its income and the prices of the goods that it buys.

- The position of the budget line depends on real income and its slope depends on the relative price.
- A change in the price of one good changes the relative price and changes the slope of the budget line. If the price of the good measured on the horizontal axis rises, the budget line becomes steeper.
- A change in income changes real income and shifts the budget line but its slope does not change. An increase in income shifts the budget line outward.

We've studied the limits to which a household's consumption can go. Let's now see how we can describe the household's preferences.

Preferences and Indifference Curves

Preferences are a person's likes and dislikes. A key assumption about preferences is that they do not depend on what you can afford. When a price changes, or when your income changes, you make a new choice, but the preferences that guide that choice don't change. We are going to discover a neat idea – that of drawing a map of a person's preferences.

A preference map is based on the intuitively appealing assumption that people can sort all the possible combinations of goods they might consume into three groups: preferred, not preferred and indifferent. To make this idea more concrete, we'll ask Lisa to say how she ranks various combinations of films and cola. Figure 9.3 illustrates part of her answer.

Lisa tells us that she currently consumes 2 films and 6 six-packs a month at point c in Figure 9.3. She then lists all the combinations of films and cola that she regards as equally acceptable to her as her current consumption. When we plot the combinations of films and cola that Lisa tells us she likes just as much as the combination at point c, we get the green curve shown in Figure 9.3. This curve is the key element in a map of preferences and is called an indifference curve.

An **indifference curve** is a line that shows combinations of goods among which a consumer is

Figure 9.3 A Preference Map 

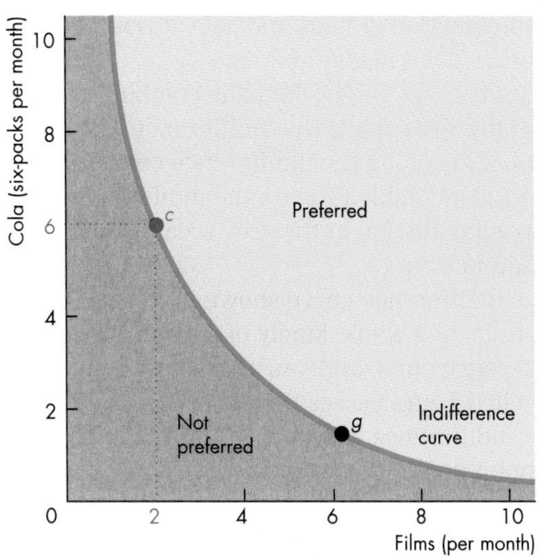

(a) An indifference curve

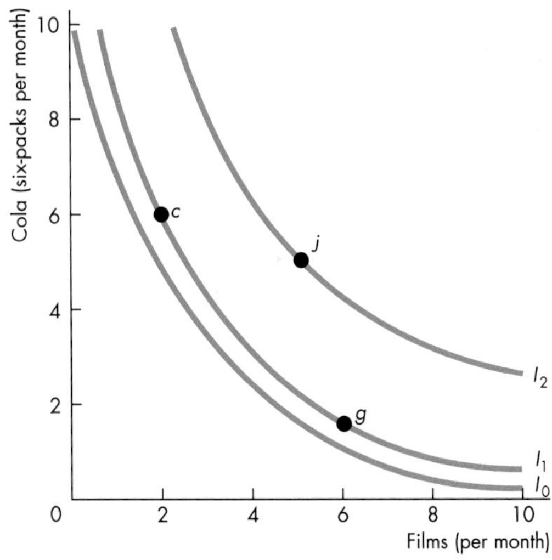

(b) Lisa's preference map

In part (a), Lisa consumes 6 six-packs of cola and 2 films a month at point *c*. She is indifferent between all the points on the green indifference curve such as *c* and *g*. She prefers any point above the indifference curve (yellow area) to any point on it, and she prefers any point on the indifference curve to any point below it (grey area). A preference map is a number of indifference curves. Part (b) shows three – I_0, I_1, and I_2 – that are part of Lisa's preference map. She prefers point *j* to point *c* or *g*, so she prefers any point on I_2 to any point on I_1.

indifferent. The indifference curve in Figure 9.3(a) tells us that Lisa is just as happy to consume 2 films and 6 six-packs a month at point c as to consume the combination of films and cola at point g or at any other point along the curve.

Lisa also says she prefers any combination in the yellow area above the indifference curve to any combination along the indifference curve. And she prefers any combination on the indifference curve to any combination in the grey area below the indifference curve.

The indifference curve shown in Figure 9.3(a) is just one of a whole family of such curves. This indifference curve appears again in Figure 9.3(b). It is labelled I_1 and passes through points c and g. Two other indifference curves are I_0 and I_2. Lisa prefers any point on indifference curve I_2 to any point on indifference curve I_1, and she prefers any point on I_1 to any point on I_0. We refer to I_2 as being a higher indifference curve than I_1 and I_1 as being higher than I_0.

Indifference curves never intersect each other. To see why, consider indifference curves I_1 and I_2 in Figure 9.4. We know that Lisa prefers point j to point c. We also know that Lisa prefers any point on indifference curve I_2 to any point on indifference curve I_1. If these indifference curves did intersect, Lisa would be indifferent between the combination of goods at the intersection point and combinations c and j. But we know that Lisa prefers j to c, so there cannot be an intersection point. Hence the indifference curves never intersect.

A preference map is a series of indifference curves. The indifference curves shown in Figure 9.4 are only a part of Lisa's household preference map. Her entire map consists of an infinite number of indifference curves; each one slopes downward and none of them intersect. Each indifference curve joins points representing combinations of goods among which Lisa is indifferent in much the same way that contour lines on a map join points of equal height above sea level. By looking at the shape of the contour lines on a map, we can draw conclusions about the terrain. In the same way, by looking at the shape of a person's indifference curves we can draw conclusions about preferences. But interpreting a preference map requires a bit of work. It also requires some way of describing the shape of the indifference curves. In the next two sections, we'll learn how to 'read' a preference map.

Figure 9.4 The Marginal Rate of Substitution 

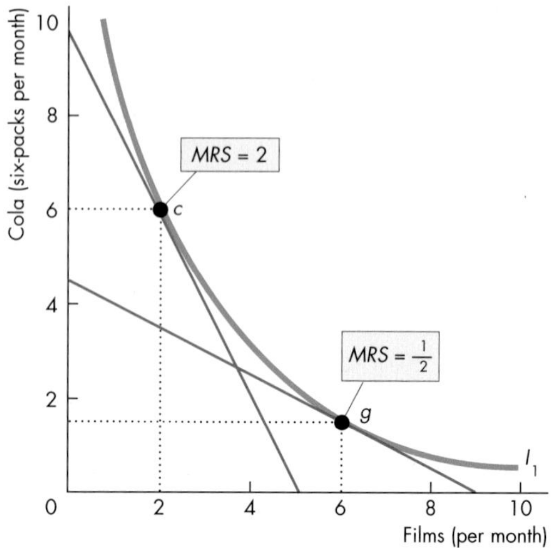

The magnitude of the slope of an indifference curve is called the marginal rate of substitution, *MRS*. The marginal rate of substitution tells us how much of one good a person is willing to give up to gain more of another good, while remaining indifferent. The marginal rate of substitution at point *c* is 2; at point *g* it is ½.

Marginal Rate of Substitution

The **marginal rate of substitution** (or *MRS*) is the rate at which a person will give up good y (the good measured on the y-axis) in order to get more of good x (the good measured on the x-axis) and at the same time remain indifferent. The marginal rate of substitution is measured from the slope of an indifference curve. If the indifference curve is steep, the marginal rate of substitution is high. The person is willing to give up a large quantity of good y in exchange for a small quantity of good x while remaining indifferent. If the indifference curve is flat, the marginal rate of substitution is low. The person is willing to give up only a small amount of good y in exchange for a large amount of good x to remain indifferent.

Figure 9.4 shows you how to calculate the marginal rate of substitution. The curve labelled I_1 is one of Lisa's indifference curves. Suppose that Lisa drinks 6 six-packs and watches 2 films at point c in the figure. Her marginal rate of substitution is calculated by measuring the absolute magnitude of the slope of the indifference curve at point *c*. To measure this magnitude, place a straight line against, or tangent to, the indifference curve at point *c*. The slope of that line is the change in the quantity of cola divided by the change in the quantity of films as we move along the line. As cola consumption decreases by 10 six-packs, film consumption increases by 5. So at point *c* Lisa is willing to give up cola for films at the rate of 2 six-packs per film. Her marginal rate of substitution is 2.

Now, suppose that Lisa consumes 6 films and 1.5 six-packs at point *g* in Figure 9.4. Her marginal rate of substitution at this point is found by calculating the absolute magnitude of the slope of the indifference curve at point *g*. That slope is the same as the slope of the tangent to the indifference curve at point *g*. Here, as cola consumption decreases by 4.5 six-packs, film consumption increases by 9. So at point *g* Lisa is willing to give up cola for films at the rate of 0.5 a six-pack per film. Her marginal rate of substitution is 0.5.

Notice that if Lisa drinks a lot of cola and does not see many films (point *c*), her marginal rate of substitution is large. If she watches a lot of films and does not drink much cola (point *g*), her marginal rate of substitution is small. This feature of the marginal rate of substitution is the central assumption of the theory of consumer behaviour and is referred to as the diminishing marginal rate of substitution. The assumption of **diminishing marginal rate of substitution** is a general tendency for the marginal rate of substitution to diminish as the consumer moves along an indifference curve, increasing consumption of good x and decreasing consumption of good y.

Your Own Diminishing Marginal Rate of Substitution You might be able to appreciate why we assume the principle of a diminishing marginal rate of substitution by thinking about your own preferences for films and cola. Suppose in one month you consumed 10 six packs of cola but you didn't see any films. You would probably be happy to give up lots of cans of cola just to see one film. On the other hand, suppose you saw 6 films this month and consumed only 1 six pack of cola. You would probably only give up a few cans of cola to see an extra film. Generally, the greater the number of films you see, the smaller is the quanity of cola you will give up to see an extra film.

The shape of the indifference curves incorporates the principle of the diminishing marginal rate of substitution because the curves are bowed towards the origin. The tightness of the bend of an indifference curve tells us how willing a person is to substitute one good for another while remaining indifferent. Let's look at some examples that will clarify this point.

Degree of Substitutability

Most of us would not regard films and cola as being close substitutes for each other. We probably have some fairly clear ideas about how many films we want to see each month and how many cans of cola we want to drink. Nevertheless, to some degree, we are willing to substitute between these two goods. No matter how big a cola freak you are, there is surely some increase in the number of films you can see that will compensate you for being deprived of a can of cola. Similarly, no matter how addicted you are to films, surely some number of cans of cola will compensate you for being deprived of seeing one film. A person's indifference curves for films and cola might look something like those shown in Figure 9.5(a).

Close Substitutes Some goods substitute so easily for each other that most of us do not even notice which we are consuming. A good example concerns different brands of personal computers. Dell, Compaq and Elonex are all clones of the IBM PC – but most of us can't tell the difference between the clones and the IBM. The same holds true for marker pens. Most of us don't care whether we use a marker pen from the university bookshop or the local supermarket. When two goods are perfect substitutes for each other, their indifference curves are straight lines that slope downward, as Figure 9.5(b) illustrates. The marginal rate of substitution between perfect substitutes is constant.

Complements Some goods cannot substitute for each other at all. Instead they are complements. The complements in Figure 9.5(c) are left and right running shoes. Indifference curves of perfect complements are L-shaped. For most of us, one left running shoe and one right running shoe are as good as one left shoe and two right ones.

Figure 9.5 The Degree of Substitutability

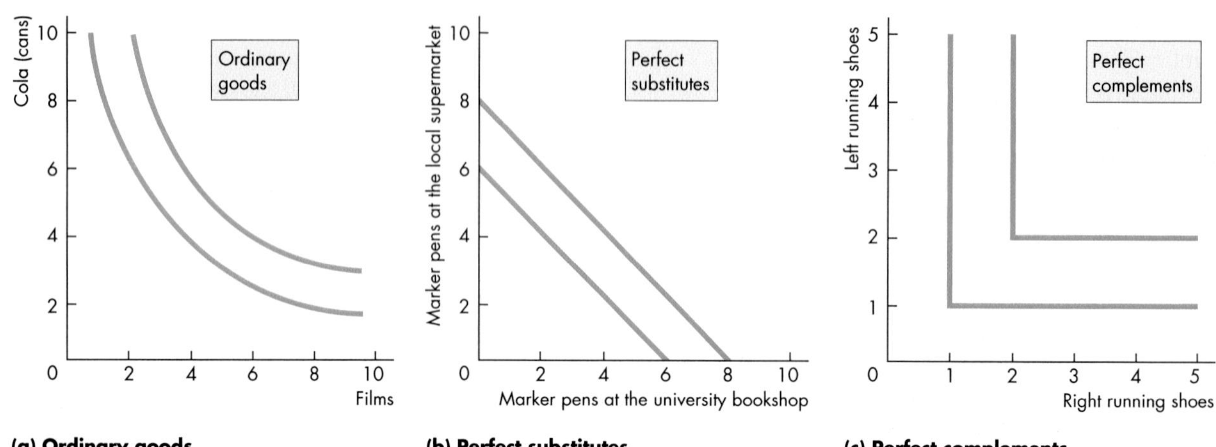

(a) Ordinary goods **(b) Perfect substitutes** **(c) Perfect complements**

The shape of the indifference curves reveals the degree of substitutability between two goods. Part (a) shows the indifference curves for two ordinary goods: films and cola. To consume less cola and remain indifferent, one must see more films. The number of films that compensates for a reduction in cola increases as less cola is consumed. Part (b) shows the indifference curves for two perfect substitutes. For the consumer to remain indifferent, one fewer marker pen from the local supermarket must be replaced by one extra marker pen from the university bookshop. Part (c) shows two perfect complements – goods that cannot be substituted for each other at all. Two left running shoes with one right running shoe is no better than one of each. But two of each is preferred to one of each.

Two of each is preferred to one of each, but two of one and one of the other is no better than one of each.

The extreme cases of perfect substitutes and perfect complements shown here don't often happen in reality. They do, however, illustrate that the shape of the indifference curve shows the degree of substitutability between two goods. The more any pair of goods become close substitutes, the less bowed the indifference curves and the more the indifference curves look like straight lines. A high degree of substitutability means that the marginal rate of sustitution falls less quickly. The more any pair of goods become poor substitutes for each other, or become complementary, the more the indifference curves become bowed and tightly curved. At the extreme, the indifference curves become 'L' shaped like those shown in Figure 9.5(c). A low degree of sustitutability, or a high degree of complementarity, means that the marginal rate of substitution falls more quickly.

Review

- Preferences can be represented by a preference map, which is a series of indifference curves.
- Indifference curves slope downward, bow toward the origin, and do not intersect each other.
- The magnitude of the slope of an indifference curve is called the marginal rate of substitution. The marginal rate of substitution diminishes as a person consumes less of the good measured on the y-axis and more of the good measured on the x-axis.
- The degree of substitutability between any pair of goods is shown by the shape of the indifference curves.

The two components of the model of household choice are now in place: the budget line and the preference map. We will use these components to work out the consumer's choice.

Predicting Consumer Behaviour

We are now going to bring Lisa's budget line and indifference curves together to model her best affordable choice of films and cola. We can use the model to predict the quantities of films and cola that Lisa *chooses* to consume? In Figure 9.6 you can see her budget line from Figure 9.1 and her indifference curves from Figure 9.3(b). We assume that Lisa wants to consume as much of both goods as she can afford – her best affordable point. This is point *c* in Figure 9.6. Where she consumes 2 films and 6 six-packs of cola. Is there any affordable point that Lisa prefers to point *c*? There is not. All Lisa's other affordable consumption points – all the other points on or below her budget line – lie on indifference curves that are below I_1. Indifference curve I_1 is the highest indifference curve on which Lisa can afford to consume.

Let's look more closely at Lisa's best affordable choice. It is:

- On the budget line
- On the highest attainable indifference curve
- Has a marginal rate of substitution between films and cola equal to the relative price of films and cola.

The best affordable point is *on* the budget line. If Lisa chooses a point inside the budget line like *i*, there are other affordable point on the budget line at which she can consume more of at least one good, if not both goods. Lisa prefers points like *c* and *h* to the one inside the budget line. The best affordable point cannot be outside the budget line because Lisa cannot afford such a point.

Lisa's preferred point is also on the highest attainable indifference curve. She prefers all points on I_2 to any point on I_1, and all points on I_1 to any point on I_0. Point *c* is on the highest attainable indifference curve and is also on the budget line. At this point, the indifference curve has the same slope as the budget line. To see why this describes the best affordable point, consider point *h*.

Figure 9.6 The Best Affordable Point

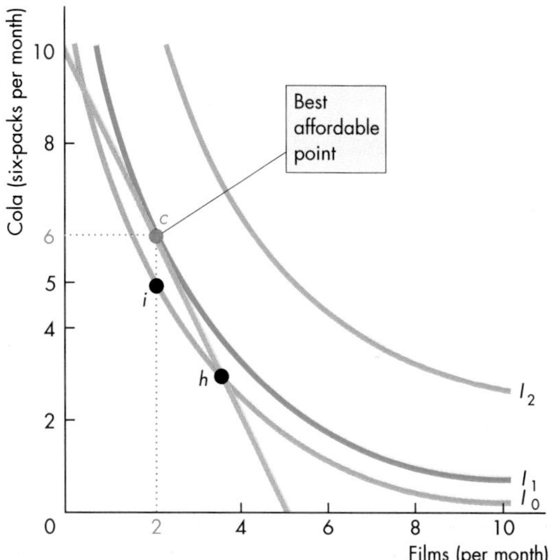

Lisa's best affordable point is *c*. At that point, she is on her budget line and so spends her entire income on the two goods. She is also on the highest attainable indifference curve. Higher indifference curves (such as I_2) do not touch her budget line, so she cannot afford any point on them. At point *c*, the marginal rate of substitution (the magnitude of the slope of the indifference curve) equals the relative price of a film (the magnitude of the slope of the budget line). A point such as *h* on the budget line is not Lisa's best affordable point because at that point she is willing to give up seeing more films in exchange for cola than she has to. She can move to point *i*, which she regards as being just as good as point *h* and which leaves her with some unspent income. She can spend that income and move to *c*, a point that she prefers to point *i*.

At point *h*, Lisa's marginal rate of substitution (the magnitude of the slope of the indifference curve) is less than the relative price (the magnitude of the slope of the budget line). The slope of the indifference curve I_0 at *h* shows Lisa is willing to give up approximately one film for one cola six-pack whereas the budget line slope shows Lisa will get 2 cola six-packs if she gives up one film. Lisa has an incentive to give up films for cola and move along the budget line towards point *c*.

As Lisa moves, she reaches points on the budget line which are on higher indifference curves (not shown) and so are preferred to *h* on I_0. If Lisa moves beyond point c she will reach points on indifference curves which are lower than I_1 and her marginal rate of substitution will be more than the relative price. She will have an incentive to give up cola and move back towards point c. The best affordable point at c, is where the marginal rate of substitution is equal to the relative price.

Let's now use this model of household choice to predict the effects on consumption of changes in prices and income. We'll begin by studying the effects of a price change.

A Change in Price

The effect of a change in price on the quantity of a good consumed is called the **price effect**. We will use Figure 9.7(a) to work out the price effect of a fall in the price of a cinema ticket. We start with tickets costing £6 each, cola costing £3 a six-pack, and with Lisa's income at £30 a month. In this situation, she consumes at point c, where her budget line is tangent to her highest attainable indifference curve, I_1. She consumes 6 six-packs and 2 films a month.

Now suppose that the price of a cinema ticket falls to £3. We've already seen how a change in Figure 9.2(a) affects the budget line. With a lower price of a ticket, the budget line rotates outward and becomes flatter. On the new budget line in Figure 9.7(a), Lisa's best affordable point is j, where she consumes 5 films and 5 six-packs of cola. As you can see, Lisa drinks less cola and sees more films now that films cost less. She reduces her cola consumption from 6 to 5 six-packs, and increases the number of films she sees from 2 to 5 a month. Lisa substitutes films for cola when the price of a cinema ticket falls, and the price of cola and her income remain constant.

The Demand Curve In Chapter 4, we asserted that the demand curve slopes downward and that it shifts when the consumer's income changes, or when the price of another good changes. We can now derive a demand curve from a consumer's budget line and indifference curves. By doing so, we can see that the law of demand and the downward-sloping demand curve are consequences of the consumer choosing his or her best affordable combination of goods.

Figure 9.7 Price Effect and Demand Curve

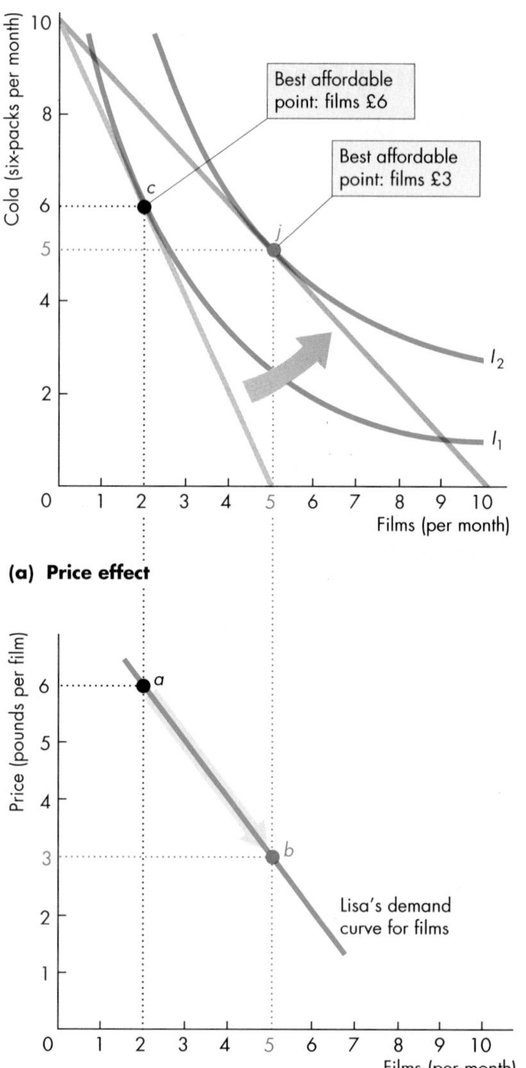

Initially, Lisa consumes at point c (part a). If the price of a cinema ticket falls from £6 to £3, she consumes at point j. The increase in films from 2 to 5 per month and the decrease in cola from 6 to 5 six-packs is the price effect. When the price of a cinema ticket falls, Lisa sees more films. She also consumes less cola. Part (b) shows Lisa's demand curve for films. When the price of a ticket is £6, she sees 2 a month, at point a. When the price of a ticket falls to £3, she sees 5 a month, at point b. Lisa's demand curve traces out her best affordable quantity of films as the price of a cinema ticket varies.

Figure 9.8 Income Effect and Change in Demand

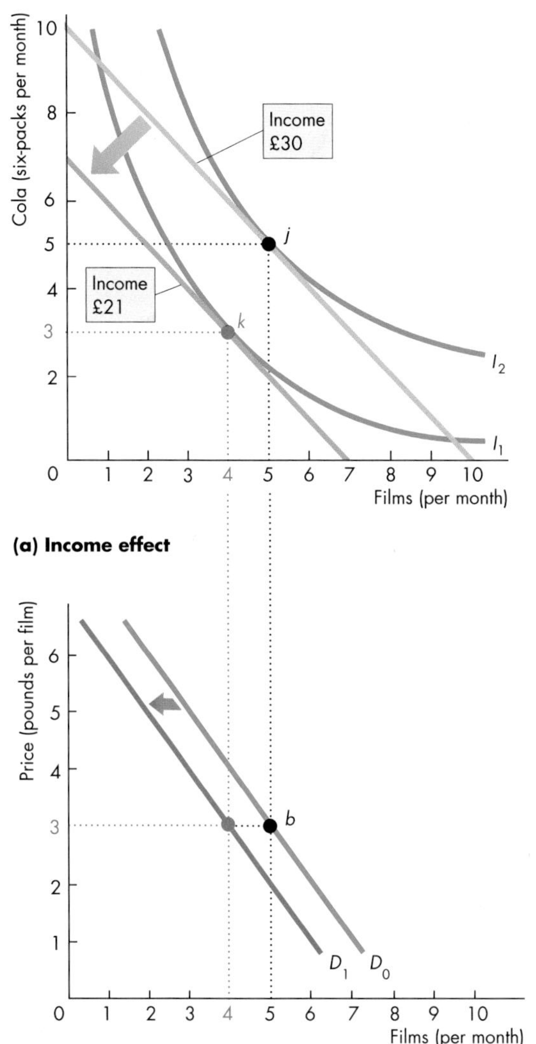

A change in income shifts the budget line and changes consumption. In part (a), when Lisa's income decreases, she consumes less of both films and cola. In part (b), when Lisa's income decreases, her demand curve for films shifts leftward. Lisa's demand for films decreases because she will now see fewer films at each price.

To derive Lisa's demand curve for films, we lower the price of a cinema ticket and finding her best affordable point at different prices, holding all other things constant. We just did this for two ticket prices in Figure 9.7(a). Figure 9.7(b) highlights these two prices and two points that lie on Lisa's demand curve for films. When the price of a cinema ticket is £6, Lisa sees 2 films a month at point *a*. When the price falls to £3, she increases the number of films she sees to 5 a month at point *b*. The entire demand curve is made up of these two points plus all the other points that tell us Lisa's best affordable consumption of films at each ticket price – more than £6, between £6 and £3, and less than £3 – given the price of cola and Lisa's income. As you can see, Lisa's demand curve for films slopes downward – the lower the price of a cinema ticket, the more films she watches each month. This is the law of demand.

Next, let's examine how Lisa adjusts her consumption when her income changes.

A Change in Income

The effect of a change in income on consumption is called the **income effect**. Let's work out the income effect by examining how consumption changes when income changes and prices remain constant. Figure 9.8(a) shows the income effect when Lisa's income falls. With an income of £30 and with a cinema ticket costing £3 and cola £3 a six-pack, she consumes at point *j* – 5 films and 5 six-packs. If her income falls to £21, she consumes at point *k* – 4 films and 3 six-packs. Thus when Lisa's income falls, she consumes less of both goods[2].

The Demand Curve and the Income Effect

A change in income leads to a shift in the demand curve, as shown in Figure 9.8(b). With an income of £30, Lisa's demand curve is D_0, the same as in Figure 9.8. But when her income falls to £21, she plans to see fewer films at each price, so her demand curve shifts leftward to D_1.

Substitution Effect and Income Effect

Films and cola are *normal goods*. For normal goods, a fall in price always increases the quantity bought. We can prove this assertion by dividing the price effect into two parts:

2 For Lisa, films and cola are *normal* goods. When her income falls, she consumes less of both goods and when her income rises, she consumes more of both goods. Some goods are *inferior* goods. When income rises, the consumption of an *inferior* good decreases. Try to draw some indifference curves that illustrate an inferior good.

1 The substitution effect.

2 The income effect.

Figure 9.9(a) shows the price effect and Figure 9.9(b) separates the price effect into the substitution effect and the income effect.

Substitution Effect The **substitution effect** is the effect of a change in price on the quantities consumed when the consumer (hypothetically) remains indifferent between the original and the new combinations of goods consumed. To work out Lisa's substitution effect, we have to imagine that when the price of a cinema ticket falls, Lisa's income also decreases by an amount that is just enough to leave her on the same indifference curve.

When the price of a cinema ticket falls from £6 to £3, let's suppose (hypothetically) that Lisa's income decreases to £21. What's special about £21? It is the income that is just enough, at the new price of a ticket, to keep Lisa's best affordable point on the same indifference curve as her original consumption point *c*. Lisa's budget line in this situation is the light orange line shown in Figure 9.9(b). With the new price of a cinema ticket and the new lower income, Lisa's best affordable point is *k* on indifference curve I_1. The move from *c* to *k* isolates the substitution effect of the price change. The substitution effect of the fall in the price of a cinema ticket is an increase in the consumption of films from 2 to 4 and a decrease in the consumption of cola. The direction of the substitution effect never varies; when the relative price of a good falls, the consumer substitutes more of that good for the other good.

Income Effect To calculate the substitution effect, we gave Lisa a £9 pay cut. Now let's give Lisa her £9 back. The £9 increase in income shifts Lisa's budget line outward, as shown in Figure 9.9(b). The slope of the budget line does not change because both prices remain constant. This change in Lisa's budget line is similar to the one illustrated in Figure 9.8, where we study the effect of income on consumption. As Lisa's budget line shifts outward, her consumption possibilities expand and her best affordable point becomes *j* on indifference curve I_2. The move from *k* to *j* isolates the income effect of the price change. In this example, as Lisa's income increases, she increases her consumption of both films and cola. For Lisa, films and cola are normal goods. The income effect always reinforces the substitution effect for normal goods.

Figure 9.9 Substitution Effect and Income Effect

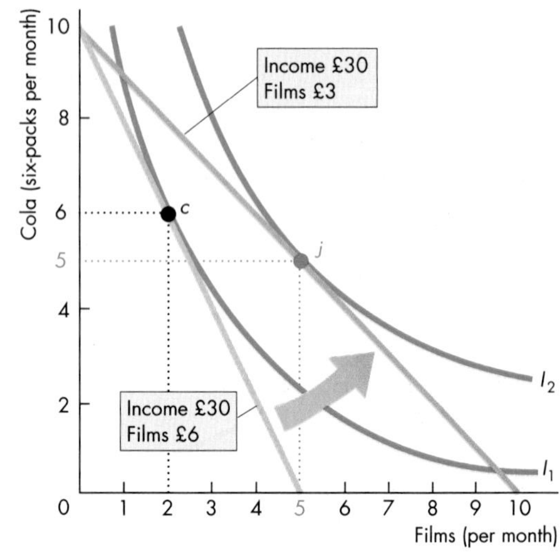

(a) Price effect

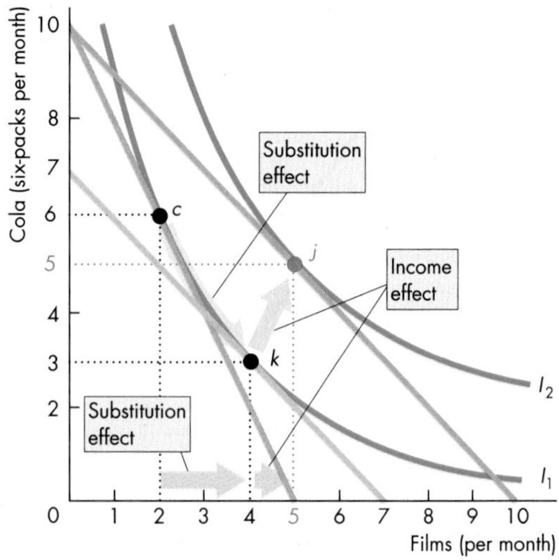

(b) Substitution effect and income effect

The price effect in part (a) can be separated into a substitution effect and an income effect in part (b). To isolate the substitution effect, we confront Lisa with the new price but keep her on her original indifference curve, I_1. The substitution effect is the move from *c* to *k*. To isolate the income effect, we confront Lisa with the new price of films but increase her income so that she can move from the original indifference curve, I_1, to the new one, I_2. The income effect is the move from *k* to *j*.

You can read about how income and substitution effects explain market reactions after the Belgian food scare involving cancer inducing dioxin contamination in *Reading Between the Lines* on pp. 208–209.

Inferior Goods The example that we have just studied is that of a change in the price of a normal good. The effect of a change in the price of an inferior good is different. Recall that an inferior good is one whose consumption decreases as income increases. For an inferior good, the income effect is negative. Thus for an inferior good a lower price does not always lead to an increase in the quantity demanded. The lower price has a substitution effect that increases the quantity demanded. But the lower price also has a negative income effect, which reduces the demand for the inferior good. Thus the negative income effect offsets the substitution effect to some degree. Even so, the substitution effect usually dominates so that the quantity demanded rises when the price falls – confirming the law of demand.

It has been suggested that some goods defy the law of demand – the quantity demanded increases when price increases. In fact, they are the exception that proves the rule. These goods have become known as 'Giffen' goods, named after a nineteenth century economist who suggested the quantity of potatoes demanded increased as the price of potatoes increased during the Irish potato famine. Giffen goods are types of inferior goods, where consumption decreases as income increases. They are rare because the income effect is negative *and* strong enough to offset the positive substitution effect. They arise when the total expenditure on a good is a high proportion of total income – as in the potato famine example. They do not defy the law of demand because it is based on preference theory which allows for these exceptions. The law of demand holds for all normal goods and for inferior goods, providing they account for a small proportion of total expenditure.

Back to the Facts

We started this chapter by observing how consumer spending has changed over the years. The indifference curve model explains these changes. Spending patterns are determined by best affordable choices and these choices change over time as incomes and prices change.

Labour Supply and Leisure Choices

Households make many choices other than those about how to spend their income on the various goods and services available. We can use the model of consumer choice to explain a wide range of other household choices such as how much labour to supply and how much time to spend on leisure rather than work. Some of these are discussed in *Economics in History* on pp. 210–211. Here we'll study household choices about labour supply and leisure.

Labour Supply

Every week, we allocate our 168 hours between working – called *labour* – and all other activities – called *leisure*. How do we decide how to allocate our time between labour and leisure? We can answer this question by using the theory of household choice.

The more hours we spend on leisure, the smaller is our income. The relationship between leisure and income is described by an *income–time budget line*. The orange lines in Figure 9.10(a) show Lisa's income–time budget lines. If Lisa devotes the entire week to leisure – 168 hours – she has no income and is at point z. By supplying labour in exchange for a wage, she can convert hours into income along the time–budget line. The slope of that line is determined by the hourly wage rate. If the wage rate is £2 an hour, Lisa faces the lowest budget line. If she worked for 68 hours a week, she would make an income of £136 a week. If the wage rate is £4 an hour, she faces the middle budget line. If the wage rate is £6 an hour, she faces the highest budget line. Lisa buys time by not supplying labour and by foregoing income. The opportunity cost of an hour of leisure is the hourly wage rate foregone.

Let's assume Lisa is a student who has some time available for part-time work. She must choose a point on a time–budget line. That is, she must choose how many hours of labour to supply. We can study this choice by looking at Lisa's indifference curves. Income and leisure are goods, just like films and cola, and Lisa has indifference curves for income and leisure.

Figure 9.10(a) also shows Lisa's indifference curves for income and leisure. The magnitude of the slope of an indifference curve tells us Lisa's

Figure 9.10 The Supply of Labour

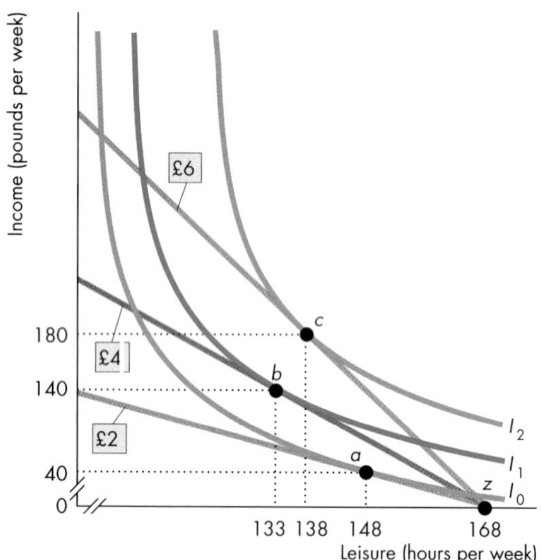

(a) Time allocation decision

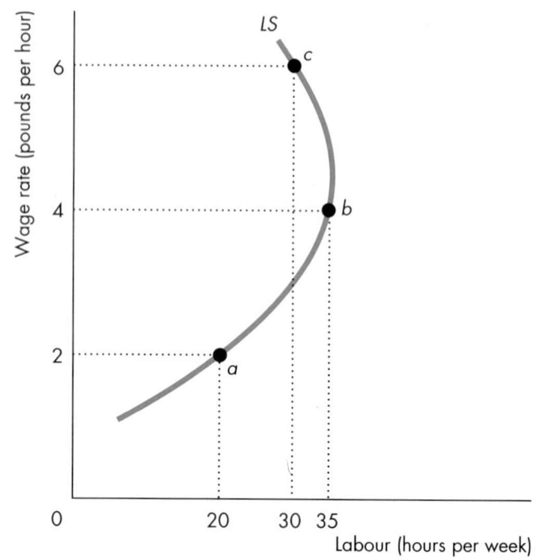

(b) Labour supply curve

In part (a), at a wage rate of £2 an hour, Lisa takes 148 hours of leisure (works 20 hours) a week at point *a*. If the wage rate increases from £2 to £4, she decreases her leisure to 133 hours (increases her work to 35 hours) a week at point *b*. But if the wage rate increases from £4 to £6, Lisa *increases* her leisure to 138 hours (*decreases* her work to 30 hours) a week at point *c*.

Part (b) shows Lisa's labour supply curve – the change in Lisa's hours of work as the wage rate changes. Lisa's labour supply curve slopes upward between points *a* and *b* and then bends back between points *b* and *c*. The reason is that leisure is a normal good and at a high enough wage rate, the positive income effect of a higher wage rate outweighs the negative substitution effect.

marginal rate of substitution – the rate at which she is willing to give up income to get one more hour of leisure, while remaining indifferent.

Lisa chooses her best attainable point. This choice of income and time allocation is just like her choice of films and cola. She gets onto the highest possible indifference curve by making her marginal rate of substitution between income and leisure equal to her wage rate. The choice depends on the wage rate Lisa can earn. At a wage rate of £2 an hour, Lisa chooses point *a* and works 20 hours a week (168 – 148) for an income of £40 a week. At a wage rate of £4 an hour, she chooses point *b* and works 35 hours a week (168 – 133) for an income of £140 a week. At a wage rate of £6 an hour, she chooses point *c* and works 30 hours a week (168 – 138) for an income of £180 a week.

Figure 9.10(b) shows Lisa's choices of hours to work at different wage rates in the form of her labour supply curve. This curve shows that as the wage rate increases from £2 an hour to £4 an hour, Lisa increases the quantity of labour supplied from 20 hours a week to 35 hours a week. But when the wage rate increases to £6 an hour, she decreases her quantity of labour supplied to 30 hours a week.

Lisa's supply of labour is similar to that described for the economy as a whole at the beginning of this chapter. As wage rates have increased, work hours have decreased. At first, this pattern seems puzzling. We've seen that the hourly wage rate is the opportunity cost of leisure. So a higher wage rate means a higher opportunity cost of leisure. This fact on its own leads to a decrease in leisure and an increase in work hours. But instead, we've cut our work hours. Why? Because our incomes have increased. As the real wage rate increases, real incomes increase, so people demand more of all normal goods. Leisure is a normal good, so as incomes increase, people demand more leisure.

The higher wage rate has both a *substitution effect* and an *income effect*. The higher wage rate

Figure 9.11 Utility and Indifference Curves

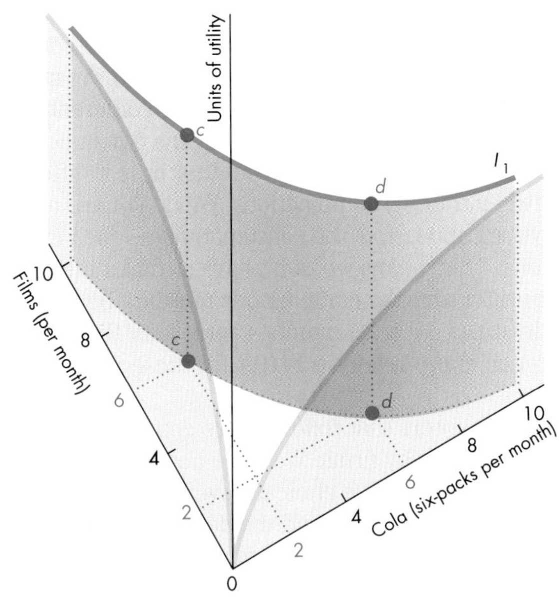

(a) Total utility from films and cola

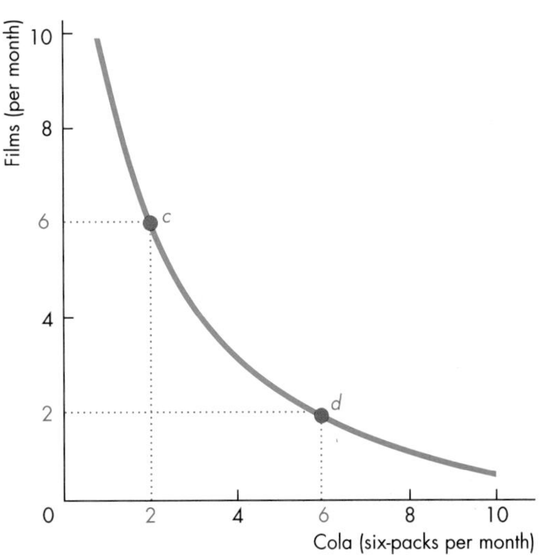

(b) Indifference curve for films and cola

Part (a) shows the total utility received from films when no cola is consumed (left-hand yellow curve) and the total utility received from cola when no films are seen (right-hand yellow curve). It also shows an indifference curve as a contour that maps all the choices that give equal (constant) utility – the blue curve.

Part (b) shows an indifference curve for films and cola. It is the same as the blue curve in part (a). Points *c* and *d* represent the same choices and utility as in part (a). The indifference curve in part (b) is what you would see if you looked straight down on top of the three-dimensional diagram shown in part (a).

increases the opportunity cost of leisure and so leads to a substitution effect away from leisure. The higher wage rate increases income and so leads to an income effect towards more leisure.

This theory of household choice can explain the facts about work patterns described at the beginning of this chapter. First, it can explain why the average working week has fallen steadily from 70 hours a week in the nineteenth century to 35 hours a week today. The reason is that as wage rates have increased, although people have substituted work for leisure, they have also decided to use their higher incomes in part to consume more leisure. Second, the theory can explain why more women now have jobs in the labour market. The reason is that increases in their wage rates and improvements in their job opportunities have led to a substitution effect away from working at home and towards working in the labour market.

Marginal Utility and Indifference Curves

Each theory of choice describes consumer's preferences. Marginal utility theory describes preferences in terms of the utility derived from consumption, and indifference curve theory uses indifference curves to represent preferences. You can understand how the two models relate to each other by thinking of an indifference curve as connecting points of equal utility. If Lisa is indifferent between consuming 2 films and 6 six-packs of cola or 6 films and 2 six-packs of cola, we are also saying she gets equal utility from the two choices.

You can see the connection between utility and indifference curves by looking at the two parts of Figure 9.11. Part (a) has three dimensions – the quantity of cola, the quantity of films and the level of total utility.

Part (b) has just two dimensions – the quantities of cola and films consumed. In part (a), the utility that Lisa gets from cola alone (with no films) appears as the right-hand yellow line. It shows that as Lisa's consumption of cola rises, so does the total utility she gets from cola. Lisa's total utility from films, which appeared in Figure 8.3, appears here as the left-hand yellow line. It shows that as Lisa's consumption of films increases, so does the total utility she gets from films. Lisa's indifference curve for films and cola is the blue line in part (b). But it also appears in part (a) as the blue contour line which maps points of equal utility. Points *c* and *d* in part (a) are the same as points *c* and *d* in part (b). Viewed in this way, an indifference curve can be interpreted as a contour curve that measures equal levels of total utility.

We can work either with total utility curves, as we did in Chapter 8, or with indifference curves, as we did in this chapter. They each give the same answer. You will find a mathematical interpretation of this equivalence on the Parkin, Powell and Matthews Web site. So why do we have two theories? Is one better than the other?

Differences between Theories of Choice

The key difference between our two models of consumer choice is that we do not need to use the concept of utility in the indifference curve approach. We merely have to talk about preferences between different pairs of goods. We have to say whether the consumer prefers one combination to another or is indifferent between the two combinations. We don't have to say anything about *how* the consumer makes such evaluations. This means we don't have to find a measure for utility to make comparisons of utility between individuals. Most economists agree that the indifference curve theory is better for these reasons.

In the chapters that follow, we're going to study the choices made by firms. We'll see how, in the pursuit of profit, firms make choices governing the supply of goods and services and the demand for factors of production (inputs). After completing these chapters, we'll then bring the analysis of households and firms together and study their interactions in markets for goods and services and factors of production.

Summary

Key Points

Consumption Possibilities (pp. 190–193)

- The budget line shows the limits to a household's consumption given its income and the prices of goods. The budget line is the boundary between what the household can and cannot afford.
- The point at which the budget line intersects the y-axis is the household's real income in terms of the good measured on that axis.
- The magnitude of the slope of the budget line is the relative price of the good measured on the x-axis in terms of the good measured on the y-axis.
- A change in price changes the slope of the budget line. The lower the price of the good measured on the x-axis, the flatter is the budget line. A change in income shifts the budget line (rightward for an increase and leftward for a decrease) but does not change its slope.

Preferences and Indifference Curves (pp. 193–197)

- A consumer's preferences can be represented by indifference curves. An indifference curve joins all the combinations of goods to which the consumer is indifferent.
- A consumer prefers any point above an indifference curve to any point on it and any point on an indifference curve to any point below it. Indifference curves bow towards the origin.
- The magnitude of the slope of an indifference curve is called the marginal rate of substitution.
- The marginal rate of substitution diminishes as consumption of the good measured on the y-axis decreases and consumption of the good measured on the x-axis increases.

Predicting Consumer Behaviour (pp. 197–201)

- A household consumes at its best affordable point. This point is on the budget line and on the highest attainable indifference curve and has a marginal rate of substitution equal to the relative price.
- The price effect can be divided into a substitution effect and an income effect.
- The substitution effect is the effect of a change in price on consumption when the consumer (hypothetically) remains indifferent between the original situation and the new situation.
- The substitution always results in an increase in consumption of the good whose relative price has decreased.
- The income effect is the effect of change in income on consumption.
- For a normal good, the income effect reinforces the substitution effect. For an inferior good, the income effect offsets the substitution effect.

Labour Supply and Leisure Choices (pp. 201–204)

- The indifference curve model of household choice enables us to understand how a household allocates its time between leisure and work.
- Work hours have increased and leisure hours have increased because the income effect on the demand for leisure has been greater than the substitution effect.

Key Figures

Key Terms

Review Questions

1. What determines the limits to a household's consumption choices?
2. What is the budget line?
3. What determines the intercept of the budget line on the y-axis?
4. What determines the slope of the budget line?
5. If the price of books is \$5 each and the price of CDs is \$10 each and you have \$50 to spend on books and CDs, write a mathematical equation for the budget line.
6. What happens to the equation in review question 5 if your income rises to \$60?
7. What happens to the equation in review question 5 if the price of CDs falls to \$5?
8. What is an indifference curve?
9. What do all the points on an indifference curve have in common?
10. Why do individuals prefer to be on a higher indifference curve?
11. What is the marginal rate of substitution?
12. What determines the shape of an indifference curve?
13. What is meant by diminishing rate of marginal substitution?

14 What two conditions are satisfied when a consumer makes the best affordable consumption?

15 What is the effect of a change in income on consumption?

16 What is the effect of a change in price on consumption?

17 What is the price effect?

18 Define the income effect of a price change.

19 Distinguish between the income effect and the substitution effect of a price change.

20 What is the opportunity cost of leisure?

21 What is the effect of reducing the wage rate on the opportunity cost of leisure?

22 Why might the labour supply curve bend backward?

Problems

1 Sara has an income of £12 a week. Pizzas costs £3 each and beer costs £3 a bottle.

a What is Sara's real income in terms of beer?
b What is her real income in terms of pizzas?
c What is the relative price of beer in terms of pizzas?
d What is the opportunity cost of a bottle of beer?
e Calculate the equation for Sara's budget line (placing pizzas on the left side).
f Draw a graph of Sara's budget line with beer on the x-axis.
g What is the slope of Sara's budget line? What is it equal to?

2 Sara's income and the prices she faces are the same as in Problem 1. Her preferences are shown by her indifference curves in the figure.

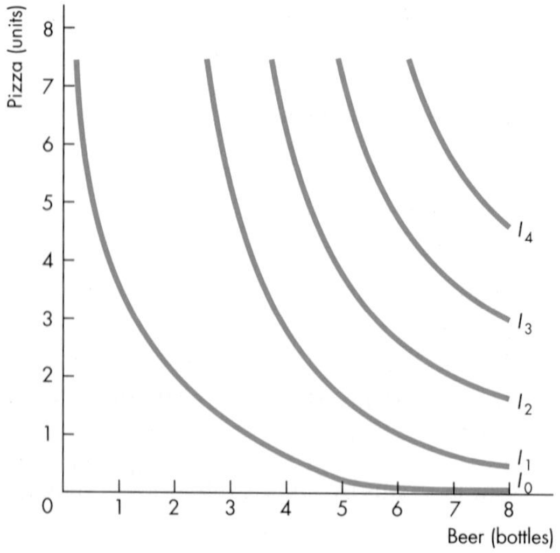

a What are the quantities of pizzas and beer that Sara buys?
b What is Sara's marginal rate of substitution of pizzas for beer at the point at which she consumes?

3 Now suppose that in the situation described in Problem 2, the price of beer halves to £1.50 per can and the price of pizzas and Sara's income remain constant.

a Find the new quantities of beer and pizzas that Sara buys.
b Find two points on Sara's demand curve for beer.
c Find the substitution effect of the price change.
d Find the income effect of the price change.
e Is beer a normal good or an inferior good for Sara?
f Is pizza a normal good or an inferior good for Sara?

4 Gerry buys cakes that cost £1 each and comic books that cost £2 each. Each month Gerry buys 20 cakes and 10 comic books. He spends all of his income. Next month the price of cakes will fall to 50 pence, but the price of a comic book will rise to £3.

a Will Gerry be able to buy 20 cakes and 10 comic books next month?
b Will he want to?
c If he changes his consumption, which good will he buy more of and which less?
d Which situation does Jerry prefer: cakes at £1 and comic books at £2 or cakes at 50 pence and comic books at £3?

e When the prices change next month will there be an income effect and a substitution effect at work or just one of them? If there is only one effect at work, which one will it be?

5 Now suppose that in the situation described in Problem 4, the prices of cakes and comic books next month remain at £1 and £2 respectively. Gerry gets a pay rise of £10 a month. He now buys 16 comic books and 18 cakes. For Gerry are cakes and comic books normal goods or inferior goods?

6 Jane is a student. She has worked out that she can spend £50 on recorded music tapes and CDs this term. If tapes cost £5 and CDs cost £10:

a Write out an equation for the budget line between tapes and CDs.
b Draw the budget line as a graph.

7 If Jane chooses to buy 6 tapes this term on the basis of the information in Problem 6:

a How much does she spend on CDs this term?
b How many CDs does she buy this term?
c Draw an indifference curve on your graph of the budget from Problem 6 to illustrate the choice between tapes and CDs which maximizes Jane's utility.
d What is Jane's marginal rate of substitution between tapes and CDs at her preferred choice?

8 Suppose Jane's grandmother sends her a cheque for £20 for her birthday. Jane decides to spend this on tapes or CDs.

a Draw the new budget line on your graph from Problem 6.
b Assuming tapes and CDs are both normal goods, draw another indifference curve on the graph to illustrate the choice of tapes and CDs which maximizes Jane's utility.
c How much does Jane spend on CDs when she includes her birthday money?
d What is the substitution and income effect of her birthday money on tapes?

9 Jane now has £70 to spend on tapes and CDs this term. But when she goes shopping, she finds the price of tapes has risen to £10:

a Write an equation for Jane's new budget line.
b Draw Jane's new budget line on a graph.
c Assuming Jane's preferences have not changed, how many CDs does she buy this term?
d What is Jane's marginal rate of substitution between tapes and CDs at her preferred choice?

10 Jim spends his income on rent, food, clothing, and holidays. He gets a pay raise from £1,000 a month to £2,000 a month. At the same time, airfares and other holiday related costs increase by 50 per cent while other prices remain unchanged.

a How do you think Jim will change his spending pattern as a result of the changes in his income and prices?
b Is Jim better off or worse off in his new situation? Why or why not?
c If *all* prices rise by 50 per cent, how does Jim change his purchases? Is he now better off or worse off? Why?

11 Turn back to pp. 210–211 and read the material in *Economics in History*. Then answer the following questions:

a What is the role of technology in explaining women's increased participation in the workforce over the past 100 years?
b Use a diagram similar to Figure 9.11 to illustrate your answer to part (a) of this question.
c Gary Becker would argue that the decision to have a baby like the decision to join the workforce, can be modelled by utility maximizing behaviour. According to this model, what benefits and costs do you think parents would take into account in the decision to start a family?
d On the basis of your experience and the economics you have studied, do you think that family decisions are in any part economic decisions? Explain your answer.

12 Read the article in *Reading Between the Lines* on pp. 208–209 and then answer the following questions:

a Why does the Belgium food scare affect the shape of the indifference curves between Belgian and UK egg-based mayonnaises?
b Use an indifference curve diagram to show how the Belgian food scare could lead to a fall in the consumption of all manufactured foods containing animal products relative to strictly vegetarian alternatives.

Indifference Curves: The Belgian Food Scare

The Guardian, 4 June 1999

Contaminated food crisis spreads across Europe

Stephen Bates in Brussels, **James Meikle** and **Vikram Dodd**

The European food industry was in turmoil last night, with stores clearing thousands of products from their shelves as the list of potentially contaminated foodstuffs seemed to grow almost by the hour.

The crisis that began in Belgium over the weekend was spreading rapidly across other countries as the Belgian authorities revealed that animal feed contaminated with carcinogenic dioxins might have been fed to cattle as well as pigs and chickens.

The likelihood emerged that millions of consumers across the continent — and perhaps some in Britain — had been eating contaminated food for the past four months as European commission officials admitted they could not exclude the possibility that other animal species or dairy products had been affected as well.

The ministry of agriculture and the food industry were last night trying to reassure the public, but British supermarket bosses are to hold an emergency meeting today to try to pool their resources in tracing affected supplies and products.

Nick Brown, the agriculture minister, said he was "pretty confident" that contaminated products imported into Britian could be traced.

He added: "The only way to guarantee not being at risk from eggs, poultry or pork from Belgium would be not to eat it. I wouldn't."

Supermarkets that have spent two days checking the exact source of Belgian-supplied ingredients based on poultry, egg or pork products were last night turning their attention to other foods and suppliers in Germany, the Netherlands and France.

Tesco has withdrawn 15 pates, eight mayonnaises and a line of Belgian croissants, Sainsbury's two pates, and Waitrose five lines of cooked poultry. Asda and Somerfield also withdrew lines.

The European commission last night ordered a ban on pork and beef, milk and dairy products produced on affected farms since mid-January. More than 1,000 farms in Belgium and 350 in Holland have been closed.

The Essence of the Story

- The Belgian food scare began when the Belgian authorities reported that animal feed contaminated with cancer forming dioxins had been fed to cattle, pigs and chickens in Belgium, the Netherlands and Germany. The authorities had found dioxin levels up to 700 times the permitted health levels in Belgian eggs, chickens and pigs.

- Millions of consumers across Europe may have eaten food products contaminated by dioxins of the past four months.

- Nick Brown, UK agriculture minister tried to reassure the public, saying that contaminated products imported into Britain could be traced. However, consumers were advised to avoid products that might contain Belgian animal products.

- Supermarkets have been taking products such as pâtés, mayonnaises, croissants, cooked poultry and Belgian chocolates, off the shelves because they contain Belgian poultry, egg or pork products. Supermarkets have also said that they may consider removing products supplied by other European countries.

■ More than 1000 farms in Belgian and the Netherlands have been closed and their products have been banned. As the cartoon implies, even when the ban is lifted, the long-term effect may be to reduce demand for Belgian animal foods if consumers have less faith in the safety of the animal food industry following the BSE crisis three years ago.

Economic Analysis

■ Figure 1 shows a consumer's choice of mayonnaise containing Belgian eggs and mayonnaise containing UK eggs before the 1999 scare.

■ The indifference curves were I_0 and I_1 and the budget line was *AB*. A typical consumer bought 10 bottles of Belgian egg mayonnaise and 12 bottles of UK egg mayonnaise. Both types of mayonnaise were good substitutes for each other.

■ The dioxin contamination scare changed people's preferences for the two types of mayonnaise. Figure 2 shows how the indifference curves changed. The new indifference curves, I_2 and I_3, are much steeper than the original ones.

■ With the new preferences, the two types of mayonnaise are poor substitutes. The marginal rate of substitution is so high that the best affordable consumption point changes to zero Belgian egg mayonnaise and 22 UK egg mayonnaise bottles.

■ The outcome shown in Figure 2 is not the end of the story. The change in preferences increased demand for the UK egg mayonnaise so its price increased.

■ Figure 3 shows the effect of the price increase on the choice of a typical UK consumer.

■ The marginal rate of substitution is so high – the indifference curves are so steep – that even at the new higher price, no Belgian egg mayonnaise is bought.

■ When the ban is eventually lifted, the situation will only return to the original one shown in Figure 1, if consumer confidence in Belgian egg mayonnaise is fully restored.

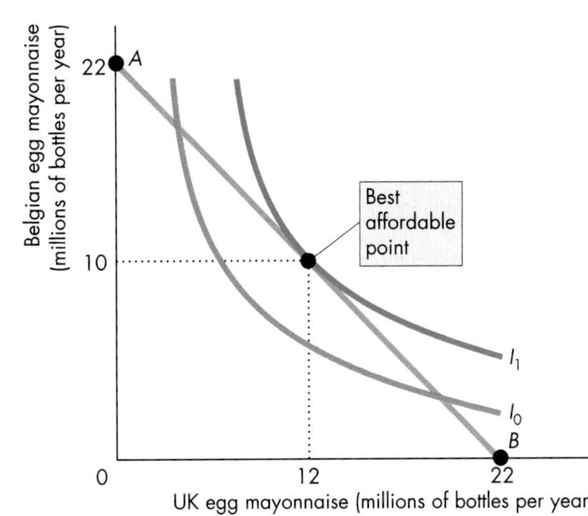

Figure 1 Consumer's choice before scare

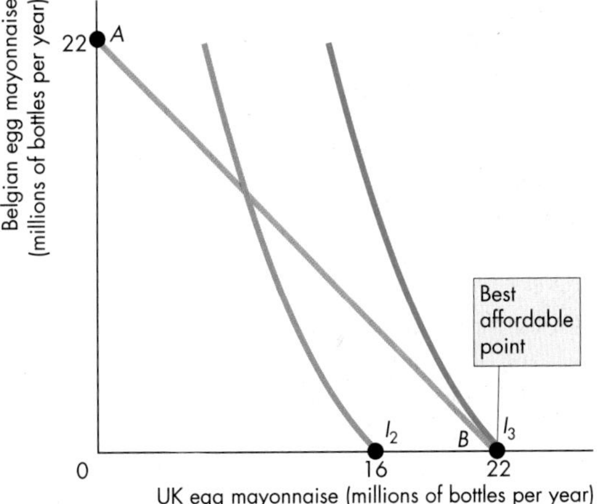

Figure 2 Consumer's choice after scare

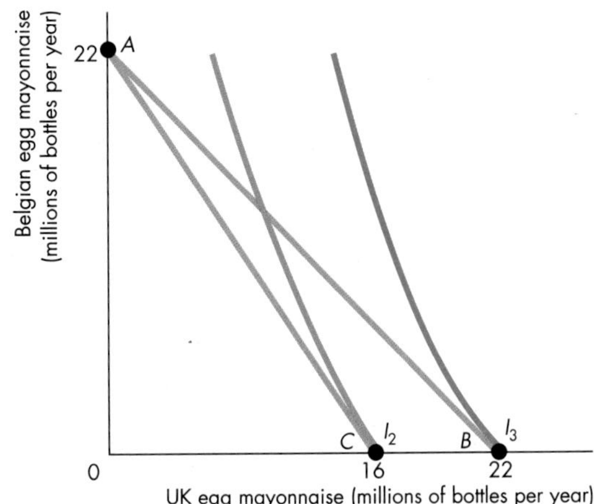

Figure 3 Consumer's choice after the price rise

Understanding Human Behaviour

". . . it is the greatest happiness of the greatest number that is the measure of right and wrong."

Jeremy Bentham, *Fragment on Government*

The Economist: Jeremy Bentham

Jeremy Bentham (1748–1832), who lived in London, was the son and grandson of a lawyer and was himself trained as a barrister. But he rejected the opportunity to maintain the family tradition and instead spent his life as a writer, activist and Member of Parliament, in the pursuit of rational laws that would bring the greatest happiness to the greatest number.

Bentham, whose embalmed body is preserved to this day in a glass cabinet at the University of London, was the first person to use the concept of utility to explain human choices. But in Bentham's day, the distinction between explaining and prescribing was not a sharp one, and Bentham was ready to use his ideas to tell people how they ought to behave. He was one of the first to propose pensions for the retired, guaranteed employment, minimum wages and social benefits such as free education and free medical care.

The Issues and Ideas

The economic analysis of human behaviour in the family, the workplace, the markets for goods and services, the markets for labour services and financial markets is based on the idea that our behaviour can be understood as a response to scarcity. Everything we do can be understood as a choice that maximizes total benefit subject to the constraints imposed by our limited resources and technology. If people's preferences are stable in the face of changing constraints, then we have a chance of predicting how they will respond to an evolving environment.

The economic approach explains the incredible change that has occurred during the past 100 years in the way women allocate their time as the consequence of changing constraints, not of changing attitudes. Technological advances have equipped the nation's farms and factories with machines that have increased the productivity of both women and men, thereby raising the wages they can earn. The increasingly technological world has increased the return to education for both women and men and has led to a large increase in the number of both sexes staying in full-time school and college education. Equipped with an ever widening array of gadgets and appliances that cut the time taken to do household jobs, an increasing proportion of women have joined the workforce.

The economic explanation might not be correct, but it is a powerful one. If it is correct, the changing attitudes are a consequence, not a cause, of the economic advancement of women.

Then . . .

Economists now explain people's actions as the consequences of choices that maximize total utility subject to constraints. Professor Gary Becker of the University of Chicago has transformed the way we think about human choices. In the 1890s, fewer than 20 per cent of women chose paid employment, and most of those who did had low-paying and unattractive jobs. The other 80 per cent of women chose unpaid work in the home. Professor Becker would explain this as the rational result of women's choices, given the constraints at the time.

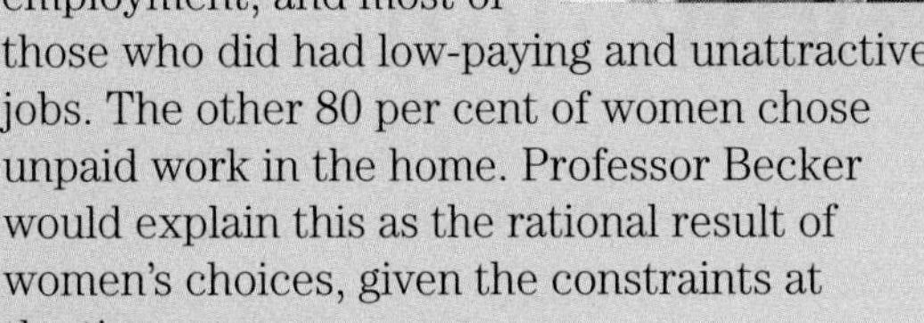

. . . And Now

By 1997, more than 60 per cent of women were in the workforce, and, although many had low-paying jobs, women were increasingly found in the professions and in executive positions. What brought about this dramatic change compared with 100 years earlier? Was it a change in preferences or a change in the constraints that women face?

Trying These Ideas Today

Using what you have learned about utility and choice in Chapter 9, and what you know about the participation of women in the workforce, you should be able to answer the following questions:

- Professor Gary Becker would argue that the decision to have a baby, like the decision to join the workforce, can be modelled as utility maximizing behaviour. Using this model, what costs and benefits do you think parents would take into account in the decision to start a family?
- Use the utility maximizing behaviour model to explain the falling birth rate in industrialized countries.

CHAPTER 10

Organizing Production

After studying this chapter you will be able to:

- Explain what a firm is and describe the economic problems that all firms face
- Define and explain the principal–agent problem
- Describe and distinguish between different forms of business organization
- Explain how firms raise the funds to finance their operations
- Calculate a firm's opportunity cost and economic profit
- Explain why firms coordinate some economic activities and markets coordinate others

An Apple a Day

On a July day in 1977, a tiny new firm was born that grew into a giant – Apple Computer. But that day was not unusual. Every day a new successful firm is born. Apple began its life when two students at Stanford University in the United States produced the world's first commercially successful personal computer in a garage. From that modest start, Apple has grown into one of the world's multinational giants. But most new firms remain small, like family restaurants and corner shops. Although three-quarters of all firms are operated by their owners, as Apple once was, giant corporations now account for the majority of direct investment and trade in Europe. What are the different forms a firm can take? Why do some remain small while others become giants? Why are most firms owner-operated? ◆ Firms spend millions of pounds on buildings and production lines and on developing and marketing new products. How does a firm get the funds needed to pay for all these activities? What do investors expect in return when they put funds into a firm? And how do we measure a firm's economic health? ◆ Most of the components of an IBM personal computer are made by other firms such as Microsoft, which created the operating system. Microsoft has now outgrown IBM, and its products such as DOS and Windows have become household names all over the world. Why doesn't IBM make its own computer components? Why didn't it create its own operating system? Why did it leave these activities to other firms? How do firms decide what to make themselves and what to buy in the marketplace from other firms?

◆ ◆ ◆ ◆ In this chapter, we are going to learn about firms and the choices they make to cope with scarcity. We begin by studying the economic problems and choices that all firms face.

The Firm and its Economic Problem

A **firm** is an institution that hires factors of production and that organizes those factors to produce and sell goods and services. There are 2.8 million firms in the United Kingdom, and they differ enormously in size and in the scope of what they do. Despite this diversity, each firm faces the same fundamental economic problem. How can it get the most out of the scarce resources it has under its control? For the majority of firms, this means making the maximum possible profit. For every firm, whether it is motivated by profit or some other goal, getting the most out of its resources means operating efficiently. A firm is efficient when it produces its output at the lowest possible cost.

In this chapter and in Chapters 11 to 14 we're going to study what decisions a firm must must take to be efficient. We'll see how to predict a firm's behaviour by working out its efficient response to a change in circumstances. Before we start, let's look at the main forms of business organization which apply throughout Europe and North America.

The Main Types of Firm

The three main types of firm are:

1 Proprietorship.

2 Partnership.

3 Company.

The form of organization influences the management structure of a firm. It determines how factors of production are paid, how much tax its owners pay, who receives its profits and who is liable for its debts if it goes out of business.

Proprietorship A *proprietorship*, sometimes called a sole trader, is a firm with a single owner – the proprietor – who has unlimited liability for the business. *Unlimited liability* is the legal responsibility for all the debts of a firm up to an amount equal to the entire wealth of the owner. If a proprietorship cannot pay its debts, the personal property of the owner can be claimed by those to whom the firm owes money. Corner shops, self-employed computer programmers, window cleaners and many small businesses are all examples of proprietorships.

The proprietor makes the management decisions and is the firm's sole residual claimant. A firm's *residual claimant* is the person who receives the firm's profits and is responsible for its losses. The profits of a proprietorship are part of the income of the owner and are taxed as personal income.

Partnership A *partnership* is a firm with two or more owners who have unlimited liability for the business. Partners must agree on an appropriate management structure and on how to divide the firm's profits among themselves. As in a proprietorship, the profits of a partnership are taxed as the personal income of the owners. But each partner is legally liable for all the debts of the partnership (only limited by the wealth of an individual partner). Liability for the full debts of the partnership is called *joint unlimited liability.* Most solicitors, consultancies and accounting firms are set up as partnerships.

Companies A **company** is a firm owned by one or more limited liability shareholders. *Limited liability* means the owners have legal liability only for the value of their initial investment. This limitation of liability means that if the company becomes bankrupt, the owners of the company, unlike the owners of a proprietorship or a partnership, cannot be forced to use their personal wealth to pay the company's debts. A large-scale limited liability company is often called a corporation. Most large companies are owned by groups of individual and company shareholders who have invested in the company through the stock market. If a company makes a profit, the residual claimants to that profit are the shareholders who receive dividends. If a company becomes bankrupt, the residual loss is absorbed by the banks and the company's other creditors.

Some small companies, no bigger than a proprietorship, have just one main owner and are managed in the same way as a proprietorship. Larger companies have elaborate management structures headed by a board of directors, executive officers and senior managers responsible for such areas as production, finance, marketing and research. These senior managers are in turn served by a series of specialist managers. Each layer in the management structure knows enough about what happens in the layer below it to exercise control, but the entire management consists of specialists

Figure 10.1 Relative Importance of Firms by Size

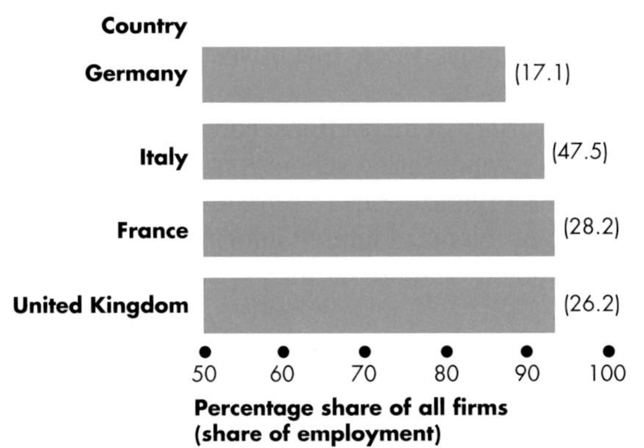

(a) Importance of small firms

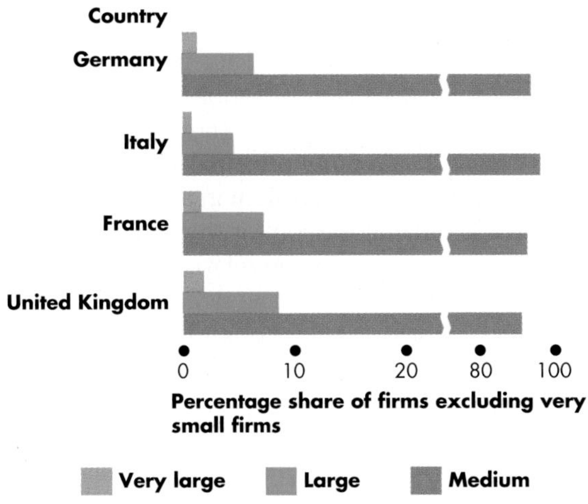

(b) Importance of medium, large and very large firms

Very small firms employing less than 10 employees account for over 90 per cent of all firms in most western European countries, but usually account for less than 30 per cent of employment. Of the remainder, medium-sized firms are the most important. Very large firms employing more than 500 employees account for less than 2 per cent of medium and large scale firms, but account for about 40 per cent of all employment.

Source: *Enterprises in Europe*, Commission of the European Communities, Office for Official Publications of the European Communities, Luxembourg, 1992.

who concentrate on a narrow aspect of the company's activities.

The Relative Importance of Different Sizes of Firm

The total number of businesses in the United Kingdom increased from 1.9 million to 2.8 million between 1979 and 1993. This was largely owing to an increase in the number of one-person and two-person businesses – many of them family businesses. Over 26 per cent of employees in the private sector are employed in small businesses with fewer than 10 employees. The majority of single proprietorships and partnerships are small firms of this type.

Figure 10.1(a) shows the importance of very small firms in a selection of Western European countries. Firms employing less than 10 employees account for more than 90 per cent of all firms in most European countries. These firms can account for as little as 17 per cent of employment in Germany or as much as 47 per cent of employment in Italy. The majority of employment in very small firms is in the services, construction and agriculture sectors. Part (b) shows the importance of the remaining medium and larger firms in a selection of European countries. The pattern is similar across most European countries. Medium-sized firms consititute the largest proportion of this group. Whilst very large corporations employing more than 500 employees only account for just over 1 per cent of firms in most European countries, they account for about 40 per cent of employment.

Now we know about the size and types of firm, let's look at their goals and how they differ.

It is easy to think that all firms aim to be efficient and maximize profits. Although firms strive to be efficient, they operate in a hostile environment and two pervasive facts of life make the profit maximizing decision difficult. They are:

1 Uncertainty about the future.

2 Incomplete information.

Uncertainty About the Future

Management is about planning and strategic thinking. This means making decisions today about what to do tomorrow. Even if managers base every decision on the presumption that it will make the maximum possible contribution to the firm's profits – expectations often turn out to be wrong. The main reason is that a firm must commit itself to a project and spend huge amounts on it *before* it knows whether it will be able to sell enough output at a high enough price to cover its outlays. For example, 30 years ago French and British aircraft makers spent several years and millions of pounds building a supersonic transatlantic passenger plane – the Concorde. They expected to be able to sell enough of these technologically sophisticated aircraft to recover their costs. It turned out that too few people valued the Concorde's extra speed for it to generate sales revenues equal to its cost. On a smaller scale, millions of people try their luck at opening coffee shops and other small businesses by estimating future demand and costs. If they need to borrow the initial capital, lenders will scrutinize their business plans and forecasts carefully. However, many of them turn out to be too optimistic – revenue falls short of the cost – and the business fails.

The fact that uncertainty exists has led to the development of many ingenious devices for limiting and spreading risk, including different types of corporate structures. We'll look at some of these later in this chapter.

Incomplete Information

The future is not the only unknown. Firms have limited information even about the past and present. It is simply not possible for a firm's owners and managers to know everything that is relevant to the efficient operation of their business. Firms do not know all the possible suppliers of inputs and all the available prices. In particular, firms do not always know the productivity of their employees. What has Jan Leschly, the chief executive officer (CEO), really done for pharmaceutical giant, SmithKline Beecham? Did his actions warrant raising his pay package to £90 million in 1999 – an 18 per cent rise? These questions cannot be answered with certainty, even long after the event. Yet companies like SmithKline Beecham must put CEOs in charge of operations and give them *incentives* to succeed, even when the contribution they make cannot be measured directly.

Similarly, some workers are more productive than others and it is often difficult for managers to know who is productive and who is not. Did sales fall last month because the sales-force took things easy or because of a general fall in demand for the product? Again, firms must devise incentives to motivate their sales-forces.

A rich variety of institutions, contractual relationships and compensation schemes have been devised in business organizations to raise efficiency and avoid the problems of limited information. Let's look at this problem in more detail.

The Principal–Agent Problem

Because of uncertainty and incomplete information, firms do not simply demand factors of production and pay for them as if they were buying toothpaste in a supermarket. Instead, they enter into contracts and devise compensation packages that strengthen the incentives to raise productivity and spread risks. These contracts and compensation packages are called agency relationships and they are an attempt to solve what is called the principal–agent problem. The **principal–agent problem** in a firm occurs because it is difficult to monitor the activities of all employees. For example, the relationship between the shareholders of SmithKline Beecham and its managers is an agency relationship. The shareholders (the principals) want the managers (agents) to act in the shareholders' best interest. Another example of an agency relationship is that between Microsoft Corporation senior managers (the principals) and programmers working on the next version of Windows (agents). Microsoft managers wants the programmers to work towards their managerial goals.

We have already seen that some forms of business organization are complex. There is a long chain of interests in large companies from the shareholders, through the board of directors, to divisional and functional managers, and through to production workers. This generates two principal–agent problems:

1 Separation of ownership and control.
2 Monitoring and motivation problems.

Separation of ownership and control The owners of modern large companies have become separated from the managers who control decision making. The *separation of ownership from control* is a problem if managers pursue different goals from shareholders. For example, shareholders (the principals) want the firm to maximize profit. But the firm's profit depends on the actions of its managers (agents), who may have their own goals such as maximizing salaries and perks.

Why might managers and employees have different goals from shareholders? Is there any reason to believe that managers do not seek efficiency and profit maximization? We can use our model of utility maximization to explain this. If managers are rational utility maximizers, their utility will increase as they get more power, prestige and pay. The best way to increase utility is to maximize sales or the size of the division that they run because power, prestige and pay tend to increase with sales and division size. If managers divert some of the profits into expanding their division and increasing their pay, less profit will be available to shareholders.

Monitoring and Motivation It is more difficult for managers (principals) to monitor their workforce (agents) in complex organizations. The workforce may be spread across many different buidlings or countries. Workers are also rational utility maximizers, and their utility falls as they do more work for a given weekly wage. So workers (agents) might do less work if they are not closely monitored by their managers (principals). This monitoring and motivation problem raises costs and reduces profits.

Business organizations have devised a number of innovative schemes to reduce the principal–agent problem, as a way to increase efficiency. Let's look at these more closely.

Coping with the Principal–Agent Problem

The perfect incentive scheme does not exist. Agents, whether they are managers or workers, can pursue their own goals and often impose costs on a principal. The principal–agent problem cannot be solved just by giving orders and having them obeyed. In most firms, it isn't possible for the shareholders to monitor the managers, or even for the managers to monitor the workers. To achieve their goal, the firm's owners (principals) must find a way to induce the managers (agents) to pursue the maximum possible profit, and the managers (principals) must induce the workers (agents) to work efficiently. Each principal does this by creating incentives to persuade each agent to work in the interests of the principal. The four main ways of coping with the principal–agent problem are:

1 Ownership.

2 Incentive pay.

3 Long-term contracts.

4 Internal restructuring.

Ownership Giving a manager or worker ownership (or part-ownership) of a business is a way of improving job performance and increasing a firm's profits. The manager (agent) becomes more like the owner (principal) and profit maximization will become a more important management goal. Part-ownership schemes for senior managers are quite common, and are becoming more common for staff. The two largest UK employee share ownership schemes are run by Baxi Partnership Ltd, which makes heating systems, and Tullis Russell Group, which makes paper. Both companies belonged to the same family firm, which decided to distribute over 50 per cent of the shares to employees to raise motivation and profitability. Many large retail stores now offer staff cheap share purchase options.

Incentive pay Incentive pay schemes are very common. Most middle managers are assessed annually against a wide variety of performance criteria. If they work on a performance related pay scheme, their pay increments will be based on their performance in the previous year. In addition, many companies reward managers and workers by offering separate bonuses for meeting production or sales targets. These types of incentive pay schemes help to focus the goals of all employees on profit maximization, reducing the principal–agent problem.

Long-term contracts Long-term contracts are another way of coping with the principal–agent problem because they tie the long-term fortunes of managers and workers (agents) to the success of the principal(s) – the owner(s) of the firm.

Internal restructuring Monitoring and motivating your workforce is easier in a small organization where the owner is also the manager and knows all

Figure 10.2 Corporate Structures

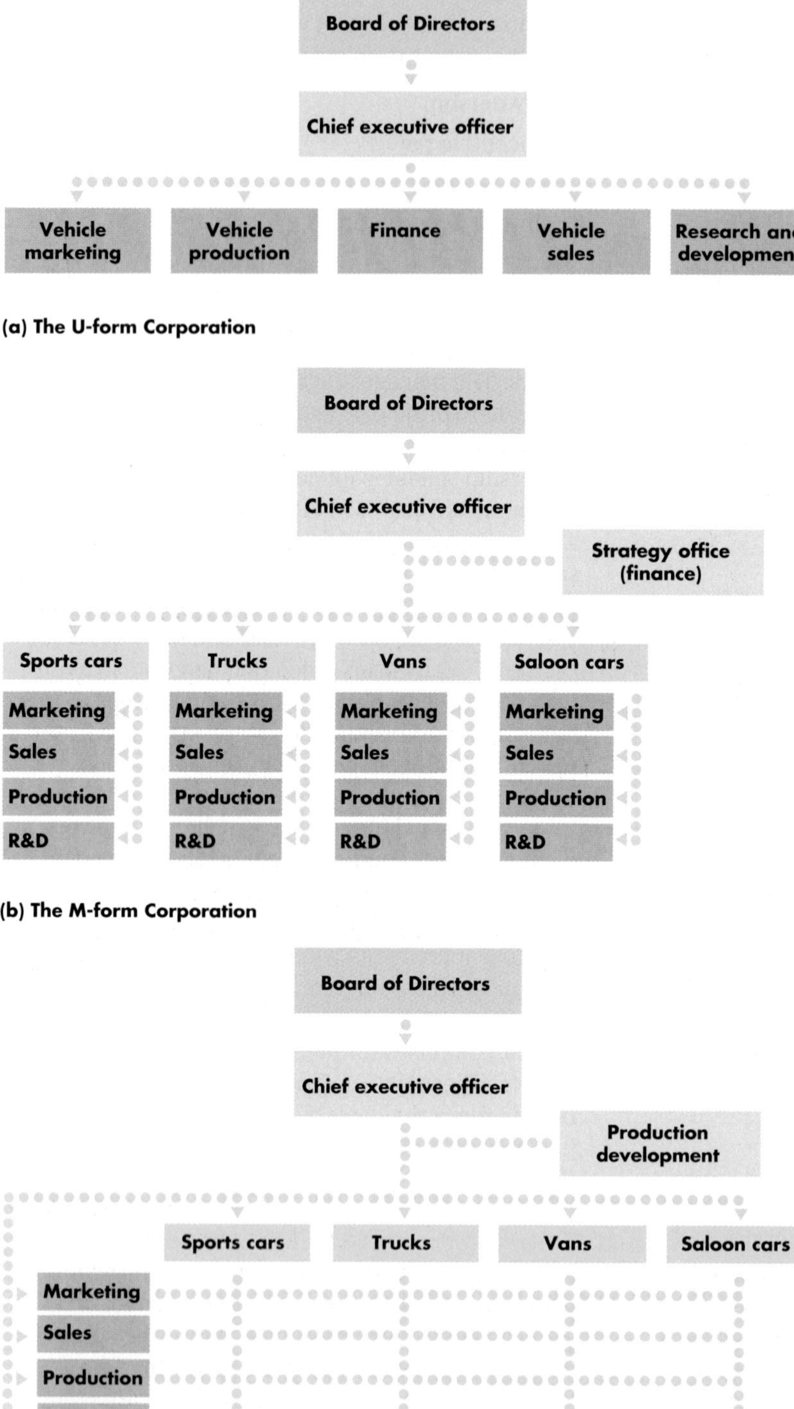

Large car companies can be set up as unitary divisional (U-form), multi-divisional (M-form) or matrix-form (X-form) structures. The functional divisions cover work for all products produced in the U-form and X-form structures. But in an M-form structure, there is a separate set of functional staff under each division. The U-form is efficient for medium-sized companies with few products. The M-form and X-form are better suited to large and very large scale multinational corporations where the flow of information is more complex.

the staff personally. In a large company, the flow of information can be slow and misleading. The flow of information and the benefits of team work and specialization can be increased by changing the internal structure of the firm. The internal structures of large corporations are organized in one of three ways:

1 Unitary divisional form (U-form).
2 Multi-divisional form (M-form).
3 Matrix form (X-form).

Figure 10.2 compares the three structures for a motor vehicle corporation such as Ford. In the U-form structure, the directors appoint managers to run separate divisions specializing in a function of business organization – finance, production and marketing, for example. Each division will deal with all the vehicles that the company produces. In the M-form structure, each vehicle type is allocated to a separate division, serviced by its own U-form structure underneath. There is also a separate executive office to develop general strategy and overall finance. Ford combined its European and US divisions into a matrix structure in 1996. In the matrix structure, some functions are separated out to operate across many vehicles and several countries.

The U-form structure is an improvement on proprietorship, when it generates savings from staff specialization. The Chief Executive Officer (CEO) can hire specialist accountants, marketing staff and engineers, who spread their specialist knowledge across all the products, reducing unit costs. But there comes a point as the organization grows when the CEO can no longer tell which product is doing well and which should be discontinued. Divisional managers are recommending strategies to protect their own divisions. Restructuring to the M-form can cut the costs of monitoring and increase manager motivation to maximize profits. The M-form structure has the separate strategy office whose staff can look dispassionately at the information on divisions. Divisional managers are made to compete for project bids to raise profits and cut costs. The M-form structure is now the most common structure for large, complex multinational corporations. The matrix-form structure increases the potential for team specialization across divisions and is increasingly adopted by multinational firms producing similar products in many countries. Ford have used new communications technology and the introduction of the world car to introduce team work systems that not only span national boundaries but also vehicle types.

Reducing Risk

Part of the reason why incentive schemes and restructuring raise efficiency lies in the difference between principals and agents in their attitude to risk. In general, principals (shareholders) are less risk averse than agents (employees). Shareholders can spread the risk of poor performance by employees by holding many shares in many firms. Employees are more risk averse about a low future income because they have one main source of income – their salary. In an uncertain environment with poor information, incentive schemes and restructuring pool these risks and raise efficiency. For example, incentive schemes raise profitability but expose more risk averse employees to greater variability of future income. An employee may work much harder but fail to get a pay increase if output does not rise. Output is affected by many things which employees cannot control – market demand, the efforts of colleagues and local suppliers. So to be efficient, an incentive scheme must balance the cost of exposing the agent to higher risk against the benefit of reducing risk for the principal. We'll look at risk again in more detail in Chapter 18.

The principal–agent problem seems to be mainly a problem of larger firms. So why isn't all production organized by single proprietors and partnerships? The answer lies in the balance of the benefits of size against the costs of monitoring and control.

The Pros and Cons of Different Types of Firm

Why do large companies dominate trade? Why do the other types of businesses survive? Why are proprietorships and partnerships more prominent in some sectors? The answer to these questions lies in the pros and cons of the different types of business organizations that are summarized in Table 10.1. Each firm type has its disadvantages, but companies dominate because most businesses use a large amount of capital. Proprietorships and partnerships operate where flexibility in decision making is critical.

Table 10.1 The Pros and Cons of Different Types of Firm

Type of firm	Pros	Cons
Proprietorship	◆ Easy to set up ◆ Simple decision making ◆ Profits taxed only once as owner's income	◆ Bad decisions not checked by need for consensus ◆ Owner's entire wealth at risk ◆ Firm dies with owner ◆ Capital is expensive ◆ Labour is expensive
Partnership	◆ Easy to set up ◆ Diversified decision making ◆ Can survive withdrawal of partner ◆ Profits taxed only once as owners' incomes	◆ Achieving consensus may be slow and expensive ◆ Owners' entire wealth at risk ◆ Withdrawal of partner may create capital shortage ◆ Capital is expensive
Corporation	◆ Owners have limited liability ◆ Large-scale, low-cost capital available ◆ Professional management not restricted by ability of owners ◆ Perpetual life ◆ Long-term labour contracts cut labour costs	◆ Complex management structure can make decisions slow and expensive ◆ Profits taxed twice as company profit and as shareholders' income

Review

- A firm is an institution that hires factors of production and organizes the production and sale of goods and services.
- Firms strive to be efficient and most firms aim to maximize profit, but they face uncertainty and have incomplete information. To cope with these problems, firms enter into relationships – agency relationships – with owners, managers, workers and other firms and devise efficient legal structures and compensation schemes.
- Each main type of firm – proprietorship, partnership and company – has its advantages and disadvantages, and each plays a role in every sector of the economy.

Business Finance

Every year firms raise billions of pounds to enable them to buy capital equipment and to finance their stocks of goods. For example, an airline may raise hundreds of millions of pounds to buy a bigger fleet of jets. A steel manufacturer may raise hundreds of millions of pounds to build a new plant. A software producer may raise millions of pounds to pay programmers to develop a new computer game. Let's see how firms raise funds.

How Firms Raise Funds

All firms get some of their funds from their owners. The owner's stake in a business is called **equity**. Firms also borrow some of the funds they need from banks. Proprietorships and partnerships raise additional funds by borrowing from friends. The more permanent structure of companies gives them two ways of raising large amounts of money that are not generally available to households and proprietorships and partnerships. They are:

1 Selling shares.
2 Selling bonds.

Selling Shares

One major way in which a company can raise funds is by selling shares. A **share** is a long term debt certificate issued by a company, which can never be repaid. Funds raised in this way are the company's *equity* because the shareholders of a company are its owners. They have bought shares of the company's stock. PLCs can sell new issues of their shares and current owners can sell their existing shares on the stock exchange. A *stock exchange* is an organized market for trading in shares. There are stock markets in many major European cities, and the London Stock Exchange is one of the biggest stock exchanges in the world. Shares in private limited companies can only be sold by private agreement.

Figure 10.3 shows an example of a firm raising funds by selling stock. In June 1996, Monument Oil

Figure 10.3 Selling Shares

MONUMENT OIL AND GAS (HOLDINGS) PLC

(Incorporated in England and Wales under the Companies Act 1985 with registration no. 3211318)

Introduction
of up to
800,000,000 Ordinary Shares of 25 pence each
and
admission to listing on the
London Stock Exchange

Share capital following the introduction

Authorised			Issued and fully paid	
Nominal Value	Number		Nominal Value	Number
£200,000,000	800,000,000	Ordinary Shares of 25 pence each	£167,018,021	668,072,083

(Assuming no elections under the mix and match provisions of the Scheme of Arrangement)

Monument's principal business is in the exploration for and production of oil and gas.

Monument Oil and Gas (Holding) PLC
80 Petty France
London SW1H 9EX

June 25, 1996

NatWest Wood Mackenzie & Co. Limited
135 Bishopsgate
London EC2M 3XT

A share in a company entitles its holder to vote at shareholders' meetings, to participate in the election of directors and to a dividend (if the directors vote to pay one). Monument Oil and Gas (Holdings) PLC, an oil and gas exploration company, announced the issue of 800 million shares at 25 pence each, to raise £200 million of additional funds.

Figure 10.4 Selling Bonds

Halifax Building Society

(Incorporated in England under the Building Societies Act 1986)

Issue of up to an aggregate of
£200,000,000
Subordinated Variable Rate Notes
with a maturity of 12 years

(Formerly Subordinated Variable Rate Notes issued by Leeds Permanent Building Society)

Notice is hereby given that the three months interest period from June 27, 1996 to September 27, 1996 (92 days) the Subordinated Notes will carry an interest rate of 6.275%. The interest payable on September 27, 1996 for the Subordinated Notes will be £157.73.

By: The Chase Manhattan Bank, N.A.
London, Principal Paying Agent
July 1, 1996

A bond is an obligation to make a stated dividend payment and a redemption payment on a given date. The Halifax Building Society announced an issue of 12-year bonds to raise £200 million. It promised to pay an interest rate of 6.275 per cent for the three-month period ending on 27 September 1996.

and Gas (Holdings) PLC, a gas and oil exploration company, announced the issue of 800 million shares at 25 pence a share to raise £200 million. There is no obligation for a firm to make dividend payments to its shareholders just because it raises funds by selling stock. But shareholders expect a dividend or a capital gain – otherwise no one will buy the shares.

Selling Bonds

A **bond** is a legally enforceable debt obligation to pay specified amounts of money at specified future dates. Usually a bond specifies that a certain amount of money called the *redemption value* of the bond will be paid at a certain future date called the *maturity date*. In addition, another amount will be paid each year between the date of sale of the bond and the maturity date. The amount of money paid each year is called the *dividend payment*.

An example of bond financing is shown in Figure 10.4. The Halifax Building Society announced the issue of £200 million of bonds (called subordinated variable rate notes) in June 1996. The bonds mature over a period of 12 years and carried an interest rate of 6.275 per cent for the three-month period ending on 27 September 1996.

When it makes a financing decision, a firm tries to minimize its cost of funds. If it can raise funds by selling bonds at a lower cost than from any other source, that is the method of financing it chooses. But how does it decide how much to borrow? To answer this question, we need to understand a key principle of business and personal finance.

Discounting and Present Value

When a firm raises funds, it receives money in the current period and takes on an obligation to make a series of payments in *future* periods. But a firm also raises funds, because it plans to use them to generate a future net inflow of cash from its business operations.

To decide whether to borrow and how much to borrow, a firm must somehow compare money today with money in the future. If you are given a choice between a pound today and a pound a year from today, you will choose a pound today. A pound today is worth more to you than a pound in the future because you can invest today's pound to earn interest. The same is true for a firm. To compare an amount of money in the future with an amount of money in the present, we calculate the present value of the future amount of money. The **present value** of a future amount of money is the amount which, if invested today, will grow to be as large as that future amount, taking into account the interest that it will earn. Let's express this idea with an equation:

$$\text{Future amount} = \text{Present value} + \text{Interest income}$$

But the interest income is equal to the present value multiplied by the interest rate, r, so:

$$\text{Future amount} = \text{Present value} + (r \times \text{Present value})$$

or

$$\text{Future amount} = \text{Present value} \times (1 + r)$$

If you have £100 today and the interest rate is 10 per cent a year ($r = 0.1$), one year from today you will have £110, the original £100 plus £10 interest. Check that the above formula delivers that answer: £100 × 1.1 = £110.

The formula that we have just used calculates a future amount from the present value and an interest rate. To calculate the present value, we just work backwards. Instead of multiplying the present value by $(1 + r)$, we divide the future amount by $(1 + r)$. That is:

$$\text{Present value} = \frac{\text{Future amount}}{(1 + r)}$$

You can use this formula to calculate present value. Calculating present value is called discounting. **Discounting** is the conversion of a future amount of money to its present value. Let's check that we can use the present value formula by calculating the present value of £110 one year from now when the interest rate is 10 per cent a year. You'll be able to guess that the answer is £100 because we just calculated that £100 invested today at 10 per cent a year becomes £110 in one year. Thus it follows immediately that the present value of £110 in one year's time is £100. But let's use the formula. Putting the numbers into the above formula we have:

$$\begin{aligned}\text{Present value} &= \frac{\pounds 110}{(1 + 0.1)} \\ &= \frac{\pounds 110}{(1.1)} \\ &= \pounds 100\end{aligned}$$

Calculating the present value of an amount of money one year from now is the easiest case. But we can also calculate the present value of an amount any number of years in the future. As an example, let's see how we calculate the present value of an amount of money available two years from now.

Suppose that you invest £100 today for two years at an interest rate of 10 per cent a year. The money will earn £10 in the first year, which means that by the end of the first year you will have £110. If the interest of £10 is invested, then the interest earned in the second year will be a further £10 on the original £100 plus £1 on the £10 interest. Thus the total interest earned in the second year will be £11. The total interest earned overall will be £21 (£10 in the first year and £11 in the second year). After two years, you will have £121. From the definition of present value, you can see that the present value of £121 two years hence is £100. That is, £100 is the present amount which, if invested at 10 per cent interest, will grow to £121 two years from now.

To calculate the present value of an amount of money two years in the future we use the formula:

$$\text{Present value} = \frac{\text{Amount of money in future}}{(1 + r)^2}$$

Let's check that the formula works by calculating the present value of £121 two years in the future when the interest rate is 10 per cent a year. Putting these numbers into the formula gives:

$$\begin{aligned}\text{Present value} &= \frac{\pounds 121}{(1 + 0.1)^2} \\ &= \frac{\pounds 121}{(1.1)^2} \\ &= \frac{\pounds 121}{1.21} \\ &= \pounds 100\end{aligned}$$

We can calculate the present value of an amount of money any number of years in the future by using a formula based on the two that we've already used. The general formula is:

$$\text{Present value} = \frac{\text{Money available } n \text{ years in future}}{(1 + r)^n}$$

For example, if the interest rate is 10 per cent a year, £100 to be received 10 years from now has a present value of £38.55. That is, if £38.55 is invested today at an interest rate of 10 per cent, it will accumulate to £100 in 10 years. (You might check this calculation on your pocket calculator.)

Present Value and Marginal Analysis

Firms use the concept of present value to make their financing decisions. But they use it together with another fundamental principle, marginal analysis. In making any decision, only the additional benefit

– *marginal benefit* – and additional cost – *marginal cost* – resulting from that decision are relevant. By evaluating the marginal benefit and marginal cost of borrowing, a firm is able to maximize its profit. Marginal benefit minus marginal cost is net benefit, and the present value of net benefit is called *net* present value.

The firm decides how much to borrow by calculating the net present value of borrowing one additional pound – the marginal pound borrowed. If the present value of the marginal pound borrowed is positive, then the firm increases its profit by increasing the amount it borrows. If the present value of the marginal pound borrowed is negative, then the firm increases its profit by *decreasing* its borrowing. When the present value of the marginal pound borrowed is zero, then the firm is maximizing its profit.

Review

- Firms finance capital equipment purchases by selling bonds – promises of a fixed income independent of the firm's profit, and selling shares – opportunities to share in the firm's profit.
- Firms borrow if doing so increases the net present value of their cash flow.

We've seen how firms pursue maximum profits by establishing appropriate types of business organizations and by raising funds in the most profitable way. But how do firms measure their performance? How do they calculate their costs and profits? These are the questions we now study.

Opportunity Cost and Economic Profit

A firm's *opportunity cost* of producing a good is the best alternative action that the firm foregoes to produce it. Equivalently, it is the firm's best alternative use for the factors of production it employs to produce a good. Opportunity cost is a real alternative foregone. But so that we can compare the opportunity cost of one action with that of another action, we often express opportunity cost in units of money. Even though we sometimes express opportunity cost in money units, it is the real alternative foregone and not the money value of that alternative.

A firm's opportunity cost of production has two components:

1 Explicit costs.
2 Implicit costs.

Explicit and Implicit Costs

Explicit costs are paid directly in money – *money costs*. It is easy to measure explicit costs using accountancy standards.

A firm incurs explicit costs when it pays for a factor of production at the same time as it uses it. The money cost is the amount paid for the factor of production, but this same amount could have been spent on something else, so it is also the opportunity cost (expressed in pounds) of using this factor of production. For example, if a pizza restaurant hires a waiter, the wages paid are both the money cost and the opportunity cost of hiring the waiter – the firm pays the waiter at the same time as it uses the services of the waiter. Labour is the factor of production whose money cost typically equals its opportunity cost. Implicit costs are measured in units of money but they are not paid for directly in money. Like explicit costs, implicit costs are the value of foregone opportunities. A firm incurs implicit costs when it uses the following factors of production:

- Capital.
- Stocks.
- Owner's resources.

Cost of Capital

The cost of using capital equipment is an implicit cost because a firm usually buys its equipment – lays out some money – and then uses the equipment over a future period. For example, Ford (UK) buys an assembly line, pays for it this year and uses it for several years. What is the opportunity cost of using capital equipment bought several years earlier? This opportunity cost has two components:

1 Depreciation.
2 Interest.

Economic Depreciation

Economic depreciation is the change in the market price of a capital asset over a given period. It is calculated as the market price of the capital at the beginning of the period minus its market price at the end of the period. For example, suppose that British Airways has a Boeing 747 jumbo jet that it could have sold on 31 December, 1997 for £5 million. Suppose also that it could sell the same aircraft on 31 December 1998 for £4 million. The £1 million fall in the market value is an implicit cost of using the aircraft during 1998. Notice that the original cost of the aircraft is not directly relevant to this calculation.

Economic depreciation occurs for a variety of reasons. The most common is that an older piece of equipment has a shorter future life, and it is often more costly to maintain in good working order. But economic depreciation also occurs simply because a piece of equipment has become obsolete. It still works well and might do so for many years, but there is something new that works even better. For example, suppose your university library bought some new photocopiers on 1 January 1998 which it expected to operate for three years. Then, during 1998, a faster photocopier became available and the market price of the slower copiers fell by 90 per cent. This 90 per cent price fall is the opportunity cost of using the photocopiers in 1998. Even though the copiers are new and still work well, their economic depreciation – and opportunity cost – during 1998 is large.

Interest The funds used to buy a capital asset could have been used for some other purpose. In their next best alternative use, they would have yielded a return – an interest income. This foregone interest is part of the opportunity cost of using the capital asset. And it is an opportunity cost regardless of whether a firm borrows the funds it uses to buy its capital (its buildings, plant and equipment). To see why, think about two cases: the firm borrows or uses its previous earnings.

If a firm borrows the money, then it makes an explicit interest payment, so the interest cost is an explicit cost. If the firm uses its own funds, then the opportunity cost is the amount that could have been earned by allocating those funds to their best alternative use. Suppose the best alternative is for the firm to put the money in a bank deposit. The bank deposit interest foregone is the opportunity cost of buying and using the capital asset.

Implicit Rental Rate To measure the opportunity cost of using capital (buildings, plant and equipment), we calculate the sum of economic depreciation and interest costs. This opportunity cost is the income that the firm foregoes by using the assets itself and not renting them to another firm instead. The firm actually rents the assets to itself. When a firm rents assets to itself, it pays an **implicit rental rate** for their use.

People commonly rent houses, flats, cars, televisions, VCRs and videotapes. Firms commonly rent photocopiers, earth-moving equipment, satellite launching services, and so on. If a piece of equipment is rented, a pound payment called an *explicit* rental rate is made. If a piece of equipment is bought and used by its owner rather than rented to someone else, an *implicit* rental rate is paid. The owner–user of a piece of equipment could have rented the equipment to someone else instead. The income foregone is the opportunity cost of using the equipment. That opportunity cost is the implicit rental rate.

In the absence of transactions costs, market forces make explicit rental rates equal to implicit rental rates. If renting had a lower opportunity cost than buying, everyone would want to rent and no one would want to buy. So renters would not be able to find anyone to rent from and the (explicit) rental rate would rise. If renting had a higher opportunity cost than buying, everyone would want to buy and no one would want to rent. So owners would not be able to find anyone to rent to and the (explicit) rental rate would fall. Only when the opportunity cost of renting and buying are equal is there no incentive to switch between buying and renting.

Sunk Cost A **sunk cost** is the *past economic depreciation* of a capital asset (building, plant or equipment). When the asset was purchased, an opportunity was foregone. But that past foregone opportunity is a bygone. The opportunity cannot be retrieved. Sunk cost is not an *opportunity cost*. In the photocopier example, your university library incurred a high opportunity cost during 1998 when the market price of its slow copiers fell. But as the library's planners look forward to 1999, the fall in the value of its photocopiers in 1998 is a sunk cost. The opportunity cost of using the copiers during 1999 does *not* include that fall in value.

Accounting Depreciation Accountants measure depreciation, but they do not usually measure *economic depreciation*. Instead, they assess this fall in the value of a capital asset by applying a conventional depreciation rate to the original purchase price. The conventions used are based on standardized accounting schedules. For buildings, a conventional depreciation period is 20 years. Thus if a firm buys a new office building for £100,000, its accounts show one-twentieth of that amount, £5,000, as a cost of production each year. At the end of the first year, the firm's accounts record the value of the building as £95,000 (the original cost minus the £5,000 depreciation). Different depreciation rates are used for different types of capital. For example, for cars and computers, the conventional depreciation period is three years.

These accounting measures of depreciation do not measure economic depreciation and are not a correct measure of the depreciation component of the opportunity cost of using capital.

Cost of Stocks

The opportunity cost of using an item from stocks is its current replacement cost. If an item is taken out of stocks, it will have to be replaced by a new item. The cost of that new item is the opportunity cost of using the item taken from stocks.

Stocks are stores of raw materials, semi-finished goods and finished goods held by firms. Some firms carry small stocks and some have stocks that turn over quickly. In such cases, the money cost of using an item from stocks and its opportunity cost are the same. When a production process requires stocks to be held for a long time, the two costs might differ.

To measure the cost of using stocks, accountants frequently use a money cost method called FIFO, which stands for 'First In, First Out'. This method of calculating the cost of an item taken from stocks assumes that the first item placed into stocks is the first one taken out. An alternative accountant's measure is called LIFO, which stands for 'Last In, First Out'. The opportunity cost of an item taken from stocks is the cost of replacing it. If prices are constant over long periods of time, FIFO and LIFO measure opportunity cost. But if prices are changing, FIFO is not a measure of opportunity cost, although LIFO is a good approximation to it if the price most recently paid is similar to the price paid to replace the used item.

Cost of Owner's Resources

The owner of a firm often puts a great deal of time and effort into organizing the firm. But the owner could have worked at some other activity and earned a wage. The opportunity cost of the owner's time spent working for the firm is the wage income foregone by not working in the best alternative job.

In addition to supplying labour to the firm, its owner also supplies *entrepreneurial ability* – the factor of production that organizes the business, makes business decisions, innovates and bears the risk of running the business. These activities would not be undertaken without the expectation of a return. The expected return for supplying entrepreneurial ability is called **normal profit**. Normal profit is part of a firm's opportunity cost because it is the cost of a foregone alternative. The foregone alternative is running another firm.

Usually, the owner of a firm withdraws cash from the business to meet living expenses. Accountants regard such withdrawals of cash as part of the owner's profit from the business, rather than as part of the opportunity cost of the owner's time and entrepreneurial ability. But to the extent that they compensate for wages foregone and risk, they are part of the firm's opportunity cost.

Economic Profit

What is the bottom line – the profit or loss of the firm? A firm's economic profit is equal to its total revenue minus its opportunity cost. Its opportunity cost is the explicit and implicit cost of the best alternative actions foregone, including normal profit.

Economic profit is not the same as what accountants call profit. For the accountant, a firm's profit is equal to its total revenue minus its money cost and its conventional depreciation.

An Example

To help you get a clearer picture of the concepts of a firm's opportunity cost, normal profit and economic profit, we'll look at a concrete example. And we'll contrast the economic concepts of cost and profit with the accounting concepts.

Mike owns Mike's Bikes – a shop that sells bikes. His revenue, cost and profit appear in Table 10.2. The accountant's cost calculations are on the left side and the economist's opportunity cost calculations are on the right.

Mike sold £300,000 worth of bikes during the year. This amount appears as his total revenue. The

Table 10.2 Mike's Mountain Bikes, Revenues, Costs and Profit Statement 

The accountant

Item	Amount
Total revenue	£300,000
Costs:	
Wholesale cost of bikes	150,000
Utilities and other services	20,000
Wages	50,000
Depreciation	22,000
Bank interest	12,000
Total cost	£254,000
Profit	£46,000

The economist

Item	Amount
Total revenue	£300,000
Costs:	
Wholesale cost of bikes	150,000
Utilities and other services	20,000
Wages	50,000
Fall in market value of assets[1]	10,000
Mike's wages (implicit)[2]	40,000
Bank interest	12,000
Interest on Mike's money invested in firm (implicit)[3]	11,500
Normal profit (implicit)[4]	6,000
Opportunity cost	£299,500
Economic profit	£500

Notes

1 The fall in the market value of the assets of the firm gives the opportunity cost of not selling them one year ago. That is part of the opportunity cost of using them for the year.

2 Mike could have worked elsewhere for £40 an hour, but he worked 1,000 hours on the firm's business, which means that the opportunity cost of his time is £40,000.

3 Mike has invested £115,000 in the firm. If the current interest rate is 10 per cent a year, the opportunity cost of those funds is £11,500.

4 Mike could avoid the risk of running his own business and he would be unwilling to take on the risk for a return of less than £6,000. This is his *normal profit*. (The magnitude of normal profit is assumed.)

wholesale cost of bikes was £150,000, he bought £20,000 worth of utilities and other services, and paid out £50,000 in wages to his mechanic and sales assistant. Mike also paid £12,000 in interest to the bank. All of the items just mentioned appear in both the accountant's statement and the economist's statement. The remaining items differ between the two statements and some notes at the foot of the table explain the differences.

The accountant's depreciation calculation is based on conventional life assumptions for Mike's capital. The economist calculates the cost of Mike's time, funds invested in the firm and risk-bearing, and also calculates economic depreciation. The accountant says Mike's costs are £254,000 and his profit is £46,000. In contrast, the economist says that Mike's year in business had an opportunity cost of £299,500 and yielded an economic profit of £500.

The accountant's calculation of Mike's profit does not tell Mike his economic profit because it omits some components of opportunity cost and measures others incorrectly. The economist's measure of economic profit tells Mike how his business is doing compared with what he can normally expect. Any positive economic profit is good news for Mike because his normal profit – the normal return for his entrepreneurial ability – is part of the opportunity cost of running his business. *Reading Between the Lines* on pp. 234–235 explores an example of the difference between economic and accounting cost.

Review

- A firm's economic profit is equal to its total revenue minus its opportunity cost of production.
- Opportunity cost differs from money cost. Money cost measures cost as the money spent to hire inputs. Opportunity cost measures cost as the value of the best alternative foregone.

- The main differences between money cost and opportunity cost arise from the cost of capital and stocks and the cost of the resources supplied directly by the owner. Normal profit is part of opportunity cost.

We are interested in measuring the opportunity cost of production, not for its own sake, but so that we can compare the efficiency of alternative methods of production. What do we mean by efficiency?

Economic Efficiency

How does a firm choose among alternative methods of production? What is the most efficient way of producing? There are two concepts of efficiency: technological efficiency and economic efficiency. **Technological efficiency** occurs when it is not possible to increase output without increasing inputs. **Economic efficiency** occurs when the cost of producing a given output is as low as possible.

Technological efficiency is an engineering matter. Given what is technologically feasible, something can or cannot be done. Economic efficiency depends on the prices of the factors of production. Something that is technologically efficient may not be economically efficient. But something that is economically efficient is always technologically efficient. Let's study technological efficiency and economic efficiency by looking at an example.

Suppose that there are four methods of making TV sets:

a *Robot production*. One person monitors the entire computer-driven process.

b *Production line*. Workers specialize in a small part of the job as the emerging TV set passes them on a production line.

c *Human production*. Workers specialize in a small part of the job but walk from bench to bench to perform their tasks.

d *Hand-tool production*. A single worker uses a few hand tools to make a TV set.

Table 10.3 sets out the amount of labour and capital required to make 10 TV sets a day by each of these four methods. Are all of these alternative methods technologically efficient? By inspecting the numbers in the table you will be able to see that method *c* is not technologically efficient. It requires 100 workers and 10 units of capital to produce 10 TV sets. Those same 10 TV sets can be produced by method *b* with 10 workers and the same 10 units of capital. Therefore method *c* is not technologically efficient.

Are any of the other methods not technologically efficient? The answer is no: each of the other three methods is technologically efficient. Method *a* uses less labour and more capital than method *b*, and method *d* uses more labour and less capital than method *b*.

What about economic efficiency? Are all three methods economically efficient? To answer this question, we need to know the labour and capital costs. Let's suppose that labour costs £75 per person–day and that capital costs £250 per machine–day. Recall that economic efficiency occurs with the least expensive production process. Table 10.4 calculates the costs of using the four different methods of production. As you can see, the least expensive method of producing a TV set is *b*. Method *a* uses less labour but more capital. The combination of labour and capital needed by method *a* costs much more than in method *b*. Method *d*, the other technologically efficient method, uses much more labour and hardly any capital. Like method *a*, it costs far more to make a TV set using method *d* than method *b*.

Method *c* is technologically inefficient. It uses the same amount of capital as method *b* but 10 times as much labour. It is interesting to notice that although method *c* is technologically inefficient, it costs less to produce a TV set using method *c* than it does using methods *a* and *d*. But method *b* dominates method *c*. Because method *c* is not technologically efficient, there is always a lower-cost method available. That is, a technologically inefficient method is never economically efficient.

Table 10.3 Four Ways of Making 10 TV Sets a Day

	Method	Quantities of inputs: Labour	Capital
a	Robot production	1	1,000
b	Production line	10	10
c	Human production	100	10
d	Hand-tool production	1,000	1

Table 10.4 Costs of Four Ways of Making 10 TV Sets a Day

Method	Labour cost (£75 per day)		Capital cost (£250 per day)		Total cost	Cost per TV set
a	£75	+	£250,000	=	£250,075	£25,007.50
b	750	+	2,500	=	3,250	325.00
c	7,500	+	2,500	=	10,000	1,000.00
d	75,000	+	250	=	75,250	7,525.00

A firm that does not use the economically efficient method of production makes a smaller profit. Natural selection favours firms that choose the economically efficient method of production and goes against firms that do not. In extreme cases, an inefficient firm may go bankrupt or be taken over by another firm that can see the possibilities for lower cost and greater profit. Efficient firms will be stronger and better able to survive temporary adversity than inefficient ones.

Firms and Markets

At the beginning of this chapter, we defined a firm as an institution that hires factors of production and organizes them to produce and sell goods and services. To organize production, firms coordinate the economic decisions and activities of many individuals. But firms are not the only coordinators of economic decisions. As we learned in Chapter 4, markets also coordinate decisions. By adjusting prices, markets make the decisions of buyers and sellers consistent – make the quantities demanded equal to the quantities supplied of the many different goods and services.

An example of market coordination is the production of a rock concert. A promoter hires a stadium, some stage equipment, audio and video recording engineers and technicians, some rock groups, a superstar, a publicity agent and a ticket agent – all market transactions – and sells tickets to thousands of rock fans, audio rights to a recording company and video and broadcasting rights to a television network – another set of market transactions. If rock concerts were produced like cornflakes, the firm producing them would own all the capital used (stadiums, stage, sound and video equipment) and would employ all the labour needed (singers, engineers, sales persons, and so on).

What determines whether a firm or markets coordinate a particular set of activities? Why is the production of cornflakes coordinated by a firm and the production of a rock concert coordinated by markets? The answer is cost. Taking account of the opportunity cost of time as well as the costs of the other inputs, people use the method that costs least. In other words, they use the economically efficient method.

Firms coordinate economic activity when they can perform a task more efficiently than markets. In such a situation, it is profitable to set up a firm. If markets can perform a task more efficiently than a firm, people will use markets, and any attempt to set up a firm to replace such market coordination will be doomed to failure.

Why Firms?

There are four key reasons why, in many instances, firms are more efficient than markets as coordinators of economic activity. Firms achieve:

1 Lower transactions costs.
2 Economies of scale.
3 Economies of scope.
4 Economies of team production.

Transactions Costs The idea that firms exist because there are activities in which they are more efficient than markets was first suggested by a University of Chicago economist and Nobel Laureate, Ronald Coase[1]. Coase focused on the firm's ability to reduce or eliminate transactions costs. **Transactions costs** are the costs arising

1 Ronald H. Coase 'The Nature of the Firm', *Economica*, (November 1937) 386–405.

from finding someone with whom to do business, of reaching an agreement about the price and other aspects of the exchange, and of ensuring that the terms of the agreement are fulfilled. *Market* transactions require buyers and sellers to get together and to negotiate the terms and conditions of their trading. Sometimes lawyers have to be hired to draw up contracts. A broken contract leads to still more expenses. A *firm* can lower such transactions costs by reducing the number of individual transactions undertaken.

Consider, for example, two ways of getting your creaking car fixed.

1 *Firm coordination*. You take the car to the garage. Parts and tools as well as the mechanic's time are coordinated by the garage owner and your car gets fixed. You pay one bill for the entire job.
2 *Market coordination*. You hire a mechanic who diagnoses the problems and makes a list of the parts and tools needed to fix them. You buy the parts from the local breaker's yard and rent the tools from ABC Rentals. You hire the mechanic again to fix the problems. You return the tools and pay your bills – wages to the mechanic, rental to ABC and the cost of the parts used to the breaker.

What determines the method that you use? The answer is cost. Taking account of the opportunity cost of your own time as well as the costs of the other inputs that you'd have to buy, you will use the method that costs least. In other words, you will use the economically efficient method.

The first method requires that you undertake only one transaction with one firm. It's true that the firm has to undertake several transactions – hiring the labour and buying the parts and tools required to do the job. But the firm doesn't have to undertake those transactions simply to fix your car. One set of such transactions enables the firm to fix hundreds of cars. Thus there is an enormous reduction in the number of individual transactions that take place if people get their cars fixed at the garage rather than going through an elaborate sequence of market transactions.

Economies of Scale When the cost of producing a unit of a good falls as its output rate increases, **economies of scale** exist. Many industries experience economies of scale; car manufacturing is an example. One firm can produce 4 million cars a year at a lower cost per car than 200 firms each producing 20,000 cars a year. Economies of scale arise from specialization and the division of labour that can be reaped more effectively by firm coordination rather than market coordination.

Economies of Scope Economies which are derived from the size of the firm rather than the amount of plant or machinery available are called **economies of scope**. Today's large companies face high costs when developing, financing and marketing a new good – costs which must be recouped from sales of the new product. The bigger a firm's potential volume of sales, the less each unit sold of a new good must contribute to its development costs. So the price of a new good produced by a large firm, which already has a large-scale sales-force and retail outlets, will be less than a similar product launched by a smaller firm.

Team Production A production process in which a group of individuals each specializes in mutually supportive tasks is *team production*. Sport provides the best example of team activity. Some team members specialize in striking and some in defending, some in speed and some in strength. The production of goods and services offers many examples of team activity. For example, production lines in car plants and TV manufacturing plants work most efficiently when individual activity is organized in teams, each specializing in a small task. You can also think of an entire firm as being a team. The team has buyers of raw materials and other inputs, production workers and sales persons. There are even specialists within these various groups. Each individual member of the team specializes, but the value of the output of the team and the profit that it earns depend on the coordinated activities of all the team's members. The idea that firms arise as a consequence of the economies of team production was first suggested by Armen Alchian and Harold Demsetz of the University of California at Los Angeles[2].

Because firms can economize on transactions costs, reap economies of scale and scope, and

2 Armen Alchian and Harold Demsetz, 'Production, Information Costs, and Economic Organization', *American Economic Review* (December 1972) 57, 5, 777–795.

organize efficient team production, it is firms rather than markets that coordinate most of our economic activity. Reductions in transactions costs explain why Ford, which started hand-building cars in the early 1900s, created a U-form structured company based on production line technology. But there are limits to the economic efficiency of firms. If a firm becomes too big or too diversified in the things that it seeks to do, the cost of management and monitoring per unit of output begins to rise and, at some point, the market becomes more efficient at coordinating the use of resources. This explains why Ford restructured into a global M-form TNC, effectively creating a set of smaller, more independent companies. It also explains why companies such as Hanson Trust target segments of large, ailing TNCs to run as separate, more profitable companies.

Sometimes firms enter into long-term relationships with each other that effectively cut out ordinary market transactions and make it difficult to see where one firm ends and another begins. For example, when Rover became part of BMW, it had a long-term relationship with Honda as a supplier of gearboxes. These long-term relationships are also common between supermarkets and manufacturers. Famous cereal manufacturers produce supermarket own-label brands as well as their own more established brands.

In this chapter we examined why different firms exist, their objectives and how they cope with the problems of uncertainty and limited information. We have used our concepts of marginal decisions and opportunity costs to explain the decisions that firms make. In the next chapter, we are going to study more choices of firms. We will study their production decisions, how they minimize cost, and how they choose the amounts of labour and capital to employ.

Summary

Key Points

The Firm and its Economic Problem (pp. 214–220)

- Firms hire and organize factors of production to produce and sell goods and services. The main types of firm are: proprietorships, partnerships and companies.
- The vast majority of firms are small scale but corporations are responsible for most employment and output.
- Firms strive to be efficient – to produce output at the lowest possible cost and to maximize profit. Uncertainty and incomplete information place limits on what a firm can attain.
- Firms devise incentive schemes and internal structures which reduce the costs of the principal–agent problem and encourage employees and managers to perform in ways which are consistent with profit maximizing.

Business Finance (pp. 220–223)

- Firms get funds from their owners and from the sale of shares and bonds. A firm gets its funds from the least cost source.
- A firm decides how much to borrow by calculating the *net present value* of borrowing one additional pound – the marginal pound borrowed.
- A firm increases its borrowing up to the point at which the present value of the marginal pound borrowed is zero. At this amount of borrowing, the firm is maximizing its profit.

Opportunity Cost and Economic Profit (pp. 223–227)

- Economic profit is calculated as total revenue minus opportunity cost.
- Opportunity cost has two components: explicit costs and implicit costs. Explicit costs are paid directly in money – money costs. Implicit costs (measured in units of money) are opportunities

foregone but not paid for directly in money. They arise from the use of capital, stocks and the owner's own resources.

- The opportunity cost of the resources supplied by a firm's owner, including normal profit for supplying entrepreneurial ability, is part of a firm's costs.

Economic Efficiency (pp. 227–228)

- A method of production is technologically efficient when to produce a given output, it is not possible to increase output without using more inputs.
- A method of production is economically efficient when the cost of producing a given output is as low as possible.

Firms and Markets (pp. 228–230)

- Firms coordinate economic activities when they can achieve lower costs than coordination through markets.
- Firms economize on transactions costs and achieve the benefits of economies of scale, economies of scope and of team production.

Key Figure and Tables 

Key Terms

Review Questions

1. What is a firm and what are the economic problems that all firms face?
2. What factors make it difficult for a firm to get the most out of its resources?
3. What are the principal–agency relationships?
4. Why do principal–agency relationships arise?
5. What is the difference between an M-form and a U-form structured firm?
6. What are the main forms of business organization and the advantages and disadvantages of each?
7. What is the most common form of business?
8. What are the main ways in which firms can raise funds?
9. Describe and contrast a bond and a share.
10. What do we mean by net present value?

11 What determines the value of a bond?

12 Distinguish between money cost and opportunity cost.

13 What are the main items of opportunity cost and opportunity cost that don't get counted as part of money cost?

14 Explain how a firm uses marginal analysis when it makes a financial decision.

15 Distinguish between profit as defined by accountants, normal profit and economic profit.

16 Distinguish between implicit costs and explicit costs.

17 Distinguish between technological efficiency and economic efficiency.

18 Why do firms, rather than markets, coordinate such a large amount of economic activity?

Problems

1 Soap Bubbles PLC has a bank loan of £1 million on which it is paying an interest rate of 10 per cent a year. The firm's financial adviser suggests paying off the loan by selling bonds. To sell bonds valued at £1 million, Soap Bubbles must offer the following deal: one year from today, pay the bondholders £9 for each £100 of bonds; two years from today, redeem the bonds for £114 per £100 of bonds.

a Does it pay Soap Bubbles to sell the bonds to repay the bank loan?
b What is the present value of the profit or loss that would result from repaying the bank loan and selling the bonds?

2 One year ago, Jack and Jill set up a vinegar bottling firm (called JJVB).

- Jack and Jill put £50,000 of their own money into the firm.
- They bought equipment for £30,000 and an inventory of bottles and vinegar for £15,000.
- They hired one employee to help them for an annual wage of £20,000.
- JJVB's sales for the year were £100,000.
- Jack gave up his previous job, at which he earned £30,000, and spent all his time working for JJVB.
- Jill kept her old job, which paid £30 an hour, but gave up 10 hours of leisure each week (for 50 weeks) to work for JJVB.
- The cash expenses of JJVB were £10,000 for the year.
- The stock at the end of the year was worth £20,000.
- The market value of the equipment at the end of the year was £28,000.
- JJVB's accountant depreciated the equipment by 20 per cent a year.

a Construct JJVB's profit and loss account as recorded by its accountant.
b Construct JJVB's profit and loss account based on opportunity cost rather than money cost concepts.

3 There are three methods of completing your income tax return: using a personal computer, using a pocket calculator, or using a pencil and paper. With a PC, you complete the task in an hour; with a pocket calculator, it takes 12 hours; and with a pencil and paper, it takes two days. The PC and its software cost £1,000, the pocket calculator costs £10, and the pencil and paper cost £1.

a Which, if any, of the above methods is technologically efficient?
b Suppose that your wage is £5 an hour. Which of the above methods is economically efficient?
c Suppose your wage is £50 an hour. Which of the above methods is economically efficient?
d Suppose your wage is £500 an hour. Which of the above methods is economically efficient?

4 Imagine you operate and own a small petrol station, and the following facts describe some aspects of your business:

i) Your petrol tanks hold 2 million litres and once a week you get them filled to capacity.
ii) You sell 2 million litres of petrol per week and your sales are the same each day.
iii) You buy your petrol from a wholesale company that charges you 20 pence per litre.
iv) You sell petrol for 60 pence per litre.
v) On each litre you sell, you pay taxes to the government of 30 pence per litre.
vi) Your wholesaler has tanks that hold a month's supply of petrol.
vii) Your wholesaler gets its tanks filled once a month from the refinery.
viii) The refinery buys crude oil by the tanker load, and it agrees the price of each load as it leaves port in Saudi Arabia. The journey from Saudi Arabia takes two weeks.
ix) On the average, it takes two months for crude oil on a tanker in Saudi Arabia to become refined petrol in your tanks.
x) One day, the price of crude oil jumps by an amount that is equivalent to doubling the price you will pay your wholesaler. On the day after the price of crude oild has increased:

a What is the opportunity cost of crude oil in Saudi Arabia?
b What is your wholesaler's opportunity cost of refined oil?
c What is your opportunity cost of selling a litre from your stocks?
d When will your price change?

Explain each part of your answer.

5 It is January 1, 2000, and Michael Schumacher is trying to decide which of two alternative contracts to accept. Contract A pays the following amounts:

On December 31	Amount £
2000	2,000,000
2001	2,500,000
2002	3,000,000
2003	3,500,000
2004	4,000,000
2005	4,500,000

Contract B pays £5,000,000 now (on January 1, 2000) and £14,500,000 on December 31, 2005. Michael Schumacher's financial advisor points out that under both contracts, the racing driver is paid £19,500,000. However, he says that Contract B is better because it put £5 million in Michael Schumacher's pocket right away. The interest rate is 10 per cent a year. What is your advice?

a Is Michael Schumacher better off with Contract A or Contract B?
b Try to convince Michael Schumacher that his financial advisor is wrong.
c Thinking more broadly about the principal-agent problem, if you were offering Michael Schumacher one of these contracts, which would you offer and why?

6 Study *Reading Between the Lines* on pp. 234–235.

a Identify the main factors which make two horses cheaper to run than a lorry.
b Explain the difference between the opportunity cost and the accounting cost of two horses compared to one lorry.
c Explain why using two horses rather than one lorry is economically efficient.

7 Use the links on the Parkin, Powell and Matthews Web site to obtain information about the car industry.

a What are the main economic problems faced by car producers?
b Why are car producers merging?

8 Use the links on the Parkin, Powell and Matthews Web site to obtain information about the steel industry.

a What are the main economic problems faced by steel producers?
b Is the number of steel producers likely to increase or decrease during the next few years? Why?

W http://www.econ100.com

Cutting Costs with Old Technology

The Essence of the Story

- Bracknell Forest Borough Council has replaced a worn-out tractor with two shire horses rather than a new tractor.
- The attractions to the council of doing this are economic: two horses have lower running costs than a tractor.
- Data from the Shire Horse Society suggests that the cost of purchasing and maintaining two horses is about a fifth lower than that for a lorry.
- The working life of a horse is twice that of a tractor.
- Moreover, the two horses would produce manure worth £90 a year which could be sold or used in the council's gardens.
- Horse-drawn vehicles are slower than tractors and lorries, but for tasks where time and distance are not important factors, horses cost less.

The Times, 13 May 1992

Horsepower pulls ahead of tractors

David Young

The two newest members of Bracknell Forest Borough Council gardening department will clock on for the first time next Monday to be rewarded for an eight hour shift with a handful of carrots, a bale of hay and a bucket of oats.

The council in Berkshire has gone green. Instead of spending £20,000 or more to replace a worn-out tractor, it has bought two £4,000 Shire horses who will pull trailers around the town's gardens, and lug tankers used for watering its hanging baskets. Their working life could span 15 years, double the average tractor's. The council will save on a road fund licence and the insurance premiums will be lower.

Alan Stanton, environmental health officer, said: 'We looked at the figures very closely and, on the economics, are in favour of the horses. We have drawn on the experience of other horse users, such as the brewers, who have found them to be more economical for local work than lorries.'

Several authorities are considering heavy horses. Aberdeen has bought 14 Clydesdales for the parks department, Luton, whose fortunes owe much to the internal combustion engine, has bought a Shire horse. Bradford, West Yorkshire, uses three to pull flower-watering machines, street-cleaning equipment and mowers at its industrial museum.

Winning ride: research for the Shire Horse Society shows that, in most cases, horsepower can work out cheaper than motor power, with horses also earning unquantifiable amounts of goodwill for their users. The society can provide figures which show that horses win over lorries by a short neck when used for local journeys during an eight-hour day. In addition, each horse produces £45 worth of manure each year.

How the Costs Compare

Two Horses	£8,000	Lorry	£14,400
Stabling	£2,223	Garaging	£1,332
Insurance	£216	Insurance	£270
Tax	Nil	Tax	£427
Wages	£12,600	Wages	£10,800
Keep	£3,481	Fuel	£792
Depreciation	£436	Depreciation	£2,876
Maintenance	£540	Maintenance	£2,605
		Tyres	£243

All costs are based on 1981 prices supplied by The Shire Horse Society (adjusted to 1991 prices)

Economic Analysis

■ A number of councils have identified tasks for which shire horses could be employed more cheaply than tractors and other mechanical alternatives.

■ The data from the Shire Horse Society indicates a number of areas where costs for two horses are lower than the cost of a lorry.

■ The initial purchase cost of two horses is lower than that of one lorry and the depreciation of horses is also significantly lower. These differences are further amplified by the councils' prediction that two horses will have twice the operational life of a lorry.

■ All other figures for the annual running costs indicate that it will cost the councils about the same to operate two horses as to operate one lorry.

■ By changing the technology employed, the councils are able to make economic efficiency gains by lowering the costs of producing the same output.

■ The figure compares the costs for two horses with those for a lorry.

Costs of Horse and Lorry

Accountant's costs

Item	Two horses	Lorry
Purchase	£8,000	£14,400
Depreciation	£436	£2,876
Housing	£2,223	£1,332
Insurance	£216	£270
Tax	£0	£427
Fuel	£3,487	£792
Maintenance	£540	£2,605
Tyres	£0	£243
Totals	£14,902	£22,945

Economist's opportunity costs

Item	Two horses	Lorry
Purchase price	£8,000	£14,400
less		
Market value at year end	£7,000	£10,000 (assumed)
equals		
Economic depreciation	£1,000	£4,400
Interest (at 5% pa)	£400	£720
Housing	£2,223	£1,332
Insurance	£216	£270
Tax	£0	£427
Fuel	£3,487	£792
Maintenance	£540	£2,605
Tyres	£0	£243
Totals	£7,866	£10,789

Output and Costs

After studying this chapter you will be able to:

- Explain what limits the profitability of a firm
- Explain the relationship between a firm's output and its costs
- Derive a firm's short-run cost curves
- Explain how cost changes when a firm's plant size changes
- Derive a firm's long-run average cost curve

Survival of the Fittest

Large size does not guarantee survival in business. While some of Europe's large firms – such as Shell and BMW – have been operating for many years, most of their contemporaries from 30 years ago have disappeared. But remaining small does not guarantee survival either. Every year, millions of small businesses close down. Phone a random selection of restaurants and plumbers from last year's Yellow Pages and see how many have vanished. So what does a firm have to do to be one of the survivors? ◆ Firms differ in lots of ways – from the local corner shop to multinational giants producing high-tech goods. But regardless of their size or what they produce, all firms must decide how much to produce and how to produce it. How do firms make these decisions? ◆ Most European car makers can produce far more cars than they can sell. Why do car makers have expensive equipment lying around that isn't fully used? Many electrical suppliers in the United Kingdom don't have enough production equipment on hand to meet demand on the coldest and hottest days and have to buy power from the central pool. Why don't such firms have a bigger production plant so that they can supply the market themselves?

◆ ◆ ◆ ◆ We are going to answer these questions in this chapter. To do so, we are going to model the economic decisions of a small, imaginary firm – Neat Knits Ltd, a producer of knitted jumpers. The firm is owned and operated by Sam. By studying Neat Knits' economic problems and the way Sam solves them, we will be able to get a clear view of the problems that face all firms. We will be able to understand and predict the behaviour of small firms as well as the giants.

The Firm's Objective and Constraints

The first step in modelling a firm's behaviour is to start by describing a firm's objective – what it is trying to achieve.

The Objective: Profit Maximization

We will assume that the firm that we will study has a single objective: profit maximization. *Profit maximization* means striving for the largest possible profit. A firm that seeks the largest possible profit is one that tries to use its scarce resources efficiently. And a firm that maximizes profit has the best chance of surviving in a competitive environment and of avoiding being taken over by another firm.

Two types of constraint limit the profit a firm can make. They are:

1 Market constraints.

2 Technology constraints.

Market Constraints A firm's market constraints are the conditions under which it can buy its inputs and sell its output. On the output side, people have a limited demand for each good or service and will buy additional quantities only at lower prices. On the input side, people have a limited supply of the factors of production that they own and will supply additional quantities only at higher prices.

We'll study these market constraints on firms in Chapters 12–15. Neat Knits, the firm that we'll study in this chapter, is small and cannot influence the prices at which it sells its output or buys its inputs. For such a firm, the market constraints are a given set of market prices.

Technology Constraints Firms combine inputs – factors of production like capital and labour – to produce output. A firm's technology constraints are the limits to the quantity of output that can be produced from given quantities of inputs. To maximize profit, a firm chooses a *technologically efficient* method of production. This means it does not use more inputs than necessary to produce its chosen output. Equivalently, it does not waste resources. But a firm must also choose how to combine its inputs – its technique. It must choose the *economically efficient* technique – the combination of inputs that produces its chosen output at the lowest possible cost (see Chapter 10, pp. 212–235). This might be a labour-intensive technique which uses relatively more labour than capital, or a capital-intensive technique which uses relatively more capital than labour.

The possibilities open to a firm depend on the length of the planning period over which it is making its decisions. A firm that wants to change its output overnight has fewer options than one that plans to change its output several months in the future. In studying the way a firm's technology constrains its actions, we distinguish between two planning horizons: the short run and the long run.

The Short Run and the Long Run The **short run** is a period of time in which the quantity of at least one input is fixed and the quantities of the other inputs can be varied. The **long run** is a period of time in which the quantities of all inputs can be varied. Inputs whose quantity can be varied in the short run are called *variable inputs*. Inputs whose quantity cannot be varied in the short run are called *fixed inputs*.

There is no specific time that can be marked on the calendar to separate the short run from the long run. In some cases, such as a photocopying service, the short run is a month or two. New premises can be rented and new machines installed quickly. In other cases, for example an electricity power company, the short run is several years. Bigger power generators take several years to build.

Let's go back to our small company, Neat Knits. It has a fixed amount of capital – knitting machines – so to vary its output in the short run it must vary the quantity of labour employed. For Neat Knits, the knitting equipment is the fixed input and labour is the variable input. In the long run, Neat Knits can vary the quantity of both inputs – knitting machines and labour employed.

Let's look more closely at the short-run technology constraint.

Short-run Technology Constraint

To increase output in the short run, a firm must increase the quantity of a variable input. To make a decision about the quantity of a variable input to use, the firm must calculate the effect on output of making a small change – a marginal change – in the quantity of the variable input used, when the fixed inputs remain unchanged. To make such a calcula-

Figure 11.1 Total Product

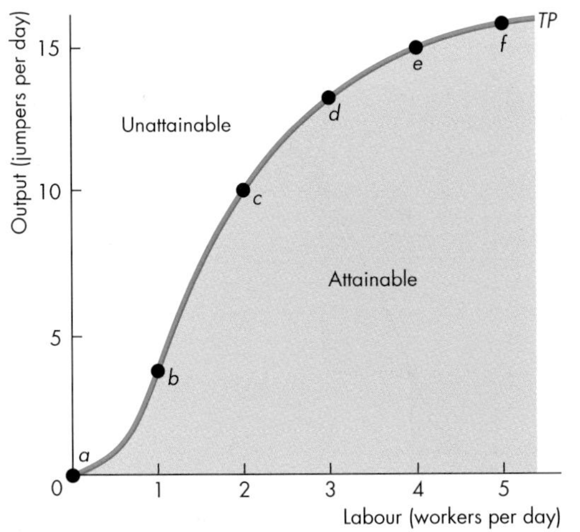

	Labour (workers per day)	Output (jumpers per day)
a	0	0
b	1	4
c	2	10
d	3	13
e	4	15
f	5	16

The table shows how many jumpers Neat Knits can produce when it uses 1 knitting machine and different amounts of labour. For example, using 1 knitting machine, 2 workers can produce 10 jumpers a day (row *c*). The total product curve, *TP*, is based on these data. Points *a* to *f* on the curve correspond to the rows of the table. The total product curve separates the attainable output from the unattainable output.

tion, the firm uses its short-run technology constraint. A firm's short-run technology constraint can be described using three related concepts:

1 Total product.
2 Marginal product.
3 Average product.

Total Product

The total output produced with a given quantity of a fixed input is called **total product**. The *total product curve* shows the maximum output attainable with a given amount of capital as the amount of labour employed is varied. Equivalently, the relationship between total product and the amount of labour employed can be described by a schedule that lists the amounts of labour required with the given amount of capital to produce given amounts of output. Neat Knits' total product schedule and curve are shown in Figure 11.1. Labour is the variable input used with 1 machine. As you can see, when employment is zero, no jumpers are knitted. As employment increases, so does the number of jumpers knitted. Neat Knits' total product curve with 1 machine, *TP*, is based on the schedule in the figure. Points *a* to *f* on the curve correspond to the same rows in the table.

The total product curve is similar to the *production possibility frontier* (explained in Chapter 3). It separates the attainable output levels from those that are unattainable. All the points that lie above the curve are unattainable. Points that lie below the curve, in the orange area, are attainable. But they are inefficient – they use more labour than is necessary to produce a given output. Only the points *on* the total product curve are technologically efficient.

Marginal Product

The **marginal product** of an input is the increase in total product divided by the increase in the quantity of the input employed, when the quantity of all other inputs is constant. For example, the marginal product of labour is the increase in total product divided by the increase in the quantity of labour employed, when the quantity of capital is constant. Equivalently, it is the change in total product resulting from a 1-unit increase in the quantity of labour employed.

Table 11.1 shows the calculation of Neat Knits' marginal product of labour with 1 machine. For example, when the quantity of labour increases from 2 to 3 workers, total product increases from 10 to 13 jumpers. The change in total product – 3 jumpers – is the marginal product of going from 2 to 3 workers.

Figure 11.2 illustrates Neat Knits' marginal product of labour with 1 machine. Part (a) reproduces the total product curve that you met in Figure 11.1. Part (b) shows the marginal product curve, *MP*. In part (a), the height of the orange bars illustrate the marginal product of labour. Marginal product is also measured by the slope of the total

Table 11.1 Calculating Marginal Product and Average Product

	Labour (workers per day)	Output (jumpers per day)	Marginal product (jumpers per day)	Average product (jumpers per worker)
a	0	0		
			4	
b	1	4		4.00
			6	
c	2	10		5.00
			3	
d	3	13		4.33
			2	
e	4	15		3.75
			1	
f	5	16		3.20

Marginal product of an input is the change in total product resulting from a 1-unit increase in an input. For example, when labour increases from 2 to 3 workers a day (row *c* to row *d*), total product increases from 10 to 13 jumpers a day. The marginal product of going from 2 to 3 workers is 3 jumpers.

Average product of an input is total product divided by the quantity of an input employed. For example, 3 workers produce 13 jumpers a day, so the average product of 3 workers is 4.33 jumpers per worker.

Figure 11.2 Marginal Product 

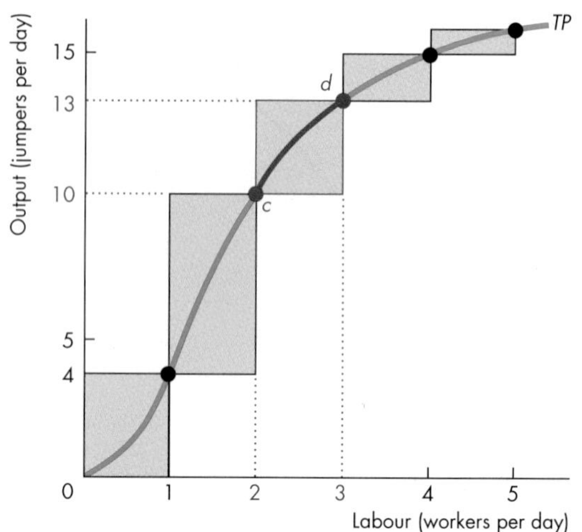

(a) Total product

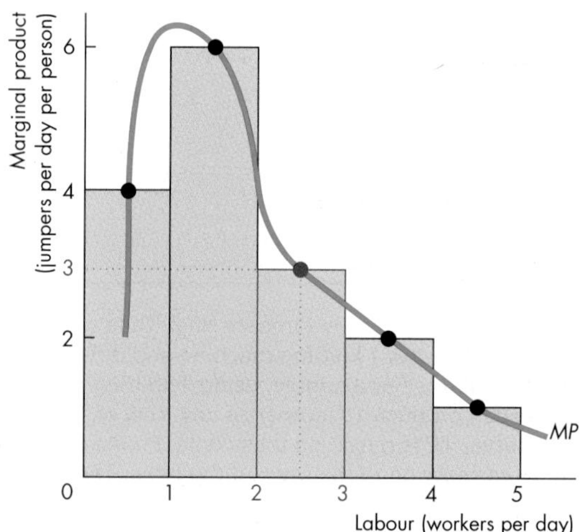

(b) Marginal product

Marginal product is illustrated in both parts of the figure by the orange bars. The height of each bar indicates the size of the marginal product. For example, when labour increases from 2 to 3, marginal product is the orange bar whose height is 3 jumpers. (Marginal product is shown midway between the labour inputs to emphasize that it is the result of *changing* inputs – moving from one level to the next.) The steeper the slope of the total product curve (*TP*) in part (a), the larger is marginal product (*MP*) in part (b). Marginal product increases to a maximum (when 1 worker is employed in this example) and then declines – diminishing marginal product.

product curve. Recall that the slope of a curve is the change in the value of the variable measured on the y-axis – output – divided by the change in the variable measured on the x-axis – labour input – as we move along the curve. A 1-unit increase in labour input, from 2 to 3 workers, increases output from 10 to 13 jumpers, so the slope from point c to point d is 3, the same as the marginal product that we've just calculated.

We've calculated the marginal product of labour for a series of unit increases in the amount of labour. But labour is divisible into smaller units than one person. It is divisible into hours and even minutes. By varying the amount of labour in the smallest imaginable units, we can draw the marginal product curve shown in Figure 11.2(b). The *height* of this curve measures the *slope* of the total product curve at a point. The total product curve in part (a) shows that an increase in employment from 2 to 3 workers increases output from 10 to 13 jumpers (an increase of 3). The increase in output of 3 jumpers appears on the vertical axis of part (b) as the marginal product of going from 2 to 3 workers. We plot that marginal product at the midpoint between 2 and 3 workers. Notice that marginal product shown in Figure 11.2(b) reaches a peak at 1 unit of labour and at that point marginal product is more than 6. The peak occurs at 1 unit of labour because the total product curve is steepest at 1 unit of labour.

The total, marginal and average product curves are different for different firms and different types of goods. BMW's product curves are different from those of your local supermarket, which in turn are different from those of Sam's jumper factory. But the shapes of the product curves are similar, because almost every production process incorporates two features:

1 Increasing marginal returns initially.
2 Diminishing marginal returns eventually.

Increasing Marginal Returns **Increasing marginal returns** occur when the marginal product of an additional worker exceeds the marginal product of the previous worker. If Sam employs just one worker at Neat Knits, that person has to learn all the different aspects of jumper production, running the knitting machines, fixing breakdowns, packaging and mailing jumpers, buying and checking the type and colour of the wool. All of these tasks have to be done by that one person. If Sam employs a second person, the two workers can specialize in different parts of the production process. As a result, two workers produce more than twice as much as one. The marginal product of the second worker is greater than the marginal product of the first worker. Marginal returns are increasing.

Diminishing Marginal Returns Increasing marginal returns do not always occur, but all production processes eventually reach a point of diminishing marginal returns. **Diminishing marginal returns** occur when the marginal product of an additional worker is less than the marginal product of the previous worker. If Sam employs a third worker, output increases but not by as much as it did when he added the second worker. In this case, after two workers are employed, all the gains from specialization and the division of labour have been exhausted. By employing a third worker, the factory produces more jumpers, but the equipment is being operated closer to its limits. There are even times when the third worker has nothing to do because the plant is running without the need for further attention. Adding yet more and more workers continues to increase output but by successively smaller amounts. Marginal returns are diminishing. This phenomenon is such a pervasive one that it is called 'the law of diminishing returns'. The **law of diminishing returns** states that:

> As a firm uses more of a variable input, with a given quantity of fixed inputs, the marginal product of the variable input eventually diminishes.

Because marginal product eventually diminishes, so does average product. Recall that average product decreases when marginal product is less than average product. If marginal product is diminishing it must eventually become less than average product and, when it does so, average product begins to decline.

Average Product

The **average product** of an input is equal to total product divided by the quantity of the input employed. Average product tells us how productive, on the average, a factor of production is. Table 11.1 shows Neat Knits' average product of labour with 1 machine. For example, 3 workers can knit 13 jumpers a day, so the average product of labour is 13 divided by 3, which is 4.33 jumpers per worker.

Figure 11.3 illustrates Neat Knits' average product of labour, *AP*, and marginal product of labour, *MP*, and shows the relationship between average product and marginal product. Points *b* to *f* on the average product curve are plotted from the same rows in Table 11.1. Average product increases from 1 to 2 workers (its maximum value is at point *c*) but then decreases as yet more workers are employed. Notice that average product is largest when average product and marginal product are equal. That is, the marginal product curve cuts the average product curve at the point of maximum average product. For employment levels at which marginal product is less than average product, average product is decreasing.

The relationships between the average and marginal product curves that you've just seen are a general feature of the relationship between the average and marginal values of any variable. Let's look at a familiar example.

Figure 11.3 Average Product

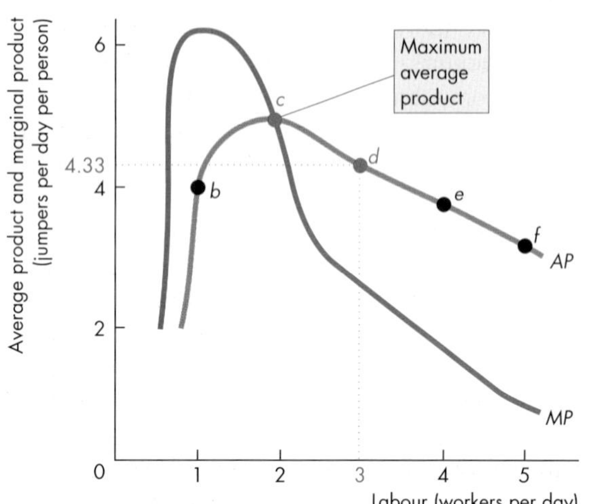

The figure shows the average product of labour, *AP*, and the marginal product of labour, *MP*, and the relationship between the shape of the two curves. With 1 worker per day, marginal product exceeds average product, so average product is increasing. With 2 workers per day, marginal product equals average product, so average product is at its maximum. With more than 2 workers per day, marginal product is less than average product, so average product is decreasing.

Figure 11.4 Marginal Mark and Average Mark

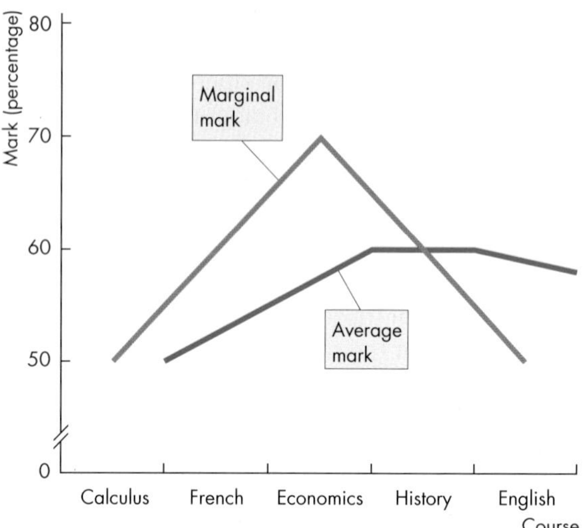

Sam's first course is calculus for which he gets 50 per cent. His marginal grade is 50 per cent and his average is 50 per cent. He then gets 60 per cent for French, which pulls his average up to 55 per cent. Next he gets 70 per cent for economics, which pulls his average up again to 60 per cent. On his next course, history, he gets 60 per cent, which maintains his average. Then his mark drops to 50 per cent for English. This marginal mark is below his previous average and so it pulls his average down.

Marginal Marks and Average Marks

Sam is also a part-time student who takes one course per term. (He's too busy at the jumper factory to do more than one course.) Figure 11.4 shows Sam's performance over five terms. He gains a mark of 50 per cent in his first exam for calculus. This is his marginal mark and it is his average mark as it is the first course taken. Sam takes French in the second term and gets 60 per cent in the exam. As French is Sam's marginal course, his marginal mark is 60 per cent, but his average mark rises to 55 per cent, the average of 50 and 60. His average mark rises because his marginal mark is greater than his previous average mark – it pulls his average up. In the third term, Sam takes economics, his best subject. His marginal mark is 70 per cent, which is higher than his previous average. His marginal mark pulls his average up, this time to 60 per cent, the average of 50, 60 and 70. In the fourth term, Sam takes history. Unfortunately, he achieves only 60 per cent in the exam. This time, his marginal mark is equal to his previous average – so his average does not change. In the fifth term, Sam takes English but achieves only 50 per cent in the exam. This time his marginal mark is below his previous average, and drags his average down to 55 per cent, the average of 50, 60, 70, 60, and 50 per cent.

This example of an everyday relationship between marginal and average values agrees with the relationship between marginal and average product that we have just discovered. Sam's average mark increases when the mark on the last course taken, the marginal mark, exceeds his previous average. The average mark falls when the mark on the marginal course is below his previous average. His average mark is constant (it neither increases nor decreases) when the mark for the marginal course equals his previous average.

Review

- Three curves – total product, marginal product and average product – show how the output rate of a firm varies as the variable input – labour – varies with fixed capital.
- Initially, as the labour input increases, marginal product and average product might increase.
- But as the labour input increases further, first marginal product and later average product decline.
- When marginal product exceeds average product, average product increases; when marginal product is less than average product, average product decreases; and when marginal product and average product are equal, average product is at its maximum.

Why does Sam care about Neat Knits total product, marginal product and average product, and whether marginal product and average product are increasing or decreasing? He cares because the product curves influence costs and the way costs change with the quantity of jumpers produced.

Short-run Cost

To produce more output in the short run, a firm must employ more labour. But if the firm employs more labour, its costs increase. Thus to produce more output, a firm must increase its costs. Let's study Neat Knits' costs to see how a firm's costs change with the level of production.

Neat Knits is a small firm and we'll assume that it cannot influence the prices it pays for its inputs. Given the prices of its inputs, Neat Knits' lowest attainable cost of production for each output level is determined by its technology constraint. Let's see how.

Total Cost

A firm's **total cost** is the sum of the costs of all the inputs it uses in production. It includes the cost of renting land, buildings and equipment, the wages paid to the firm's workforce and normal profit. Total cost is divided into two categories: fixed cost and variable cost.

A **fixed cost** is the cost of a fixed input. Because the quantity of a fixed input does not change as output changes, a fixed cost is a cost that is independent of the output level. For example, BMW can change its output of cars without changing the amount it spends on advertising. The cost of advertising is a fixed cost.

A **variable cost** is a cost of a variable input. Because to change its output a firm must change the quantity of variable inputs, a variable cost is a cost that varies with the output level. For example, to produce more cars, BMW must run its assembly lines for longer hours and hire more labour. The cost of this labour is a variable cost.

Total fixed cost is the total cost of the fixed inputs. **Total variable cost** is the total cost of the variable inputs. We call total cost *TC*, total fixed cost *TFC* and total variable cost *TVC*. The total cost of production is the sum of total fixed cost and total variable cost. That is:

$$TC = TFC + TVC$$

Table 11.2 shows Neat Knits' total cost and its division into total fixed cost and total variable cost. Neat Knits has 1 knitting machine and this is its fixed input. To produce more jumpers Sam must employ more labour, and the first two columns of the table show how many jumpers can be produced at each level of employment. This is Neat Knits' technology constraint.

Neat Knits rents its knitting machine for £25 a day. This amount is its total fixed cost. It employs workers at a wage rate of £25 a day and its total variable cost is equal to the total wage bill. For example, if Neat Knits employs 3 workers, its total variable cost is (3 × £25), which equals £75. Total cost is the sum of total fixed cost and total variable cost. For example, when Neat Knits employs 3 workers, its total cost is £100 – total fixed cost of £25 plus total variable cost of £75.

Marginal Cost

A firm's **marginal cost** is the increase in its total cost divided by the increase in its output. Equivalently, it is the change in total cost that results from a unit increase in output. For example, when output increases from 10 to 13 jumpers, total cost increases from £75 to £100. The change in output is 3 jumpers and the change in total cost is £25. The

Table 11.2 Calculating a Firm's Costs

Labour (workers per day)	Output (jumpers per day)	Total fixed cost (*TFC*)	Total variable cost (*TVC*)	Total cost (*TC*)	Marginal cost (*MC*)	Average fixed cost (*AFC*)	Average variable cost (*AVC*)	Average total cost (*ATC*)
		(pounds per day)			(pounds per day)			
0	0	25	0	25				
					6.25			
1	4	25	25	50		6.25	6.25	12.50
					4.17			
2	10	25	50	75		2.50	5.00	7.50
					8.33			
3	13	25	75	100		1.92	5.77	7.69
					12.50			
4	15	25	100	125		1.67	6.00	78.33
					25.00			
5	16	25	125	150		1.56	7.81	9.38

marginal cost of one of these 3 jumpers is (£25 ÷ 3), which equals £8.33.

Notice that when Neat Knits hires a second worker, marginal cost decreases but when a third, fourth and fifth worker are employed, marginal cost successively increases. Marginal cost eventually increases because each additional worker produces a successively smaller addition to output – *the law of diminishing returns*. The law of diminishing returns means that each additional worker produces a successively smaller addition to output. So to get an additional unit of output, ever more workers are required. Because more workers are required to produce one additional unit of output, the cost of the additional output – marginal cost – must eventually increase.

Average Cost

Average cost is the cost per unit of output. There are three average costs:

1 Average fixed cost.

2 Average variable cost.

3 Average total cost.

Average fixed cost (*AFC*) is total fixed cost per unit of output. **Average variable cost** (*AVC*) is total variable cost per unit of output. **Average total cost** (*ATC*) is total cost per unit of output.

The average cost concepts are calculated from the total cost concepts as follows:

$$TC = TFC + TVC$$

Divide each total cost term by the quantity produced, Q, to give:

$$\frac{TC}{Q} = \frac{TFC}{Q} + \frac{TVC}{Q}$$

or:

$$ATC = AFC + AVC$$

Average total cost equals average fixed cost plus average variable cost.

Table 11.2 shows the calculation of average total cost. For example, when output is 10 jumpers, average fixed cost is (£25 ÷ 10), which equals £2.50, average variable cost is (£50 ÷ 10), which equals £5.00, and average total cost is (£75 ÷ 10), which equals £7.50. Equivalently, average total cost is equal to average fixed cost (£2.50) plus average variable cost (£5.00).

Short-run Cost Curves

Figure 11.5(a) illustrates Neat Knits' short-run costs as the total cost curves. Total fixed cost is a constant £25. It appears in the figure as the horizontal green curve *TFC*. Total variable cost and total cost both increase with output. They are graphed as the

Figure 11.5 Short-run Costs

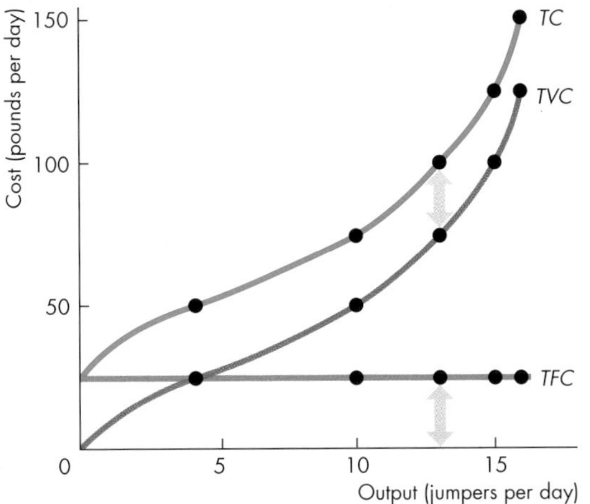

(a) Total costs

The short-run costs are calculated in Table 11.2 and illustrated in the graphs. Part (a) shows the total cost curves. Total cost (*TC*) increases as output increases. Total fixed cost (*TFC*) is constant – it graphs as a horizontal line – and total variable cost (*TVC*) increases in a similar way to total cost. The vertical distance between the total cost curve and the total variable cost curve is total fixed cost.

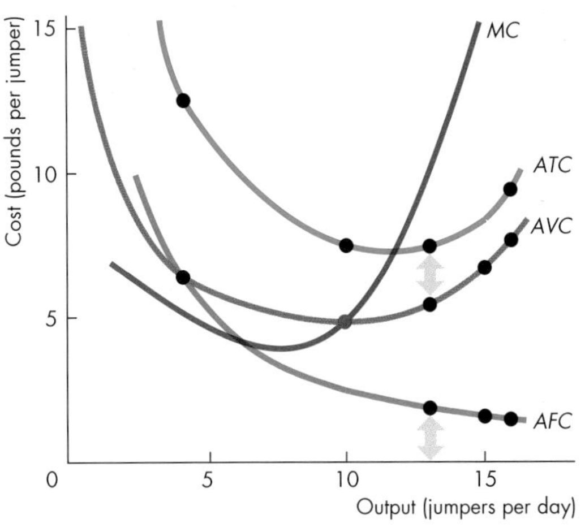

(b) Marginal cost and average costs

Part (b) shows the average and marginal cost curves. Average fixed cost (*AFC*) decreases as output increases. The average total cost curve (*ATC*) and average variable cost curve (*AVC*) are U-shaped. The vertical distance between these two curves is equal to average fixed cost. The marginal cost curve (*MC*) is also U-shaped. It intersects the average variable cost curve and the average total cost curve at their minimum points.

purple total variable cost curve (*TVC*) and the blue total cost curve (*TC*). The vertical distance between those two curves is equal to total fixed cost – as indicated by the arrows. Because total fixed cost is a constant £25, the distance between the purple total variable cost curve and the blue total cost curve is a constant £25. Use your ruler to check that the distance is a constant £25.

Figure 11.5(b) shows the average cost curves. The green average fixed cost curve (*AFC*) slopes downward. As output increases, the same constant fixed cost is spread over a larger output. When Neat Knits produces 4 jumpers, average fixed cost is £6.25; when total product increases to 16 jumpers, average fixed cost decreases to £1.56.

The blue average total cost curve (*ATC*) and the purple average variable cost curve (*AVC*) are U-shaped. The vertical distance between the average total cost and average variable cost curves is equal to average fixed cost – as indicated by the arrows. That distance shrinks as output increases because average fixed cost declines with increasing output.

Figure 11.5(b) also illustrates the marginal cost curve. It is the red curve *MC*. This curve is also U-shaped. The marginal cost curve intersects the average variable cost curve and the average total cost curve at their minimum points. That is, when marginal cost is less than average cost, average cost is decreasing, and when marginal cost exceeds average cost, average cost is increasing. This relationship holds for both the *ATC* and the *AVC* curves and is just another example of the relationship you saw in Figure 11.4 for Sam's course marks.

Why the Average Total Cost Curve is U-shaped

Average total cost, *ATC*, is the sum of average fixed cost, *AFC*, and average variable cost, *AVC*. So the shape of the *ATC* curve combines the shapes of the *AFC* and *AVC* curves. The U-shape of the average total cost curve arises from the influence of two opposing forces:

1 Spreading fixed cost over a larger output.
2 Eventually diminishing returns.

When output increases, the firm spreads its fixed costs over a larger output and its average fixed cost decrease – its average fixed cost curve slopes downward.

When output increases, diminishing returns eventually set in. That is, to produce an additional unit of output, ever larger amounts of labour are required. So average variable cost eventually increases and the firm's *AVC* curve eventually slopes upward.

The shape of the average total cost curve combines these two effects. Initially, as output increases, both average fixed cost and average variable cost decrease, so average total cost decreases and the *ATC* curve slopes downward. But as output increases further and diminishing returns set in, average variable cost begins to increase. Eventually, average variable cost increases more quickly than average fixed cost decreases, so average total cost increases and the *ATC* curve slopes upward. At the output level at which declining average fixed cost offsets increasing average variable cost, average total cost is constant and at its minimum.

Cost Curves and Product Curves

A firm's cost curves are determined by its technology and its product curves. Figure 11.6 shows the links between the product curves and the cost curves. The upper part of the figure shows the average product curve and the marginal product curve – like those in Figure 11.3. The lower part of the figure shows the average variable cost curve and the marginal cost curve – like those in Figure 11.5(b).

Notice that at over the output range in which marginal product and average product are rising, marginal cost and average variable cost are falling. Then, at the point of maximum marginal product, marginal cost is a minimum. At output levels above this point, marginal product diminishes and marginal cost increases. But there is an intermediate range of output over which average product is still rising and average variable cost is falling. Then an output is reached at which average product is a maximum and average variable cost is a minimum. At outputs above this level, average product diminishes and average variable cost increases.

Figure 11.6 Product Curves and Cost Curves

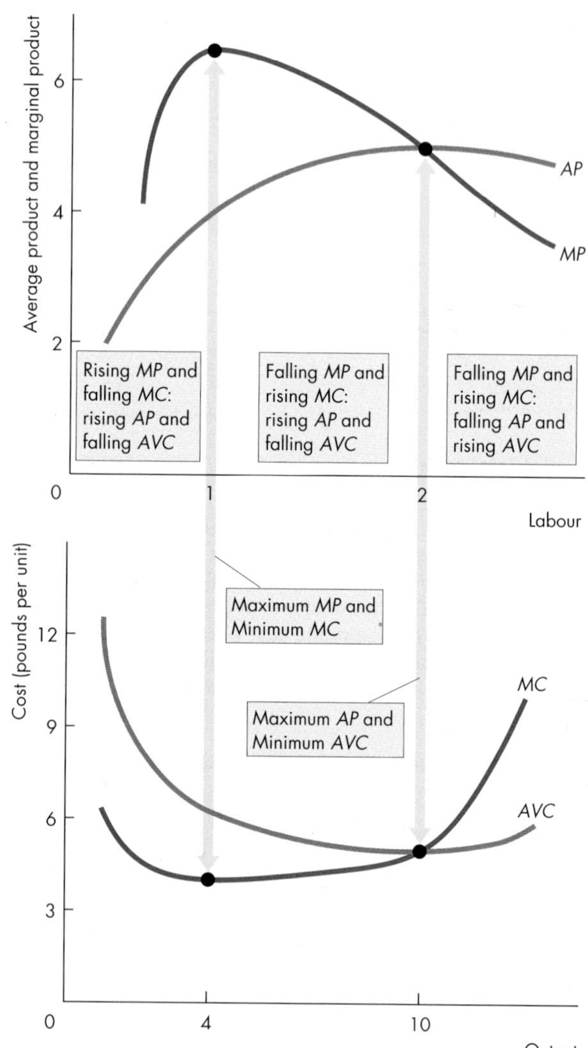

A firm's cost curves are linked to its product curves. Over the range of rising marginal product, marginal cost is falling. When marginal product is a maximum, marginal cost is a minimum. Over the range of rising average product, average variable cost is falling. When average product is a maximum, average variable cost is a minimum. Over the range of diminishing marginal product, marginal cost is rising. And over the range of diminishing average product, average variable cost is rising.

Table 11.3 A Compact Glossary of Costs

Term	Symbol	Equation	Definition
Fixed cost			Cost that is independent of the output level
Variable cost			Cost that varies with the output level
Total fixed cost	*TFC*		Cost of the fixed inputs (equals their number times their unit price)
Total variable cost	*TVC*		Cost of the variable inputs (equals their number times their unit price)
Total cost	*TC*	$TC = TFC + TVC$	Cost of all inputs (equals fixed costs plus variable costs)
Output (total product)	*TP*		Output produced
Marginal cost	*MC*	$MC = \Delta TC \div \Delta TP$	Change in total cost resulting from a one-unit increase in total product (equals the change in total cost divided by the change in total product)
Average fixed cost	*AFC*	$AFC = TFC \div TP$	Total fixed cost per unit of output (equals total fixed cost divided by total product)
Average variable cost	*AVC*	$AVC = TVC \div TP$	Total variable cost per unit of output (equals total variable cost divided by total product)
Average total cost	*ATC*	$ATC = AFC + AVC$	Total cost per unit of output (equals average fixed cost plus average variable cost)

Shifts in the Cost Curves

The position of a firm's short-run cost curves depend on technology, described by its product curves, and by the prices it pays for its factors of production. If technology changes or if factor prices change, the firm's costs change and its cost curves shift. You can read about the effects of new technology on company costs in *Reading Between the Lines* on pp. 264–265.

A technological change that increases productivity shifts the product curves upward and shifts the cost curves downward. For example, advances in robotic production techniques have increased productivity in the car industry. As a result, the product curves of BMW, Renault and Volvo have shifted upward and their cost curves have shifted downward. But the relationships between their product curves and cost curves have not changed. The curves are still linked in the way shown in Figure 11.6.

An increase in factor prices increases costs and shifts the cost curves. But the way the curves shift depends on which factor prices change. A change in rent or some other component of *fixed* cost shifts the fixed cost curves (*TFC* and *AFC*) and the total cost curve (*TC*) upward, but leaves the variable cost curves (*AVC* and *TVC*) and the marginal cost curve (*MC*) unchanged. A change in wages or some other component of *variable* cost shifts the variable curves (*TVC* and *AVC*), the total cost curve (*TC*) and the marginal cost curve (*MC*) upward, but leaves the fixed cost curves (*AFC* and *TFC*) unchanged.

We've studied the way costs change when a firm changes its output by changing the quantity of labour it employs in a fixed plant. All the concepts that you've met are summarized in a compact glossary in Table 11.3. But what happens if the firm changes its plant? Let's answer this question by seeing what happens if Neat Knits installs more knitting machines.

Review

- Tables 11.2 and Figures 11.5 and 11.6 define the key concepts and explain the key relationships between short-run cost and output.
- Marginal cost eventually increases because of diminishing returns – each additional worker produces a successively smaller addition to output.

- Average fixed cost decreases because as output increases, fixed costs are spread over a larger output.
- The average total cost curve is U-shaped because it combines the influences of falling average fixed cost and eventually diminishing returns.

Plant Size and Cost

We have studied how the cost of production varies for a given jumper plant when different quantities of labour are used. We are now going to see how the cost of production varies when both plant size – the number of machines – and the quantity of labour are varied. That is, we are going to study a firm's long-run costs. **Long-run cost** is the cost of production when a firm uses the economically efficient quantity of labour and plant size.

The behaviour of long-run cost depends on the firm's production function. A **production function** is the relationship between the maximum output attainable and the quantities of *all* inputs used.

The Production Function

Figure 11.7 shows Neat Knits' production function. The table lists the total product for four different plant sizes and five different quantities of labour. The numbers for Plant 1 are for the jumper factory whose short-run product and cost curves we've just studied. The other three plants have 2, 3 and 4 machines. If Sam doubles the plant size to 2 knitting machines, the various amounts of output that labour can produce are shown in the third column of the table. The other two columns show the outputs of yet larger plants.

The numbers in the table are graphed as the four total product curves in Figure 11.7. Each total product curve has the same basic shape, but the larger the number of knitting machines, the larger is the number of jumpers knitted each day by a given number of workers.

Diminishing Returns

Diminishing returns occur in all four plants as the labour input increases. You can check that fact by doing similar calculations for the larger plants to those you've already done for a plant with one

Figure 11.7 The Production Function

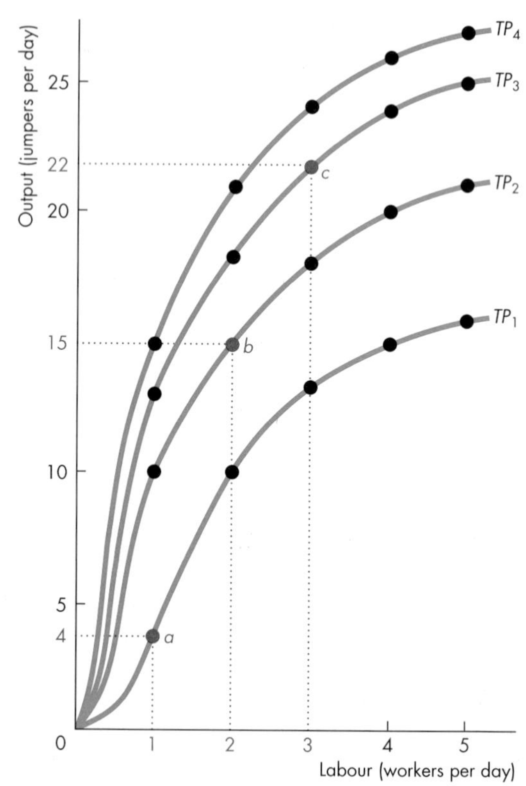

Labour (workers per day)	Output (jumpers per day)			
	Plant 1	Plant 2	Plant 3	Plant 4
1	4	10	13	15
2	10	15	18	21
3	13	18	22	24
4	15	20	24	26
5	16	21	25	27
Knitting machines (number)	1	2	3	4

The table shows the short-run total product data for four plant sizes with different numbers of machines. These numbers are graphed as the total product curves, TP_1, TP_2, TP_3 and TP_4. The bigger the plant, the larger is the total product for any given amount of labour employed. But each total product curve displays diminishing marginal product. The highlighted numbers show what happens. If Neat Knits doubles its scale from 1 machine and 1 worker to 2 machines and 2 workers, its output more than doubles – increasing returns to scale are shown between *a* and *b*. But increasing the scale again from 2 workers and 2 machines to 3 workers and 3 machines or to 4 workers and 4 machines increases output by a smaller percentage than the increase in inputs – decreasing returns to scale are shown from *b* to *c*.

machine. Regardless of the plant size, as the labour input increases, its marginal product (eventually) decreases.

Diminishing Marginal Product of Capital

Just as we can calculate the marginal product of labour for each plant size, we can also calculate the marginal product of capital for each quantity of labour. The *marginal product of capital* is the change in total product divided by the change in capital employed when the amount of labour employed is constant. Equivalently, it is the change in output resulting from a one-unit increase in the quantity of capital employed. For example, if Neat Knits employs 3 workers and increases the number of machines from 1 to 2, output increases from 13 to 18 jumpers a day. The marginal product of capital is 5 jumpers a day. The marginal product of capital diminishes, just like the marginal product of labour. For example, if with 3 workers Neat Knits increases the number of machines from 2 to 3, output increases from 18 to 22 jumpers a day. The marginal product of the third machine is 4 jumpers a day, down from 5 jumpers a day for the second machine.

The law of diminishing returns tells us what happens to output when a firm changes one input, either labour or capital, and holds the other input constant. But what happens to a firm's output if it changes both labour and capital?

Returns to Scale

A change in scale occurs when there is an equal percentage change in the use of all the firm's inputs. For example, if Neat Knits has been employing one worker and has one knitting machine and then doubles its use of both inputs (to use two workers and two knitting machines), the scale of the firm will double. **Returns to scale** are the increases in output that result from increasing all inputs by the same percentage. There are three possible cases:

1 Constant returns to scale.

2 Increasing returns to scale.

3 Decreasing returns to scale.

Constant Returns to Scale **Constant returns to scale** occur when the percentage increase in a firm's output is equal to the percentage increase in its inputs. If constant returns to scale are present and a firm doubles all its inputs, its output exactly doubles. Constant returns to scale occur if an increase in output is achieved by replicating the original production process. For example, BMW can double its production of its 5-series by doubling its production facility for those cars. It can build an identical production line and hire an identical number of workers. With the two identical production lines, BMW produces exactly twice as many cars.

Increasing Returns to Scale **Increasing returns to scale** occur when the percentage increase in output exceeds the percentage increase in inputs. If increasing returns to scale are present and a firm doubles all its inputs, its output more than doubles. Increasing returns to scale occur in production processes where increased output enables a firm to increase the division of labour and to use more specialized labour and capital. For example, if BMW produces only 100 cars a week, each worker and each machine must be capable of performing many different tasks. But if it produces 10,000 cars a week, each worker and each piece of equipment can be highly specialized. Workers specialize in a small number of tasks at which they become highly proficient. BMW might use 100 times more capital and labour, but the number of cars produced increases by more than a hundredfold. In this case, BMW experiences increasing returns to scale. Another source of increasing returns is technological. A doubling of the surface area of an oil pipe (a doubling of inputs), more than doubles the volume of oil that can flow through the pipe.

Decreasing Returns to Scale **Decreasing returns to scale** occur when the percentage increase in output is less than the percentage increase in inputs. If decreasing returns to scale are present and a firm doubles all its inputs, its output less than doubles. Decreasing returns to scale occur in all production processes at some output rate, but may not appear until a very large output rate is achieved. The most common source of decreasing returns to scale is the increasingly complex management and organizational structure required to control a large international firm. The larger the organization, the larger are the number of layers in the management pyramid and the greater are the costs of monitoring and maintaining control of the production and marketing process.

Figure 11.8 Short-run and Long-run Costs

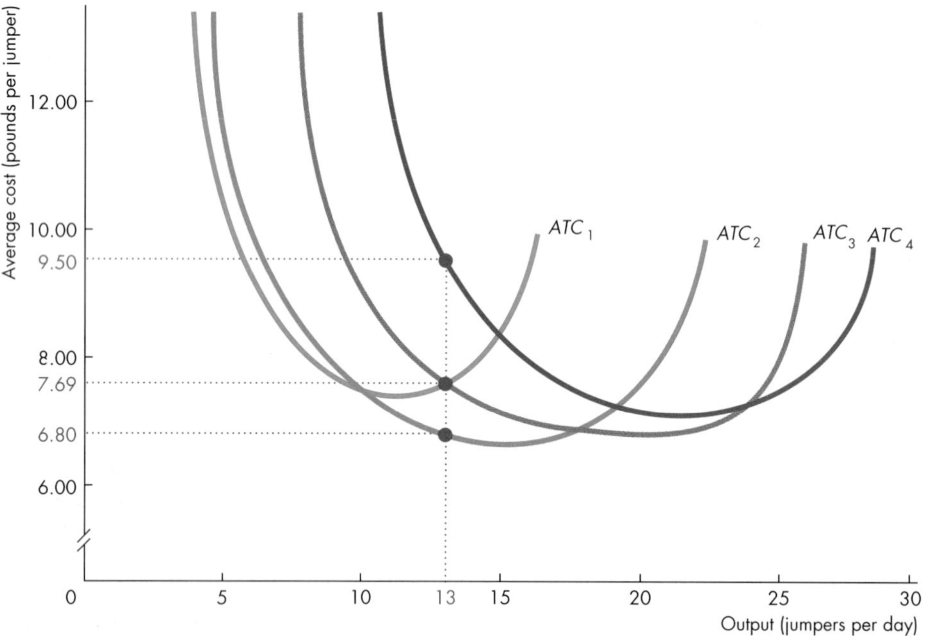

The figure shows short-run average total cost curves for four different plants. Neat Knits can produce 13 jumpers a day with 1 knitting machine on ATC_1 or with 3 knitting machines on ATC_3 for an average cost of £7.69 per jumper. It can produce the same number of jumpers by using 2 knitting machines on ATC_2 for £6.80 per jumper or with 4 machines on ATC_4 for £9.50 per jumper. If Neat Knits produces 13 jumpers a day, the least-cost method of production – the long-run method – is with 2 machines on ATC_2.

Returns to Scale at Neat Knits Neat Knits' production possibilities, set out in Figure 11.7, display both increasing returns to scale and decreasing returns to scale. If Sam has 1 knitting machine and employs 1 worker, his factory will produce 4 jumpers a day at point *a*. If he doubles the firm's inputs to 2 knitting machines and 2 workers, the factory's output increases almost fourfold to 15 jumpers a day at point *b*. If he increases the firm's inputs by another 50 per cent to 3 knitting machines and 3 workers, output increases to 22 jumpers a day at point *c* – an increase of less than 50 per cent. Doubling Neat Knits' scale from 1 to 2 units of each input gives rise to increasing returns to scale from point *a* to point *b*, but the further increase from 2 to 3 units of each input gives rise to decreasing returns to scale from point *b* to point *c*.

Whether a firm experiences increasing, constant, or decreasing returns to scale affects its long-run costs. Let's see how.

Short-run Cost and Long-run Cost

The cost curves in Figure 11.5 apply to a plant with 1 knitting machine. There is a set of short-run cost curves like those shown in Figure 11.5 for each different plant size. Let's look at the short-run costs for the four plants set out in Figure 11.7 and see how plant size affects the cost curves.

We've already studied the costs of a plant with 1 knitting machine. We'll call the average total cost curve for that plant ATC_1 in Figure 11.8. The average total cost curve for larger plants (with 2, 3 and 4 knitting machines respectively) are also

Figure 11.9 The Long-run Average Cost Curve

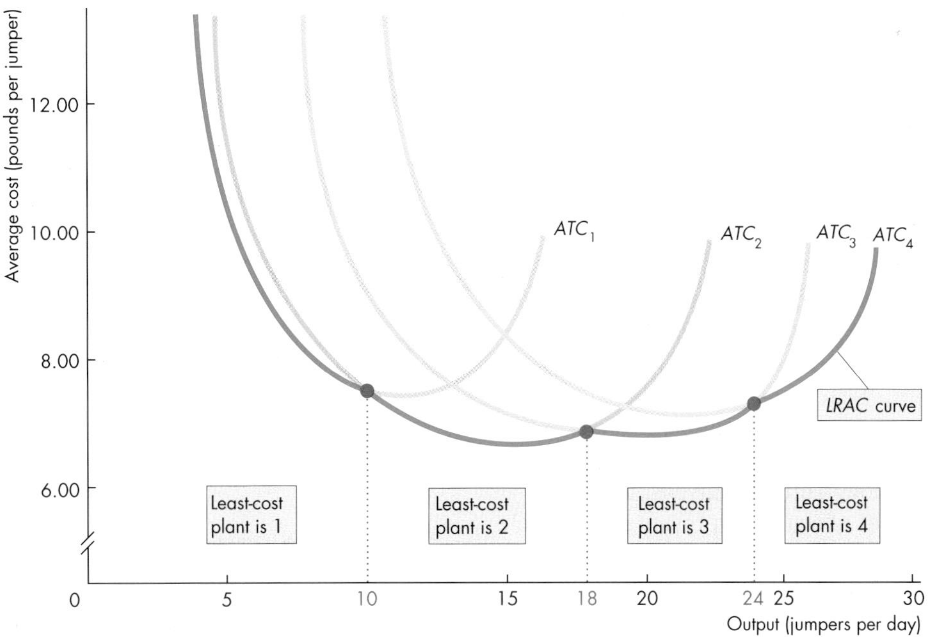

The figure shows the construction of the long-run average cost curve. The curve traces the lowest attainable costs of production at each output when both capital and labour inputs are varied. On the long-run average cost curve, Neat Knits uses 1 machine to produce up to 10 jumpers a day, 2 machines to produce between 11 and 18 jumpers a day, 3 machines to produce between 19 and 24 jumpers a day, and 4 machines to produce more than 24 jumpers a day.

shown in Figure 11.8 as ATC_2 (for 2 machines), ATC_3 (for 3 machines) and ATC_4 (for 4 machines). The average total cost curve for each plant size has the same basic U-shape. And because larger plants produce larger outputs with the same amount of labour, the *ATC* curves for successively larger plants lie farther to the right. Which of these cost curves Neat Knits operates on depends on its plant size. For example, if Neat Knits has 1 machine, then its average total cost curve is ATC_1 and it costs £7.69 per jumper to knit 13 jumpers a day. But Neat Knits can produce 13 jumpers a day with any of these four plant sizes. If it uses 2 machines, the average total cost curve is ATC_2 and the average total cost of a jumper is £6.80. If it uses 4 machines, the average total cost curve is ATC_4, and the average total cost of a jumper is £9.50. If Neat Knits wants to produce 13 jumpers a day, the economically efficient plant size is 2 machines – the one with the lowest average total cost of production.

The Long-run Average Cost Curve

The *long-run average cost curve* traces the relationship between the lowest attainable average total cost and output when both capital and labour inputs can be varied. This curve is illustrated in Figure 11.9 as *LRAC*. It is derived directly from the short-run average total cost curves that we have just reviewed in Figure 11.8. As you can see, ATC_1 has the lowest average total cost for all output rates up to 10 jumpers a day. ATC_2 has the lowest average total cost for output rates between 10 and 18 jumpers a day. ATC_3 has the lowest average total cost for output rates between 18 and 24 jumpers a day. And ATC_4 has the lowest average total cost for output rates in excess of 24 jumpers a day. The segment of each of the four average total cost curves for which that plant has the lowest average total cost is shown as dark blue in Figure 11.9. The scallop-shaped curve made up of these four segments is the long-run average cost curve.

Neat Knits will be on its long-run average cost curve if it does the following: to produce up to 10 jumpers a day it uses 1 machine; to produce between 11 and 18 jumpers a day it uses 2 machines; to produce between 19 and 24 jumpers it uses 3 machines; and, finally, to produce more than 24 jumpers it uses 4 machines. Within these ranges, Neat Knits varies its output by varying only the amount of labour employed.

Economies and Diseconomies of Scale

Economies of scale are present when, as output increases, long-run average cost decreases. When economies of scale are present, the *LRAC* curve slopes downward. Neat Knits experiences economies of scale for outputs up to 15 jumpers a day. **Diseconomies of scale** are present when, as output increases, long-run average cost increases. When diseconomies of scale are present, the *LRAC* curve slopes upward. At outputs greater than 15 jumpers a day, Neat Knits experiences diseconomies of scale. Between the regions of economies of scale and diseconomies of scale, at an output of 15 jumpers a day, Neat Knits' long-run average cost is at a minimum.

Neat Knits' long-run average cost curve has two special features that are not always found. First, Neat Knits can adjust its plant size only in big jumps by adding another knitting machine per day. In general, we can imagine varying the plant size in smaller increments by adding another knitting machine for part of a day so that there is an infinite number of plant sizes. In such a situation, there is an infinite number of short-run average total cost curves, one for each plant size. Second, Neat Knits' long-run average cost curve is U-shaped – it slopes either downward (economies of scale) or upward (diseconomies of scale). In contrast, many production processes have been shown to have constant long-run average cost over some intermediate range of output. The long-run average cost curve is horizontal over this range.

Figure 11.10 illustrates this situation. Here there is an infinite number of plant sizes so the long-run average cost curve is smooth, not scalloped like Neat Knits'. For outputs up to Q_1, there are economies of scale and long-run average cost is decreasing. For outputs that exceed Q_2, there are diseconomies of scale and long-run average cost is increasing. And for outputs between Q_1 and Q_2, long-run average cost is constant.

Figure 11.10 Economies of Scale

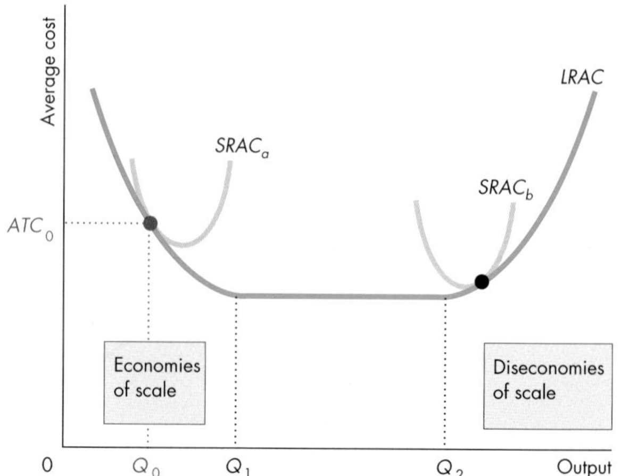

If capital can be varied in small units, there is an infinitely large number of plant sizes and an infinitely large number of short-run average total cost curves. Each short-run average total cost curve touches the long-run average cost curve at a single point. For example, the short-run average total cost curve ($SRAC_a$) touches the long-run average cost curve (*LRAC*) at the output rate Q_0 and average total cost ATC_0. For outputs up to Q_1, there are economies of scale; for outputs between Q_1 and Q_2, there are constant costs; and for outputs greater than Q_2, there are diseconomies of scale. For firms that face constant factor prices, economies of scale and returns to scale are linked. For outputs up to Q_1, there are increasing returns to scale; for outputs between Q_1 and Q_2, there are constant returns to scale; and for outputs greater than Q_2, there are decreasing returns to scale.

To keep the figure clear, only two of the infinite number of short-run average total cost curves, $SRAC_a$ and $SRAC_b$, are shown. Each short-run average total cost curve touches the long-run average cost curve, *LRAC*, at a single point – at a unique level of output. Thus for each output, there is a unique, economically efficient plant size. The short-run average total cost curve $SRAC_a$ is for the plant that can produce the output rate Q_0 at minimum average total cost, ATC_0.

The first time the long-run average cost curve appeared in print, it was drawn incorrectly. Take a look at *Economics in History* (pp. 266–267) to see why. You will understand the connection between the short-run and long-run average cost curves more thoroughly after you have studied that material.

Returns to Scale and Economies of Scale

A firm can experience economies (or diseconomies) of scale for two reasons:

1 Factor prices might change with scale.

2 Returns to scale.

A small firm might pay a higher price for its inputs than a large firm. For example, a large farmer can buy seeds and fertilizer in bulk for a lower price than a small farmer who buys in small batches. In this case, as scale increases, average cost decreases – there are economies of scale. The opposite case might also arise. A small firm might be able to buy its inputs for a lower price than a large firm. For example, a small car-hire firm might operate with part-time labour, while a large firm must hire full-time labour and operate for 24 hours a day. The large firm pays a much higher wage rate and possibly faces a diseconomy of scale.

But most firms face the same factor prices and are price takers. Even in this case, there are economies and diseconomies of scale. But they arise from the firm's production function and from its returns to scale. With constant factor prices, economies of scale occur – the *LRAC* curve is downward-sloping – when there are increasing returns to scale. Diseconomies of scale occur – the *LRAC* curve is upward-sloping – when there are decreasing returns to scale. And constant average costs occur – the *LRAC* curve is horizontal – when there are constant returns to scale.

To see why returns to scale and economies of scale are linked, think about what happens if a firm doubles all its inputs. Because its inputs double, total cost also doubles. If the firm has constant returns to scale output doubles, so average cost is constant. If the firm has increasing returns to scale output more than doubles, so average cost falls. If the firm has decreasing returns to scale output less than doubles, so average cost rises.

You've now studied the principles of long-run cost. Let's use what you've learned to answer some questions about real businesses.

Producing Cars and Generating Electric Power

At the beginning of this chapter, we noted that most car makers can produce far more cars than they can sell. We posed the question: why do car makers have expensive equipment lying around that isn't fully used? You can see the answer in Figure 11.10. Car producers experience economies of scale. The minimum cost of production occurs on a short-run average total cost curve that looks like $SRAC_a$.

We also noted that many electrical suppliers don't have enough production equipment on hand to meet demand on the coldest and hottest days and have to buy power from other producers. You can now see why this occurs and why they don't build a bigger plant. Power producers experience diseconomies of scale. They have short-run average total cost curves like $SRAC_b$. If they had larger plants, their average total costs of producing their normal output would increase.

Long-run Costs are Variable Costs For short-run costs, we distinguish between fixed costs and variable costs. We do not make this distinction for long-run costs. All inputs vary in the long run, so there are only variable costs. The long-run average cost curve is also the long-run average variable cost curve.

There is a long-run marginal cost curve that goes with the long-run average cost curve. The relationship between the long-run average cost curve and the long-run marginal cost curve is similar to that between the short-run average total cost curve and the short-run marginal cost curve. When long-run average cost is decreasing, long-run marginal cost is less than long-run average cost. When long-run average cost is increasing, long-run marginal cost exceeds long-run average cost. And when long-run average cost is constant, long-run marginal cost is equal to long-run average cost.

We've now studied the way in which a firm's costs vary as the firm changes its inputs and its output. We've seen that diminishing marginal product gives rise to increasing marginal and average costs. We've also seen how the long-run cost curve takes its shape from economies and diseconomies of scale – long-run average cost decreases as output increases with economies of scale, and long-run average cost increases as output increases with diseconomies of scale. Our next task is to study the interactions of firms and households in markets for goods and services and see how prices, output levels and profits are determined.

Summary

Key Points

The Firm's Objective and Constraints (p. 238)

- Firm's aim to maximize profit, constrained by the demand for its product, the technology available, and the prices of inputs into production.
- In the short run, the quantity of at least one input – usually capital – is fixed and the quantities of the other inputs – usually labour – can be varied. In the long run, the quantities of all inputs can be varied.

Short-run Technology Constraint (pp. 238–243)

- A total product curve shows how much output a firm can produce using a given quantity of capital and different quantities of labour.
- Initially, marginal product increases as the quantity of labour increases. But eventually, marginal product diminishes – the law of diminishing marginal returns.
- Average product increases initially and eventually diminishes.

Short-run Cost (pp. 243–248)

- As output increases, total fixed cost is constant, and total variable cost and total cost increase.
- As output increases, average fixed cost decreases.
- As output increases, average variable cost, average total cost, and marginal cost decrease at small outputs and increase at large outputs. These costs curves are U-shaped.

Plant Size and Cost (pp. 248–253)

- Long-run cost is the cost of production when all inputs – labour as well as plant and equipment – have been adjusted to their economically efficient levels.
- There is a set of short-run cost curves for each different plant size. There is one least-cost plant for each output. The larger the output, the larger is the plant that will minimize average total cost.
- The long-run average cost curve traces the relationship between the lowest attainable average total cost and output when both capital and labour inputs can be varied.
- With increasing returns to scale, the long-run average cost curve slopes downward. With decreasing returns to scale, the long-run average cost curve slopes upward.

Key Figures and Tables 

Key Terms

Long run, 238
Long-run cost, 248
Marginal cost, 243
Marginal product, 239
Production function, 248
Returns to scale, 249
Short run, 238
Total cost, 243
Total fixed cost, 243
Total product, 239
Total variable cost, 243
Variable cost, 243

Review Questions

1 Why do firms try to maximize profit?

2 What are the constraints on a firm's ability to maximize profit?

3 Distinguish between the short run and the long run.

4 What does a firm's total product curve show?

5 What does a firm's marginal product curve show?

6 What does a firm's average product curve show?

7 Explain the relationships between the shape of a firm's total product curve and its marginal product curve.

8 Explain the relationship between the shape of a firm's average product curve and its marginal product curve.

9 What is the law of diminishing returns? What does this law imply about the shapes of the total, marginal and average product curves?

10 Why does a firm's marginal product at first increase and eventually diminish?

11 What is the relationship between average total cost, average variable cost and marginal cost?

12 What is the relationship between the long-run average cost curve and the short-run average total cost curves?

13 What effects do economies of scale and diseconomies of scale have on the shape of the long-run average cost curve?

Problems

1 The total product schedule of Small Toys Ltd, a firm making plastic boats, is described by the following:

Labour (number of persons employed per week)	Output (plastic boats per week)
1	1
2	3
3	6
4	10
5	15
6	21
7	26
8	30
9	33
10	35

a Draw the total product curve.
b Calculate the average product of labour and draw the average product curve.
c Calculate the marginal product of labour and draw the marginal product curve.
d What is the relationship between average product and marginal product when Small Toys Ltd produces fewer than 30 boats a week? Why?
e What is the relationship between average and marginal product when Small Toys Ltd produces more than 30 boats a week? Why?

2 Suppose that the cost of labour is £400 a week, the total fixed cost is £1,000 a week and the total product schedule is the same as in Problem 1.

a Calculate total cost, total variable cost and total fixed cost for each level of output.
b Draw the total cost, total variable cost and total fixed cost curves.
c Calculate average total cost, average fixed cost, average variable cost and marginal cost at each level of output.
d Draw the following cost curves: average total cost, average variable cost, average fixed cost and marginal cost.

3 Suppose that total fixed cost increases to £1,100 a week. How will this affect the firm's short-run cost curves in Problem 2?

4 Suppose that total fixed cost remains at £1,000 a week, but that the cost of labour increases to £450 a week. Using these new costs, rework Problem 2.

5 Small Toys Ltd can buy an additional factory. If it does so and operates two factories, its total product schedule is:

Labour (workers per week)	Output (plastic boats per week)
1	2
2	6
3	12
4	20
5	30
6	42
7	52
8	60
9	66
10	70

The total fixed cost of operating its current factory is £1,000 a week and the total fixed cost of operating the additional factory is also £1,000 a week. The wage rate is £400 a week.

a Calculate the total cost for each of the outputs given for the new factory.
b Calculate Small Toys' average total cost of each output given.
c Draw Small Toys' long-run average cost curve.
d Over what output range would it be efficient for Small Toys to operate one factory?
e Over what output range would it be efficient for Small Toys to operate two factories?

6 Read the story about the introduction of teleworking in *Reading Between the Lines* on pp. 264–265 and then answer the following questions:

a What is the short-run impact of introducing teleworking on company costs?
b Why does teleworking involve investing in new technology?
c What is the long-run impact of introducing teleworking on company costs?
d What do you think are the advantages and disadvantages for employees of teleworking?
e Why do you think companies thought that employees would take more time off when working?
f Why might employees tend to work harder as a result of teleworking from home as opposed to working from an office or depot?

Appendix to Chapter 11
Producing at Least Cost

Least Cost and Input Substitution

Whatever goods and services we produce – cars, financial services, telecommunication services – we could use a variety of production techniques ranging from highly labour intensive to highly capital intensive methods. For example, financial services can be sold in a labour intensive way by financial advisers meeting clients, or in a capital intensive way by providing interactive information and application forms on the internet. Some specialist cars like the TVR are produced by hand while other cars, like Ford and Rover, are produced using computer-controlled robotic assembly. This movement from one technique to another is achieved through input substitution – changing the combination of inputs in the production process. A firm's long-run production function describes all the technically feasible combination of inputs.

Figure A11.1 shows Neat Knits' long-run production function. The figure highlights the fact that Neat Knits can use three different combinations of labour and capital to produce 15 jumpers a day, and two different combinations to produce 10 and 21 jumpers a day. But which combination should Neat Knits use? To be efficent,

Figure A11.1 Neat Knits' Production Function

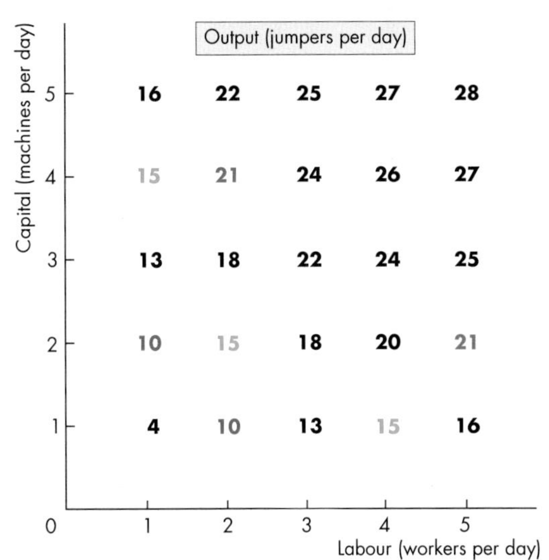

The figure shows how many jumpers can be produced per day by various combinations of labour and capital inputs. For example, by using 1 worker and 2 machines, Neat Knits can produce 10 jumpers a day; and by using 4 workers and 2 knitting machines, Neat Knits can produce 20 jumpers.

Neat Knits should use the least-cost combination. In this appendix we are going to use a new model to find the least-cost combination of these inputs. The first step is to illustrate the combinations shown in the figure (and many more are not shown), as an isoquant map.

An Isoquant Map

An **isoquant** is a curve that shows the different combinations of labour and capital required to produce a given quantity of output. The word isoquant means 'equal quantity' – *iso* meaning equal and *quant* meaning quantity. There is an isoquant for each output level. A series of isoquants is called an **isoquant map**. Figure A11.2 shows an isoquant map for Neat Knits with three isoquants: one for 10 jumpers, one for 15 jumpers and one for 21 jumpers. Each isoquant shown is based on the production function in Figure A11.1.

Although all goods and services can be produced by using a variety of alternative methods of production or techniques, the ease with which capital and labour can be substituted for each other varies from industry to industry. The production function reflects the ease with which inputs can be substituted for each other. The production function can also be used to calculate the degree of substitutability between inputs. Such a calculation involves the marginal rate of substitution of labour for capital. The marginal rate of substitution of labour for capital is the increase in labour needed per unit decrease in capital so that output remains constant. Let's look at this in more detail.

Figure A11.2 An Isoquant Map

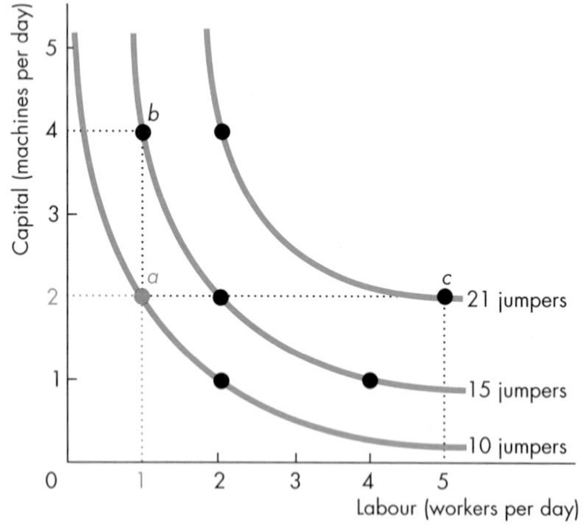

The figure illustrates an isoquant map, but one that shows only 3 isoquants – those for 10, 15 and 21 jumpers a day. These curves correspond to the production function shown in Figure A11.1. If Neat Knits uses 2 machines and 1 worker (point *a*), it produces 10 jumpers. If it uses 4 machines and 1 worker (point *b*), it produces 15 jumpers. And if it uses 2 machines and 5 workers (point *c*), it produces 21 jumpers.

Marginal Rate of Substitution

The marginal rate of substitution is the absolute magnitude of the slope of the isoquant. Figure A11.3 illustrates this relationship. The figure shows the isoquant for 13 jumpers a day. Pick any point on this isoquant and imagine decreasing capital by the smallest conceivable amount and increasing labour

Figure A11.3 The Marginal Rate of Substitution

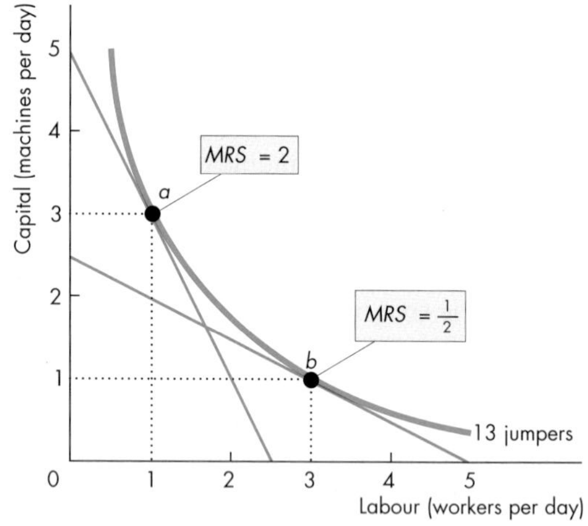

The marginal rate of substitution is measured by the absolute magnitude of the slope of the isoquant. To calculate the marginal rate of substitution at point *a*, use the red line that is tangential to the isoquant at point *a*. Calculate the slope of that line to find the slope of the isoquant at point *a*. The magnitude of the slope at point *a* is 2. Thus at a point *a*, the marginal rate of substitution of labour for capital is 2. The marginal rate of substitution at point *b* is found from the slope of the red line tangential to the isoquant at that point. That slope is $^1/_2$. Thus the marginal rate of substitution of labour for capital at point *b* is $^1/_2$.

by the amount necessary to keep output constant at 13 jumpers. As we decrease the capital input and increase the labour input so as to keep output constant at 13 jumpers a day, we travel down along the isoquant.

The marginal rate of substitution at point *a* is the absolute magnitude of the slope of the straight red line that is tangent to the isoquant at point *a*. The slope of the isoquant at point *a* equals the slope of the line. To calculate that slope, let's move along the red line from 5 knitting machines and no workers to 2.5 workers and no knitting machines. Capital decreases by 5 knitting machines and labour increases by 2.5 workers. The magnitude of the slope is 5 divided by 2.5, which equals 2. Thus when using technique *a* to produce 13 jumpers a day, the marginal rate of substitution of labour for capital is 2.

The marginal rate of substitution at point *b* is the absolute magnitude of the slope of the straight red line that is tangent to the isoquant at point *b*. Along this red line, if capital decreases by 2.5 knitting machines, labour increases by 5 workers. The magnitude of the slope is 2.5 knitting machines divided by 5, which equals 1/2. Thus when using technique *b* to produce 13 jumpers a day, the marginal rate of substitution of labour for capital is 1/2.

The marginal rates of substitution we've just calculated obey the law of diminishing marginal rate of substitution which states that:

> The marginal rate of substitution of labour for capital diminishes as the amount of labour increases and the amount of capital decreases.

You can now see that the law of diminishing marginal rate of substitution determines the shape of the isoquant. When the capital input is large and the labour input is small, the isoquant is steep and the marginal rate of substitution of labour for capital is large. As the capital input decreases and the labour input increases, the isoquant becomes flatter and the marginal rate of substitution of labour for capital diminishes. Only curves that are bowed towards the origin have this feature; hence isoquants are always bowed towards the origin.

Isoquants are very nice, but what do we do with them? The answer is that we use them to work out a firm's least-cost technique of production. But to do so, we need to illustrate the firm's costs in the same sort of figure that contains the isoquants.

Isocost Lines

An **isocost line** shows all the combinations of capital and labour that can be bought for a given total cost. For example, suppose Neat Knits is going to spend £100 a day producing jumpers. Knitting-machine operators can be hired for £25 a day, and knitting machines can be rented for £25 a day. The points *a*, *b*, *c*, *d* and *e* in Figure A11.4 show five possible combinations of labour and capital that Neat Knits can employ for £100. For example, point *b* shows that Neat Knits can use 3 machines (costing £75) and 1 worker (costing £25). If Neat Knits can employ workers and machines for fractions of a day, then any combination along the line *ae* will cost Neat Knits £100 a day. This line is Neat Knits' isocost line for a total cost of £100.

Figure A11.4 Neat Knits' Input Possibilities

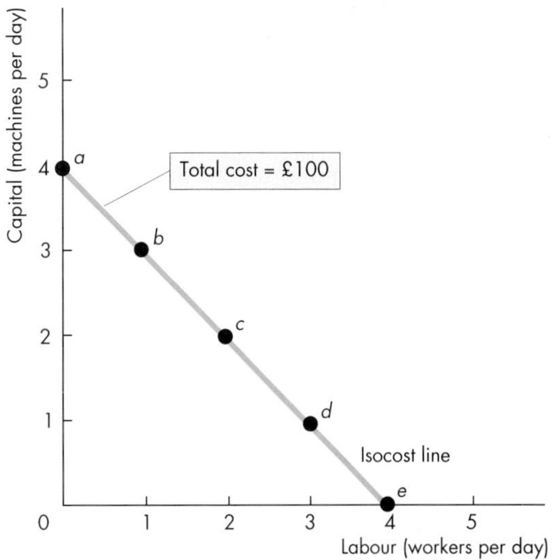

For a given total cost, Neat Knits' input possibilities depend on input prices. If labour and capital each cost £25 a day, for a total cost of £100 Neat Knits can employ the combinations of capital and labour shown by points *a* to *e*. The line passing through these points is an isocost line. It shows all possible combinations of capital and labour that Neat Knits can hire for a total cost of £100 when capital and labour cost £25 a day each.

The Isocost Equation

The isocost line can be described by an equation. We'll work out the isocost equation by using symbols that apply to any firm and numbers that describe Neat Knits' situation.

The variables that affect the firm's total cost (TC) are the prices of the inputs – the price of labour (P_L) and the price of capital (P_K) – and the quantities of the inputs employed – the quantity of labour (L) and the quantity of capital (K). In Neat Knits' case, we're going to look at the amount of labour and capital that can be employed when each input costs £25 a day and the total cost is £100. The cost of the labour employed ($P_L \times L$) plus the cost of the capital employed ($P_K \times K$) is the firm's total cost (TC). That is:

$$P_L L + P_K K = TC$$

and, in Neat Knits' case:

$$25L + 25K = 100$$

To calculate the isocost equation, divide the firm's total cost by the price of capital and then subtract $(P_L/P_K)L$ from both sides of the resulting equation. The isocost equation is:

$$K = \frac{TC}{P_K} - \frac{P_L}{P_K}$$

It tells us how the firm can vary its capital input as it varies its labour input, holding total cost constant. Neat Knits' isocost equation is:

$$K = 4 - L$$

This equation corresponds to the isocost line in Figure A11.4.

The Effect of Input Prices

Along the isocost line that we have just calculated, capital and labour each cost £25 a day. Therefore, in order to decrease its capital input by 1 unit and keep its total cost at £100 a day, the firm must increase the labour input by 1 unit. The absolute magnitude of the slope of the isocost line shown in Figure A11.4 is 1. The slope tells us that 1 unit of labour costs 1 unit of capital.

If factor prices change, the slope of the isocost line changes. If the wage rate rises to £50 and the rental rate of a machine remains at £25, then 1 worker costs 2 machines and the isocost line becomes steeper – line B in Figure A11.5. If the wage rate remains at £25 and the rental rate of a machine rises to £50, then 1 machine costs 2 workers and the isocost line becomes less steep – line C in Figure A11.5.

The higher the relative price of labour, the steeper is the isocost line. The magnitude of the slope of the isocost line measures the relative price of labour in terms of capital – that is, the price of labour divided by the price of capital.

The Isocost Map

An **isocost map** shows a series of isocost lines, each for a different total cost when the price of each input is constant. With a larger total cost, larger quantities of all the inputs can be employed. Figure A11.6 illustrates an isocost map. In the figure, the middle isocost line is the original one that appears in Figure A11.4. It is the isocost line for a total cost of £100 when capital and labour cost

Figure A11.5 Input Prices and Isocost Lines

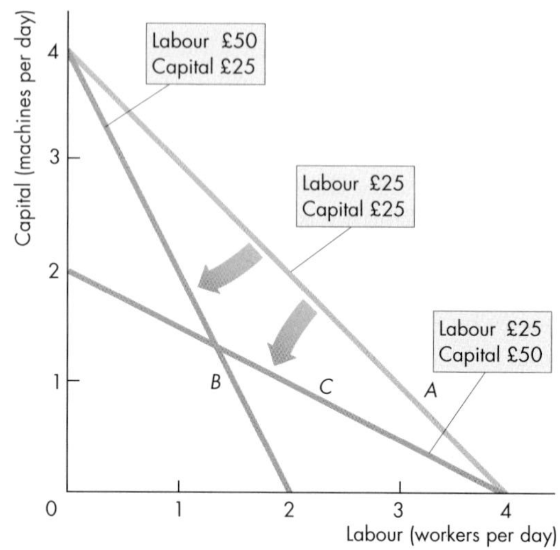

The slope of the isocost line depends on the relative input prices. Three cases are shown (each for a total cost of £100). If both labour and capital have a price of £25 a day, the isocost line is line *A*. If the price of labour rises to £50 but the price of capital remains £25, the isocost line becomes steeper and is line *B*. If the price of capital rises to £50 and the price of labour remains constant at £25, the isocost line becomes flatter and is line *C*.

Figure A11.6 An Isocost Map

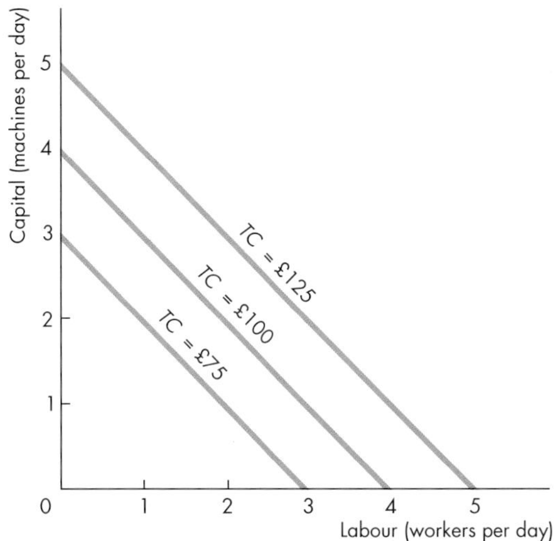

There is an isocost line for each total cost. This isocost map shows three isocost lines, one for a total cost of £75, one for £100 and one for £125. For each isocost line, the prices of capital and labour are £25 each. The slope of an isocost line is determined by the relative price of the two inputs – the price of labour divided by the price of capital. The larger the total cost, the farther is the isocost line from the origin.

£25 a day each. The other two isocost lines in Figure A11.6 are for a total cost of £125 and £75, holding constant the input prices at £25 each.

The Least-cost Technique

The **least-cost technique** is the combination of inputs that minimizes the total cost of producing a given output. Let's suppose that Neat Knits wants to produce 15 jumpers a day. What is the least-cost way of doing this? The answer can be seen in Figure A11.7. The isoquant for 15 jumpers is shown and the three points on that isoquant (marked *a*, *b* and *c*) illustrate the three techniques of producing 15 jumpers. The figure also contains two isocost lines – each drawn for a price of capital and labour of £25. One isocost line is for a total cost of £125 and the other is for a total cost of £100.

First, consider point *a*. Neat Knits can produce 15 jumpers at point *a* by using 1 worker and

Figure A11.7 The Least-cost Technique of Production

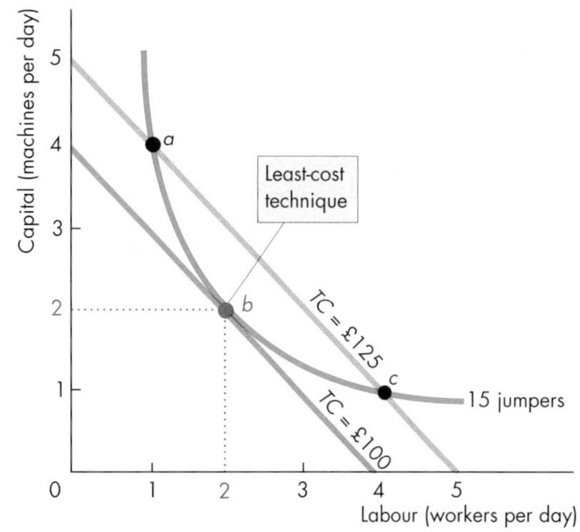

The least-cost technique of producing 15 jumpers is 2 machines and 2 workers (point *b*). The total cost of 15 jumpers is £100. An output of 15 jumpers can be produced by using 4 machines and 1 worker (point *a*) or by using 1 machine and 4 workers (point *c*). But with either of these techniques the total cost is greater at £125. At *b*, the isoquant for 15 jumpers is tangential to the isocost line for £100. The isocost line and the isoquant have the same slope. If the isoquant intersects the isocost line – for example, at *a* and *c* – the least-cost technique has not been found. With the least-cost technique, the marginal rate of substitution (slope of isoquant) equals the relative price of the inputs (slope of isocost line).

4 machines. The total cost, is £125. Point *c*, which uses 4 workers and 1 machine to produce 15 jumpers shows another technique for a cost of £125.

At point *b*, Neat Knits uses 2 machines and 2 workers to produce 15 jumpers at a cost of £100. Point *b* is the *least-cost technique* or the *economically efficient technique* for producing 15 jumpers, when knitting machines and workers each cost £25 a day.

Notice that although there is only one way that Neat Knits can produce 15 jumpers for £100, there are several ways of producing 15 jumpers for more than £100. Techniques shown by points *a* and *c* are two examples. All the points between *a* and *b* and all the points between *b* and *c* are also ways of producing 15 jumpers for a cost that exceeds £100 but is less than £125. That is, there are isocost lines between those shown, for total costs falling between £100 and £125. Neat Knits can also produce 15 jumpers for a cost that exceeds £125. That is, the firm can change its technique of production by moving to a point on the isoquant higher than point *a*. All of these ways of producing 15 jumpers are economically inefficient.

You can see that Neat Knits cannot produce 15 jumpers for less than £100 by imagining the isocost line for £99. That isocost line will not touch the isoquant for 15 jumpers. At £25 for a unit of each input, £99 will not buy the inputs required to produce 15 jumpers.

Marginal Rate of Substitution Equals Relative Input Price

At the least-cost technique point *b*, the slope of the isoquant on which Neat Knits is producing is equal to the slope of the isocost line. Equivalently, when a firm is using the least-cost technique of production, the marginal rate of substitution between the inputs equals their relative price. Recall that the marginal rate of substitution is the magnitude of the slope of an isoquant. Relative input prices are measured by the magnitude of the slope of the isocost line. We've just seen that producing at least cost means producing at a point where the isocost line is tangential to the isoquant. Because the two curves are tangential, their slopes are equal. Hence the marginal rate of substitution (the magnitude of the slope of isoquant) equals the relative input price (the magnitude of the slope of isocost line).

Marginal Product and Marginal Cost in the Long Run

When we studied short-run cost in Chapter 10, we learned that marginal cost is the change in total cost per unit change in total product. In the short run, a change in total cost occurs when the quantity of the variable input, labour, changes. But there is a long-run marginal cost concept for a change in the capital input. When long-run cost is minimized, the marginal cost of increasing output by using one more unit of capital is equal to the marginal cost of increasing output by using one more unit of labour. To see why, we're first going to learn about the relationship between the marginal rate of substitution and marginal product.

Marginal Rate of Substitution and Marginal Products

The marginal rate of substitution and the marginal products are linked together in a simple formula:

> The marginal rate of substitution of labour for capital equals the marginal product of labour divided by the marginal product of capital.

A few steps of reasoning are needed to establish this fact. First, we know that output changes when a firm changes the amounts of labour and capital employed. Furthermore, we know that the change in output resulting from a change in one of the inputs is determined by the marginal product of the input. That is:

$$\text{Change in output} = (MP_L \times \Delta L) + (MP_K \times \Delta K)$$

That is, the change in output equals the marginal product of labour, MP_L, multiplied by the change in labour, ΔL, plus the marginal product of capital, MP_K, multiplied by the change in capital, ΔK.

Suppose that Neat Knits wants to change its inputs but remain on an isoquant – that is, it wants to change its inputs of labour and capital but produce the same number of jumpers. To remain on an isoquant, the change in output must be zero. We can make the change in output zero in the above equation, and doing so yields the equation:

$$MP_L \times \Delta L = MP_K \times \Delta K$$

To stay on an isoquant when labour increases, capital must decrease. That is, when labour increases by ΔL, capital must decrease by $-\Delta K$. We can write the above equation as:

$$MP_L \times \Delta L = MP_K \times -\Delta K$$

which states that the marginal product of labour multiplied by the *increase* in labour equals the marginal product of capital multiplied by the *decrease* in capital. Divide both sides of this equation by the increase in labour (ΔL), and also divide both sides by the marginal product of capital (MP_K), to give:

$$\frac{MP_L}{MP_K} = \frac{-\Delta K}{\Delta L}$$

This equation tells us that, when Neat Knits remains on an isoquant, the decrease in its capital input ($-\Delta K$) divided by the increase in its labour input (ΔL) is equal to the marginal product of labour (MP_L) divided by the marginal product of capital (MP_K). The decrease in capital divided by the increase in labour when we remain on a given isoquant is the marginal rate of substitution of labour for capital. What we have discovered, then, is that the marginal rate of substitution of labour for capital equals the ratio of the marginal product of labour to the marginal product of capital.

Marginal Cost

We can use the fact that the marginal rate of substitution of labour for capital equals the ratio of the marginal product of labour to the marginal product of capital to work out a key implication of cost minimization. A few steps are needed.

Part (a) defines some symbols. Part (b) reminds us that the marginal rate of substitution of labour for capital is the slope of the isoquant, which in turn equals the ratio of the marginal product of labour (MP_L) to the marginal product of capital (MP_K). Part (b) also reminds us that the magnitude of the slope of the isocost line equals the ratio of the price of labour (P_L) to the price of capital (P_K). Part (c) of the table summarizes some propositions about a firm that is using the least-cost technique of production.

The first of these propositions is that when the least-cost technique is employed, the slope of the isoquant and the isocost line are the same. That is:

$$\frac{MP_L}{MP_K} = \frac{P_L}{P_K}$$

The second proposition is that total cost is minimized when the marginal product of labour per pound spent on labour equals the marginal product of capital per pound spent on capital. To see why, just rearrange the above equation in the following way. First, multiply both sides by the marginal product of capital and then divide both sides by the price of labour. We then get:

$$\frac{MP_L}{P_L} = \frac{MP_K}{P_K}$$

This equation says that the marginal product of labour per pound spent on labour is equal to the marginal product of capital per pound spent on capital. In other words, the extra output from the last pound spent on labour equals the extra output from the last pound spent on capital. This makes sense if the extra output from the last pound spent on labour exceeds the extra output from the last pound spent on capital, it will pay the firm to use less capital and more labour. By doing so, it can produce the same output at a lower total cost. Conversely, if the extra output from the last pound spent on capital exceeds the extra output from the last pound spent on labour the firm can lower its cost of producing a given output by using less labour and more capital. A firm achieves the least-cost technique of production only when the extra output from the last pound spent on all the inputs is the same.

The third proposition is that marginal cost with fixed capital and variable labour equals marginal cost with fixed labour and variable capital. To see this proposition, simply flip the last equation over and write it as:

$$\frac{P_L}{MP_L} = \frac{P_K}{MP_K}$$

This equation says that the price of labour divided by its marginal product must equal the price of capital divided by its marginal product. The price of labour divided by the marginal product of labour is marginal cost when the capital input is held constant. To see why, first recall the definition of marginal cost. *Marginal cost* is the change in total cost resulting from a unit increase in output. If output increases because one more unit of labour is employed, total cost increases by the cost of the extra labour, and output increases by the marginal product of the labour. So marginal cost is the price of labour divided by the marginal product of labour. For example, if labour costs £25 a day and the marginal product of labour is 2 jumpers, then the marginal cost of a jumper is £12.50 (£25 divided by 2).

The price of capital divided by the marginal product of capital has a similar interpretation. The price of capital divided by the marginal product of capital is marginal cost when the labour input is constant. As you can see from the above equation, with the least-cost technique of production, marginal cost is the same regardless of whether the capital input is constant and more labour is used, or the labour input is constant and more capital is used.

Output and Costs: Teleworkers

Financial Times, 13 May 1999

At home with the 'virtual' workers

An increasing number of companies and staff are finding teleworking is good for business, writes **Deborah Hargreaves**

British Telecommunications said this week it would have 10 per cent of its workforce based at home by next year.

The CBI employment trends survey published yesterday found that 10 per cent of the companies in its sample of 830 private sector employers were using teleworkers – those connected to the office by computer and telephone – and 21 per cent employed other types of home worker. Neil McLocklin, head of BT's workstyle consultancy group, predicts there will be 4m teleworkers in the UK by the end of next year compared with 1.8m last year.

This has big implications for the future of work and where people live.

'The increase in efficiency is staggering. It has made a significant difference to our return to profit'.

British Gas moved 5,000 of its service engineers to teleworking four years ago, enabling it to close 440 depots and reporting stations. Engineers are now all based at home and receive their appointments for the day on a laptop computer. They keep in touch via mobile phones and e-mail.

The company invested £30m in the hardware and back-up for the changeover, but has recouped that many times in savings. "The increase in efficiency is staggering. It has made a significant and material difference to our return to profitability," said Chris Wright at British Gas Services.

There are tangible advantages for companies in using teleworkers, but staff working from home could lose out in terms of the social contact they get at the office.

BT says there could be a move in future to set up local teleworking centres where people employed by different companies would go to work, so maintaining social contact with other workers.

Many managers thought people might take advantage of teleworking to shirk their duties, Mr McLocklin says. "But we've found the opposite, people are prepared to work much harder." Mr Wright says: "It's not big brother. But we do have systems in place to let us know where an engineer is at any given time."

Organisations that use teleworkers in the UK

Organisation	
British Gas	7,000
BT	825
Cable & Wireless	2,000
Canon UK	1,100
CocaCola/Schweppes	250
Digital Electronic	1,500
Lloyds TSB	180

Sources: Office for National Statistics, TCA

The Essence of the Story

- British Telecommunications (BT) intends to persuade 10 per cent of its 100,000 UK workforce to work as teleworkers by the year 2,000. Teleworkers work from home, communicating with customers, managers and colleagues by the internet, fax and telephone.

- The Confederation of British Industries estimate that 10 per cent of companies are already using teleworkers to some extent. If companies like BT expand teleworking, the number of teleworkers could rise from 1.8 million to 4 million by the end of 2000.

- BT is following the initiative of British Gas, which moved 5,000 of its service engineers to teleworking four years ago, allowing it to close 440 depots to save on property and office costs.

- British Gas invested £30 million in providing new technology to enable its engineers to telework, but has recouped the investment many times over since then. A spokesman described the increase in efficiency as 'staggering'.

■ A major disadvantage of teleworking for employees is the loss of social contact in the office. BT suggests this could be resolved by companies setting up joint teleworking centres where teleworkers can meet.

Economic Analysis

■ Figure 1 shows the costs curve for British Gas domestic services in 1995 when it first introduced teleworking, ATC_{95}. The company invests £30 million in new technology for its service engineers raising initial costs for current output from ATC_1 to ATC_2 on ATC'_{95}.

■ Over the next four years, British Gas sold the offices and depots which were no longer needed. The capital value realized and the reduction in running costs more than covered the inital investment cost.

■ By 1999, the investment in new technology had shifted the British Gas cost curve to ATC_{99}. Costs fell by £100 million, allowing the value of output to increase from Q_1 to Q_2, with the same number of employees. British Gas has increased efficiency and reaped economies of scale from the introduction of new technology.

■ BT has 100,000 employees. By moving 10,000 employees to teleworking, BT can save £134 million each year in costs, selling off surplus properties.

■ In addition to cost savings, BT will have a better equipped and more efficient workforce which could generate economies of scale.

■ Figure 2 shows the long-run production function for British Telecommunications. The total product curve for 1999 is TP_{99} and the total product curve for 2000 is TP_{00}. By investing in technology, BT could create a more than proportionate increase in the value of output. Output increases from point *a* to point *b*, with the same size workforce. Other companies are switching to teleworking for similar reasons.

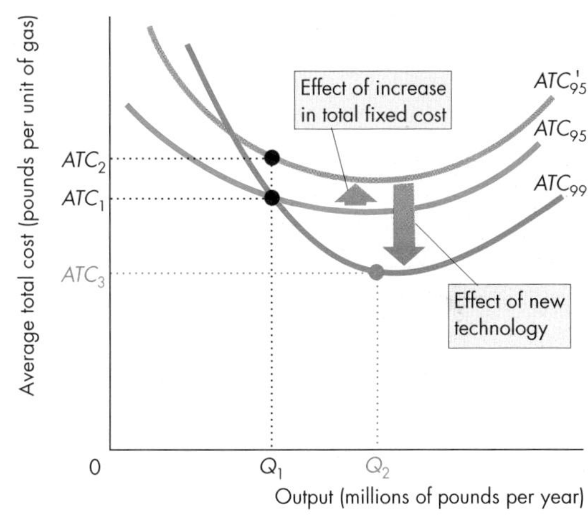

Figure 1 British Gas

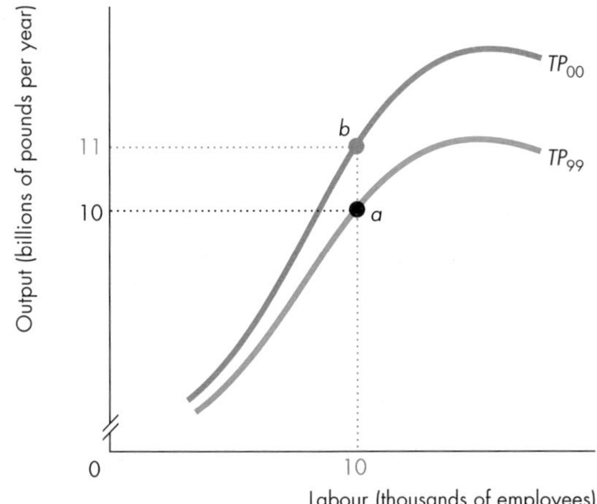

Figure 2 British Telecommunications

Part 4

Competition v Monopoly

Talking with **Peter Mackie**

Peter Mackie is Professor of Transport Studies at the Institute for Transport Studies (ITS) University of Leeds. ITS is a top-rated international research institute which conducts research into transport policy and economics, traffic and network management, traveller behaviour and safety and environmental aspects of transport. Peter Mackie's research interests are in the fields of transport regulation and economic appraisal of transport projects and policies. He is author of three books, most recently (with John Preston) The Local Bus Market: A Case Study in Regulatory Change, Avebury 1996.

He is a member of the Government's Standing Advisory Committee on Trunk Road Assessment (SACTRA) which has produced influential reports during the 1990s on environmental appraisal of roads, on whether new road capacity induces additional traffic, and most recently the 1999 report on Transport and the Economy. He has carried out research, consultancy and advisory work for private sector transport operators and for all levels of agency from local authorities to the EU and the World Bank.

What do you think is the most powerful concept in economics and why?

Prices matter. Prices are signals and if prices reflect resource costs, the signals are set correctly. If prices diverge from resource costs because of market failures, whether caused by imperfect markets driving prices higher than marginal costs or by failure to account for externalities such as environmental and congestion costs, then the signals for the allocation of resources and for investment decisions will be wrong. In areas like transport, energy and water, getting the prices right – and defining what that means in practice – is the big problem.

Economists talk about 'perfect competition' but it is hard to find examples. What do you think are the most competitive markets and why?

In my field, which is the transport sector, parts of the road haulage market remain highly competitive. Activities like tipper haulage serving the aggregates and construction industries are not very specialized and offer few economies of scale. As a result they are easy to enter, low margin businesses with many owner-operators, even in these days of big business. So there are highly competitive markets, but what is not so easy to find are markets in competitive equilibrium. In real life, the process of entry and exit is continuous, and such markets are in disequilibrium most of the time.

Why is it so important for governments to regulate the abuse of monopoly power?

Governments and monopolists have opposing interests. Monopolists have strong incentives to earn monopoly rents and protect or develop their monopoly by all legal means. Governments must act for the people by regulating firms' behaviour and/or promoting competition where feasible. A key issue for policy is to decide when to rely on market competition backed up by legislation to outlaw anti-competitive practices, and when to conclude that competition either will not happen or will not produce a good social result if it does. Sometimes economies of scale, for example in the utility industry networks, are so powerful that competition is just not feasible. Then the emphasis is on regulation of the monopoly resource such as the gas, water or electricity distribution networks, and ensuring that terms of access to those networks are even-handed for competing suppliers.

To what extent has government been successful in its attempt to control predatory pricing and abuses of monopoly power?

The British approach has tended to be rather *laissez-faire*. Whatever is in the commercial interest is deemed to be in the public interest unless there is overwhelming evidence to the contrary. Examples from the local bus and national newspaper industries come to mind. We have a lot to learn from the US regulatory system which is faster, sharper and more punitive of anti-competitive behaviour. In the UK by the time the Office of Fair Trading has investigated and recommended action to the (Monopolies and Mergers) Commission, who then report to the Secretary of State for Trade and Industry, whose decision may lead to court action, the events complained about will be far in the past.

Has the privatization programme in Britain and Europe been a success?

It's a mixed picture. Changing the ownership of industries from public to private has been less important than the structural reforms which have taken place. Where these have been sensible, as in telecommunications, electricity, and after a very slow start, gas, the results have been good in terms of the prices, quality and range of services offered. Where there are few opportunities for reform (water) or the structure is not right (railways), the outcome is not so good. One difficulty is that once a mistake has been made, there is no going back. Private capital has been invested and risks have been taken. So there is a high premium on being able to predict the effect of structuring public industries in particular ways. We see this currently in the debate about the likely impact of privatizing the Royal Mail.

Since privatization, British Telecommunication (BT) has recorded increasing profits? To what extent is this the result of a continuation of its monopoly power and a failure of regulation?

We shouldn't succumb to the disease of profit envy. Let's look at the picture as a whole – the price of phone calls, the range of services offered, the creation of competition, the mobile and cable sectors. BT needs to be compared with its counterparts in France, Germany and the US. You can argue about whether, with the important benefit of hindsight, regulation should have been tighter, but given the overall impact of telecoms, privatization and the accompanying regulatory regime has been positive.

What do you think is the most pressing problem facing European governments in their attempt to regulate competition and monopoly in the next millennium?

The most pressing problem will be regulation across boundaries; dealing with multi-industry firms such as United Utilities and dealing with multinational utilities operating under the regulatory regimes of different countries. The European Union will become an increasingly important player in this policy area.

After studying this chapter you will be able to:

- Define perfect competition
- Explain how price and output are determined in a competitive industry
- Explain why firms sometimes shut down temporarily and lay off workers
- Explain why firms enter and leave an industry
- Predict the effects of a change in demand and of a technological advance
- Explain why perfect competition is efficient

Rivalry in Personal Computers

Personal computers are big business in Europe. Millions of PCs are bought and sold each year in a multibillion pound market. Competition in supply is strong. National names such as Elonex and Gateway compete with international contenders such as Dell and IBM. New firms enter and try their luck while other firms are squeezed out of the industry. How does competition affect prices and profits? What causes some firms to enter an industry and others to leave it? What are the effects on profits and prices of new firms entering and old firms leaving an industry? ◆ In 1997, 16.5 million people were unemployed in the European Union. Of these, a large proportion were unemployed because they had been laid off by firms seeking to trim their costs and avoid bankruptcy. PC suppliers, ice cream producers and firms in almost every sector of the economy laid off workers in 1994. Why do firms lay off workers? When will a firm temporarily shut down, laying off its workers? ◆ Over the past few years, there has been a dramatic fall in the prices of PCs. For example, a slow 486 computer cost almost £3,000 a few years ago and a much faster Pentium III costs only £1,200 today. What goes on in an industry when the price of its output decreases sharply? What happens to the profits of the firms producing such goods?

◆ ◆ ◆ ◆ Computers, like most other goods, are produced and supplied by more than one firm and these firms compete with each other. In order to study competitive markets, we are going to build a model of a market in which competition is as fierce and extreme as possible. We call this case perfect competition.

Perfect Competition

Perfect competition is an extreme form of competition that arises when:

- There are many firms, each selling an identical product.
- There are many buyers.
- There are no restrictions on entry into the industry.
- Firms in the industry have no advantage over potential new entrants.
- Firms and buyers are completely informed about the prices of the products of each firm in the industry.

An industry can have a large number of firms only if the demand for its product is large relative to the minimum efficient scale of producing it. Minimum efficient scale is the output level at which average total cost is at a minimum. For example, the world-wide demand for wheat, rice and other basic grains is many thousands of times larger than the output that can be produced by a single farm at minimum average cost.

The conditions that define perfect competition imply that no individual firm can influence the price at which it sells its output. Firms in perfect competition are said to be price takers. A **price taker** is a firm that cannot influence the price of a good or service.

The key reasons why a perfectly competitive firm is a price taker are that it produces a tiny fraction of the total output of a particular good and buyers are well informed about the prices of other firms. Imagine for a moment that you are a carrot farmer in East Anglia in the United Kingdom. You have a thousand acres under cultivation – which sounds like a lot. But when you take a drive around East Anglia you see thousands more acres like yours full of carrots. Your thousand acres is just a drop in an ocean of carrots.

Nothing makes your carrots any better than any other farmer's, and all the buyers of carrots know the price at which they can do business. If everybody else sells their carrots for 50 pence a kilogram, and you want 60 pence, why would people buy from you? They can simply go to the next farmer, and the one after that, and the next, and buy all they need for 50 pence a kilogram. You are a price taker. A price-taking firm faces a demand curve that is perfectly elastic.

The market demand for carrots is not perfectly elastic. The market demand curve is downward-sloping, and its elasticity depends on the substitutability of carrots for other vegetables such as parsnips, cabbage and peas. The demand for carrots from farm A is perfectly elastic because carrots from farm A are a *perfect substitute* for carrots from farm B.

Perfect competition does not occur frequently in the real world. But competition in many industries is so fierce that the model of perfect competition we're about to study is of enormous help in predicting the behaviour of the firms in these industries. Assembling and retailing PCs, ice cream making, producing all kinds of agricultural goods, fishing, wood pulping and paper milling, the manufacture of paper cups and plastic shopping bags, photo-processing, plant growing and retailing, plumbing, painting and dry cleaning are all examples of industries that are highly competitive.

Profit and Revenue

The goal of a firm is to maximize profit, which is the sum of normal profit and economic profit. **Normal profit** is the return that a firm's owner could obtain in the best alternative business. So it is a foregone alternative or *opportunity cost* and part of the firm's total cost. **Economic profit** is equal to total revenue minus total cost.

Total revenue is the value of a firm's sales. It equals the price of the firm's output multiplied by the number of units of output sold (price × quantity). **Average revenue** is total revenue divided by the total quantity sold – revenue per unit sold. Because total revenue equals price multiplied by quantity sold, average revenue (total revenue divided by quantity sold) equals price. **Marginal revenue** is the change in total revenue divided by the change in quantity. That is, marginal revenue is the change in total revenue resulting from a one-unit increase in the quantity sold. In the case of perfect competition, the price remains constant when the quantity sold changes. So the change in total revenue resulting from a one-unit increase in the quantity sold equals price. Therefore, in perfect competition, marginal revenue equals price and marginal revenue does not vary with quantity.

An example of these revenue concepts is set out for Neat Knits Ltd in Figure 12.1. The table shows

Figure 12.1 Demand, Price and Revenue in Perfect Competition

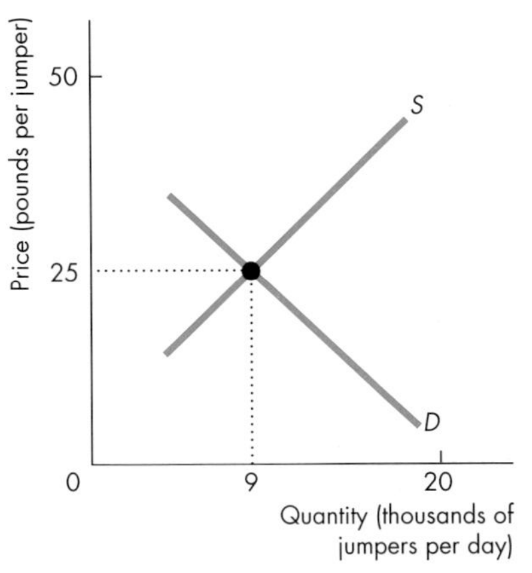

(a) Jumper industry

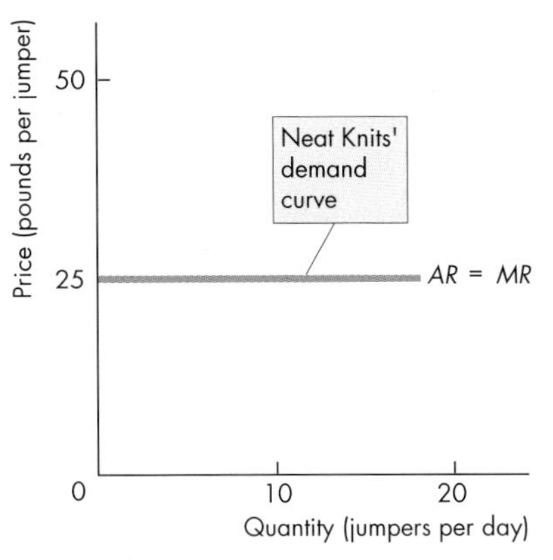

(b) Neat Knits' demand, average revenue and marginal revenue

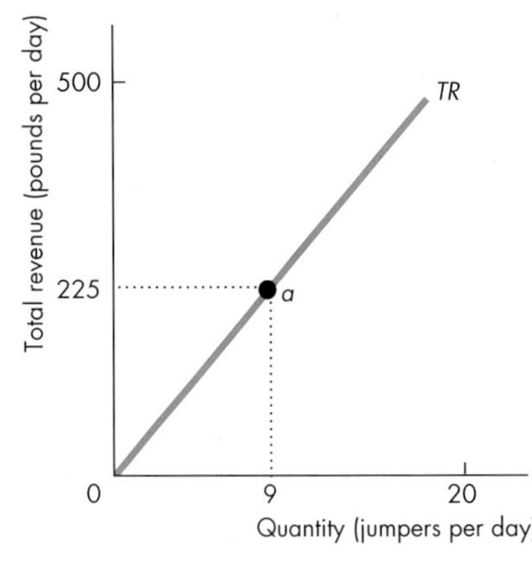

(c) Neat Knits' total revenue

Quantity sold (*Q*) (jumpers per day)	Price (*P*) (pounds per jumper)	Total revenue (*TR* = *P* × *Q*) (pounds)	Average revenue (*AR* = *TR*/*Q*) (pounds per jumper)	Marginal revenue (*MR* = Δ*TR*/Δ*Q*) (pounds per jumper)
8	25	200	25	
				25
9	25	225	25	
				25
10	25	250	25	

In perfect competition, price is determined where the industry demand and supply curves intersect. Such an equilibrium is illustrated in part (a) where the price is £25 and 9,000 jumpers are bought and sold. Neat Knits, a perfectly competitive firm, faces a fixed price, £25 in this example, regardless of the quantity it produces. The table calculates Neat Knits' total revenue, average revenue and marginal revenue. For example, when 9 jumpers are sold, total revenue is £225 and average revenue is £25. When sales increase from 9 jumpers to 10 jumpers, marginal revenue equals £25. The demand curve faced by Neat Knits is perfectly elastic at the market price and is shown in part (b) of the figure. Neat Knits' demand curve is also its average revenue curve and marginal revenue curve (*AR* = *MR*). Neat Knits' total revenue curve (*TR*) is shown in part (c). Point *a* on the total revenue curve corresponds to the second row of the table.

three different quantities of jumpers sold. For a price taker, as the quantity sold varies, the price stays constant – in this example at £25. Total revenue is equal to price multiplied by quantity. For example, if Neat Knits sells 8 jumpers, total revenue is 8 times £25, which equals £200. Average revenue is total revenue divided by quantity. Again, if Neat Knits sells 8 jumpers, average revenue is total revenue (£200) divided by quantity (8), which equals £25. Marginal revenue is the change in total revenue resulting from a 1-unit change in quantity. For example, when the quantity sold increases from 8 to 9, total revenue increases from £200 to £225, so marginal revenue is £25. (Notice that in the table, marginal revenue appears *between* the lines for the quantities sold. This arrangement presents a visual reminder that marginal revenue results from the *change* in the quantity sold.)

Suppose that Neat Knits is one of a thousand similar small producers of jumpers. Figure 12.1(a) shows the demand and supply curves for the entire jumper industry. Demand curve *D* intersects supply curve *S* at a price of £25 and a quantity of 9,000 jumpers. Figure 12.1(b) shows Neat Knits' demand curve. Because the firm is a price taker, its demand curve is perfectly elastic – the horizontal line at £25. The figure also illustrates Neat Knits' total, average and marginal revenues, calculated in the table. The average revenue curve and marginal revenue curve are the same as the firm's demand curve. That is, the firm's demand curve tells us the revenue per jumper sold and the change in total revenue that results from selling one more jumper. Neat Knits' total revenue curve (part c) shows the total revenue for each quantity sold. For example, when Neat Knits sells 9 jumpers, total revenue is £225 (point *a*). Because each additional jumper sold brings in a constant amount – in this case £25 – the total revenue curve is an upward-sloping straight line.

The Firm's Decisions in Perfect Competition

Firms in a perfectly competitive industry face a given market price and have the revenue curves that you've just studied. These revenue curves summarize the market constraint faced by a perfectly competitive firm.

Firms also have a technology constraint, which is described by the product curves (total product, average product and marginal product) that you studied in Chapter 10. The technology available to the firm determines its costs, which are described by the cost curves (total cost, average cost and marginal cost) that you also studied in Chapter 10.

The task of the competitive firm is to make the maximum profit possible, given the constraints it faces. To achieve this objective, a firm must make four key decisions, two in the short run and two in the long run.

Short-run Decisions The short run is a time-frame in which each firm has a given plant and the number of firms in the industry is fixed. But many things can change in the short run and the firm must react to these changes. For example, the price for which the firm can sell its output might have a seasonal fluctuation, or it might be affected by general business fluctuations.

The firm must react to such short-run price fluctuations and decide:

1 Whether to produce or to temporarily shut down.
2 If the decision is to produce, what quantity to produce.

Long-run Decisions The long run is a time-frame in which each firm can change the size of its plant and can decide whether to enter or leave an industry. So in the long run, both the plant size of each firm and the number of firms in the industry can change. Many additional things can change in the long run to which the firm must react. For example, the demand for a good can permanently fall. Or a technological advance can change an industry's costs.

The firm must react to such long-run changes and decide:

1 Whether to increase or decrease its plant size.
2 Whether to stay in the industry or leave it.

The Firm and the Industry in the Short Run and the Long Run To study a competitive industry, we begin by looking at an individual firm's short-run decisions. We then see how the short-run decisions of all the firms in a competitive industry combine to determine the industry price, output and economic profit. Then we turn to the long run and study the effects of long-run decisions on the industry price, output and economic profit.

All the decisions we study are driven by the single objective: to maximize profit.

Profit-maximizing Output

A perfectly competitive firm cannot influence profit by choosing a price. But it can maximize profit in the short run by choosing its output level. One way of finding the profit-maximizing output is to study a firm's total revenue and total cost curves and to find the output level at which total revenue exceeds total cost by the largest amount. Figure 12.2 shows you how to do this for Neat Knits. The table lists Neat Knits' revenue and total cost at different outputs, and part (a) of the figure shows Neat Knits' total revenue and total cost curves. These curves are graphs of the numbers shown in the first three columns of the table. The total revenue curve (*TR*) is the same as that in Figure 12.1(c). The total cost curve (*TC*) is similar to the one that you met in Chapter 10. As output increases, so does total cost.

Economic profit equals total revenue minus total cost. The fourth column of the table in Figure 12.2 shows Neat Knits' economic profit and part (b) of the figure illustrates these numbers as Neat Knits' profit curve. This curve shows that Neat Knits makes an economic profit at outputs greater than 4 and fewer than 12 jumpers a day. At outputs of fewer than 4 jumpers a day, Neat Knits incurs a loss. It also incurs a loss if output exceeds 12 jumpers a day. At outputs of 4 jumpers and 12 jumpers a day, total cost equals total revenue and Neat Knits' economic profit is zero. An output at

Figure 12.2 Total Revenue, Total Cost and Profit

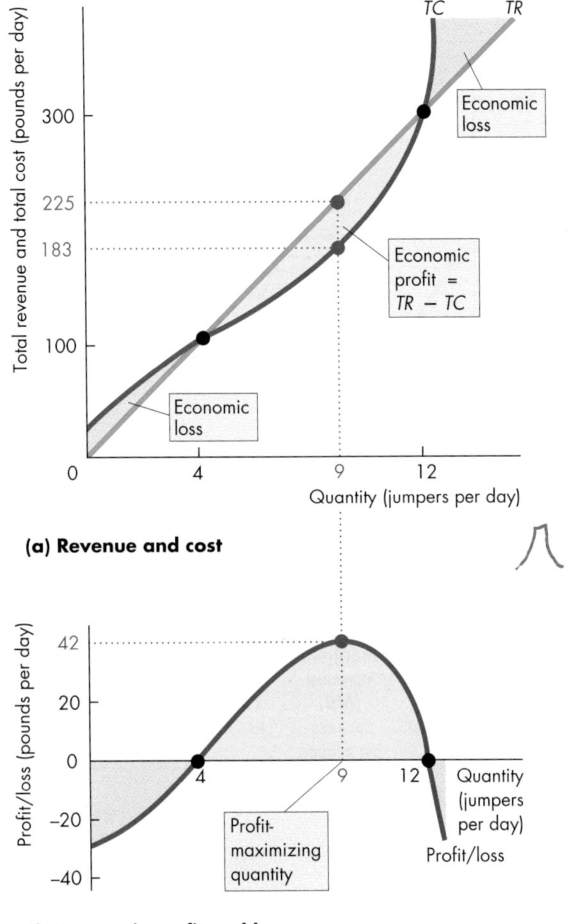

Quantity (Q) (jumpers per day)	Total revenue (TR) (pounds)	Total cost (TC) (pounds)	Economic profit ($TR - TC$) (pounds)
0	0	22	–22
1	25	45	–20
2	50	66	–16
3	75	85	–10
4	100	100	0
5	125	114	11
6	150	126	24
7	175	141	34
8	200	160	40
9	225	183	42
10	250	210	40
11	275	245	30
12	300	300	0
13	325	360	–35

The table lists Neat Knits' total revenue, total cost and economic profit. Part (a) graphs the total revenue and total cost curves. Economic profit is seen in part (a) as the blue area between the total cost and total revenue curves. The maximum economic profit, £42 a day, occurs when 9 jumpers are produced – where the vertical distance between the total revenue and total cost curves is at its largest. At outputs of 4 jumpers a day and 12 jumpers a day, Neat Knits makes zero economic profit – these are break-even points. At outputs fewer than 4 and greater than 12 jumpers a day, Neat Knits incurs a loss. Part (b) of the figure shows Neat Knits' profit curve. The profit curve is at its highest when profit is at a maximum and cuts the horizontal axis at the break-even points.

which total cost equals total revenue is called a *break-even point*. Because normal profit is part of total cost, a firm makes normal profit at a break-even point.

Neat Knits' economic profit, calculated in the final column of the table, is graphed in part (b) of the figure. Notice the relationship between the total revenue, total cost and profit curves. Economic profit is measured by the vertical distance between the total revenue and total cost curves. When the total revenue curve in part (a) is above the total cost curve, between 4 and 12 jumpers, the firm is making an economic profit and the profit curve in part (b) is above the horizontal axis. At the break-even point, where the total cost and total revenue curves intersect, the profit curve intersects the horizontal axis.

The profit curve is at its highest when the distance between *TR* and *TC* is greatest. In this example, profit maximization occurs at an output of 9 jumpers a day. At this output, Neat Knits' economic profit is £42 a day.

Marginal Analysis

Another way of finding the profit-maximizing output is to use *marginal analysis*. To use marginal analysis, a firm compares its marginal cost, *MC*, with its marginal revenue, *MR*. As we have seen, marginal revenue in perfect competition is constant and marginal cost increases as output increases. If marginal revenue exceeds marginal cost (if $MR > MC$), then the extra revenue from selling one more unit exceeds the extra cost incurred to produce it, so profit increases if output increases. If marginal revenue is less than marginal cost (if $MR < MC$), then the extra revenue from selling one more unit is less than the extra cost incurred to produce it, so profit increases if output *decreases*. If marginal revenue equals marginal cost (if $MR = MC$), profit is maximized. The rule $MR = MC$ is a prime example of marginal analysis. Let's check that this rule works to find the profit-maximizing output by returning to Sam's jumper factory.

Look at Figure 12.3. The table records Neat Knits' marginal revenue and marginal cost. Focus on the highlighted rows of the table. If output increases from 8 jumpers to 9 jumpers, marginal revenue is £25 and marginal cost is £23. Because marginal revenue exceeds marginal cost, profit increases. The last column of the table shows that profit increases from £40 to £42, an increase of £2. This profit from the ninth jumper is shown as the blue area in the figure.

If output increases from 9 jumpers to 10 jumpers, marginal revenue is still £25, but marginal cost is £27. Because marginal revenue is less than marginal cost, profit decreases. The last column of the table shows that profit decreases from £42 to £40. This loss from the tenth jumper is shown as the red area in the figure.

Neat Knits maximizes profit by producing 9 jumpers a day, the quantity at which marginal revenue equals marginal cost.

Economic Profit in the Short Run

In the short run, when a firm has set its marginal cost equal to its marginal revenue and maximized profit, it might make an economic profit, break even (making normal profit), or incur an economic loss. Maximizing profit is not the same as making a profit. To determine which of these three possible outcomes occurs, we need to compare the firm's total revenue and total cost. Alternatively, we can compare price with average total cost. If price exceeds average total cost, a firm makes an economic profit. If price equals average total cost, a firm breaks even – makes a normal profit. If price is less than average total cost, a firm incurs an

Figure 12.3 Marginal Revenue, Marginal Cost and Profit-maximizing Output

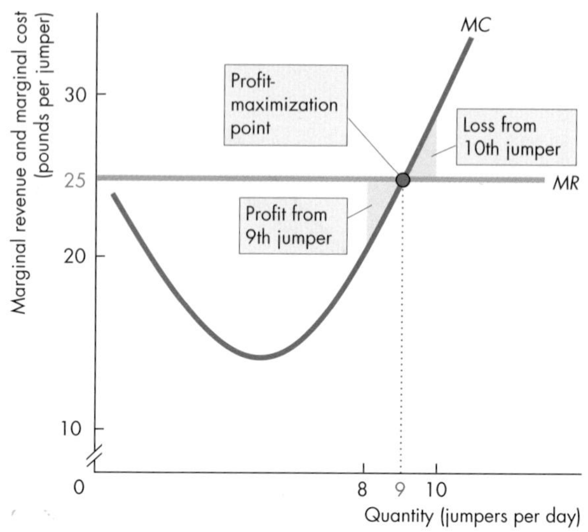

Quantity (Q) (jumpers per day)	Total revenue (TR) (pounds)	Marginal revenue (MR) (pounds per jumper)	Total cost (TC) (pounds)	Marginal cost (MC) (pounds per jumper)	Economic profit ($TR - TC$) (pounds)
7	175		141		34
		25		19	
8	200		160		40
		25		23	
9	225		183		42
		25		27	
10	250		210		40
		25		35	
11	275		245		30

Another way of finding the profit-maximizing output is to determine the output at which marginal revenue equals marginal cost. The table shows that if output increases from 8 to 9 jumpers, marginal cost is £23, which is less than the marginal revenue of £25. If output increases from 9 to 10 jumpers, marginal cost is £27, which exceeds the marginal revenue of £25. The figure shows that marginal cost and marginal revenue are equal when Neat Knits produces 9 jumpers a day. If marginal revenue exceeds marginal cost, an increase in output increases profit. If marginal revenue is less than marginal cost, an increase in output decreases profit. If marginal revenue equals marginal cost, economic profit is maximized.

Figure 12.4 Three Possible Profit Outcomes in the Short-run

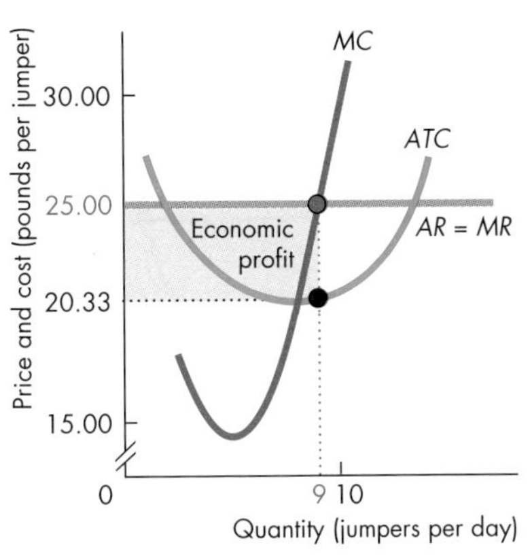

(a) Economic profit

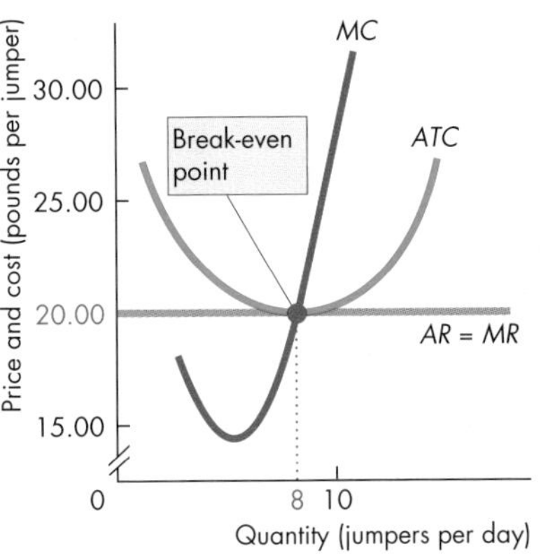

(b) Normal profit

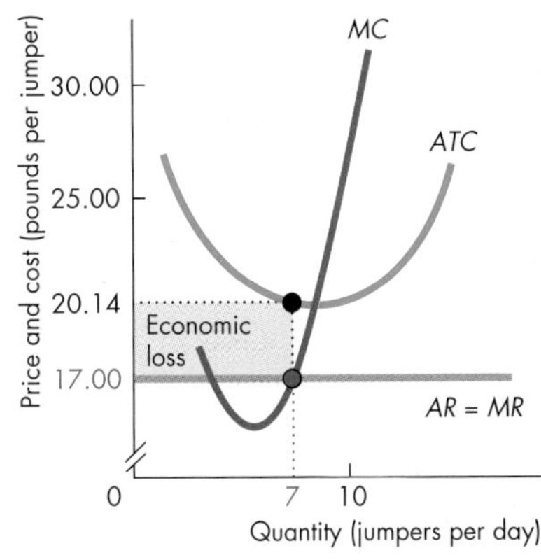

(c) Economic loss

In the short run, firms might make an economic profit, break even (making a normal profit), or incur a loss. If the market price is higher than the average total cost of producing the profit-maximizing output, the firm makes an economic profit (part a). If price equals minimum average total cost, the firm breaks even and makes a normal profit (part b). If the price is below minimum average total cost, the firm incurs an economic loss (part c). The firm's economic profit is shown as the blue rectangle and the firm's economic loss is the red rectangle.

economic loss. But the economic loss incurred is its minimum possible loss. Profit maximization implies loss minimization. Let's look more closely at these three possible outcomes for a firm.

Three Possible Profit Outcomes Figure 12.4 shows the three possible profit outcomes in the short run. In part (a), price exceeds average total cost and Neat Knits makes an economic profit. Price and marginal revenue are £25 a jumper and the profit-maximizing output is 9 jumpers a day. Neat Knits' total revenue is £225 a day (9 × £25). Average total cost is £20.33 a jumper and total cost is £183 a day (9 × £20.33). Neat Knits' economic profit is £42 a day. Economic profit equals total revenue minus total cost, which is £225 – £183 or £42 a day. Economic profit also equals economic profit per jumper, which is £4.67 (£25.00 – £20.33), multiplied by the number of jumpers (£4.67 × 9 = £42). The blue rectangle in the figure shows this economic profit. The height of the rectangle is profit per jumper, £4.67, and the length is the quantity of jumpers produced, 9 a day, so the area of the rectangle measures Neat Knits' economic profit of £42 a day.

In part (b), price equals average total cost and Neat Knits breaks even – makes normal profit and zero economic profit. Price and marginal revenue are £20 a jumper and the profit-maximizing output is 8 jumpers a day. At this output, average total cost is at its minimum.

In part (c), price is less than average total cost and Neat Knits incurs an economic loss. Price and marginal revenue are £17 a jumper and the profit-maximizing (loss-minimizing) output is 7 jumpers a day. Neat Knits' total revenue is £119 a day (7 × £17). Average total cost is £20.14 a jumper and total cost is £141 a day (7 × £20.14). Neat Knits' economic loss is £22 a day. Economic loss equals total revenue minus total cost, which is £119 – £141 = –£22 a day. The economic loss, £22, also equals economic loss per jumper, £3.14 (£20.14 – £17.00), multiplied by the number of jumpers (£3.14 × 7 = £22). The red rectangle in the figure shows this economic loss. The height of the rectangle is economic loss per jumper, £3.14, and the length is the quantity of jumpers produced, 7 a day, so the area of the rectangle measures Neat Knits' economic loss of £22 a day.

The Firm's Short-run Supply Curve

A perfectly competitive firm's supply curve shows how the firm's profit-maximizing output varies as the market price varies, other things remaining the same. Figure 12.5 shows you how to derive Neat Knits' entire supply curve. Part (a) shows Neat Knits' marginal cost and average variable cost curves and part (b) shows its supply curve. Let's look at the link between the marginal cost and average variable cost curves and the supply curve.

Temporary Plant Shutdown A firm can avoid only variable costs. Fixed costs are incurred even at zero output, and a firm that shuts down and produces no output incurs a maximum loss equal to its total fixed cost. If the price falls below average variable cost, the firm's profit-maximizing action is to shut down temporarily, lay off its workers and produce nothing. A firm's **shutdown point** is the level of output and price where the firm is just covering its total *variable* cost incurring a loss equal to its total fixed cost. If a firm did produce and sell its output for less than its average variable cost, its loss would exceed its total fixed cost. Such a firm would not be maximizing profit (minimizing loss).

The shutdown point is shown in Figure 12.5(a). When the marginal revenue curve is MR_0, price is £17 and the firm produces 7 jumpers a day at the shutdown point *s*. If the price falls just a penny below £17, profit is maximized (loss is minimized) by producing nothing.

Production Decisions If the price is above minimum average variable cost, Neat Knits maximizes profit by producing the output at which marginal cost equals price. We can determine the quantity produced at each price from the marginal cost curve. At a price of £25, the marginal revenue curve is MR_1 and Neat Knits maximizes profit by producing 9 jumpers. At a price of £31, the marginal revenue curve is MR_2 and Neat Knits produces 10 jumpers.

The Supply Curve The supply curve is shown in Figure 12.5(b). In the range of prices that exceed minimum average variable cost, the supply curve is the same as the marginal cost curve above the shutdown point (*s*). At prices below minimum average variable cost, Neat Knits shuts down and produces nothing. Its supply curve runs along the vertical axis. At a price of £17, Neat Knits is indifferent between shutting down and producing 7 jumpers a day. Either way, it incurs a loss of £25 a day.

Figure 12.5 Neat Knits' Supply Curve

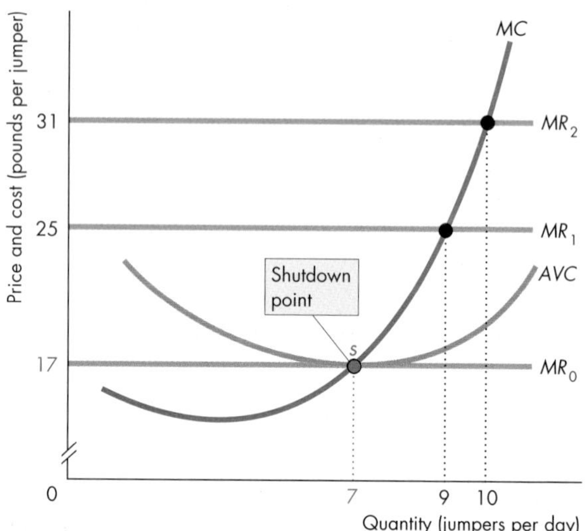

(a) Marginal cost and average variable cost

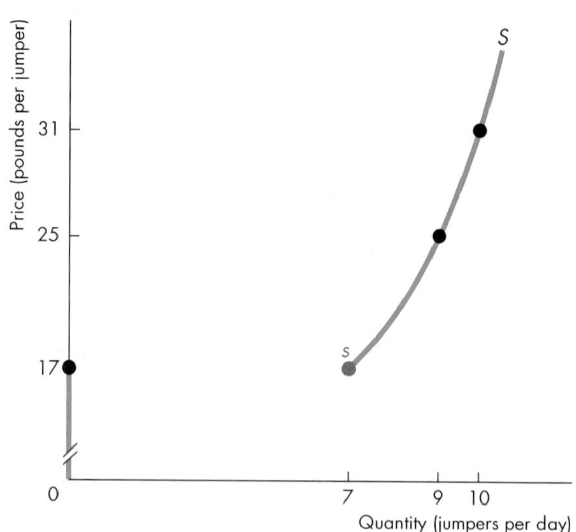

(b) Neat Knits' supply curve

Part (a) shows Neat Knits' profit-maximizing output at each market price. At £25 a jumper, Neat Knits produces 9 jumpers. At £17 a jumper, Neat Knits produces 7 jumpers. At any price below £17 a jumper, Neat Knits produces nothing as Neat Knits' shutdown point is *s*. Part (b) shows Neat Knits' supply curve – the number of jumpers Neat Knits will produce at each price. Neat Knits' supply curve is made up of its marginal cost curve (part a) at all points above the average variable cost curve, and the vertical axis at all prices below minimum average variable cost.

Review

- In perfect competition, a firm is a price taker and its marginal revenue equals the market price.
- If price exceeds average variable cost, a firm maximizes profit by producing the output at which marginal cost equals marginal revenue (equals price). The lowest price at which a firm produces is equal to its minimum average variable cost.
- If price falls below minimum average variable cost, the firm stops producing and incurs an economic loss equal to its total fixed cost.
- In the short run, a firm can make an economic profit, break even (make zero economic profit and earn normal profit), or incur an economic loss. The maximum economic loss that a firm incurs is equal to its total fixed cost.

So far, we have seen that the firm's profit-maximizing actions depend on the market price. But how is the market price determined? Let's find out.

Figure 12.6 Industry Supply Curve

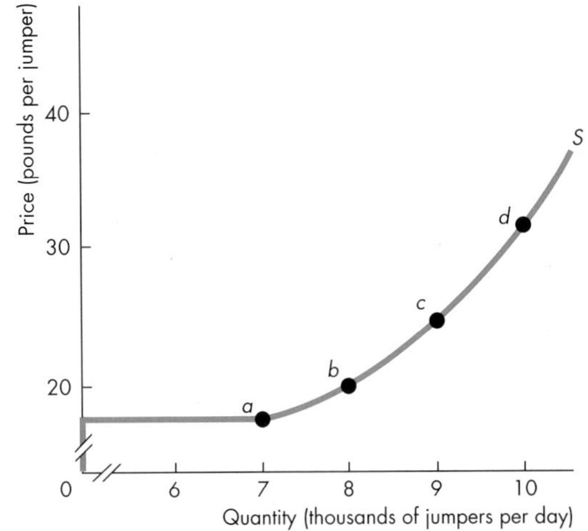

	Price (pounds per jumper)	Quantity supplied by Neat Knits (jumpers per day)	Quantity supplied by industry (jumpers per day)
a	17	0 or 7	0 to 7,000
b	20	8	8,000
c	25	9	9,000
d	31	10	10,000

The industry supply schedule is the sum of the supply schedules of all individual firms. An industry that consists of 1,000 identical firms will supply a quantity 1,000 times as large as that of the individual firm (see table). The industry supply curve is *S*. Points *a*, *b*, *c* and *d* correspond to the rows of the table. At the shutdown price of £17, each firm produces either 0 or 7 jumpers per day. The industry supply curve is perfectly elastic at the shutdown price.

Output, Price and Profit in the Short Run

To determine the market price and the quantity bought and sold in a perfectly competitive market, we need to study how market demand and market supply interact. We begin this process by studying a perfectly competitive market in the short run.

Short-run Industry Supply Curve

The **short-run industry supply curve** shows how the quantity supplied by the industry varies as the market price varies when the plant size of each firm and the number of firms in the industry remain the same. The quantity supplied by the industry at a given price is the sum of the quantities supplied by all firms in the industry at that price. To construct the industry supply curve, we sum horizontally the supply curves of the individual firms. Let's see how we do that.

Suppose that the competitive jumper industry consists of 1,000 firms exactly like Neat Knits. The relationship between a firm's supply curve and the industry supply curve, for this case, is illustrated in Figure 12.6. Each of the 1,000 firms in the industry has a supply schedule like Neat Knits', set out in the table. At a price below £17, every firm in the industry will shut down production so that the industry will supply nothing. At £17, each firm is indifferent between shutting down and producing 7 jumpers. Because each firm is indifferent, some firms will produce and others will shut down. Industry supply can be anything between 0 (all firms shut down) and 7,000 (all firms producing 7 jumpers a day

Figure 12.7 Three Short-run Equilibrium Positions for a Competitive Industry

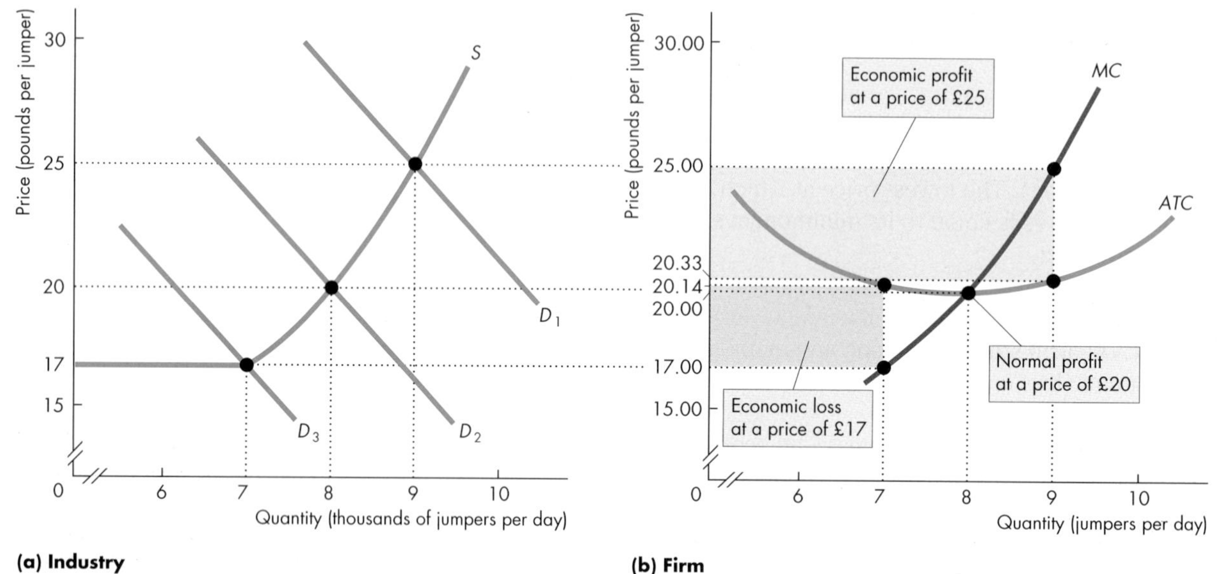

(a) Industry

(b) Firm

In part (a), the competitive jumper industry's supply curve is *S*. If demand is D_1, the price is £25 and the industry produces 9,000 jumpers. If demand is D_2, the price is £20 and industry output is 8,000 jumpers. If demand is D_3, the price is £17 and industry output is 7,000 jumpers.

In part (b), when the price is £25, an individual firm is making an economic profit; when the price is £20, it is breaking even (making normal profit), and when the price is £17 it is incurring an economic loss.

each). Thus at £17, the industry supply curve is horizontal – it is perfectly elastic. As the price rises above £17, each firm increases its quantity supplied and the quantity supplied by the industry also increases, but by 1,000 times that of each individual firm.

The supply schedules set out in the table form the basis of the industry supply curve in Figure 12.6. At each price, the quantity supplied by the industry is 1,000 times the quantity supplied by a single firm. At a price of £17 a jumper, a firm supplies either nothing or 7 jumpers a day, so the industry supplies any quantity between zero and 7,000 jumpers. The industry supply curve is perfectly elastic over that range.

Short-run Equilibrium

Market price and industry output are determined by industry demand and supply. Figure 12.7(a) shows three different possible short-run equilibrium positions in a perfectly competitive market. The industry supply curve is *S* and the industry demand curve is D_1, the equilibrium price is £25 and industry output is 9,000 jumpers a day. If the demand curve is D_2, the price is £20 and industry output is 8,000 jumpers a day. If the demand curve is D_3, the price is £17 and industry output is 7,000 jumpers a day.

Figure 12.7(b) shows the situation facing each of the 1,000 individual firms. With demand curve D_1, the price is £25 a jumper, so each firm produces 9 jumpers a day and makes an economic profit (the blue rectangle); if the demand curve is D_2, the price is £20 a jumper, so each firm produces 8 jumpers a day and makes zero economic profit (normal profit); and if the demand curve is D_3, the price is £17 a jumper, so each firm produces 7 jumpers a day and incurs a loss (the red rectangle).

If the demand curve shifts farther leftward than D_3, the price remains constant at £17 because the industry supply curve is horizontal at that price. Some firms continue to produce 7 jumpers a day and others shut down. Firms are indifferent between these two activities and, whichever they choose, they incur a loss equal to total fixed cost. The number of firms continuing to produce is just enough to satisfy the market demand at a price of £17.

In the short-run, the number of firms and plant size of each firm is fixed. In the long run, each of these features of an industry can change. Also, as you are about to discover, there are forces at work that will disturb some of the short-run situations we've just examined. Let's now look at the forces that operate in the long run.

Output, Price and Profit in the Long Run

In short-run equilibrium, a firm might make an economic profit, incur an economic loss, or break even (make normal profit). Although each of these three situations is a short-run equilibrium, only one of them is a long-run equilibrium. To see why, we need to examine the forces at work in a competitive industry in the long run.

In the long run, an industry adjusts in two ways: the number of firms in the industry changes and firms change the scale of their plants. The number of firms in an industry changes as a result of entry and exit. *Entry* is the act of setting up a new firm in an industry. *Exit* is the act of a firm leaving an industry. Let's first see how economic profit and loss trigger entry and exit.

Economic Profit and Economic Loss as Signals

An industry in which firms are making an economic profit attracts new entrants; one in which firms are incurring an economic loss induces exits; and an industry in which firms are making normal profit (zero economic profit) induces neither entry nor exit. Thus economic profit and economic loss are the signals to which firms respond in making entry and exit decisions.

Temporary economic profits and temporary losses that are random, like the winnings and losses at a casino, do not trigger entry or exit. But the prospect of persistent economic profit or loss does.

Entry and exit influence market price, the quantity produced and economic profit. The immediate effect of entry and exit is to shift the industry supply curve. If more firms enter an industry, the industry supply curve shifts rightward: supply increases. If firms exit an industry, the industry supply curve shifts leftward: supply falls. Let's see what happens when new firms enter an industry.

Figure 12.8 Entry and Exit

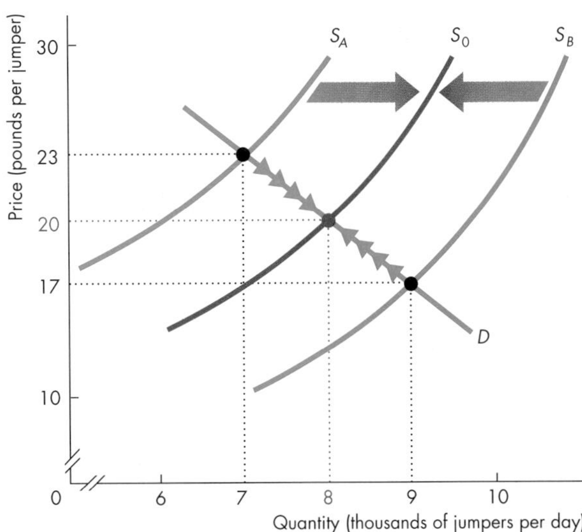

When new firms enter the jumper industry, the industry supply curve shifts rightward, from S_A to S_0. The equilibrium price falls from £23 to £20, and the quantity produced increases from 7,000 to 8,000 jumpers. When firms exit the jumper industry, the industry supply curve shifts leftward, from S_B to S_0. The equilibrium price rises from £17 to £20, and the quantity produced decreases from 9,000 to 8,000 jumpers.

The Effects of Entry

Figure 12.8 shows the effects of entry. Suppose that the demand curve for jumpers is D and the industry supply curve is S_A, so jumpers sell for £23 and 7,000 jumpers are being produced. Firms in the industry are making an economic profit. Some new firms enter the industry. As they do so, the industry supply curve shifts rightward to S_0. With the greater supply and unchanged demand, the market price falls from £23 to £20 a jumper and the quantity produced increases from 7,000 to 8,000 jumpers a day.

As the price falls, Neat Knits and every other firm in the industry moves down along its supply curve and decreases output. That is, for each existing firm in the industry, the profit-maximizing output decreases. Because the price falls and each firm sells less, economic profit decreases. When the price falls to £20, economic profit disappears and each firm makes a normal profit.

You have just discovered a key proposition:

As new firms enter an industry, the price falls and the economic profit of each existing firm decreases.

A good example of this process has occurred in the last few years in the personal computer industry. When IBM introduced its first personal computer in the early 1980s, there was little competition and the price of PCs gave IBM a big profit. But new firms such as Amstrad, Dell, Elonex and a host of others soon entered the industry with machines technologically identical to the IBM PC. In fact, they were so similar that they came to be called 'clones'. The massive wave of entry into the personal computer industry shifted the supply curve rightward and lowered the price and the economic profit for all firms. You can read about the effects of entry on car retail franchises in *Reading Between the Lines*, pp. 292–293.

Let's now see what happens when firms leave an industry.

The Effects of Exit

Figure 12.8 shows the effects of exit. Suppose that the demand curve is D and the supply curve is S_B, so the market price is £17 and 9,000 jumpers are being produced. Firms in the industry are incurring an economic loss. As firms leave the industry, the supply curve shifts leftward to S_0. With the decrease in supply, industry output decreases from 9,000 to 8,000 jumpers and the price rises from £17 to £20.

As the price rises, Neat Knits and every other firm in the industry moves up along its supply curve and increases output. That is, for each existing firm in the industry, the profit-maximizing output increases. Because the price rises and each firm sells more, economic loss decreases. When the price rises to £20, economic loss disappears and each firm makes a normal profit.

You have just discovered a second key proposition:

As firms leave an industry, the price rises and so do the economic profits of the remaining firms.

An example of a firm leaving an industry is Escom UK – the United Kingdom's largest high street specialist computer chain in 1996. Escom's German parent company, Escom AG, also went bankrupt after making losses of £76 million in 1995. Escom entered the UK market in 1993, and expanded in 1995 when it took over 231 Rumbelows shops. Its agressive price-cutting strategy did not generate sufficient revenue as other retailers also reduced their prices. Profit margins in the industry were squeezed. Escom eventually exited the industry because it made persistent economic losses. When it exited the industry, it had already closed down many of its outlets. This decrease allowed the remaining retailers to break even or regain some economic profit.

Long-run Equilibrium

Long-run equilibrium occurs in a competitive industry when firms are earning normal profit and economic profit is zero. If the firms in a competitive industry make an economic profit, new firms enter the industry and the supply curve shifts rightward. As a result, the market price falls and so does economic profit. Firms continue to enter and economic profit continues to decrease as long as the industry is earning positive economic profits. Only when the economic profit has been eliminated and normal profit is being made do firms stop entering.

If the firms in a competitive industry incur an economic loss, some of the firms exit the industry and the supply curve shifts leftward. As a result, the market price rises and the industry's economic loss shrinks. Firms continue to leave and economic loss shrinks as long as the industry is incurring an economic loss. Only when the economic loss has been eliminated and normal profit is being made do firms stop exiting.

So, in long-run equilibrium in a competitive industry, firms neither enter nor exit the industry.

Let's now examine the second way in which the competitive industry adjusts in the long run – by existing firms changing their plant size.

Changes in Plant Size

A firm changes its plant size if, by doing so, its profit increases. Figure 12.9 shows a situation in which Neat Knits can increase its profit by increasing its plant size. With its current plant, Neat Knits'

Figure 12.9 Plant Size and Long-run Equilibrium

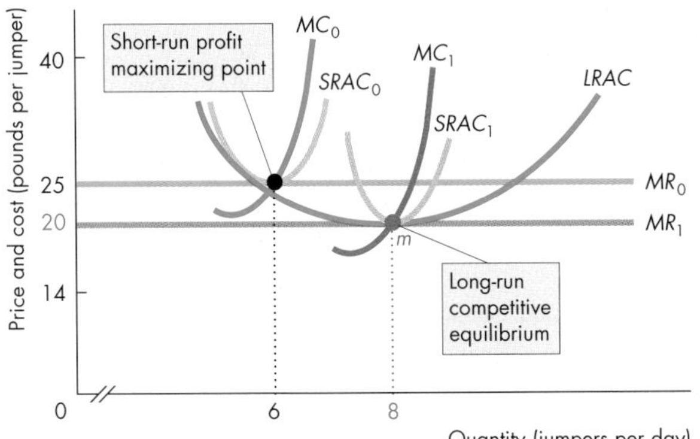

Initially, Neat Knits' plant has marginal cost curve MC_0 and short-run average total cost curve $SRAC_0$. The market price is £25 a jumper and Neat Knits' marginal revenue is MR_0. The short-run profit-maximizing quantity is 6 jumpers a day. Neat Knits can increase its profit by increasing its plant size. If all firms in the jumper industry increase their plant sizes, the short-run industry supply increases and the market price falls.

In long-run equilibrium, a firm operates with the plant that minimizes its average cost. Here, Neat Knits operates the plant with short-run marginal cost MC_1 and short-run average total cost $SRAC_1$. Neat Knits is also on its long-run average cost curve *LRAC* and produces at point *m*. Output is 8 jumpers a day and average total cost equals the price of a jumper at £20.

marginal cost curve is MC_0 and its short-run average total cost curve is $SRAC_0$. The market price is £25 a jumper, so Neat Knits' marginal revenue curve is MR_0 and Neat Knits maximizes profit by producing 6 jumpers a day.

Neat Knits' long-run average cost curve is *LRAC*. By increasing its plant size – installing more knitting machines – Neat Knits can move along its long-run average cost curve. As Neat Knits increases its plant size, its short-run marginal cost curve shifts rightward.

Recall that a firm's short-run supply curve is linked to its marginal cost curve. As Neat Knits' marginal cost curve shifts rightward, so does its supply curve. If Neat Knits and the other firms in the industry increase their plants, the short-run industry supply curve shifts rightward and the market price falls. The fall in the market price limits the extent to which Neat Knits can profit from increasing its plant size.

Figure 12.9 also shows Neat Knits in a long-run competitive equilibrium. This situation arises when the market price has fallen to £20 a jumper. Marginal revenue is MR_1, and Neat Knits maximizes profit by producing 8 jumpers a day. In this situation, Neat Knits cannot increase its profit by changing its plant size. It is producing at minimum long-run average cost (point m on $LRAC$).

Because Neat Knits is producing at minimum long-run average cost, it has no incentive to change its plant size. Either a bigger plant or a smaller plant has a higher long-run average cost.

If all firms in the jumper industry are in the situation described in Figure 12.9, the industry is in long-run equilibrium. No firm has an incentive to change its plant size. Also, because each firm is making zero economic profit (normal profit), no firm has an incentive to enter the industry or to leave it.

Review

Long-run competitive equilibrium is described by three conditions:

1. Firms maximize short-run profit by producing the quantity that makes marginal cost equal to marginal revenue and price.
2. Economic profits are zero, so no firm has an incentive to enter or to leave the industry.
3. Long-run average cost is at a minimum, so no firm has an incentive to change its plant size.

We've seen how economic loss triggers exit, which eventually eliminates the loss, and we've seen how economic profit triggers entry, which eventually eliminates the profit. In the long run, normal profit is earned. But a competitive industry is rarely in a long-run equilibrium. It is restlessly evolving towards such an equilibrium and the conditions the industry faces are constantly changing. The two most persistent sources of change are in tastes and technology. Let's see how a competitive industry reacts to such changes.

Figure 12.10 A Decrease in Demand

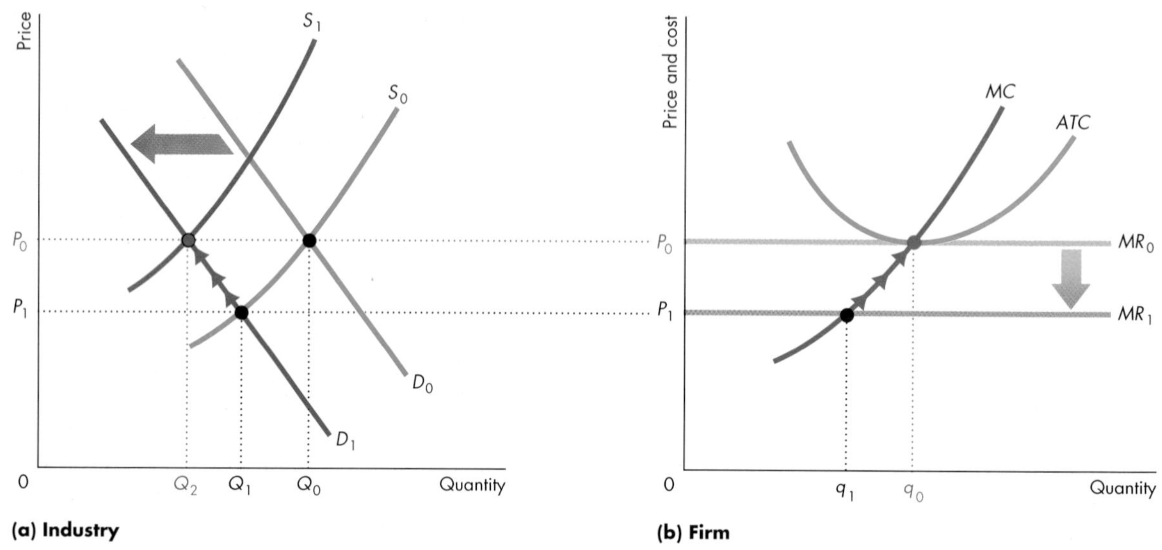

An industry starts out in long-run competitive equilibrium. Part (a) shows the industry demand curve D_0 and the industry supply curve S_0, the equilibrium quantity Q_0 and the market price P_0. Each firm sells at price P_0, so its marginal revenue curve is MR_0 in part (b). Each firm produces q_0 and makes a normal profit. Demand decreases from D_0 to D_1 (part a). The equilibrium price falls to P_1, each firm decreases its output to q_1 (part b) and industry output decreases to Q_1 (part a). In this new situation, firms are incurring losses and some firms leave the industry. As they do so, the industry supply curve gradually shifts leftward, from S_0 to S_1. This shift gradually raises the industry price from P_1 back to P_0. While the price is below P_0, firms are incurring losses and some leave the industry. Once the price has returned to P_0, each firm makes a normal profit. Firms have no further incentive to leave the industry. Each firm produces q_0 and industry output is Q_2.

Changing Tastes and Advancing Technology

Increased awareness of the health hazard of smoking has caused a decrease in the demand for tobacco and cigarettes. The development of cheap cars and air travel has caused a huge decrease in the demand for long-distance trains and buses. Solid-state electronics have caused a large decrease in the demand for TV and radio repair. The development of good quality budget clothing has decreased the demand for sewing machines. What happens in a competitive industry when there is a permanent decrease in the demand for its products?

The development of the microwave oven has produced an enormous increase in demand for paper, glass and plastic cooking utensils, and for plastic wrap. The demand for almost all products is steadily increasing as a result of increasing population and increasing incomes. What happens in a competitive industry when the demand for its product increases?

Advances in technology are constantly lowering the costs of production. New biotechnologies have dramatically lowered the costs of many food and pharmaceutical products. New electronic technologies have lowered the cost of producing just about every good and service. What happens in a competitive industry when technological change lowers its production costs?

Let's use the theory of perfect competition to answer these questions.

A Permanent Change in Demand

Figure 12.10(a) shows an industry that initially is in long-run competitive equilibrium. The demand curve is D_0, the supply curve is S_0, the market price is P_0 and industry output is Q_0. Figure 12.10(b) shows a single firm in this initial long-run equilibrium. The firm produces q_0 and makes a normal profit and zero economic profit.

Now suppose that demand decreases and the demand curve shifts leftward to D_1, as shown in part (a). The price falls to P_1 and the quantity supplied by the industry decreases from Q_0 to Q_1 as the industry slides down its short-run supply curve S_0. Part (b) shows the situation facing a firm. Price is now below minimum average total cost so the firm incurs an economic loss. But to keep its loss to a minimum, the firm adjusts its output to keep price equal to marginal cost. At a price of P_1 each firm produces an output of q_1.

The industry is now in short-run equilibrium but not long-run equilibrium. It is in short-run equilibrium because each firm is maximizing profit. But it is not in long-run equilibrium because each firm is incurring an economic loss – its average total cost exceeds the price.

In this situation, some firms leave the industry. As they do so, short-run industry supply decreases and the supply curve shifts leftward. As supply decreases, the price rises. At each higher price a firm's profit-maximizing output is greater, so those remaining in the industry increase their output as the price rises. Each slides up its marginal cost or supply curve (part b). That is, as firms exit the industry, industry output decreases but the output of the firms that remain in the industry increases. Eventually, enough firms leave the industry for the supply curve to have shifted to S_1 (part a). At this time, the price has returned to its original level, P_0. At this price, the firms remaining in the industry produce q_0, the same quantity as they produced before the decrease in demand. Because firms are now making normal profits and zero economic profit, no firm wants to enter or exit the industry. The industry supply curve remains at S_1 and industry output is Q_2. The industry is again in long-run equilibrium.

The difference between the initial long-run equilibrium and the final long-run equilibrium is the number of firms in the industry. A permanent decrease in demand has decreased the number of firms. Each remaining firm produces the same output in the new long-run equilibrium as it did initially and earns a normal profit. In the process of moving from the initial equilibrium to the new one, firms that remain in the industry incur losses.

The market for mainframe computers is one that has experienced a decrease in demand in recent years. As personal computers have become faster and cheaper, more and more data processing has been done on people's desktops rather than in big computer laboratories. The effects of this decrease in demand have been similar to those we have just studied.

We've just worked out how a competitive industry responds to a permanent *decrease* in demand. A permanent increase in demand triggers a similar response, except in the opposite direction. The increase in demand brings a higher price, profit and entry. Entry increases supply and eventually lowers the price to its original level.

We've now studied the effects of a permanent change in taste that brings a permanent change in demand for a good. We began and ended in a long-run equilibrium and examined the *process* that gets a market from one equilibrium to another. It is this process that describes the real world, not the equilibrium points.

One feature of the predictions that we have just generated seems odd: in the long run, regardless of whether demand increases or decreases, the price returns to its original level. Is this outcome inevitable? In fact, it is not. It is possible for the long-run equilibrium price to remain the same, rise, or fall.

External Economies and Diseconomies

Whether the long-run equilibrium price remains the same, rises, or falls depends on external economies and external diseconomies. **External economies** are factors beyond the control of an individual firm that lower its costs as *industry* output increases. **External diseconomies** are factors outside the control of a firm that raise its costs as industry output increases. With no external economies or external diseconomies, a firm's costs remain constant as industry output changes.

Figure 12.11 illustrates these three cases and introduces a new supply concept, the long-run industry supply curve. **A long-run industry supply curve** shows how the quantity supplied by an industry varies as the market price varies after all the possible adjustments have been made, including changes in plant size and changes in the number of firms in the industry.

Part (a) shows the case we have just studied – no external economies or diseconomies. The long-run industry supply curve (LS_A) is perfectly elastic. In

Figure 12.11 Long-run Changes in Price and Quantity

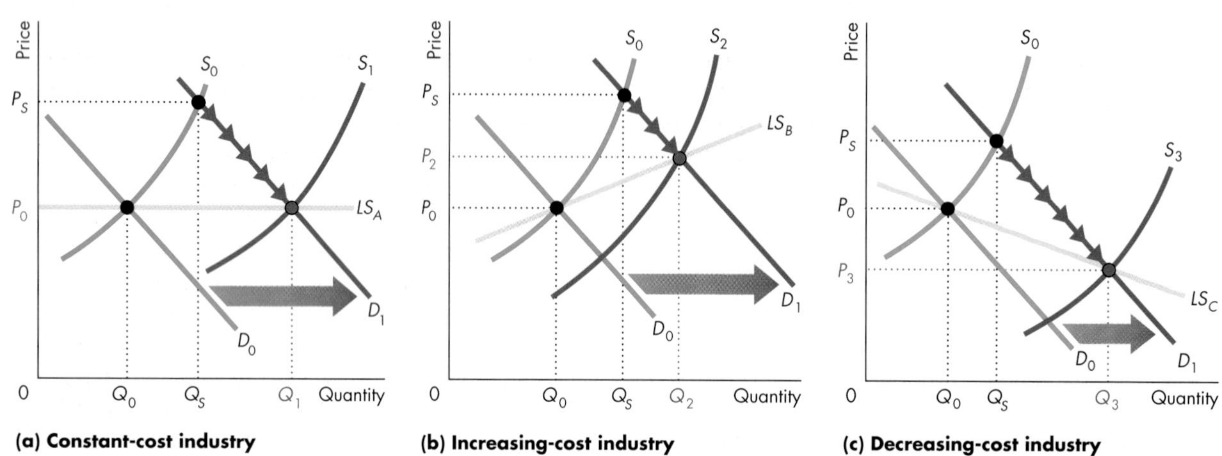

Three possible long-run changes in price and quantity are illustrated. When demand increases from D_0 to D_1, entry occurs and the industry supply curve shifts from S_0 to S_1. In part (a), the long-run supply curve LS_A is horizontal. The quantity increases from Q_0 to Q_1 and the price remains constant at P_0. In part (b), the long-run supply curve is LS_B; the price increases to P_2 and the quantity increases to Q_2. This case occurs in industries with external diseconomies. In part (c), the long-run supply curve is LS_C; the price decreases to P_3 and the quantity increases to Q_3. This case occurs in an industry with external economies.

this case, a permanent increase in demand from D_0 to D_1 has no effect on the price in the long run. The increase in demand brings a temporary increase in price to P_S, and a short-run quantity increase from Q_0 to Q_S. Entry increases short-run supply from S_0 to S_1, which lowers the price to its original level, P_0, and increases the quantity to Q_1.

Part (b) shows the case of external diseconomies. In this case, the long-run supply industry curve (LS_B) slopes upward. A permanent increase in demand from D_0 to D_1 increases the price in both the short run and the long run. As in the previous case, the increase in demand brings a temporary increase in price to P_S, and a short-run quantity increase from Q_0 to Q_S. Entry increases short-run supply from S_0 to S_1, which lowers the price to P_2 and increases the quantity to Q_2.

One source of external diseconomies is congestion. The airline industry provides a good illustration. With bigger airline industry output, there is more congestion of both airports and airspace, which results in longer delays and extra waiting time for passengers and aircraft. These external diseconomies mean that as the output of air travel services increases (in the absence of technological advances), average cost increases. As a result, the long-run supply curve is upward-sloping. So a permanent increase in demand brings an increase in quantity and a rise in the price. Technological advances decrease costs and *shift* the long-run supply curve downward. So even an industry that experiences external diseconomies might have falling prices over the long run.

Part (c) shows the case of external economies. In this case, the long-run industry supply curve (LS_C) slopes downward. A permanent increase in demand from D_0 to D_1, increases the price in the short run and lowers it in the long run. Again, the increase in demand brings a temporary increase in price to P_S, and a short-run quantity increase from Q_0 to Q_S. Entry increases short-run supply from S_0 to S_3, which lowers the price to P_3 and increases the quantity to Q_3.

One of the best examples of external economies is the growth of specialist support services for an industry as it expands. As farm output increased in the nineteenth and early twentieth centuries, the services available to farmers expanded and their costs fell. For example, markets developed in farm machinery and fertilizers that lowered farm costs.

Farms enjoyed the benefits of external economies. As a consequence, as the demand for farm products increased, the quantity produced increased but the price fell.

Over the long term, the prices of many goods and services have fallen, not because of external economies but because of technological change. Let's now study this influence on a competitive market.

Technological Change

Industries are constantly discovering lower-cost techniques of production. Most cost-saving production techniques cannot be implemented, however, without investing in new plant and equipment. As a consequence, it takes time for a technological advance to spread through an industry. Some firms whose plants are on the verge of being replaced will be quick to adopt the new technology, while other firms whose plants have recently been replaced will continue to operate with an old technology until they can no longer cover their average variable cost. Once average variable cost cannot be covered, a firm will scrap even a relatively new plant (embodying an old technology) in favour of a plant with a new technology.

New technology allows firms to produce at a lower cost and to make a larger profit than the existing technology. As a result, as firms adopt a new technology, their cost curves shift downward. With lower costs, firms are willing to supply a given quantity at a lower price or, equivalently, they are willing to supply a larger quantity at a given price. In other words, supply increases and the supply curve shifts rightward. With a given demand, the quantity produced increases and the price falls.

Two forces are at work in an industry undergoing technological change. Firms that adopt the new technology make an economic profit. So there is entry by new-technology firms. Firms that stick with the old technology incur economic losses. They either exit the industry or switch to the new technology.

As old-technology firms disappear and new-technology firms enter, the price falls and the quantity produced increases. Eventually, the industry arrives at a long-run equilibrium in which all the firms use the new technology, produce at minimum long-run average cost and make zero economic profit (a normal profit). Because in the long run competition eliminates economic profit, technological change brings only temporary gains to producers. But the lower prices and better products that technological advances bring are permanent gains for consumers.

The process that we've just described is one in which some firms experience economic profits and others experience economic losses. It is a period of dynamic change for an industry. Some firms do well and others do badly. Often the process has a geographical dimension – the expanding new-technology firms bring prosperity to the 'rust-belt' regions where traditional industries have gone into decline. Sometimes the new-technology firms are in a foreign country, while the old-technology firms are in the domestic economy. Scotland's 'silicon glen' is an example of a high-tech industry which has located in a traditionally agricultural area. The information revolution of the 1990s has produced many examples of changes like these. Technological advances are not confined to the information industry. Even milk production is undergoing a major technological change, which arises from the use of hormones in cattle.

Review

- A fall in demand in a competitive industry brings a fall in price, economic loss and exit. Exit decreases supply, which brings a rise in price. In the long run, enough firms exit for those remaining to make a normal profit.
- A rise in demand in a competitive industry brings a rise in price, economic profit, and entry. Entry increases supply, which brings a fall in price. In the long run, enough firms enter to compete away the economic profit and leave firms making a normal profit.
- A new technology lowers costs, increases supply, and lowers price. New-technology firms make an economic profit and enter. Old-technology firms incur an economic loss and exit. In the long run, all firms adopt the new technology and make normal profits.

You've now studied how a competitive market works and have used the model of perfect competition to interpret and explain a variety of aspects of real-world economic behaviour. The last topic that we'll study in this chapter is efficiency in our model of perfect competition.

Competition and Efficiency

Is perfect competition efficient? To answer this question, we need to describe the conditions that prevail when efficiency has been achieved.

Allocative Efficiency

Allocative efficiency occurs when no resources in the economy are wasted. It is a point where society's welfare is maximized. If someone can be made better off – gain more utility – without making someone else worse off, resources are being wasted, and efficiency has not been achieved. To achieve allocative efficiency, three conditions must be satisfied. They are:

1 Producer efficiency.
2 Consumer efficiency.
3 Exchange efficiency.

Producer Efficiency **Producer efficiency** occurs when firms cannot decrease the cost of producing a given output by changing the factors of production used. An individual firm achieves producer efficiency if it produces at a point on its marginal cost curve, or equivalently, on its supply curve. An industry achieves producer efficiency if it produces at a point on the industry supply curve. If all firms in all industries minimize cost, the economy is at a point on its *production possibility frontier* (see Chapter 3, pp. 43–44).

Consumer Efficiency **Consumer efficiency** occurs when consumers cannot make themselves better off – they cannot increase their utility by reallocating their budgets. Consumer efficiency is achieved at all points along a demand curve.

Exchange Efficiency **Exchange efficiency** occurs when the price at which trade takes place equals marginal social cost and also equals marginal social benefit. **Marginal social cost** is the full cost to society of producing one additional unit of output. **Marginal social benefit** is the full benefit to society from one additional unit of consumption.

Society's welfare is the sum of total social benefit minus total social cost to all individuals, whether they are producers or consumers.
Total social welfare is maximized with allocative efficiency.

Figure 12.12(a) illustrates allocative efficiency. The marginal social benefit curve is *MSB* and the marginal social cost curve is *MSC*. If output is 1 unit, *MSC* at £10 is less than *MSB* at £70, and producers could supply more for less than the value people place on additional output. This means resources are being wasted and total social welfare (*TSW*) is not maximized. The value of *TSW* at each unit of output is shown in part (b). The addition to *TSW* is total social benefit for each unit (blue plus red area) minus total social cost for each unit (red area), shown in part (a). Let's see why. If output is 2 units, *MSB* is £60 and *MSC* is £20, adding a further £40 (£60 – £20) to *TSW*. So producing the second unit increases *TSW* from £60 to £100 (£60 + £40).

At the allocatively efficient quantity and price, the marginal benefit to society of the last unit produced exactly equals the marginal cost to society of the last unit. If output is 4 units and price is £40 a unit as shown in part (a), allocative efficiency is achieved – no resources are wasted – and total social welfare shown in part (b) is at its highest level at £130. The market could not reallocate resources through trade, production and consumption in any way that would make at least one person better off without making anyone else worse off. Allocative efficiency is also known as **Pareto efficiency**. The three types of efficiency required for allocative efficiency can only occur if markets work perfectly. Let's see what happens when markets fail to work perfectly.

Market Failure

The kinds of problem which prevent markets working perfectly are called **market failure**. Market failure means that markets will not allocate resources efficiently. There are five main types of market failure.

1 Limited information.
2 Poor definition of property rights.
3 External costs and external benefits.
4 Monopoly power.
5 Public goods.

Figure 12.12 Allocative Efficiency

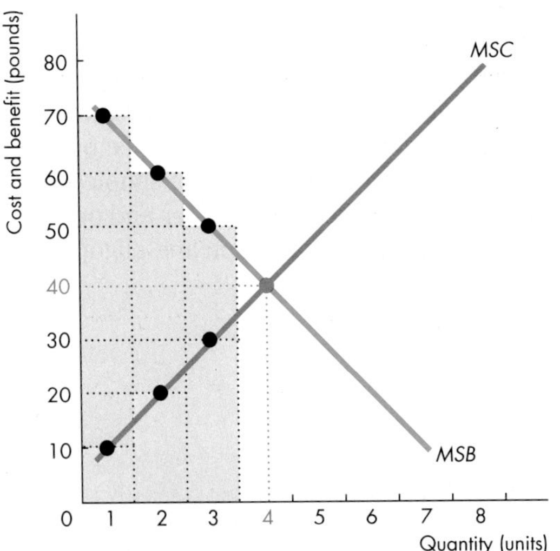

(a) Allocative efficiency

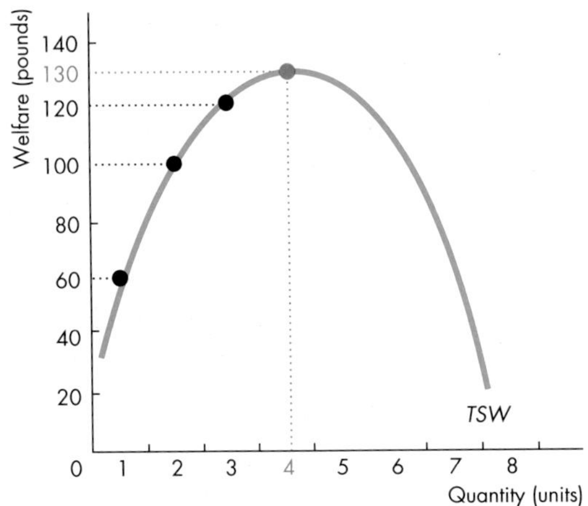

(b) Maximizing welfare

Allocative efficiency requires producer efficiency, consumer efficiency and exchange efficiency. Exchange efficiency occurs when 4 units are produced, where marginal social cost (*MSC*) equals marginal social benefit (*MSB*) as shown in part (a). If the second unit is produced, *MSB* is greater than *MSC* – total social welfare (*TSW*) increases but is not maximized as shown in part (b). *TSW* is total social benefit minus total social cost. Producing the second unit raises *TSW* to £100 – an increase of £40 (£60 – £20). Allocative efficiency only occurs at 4 units of output and a price of £40 a unit where *MSB* = *MSC*. At this point no resources are wasted and total social welfare is maximized at £130.

You have already discovered in Chapter 10 that **limited information** leads firms to devise agency relationships to resolve the *principal–agent* problem. Firms enter into contracts and offer compensation packages to their employees to strengthen incentives and raise productivity when information about the actions of the agent are limited. You also learned that another form of limited information, *transaction costs*, explains why organizing production within a firm can be more efficient than individuals trading in many markets.

Poor definition of property rights occurs if ownership rights of goods and resources are in doubt. If there are no clear rights of individual or company ownership, you could not rightfully buy or sell a resource or product in a market. That is why governments must provide a legal system to help market systems work properly.

External costs are costs not borne by the producer or consumer but by other members of society. Pollution and road traffic accidents are examples. **External benefits** are benefits accruing to people other than the buyer of a good. These include the pleasure we get from well-designed buildings and beautiful works of art in public galleries. Producing energy and well-designed buildings also produces other goods and services – pollution and pleasure – that people suffer or enjoy without payment. External costs and benefits are not priced because they are goods and services that do not have a market. We'll look at the inefficiency caused by external costs and benefits, and the impact of government policy in Chapter 20.

Monopoly power is created when there are barriers to entry into a market. The result of monopoly is inefficiency in the form of lost consumer surplus. You are going to learn about the problems of monopoly in more detail in the next chapter and then look at how government regulation of monopoly can improve market efficiency in Chapter 19.

Public goods are the type of goods and services that the market sector will not supply. These goods and services have special characteristics. In particular, the marginal cost of providing an extra unit is close to zero as in the case of national defence. This makes supply by private firms unprofitable. But if the goods and services are not supplied, the benefits from consumption are lost. The argument that governments should supply these goods is set out in Chapter 18.

Efficiency of Perfect Competition

Perfect competition delivers allocative efficiency if there is no market failure. In such a case, all the benefits and costs are taken into account. The marginal social benefit curve is the same as the industry demand curve and the marginal social cost curve is the same as the industry supply curve. Private benefits and costs are the same as social benefits and costs. If there is no market failure with perfect competition, price and quantity are determined at the point of intersection of the demand and supply curves. This is also the allocatively efficient price and quantity shown in Figure 12.12 which maximizes social welfare.

We have now completed our study of the model of perfect competition. It has given us an insight into the way that firms make choices when competition is strong and firms have little influence over price. However, perfect competition is not an appropriate model for every market and our next task is to study markets where there is a significant amount of market failure. We'll start by studying a model where firms have the power to influence prices by restricting output. We study the simplest case, monopoly, in the next chapter and other cases, monopolistic competition and oligopoly, in Chapter 14.

Summary

Key Points

Perfect Competition (pp. 270–277)

- A perfectly competitive firm is a price taker.
- The firm produces the output at which marginal revenue (price) equals marginal cost.
- If price is less than minimum average variable cost, the firm temporarily shuts down.
- A firm's supply curve is the upward-sloping part of its marginal cost curve above minimum average variable cost.
- An industry supply curve shows the sum of the quantities supplied by each firm at each price.

Output, Price and Profit in the Short Run (pp. 277–279)

- Market demand and market supply determine price.
- The firm takes market price as given and produces the output at which price, which is equal to marginal revenue, equals marginal cost.
- In short-run equilibrium, a firm can make an economic profit, incur an economic loss, or break even.

Output, Price and Profit in the Long Run (pp. 279–281)

- Economic profit induces entry. Economic loss induces exit.
- Entry and plant expansion increase supply and lower price and profit. Exit and plant contraction decrease supply and raise price and profit.
- In long-run equilibrium, economic profit is zero (firms earn normal profit). There is no entry, exit, plant expansion or contraction.
- In long-run equilibrium, firms produce at minimum long-run average cost.

Changing Tastes and Advancing Technology (pp. 282–286)

- A permanent decrease in demand leads to a smaller industry output and a smaller number of firms.
- A permanent increase in demand leads to a larger industry output and a larger number of firms.
- The long-run effect of a change in demand on price depends on whether there are external economies (price falls), external diseconomies, (price rises) or neither (price remains constant).

Competition and Efficiency (pp. 286–287)

- Resources are used efficiently when no one can be made better off without making someone else worse off.
- Three conditions for efficient use of resources – producer efficiency, consumer efficiency, and exchange efficiency – occur in perfect competition when there is no market failure.
- The main forms of market failure (obstacles to achieving allocative efficiency) are poor information and uncertainty, poor definition of property rights, external costs and benefits, monopoly and public goods.

Key Figures

Key Terms

Allocative efficiency, 286
Average revenue, 270
Consumer efficiency, 286
Economic profit, 270
Exchange efficiency, 286
External benefits, 287
External costs, 287
External diseconomies, 283
External economies, 283
Limited information, 287
Long-run industry supply curve, 283
Marginal revenue, 270
Marginal social benefit, 286
Marginal social cost, 286
Market failure, 286
Monopoly power, 287
Normal profit, 270
Pareto efficiency, 286
Perfect competition, 270
Poor definition of property rights, 287
Price taker, 270
Producer efficiency, 286
Public goods, 287
Short-run industry supply curve, 277
Shutdown point, 276
Total revenue, 270

Review Questions

1 What are the main features of a perfectly competitive industry?

2 Why can't a perfectly competitive firm influence the industry price?

3 List the three key decisions that a firm in a perfectly competitive industry has to make in order to maximize profit.

4 Why is marginal revenue equal to price in a perfectly competitive industry?

5 When will a perfectly competitive firm temporarily stop producing?

6 What is the connection between the supply curve and marginal cost curve of a perfectly competitive firm?

7 What is the relationship between a firm's supply curve and the short-run industry supply curve in a perfectly competitive industry?

8 When will firms enter an industry and when will they leave it?

9 What happens to the short-run industry supply curve when firms enter a competitive industry?

10 What is the effect of entry on the price and quantity produced?

11 What is the effect of entry on economic profit?

12 Trace the effects of a permanent increase in demand on price, quantity sold, number of firms and economic profit.

13 Trace the effects of a permanent decrease in demand on price, quantity sold, number of firms and economic profit.

14 Under what circumstances will a perfectly competitive industry have:

a A perfectly elastic long-run supply curve?
b An upward-sloping long-run supply curve?
c A downward-sloping long-run supply curve?

15 What is allocative efficiency and under what circumstances does it arise?

Problems

1 Pat's Pottery is a price taker. It has the following hourly costs:

Output (glazed pots per hour)	Total cost (pounds per hour)
0	10
1	21
2	30
3	41
4	54
5	79
6	96

a If glazed pots sell for £14, what is Pat's profit-maximizing output per hour? How much economic profit does she make?
b What is Pat's shutdown point?
c Derive Pat's supply curve.
d What range of prices will cause Pat to leave the craft pottery industry?
e What range of prices will cause other firms with costs identical to Pat's to enter the industry?
f What is the long-run equilibrium price of glazed pots?

2 Why have the prices of pocket calculators and VCRs fallen?

3 What has been the effect of an increase in world population on the wheat market and the individual wheat farmer?

4 Lucy's Seafood Bar is a price taker that has the following costs:

Output (Seafood plates per hour)	Total cost (pounds per hour)
0	5
1	20
2	26
3	35
4	46
5	59

a If a plate of seafood sells for £7.50, what is Lucy's profit-maximizing output?
b What is Lucy's shutdown point?
c Over what price range will Lucy leave the Seafood Bar industry?
d Over what price range will other firms with costs identical to Lucy's enter the industry?
e What is the price of a plate of seafood in the long run?

5 The market demand schedule for pop CDs is as follows:

Price (pounds per CD)	Quantity demanded (CDs per week)
3.65	500,000
4.40	475,000
5.20	450,000
6.00	425,000
6.80	400,000
7.60	375,000
8.40	350,000
9.20	325,000
10.00	300,000
10.80	275,000
12.60	250,000

Price (pounds per CD)	Quantity demanded (CDs per week)
12.40	225,000
13.20	200,000
14.00	175,000
14.80	150,000

The market is perfectly competitive and each firm has the same cost structure described by the following table:

Output (CDs per week)	Marginal cost	Average variable cost (pounds per CD)	Average total cost
150	6.00	8.80	15.47
200	6.40	7.80	12.80
250	7.00	7.00	12.00
300	7.65	7.10	10.43
350	8.40	7.20	10.06
400	10.00	7.50	10.00
450	12.40	8.00	10.22
500	12.70	9.00	12.00

There are 1,000 firms in the industry.

6 The same demand conditions as those in Problem 5 prevail and there are still 1,000 firms in the industry, but fixed costs increase by £980.

a What is the short-run profit-maximizing output for each firm?
b Do firms enter or exit the industry in the long run?
c What is the new long-run equilibrium price?
d What is the new long-run equilibrium number of firms in the industry?

7 In problem 5, a fall in the price of digital tapes decreases the demand for CDs and demand schedule becomes:

Price (pounds per CD)	Quantity demanded (CDs per week)
2.95	500,000
4.13	450,000
5.30	400,000
6.48	350,000
7.65	300,000
8.83	250,000
10.00	200,000
11.18	150,000

Rework your answers for the questions in problem 5 using this demand schedule.

8 In problem 6, the price of digital tapes decreases the demand for CDs and the demand schedule becomes that given in the table for problem 7.

Rework your answers to the questions in problem 6.

9 Study *Reading Between the Lines* on pp. 292–293 and then answer the following questions:

a What is meant by a 'grey import'?
b Why do restrictions on grey imports affect competition amongst dealerships?
c Why do you think the Competition Commission is investigating new car prices in Britain?
d Why does government need to impose a 'test' on the quality of imported vehicles?

Competition: Lifting Restrictions on Grey Car Imports

The Essence of the Story

- Motorists in the UK will save up to £3,000 on the price of a new car as government lifts the tight restrictions on foreign car imports which protect UK car producers from foreign competition.
- The UK allows only 50 cars of any particular model built outside the European Union to enter the country each year, mainly from Japan, Korea and the Far East.
- The independent dealers who sell these 'grey imports' will be able to import up to 55,000 vehicles in December 2000, and then as many as demanded by 2001.
- A European Commission survey showed that car prices are generally higher in Britain than in other EU countries. The table in the article shows the current franchise price and the grey market or independent price, and potential savings of up to 35 per cent on some models.
- There is pressure for further price cuts as the Competition Commission has announced a further investigation into anti-competitive practices by franchise dealers over new car prices.

The Guardian, 26 May 1999

Car buyers glad to be grey

David Gow

Motorists will save thousands of pounds on new cars when a government scheme to relax tight limits on some foreign models comes into effect in March next year.

Ministers, promising savings of up to £3,000 a car, yesterday drove a further nail in the coffin of excessive British prices by removing all restrictions on so-called "grey imports" from the end of 2000.

John Reid, transport minister, held out the prospect of even greater savings after the competition commission inquiry into new car prices is published in December.

Currently, Britain allows only 50 models a year of foreign cars not built for the European market to enter the country. These cars, sold through independent dealers, originate mainly in Japan, Korea and elsewhere in the Far East and cost up to 35% less than those bought through franchised dealers. But the scheme will also cover imported and re-imported cars which have been produced in Europe.

Under the revised scheme, these limits will gradually be relaxed so that 1,000 can be bought in March next year. The quota will be expanded throughout the year to 55,000 in December and lifted entirely from January 2001.

Dr Reid said the decision paved the way for cheaper cars for all and increased choice for consumers. Stephen Byers [trade and industry secretary] said: "We expect that many cars will cost thousands of pounds less as a result."

A European Commission survey comparing prices for 76 models in the 15 EU countries showed them highest in Britain in 57 cases — with some models up to £4,000 more expensive than on the Continent.

Under the present scheme "grey imports" must undergo a £165 vehicle approval test to make sure they conform with EU safety, security (anti-theft) and emissions standards. These standards will be enhanced under a tougher test in the new scheme.

The grey price

Make	Franchise price £	Independent price £
Toyota Landcruiser 4.2 VX	44,990	29,995
Nissan Skyline	50,000	40,000
Mazda MX5 1.6i	15,520	13,000
Porsche 911 Carrera Tiptronic	67,950	59,995
Mercedes Benz E300 Elegance	34,765	29,995
BMW 328i SE	29,140	24,995
Chrysler Voyager 3.3 LE	23,545	19,995
Rover MGF 1.81 VVC	20,395	17,995
Alfa Romeo 146 2.1 Ti	17,076	11,995
VW Golf 1.9tdi GT	16,495	14,995
Fiat Punto Cabriolet	15,309	11,995
Ford 1.3 Ka 2	8,845	6,995

Source: Press Association

Economic Analysis

■ Lifting the ban on grey imports has opened up the UK market to competition from non-EU makers of vehicles. UK franchise dealers will no longer be able to set the price, but will act more like price takers.

■ Figure 1 uses the example of Nissan's Skyline model from the table in the article. It shows a Nissan UK franchise dealer in a competitive environment, with marginal cost, MC_0, average total cost, ATC_0, and marginal revenue, MR_0.

■ The franchise maximizes profit by setting MR_0 equal to MC_0, selling three Skyline vehicles per month at a price of £50,000 each. The franchise (and/or producer) makes an economic profit of £8,000 on each vehicle and a total profit of £24,000 per month (numbers are hypothetical).

■ Figure 2 shows the total UK market for Nissan Skylines before the restrictions are lifted. Demand is D_0 and supply is S_0, and the equilibrium price is £50,000 with 100 vehicles sold each month.

■ Lifting restrictions allows foreign producers to enter the market through independent dealers and shifts the supply curve rightwards over time towards S_1. Price eventually falls to £40,000 per vehicle and quantity increases to 120 vehicles per month.

■ Figure 3 shows that as price falls, the marginal revenue curve for the Skyline at the franchise dealer falls to MR_1 and all economic profits are competed away. Franchise dealers now sell the Skyline at £40,000, sell fewer vehicles each month, and make zero economic profit.

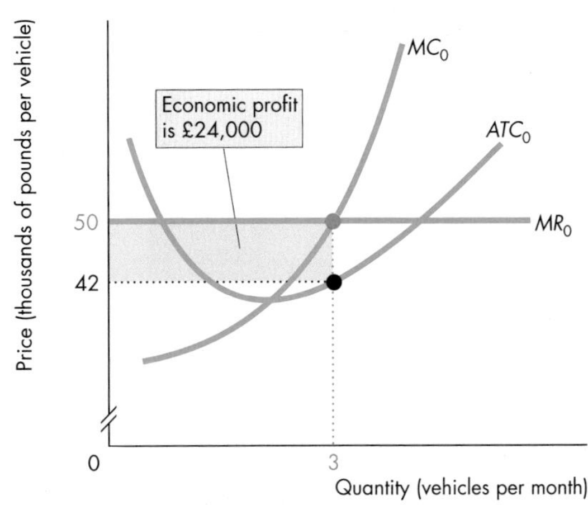

Figure 1 Nissan Franchise Dealer with restrictions on foreign imports

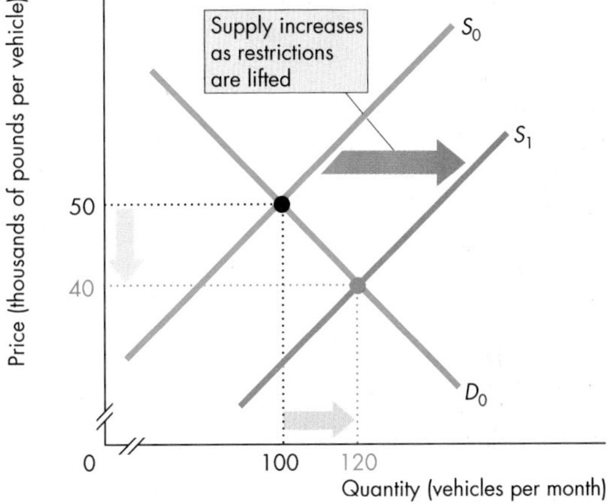

Figure 2 The UK market for Nissan Skylines

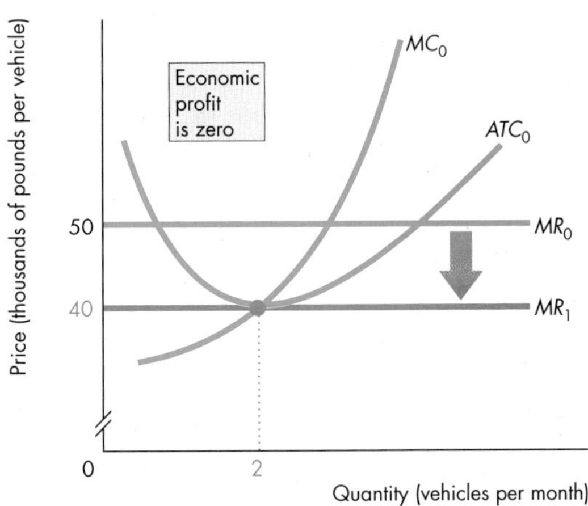

Figure 3 Nissan Franchise Dealer after restrictions lifted

CHAPTER 13

Monopoly

After studying this chapter you will be able to:

- Define monopoly and explain the conditions under which it arises
- Distinguish between legal monopoly and natural monopoly
- Explain how a monopoly determines its price and output
- Define price discrimination and explain why it leads to a bigger profit
- Compare the performance of a competitive and a monopolistic industry
- Define rent seeking and explain why it arises
- Explain the conditions under which monopoly is more efficient than competition

The Profits of Generosity

We've talked a lot about firms that want to maximize profit. But are all firms really so intent on maximizing profit? After all, you have probably been offered a student's discount at some bookshops, theatres and record shops. Airlines often give a discount for buying a ticket in advance and rail companies offer discounts for student travel. Are all these firms simply being generous? Are they throwing money away? Or perhaps the perfectly competitive model does not apply in all cases. ◆ When you buy water, you don't shop around. You buy from your water utility, which is your only available supplier. If you live in Leeds and want a water supply, you only have one option: buy from Yorkshire Water. These are examples of a single producer of a good or service controlling its supply. Such firms are obviously not like firms in perfectly competitive industries. They don't face a market-determined price. They can choose the price they charge. How do such firms behave? How do they choose the quantity to produce and the price at which to sell it? How does their behaviour compare with firms in perfectly competitive industries? Do such firms charge prices that are too high and that damage the interests of consumers? Do such firms bring any benefits?

◆ ◆ ◆ ◆ In this chapter we are going to build a model of a monopoly supplier. We will use this model to study markets in which an individual firm can influence the quantity of goods supplied and can also determine price. We can then compare the performance and efficiency of a monopoly market with our model of a competitive market.

How Monopoly Arises

A monopoly is an industry that produces a good or service for which no close substitute exists and in which there is one supplier that is protected from competition by a barrier preventing the entry of new firms. The lack of close substitutes and the barriers to entry are the reasons why monopoly is a form of market failure. Monopolies can operate locally, such as electricity suppliers, nationally, such as Royal Mail stamps, or globally, like Microsoft and its world dominating PC operating system. A monopoly has two key features:

1 No close substitutes.

2 Barriers to entry.

No Close Substitutes

If a good does have a close substitute, even though only one firm produces it, that firm effectively faces competition from the producers of substitutes. Electricity supplied by a local public utility is an example of a good that does not have close substitutes. While mains gas and oil are substitutes for domestic heating, there is no realistic substitute for domestic electrical appliances.

Monopolies are constantly under attack from new products and ideas that substitute for products produced by monopolies. For example, the spread of international courier services such as DHL, the development of the fax machine and e-mail, have weakened the first-class letter monopoly of the UK Post Office. Advances in telecommunications technology have weakened British Telecommunication's telephone monopoly. In particular, cell-phones have begun to undermine the monopoly in local calls.

So monopolies are constantly looking for new products. The development of the computer has created monopolies, the most obvious of which is Microsoft's PC operating system – DOS. Similarly, research in the pharmaceuticals industry is constantly creating new monopolies in drugs.

Barriers to Entry

Barriers to entry are legal or natural impediments protecting a firm from competition from potential new entrants. Firms can sometimes create barriers to entry by owning a unique and natural resource such as diamonds, but most monopolies arise because of legal and natural barriers.

Legal Barriers to Entry Legal barriers to entry create legal monopoly. A **legal monopoly** is a market in which competition and entry are restricted by the granting of a franchise, licence, patent or copyright, or in which a firm has acquired ownership of a significant proportion of a key resource.

A *monopoly franchise* is an exclusive right granted to a firm to supply a good or service. An example of a monopoly franchise is the UK Post Office, which has been granted the exclusive right to provide some letter-carrying services.

A *government licence* controls entry into particular occupations, professions and industries. Government licensing in the professions is the most common example of this type of barrier to entry. For example, a licence is required to practise medicine, law and dentistry among many other professional services. Licensing need not create monopoly, but it does restrict competition. When a new TV channel is offered for franchise, the successful bidder gains a licence to broadcast for a limited period. In this case, it confers a monopoly on the channel broadcaster. Where the number of channels is restricted, competition in broadcasting will be limited.

A **patent** is an exclusive right granted to the inventor of a product or service. A **copyright** is an exclusive right granted to the author or composer of a literary, musical, dramatic or artistic work. Patents and copyrights are valid for a limited time period that varies from country to country. In the United Kingdom, a patent is valid for 16 years. Patents protect inventors by creating a property right and thereby encourage invention by preventing others from copying an invention until sufficient time has elapsed for the inventor to have reaped some benefits. They also stimulate *innovation* – the use of new inventions – by increasing the incentives for inventors to publicize their discoveries and offer them for use under licence.

Natural Barriers to Entry Natural barriers to entry give rise to natural monopoly. **Natural monopoly** occurs when one firm can supply the entire market at a lower price than two or more firms can. This situation arises when demand limits sales to a quantity at which economies of scale exist.

Figure 13.1 shows a natural monopoly in the distribution of electric power. The demand for electric power is D and the average total cost curve is ATC. Because average total cost decreases as output increases, economies of scale prevail over the entire

Figure 13.1 Natural Monopoly

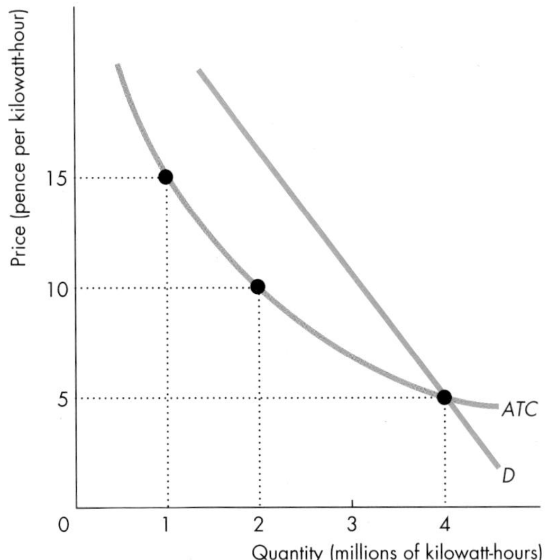

The demand curve for electric power is *D* and the average total cost curve is *ATC*. Economies of scale exist over the entire *ATC* curve. One firm can produce a total output of 4 million kilowatt-hours at a cost of 5 pence a kilowatt-hour. This same total output costs 10 pence a kilowatt-hour with two firms and 15 pence a kilowatt-hour with four firms. So one firm can meet the demand in this market at a lower cost than two or more firms can and the market is a natural monopoly.

length of the *ATC* curve. One firm can produce 4 million kilowatt-hours at 5 pence a kilowatt-hour. At this price, the quantity demanded is 4 million kilowatt-hours. So if the price was 5 pence, one firm could supply the entire market. If two firms shared the market, it would cost each of them 10 pence a kilowatt-hour to produce a total of 4 million kilowatt hours. If four firms shared the market, it would cost each of them 15 pence a kilowatt-hour to produce a total of 4 million kilowatt hours. So in conditions like those shown in Figure 13.1, one firm can supply the entire market at a lower cost than two or more firms can. Electricity generating utilities are an example of natural monopoly. Another example is natural gas distribution.

Most monopolies in the real world, whether legal or natural, are regulated in some way by government or by government agencies. We will study such regulation in Chapter 19. Here we will study unregulated monopoly for two reasons. First, we can better understand why governments regulate monopolies and the effects of regulation if we also know how an unregulated monopoly behaves. Second, even in industries with more than one producer, firms often have a strong degree of monopoly power, arising from locational advantages or from differences in product quality protected by patents. The theory of monopoly sheds light on the behaviour of many of these firms and industries.

We begin by studying the behaviour of a single-price monopoly. A *single-price monopoly* is a monopoly that charges the same price for each and every unit of its output. How does a single-price monopoly determine the quantity to produce and the price to charge for its output?

Single-price Monopoly

The starting point for understanding how a single-price monopoly chooses its price and output is to work out the relationship between the demand for the good produced by the monopoly and the monopoly's revenue.

Demand and Revenue

Because in a monopoly there is only one firm, the demand curve facing that firm is the industry demand curve. Let's look at an example of a local monopoly: Cut and Dry, the only hairdressing salon in a 15-mile radius in a small town in North Yorkshire. The demand schedule that the owner faces is set out in Table 13.1. At a price of £20, Cut and Dry sells no haircuts. The lower the price, the more haircuts per hour it can sell. For example, at a price of £12, consumers demand 4 haircuts per hour (row *e*), and at a price of £4, they demand 8 haircuts per hour (row *i*).

Total revenue (*TR*) is the price (*P*) multiplied by the quantity sold (*Q*). For example, in row *d*, Cut and Dry sells 3 haircuts at £14 each, so total revenue is £42. *Marginal revenue* (*MR*) is the change in total revenue (ΔTR) resulting from a 1-unit increase in the quantity sold. For example, if the price falls from £18 (row *b*) to £16 (row *c*), the quantity sold increases from 1 to 2 haircuts. Total revenue rises from £18 to £32, so the change in total revenue is £14. Because the quantity sold increases by 1 haircut, marginal revenue equals the change in total revenue and is £14. When recording marginal revenue, it is written between the two

Table 13.1 A Single-price Monopoly's Revenue

	Price P (pounds per haircut)	Quantity demanded Q (haircuts per hour)	Total revenue $TR = P \times Q$ (pounds)	Marginal revenue $MR = \Delta TR/\Delta Q$ (pounds per haircut)
a	20	0	0	
				18
b	18	1	18	
				14
c	16	2	32	
				10
d	14	3	42	
				6
e	12	4	48	
				2
f	10	5	50	
				−2
g	8	6	48	
				−6
h	6	7	42	
				−10
i	4	8	32	
				−14
j	2	9	18	
				−18
k	0	10	0	

The table shows Cut and Dry's demand schedule – the number of haircuts demanded per hour at each price. Total revenue (*TR*) is price multiplied by quantity sold. For example, row *c* shows that when the price is £16 a haircut, two haircuts are sold for a total revenue of £32. Marginal revenue (*MR*) is the change in total revenue resulting from a 1-unit increase in the quantity sold. For example, when the price falls from £16 to £14 a haircut, the quantity sold increases from 2 to 3 haircuts and total revenue increases by £10. The marginal revenue of the third haircut is £10. Total revenue rises to row *f*, where 5 haircuts are sold for £10, and it falls thereafter. In the output range over which total revenue is increasing, marginal revenue is positive; in the output range over which total revenue is decreasing, marginal revenue is negative.

Figure 13.2 Demand and Marginal Revenue for a Single-price Monopoly

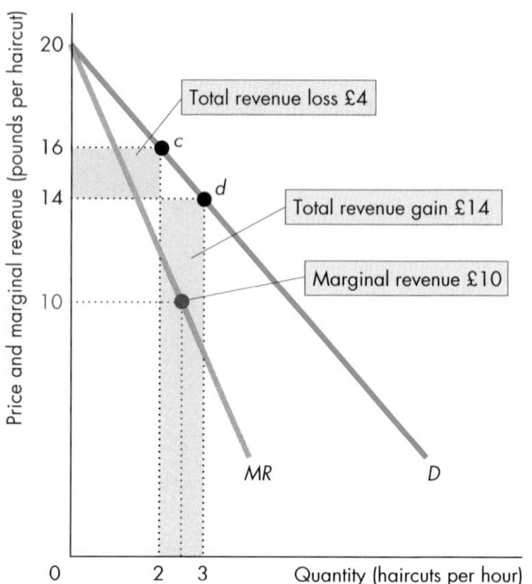

The monopoly demand curve (*D*) is based on the numbers in Table 13.1. At a price of £16 a haircut, Cut and Dry sells 2 haircuts an hour. If the price is cut to £14, 3 haircuts an hour are sold. The sale of the third haircut brings a revenue gain of £14 (the price charged for the third haircut). But there is a revenue loss of £4 (£2 per haircut) on the initial 2 haircuts that could have been sold for £16 each. The marginal revenue (extra total revenue) from the third haircut is the difference between the revenue gain and the revenue loss – £10. The marginal revenue curve (*MR*) shows the marginal revenue at each level of sales. Marginal revenue is lower than price.

rows to emphasize that marginal revenue relates to the *change* in the quantity sold.

Figure 13.2 shows the demand curve (*D*) for the Cut and Dry salon. Each row of Table 13.1 corresponds to a point on the demand curve. For example, row *d* in the table and point *d* on the demand curve tell us that at a price of £14, it sells 3 haircuts. The figure also shows the marginal revenue curve (*MR*). Notice that the marginal revenue curve is below the demand curve. That is, at each level of output marginal revenue is less than price. Why is marginal revenue less than price? It is because when the price is lowered to sell one more unit, there are two opposing effects on total revenue. The lower price results in a revenue loss and the increased quantity sold results in a revenue gain. For example, at a price of £16, the salon sells 2 haircuts (point *c*). If the price is reduced to £14, it sells 3 haircuts and revenue increases by £14 on the third haircut. But if all haircuts are sold at the same price, the salon receives only £14 on the first two as well – £2 less than before. As a result, the salon

Figure 13.3 A Single-price Monopoly's Revenue Curves

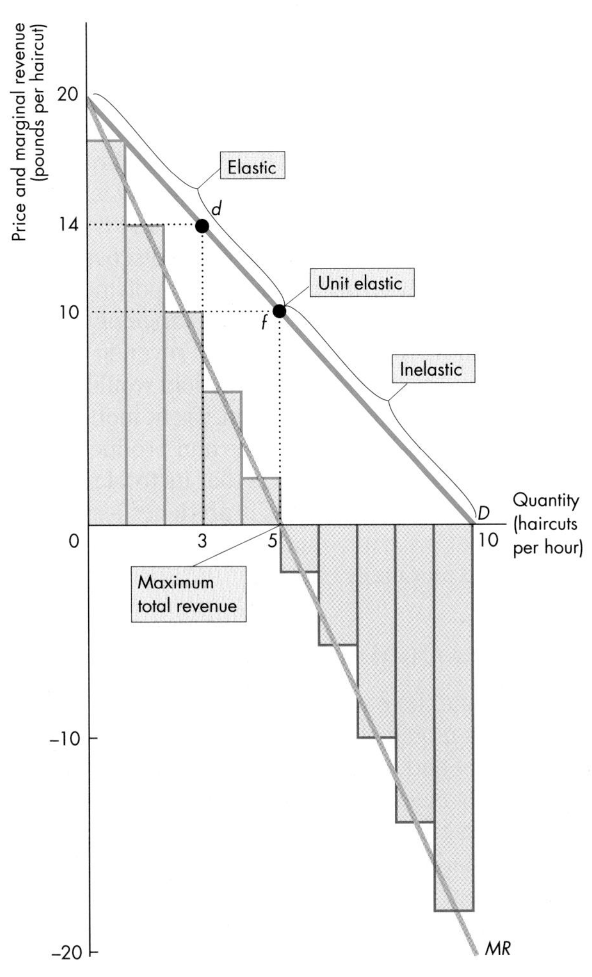

(a) Demand and marginal revenue curves

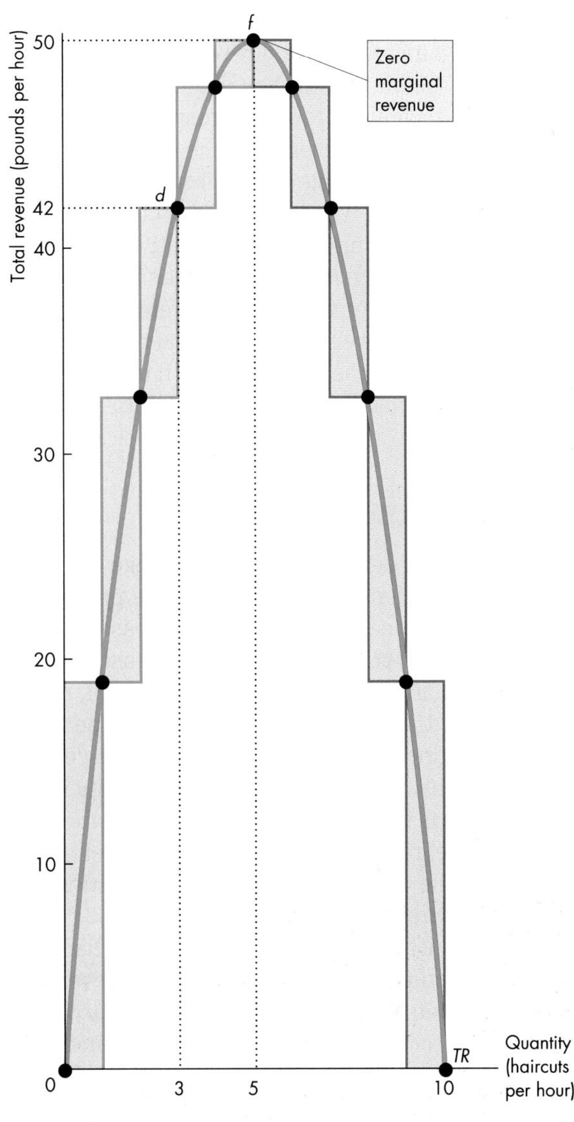

(b) Total revenue curve

Cut and Dry's demand curve (*D*) and marginal revenue curve (*MR*), shown in part (a), and total revenue curve (*TR*), shown in part (b), are based on the numbers in Table 13.1. For example, at a price of £14, the salon sells 3 haircuts an hour (point *d* in part (a)) for a total revenue of £42 (point *d* in part (b)). Over the range 0–5 haircuts an hour, total revenue is increasing and marginal revenue is positive, as shown by the blue bars. Over the range 5–10 haircuts an hour, total revenue declines – marginal revenue is negative, as shown by the red bars. Over the range of output for which marginal revenue is positive, demand is elastic. At the level of output at which marginal revenue is zero, demand is unit elastic. Over the range of output for which marginal revenue is negative, demand is inelastic.

loses £4 of revenue on the first 2 haircuts. This is deducted from the revenue gain of £14. Marginal revenue – the difference between the revenue gain and the revenue loss – is £10.

Figure 13.3 shows the demand curve, marginal revenue curve (*MR*) and total revenue curve (*TR*) for the Cut and Dry salon, and illustrates the connections between them. Again, each row in Table 13.1

corresponds to a point on the curves. For example, row *d* in the table and point *d* on the graphs tell us that when 3 haircuts are sold for £14 each (part a) total revenue is £42 (part b). Notice that as the quantity sold increases, total revenue rises to a peak of £50 (point *f*) and then declines. To understand the behaviour of total revenue, notice what happens to marginal revenue as the quantity sold increases. Over the range 0–5 haircuts, marginal revenue is positive. When more than 5 haircuts are sold, marginal revenue becomes negative. The output range over which marginal revenue is positive is the same as that over which total revenue is rising. The output range over which marginal revenue is negative is the same as that over which total revenue declines. When marginal revenue is 0, total revenue is at a maximum.

Revenue and Elasticity

The elasticity of demand is the percentage change in the quantity demanded divided by the percentage change in price. If a 1 per cent decrease in price results in a greater than 1 per cent increase in the quantity demanded, the elasticity of demand, is greater than 1 and demand is *elastic*. If a 1 per cent decrease in price results in a less than 1 per cent increase in the quantity demanded, the elasticity of demand is less than 1 and demand is *inelastic*. If a 1 per cent decrease in price results in a 1 per cent increase in the quantity demanded, the elasticity of demand is 1 and demand is *unit elastic*.

The elasticity of demand influences the change in total revenue. If demand is elastic total revenue increases when the price decreases. The reason is that the positive effect on revenue from an increase in the quantity sold outweighs the negative effect from a lower price. If demand is inelastic total revenue decreases when the price decreases. In this case, the positive effect on revenue from an increase in the quantity sold is outweighed by the negative effect from a lower price. If demand is unit elastic total revenue does not change when the price changes. In this case, the positive effect on revenue from an increase in the quantity sold is offset by an equal negative effect from a lower price. (Chapter 5, pp. 104–106, explains the relationship between revenue and elasticity more fully.)

The output range over which total revenue increases when the price decreases is the same as the range where marginal revenue is positive – shown in Figure 13.3. This is also the output range where demand is elastic – where the elasticity of demand is greater than 1. The output range over which total revenue decreases when price decreases is the same as the range where marginal revenue is negative. This is also the output range where demand is inelastic – where the elasticity of demand is less than 1. The output at which total revenue remains constant when the price decreases is where marginal revenue is zero. Thus the output at which marginal revenue is zero is also the output at which demand is unit elastic – at which the elasticity of demand is 1.

The relationship that you have just discovered implies that a profit-maximizing monopoly never produces an output in the inelastic range of its demand curve. If it did so, marginal revenue would be negative – each additional unit sold would lower total revenue. In such a situation, profit increases if the firm charges a higher price and produces a smaller quantity. The reason is that its total revenue rises and its total cost falls as it produces less. But exactly what price and quantity does a profit-maximizing monopoly choose?

Price and Output Decision

To determine the output level and price that maximize a monopoly's profit, we need to study the behaviour of both revenue and costs as output varies. A monopoly faces the same types of technology and cost constraints as a competitive firm. But it faces a different market constraint. The competitive firm is a price taker, whereas the monopoly's production decision influences the price it receives. Let's see how.

The revenue for the Cut and Dry salon studied in Table 13.1 and Figures 13.2 and 13.3 is shown again in Table 13.2. The table also contains information on the salon's costs and economic profit. Total cost (*TC*) rises as output increases and so does total revenue (*TR*). Economic profit equals total revenue minus total cost. As you can see in the table, the maximum profit (£12) occurs when the salon sells 3 haircuts for £14 each. Selling 2 haircuts for £16 each or 4 haircuts for £12 each would mean less economic profit at only £8.

You can see why 3 haircuts is the profit-maximizing output by looking at the marginal revenue and marginal cost columns. When the salon increases output from 2 to 3 haircuts, the marginal revenue is £10 and the marginal cost is £6. Profit increases by the difference – £4 an hour. If the salon increases output yet further, from 3 to 4 haircuts,

Table 13.2 A Monopoly's Output and Price Decision

Price (*P*) (pounds per haircut)	Quantity demanded (*Q*) (haircuts per hour)	Total revenue (*TR* = *P* × *Q*) (pounds)	Marginal revenue (*MR* = Δ*TR*/Δ*Q*) (pounds per haircut)	Total cost (*TC*) (pounds)	Marginal cost (*MC* = Δ*TC*/Δ*Q*) (pounds per haircut)	Profit (*TR* – *TC*) (pounds)
20	0	0		20		–20
			18		1	
18	1	18		21		–3
			14		3	
16	2	32		24		+8
			10		6	
14	3	42		30		+12
			6		10	
12	4	48		40		+8
			2		15	
10	5	50		55		–5

The table adds information about total cost (*TC*), marginal cost (*MC*) and economic profit to the information on demand and revenue in Table 13.1. Total profit (*TR* – *TC*) equals total revenue (*TR*) minus total cost (*TC*). Profit is maximized at a price of £14 when 3 haircuts are sold – the row highlighted in red. Total revenue is £42, total cost is £30 and economic profit is £12 (£42 – £30).

marginal revenue is £6 and marginal cost is £10. In this case, marginal cost exceeds marginal revenue by £4, so profit decreases by £4 an hour. When marginal revenue exceeds marginal cost, profit increases if output increases. When marginal cost exceeds marginal revenue, profit increases if output decreases. When marginal cost and marginal revenue are equal, profit is maximized.

The information set out in the table is shown graphically in Figure 13.4. Part (a) shows the Cut and Dry salon's total revenue curve (*TR*) and total cost curve (*TC*). Economic profit is the vertical distance between *TR* and *TC*. Profit is maximized at 3 haircuts an hour – economic profit is £42 minus £30, or £13.

Figure 13.4(b) shows the salon's demand curve (*D*) and the marginal revenue curve (*MR*) along with the marginal cost curve (*MC*) and average total cost curve (*ATC*). To maximize profit, a monopolist, like a competitive firm, sets marginal cost equal to marginal revenue. In the case of the Cut and Dry salon, marginal cost equals marginal revenue when output is 3 haircuts a day. But for a monopoly, price is greater than marginal cost. To find the price, the monopolist uses the demand curve. In the case of the Cut and Dry salon, the price at which it can sell 3 haircuts a day is £14 a cut.

A firm maximizes profit when marginal cost equals marginal revenue. But whether the maximum profit is an economic profit, normal profit (zero economic profit), or an economic loss depends on price and average total cost. If price exceeds average total cost, an economic profit is made. If price equals average total cost, zero economic profit is made, and if price is less than average total cost, an economic loss is incurred.

When the Cut and Dry salon produces 3 haircuts an hour, the average total cost is £10 (read from the *ATC* curve) and the price is £14 (read from the *D* curve). The profit per haircut is £4 (£14 minus £10). The economic profit is indicated by the blue rectangle, which equals the profit per haircut (£4) multiplied by the number of haircuts (3), making a total of £13.

The salon makes a positive economic profit. But suppose that the owner of the salon rents the premises. If the rent is increased by £12 an hour, the fixed cost increases by £12 an hour. The marginal cost and marginal revenue don't change, so her profit-maximizing output remains at 3 haircuts an hour. However, profit has fallen by

Figure 13.4 A Single-price Monopoly's Output and Price

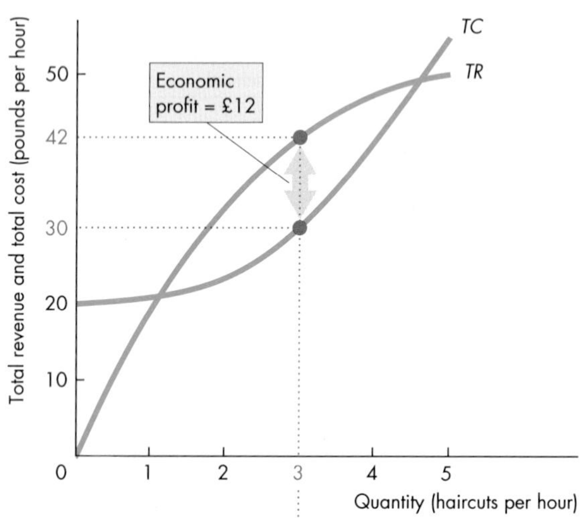

(a) Total revenue and total cost curves

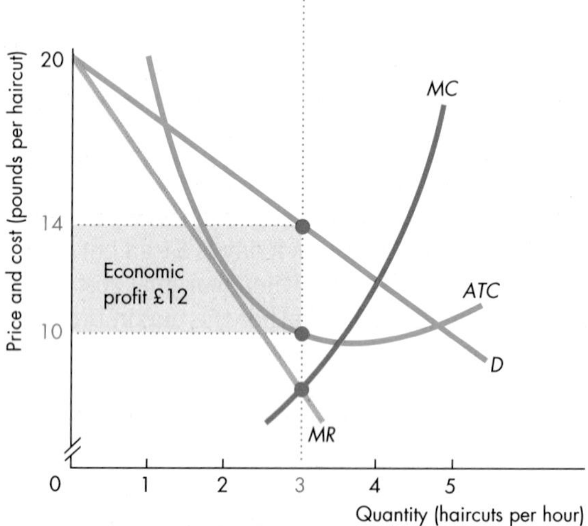

(b) Demand and marginal revenue and cost curves

This figure graphs the numbers in Table 13.2. The vertical distance between total revenue (*TR*) and total cost (*TC*) in part (a) determines the maximum economic profit output. Maximum profit occurs at 3 haircuts an hour. In part (b), economic profit is maximized where marginal cost (*MC*) equals (*MR*). The monopoly sells its profit-maximizing output for the highest price that buyers are willing to pay, which is determined by the demand curve (*D*). In this case, that price is £14. The monopoly's economic profit is illustrated in part (b) by the blue rectangle. That economic profit is £12 – the profit per haircut (£4) multiplied by 3 haircuts.

£12 an hour to zero. If the salon owner pays more than an additional £12 an hour for the shop lease, the salon makes an economic loss. If this situation was permanent, the owner would go out of business. But entrepreneurs are a hardy lot, and it might pay to find another shop where the rent is lower.

If firms in a perfectly competitive industry are making a positive economic profit, new firms enter. This does not happen in a monopolistic industry. Barriers to entry prevent new firms from entering. So in a monopolistic industry, a firm can make a positive economic profit and continue to do so indefinitely. Sometimes that profit is large, as in the international diamond business.

Review

- A single-price monopoly maximizes profit, like all other firms, by producing an output at which marginal cost equals marginal revenue.
- At the profit-maximizing output, the monopoly charges the price that consumers are willing to pay, which is determined by the demand curve.
- Because in a monopoly price exceeds marginal revenue, price also exceeds marginal cost.
- A monopoly can make a positive economic profit even in the long run because barriers prevent the entry of new firms.

Price Discrimination

Price discrimination is the practice of charging some customers a lower price than others for an identical good or of charging an individual customer a lower price on a large purchase than on a small one, even though the cost of servicing all customers is the same. An example of price discrimination is the practice of charging children or students a lower price than others to travel by train. Another example is the common practice of hairdressers giving discounts to senior citizens and students. Price discrimination can be practised in varying degrees. *Perfect price discrimination* occurs when a firm charges a different price for each unit sold and charges each consumer the maximum price that he or she is willing to pay for the unit. Although perfect price discrimination does not happen in the real world, it shows the limit to which price discrimination can be taken.

Not all price *differences* imply price discrimination. In many situations, goods that are similar but not identical have different costs and sell for different prices *because* they have different costs. For example, the marginal cost of producing electricity depends on the time of day. If an electric power company charges a higher price for consumption between 7.00 and 9.00 in the morning and between 4.00 and 7.00 in the evening than it does at other times of the day, this practice is not called price discrimination. Price discrimination charges varying prices to consumers, not because of differences in the cost of producing the good, but because of differences in consumers' elasticities of demand for the good.

At first sight, it appears that price discrimination contradicts the assumption of profit maximization. Why would a railway company give a student discount? Why would a hairdresser charge students and senior citizens less? Aren't these producers losing profit by being so generous?

Deeper investigation shows that far from losing profit, price discriminators actually make a bigger profit than they would otherwise. Thus a monopoly has an incentive to try to find ways of discriminating among groups of consumers and charging each group the highest possible price. Some people may pay less with price discrimination, but others pay more. How does price discrimination bring in more total revenue?

Figure 13.5 Total Revenue and Price Discrimination

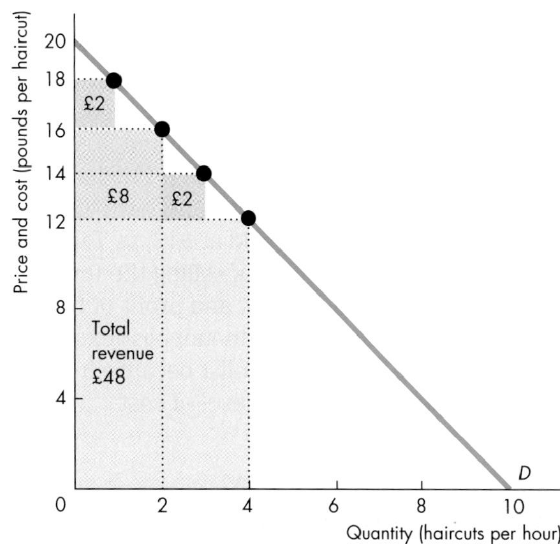

If Cut and Dry sells 4 haircuts for the same price – £12 each – total revenue is £48, as shown by the blue rectangle. If the salon charges two prices – £16 each for the first 2 haircuts and £12 each for the next 2 – total revenue will be £56 (the blue rectangle plus the the red rectangle). If the salon charges four different prices – £18 for the first haircut, £16 for the second haircut, £14 for the third haircut and £12 for the fourth haircut – total revenue will be £60 (the blue rectangle plus the red rectangle plus the two orange areas). The more finely a monopoly can price discriminate, the larger is its total revenue from a given level of sales.

Price Discrimination and Total Revenue

The total revenue received by a single-price monopoly equals the quantity sold multiplied by the single price charged. Let's look at the relationship between total revenue and price discrimination using our hair salon example. Figure 13.5 shows the demand curve, *D*, for Cut and Dry Salon haircuts, and the shaded areas show total revenue. Suppose that the Cut and Dry salon sells 4 haircuts for a single price of £12 each. The area of the blue rectangle shows total revenue is £48 – the quantity sold, 4 haircuts, multiplied by the price of a haircut, £13.

Now suppose that the salon can discriminate between its customers so that it can sell some haircuts for one price and some for another, higher price. If the first 2 haircuts are sold for £16 each and then 2 more are sold for the original price, £12, the salon makes greater total revenue than when it charged a single price.The salon gets the extra revenue earned on the first 2 haircuts (the area of the red rectangle) added to the original revenue (the blue rectangle). Total revenue is now £56 (£48 + £8).

What would happen if the salon could find a way to perfectly discriminate among customers by selling each haircut for the maximum possible price each customer is willing to pay? Let's look again at Figure 13.5. The first haircut sells for £18, the next for £16, the third for £14 and the fourth for £13. Total revenue is £60 – the blue area plus the red area plus the two orange areas – £12 more than if it sold all four haircuts for the single price of £13.

So how many haircuts will the perfectly discriminating salon sell? To answer this question, we must look at the marginal cost of each haircut relative to the price charged. Figure 13.4(b) showed that the maximum profit for the single price monopolist is £12, when 3 haircuts are sold for £14 each. The perfectly price discriminating monopolist earns an extra £4 on the first haircut sold at £18, an extra £2 on the second haircut sold at £16, and no extra profit on the third haircut sold at £14. But unlike the single price monopolist it can also earn extra profit on the fourth haircut sold at £12, as Table 13.2 shows the marginal cost of selling the fourth haircut is only £10. The output and profit of the perfectly price discriminating monopolist exceeds that of the single price monopolist because it earns greater revenue for the same level of cost.

Price Discrimination and Consumer Surplus

Demand curves slope down because the value that an individual places on a good falls as the quantity consumed of that good increases. When all the units consumed can be bought for a single price, consumers benefit. We call this benefit *consumer surplus*. (If you need to refresh your understanding of consumer surplus, flip back to Chapter 8, p. 180.) Price discrimination can be seen as an attempt by a monopoly to capture the consumer surplus (or as much of the surplus as possible) for itself.

Discriminating Among Units of a Good

One form of price discrimination charges each single buyer a different price on each unit of a good bought. An example of this type of discrimination is a discount for bulk buying. The larger the order, the larger is the discount – and the lower is the price. This type of price discrimination works because each individual's demand curve slopes downward. Some discounts for bulk arise from lower costs of production for greater bulk. In these cases, such discounts are not price discrimination.

To extract every pound of consumer surplus from every buyer, a monopolist would have to offer each individual customer a separate price schedule based on that customer's own demand curve. Clearly such price discrimination cannot be carried out in practice because a firm does not have enough information about each consumer's demand curve.

Discriminating Among Individuals

Even when it is not possible to charge each individual a different price for each unit bought, it may still be possible to discriminate among individuals. This possibility arises from the fact that some people place a higher value on consuming one more unit of a good than do other individuals. By charging such an individual a higher price, the producer can obtain some of the consumer surplus that would otherwise accrue to its customers.

Discriminating Between Groups

Price discrimination often takes the form of discriminating between different groups of consumers on the basis of age, employment status or some other easily distinguished characteristic. This type of price discrimination works only if each group has a different price elasticity of demand for the product. But this situation is a common one. For example, the elasticity of demand for haircuts is lower for business people than for students, and the elasticity of demand for air travel is lower for business travellers than for holiday-makers. Let's see how an airline exploits the differences in demand by business travellers and holiday-makers and increases its profit by price discriminating.

Global Air has a monopoly on an exotic route. Figure 13.6(a) shows the demand curve (*D*) and the marginal revenue curve (*MR*) for travel on this route. It also shows Global Air's marginal cost curve (*MC*). Marginal cost is constant, and fixed cost is zero[1]. Global Air is a single-price monopoly and maximizes its profit by producing the output at which marginal revenue equals marginal cost. This output is 10,000 trips a year. The price at which Global can sell 10,000 trips is £1,500 per trip. Global Air's total revenue is £15 million a year. Its total cost is £10 million a year, so its economic profit is £5 million a year, as shown by the blue rectangle in part (a).

Global is struck by the fact that most of its customers are business travellers. Global knows that its exotic route is ideal for holidays, but it also knows that to attract more holiday-makers, it must offer a lower fare than £1,500. At the same time,

1 The more usual case in which marginal cost increases when output increases (such as Cut and Dry's) is harder to analyse. All the key principles are shown by this special situation in which marginal cost is constant.

Figure 13.6 A Single-price Monopoly

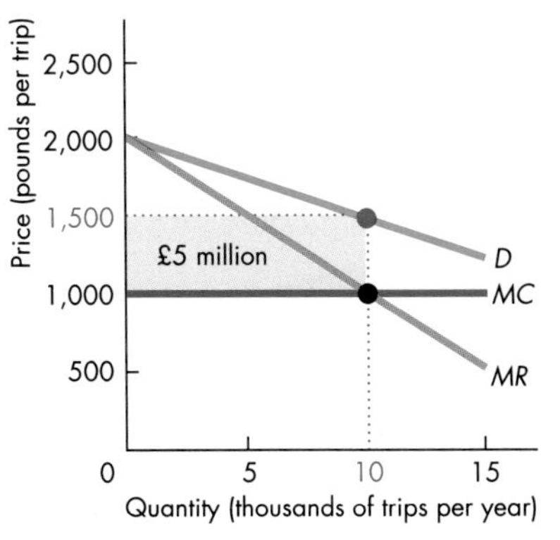

(a) All travellers

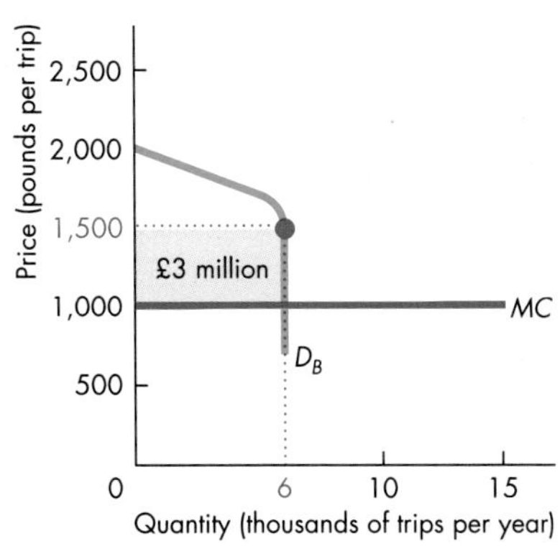

(b) Business travellers

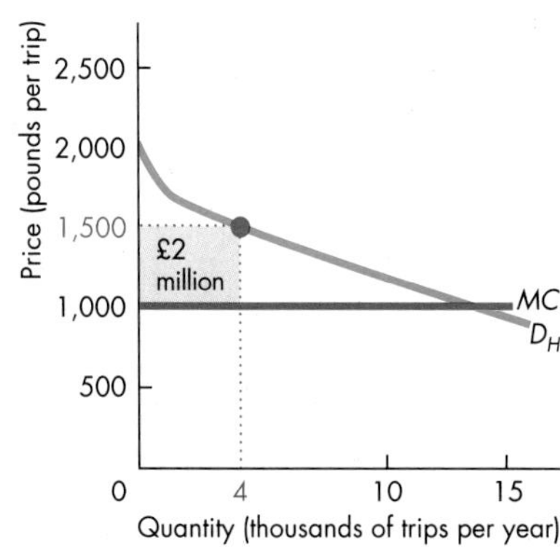

(c) Holiday-makers

Part (a) shows the demand curve (*D*), marginal revenue curve (*MR*) and marginal cost curve (*MC*), for a route on which Global Airlines has a monopoly. As a single-price monopoly, Global maximizes profit by selling 10,000 trips a year (the quantity at which *MC* = *MR*) at a fare of £1,500 a trip. Its profit is £5 million, which is shown by the blue rectangle in part (a). The demand curve in part (a) is the horizontal sum of the demand curves for business travel (D_B) in part (b) and for holiday travel (D_H) in part (c). Global sells 6,000 trips to business travellers for a profit of £3 million and 4,000 trips to holiday-makers for a profit of £2 million.

Global knows that if it cuts the fare, it will lose revenue on its business travellers. So Global decides to price discriminate between the two groups.

Global's first step is to determine the demand curve of business travellers and the demand curve of holiday-makers. The market demand curve *D* (in Figure 13.6a) is the horizontal sum of the demand curves for these two types of traveller (see Chapter 8, p. 170). Global determines that the demand curve for business travel is D_B in Figure 13.6(b) and the demand curve for holiday-makers is D_H in Figure 13.6(c). At the single fare of £1,500, the 10,000 trips that Global sells is made up of 6,000 to business travellers and 4,000 to holiday-makers. At £1,500 a trip, business travellers buy more trips than holiday-makers – but at this price, the demand for business travel is much less elastic than holiday travel. As the price decreases below £1,500, the demand for business travel becomes perfectly inelastic while the demand for holiday travel is more elastic.

Profiting by Price Discrimination

Global uses the profit-maximization rule: produce the quantity at which marginal revenue equals marginal cost and set the price at the level the consumer is willing to pay. But now that Global has separated its market into two parts, it has two marginal revenue curves. Global's marginal revenue curve for business travel is MR_B as shown in Figure 13.7(a) and its marginal revenue curve for holiday travel is MR_H as shown in Figure 13.7(b).

In Figure 13.7(a), marginal revenue from business travel equals marginal cost of £1,000 at 5,000 trips a year. The price that business travellers are willing to pay for this quantity of trips is £1,700 a trip, up £200 on the current price. In Figure 13.7(b), marginal revenue from holiday travel equals marginal cost of £1,000 at 7,000 trips a year. The price that holiday-makers are willing to pay for this quantity of trips is £1,350 a trip, *down* £150 on the current price.

If Global can charge its business travellers a fare of £1,700 and its holiday-makers a fare of £1,350, it can increase its sales from 10,000 to 13,000 trips a year and can increase its economic profit from £5 million to £5.95 million a year. On business travellers, it can make £3.5 million a year, which is £700 per trip on 5,000 trips. This economic profit is shown by the blue rectangle in Figure 13.7(a). On holiday-makers, Global can make £2.45 million a year, which is £350 per trip on 7,000 trips. The blue rectangle in Figure 13.6(b) illustrates this economic profit.

Figure 13.7 Global's Price Discriminating Strategy

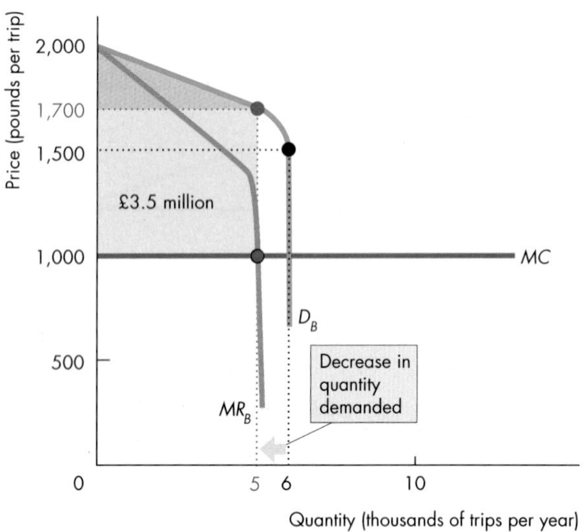

(a) Business travellers

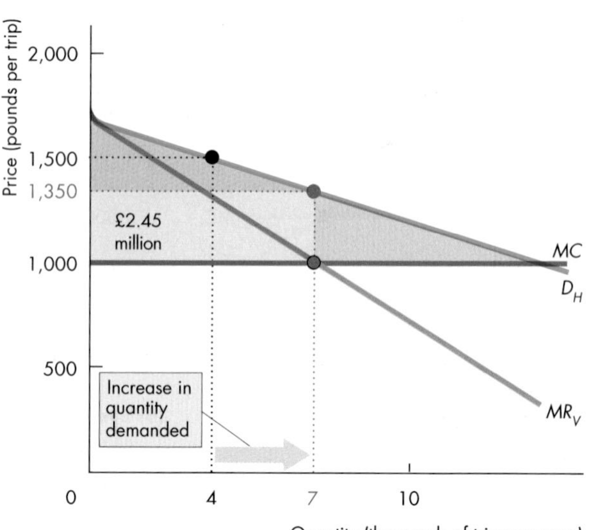

(b) Holiday-makers

The marginal revenue curve for business travel is (MR_B) in part (a) and for holiday travel is (MR_H) in part (b). Profit is maximized by making marginal revenue equal to marginal cost for each type of travel. By increasing the fare for business travel (part a) to £1,700 and by cutting the fare for holiday travel (part b) to £1,350, Global increases its economic profit. It now makes £3.5 million on business travel (the blue rectangle in part (a)) and £2.45 million on holiday travel (the blue rectangle in part (b)). Total profit is £5.95 million, up £950,000 on its single-price strategy.

How can Global get its business travellers to pay £1,700? If it offers fares to holiday-makers for £1,350, won't business travellers claim to be on holiday to get the lower fare? Not with the deal that Global comes up with.

Global has noticed that its business travellers never make reservations more than three weeks in advance. It conducts a survey, which reveals that these travellers never know more than a month in advance when they will need to travel. Its survey also reveals that holiday-makers always know at least a month in advance of their travel plans. So Global offers a deal to all travellers. The basic fare is increased from £1,500 to £1,700. But if a traveller buys a non-refundable ticket one month in advance of the date of travel, the fare is discounted by £350 to £1,350. By price discriminating between business travellers and holiday-makers, Global increases the quantity of trips sold from 10,000 to 12,000 and increases its profit by £950,000 a year.

More Perfect Price Discrimination

Global can do even better. Some of the business travellers are willing to pay more than £1,700 a trip – their consumer surplus is shown by the green triangle in Figure 13.7(a). Most holiday-makers, paying £1,350 a trip, are also willing to pay more – their consumer surplus is shown by the green triangle in Figure 13.7(b). Some potential holiday-makers are not willing to pay £1,350, but are willing to pay at least £1,000. With a marginal cost of £1,000 a trip, there is a consumer surplus for potential holiday-makers, as shown by the orange triangle in Figure 13.7(b).

Global gets creative. It comes up with a host of special deals. For higher prices, it offers priority reservations and frills to business travellers. (These deals don't change Global's marginal cost.) It refines the list of restrictions on its discount fares and creates many different fare categories, the lowest of which has lots of restrictions but is £1,000 a trip.

The quantity of seats sold increases until Global is selling 20,000 trips year – 6,000 to business travellers at various prices between £1,500 and almost £2,000 and 14,000 to holiday-makers at prices ranging between £1,000 and £1,700 a trip. Global is now almost a perfect price discriminator – capturing virtually the entire consumer surplus as profit.

Price Discrimination in Practice

You can now see why price discrimination is profitable. Global's special offer – 'Normal fare, £1,700, 30-day advance purchase special, £1,300' – is no generous gesture. It is profit-maximizing behaviour. The model of price discrimination that you have just studied explains a wide variety of familiar pricing practices where firms have the ability to set prices, even if they are not pure monopolies.

For example, real airlines, not just the imaginary Global that we've just studied, offer lower fares for advance-purchase tickets than for last-minute travel. Last-minute travellers usually have a lower elasticity of demand, while holiday-makers who can plan ahead have a higher elasticity of demand. Retail shops of all kinds hold seasonal 'sales' when they reduce their prices, often by substantial amounts. These 'sales' are a form of price discrimination. Each season, the newest fashions carry a high price tag but retailers do not expect to sell all their stock at such high prices. At the end of the season, they sell off what is left at a discount. These stores discriminate between buyers who have an inelastic demand (for example, those who want to be instantly fashionable) and buyers who have a more elastic demand (for example, those who pay less attention to up-to-the-minute fashion and more attention to price).

Limits to Price Discrimination

If price discrimination is profitable, why don't more firms do it? Why doesn't every air passenger have a separately discounted ticket? What are the limits to price discrimination?

Profitable price discrimination can take place only under certain conditions. First, it is possible to price discriminate only if the good cannot be resold. If a good can be resold, then customers who get the good for the low price can resell it to someone willing to pay a higher price. Price discrimination breaks down. It is for this reason that price discrimination usually occurs in markets for services rather than in markets for storable goods. One major exception, price discrimination in the sale of fashion clothes, works because at the end of the season when the clothes go on sale, fashion-conscious people are looking for next season's fashions. People buying on sale have no one to whom they can resell the clothes at a higher price.

Second, a price-discriminating monopoly must be able to identify groups with different elasticities of demand. The characteristics used for discrimination must also be within the law. These requirements usually limit price discrimination to cases based on age, employment status, or the timing of the purchase.

Review

- Price discrimination can increase a monopoly's profit.
- By charging the highest price for each unit of the good that each person is willing to pay, a monopoly perfectly price discriminates and captures all of the consumer surplus.
- Most price discrimination takes the form of discriminating among different groups of customers with different elasticities of demand.
- People with a lower elasticity of demand pay a higher price, and people with a higher elasticity of demand pay a lower price.
- A price-discriminating monopoly produces a larger output than a single-price monopoly.

Comparing Monopoly and Competition

We have now studied a variety of ways in which firms and households interact in markets for goods and services. In Chapter 12, we saw how perfectly

Figure 13.8 Monopoly and Competition Compared

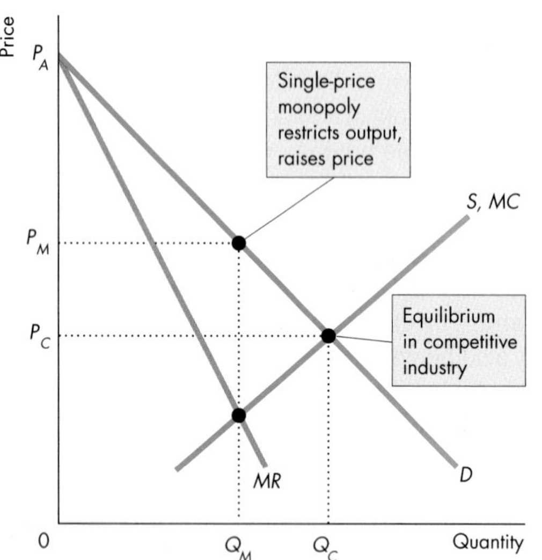

A competitive industry has a demand curve *D* and a supply curve *S*. Equilibrium occurs where the quantity demanded equals the quantity supplied at quantity Q_C and price P_C. If all the firms in the industry are taken over by a single producer that sells the profit-maximizing output for a single price, marginal revenue is *MR* and the competitive industry supply curve, *S*, becomes the monopoly's marginal cost curve, *MC*. The monopoly produces the output at which marginal revenue equals marginal cost. A single-price monopoly produces Q_M and sells that output for the price P_M. A perfectly price-discriminating monopoly produces Q_C and charges a different price for each unit sold. The prices charged range from P_A to P_C.

Monopoly restricts output and raises the price. But the more perfectly a monopoly can price discriminate, the closer its output gets to the competitive output.

competitive firms behave and discovered the price and output at which they operate. In this chapter, we have studied the price and output of a single-price monopoly and a monopoly that price discriminates. How do the quantities produced, prices and profits of these different types of firm compare with each other?

To answer this question, let's imagine an industry made up of a large number of identical competitive firms. We can work out what the price charged and quantity produced will be in that industry. Then we can imagine that a single firm buys out all the individual firms and creates a monopoly. We will then work out the price charged and quantity produced by the monopoly, first when it charges a single price and second when it price discriminates.

Price and Output Comparison

Figure 13.8 shows the industry for comparison. The industry market demand curve is D and the industry supply curve is S. In perfect competition, the market equilibrium occurs where the supply curve and the demand curve intersect.

In Perfect Competition The quantity produced by the industry is Q_C and the price is P_C. Each firm takes the price P_C and maximizes its profit by producing the output at which its own marginal cost equals the price. Because each firm is a small part of the total industry, there is no incentive for any firm to try to manipulate the price by varying its output.

With Single-price Monopoly Now suppose that this industry is taken over by a single firm. No changes in production techniques occur, so the new combined firm has identical costs to the original separate firms. Recall that an industry supply curve is the sum of all the supply curves of the firms in the industry and that a firm's supply curve is its marginal cost curve (see Chapter 12, pp. 276–277). So when the industry is taken over by a single firm, that firm's marginal cost curve is the competitive industry's supply curve. (The supply curve has also been labelled MC to remind you of this fact.)

The new single firm maximizes its profit by producing Q_M, where marginal revenue equals marginal cost. Because marginal revenue is below the demand curve, output Q_M is smaller than output Q_C. The monopoly charges the highest price for which output Q_M can be sold, and that price is P_M. We have just established that:

> Compared with a perfectly competitive industry, a single-price monopoly restricts its output and charges a higher price.

With Perfect Price Discrimination If a monopoly can perfectly price discriminate, it will charge a different price on each unit sold and increase output to Q_C. The highest price charged is P_A and the lowest price charged is P_C, the price in a competitive market. The price P_A is the highest that is charged because at yet higher prices nothing can be sold. The price P_C is the lowest price charged because when a monopoly perfectly price discriminates, its marginal revenue curve is the same as the demand curve and at prices below P_C marginal cost exceeds marginal revenue. We have just established a second key proposition:

> The more perfectly the monopoly can price discriminate, the closer its output gets to the competitive output.

We've seen how the output and price of a monopoly compare with those in a competitive industry. Let's now compare the efficiency of the two types of market.

Allocative Efficiency

Except for the case of a perfect price-discriminating monopoly, monopoly is a form of market failure and is less efficient than competition. Market failure prevents some of the gains from trade from being achieved. To see why, look at Figure 13.9. The maximum price that consumers are willing to pay for each unit is shown by the demand curve. This price measures the *value* of the good to the consumer. The difference between the value of a good and its price is **consumer surplus**. (See Chapter 8, p. 180, for a more detailed explanation of consumer surplus.)

Under perfect competition (part a), consumers pay P_C for each unit bought and obtain a consumer surplus represented by the green triangle. A single-price monopoly (part b) restricts output to Q_M and sells that output for P_M. Consumer surplus is decreased to the smaller green triangle. Consumers lose partly by having to pay more for what is available and partly by getting less of the good. But is the consumers' loss equal to the monopoly's gain? Is there simply a redistribution of the gains from trade and hence no loss in overall efficiency? A closer look at Figure 13.9(b) will convince you that there is a reduction in the gains from trade. It is true that some of the loss in consumer surplus does accrue to the monopoly – the monopoly gets the difference between the higher price (P_M) and P_C on the quantity sold (Q_M). So the monopoly has taken the blue rectangle part of the consumer surplus. This portion of the loss of consumer surplus is not a loss to society and hence not a loss of efficiency. It is a redistribution from consumers to the monopolist.

Figure 13.9 Allocative Efficiency of Monopoly

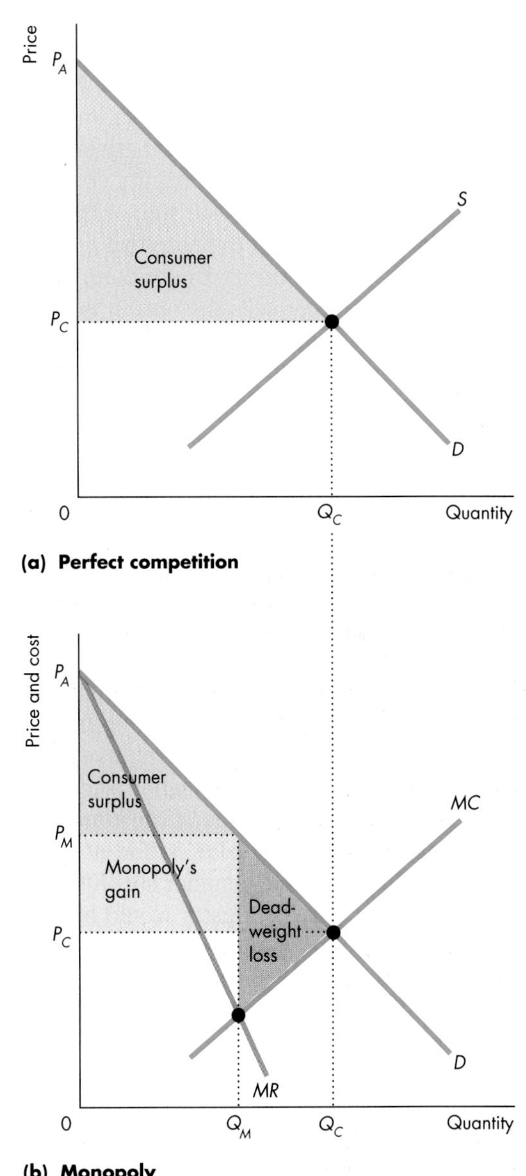

In perfect competition (part a), quantity is Q_C, price is P_C and consumer surplus is the green triangle. With free entry, firms' economic profits in long-run equilibrium are zero. Consumer surplus is maximized. Under a single-price monopoly (part b), output is restricted to Q_M and the price increases to P_M. Consumer surplus is reduced to the smaller green triangle. The monopoly takes the blue rectangle for itself, but the grey triangle is a deadweight loss. Part of the deadweight loss (above P_C) is a loss of consumer surplus, and part (below P_C) is a loss of producer surplus.

But where is the rest of the consumer surplus? The answer is that because output has been restricted, it is lost. But more than that has been lost. The total loss resulting from the lower monopoly output (Q_M) is the grey triangle in Figure 13.9(b). The part of the grey triangle above P_C is the loss of consumer surplus and the part of the triangle below P_C is a loss to the producer – a loss of producer surplus. **Producer surplus** is the difference between a producer's revenue and the opportunity cost of production. It is calculated as the sum of the differences between price and the marginal cost of producing each unit of output. Under competitive conditions, the producer sells the output between Q_M and Q_C for a price of P_C. The marginal cost of producing each extra unit of output through that range is shown by the marginal cost (supply) curve. Thus the vertical distance between the marginal cost curve and price represents a producer surplus. Part of the producer surplus is lost when a monopoly restricts output to less than its competitive level.

The grey triangle, which measures the total loss of both consumer and producer surplus, is called the deadweight loss. **Deadweight loss** measures the loss of allocative efficiency as the reduction in consumer and producer surplus resulting from a restriction of output below its efficient level. A monopoly's reduced output and higher price results in the monopoly capturing some of the consumer surplus. It also results in the elimination of the producer surplus and the consumer surplus on the output that a competitive industry would have produced but that the monopoly does not. Deadweight loss measures the degree of market failure or allocative inefficiency created by a monopoly. *Reading Between the Lines* on pp. 318–319 explores the efficiency loss arising from monopoly pricing in satellite and cable broadcasting.

Usually a monopoly produces an output well below that at which average total cost is at a minimum. It has far more capacity than it uses. But even if a monopoly produces the quantity at which average total cost is a minimum, which it might, the consumer does not have the opportunity of buying the good at that price. The price paid by the consumer always exceeds marginal cost.

We have seen that a single-price monopoly creates a deadweight loss by restricting output. What is the deadweight loss if the monopoly practises perfect price discrimination? The answer is zero. A perfect price discriminator produces the same output as the competitive industry. The last item sold costs P_C, the same as its marginal cost. Thus from the point of view of allocative efficiency, a perfect price-discriminating monopoly achieves the same result as perfect competition.

Redistribution

Under perfect competition, the consumer surplus is the green triangle in Figure 13.9(a) and the long-run equilibrium economic profit is zero. We've just seen that the creation of monopoly reduces consumer surplus and may lead to a deadweight loss. But what happens to the distribution of surpluses between producers and consumers? The answer is that the monopoly always wins. In the case of a single-price monopoly (Figure 13.9b), the monopoly gains the blue rectangle at the expense of the consumer, but it loses part of its producer surplus – its share of the deadweight loss. This loss reduces its gain. But there is always a net gain for the monopoly and a net loss for the consumer. We also know that because there is a deadweight loss, the consumer loses more than the monopoly gains.

In the case of a perfect price-discriminating monopoly, there is no deadweight loss but there is an even larger redistribution of the gains from trade away from consumers to the monopoly. In this case, the monopoly captures the entire consumer surplus, the green triangle in Figure 13.9(a).

It is because it creates a deadweight loss that monopoly is inefficient. It imposes a cost on society. This cost might be avoided by the break-up of a monopoly, using law and regulation. We look at ways of avoiding this cost in Chapter 19.

Review

- The creation of a monopoly results in a redistribution of economic gains away from consumers and to the monopoly producer.
- If a monopoly can perfectly price discriminate, it produces the same output as a competitive

industry and achieves allocative efficiency, but it captures the entire consumer surplus.

- A monopoly cannot usually perfectly price discriminate, so it restricts output below the level that a competitive industry would produce and creates a deadweight loss. The monopoly creates allocative inefficiency – the consumers' loss exceeds the monopoly's gain.

Rent Seeking

The activity of creating a monopoly from which an economic profit can be made is called **rent seeking**. The term 'rent seeking' is used because 'rent' (or 'economic rent') is another name for consumer surplus plus producer surplus. We've seen that a monopoly makes its economic profit by diverting part of the consumer surplus to itself. Thus the pursuit of an economic profit by a monopolist is rent seeking. It is the attempt to capture some consumer surplus.

Rent seekers pursue their goals in two main ways. They can:

1. Buy a monopoly.
2. Create a monopoly.

Buy a Monopoly This type of rent seeking is the searching out of existing monopoly rights that can be bought for a lower price than the monopoly's economic profit – that is, seeking to acquire existing monopoly rights. An example is the purchase of taxi licences. In most cities, taxis are regulated. The city restricts both the fares and the number of taxis that are permitted to operate. Operating a taxi results in economic profit or rent. A person who wants to operate a taxi must buy the right to do so from someone who already has that right.

But buying an existing monopoly does not assure an economic profit. The reason is that there is freedom of entry into the activity of rent seeking. Rent seeking is like perfect competition. If an economic profit is available, a new entrant will try to get some of it. Competition among rent seekers pushes the price that must be paid for a monopoly right up to the point at which only a normal profit can be made by operating the monopoly. The economic profit – the rent – goes to the person who created the monopoly in the first place. For example, competition for the right to operate a taxi in UK cities leads to a price of more than £10,000, which is sufficiently high to eliminate long-run economic profit for the taxi operator. But the person who acquired the right in the first place collects the economic rent. This type of rent seeking transfers wealth from the buyer to the seller of the monopoly.

Create a Monopoly This type of rent seeking activity takes the form of lobbying and seeking to influence the political process. Such influence is sometimes sought by making political contributions in exchange for legislative support or by indirectly seeking to influence political outcomes through publicity in the media or more direct contacts with politicians and bureaucrats. An example would be the donations to political parties that the alcohol and tobacco companies make in an attempt to avoid a tightening of legislation on activities such as advertising and licensing, which might affect their profits.

This type of rent seeking is a costly activity that uses up scarce resources. In aggregate, firms spend millions of pounds lobbying Parliament in the pursuit of licences and laws that create barriers to entry and establish a monopoly right. Everyone has an incentive to rent seek, and because there are no barriers to entry into the rent-seeking activity, there is a great deal of competition for new monopoly rights.

What determines the value of the resources that a person will use to obtain a monopoly right? The answer is the monopoly's economic profit. If the value of resources spent trying to create a monopoly exceeds the monopoly's economic profit, the result is an economic loss. But as long as the value of the resources used to create a monopoly falls short of the monopoly's economic profit, there is an economic profit to be earned. With no barrier to entry into rent seeking, the value of the resources used up in rent seeking equals the monopoly's economic profit.

Because of rent seeking, monopoly imposes social costs that exceed the deadweight loss that we calculated earlier. To calculate that cost, we must add to the deadweight loss the value of resources used in rent seeking. That amount equals the monopoly's entire economic profit, because that is the value of the resources that it pays to use in rent seeking. Thus the social cost of monopoly is the deadweight loss plus the monopoly's economic profit.

Gains from Monopoly

So far, compared with perfect competition, monopoly has come out in a pretty bad light. If monopoly is so bad, why do we put up with it? Why don't we have laws that crack down on monopoly so hard that it never rears its head? We do indeed have laws that limit monopoly power (see Chapter 19). We also have laws that regulate these monopolies that exist. But monopoly is not all bad. Let's look at its potential advantages and some of the reasons for its existence.

The main reasons why monopoly might have some advantages are:

- Economies of scale and economies of scope.
- Incentives to innovate.

Economies of Scale and Scope A firm experiences *economies of scale* when an increase in its production of a good or service brings a decrease in the average total cost of producing it – see Chapter 11, pp. 252–253. **Economies of scope** arise when an increase in the *range of goods produced* brings a decrease in average total cost. Economies of scope occur when highly specialized (and usually expensive) technical inputs can be shared by different goods. For example, McDonald's can produce both hamburgers and chips at an average total cost that is lower than what it would cost two separate firms to produce the same goods because hamburgers and chips share the use of specialized food storage and preparation facilities. Firms producing a wide range of products can hire specialist computer programmers, designers and marketing experts whose skills can be used across the product range, thereby spreading their costs and lowering the average total cost of production of each of the goods.

Economies of scale and scope can lead to natural monopoly, where a single firm in the industry can produce at a lower average cost than a larger number of firms can achieve.

Large-scale firms that have control over supply and can influence price – and that therefore behave like the monopoly firm that we've been studying in this chapter – can reap these economies of scale and scope; small, competitive firms cannot. As a consequence, there are situations in which the comparison of monopoly and competition that we made earlier in this chapter is not a valid one. Recall that we imagined the takeover of a large number of competitive firms by a single monopoly firm. But we also assumed that the monopoly would use exactly the same technology as the small firms and have the same costs. But if one large firm can reap economies of scale and scope, its marginal cost curve will lie below the supply curve of a competitive industry made up of thousands of small firms. It is possible for such economies of scale and scope to be so large as to result in a higher output and lower price under monopoly than a competitive industry would achieve.

Examples of industries in which economies of scale are so significant that they lead to natural monopolies are becoming more rare. Public utilities such as gas and electric power were once natural monopolies, but customers can now buy their gas and electricity from a number of different suppliers. Water distribution, however, remains a local natural monopoly. There are many examples where a combination of economies of scale and economies of scope arise. These include the brewing of beer, the manufacture of refrigerators, other household appliances and pharmaceuticals, and the refining of petroleum.

Incentives to Innovate

Innovation is the first-time application of new knowledge in the production process. Innovation may take the form of developing a new product or a lower-cost way of making an existing product. Controversy has raged among economists over whether large firms with monopoly power or small competitive firms lacking such monopoly power are the more innovative. It is clear that some temporary monopoly power arises from innovation. A firm that develops a new product or process and patents it obtains an exclusive right to that product or process for the term of the patent.

But does the granting of a monopoly, even a temporary one, to an innovator increase the pace of innovation? One line of reasoning suggests that it does. With no protection, an innovator is not able to enjoy the profits from innovation for long. Thus the incentive to innovate is weakened. A contrary argument is that monopolies can afford to be lazy while competitive firms cannot. Competitive firms must strive to innovate and cut costs even though they know that they cannot hang on to the benefits of their innovation for long. But that knowledge spurs them on to greater and faster innovation.

The evidence on whether monopoly leads to greater innovation than competition is mixed. It shows that large firms do much more research and development than small firms. But measuring research and development is measuring the volume of inputs into the process of innovation. What matters is not input but output. Two measures of the output of research and development are the number of patents and the rate of productivity growth. On these measures, there is no clear evidence that big is better. But there is a clear pattern in the process of diffusion of technological knowledge. After innovation, a new process or product spreads gradually through the industry. Whether an innovator is a small firm or a large firm, large firms jump on the bandwagon more quickly than do the remaining small firms. Thus large firms speed the process of diffusion of technological advances.

- Monopoly produces a smaller quantity at a higher price than a competitive industry.
- A perfectly discriminating monopoly produces the same output as a competitive industry, but sells each unit for the highest possible price.
- Monopoly is inefficient because it creates a deadweight loss and expenditure on rent seeking.
- Monopoly can be efficient if it achieves economies of scale or scope.

We've now studied two models of market structure – perfect competition and monopoly. We've discovered the conditions under which perfect competition achieves allocative efficiency and we've compared the efficiency of competition with that of monopoly. Although there are examples of markets in the European economies that are highly competitive or highly monopolistic, the markets for most goods and services lie somewhere between these two extremes. In the next chapter, we're going to study this middle ground between monopoly and competition. We're going to discover that many of the lessons that we learned from these two extreme models are still relevant and useful in understanding behaviour in real-world markets.

Summary

Key Points

How Monopoly Arises (pp. 296–297)

- A monopoly is an industry in which there is a single supplier of a good, service or resource. Monopoly arises because of barriers to entry that prevent competition.
- Barriers to the entry of new firms may be legal or natural and can arise when a firm owns control of a resource.
- Legal barriers take the form of public franchise, government licence, patent and copyright.
- Natural barriers exist when economies of scale exist.

Single-price Monopoly (pp. 297–302)

- A monopoly's demand curve is the market demand curve, (downward sloping) and a single price monopoly's marginal revenue is less than price.
- A monopoly maximizes profit by producing the output at which marginal revenue equals marginal cost and by charging the highest price that consumers are willing to pay for that output.

Price Discrimination (pp. 302–307)

- Price discrimination is an attempt by the monopoly to convert consumer surplus into economic profit.

- Perfect price discrimination extracts all the consumer surplus. Such a monopoly charges a different price for each unit sold and obtains the maximum price that each consumer is willing to pay for each unit bought.
- With perfect price discrimination, the monopoly produces the same output as would a perfectly competitive industry.
- A monopoly that discriminates between different groups of customers produces that output for each group at which the marginal cost equals marginal revenue and charges each group the most it is willing to pay.
- Price discrimination can be practised only when it is impossible for a buyer to resell the good and when consumers with different elasticities can be identified.

Comparing Monopoly and Competition (pp. 307–313)

- A single-price monopoly charges a higher price and produces a smaller quantity than does a perfectly competitive industry.
- A perfect price-discriminating monopoly produces the competitive quantity and sells the last unit for the competitive price.
- A single-price monopoly restricts output and creates a deadweight loss. A perfectly-discriminating monopoly is efficient but captures all the surplus.
- Monopoly imposes costs that equal its deadweight loss plus the cost of the resources used for rent seeking (creating and maintaining barriers to entry).
- Monopolies with large economies of scale and scope can produce a larger quantity at a lower price than a competitive industry, and monopoly might be more innovative than competition.

Key Figures

Key Terms

Review Questions

1 What is a monopoly? What are some examples of monopoly in your region?

2 How does monopoly arise?

3 Distinguish between a legal monopoly and a natural monopoly. Give examples of each type.

4 Explain why marginal revenue is always less than price for a single-price monopoly.

5 Why does a monopoly's economic profit increase as output increases initially but eventually decrease when output gets too big?

6 Does a single-price monopoly operate on the inelastic part of its demand curve? Explain why it does or does not.

7 Explain how a single-price monopoly chooses its output and price.

8 Can any monopoly price discriminate? If yes, why? If no, why not?

9 Explain why a single-price monopoly produces a smaller output than an equivalent competitive industry.

10 Is a single-price monopoly as efficient as competition?

11 What is deadweight loss?

12 Show graphically the deadweight loss under perfect price discrimination.

13 As far as allocative efficiency is concerned, is a single-price monopoly better or worse than perfect price discrimination? Why?

14 Monopoly redistributes consumer surplus. Explain why the consumer loses more under perfect price discrimination than under single-price monopoly.

15 Explain why people indulge in rent-seeking activities.

16 When taking account of the cost of rent seeking, what is the social cost of monopoly?

17 What are economies of scale and economies of scope? What effects, if any, do they have on allocative efficiency of monopoly?

Problems

1 Cool Condiments, a single-price monopoly, faces the following demand schedule for bottled balsamic vinegar:

Price (pounds per bottle)	Quantity demanded (bottles)
10	0
8	1
6	2
4	3
2	4
0	5

a Calculate the company's total revenue schedule.
b Calculate its marginal revenue schedule.
c At what price is the elasticity of demand equal to 1?

2 Dan's Diamond Mines, a single-price monopoly, faces the following demand schedule for industrial diamonds:

Price (pounds per kilo)	Quantity demanded (kilos per day)
2,200	5
2,000	6
1,800	7
1,600	8
1,400	9
1,200	10

a Calculate the company's total revenue schedule.
b Calculate its marginal revenue schedule.
c At what price is the elasticity of demand for diamonds equal to 1?

3 Cool Condiments has the following total cost:

Quantity produced (bottles)	Total cost (pounds)
0	1
1	3
2	7
3	13
4	21
5	31

Calculate the profit-maximizing levels of:

a Output.
b Price.
c Marginal cost.
d Marginal revenue.
e Economic profit.

4 Dan's Diamond Mines in problem 2, has the following total cost:

Quantity produced (kilos per day)	Total cost (pounds)
5	8,000
6	9,000
7	10,200
8	11,600
9	13,200
10	15,000

Calculate the profit-maximizing levels of

a Output
b Price
c Marginal cost
d Marginal revenue
e Economic profit
f Does Dan's Diamond Mines use resources efficiently? Explain your answer.

5 Suppose that Cool Condiments can perfectly price discriminate. Calculate its profit-maximizing

a Output.
b Total revenue.
c Economic profit.

6 What is the maximum price that someone would be willing to pay the company for a licence to operate its balsamic vinegar cellars?

7 Two demand schedules for round-trip flights between London and New York are set out below. The schedule for weekday travellers is for those making round-trips on weekdays and returning within the same week. The schedule for weekend travellers is for those who stay over the weekend. (The former tend to be business travellers and the latter holiday and pleasure travellers.)

Weekday travellers		Weekend travellers	
Price (pounds per round-trip)	Quantity demanded (thousands of round-trips)	Price (pounds per round-trip)	Quantity demanded (thousands of round-trips)
1,500	0	750	0
1,250	5	500	5
1,000	10	250	10
750	15	0	15
500	15		
250	15		

The marginal cost of a round-trip is £500. If a single-price monopoly airline controls the London–New York route, use a graph to find out the following:

a What price is charged?
b How many passengers travel?
c What is the consumer surplus for weekday travellers?
d What is the consumer surplus for weekend travellers?

8 Barbara runs a café in the Scottish Highlands, miles from anywhere. She has a monopoly and faces the following demand schedule for meals:

Price (pounds per meal)	Quantity demanded (meals per week)
1.00	160
1.50	140
2.00	120
2.50	100
3.00	80
3.50	60
4.00	40
4.50	20
5.00	0

Barbara's marginal cost and average total cost are a constant £2 per meal.

a If Barbara charges all customers the same price for a meal, what price is it?
b What is the consumer surplus of all the customers who buy a meal from Barbara?
c What is the producer surplus?
d What is the deadweight loss?

9 Barbara discovers that some of the people stopping for meals are truck drivers and some of them are tourists. She estimates that the demand schedules for the two groups are:

Price (pounds per meal)	Quantity demanded (meals per week) Truck Drivers	Tourists
1.00	70	90
1.50	65	75
2.00	60	60
2.50	55	45
3.00	50	30
3.50	45	15
4.00	40	0
4.50	20	0
5.00	0	0

If Barbara price discriminates between the two,

- a What price does she charge truck drivers?
- b What price does she charge tourists?
- c What is her output per week and is it higher, lower, or the same as when she did not price discriminate?
- d What is her weekly economic profit and is it higher, lower, or the same as when she did not price discriminate?
- e What is the consumer surplus for truck drivers?
- f What is the consumer surplus for tourists?

10 Study *Reading Between the Lines* on pp. 318–319 and then answer the following:

- a How does BSkyB create a barrier to entry for new channels?
- b Why has BSkyB excluded the Sky One channel from its rate card to cable companies?
- c What is the long-run impact on consumers of BSkyB's tariff strategy?
- d Explain why cable companies are also offering a package of cheap telephone rates and pay-television to their customers.

11 Use the links on the Parkin, Powell and Matthews Web site to study the market for computer chips.

- a Is it correct to call Intel a monopoly? Explain why or why not?
- b How does Intel try to raise barriers to entry in this market?

12 Use the links on the Parkin, Powell and Matthews Web site to obtain information on Microsoft. Then answer the following questions.

- a Is it correct to call Microsoft a monopoly? Explain why or why not.
- b How do you think that Microsoft sets the price of Windows 98 and decides how many copies of the program to produce?
- c How would the arrival of a viable alternative operating system to Windows affect Microsoft?
- d How would you regulate the software industry to ensure that resources are used efficiently?
- e 'Anyone is free to buy shares in Microsoft, so everyone is free to share in Microsoft's economic profit, and the bigger that economic profit, the better for all.' Evaluate this statement.

Monopoly in Action: BSkyB Raises Barriers to Entry

The Essence of the Story

- The Independent Television Commission, the broadcasting regulator, is to investigate British Sky Broadcasting's (BSkyB's) tarrif charge system.
- The Commission believes the tariff structure may price competitors out of the market, creating a barrier to entry and monopoly power.
- The tariff structure charges a high price for the premium channels such as Sky Sports One and then gives deep discounts for adding similar channels.
- The deep discounting makes it impossible for other broadcasters to launch a new channel to rival the channel package at a profitable rate.
- BSkyB has also been accused of excluding high priced channels from the discounted rate charged to cable companies that transmit BSkyB channels.

The Guardian, 23 January 1999

BSkyB faces price inquiry

Watchdog fears rivals are being forced out of pay-television market

Chris Barrie, Media Business Correspondent

British Sky Broadcasting faces an official inquiry into the way it charges customers for its top sports and movie channels.

The Independent Television Commission is to scrutinise the tariffs for Sky's premium channels amid concerns that other TV channels may be unfairly excluded.

The ITC fears BSkyB's tariff structure is pricing rivals out of the market. BSkyB's premium channels are available at an expensive rate for the first channel selected, with subsequent channels in the genre then available at much lower rates.

Sky MovieMax costs a subscriber to digital television £18.99 a month, and Sky Premier £22.99. Combining the two costs just £24.99, and the Disney and Sky Cinema channels are thrown in for free.

BSkyS charges £20.99 for Sky Sports One and Three, but only £24.99 for all its sports channels. The ITC is to consider whether this "deep discount and margin squeeze", makes it impossible for a rival sports or movie channel to launch at a profitable rate.

The watchdog has been considering the issues for some time, and the decision to issue a public consultation document in the near future indicates that officials feel there is a serious case to answer.

It has also emerged that BSkyB is revising its wholesale rate card, the charges levied on cable companies for transmitting BSkyB channels.

Cable companies, among them Cable and Wireless Communications, are complaining that the rate card does not allow them a reasonable return, and are concerned that BSkyB has excluded Sky One from the card — allowing BSkyB to charge what it wants for the channel.

Sir Robin Biggam [ITC chairman] also disclosed that the ITC and its counterpart in telecommunications, Oftel, are to scrutinise the way cheap telephone rates and pay-television are bundled together by cable companies.

The inquiry will focus on whether income from telephone calls is being used to cross-subsidise television services, causing a serious distortion of the market.

Economic Analysis

- BSkyB is accused of using its pricing system to create a barrier to entry and increase monopoly power.

- Figure 1 shows the situation for BSkyB if it can generate a monopoly channel in a popular area such as sports television. It faces a downward sloping demand curve. Average total cost is *ATC*, marginal cost is *MC* and marginal revenue is *MR*.

- To maximize profits, BSkyB sets the price of its premium popular Sky Sports One at £20.99 and then adds the other sports channels for just £3.01 extra. The majority of sports lovers purchase Sky Sports One and pay the extra for the complete sports package.

- Rival broadcasters cannot produce a new sports channel at a price that is profitable. BSkyB now has an effective monopoly as shown in Figure 1. The profit maximizing price for the sports channel package is £24, where *MR* equals *MC*, generating an economic profit shown by the blue area.

- The Commission regulates against monopoly because it is inefficient as shown in Figure 2. At a price of £24 – the price is higher than the competitive price, £16, and some consumer and producer surplus is lost in the deadweight loss (red plus grey area). BSkyB also captures some consumer surplus as additional profit shown as the monopoly gain.

- If BSkyB is forced to price each channel competitively, prices for premium channels will fall to £16 as shown in Figure 2, and the discounts for other channels will be removed. The quantity of customers will rise from Q_M to Q_C, and the deadweight loss is removed.

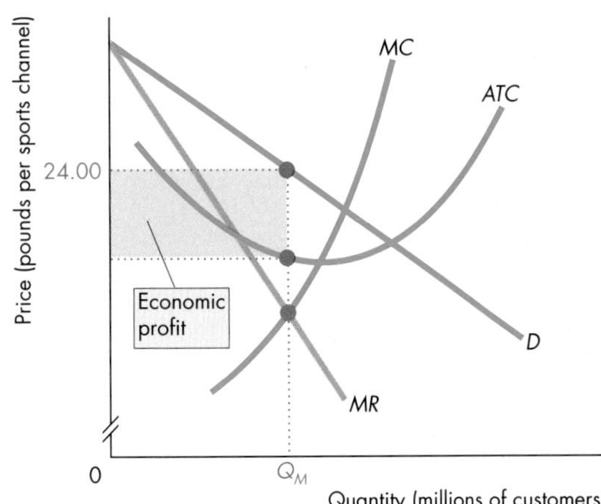

Figure 1 BSkyB makes monopoly profit

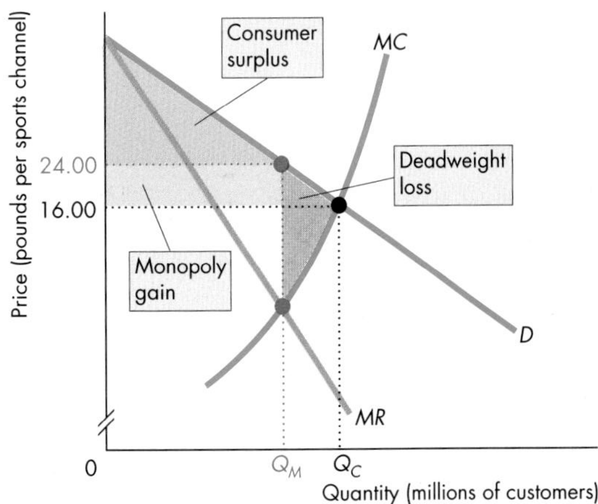

Figure 2 Monopoly gain and inefficiency

CHAPTER 14

Monopolistic Competition and Oligopoly

After studying this chapter you will be able to:

- Define monopolistic competition and oligopoly
- Explain how price and output are determined in a monopolistically competitive industry
- Explain why the price may be sticky in an oligopoly industry
- Explain how price and output are determined when there is one dominant firm and several small firms in an industry
- Use game theory to make predictions about price wars and competition among small numbers of firms

Fliers and War Games

Every week, we receive a newspaper stuffed with supermarket fliers describing this week's 'specials', providing coupons and other enticements. They are all designed to persuade us that Tesco, Safeway, Sainsbury's, Asda, Kwik Save and Aldi have the best deals in town. One claims the lowest price, another the best brands, yet another the best value for money even if its prices are not the lowest. How do firms locked in such fierce competition set their prices, pick their goods and services and choose the quantities to produce? How are the profits of such firms affected by the actions of other firms? ◆ Until 1994, only one firm made the chips that drive IBM and compatible PCs – Intel Corporation. Then prices of powerful personal computers based on Intel's fast 486 and Pentium chips collapsed. The reason: Intel suddenly faced competition from new chip producers. The price of Intel's Pentium processor, set at more than £1,500 when it was launched in 1993, fell to less than £150 by spring 1998, and the price of Pentium II-based computers fell to less than £900. How did competition among a small number of chip makers bring such a rapid fall in the price of chips and computers?

◆ ◆ ◆ ◆ The theories of monopoly and perfect competition do not predict the kind of behaviour just described. There are no adverts and discounts, best brands or price wars in perfect competition because each firm produces an identical product and is a price taker. Similarly, there are none in monopoly because each monopoly firm has the entire market to itself. To understand discounts, adverts and price wars, we need the more complex models explained in this chapter.

Varieties of Market Structure

We have studied two types of market structure – perfect competition and monopoly. In perfect competition, a large number of firms produce identical goods and there are no barriers to the entry of new firms into the industry. In this situation, each firm is a price taker and, in the long run, there is no economic profit. In monopoly, there is just one firm in the industry which is protected by barriers, preventing the entry of new firms. The firm sets its price to maximize profit and might enjoy economic profit even in the long run.

Many real-world industries are not well described by the models of perfect competition and monopoly because they lie between the two cases. Two other market models have been developed to study the industries that lie between perfect competition and monopoly. They are:

1 Monopolistic competition.
2 Oligopoly.

Monopolistic competition is a market structure in which a large number of firms compete with each other by making similar but slightly different products. Making a product slightly different from the product of a competing firm is called **product differentiation**. Because of product differentiation, a monopolistically competitive firm has an element of monopoly power. The firm is the sole producer of the particular version of the good in question. For example, in the breakfast cereal market, only Weetabix Ltd makes Weetabix and only the Kellogg Company makes All Bran. Differentiated products are not necessarily different in an objective sense. For example, there are many cereals which are similar to Weetabix and All Bran in shape, content and production. Many supermarkets sell their own brands of these cereals under different names. The differences are mainly in the packaging and name. What matters is that consumers perceive products to be different.

In some markets, there are few firms but entry and exit is so easy that competition from *potential* new firms is fierce. A market in which potential entry is free is called a **contestable market**. Even if there are some small costs to entry and exit, a market can still be highly contestable. An example of a virtually contestable market is that of local private bus routes. Firms can easily switch their buses from one route to another with virtually no entry and exit costs. Contestable markets can also be studied using the model of monopolistic competition.

Oligopoly is a market structure in which a small number of producers compete with each other. There are hundreds of examples of oligopolistic industries. Computer software, aircraft and car manufacture are but a few. In some oligopolistic industries, each firm produces an almost identical product. In others, products are differentiated. For example, oil and petrol are essentially the same whether they are made by Shell or Esso. But in the European car market, the Volkswagen Golf is a differentiated commodity from the Renault Clio or Peugeot 205.

Measures of Concentration

In order to tell which of our market models best describes a particular industry, and hence how much market power firms in the industry might have, economists use measures of industrial concentration. Industrial concentration measures the proportion of output or employment accounted for by a specified number of the largest firms in the industry. The most commonly used measure is the five-firm concentration ratio, but there is no reason why a three- or four-firm ratio could not be used.

Five-firm concentration ratio The **five-firm concentration ratio** is the percentage of the industry's output accounted for by the five firms with the largest output in the industry. Output could be measured by volume or the value of sales. The range of the concentration ratio is from almost zero for perfect competition to 100 for monopoly. This ratio is the main measure used to assess market structure.

Table 14.1 sets out two hypothetical concentration ratio calculations, one for shoe manufacturing and one for egg farming. In this example, there are 15 firms in the shoe manufacturing industry. The largest five have 81 per cent of the sales of the industry, so the five-firm concentration ratio for that industry is 81 per cent. In the egg industry, with 1,005 firms, the top five firms account for only 0.8 per cent of total industry sales. In this case, the five-firm concentration ratio is 0.8 per cent.

The idea behind calculating five-firm concentration ratios is to get information about the degree of competitiveness of a market. A low concentration

Table 14.1 Concentration Ratio Calculations (Hypothetical)

Shoemakers		Egg farmers	
Firm	**Sales (£ million)**	**Firm**	**Sales (£ million)**
Lace-up plc	250	Bills's	0.9
Finefoot plc	200	Sue's	0.7
Easyfit plc	180	Jane's	0.5
Comfy plc	120	Tom's	0.4
Loafers plc	70	Jill's	0.2
Top 5 sales	820	Top 5 sales	2.8
Other 10 firms	190	Other 1,000 firms	349.2
Industry sales	1,010	Industry sales	352.0

Five-firm concentration ratios:

Shoemakers: $\frac{820}{1,010} = 81\%$ Printers: $\frac{2.80}{352} = 0.8\%$

ratio indicates a high degree of competition, and a high concentration ratio indicates an absence of competition. In the extreme case of monopoly, the concentration ratio is 100 per cent as the largest (and only) firm makes the entire industry sales. Between these extremes, the five-firm concentration ratio is regarded as being a useful indicator of the likelihood of collusion among firms in an oligopoly. If the ratio exceeds 60 per cent, it is likely that firms in that industry will have a high degree of market power. They are likely to collude and behave like a monopolist. If the ratio is less than 40 per cent, it is likely that the firms will compete effectively. Between the ratios of 40 and 60 per cent, the industries have oligopolistic and monopolistic competitive structures. But the degree of market power for firms in these industries is likely to be limited by some form of competition.

Limitations of Concentration Measures

Although concentration ratios are useful, they have some limitations. They must be supplemented by other information to determine the structure of an industry and the degree of market power of firms in that industry. The three key problems are:

1 The geographical scope of the market.

2 Barriers to entry and firm turnover.

3 The correspondence between a market and an industry.

Geographical Scope of Market Concentration ratio data are based on a national view of the market. Many goods are sold on a national market, but some are sold on a regional market and some on a global one. The brewing industry is a good example of one in which the local market is more relevant than the national market. Thus although the national concentration ratio for brewers is in the middle range, there is nevertheless a high degree of concentration in the brewing industry in most regions. The automobile industry is an example of one for which there is a global market. Thus although the largest five car producers in the United Kingdom account for 80 per cent of all cars sold by UK producers, they account for a smaller percentage of the total UK car market, which includes imports, and an even smaller percentage of the global market for cars.

Barriers to Entry and Turnover Measures of concentration do not indicate the severity of any barriers to entry in a market. Some industries, for example, are highly concentrated but their markets have virtually free entry and a high turnover of firms. A good example is the market for local restaurants. Many small towns have few restaurants, but there are few restrictions on entering the restaurant industry. So firms enter and exit with great regularity.

Even if the turnover of new firms in a market is limited, an industry might be competitive because of potential entry. This will be the case if the market

Table 14.2 Market Structure

Characteristics	Perfect competition	Monopolistic competition	Contestable	Oligopoly	Monopoly
Number of firms in industry	Many	Many	Few	Few	One
Product	Identical	Differentiated	Differentiated	Either identical or differentiated	No close substitutes
Barriers to entry	None	None	None	Scale and scope economies	Scale and scope or legal barriers
Firm's control over price	None	Some	Some	Considerable	Considerable or regulated
Concentration ratio (0–100)	0	Low	Low	High	100
Examples	Agricultural goods	Corner shops, bread, car mechanics	Local restaurants, buses	Washing powders, disposable nappies	Local water utility, postal letter service

is *highly contestable*. Table 14.2 summarizes the characteristics of different market structures and their concentration ratios.

Market and Industry The classifications used to calculate UK concentration ratios allocate every firm in the economy to a particular industry. But markets for particular goods do not usually correspond to these industries.

The main problem is that markets are often narrower than industries. For example, the basic industrial chemicals industry, which has a medium concentration ratio, operates in many separate markets for individual products (for instance tobacco and cement), each one of which has few substitutes. So this industry, which looks relatively competitive, operates in some monopolistic markets.

Another problem arises from the fact that firms make many products. For example, the tobacco firms also operate in insurance. The privatized water companies operate hotels and printing works. The value of sales for each firm can overestimate their contribution to the industry to which they have been assigned.

If concentration ratios are combined with information about the geographical scope, barriers to entry and the extent to which large, multi-product firms straddle a variety of markets, they can provide a basis for classifying industries. The less concentrated an industry and the lower its barriers to entry, the more closely it approximates the perfect competition case. The more concentrated an industry and the higher the barriers to entry, the more it approximates the monopoly case.

Concentration in the UK Economy

Concentration ratios for the United Kingdom can be derived from the regular census of manufacturing companies known as the Census of Production. The census is undertaken every year and provides information on the sales, employment and structure of every manufacturing firm in the United Kingdom. Figure 14.1 shows a selection of the five-firm concentration ratio calculations using sales data. As you can see, some industries such as plastics, printing, metal foundries and wool have low concentration ratios – implying firms in these industries are competitive. At the other extreme are industries with high concentration ratios such as tobacco, man-made fibres, wines and ciders, and motor vehicles. These industries appear to have a high degree of monopoly power. Medium concentration ratios are found in industries like mineral oils, water supply and basic chemicals. Firms in these industries have a limited amount of market power.

Market Structures in the UK

The majority of markets for goods and services in Europe are highly competitive and only a few markets are monopolized. For example, more than 70 per cent by value of UK goods and services are traded in highly competitive markets. Where pure monopoly does arise it is usually in the public services although this has declined with privatization. But monopoly power can still be strong in markets like telecommunications when privatization attracts few new entrants. Less than 6 per cent of

Figure 14.1 Some Concentration Measures in the United Kingdom

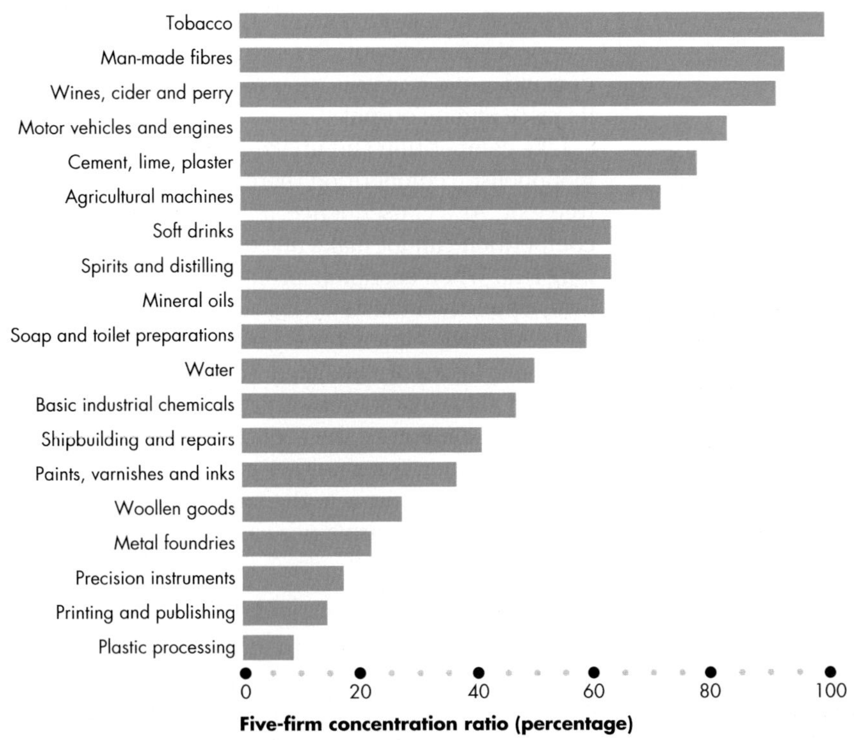

Using the five-firm concentration ratio, tobacco, man-made fibres, wines, ciders and perry are all highly concentrated. Water, chemicals and shipbuilding and repairs have medium concentration. Industries producing woollen goods, precision instruments, plastics and printed products are highly competitive.

Source: Central Statistical Office, *Report of the Census of Production, Business Monitor,* London, HMSO, 1998.

the value of goods and services traded in the UK are in highly monopolized markets. Oligopoly is more common in manufacturing than in the services sector, but more than 55 per cent of UK manufacturing industries have a concentration ratio of less than 40 per cent.

The overall level of concentration across an economy can be measured by the proportion of total output accounted for by the largest 100 firms. Figure 14.2 shows the UK aggregate concentration ratio in manufacturing since 1949. Aggregate concentration increased in the post-war period indicating an increase in market power, but it levelled off in the 1970s and 1980s and has fallen in recent years. The increase in concentration resulted from several waves of merger activity and the growth of transnational corporations serving new global markets. This is not surprising given the growth in world trade, and advances in telecommunications and low-cost transport. So although the United Kingdom's national aggregate concentration has increased, many of its markets are now globalized and highly competitive.

Monopolistic Competition

Monopolistic competition arises in an industry in which:

1 A large number of firms compete with each other.

2 Each firm produces a differentiated product, which is a close but not a perfect substitute for the products of the other firms.

3 Firms are free to enter and exit.

Local corner shops and bakers, family restaurants, service garages and makers of running shoes are all examples of firms that operate in monopolistic competition. In monopolistic competition, as in perfect competition, the industry consists of a large

Figure 14.2 Aggregate Concentration Ratios

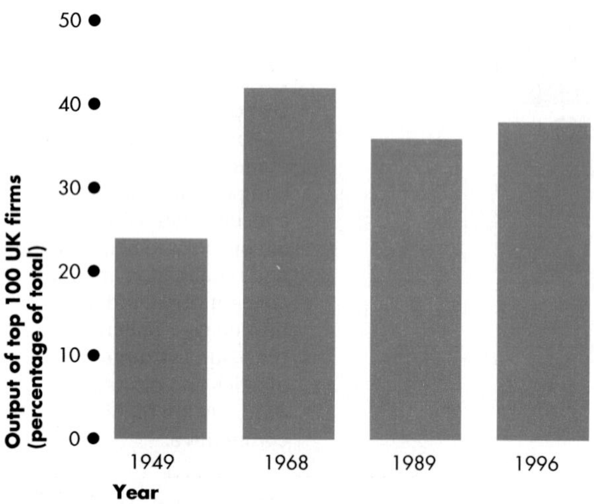

The output of the top 100 manufacturing firms as a percentage of total UK output in manufacturing is a measure of concentration in the manufacturing sector. The concentration ratio as a percentage increased from 22 per cent in 1949 to 43 per cent in 1968, indicating an increase in market power in manufacturing. Concentration has declined since then. The ratio fell to 35 per cent in 1989 and increased slightly in 1996.

Source: Central Statistical Office, *Report of the Census of Production, Business Monitor*, London, HMSO, 1998.

number of firms and each firm supplies a small part of the total industry output. Because each firm is small, no one firm can effectively influence what other firms do. If one firm changes its price, this action has no effect on the actions of the other firms.

Unlike perfect competition and like monopoly, a firm in monopolistic competition faces a downward-sloping demand curve. The reason is that the firm's product is differentiated from the products of its competitors. Some people will pay more for one variety of the product, so when its price rises, the quantity demanded falls but it does not (necessarily) fall to zero. For example, Adidas, Asics, New Balance, Nike, Puma and Reebok all make differentiated running shoes, as do many other firms. Other things remaining the same, if the price of Adidas running shoes rises and the prices of the other shoes remain constant, Adidas sells fewer shoes and the other producers sell more. But Adidas shoes don't disappear from the market unless the price rises by a large amount. Because a firm in monopolistic competition faces a downward-sloping demand curve it maximizes profit by choosing both its price and its output.

Like competition and unlike monopoly, in monopolistic competition there is free entry and free exit. As a consequence, a firm in monopolistic competition cannot make an economic profit in the long run. When economic profit is being made, new firms enter the industry. This entry lowers prices and eventually eliminates economic profit. When economic losses are incurred, some firms leave the industry. This exit increases prices and profits and eventually eliminates the economic loss. In long-run equilibrium, firms neither enter nor leave the industry, and the firms in the industry make zero economic profit – earn a normal profit.

Price and Output in Monopolistic Competition

Figure 14.3 shows how price and output are determined by a firm in a monopolistically competitive industry. Part (a) deals with the short run and part (b) the long run. Let's concentrate initially on the short run. The demand curve D is the demand curve for the firm's own variety of the product. For example, it is the demand for Disprin rather than for aspirin in general; or for McDonald's hamburgers rather than for hamburgers in general. The curve MR is the marginal revenue curve associated with the demand curve. The figure also shows the firm's average total cost (ATC) and marginal cost (MC). The firm maximizes profit in the short run by producing output Q_S, where marginal revenue equals marginal cost, and charging the price P_S. The firm's average total cost is C_S and the firm makes a short-run economic profit, as measured by the blue rectangle.

So far, the monopolistically competitive firm looks just like a monopoly. It produces the quantity at which marginal revenue equals marginal cost and then charges the price that buyers are willing to pay for that quantity, determined by the demand curve. The key difference between monopoly and monopolistic competition lies in what happens next.

There is no restriction on entry in monopolistic competition so economic profit attracts new entrants. As new firms enter the industry, the

Figure 14.3 Monopolistic Competition

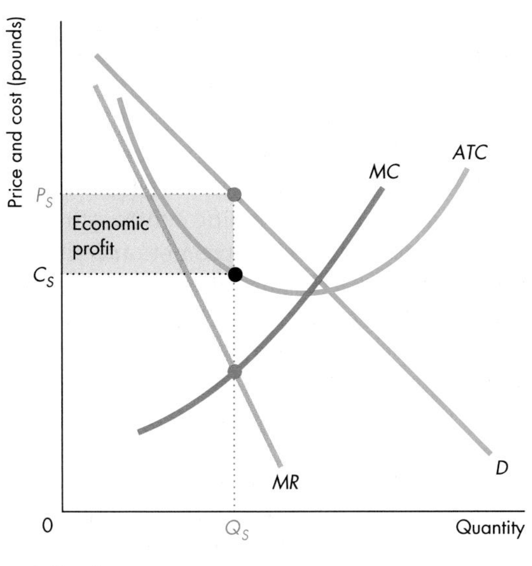

(a) Short run

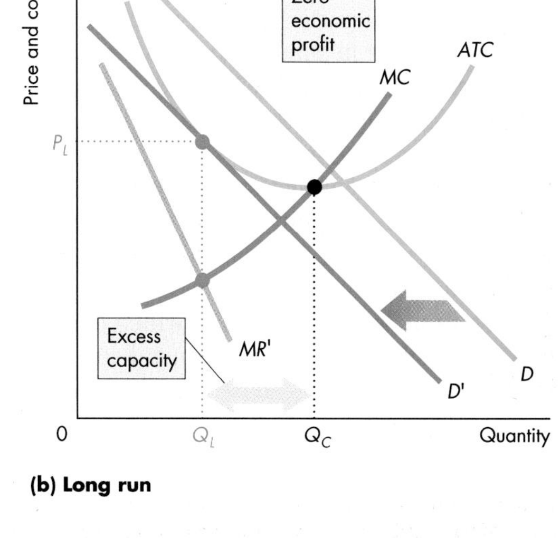

(b) Long run

In monopolistic competition, because it produces a differentiated product, a firm faces a downward-sloping demand curve. Part (a) shows the short run. Profit is maximized where marginal revenue equals marginal cost. In the short run profit is maximized by producing the quantity Q_S and selling it for the price P_S. Average total cost is C_S, and the firm makes an economic profit represented by the blue rectangle. Economic profit encourages new entrants in the long run. Part (b) shows the long-run outcome. The entry of new firms decreases each firm's demand and the demand curve and marginal revenue curve shift leftward. When the demand curve has shifted from *D* to *D'*, the marginal revenue curve is *MR'* and the firm is in a long-run equilibrium. The output that maximizes profit is Q_L and the price is P_L. In long-run equilibrium, economic profit is zero and there is no further entry. Each firm has excess capacity.

firm's demand curve and marginal revenue curve start to shift leftward. At each point in time, the firm maximizes its short-run profit by producing the quantity at which marginal revenue equals marginal cost, and by charging the price that buyers are willing to pay for this quantity. But as the demand curve shifts leftward, the profit-maximizing quantity and price fall.

Figure 14.3(b) shows the long-run equilibrium. The firm produces Q_L and sells it at a price of P_L. In this situation, the firm is making a zero economic profit. Average total cost equals price. There is no incentive for firms to enter or exit.

Excess Capacity A firm's *capacity* output is the output produced when average total cost is at its minimum point – the output at the bottom of the U-shaped *ATC* curve (point Q_c in Figure14.3b). In monopolistic competition, in the long run, firms always have *excess capacity.* That is, they produce less output than that which minimizes average total cost. As a consequence, the consumer pays more than the minimum average total cost. This result arises from the fact that the firm faces a downward-sloping demand curve. The demand curve slopes down because of product differentiation – because one firm's product is not a perfect substitute for another firm's product. Thus it is product differentiation that produces excess capacity.

You can see the excess capacity in monopolistic competition all around you. Family restaurants (except for the truly outstanding ones) almost always have a few empty tables. You can always get a pizza delivered in less than 30 minutes and many local service garages will offer an exhaust emission test on the spot without an appointment. It is rare for the bakery to have no leftover bread and cakes at the end of the day.

Monopolistic Competition and Efficiency

When we studied a perfectly competitive industry, we discovered that in some circumstances such an industry achieves allocative efficiency. A key feature of allocative efficiency is that price equals marginal cost. Recall that price measures the value placed on the last unit bought by the consumer and marginal cost measures the firm's opportunity cost of producing the last unit. We also discovered that monopoly is allocatively inefficient because it restricts output below the level at which price equals marginal cost. As we have just discovered, monopolistic competition shares this feature with monopoly. Even though there is zero economic profit in long-run equilibrium, the monopolistically competitive industry produces an output at which price equals average total cost but exceeds marginal cost.

Because price exceeds marginal cost, monopolistic competition, like monopoly, is allocatively inefficient. The marginal cost of producing one more unit of output is less than the marginal benefit to the consumer – the price the consumer is willing to pay. But the inefficiency of monopolistic competition arises from product differentiation – product variety. This variety is valued by consumers, but it is only achievable if firms make differentiated products. So the loss in allocative efficiency that occurs in monopolistic competition must be weighed against the gain of greater product variety.

Product Innovation and Differentiation

Another source of gain from monopolistically competitive industries is product innovation and differentiation. Monopolistically competitive firms are constantly looking for new products that will provide them with a competitive edge, even if only temporarily. These firms also look for small changes in design or technology to differentiate their existing products. You can see this in the use of new shock absorbing gel's in the soles of sports shoes, or special fibres in sports raquets. A firm that manages to introduce a new and differentiated variety will temporarily face a steeper demand curve than before and will be able temporarily to increase its price. New firms that make close substitutes for the new product will enter and eventually compete away the economic profit arising from this initial advantage.

Selling Costs

A large proportion of the price charged by firms in monopolisitc competion covers the cost of selling the good, rather than making it or designing it. When you visit a major shopping centre, you are bombarded with advertising, promotional offers and gimmicks. The costs of these items are just a part of selling costs. Others costs arise from the production of glossy catalogues and brochures, magazine and television advertising, and from the salaries, air fares and hotel bills of sales staff. These costs arise because monopolistically competitive firms have to maintain the perception in the consumer's mind that the product is different from competing products. This is one of the main roles of marketing and advertising. Selling costs increase a monopolistically competitive firm's costs above those of a competitive firm or a monopoly, which do not generate selling costs.

To the extent that selling costs provide consumers with services that are valued and with information about the precise nature of the differentiation of products, they serve a valuable purpose to the consumer and enable a better product choice to be made. But the opportunity cost of the additional services and information must be weighted against the gain to the consumer.

The bottom line on the question of allocative efficiency of monopolistic competition is ambiguous. In some cases, the gains from extra product variety unquestionably offset the selling costs and the extra cost arising from excess capacity. The tremendous varieties of books and magazines, of clothing, food and drink are examples of such gains. It is less easy to see the gains from being able to buy brand-name drugs and cleaning products that have a chemical composition identical to a generic alternative. But some people willingly pay more for the brand-name alternative.

Contestable Markets

In a contestable market, potential entry is so easy that the firms in the market, even if few in number, must behave in a way that deters entry. To prevent entry, the firms in the market set a price and produce a quantity that leaves zero economic profit for new entrants. This price is determined by the minimum average cost of the potential entrant. The lower the costs of entry and exit, the closer are the price and quantity to those in perfect competition.

Review

- In monopolistic competition, a large number of firms compete by producing differentiated products. Each firm faces a downward-sloping demand curve.
- In long-run equilibrium, price equals average total cost (economic profit is zero) and price exceeds marginal cost. The quantity produced is less than the quantity associated with minimum average cost.
- The cost of monopolistic competition is excess capacity and high selling costs; the gain is a wide product variety and consumer information.

You've seen that monopolistic competition is a blend of monopoly and competition. As in monopoly, each firm faces a downward-sloping demand curve and is a price setter. But as in competiton, economic profit triggers entry, so that firms only make economic profit in the long run. We're now going to look at a completely different market type – oligopoly – where excess profits might be maintained.

Oligopoly

In oligopoly, a small number of producers compete with each other. The quantity sold by any one producer depends on that producer's price *and* the prices and quantities sold by the other producers. The main feature of oligopoly is that each firm must take into account the effects of its own actions on the actions of other firms.

To see the interplay between prices and sales, suppose you run one of the three service garages in a small town. If you lower the price you charge for an hour's work and your two competitors don't lower theirs, you will get more hours of work, but the other two firms will get less work. In such a situation, the other firms are likely to lower their prices too. If they do cut their prices, hours of work and profits will fall again. So before deciding to cut your price, you try to predict how the other firms will react and you attempt to calculate the effects of those reactions on your own profit.

Several models have been developed to explain the determination of price and quantity in oligopoly markets. No one theory has been found that can explain all the different types of behaviour that we observe in such markets. The models fall into two broad groups: traditional models and game theory models. We'll look at examples of both types, starting with two traditional models.

The Kinked Demand Curve Model

The kinked demand curve model is based on assumptions about the reaction of other firms. Each firm believes that:

1. If it raises its price, other firms will not.
2. If it cuts its price, so will all other firms.

Figure 14.4 shows a demand curve, D, that reflects these beliefs. The demand curve has a kink occurring at the current price, P. A small price rise above P, leads to a big fall in quantity demanded as the firm loses its market share to other firms that do not raise price. So the demand curve is relatively elastic above P. Even a large price cut below P only leads to a small increase in quantity. In this case, other firms match the price cut, so the firm gets very little price advantage over its competitors. So demand is relatively inelastic below P.

The kink in demand curve D creates a break in the marginal revenue curve (MR). To maximize profit, the firm produces the quantity that makes marginal cost and marginal revenue equal. But that output, Q, is where the marginal cost curve passes through the discontinuity in the marginal revenue curve – the gap ab. If marginal cost fluctuates between a and b, like the marginal costs curves MC_0 and MC_1, the firm does not change price or output. Only if marginal cost fluctuates outside the range ab will the firm change its price and output levels. So, the kinked demand curve model predicts that price and quantity are insensitive to small changes in cost. Prices and quantities will fluctuate less as a result of small changes in costs in oligopoly markets.

Figure 14.4 The Kinked Demand Curve

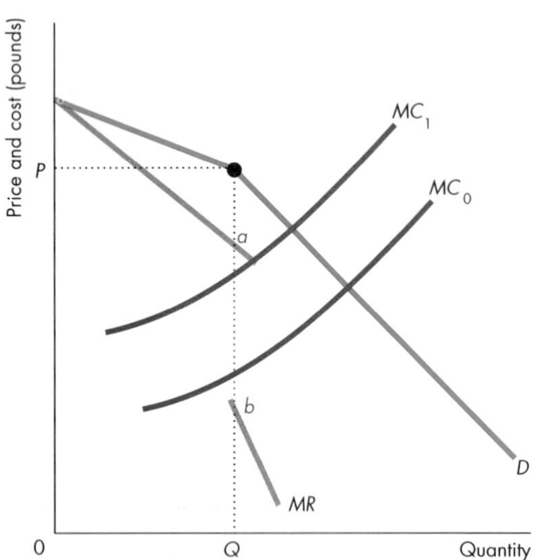

The price in an oligopoly market is *P*. Each firm believes it faces the demand curve *D*. At prices above *P*, demand is highly elastic because the firm believes that its price increases will not be matched by other firms. At prices below *P*, demand is less elastic because the firm believes its price cuts will be matched. Because the demand curve is kinked, the marginal revenue curve, *MR*, has a break *ab*. Profit is maximized by producing *Q*. Marginal cost changes inside the range *ab* leave the price and quantity unchanged.

One problem with the kinked demand curve model is that it does not tell us how price is set. Another problems is that the firm's beliefs about how competitors will react are not always correct, and firms will work this out for themselves. If marginal cost increases by enough to cause the firm to increase it price, and all other firms experience the same cost rise, all firms will increase prices together. Each firm will quickly realize that its previous belief that other firms will not follow a price rise, is false. Any firm that bases its actions on beliefs that are wrong will not maximize profit and may even make economic losses.

The kinked demand curve model is an attempt to understand price and output determination in an oligopoly in which the firms are of similar size. Another traditional model deals with the case in which firms differ in size and one firm dominates the industry.

Dominant Firm Oligopoly

A dominant firm oligopoly arises when one firm – the dominant firm – has a substantial cost advantage over the other firms and produces a large part of the industry output. The dominant firm sets the market price and the other firms are price takers. An example of a dominant firm oligopoly is a large petrol retailer or a big video rental company that dominates its local market.

To see how a dominant firm oligopoly works, suppose that 11 firms operate petrol stations in a city. Big-G is the dominant firm. It sells 50 per cent of the city's petrol. The other firms are small and each sells 5 per cent of the city's petrol.

Figure 14.5 shows the market for petrol in this city. In part (a), the demand curve D tells us how the total quantity of petrol demanded in the city is influenced by its price. The supply curve S_{10} is the supply curve of the 10 small suppliers. These firms are price takers.

Part (b) shows the situation facing Big-G. Its marginal cost curve is MC, its demand curve is XD, and its marginal revenue curve is MR. Big-G's demand curve shows the excess demand not met by the 10 other small firms. For example, at a price of 50 pence a litre, the market quantity demanded is 20,000 litres per week. The 10 small firms supply 10,000 litres, and the excess quantity demanded is 10,000 litres, measured by the distance ab in part (a). The distance ab determines Big-G's demand at the price 50 pence a litre as shown in part (b).

To maximize its profit, Big-G operates like a monopoly. It sells 10,000 litres of petrol for 50 pence a litre. This price and quantity of sales gives Big-G the biggest possible profit. The 10 small firms take the price of 50 pence a litre and behave like firms in perfect competition. The quantity of petrol demanded in the entire city at 50 pence a litre is 20,000 litres, as shown in part (a). Of this amount, 10,000 litres are sold by Big-G and 10,000 litres are sold by the 10 small firms which sell 1,000 litres each.

The dominant firm model of oligopoly works for markets in which there is a producer that has a cost advantage over all the other firms. But the model doesn't explain why the dominant firm has a cost advantage or what happens if some of the smaller firms acquire the same technology and costs as the dominant firm. Also it does not predict prices and quantities in markets in which firms are of similar size.

Figure 14.5 A Dominant Firm Oligopoly

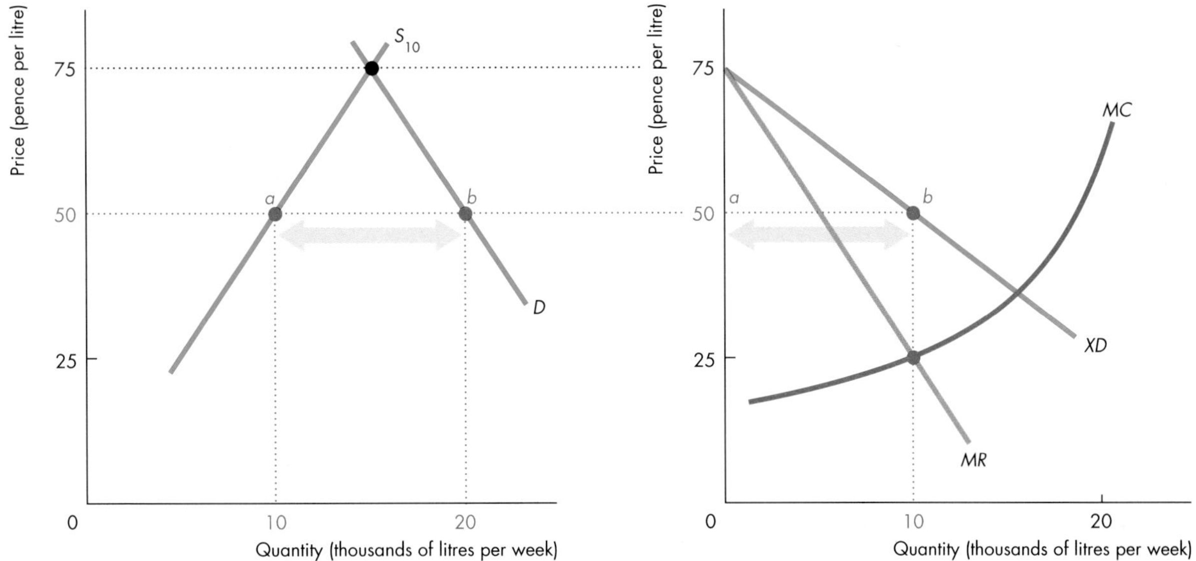

(a) Ten small firms and market demand

(b) Big-G's price and output decision

The demand curve for petrol in a city is *D* in part (a). There are 10 small competitive firms which together have a supply curve of S_{10}. In addition, there is one large firm, Big-G, shown in part (b). Big-G faces the demand curve, *XD*, determined as market demand *D* minus the supply of the other firms S_{10} – the demand that is not satisfied by the small firms. Big-G's marginal revenue is *MR* and marginal cost is *MC*. Big-G sets its output to maximize profit by equating marginal cost, *MC*, and marginal revenue, *MR*. This output is 10,000 litres. The price at which Big-G can sell this quantity is 50 pence a litre. The other 10 firms take this price and each firm sells 1,000 litres.

Review

- In the kinked demand curve model, the firm faces a demand curve with a kink at the current price, and a break in the marginal revenue schedule. The model predicts that price and output are insensitive to small changes in costs.
- In the dominant firm model, the dominant firm acts like a monopoly and sets its price. The other firms take this price and act like competitive firms.

The traditional theories of oligopoly are limited and do not enable us to understand all oligopoly markets. In recent years, economists have developed some interesting new oligopoly models based on game theory. Let's look at these now.

Game Theory

Game theory is a method of analysing *strategic behaviour* – behaviour that takes into account the expected behaviour of others and the mutual recognition of interdependence. Game theory was invented by John von Neumann in 1937 and extended by von Neumann and Oskar Morgenstern in 1944. Today it is a major research field in economics. You can read about John von Neumann in *Economics in History* on pp. 348–349.

Game theory seeks to understand oligopoly as well as political and social rivalries by using a method of decision analysis specifically designed to understand games of all types, including the familiar games of everyday life. We will begin our study of game theory, and its application to the behaviour of firms, by considering those familiar games.

Familiar Games: What They Have in Common

What is a game? At first thought, the question seems silly. After all, there are many different games. There are ball games and board games, games of chance and games of skill. What do games of such diversity and variety have in common? In answering this question, we will focus on those features of games that are relevant for game theory and for analysing oligopoly as a game. All games have three things in common:

1 Rules.

2 Strategies.

3 Payoffs.

Let's see how these common features of games apply to a game called 'the prisoners' dilemma'. This game, it turns out, captures some of the essential features of oligopoly and it gives a good illustration of how game theory works and how it leads to predictions about the behaviour of the players.

The Prisoners' Dilemma

John and Bob have been caught red-handed stealing a car. Facing airtight cases, they will receive a sentence of 2 years each for their crime. During her interviews with the prisoners, the arresting police officer begins to suspect the two men were responsible for a multimillion-pound bank robbery some months earlier. But, the police officer knows she cannot charge the suspects of the greater crime unless she can get each of them to confess to it. She decides to adopt a new interview strategy that can be represented by a game with the following rules.

Rules Each prisoner (player) is placed in a separate room and there is no communication between them. Each is told that he is suspected of having carried out the bank robbery and that if both he and his accomplice confess to the larger crime, each will receive sentences of 3 years; if he alone confesses and his accomplice does not, he will receive an even shorter sentence of 1 year while his accomplice will receive a 10-year sentence.

Strategies In game theory, as in ordinary games, **strategies** are all the possible actions of each player. The strategies in the prisoners' dilemma game are very simple. Each prisoner (player) can do only one of two things:

1 Confess to the bank robbery.

2 Deny having committed the bank robbery.

Payoffs Because there are two players, each with two strategies, there are four possible outcomes.

1 Neither player confesses.

2 Both players confess.

3 John confesses but Bob does not.

4 Bob confesses but John does not.

Each prisoner can work out exactly what will happen to him – his *payoff* – in each of these four situations. We can tabulate the four possible payoffs for each of the prisoners in what is called a payoff matrix for the game. A **payoff matrix** is a table that shows the payoffs for every possible action by each player for every possible action by each other player.

Table 14.3 shows a payoff matrix for John and Bob. The squares show the payoffs for each prisoner – the red triangle in each square shows John's and the blue triangle Bob's. If both prisoners confess (top-left), they each get a prison term of 3 years. If Bob confesses but John denies (top-right), John gets a 10-year sentence and Bob gets a 1-year sentence. If John confesses and Bob denies (bottom-left), John gets a 1-year sentence and Bob gets a 10-year sentence. Finally, if both of them deny (bottom-right), neither can be convicted of the bank robbery charge but both are sentenced for the car theft – a 2-year sentence.

The Dilemma The dilemma arises as each prisoner contemplates the consequences of denying. Each prisoner knows that if both of them deny, they will only be sentenced to 2 years. But neither prisoner has any way of knowing that his accomplice will deny. Each prisoner asks himself the following question: should I deny and rely on my acomplice to deny in the hope that we both get 2 years? Or should I confess in the hope that if my accomplice denies, I will only get 1 year, but knowing that if he confesses as well, we will both get 3 years in prison. The dilemma is resolved by finding the equilibrium for the game.

Equilibrium The equilibrium of a game is when player A takes the best possible action given the action of player B, and player B takes the best possible action given the action of player A. In the prisoners' dilemma, the equilibrium occurs when John makes his best choice, given Bob's choice, and

Table 14.3 Prisoners' Dilemma Payoff Matrix

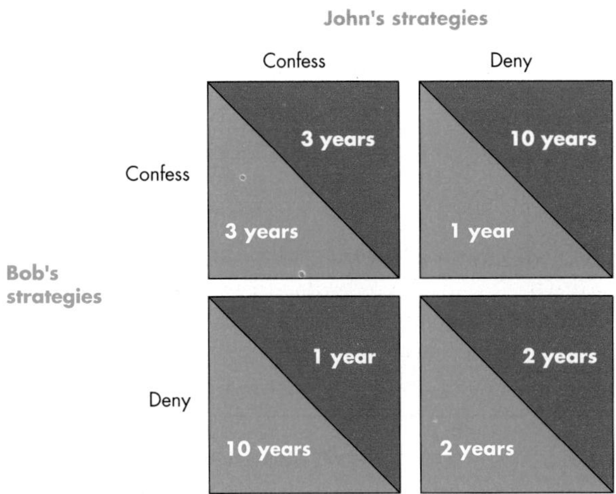

Each square shows the payoffs for the two players, John and Bob, for each possible pair of actions. In each square, John's payoff is shown in the red triangle and Bob's in the blue triangle. For example, if both confess, the payoffs are in the top-left square. John reasons as follows: if Bob confesses, I should confess because then I get 3 years rather than 10. If Bob denies, I should confess because then I get 1 year rather than 2. Regardless of what Bob does, I should confess. John's dominant strategy is to confess. Bob reasons similarly. Since each player's dominant strategy is to confess, the equilibrium of the game is for both players to confess and each to get 3 years.

Bob makes his best choice, given John's choice. Let's find the equilibrium of the prisoners' dilemma game.

Look at the situation from John's point of view. John realizes that his outcome depends on the action Bob takes. If Bob confesses, it pays John to confess also, for in that case, he will be sentenced to 3 years rather than 10 years. But if Bob does not confess, it still pays John to confess for in that case he will receive 1 year rather than 2 years. John reasons that regardless of Bob's action, his own best action is to confess.

Now look at the dilemma from Bob's point of view. Bob knows that if John confesses, he will receive 10 years if he does not confess or 3 years if he does. Therefore if John confesses, it pays Bob to confess. Similarly, if John does not confess, Bob will receive 2 years for not confessing and 1 year if he confesses. Again, it pays Bob to confess. Bob's best action, regardless of John's action, is to confess.

Each prisoner's best action is to confess. The equilibrium of the game is that both prisoners confess. The crime is solved and both prisoners get a 3-year sentence.

Nash Equilibrium and Dominant Strategies

An equilibrium when each player takes the best possible action, given the action of the other player, is called a **Nash equilibrium**. It is named after Nobel Prize winner, John Nash, who proposed the equilibrium for this game. The prisoners' dilemma has a special kind of Nash equilibrium called a dominant strategy equilibrium. A *dominant strategy* is a strategy that is the same regardless of the action taken by the other player. In other words, there is a unique best action regardless of what the other player does. A **dominant strategy equilibrium** occurs when there is a dominant strategy for each player.

A Bad Outcome For the prisoners, the equilibrium of the game, with each confessing, is not the best outcome. If neither of them confesses, each will get only 2 years for the lesser crime. Isn't there some way in which this better outcome can be achieved? It seems that there is not, because the players cannot communicate with each other since they are interviewed separately. Each player can put himself in the other player's place, and so each player can figure out that there is a dominant strategy for each of them. The prisoners are indeed in a dilemma. Each knows that he can serve 2 years only if he can trust the other not to confess. But each prisoner also knows that it is not in the best interest of the other not to confess. Thus each prisoner knows that he has to confess, thereby delivering a bad outcome for both.

Let's now see how we can use the ideas we've just developed to understand price fixing, price wars and the behaviour of firms in oligopoly.

Oligopoly Price Fixing Game

To understand how oligopolies fix price, we are going to study a special case of oligopoly, called duopoly. **Duopoly** is a market structure in which there are two producers of a commodity competing with each other. There are few cases of duopoly on a national and international scale but many cases of local duopolies, such as, two car rental firms or two university bookshops. But the main reason for studying duopoly is not its 'realism'. It is the fact

Figure 14.6 Costs and Demand

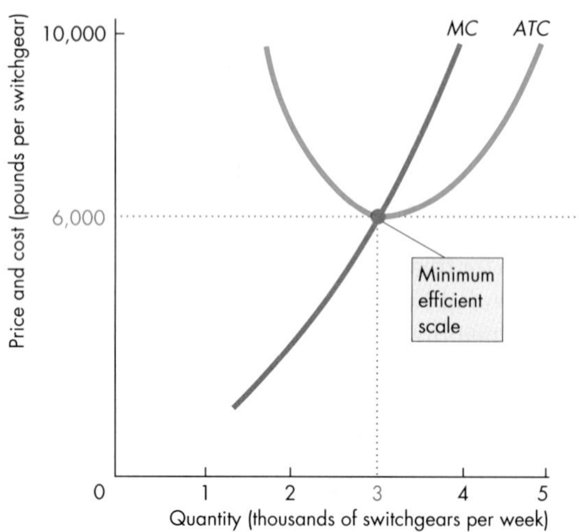

(a) Individual firm

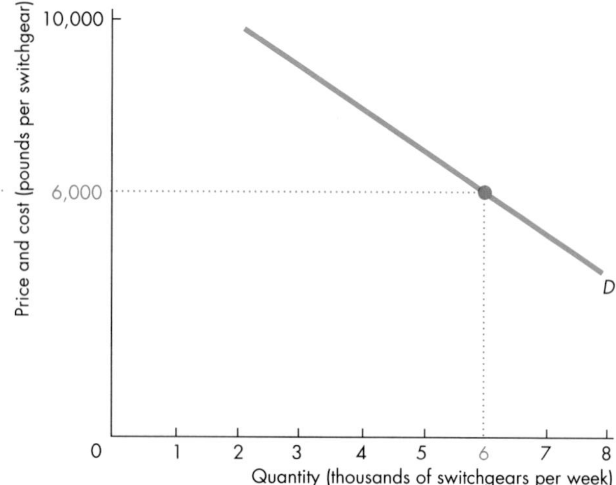

(b) Industry

Part (a) shows the costs facing Trick and Gear, two duopolists which make switchgears. Each firm faces identical costs. The average total cost curve for each firm is *ATC* and the marginal cost curve is *MC*. For each firm the minimum efficient scale of production is 3,000 switchgears a week and the average total cost of producing that output is £6,000 a unit. Part (b) shows the industry demand curve. At a price of £6,000, the quantity demanded is 6,000 switchgears per week. There is room for only two firms in this industry.

that it captures all the essential features of oligopoly, but remains simple.

We want to be able to predict prices charged and quantities produced by two firms in a duopoly. We'll do this by building a model of a duopoly industry and then creating a duopoly game.

Suppose that only two firms, Trick and Gear, make a particular kind of electric switchgear. Both firms enter into a collusive agreement. A **collusive agreement** is an agreement between two (or more) producers to restrict output to raise prices and profits. Such an agreement is illegal in the United Kingdom and under EU rules and is undertaken in secret. A group of firms that has entered into a collusive agreement to restrict output and increase prices and profits is called a **cartel**. The strategies that firms in a cartel can pursue are to:

1 Comply.
2 Cheat.

Complying simply means sticking to the agreement. Cheating means breaking the agreement in a manner designed to benefit the cheating firm.

Because each firm has two strategies, there are four possible combinations of actions for the two firms:

1 Both firms comply.
2 Both firms cheat.
3 Trick complies and Gear cheats.
4 Gear complies and Trick cheats.

We need to work out the payoffs to each firm from each of these four possible sets of actions. To do that we need to explore the costs and demand conditions in the industry.

Cost and Demand Conditions

Trick and Gear face identical costs and Figure 14.6(a) shows their average total cost curve (*ATC*) and the marginal cost curve (*MC*). The market demand curve for switchgears (*D*) is shown in Figure 14.6(b). Each firm produces an identical switchgear product, so one firm's switchgear is a perfect substitute for the other's. The market price of each firm's product, therefore, is identical. The quantity

Figure 14.7 Colluding to Make Monopoly Profits

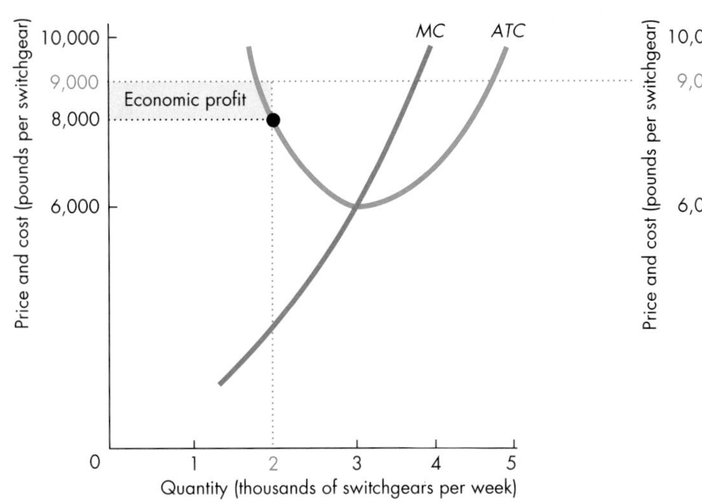

(a) Individual firm

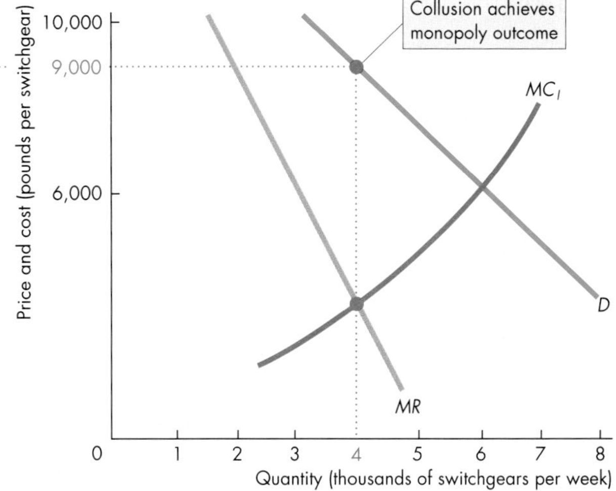

(b) Industry

If Trick and Gear come to a collusive agreement, they can act as a single monopolist and maximize profit. To maximize profit, the firms first calculate the industry marginal cost curve, MC_I (part b), which is the horizontal sum of the two firms' marginal cost curves, *MC* (part a). Next they calculate the industry marginal revenue, *MR*. They then choose the output rate that makes marginal revenue equal to marginal cost (4,000 switchgears per week). They agree to sell that output for a price of £9,000, the price at which 4,000 switchgears are demanded.

Each firm has the same costs, so each produces half the total output – 2,000 switchgears per week. Average total cost is £8,000 per unit, so each firm makes an economic profit of £2 million (blue rectangle) – 2,000 switchgears multiplied by £1,000 profit per unit.

demanded depends on that price – the higher the price, the lower is the quantity demanded.

In our example, there is room for only two firms in the industry. For each firm the *minimum efficient scale* of production is 3,000 switchgears a week. When the price equals the average total cost of production at the minimum efficient scale, total industry demand is 6,000 switchgears a week.

Colluding to Maximize Profits

We can now work out the payoffs to the two firms. Let's start by looking at the payoff if they both collude to make the maximum industry profit by acting like a monopoly. The calculations that the two firms will perform are exactly the same calculations that a monopoly performs. (You studied these calculations in Chapter 13, pp. 294–302.) The only additional thing that the duopolists have to do is to agree on how much of the total output each of them will produce.

Figure 14.7 shows the price and quantity that maximizes industry profit for the duopolists. Part (a) shows the situation for each firm and part (b) for the industry as a whole. The curve labelled *MR* is the industry marginal revenue curve. The curve labelled MC_I is the industry marginal cost curve if each firm produces the same level of output. That curve is constructed by adding together the outputs of the two firms at each level of marginal cost. That is, at each level of marginal cost, industry output is twice as much as the output of each individual firm. Thus the curve MC_I in part (b) is twice as far to the right as the curve *MC* in part (a).

To maximize industry profit, the duopolists agree to restrict output to the rate that makes the industry marginal cost and marginal revenue equal. That output rate, as shown in part (b), is 4,000 switchgears a week. The highest price for which the 4,000 switchgears can be sold is £9,000 each. Let's suppose that Trick and Gear agree to split the market equally so that each firm produces 2,000 switchgears a week. The average total cost (*ATC*) of producing 2,000 switchgears a week is £8,000, so the profit per unit is £1,000 and economic profit is

Figure 14.8 One Firm Cheats

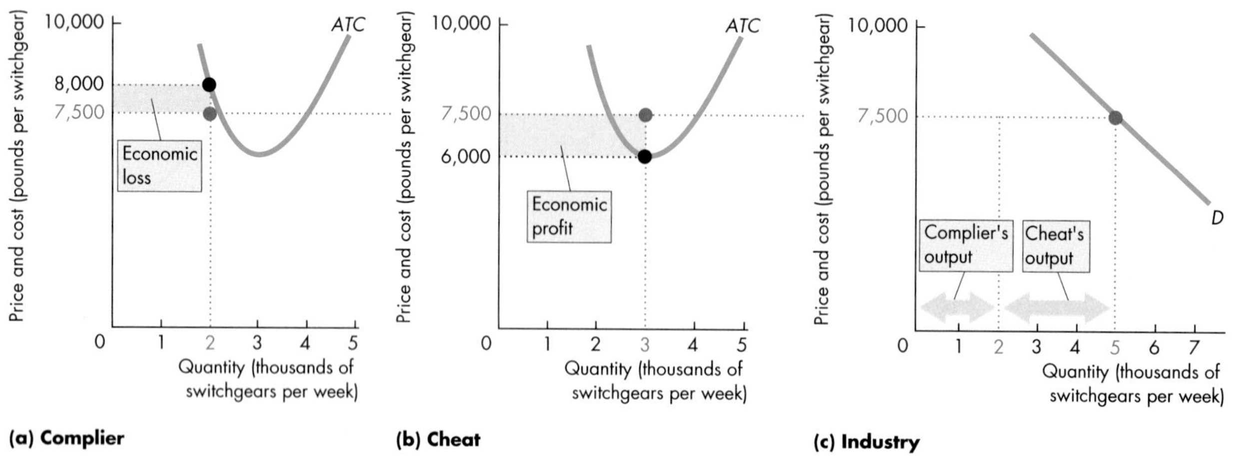

One firm, shown in part (a), complies with the agreement and produces 2,000 switchgears. The other firm, shown in part (b), cheats on the agreement and increases production to 3,000 switchgears. Given the market demand curve, shown in part (c), and with a total production of 5,000 switchgears a week, the market price falls to £7,500. At this price, the complier in part (a) incurs an economic loss of £1 million (£500 × 2,000 units) shown as the red rectangle. In part (b), the cheat makes an economic profit of £4.5 million (£1,500 × 3,000 units), shown as the blue rectangle.

£2 million (2,000 switchgears × £1,000 per unit). The economic profit of each firm is represented by the blue rectangle in Figure 14.7(a).

We have just described one possible outcome for the duopoly game: the two firms collude to produce the monopoly profit-maximizing output and divide that output equally between themselves. From the industry point of view, this solution is identical to a monopoly. A duopoly that operates in this way is indistinguishable from a monopoly. The economic profit that is made by a monopoly is the maximum total profit that can be made by colluding duopolists.

One Firm Cheats on a Collusive Agreement

In any a collusive agreement, there is often an incentive to cheat. For example, if one firm can cut its price when the other firm does not, more will be added to revenue than to costs, so profit for the cheating firm will increase. Let's look at how this might happen.

Suppose Trick convinces Gear that industry demand has fallen and that it cannot sell its share of the output at the agreed price. It tells Gear that it plans to cut its price in order to sell the agreed 2,000 switchgears each week. Because the two firms produce a virtually identical product, Gear matches Trick's price cut, but still produces just 2,000 units a week.

In fact, there has been no fall in demand. Trick plans to increase output, which it knows will lower the price, and Trick wants to ensure that Gear's output remains at the agreed level of 2,000 units.

Figure 14.8 illustrates the consequences of Trick cheating in this way. Suppose that Trick decides to cheat. Trick raises output from 2,000 to 3,000 switchgears a week – the output at which average total cost is minimized. If Gear sticks to the agreement and produces only 2,000 switchgears a week, total output will be 5,000 a week. Given the industry demand shown in part (c), the price will have to be cut to £7,500 a unit.

Gear continues to produce 2,000 switchgears a week at a cost of £8,000 a unit, and incurs a loss of £500 a unit or £1 million a week. This loss is shown as the red rectangle in part (a). Trick produces 3,000 switchgears a week at an average total cost of £6,000 each. With a price of £7,500, Trick makes a profit of £1,500 a unit and an economic profit of £4.5 million. This economic profit is shown as the blue rectangle in part (b).

We've now described a second possible outcome for the duopoly game – one of the firms cheats on the collusive agreement. In this case, the industry

Figure 14.9 Both Firms Cheat

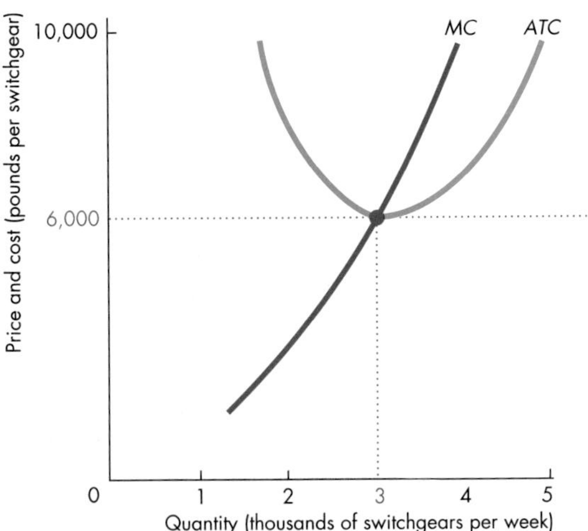

(a) Individual firm

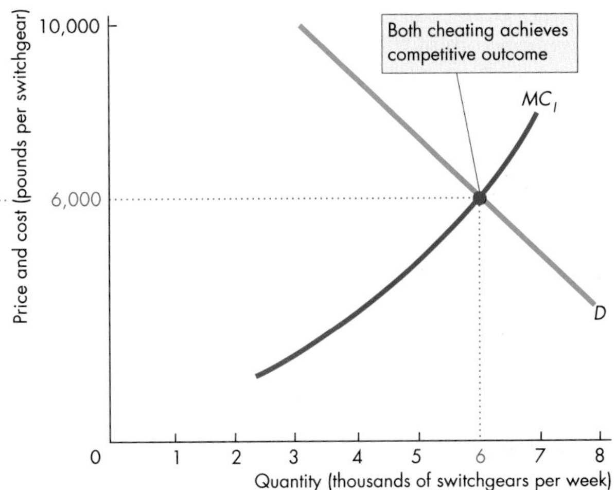

(b) Industry

If both firms cheat by raising their output and lowering the price, the collusive agreement completely breaks down. The limit to the breakdown of the agreement is the competitive equilibrium. Neither firm will want to cut the price below £6,000 (minimum average total cost), for to do so will result in losses. Part (a) shows the situation facing each firm. At a price of £6,000, the firm's profit-maximizing output is 3,000 switchgears per week. At that output rate, price equals marginal cost, and it also equals average total cost. Economic profit is zero. Part (b) describes the situation in the industry as a whole. The industry marginal cost curve (MC_I) – the horizontal sum of the individual firms' marginal cost curves (MC) – intersects the demand curve at 6,000 switchgears per week and at a price of £6,000. This output and price is the one that would prevail in a competitive industry.

output is larger than the monopoly output and the industry price is lower than the monopoly price. The total economic profit made by the industry is also smaller than the monopoly's economic profit. Trick (the cheat) makes an economic profit of £4.5 million and Gear (the complier) incurs a loss of £1 million. The industry makes an economic profit of £3.5 million, which is £0.5 million less than the economic profit a monopoly would make. But that profit is distributed unevenly. Trick makes an even bigger profit than it would under the collusive agreement, while Gear incurs a loss.

A similar outcome that would arise if Gear cheated and Trick complied with the agreement. The industry profit and price would be the same but in this case Gear (the cheat) would make an economic profit of £4.5 million and Trick (the complier) would incur a loss of £1 million.

Both Firms Cheat on a Collusive Agreement

Suppose that instead of just one firm cheating on the collusive agreement, both firms cheat. In particular, suppose that each firm behaves in exactly the same way as the cheating firm that we have just analysed. Each tells the other that it is unable to sell its output at the going price and that it plans to cut its price. But because both firms cheat, each will propose a successively lower price. So long as price exceeds marginal cost, each firm has an incentive to increase its production – to cheat. Only when price equals marginal cost is there no further incentive to cheat. This situation arises when the price has reached £6,000. At this price, marginal cost equals price. Also price equals minimum average cost. At a price of less than £6,000, each firm incurs a loss. At a price of £6,000, each firm covers all its costs and makes zero economic profit – makes normal profit. Also at a price of £6,000, each firm wants to produce 3,000 switchgears a week, so that the industry output is 6,000 switchgears a week. Given the demand conditions, 6,000 switchgears can be sold at a price of £6,000 each.

Figure 14.9 shows the situation just described. Each firm, shown in part (a), is producing 3,000 switchgears a week, and this output level occurs at the point of minimum average total cost (£6,000 per unit). The market as a whole, shown in part (b), operates at the point at which the demand curve (*D*) intersects the industry marginal cost curve. This marginal cost curve is constructed as the horizontal sum of the marginal cost curves of the two firms. Each firm has lowered its price and increased its output in order to try to gain an advantage over the other firm. They have each pushed this process as far as they can without incurring an economic loss.

We have now described a third possible outcome of this duopoly game – both firms cheat. If both firms cheat on the collusive agreement, the output of each firm is 3,000 switchgears a week and the price is £6,000. Each firm makes zero economic profit.

Duopoly Game Payoff Matrix

Now that we have described the strategies and payoffs in the duopoly game, let's summarize the strategies and the payoffs in the form of the game's payoff matrix and then calculate the equilibrium.

Table 14.4 sets out the payoff matrix for this game. It is constructed in exactly the same way as the payoff matrix for the prisoners' dilemma in Table 14.3. The squares show the payoffs for the two firms – Gear and Trick. In this case, the payoffs are profits. (In the case of the prisoners' dilemma, the payoffs were losses.)

The table shows that if both firms cheat (top-left), they achieve the perfectly competitive outcome – each firm makes zero economic profit. If both firms comply (bottom-right), the industry makes the monopoly profit and each firm earns an economic profit of £2 million. The top-right and bottom-left squares show what happens if one firm cheats while the other complies. The firm that cheats collects an economic profit of £4.5 million and the one that complies incurs a loss of £1 million.

This duopoly game is, in fact, the same as the prisoners' dilemma that we examined earlier in this chapter; it is a duopolist's dilemma. You will see this once you have determined what the equilibrium of this game is.

Duopoly Game Equilibrium

To find the equilibrium, let's look at things from the point of view of Gear. Gear reasons as follows. Suppose that Trick cheats. If we comply with the agreement, we incur a loss of £1 million. If we also cheat, we make zero economic profit. Zero economic profit is better than a £1 million loss, so it will pay us to cheat. But suppose Trick complies with the agreement. If we cheat, we will make a profit of £4.5 million, and if we comply, we will make a profit of £2 million. A £4.5 million profit is better than a £2 million profit so it would again pay us to cheat. Thus regardless of whether Trick cheats or complies, it pays us to cheat. Gear's dominant strategy is to cheat.

Trick comes to the same conclusion as Gear. Therefore both firms will cheat. The equilibrium of this game is that both firms cheat on the agreement. Although there are only two firms in the industry, the price and quantity are the same as in a competitive industry. Each firm makes zero economic profit.

Although we have done this analysis for only two firms, it would not make any difference (other than to increase the amount of arithmetic) if we were to play the game with three, four, or more firms. In other words, although we have analysed duopoly,

Table 14.4 Duopoly Payoff Matrix

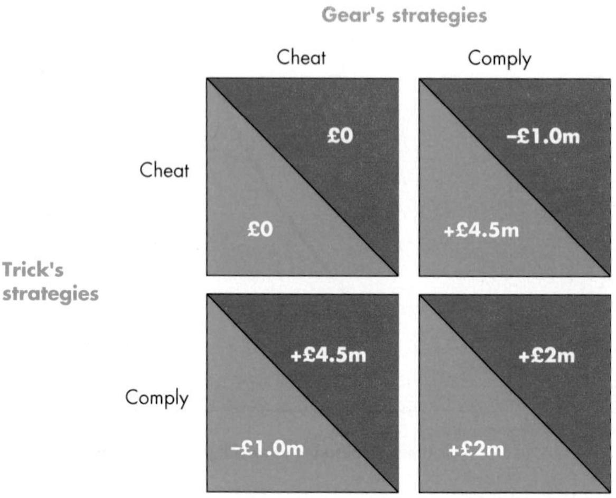

Each square shows the payoffs from a pair of actions. For example, if both firms comply with the collusive agreement, the payoffs are recorded in the square at the bottom-right corner of the table. The red triangle shows Gear's payoff and the blue triangle shows Trick's. The equilibrium is a Nash equilibrium in which both firms cheat.

the game theory approach can also be used to analyse oligopoly. The analysis of oligopoly is much harder, but the essential ideas that we have learned also apply to oligopoly.

Repeated Games

The games we've studied were just played once. By contrast, most real-world duopolists get opportunities to play repeatedly against each other. In fact, real-world duopolists might find some way of learning to cooperate so that their efforts to collude are more effective.

If a game is played repeatedly, one player always has the opportunity to penalize the other player for previous 'bad' behaviour. If Trick refuses to cooperate this week, then Gear can refuse to cooperate next week (and vice versa). If Gear cheats this week, perhaps Trick will cheat next week. Before Gear cheats this week, shouldn't it take account of the possibility of Trick cheating next week? What is the equilibrium of this more complicated prisoners' dilemma game when it is repeated indefinitely?

Actually there is more than one possibility. One is the Nash equilibrium that we have just analysed. Both players cheat with each making zero economic profit forever. In such a situation, it will never pay one of the players to start complying unilaterally, for to do so would result in a loss for that player and a profit for the other. The price and quantity will remain at the competitive levels forever.

But another equilibrium is possible – one in which the players make and share the monopoly profit. How might this equilibrium come about? The key to answering this question is the fact that when a prisoners' dilemma game is played repeatedly, the players have an increased array of strategies. Each player can punish the other player for previous actions.

There are two extremes of punishment. The smallest penalty that one player can impose on the other is what is called 'tit-for-tat'. A *tit-for-tat strategy* is one in which a player cooperates in the current period if the other player cooperated in the previous period, but cheats in the current period if the other player cheated in the previous period. The most severe form of punishment that one player can impose on the other arises in what is called a trigger strategy. A *trigger strategy* is one in which a player cooperates if the other player cooperates, but plays the Nash equilibrium strategy forever thereafter if the other player cheats. Because a tit-for-tat strategy and a trigger strategy are the extremes of punishment – the most mild and most severe – there are evidently other intermediate degrees of punishment. For example, if one player cheats on the agreement, the other player could punish by refusing to cooperate for a certain number of periods. In the duopoly game between Gear and Trick, a tit-for-tat strategy keeps both players cooperating and earning monopoly profits. Let's see why.

If both firms stick to the collusive agreement in period 1, they make an economic profit of £2 million each. Suppose that Trick contemplates cheating in period 2. The cheating produces a quick £4.5 million profit and inflicts a £1 million loss on Gear. Adding up the profits over two periods of play, Trick comes out ahead by cheating (£6.5 million compared with £4 million if it did not cheat). In the next period Gear will hit Trick with its tit-for-tat response and cheat. Both will make zero economic profit in period 3. If Trick reverts to cooperating, to induce Gear to cooperate in period 4, Gear now makes a profit of £4.5 million and Trick incurs a loss of £1 million. Adding up the profits over four periods of play, Trick would have made more profit by cooperating. In that case, its profit would have been £8 million compared with £5.5 million from cheating and generating Gear's tit-for-tat response.

What is true for Trick is also true for Gear. Because each firm makes a larger profit by sticking with the collusive agreement, both firms do so and the monopoly price, quantity and profit prevail in the industry. This equilibrium is called a *cooperative equilibrium* – an equilibrium resulting from each player responding rationally to the credible threat of the other player to inflict heavy damage if the agreement is broken. For this strategy to be credible, each player must recognize that it is in the interest of the other player to respond with a tit-for-tat. The tit-for-tat strategy is credible because if one player cheats, it clearly does not pay the other player to continue complying. So the threat of cheating in the next period is credible and sufficient to support the monopoly equilibrium outcome.

In reality, whether a cartel works like a one-play game or a repeated game, depends primarily on the number of players and the ease of detecting and punishing cheating. The larger the number of players, the more opportunities there are to cheat and not be detected immediately, so the cartel will work more like a repeated game sequence. *Reading*

Between the Lines on pp. 346–347 explores a tit-for-tat strategy as part of a repeated game in supermarket pricing.

Games and Price Wars

The theory of price and output determination under duopoly can help us understand real-world behaviour and, in particular, price wars. Some price wars can be interpreted as the implementation of a tit-for-tat strategy. We've seen that with a tit-for-tat strategy in place, firms have an incentive to stick to the monopoly price. But fluctuations in market demand lead to fluctuations in the monopoly price. This type of price change can be seen by one firm, mistakenly, to be the result of the other firm cheating. To avoid unnecessary cheating, firms might decide to ignore small reductions in price up to a certain level. If a large change in demand occurs and the price falls below the critical value for one firm, that firm will break the agreement and cut the price further. This triggers a retaliation from the other firm. In this case, a type of price war breaks out. The price war ends only when each firm has satisfied itself that the other is ready to cooperate again. The price war is not damaging to the collusive agreement because it maintains the credibility of the tit-for-tat threat. We often see cycles of price wars and the restoration of collusive agreements. Fluctuations in the world price of oil can be interpreted in this way.

Some price wars arise from the entry of a small number of firms into an industry that had been a monopoly. Although the industry has a small number of firms, the firms are in a prisoners' dilemma and they cannot impose effective penalties for price cutting. The behaviour of prices and outputs in the computer chip industry during 1994 and 1995 can be explained in this way. Until 1994, the market for PC chips was dominated by one firm, Intel Corporation, which was able to make maximum economic profit by producing the quantity of chips at which marginal cost equalled marginal revenue. The price of Intel's chips was set to ensure that the quantity demanded equalled the quantity produced. Then, in 1994 and 1995, with the entry of a small number of new firms, the industry became an oligopoly. If the firms had maintained Intel's price and shared the market, together they could have made economic profits equal to Intel's profit. But the firms were in a prisoners' dilemma. So prices tumbled to competitive levels.

Review

- As price exceeds marginal cost, each firm can raise its profit at the expense of the other by cheating on the agreement, and increasing production.
- A collusive agreement to restrict output and raise price (a cartel) can be modelled using a game like the prisoners' dilemma.
- If the game is played once, the cartel agreement breaks down because the equilibrium is the dominant strategy where each firm cheats.
- If the game is played repeatedly, punishment strategies such as tit-for-tat can be used to keep the agreement going.

The game theory model can be extended to deal with a much wider choice of strategies for firms in oligopoly or duopoly industries. Let's look at some examples of these other games.

Other Strategic Variables

Firms have to decide whether to mount expensive advertising campaigns; whether to modify products; whether to improve product reliability; whether to price discriminate and, if so, among which groups of customers and to what degree; whether to undertake a large research and development (R&D) effort aimed at lowering production costs; or whether to enter or leave an industry. All of these choices can be analysed by using game theory. All of these strategic choices can be modelled using game theory. The basic method you have studied can be applied to these problems by working out the payoff for each of the alternative strategies and then finding the equilibrium of the game.

We'll look at two examples: an R&D game and an entry-deterrence game.

An R&D Game

There are two big players in the European disposable nappy market – Procter & Gamble (the maker of Pampers) and Kimberly-Clark (the maker of

Huggies). Procter & Gamble has the largest share, but both firms have about one third of the market. The disposable nappy industry is fiercely competitive. When the product was first introduced, it had to be cost-effective in competition against reusable, laundered nappies. A costly research and development effort resulted in the development of machines that could make disposable nappies at a low enough cost to achieve that initial competitive edge. But as the industry has matured, a large number of firms have tried to get into the business and take market share away from the two industry leaders, and the industry leaders themselves have battled against each other to maintain or increase their own market share.

During the 1990s, Kimberly-Clark was the first to introduce Velcro fasteners. Later on, Procter & Gamble introduced 'breathable' nappies. The key to success in the industry is to design products that parents value highly relative to the cost of producing them. The firm that develops and uses the least-cost technology gains a competitive edge, undercutting the rest of the market, increasing its market share and increasing its profit. But the research and development effort that has to be undertaken to achieve even small cost reductions is itself very costly. The cost of R&D has to be deducted from the profit resulting from the increased market share that lower costs achieve. If no firm conducts R&D, every firm can be better off, but if one firm initiates the R&D activity, all must.

Each firm is in a research and development dilemma that is similar to the game played by John and Bob. Although the two firms play an ongoing game against each other, it has more in common with the one-play game than a repeated game. The reason is that R&D is a long-term process. Effort is repeated, but payoffs occur only infrequently and uncertainly.

Table 14.5 illustrates the dilemma (with hypothetical numbers) for the R&D game that Kimberly-Clark and Procter & Gamble are playing. Each firm has two strategies: to spend £25 million a year on R&D or to spend nothing on R&D. If neither firm spends on R&D, they make a joint profit of £100 million, £30 million for Kimberly-Clark and £70 million for Procter & Gamble (bottom-right square of payoff matrix). If each firm conducts R&D, market shares are maintained but each firm's profit is lower, by the amount spent on R&D (top-left square of payoff matrix). If Kimberly-Clark pays for R&D but Procter & Gamble does not,

Table 14.5 Pampers versus Huggies: An R&D Game

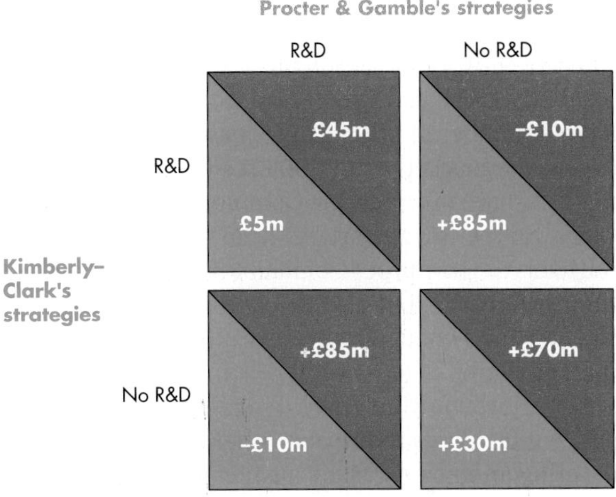

If both firms undertake R&D, their payoffs are those shown in the top-left square. If neither firm undertakes R&D, their payoffs are in the bottom-right square. When one firm undertakes R&D and the other one does not, their payoffs are in the top-right and bottom-left squares. The red triangle shows Procter & Gamble's payoff and the blue triangle shows Kimberly-Clark's. The dominant strategy equilibrium for this game is for both firms to undertake R&D. The structure of this game is the same as that of the prisoners' dilemma.

Kimberly-Clark gains a large part of Procter & Gamble's market. Kimberly-Clark profits and Procter & Gamble loses (top-right square of payoff matrix). Finally, if Procter & Gamble invests in R&D and Kimberly-Clark does not, Procter & Gamble gains market share from Kimberly-Clark, increasing its profit, while Kimberly-Clark incurs a loss (bottom-left square).

Confronted with the payoff matrix in Table 14.5, the two firms calculate their best strategies. Kimberly-Clark reasons as follows. If Procter & Gamble does not undertake R&D, we make £85 million if we do and £30 million if we do not; therefore it pays to conduct R&D. If Procter & Gamble conducts R&D, we lose £10 million if we don't and make £5 million if we do. Again, R&D pays off. Thus conducting R&D is a dominant strategy for Kimberly-Clark. Doing it pays regardless of Procter & Gamble's decision.

Procter & Gamble reasons similarly. So R&D is the dominant strategy for both companies.

Because R&D is a dominant strategy for both players, it is the Nash equilibrium. The outcome of this game is that both firms conduct R&D. They make lower profits than they would if they could collude to achieve the cooperative outcome of no R&D.

The real-world situation has more players than Kimberly-Clark and Procter & Gamble. There are a large number of other firms sharing a small portion of the market, all of them ready to eat into the market share of Procter & Gamble and Kimberly-Clark. So the R&D effort by these two firms not only serves the purpose of maintaining shares in their own battle, but also helps to keep barriers to entry high enough to preserve their joint market share.

Let's now study an entry-deterrence game in which a firm tries to prevent other firms from entering an industry. Such a game is played in a type of market called a contestable market.

Contestable Markets

A **contestable market** is a market in which one firm (or a small number of firms) operates but in which both entry and exit are free so that the firm (or firms) in the market faces perfect competition from *potential* entrants. Examples of contestable markets are routes served by airlines and by private bus companies. These markets are contestable because even though only one or a few firms actually operate on a particular air or bus route, other firms could enter those markets if an opportunity for economic profit arose and could exit those markets if the opportunity for economic profit disappeared. The potential entrance prevents the single firm (or small number of firms) from making an economic profit.

If the five-firm concentration ratio is used to determine the degree of competition, a contestable market appears to be uncompetitive. It looks like an oligopoly or monopoly. But a contestable market behaves as if it were perfectly competitive. You can see why by thinking about a game that we'll call an entry-deterrence game.

Entry-deterrence game In the entry-deterrence game we'll study, there are two players. One player is Better Bus, the only firm operating on a particular route. The other player is Wanabe Co., a potential entrant. The strategies for Better Bus are to set its price at the monopoly profit-maximizing level or at the competitive (zero economic profit) level. The strategies for Wanabe are to enter and set a price just below that of Better Bus or not to enter.

If Wanabe does not enter, Better Bus earns a normal profit by setting a competitive price and earns maximum monopoly profit (a positive economic profit) by setting the monopoly price. If Wanabe does enter and undercuts Better Bus' price, Better Bus incurs an economic loss regardless of whether it sets its price at the competitive or monopoly level. The reason is that Wanabe takes the market with the lower price, so Better Bus incurs a cost but has zero revenue. If Better Bus sets a competitive price, Wanabe earns a normal profit if it does not enter, but incurs an economic loss if it enters and undercuts Better Bus by setting a price that is less than average total cost. If Better Bus sets the monopoly price, Wanabe earns a positive economic profit by entering and a normal profit by not entering.

The Nash equilibrium for this game is a competitive price at which Better Bus earns a normal profit and Wanabe does not enter. If Better Bus raised the price to the monopoly level, Wanabe would enter and by undercutting Better Bus' price would take all the business, leaving Better Bus with an economic loss equal to total cost. Better Bus avoids this outcome by sticking with the competitive price and deterring Wanabe from entering.

Limit Pricing **Limit pricing** is the practice of charging a price below the monopoly profit-maximizing price and producing a quantity greater than that at which marginal revenue equals marginal cost in order to deter entry. The game that we've just studied is an example of limit pricing, but the practice is more general. For example, a firm can use limit pricing to try to convince potential entrants that its own costs are so low that new entrants will incur an economic loss if they enter the industry.

We have now studied the four main market structures – perfect competition, monopolistic competition, oligopoly and monopoly – and discovered how prices and output, revenue, cost and economic profit are determined in these industries. We have used the various models to make predictions about behaviour and to assess the efficiency of alternative market structures. A key element in our analysis of the markets for goods and services is the behaviour of costs. Costs are determined partly by technology and partly by the prices of factors of production. We have treated those factor prices as given. We are now going to see how factor prices are themselves determined. Factor prices interact with the goods market that we have just studied in two ways. First, they determine the firm's production costs. Second, they determine household incomes and therefore influence the demand for goods and services. Factor prices also affect the distribution of income.

The firms that we've been studying in the last four chapters decide *how* to produce; the interactions of households and firms in the markets for goods and services decide *what* will be produced. But the factor prices determined in the markets for factors of production determine *for whom* the various goods and services are produced. We'll study these interactions in the next three chapters.

Summary

Key Points

Varieties of Market Structure (pp. 322–325)

- Monopolistic competition occurs when a large number of firms compete with each other by product differentiation.
- Oligopoly is a market where there are only a small number of producers competing with each other.
- Monopoly power can be measured using a five-firm concentration ratio.

Monopolistic Competition (pp. 325–329)

- Under monopolistic competition, each firm faces a downward-sloping demand curve and sets price.
- In long-run equilibirum, economic profit is zero and firms operate with excess capacity.
- Monopolistic competition is inefficient because marginal cost is less than price, but the inefficiency must be weighed against product variety.

Oligopoly (pp. 329–331)

- If competing firms match price cuts but do not match price increases, firms face a kinked demand curve. Their marginal revenue curve will have a break at the current quantity.
- Fluctuations in marginal cost inside the break in marginal revenue has no effect on price or quantity.
- If one firm dominates the market, it acts like a monopoly and the small firms take its price and act like perfectly competitive firms.

Game Theory (pp. 331–333)

- Game theory is a method of analysing strategic behaviour.
- In the prisoners' dilemma game, two prisoners, each adopt the strategy in their own best interest, but end up not acting in their joint best interest.

Oligopoly Price Fixing Game (pp. 333–340)

- An oligopoly price fixing game is like the prisoners' dilemma game.
- The outcomes are that both firms might collude, one firm might cheat, or both firms might cheat.
- If the game is played just once, the equilibrium is that both firms cheat and the industry output and price are the same as in perfect competition.
- In a repeated game, a tit-for-tat punishment strategy can produce a cooperative equilibrium in which price and output are the same as in a monopoly.

Other Strategic Variables (pp. 340–343)

- Firms face many strategic decisions such as when to enter or leave an industry, and whether to modify a product, which can also be modelled using game theory.

Key Figures and Tables 

Key Terms

Review Questions

1 What are the main varieties of market structure? What are the main characteristics of each of those market structures?

2 What is a five-firm concentration ratio? If the five-firm concentration ratio is 90 per cent, what does that mean?

3 Give some examples of UK industries that have a high concentration ratio and of UK industries that have a low concentration ratio.

4 Explain how a firm can differentiate its product.

5 What is the difference between monopolistic competition and perfect competition?

6 Is monopolistic competition efficient? Explain your answer.

7 What is the difference between duopoly and oligopoly?

8 In what circumstances might the dominant firm model of oligopoly be relevant?

9 List the key features that all games have in common with each other.

10 Why might the demand curve facing an oligopolist be kinked, and what happens to a firm's marginal revenue curve if its demand curve is kinked?

11 What is the prisoners' dilemma?

12 What is a dominant strategy equilibrium?

13 What is the essential feature of both duopoly and oligopoly?

14 What are the features of duopoly that make it reasonable to treat duopoly as a game between two firms?

15 What is meant by a repeated game?

16 Explain what a tit-for-tat strategy is.

17 What is a price war? What is the effect of a price war on the profit of the firms in the industry and on the profitability of the industry itself?

18 What is a contestable market? Will a concentration ratio reveal such a market? How does a contestable market operate?

19 What is limit pricing? How might a firm try to use limit pricing to increase its economic profit?

Problems

1 A monopolistically competitive industry is in long-run equilibrium as illustrated in Figure 14.3(b). Demand for the industry's product increases, increasing the demand for each firm's output. Using diagrams similar to those in Figure 14.3, analyse the short-run and long-run effects on price, output and economic profit of this increase in demand.

2 Another monopolistically competitive industry is in long-run equilibrium, as illustrated in Figure 14.3(b), when it experiences a large increase in wages. Using diagrams similar to those in Figure 14.3, analyse the short-run and long-run effects on price, output and economic profit of this increase in wages.

3 A firm with a kinked demand curve experiences an increase in its variable cost. Explain the effects on the firm's price, output and economic profit/loss.

4 An industry with one large firm and 100 small firms experiences an increase in the demand for its product. Use the dominant firm model to explain the effects on:

a The price, output and economic profit of the large firm.
b The price, output and economic profit of a typical small firm.

5 Describe the game known as the prisoners' dilemma. In describing the game:

a Make up a story that motivates the game.
b Work out a payoff matrix.
c Describe how the equilibrium of the game is arrived at.

6 Consider the following game. There are two players and they are each asked a question. They can answer the question honestly or they can lie. If they both answer honestly, they each receive a payoff of £100. If one answers honestly and the other lies, the liar gains at the expense of the honest player. In that event, the liar receives a profit of £500 and the honest player gets nothing. If they both lie then they each receive a payoff of £50.

a Describe this game in terms of its players, strategies and payoffs.
b Construct the payoff matrix.
c What is the equilibrium for this game?

7 Two firms, Soapy Plc and Suddies Plc, are the only two producers of soap powder. They collude and agree to share the market equally. If neither firm cheats on the agreement, they can each make £1 million profit. If either firm cheats, the cheater can increase its profit to £1.5 million, while the firm that abides by the agreement incurs a loss of £500,000. Neither firm has any way of policing the actions of the other.

a Describe the best strategy for each firm in a game that is played once.
b What is the payoff matrix and equilibrium of a game that is played just once?
c What is the economic profit for each firm if they both cheat?
d If this duopolist game can be played many times, describe some of the strategies that each firm may adopt.

8 Explain the behaviour of the prices of computer chips in 1994 and 1995 by using the prisoners' dilemma game. Describe the types of strategies that individual firms in the industry have adopted.

9 Use the model of oligopoly to explain why producers of pet foods spend so much on advertising.

10 Read the analysis in *Reading Between the Lines*, pp. 346–347, and then explain:

a Why do Procter and Gamble spend huge amounts of money on advertising?
b Do the two companies benefit from adverstising and if so in what way?
c Do consumers benefit from advertising and if so in what way?
d Would there be an efficiency gain from eliminating this type of advertising?

11 Suppose that Netscape and Microsoft each develop their own versions of a great new Web browser that allows advertisers to target consumers with great precision. Also, the new browser is easier and more fun to use than existing browsers. Each firm is trying to decide whether to sell the browser or to give it away free. Explain what the benefits from each action are likely to be and which is more likely to occur.

Oligopoly in Action: Soap Wars

Financial Times, 10 May 1999

Procter & Gamble launches 'soap war' offensive

By John Willman, Consumer Industries Editor

Procter & Gamble will today launch a counter-attack in the UK's long-running soap war with Unilever by announcing the debut of its version of the solid detergent tablets that have restored the fortunes of its archrival Persil.

Ariel Tablets, fresh from a year-long test in Grimsby and Cleethorpes, will be unleashed on the nation's washing machines with a £17.5m marketing campaign designed to show consumers their superiority over Persil Tablets and supermarket own-label versions.

The main purpose of the campaign will be to persuade consumers that Ariel Tablets are so much better than Persil's that they should pay 25 per cent extra for them. This is to help Procter recoup the cost of making what it says is a superior product and not just standard soap powder compressed into a solid version.

Persil Tablets, launched a year ago by Lever Brothers, Unilever's soap powder operation, proved an instant success for the Anglo-Dutch consumer giant. They took almost 10 per cent of the UK detergent market and restored Persil as the number one soap brand. Lever Bros has since added solid versions of its other detergents and launched tablets in other European markets.

The success has been all the sweeter because five years ago the company had been forced to withdraw Persil Power after Procter claimed the reformulated powder damaged fabrics and caused colours to fade.

Tablet detergents have now taken about 15 per cent of the UK market and their success was blamed in January by Procter for falling sales in Europe. But the US group has refused to be panicked and has been quietly working on a reply it believes will outgun Unilever's version.

The Essence of the Story

- Proctor & Gamble and Unilever are engaged in a long running 'soap war', each company trying to capture a larger proportion of the detergent market.
- Proctor & Gamble have just started a £17.5 million marketing campaign to launch their new Ariel tablets. The campaign aims to persuade consumers that Ariel tablets are better than Persil and supermarket label tablets.
- Persil tablets were launched a year ago and took 10 per cent of the detergent market. The new Ariel tablets will cost 25 per cent more than the Persil version.
- Unilever's Persil became the leading brand last year after the Persil tablets were launched. Before this, Ariel was the leading brand following a successful campaign to persuade consumers that Persil rotted clothing.
- Proctor & Gamble have lost market share in the UK and Europe as a result of their late start in the tablet market. But the company believes it will recoup its share and profits because customers will find their version is better.

Economic Analysis

■ Proctor & Gamble and Unilever have duopoly control of the UK detergent markets and do not produce supermarket brands. One other company, Roberts, makes products for the supermarket brands which have less than 10 per cent of the market.

■ Figure 1 shows the share of the two main companies in 1995 after Proctor & Gamble ran a campaign to persuade consumers that Percil damaged clothes and faded colours. As a result, Percil was withdrawn and had to be relaunched. Unilever's market share fell to 37 per cent.

■ Figure 1 also shows that launching the new Percil tablets in 1998 boosted Unilever's share to 50 per cent and cut Proctor & Gamble's share to 40 per cent.

■ The two companies are constantly looking for strategies to raise market share and profits. This is represented as a strategic game in Table 1.

■ If neither company introduces tablets, both save on advertising revenue, market shares are equal and profits rise for both companies by 8 per cent (top-left box). Advertising reduces profits, so if both companies introduce tablets, market shares are equal and economic profits are cut to a 4 per cent (bottom-right box).

■ When Unilever introduced tablets, Proctor & Gamble did not follow and lost market share. Profits increased by 12 per cent for Unilever and fell by 4 per cent for Proctor & Gamble.

■ Proctor & Gamble hope to eliminate Unilever's lead in their new battle in the soap war. All they have to do is make consumers believe that Ariel tablets wash clothes better and are worth the paying 25 per cent more for. This is an example of a tit-for-tat strategy in an ongoing repeated game.

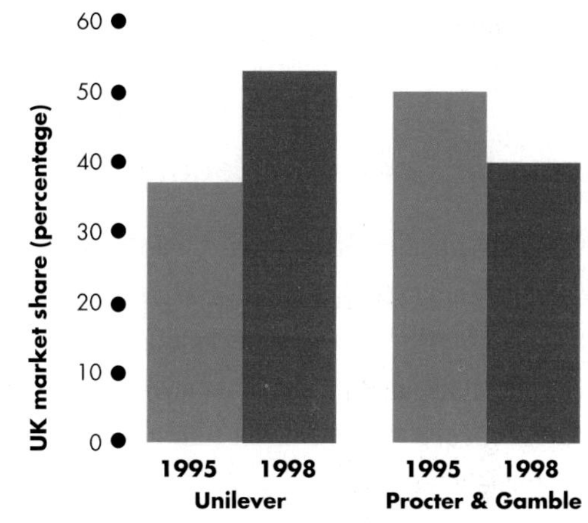

Figure 1 UK detergent market

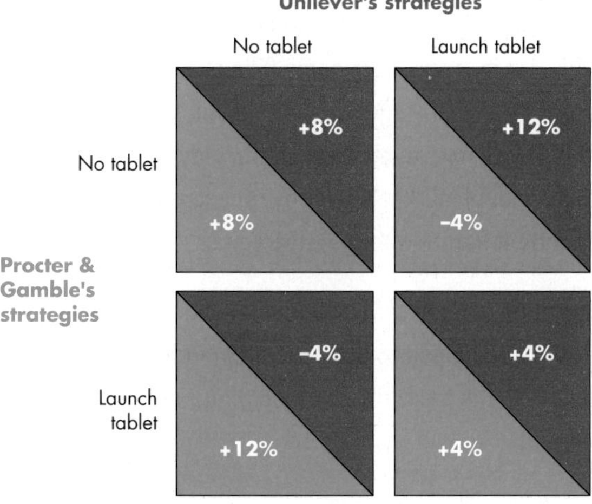

Table 1 A strategic game

Understanding Market Power

"Real life consists of bluffing, of little tactics of deception, of asking yourself what is the other man going to think I mean to do."

John von Neumann *told to Jacob Bronowski (in a London taxi) and reported in The Ascent of Man*

The Economist: John von Neumann

John von Neumann was one of the great minds of the twentieth century. Born in Budapest, Hungary, in 1903, Johnny, as he was known, showed early mathematical brilliance. His first mathematical publication was an article that grew out of a lesson with his tutor, which he wrote at the age of 18.

By the age of 25, in 1928, von Neumann published the article that began a flood of research on game theory – a flood that has still not receded today. In that article, he proved that in a zero-sum game (like sharing a pie), there exists a best strategy for each player. Von Neumann's work has revolutionized the way that economists model market power by focusing on the interdependent nature of firms' strategies.

Von Neumann's brilliance was not confined to economics. He invented and helped to build the first modern practical computer, the basis for so much of our modern technology.

Von Neumann believed that the social sciences would progress only if they used mathematical tools. But he believed that they needed different tools than those developed from the physical sciences.

The Issues and Ideas

It is not surprising that firms with market power will charge higher prices than those charged by competitive firms. But how much higher?

This question has puzzled generations of economists. Adam Smith said "The price of a monopoly is upon every occasion the highest which can be got". But he was wrong. Antoine-Augustin Cournot first worked out the price a monopoly will charge. It is not the "highest which can be got", but the price that maximizes profit. Cournot's work was not appreciated until almost a century later when Joan Robinson explained how a monopoly sets its price.

Questions about monopoly became urgent and practical during the 1870s, a time when rapid technological change and falling transport costs enabled huge monopolies to emerge all over Europe. Monopolies dominated oil, steel, railways, tobacco and even sugar. Industrial empires grew ever larger.

The success of the nineteenth century monopolies led to the creation of our competition laws – laws that limit the use of monopoly power. Those laws have been used to prevent monopolies from being set up and to break up existing monopolies. These laws have been used to investigate the big monopolies in the oil and tobacco industries, the sugar industry and more recently in the 1990s the pharmaceutical industry. They have formed the basis of regulating the privatized state monopolies such as telecommunications and electricity. Despite these efforts, near monopolies still exist. Among the most prominent today are those in computer chips and operating systems. Like their forerunners, today's near monopolies make huge profits. But unlike the situation in the nineteenth century, the technological change taking place today is strengthening the forces of competition. Today's information technologies are creating substitutes for services that previously had none. Direct satellite TV is competing with cable and new phone companies are competing with the traditional phone monopolies.

Then . . .

Ruthless greed, exploitation of both workers and customers – these are the traditional images of monopolies and the effects of their power. These images appeared to be an accurate description during the 1880s, when monopolies were at their peak of power and influence. The power of some monopolies, like British Sugar, was based on exclusive and protected access to colonial resources within the British Empire at the time. The earlier trade in slaves and control of overseas lands brought power and wealth to the monopolies.

. . . And Now

In spite of competition laws that regulate monopolies, monopoly power still exists. British Sugar still controls the vast majority of sugar beet production, sugar processing and refining. The large pharmaceutical companies may only control a 20 per cent share of the total world market, but they exercise complete monopoly over their patented drugs. National telecommunications companies like British Telecommunications (BT) are recording record profits associated with their virtual monopoly control of access lines to the internet. Internet lines are the fastest growing traffic for telecommunications networks and an easy source of monopoly profit in countries with monopoly suppliers of residential local lines. In 1998, The British Monopolies and Merger Commission ordered Vodaphone, Cellnet and BT to cut their prices for calls from BT phones to mobile phones. The regulator believed that consumers were being cheated out of £200 million by the network operators price strategy. But already, competition in these markets is increasing. Computer retailers are moving into the telephone line supply market to offer free internet access and free internet calls. This will start to erode BT's monopoly profit. So BT and other large telecommunications companies have anticipated the threat and are now looking for new ways to maintain profits. The last few years have seen a tide of mergers and merger proposals between telecommunications companies across the world, as well as joint inititiatives between telecommunications companies and software giants like Microsoft. These moves can all be seen as part of an ongoing strategic war for monopoly profit.

Trying These Ideas Today

Using what you have learned about monopoly and oligopoly games in Chapters 13 and 14, and what you know about the development of monopoly power, you should be able to answer the following questions:

- In 1998, BT tried to build a strategic alliance with the US telecommunications giant, AT&T, to pool their resources to become the world's leading provider of services to multinational companies. What do you think was the advantage to BT?
- Why do you think that the European Commission said that it would be investigating the proposed alliance?

Part 5

Resource Markets

Talking with **Frans Somers**

Frans Somers studied Economics and Law at the State University of Groningen, The Netherlands. Since graduation in 1973 he has worked mainly in the field of education. He is now a lecturer in economics and strategic management and also the manager of international projects at the International Business School of the Hanzehogeschool, Groningen. His work involved the setting up of the European Studies Programmes at the Budapest University of Economic Sciences and the Prague University of Economics, as well as the setting up educational establishments and development of economic faculties in Vietnam, Indonesia and Eritrea. He has published several books, amongst others, on political economy, macroeconomics, public finance and government policy. He is the editor of *European Union Economies, a comparative study,* Addison Wesley Longman, 1998.

What are the main microeconomic ideas that you apply in your work?

I am especially interested in economic systems and the role of the market in such systems. How should an economy be run? What is or should be the role of markets in an economy, and to what extent should a government intervene? What conditions should be fulfilled so that markets can produce optimal results? How will the structure of the market affect the business environment? The European Union for instance, an economic entity still under construction, is constantly confronted by these kind of questions.

Do you think that markets are a good way to allocate resources in general?

The market is in principle by far the best and most efficient way to allocate resources. All other methods, turn out to be inferior. According to economic theory, the only justification for government intervention in the economy is market failure, caused by externalities, free-rider problems and monopolies. In reality, many governments – especially in EU countries – went far beyond this idea. They established, took over, or supported industries for other reasons – mainly to get control over the economy or for maintaining employment (in the case of loss-making companies). In most cases this has lead to inefficiencies, distortion of competition, and a waste of government money.

In a way a market economy should be a kind of survival of the fittest: weak companies should disappear and strong ones survive, leading to an efficient economy and an efficient allocation of resources. Governments should not frustrate this process. That is also the whole idea behind the European integration. The EU should be a free and single market, with basically the same rules for all companies.

As taxes can create inefficiency, is there an argument for harmonizing taxes across the European Union?

Fiscal policy is pre-eminently accepted as a matter of national sovereignty in the EU. Whilst markets should not be constrained by taxation, taxes are needed because government has a role in preventing poverty, too much inequality and supplying public goods. To what extend governments should do this, depends on national (political) preferences. The Single Market, nevertheless, requires that the differences in individual tax systems of the member states do not influence the international 'free movement of goods, persons, services and capital'. So some co-ordination of indirect taxation is required.

For direct taxes (taxes on wealth and income), the situation is more complicated. On the one hand, direct taxes affect international competitiveness by increasing the costs of production and influencing the movement of factors of production. On the other hand, revenues from these taxes enable governments to supply a range of public goods and services (for example education, infrastructure and health service), which benefit both individuals and businesses in a country. High levels of taxes may be compensated by high levels of public provision, if public goods are provided efficiently. It can be questioned, therefore, whether a substantial convergence in this field is needed. The Single Market should expose both companies and governments to increased competition, improving the efficiency of both in the long run.

To what extent is the European Union's desire to regulate Europe's labour markets justified?

The single market has led to strongly increased competition and the potential for some governments to encouraging 'social dumping' – the shift of production to places with minimal social standards – by cutting regulation in labour markets. Strongly diverging rules and regulations in this field can distort competition, in a similar way to diverging tax systems. That is why the EU has adopted the Social Charter, which gives guidelines for minimum requirements, such as a maximum working week, a national minimum wage, health protection and safety at the working place and the right of freedom of movement. Some member states, like the UK, are very reluctant to implement these rules, saying that they infringe national sovereignty or that they simply cannot afford them. But even the most ardent supporters of the free market should admit that large differences in social policy contributes to unfair competition. That is why at least some regulation of the labour market is required.

As inequality is a reflection of how markets determine factor incomes, should income be determined by markets?

Factor incomes need to be determined by the market, if we want to have an efficient allocation of resources. The resulting distribution of income will be – by nature – unequally divided. Natural abilities are clearly not the same for everybody, the ownership of assets is unequally spread and chance also plays an important role as well. From an efficiency point of view the market may be superior, but that does not mean that the fairness of the resulting income distribution cannot be questioned. The discussion – in my opinion – should not be whether governments should redistribute incomes, but to what extent and in what way.

What do you think are the most pressing problems facing the European Union in its factor resource markets for the next millennium?

Clearly the most pressing problem for the European Union at the moment is the exceptional high unemployment rate of about 11% (on average); far higher than in the USA (less than 5%) or Japan (3%). It is an enormous waste of resources and a major source of social deprivation. The most important reason for this phenomenon is that the European labour markets do not function properly. Wages do not adjust (in the short term) to demand and supply conditions, for people to find jobs and the system also lacks incentives. Europe gets into a kind of vicious circle: high unemployment coupled with relatively generous benefits result in rising labour costs, which generally lead in turn to higher unemployment. It is in the interest of both employers and employees to break that circle.

Demand and Supply in Factor Markets

After studying this chapter you will be able to:

- Explain how firms choose the quantities of labour, capital and land and natural resources to employ
- Explain how people choose the quantities of labour, capital, land and entrepreneurship to supply
- Explain how wages, interest, rent and normal profit are determined in competitive factor markets
- Explain the concept of economic rent and distinguish between economic rent and opportunity cost

Many Happy Returns

It may not be your birthday, and even if it is chances are you are spending most of it working. But at the end of the week or month (or, if you're devoting all your time to college, when you graduate), you will receive the *returns* from your labour. These returns vary a lot. Julie Adams, who spends her working days as a professional nurse, earns a happy return of £8.20 an hour, about £16,000 a year. Jan Leschly, the chief executive of the pharmaceutical giant, SmithKline Beecham, made a very happy return by increasing his reward package by £20 million in 1999, more than £7,500 an hour! Students working at what have been called McJobs – serving fast food, labouring, or cleaning – earn just a few pounds an hour. Why aren't *all* jobs well-paid? ◆ Most of us have little trouble spending our pay. But most of us do manage to save some of what we earn. What determines the amount of saving that people do and the returns they make on that saving? How do the returns on saving influence the allocation of savings across the many industries and activities that use our capital resources? ◆ Some people receive income from supplying land, but the amount earned varies enormously with its location and quality. For example, an acre of farm land in Devon or Brittany rents for about £1,000 a year while a block of offices in London or Paris rents for several million pounds a year. What determines the rent that people are willing to pay for different blocks of land? Why are rents so enormously high in big cities and so relatively low in the great farming regions of the European Union?

◆ ◆ ◆ ◆ In this chapter we study the markets for resources – the factors of production – labour, capital, land and entrepreneurship. We'll learn how their prices are set and people's incomes are determined.

Factor Prices and Incomes

Goods and services are produced by using the four factors of production – *labour, capital, land* and *entrepreneurship*. (These factors of production are defined in Chapter 3, p. 42) Incomes are determined by the combination of factor prices – the wage rate for labour, the interest rate for capital, the rental rate for land and the rate of normal profit for entrepreneurship – and the quantities of factors used.

In addition to the four factor incomes, a residual income, *economic profit* (or *economic loss*) is paid to (or borne by) firms' owners. A firm's owners might be the suppliers of any of the four factors of production. For a small firm, the owner is usually the entrepreneur. For a large corporation, the owners are the shareholders, who supply the capital.

An Overview of a Competitive Factor Market

We're going to learn how a competitive factor market determines the prices, the quantities used and the incomes of factor suppliers. The tool that we will use is the demand and supply model.

The quantity demanded of a factor depends on its price, and the law of demand applies to factors just as it does to goods and services. The lower the price of a factor, other things remaining the same, the greater is the quantity demanded. Figure 15.1 shows the demand curve for a factor of production as the curve labelled *D*.

The quantity supplied of a factor also depends on its price. With a possible exception that we'll identify later in this chapter, the law of supply applies to factors of production. The higher the price of a factor of production, other things remaining the same, the greater is the quantity supplied of the factor. Figure 15.1 shows the supply curve of a factor as the curve labelled *S*.

The equilibrium factor price is determined at the point of intersection of the factor demand and factor supply curves. Figure 15.1 shows such an equilibrium. *PF* is the factor price and *QF* is the quantity of the factor used.

The income earned by a factor of production is its price multiplied by the quantity used. In Figure 15.1 factor income is the blue rectangle in the figure. This income is the total income received by the factor. Each person supplying a factor receives the resource price multiplied by the quantity supplied. Changes in demand and supply change the equilibrium price and quantity, and also change the income received.

An increase in demand for a factor shifts the demand curve rightward, increasing price, quantity and income. An increase in supply shifts the supply curve rightward and decreases price. The quantity used increases and factor income can increase, decrease or remain constant. The change in income that results from an increase in supply depends on the elasticity of demand for the factor. If demand is elastic, income rises; if demand is inelastic, income falls, and if demand is unit elastic, income remains constant (see Chapter 5, pp. 96–106).

The rest of this chapter explores more closely the impact of changes in demand and supply on factors of production. We're also going to study the influences on the elasticities of supply and demand for factors. These elasticities are important because of their effects on factor prices and the incomes earned.

Let's begin by studying the market for labour. Most of what we learn about the market for labour

Figure 15.1 Demand and Supply in a Factor Market

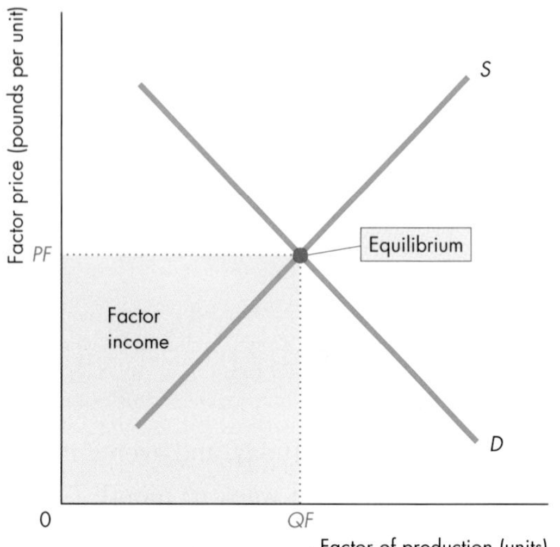

The demand curve for a factor of production (*D*) slopes downward and the supply curve (*S*) slopes upward. Where the demand and supply curves intersect, the factor price (*PF*) and the quantity of a factor used (*QF*) are determined. The factor income is the product of the factor price and the quantity of the factor, as represented by the blue rectangle.

Table 15.1 Real Wage Rate Growth in Europe (%)

Year	France	Italy	Spain	Sweden	UK
1965	3	4	6	–	3
1970	5	7	3	7	6
1975	5	2	5	–4	4
1980	3	1	3	–4	0
1985	1	1	–1	1	3
1990	2	1	1	–2	2
1994	0	0	0	1	0

Real wage growth rates have been positive in most years in most countries. Real wages have risen but the rate of increase has slowed to almost zero.

Source: Adapted from G. Bertola and A. Ichino (1995), *Economic Policy*, Vol. 21, October, 1995.

Figure 15.2 Labour Market Trends in Europe

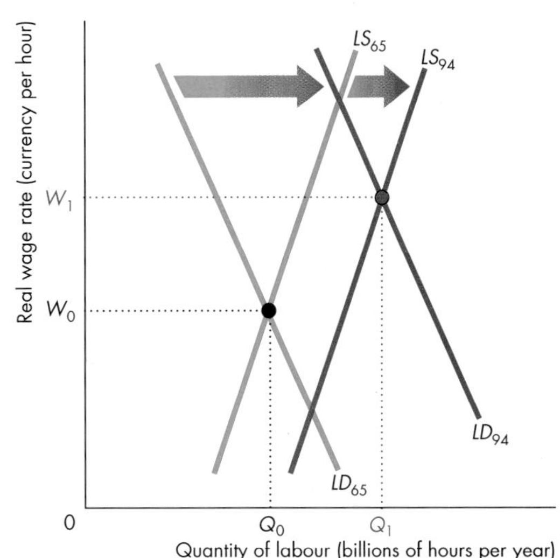

Between 1965 and 1994, the real wage rate has risen in most Western European countries. The quantity of labour employed has also risen. This is the result of an increase in labour demanded and a smaller increase in labour supplied.

will also apply to other factor markets considered later in the chapter.

Labour Markets

Most people get the majority of their income from labour markets, so changes in the price of labour, or the wage, have an important effect on household incomes and expenditure. We expect wages to rise over time to keep pace with inflation. In fact real wages, taking out the effect of inflation, have risen in most European countries over the past 30 years. Table 15.1 shows the annual growth rates of real wages in different European countries has been positive in most years. Real wages have risen over time, but the rate of increase has slowed to almost zero in some countries in recent years. In most countries, the total number of hours worked has increased, but in others, like the UK, the total number of hours worked has not risen on average over the period.

Figure 15.2 shows why these trends have occurred in most European countries. The demand for labour has increased from LD_{65} to LD_{94}, and the labour supply increased, but by much less, from LS_{65} to LS_{94}. The combined effect is that the real wage rises over time, but the number of hours worked increased by a smaller proportion.

Of course, these figures are average wages. Not all labour markets have rising real wages. Real wages have fallen for some types of worker. To understand the trends in labour markets, we must investigate the forces that influence the demand and supply of labour. This chapter studies these forces (and we take a deeper look in Chapter 16). Let's begin with the demand for labour.

The Demand for Labour

The demand for labour is a derived demand. A **derived demand** is a demand for an item not for its own sake but in order to use it in the production of goods and services. A firm's demand for labour (and its demand for all other factor inputs) stems from its profit-maximization decision. The demand for a rock musician is derived from the demand for recordings and performances. However, as the cartoon shows, you may have to wait many years to achieve the marginal revenue of a rock star.

You learned in Chapters 12, 13, and 14 that a profit-maximizing firm produces the output at which marginal cost equals marginal revenue.

Source: *The Guardian*, 12 June 1999.

This principle holds true whether the firm is in a perfectly competitive industry, in monopolistic competition, in oligopoly or a monopoly.

A firm that maximizes profit hires the quantity of labour that can produce the profit maximizing output. What is that quantity of labour and how does it change as the wage rate changes? We can answer these questions by comparing the marginal revenue earned by hiring an extra worker with the marginal cost of hiring that worker. Let's look first at the marginal revenue side of this comparison.

Marginal Revenue Product

The change in total revenue resulting from employing one worker, holding the quantity of all other factors constant, is called **marginal revenue product**. Table 15.2 shows you how to calculate marginal revenue product for a perfectly competitive firm.

The first two columns show the total product schedule for Max's Wash 'n' Wax car wash business. (Look back to p. 239 to refresh your memory on total product.) The total product schedule tells us how the number of car washes per hour varies as the quantity of labour increases.

The third column shows the marginal product of labour. This is the change in output that results when an extra unit of labour is employed. (Look back at p. 239 to refresh your memory on marginal product.)

The car wash market is perfectly competitive, and let's assume the market price is £4. Max can sell as many washes as he chooses at the price of £4. Given this information, we can calculate Max's total revenue (fourth column) by multiplying the number of cars washed each hour by £4. For example, if 9 cars are washed each hour (row *c*), total revenue is £36.

The fifth column shows the calculation of marginal revenue product of labour – the change in total revenue per unit change in labour. For example, if Max hires a second worker (row *c*), total revenue increases from £20 to £36, so the marginal revenue product of labour is £16.

There is another way to calculate the marginal revenue product of labour. The marginal product of labour tells us how many washes an additional worker produces. Marginal revenue tells us the change in total revenue from selling one more wash. So an additional worker changes total revenue by an amount that equals marginal product multiplied by marginal revenue. That is, marginal revenue product equals marginal product multiplied by marginal revenue. For a perfectly competitive firm, marginal revenue equals price, so marginal revenue product equals marginal product multiplied by price.

To see that this method works, let's use the numbers in Table 15.2. Multiply the marginal product of hiring a second worker – 4 cars an hour – by marginal revenue – £4 a car – and notice that the answer is £16, the same as we have already calculated.

Diminishing Marginal Revenue Product As the quantity of labour rises, the marginal revenue product of labour falls. When Max hires the first worker, the marginal revenue product of labour is £20. If Max hires a second worker, the marginal revenue product of labour is £16. Marginal revenue product of labour continues to decline as Max hires more workers.

Marginal revenue product diminishes as Max hires more workers because of the principle of diminishing returns that we first studied in Chapter 11. With each additional worker hired, the marginal product of labour falls and so brings in a smaller marginal revenue product. Because Max's Wash 'n' Wax is a perfectly competitive firm, the price of each additional car wash is the same and brings in the same marginal revenue.

If Max had a monopoly in car washing, he would have to lower his price to sell more washes. In the monopoly case, the marginal revenue product of labour diminishes even more quickly than in perfectly competitive conditions.

Table 15.2 Marginal Revenue Product at Max's Wash 'n' Wax

	Quantity of labour L (workers)	Output Q (cars washed per hour)	Marginal product $MP = \Delta Q/\Delta L$ (washes per worker)	Total revenue $TR = P \times Q$ (pounds)	Marginal revenue product $MRP = \Delta TR/\Delta L$ (pounds per worker)
a	0	0		0	
			5		20
b	1	5		20	
			4		16
c	2	9		36	
			3		12
d	3	12		48	
			2		8
e	4	14		56	
			1		4
f	5	15		60	

The marginal revenue product of labour is the change in total revenue that results from a unit increase in labour. Max operates in a perfectly competitive car wash market and can sell any quantity of washes at £4 a wash. To calculate marginal revenue product, first work out total revenue. If Max hires 1 worker (row *b*), output is 5 washes an hour, and total revenue is £20. If he hires 2 workers (row *c*), output is 9 washes an hour and total revenue is £36. By hiring the second worker, total revenue rises by £16 – the marginal revenue product of labour is £16.

The Labour Demand Curve

Figure 15.3 shows how the labour demand curve is derived from the marginal revenue product curve. The *marginal revenue product curve* graphs the marginal revenue product of a factor at each quantity of the factor hired. Figure 15.3(a) illustrates the marginal revenue product curve for workers employed by Max. The horizontal axis measures the number of workers that Max hires and the vertical axis measures the marginal revenue product of labour. The blue bars show the marginal revenue product of labour as Max employs more workers. These bars correspond to the numbers in Table 15.2. The curve *MRP* is Max's marginal revenue product curve.

The firm's demand for labour curve is based on its marginal revenue product curve. You can see Max's demand for labour curve (*D*) in Figure 15.3(b). The horizontal axis measures the number of workers hired – the same as part (a). The vertical axis measures the wage rate in pounds per hour. The demand for labour curve is exactly the same as the firm's marginal revenue product curve. For example, when Max employs 3 workers an hour, his marginal revenue product is £10 an hour, as in Figure 15.3(a); and at a wage rate of £10 an hour, Max hires 3 workers an hour, as in Figure 15.3(b).

Why is the demand for labour curve identical to the marginal revenue product curve? Because the firm hires the profit-maximizing quantity of labour. If the cost of hiring one more worker – the wage rate – is less than the additional revenue that the worker brings in – the marginal revenue product of labour – then the firm can increase its profit by employing one more worker. Conversely, if the cost of hiring one more worker is greater than the additional revenue that the worker brings in – the wage rate exceeds the marginal revenue product – then the firm can increase its profit by employing one fewer worker. But if the cost of hiring one more worker is equal to the additional revenue that the worker brings in – the wage rate equals the marginal revenue product – then the firm cannot increase its profit by changing the number of workers it employs. The firm is making the maximum possible profit. This situation occurs when the wage rate equals the marginal revenue product of labour. Thus the quantity of labour demanded by the firm is such that the wage rate equals the marginal revenue product of labour.

Figure 15.3 The Demand for Labour at Max's Wash 'n' Wax

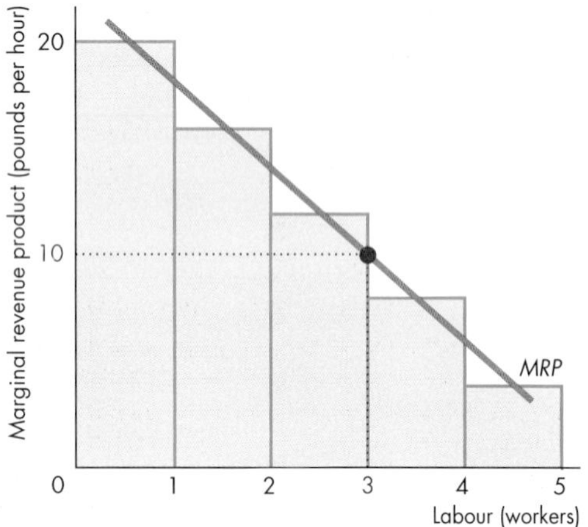

(a) Marginal revenue product

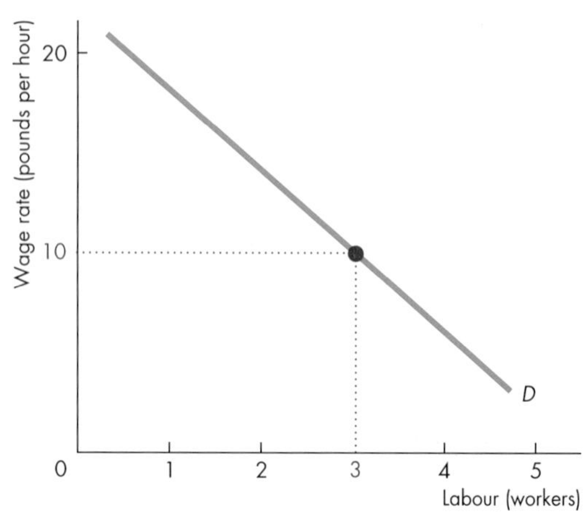

(b) Demand for labour

Max's Wash 'n' Wax operates in a perfectly competitive car wash market and can sell any quantity of washes at £4 a wash. The blue bars in part (a) represent the firm's marginal revenue product of labour. They are based on the numbers in Table 15.1. The orange line is the firm's marginal revenue product of labour curve. (Each point is plotted midway between the quantity of labour used in its calculation.) Part (b) shows Max's demand for labour curve. This curve is identical to Max's marginal revenue product curve. Max demands the quantity of labour that makes the wage rate, which is the marginal cost of labour, equal to the marginal revenue product of labour.

You already know one condition for maximizing profit-producing the output level where marginal revenue equals marginal cost. You've now discovered another condition for maximizing profit, where marginal revenue product of labour equals the wage. This condition holds for all other factor inputs into the firm. Let's now study the connection between these two conditions.

Two Conditions for Profit Maximization

Marginal revenue product and marginal revenue sound very similar. But what is the difference? These two concepts are related but not the same. Marginal revenue product is the extra revenue generated by employing an extra worker and marginal revenue is the extra revenue generated by selling an extra unit of output.

When a firm produces the output that maximizes profit, marginal revenue equals marginal cost. But the firm is also employing the amount of labour that makes the marginal revenue product equal the wage rate. These two conditions for profit maximization are equivalent, as Table 15.3 shows.

We've just derived the law of demand as it applies to the labour market. We've discovered that the same principles that apply to the demand for goods and services apply here as well. The demand for labour curve slopes downward. Other things remaining the same, the lower the wage rate (the price of labour), the greater is the quantity of labour demanded. Let's now study the influences that change in the demand for labour and shift in the demand for labour curve.

Changes in the Demand for Labour

The position of a firm's demand for labour curve depends on three factors:

1 The price of the firm's output.
2 The prices of other factors of production.
3 Technology.

Because the firm's demand for labour is a derived demand, the amount of labour a firm plans to hire depends on the price of the firm's output. The higher the price of a firm's output, the greater is the

Table 15.3 Two Conditions for Maximum Profit

SYMBOLS

Marginal product	*MP*
Marginal revenue	*MR*
Marginal cost	*MC*
Marginal revenue product	*MRP*
Factor price	*PF*

TWO CONDITIONS FOR MAXIMUM PROFIT

1.	$MR = MC$	2.	$MRP = PF$

EQUIVALENCE OF CONDITIONS

1.	$MRP/MP = MR$	=	$MC = PF/MP$
	Multiply by *MP* to give		Multiply by *MP* to give
	$MRP = MR \times MP$		$MC = MP \times PF$
	Flipping the equation over		Flipping the equation over
2.	$MR \times MP = MRP$	=	$PF = MC \times MP$

Marginal revenue product (*MR*) equals marginal cost (*MC*), and marginal revenue product (*MRP*) equals the price of the factor (*PF*). The two conditions for maximum profit are equivalent because marginal revenue product (*MRP*) equals marginal revenue (*MR*) multiplied by marginal product (*MP*), and the factor price (*PF*) equals marginal cost (*MC*) multiplied by marginal product (*MP*).

Table 15.4 A Firm's Demand for Labour

THE LAW OF DEMAND

The quantity of labour demanded by a firm

Decreases if:	*Increases if:*
◆ The wage rate increases	◆ The wage rate decreases

CHANGES IN DEMAND

A firm's demand for labour

Decreases if:	*Increases if:*
◆ The firm's output price decreases	◆ The firm's output price increases
◆ The prices of other factors decrease	◆ The prices of other factors increase
◆ A technological change decreases the marginal product of labour	◆ A technological change increases the marginal product of labour

quantity of labour demanded by the firm, other things remaining the same. The price of output affects the demand for labour through its influence on marginal revenue product. A higher price for the firm's output increases marginal revenue which, in turn, increases the marginal revenue product of labour. A change in the price of a firm's output leads to a shift in the firm's demand for labour curve. If the output price increases, the demand for labour increases.

The other two influences on the demand for labour have their main effects not in the short run but in the long run. The short-run demand for labour is the relationship between the wage rate and the quantity of labour demanded when the firm's capital is fixed and labour is the only variable factor. The long-run demand for labour is the relationship between the wage rate and the quantity of labour demanded when all factors can be varied. A change in the relative price of factors of production – such as the relative price of labour and capital – leads to a substitution away from the factor whose relative price has increased and towards the factor whose relative price has decreased. Thus if the price of using capital decreases relative to that of using labour, the firm substitutes capital for labour, increasing the quantity of capital demanded and decreasing its demand for labour.

Finally, a new technology that influences the marginal product of labour also affects the demand for labour. For example, the development of electronic telephones with memories and a host of clever features decreased the marginal product of telephone operators and so decreased the demand for telephone operators. This same technological change increased the marginal product of telephone engineers and so increased the demand for telephone engineers. Again, these effects are felt in the long run when the firm adjusts all its factors and incorporates new technologies into its production process.

As we saw earlier, in Figure 15.2, the demand for labour curve has increased over time, shifting rightward. We can now give some reasons for the demand curve shifting rightward over time. The main factors are advances in technology and investment in new capital that increases the marginal product of labour. Both of these factors have increased the demand for labour.

Table 15.4 summarizes the influences on a firm's demand for labour.

You can read about the marginal revenue product of top-class football managers and players in *Reading Between the Lines* on pp. 378–379.

Market Demand

So far we've studied only the demand for labour by an individual firm. The market demand for labour is the total demand by all firms. The market demand curve for labour is found by adding together the quantities demanded by all firms at each wage rate. Because each firm's demand for labour slopes downward, so does the market demand for labour.

Elasticity of Demand for Labour

The elasticity of demand for labour measures the responsiveness of the quantity of labour demanded to the wage rate. We calculate this elasticity in the same way that we calculate a price elasticity. The elasticity of demand for labour equals the magnitude of the percentage change in the quantity of labour demanded divided by the percentage change in the wage rate.

The demand for labour is less elastic in the short run, when only labour can be varied, than in the long run, when labour and other factors can be varied. The elasticity of demand for labour depends on:

- The labour intensity of the production process.
- How rapidly the marginal product of labour diminishes.
- The elasticity of demand for the product.
- The substitutability of capital for labour.

Labour Intensity A labour-intensive production process is one that uses a lot of labour and little capital – a process that has a high ratio of labour to capital. Home building is an example. The larger the labour–capital ratio, the more elastic is the demand for labour, other things remaining the same. Let's see why.

If wages are 90 per cent of total cost, a 10 per cent increase in the wage rate increases total cost by 9 per cent. Firms will be extremely sensitive to such a large change in total cost. If the wage rate increases, firms will decrease the quantity of labour demanded by a large amount. If wages are 10 per cent of total cost, a 10 per cent increase in the wage rate increases total cost by 1 per cent. Firms will be less sensitive to this increase in cost. If wage rates increase in this case, firms will decrease the quantity of labour demanded by a small amount.

How Rapidly Marginal Product Diminishes
The more rapidly the marginal product of labour diminishes, the less elastic is the demand for labour, other things remaining the same. In some activities marginal product diminishes quickly. For example, the marginal product of one bus driver is high, but the marginal product of a second driver on the same bus is close to zero. In other activities marginal product diminishes slowly. For example, hiring a second window cleaner on a team almost doubles the amount of glass that can be cleaned in an hour – the marginal product of the second window cleaner is almost the same as the first.

The Elasticity of Demand for the Product The greater the elasticity of demand for the good, the larger is the elasticity of demand for the factors of production used to produce it. To see why, think about what happens when the wage rate increases. An increase in the wage rate increases marginal cost and decreases the supply of the good. The decrease in the supply of the good increases the price of the good and decreases the quantity demanded of the good and the factors that produce it. The greater the elasticity of demand for the good, the larger is the decrease in the quantity demanded of the good and so the larger is the decrease in the quantities of the factors of production used to produce it.

The Substitutability of Capital for Labour
The substitutability of capital for labour influences the long-run elasticity of demand for labour but not the short-run elasticity. In the short run, capital is fixed. In the long run, capital can be varied, and the more easily capital can be substituted for labour in production, the more elastic is the long-run demand for labour. For example, it is fairly easy to substitute robots for assembly-line workers in car factories and automatic picking machines for labour in vineyards and orchards. At the other extreme, it is difficult (though not impossible) to substitute robots for newspaper reporters, bank loan officers and teachers. The more readily capital can be substituted for labour, the more elastic is the firm's demand for labour in the long run.

Supply of Labour

The supply of factors is determined by the decisions of households. Households allocate the factors of production that they own to their most rewarding uses. The quantity supplied of any factor of production depends on its price. Usually, the higher the price of a factor of production, the larger is the quantity supplied. There is a possible exception to this general law of supply concerning the supply of labour. It arises from the fact that people have preferences about how they use their time. A household chooses the number of hours per week of labour to supply as part of its time allocation decision. Time is allocated between two broad activities:

1 Market activity.

2 Non-market activity.

Market activity is the same thing as supplying labour. **Non-market activity** consists of everything else: leisure, non-market production activities including education and training, shopping, cooking and other activities in the home. The household obtains a return from market activity in the form of a wage. Non-market activities generate a return in the form of goods and services produced in the home, a higher future income, or leisure, which is valued for its own sake and which is classified as a good.

In deciding how to allocate its time between market activity and non-market activity, a household weighs the returns that it can get from the different activities. We are interested in the effects of the wage rate on the household's allocation of its time and on how much labour it supplies.

Wages and Quantity of Labour Supplied

To induce a household to supply labour, it must be offered a high enough wage rate. Non-market activities are valued by households either because the time is used in some productive activity or because of the value they attach to leisure. In order for it to be worthwhile to supply labour, a household has to be offered a wage rate that is at least equal to the value it places on the last hour it spends in non-market activities. This wage rate – the lowest one for which a household will supply labour to the market – is called its **reservation wage**. At wage rates below the reservation wage, the household supplies no labour. Once the wage rate reaches the reservation wage, the household begins to supply labour. As the wage rate rises above the reservation wage, the household varies the quantity of labour that it supplies. But a higher wage rate has two offsetting effects on the quantity of labour supplied – a *substitution effect* and an *income effect.*

Substitution Effect Other things remaining the same, the higher the wage rate, the more time people allocate to market activity and the less they allocate to non-market activities. Suppose, for example, that the market price of a duvet cleaning laundry service is £10 an hour. If the wage rate available to a household is less than £10 an hour, the household will provide its own laundry service – a non-market activity. If the household's wage rate rises above £10 an hour, it will be worthwhile for the household to work more hours and use part of its income to buy laundry services. The higher wage rate induces a switch of time from non-market activities to market activities.

Income Effect The higher the household's wage rate, the higher is its income. A higher income, other things remaining the same, induces a rise in demand for most goods. Leisure, a component of non-market activity, is one of these goods. Because an increase in income creates an increase in the demand for leisure, it also creates a decrease in the amount of time allocated to market activities and, therefore, to a fall in the quantity of labour supplied.

Backward-bending Household Supply of Labour Curve The substitution effect and the income effect operate in opposite directions. The higher the wage rate, the higher is the quantity of labour supplied via the substitution effect, but the lower is the quantity of labour supplied via the income effect. At low wage rates, the substitution effect is larger than the income effect. As the wage rate rises, the household supplies more labour. But as the wage rate continues to rise, there comes a point at which the substitution effect and the income effect just offset each other. At that point, a change in the wage rate has no effect on the quantity of labour supplied. If the wage rate continues to rise, the income effect begins to dominate the substitution effect and the quantity of labour supplied declines. The household's supply of labour curve does not slope upward throughout its entire length but begins to bend back on itself. It is called a backward-bending supply curve.

Three individual household labour supply curves are shown in Figure 15.4(a). Each household has a different reservation wage. Household *A* has a

Figure 15.4 The Supply of Labour

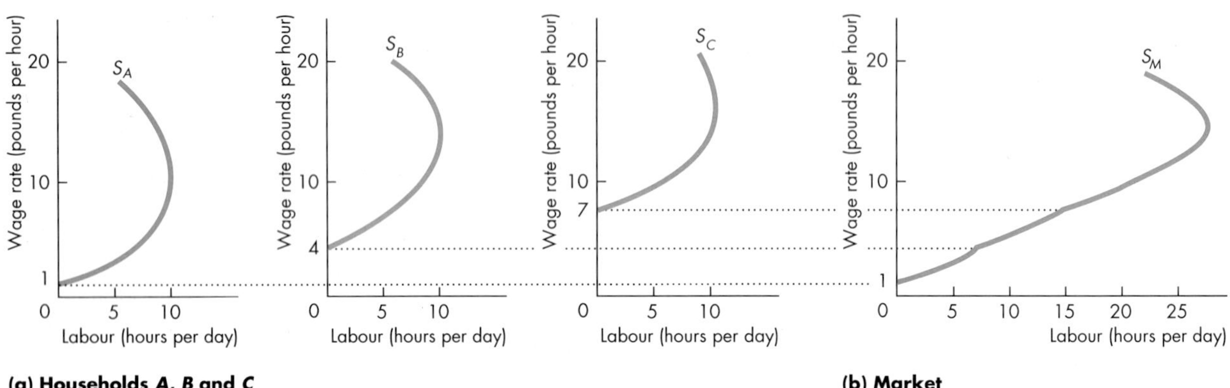

(a) Households *A, B* and *C*

(b) Market

Part (a) shows the labour supply curves of three households (S_A, S_B, and S_C). Each household has a reservation wage below which it will supply no labour. As the wage rises above the reservation wage, the quantity of labour supplied rises to a maximum. If the wage continues to rise, the quantity of labour supplied begins to decline. Each household's supply curve eventually bends backward.

Part (b) shows how, by adding together the quantities of labour supplied by the individual households at each wage rate, we derive the market supply curve of labour (S_M). The market supply curve also eventually bends backward, but has a long upward-sloping region before it bends backward.

reservation wage of £1 an hour, household *B* of £4 an hour and household *C* of £7 an hour. Each household's labour supply curve is backward-bending.

Market Supply The market supply of labour curve is the sum of the supply curves of all the individual households. Figure 15.4(b) shows the market supply curve (S_M) derived from the supply curves of the three households (S_A, S_B, S_C) in Figure 15.4(a). At wage rates of less than £1 an hour, the three households do only non-market activities such as laundry and cooking, and they do not supply any market labour. The household most eager to supply market labour has a reservation wage of £1 an hour. As the wage rate rises from £1 to £4 an hour, household *A* increases the quantity of labour that it supplies to the market. The reservation wage of household *B* is £4 an hour, so as the wage rate rises above £4 an hour, the quantity of labour supplied in the market is the sum of the labour supplied by households *A* and *B*. When the wage rate reaches £7 an hour, household *C* begins to supply some labour to the market. At wage rates above £7 an hour, the quantity supplied in the market is equal to the sum of the quantities supplied by the three households.

Notice that the market supply curve S_M, like the individual household supply curves, eventually bends backward. But the market supply curve has a long upward-sloping section. The reason why the market supply curve slopes up for such a long stretch is that the reservation wage rates of individual households are not equal and at higher wage rates additional households reach their reservation wage and so begin to supply labour.

Changes in the Supply of Labour

The supply of labour changes when influences other than the wage rate change. The main factors affecting the supply of labour over time are:

- Demographic changes.
- Social attitudes to work.

Any increase in the adult population will increase the supply of labour and any fall in the birth rate will decrease the supply of labour in the future, if there is no change in immigration rates. Another important factor is changing social attitudes to women, children and work. As more and more women enter traditional male areas of work, labour supply in these markets increases. Changes in the law prohibiting child labour, reduce labour supply. Changing attitudes to men caring for children, and greater awareness about work stress and health, have also reduced the male labour supply for traditional full time jobs.

Labour Market Equilibrium

Wages and employment are determined by equilibrium in the labour markets. You saw, in Figure 15.2, that the wage rate has risen and that total hours of employment in most European countries have also risen. But this picture hides some important differences between different types of labour market. Lets' see why.

Trends in Labour Demand The demand for labour had increased in most European countries because of technological change. As a result, the demand for labour in the UK has shifted to the right.

Some people think that technological improvements destroy jobs rather than increase labour demand. Of course, some technology changes destroy some types of job. For example, banks are cutting the number of tellers and middle managers because telephone and internet banking are lower cost ways of providing banking services. However, technology also creates jobs. Thousands of jobs have been created in telephone centres by the introduction of telephone banking. On average, the demand for labour will shift to the right if more jobs are created than destroyed by telephone banking. The demand for labour in high-skilled technology-based jobs has definitely increased with the invention of the computer 'chip', but most of the new jobs, have been for less skilled work in the service sector.

Trends in Labour Supply The supply of labour increased in the 1970s and 1980s but has started to decrease with the falling birthrate. Changes in attitudes to women working and the provision of child care outside the home, have increased the supply of labour by women over time, but mainly in the market for less skilled part-time labour. Changing attitudes to men doing housework and child care have also reduced the full-time male labour supply. So as with the demand for labour, trends in the supply of labour are different in different types of labour market. The main types of labour market are for skilled and unskilled work and for part-time and full-time work.

Trends in Labour Supply To understand the underlying causes of the changes shown in Figure 15.2, we need to understand the different trends in different labour markets, particularly in the UK. The overall effect on full-time, high-skilled jobs is for the demand for labour to increase with new technology and the supply of labour to remain constant. This has the effect of raising the real wage for labour in these markets and increasing the quantity of hours worked. However, more people are working fewer hours in these labour markets, which reduces the hours worked per week on average. In the UK, the average hours worked per week has fallen from 42 to 40 hours over the 30-year period illustrated in the figure.

However, a different picture emerges if we look at the market for less skilled part-time work. The demand for labour has also increased with new technology, but the supply of labour has also increased substantially as more women enter the labour market. This has the effect of shifting both the demand and the supply of labour rightwards. The overall impact is a smaller rise in real wages in these markets but an increase in the number of part-time hours worked. Overall, the total number of hours worked in the UK has fluctuated around a constant level of 48 billion hours per year. You will study this in more detail again in Chapter 23, pp. 552–572.

Review

- Wage rates and employment levels are determined by demand and supply in labour markets.
- The quantity of labour demanded is greater, the lower the wage rate (because the marginal revenue product of labour diminishes). An increase in the price of the good produced increases the demand for labour.
- The quantity of labour supplied is greater, the higher the wage rate (but labour supply curves may eventually bend backward). Demographic changes, social attitudes to work and the relative price of leisure to work will cause the labour supply to shift.

- Wages have increased as the demand for labour has increased more than the supply of labour in most European countries.

Capital Markets

Capital markets are the channels through which household savings flow into firms and governments. They are markets for financial capital assets. Financial assets are simply claims against another household, firm or government – a form of IOU. The financial assets obtained in capital markets are used to buy physical and natural capital goods. Physical capital such as plant and machinery, and natural capital goods, such as oil and coal, are bought and sold, or rented in goods and service markets. The price of financial capital, which adjusts to make the quantity of financial capital supplied equal to the quantity demanded, is the interest rate.

Capital markets are where we make our biggest transactions. We borrow in a capital market to get a mortgage to buy a home. We lend in capital markets to build up a pension fund for income in retirement. Do rates of return in capital markets follow a similar pattern to the return to labour, the wage rate? Table 15.5 shows you a selection of real interest rates for a selection of European countries. Our measure of real interest rates means we have subtracted the loss of the value of money caused by inflation. You can see that interest rates fluctuate and that they can even be negative in years when inflation has been very high. Over the past 30 years, there has been a tendency for the value of real interest rates to fluctuate widely in most European countries around a rising trend.

Table 15.5 Trends in Real Interest Rates in Europe (%)

Year	France	Germany	Potrugal	UK
1965	2.5	3.6	–1	1.1
1970	3.6	1	0.8	2.2
1975	–4.5	–1.2	–10.0	–12.4
1980	–1.5	3.6	5.3	0.4
1985	–1.9	3.3	1.6	6.9
1990	7.1	5.7	4.3	7.0
1994	4.7	5.5	9.5	5.0

Real short-term interest rates have been positive in most years in most countries and have tended to rise over time.

Source: Adapted from Eurostat figures.

Figure 15.5 Capital Market Trends

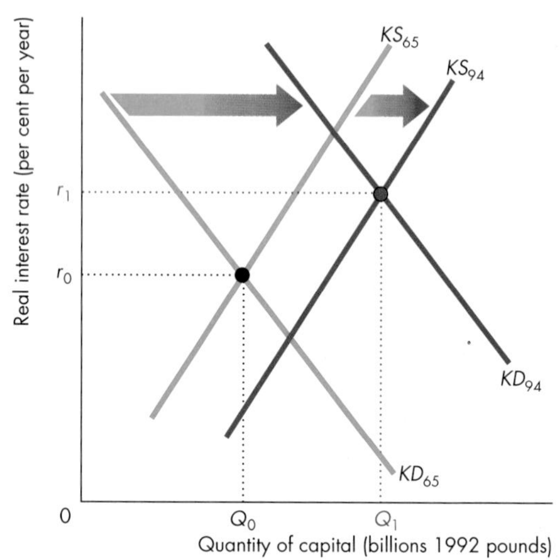

Between 1965 and 1994, the real interest rate has risen in most western European countries. The quantiry of capital employed has also risen. This is the result of an increase in the demand for financial capital a smaller increase in the supply of financial capital.

Figure 15.5 shows why the rising trend in real interest rates has occurred. Demand for financial capital has increased from KD_{65} to KD_{94} and similarly, supply of financial capital has also increased from KS_{65} to KS_{94}. The result is an increase in the price of capital, the real interest rate, and an increase in the quantity of financial capital supplied.

To understand the trends in capital markets, we must examine the forces of demand and supply in more detail. Many of the ideas you have already met in your study of demand and supply in labour markets apply to the capital markets as well. But there are some special features of capital markets. Its main feature is that people compare *present* costs with *future* benefits when making decisions in capital markets. Let's discover how these comparisons are made by studying the demand for capital.

The Demand for Capital

A firm's demand for *financial* capital stems from its demand for *physical* capital, and the amount that a firm plans to *borrow* in a given time period is determined by its planned investment – purchases of new capital. Decisions about the quantity of financial capital needed are driven by profit maximization. As a firm increases the quantity of physical capital employed, other things remaining the same, the marginal revenue product of physical capital eventually diminishes. To maximize profit, a firm will increase the quantity of physical capital, usually in the form of plant and machinery, only if the marginal revenue product of the capital exceeds the cost of capital. But the marginal revenue product comes in the *future*, and the capital cost must be paid for in the *present*. So the firm must convert what it expects will be the marginal revenue product in the future, into a present value, so that it can be compared with the present price of new equipment. You should look back at Chapter 10 (pp. 221–223) to remind yourself of the concept of present value.

Table 15.6 Net Present Value of an Investment – Taxfile plc

(a) Data

Price of workstation	£10,000
Life of workstation	2 years
Marginal revenue product	£5,900 at end of each year
Interest rate	4% a year

(b) Present value of the flow of marginal revenue product:

$$P = \frac{MRP_1}{(1+r)} + \frac{MRP_2}{(1+r)^2}$$
$$= \frac{£5{,}900}{1.04} + \frac{£5{,}900}{(1.04)^2}$$
$$= £5{,}673 + £5{,}455$$
$$= £11{,}128$$

(c) Net present value of investment:

$NPV = PV$ of marginal revenue product – Cost of workstation
$= £11{,}128 - £10{,}000$
$= £1{,}128$

The Net Present Value of a Computer

Let's see how a firm decides how much capital to buy by calculating the present value of a new computer.

Tina runs Taxfile plc, a firm that sells advice to taxpayers. Tina is considering buying a new high-power computer workstation that costs £10,000 in total. The workstation has a life of two years, after which it will be worthless. If Tina buys the workstation, she will pay out £10,000 now and she expects to generate business that will bring in an additional £5,900 at the end of each of the next two years.

To calculate the present value, *PV*, of the marginal revenue product of a new computer, Tina uses the formula:

$$PV = \frac{MRP_1}{(1+r)} + \frac{MRP_2}{(1+r)^2}$$

Here, MRP_1 is the marginal revenue product received by Tina at the end of the first year. It is converted to a present value by dividing it by $(1 + r)$. The term MRP_2 is the marginal revenue product received at the end of the second year. It is converted to a present value by dividing it by $(1 + r)^2$. Table 15.6 summarizes the data. Part (b) puts Tina's numbers into the present value formula and calculates the present value of the marginal revenue product of a workstation.

The first calculation in Table 15.6 is for the case in which Tina can borrow or lend at an interest rate of 4 per cent a year. The present value (*PV*) of £5,900 one year in the future is £5,900 divided by 1.04 (4 per cent as a proportion is 0.04). The present value of £5,900 two years in the future is £5,900 divided by $(1.04)^2$. Working out these two present values and then adding them gives Tina the present value of the future stream of marginal revenue products, which is £11,128.

Tina's Decision to Buy

Tina decides whether to buy the workstation by comparing the present value of its stream of marginal revenue product with its purchase price. She makes this comparison by calculating the net present value (*NPV*) of the computer. **Net present value** is the present value of the future return – the future stream of marginal revenue product generated by the capital minus the cost of buying the capital. If net present value is positive, the firm should buy additional capital. If net present value is negative, the firm should not buy additional capital. Table 15.6(c) shows the calculation of Tina's net present value of a workstation. The net present value is £1,128 – greater than zero – so Tina buys the workstation.

Table 15.7 Taxfile's Investment Decision

(a) Data

Price of workstation	£10,000
Life of workstation	2 years
Marginal revenue product:	
Using 1 workstation	£ 5,900 a year
Using 2 workstations	£ 5,600 a year
Using 3 workstations	£ 5,300 a year

(b) Present value of the stream of marginal revenue product

If $r = 0.04$ (4% a year):

Using 1 workstation: $$PV = \frac{£5{,}900}{1.04} + \frac{£5{,}900}{(1.04)^2} = £11{,}128$$

Using 2 workstations: $$PV = \frac{£5{,}600}{1.04} + \frac{£5{,}600}{(1.04)^2} = £10{,}562$$

Using 3 workstations: $$PV = \frac{£5{,}300}{1.04} + \frac{£5{,}300}{(1.04)^2} = £9{,}996$$

If $r = 0.08$ (8% a year):

Using 1 workstation: $$PV = \frac{£5{,}900}{1.08} + \frac{£5{,}900}{(1.08)^2} = £10{,}521$$

Using 2 workstations: $$PV = \frac{£5{,}600}{1.08} + \frac{£5{,}600}{(1.08)^2} = £9{,}986$$

If $r = 0.12$ (12% a year):

Using 1 workstation: $$PV = \frac{£5{,}900}{1.12} + \frac{£5{,}900}{(1.12)^2} = £9{,}971$$

Tina can buy any number of workstations that cost £10,000 and have a life of two years. But like all other factors of production, capital is subject to diminishing marginal returns. The greater the amount of capital employed, the smaller is its marginal revenue product. So if Tina buys a second workstation or a third one, she gets successively smaller marginal revenue products from the additional workstations.

Table 15.7(a) sets out Tina's marginal revenue products for one, two and three workstations. The marginal revenue product of one computer workstation (the case just reviewed) is £5,900 a year. The marginal revenue product of a second workstation is £5,600 a year, and the marginal revenue product of a third computer is £5,300 a year. Table 15.7(b) shows the calculations of the present values of the marginal revenue products of the first, second and third computers workstations.

You've seen that with an interest rate of 4 per cent a year, the net present value of one workstation is positive. At an interest rate of 4 per cent a year, the present value of the marginal revenue product of a second workstation is £10,562, which exceeds its price by £562. So Tina buys a second computer workstation. But at an interest rate of 4 per cent a year, the present value of the marginal revenue product of a third workstation is £9,996, which is £4 less than the price of the computer. So Tina does not buy a third workstation.

A Change in the Interest Rate We've seen that at an interest rate of 4 per cent a year, Tina buys two computer workstations but not three. Suppose that the interest rate is 8 per cent a year. In this case, the present value of the first computer is £10,521 (see Table 15.7(b)), so Tina still buys one workstation because it has a positive net present value. At an interest rate of 8 per cent a year, the net present value of the second workstation is £9,986, which is less than £10,000, its price. So, at an interest rate of 8 per cent a year, Tina buys only one computer workstation.

Suppose that the interest rate is even higher at 12 per cent a year. In this case, the present value of the marginal revenue product of one workstation is £9,971 (see Table 15.7(b)). At this interest rate, Tina buys no computer workstations.

These calculations trace Taxfile's demand schedule for capital. They show the number of computer workstations demanded – and the value of funds – at each interest rate. Other things remaining the same, the higher the interest rate, the smaller is the quantity of *physical* capital demanded. But to finance the purchase of physical capital, firms demand financial capital. So the higher the interest rate, the smaller is the quantity of *financial* capital demanded.

Demand Curve for Capital

A firm's demand curve for capital shows the relationship bewteen the quantity of physical capital demanded by the firm and the interest rate, other things remaining the same. The quantity of capital demanded by a firm depends on the marginal revenue product of capital and the interest rate. The market demand curve for capital (as shown in Figure 15.5) shows the relationship beween the total quantity of capital demanded and the interest rate, other things remaining the same.

Changes in the Demand for Capital Figure 15.5 showed that the demand for capital has increased over the past 30 years in European countries. The demand for capital changes when expectations about the future marginal revenue production of capital change. The two main factors affecting the marginal revenue product of capital, and hence demand, are:

1 Population growth.
2 Technological change.

An increase in population size increases in the demand for goods and services, and so increases the demand for capital to produce them. Technological change leads to fluctuations in the demand for capital. Technological advances increase the demand for some types of physical capital and decrease the demand for other types. For example, the development of diesel engines for railway transport decreased the demand for steam engines and increased the demand for diesel engines. In this case, the railway industry's overall demand for capital did not change much. In contrast, the development of desktop computers increased the demand for office computing equipment, decreased the demand for electric typewriters and increased the overall demand for capital in the office.

Let's now look at the supply side of the capital market.

The Supply of Capital

The quantity of capital supplied results from people's saving decisions. The main factors that determine household savings are:

- Current income.
- Expected future income.
- The interest rate.

Current Income Saving is the act of converting current income into future consumption. Typically, the higher your income, the more you plan to consume both in the present and in the future. If you want to increase your future income, you must save. So, other things remaining the same, the higher your income, the more you save. The relationship between saving and income is remarkably stable. Most people save a constant proportion of any extra income earned.

Expected Future Income Because a major reason for saving is to increase future consumption, the amount you save depends on your current income, but also on your expected future income. A person with a low current income compared with expected future income, saves little and might even have negative saving. A person with high current income compared with expected future income saves a great deal in the present in order to be able to consume more in the future.

Young people typically have a low current income compared with their expected future income, while older working people have a high current income relative to their expected future income. The consequence of this pattern in income over the life cycle is that young people have negative saving and older working people have positive saving. Thus the young incur debts (such as consumer credit) to acquire durable goods and to consume more than their income, while older working people save and accumulate assets (often in the form of pension and life insurance arrangements) to provide for their retirement years.

The Interest Rate The interest rate measures the opportunity cost of consuming this year rather than next year. The higher the interest rate, the greater is the amount that a pound saved today becomes in the future. So the higher the interest rate, the greater is the opportunity cost of current consumption. With a higher opportunity cost of current consumption, people cut their consumption and increase their saving.

The Supply Curve of Capital

The supply curve of capital, as shown in Figure 15.5, shows the relationship between the quantity of capital supplied and the interest rate, other things remaining the same. It is worth remembering that capital is the total value of accumulated saving. For an economy, that capital is measured as the sum of all its physical and natural capital. An increase in the interest rate leads to an increase in the quantity of capital supplied and a movement along the supply curve. The supply curve of capital is inelastic in the short run and more elastic in the long run. The reason is that in any one year, the total amount of savings is small relative to the size of the capital stock. So even a large change in the amount of saving, in response to a change in the interest rate, will only bring a small change in the quantity of capital supplied.

Changes in the Supply of Capital A change in any influence on saving, other than the interest rate, changes the amount of saving and shifts the supply curve of capital. The main influences on the supply of capital are income and its distribution and the size and age distribution of the population.

Other things remaining the same, an increase in income or an increase in the population bring an increase in the supply of capital. Also, other things remaining the same, the more unequally income is distributed, the higher is the saving rate. The reason is that low-income and middle-income families have low saving rates, while high-income families have high saving rates. So the larger the proportion of total income earned by the highest-income families, the greater is the amount of saving. Finally, and again other things remaining the same, the larger the proportion of middle-aged people, the higher is the saving rate. The reason is that middle-aged people do most of the saving as they build up a pension fund to provide an income in their retirement.

Let's use what we have learned about the demand and supply of capital to see how the interest rate is determined.

Figure 15.6 Capital Market Equilibrium

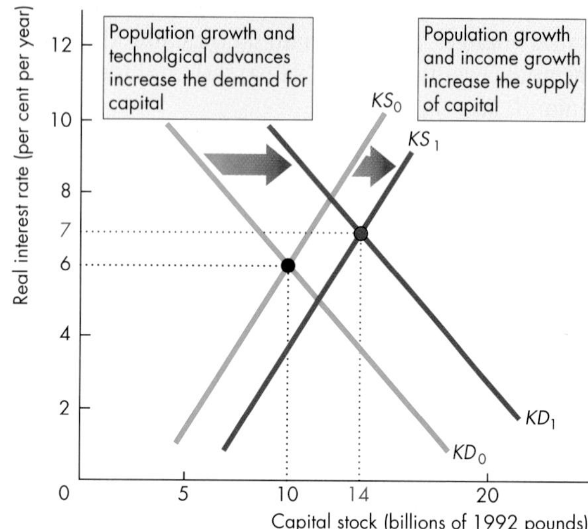

Initially, the demand for capital is KD_0 and the supply of capital is KS_0. The equilibrium interest rate is 6 per cent a year, and the capital stock is £10 billion. Over time, demand and supply increase, to KD_1 and KS_1. The capital stock and the real interest rate increase. Demand and supply increase because they are influenced by common factors.

The Interest Rate

Saving plans and investment plans are coordinated through capital markets and interest rates adjust to make these plans compatible.

Figure 15.6 shows the capital market. Initially, the demand for capital is KD_0 and the supply of capital is KS_0. The equilibrium real interest rate is 6 per cent and the quantity of capital is £10 billion at 1992 prices. The market forces that bring about this equilibrium are the same as those that we studied in the markets for goods and services. If the interest rate exceeds 6 per cent a year, the quantity of financial capital demanded is less than the quantity supplied. There is a surplus of funds in the capital market. In such a situation, as lenders compete to make loans, interest rates fall. The quantity of financial capital demanded increases as firms increase their borrowing and buy more capital goods. The interest rate continues to fall until lenders are able to lend all the funds they wish at that interest rate.

Similarly, if the interest rate is below 6 per cent a year, the quantity of financial capital supplied is less than the quantity demanded. There is a shortage of funds in the capital market. Borrowers are unable to borrow all the funds they wish so they offer a higher interest rate. Interest rates increase until there are no unsatisfied borrowers. In either case, the interest rate converges on 6 per cent a year, the equilibrium interest rate.

Over the past 30 years, both the demand for capital and the supply of capital have increased in European countries. The demand curve shifts rightwards to KD_1, and the supply curve also shifts rightward to KS_1. Both curves shift because technological advances increase both demand and supply, leading to a rising trend in real interest rates. The reason why real interest rates fluctuate over time is because the demand and supply of capital do not change uniformly. Sometimes rapid technological change leads to an increase in demand for capital before it brings rising incomes that will increase the supply of capital. When this happens, as in the 1990s, the real interest rate rises.

At other times, the demand for capital grows slowly or even decreases temporarily. In this situation, supply outstrips demand and the real interest rate falls and may even become negative. This is what happend in the mid-1970s.

Review

- The real interest rate and the capital stock are determined by the demand for financial capital and the supply of financial capital.

- The demand for financial capital is derived from the marginal revenue product of physical capital. Firms compare the net present value of the expected future marginal revenue product with the current cost of the physical capital. The lower the interest rate, the greater is the quantity of capital demanded. The demand for capital increases with technological advances and fluctuates because expectations about future marginal revenue product fluctuate.

- The supply of financial capital arises from savings decisions. The higher the interest rate, the greater is the quantity of capital supplied. The supply of capital increases because of income growth and population growth.

We can now use what we have learned about capital markets to understand how the prices of natural resources (natural capital) change over time. Let's see how.

Land and Exhaustible Natural Resource Markets

Land is the stock or quantity of natural resources. All natural resources are called *land*, and they fall into two categories:

1 Non-exhaustible.
2 Exhaustible.

Non-exhaustible natural resources are natural resources that can be used repeatedly without depleting the potential stock available for future use. Examples of non-exhaustible natural resources are land (in the everyday sense of the word), seas, rivers, lakes, rain and sunshine.

Exhaustible natural resources are natural resources that can be used only once and that cannot be replaced once used. Examples of exhaustible natural resources are coal, natural gas and oil – the so-called hydrocarbon fuels.

The demand for natural resources as inputs into production is based on exactly the same principles of marginal revenue product as for labour and capital. But the supply of natural resources is quite different. Let's look first at the supply of non-exhaustible natural resources.

The Supply of Land (Non-exhaustible Natural Resources)

The quantity of land and other non-exhaustible natural resources is fixed. The quantity supplied cannot be changed by individual decisions. People can vary the amount of land they own, but when one person sells land, another person buys it. People cannot vary the total quantity available. The total quantity of land supplied of any particular type and in any particular location is fixed, regardless of the decisions of any one individual. The rare exception is when new land is reclaimed from the sea or from old lakes. So the supply of any particular piece of land is perfectly inelastic. Figure 15.7 illustrates this case. Regardless of the rent available, that quantity of land supplied in the centre of Paris, London or Bonn is a fixed number of square feet.

As the supply of any piece of land is fixed, regardless of its price, price is determined by demand. The greater the demand for a particular piece of land, the higher is its price.

Expensive land can be, and is, used more intensively than inexpensive land. For example, high-rise buildings enable land to be used more intensively. However, to use land more intensively, it has to be combined with another factor of production – capital. Increasing the amount of capital per block of land does not change the supply of land itself. But it does enable land to become more productive. A rising price of land strengthens the incentive to find ways of increasing its productivity. These issues are explored more fully in *Economics in History* on pp. 380–381.

Figure 15.7 The Supply of Land

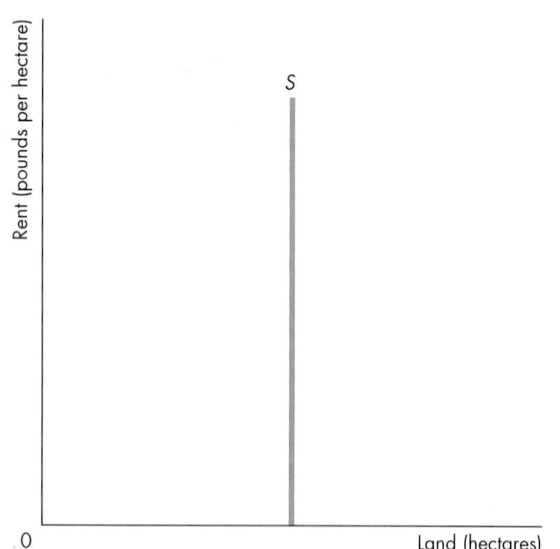

The supply of a given piece of land is perfectly inelastic. No matter what the rent, no more land than exists can be supplied.

Although the supply of each type of land is fixed and its supply is perfectly inelastic, each individual firm, operating in competitive land markets, faces an elastic supply of land. For example, Oxford Street in London has a fixed amount of land, but Waterstones, a bookshop, could rent some space from John Lewis, a department store. Each firm can rent the quantity of land that it demands at the going rent, which is determined in the marketplace. So provided land markets are highly competitive, firms are price takers in these markets, just as they are in the markets for other factors of production.

The Supply of Exhaustible Natural Resources

To understand the supply of an exhaustible natural resource, we must distinguish between three supply concepts:

1 The stock supply.
2 The known stock supply.
3 The flow supply.

The *stock supply* of a natural resource is the quantity in existence at any given time. This supply is *perfectly inelastic*, just like land. No matter what its price, the quantity cannot be changed at that time.

The *known stock supply* is the quantity of a natural resource that has been discovered. This supply is *elastic*. If the price of a natural resource rises, other things remaining the same, the known quantity increases. This is because an increase in the price of the resource, increases the potential profit from selling the resource, and raises the incentive to search for additional resources. The known supply also increases over time at any given price – the supply curve shifts rightward. This is because advances in technology enable the more inaccessible resources to be discovered.

The *flow supply* is the quantity of a natural resource that is offered for use during a given time period. This supply is *perfectly elastic* at a price that equals the present value of the next period's expected price. Let's look at this in more detail.

The Flow Supply of Exhaustible Natural Resources

Why is the flow supply of an exhaustible natural resource perfectly elastic at the price that equals the present value of the next period's expected price? It is because not supplying the resource means holding it and selling it later. If next year's expected price exceeds this year's price by a percentage that exceeds the interest rate, then it pays to hold onto the resource. It pays to sell it next year rather than this year. The reason is that the rate of return from holding the resource exceeds the interest rate. Equivalently, if this year's price is less than the present value of next year's expected price, it pays to hold onto the resource and sell it next year. This year's price is too low relative to next year's expected price.

Similarly, if this year's price exceeds the present value of next year's expected price, it pays to sell the resource now rather than wait until next year. This year's price is too high relative to next year's expected price.

What happens if this year's price equals the present value of next year's expected price? In this case, it makes no difference whether the owner of the resource sells it now or sells it next year. A pound today is worth the same value as the present value of a pound plus the interest on a pound, a year from today. Because the two amounts are equal, a resource owner is indifferent between supplying

Figure 15.8 An Exhaustible Natural Resource

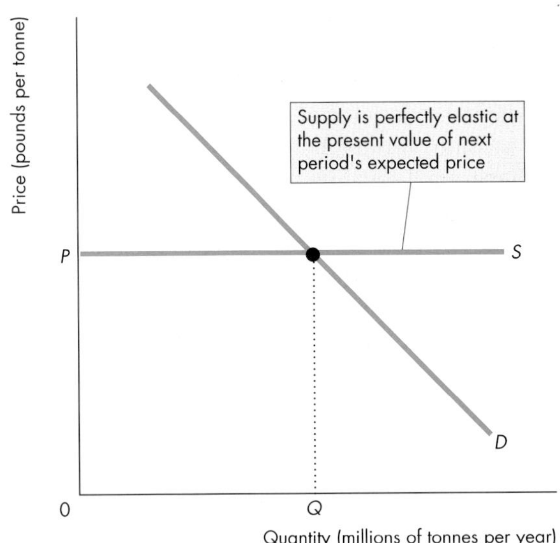

The supply of an exhaustible natural resource is perfectly elastic at the *present value* of next period's expected price. The demand for an exhaustible natural resource is determined by its marginal revenue product. The price is determined by supply and equals the *present value* of next period's expected price.

Figure 15.9 Falling Metal Prices

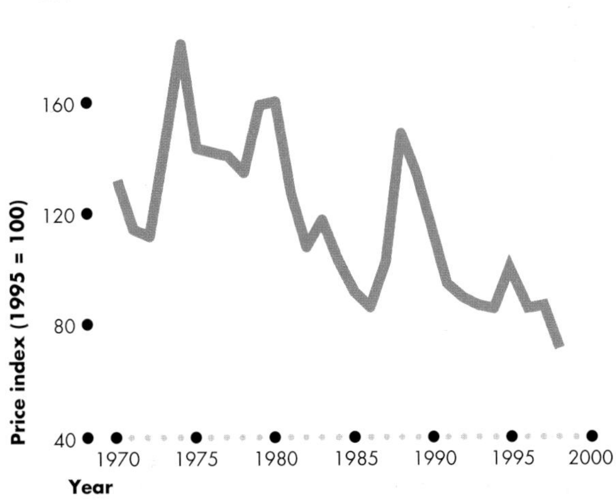

The prices of metals (here an average of the prices of aluminium, copper, iron ore, lead, manganese, nickel, silver, tin and zinc) have tended to fall over time, not rise as predicted by the Hotelling Principle. The reason is that unanticipated advances in technology have decreased the cost of extracting metals and greatly increased the exploitable known reserves.

Source: *International Financial Statistics*, International Monetary Fund, Washington, DC (various issues).

and not supplying. Supply is perfectly elastic at the present value of the next period's expected price.

As supply is perfectly elastic at the present value of the next period's expected price, the actual price of the natural resource also equals the present value of the next period's expected price. Figure 15.8 shows the equilibrium in the market for metals. Any change in the present value of the next period's expected metal price will lead to a shift in the supply curve, and a change in the actual price of metals.

The Price of Exhaustible Natural Resources

The idea that the price of an exhaustible natural resource is expected to rise at a rate equal to the interest rate is called the **Hotelling Principle**. It was first proposed by Harold Hotelling, a mathematician and economist at Columbia University.

The price of a natural resource is expected to grow at a rate equal to the interest rate on similarly risky financial capital because it makes the expected interest rate on the natural resource equal to the interest rate on similarly risky financial capital. Firms look for the highest returns they can find, holding risk constant. So if the expected interest rate on a stock of a natural resource exceeds that on similarly risky financial capital, firms buy the stocks of natural resources and sell financial capital. Conversely, if the expected interest rate on a natural resource is less than that on similarly risky financial capital, firms buy financial capital and sell stocks of natural resources.

Equilibrium occurs in the market for the stock of a natural resource when prices and expectations about future prices for the stock have adjusted to make the *expected* interest rate earned on the natural resource equal to the interest rate on similarly risky financial capital. Figure 15.9 shows that the prices of exhaustible natural resources do not follow the Hotelling Principle. The real price of metals has fallen over time. So how can we explain this?

The answer lies in the fact that the future is unpredictable. Expected technological change is reflected in the price of a natural resource. But what happens when an unexpected technological change leads to the discovery of new stocks or allows firms and households to use known stocks more efficiently? Unexpected technological change leads to a fall in the price of an exhaustible natural resource. This is the explanation for falling world oil prices and falling world metal prices.

Review

- The supply of land (and other non-exhaustible natural resources) is inelastic. Price is determined by demand.
- The flow supply of an exhaustible natural resource is perfectly elastic at a price equal to the present value of the expected future price.
- The price of an exhaustible natural resource is expected to rise at a rate equal to the interest rate on financial capital.
- Exhaustible resource prices fluctuate and even fall because of unpredictable technological change.

People supply resources to earn income. But some people earn enormous incomes whilst other people earn tiny incomes. How does income affect people's desire to work and supply other resources? Let's now answer this question.

Income, Economic Rent and Opportunity Cost

We've seen how the price of factors such as labour, capital and land are determined by the interaction of demand and supply. We've seen that demand is determined by marginal productivity and supply is determined by the resources available and by peoples' choices about their use. The interaction of demand and supply in factor markets determines who receives a large income and who receives a small income.

Large and Small Incomes

Why does the director of a large corporation earn a large income? It must be because such a person has a high marginal revenue product. This is reflected in the demand curve for his or her services. The supply of people with the combination of talents needed for this kind of job is also small and this is reflected in the supply curve. Equilibrium occurs at a high wage rate and a small quantity employed.

Why do McJobs pay low wages? It is because they have a low marginal revenue product – reflected in the demand curve – and there are many households able and willing to supply their labour for these jobs. Equilibrium occurs at a low wage rate and large quantity employed.

If the demand for news readers increases, their incomes increase by a large amount and the number of news readers barely changes. If the demand for workers in McJobs increases, the number of people doing these jobs increases by a large amount and the wage rate barely changes.

You can get a further insight into people's incomes by learning about the distinction between economic rent and opportunity cost.

Economic Rent and Opportunity Cost

The total income of a factor of production is made up of its economic rent and its opportunity cost. **Economic rent** is an income received by the owner of a factor over and above the amount required to induce that owner to offer the factor for use. Any factor of production can receive an economic rent. The income required to induce the supply of a factor of production is the opportunity cost of using a factor of production – the value of the factor in its next best use.

Figure 15.10 illustrates the concepts of economic rent and opportunity cost. Figure 15.10(a) shows the market for rock singers. It could be *any* factor of production – labour, capital, land or entrepreneurship. The demand curve for the factor of production is D and its supply curve is S. The factor price in this case is the wage, W, and the quantity of the factor used is C. The income of the factor is the sum of the yellow and blue areas. The yellow area below the supply curve measures opportunity cost

Figure 15.10 Economic Rent and Opportunity Cost

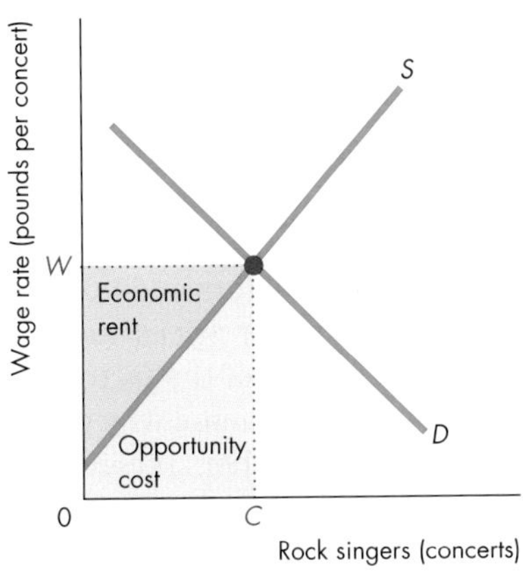

(a) Intermediate case

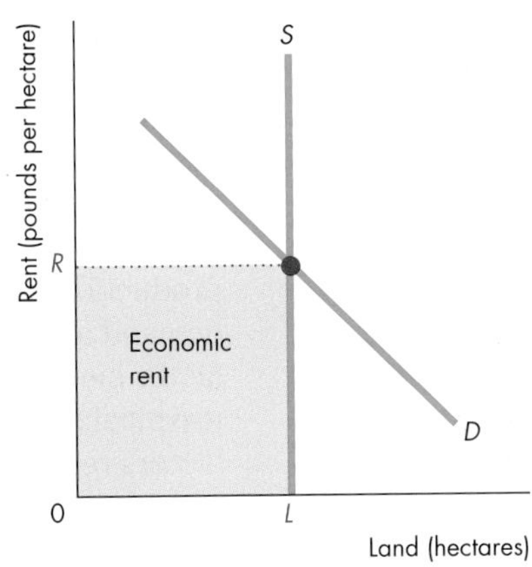

(b) All economic rent

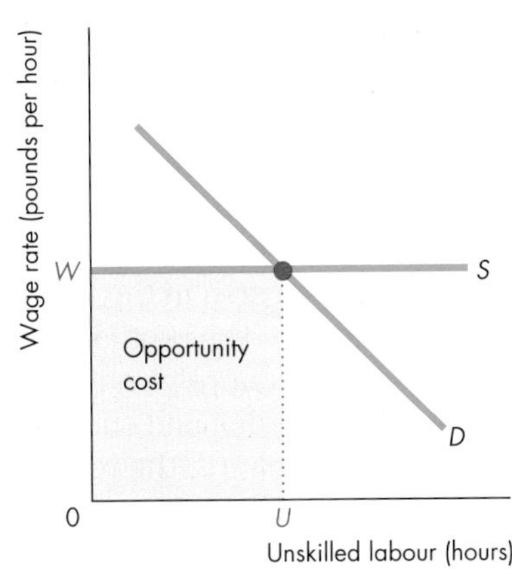

(c) All opportunity cost

When a factor supply curve slopes upward – the general case – as in part (a), part of the factor income is rent (green) and part is opportunity cost (yellow). When the supply of a factor is perfectly inelastic (vertical), as in part (b), the entire factor income is economic rent. When the supply of a factor is perfectly elastic (horizontal), as in part (c), the entire factor income is opportunity cost.

and the green area below the factor price but above the supply curve measures economic rent.

To see why the area below the supply curve measures opportunity cost, recall that a supply curve can be interpreted in two different ways. One interpretation is that a supply curve indicates the quantity supplied at a given price. But the alternative interpretation of a supply curve is that it shows the minimum price at which a given quantity is willingly supplied. If suppliers receive only the minimum amount required to induce them to supply each unit of the factor of production, they will be paid a different price for each unit. The prices will trace the supply curve and the income received is entirely opportunity cost – the yellow area in Figure 15.10(a).

The concept of economic rent is similar to the concept of consumer surplus that you met in Chapter 6, pp. 122–124. Remember that consumer surplus is the difference between the price the household pays for a good and the maximum price it would be willing to pay, as indicated by the demand curve. In a parallel sense, economic rent is the difference between the factor price a household actually receives and the minimum factor price at which it would be willing to supply a given amount of a factor of production.

Economic rent is not the same thing as *rent*. Rent is the price paid for the services of land. Economic rent is a component of the income received by any factor of production.

The portion of the income of a factor of production that consists of economic rent depends on the elasticity of the supply of the factor of production. When the supply of a factor of production is perfectly inelastic, its entire income is economic rent. Most of Madonna's income is economic rent. Also, a large part of the income of an international football player is economic rent. When the supply of a factor of production is perfectly elastic, none of its income is economic rent. Most of the income of a babysitter is opportunity cost. In general, when the supply curve is neither perfectly elastic nor perfectly inelastic (like that illustrated in Figure 15.10(a), some part of the factor income is economic rent and the other part opportunity cost.

Part (b) of Figure 15.10 shows the market for a particular parcel of land in London. The land is fixed in size at L hectares. Therefore the supply curve of the land is vertical – perfectly inelastic. No matter what the rent on the land is, there is no way of increasing the quantity that can be supplied.

The demand for that block of land is determined by its marginal revenue product. The marginal revenue product in turn depends on the uses to which the land can be put. In a central business district such as Canary Wharf, the marginal revenue product is high because a large number of people are concentrated in that area, making it a prime place for conducting business. Suppose that the marginal revenue product of this block of land is shown by the demand curve in Figure 15.10(b). The entire income accruing to the owner of the land is the green area in the figure. This income is economic rent. The rent charged for this piece of land depends entirely on its marginal revenue product – on the demand curve. If the demand curve shifts rightward, the rent rises. If the demand curve shifts leftward, the rent falls. The quantity of land supplied remains constant at *L*.

Figure 15.9(c) shows the market for a factor of production that is in perfectly elastic supply. An example of such a market might be that for unskilled labour in a poor country such as India or China. In these countries, large amounts of labour flock to the cities and are available for work at the going wage rate (in this case, *W*). Thus in these situations, the supply of labour is almost perfectly elastic. The entire income earned by this labour is opportunity cost. They receive no economic rent.

We've now studied the markets for factors of production, the returns to these factors and how demand and supply determine factor prices and factor incomes. We've seen the role of the factor's marginal revenue product in determining why some factors receive large incomes and others receive small incomes. Finally, we've distinguished between economic rent and opportunity cost. In the next chapter, we're going to examine labour markets more closely and explain differences in wage rates among skilled and unskilled workers, males and females, and racial and ethnic minorities.

Summary

Key Points

Factor Prices and Incomes (pp. 354–355)

- An increase in the demand for a factor of production increases its price and total income; a decrease in the demand for a factor of production decreases its price and total income.
- An increase in the supply of a factor of production increases the quantity used but decreases its price and might increase or decrease its total income, depending on whether demand is elastic or inelastic.

Labour Markets (pp. 355–364)

- The demand for labour is determined by the marginal revenue product of labour.
- The demand for labour increases because of technological change.
- The elasticity of demand for labour depends on labour intensity in production, the elasticity of demand for the product, and the ease with which labour can be substituted for capital.
- The quantity of labour supplied increases as the real wage rate increases, but at high wage rates, the supply curve may bend backwards.
- The supply of labour increases as the population increases and with changes in social attitudes towards the paid work of women and children.

Capital Markets (pp. 364–369)

- The demand for financial capital is determined by the marginal revenue product of physical capital.
- To make an investment decision, firms compare the present value of the expected marginal revenue product of capital with the current price of capital.
- Population growth and technological change increase the demand for capital.

- The higher the interest rate, the greater are the amount of saving and the quantity of capital supplied.
- The supply of capital increases as incomes increase.
- Capital market equilibrium determines interest rates.

Land and Exhaustible Natural Resource Markets (pp. 369–372)

- The demand for natural resources is determined by its marginal revenue product.
- The supply of land is inelastic.
- The supply of exhaustible natural resources is perfectly elastic at a price equal to the present value of the expected future price.
- The price of exhaustible natural resources is expected to rise at a rate equal to the interest rate but fluctuates and sometimes falls because of unexpected changes in technology.

Income, Economic Rent and Opportunity Cost (pp. 372–374)

- Economic rent is the income received by a factor over and above the amount needed to induce the factor owner to supply the resource for use.
- The rest of a resource's income is opportunity cost.
- When the supply of a factor is perfectly inelastic, its entire income is made up of economic rent. When the supply of a factor is perfectly elastic, its entire income is made up of opportunity cost.

Key Figures and Tables 

Key Terms

Review Questions

1 Explain what happens to the price of a factor of production and its income if the following occurs:

a There is an increase in demand for the factor.
b There is an increase in supply of the factor.
c There is a decrease in demand for the factor.
d There is a decrease in supply of the factor.

2 Explain why the effect of a change in supply of a factor on a factor's income depends on the elasticity of demand for the factor.

3 Define marginal revenue product and distinguish between marginal revenue product and marginal revenue.

4 Why does marginal revenue product decline as the quantity of a factor employed increases?

5 What is the relationship between the demand curve for a factor of production and its marginal revenue product curve? Why?

6 Show that the condition for maximum profit in the product market – marginal cost equals marginal revenue – is equivalent to the

condition for maximum profit in the factor market – marginal revenue product equals marginal cost of factor (equals factor price in a competitive factor market).

7 Review the main influences on the demand for a factor of production – the influences that shift the demand curve for a factor.

8 What determines the short-run and the long-run elasticity of demand for labour?

9 What determines the supply of labour?

10 Why might the supply of labour curve bend backward at a high enough wage rate?

11 Why might real wages rise over time?

12 What is present value and how is it calculated?

13 What determines the supply of capital?

14 How are interest rates determined?

15 Why is the price of a particular piece of land determined by its marginal revenue product?

16 Why is the price of an exhaustible natural resource determined by the present value of its expected future price?

17 Why do national news readers receive large incomes and cleaners low incomes?

18 Define economic rent and opportunity cost and distinguish between these two components of income.

19 Suppose that a factor of production is in perfectly inelastic supply. If the marginal revenue product of the factor decreases, what happens to the price, quantity used, income, opportunity cost and rent of the factor?

Problems

1 Wanda owns a fish shop and employs students to pack the fish. Students can pack the following amounts of fish in an hour:

Number of students	Quantity of fish (Kilograms)
1	20
2	50
3	90
4	120
5	145
6	165
7	180
8	190

a Draw the average and marginal product curves of these students.
b If Wanda can sell her fish for 50 pence a kilogram, draw the average and marginal revenue product curves.
c Draw Wanda's demand for labour curve.

2 The price of fish falls to 33 pence a kilogram, and fish packers' wages remain at £7.50 an hour.

a What happens to Wanda's average and marginal product curves?
b What happens to her average and marginal revenue product curves?
c What happens to her demand for labour curve?
d What happens to the number of students that she hires?

3 Fish packers' wages increase to £10 an hour but the price of fish remains at 50 pence a kilogram.

a What happens to Wanda's average and marginal revenue product curves?
b What happens to her demand curve for labour?
c How many packers does Wanda hire?

4 Using the information provided in Problem 1, calculate Wanda's marginal revenue and marginal cost, marginal revenue product and marginal cost of labour. Show that when Wanda is making maximum profit, marginal cost equals marginal revenue and marginal revenue product equals the marginal cost of labour.

5 You are given the following information about the labour market in an isolated town in the Amazon rain forest. Everyone works for logging companies, but there are many logging companies in the town. The market for logging workers is perfectly competitive. The town's labour supply is given as follows:

Wage rate (cruzeiros per hour)	Quantity of labour supplied (hours)
200	120
300	160
400	200
500	240
600	280
700	320
800	360

The market demand for labour from all the logging firms in the town is as follows:

Wage rate (cruzeiros per hour)	Quantity of labour demanded (hours)
200	400
300	360
400	320
500	280
600	240
700	200
800	160

a What is the competitive equilibrium wage rate and the quantity of labour employed?
b What is total labour income?
c How much of that labour income is economic rent and how much is opportunity cost? (You may find it easier to answer this question by drawing graphs of the demand and supply curves and then finding the economic rent and opportunity cost as areas on the graph as was done in Figure 15.8.)

6 Study *Reading Between the Lines* on pp. 378–379 and answer the following questions:

a Why is it easier to value the marginal revenue product of a football manager than a manager in commercial business?
b How does a manager decide on the profit maximizing number of players to buy each year?
c Given that the evidence shows that 80–90 per cent of the difference between club league rankings is due to their wage bill, do you think that football managers are worth having?
d What does a top-class manager do for a football club that an average manager does not?

7 'We are running out of natural resources and must take urgent action to conserve our precious reserves.' 'There is no shortage of resources that the market cannot cope with.' Identify the pros and cons for each view, and discuss each in turn. What is your view and why?

8 Why do we keep finding new reserves of oil? Why don't we do a big once-and-for-all survey to catalog the earth's entire inventory of natural resources?

Factor Incomes: What's a Football Manager Worth?

The Observer, 1 November 1998

Suits in a league of their own

Stefan Szymanski

Managers are the heroes of the corporate economy. But do they make a difference?

In theory a successful manager is simply someone who can take the same set of inputs and turn them into something of greater value than anyone else. Measuring the impact of managers in practice is difficult because in most industries both the inputs and outputs come in non-standard forms and because the evaluation of performance so often depends on the context.

The football industry is different. In England and Wales the leading clubs compete in a league system. This provides a controlled set of contests, which renders the outcome of competition comparable for each team, an unassailable indicator of relative performance.

Of course, the equality of opportunity of each club is limited by its resources, which are devoted primarily to buying players. Human inputs are notoriously unpredictable in their performance and the market for labour is often a lottery.

Again, the football industry is different. The characteristics of players are generally well known, and the most important work the player does (playing in cup or league matches) can be fully monitored.

Because of this there is a more or less perfect market for players. Players are paid what they are worth, which can be measured by their contribution to enhancing league performance.

Econometric analysis of the performance of 41 clubs over the past 16 years shows that the wage spending of clubs can account for 80–90 per cent of the variation in league performance over time. Disgruntled fans notwithstanding, in football you generally get what you pay for.

The first question to ask about a football manager is this: is he or she capable of raising the performance of the club above the level implied by the wage spend alone?

The analysis allows us to place a value on a good manager, by measuring the difference in league position that would be expected with an average manager compared to that under a top manager. The gap in expected league position could always be made up by buying more players, and from this we can estimate the worth of the manager.

For example, at present a club with an average manager and £15m to spend on salaries could expect to achieve a mid-table position in the Premier League. In the hands of Alex Ferguson, £15m would be expected to yield a league position of third. Coming third with an average manager would require a wage bill of £32m, so the added value of Alex Ferguson in today's money is about £17m.

The strongest predictor of success as a manager is to have won international honours as a player. Forwards are also more likely to have successful careers. But overall, successful managers are extremely difficult to predict.

Stefan Szymanski lectures in economics at Imperial College Management School.

The Essence of the Story

- Measuring the impact of a manager in business is difficult, but this is not the case in football. A better manager is someone who takes the same set of inputs and turns them into greater value.
- Football clubs compete in leagues and their success is a combination of the scoring capability of players and the effect of the manager.
- Human inputs are normally difficult to measure in business, but the characteristics and output of football players is easily observed. So football players are paid what they are worth, measured by their contribution to league performance.
- The wage bill for players wages accounts for 80–90 per cent of differences in league performance.
- The value of a good manager is measured by the difference in the league position expected with an average manager compared to a top manager. The extra player wage bill that would be needed to fill the league position gap is the market value of the manager.

Economic Analysis

- Football players and managers are factors of production for football clubs. Demand for players and managers is derived from their marginal revenue product (*MRP*), a measure of their performance.

- Players are paid according to their marginal revenue product, *MRP*, in a competitive market. *MRP* is the marginal product (the extra league points gained) times the marginal revenue (the extra sales from one extra league point gained).

- Figure 1 shows a football club's marginal revenue product, *MRP*, for players. *MRP* equals the club's demand for players, *D*. A better manager would gain more league points from the same 5 players so would shift *MRP* to *MRP*'.

- At a factor price of £3 million for players, the manager maximizes profit by buying additional players up to the point where *MRP*' equals factor price at 5 players per year. A better manager will employ more players.

- The value of the extra players that could be bought with a better manager, gaining higher league points and higher sales revenue, is a measure of the manager's worth.

- Figure 2 shows the marginal revenue product for an average club manager, MRP_1, achieving mid-league status compared to the the marginal revenue product for achieving third position league status, MRP_2.

- The average manager achieves a mid-league table position with a wage bill of £15 million. A top manager achieves a league position of third with £15 million. But an average manager would have to spend £32 million (£17 million more) to achieve third position, buying more expensive players.

- The blue shaded area in Figure 2 shows the value of a top-class manager as the difference in the wage bill of £17 million. If the club has sufficient funds, it would pay up to £17 million more for a top manager to achieve third position in the league.

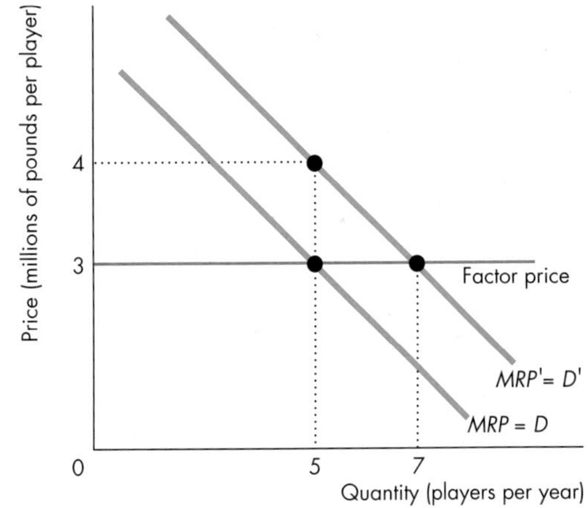

Figure 1 Demand for new players

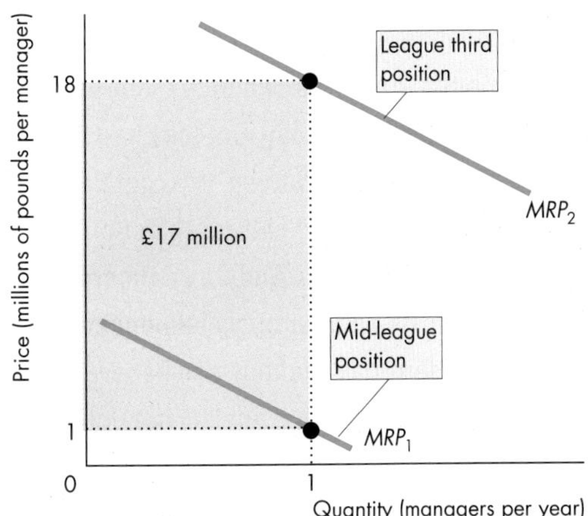

Figure 2 Demand for managers

Running Out?

"The passion between the sexes has appeared in every age to be so nearly the same, that it may always be considered, in algebraic language as a given quantity."

Thomas Robert Malthus
An Essay on the Principle of Population

The Economist: Thomas Robert Malthus

Thomas Robert Malthus (1766–1834), an English parson and economist, was an extremely influential social scientist. In his best-selling *Essay on the Principle of Population*, published in 1798, he predicted that population growth would outstrip food production and said that wars, famine and disease were inevitable unless population growth was held in check by what he called "moral restraint". By "moral restraint" he meant marrying at a late age and living a celibate life. At the age of 38 he married a wife of 27, marriage ages that he recommended for others. Malthus's ideas were regarded as too radical in their day. But they had a profound influence on Charles Darwin, who got the key idea that led him to the theory of natural selection from reading the *Essay on Population*. And David Ricardo and the classical economists were strongly influenced by Malthus's ideas. Modern-day Malthusians believe that his basic idea was right and that it applies not only to food but also to every natural resource.

The Issues and Ideas

Is there a limit to economic growth, or can we expand production and population without effective limit? Thomas Malthus gave one of the most influential answers to these questions in 1798. He reasoned that population, unchecked, would grow at a geometric rate – 1, 2, 4, 8, 16, . . . , while the food supply would grow at an arithmetic rate – 1, 2, 3, 4, 5, ... To prevent the population from outstripping the available food supply, there would be periodic wars, famines and plagues. In Malthus's view, only what he called moral restraint could prevent such periodic disasters.

As industrialization proceeded through the nineteenth century, Malthus's idea came to be applied to all natural resources, especially those that are exhaustible. A modern-day Malthusian, ecologist Paul Ehrlich, believes that we are sitting on a "population bomb" and that the government must limit both population growth and the resources that may be used each year.

In 1931, Harold Hotelling developed a theory of natural resources with different predictions from those of Malthus. The Hotelling Principle is that the relative price of an exhaustible natural resource will steadily rise, bringing a decline in the quantity used and an increase in the use of substitute resources.

Julian Simon, a contemporary economist, has challenged both the Malthusian gloom and the

Hotelling Principle. He believes that people are the "ultimate resource" and predicts that a rising population lessens the pressure on natural resources. A bigger population provides a larger number of resourceful people who can work out more efficient ways of using scarce resources. As these solutions are found, the prices of exhaustible resources actually fall. To demonstrate his point, in 1980, Simon bet Ehrlich that the prices of five metals – copper, chrome, nickel, tin and tungsten – would fall during the 1980s. Simon won the bet!

Then . . .

No matter whether it is agricultural land, an exhaustible natural resource, or the space in the centre of Manchester, and no matter whether it is 1998 or, as shown opposite, 1914, there is a limit to what is available, and we persistently push against that limit. Economists see urban congestion as a consequence of the value of doing business in the city centre relative to the cost. They see the price mechanism, bringing ever-higher rents and prices of raw materials, as the means of allocating and rationing scarce natural resources. Malthusians, in contrast, explain congestion as the consequence of population pressure, and they see population control as the solution.

. . . And Now

In Tokyo, the pressure on space is so great that in some residential neighbourhoods, a parking space costs £1,000 a month. To economize on this expensive space – and to lower the cost of car ownership and hence boost the sale of cars – Honda, Nissan and Toyota, three of Japan's big car producers, have developed a parking machine that enables two cars to occupy the space of one. The most basic of these machines costs a mere £7,500, less than 6 months' worth of parking fees.

Trying These Ideas Today

Using what you have learned about factor markets in Chapter 15 and what you have read about Malthus and the challenge to Malthusian ideas, you should be able to answer the following questions:

- London's roads, like those of most modern cities, are highly congested. The average speed is just 3 miles an hour! We don't pay for road use directly, so what is the price that motorists have to pay for ever more congested roads, and is it rising or falling over time?
- In what ways do you think that technology could resolve this 'overcrowding' problem?

CHAPTER 16

Labour Markets

After studying this chapter you will be able to:

- Explain why skilled workers earn more, on the average, than unskilled workers
- Explain why university graduates earn more, on the average, than school leavers
- Explain why union workers earn higher wages than non-union workers
- Explain why, on the average, men earn more than women and whites earn more than minorities
- Predict the effects of equal pay and equal worth laws

The Sweat of Our Brows

As you well know, studying is not a party. Those exams and problem-sets require a lot of time and effort. Are they worth the sweat that goes into them? What is the payoff? Is it sufficient to make up for the years of tuition, rents and lost wages? (You could, after all, be working now instead of slogging through this economics course.) ◆ Many workers belong to trade unions. Usually, union workers earn a higher wage than non-union workers in comparable jobs. Why? How are unions able to get higher wages for their members than non-union workers? ◆ Among the most visible and persistent differences in earnings are those between men and women and between whites and ethnic minorities. Women, on the average, earn hourly incomes that are 78 per cent of men's incomes in the United Kingdom. Non-white workers, on the average, earn hourly incomes that are 92 per cent of white workers' incomes in the United Kingdom. Why do minorities and women so consistently earn less than white men? Is it because of discrimination and exploitation? Or is it because of economic factors? Or is it a combination of the two? ◆ Equal pay legislation was introduced in the United Kingdom in 1970. Since 1976, the law has required men and women who perform similar tasks to be paid the same rate. Does this type of legislation bring economic help to women and minorities?

◆ ◆ ◆ ◆ In this chapter, we answer these questions by continuing our study of labour markets. We begin by extending the competitive labour market model developed in Chapter 15 to analyse the effects of education and training on wages. We then study differences in union and non-union wages and in pay among men, women and minorities. Finally, we analyse the effects of equal pay legislation.

Skill Differentials

Differences in earnings between workers with varying levels of education and training can be explained using a model of competitive labour markets. In the real world, there are many different levels and varieties of education and training. To keep our analysis as clear as possible, we'll study a model economy in which there are just two different levels that result in two types of labour, which we will call skilled labour and unskilled labour. We'll study the demand for and supply of these two types of labour and see why there is a difference in their wages and what determines that difference. Let's begin by looking at the demand for the two types of labour.

The Demand for Skilled and Unskilled Labour

Skilled workers can perform a wide variety of tasks that unskilled workers would perform badly or perhaps could not even perform at all. Imagine an untrained, inexperienced person performing surgery or piloting a plane. Skilled workers have a higher marginal revenue product than unskilled workers. As we learned in Chapter 15, the demand for labour curve is derived from the marginal revenue product curve. Other things remaining the same, the higher the marginal revenue product of labour, the greater is the demand for labour.

Figure 16.1(a) shows the demand curves for skilled and unskilled labour. At any given level of employment, firms are willing to pay a higher wage to a skilled worker than to an unskilled worker. The gap between the two wages is the difference between the marginal revenue products of a given number of skilled and unskilled workers. This difference is the marginal revenue product of skill. For example, at an employment level of 2,000 hours, firms are willing to pay £12.50 for a skilled worker and only £5 for an unskilled worker. The difference in the marginal revenue product of the two workers is £7.50 an hour. Thus the marginal revenue product of skill is £7.50 an hour.

Figure 16.1 Skill Differentials

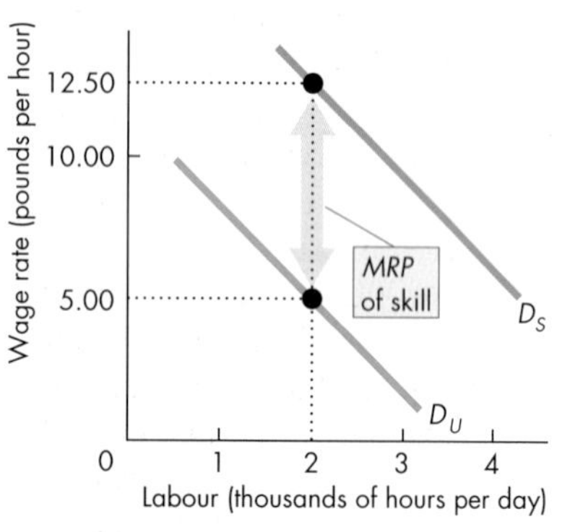

(a) Demand for skilled and unskilled labour

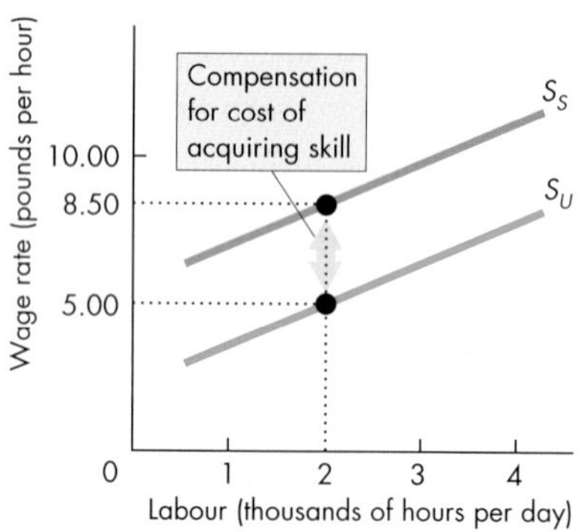

(b) Supply of skilled and unskilled labour

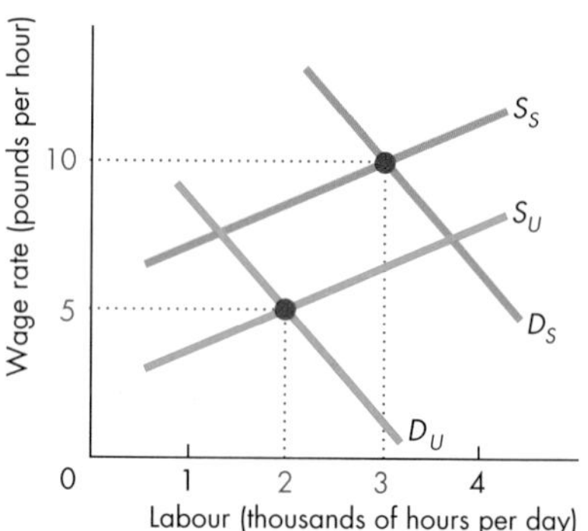

(c) Markets for skilled and unskilled labour

Part (a) illustrates the marginal revenue product of skill. Unskilled workers have a marginal revenue product that gives rise to the demand curve marked D_U. Skilled workers have a higher marginal revenue product than unskilled workers. Therefore the demand curve for skilled workers, D_S, lies to the right of D_U. The vertical distance between these two curves is the marginal revenue product of the skill.

Part (b) shows the effects of the cost of acquiring skills on the supply curves of labour. The supply curve for unskilled workers is S_U. Skilled workers have to incur costs in order to acquire their skills. Therefore they would only supply labour services at a wage rate that exceeds that of unskilled labour. The supply curve for skilled workers is S_S. The vertical distance between these two curves is the required compensation for the cost of acquiring a skill.

Part (c) shows the determination of the equilibrium levels of employment and the skilled/unskilled wage differential. Unskilled workers earn a wage rate of £5 an hour, at which the quantities demanded and supplied of unskilled workers are equal. The employment level of unskilled workers is 2,000 hours. Skilled workers earn the wage rate £10 an hour where the quantities demanded and supplied of skilled workers are equal. The employment level of skilled workers is 3,000 hours. Wages for skilled workers are always greater than those for unskilled workers.

The Supply of Skilled and Unskilled Labour

Skills are costly to acquire. Furthermore, a worker usually pays the cost of acquiring a skill before benefiting from a higher wage. For example, attending university usually leads to a higher income, but the higher income is not earned until after graduation. These facts imply that the acquisition of a skill is an investment. To emphasize the investment nature of acquiring a skill, we call that activity an investment in human capital. **Human capital** is the accumulated skill and knowledge that individuals acquire through learning, training, work and life experiences.

The opportunity cost of acquiring a skill includes actual expenditures on such things as tuition and room and board, and also costs in the form of lost or reduced earnings while the skill is being acquired. When a person studies full time, that cost is the total earnings foregone. However, some people acquire skills on the job. Such skill acquisition is called on-the-job training. Usually a worker undergoing on-the-job training is paid a lower wage than one doing a comparable job but not undergoing training. In such a case, the cost of acquiring the skill is the difference between the wage paid to a person not being trained and that paid to a person being trained.

Supply Curves of Skilled and Unskilled Labour

The position of the supply curve of skilled workers reflects the cost of acquiring the skill. Figure 16.1(b) shows two supply curves, one for skilled workers and the other for unskilled workers. The supply curve for skilled workers is S_S and for unskilled workers S_U.

The skilled worker's supply curve lies above the unskilled worker's supply curve. The vertical distance between the two supply curves is the compensation that skilled workers require for the cost of acquiring the skill. For example, suppose that the quantity of unskilled labour supplied is 2,000 hours at a wage rate of £5 an hour. This wage rate compensates the unskilled workers purely for their time on the job. Consider next the supply of skilled workers. To induce 2,000 hours of skilled labour to be supplied, firms must pay a wage rate of £8.50 an hour. This wage rate for skilled labour is higher than that for unskilled labour because skilled labour must be compensated not only for the time on the job but also for the time and other costs of acquiring the skill.

Wage Rates of Skilled and Unskilled Labour

To work out the wage rates of skilled and unskilled labour, all we have to do is bring together the effects of skill on the demand and supply of labour. Figure 16.1(c) shows the demand curves and the supply curves for skilled and unskilled labour. These curves are exactly the same as those plotted in parts (a) and (b). Equilibrium occurs in the market for unskilled labour where the supply and demand curves for unskilled labour intersect. The equilibrium wage rate is £5 an hour and the quantity of unskilled labour employed is 2,000 hours. Equilibrium in the market for skilled workers occurs where the supply and demand curves for skilled workers intersect. The equilibrium wage rate is £10 an hour and the quantity of skilled labour employed is 3,000 hours.

As you can see in part (c), the equilibrium wage rate of skilled labour is higher than that of unskilled labour. There are two reasons why this occurs. First, skilled labour has a higher marginal revenue product than unskilled labour, so at a given wage rate the demand for skilled labour is greater than the demand for unskilled labour; second, skills are costly to acquire so that at a given wage rate the supply of skilled labour is less than the supply of unskilled labour. The wage differential (in this case £5 an hour) depends on both the marginal revenue product of the skill and the cost of acquiring it. The higher the marginal revenue product of the skill, the larger is the vertical distance between the demand curves for skilled and unskilled labour. The more costly it is to acquire a skill, the larger is the vertical distance between the supplies of skilled and unskilled labour. The higher the marginal revenue product of the skill and the more costly it is to acquire, the larger is the wage differential between skilled and unskilled workers.

UK MPs voted themselves a 26 per cent pay rise in July 1996, raising their salaries to £43,000 a year. They argued that their pay did not reflect differentials seen in the private sector. The increase would reward the high level of marginal revenue product from the specialist skills needed by an MP and the high cost of gaining those skills – an alternative career foregone. Of course, not all of the duties of an MP require a great deal of skill as you can see from the cartoon.

'I earn too much to kiss babies'

Do Education and Training Pay?

There are large and persistent differences in earnings based on the degree of education and training. An indication of those differences in the United Kingdom can be seen in part (a) of Figure 16.2. It shows that the higher the level of education, other things remaining the same, the higher are earnings for both men and women. The percentages indicate women's earnings as a percentage of men's earnings. Men earn more than women on average at all qualification levels but the gap between men's and women's earnings is less at higher levels of qualification. Most people finish their education by the time they are 25, so do earnings increase with age? The link between age and earnings is shown in part (b) of Figure 16.2. You can see that earnings rise with age up to middle age and then decline. Men earn more than women in all age groups but the gap is greatest between the ages of 40 and 49. This is because age is also correlated with experience and the degree of on-the-job training up to middle age. The gap between men's and women's earnings increases because women take periods away from work to raise children, reducing their years of experience and on-the-job training in middle age.

We can see from part (a) of Figure 16.2 that going through school, university and postgraduate education leads to higher incomes. But do they pay in the sense of yielding a higher income that

Figure 16.2 Education, Age and Real Earnings

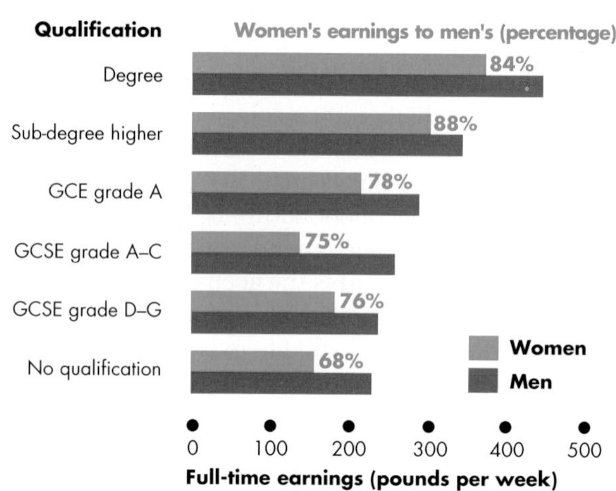

(a) Qualifications and earnings for men and women

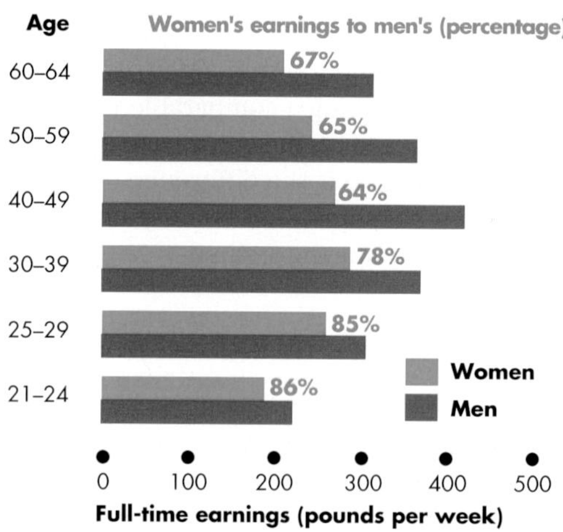

(b) Age and earnings for men and women

Part (a) shows full-time weekly earnings for men and women in 1995 by qualification. Earnings increase with the amount of education for men and women. The gap between men's and women's earnings declines with higher levels of qualifications. Part (b) shows full-time weekly earnings for men and women in full-time work in 1997 by age. Men earn more than women at all ages but the gap widens with age up to middle age. Beyond that age, earnings decrease for both men and women more equally.

Source: (a) Office of Population Censuses and Surveys, *General Household Survey, 1997*, London, HMSO, 1997. (b) Department of Employment, 'Labour Force Survey', *Employment Gazette*, March 1998.

Table 16.1 A Compact Glossary on Labour Relations 

Arbitration	When parties to a dispute accept the determination of wages and other employment conditions by a third party (an arbitrator)
Collective bargaining	Negotiations between representatives of employers and unions on wages and conditions
Corporatist bargaining	Collective bargaining at the national level between unions and employer federations, with government, for national wages and conditions
Decentralized bargaining	Collective bargaining, at the local level between unions and employers, for local wages and conditions
Employer federation	An organization of employer representatives which provides a service to its members and acts as the national voice of employers. The Confederation of British Industries is an example
Industrial union	An organized group of workers with different skills and job types that attempts to increase wages and improve conditions for its members within that industry
Lockout	When a firm will not allow its employees access to the workplace
Trade union	An organized group of workers with similar skills and job types that attempts to increase wages and improve conditions for its members in that trade
Open shop	A place of work that has no union restriction on who can work in it; here, the union bargains for its members but not for non-members
Strike	When a group of employees refuse to work under the exisiting conditions
Union federation	An organization of union representatives which provides a service to its members and acts as the national voice of unions. The Trades Union Congress is an example

compensates for the cost of education and for the delay in the start of earnings? For most people, college or university does pay. Rates of return have been estimated to be in the range of 5–10 per cent a year after allowing for inflation, which suggests that a university degree is a better investment than almost any other.

Education is an important source of earnings differences. But there are others. One is the activities of trade unions. Let's see how unions affect wages and why, on the average, union wages exceed non-union wages.

Union–Non-union Wage Differentials

A union is an organized group of workers who aim to increase wages and influence other job conditions. A union acts in the labour market like a monopolist in the product market. The union seeks to restrict competition and, as a result, increases the price at which labour is traded. A compact glossary on labour relations can be found in Table 16.1.

There are two main types of union: trade (or craft) unions and industrial unions. A **trade union** is a group of workers who have similar skills, but may work in many different firms and in different industries. This is the most common type of union in the United Kingdom. Because of this, a large-scale employer may have to deal with many unions at a time during negotiation. An industrial union is a group of workers who have a variety of skills and job types but work for the same firm or industry. Industrial unions are most commonly found in the United States and in Germany. They allow an industry-wide agreement to be made through negotiation with just one union.

A union can be organized as an open shop or a closed shop. An *open shop* is an arrangement in which workers can be employed without joining the union – there is no union restriction on who can work in the 'shop'. In an open shop, non-union members may belong to other professional organizations and are not represented by the union. However, non-union staff usually receive the same benefits as union staff after a dispute, even if they have not participated in any action. A closed shop is an arrangement in which only union members can be employed by a firm. This arrangement was preferred by unions as it strengthened the power of the union in a dispute with employers. Closed shops virtually disappeared in the United Kingdom as a result of the 1980 Employment Act.

Unions negotiate with employers or their representatives in a process called **collective bargaining**. Countries like the United Kingdom

Figure 16.3 Union Numbers and Union Membership

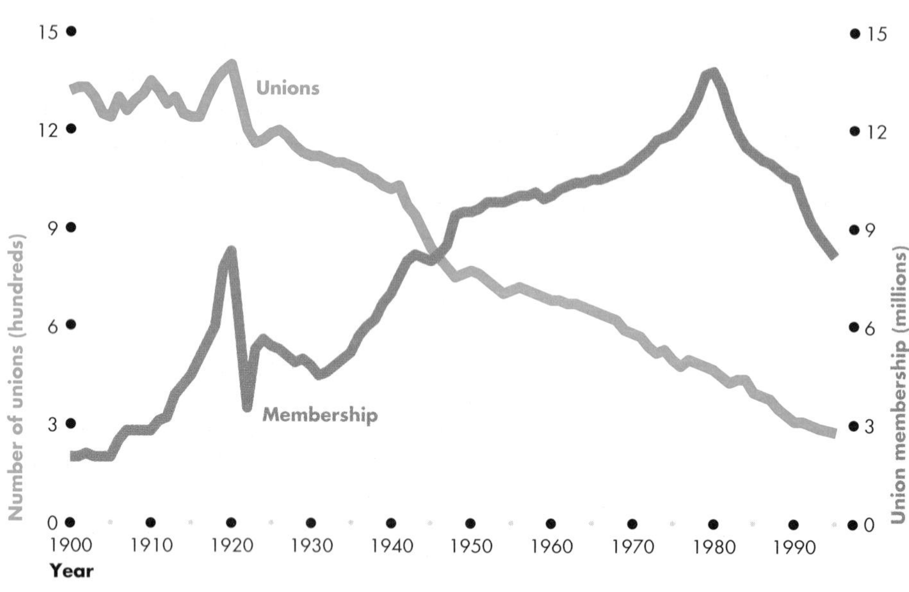

The number of unions in the United Kingdom has declined steadily over this century, peaking in the early 1920s when there were more than 1,300 individual unions compared with just 235 in 1997. By contrast, union membership increased steadily to a peak in 1979 with 13.3 million, but then declined to its current level of 8.3 million members. The number of unions has declined as smaller unions have merged, and the largest seven unions now account for 59 per cent of union membership.

Source: Central Statistical Office, *Labour Market Trends*, p. 50, London, HMSO, February 1998.

use a process of *decentralized bargaining*, where individual employers and local union representatives negotiate local wages and conditions. Countries like Sweden adopt a *corporatist bargaining* process. In this process, the government brings employer and union representatives together at the national level to negotiate national wage structures and conditions. The parties in corporatist bargaining are employer federations, union federations and government. Federations have affiliated members and aim to represent their views to the public and in national negotiation, as well as providing information services to their members. The Confederation of British Industries (CBI) is the main employer federation and the Trades Union Congress (TUC) is the union federation in the United Kingdom.

The main weapons available to the union and the employer in collective bargaining are the strike and the lockout. A *strike* is a group decision to refuse to work under prevailing conditions. A *lockout* is a firm's refusal to operate its plant and pay its workers. Each party uses the threat of a strike or a lockout to try to get an agreement in its own favour. Sometimes when the two parties in the collective bargaining process cannot agree on the wage rate and other conditions of employment, they agree to submit their disagreement to binding arbitration. *Arbitration* is a process in which a third party – an arbitrator – determines wages and other employment conditions on behalf of the negotiating parties. The decision of the arbitrator may be binding or subject to voluntary agreement.

There are about 243 unions in the United Kingdom. The smallest has fewer than 100 members and the largest, Unison, the public sector union, has nearly 1.4 million members. Most of the larger unions are members of the TUC. Figure 16.3 shows that the number of unions in the United Kingdom has declined during this century. At its peak, in 1921, there were more than 1,300 separate unions. Union membership, by contrast, has increased over most of this century. It was at its highest in the United Kingdom in 1979, when more than half the labour force, 13.3 million people, were members of trade unions. Since then, there has been a steady decline in union membership to its current level of 8.3 million members. There are two main reasons for the recent decline in membership. The first is the decline in the proportion of total employment of the traditional industries such as shipbuilding, coal and steel on which the union movement developed.

New jobs have been created in the expanding services sectors, but many of these are part-time and taken up by women. Part-timers and women did not believe unions served their interests in the past. The second is the impact of technology on production processes. Robotics and computer-controlled production have cut employment and reduced the power of union members to halt production in a dispute. The introduction of flexible work practices and no-union agreements have also undermined traditional union practices.

Professional associations are not unions in a legal sense, but they act like unions. A *professional association* is an organized group of professional workers such as doctors, lawyers and accountants (an example is the British Medical Association – BMA). Professional associations control entry into the professions and license practitioners, ensuring the adherence to minimum standards of competence. They also influence the level of wages and conditions for their members.

Unions' Objectives and Constraints

A union has three broad objectives that it strives to achieve for its members:

1 To increase compensation.
2 To improve working conditions.
3 To expand job opportunities.

Each of these objectives contains a series of more detailed goals. For example, in seeking to increase the compensation of its members, a union operates on a variety of fronts: wage rates, fringe benefits, retirement pay and such things as holiday allowances. In seeking to improve working conditions, a union is concerned with occupational health and safety as well as the environmental quality of the workplace. In seeking to expand job opportunities, a union tries to obtain greater job security for existing union members and to find ways of creating additional jobs for them.

A union's ability to pursue its objectives is restricted by two sets of constraints – one on the supply side and the other on the demand side of the labour market. On the supply side, the union's activities are limited by how well it can restrict non-union workers from offering their labour in the same market. The larger the fraction of the workforce controlled by the union, the more effective the union can be. If the union is unable to restrict entry, such as in the market for bar and nightclub staff, it cannot have any effect. At the other extreme, unions in the construction industry can influence the number of people obtaining skills as electricians, plasterers and carpenters, and so can better pursue their goals. Those best able to restrict supply are the professional associations for such groups as doctors, lawyers and accountants. These groups control the number of qualified workers by controlling either the examinations that new entrants must pass or entrance into professional degree programmes.

On the demand side of the labour market, the constraint facing a union is the fact that it cannot force firms to hire more labour than the quantity that maximizes their profits. Anything that increases the wage rate or other employment costs decreases the quantity of labour demanded. Unless the union can take actions that shift the demand curve for the labour that it represents, it has to accept the fact that a higher wage rate can be obtained only at the price of lower employment. For this reason, unions try to make the demand for their union labour inelastic as well as to increase the demand for it. Some of the methods employed by unions are:

- To encourage import restrictions.
- To support minimum wage laws.
- To increase demand for the good produced.
- To increase the marginal product of union members.

One of the best examples of import restrictions in the United Kingdom is the support by the National Union of Mineworkers for restrictions on imports of foreign coal. Unions support minimum wage laws in order to increase the cost of employing unskilled labour. An increase in the wage rate of unskilled labour leads to a decrease in the quantity demanded of unskilled labour and to an increase in demand for skilled union labour, a substitute for unskilled labour. An increase in the demand for the good produced increases the demand for union labour because the demand for labour is a derived demand. Good examples are attempts by textiles and car unions to encourage their own workers as well as the public to buy British. Increasing the marginal product of union members directly shifts the demand curve for their services. Unions use apprenticeship, training and professional certification to increase the marginal product of their members.

Figure 16.4 A Union in a Competitive Labour Market

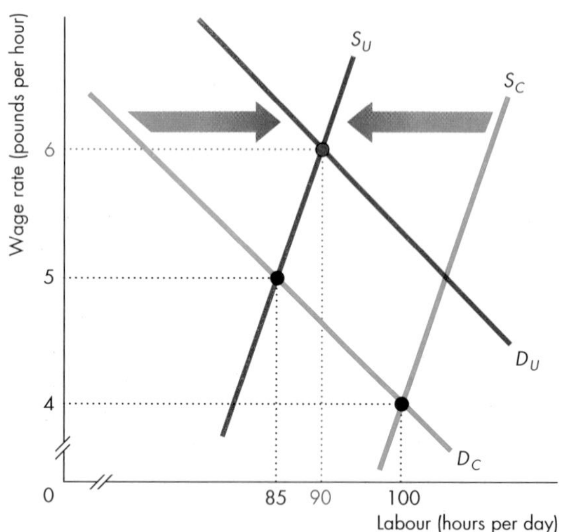

In a competitive labour market, the demand curve is D_C and the supply curve is S_C. Competitive equilibrium occurs at a wage rate of £4 an hour with 100 hours employed. By restricting employment below its competitive level, the union shifts the supply of labour to S_U. If the union can do no more than that, the wage rate will increase to £5 an hour, but employment will fall to 85 hours. If the union can increase the demand for labour (by increasing the demand for the good produced by the union members or by raising the price of substitute labour) and shift the demand curve to D_U, then it can increase the wage rate still more to £6 an hour and achieve employment of 90 hours.

Unions in a Competitive Labour Market

When a union operates in an otherwise competitive labour market, it seeks to increase wages and other compensation and to limit employment reductions by increasing demand for the labour of its members.

Figure 16.4 illustrates a labour market. The demand curve is D_C and the supply curve is S_C. If the market is a competitive one with no union, the wage rate is £4 an hour and 100 hours of labour will be employed. Suppose that a union is formed to organize the workers in this market and that the union has sufficient control over the supply of labour to be able to artificially restrict that supply below its competitive level – to S_U. If that is all the union does, employment will fall to 85 hours of labour and the wage rate will rise to £5 an hour. If the union can also take steps that increase the demand for labour to D_U, it can achieve an even bigger increase in the wage rate with a smaller fall in employment. By maintaining the restricted labour supply at S_U, the union increases the wage rate to £6 an hour and achieves an employment level of 90 hours of labour.

Because a union restricts the supply of labour in the market in which it operates, its actions increase the supply of labour in non-union markets. Those who can't get union jobs must look elsewhere for work. This increase in supply in non-union markets lowers the wage rate in those markets and further widens the union–non-union differential. But low non-union wages decrease the demand for union labour and limit the increase in wages that unions can achieve. For this reason, unions are strong supporters of minimum wage laws that keep non-union wages high and limit the incentive to use non-union labour.

Let's now turn our attention to the case in which employers have considerable influence in the labour market.

Monopsony

A **monopsony** is a market structure in which there is just a single buyer. With the growth of large-scale production over the last century, large organizations such as coal mines, steel and textile mills, and car manufacturers became the major employer of labour in some regions, and in some places a single firm employed almost all the labour. Such a firm has some monopsony power.

A monopsony can make a bigger profit than a group of firms that have to compete with each other for their labour. Figure 16.5 illustrates how a monopsony operates. The monopsony's marginal revenue product curve is *MRP*. This curve tells us the extra revenue from selling the output produced by the last hour of labour hired. The curve labelled *S* is the supply curve of labour. This curve tells us how many hours are supplied at each wage rate. It also tells us the minimum wage that is acceptable at each level of labour supplied.

In deciding how much labour to hire, the monopsony recognizes that to hire more labour it must pay a higher wage or, equivalently, by hiring less labour the monopsony can get away with paying a lower wage. The monopsony takes account of this fact when calculating its marginal cost of labour.

Figure 16.5 A Monopsony Labour Market

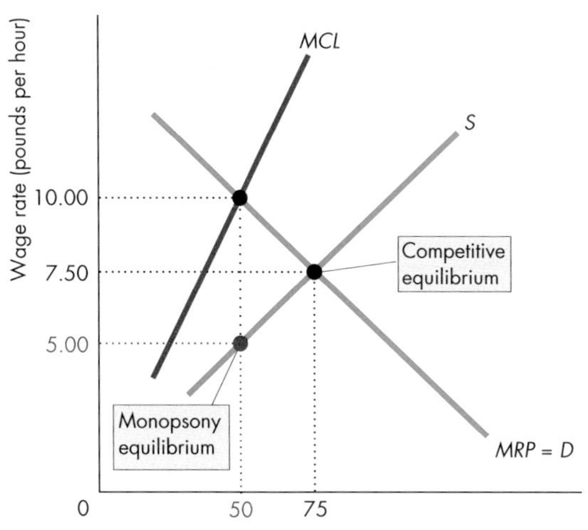

A monopsony is a market structure in which there is a single buyer. A monopsony in the labour market which has a marginal revenue product curve *MRP* faces a labour curve *S*. The marginal cost of labour curve is *MCL*. Profit is maximized by making the marginal cost of labour equal to marginal revenue product. The monopsony hires 50 hours of labour and pays the lowest wage for which that labour will work, £5 an hour.

If a union enters the market, it will attempt to increase the wage rate to above £5 an hour. If the union is all powerful, the highest wage it can achieve is £10 an hour. If the union and the firm are equally powerful they will bargain and agree to a wage rate of £7.50 an hour – the wage rate that equally splits the difference between marginal revenue product and the lowest wage for which labour will work.

The marginal cost of labour is shown by the curve *MCL*. The relationship between the marginal cost of labour curve and the supply curve is similar to the relationship between the marginal cost and average total cost curves that you studied in Chapter 11. The supply curve is like the average total cost of labour curve. For example, in Figure 16.5 the firm can hire 50 hours of labour at £5 an hour, so its average total cost is £5 an hour. The total cost of labour is £5 an hour multiplied by 50 hours, which equals £250 an hour. But suppose that the firm hires slightly less than 50 hours of labour, say 49 hours. The wage rate at which 49 hours of labour can be hired is just below £4.90 an hour. The firm's total labour cost is £240. Hiring the fiftieth hour of labour increases the total cost of labour from £240 to £250, which is £10. The curve *MCL* shows the £10 marginal cost of hiring the fiftieth hour of labour.

To calculate the profit-maximizing quantity of labour to hire, the firm sets the marginal cost of labour equal to the marginal revenue product of labour. That is, the firm wants the cost of the last worker hired to equal the extra revenue brought in. In Figure 16.5, this outcome occurs when the monopsony employs 50 hours of labour. What is the wage rate that the monopsony pays? To hire 50 hours of labour, the firm must pay £5 an hour, as shown by the supply of labour curve. The marginal revenue product of labour, however, is £10 an hour, which means that the firm makes an economic profit of £5 on the last hour of labour that it hires. Each worker is paid £5 an hour.

Compare this outcome with that in a competitive labour market. If the labour market shown in Figure 16.5 were competitive, equilibrium would occur at the point of intersection of the demand curve and the supply curve. The wage rate would be £7.50 an hour and 75 hours of labour a day would be employed. So, compared with a competitive labour market, a monopsony decreases both the wage rate and the level of employment.

The ability of a monopsony to lower the wage rate and employment level and make an economic profit depends on the elasticity of labour supply. The more elastic the supply of labour, the less opportunity a monopsony has to cut wages and employment and make an economic profit.

Monopsony Tendencies With today's low costs of transport, it is unlikely that many pure monopsonies remain. Workers can easily commute long distances to a job, and so for most people there is not just one potential employer. But some firms do have a monopsony tendency. That is, while they are not pure monopsonies, they face an upward-sloping supply of labour curve and their marginal cost of labour exceeds the wage rate. Monopsony tendencies arise in isolated communities in which a single firm is the main employer. But in such situations there is also, usually, a union. Let's see how a union interacts with a monopsony.

Monopsony and Unions When we studied monopoly in Chapter 13, we discovered that a single seller in a market is able to determine the price in that market. We have just studied monopsony – a market with a single buyer – and discovered that in such a market the buyer is able to determine the price. Suppose that a union starts to operate in a monopsony labour market. A union is like a monopoly. It controls the supply of labour and acts like a single seller of labour. If the union (monopoly seller) faces a monopsony buyer, the situation is one of **bilateral monopoly**. In bilateral monopoly, the wage rate is determined by bargaining between the two sides. Let's study the bargaining process.

In Figure 16.5, if the monopsony is free to determine the wage rate and the level of employment, it hires 50 hours of labour for a wage rate of £5 an hour. But suppose that a union represents the workers and can, if necessary, call a strike. Also suppose that the union agrees to maintain employment at 50 hours, but seeks the highest wage rate the employer can be forced to pay. That wage rate is £10 an hour. That is, the wage rate equals the marginal revenue product of labour. It is unlikely that the union will get the wage rate up to £10 an hour. But it is also unlikely that the firm will keep the wage rate down to £5 an hour. The monopsony firm and the union will bargain over the wage rate and the result will be an outcome between £10 an hour (the maximum that the union can achieve) and £5 an hour (the minimum that the firm can achieve).

The actual outcome of the bargaining depends on the costs that each party can inflict on the other as a result of a failure to agree on the wage rate. The firm can shut down the plant and lock out its workers, and the workers can shut down the plant by striking. Each party knows the strength of the other and knows what it will lose if it does not agree to the demands of the other. If the two parties are equally strong, and they realize it, they will split the difference and agree to a wage rate of £7.50 an hour. If one party is stronger than the other – and both parties know it – the agreed wage will favour the stronger party. Usually, an agreement is reached without a strike or a lockout. The threat – the knowledge that such an event can occur – is usually enough to bring the bargaining parties to an agreement. When strikes or lockouts do occur, it is usually because each party has misjudged the costs the other can inflict.

Monopsony has an interesting implication for the effects of minimum wage laws. Let's now study these effects.

Figure 16.6 Minimum Wage in Monopsony

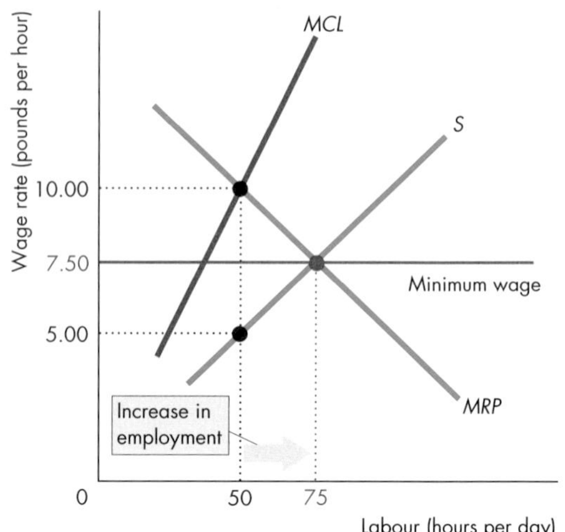

In a monopsony labour market the wage rate is £5 an hour. If a minimum wage law increases the wage rate to £7.50 an hour, employment increases to 75 hours.

Monopsony and the Minimum Wage

A **minimum wage** that exceeds the equilibrium wage in a competitive labour market decreases employment (see Chapter 7, pp. 146–148). A minimum wage in a monopsony labour market can *increase* both the wage rate and employment. Let's see how.

Minimum Wages and Monopsony Suppose that the labour market is that shown in Figure 16.6 and that the wage rate is £5 an hour with 50 hours of labour employed. The government now passes a minimum wage law that prohibits anyone from hiring labour for less than £7.50 an hour. Firms can hire labour for £7.50 an hour or more but not for less than that wage. The monopsony in Figure 16.6 now faces a perfectly elastic supply of labour at £7.50 an hour up to 75 hours. Above 75 hours, a higher wage than £7.50 an hour must be paid to hire additional hours of labour. Because the wage rate is a fixed £7.50 an hour up to 75 hours, the marginal cost of labour is also constant at £7.50 up to 75 hours. Beyond 75 hours, the marginal cost of labour rises above £7.50 an hour. To maximize profit, the monopsony sets the marginal cost of labour equal to its marginal revenue product. That is, the monopsony hires 75 hours of labour at £7.50 an hour. The minimum wage law has made the supply of labour perfectly elastic and made the marginal cost of labour the same as the wage rate up to 75 hours. The law has not affected the supply of labour curve or the marginal cost of labour at employment levels above 75 hours. The minimum wage law has succeeded in raising the wage rate by £2.50 an hour and raising the amount of labour employed by 25 hours.

The Scale of Union–Non-union Wage Differentials

We have seen that unions can influence the wages of their members partly by restricting the supply of labour and partly by increasing the demand for labour. How much of a difference to wage rates do unions make in practice? How big is the union mark-up over non-union wages?

Estimates of the union mark-up in the United Kingdom suggest that it was about 3.8 per cent in the early 1960s but increased steadily to a peak of 8.8 per cent in 1982. Since then the mark-up has remained positive but has decreased to between 5 and 6 per cent. It is not clear that all of this mark-up is a result of union activities. In times of high unemployment, union workers lose their jobs and add to the non-union labour supply. This reduces wages in the non-union sector and increases the mark-up. Also, in some industries, union wages are higher than non-union wages because union members do jobs that involve greater skill. Even without a union, those who perform such tasks receive a higher wage.

Review

- Differences in earnings based on skill or education level arise because skilled labour has a higher marginal revenue product than unskilled labour and because skills are costly to acquire.
- Union workers have higher wage rates than non-union workers because a union is able to control the supply of labour and, indirectly, influence the marginal revenue product of its members.

Wage Differentials Between Sexes and Races

We have already seen from Figure 16.2 that men earn more than women across all age groups and qualification levels. White male workers earn more on average than all other workers whatever their gender or race. White male full-time workers earned £8 an hour on average in 1994, 12 per cent more than men from ethnic minorities. While white female full-time workers earned more than their female ethnic minority counterparts, the differential was much smaller than for men.

Why do these differentials exist? Do they arise because there is discrimination against women and members of minority races, or is there some other explanation? These controversial questions generate an enormous amount of passion. It is not our intention to make you angry, but that may happen as an unintended consequence of this discussion. The objective of this section is to show you how to use economic analysis to address controversial and emotionally charged issues.

We are going to examine four possible explanations for these earnings differences:

1 Job types.
2 Discrimination.
3 Human capital differences.
4 Degrees of specialization.

Job Types

Some of the sex difference in wages arises from the fact that men and women do different jobs and, for the most part, men's jobs are better paid than women's jobs. But there are increasing numbers of women entering areas that were traditionally the preserve of men. This trend is particularly clear in professions such as architecture, medicine, management, law and accounting. The percentage of total enrolments in university courses in these subjects for women has increased from less than 20 per cent in 1970 to 50 per cent in some cases, such as medicine, today. Women are also increasingly seen as bus drivers, police officers and construction workers, all jobs that traditionally were done mainly by men.

The pattern of occupational structures over time is shown in Figure 16.7. One reason why men have earned more than women on the average is that a higher proportion of men had higher-paid work in

Figure 16.7 Occupational Differences

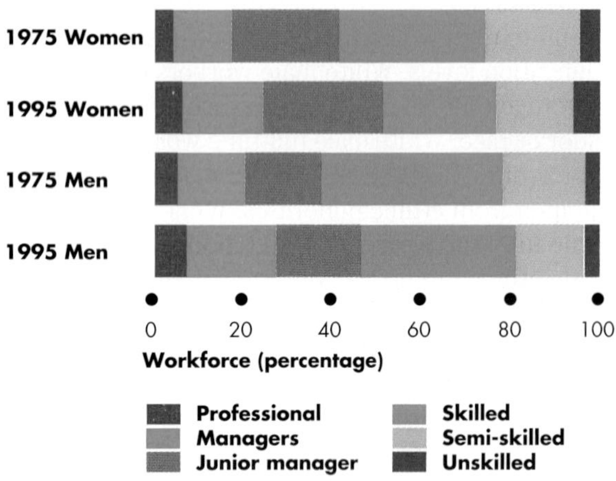

In 1975 a higher proportion of men had higher-paid work in professional or senior managerial jobs and skilled work than women. A smaller proportion of men had poorly paid unskilled work. By 1995, a larger proportion of women had higher-paid managerial jobs and a smaller proportion of women than men had low-paid skilled or unskilled work. This has reduced the gap between men's and women's earnings since 1975.

Source: Office of Population Censuses and Surveys, *General Household Survey, 1995*, London, HMSO, 1997.

professional or senior managerial jobs and skilled work. As a result, a smaller proportion of men had poorly paid unskilled work. However, the pattern is changing. A growing proportion of women now have higher-paid managerial jobs compared with 1975. As a result, a smaller proportion of women than men now have low-paid skilled or unskilled work. This has had an impact – reducing the gap between men's and women's earnings since 1975.

But there are many situations in which women and minorities earn less than white men, even when they do essentially the same job. One possible reason is that women and minorities are discriminated against. Let's see how discrimination might affect wage rates.

Discrimination

Suppose that there are two groups of investment advisers who are identical in their skills at picking good investments. One group consists of black females and the other of white males. Figure 16.8(a) shows the supply curve of black females, S_{BF}, and Figure 16.8(b) shows the supply curve of white males, S_{WM}. These supply curves are identical. The marginal revenue product of investment advisers, whether they are black female or white male, is also identical, as shown by the two curves labelled *MRP* in parts (a) and (b). (Their revenues are the fees their customers pay for investment advice.)

If everyone is free of prejudice about race and sex, the market determines a wage rate of £40,000 a year for both groups of investment advisors. But if the customers of investment houses are prejudiced, this is reflected in the wages of women and racial minority groups.

Suppose that the marginal revenue product of black females, when discriminated against, is the line labelled $MRP_{DA} - DA$ standing for discriminated against. Suppose that the marginal revenue product of white males, the group discriminated in favour of, is $MRP_{DF} - DF$ standing for discriminated in favour of. Given these marginal revenue product curves, the markets for the two groups of investment advisers will now determine very different wages and employment levels. Black females will earn £20,000 a year and only 1,000 will work as investment advisers. White males will earn £60,000 a year and 3,000 of them will work as investment advisers. Thus, purely on the basis of the prejudice of the demanders of investment advice, black women will earn one-third of the wages of white men, and three-quarters of all investment advisers will be white men and only one-quarter will be black women.

Economists disagree about whether prejudice actually causes wage differentials, and one line of reasoning suggests that it does not. In the example, the customers who buy from white men pay a higher service charge for investment advice than the customers who buy from black women. This price difference acts as an incentive to limit discrimination and encourages people who are prejudiced to buy from the people whom they are prejudiced against. This force could be so strong as to eliminate the effects of discrimination altogether. Suppose, as is true in manufacturing, that a firm's customers never meet its workers. If a manufacturing firm discriminated against women or minorities, it would not be able to compete with firms which hired these groups. So only those firms that do not discriminate are able to survive in a competitive industry. You can read about different explanations of pay

Figure 16.8 Discrimination

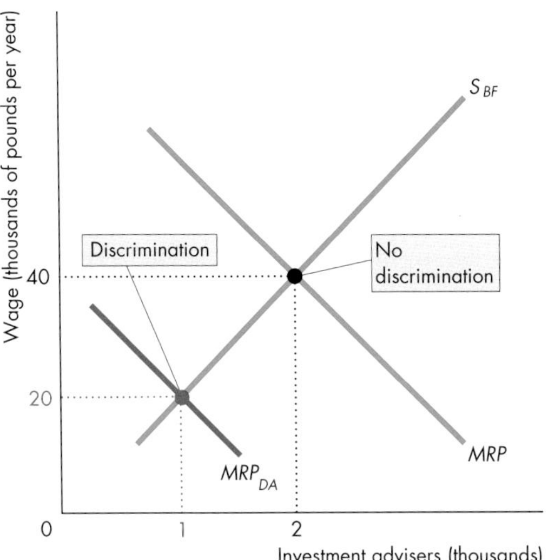

(a) Black females

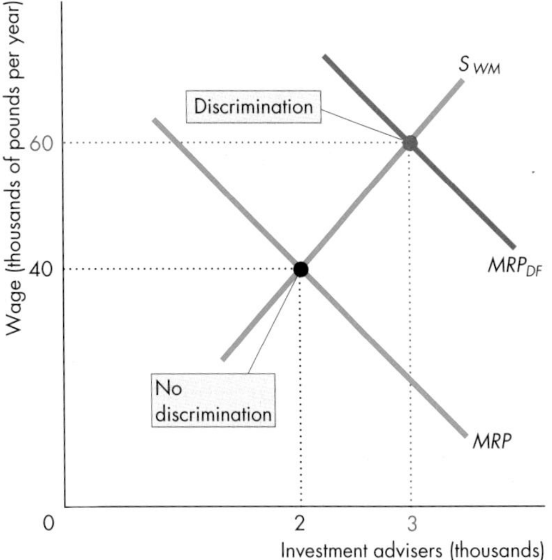

(b) White males

The supply curve for black female investment advisers is S_{BF} in part (a), and the supply curve for white male investment advisers is S_{WM} in part (b). If the marginal revenue product of both groups of investment advisers is *MRP* (the same curve in each part), then the equilibrium wage rate for each group is £40,000 a year and 2,000 of each type of adviser are employed. If there is discrimination against blacks and women, the marginal revenue product curve is to the left of the original curve. It is the curve labelled MRP_{DA} – *DA* standing for discriminated against. There is discrimination in favour of white males, so their marginal revenue product curve is MRP_{DF} – *DF* standing for discriminated in favour of. The wage rate for black women falls to £20,000 a year and only 1,000 are employed. The wage rate for white males increases to £60,000 a year and 3,000 are employed.

differentials between men and women in *Reading Between the Lines* on pp. 402–403.

A further source of wage rate differences lies in differences in human capital. Let's now examine the effects of human capital on wage rates.

Human Capital Differences

Wages are compensation in part for time spent on the job and in part for the cost incurred in acquiring skill – *human capital*. The more human capital a person possesses, the more that person earns, other things remaining the same. It is impossible to measure human capital precisely but there are some rough indicators. The three most useful indicators are:

1 Years of schooling.
2 Years of work experience.
3 Number of job interruptions.

In the past, it has been the case that women and minority groups had less formal education than white males. These differences in education are becoming smaller but have not been eliminated.

The more years of work experience and the fewer the number of job interruptions, the higher is a person's wage. Historically and today, job interruptions are more serious for women than for men. Traditionally, women's careers have been interrupted by bearing and rearing children. It is estimated that women give up £200,000 of income, on the average, over their working lives rearing two children at home. This factor is a possible source of lower wages, on the average, for women. But just as education differences are disappearing, so career interruptions for women are becoming less important. Maternity leave and day-care facilities are providing an increasing number of women with uninterrupted employment that makes their human capital accumulation more similar to that of men.

There is one final source of earnings differences that still affects women's incomes adversely: the relative degree of specialization of women and men.

Degrees of Specialization

People must choose how to allocate their time between paid work and doing jobs in the home, such as cleaning, cooking, decorating, repairing the house, and most importantly, looking after children. Let's look at the choice for a typical couple, Bob and Sue.

Bob and Sue have to decide how they will allocate their time. Bob might specialize in market activity and Sue specialize in non-market activity, or Sue might specialize in market activity and Bob in non-market activity. Alternatively, one or both of them can earn an income and work in the home.

The particular allocation they choose depends on their preferences and on their market earning potential. An increasing number of households are choosing the egalitarian allocation with each person diversified between non-market household production and market activity. Most households, however, still choose an allocation in which Bob almost fully specializes in market activity and Sue covers a greater diversity of tasks in both the job market and the household.

What are the effects of this common assignment of market and non-market tasks? Although there will always be exceptions, on average, it seems likely that if Bob specializes in market production and Sue diversifies between market and non-market production, Bob will have higher earning potential in the marketplace than Sue. If Sue is devoting a great deal of productive effort to ensuring Bob's mental and physical well-being, the quality of Bob's market labour will be higher than if he were undertaking his household production tasks on his own. If the roles were reversed, Sue would be able to supply market labour capable of earning more than Bob.

To test whether the degree of specialization accounts for earning differentials between the sexes, economists have studied two groups: 'never-married' men and 'never-married' women.

The available evidence suggests that, on the average, when they have the same amount of human capital – measured by years of schooling, work experience and career interruptions – the wages of these two groups differ by only a small margin, about 5 per cent.

Review

- Wage differences might arise from differences in the types of job done, discrimination and differences in human capital.
- Wage differences might also arise from differences in the degree of specialization.

Because labour markets do not seem to treat everyone in the same way, governments intervene in these markets to modify the wages and employment levels that they determine. One potentially far-reaching intervention is equal pay laws. Let's see how these laws work.

Equal Pay and Equal Worth Laws

The Equal Pay Act of 1970, the Sex Discrimination Act of 1975 and the Race Discrimination Act of 1980 were designed to promote *equal pay* and equality of opportunity between men and women and between people of different ethnic origin. They are attempts to remove the most blatant forms of discrimination between men and women and whites and minorities. But many people believe that these acts do not go far enough. In their view, getting paid the *same* wage for doing the *same* job is just the first tiny step that has to be taken. What the law should state is that jobs of *equal worth* receive the same wages regardless of whether they are done by men or women or by blacks or whites. Paying the same wage for different jobs that are judged to be comparable is called **equal pay for equal worth**.

Advocates of equal worth laws argue that wages should be determined by analysing the characteristics of jobs and determining their worth on objective grounds. However, such a method of determining wage rates does not achieve the objectives sought by supporters of wage equality. Let's see why.

Figure 16.9 shows two markets: that for oil rig operators in part (a) and that for school teachers in part (b). The marginal revenue product curves (MRP_R and MRP_T) and the supply curves (S_R and S_T) are shown for each type of labour. Competitive equilibrium generates a wage rate W_R for oil rig operators and W_T for teachers.

Suppose that the knowledge and skills required in these two occupations – the mental and physical

Figure 16.9 The Problem with Equal Worth

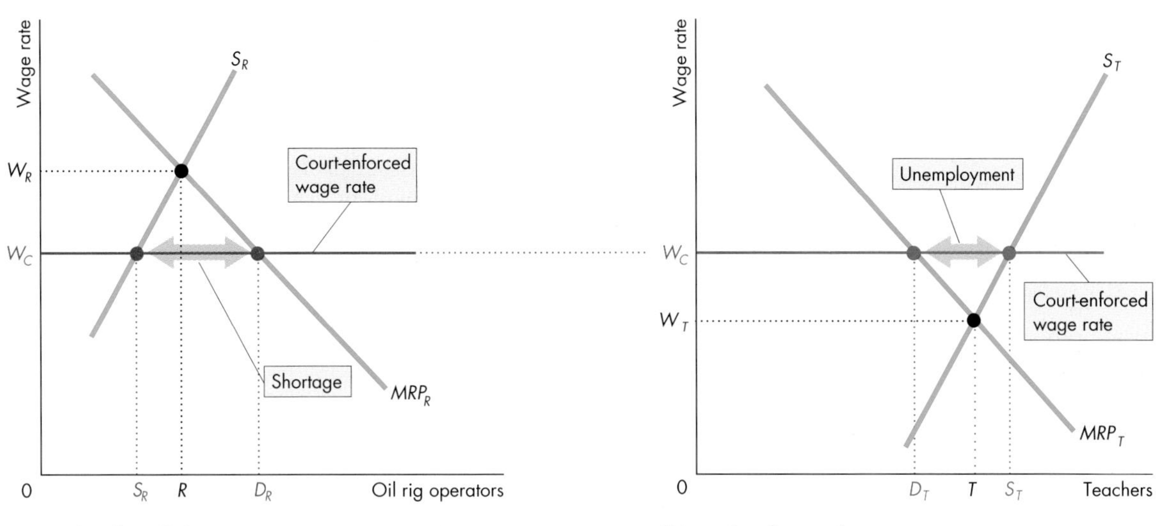

(a) Market for oil rig operators

(b) Market for teachers

The demand for and supply of oil rig operators, MRP_R and S_R, are shown in part (a), and those for school teachers, MRP_T and S_T, in part (b). The competitive equilibrium wage rate for oil rig operators is W_R, and that for teachers is W_T. If an evaluation of the two jobs finds that they have equal worth and rules that the wage rate W_C be paid to both types of workers, there is an excess of demand for oil rig operators and an excess supply of teachers. There are $S_T - D_T$ teachers unemployed and a shortage of $D_R - S_R$ oil rig operators. Oil producers search for other labour-saving ways of producing oil (that are more expensive) and teachers search for other jobs (that are less desirable to them and probably less well paid).

demands, the responsibilities and the working conditions – result in a judgement that these two jobs are of equal worth. The wage rate that is judged to apply to each of them is W_C, and the courts enforce this wage rate. What happens? First, there is a shortage of oil rig operators. Oil rig companies are able to hire only S_R workers at the wage rate W_C. They cut back their production or build more expensive labour-saving oil rigs. Second the number of teachers employed decreases. But this decrease occurs because school governors demand fewer teachers. At the higher wage W_C, school governors demand only D_T teachers. The quantity of teachers supplied is S_T and the difference between S_T and D_T is the number of unemployed teachers looking for jobs. These teachers eventually accept non-teaching jobs (which they don't like as much as teaching jobs), and probably at a lower rate of pay than that of teachers.

Thus equal worth laws may have serious and costly unintended consequences.

Review

- Equal pay laws require equal pay for work requiring the same levels of skill and responsibility.
- Equal worth laws cannot, themselves, eliminate wage differences.
- Wage differences will be reduced only if differences in actual and perceived marginal revenue product are reduced.

In this chapter, we extended and applied the factor market model to understand a variety of phenomena in labour markets such as wage differentials. In the next chapter, we apply and extend the factor market model to deal with markets for capital and for natural resources.

Summary

Key Points

Skill Differentials (pp. 384–387)

- Skill differentials arise partly because skilled labour has a higher marginal product than unskilled labour and partly because skills are costly to acquire.
- Wage rates of skilled and unskilled labour are determined by demand and supply in the two labour markets. The equilibrium wage rate for skilled labour exceeds that for unskilled labour.

Union–Non-union Wage Differentials (pp. 387–393)

- Labour unions influence wages by controlling the supply of labour.
- In competitive labour markets, unions obtain higher wages only at the expense of lower employment, but they try to influence the demand for labour.
- In a monopsony – a market in which there is a single buyer – a union can increase the wage rate without sacrificing employment.
- Bilateral monopoly occurs when the union is a monopoly seller of labour, the firm is a monopsony buyer of labour and the wage rate is determined by bargaining between the two parties.
- In practice, union workers earn an estimated 5–6 per cent more than comparable non-union workers.

Wage Differentials Between Sexes and Races (pp. 393–396)

- Earnings differentials between men and women and between whites and minorities arise from differences in types of job, discrimination, differences in human capital and differences in degree of specialization.
- Well-paid jobs such as those in the legal, medical and other professions, and in higher ranks of management are more likely to be held by white men than by women and minorities. But discrimination is hard to measure.
- Historically, white males have had more human capital than other groups, but human capital differences arising from schooling differences have been falling and have almost been eliminated.
- Differentials arising from different degrees of specialization have kept women's pay below that for men because women's careers have been interrupted more frequently than those of men. This difference is smaller today than in the past.
- Attempts to test for the importance of the degree of specialization suggest that it is still a source of the difference between the earnings of men and women.

Equal Pay and Equal Worth Laws (pp. 396–397)

- Equal worth laws would determine wages by using objective characteristics rather than what the market will pay to assess the value of different types of job.
- Determining wages through equal worth will result in a decrease in the number of people employed in those jobs on which the market places a lower value and shortages of those workers that the market values more highly.
- Attempts to achieve equal wages for comparable work have costly, unintended consequences.

Key Figures and Table 

Key Terms

Review Questions

1 Explain why skilled workers are paid more than unskilled workers.

2 Explain why the demand curve for high-skilled workers lies to the right of the demand curve for low-skilled workers.

3 Explain why the demand curve for high-skilled workers lies to the left of the supply curve for low-skilled workers.

4 What is the influence of education and on-the-job training on earnings?

5 Explain why skilled workers are paid more than low-skilled workers.

6 What are the main types of trade union?

7 What is corporatist bargaining and how does it differ from decentralized bargaining?

8 What are the main weapons available to a union and to employers.

9 How does a union try to influence wages?

10 What can a union do in a competitive labour market?

11 How might a union increase the demand for its members' labour?

12 Explain why the elasticity of supply of labour influences how much the union can raise the wage rate paid to union members.

13 What is a monopsony?

14 Explain why the supply of labour facing a monopsony is not the marginal cost of labour.

15 Explain why a monopsony maximizes its profit by paying labour a wage rate that is less than the marginal revenue product of labour.

16 Under what circumstances will the introduction of a minimum wage increase employment?

17 Describe the differences in male and female earnings in the United Kingdom today?

18 What are the main reasons for the existence of sex and race differentials in earnings?

19 How would equal worth laws work?

20 What are the predicted effects of equal worth laws?

Problems

1 The demand for and supply of unskilled labour is given by the following schedules:

Hourly wage rate (pounds per hour)	Quantity supplied (hours)	Quantity demanded (hours)
9	9,000	1,000
8	8,000	2,000
7	7,000	3,000
6	6,000	4,000
5	5,000	5,000
4	4,000	6,000
3	3,000	7,000
2	2,000	8,000

a What is the wage rate of unskilled labour?
b What is the quantity of unskilled labour employed?

2 The workers in Problem 1 can be trained to obtain a skill – and their marginal productivity doubles. (The marginal product at each employment level is twice the marginal product of an unskilled worker.) The compensation for the cost of acquiring skill adds £2 an hour to the wage that must be offered to attract skilled labour.

a What is the wage rate of skilled labour?
b What is the quantity of skilled labour employed?

3 Suppose that skilled workers in Problem 1 become unionized and the union restricts the amount of high-skilled labour to 5,000 hours.

a What is the wage rate of skilled workers?
b What is the wage differential between low-skilled and high-skilled workers?

4 If in Problem 1, the government introduces a minimum wage rate of £6 an hour for low-skilled workers.

a What is the wage rate paid to low-skilled workers?
b How many hours of low-skilled labour gets hired each day?

5 Look again at the information in Figure16.2 of this chapter. Use diagrams similar to those in Figure 16.1 to explain the fact that both men and women with a degree earn more on average than both men and women with no qualifications.

6 Look again at the cartoon on p. 386 of this chapter. What is implied about the marginal revenue products associated with the range of skills demanded of an MP?

7 Following on from Problem 6, if an MP is required to have a wide range of skills with different marginal revenue products, which of the following do you think the wage rate should reflect:

a The highest level of skill – if so why?
b The average level of skill – if so why?
c The lowest level of skill – if so why?

8 In a small, isolated town in Yorkshire, the only firm hiring workers is a cloth manufacturer. The firm's demand for labour and the town's supply of labour are as follows:

Wage rate (pounds per hour)	Quantity supplied (hours per day)	Quantity demanded (hours per day)
1	20	220
2	40	200
3	60	180
4	80	160
5	100	140
6	120	120
7	140	100
8	160	80
9	180	60
10	200	40

a Draw both the supply of labour and the marginal revenue product of labour on the same graph.

b Write down the total cost of labour for each level of supply.
c What is the wage rate?
d How much labour does the firm hire?
e How much labour does the firm hire?
f What would the wage rate be if there was a competitive labour market in the town?

9 The people from the town in Problem 8 form a union. The union and the firm agree that the level of employment will not change and the union gets the highest wage rate acceptable to the firm. What is that wage rate?

10 In Problem 8, the government imposes a minimum wage rate at the competitive equilibrium wage.

a What is the impact of the minimum wage law on the supply of labour below the minimum wage?
b What is the impact of the minimum wage law on the supply of labour above the minimum wage?
c By how much has the amount of labour employed increased?
d By how much has the wage rate risen?

11 A nationwide investigation determines that on the basis of equal worth, a loom operator should be paid £7 an hour. In the cloth making village in Problem 4 and before the union described in Problem 5 is formed:

a What is the actual hourly wage rate paid?
b How much labour does the cloth manufacturer hire at this wage?
c How much labour is unemployed?

12 Read the story in *Reading Between the Lines* on pp. 402–403 and then:

a Identify all the different explanations you can think of as to why men might earn more on average than women in similar jobs.
b Explain why women earn more than men as authors.
c If discrimination is due to incorrect information, are pay differentials likely to continue? Explain your answer.
d Why do you think the pay gap tends to get bigger at higher ends of salary scales and career paths.

13 Use the link on the Parkin, Powell and Matthews Web site to visit the Department of Employment and obtain data on graduate earnings in Britain.

a Explain using demand and supply, why wage returns for graduate earnings have risen betwen 1974 and 1995.
b Explain why the wages of the more highly qualified have risen faster than the wages of the less well qualified.
c Why do you think the wages of science and engineering graduates have risen faster than those of arts graduates?

W http://www.econ100.com

Pay Differentials Between Men and Women

The Essence of the Story

The Independent on Sunday, 27 June 1999

Women still earn less than men

Jeremy Kay and Jane Hughes

Across the upper echelons of showbusiness, academia, industry and the judiciary, and with a few notable exceptions, women are still banging their heads against the glass ceiling as it affects incomes.

The Bett report on academic pay found that women lecturers receive, on average, less than £29,000 a year compared to more than £32,000 for their male counterparts. The report's all-male review panel warned that universities could face legal action from women employees unless they took steps to redress the balance.

Among big-screen stars, women also appear to trail. Sean Connery, the country's highest grossing male actor, commands around £8m a movie, with Anthony Hopkins trailing on less than £3m.

Middle-ranking female actors still face an uphill battle, according to research by the actors' union Equity. It found that, on average, they receive 34 per cent less for lead roles.

Sometimes the remedy lies in the women's hands. When Caroline Quentin and Leslie Ash found they were being paid £25,000 less per series than their *Men Behaving Badly* co-stars Martin Clunes and Neil Morrissey, their threat to walk out was rewarded with a pay rise.

According to Nicholas Clee, editor of the *Bookseller*, things are different in publishing, where there is a clear relationship between author popularity and prestige and reward.

"There is no difference in royalties between the sexes," he said. "In commercial fiction, my guess is that higher advances are going to women than men."

The chief executive of Pearson, Marjorie Scardino, is the only woman in the top 20 highest paid people in quoted companies.

Philip Beresford, who compiled the list is optimistic about more women reaching the top because of the growing importance of "female" skills needed for better communication and motivation.

- A recent report found that women lecturers receive £3,000 per annum less on average than male lecturers.
- Similar cases of women being paid less than their male counterparts are still found in television, radio, the film and music industry, in business management and in the legal profession.
- In one case when two female actors took direct action and walked out on their roles in a popular television comedy, their pay was increased.
- One example of an industry where women are paid more than men is in authorship in publishing.
- The compiler of the top 20 list of highest paid executives believes more women will reach the top because of the growing desire for 'female' skills of better communication and motivation in business.

Economic Analysis

■ The pay differentials of male and female actors might be caused by discrimination as shown in Figure 1. If male and female actors are equivalent, their combined marginal revenue product will be MRP_{mf} and the supply of actors will be S_{mf}. Actors are paid £30,000 and 2,000 male and 2,000 female actors are hired each year.

■ If broadcasters believe that male lead actors generate higher revenues than female lead actors, the marginal revenue product of male actors, MRP_m is higher than the marginal revenue product of female actors, MRP_f, as shown in Figure 1. Broadcasters hire 3,000 male actors at £40,000 a year and only 1,000 female actors at £20,000 a year.

■ When the two female lead actors walked out, they proved to broadcasters that their marginal revenue product was as high as their male co-lead actors. The programme only generates revenue with all four actors and so broadcasters raised the pay of the female actors.

■ Another explanation of some pay differentials is that males and females bring different skills, on average, to the same job. Most management research suggests that male and female managers have different skills and manage in different ways. If male managerial skills are valued more highly than female managerial skills, then male managers will have higher marginal revenue product.

■ Figure 2 shows the marginal revenue product of male managers in 1998 as MRP_{m98} and for female managers as MRP_{f98}. For the same quantity of hours, Q_0, top male executives earn £3.2 million and top female executives earn £1 million. If female skills become more highly valued over the next five years, male marginal revenue product falls to MRP_{m03} and female marginal revenue product rises to MRP_{f03}, and the pay gap will close.

■ A further explanation for continuing pay differentials is institutional discrimination, where traditional practices create barriers to female promotion and salary advancement.

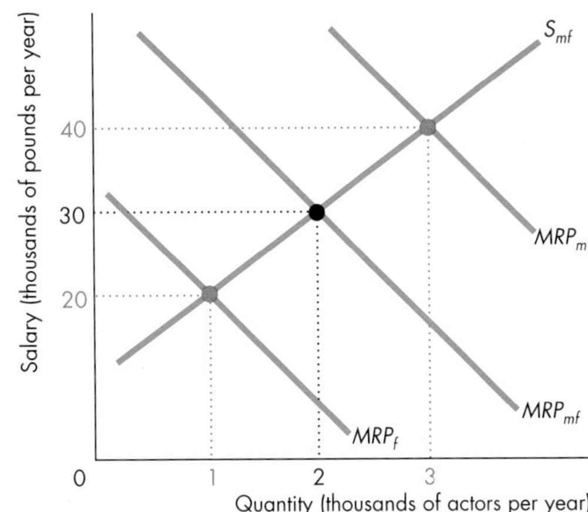

Figure 1 Discrimination in the market for actors

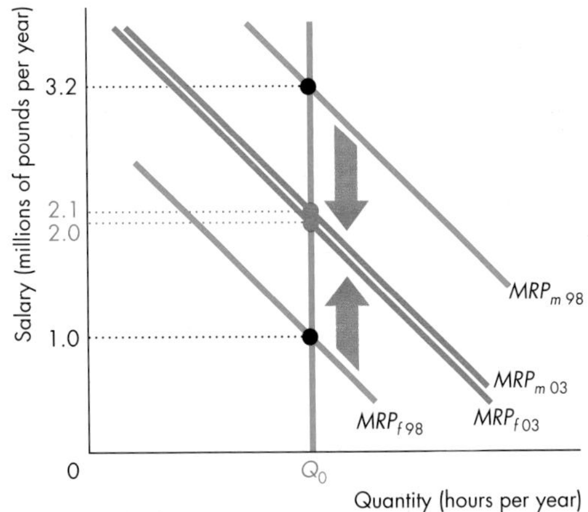

Figure 2 The market for managers

Inequality, Redistribution and Welfare

After studying this chapter you will be able to:

- Describe inequality in income and wealth
- Explain why wealth inequality is greater than income inequality
- Explain how economic inequality arises
- Explain the effects of taxes and cash benefits on economic inequality
- Explain the effects of health care as a benefit in kind on economic inequality
- Compare different forms of health-care provision

Riches and Rags

Walk through the leafy suburbs of any major city and you will find plenty of evidence of conspicuous consumption, clear signs that some people are very rich. Walk down some private road and you'll find 10-bedroom mansions for families of four, immaculate lawns tended by gardeners, heated swimming pools and several double garages. Outside the garages there'll be not one, not two, but three or more cars – a Porsche for fun, a 4-wheel drive Land Rover for shopping and a large, powerful BMW as a family saloon car. It's what people wish for when they play the National Lottery. Walk into the centre of the city and you'll pass people who are cold and miserable huddled in doorways. You'll see the homeless – living in cardboard boxes, unemployed and begging for change – owning nothing more than the clothes they stand in. ◆ Why are some people exceedingly rich while others are very poor and own almost nothing? Are the rich getting richer and the poor poorer? Does the information we have about the inequality of income and wealth paint an accurate picture or a misleading one? How do taxes, social security benefits and the health service influence economic inequality? What is an equitable distribution of economic well-being?

◆ ◆ ◆ ◆ In this chapter, we study economic inequality – its extent, its sources and its potential remedies. We look at taxes and government policies that redistribute incomes, and study their effects on economic inequality. We also study the different ways in which health care can be delivered and its effects on economic efficiency and equality. Let's begin by looking at some facts about economic inequality.

Economic Inequality in the United Kingdom

We can study inequality by looking at the distribution of income or wealth. A family's income is the amount that it receives in a given period of time. A family's wealth is the value of the things it owns at a point in time. We can measure family income inequality by looking at the percentage of total income received by a given percentage of households. We measure wealth inequality by looking at the percentage of total wealth owned by a given percentage of individuals, as household figures are not recorded.

In 1996, the average income in the United Kingdom was £421 a week. But there was considerable inequality around that average. The poorest 20 per cent received only 3 per cent of total income. Their incomes were just one-fifth of the average. The next poorest 20 per cent received just 5 per cent of total income. But the richest 20 per cent received over 50 per cent of total income, their incomes being more than twice the average.

The wealth distribution shows even greater inequality. Average individual wealth in 1996 was £50,500. But the range was enormous. The wealthiest 10 per cent of the population owned 38 per cent of the nation's wealth and the wealthiest 25 per cent owned a staggering 74 per cent of the nation's wealth. The poorest half of the population owned just 7 per cent of the nation's wealth.

Lorenz Curves

Income and wealth distributions are shown in Figure 17.1. Part (a) of the table divides households into five income groups, called *quintiles*, ranging

Figure 17.1 Lorenz Curves for Income and Wealth

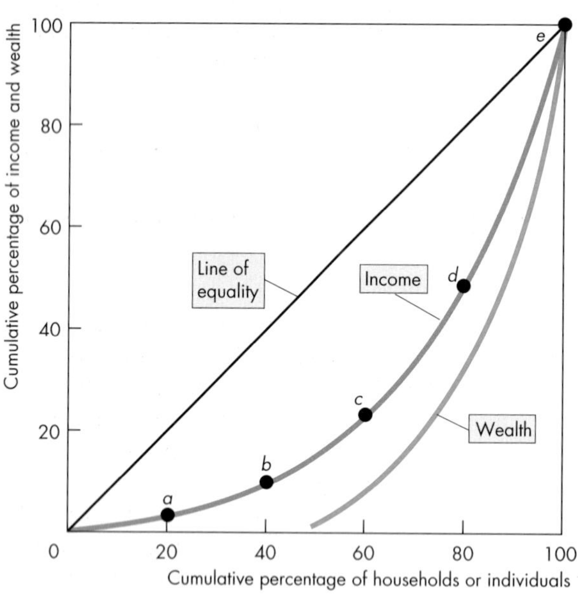

Part (a)	Households		Income	
	Percentage	Cumulative percentage	Percentage	Cumulative percentage
a	Lowest 20	20	3	3
b	Second 20	40	5	8
c	Third 20	60	14	22
d	Fourth 20	80	25	47
e	Highest 20	100	53	100

Part (b)	Individuals		Wealth	
	Percentage	Cumulative percentage	Percentage	Cumulative percentage
a'	Lowest 50	50	7	9
b'	Next 25	75	19	26
c'	Next 10	85	23	49
d'	Next 5	90	13	62
e'	Next 8	98	12	74
f'	Highest 2	100	26	100

The cumulative percentages of income are graphed against the cumulative percentage of households. If income were distributed equally, each 20 per cent of households would have 20 per cent of the income – the line of equality. Points *a* to *e* on the Lorenz curve for income correspond to the rows in part (a) of the table. The Lorenz curve for wealth plots the cumulative percentage of wealth against the cumulative percentage of adults from part (b) of the table. The distribution of wealth is more unequal than the distribution of income.

Sources: Income: Central Statistical Office, *Economic Trends, 1999,* London, HMSO. Wealth: Inland Revenue, *Inland Revenue Statistics, 1998,* London, HMSO.

from the income of the lowest 20 per cent (row *a*) to the income of the top 20 per cent (row *e*). It shows the percentage share of total income taken by each of these income groups. For example, row *a* tells us that the lowest quintile of households received 3 per cent of total income. The table also shows the *cumulative* percentages of households and original income. Original income is income before any taxes are deducted and before any government benefits are received. For example, row *b* tells us that the lowest two quintiles (lowest 40 per cent) received 8 per cent of total income (3 per cent for the lowest quintile and 5 per cent for the next lowest). The data on cumulative income shares are illustrated by a Lorenz curve. A **Lorenz curve** graphs the cumulative percentage of income against the cumulative percentage of households.

If income was distributed equally to every household, the cumulative percentages of income received by the cumulative percentages of households would fall along the straight line labelled 'Line of equality' in Figure 17.1. The actual distribution of income is shown by the Lorenz curve labelled 'Income'.

The Lorenz curve shows the degree of inequality. The closer the Lorenz curve is to the line of equality, the more equal is the distribution. Figure 17.1 also shows a Lorenz curve for wealth, based on the distribution in part (b) of the table. As you can see from the two Lorenz curves, the Lorenz curve for wealth is much farther away from the line of equality than the Lorenz curve for income. As the data for income are based on households and the data for wealth are based on individuals, the two Lorenz curves for the United Kingdom are not directly comparable. For example, an unemployed 21 year-old may have little personal wealth but be living in a household with a high income. Despite this, the two Lorenz curves show the basic pattern found in most market economies – the distribution of wealth is much more unequal than the distribution of income.

Inequality Over Time

The Lorenz curve picture of inequality can be converted into a measure of inequality called the Gini coefficient. This measure lets us look at how inequality changes over time. The Gini coefficient is calculated by dividing the value of the area under the Lorenz curve (the area under the green line in Figure 17.1), by the value of the area under the line of total equality (the area under the black diagonal line) and multiplying by 100. The closer the Gini coefficient is to 0, the closer the distribution is to total equality. The closer the Gini coefficient is to 100 per cent, the closer the distribution is to total inequality.

Changes in the distribution of income in the United Kingdom are shown in Figure 17.2. Original income is income from wages and investments before tax and gross income is original income plus any government benefits. You can see that inequality (the value of Gini coefficient) has risen steadily for the past 20 years using both measures. Also, government benefits reduces inequality because the gross income line always lies below original income. Benefits have a stronger effect on reducing inequality when the gap between original and gross income becomes larger, for example between 1990 and 1996.

Figure 17.2 UK Income Inequality: 1978–1998

Changes in the distribution of income can be measured using the Gini coefficient. The Gini coefficient is a numerical measure of the Lorenz curve for each year. The distribution of income in the United Kingdom became more equal in the late 1980s and early 1990s. Inequality in income has been steadily increasing since 1978.

Source: Economic Trends, May 1998. Office for National Statistics, London, The Stationery Office.

Figure 17.3 The Distribution of Income by Selected Household Characteristics in 1996

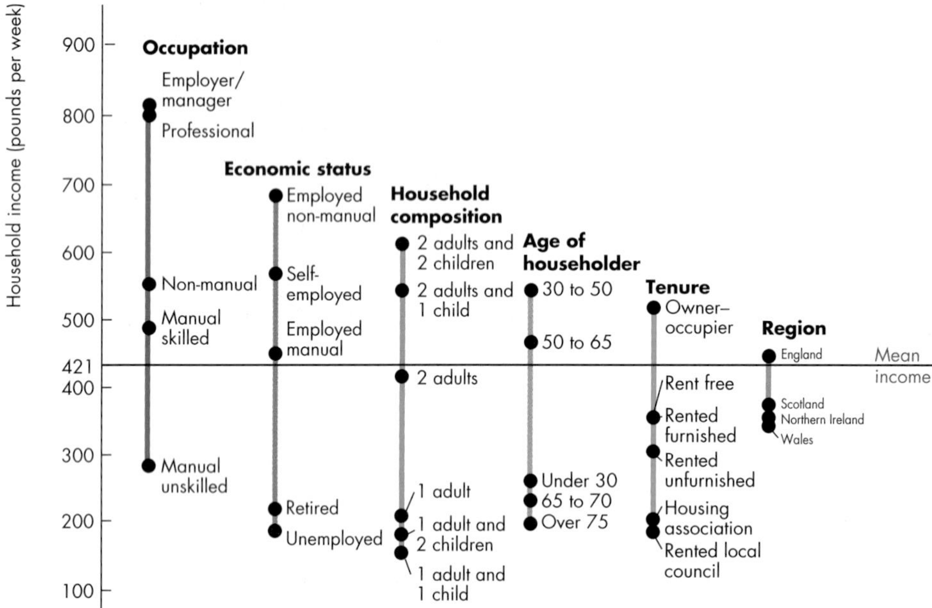

The figure shows that being a single adult household or one parent family, being unemployed or aged over 75 are common characteristics of poor households in the United Kingdom. You are also likely to be poor if you are employed as a manual worker, if you are living in local council accommodation, or if you live in Wales.

Source: Office for National Statistics, *Family Spending: A Report on the 1997/98 Family Expenditure Survey, 1998*, London, The Stationery Office.

Who are Rich and Who are Poor?

What are the characteristics of poor and rich households? The lowest-income household in the United Kingdom today is likely to comprise a retired person over 75 years of age, living alone in local council accommodation, somewhere in Wales. The highest-income household in the United Kingdom today is likely to comprise two adults aged between 30 and 50, both graduates with professional or managerial jobs, living together with two children somewhere in the south east of England.

These snapshot profiles are the extremes in Figure 17.3. The figure shows how incomes vary around the mean household income of £421 a week by different characteristics. The mean (average) income is higher than the most commonly occuring income because it is inflated by a few households with very high incomes. Figure 17.3 illustrates the importance of household size, the age, education and economic status of the householder, and the region of residence, in influencing the size of a household's income.

The households most likely to be on low incomes are usually those with just one adult. This person might be a pensioner living alone, or a single parent with children. He, or more likely she, is probably unemployed or retired, has few qualifications and is likely to be over the age of 65 years. Incomes are also higher on average in England than in the other regions of the United Kingdom.

Poverty

Households at the low end of the income distribution are so poor that they are considered to be living in poverty. **Poverty** is a state in which a household's income is too low for it to be able to buy the quantities of food, shelter and clothing that are deemed necessary. Poverty is a relative concept: so poverty in one country might be considered an acceptable standard of living in another. Because poverty is relative, it is necessary to decide on a *poverty line* – an imaginary benchmark which distinguishes poor people from everyone else. There are two widely used definitions of the poverty line:

1. People living on an income less than 50 per cent of average income.
2. People living on an income at or below the current means-tested benefit level.

Figure 17.4 Poverty in the European Union

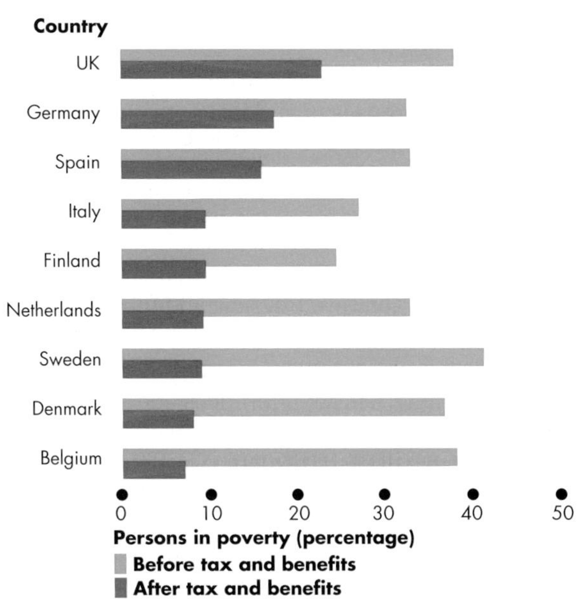

The figure shows comparable EU poverty rates for the latest available year, 1991. The poverty line is 50 per cent of national average household income adjusted for family size. Poverty rates were highest in the UK, Germany and Spain. The tax and benefit system reduces poverty in all countries, but more effectively in some than others.

Source: R. Walker, 1997. Poverty and Social Exclusion in Europe, in A. Walker and C. Walker, 1997, (eds) *Britain Divided*, Child Poverty Action Group, London.

According to government figures, 13.7 million people in the United Kingdom had an income below 50 per cent of average income in 1994 – nearly one-quarter of the population. Using the second definition, 14.8 million people – 26 per cent of the population – had an income at or below the level of income support in 1994. There are significant differences in poverty rates among countries – even within the European Union. Figure 17.4 shows the latest comparable figures using a poverty line of 50 per cent of national average income. The UK rate is the highest shown. Other European countries have higher rates but are mainly those with heavier dependence on agriculture for income.

Looking back at the factors which determine low income in Figure 17.3, we can see that within any one country, poverty results from two main factors – limited access to high-paid employment and the extra costs associated with having children – which may vary through someone's lifetime. There is more poverty among women and racial minorities because they tend to have less well-paid jobs. Women still take a larger share of domestic responsibilities, leading to more time out of work and lower pensions when they retire. However, another factor is the availability of benefits and the effect of taxes to pay for them. Figure 17.4 shows that the reduction in poverty resulting from benefits and taxes is greater in other countries than in the United Kingdom. We will look at the effect of taxes and benefits in more detail later in this chapter.

Review

- Income and wealth are distributed unequally, but wealth is more unequal than income.
- The distribution of income became more equal in two short periods in the early 1960s and 1970s but has become steadily more unequal since 1977.
- The main influences on a household's income are: family size, economic status, age of householder, occupation and related skill, and region of residence. Gender and race are also contributing factors.

Factor Prices, Endowments and Choices

A household's income depends on the prices of the factors of production supplied, the endowment of the factors owned by the household, and the choices the household members make. To what extent do differences in income arise from differences in factor prices and from differences in the quantities of factors that people supply?

Labour Market and Wages

Wages are the biggest single source of income. To what extent do variations in wage rates account for the unequal distribution of income? Figure 17.5

Figure 17.5 Growth in Occupational Wage Rates1978–1998

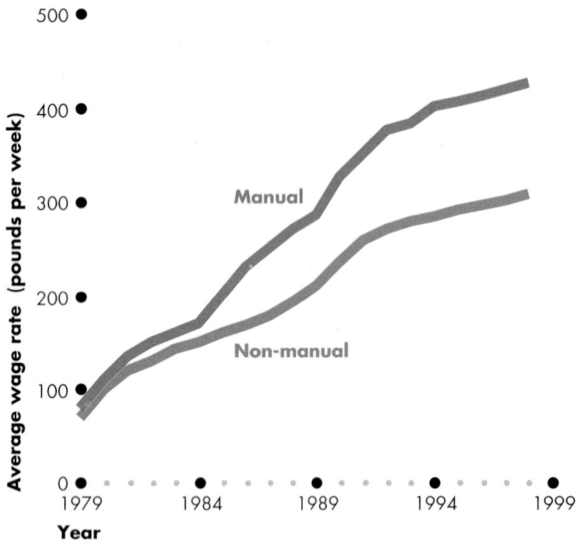

The figure shows current weekly wages for manual and non-manual workers over time. During the 1980s, wages of higher paid non-manual workers increased faster than those of lower-paid workers. When wages of higher-paid workers increase faster than the wages of lower-paid workers, income inequality tends to increase.

Source: *Labour Market Trends*, December 1998. Office of National Statistics. London, The Stationery Office.

helps answer this question. It shows the growth in weekly wage rates for manual and non-manual workers. It is clear that non-manual workers have earned consistently more than manual workers – and these differentials have increased over time. Non-manual workers earned 38 per cent more than manual workers in 1998. In the 1980s, wages of higher-paid workers increased faster than those of lower-paid workers. But by the 1990s, the wages of lower-paid workers were growing as fast as those of higher-paid workers. One of the things that wage rate differences reflect is differences in skills or human capital, as we saw in Chapter 15. So one explanation for the faster rate of growth of wages for higher-paid non-manual workers may be the increasing amount of training and education undertaken by these workers.

Changes in the rate of growth of wages between occupational groups partly explains the overall changes in income inequality. When the wages of the lower-paid groups are growing faster than those of the higher-paid groups, income inequality tends to fall. When the wages of higher-paid groups rise faster than those of the lower-paid groups, income inequality tends to fall.

Differences in wage rates are one source of income inequality. Differences in endowments of factors of production are another.

Distribution of Endowments

There is a large amount of variety in a household's endowments of abilities. Physical and mental differences (some inherited, some learned) are such an obvious feature of human life that they hardly need mentioning. These differences across individuals have a normal, or bell-shaped distribution – like the distribution of heights or weights.

The distribution of individual ability across individuals is a major source of inequality in income and wealth. But it is not the only source. If it were, the distributions of income and wealth would look like the bell-shaped curve that describes the distribution of heights. In fact, these distributions are skewed towards high incomes and look like the curve in Figure 17.6. This figure shows income on the horizontal axis and the percentage of households receiving each income on the vertical axis. The median income is £382 per week. The most common income – called the modal income – is less than the median income and is £160. The mean income – also called the average income – is greater than the median income and is £421. A skewed distribution like the one shown in Figure 17.6 is one in which many more people have incomes below the average than above it, a large number of people have very low incomes, and a small number of people have very high incomes. The distribution of (non-human) wealth has a similar shape to the distribution of income but is even more skewed.

The skewed shape of the distribution of income cannot be explained by the bell-shaped distribution of individual abilities. It results from the choices that people make.

Choices

A household's income and wealth depend partly on the choices that its members make. People choose how much to supply of each of the factors of production they own. They also choose whether to

Figure 17.6 The Distribution of Income

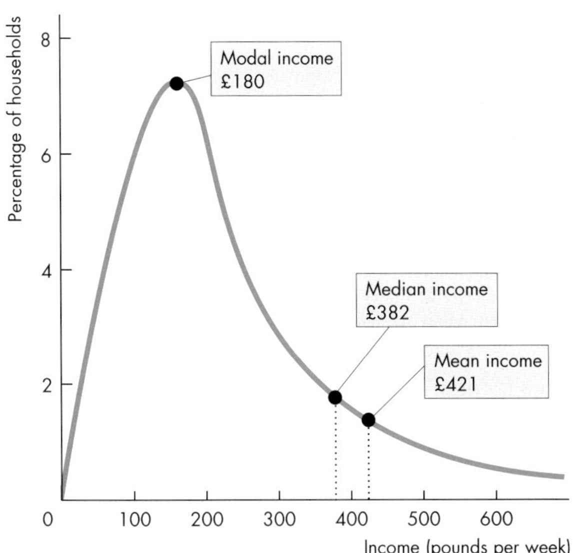

The distribution of income is unequal and is not symmetric around the mean. There are many more people below the mean than above the mean. Also, the distribution has a long thin upper tail representing a small number of people earning very large incomes.

babysit or look for a job in a bank, whether to put their savings in the bank or in shares. We are going to discover that the choices people make exaggerate the differences among households. Their choices make the distribution of income more unequal than the distribution of abilities and they make the distribution of income skewed.

Wages and the Supply of Labour Other things remaining the same, the quantity of labour that a person supplies increases as that person's wage rate increases. A person who has a low wage rate chooses to work fewer hours than a person who has a high wage rate. Compare two people, one whose wage rate is £5 an hour and another whose wage rate is £10 an hour. If each person works the same number of hours, one has an income that is twice as much as the other. But a higher wage rate can induce a greater number of hours of work. So if the person whose wage is £10 an hour chooses to work more hours, she earns an income that exceeds twice the income of the other person.

Thus because the quantity of labour supplied increases as the wage rate increases, the distribution of income is more unequal than the distribution of hourly wages. It is also skewed. People whose wage rates are below the average tend to work fewer hours than the average, and their incomes bunch together much below the average. People whose wage rates are above the average tend to work more hours than the average, and their incomes stretch out above the average.

Saving and Bequests Another choice that results in unequal distributions in income and wealth is the decision to save and make bequests. A *bequest* is a gift from one generation to the next. The higher a family's income, the more that family tends to save and bequeath to later generations. By making a bequest, a family can spread consumption across the generations. One common way in which people make bequests is to provide educational resources for their children and grandchildren.

Saving and bequests are not inevitably a source of increased inequality. If a family saves to redistribute an uneven income over the life cycle and enable consumption to be constant, the act of saving decreases the degree of inequality. If a lucky generation that has a high income saves a large amount and makes a bequest to a generation that is unlucky, this act of saving also decreases the degree of inequality. But there are two important features of bequests that do make inter-generational transfers of wealth a source of increased inequality:

1 Debts cannot be bequeathed.
2 Mating is assortative.

Debts Cannot be Bequeathed Although a person may die with debts that exceed assets – with negative wealth – debts cannot be forced on to other family members. Because a zero inheritance is the smallest inheritance that anyone can receive, bequests can only add to future generations' wealth and income potential.

The vast majority of people inherit nothing or a very small amount. A few people inherit enormous fortunes. As a result, bequests make the distribution of income and wealth not only more unequal than the distribution of ability and job skills but also more persistent. A family that is poor in one generation is more likely to be poor in the next. A family that is wealthy in one generation is likely to be wealthy in the next. Even so, there is also a tendency for income and wealth to converge, across generations, to the average. One feature of human behaviour that slows down convergence and makes inequalities persist is assortative mating.

Assortative Mating *Assortative mating* is the tendency for people to marry within their own socioeconomic class – like attracts like. Although there is a good deal of folklore that 'opposites attract', perhaps such Cinderella tales appeal to us because they are so rare in reality. Marriage partners tend to have similar socioeconomic characteristics. Wealthy individuals seek wealthy partners. The consequence of assortative mating is that inherited wealth becomes more unequally distributed.

Review

- Income inequality arises from unequal wage rates, unequal endowments and choices.
- Wage rates are unequal because of differences in skills or human capital.
- Endowments are unequal and have a bell-shaped distribution.
- The distribution of income is skewed because people with higher wage rates tend to work longer hours and so make a disproportionately larger income.
- The distribution of wealth is skewed because people with higher incomes save more, bequeath more to the next generation and marry people with similar wealth.

We've now described the extent of inequality and examined some of the reasons it exists. Next we're going to see how government policy modifies the outcome of the market economy and changes the distributions of income and wealth.

Income Redistribution

Governments use three main types of policies to redistribute income and relieve poverty. They are:

1 Income taxes.
2 Transfer payments.
3 Goods and services in kind.

Income Taxes

The scale of redistribution of income achieved through income taxes depends on the form that the income taxes take. Income taxes may be progressive, regressive or proportional. A **progressive income tax** is one that taxes income at a marginal rate which increases with the level of income. The term 'marginal', applied to income tax rates, refers to the fraction of the last pound earned that is paid in taxes. A **regressive income tax** is one that taxes income at a marginal rate which decreases with the level of income. A **proportional income tax** (also called a *flat-rate income tax*) is one that taxes income at a constant rate regardless of the level of income.

The income tax rates that apply in the United Kingdom are progressive. The poorest households pay no income tax as everyone is allowed to earn a certain amount before paying any tax at all. Middle-income households pay 10 per cent initially and then 20 and 24 per cent of each additional pound they earn, and richer households pay 40 per cent of each additional pound earned above the middle-income tax band.

Transfer Payments

Transfer payments redistribute income by making direct payments to people in the lower part of the income distribution. In 1997, the UK government paid out £131 billion in transfer payments, 40 per cent of total government expenditure. The main types of payments are:

- Income support payments.
- Unemployment benefits.
- State pensions.

Income Support Payments The UK government uses two main forms of income support payments to raise household incomes and reduce poverty. Family credit helps families where at least one person is in work, but the family wage is very low. Income support helps people whose incomes are low because they are not working. These people may also be claiming other sorts of income support payments such as incapacity benefit – a benefit for those who cannot work because of a disability. In 1999, income support was £50.00 a week for a single person over 25 years old. The average amount claimed under family credit was £55.06 a week.

Unemployment Benefits The job seekers allowance is a payment for individuals who have lost their jobs involuntarily and have no other main source of income. It is available for six months and is awarded on the condition that individuals register as unemployed and are actively seeking work. They may also be required to attend training courses and attend for interviews for suitable jobs. The allowance was £51.40 for those aged over 25 in 1999.

State Pensions State pensions are a major component of transfer payments. All European economies operate a system whereby the current taxpayers pay for the pensions of the current elderly people. In the United Kingdom state pensions are a contributory benefit – you must have made sufficient National Insurance tax contributions to be eligible. The full basic pension was £66.75 a week in 1999 and was paid to 7 million people, 70 per cent of people of pensionable age. Many women do not get a full state pension because part-time work generates insufficient contributions.

Comparing expenditure on transfer payments across EU countries, spending is higher in northern countries, with the exception of Northern Ireland. In 1996, Denmark spent the most on transfer payments at £5,000 per head, three times the amount spent by Portugal. The UK ranked 9 out of 15, spending just £3,000 per head on transfer payments.

So what is the impact of transfer payments? They certainly relieve poverty because they raise the income of the poorest people. But do they remove poverty? The answer depends on how the poverty line is defined and the value of the benefits. If we define the poverty line as 50 per cent of average UK income, then a single person needed at least £80 a week after housing costs to stay above the poverty line in 1999. The income support paid, after housing costs, was less than £50 a week – not enough to remove poverty using this definition.

Benefits in Kind

A great deal of redistribution takes place in most European countries through the provision of benefits in kinds. These are the goods and services provided by the government at prices below marginal cost. The taxpayers who consume these goods and services receive a transfer in kind from the taxpayers who do not consume them. The two most important areas in which this form of redistribution takes place are education – from nursery care through to university – and health care.

In the United Kingdom, 50 per cent of government expenditure is on benefits in kind – 24 per cent on the National Health Service (NHS), 21 per cent on education, the remainder on other services. The NHS provides almost all health care free at the point of demand. Primary and secondary education are provided free for all children in the United Kingdom. Vouchers are available to help parents pay for the cost of nursery care and, although student grants are being withdrawn, the government still subsidizes the cost of university education by paying tuition fees for most undergraduate students.

Because the NHS and free basic education ensure that everyone can gain access to good-quality health care and education, benefits in kind help to reduce inequality in health status and basic human capital. They also help to reduce inequality in income. Although rich households receive the value of the benefits in kind as well as poor households, rich households pay more in tax – reducing income inequality. Richer households often pay for these services privately, without any compensatory tax rebate.

Take-up and Targeting Benefits

Up to 30 per cent of people eligible for income support and family credit benefits do not claim them, whereas virtually everyone eligible for child benefit claims this benefit. Why are these *take-up* rates so different? Child benefit, the NHS and primary and secondary schooling are universal benefits, available to anyone without a means test or an eligibility test. As a result, there is no stigma attached to claiming these benefits and take-up is high. Other benefits are means tested on income. Only those people with very low incomes and wealth are eligible. Means testing involves filling in complex forms and generates a high level of stigma for recipients. This stops many people claiming and so take-up is poor.

If government wants to redistribute income efficiently, it needs to achieve a high level of take-up. So why are so many benefits means tested rather than universal benefits? The answer lies in the problem of *targeting* and its opportunity cost. Universal benefits are paid to everyone, rich and poor. The high level of take-up has an opportunity cost – the waste involved in taxing the rich to pay benefits back to the rich. Means-tested benefits have low take-up but they reach only the poor – targeting is high.

Because the NHS is such an important benefit, we'll study it more fully later in this chapter. But before doing so, let's bring all the different methods of redistribution together and look at their impact on incomes.

The Impact on Income Redistribution

You saw the impact of the tax and benefit system on poverty rates in Figure 17.4. The tax and benefit system reduces poverty because it works as a redistributive mechanism, making income more equally distributed. Taxes are paid by richer people to pay for benefits to poorer people. Let's look at the impact of taxes and benefits on income distribution in more detail.

Figure 17.7 shows the impact of taxes and benefits for the five quintile income groups, from bottom fifth (the poorest) to top fifth (the richest). You can see that the value of cash benefits received by the poorest group is much higher than the value of cash benefits received by the richest group. On average, the poorest fifth received £4,700 of cash benefits each year, while the richest fifth received only £1,000. The richest group receives a small amount of benefit because some are universally available. The impact on income of benefits in kind – the NHS and education – is more evenly distributed across all income groups, but the poorest groups still receive more in total. Benefits in kind are strongly progressive as they are worth over 70 per cent of post-tax income to the poorest fifth, but just 7 per cent for the richest fifth.

Direct taxes also have a strong effect on the distribution of income. Figure 17.7 shows that the richest fifth pay £10,000 in direct taxes on income each year and the poorest fifth pay just £800 each year. Indirect taxes on expenditure have a less dramatic redistributive effect because the poorest groups spend proportionately more of their total income on goods. Overall, the net impact on income distribution as shown in Figure 17.7 is to redistribute income from the top 40 per cent to the bottom 40 per cent, with no net gain to the middle 20 per cent.

Figure 17.7 The Effect of Taxes and Benefits on the Distribution of Income

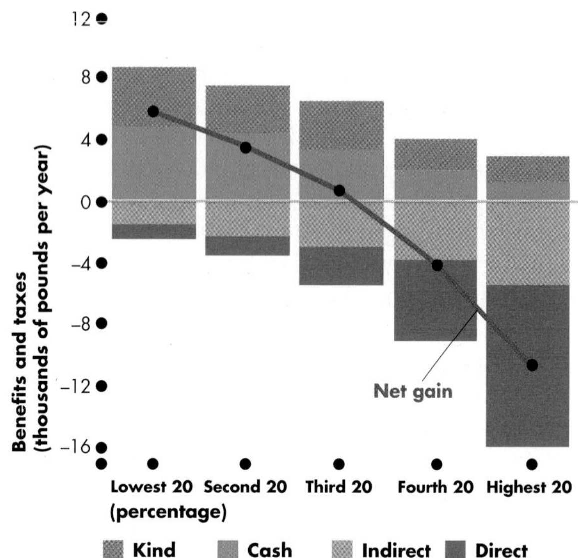

The impact of taxes and benefits in 1997 was to redistribute income from the richest (top) 40 per cent to the poorest (bottom) 40 per cent. The poorest groups receive more income as cash benefits and benefits in kind than the richest groups and the poorest groups pay less tax than the richest groups. Cash benefits and direct taxes on income have the strongest redistributive effects on income.

Source: Office of National Statistics, *Social Trends, 1999*, London, The Stationery Office, Figure 5.13.

The Big Trade-off

You learned about the Big Trade-off between equity and efficiency in Chapter 6, pp. 131–132. Any redistribution policy requires the use of skilled labour and other scarce resources. The bigger the redistributive policy, the greater is the opportunity cost of running it and the greater is the efficiency trade-off. Government can only introduce redistributive policies by taxing richer people to pay for benefits to poorer people. This reduces the income of richer people so they work and save less, resulting in less output and consumption for everybody – rich and poor. The taxes also create inefficiency through them deadweight loss. A final source of inefficiency in most benefit systems is the benefit trap. This has been the main reason for reforming the benefits system in Australia, the United Kingdom and the United States. Let's look at benefit traps in more detail.

The Benefit Trap The benefit system has been criticized for creating disincentives to work by catching people in the *benefit trap*. Benefit traps arise when people who are receiving benefits do not think it is worthwhile taking up employment or working longer hours. If people lose £1 of benefit for every extra £1 that they earn – a *withdrawal rate* of 100 per cent – they will be no better off. They are facing a marginal tax rate of 100 per cent, much higher than all other taxpayers! This problem is unavoidable if benefits are withdrawn as people earn additional income.

There are two main types of benefit trap – the unemployment trap and the poverty trap. In the unemployment trap, people make decisions based on the replacement ratio – the ratio of the expected wage to the benefits received. If the expected wage is only marginally higher than the level of unemployment benefit, the rational choice for most people is to remain unemployed. In the poverty trap, people are already in low-paid work but still receiving benefit. They may want to work longer hours to earn an extra £10, but they will pay tax on the extra £10 and lose up to £10 of benefit. As a result, they are facing a marginal tax rate in excess of 100 per cent! The rational choice is not to work more hours.

Reform Proposals

There are two broad ways in which the problem of the benefit traps can be tackled. They are:

1 Piecemeal reforms.

2 Radical reform.

Piecemeal Reforms For practical reasons, most reforms that actually get implemented are piecemeal. They are a response to the most pressing problems of the day. The process of reform in the United Kingdom began in 1988 when the Social Security Act of 1986 was implemented. At the time, some people faced marginal tax rates of up to 120 per cent in the poverty trap. Although the number of people facing such extreme marginal tax rates was not high – about 100,000 – the idea that anyone could earn an extra pound and actually be worse off as a result was unacceptable.

The UK reforms removed the worst aspect of the benefit trap by calculating benefit on income after tax, rather than income before tax. This has eliminated marginal tax rates in excess of 100 per cent. But many more people now face extremely high marginal tax rates of between 60 and 90 per cent.

The 1998 Labour Government reforms raised benefit levels, cut the rate at which benefit is withdrawn as extra income is earned, and introduced a system of paying benefit as a tax credits for working families. The lower withdrawal rate and higher levels of benefit will reduce the poverty trap and the tax credit system will increase uptake.

Radical Reform A more radical reform proposal is a negative income tax. A **negative income tax** gives every household a *guaranteed annual income* and decreases the household's benefit at a specified *withdrawal rate* as the household's original income increases. For example, suppose the guaranteed annual income is £10,000 and the withdrawal rate and the income tax rate are set at 25 per cent. A household with no earnings receives the £10,000 guaranteed income. A household with earnings of £8,000 loses 25 per cent of that amount – £2,000 – and receives a total income of £16,000 (£8,000 earnings plus £10,000 guaranteed income minus £2,000 benefit loss). A household earning £40,000 receives an income of £40,000 (£40,000 earnings plus £10,000 guaranteed income minus £10,000 benefit loss). Such a household is at the break-even income level. Households with earnings exceeding £40,000 pay more in taxes than they receive in benefits.

A negative income tax is illustrated and compared with our current arrangements in Figure 17.8. In both parts of the figure, the horizontal axis measures *original income* – that is, income *before* taxes are paid and benefits received – and the vertical axis measures net income *after* taxes are paid and benefits received. The 45° line shows the hypothetical case of 'no redistribution'.

Part (a) shows the current redistribution arrangements – the blue line. Benefits of G are paid to those with no income. As original incomes increase from zero to A, benefits are withdrawn, *lowering* net income below G. This arrangement creates a *benefit trap* shown as the grey triangle. Over the income range A to C, each additional pound of

Figure 17.8 Comparing the Current Benefit System and a Negative Income Tax

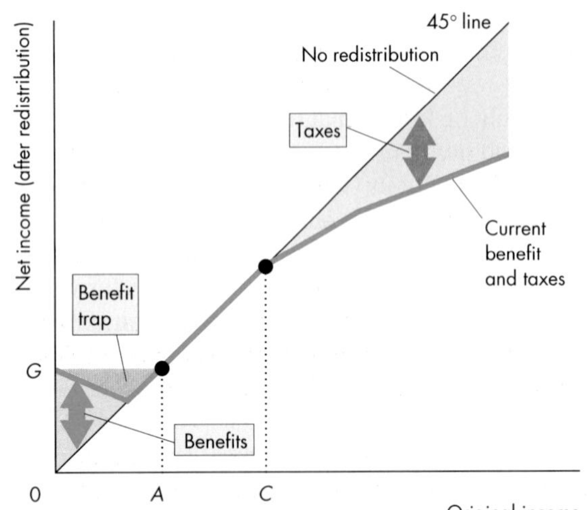

(a) Current redistribution arrangements

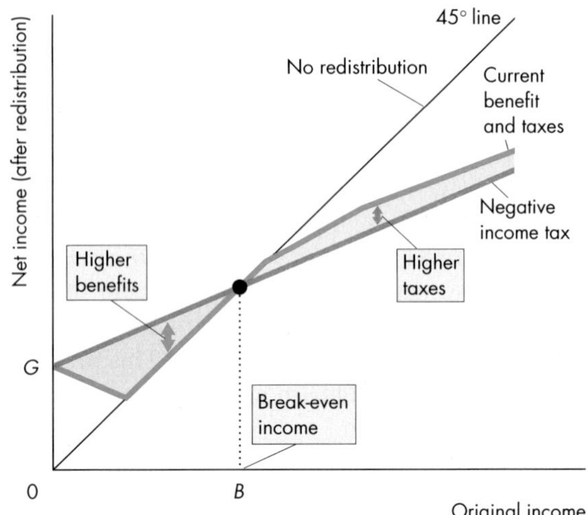

(b) A negative income tax

Part (a) shows the current redistribution arrangements – the blue line. Benefits of *G* are paid to those with no income. As incomes increase from zero to *A*, benefits are withdrawn, *lowering* income after redistribution below *G* and creating a welfare trap – the grey triangle. As incomes increase from *A* to *C*, there is no redistribution. As incomes increase above *C*, income taxes are paid at successively higher rates.

In part (b), a negative income tax gives a guaranteed annual income of *G* and decreases benefits at the same rate as the tax rate on incomes. The red line shows how market incomes translate into income after redistribution. Households with market incomes below *B*, the break-even income, receive net benefits. Those with market incomes above *B* pay net taxes.

original income increases net income by a pound. At incomes greater than *C*, income taxes are paid at successively higher rates, and net income is smaller than original income.

Part (b) shows the negative income tax. The guaranteed annual income is *G* and the break-even income is *B*. Households with original incomes below *B* receive a net benefit (blue area) and those with incomes above *B* pay taxes (red area). You can see why such a scheme is called a negative income tax. Every household receives a guaranteed minimum income and every household pays a tax on its earnings – losing benefits is like paying a tax – but households with incomes below the break-even income receive more than they pay and so, in total, pay a negative amount of tax.

A negative income tax removes the benefit trap (the grey triangle) and gives greater encouragement to low-income households to seek additional employment, even at a low wage. But it has a high cost. Basic tax rates would have to rise above 50 per cent to achieve a guaranteed income of just £6,000 a year.

It has been suggested that a small level of guaranteed annual income supported by the existing system of means-tested benefit could improve both equity and the efficiency of the existing system. A computerized negative income tax system would contain details of everyone's income on a database – rich and poor. The system could be used to identify who should be receiving means-tested benefits and these could be sent out automatically, avoiding the stigma of claiming. The guaranteed income received would be negligible, but take-up and targeting of existing benefits would be radically improved.

Review

- Government redistributes income in the United Kingdom by using transfer payments, income taxes and benefit payments – and benefits in kind of goods and services provided below cost.
- The overall impact of the tax and benefit system is progressive, redistributing income from the richest 40 per cent to the poorest 40 per cent.
- Increasing equity implies a reduction in efficiency as benefit traps create disincentives to work.
- Welfare reform aims to reduce the problems of benefit traps.

Health and the cost of health care are major sources of inequality. We are now going to study the economics of health care, public provision of health care to reduce inequality and how market mechanisms can be used to improve the efficiency of public health services.

Health-care Provision

Health-care provision is one of the most widely used methods of improving redistribution in European economies – but at a cost. Rising health-care costs and increasing government expenditure have led many economists to consider the alternative – a private market in health care. But would we be better off with private health-care systems modelled on the United States? Is a national health service the best method of producing health care? We'll try to answer these questions by comparing the benefits of different systems in terms of equity and efficiency. Before that we need to look at the different systems and the problem of rising health-care costs.

Health-care Systems

There are three basic types of health-care system:

1 Mainly private finance and private supply.
2 Mainly government finance and private supply.
3 Mainly government finance and government supply.

The private finance and supply system is one where people buy and sell health care in health-care markets, like in the United States. Many European countries like Belgium, France, Germany, Italy and the Netherlands have a system of private suppliers, financed by government expenditure rather than private individuals. Finally, countries like the United Kingdom, Greece and Portugal have national health services, while Scandinavian countries have local government health services. These are all mainly government financed and supplied. All of these systems have some mix of private and government provision.

So which of these systems is better? Which system will maximize social welfare? The answer lies in our model of market failure and efficiency and in the preferences of voters for equity. The best system is the most efficient system which also maximizes voters' preferences for equity. We can start by comparing systems in terms of the cost of producing health care.

Health-care Costs

Health-care costs have increased more rapidly than consumer prices on the average in most developed countries as shown in Figure 17.9. The percentage growth in health-care costs relative to other prices is highest in the United States, Ireland and Canada. There appears to be a cost crisis in health care in these countries, and there is evidence of rising real costs in many other European countries. Why has this happened? First, health care is labour-intensive with limited scope for labour-saving technological change. Health-care labour costs generally increase at a faster rate than do prices. Because there is limited scope for labour-saving changes higher labour costs lead to higher prices for final health-care services.

Second, the main effect of any technological change in health care is to improve the quality of the service. For example, the application of computer technology and advances in drugs have broadened the range of conditions that can be treated. Costs rise steadily as we constantly improve quality and use new technologies to treat previously untreatable conditions.

Figure 17.10 shows the market for health care. Initially, the demand curve is D_0, the supply curve is S_0, the quantity is Q_0 and the price is P_0. Increasing incomes and advances in medical technology increase the demand for health-care services and

Figure 17.9 Health Care Costs

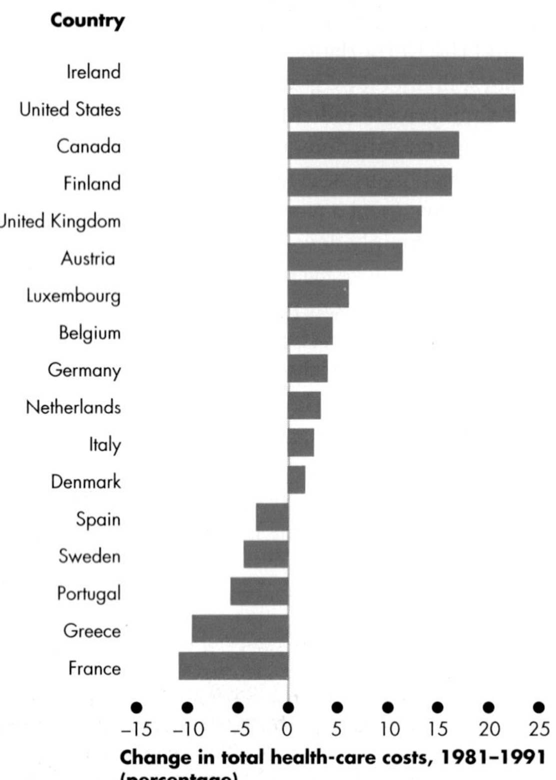

Health-care costs have increased relative to consumer prices in most developed countries. The percentage growth in health-care costs between 1981 and 1991 is highest in the United States, Ireland and Canada, and positive in many other European countries.

Source: T. Besley and M. Gouveia, 'Alternative systems of health care provision', *Economic Policy*, October 1994, 19.

Figure 17.10 The Market for Health Care

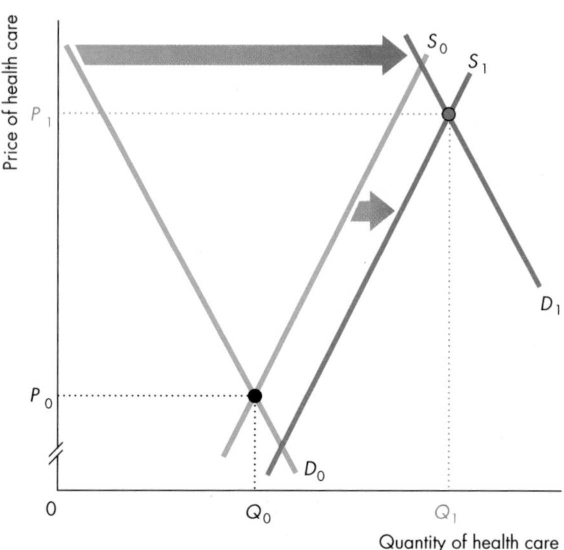

Initially (say in 1980), demand was D_0, supply was S_0, the quantity was Q_0, and the price was P_0. Increasing incomes and technological advances that expand the range of conditions that can be treated increase demand and shift the demand curve rightward to D_1. Advancing technology also increases supply but increasing wages and more costly equipment and drugs counteract this increase in supply. The result is that the supply curve moves rightward to S_1. The quantity increases by a small amount to Q_1 and the price increases steeply to P_1.

the demand curve shifts rightward to D_1. Technological advances also increase supply, but by a smaller amount than the increase in demand because some factors have worked to decrease supply. One of these factors is the increasing wage rates of health-care workers and another is the increasing cost of health-care technologies. The net effect of the positive and negative influences on supply over time is a rightward shift in the supply curve to S_1. The quantity of health care increases to Q_1 – a relatively small increase, and the price rises to P_1 – a relatively large increase.

The forces at work that produce the changes shown in Figure 17.10 do not appear to be temporary, and appear to work in all health-care systems. So do we have any reason to believe that introducing more competition and private provision can improve health-care efficiency in Europe. Or will introducing more government finance improve efficiency in North America? Let's look at our model of market failure to see if there are any reasons to prefer one system over another in terms of efficiency.

Private Health Care and Insurance

Everyone demands health care at some point in their life, but the people with the largest demands are the elderly, the very young and the chronically sick. The costs for most people are high and the frequency of use is low. Uncertainty about your future income makes planning health-care expenditure difficult, so in a purely private market system most people choose to finance their health care by insurance. Let's look at the problem of health-care insurance.

Health-care insurance, like all types of insurance, faces two problems: *moral hazard* and *adverse selection*. Moral hazard is the tendency for people who are covered by insurance to use more health services or to be less careful about avoiding health risks than they otherwise would. Adverse selection is the tendency for people who know they have a greater chance than the average of falling ill to be the ones more likely to buy health insurance.

Insurance companies set their premium levels sufficiently high to cover claims arising from people who have been adversely selected and who face moral hazard. But to attract profitable business from low-risk customers, insurance companies give preference to healthy and employed people.

Insurance markets work well if the probabilities of getting a certain type of illness can be estimated by insurance companies, and if the probabilities are independent of other people getting the disease. Some diseases are so rare that probabilities cannot be estimated. The probability of my getting flu (an infectious disease) is clearly linked to the probability of your getting flu if we live or work together. Also, there is no profit in insuring people against a disease they already have – perhaps one they were born with. So, many people will not be able to buy health-care insurance even if they want it in a private system. Many of the economic benefits of health care will be lost. To avoid this problem, governments can provide health insurance.

Private Health Care and Government Insurance

Many countries have a mixed system of compulsory social insurance (taxation) to pay for privately provided health care. This removes the market failure problem in insurance. But private provision may still be inefficient. Economies of scale in local hospital services may lead to monopoly supply where the quantity of health care is cut back below the efficient level and price is raised above marginal cost. Although government can determine the price it pays private suppliers, the private sector will only provide health care if the return is at least as good as that available in other industries. Some high-cost health care – heart transplants and specialized brain scanners – may never be provided.

Introducing a third party – government – to pay for costs generates another type of inefficiency shown in Figure 17.11. For simplicity, we'll assume there are no benefits from health care, so the marginal social benefit, *MSB*, equals demand, *D*. Marginal social cost is shown by the line *MSC*. The efficient quantity of health care is at Q_e where $MSC = MSB$. If doctors are paid a fee for their private service, neither doctor nor patient has to bear the cost directly. The marginal private cost (*MPC*) will appear to be zero and they provide and consume the maximum quantity of health care at Q_m. Doctors maximize their income and patients maximize their total benefit. The result of third party payment is inefficiency – overconsumption and high cost.

Figure 17.11 Third Party Payments Inefficiency

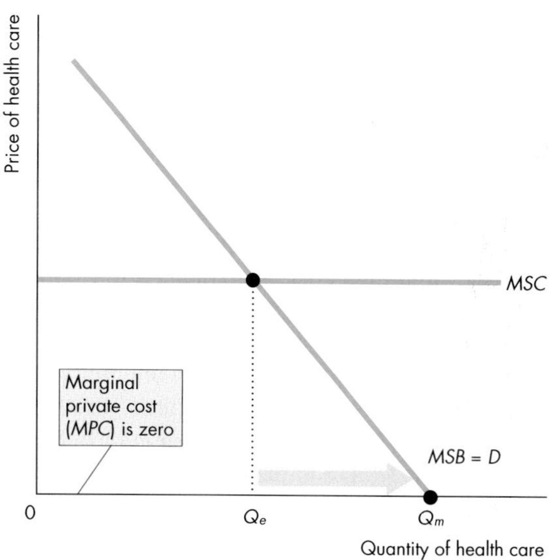

The efficient quantity of health-care provision is where $MSB = MSC$ at Q_e. In a health-care system where government pays private sector doctors a fee for service, there is a third party payments problem. The marginal private cost to doctors and patients is zero. Doctors have an incentive to maximize income and total patient benefit at Q_m. This leads to over consumption of $Q_m - Q_e$, and inefficiency.

Third party problems can be removed through the introduction of a national health service, where government finances and supplies health care.

National Health Services

A national health service avoids the problems of third party payments, economies of scale and insurance markets. But other forms of inefficiency tend to arise. One major criticism of a national health service is that it is a monopoly. Monopoly provision on a national scale can result in bureaucratic inefficiency and high cost, as explained in Chapter 18. The National Health Service (NHS) in the United Kingdom is one of the world's largest organizations, employing more than one million people. Rising costs led real expenditure on the NHS to increase by more than 33 per cent between 1987 and 1997, from £33 billion to £44 billion at 1997 prices.

Another problem arises in the allocation of resources among different forms of health care. If there are no prices, there is no information on cost. The forces of demand and supply are not working and there are no incentives to allocate resources efficiently among different types of care. Decisions about the allocation of resources between prevention and treatment, between care for the chronically sick and emergency treatment, and between hospitals and general practitioners, are made by NHS managers from politically determined budgets. As most voters do not have access to this information, voting behaviour is unlikely to reflect preferences for different political allocations.

Some economists also believe that monopoly restricts patient choice. While patients are free to choose a private alternative, only 15 per cent of households in the United Kingdom had private insurance in 1997. Private insurance does not cover chronic illness or maternity care, and deals mainly with non-life-threatening illnesses. So there is little alternative choice in many areas of health care.

We have looked at the different forms of health-care provision and seen that they all generate inefficiency and all face rising costs. Let's look at the policies that have been used to contain costs and reduce inefficiency in health care.

Reforming Private Systems

The pressure for reform is greatest in those countries that operate mainly private systems. In the United States, government pays the health-care costs of people on low incomes through the Medicaid and Medicare programmes. Although it is a private system, half of all health-care expenditure is paid for by government. Removing the effects of inflation, US government expenditure on health has increased more than fourfold since 1970, while the cost of private health care has less than doubled. One reason for this might be the third party payment problem generated by the government support element.

An attempt by the Clinton administration to expand the role of government in health-care provision failed in 1993. It included capping insurance premiums, creating universal cover and raising more funds through taxation. These changes would have made the system more like those in Canada and Europe but its critics say it would do no more than swap one form of inefficiency for another. For example, capping insurance premiums creates shortages which lead to quantity rationing. This form of rationing – waiting lists – is common in most European systems.

Reforming Mixed Systems and the NHS

Third party payment problems are also a source of inefficiency in mixed systems of government finance with private supply. Some countries such as Germany and the Netherlands have introduced a per-head fee, replacing a fee-for-service system. A per-head fee removes any incentive to maximize earnings through increasing treatment. Introducing co-payments – making patients pay part of the cost at the point of demand – makes patients more aware of costs and reduces the incentive to maximize total benefits. Co-payments have been introduced in Germany and in the NHS for dental care and prescriptions. Other European countries have implemented stringent regulation of prices and quantities and imposed annual health-care spending budgets to contain costs.

The problem of bureaucratic inefficiency in national health services can be tackled through privatization and the introduction of internal markets. An internal market is a system that generates prices within government-provided services by creating separate and independent groups of purchasers and providers. Each group is given a budget – providers set prices and market their services and purchasers look for the best buys.

Competition between purchasers and providers is intended to reduce costs and increase producer efficiency. It cannot improve allocative efficiency as the proportion spent on health care is determined by political choice at any point in time. Producer efficiency will increase if the monopoly of the NHS can be broken without raising other costs. The problem with the internal market is that it may generate more inefficiency than it removes. Let's see why.

To compete, purchasers and providers in the NHS must have good information. They must put prices on all goods and services and create contracts among themselves. This is time consuming and expensive. If these transactions costs are high in the new internal market it will be less efficient than the old monopoly NHS. Uncertainty about future demand for health care is also likely to increase the transactions costs of contracting in an internal market. Finally, many health professionals use their professional organizations to negotiate for wages. The old NHS was a monopsonist – a monopoly buyer of labour – whose power balanced the power of professional organizations in setting wages. The internal market reforms changed the NHS into a monopoly buyer of services without the power to control labour costs – the vast majority of its expenditure. In 1999, the Labour government introduced a new system of community care groups which will allow care givers to work together to increase patient choice and reduce costs. The purchaser–provider split has been dismantled but strict budgetary controls will be placed on the new community care groups.

The Impact of Reforms

Figure 17.12 shows the change in government expenditure on health as a percentage of all health expenditure between 1980 and 1991. It is clear that health-care reforms in most countries have reduced the share of health-care spending paid for by government. In particular, the biggest cuts have been made by those countries with national health services – the United Kingdom, Greece and Portugal. However, total spending on health care (government and private) is rising as a proportion of total expenditure in most countries as predicted in Figure 17.10. So private finance and supply is becoming more common in countries with national health services and mixed systems. Health-care systems are slowly becoming more similar, but there is no reason to believe that the systems are converging on the most efficient model.

So which system is better? Is the NHS doomed? It depends upon voter preferences for equity. A national health service is a benefit in kind and has an important redistributive effect as we saw in Figure 17.7. Comparative studies have shown that national health services are highly progressive – redistributing incomes from richer households to poorer households[1]. Private supply systems that are financed by governments are slightly regressive –

Figure 17.12 Changing Government Expenditure on Health Care

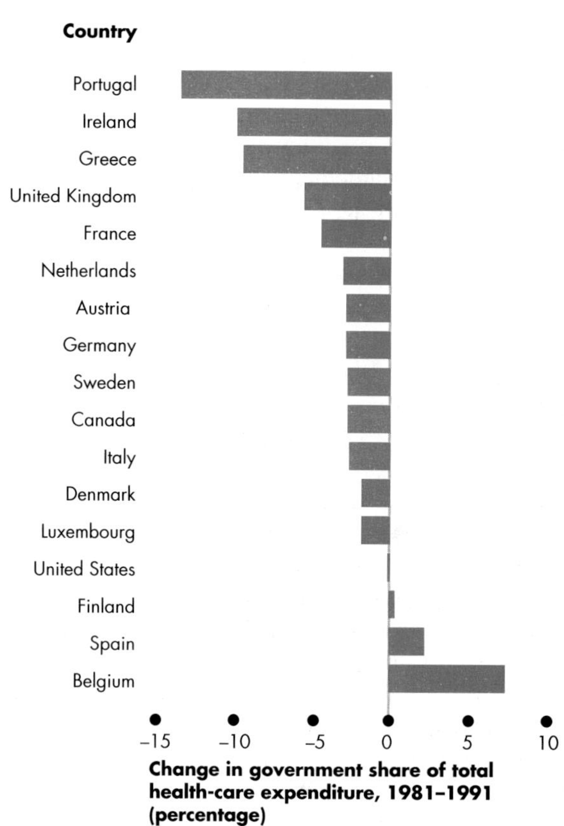

Over the period 1981–1991, governments have succeeded in reducing the proportion of government expenditure in total health-care expenditure in most countries. Government expenditure on health care as a percentage of total health-care expenditure has increased in only three countries. Some of the largest reductions are in those countries with national health services.

Source: T. Besley and M. Gouveia, 'Alternative systems of health care provision', *Economic Policy*, October 1994, 19.

1 The study is by E. Van Doorslaer and A. Wagstaff, 'Equity in the Delivery of Health Care: Some International Comparisons', *Journal of Health Economics*, 1992.

redistributing incomes from poorer households to richer households. Private systems, like the one operated in the United States, are highly regressive.

Private systems are less able to control rising costs driven by technology change, while systems with rigid budget controls like the NHS are better able to contain these costs. This may also make the relative efficiency of the NHS appear more certain to the median voter in the longer run. You can read about the publication of hospital cost figures as a method of controlling divergent costs in the NHS in *Reading Between the Lines* on pp. 426–427.

Review

- There are three types of health-care system: mostly private supply and finance, mostly private supply and government finance, and mostly government supply and finance.
- Health-care costs are high and rising in all systems.
- Health-care costs increase more quickly than average prices because health care is a labour-intensive personal service and it experiences continuous improvements in product quality.
- All health-care systems suffer from some form of inefficiency. Private insurance (like all types of insurance) faces moral hazard and adverse selection problems. Mixed systems face a third party payment problem and national health services face monopoly problems.
- Health-care reforms have tried to reduce inefficiency in all systems and systems are more similar as a result.
- Key differences still exist in terms of equity. National health services are the most equitable – progressive, mixed systems are slightly regressive and private systems are highly regressive in their impact.

We've examined economic inequality in the United Kingdom, and we've seen that there is a large amount of inequality across households and individuals. Some of that inequality arises from comparing households at different stages in the life cycle. But even taking a lifetime view, inequality remains. Some of that inequality arises from differences in wage rates. Economic choices accentuate these differences. We've seen that government policy can redistribute income to alleviate the worst aspects of poverty and to improve equality of access and outcomes in health care. Our next task is to take a closer look at the ways in which government policy can affect the outcome of a market economy. In the next three chapters we will look at sources of market failure and the ways that government policy can overcome it. We also look at the ways in which government and the political marketplace can fail.

Summary

Key Points

Economic Inequality in the United Kingdom (pp. 406–409)

- The richest one per cent of the population own almost one-third of the total wealth in the United Kingdom.
- Income is distributed less unevenly than wealth. Income inequality was reduced in the early 1960s and 1970s but increased in all other periods.
- The poorest people in the United Kingdom are likely to be single retired women over the age of 75, with no qualifications, living in Wales. The richest are university-educated couples, aged between 30 and 50, who live in the South East.

Factor Prices, Endowments and Choices (pp. 409–412)

- Differences in income and wealth arise partly from differences in individual endowments and partly from differences in factor prices.

- People who face a high hourly wage rate generally choose to work longer than those who face a low wage rate. As a result, the distribution of income becomes more unequal than the distribution of wage rates.
- Bequests accentuate inequality because of assortative mating.

Income Redistribution (pp. 412–417)

- Governments redistribute income through transfer payments such as income taxes, cash benefits and benefits in kind.
- Income taxes are progressive.
- Redistribution suffers from the big trade-off problem between equity and efficiency. The trade-off arises because the process of redistribution uses resources and weakens incentives to work and save.
- Benefit system reforms try to lessen the severity of the benefit traps. A more radical reform known as negative income tax would strengthen the incentives but increase the tax burden.

Health-care Provision (pp. 417–422)

- There are three types of health-care system: private supply and finance, private supply and government finance, and government supply and government finance.
- The main problems for all health-care systems are high and rising costs and inefficient production.
- All health-care systems suffer from some form of inefficiency including moral hazard, adverse selection, third party payment problems and monopoly.
- Health-care reforms in all systems have reduced inefficiency, making the different systems increasingly similar.
- National health services are the most progressive, shifting income from rich people to poor people.

Key Figures

Key Terms

Review Questions

1 Which of the following describe the distributions of personal income and wealth in the United Kingdom today?

 a The distributions of income and wealth are best represented by normal or bell-shaped curves.
 b More than 50 per cent of the population is wealthier than the average.
 c More than 50 per cent of the population is poorer than the average.

2 What is a Lorenz curve? How does a Lorenz curve illustrate inequality? Explain how the Lorenz curves for the distributions of income and wealth in the United Kingdom differ from each other.

3 Which is more unequally distributed, income or wealth? In answering this question, pay careful attention both to the way in which income and wealth are measured by official statistics and to the fundamental concepts of income and wealth.

4 How has income inequality changed over the past 30 years? What factors have contributed to changes in inequality of income over time?

5 What is a Gini-coefficient?

6 How has the Gini-coefficient changed over time and what does this indicate?

7 Why do we need a poverty line and how can it be measured?

8 What is wrong with the way in which the official statistics measure the distribution of wealth?

9 Explain why the work/leisure choices made by individuals can result in a distribution of income that is more unequal than the distribution of ability. If ability is distributed normally (bell-shaped), will the resulting distribution of income also be bell-shaped?

10 What is meant by a benefit trap?

11 Explain what is meant by transfer payments and benefits in kind.

12 Explain the difference between take-up and targetting of benefits.

13 Explain the difference between a poverty trap and an unemployment trap.

14 What is a negative income tax, and why don't we have one?

15 What are the three main types of health-care system?

16 How do different health-care systems compare in terms of efficiency and equity?

17 What factors will determine whether the NHS is retained or whether a different form of health-care system is introduced in the United Kingdom?

Problems

1 Imagine an economy in which there are five people who are identical in all respects. They each live for 70 years. For the first 14 of those years, they earn no income. For the next 35 years, they work and earn £30,000 a year from their work. For their remaining years, they are retired and have no income from labour. To make the arithmetic easy, let's suppose that the interest rate in this economy is zero; the individuals consume all their income during their lifetime and at a constant annual rate. What are the distributions of income and wealth in this economy if the individuals have the following ages:

a All are 45?
b 25, 35, 45, 55, 65?

Does case (a) show greater inequality than case (b)?

2 In the economy described in Problem 1, there is a 'baby boom'. Two people who were born in the same year are now 25. One person is 35, one 45, one 55, and no one is 65. What are the distributions of income and wealth:

a This year.
b 10 years in the future.
c 20 years in the future.
d 30 years in the future.
e 40 years in the future.
f Comment on and explain the changes in the distributions of income and wealth in this economy.

3 You are given the following information about income and wealth shares:

	Income shares (per cent)	Wealth shares (per cent)
Lowest 20%	5	0
Second 20%	11	1
Third 20%	17	3
Fourth 20%	24	11
Highest 20%	43	85

a Draw the Lorenz curves for income and wealth for this economy. Explain which of the two variables – income or wealth – is more unequally distributed.
b Compare the distributions of income and wealth in this economy with the actual

distributions in the United Kingdom. Is the UK income distribution more or less equal than the economy described here? Is the UK distribution of wealth more or less equal than the economy described here?

4 An economy consists of 10 people, each of whom has the following labour supply schedule:

Wage rate (pounds per hour)					
1	2	3	4	5	6
Hours worked per day					
0	1	2	3	4	5

The people differ in ability and earn different wage rates. The distribution of wage rates is as follows:

Wage rate (pounds per hour)				
1	2	3	4	5
Number of people				
1	2	4	2	1

a Calculate the average wage rate.
b Calculate the ratio of the highest to the lowest wage rate.
c Calculate the average daily income.
d Calculate the ratio of the highest to the lowest daily income.
e Sketch the distribution of hourly wage rates.
f Sketch the distribution of daily incomes.
g What important lesson is illustrated by this problem?

5 The table shows the distribution of market income in an economy.

Percentage of households	Income (millions of pounds)
Lowest 20%	5
Second 20%	10
Third 20%	18
Fourth 20%	28
Highest 20%	39

The government in the economy in Problem 2 redistributes income by collecting income taxes and paying benefits shown in the following table:

Percentage of households	Income taxes (percentage of income)	Benefits (millions of pounds)
Lowest 20%	5	10
Second 20%	10	8
Third 20%	18	3
Fourth 20%	28	0
Highest 20%	39	0

a Draw the Lorenz curve for this economy after taxes and benefits.
b Is the scale of redistribution of income in this economy greater or smaller than in the United Kingdom?

6 The government in the economy described in Problem 5 replaces its tax and benefit system with a negative income tax. What changes do you expect to occur in the economy?

7 Read the article about health-care spending in *Reading Between the Lines* on pp. 426–427 and then answer the following questions:

a Explain why a hospital's average total cost might exceed the average cost level for hospitals by as much as 62 per cent.
b What factors would make a hospital's average total cost fall below the average cost level for all hospitals.
c Why might the cost charged in different hospitals for cataract removal with lens implant differ between £337 and £1,659 per operation?
d Explain why the cheapest operation might not necessarily be the best operation?
e Do you think the most expensive operation is necessarily the best? Explain your answer.

8 Use the Parkin, Powell and Matthews Web site to visit the UK Department for Education and Employment to find information on graduate earnings in Britain between 1974 and 1995, and then:

a Describe what is meant by the graduate earnings premium.
b Describe the trend in the premium since 1974.
c Use demand and supply diagrams to explain the change in the graduate premium over time.

W http://www.econ100.com

Health-care Spending

The Essence of the Story

The Guardian, 3 November 1998

Health trusts defend wide cost variations

David Brindle, Social Services Correspondent

The first official tables yesterday showed huge variations in the costs of operations. Some hospitals were found to have average costs as much as 62 per cent above average, while others returned figures up to 33 per cent below — an overall difference of almost 100 per cent.

Alan Milburn, the Health Minister, said the figures revealed "unexplained and unacceptable" discrepancies in costs. Managers urged caution, however, pointing out that the figures said nothing about the quality of treatment and that "a cheap operation" was not necesarily the best.

Karen Caines, director of the Institute of Health Services Management, said: "Where costs are deemed overly high, an off-with-their-heads approach will lead to defensiveness and resentment — when what is needed is a willingness to acknowledge problems openly and deal with them."

The figures represent the Government's first attempt to iron out variations in hospital costs through public comparison, as against the competitive market discipline pursued by the Tories.

Data have been collected on almost five million surgical procedures of more than 500 different types, performed last year at all of the then 249 acute care NHS trusts in England. Nine in 10 trusts were found to fall within 20 per cent of the average.

But even with the data trimmed to exclude cases where patients stayed in hospital for exceptionally long periods, trusts' overall costs expressed as an index — where the average was 100 — varied from 67 to 162. The Walton Centre for Neurology and Neurosurgery, in Liverpool, emerged as the highest-cost trust. It said it was bound to have higher costs because of the specialised and hi-tech nature of its work.

Keith Griffiths, the trust's finance director, said: "There is always room for improvement, but we feel comfortable that we are as lean as we can be. We have the fourth lowest management costs in the north west region."

The former United Leeds Teaching Hospitals trust, which merged this April with the St James's and Seacroft University Hospitals trust, was found to be the second most costly. A spokesman for the new trust said its costs were inevitably raised by its training role and the high capital charges being incurred on a new wing at Leeds General Infirmary.

Ian Balmer, chief executive of Moorfields, the specialist eye hospital in London which was found to be the lowest-cost trust, said it carried out 83 per cent of cataract operations on a day-case basis. The national average was 59 per cent on a day basis.

Cost Variations

Cataract removal with lens implant — £337–£1,659; hip replacement — £1,834–£6,494; vasectomy — £148–£1,000; appendictomy — £468–£2,108

- An official report shows NHS hospital costs vary dramatically and that the costs of operations, such as hip replacements, could be up to two-and-a-half times more in the most expensive compared to the cheapest hospitals.
- As the figures do not compare treatments of similar quality, the cheapest operations may not be the best.
- Closing units with high costs may not be the efficient solution. The publication of the figures is an attempt to smooth out variations through public comparison rather than through market competition.
- Factors such as high investment in expensive technology and an emphasis on training in teaching hospitals will raise the costs of operations.

Economic Analysis

■ Figure 1 shows the impact of differences in the average total cost of hip replacements on NHS expenditure. Comparing two hospitals with similar demands for hip replacements, both hospitals undertake 500 hip replacements a year.

■ The average total cost in hospital 1, ATC_1, is higher than in hospital 2, ATC_2. Hospital 1 charges £6,494 for a hip replacement and hospital 2 charges £1,834. The NHS bill for 500 hip replacements is £0.9 million in hospital 2 and £3.2 million (the dark plus the light blue areas) in hospital 1.

■ Costs in hospital 2 may be lower because of more efficient practices, such as higher capacity utilization of operating theatres and staff, lower price contracts for drugs and dressings, less wastage and shorter stays in hospital.

■ But cost cutting in hospital 2 may lead to lower quality health outcomes. If success rates in hospital 2 are lower than in hospital 1, and patients have to return more frequently for further treatment, the opportunity cost of the operation and NHS expenditure will be much higher in hospital 2.

■ Some hospitals have additional responsibilities such as teaching roles, or specialize in high technology procedures which raise fixed costs and explain variations in average total costs.

■ Figure 2 shows the average variable costs, $AVC_{1 \text{ and } 2}$, for a hip replacement as the same in two hospitals. Hospital 1 is a teaching hospital and has higher average fixed costs, AFC_1, than hospital 2, AFC_2, to cover buildings and equipment for teaching. *ATC* in Figure 1 is the sum of *AVC* and *AFC* in Figure 2.

■ The internal market set up under Conservative reforms should have led to competition to reduce costs as budget holding doctors sent patients to lowest cost hospitals. Cost differences remain and the internal market has been removed by the Labour government. The new publication of cost data is intended to make hospitals more accountable to government and voters. But accountability, like the internal market, can only work if the cost indicators provide accurate information.

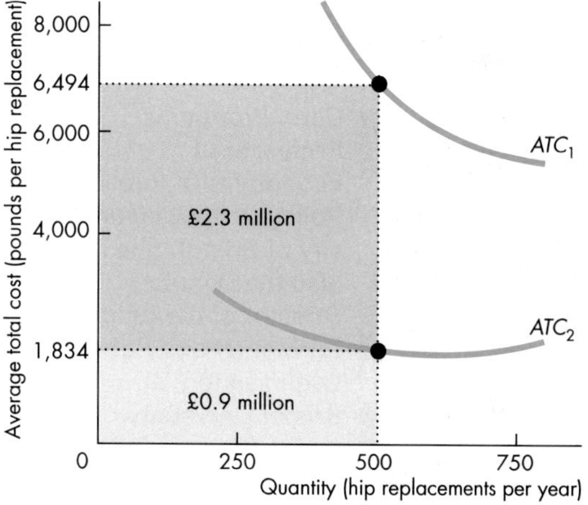

Figure 1 Cost and expenditure on hip replacements

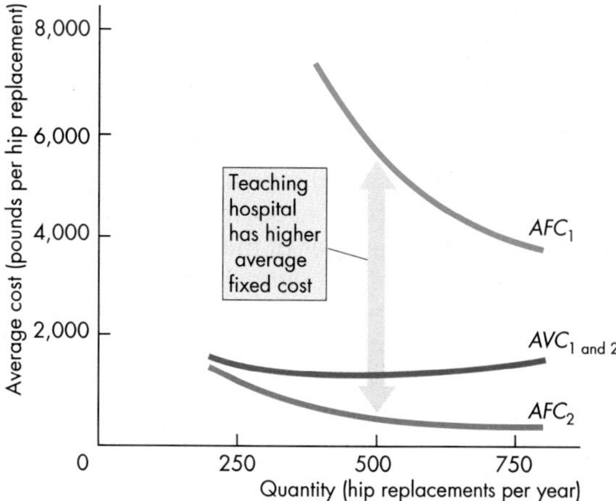

Figure 2 Average fixed and variable cost

Part 6

Market Failure and Government

Talking with **Carol Propper**

Carol Propper is Professor of Economics of Public Policy at the University of Bristol. She is also the Deputy Director of the Centre for Market and Public Organisation, at Bristol University, and the Centre for Social Exclusion at the London School of Economics, and a research Fellow at the Centre for Economic Policy research. Professor Propper was educated at Bristol, Oxford and York universities. She is currently a member of the ESRC Research Grants Board, and Chair of the Royal Economics Society Committee on Women in Economics and regularly contributes to the Royal Economic Society annual conferences. She is a member of the editorial board of *Journal of Health Economics* and *Health Economics*. Her recent research interests include the impact of competition on outcomes in health and education markets, poverty and income dynamics, models of marriage and divorce, the effect of early adult labour, neighbourhood and schooling experiences on later life outcomes. Recent advisory work includes secondment to the Department of Health 1993–94 as Senior Economic Advisor on the NHS Internal Market.

What do you find most interesting about economics?

Economics provides a structure to understand the behaviour of individuals when they make decisions about a wide range of consumption and investment activities. The structure is that all actions have costs and benefits, and that individuals take these into account when making their decisions. These terms include costs and benefits which may happen in the future (for example when people think about buying pensions) or ones which are non-monetary but important, for example, those that arise when people make decisions about having children or returning to education. In addition, the emphasis on theoretical models is a useful way of approaching a problem as it forces you to think logically about the issue.

Is government intervention always justifiable?

Standard economic analysis starts from the premise that if certain conditions hold, government intervention is needed only to redistribute income. If these conditions do not hold, then there is a case for government intervention. However, recent economics analysis has shown that even if in theory government intervention could improve matters, it does not always do so. Government is composed of groups of individuals – national and local politicians and civil servants – and influenced by pressure groups and lobbyists. All of these individuals have their own agendas, and it is not necessarily the case that their actions will bring gains to all members of society.

To what extent should governments provide services such as health care and why?

Health care and education are two of the areas in which the case for government action to overcome problems of the free market is strongest. In health care, markets fail to provide adequate levels of health care for two distinct reasons. First, health care is an area in which different groups have very different levels of information. For example, people go to a doctor when they don't know what is wrong with their health or they don't know how to make themselves better. Without government regulation, unscrupulous individuals could pretend to have this knowledge and make profit from selling inappropriate or even dangerous remedies. Second, health care is a service that most people in OECD countries think should be accessible, at some level, to all members of society. There is nothing about a market allocation that would guarantee equal access to all when in need of health care, or even access to some minimum level of health care.

Access to education is important for individuals who want to get on in society and improve their skills, and education has also been shown to be central in increasing the growth of countries, and therefore of living standards. But because the gains to education accrue to people other than the individual who has been to school, many people will under-invest in their own education. We saw this in nineteenth century Britain, when children of the poor went to work at age 7, and we see it today in countries where poor families in rural and urban areas need the money that their children can bring in. So intervention is needed to ensure that access to primary and secondary education is possible for all, not just the wealthy.

There is less of a case for government funding of university education, where most of the gains accrue to the individual. However, government intervention is needed to set up and guarantee a system of loans where the amount paid back is related to future income. Students could then borrow to fund their University education, so lack of access to funds would not deter people from going to university or taking low paid jobs initially. However, evidence suggests the free market (private banks) would not provide these loans without some government intervention, for example in underwriting bad debts.

Can economists successfully measure the efficiency of services such as health care and education?

It's difficult to measure the efficiency of services such as health and education because it's hard to measure what is being produced. To measure efficiency, we must measure both the inputs and the outputs of a production process, and find a measure that allows us to compare the relationship between inputs and outputs across different producers. While we can measure many (though not all) inputs into health care and education (for example nurses and teachers), it's a lot harder to measure the outputs, which are gains in health and additions to skills. School league tables are one example. Initially schools were ranked according to how many A level and GSCE passes were achieved. But it is known that this doesn't really measure the 'value-added' of the school, as these passes are influenced by the social composition of the pupils. So now economists try to measure the actual value added – the gain brought about by the teachers over and above what pupils get from their home environment.

Can economic theory make any contribution to the process of creating a fairer society?

The creation of a fairer society is a political and social decision, not an economic one. What economics can do is to identify which are the better and which are the poorer methods of achieving this goal. So for example, economics can help in the question of whether it is better to give cash benefits to all members of society or whether it is better just to target the poor. An example is the choice between paying child benefit to all mothers, or only those who have incomes below a certain level. Similarly, economics is helpful in thinking about the arguments for student loans to a large group of students versus free higher education for a smaller, more select group.

CHAPTER 18

Market Failure and Public Choice

After studying this chapter you will be able to:

- Describe and explain the growth in the size of government
- Explain how government policy arises from market failure and why government policy might improve the performance of the market economy
- Distinguish between public goods and private goods and explain the free-rider problem
- Explain how the quantity of public goods is determined
- Explain why government chooses to raise revenue from different sources
- Explain why some goods are taxed at a high rate

Government: Solution or Problem?

In 1998, the central and local governments in the United Kingdom spent £325 billion – 39 per cent of UK output. In other countries governments spend an even higher proportion of their national output on public sector services. Do we need this much government? Is government, as conservatives sometimes suggest, too big? Or, despite its enormous size, is government too small to do all the things it must attend to? Is government, as liberals sometimes suggest, not contributing enough to economic life? ◆ Government touches many aspects of our lives from birth to death. It supports health care when we're born and our schools, colleges and teachers. It is present throughout our working lives, taxing our incomes and employers, regulating our work environment and paying us benefits when we are unemployed. It is present throughout our retirement, paying us a small income, and when we die, taxing our bequests. Governments also create laws, and provide goods and services such as policing and national defence. ◆ But the government does not make all our choices. We decide what work to do, how much to save and what to spend our income on. Why does the government participate in some aspects of our lives but not in others? What determines the scale on which public services are provided? Is government policy really needed? Can't government services be provided equally well in the private sector?

◆ ◆ ◆ ◆ In this chapter and the next three, we study the interactions of governments and markets. We'll begin by describing the government sector, and explain why governments intervene in markets. We also explain the scale of government and examine whether their services are provided efficiently.

The Government Sector

The size of the government sector can be measured by the share of government expenditure out of total output. The share of government expenditure in the world's major industrialized countries is shown in Figure 18.1. You can see that the size of government is increasing over time. Government expenditure was just 27 per cent of the total output of major industrialized countries in 1960. By 1994, it had risen to a peak of 50 per cent. The only period of a sustained fall in the size of government expenditure in industrialized countries was between 1985 and 1990. But since 1990, the size of government expenditure in industrialized countries has increased again. In many countries the rise is due to increased expenditure on transfer payments – benefits to support income such as pensions, unemployment and sickness benefit.

The growth of government expenditure understates the growth of government influence on economic life. That influence stems not only from the government's share of expenditure but also from the increasing number of laws and regulations that affect the economic actions of households and firms.

Why does the government sector become an ever larger part of the economy in so many countries? What factors cause public expenditure as a proportion of total output to rise and fall? We'll discover the answers to these and other questions about government later in this chapter and in the following three chapters. But first let's look at the economic role that government plays.

Figure 18.1 The Size of Government in Major Industrialized Countries

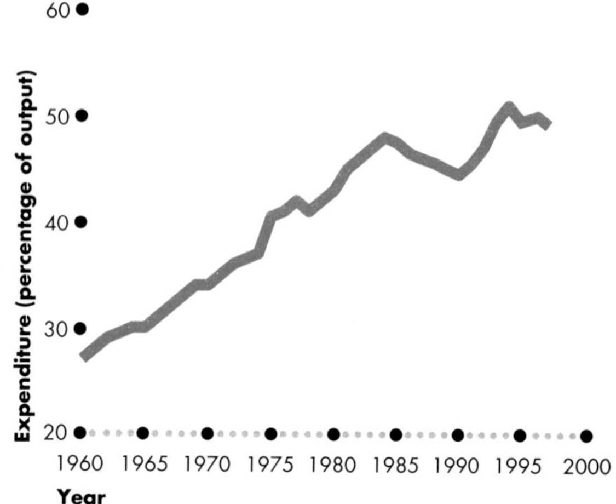

The size of the government sector is measured by graphing the share of total government expenditure out of of total output. The graph shows how the size of government in major OECD countries has changed over time. Government expenditure in major OECD countries was less than 30 per cent of total output in 1960, but has risen steadily over time, peaking at 50 per cent in 1994. Much of the increase is due to a rise in government spending on transfer payments such as pensions and unemployment benefits.

The Economic Theory of Government

Economic theory tries to predict the economic actions of government and the consequences of these actions. Governments exist to help people cope with scarcity and to provide non-market mechanisms for allocating scarce resources. So government economic activity arises when market economies do not always achieve an *efficient allocation of resources* – when there is **market failure**. In Chapter 12, we saw that markets will only be allocatively efficient when the assumptions of our basic model hold. When they don't hold, markets will be inefficient and resources will not be allocated efficiently. Market economies will produce too many of some goods and services and too few of others. Social welfare will not be maximized as the marginal social cost of each good and service will not equal its marginal social benefit.

If government policy could reallocate resources, it might be possible to make some people better off, while making no one worse off – improving market efficiency and increasing social welfare. Figure 18.2 shows that government policy has three aims. The first is to implement policies to make markets work more efficiently by reducing market failure. As we will see in this chapter and following chapters, governments can use a range of policies to achieve this. Second, since market economies do not achieve what most people regard as an *equitable distribution of income*, some government policy is needed to redistribute income and wealth, usually through the tax and benefit system. We looked at these policies in Chapter 17. Third, market economies are subject to shocks and uncertainty and these can cause macroeconomic problems such as

Figure 18.2 The Aims of Government Policy

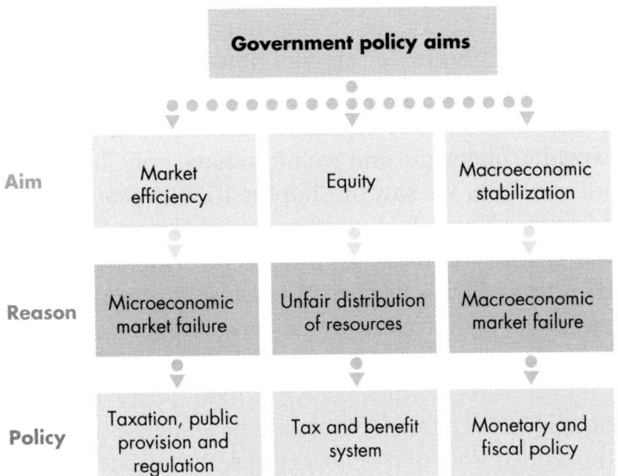

Government policy has three aims. First, governments try to improve efficiency by reducing the impact of microeconomic market failure. They can use a mixture of taxation, public provision and regulation to help individual markets work more efficiently. Second, governments try to improve equity by redistributing incomes and wealth. This can be done by designing an appropriate tax and benefit system which transfers income and wealth, for example, from the rich to the poor. Third, governments try to reduce the impact of uncertainty and limited information on macroeconomic growth by using a mixture of monetary and fiscal policies.

unemployment and inflation, so some government policy is needed to stabilize the economy over time. Macroeconomic policy is examined in Parts 6 and 7 of this book. So let's now take a closer look at market failure and government policy.

The main types of microeconomic market failure are:

- Public goods.
- Monopoly.
- Externalities.
- Poor information and uncertainty.

Public Goods

A pure **public good** is a good or service that can be consumed simultaneously by everyone and from which no one can be excluded. Public goods are

Figure 18.3 Public Goods and Private Goods

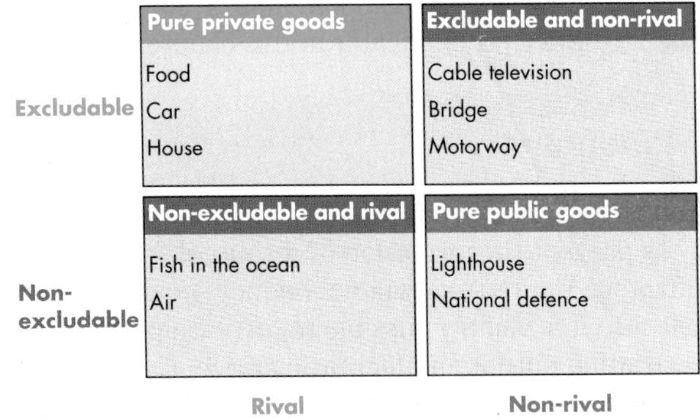

A pure public good (bottom-right) is one for which consumption is non-rival and from which it is impossible to exclude a consumer. Pure public goods pose a free-rider problem. A pure private good (top-left) is one for which consumption is rival and from which consumers can be excluded. Some goods are non-excludable but are rival (bottom-left) and some goods are non-rival but are excludable (top-right).

Source: Adapted from and inspired by E. S. Savas, *Privatizing the Public Sector,* Chatham, NJ, Chatham House Publishers Inc., 1982, p. 34.

non-rival in consumption because one person's consumption of the good does not affect the quantity available for anyone else. Most goods, by contrast, are rival in consumption. For example, if I eat a pizza, that pizza is no longer available for anyone else. Public goods are also **non-excludable** if it is impossible, or extremely costly, to prevent someone from benefiting from a good who has not paid for it. An example of a non-excludable good is national defence because government cannot refuse to protect people who may not have paid taxes towards paying for defence.

Figure 18.3 shows that many goods have a public element but are not pure public goods. An example is a motorway. A motorway is non-rival until it becomes congested. But the use of road tolls and electronic road pricing could exclude non-payers. Ocean fish are rival because a fish taken by one person is not available for anyone else. But ocean fish are non-excludable because it is difficult to stop other countries taking them if they are outside a country's territorial limits.

Public goods create a free-rider problem. A **free rider** is a person who consumes a good without paying for it. Markets fail to supply a public good because no one has an incentive to pay for it. We'll see how government can help to cope with the free-rider problem later in this chapter.

Monopoly

You already know that *rent seeking* and *monopoly* prevent the allocation of resources from being efficient. Markets fail when monopoly power exists, because it is usually possible to increase profit by restricting output and increasing price. Until a few years ago, for example, British Telecommunications had a monopoly on telephone services and the price of business and domestic telephone services was higher than it is today.

Although some monopolies arise from *legal barriers to entry* – barriers to entry created by governments – a major activity of government is to regulate monopoly and to enforce laws that prevent cartels and other restrictions on competition. We'll study competition and monopoly regulations in Chapter 19.

Externalities

An **externality** is a cost or a benefit arising from an economic transaction that falls on people who do not participate in that transaction. They cannot participate because there is no market for the cost or benefit. For example, when a chemicals factory (legally) dumps its waste into a river and kills the fish, it imposes an externality – in this case, an external cost – on the fisherman who lives downstream. External costs and benefits are not taken into account by the people whose actions create them if there are no markets – and no prices – for these costs and benefits. For example, the chemicals factory does not take the damaging effects on the fish into account when deciding whether to dump waste into the river because there is no market for waste water. When a home owner fills her garden with spring bulbs, she generates an external benefit for all the joggers and walkers who pass by. In deciding how much to spend on this lavish display, she takes into account only the benefits accruing to herself. We study externalities and the way governments and markets cope with them in Chapter 20.

Poor Information and Uncertainty

If markets are to work well, people need to have good information about what is being produced, at what price, and by whom. Firms also need to know what factors of production are available, the price of different factors and how technology has changed. Firms need to be able to predict expected future outcomes of capital investment. But the world is uncertain and we often have only limited information. We saw in Chapter 15, how our inability to predict future technologies causes the price of exhaustible natural resources to fall, rather than rise over time. This is inefficient because it encourages us to use up our natural resources too quickly. We have already seen in Chapter 17, how poor information can cause a third party payment problem in health care systems. Government policies such as those introduced in health care reforms can reduce this inefficiency.

Before we look at government policy, we need to understand the arena in which governments operate. To do this we are going to build a model of the 'political marketplace'.

Public Choice and the Political Marketplace

Government is a complex organization made up of millions of individuals, each with their *own* economic objectives. Government policy choices are the outcome of the choices made by these individuals. To analyse these choices, economists have developed a theory of the political activity called **public choice theory**. We can use this theory to build a model of the political marketplace similar to our market models.

The actors in the political marketplace model are:

- Voters.
- Politicians.
- Bureaucrats.

The choices and interactions of these actors are illustrated in Figure 18.4. Let's look at each in turn.

Voters

Voters are the consumers of the political process. In markets for goods and services, people express their demands by their willingness to pay. In the

Figure 18.4 The Political Marketplace

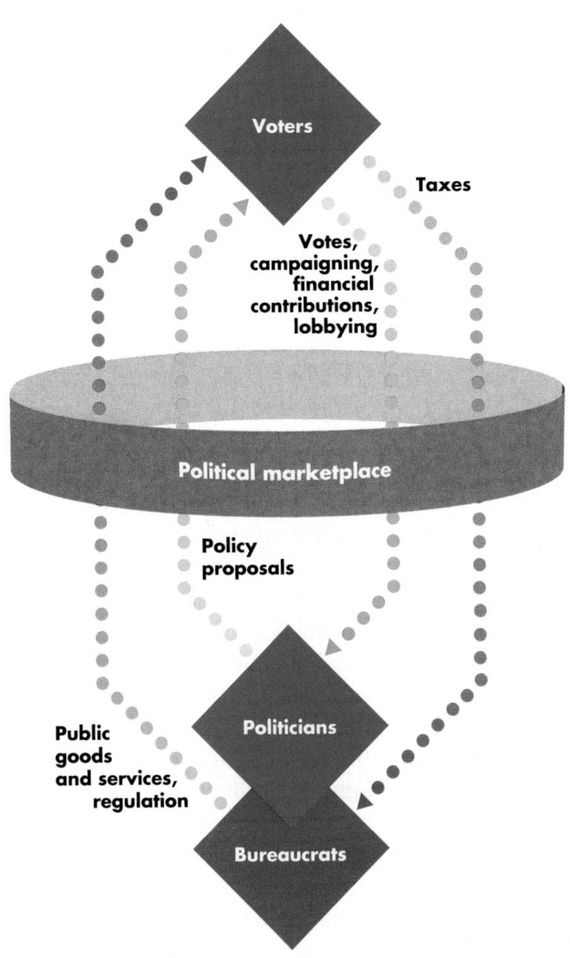

Voters express their demands for policies by voting, election campaigning, making financial contributions to political parties and joining interest groups to lobby government. Politicians propose policies to appeal to a majority of voters. Bureaucrats try to maximize the budgets of their departments or agencies. If voters are well-informed, the political equilibrium is efficient. If voters are rationally ignorant, the cost and provision of public goods exceeds the efficient level.

political marketplace, they express their demands by voting, campaigning, lobbying and making financial contributions. Public choice theory assumes that people support policies that they believe will make them better off and oppose policies that they believe will make them worse off. They neither oppose nor support – they are indifferent towards – policies that they believe have no effect on them. Voters' *perceptions* of policy outcomes are what guide their choices.

Politicians

Politicians are the elected administrators and legislators at all levels of government. Economic models of public choice assume that the objective of a politician is to get elected and to remain in office. Votes, to a politician, are like pounds to a firm. To get enough votes, politicians form coalitions – political parties – to develop policy proposals, which they expect will appeal to a majority of voters.

Bureaucrats

Bureaucrats are employed staff who work in government departments at all levels. They are responsible for enacting government policy. The most senior bureaucrats are hired by politicians. Junior bureaucrats are hired by senior bureaucrats.

Economic models of public choice assume that bureaucrats aim to maximize their own utility. To achieve this objective, they try to maximize the budget of the agency or department in which they work. This is because the bigger the budget, the greater is the prestige of the agency or department boss and the larger is the opportunity for promotion for people further down the bureaucratic ladder. To maximize their budgets, bureaucrats devise programmes that they expect will appeal to politicians and they help politicians to sell programmes to voters.

Political Equilibrium

Voters, politicians and bureaucrats make their economic choices to maximize their own objectives. But each group is constrained by the preferences of the other groups and by what is technologically feasible. The outcome of the choices of voters, politicians and bureaucrats is the **political equilibrium**, which is a situation in which the choices of voters, politicians and bureaucrats are all compatible and in which no group can improve its position by making a different choice.

Let's see how voters, politicians and bureaucrats interact to determine the quantity of public goods.

Public Goods and the Free-rider Problem

Why does the government provide public goods and services such as national defence and health services – goods and services that can be consumed simultaneously by everyone and from which no one can be excluded? Why don't we leave the provision of these goods and services to private firms that sell their output in markets? Why don't we buy our national defence from North Pole Protection plc, a private firm that competes for our pounds in the marketplace in the same way that McDonald's and Coca-Cola do? The answer to these questions lies in the *free-rider problem.*

The Free-rider Problem

Suppose that for its effective national defence, a country must launch some communication and surveillance satellites. One satellite can do part of the job required. But the larger the number of satellites deployed, the greater is the degree of security. Satellites are expensive, and to build them resources are diverted from other productive activities. The larger the number of satellites installed, the greater is their marginal cost.

Our task is to work out the number of satellites to install to achieve allocative efficiency. We'll then examine whether private provision can achieve allocative efficiency, and we'll discover that it cannot – that there is a free-rider problem.

Benefits and Costs of Satellites

Suppose that for its defense, a country must launch some surveillance satellites. The benefit provided by a satellite is the *value* of its services. The value of a *private* good is the maximum amount that the *person* is willing to pay for one more unit of the good, shown by the demand curve. Similarly, the value to an individual of a *public* good is the maximum amount that the *people* are willing to pay for one more unit of the good.

To calculate the value a person places on one more unit of a public good, we can use a total benefit curve. *Total benefit* is the total pound value that a person places on a given level of provision of a public good. The greater the quantity of the public good, the larger is a person's total benefit. The increase in total benefit resulting from a one-unit increase in the quantity of a public good is the **marginal benefit**.

Figure 18.5 shows an example of the marginal benefit that arises from defence satellites for a society of just two people, Lisa and Max. Lisa's and Max's marginal benefits are graphed as MB_L and MB_M, respectively, in parts (a) and (b) of the figure. As you can see, the greater the quantity of satellites, the smaller is the marginal benefit for both Lisa and Max. By the time four satellites are deployed, Lisa perceives no additional benefits and Max perceives only £10 worth of benefit.

Part (c) of the figure shows the economy's marginal benefit curve, *MB* (where the economy has only two people, Lisa and Max). An individual's marginal benefit curve for a public good is similar to the individual's demand curve for a private good. But the economy's marginal benefit curve for a public good is different from the market demand curve for a private good. To obtain the market demand curve for a private good, we add up the quantities demanded by each individual at each price. In other words, we sum the individual demand curves horizontally[1]. In contrast, to find the economy's marginal benefit curve of a public good, we add the marginal benefit of each individual at each quantity provided, as one person's consumption does not reduce the amount available for another. So we sum the individual marginal benefit curves of Lisa and Max vertically. The resulting marginal benefit curve for the whole economy of two people is graphed in part (c) – the curve *MB*. Lisa's marginal benefit from the first satellite gets added to Max's marginal benefit from the first satellite because they both enjoy its security value.

The Efficient Quantity of a Public Good

In reality, an economy with two people would not buy any satellites – the total benefit falls far short of the cost. But an economy with 50 million people might. To determine the efficient quantity, we need to take cost as well as benefit into account.

The cost of a satellite is based on technology and the prices of the factors of production used to produce it. It is an opportunity cost and is derived

1 The derivation of the market demand curve from the individual demand curves is explained in Figure 8.1, p. 170.

Figure 18.5 Benefits of a Public Good

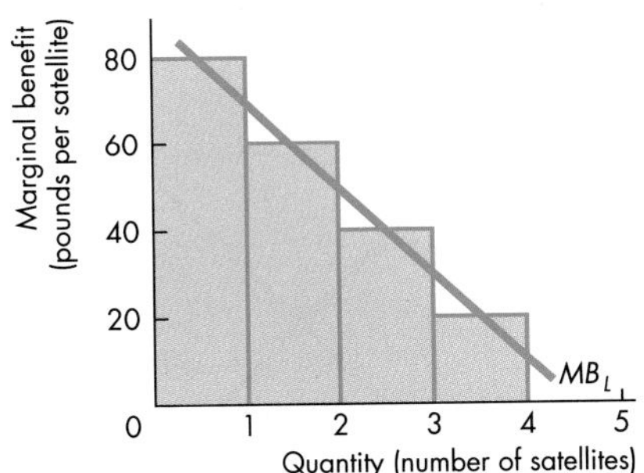

(a) Lisa's marginal benefit

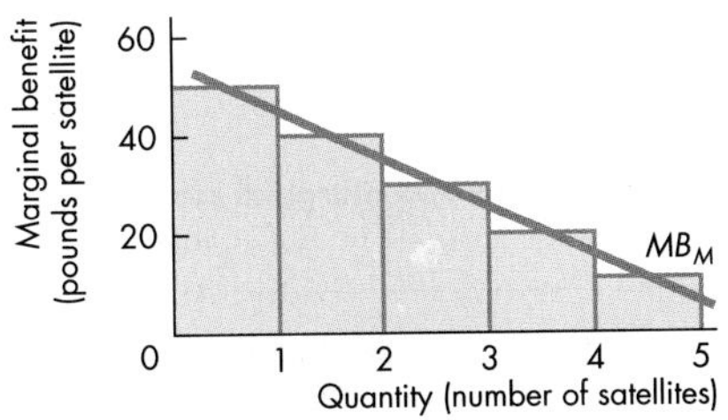

(b) Max's marginal benefit

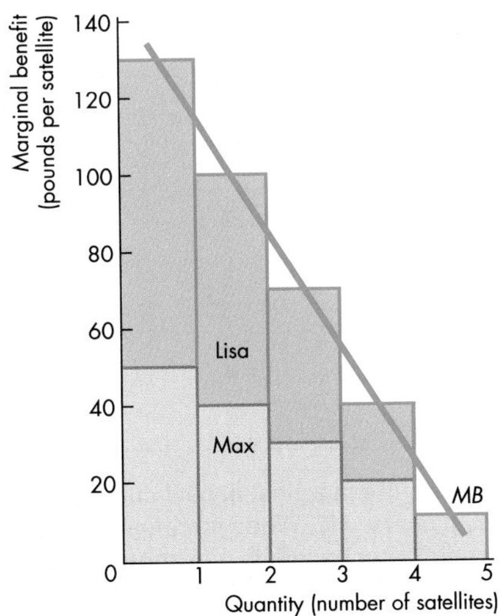

(c) Economy's marginal benefit

The figure shows the marginal benefit for two individuals, Lisa and Max, and for the whole economy (comprising only Lisa and Max) for different quantities of satellites. The marginal benefit curves are MB_L for Lisa, MB_M for Max and MB for the economy. The marginal benefit to the economy at each quantity of the public good is the sum of the marginal benefits to each individual.

in the same way as the cost of producing jumpers – explained in Chapter 11. The efficient quantity is the one that maximizes *net benefit* – total benefit minus total cost.

Figure 18.6 illustrates the efficient quantity of satellites. The first three columns of the table show the total and marginal benefits to an economy consisting of 50 million people. The next two columns show the total and marginal cost of producing satellites. The final column shows net benefit. Total benefit, *TB*, and total cost, *TC*, are graphed in part (a) of the figure. Net benefit (total benefit minus total cost) is maximized when the vertical distance between the *TB* and *TC* curves is at its largest, a situation that occurs with two satellites. This is the efficient quantity.

Another way of describing the efficient scale uses marginal benefit and marginal cost. The marginal benefit, *MB*, and marginal cost, *MC*, of satellites are graphed in part (b). When marginal benefit exceeds marginal cost, net benefit increases if the quantity produced increases. When marginal cost exceeds marginal benefit, net benefit increases if the quantity produced decreases. Marginal benefit equals marginal cost at *M* in part (b) with two satellites. So making marginal cost equal to marginal benefit maximizes net benefit and determines the allocatively efficient quantity of the public good.

Private Provision

We have now worked out the quantity of satellites that maximizes net benefit. Would a private firm – North Pole Protection plc – deliver that quantity? It would not. To do so, it would have to collect £15 million to cover its costs – or £40 from each of the 50 million people in the economy. But no one would have an incentive to buy his or her 'share' of the satellite system. Each person would reason as follows. The number of satellites provided by North Pole Protection is not affected by my £40. My consumption of other goods will be greater if I free ride and do not pay my share of the cost of the satellite system. If I do not pay and everyone else does, I enjoy the same level of security and can buy more private goods.

If everyone reasons the same way, North Pole Protection has no revenue and can't supply any satellites. The market does not provide the efficient level – two satellites – so private provision is inefficient.

Figure 18.6 The Efficient Quantity of a Public Good

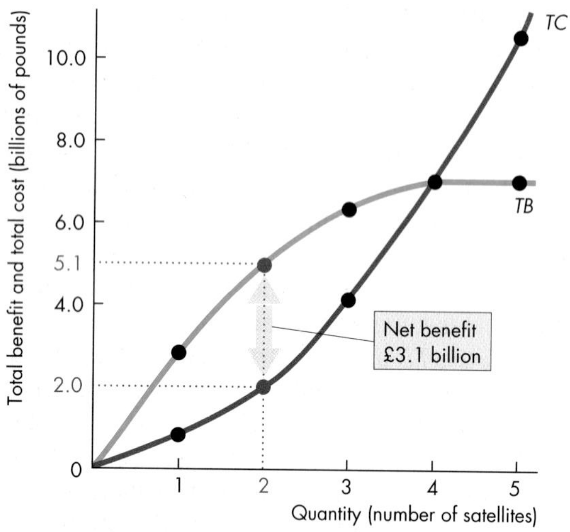

(a) Total benefit and total cost

Marginal benefit and marginal cost (billions of pounds per satellite)
3
2
M
1
0
MC
Point of allocative efficiency
MB
1
2
3
4
5
Quantity (number of satellites)

(b) Marginal benefit and marginal cost

Quantity (number of satellites)	Total benefit (billions of pounds)	Marginal benefit (billions of pounds per satellite)	Total cost (billions of pounds)	Marginal cost (billions of pounds per satellite)	Net benefit (billions of pounds)
0	0		0		0
		3		0.7	
1	3		0.7		2.3
		2.1		1.3	
2	5.1		2		3.1
		1.2		2	
3	6.3		4		2.3
		1.0		3.3	
4	7.3		7.3		0
		0		4	
5	7.3		11		−3.7

Total benefit and total cost are graphed in part (a) as the total benefit curve, *TB*, and the total cost curve, *TC*. Net benefit – the vertical distance between the two curves – is maximized when two satellites are installed.

Part (b) shows the marginal benefit curve, *MB*, and marginal cost curve, *MC*. When marginal cost equals marginal benefit, net benefit is maximized and allocative efficiency is achieved.

Public Provision

Suppose there are two political parties, the Greys and the Browns, that agree with each other on all issues except satellites. The Greys would like to provide four satellites at a cost of £7.3 billion, with benefits of £7.3 billion and a net benefit of zero, as shown in Figure 18.7. The Browns would like to provide one satellite at a cost of £0.7 billion, a benefit of £3 billion and a net benefit of £2.3 billion.

Before campaigning, the two political parties do a 'what-if' analysis. Each party reasons as follows. If each party offers the satellite programme it wants – Greys four satellites and Browns one satellite – the

Figure 18.7 Provision of a Public Good in a Political System

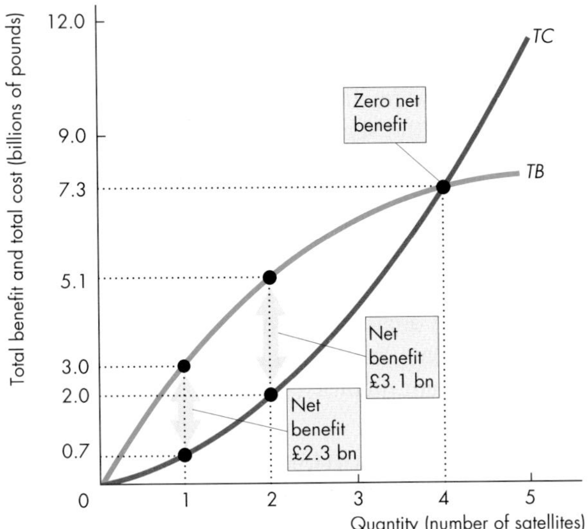

Net benefit is maximized if two satellites are installed, with a total benefit of £5.1 billion and a total cost of £2 billion. The Browns would like one satellite and the Greys would like four. But each party recognizes that its only hope of being elected is to provide two satellites – the quantity that maximizes net benefit and so leaves no room for the other party to improve on. If voters are well-informed about the cost and benefit of a public good, competition between political parties for their votes achieves the efficient outcome.

voters will get a net benefit of £2.3 billion from the Browns, zero net benefit from the Greys, and the Browns will win the election.

Contemplating this outcome, the Greys realize that their party is too grey to get elected. They figure that they must offer net benefits in excess of £2.3 billion if they are to beat the Browns. So they scale back their proposal to two satellites. At this level of provision, total cost is £2 billion, total benefit is £5.1 billion and net benefit is £3.1 billion. If the Browns stick with one satellite, the Greys will win the election.

But contemplating this outcome, the Browns realize that the best they can do is to match the Greys. They too propose to provide two satellites on exactly the same terms as the Greys. If the two parties offer the same number of satellites, the voters are indifferent between the parties. They toss coins to decide their votes and each party receives around 50 per cent of the vote.

The result of the politicians' 'what-if' analysis is that each party offers two satellites so regardless of who wins the election, this is the quantity of satellites installed. This quantity is efficient because it maximizes the perceived net benefit of the voters. Thus in this example, competition in the political marketplace results in the efficient provision of a public good. But for this outcome to occur, voters must be well-informed and able to evaluate the alternatives. We'll see below that they do not always have an incentive to do so.

In the example we've just studied, both parties eventually propose identical policies. This is called the principle of minimum differentiation. We have analysed the behaviour of politicians but not that of the bureaucrats who translate the choices of the politicians into programmes. Let's now see how the economic choices of bureaucrats influence the political equilibrium.

The Role of Bureaucrats

We've seen in Figures 18.6 and 18.7 that two satellites at a cost of £2 billion maximize net benefit and that competition between two political parties delivers this outcome. But will the Ministry of Defence's bureaucrats cooperate?

Suppose the Ministry of Defence's aim is to maximize the defence budget. To achieve its objective, the department will try to persuade Parliament that tow satellites cost more than £2 billion. As Figure 18.8 shows, it will argue if possible that they cost £5.1 billion – the entire benefit. Pressing its position even more strongly, the department will argue for more satellites. It will press for four satellites and a budget of £7.3 billion. In this situation, total benefit and total cost are equal and net benefit is zero.

But won't the politicians always control the bureaucracy and keep spending down to the efficient level – the level that maximizes the perceived net benefits of the voters? We've already seen that when there are two political parties competing for votes, the party that comes closest to maximizing net benefit gets the most votes. Don't these forces of competition for votes dominate the aims of the bureaucrats to ensure that the Ministry of Defence only gets a budget big enough to provide two satellites – to maximize net benefit?

If voters are well-informed and if their perception of their self-interest is correct, the political party

Figure 18.8 Bureaucratic Overprovision

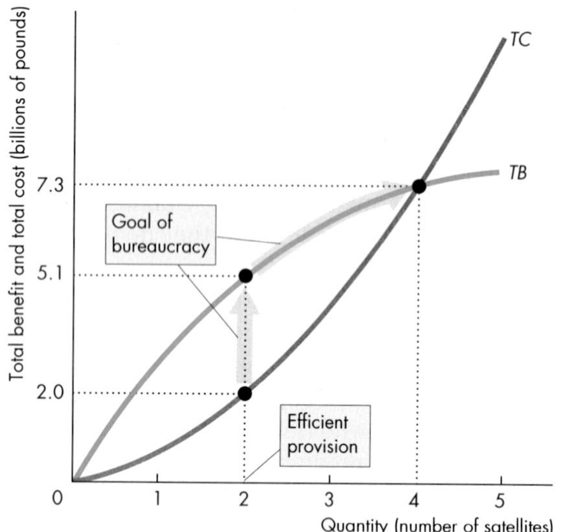

The goal of a bureaucracy is to maximize its budget. A bureau that maximizes its budget will seek to increase cost all the way to the total benefit and to expand output and expenditure as far as possible. Here, the Department of Defence tries to get £2 billion to provide two satellites and to increase the quantity of satellites to four with a budget of £7.3 billion.

that wins the election does hold the budget to the level that provides the efficient outcome. But there is another possible political equilibrium. It is one based on the principle of voter ignorance and well-informed interest groups.

Rational Ignorance A principle of public choice theory is that it is rational for a voter to be ignorant about an issue unless that issue has a perceptible effect on the voter's income. **Rational ignorance** is the decision *not* to acquire information because the cost of doing so exceeds the expected benefit. For example, each voter knows that he or she can make virtually no difference to the defence policy of the government. Each voter also knows that it would take an enormous amount of time and effort to become even moderately well-informed about alternative defence technologies. So voters remain relatively uninformed. (Though we are using defence policy as an example, the same applies to all aspects of government economic activity.)

All voters are consumers of national defence. But only a few voters are producers of national defence. Those voters who own or work for firms that produce satellites have a direct personal interest in defence because it affects their incomes. Such voters have an incentive to become well-informed about defence issues and to form or join interest groups to lobby government and further their own interests. In collaboration with the Ministry of Defence's bureaucracy, these voters exert a larger influence than the relatively uninformed voters who only consume defence.

When the rationality of the uninformed voter and special interest groups are taken into account, the political equilibrium provides public goods in excess of the efficient quantity. So in the satellite example, three or four satellites might be installed rather than the efficient quantity, which is two satellites.

Two Types of Political Equilibrium

We've seen that two types of political equilibrium are possible: efficient and inefficient. These two types of political equilibrium correspond to two theories of government:

1 Public interest theory.
2 Public choice theory.

Public Interest Theory Public interest theory predicts that governments make choices about policies to achieve efficiency. This outcome occurs in a perfect political system in which voters are fully informed about the effects of policies and refuse to vote for outcomes that can't be improved upon. The result of government policy is an improvement in efficiency and a reduction in market failure.

Public Choice Theory Public choice theory predicts that governments make choices that result in inefficiency. This outcome occurs in political markets in which voters are rationally ignorant and base their votes only on issues that they know affect their own net benefit. Voters pay more attention to their interests as producers than their interests as consumers. Public officials also act in their own interest. The result of government policy is government failure that parallels market failure.

Why Government is Large and Grows

We saw at the beginning of this chapter that the share of government expenditure out of income has grown over the years. Now that we know how the quantity of public goods is determined, we can explain part of the reason for the growth of government. Government grows in part because the demand for some public goods increases at a faster rate than the demand for private goods. There are two possible reasons for this growth:

1 Voter preferences.
2 Inefficient overprovision.

Voter Preferences The growth of government can be explained by voter preferences in the following way. As voters' incomes increase (as they usually do in most developed economies), the quantity of public goods demanded increases more quickly than income. The *income elasticity of demand* for public goods is greater than one. Many (and the most expensive) public goods are in this category. They include communication systems, such as motorways, airports and air-traffic control, public health, education and defence. If government's did not support increasing expenditure, they would not get elected. So this first reason for government growth seems convincing.

Inefficient Overprovision Inefficient overprovision is the reason given to back many attempts to control government spending. These include privatization programmes, budget cuts, the use of contracting and performance indicators in public services, and the introduction of auditing and management practice into public services. You can read about the impact of introducing target reforms to increase the efficiency of goverment provision in *Reading Between the Lines* on pp. 450–451. Inefficient overprovision might explain the *size* of government but not the *growth* of government. It only explains why government might be *larger* than its efficient scale at any point in time. It does, however, explain why governments might introduce mechanisms to make government work more efficiently, resulting in a reduction in the size of the government sector.

Voters Strike Back

If government expenditure grows too large relative to voters' preferences, there is always the possibility of a voter backlash. Governments have to pay for their spending and policies by raising revenue through taxation or borrowing. Higher taxes reduce voters' incomes – reducing voter utility – so governments must balance the increase in voter utility from spending against the decrease in voter utility from taxation.

If governments borrow too much, they will generate inflation and become equally unpopular. When governments fear they will lose the next election as a result of rising public sector expenditure, taxation or inflation, they'll start to cut expenditure. You can find examples of cuts in welfare spending for this reason all over Europe – particularly in Belgium, France, Germany, Italy, the United Kingdom and Sweden.

Review

- Governments use policies to achieve three goals: reducing inefficiency from market failure, increasing equality and stabilizing the economy to achieve macroeconomic growth.
- Private provision of a public good creates a free-rider problem and provides less than the efficient quantity of the good.
- Competition between politicians for votes can achieve an efficient quantity of a public good, provided voters are well-informed and bureaucrats do not maximize the size of their own departments.
- Private provision of a public good creates a free-rider problem and provides less than the efficient quantity of the good.

We've now seen how voters, politicians and bureaucrats interact to determine the quantity of public goods and services. But public goods must be paid for with taxes. How does the political marketplace determine the scale and variety of taxes that we pay?

Taxes

Taxes generate the financial resources that governments use to provide voters with public goods and other benefits. For the UK government in 1996, 26 per cent of total revenue came from income tax, 28 per cent from Value Added Tax and excise taxes, and 20 per cent from social security taxes. What factors affect the government's choice of revenue sources?

Taxes and Income

The amounts that people pay in tax and receive in benefits from social security payments depends mainly on their income. Other things remaining the same, the higher a person's income, the greater is the amount of income tax paid and the smaller is the amount of benefit received. As a rule high-income people prefer to vote for a political party that proposes low benefits and low income tax rates, while low-income people prefer to vote for a political party that proposes high benefits and high income tax rates. Let's build a model of the political marketplace based on the idea that politicians try to find the income tax rate and benefit level that attracts the majority of voters – the median voter theorem.

The Median Voter Theorem The **median voter theorem** states that political parties will pursue policies that appeal to the median voter. The median member of a population is the one in the middle – one-half of the population lies on one side and one-half on the other. Let's see how the median voter theorem applies to the question of how large the tax and benefit system should be.

Imagine a list of all the possible levels of benefit from government policies and the associated tax rate needed to finance them. We'll assume that the only tax is an income tax to simplify the problem. The list begins with the highest possible level of benefit and tax rate and ends with no benefit and a zero tax rate. We can identify each entry in the list by the tax rate associated with it.

Next imagine arranging all the voters along a line running from A to D, as shown in Figure 18.9. The voter who favours the highest tax rate (and the highest benefit level) is at A. The voter who favours a zero tax rate (and no benefits) is at D. All the other voters are arranged along the line based on the tax rate (and benefit level) that they favour most. The curve in the figure shows the tax rate favoured by each voter between A and D. The median voter in the example favours a tax rate of 30 per cent.

Suppose that two political parties propose slightly different tax rates. The high-tax party proposes a tax rate of 61 per cent and the low-tax party proposes a tax rate of 59 per cent. Given this choice, all the voters between A and B prefer the higher tax rate and will vote for the high-tax party. All the voters between B and D prefer the lower tax and will vote for the low-tax party. The low-tax party will win the election.

Alternatively, suppose that the high-tax party proposes a tax rate of 11 per cent and the low-tax party proposes a tax rate of 9 per cent. The voters between A and C will vote for the high-tax party and those between B and C will vote for the low-tax party. This time, the high-tax party will win the election.

Figure 18.9 Voting for Income Taxes

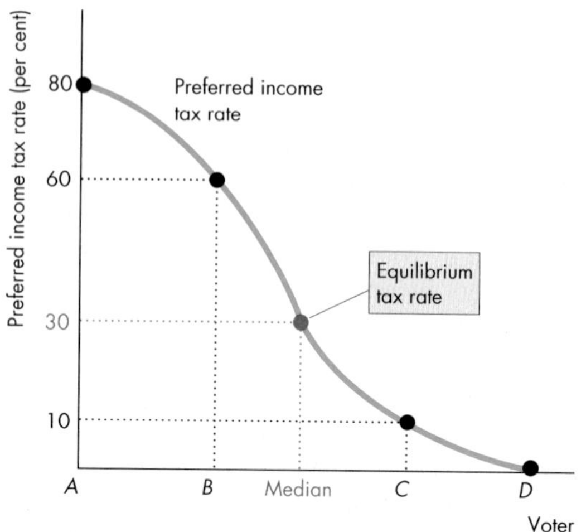

A political party can win an election by proposing policies that appeal to the median voter and to all the other voters on one side of the median. If the median voter favours a policy, that policy will be proposed. In the figure, voters have different preferences concerning the income tax rate (and benefit rate). They are ranked in descending order of their preferred tax – A's preferred tax rate is highest, B's is next highest, and so on.

There are two political parties. If one proposes a 61 per cent tax and the other a 59 per cent tax, the low-tax party will win the election – voters between A and C will vote for the high tax and those between C and B for the low tax. If both parties propose low taxes – 11 per cent and 9 per cent – the high-tax party will win. It will pick up the votes between A and D, leaving only the votes between D and B for the low-tax party. Each party has an incentive to move towards the tax rate preferred by the median voter. At that point, each party picks up half the votes and neither can improve its share.

In either of the two situations we've just examined, the party that wins the election is the one offering a tax rate closest to the tax rate preferred by the median voter. So each party can improve its election performance by moving closer to the median than the other party. But each party has the same incentive, so each moves towards the median. Once the two parties are offering the tax rate favoured most by the median voter, neither can increase its vote by changing its proposal. One party will get the votes between *A* and the median, and the other party will get the votes between the median and *D*.

All the voters except those at the median will be dissatisfied – for those between *A* and the median, the benefits and the tax rate are too low, and for those between *D* and the median, the benefits and the tax rate are too high. But no political party can propose programmes other than those that can be financed with a 30 per cent tax rate and expect to win the election. If the two parties propose identical programmes and a 30 per cent tax rate, the voters are indifferent and either don't vote or toss a coin to decide which party to vote for.

The median voter theorem implies the principle of minimum differentiation that we've already studied. The policies of different political parties will tend to converge. But this does not mean that all political parties will be identical. They may be aligned to wealthy people or to poor people and will retain a rhetoric which shows this. One party will talk about higher taxes and benefits and the other will talk about cutting taxes and benefits, but neither will actually carry such policies to excess for fear of losing the support of the median voter.

Our discussion so far has focused on income taxes, but 28 per cent of total revenue is drawn from indirect taxes – taxes on expenditure. Let's look now at the factors that determine the level of expenditure taxes and which goods are taxed by governments.

Excise Taxes

An **excise tax** is a tax on the sale of a particular commodity. We'll now study the effects of an excise tax by considering the tax on petrol shown in Figure 18.10. The demand curve for petrol is *D* and the supply curve is *S*. If there is no tax on petrol, its price is 60 pence a litre and 400 million litres of petrol a day are bought and sold.

Now suppose that a tax is imposed on petrol at the rate of 60 pence a litre. If producers are willing to supply 400 million litres a day for 60 pence when there is no tax, then they are willing to supply that same quantity in the face of a 60 pence tax only if the price increases to 120 pence a litre. That is, they want to get the 60 pence a litre they received before, plus the additional 60 pence that they now have to hand over to the government in the form of a petrol tax. As a result of the tax, the supply of petrol decreases and the supply curve shifts leftward. The magnitude of the shift is such that the vertical distance between the original and the new supply curve is the amount of the tax. The new supply curve is the red curve *S* + *tax*. The new supply curve intersects the demand curve at 300 million litres a day and 110 pence a litre. This situation is the new equilibrium after the imposition of the tax.

Figure 18.10 An Excise Tax

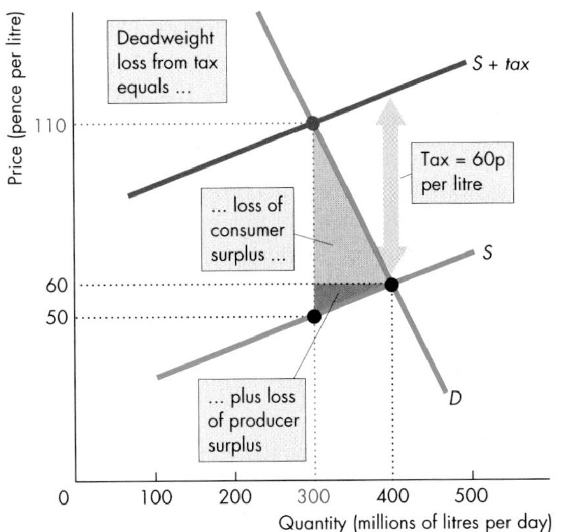

The demand curve for petrol is *D* and the supply curve is *S*. In the absence of any taxes, petrol will sell for 60 pence a litre and 400 million litres a day will be bought and sold. When a tax of 60 pence a litre is imposed, the supply curve shifts upward to become the curve *S* + *tax*. The new equilibrium price is 110 pence a litre and 300 million litres a day are bought and sold. The excise tax creates a deadweight loss represented by the grey triangle. The tax revenue collected is 60 pence a litre on 300 million litres, which is £180 million a day. The deadweight loss from the tax is £30 million a day. That is, to raise tax revenue of £180 million a day a deadweight loss of £30 million a day is incurred.

Why Excise Tax Rates Vary

Why does government tax petrol, alcohol and tobacco at high rates and some goods not at all? One reason is that taxes create deadweight losses. (You first encountered the concept of deadweight loss when you studied monopoly in Chapter 13). A **deadweight loss** is the inefficiency caused by the tax when people substitute cheaper alternatives for the more expensive taxed good. (This is the substitution effect that we met in Chapter 9, p. 200.) It is impossible to avoid deadweight losses from taxes, but they can be minimized by varying the tax rate and the goods taxed. As we'll see, minimizing deadweight loss on excise taxes is also consistent with the median voter theorem.

Minimizing the Deadweight Loss of Taxes

You can see the deadweight loss that taxes create in Figure 18.10. Without a tax, 400 million litres of petrol a day are consumed at a price of 60 pence a litre. With a 60 pence a litre tax, the price paid by the consumer rises to 110 pence a litre and the quantity consumed declines to 300 million litres a day. The consumer surplus loss arising from the change is shown by the light grey triangle. On the 300 millionth litre bought – the marginal unit bought – the consumer pays 110 pence compared with 60 pence in the absence of a tax. So 50 pence of consumer surplus is lost on this unit. On each successive unit up to the 400 millionth, there is a successively smaller loss of consumer surplus. The total amount of consumer surplus equals the area of the light grey triangle, which is £25 million a day[2].

There is also a loss of producer surplus as shown by the dark grey triangle. On the 300 millionth litre sold – the marginal unit sold – the producer receives 50 pence compared with 60 pence in the absence of a tax. So 10 pence of producer surplus is lost on this unit. On each successive unit up to the 400 millionth, there is a successively smaller loss of producer surplus. The total amount of producer surplus equals the area of the dark grey triangle, which is £5 million pounds a day[3].

The deadweight loss – the sum of consumer and producer surplus lost – is indicated by the two grey triangles in Figure 18.10. The pound value of that triangle is £30 million a day. But how much revenue is raised by this tax? Since 300 million litres of petrol are sold each day and since the tax is 60 pence a litre, total revenue from the petrol tax is £180 million a day (300 million litres multiplied by 60 pence a litre). Thus to raise tax revenue of £180 million pounds a day using the petrol tax, a deadweight loss of £30 million a day – one-sixth of the tax revenue – is incurred.

One of the main influences on the deadweight loss arising from a tax is the elasticity of demand for the product. As the demand for petrol is fairly inelastic, when a tax is imposed the quantity demanded falls by a smaller percentage than the percentage rise in price. In our example, the quantity demanded falls by 25 per cent but the price increases by 83.33 per cent.

To see the importance of the elasticity of demand, let's consider a different commodity – orange juice. To help make a direct comparison, let's assume that the orange juice market is exactly as big as the market for petrol. Figure 18.11 illustrates this market. The demand curve for orange juice is D and the supply curve is S. When orange juice is not taxed, the quantity of orange juice traded is 400 million litres a day and the price of orange juice is 60 pence a litre.

Now suppose that the government contemplates abolishing the petrol tax and taxing orange juice instead. The demand for orange juice is more elastic than the demand for petrol. It has many more good substitutes in the form of other fruit juices. The government wants to raise £180 million a day so that its total revenue is not affected by this tax change. The government's economists, armed with their statistical estimates of the demand and supply curves for orange juice that appear in Figure 18.11, work out that a tax of 90 pence a litre will do the job. This tax will shift the supply curve upward to the curve labelled $S + tax$. This new supply curve intersects the demand curve at a price of 130 pence a litre and at a quantity of 200 million litres a day. The price at which suppliers are willing to produce 200 million litres a day is 40 pence a litre. The

2 You can calculate the area of that triangle by using the formula: (base × height)/2. The base is 100 pence, the decrease in quantity. The height is the price increase – 50 pence. Multiplying 100 million litres by 50 pence and dividing by 2 gives £25 million a day.

3 The base is 100 pence, the decrease in quantity. The height is the price decrease for the producer – 10 pence. Multiplying 100 million litres by 10 pence and dividing by 2 gives £5 million a day.

Figure 18.11 Why We Don't Tax Orange Juice

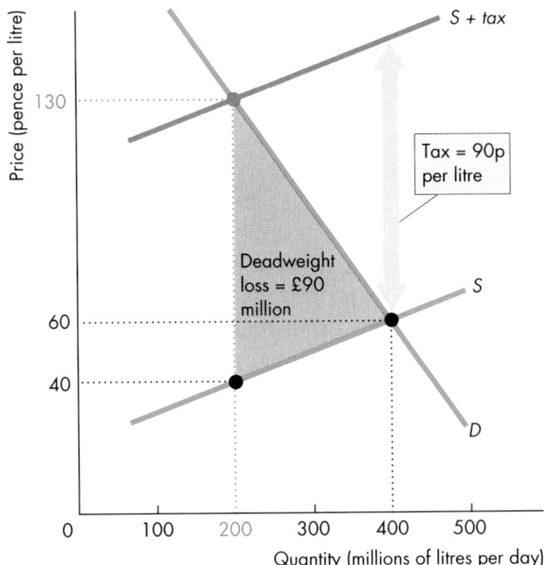

The demand curve for orange juice is *D* and the supply curve is *S*. The equilibrium price is 60 pence a litre and 400 million litres of juice a day are traded. To raise £180 million of tax revenue, a tax of 90 pence a litre will have to be imposed. The introduction of this tax shifts the supply curve to *S + tax*. The price rises to 130 pence a litre and the quantity bought and sold falls to 200 million litres a day. The deadweight loss is represented by the grey triangle and equals £90 million a day. The deadweight loss from taxing orange juice is much larger than that from taxing petrol (Figure 18.10) because the demand for orange juice is more elastic than the demand for petrol. Items that have a low elasticity of demand are taxed more heavily than items that have a high elasticity of demand.

government collects the required revenue of £180 million pounds a day – 90 pence a litre on 200 million litres a day.

But what is the deadweight loss in this case? The answer can be seen by looking at the grey triangle in Figure 18.11. The magnitude of that deadweight loss is £90 million[4]. Notice how much bigger the deadweight loss is from taxing orange juice than that from taxing petrol. In the case of orange juice, the deadweight loss is one-half of the revenue raised, while in the case of petrol it is only one-sixth. What accounts for this difference? The supply curves and the initial pre-tax prices and quantities were identical in each case. The only difference is the elasticity of demand. In the case of petrol, the quantity demanded falls by only 25 per cent when the price almost doubles. In the case of orange juice, the quantity demanded falls by 50 per cent when the price only slightly more than doubles.

You can see why taxing orange juice is not on the political agenda of any of the major parties. Vote-seeking politicians seek out taxes that benefit the median voter. Other things remaining the same, this means that they try to minimize the deadweight loss of raising a given amount of revenue. Equivalently, they tax items with poor substitutes more heavily than items with close substitutes.

Value Added Tax (VAT) was introduced throughout the European Union in 1969 to harmonize the various forms of sales and purchase taxes that were operating in different member states. In the United Kingdom, some goods such as children's clothes and food are still exempt from VAT, so that only 40 per cent of private expenditure is covered by VAT compared to 90 per cent in most other member states. Is there an economic efficiency reason for reducing exemptions? The answer lies in the degree of substitution. The more goods that are subject to VAT, the smaller is the number of tax free goods towards which consumers can switch, and so the smaller the deadweight loss associated with the VAT system as a whole. In fact the UK government argues that the exemptions are needed to relieve poverty.

Compliance and Administration Costs

When any new tax is introduced there will be some additional costs. *Compliance costs* are the costs of ensuring that people do not avoid or evade the tax. *Administration costs* are the costs of running the new tax system, including the wages of tax officials and creating new computer software. Vote-seeking politicians will tend to choose taxes which minimize compliance and administration costs. This will benefit the median voter because it reduces the total amount of revenue needed for any set of benefits. When the UK government decided to fund local

4 This deadweight loss is calculated in exactly the same way as our previous calculation of the deadweight loss from the petrol tax. The loss of consumer surplus is 200 million litres multiplied by 70 pence, divided by 2, which equals £70 million a day. The loss of producer surplus is 200 million litres multiplied by 20 pence, divided by 2, which equals £20 million a day. The deadweight loss is the sum of the two losses, which equals £90 million a day.

government using a per head tax (the Poll tax) rather than a housing tax (Rates), it found that compliance and administration costs increased dramatically. Administration costs increased because more bills and reminders had to be issued as more people pay a per head tax than a household tax. Compliance costs rose because the tax was unpopular and many people refused to pay, or delayed paying. Court costs were high and the tax rate had to be increased to cover the shortfall from non-payment. Eventually the tax was replaced by another housing tax, the Council tax. Vote-seeking politicians were forced to adopt a more efficient tax with lower costs. Whether a housing tax also has a lower deadweight loss than a per head tax is debatable, but it is likely that the gains from lower compliance and administration costs under the new Council tax outweigh any loss from a higher deadweight loss.

Review

- Taxes generate resources for government expenditure and most revenue is derived from income taxes and taxes on goods and services.
- Income taxes appeal to the median voter.
- Indirect taxes generate a deadweight loss – consumer and producer surplus is lost which is not transferred to government as revenue.
- The efficiency of a tax depends on the size of the deadweight loss, which in turn depends on the elasticity of demand.
- Minimizing deadweight loss, and administration and compliance costs appeal to the median voter.

We've seen that markets don't always achieve allocative efficiency – that there is market failure. We've looked at one example of how government policy can overcome market failure in the provision of public goods. But we've also seen that bureaucrats can overprovide a public good, creating government failure. Finally, we've seen how the political marketplace can determine the rates of income tax and excise tax, as well as which goods are taxed. In the next three chapters, we are going to look more closely at government policy to overcome other forms of market failure – monopoly, externalities, uncertainty and limited information – as well as the problem of inequality.

Summary

Key Points

The Government Sector and The Economic Theory of Government (pp. 432–434)

- The trend is for the size of the government sector to increase in all developed economies.
- Government policy is an attempt to cope with problems created by market failure – public goods, monopoly, externalities, uncertainty and limited information.
- Market failure means that markets do not provide the efficient level of some goods and services.
- Government can use policies such as public provision, taxation and regulation to improve market efficiency caused by market failure.
- In addition, governments use the tax and benefit system to make the market allocation of resources more equitable, and use monetary and fiscal policy to stabilize the economy and generate more potential for growth.

Public Choice and the Political Marketplace (pp. 434–435)

- Public choice theory is a model of the political marketplace in which voters, politicians and bureaucrats interact with each other.
- Voters are the consumers of the political process and they express their demands through their votes, political campaigning and financial contributions, and by lobbying.
- Politicians propose policies and their objective is to win elections. Bureaucrats implement

policies and their objective is to maximize their own departmental budgets.

- The outcome of the interaction of voters, politicians and bureaucrats is a political equilibrium which might or might not be efficient.

Public Goods and the Free-rider Problem (pp. 436–441)

- A public good is a good or service that is consumed by everyone and that is non-rival and non-excludable.
- A public good creates a free-rider problem where no one has an incentive to pay for their share of the cost of providing the public good.
- The efficient level of provision of a public good maximizes the value of total benefit minus total cost – where marginal benefit equals marginal cost.
- Competition between political parties, each of which tries to appeal to the maximum number of voters, can lead to the efficient scale of provision of a public good and to both parties to proposing the same policies.
- Bureaucrats try to maximize their budgets, and if voters are rationally ignorant, producer interests may result in voting to support taxes that provide public goods in quantities that exceed those that maximize net benefit.

Taxes (pp. 441–446)

- Most government revenue comes from income taxes, Value Added Tax and excise taxes on petrol, alcoholic beverages and tobacco products.
- Income taxes appeal to the median voter. The tax rate that wins elections is the one that appeals to the median voter.
- The imposition of a tax on a good creates a deadweight loss, the size of which depends on the elasticity of demand.
- High levels of tax are an efficient method of raising revenue if they tax goods with low elasticity of demand.
- Excise taxes are placed on goods with low elasticity of demand so that the deadweight loss of raising a given amount of tax revenue is minimized.

Key Figures

Key Terms

Review Questions

1 Describe the growth of the governments in industrialized economies.

2 What is market failure and from what does it arise?

3 What is a public good? Give three examples.

4 What is the free-rider problem and how does government help overcome it?

5 What is an externality?

6 Describe the three actors in the political marketplace.

7 Describe the economic functions of voters and explain how they make their economic choices.

8 Describe the economic functions of politicians and explain how they make their economic choices.

9 Describe the economic functions of bureaucrats and explain how they make their economic choices.

10 What is meant by political equilibrium?

11 How does the principle of minimum differentiation explain the policy choice of different political parties?

12 Explain why it is likely that the quantity of public goods will exceed the efficient scale.

13 Why is it rational for voters to be ignorant?

14 What is the median voter theorem?

15 What features of political choices does the median voter theorem explain?

Problems

1 You are given the following information about a sewage disposal system that a city of 1 million people is considering installing:

Capacity (thousands of litres per day)	Marginal private benefit to one person (pounds)	Total cost (millions of pounds)
0		0
1	100	10
2	80	30
3	60	60
4	40	100
5	20	150

a What is the capacity that achieves maximum net benefit?
b How much will each person have to pay in taxes in order to pay for the efficient capacity level?
c What are the total and net benefits?
d What is the political equilibrium if voters are well-informed?
e What is the political equilibrium if voters are rationally ignorant and bureaucrats achieve the highest attainable budget?

2 Your local council is contemplating upgrading its system for controlling traffic signals. It reckons that by installing a sophisticated computer with sensing mechanisms at all the major intersections, it can better adjust the timing of the changes in signals and improve the speed of the traffic flow. The bigger the computer the council buys, the better is the job it can do, and the more sensors it installs, the more intersections it can monitor and the faster will be the resulting overall traffic flow. The mayor and the other elected officials who are working on the proposal want to determine the scale and sophistication of the system that will win them the most votes. The city bureaucrats in the traffic department want to maximize the budget. Suppose that you are an economist who is observing this public choice. Your job is to calculate the quantity of this public good that maximizes net benefit – that achieves allocative efficiency.

a What data would you need in order to reach your own conclusions?
b What does the public choice theory predict will be the quantity chosen?
c How could you, as an informed voter, attempt to influence the choice?

3 An economy with 9 groups of people, identified by letters **A** to **I** has net benefits from different tax income tax levels as follows:

A	B	C	D	E	F	G	H	I
90	80	70	60	50	0	0	0	0

Suppose there are two political parties competing for office in this community. What income tax rate would the parties propose?

4 You are given the following information about a competitive market for biscuits:

Price (pounds per kilogram)	Quantity demanded (kilograms per month)	Quantity supplied (kilograms per month)
10	0	36
8	3	30
6	6	24
4	9	18
2	12	12
0	15	0

a What are the equilibrium price and quantity bought and sold?

b Suppose that a 10 per cent tax is imposed on biscuits.

1 What is the new price of biscuits?

2 What is the new quantity bought and sold?

3 What is the total amount of tax revenue raised by the government?

4 What is the deadweight loss?

5 You are given the following information about the market for ballpoint pens.

Price (pence per week)	Quantity demanded (thousands a week)	Quantity supplied
10	200	0
20	180	30
30	160	60
40	140	90
50	120	120
60	100	140
70	80	160
80	60	180
90	40	200

a Draw the demand and supply curves on a graph.

b What is the equilibrium price and quantity of ballpoint pens?

c Estimate the value of consumer surplus.

d Estimate the value of producer surplus.

6 Suppose the government decides to impose a tax of 20 pence per pen. Using your graph from Problem 5, answer the following:

a What is the new equilibrium price and quantity of ballpoint pens?

b How much revenue does the government make?

c Estimate the value of consumer surplus after tax.

d Estimate the value of producer surplus after the tax.

e Estimate the value of the deadweight loss associated with the tax.

7 Suppose the demand for pens in Problem 6 were more elastic.

a Draw an example of a more inelastic demand for pens on your graph from Problem 6. (Draw the line through the original equilibrium point before tax.)

b Using the new demand curve, shade in the area of the deadweight loss when the government imposes a tax of 20 pence per pen.

c Is the deadweight loss larger or smaller with the new, more inelastic demand curve?

d Is government revenue larger or smaller with the new, more inelastic demand curve?

8 Read the story in *Reading Between the Lines* on pp. 450–451 again and then answer the following questions:

a How will targets help to make ministers and bureaucrats more accountable?

b How will targets help to make the government sector more efficient?

c Why might targets fail to measure the performance of the government sector? Use the example of setting targets for school grade achievement to answer this question.

9 Use the Parkin, Powell and Matthews Web site to obtain data on UK government expenditure.

a Which government department accounts for the majority of expenditure?

b What proportion of government expenditure is spent on goods and services, rather than transfers such as benefits and transfers?

c What percentage of government expenditure is spent on each of the following: health, social security and defence?

d What proportion of government revenue is generated by tax receipts?

10 Use the Parkin, Powell and Matthews Web site to find out what happened in the last budget.

a By how much did government raise tax on cigarettes, wines and beer?

b What reasons did government give for raising these excise taxes?

W http://www.econ100.com

Monitoring Costs in the Government Sector

The Essence of the Story

The Guardian, 23 January 1999

Bringing business to the public sector

Charlotte Denny

In management thinking the idea of measuring performance by focusing on objectives is old hat, so obvious it hardly needs restating. But in the public sector, where the success of ministers is judged by the size of the budget they manage to secure for their departments, asking what is achieved once the money is spent is still a novelty.

The Government hopes to change this and to bring more businesslike attitudes into the public sector. Announcing more than 500 new targets for Government departments last December, the then Treasury chief secretary Stephen Byers said they would bring about a "revolution" in the public services. For too long people had focused exclusively on how much money was spent in the public sector. "It is now time to move and consider the more important question — how the money is spent and what people get in return for their money," said Mr Byers.

Each department negotiated its own public service agreement with the Treasury and was required to make its targets Specific, Measurable, Achievable, Relevant and Timed — SMART. Among those chosen include promises to quadruple the numbers of cyclists, reduce suicides by 17 per cent, ensure that three-quarters of public libraries have Internet access and lower the number of terrorist incidents.

Instead of wrangling over the size of departmental budgets once a year, the Government hopes ministers will focus their minds on how they are doing in relation to the objectives they have set for themselves.

Peter Robinson, senior economist at the Institute for Public Policy Research, says a better description of the targets most departments have chosen would be Superficial, Modest, Ambiguous, Risky and Trivial. He says, departments have committed themselves to achieving what is easily attainable. So the Department for Education and Employment has committed itself to increasing the proportion of those aged 16 who achieve five or more GCSEs at grades A-C from 45 per cent to 50 per cent.

But Mr Robinson says the pattern over the last few years has been for the proportion to rise anyway. "If you simply extrapolate the trend they will achieve their goal," he says.

The penalty for failure to meet the targets has not been spelt out so far. Financial penalties are probably out of the question. If the NHS fails to meet its target of reducing waiting lists by 100,000 over the next five years, it would be perverse to cut budgets of health trusts. But without any sanctions, what incentive is there for Whitehall managers to meet the new objectives?

The critical flaw in the new approach could be its sheer variety. Whitehall has 500 targets. "What is missing is what are the big global outcomes which the Government wants," says Mr Robinson. "Where are the targets for reducing poverty and unemployment?"

- Government is bringing management thinking to the public sector. It is introducing more than 500 new targets to help control departmental spending and make Ministers more accountable.
- The targets are negotiated and should focus attention on how the money is spent and what it is spent on rather than simply the size of the budget. Targets should be SMART – specific, measurable, achievable, relevant and timed.
- Some economists argue that the targets will have no effect because departments will only commit themselves to easily achievable targets. They will be SMART – superficial, modest, ambiguous, risky and trivial.
- In addition, there are unlikely to be any incentives to meet targets as there are no penalties for failure. There are so many targets that the most important goals for government, for example reducing poverty and unemployment, are hidden.

Economic Analysis

■ Until 1998, the success of ministers was judged by the size of their deparmental budget. Introducing the target reforms will increase the accountability of ministers to the voter, making it more efficient.

■ Figure 1 shows the total benefit to the public of government departmental provision of goods and services, *TB*, and the total cost of that provision, *TC*.

■ Government ministers and bureaucrats usually try to maximize the size of the budget in their annual negotiations with the Treasury. This leads to Q_{98} level of provision, the most costly that voters will tolerate, C_{98}. Q_{98} is inefficient as the marginal benefit of provision, *MB* is not equal to the marginal cost of provision, *MC*. *MB* is the slope of *TB* and *MC* is the slope of *TC*.

■ Ministers and bureaucrats must now identify targets which make the quality and cost of provision open to public scrutiny. It focuses decision making on the type of provision rather than the size of the budget.

■ Figure 2 shows the effect of targets. Ministers and bureaucrats are forced to make decisions which maximize the net benefit to voters, provision falls to the efficient level *Q*, and total cost and expenditure is reduced to *C*.

■ Voters receive a net benefit equal to the total benefit, *B*, minus the total cost, *C*, at *Q*. Government resources will be used efficiently as the marginal benefit of provision, *MB* equals the marginal cost of provision, *MC* as shown in Figure 2.

■ However, if there are no incentives for ministers and bureaucrats to comply, and if the targets agreed are simply those that would have arisen from maximizing the budget, the reforms will have no impact. The level of provision will remain at Q_{98}.

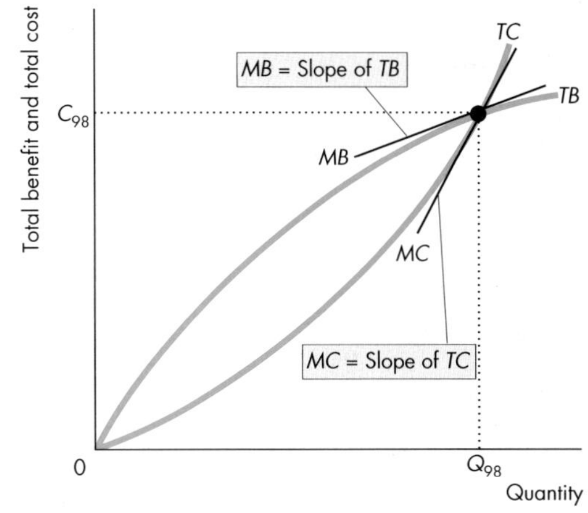

Figure 1 Inefficient provision

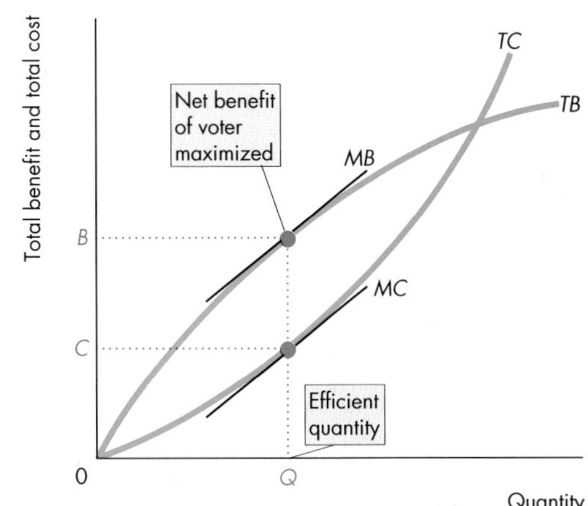

Figure 2 Efficient provision

CHAPTER 19

Regulation and Privatization

After studying this chapter you will be able to:

- Define regulation and monopoly control law
- Distinguish between the public interest and capture theories of regulation
- Explain how regulation affects prices, outputs, profits and the distribution of the gains from trade between consumers and producers
- Explain how monopoly and competition law are applied in the UK and the European Union
- Explain the case for public ownership and privatization and why privatized organizations are regulated by government

Public Interest or Special Interest

When you consume water, electric power, natural gas, or telephone services you buy from a regulated local monopoly. Why and how are the industries that produce these goods and services regulated? Do the regulations work in the public interest – the interest of all consumers and producers – or do they serve special interests – the interests – of particular groups of consumers or producers? ◆ Regulation extends beyond monopoly to oligopoly. For example, until 1987, the price of tickets and the routes that airlines could fly throughout Europe were regulated to create a cartel. EU member states agreed to deregulate airline routes in 1997 to free up access to European routes and promote cut-price tickets. Why do we regulate and then deregulate some industries? ◆ In 1995, the UK Monopolies and Mergers Commission blocked the merger of a regional bus company and a national bus company using monopoly control laws but allowed the merger of two electricity generators with electricity suppliers. What are monopoly control laws and whose interest do they serve? ◆ After 1945, many monopolies, flagship firms and major industries were bought by the government. Since 1979, many of these have been privatized. Why has government bought up firms and industries and then sold them off? Does privatization serve the public interest or the special interests of producers and shareholders?

◆ ◆ ◆ ◆ This chapter studies government regulation of markets for goods and services and identifies who stands to gain and who stands to lose from different types of regulation. It also looks at the economic behaviour of politicians and bureaucrats who supply regulation.

Market Intervention

The government intervenes in monopolistic and oligopolistic markets to influence prices, quantities produced and the distribution of the gains from economic activity. It intervenes in two main ways:

1 Regulation.

2 Monopoly control.

Regulation

Regulation consists of rules administered by a government agency to influence economic activity by determining prices, product standards and types, and the conditions under which new firms may enter an industry. To implement its regulations, government creates agencies to oversee the regulations and ensure their enforcement. Price and entry condition regulations are typically applied at the industry level to banking and financial services, telecommunications, gas and electricity suppliers, railways, airlines and buses. Many new UK regulatory agencies such as OFWAT, the water regulator, and OFTEL, the telecommunications regulator, were set up after privatization to regulate prices. Other similar industry-level regulatory organizations exist in most other countries, and EU industries are also regulated by the European Commission.

Regulation is also widely applied at the product level and is constantly developing. The identification of genetically modified food products is a recent area earmarked for new regulation at the European level. But as more regulation develops at one level, there is a tendency to deregulate at another level.

Deregulation is the process of removing restrictions on prices, product standards and types, and entry conditions. In recent years, deregulation has been introduced in European airways, and many areas of transport and telecommunications. The most important deregualation at the European Union level was the removal of border controls to create the Single European Market.

Monopoly Control

Monopoly control law regulates and prohibits certain kinds of market behaviour, such as monopoly and monopolistic practices. Monopolistic practices include restrictive practices where firms collude to act like monopolies. European firms suspected of gaining monopoly power through creating barriers to entry, restrictive practices, or through merger activity, can be investigated under European Union law or under the laws of particular member states. United Kingdom monopoly control law was first set up in 1948 with the first Monopolies and Restrictive Practices Act, and is currently regulated under the 1973 Fair Trading Act which created the Office of Fair Trading. However, all firms operating in the United Kingdom are also subject to European Union monopoly control law.

We will look at regulation and monopoly control law in more detail later in the chapter. To understand why government intervenes to control monopoly and the effect of these laws, we need to identify the gains and losses that these policies create. These gains and losses are the consumer and producer surpluses associated with different levels of output and prices. Let's start by looking at the theory of regulation.

Economic Theory of Regulation

The economic theory of regulation is part of the broader theory of public choice that is explained in Chapter 18, pp. 434–435. Here, we apply the public choice theory to regulation. We'll examine the demand for government actions, the supply of those actions and the political equilibrium that emerges.

Demand for Regulation

The *demand for regulation* is expressed through political activity – voting, lobbying and making campaign contributions. But engaging in political activity is costly and people demand political action only if the benefit that they individually receive from such action exceeds their individual costs in obtaining the action. The four main factors that affect the demand for regulation are:

1 Consumer surplus per buyer.

2 Number of buyers.

3 Producer surplus per firm.

4 Number of firms.

The larger the consumer surplus per buyer resulting from regulation, the greater is the demand for regulation by buyers. Also, as the number of buyers increases, so does the demand for regulation. But numbers alone do not necessarily translate into an effective political force. The larger the number of buyers, the greater is the cost of organizing them, so the demand for regulation does not increase proportionately with the number of buyers.

The larger the producer surplus per firm arising from a particular regulation, the larger is the demand for that regulation by firms. Also, as the number of firms that might benefit from some regulation increases, so does the demand for that regulation. But again, as in the case of consumers, large numbers do not necessarily mean an effective political force. The larger the number of firms, the greater is the cost of organizing them.

For a given surplus, consumer or producer, the smaller the number of households or firms which share that surplus, the larger is the demand for the regulation that creates it.

Supply of Regulation

Regulation is supplied by politicians and bureaucrats. Politicians choose policies that appeal to a majority of voters, thereby enabling themselves to achieve and maintain office. Bureaucrats support policies that maximize their budgets (see Chapter 18, pp. 439–440). Given these objectives of politicians and bureaucrats, the *supply of regulation* depends on the following factors:

1 Consumer surplus per buyer.

2 Producer surplus per firm.

3 The number of persons affected.

The larger the consumer surplus per buyer or producer surplus per firm generated, and the larger the number of persons affected by a regulation, the greater is the tendency for politicians to supply that regulation. If regulation benefits a large number of people significantly enough for it to be noticed and if the recipients know who is the source of the benefits, that regulation appeals to politicians and it is supplied. If regulation benefits a *small* number of people by a large amount per person, that regulation also appeals to politicians provided its costs are spread widely and are not easily identified. If regulation affects markets that benefit a large number of people but by a small amount per person, and if such benefits do not attract notice, that regulation does not appeal to politicians and is not supplied.

Political Equilibrium

In equilibrium, the regulation that exists is such that no interest group feels it is worthwhile to use additional resources to press for changes, and no group of politicians feels it is worthwhile to offer different regulations. Being in a *political equilibrium* is not the same thing as everyone being in agreement. Interest groups will devote resources to trying to change regulations that are already in place; others will devote resources to maintaining the existing regulations. But no one will feel it is worthwhile to *increase* the resources they are devoting to such activities. Also, political parties might not agree with each other. Some support the existing regulations and others propose different regulations. In equilibrium, no one wants to change the proposals that they are making.

What will a political equilibrium look like? The answer depends on whether the regulation serves the public interest or the interest of the producer. Let's look at these two possibilities.

Public Interest Theory

The **public interest theory** is that regulations are supplied to satisfy the demand of consumers and producers to maximize total surplus – that is, to attain allocative efficiency. Public interest theory implies that the political process relentlessly seeks out deadweight loss and introduces regulations that eliminate it. For example, where monopoly practices exist, the political process will introduce price regulations to ensure that outputs increase and prices fall to their competitive levels.

Capture Theory

The **capture theory** is that the regulations are supplied to satisfy the demand of producers to maximize producer surplus – that is, to maximize economic profit. The key idea of capture theory is that the cost of regulation is high and only those regulations that increase the surplus of small, easily identified groups and that have low organization costs are supplied by the political process. Such regulations are supplied even if they impose costs on others, provided these costs are spread thinly and widely enough so that they do not decrease votes.

The predictions of the capture theory are less clear cut than the predictions of the public interest theory. According to the capture theory, regulations benefit cohesive interest groups by large and visible amounts and impose small costs on everyone else. But these costs are so small, in per person terms, that no one feels it is worthwhile to incur the cost of organizing an interest group to avoid them. To make these predictions concrete enough to be useful, the capture theory needs a model of the costs of political organization.

Whichever theory of regulation is correct, according to public choice theory, the political system delivers amounts and types of regulations that best further the electoral success of politicians. Because producer-oriented and consumer-oriented regulation are in conflict with each other, the political process can't satisfy both groups in any particular industry. Only one group can win. This makes the regulatory actions of government a bit like a unique good – for example, a painting by Rembrandt. There is only one original and it will be sold to just one buyer. Normally, a unique commodity is sold through an auction; the highest bidder takes the prize. Equilibrium in the regulatory process can be thought of in much the same way: the suppliers of regulation will satisfy the demands of the higher bidder. If the producer demand offers a bigger return to the politicians, either directly through votes or indirectly through political contributions, then the producers' interests will be served. If the consumer demand translates into a larger number of votes, then the consumers' interests will be served by regulation.

Review

- The demand for regulation is expressed by both consumers and producers who spend scarce resources voting, lobbying and campaigning for regulations that best further their own interests.
- Regulation is supplied by politicians and bureaucrats. Politicians choose actions that appeal to a majority of voters, and bureaucrats choose actions that maximize their budgets.
- The regulation that exists is the political equilibrium that balances the opposing demand and supply forces. The political equilibrium either achieves efficiency – the public interest theory – or maximizes producer surplus – the capture theory.

We have now completed our study of the theory of regulation in the marketplace. Let's turn our attention to the regulations that exist in our economy today. Which of these regulations are in the public interest and which are in the interests of producers?

Regulation and Deregulation

The past 20 years have seen dramatic changes in the way in which European economies are regulated by government. We're going to examine some of these changes. To begin we'll look at what is regulated and also at the scope of regulation. Then we'll turn to the regulatory process itself and examine how regulators control prices and other aspects of market behaviour. Finally, we'll tackle the more difficult and controversial questions. Why do we regulate some things but not others? Who benefits from this regulation – consumers or producers?

The Scope of Regulation

Table 19.1 shows the hierarchy of regulatory agencies that operate in the United Kingdom. At the top are institutions created by agreement among countries. These institutions regulate firms indirectly by restricting government protection of domestic industry. The World Trade Organization (WTO), set up in 1995 to replace the General Agreement on Tariffs and Trade, oversees and monitors agreements to reduce tariffs and aims to avoid tariff wars among its 124 participating countries. Below this are the 23 Directorates General of the European Commission. The European Commission is responsible for ensuring its member states comply with EU-level regulation of industry, based on the Treaty of Rome and the Treaty of European Union. Its directives control many aspects of business activity directly and indirectly. For example, its directives determine standards of production and marketing, the pricing of agricultural products, employment practices, health and safety, pollution, monopoly power, restrictive practices and mergers.

Table 19.1 The Regulation Hierarchy

LEVEL	AGENCY	ACTIVITY	METHOD
Global	World Trade Organization	Monitors and enforces rules on tariff agreements	International agreements
European Union	European Commission	Monitors and enforces rules on member states	Directives
National Government	Departments	Monitor and control public provision in the NHS, education, and so on	Circulars
◆ General	MMC	Investigates monopoly and recommends action	Investigative reports
	Health and Safety Executive	Investigates breaches of health and safety law	Inspectorate
	Environment Agency	Monitors and enforces environmental law	Inspectorate
	Securities and Investments Board	Regulates financial investment firms and other financial agencies	Code of practice and licence
	Bank of England	Regulates banks and building societies and enforces monetary policy	Licence
	Civil Aviation Authority	Monitors and regulates airlines, airports and air-traffic control	Route and price control, code of practice
◆ Specific	OFGEM Office of Gas and Electricity Markets	Monitors and regulates gas and electricity markets	Price cap formula and licence
	OFWAT Office of Water Services	Monitors and regulates water companies	Price cap formula
	OFTEL Office of Telecommunications	Monitors and regulates British Telecom and new suppliers	Price cap formula and licence
	OFRAIL Office of Rail Transport	Monitors and regulates Railtrack and travel companies	Price cap formula
Local and Regional Government	Departments	Control and monitor planning, education, taxis, traders, and so on	Licences and bye-laws
Industry	Professional organizations	Control and monitor participating industries	Code of practice and membership

Firms are also subject to general and specific regulation by agencies at the national level. United Kingdom examples are shown in Table 19.1. General regulation agencies cover all industries for a specific issue like health and safety. Specific regulation agencies cover several aspects of regulation for a specific industry. The agencies set up to regulate the newly privatized industries – OFFER, OFWAT, OFGEM, OFTEL and OFRAIL – are industry-specific regulators.

Many firms are also subject to voluntary regulation by professional and industrial organizations, such as the British Medical Association. Local and regional government, which have responsibility for issuing planning regulations and the licensing of taxis and traders, is the lower regulatory tier.

The Regulatory Process

Although regulatory agencies vary in size and scope and in the detailed aspects of economic life that they control, there are certain features common to all agencies.

First, the bureaucrats, who are the key decision makers in the main regulatory agencies, are appointed by central and local governments. In addition, all agencies have a permanent bureaucracy made up of experts in the industry being regulated, who are often recruited from the regulated firms. Agencies are allocated financial resources by government to cover the costs of their operations.

Second, each agency adopts a set of practices or operating rules for controlling prices and other aspects of economic or professional performance. We will concentrate on the main agencies and on industry-specific economic regulation. These rules and practices are based on well-defined physical and financial accounting procedures that are quite easy to administer and to monitor.

In a regulated industry, individual firms are usually free to determine the technology that they will use in production. The exceptions are those industries whose production technology is regulated by the Environment Agency. Regulation usually involves limiting the power of firms to determine one or more of the following: the price of output, the quantities sold, the quality of the product, or the markets served. The regulatory agency grants certification to a company to serve a particular market with a particular line of products, and it determines the level and structure of prices that will be charged. In some cases, the agency also determines the scale and quality of output permitted.

To analyse the way in which industry-specific regulation works, it is convenient to distinguish between the regulation of natural monopoly and the regulation of cartels. Let's begin with natural monopoly.

Natural Monopoly

Natural monopoly was defined in Chapter 13 (p. 296) as an industry in which one firm can supply the entire market at a lower price than can two or more firms. As a consequence, a natural monopoly experiences economies of scale, no matter how high an output rate it achieves. Examples of natural monopolies include telephone and cable companies, local electricity and water companies, and rail services. It is much more expensive to have two or more competing sets of wires, pipes and railway lines serving every area than it is to have a single set. (What is a natural monopoly changes over time as technology changes. With the introduction of fibre optic cables, both telephone companies and cable television companies can compete with each other in both markets, so what was once a natural monopoly is becoming a more competitive industry.)

Let's consider the example of cable TV, which is shown in Figure 19.1. The demand curve for cable TV is *D*. The cable TV company's marginal cost curve is *MC*. That marginal cost curve is (assumed to be) horizontal at £10 per household per month – that is, the cost of providing each additional household with a month of cable programming is £10. The cable company has a heavy investment in satellite receiving dishes, cables and control equipment and so has high fixed costs. These fixed costs are part of the company's average total cost curve, shown as *ATC*. The average total cost curve slopes downward because as the number of households served increases, the fixed cost is spread over a larger number of households. (If you need to refresh your memory on how the average total cost curve is calculated, take a quick look back at Chapter 11, pp. 244–245.)

Figure 19.1 Natural Monopoly: Marginal Cost Pricing

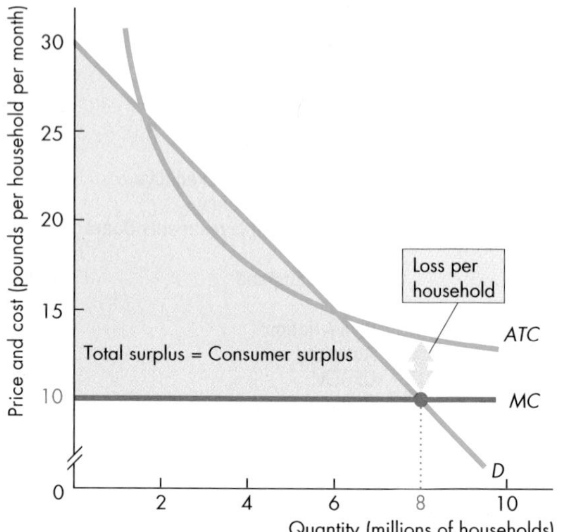

A natural monopoly is an industry in which average total cost is falling even when the entire market demand is satisfied. A cable TV operator faces the demand curve *D*. The firm's marginal cost is constant at £10 per household per month, as shown by the curve *MC*. Fixed costs are large and the average total cost curve, which includes average fixed cost, is shown as *ATC*. A marginal cost pricing rule that maximizes total surplus sets the price at £10 a month, with 8 million households being served. It also maximizes consumer surplus, shown as the green area. The firm incurs a loss on each household, indicated by the red arrow. To remain in business, the cable operator must either price discriminate or receive a subsidy.

Regulation in the Public Interest How will cable TV be regulated according to the public interest theory? In the public interest theory, regulation maximizes total surplus, which occurs if marginal cost equals price. As you can see in Figure 19.1, that outcome occurs if the price is regulated at £10 per household per month and if 8 million households are served. Such a regulation is called a marginal cost pricing rule. A **marginal cost pricing rule** sets price equal to marginal cost. It maximizes total surplus and consumer surplus in the regulated industry.

A natural monopoly that is regulated to set price equal to marginal cost incurs an economic loss. Because its average total cost curve is falling, marginal cost is below average total cost. Because price equals marginal cost, price is below average total cost. Average total cost minus price is the loss per unit produced. It's pretty obvious that a cable TV operator that is required to use a marginal cost pricing rule will not stay in business for long. How can a company cover its costs and, at the same time, obey a marginal cost pricing rule?

One possibility is price discrimination. Some natural monopolies can fairly easily price discriminate using a two-part tariff that gives consumers a bill for connection and a bill for units used. For example, a gas supply company can charge consumers a monthly fee for being connected to the gas supply and then charge a price equal to marginal cost for each unit of gas supplied. A cable TV operator can price discriminate by charging a one-time connection fee that covers its fixed cost and then charging a monthly fee equal to marginal cost.

But a natural monopoly cannot always price discriminate. It is difficult to operate a two-part tariff on a rail network. When a natural monopoly cannot price discriminate, it can cover its total cost and follow a marginal cost pricing rule only if it receives a subsidy from the government. In this case, the government raises the revenue for the subsidy by taxing some other activity. But as we saw in Chapter 18, taxes themselves generate deadweight loss. Thus the deadweight loss resulting from additional taxes must be offset against the allocative efficiency gained by forcing the natural monopoly to adopt a marginal cost pricing rule.

It is possible that deadweight loss will be minimized by permitting the natural monopoly to charge a higher price than marginal cost rather than by taxing some other sector of the economy in order to subsidize the natural monopoly. This pricing arrangement is called an average cost pricing rule. An **average cost pricing rule** sets price equal to average total cost. Figure 19.2 shows the average cost pricing solution. The cable TV operator charges £15 a month and serves 6 million households. A deadweight loss arises, which is shown by the grey triangle in the figure, and consumer surplus is less than under marginal cost pricing regulation.

Figure 19.2 Natural Monopoly: Average Cost Pricing

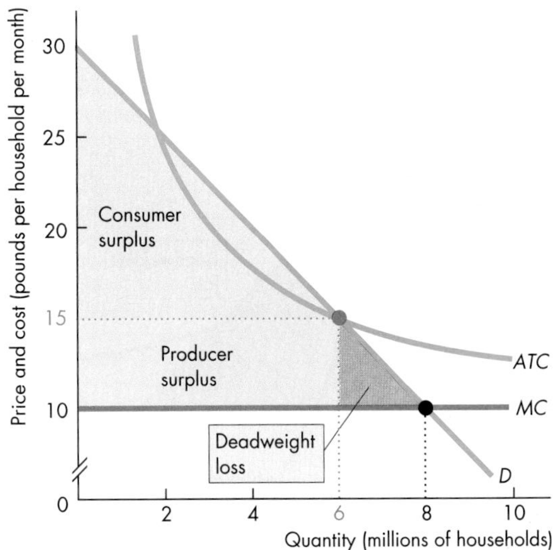

Average cost pricing sets price equal to average total cost. The cable TV operator charges £15 a month and serves 6 million households. In this situation the firm breaks even – average total cost equals price. Deadweight loss, shown by the grey triangle, is generated. Consumer surplus is reduced to the green area.

Capturing the Regulator What does the capture theory predict about the regulation of this industry? According to the capture theory, regulation serves the interests of the producer. The interests of the producer are best satisfied by maximizing profit. To work out the price that achieves this goal, we need to look at the relationship between marginal revenue and marginal cost. A monopoly maximizes profit by producing the output at which marginal revenue equals marginal cost. The monopoly's marginal revenue curve in Figure 19.3 is the curve *MR*. Marginal revenue equals marginal cost when output is 4 million households and the price is £20 a month. Thus a regulation that best serves the interest of the producer will set the price at this level.

But how can a producer go about obtaining regulation that results in this monopoly profit-maximizing outcome? To answer this question, we need to look at the way agencies determine a regulated price. A key method used is called rate of return regulation.

Rate of Return Regulation **Rate of return regulation** determines a regulated price by setting the price at a level that enables the regulated firm to earn a specified target percentage return on its capital. The target rate of return is determined with reference to what is normal in competitive

Figure 19.3 Natural Monopoly: Profit Maximization

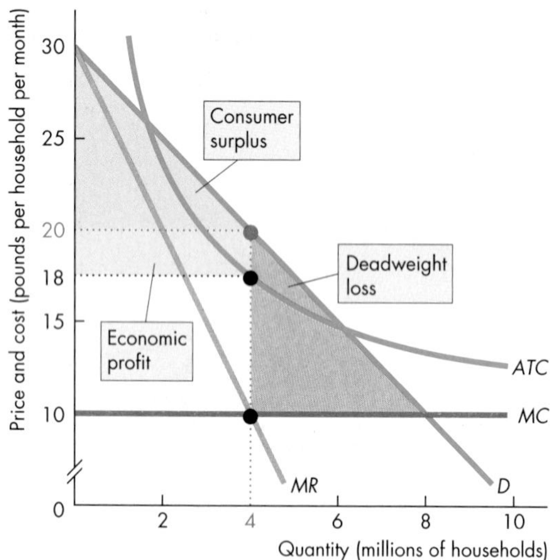

The cable TV operator would like to maximize profit. To do so, marginal revenue (*MR*) is made equal to marginal cost. At a price of £20 a month, 4 million households buy cable services. Consumer surplus is reduced to the green triangle. The deadweight loss increases to the grey triangle. The monopoly makes the profit shown by the blue rectangle. If the producer can capture the regulator, the outcome will be the situation shown here.

industries. This rate of return is part of the opportunity cost of the natural monopolist and is included in the firm's average total cost. By examining the firm's total cost, including the normal rate of return on capital, the regulator attempts to determine the price at which average total cost is covered. Thus rate of return regulation is equivalent to average cost pricing.

In the example that we have just been examining – in Figure 19.2 – average cost pricing results at a regulated price of £15 a month with 6 million households being served. Thus rate of return regulation, based on a correct assessment of the producer's average total cost curve, results in a price and quantity that favour the consumer and do not enable the producer to maximize monopoly profit. The special interest group will have failed to capture the regulator and the outcome will be closer to that predicted by the public interest theory of regulation.

But there is a feature of many real-world situations that the above analysis does not take into account – the ability of the monopoly firm to mislead the regulator about its true costs.

Inflating Costs The managers of a regulated firm might be able to inflate the firm's costs by spending part of its revenue on inputs that are not strictly required for the production of the good. By this device, the firm's apparent cost curves exceed the true cost curves. This is sometimes called X-inefficiency. On-the-job luxury in the form of sumptuous office suites, expensive company cars, free football match tickets (disguised as public relations expenses), lavish international travel and entertainment are all ways in which managers can inflate costs.

If the managers of the cable firm inflate costs and persuade the regulator that the firm's true cost curve is that shown as *ATC (inflated)* in Figure 19.4, then the regulator, applying the normal rate of return principle, will regulate the price at £20 a month. In this example, the price and quantity will be the same as in an unregulated monopoly. It might be impossible for firms to inflate their costs by as much as that shown in the figure. But to the extent that costs can be inflated, the apparent average total cost curve lies somewhere between the true *ATC* curve and *ATC (inflated)*. The greater the ability of the firm to pad its costs in this way, the closer its profit (measured in economic terms) approaches the maximum possible. The shareholders of this firm don't receive this economic profit because it gets used up in football match tickets, luxury offices and the other actions taken by the firm's managers to inflate the firm's costs.

Incentive Regulation Schemes Partly for the reasons we've just examined, rate of return regulation is increasingly being replaced by incentive regulation schemes. An **incentive regulation scheme** is a type of regulation that gives a firm an incentive to operate efficiently and keep costs under control. These new schemes take two main forms: price caps and earnings sharing plans. Under a price cap regulation, the regulators set the maximum price that may be charged and hold that price cap for a number of years. If profits are considered too high, the price cap will be lowered. Under earnings sharing regulation, if profits rise above a certain level, they must be shared with the firm's customers.

Figure 19.4 Natural Monopoly: Inflating Costs

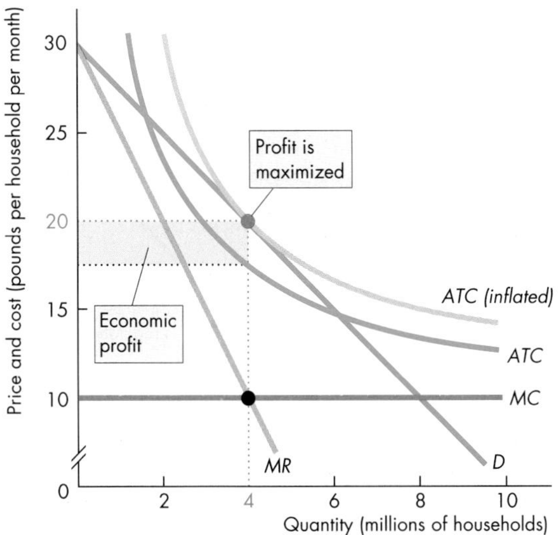

If the cable TV operator is able to inflate its costs to *ATC* (inflated) and persuade the regulator that these are genuine minimum costs of production, rate of return regulation results in a price of £20 a month – the profit-maximizing price. To the extent that the producer can inflate costs above average total cost, the price rises, output falls and deadweight loss increases. The profit is captured by the managers, not the shareholders (owners) of the firm.

Table 19.2 Rates of Return in Monopolies

	Before privatization	After privatization	
	1979	1990	1992
	(percentage)		
Regulated natural monopolies			
British Gas	5	6	7
British Telecommunications	14	24	21
Other monopolies			
British Steel	3	18	1
British Airways	14	24	12

Source: D. Parker, 'Privatization and Business Restructuring: Change and Continuity in the Privatized Industries', *The Review of Policy Issues*, 1994, 1 (2).

The newly privatized industries in the United Kingdom are all subject to a form of price cap regulation. You can read about price cap regulation in the telecom industry in *Reading Between the Lines* on pp. 476–477, and we'll look at this in more detail later in this chapter.

Public Interest or Capture?

It is not clear whether actual regulation produces prices and quantities that more closely correspond with the predictions of capture theory or public interest theory. One thing is clear, however. Price regulation does not require natural monopolies to use the marginal cost pricing rule. If it did, most natural monopolies would make losses and receive hefty government subsidies to enable them to remain in business. But there are even exceptions to this conclusion. For example, British Telecommunications does not appear to use marginal cost pricing for telephone calls. It covers its total cost by charging a flat fee each month for being connected to its telephone system but then permitting each call to be made at its marginal cost.

A test of whether natural monopoly regulation is in the public interest or the interest of the producer is to examine the rates of return earned by regulated natural monopolies. If these rates of return are significantly higher than those in the rest of the economy, then, to some degree, the regulator may have been captured by the producer. If the rates of return in the regulated monopoly industries are similar to those in the rest of the economy, then we cannot tell, for sure, whether the regulator has been captured or not for we cannot know the extent to which costs have been inflated by the managers of the regulated firms.

It is difficult to assess regulatory capture in the United Kingdom because all the regulated natural monopolies were under public ownership in the 1970s and 1980s. Some of them have been privatized in the 1990s and there is insufficient evidence to make a meaningful comparison. Table 19.2 compares the rates of return on assets before and after privatization. Two of the monopolies are natural monopolies and were subject to regulation after privatization. Rates of return had improved in all the monopolies by 1990. The improvement was small in the case of the regulated natural monopoly, gas, and the improvement was cut back substantially by 1992 in the case of the non-regulated monopoly, steel. There is no evidence to suggest that rates of return are substantially higher for regulated natural monopolies and so the evidence on capture is inconclusive.

A final test of whether regulation of natural monopoly is in the public interest or the interest of producers is to study the changes in consumer surplus and producer surplus following deregulation. Microeconomists have examined this issue in the United States. In the case of rail deregulation, which occurred during the 1980s, both consumers and producers gained, and by large amounts. The gains from deregulation of telecommunications and cable television were smaller and accrued only to the consumer. These findings suggest that rail regulation hurt everyone, while regulation of telecommunications and cable television hurt only the consumer.

We've now examined the regulation of natural monopoly. Let's turn next to regulation in oligopolistic industries – to the regulation of cartels.

Figure 19.5 Collusive Oligopoly

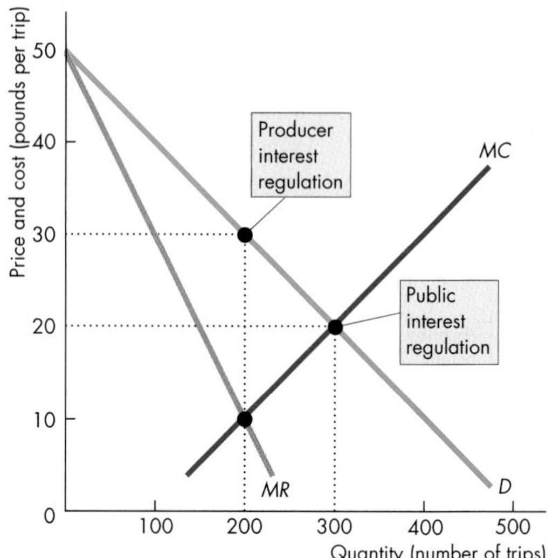

Ten road haulage firms transport carrots from East Anglia to Yorkshire. The demand curve is *D* and the industry marginal cost curve is *MC*. Under competition, the *MC* curve is the industry supply curve. If the industry is competitive, the price of a trip will be £20 and 300 trips will be made each week. Producers will demand regulation that restricts entry and limits output to 200 trips a week. This regulation raises the price to £30 a trip and results in each producer making maximum profit – as if it were a monopoly. Industry marginal revenue is equal to industry marginal cost.

Cartel Regulation

A *cartel* is a collusive agreement among a number of firms designed to restrict output and achieve a higher profit for the cartel's members. Cartels are illegal in the United Kingdom, the European Union and most other countries. But international cartels can sometimes operate legally, such as the international cartel of oil producers known as OPEC (the Organization of Petroleum Exporting Countries).

Illegal cartels can arise in oligopolistic industries. An oligopoly is a market structure in which a small number of firms compete with each other. We studied oligopoly (and duopoly – two firms competing for a market) in Chapter 14. There we saw that if firms manage to collude and behave like a monopoly, they can set the same price and sell the same total quantity as a monopoly firm would. But we also discovered that in such a situation, each firm will be tempted to 'cheat', increasing its own output and profit at the expense of the other firms. The result of such 'cheating' on the collusive agreement is the unravelling of the monopoly equilibrium and the emergence of a competitive outcome with zero economic profit for producers. Such an outcome benefits consumers at the expense of producers.

How is oligopoly regulated? Does regulation prevent monopoly practices or does it encourage those practices?

According to the public interest theory, oligopoly is regulated to ensure a competitive outcome. Consider, for example, the market for road haulage of carrots from East Anglia to Yorkshire, illustrated in Figure 19.5. The demand curve for trips is *D*. The industry marginal cost curve – and the competitive supply curve – is *MC*. Public interest regulation will regulate the price of a trip at £20 and there will be 300 trips a week.

How would this industry be regulated according to the capture theory? Regulation that is in the producer interest will maximize profit. To find the outcome in this case, we need to determine the price and quantity when marginal cost equals marginal revenue. The marginal revenue curve is *MR*. So marginal cost equals marginal revenue at 200 trips a week. The price of a trip is £30.

One way of achieving this outcome is to place an output limit on each firm in the industry. If there are 10 haulage companies, an output limit of 20 trips per company ensures that the total number of trips in a week is 200. Penalties can be imposed to ensure that no single producer exceeds its output limit.

All the firms in the industry would support this type of regulation because it helps to prevent cheating and to maintain a monopoly outcome. Each firm knows that without effectively enforced production quotas every firm has an incentive to increase output. (For each firm, price exceeds marginal cost so a greater output brings a larger profit.) So each firm wants a method of preventing output from rising above the industry profit-maximizing level and the quotas enforced by regulation achieve this end. With this type of cartel regulation, the regulator enables a cartel to operate legally and in its own best interest.

What does cartel regulation do in practice? Although there is disagreement about the matter, the consensus view is that regulation tends to favour the producer. Regulating taxis (by local authorities) and airlines (by the Civil Aviation Authority) are specific examples in which profits of producers increased as a result of regulation.

Making Predictions

Most industries have a few producers and many consumers. In these cases, public choice theory predicts that regulation will protect producer interests because a small number of people stand to gain a large amount and so they will be fairly easy to organize as a cohesive lobby. Under such circumstances, politicians will be rewarded with political contributions rather than votes. But there are situations in which the consumer interest is sufficiently strong and well-organized and thus able to prevail. There are also cases in which the balance switches from producer to consumer, as seen in the deregulation process that began in the late 1970s.

Deregulation raises some hard questions for economists seeking to understand and make predictions about regulation. Why were the bus and financial sectors deregulated? If producers gained from regulation and if the producer lobby was strong enough to achieve regulation, what happened in the 1980s to change the equilibrium to one in which the consumer interest prevailed? We do not have a complete answer to this question at the present time. But regulation had become so costly to consumers, and the potential benefits to them from deregulation so great, that the cost of organizing the consumer voice became a price worth paying.

One factor that increased the cost of regulation borne by consumers and brought deregulation in the airline and bus sectors was the large increase in energy prices in the 1970s. These price hikes made route regulation extremely costly and changed the balance in favour of consumers in the political equilibrium. Technological change was the main factor at work not only in the finance sector but also in the airline sector. Computerized accounts, automatic tellers and telephone services all made smaller producers able to offer low-cost services, forcing deregulation. Let's look at the EU airline example.

The European Union has deregulated scheduled air services within and among its member states. Until recently (1997) most governments allowed only two airlines on any one route, and regulated fares and traffic in such a way that airlines could not compete. These restrictions have been lifted to encourage competition. Now, airlines from one European country can launch domestic services in another. Ryanair and EasyJet are operating dramatic cut-price services. How can they cut prices so much? These airlines can use direct telephone sales technology, pick the cheapest airports to run from, cut red tape and can adopt a 'no frills' service approach. Of course, customers get what they pay for, as you can see in the cartoon.

If the political equilibrium has swung towards the consumer, it should lead to more consumer-oriented regulation in the future. Deregulation creates more competition, as we have seen, but it could erode consumer rights. We can expect the current emphasis on deregulation to switch regulation from serving the interests of producers to serving the interests of consumers. So deregulation does not mean less regulation overall.

© Nick Baker, *Financial Times*, 18 December 1995.

Review

- Regulation of a natural monopoly in the public interest sets price equal to marginal cost or, to avoid a tax-financed subsidy, sets price equal to average total cost.
- In practice, natural monopolies face either rate of return regulation or incentive regulation schemes.
- With rate of return regulation, firms have an incentive to inflate costs and move as closely as possible to the profit-maximizing output. Incentive regulation – price caps and earnings sharing – encourage cost cutting.
- Cartel regulation that establishes output levels for each firm can help perpetuate a cartel and work against the public interest.

Let's now leave specific industry regulation and turn to the other main methods of intervention in markets – monopoly and competition policy and public ownership.

Monopoly and Competition Policy

Monopoly and competition policy is an alternative way in which government can influence the marketplace. This is a form of general regulation, where government can control the actions of any industry. As in the case of specific regulation, monopoly and competition policy can operate in the public interest, maximizing total surplus, or in the private interest, maximizing the surpluses of particular interest groups such as producers.

The historical development of UK monopoly and competition policy is shown in Table 19.3. The initial Monopolies and Restrictive Practices Act created an agency called the Monopolies and Restrictive Practices Commission (MRPC). Its role was to investigate the activities of reported monopolies and any restrictive practices to assess whether they acted against the public interest. The Act defined a monopoly as a firm having a market share greater than 30 per cent – this was reduced to 25 per cent in the Fair Trading Act of 1973. The 1973 act also allowed the investigation of an industry where one firm has a 25 per cent share of a local market rather than a national market. As a result, monopoly investigations are focused on oligopoly industries and their abuse of monopoly power, rather than on pure monopolies and single firms. The traditional emphasis of UK policy is on the behaviour of oligopolies rather than the structure of industries.

The 1956 act removed the control of restrictive practices from the MRPC, creating the Monopolies Commission. This legislation was the direct result of the early work of the MRPC. Its reports found widespread evidence of restrictive practice agreements between firms, which tended to operate against the public interest. The Monopolies Commission became the Monopolies and Mergers Commission (MMC) as a result of the 1965 act. With its new powers, it could now investigate any merger likely to create a monopoly or lead to abuse of monopoly power which would be against 'the public interest'. The Office of Fair Trading (OFT) was set up in the

Table 19.3 The Main UK Monopoly and Competition Laws

Name of law	Year	Changes introduced
Monopolies and Restrictive (Inquiry and Control) Act	1948	Set up Monopolies and Restrictive Practices Commission (MRPC). Defined monopoly as 30 per cent of national market
Restrictive Trade Practices Act	1956	Removed restrictive practices from MRPC. Set up Monopolies Commission (MC)
Monopolies and Mergers Act	1965	Set up Monopolies and Mergers Commission (MMC). Added merger investigation to MMC
Fair Trading Act	1973	Redefined national and local monopoly. Set up Office of Fair Trading (OFT) and duties of Director General (DGFT). Competition defined as the 'public interest'
Competition Act	1980	Allows referral of individual firms and small-scale MMC reports. Public corporations included

1973 act, and its Director General (DGFT) now recommends monopolies and mergers to the government for investigation. Since the 1980 Competition Act, the DGFT has been able to recommend investigation of a single firm rather than the whole industry, including public corporations.

The criterion of 'public interest' does not have a clear definition. The interpretation of public interest is a political matter determined by the Secretary of State for Trade and Industry, making the law vague. The 1973 Fair Trading Act tried to remedy this situation and stated that the 'public interest' was any practice that maintains and promotes effective competition – or total surplus. The act suggested consumer surplus should be given a higher weighting than producer surplus in this definition.

Our historical review shows that monopoly and competition policy laws control three aspects of firm activity:

1 Monopoly.
2 Mergers.
3 Restrictive practices.

Let's look at some examples these three types of investigation in the United Kingdom and the European Union.

UK Monopoly Investigations

The MMC started to promote structural remedies to monopoly as part of the general move towards deregulation in the late 1980s and early 1990s. If an oligopoly industry could be broken up into smaller parts to operate without regulation, this was considered better than regulating the oligopoly. For example, the MMC report into the brewing industry in 1989, found evidence of monopoly in the supply of beer and recommended that brewers should sell off a large proportion of the pubs that they owned because they restricted the sale of competitors' beers in these pubs. In 1993, the MMC found that British Gas was using its monopoly control of gas pipelines and storage to reduce competition from new entrants into gas supply. But its recommendation that British Gas should sell its gas supply business was not accepted by government.

But deregulation itself can also result in an increase in concentration and monopoly power. This is shown by the MMC investigation of the supply of bus services in the north of England in 1993. Local authority-run bus services had been deregulated to allow in private competitors. After deregulation, allegations were made that Busways Travel Services Ltd, was involved in predatory pricing – starting a bus war by undercutting prices. The MMC found evidence of monopoly power as four bus companies, including Busways, supplied more than 90 per cent of local bus services. After a failed bid to buy the local authority bus company, Busways recruited the majority of the local authority's drivers, and started operating free bus services on local authority routes. The successful bidder pulled out and the local authority bus company went into liquidation, removing a potential competitor. The MMC decided that predatory pricing had reduced competition against the public interest, and recommended new regulation to improve market entry and reduce predatory pricing.

Table 19.4 Merger Investigations by the OFT

	Considered	Investigated	Referred to MMC
1993	309	197	3
1996	394	244	9

UK Merger Investigations

All mergers must be notified to the OFT. These cases are then considered by the DGFT for evidence of potential monopoly creation. A potential monopoly may exist if the merged firms control 25 per cent or more of their market, or their combined assets are worth more than £70 million. The merger investigations of the OFT are shown in Table 19.4. In 1996, the OFT considered 394 merger cases and investigated 244 of these. The DGFT eventually referred 9 cases to the MMC for a full investigation. Despite the fact that the threshold for investigation had been raised, there was a 27 per cent increase in the number of cases considered by the OFT.

Mergers investigated by the MMC are of three types:

1 Horizontal.
2 Vertical.
3 Conglomerate.

Horizontal mergers are mergers between firms operating in the same industry, producing the same types of products. They can reduce the number of competitors in the industry and create monopoly power in the new combined firm. *Vertical mergers* are mergers between suppliers and customers. A vertical merger results in forward integration when a manufacturer merges with a retailer, and backward integration when a manufacturer merges with a raw materials supplier. These mergers limit access by other manufacturers to suppliers and retailers, creating monopoly power. *Conglomerate mergers* are mergers between firms that operate in different markets with unrelated products. Conglomerate mergers are likely to reduce competition only if there is some similarity between the products produced.

In deciding whether a merger is against the public interest, the MMC must balance the benefits of merger against any total surplus loss from a reduction in competition. Mergers can improve efficiency if they reduce costs by generating economies of scale. A merger will be in the public interest if the value of the reduction in costs is greater than the value of the loss of consumer surplus. Conglomerate and vertical mergers have less effect on competition than horizontal mergers, and are more likely to be in the public interest. This explains why most of the mergers recommended to the MMC are of the horizontal type. It also explains why most are accepted with minor recommendations about the activities of the combined firm after the merger.

In 1995, two mergers were announced between electricity generators and electricity suppliers – PowerGen and Midland Electricity, and National Power and Southern Electricity. PowerGen had 24 per cent of the electricity generating market and National Power had 33 per cent. Midland Electricity and Southern Electricity were both electricity supply companies with a local monopoly. These mergers are examples of vertical integration, which would reduce the number of suppliers. The MMC found that the mergers would operate against the public interest, but that the impact was not strong enough to stop the merger. Let's see why.

Since privatization, new independent electricity producers have entered the market and reduced the share of the two big generators from 73 per cent to 57 per cent. The MMC noted that both supply companies were minority shareholders in some of these new independent producers. The mergers would make the two big producers privy to new information on the operation of the independent production market, increasing their influence. This would reduce competition in the electricity market, raising prices to consumers, and would be against the public interest. But the MMC recognized that there would be benefits from cost reductions, and suggested that the merger would not be against the public interest if the two regional electricity companies were to sell their shareholdings in the independent producers within 18 months of the mergers going ahead.

We have looked at UK monopoly and merger control and shown that it works by comparing the costs and benefits of increased market share on a case-by-case basis. Many economists believe that clearer rules defining monopoly and acceptable mergers, would remove a great deal of uncertainty for firms and cut the cost of operating the policy. Other economists argue that a flexible system is needed to ensure that beneficial mergers can go ahead, and that competitive oligopolies are not destroyed. The European Union operates a compromise system – more flexible than the UK system but not subject to political control. Let's see if it is a better system.

EU Monopolies and Mergers Investigations

National competition policy controls the actions of firms within national borders, and EU policy controls the impact of monopolies and mergers on trade among member states. EU policy is also designed to promote free competition, but it defines monopoly power in a different way. Under European law, abuse of power by a firm in a dominant position is illegal if it affects trade among member states by creating unfair trading conditions. The important aspect triggering investigation is the abuse of power, not the existence of a dominant firm as it is in the United Kingdom. Abuse includes imposing unfair price and purchase conditions, limiting production, applying different conditions in different countries and imposing restrictive contracts. The European Commission is the investigating agency. Unlike its UK counterpart, it can act on its recommendations and has wide-ranging powers to enforce its decisions with fines for offending firms. For example, in 1999, The European Competition Directorate ordered British American Tobacco to sell of some of its cigarette brands as the price for agreeing its merger with Rothmans. The merged group has a 16 per cent share of the global market and a 14 per cent share of the European market, still less than its main rival, Philip Morris.

The EU Merger Control Regulation of 1990 allows the Commission to investigate mergers which have a 'European Dimension'. This is defined as a total worldwide turnover value of 5 billion ecu or more, and where two firms have a turnover value within the European Union of at least 250 million ecu. The Commission accepts a merger providing any strengthening of the dominant position does not lead to an effective reduction in competition. By 1995, only a couple of mergers had been blocked, and 95 per cent were accepted without any conditions. The wave of mergers in 1998 led to a large number of investigations including the proposed merger between giant oil companies Mobil and Exxon which may yet be blocked.

So which is the more efficient approach – the EU system or the UK system? It depends on whether you think the administrative decision of the Commission is more accountable than the political decision of the UK Secretary of State, and whether you think an investigation triggered by abuse of power leads to better decision making than an investigation triggered by changes in industrial structure. The debate can only be settled by empirical evidence. In the meantime, the United Kingdom is considering making its monopoly control policy more like the EU policy, and has introduced a system of negotiation between the OFT and firms to cut the costs of MMC investigation. We'll find similar problems in the last element of monopoly regulation – restrictive practices.

UK Restrictive Practices Investigations

A *restrictive practice* is defined in the 1973 Fair Trading Act and covers agreements between firms on prices, terms and conditions of sale, and market share. All restrictive practices in the United Kingdom are deemed illegal unless the parties can prove to the Restrictive Practices Court that they are in the public interest. There are eight clearly defined arguments for proving this, including proving beneficial effects on trade, on unemployment and on consumer interests. The firms must prove that the agreement passes at least one argument and that, on balance, the benefits of the agreement outweigh the costs.

In 1996, over 500 new agreements were registered with the OFT, raising the total number of agreements above 12,000. Whilst the process of investigation of new agreements is slow and not always successful, an increasing number of firms are abandoning agreements because of the costs involved in proving their cases.

Retail price maintenance – where manufacturers dictate the minimum selling price to retailers – only became a restrictive practice in 1964. Firms now have to prove that retail price maintenance is in the public interest. By 1998, the only remaining agreement was in pharmaceutical products. The pharmaceuticals industry argue that price maintenance is needed to keep small chemists in business and preserve the specialist pharmacy advice service that they offer. This argument was unsucessfully challenged by Asda, the supermarket retailer, in 1999 but pressure to remove the agreement is still strong. You can go back and read about this in *Reading Between the Lines* in Chapter 6 on pp. 138–139. Some economists have suggested that the EU system would be better than the current UK system. Let's look at how it works.

EU Restrictive Practices Investigations

The purpose of EU and UK law are similar. EU law prohibits any agreement that affects trade among member states and any agreement designed to reduce competition. Firms can, but don't have to register their agreements. Agreements are exempted if they improve production and distribution or technical progress and do not reduce competition. Exemptions can be granted by the Commission as a block, for example to an industry, or for individual firms. The main difference is that EU law is concerned with the *effect* of the agreement and not its *form*, which is the basis for requiring agreements to be registered in the United Kingdom. Focusing on effect reduces the cost of investigation and increases the chance that anti-competitive agreements are identified. Also, the Commission has much greater powers of enforcement than the UK Restrictive Practices Court – imposing fines of up to 10 per cent of a firm's turnover.

EU law has been effective in identifying and removing agreements on price fixing, market sharing and the use of exclusive dealerships. It has also identified secret agreements and potential collusive cartel agreements and initiated investigations. Following this success, the Department of Trade and Industry moved towards the EU approach, allowing the OFT to investigate potential cartels and award block exemptions to cut administration costs.

Public or Special Interest?

Our discussion shows that monopoly control law has evolved to protect the public interest and to restrain profit-seeking and anti-competitive actions of producers. Although the interests of the producer can influence the way in which the law is interpreted and applied, the overall thrust of the law is towards achieving allocative efficiency and serving the public interest.

There is a key difference between EU and UK law in the way it is administered. UK monopoly control and regulation are administered by a bureaucracy and the final decisions are political. EU law is administered by a bureaucracy but interpreted and enforced by the legal process – the courts. Economists are now beginning to extend theories of public choice to include an economic analysis of the law and the way the courts interpret the law. It is interesting to speculate whether the courts are more sensitive to the public interest than politicians in interpreting monopoly control law and regulation.

We have now looked at all the aspects of EU and UK monopoly control law. There is one other form of control that has been widely used in the past – public ownership or nationalization. Let's look at this now.

Public Ownership and Privatization

After World War II, most European countries took a wide range of industries and firms into public ownership. However, many European governments are now in the process of privatizing firms and industries in public ownership. **Privatization**, in this context, means the sale of assets in public ownership to the private sector. To explain this shift, we'll compare the benefits and costs of regulation through public ownership with the benefits and costs of regulating privatized industries. The United Kingdom is an interesting example because it is extreme. The progress of the UK privatization programme of nationalized industries since 1979 is shown in Table 19.5. Before this, we need to understand what public ownership means.

Public Ownership

The main form of **public ownership** is nationalization – the compulsory purchase of major industries by government to satisfy a political belief that public ownership is better. The gas, electricity generation, transport, iron, steel and coal industries came into public ownership through nationalization. Governments also bought some firms through direct dealings on the stock market because of their importance to the economy and others because they were struggling under intense international competiton.

UK governments followed a continuous programme of nationalization and purchase after World War II. The range of firms in public ownership in 1979 included the main utilities, transport,

Table 19.5 UK Privatizations of Nationalized Industries 1979–1996

NATIONALIZED INDUSTRIES

Full privatization	Partial privatization
British Aerospace	Electricity:
British Airports Authority	England and Wales Area Boards
British Airways	PowerGen and National Power
British Coal	South of Scotland Electricity Board
British Gas	North of Scotland Hydro-Electric Board
British National Oil Corporation	National Grid Company
British Rail	Nuclear Electric and Scottish Nuclear (due 1996)
British Shipbuilders (Warships)	Water and Sewerage:
British Steel	England and Wales water boards
British Telecommunications	
National Bus Company	
National Freight Consortium	

Source: S. Bailey (1995), *Public Sector Economics: Theory, Policy and Practice*, London, Macmillan, adapted from Table 13.1.

key industries and many firms from relatively competitive industries. Among these were Jaguar Cars, Sealink Ferries, Cable and Wireless, Britoil and Unipart. So why were so many firms brought into public ownership?

Reasons for Public Ownership

There are three main reasons why firms and whole industries have been brought into public ownership. They are:

1 Social reasons.
2 Political reasons.
3 Economic reasons.

Social Reasons *Social reasons* arise from the use of public ownership to generate an equitable distribution of goods and services. For example, suppose there is no gas or electricity on a remote Scottish island. The one family living on the island decides it is time to enjoy the benefits of modern utility services. It asks for a quote. The private gas and telecommunications firms quote on the basis of the marginal cost of laying pipe connections out to the Scottish islands. This price is much higher than any one family could afford – leaving them without basic utility services. A public industry can cross-subsidize the provision of these services by spreading the cost among other customers. It can also ensure uniform quality of service by charging a flat-rate price. But equity could be achieved equally by a government subsidy – to the firm or the customer. Public ownership will be preferred if the transactions costs of achieving equity are lower under public ownership than under regulation or subsidies to private firms and individuals. Governments try to achieve this by making equity a major objective of the firm under public ownership.

Political Reasons *Political reasons* stem from the belief that public ownership is better than private ownership in major industries. The post-war UK Labour government believed that private ownership of capital led to the exploitation of labour. Public ownership of the means of production, distribution and exchange could control the exploitation of labour in major industries – wages and conditions could be fairly negotiated. This political belief no longer has prominence in the United Kingdom, but it was the major reason for post-war nationalization.

Economic Reasons There are two *economic reasons* for privatization. Generating:

1 Economic benefits for the whole economy.
2 Economic benefits for the firm or industry.

Economic benefits for the whole economy arise from controlling unemployment and wage demands through public ownership, and through saving flagging industries and their potential export markets. This was part of the reason for public ownership of shipbuilding and steel, together with car manufacturing. Public ownership means that the return on the government's investment does not leak back to shareholders, but goes back to the government. Wage control can be effective through public ownership only if a large proportion of employees are employed by the government. This is no longer the case in the United Kingdom.

Economic benefits at the firm or industry include the control of monopoly power, the promotion of economies of scale, the provision of public goods and the control of externalities. Most UK nationalized industries were subject to rate of return control and were expected to use a form of long-run marginal cost pricing. Economies of scale could be promoted through investment and the creation of natural monopolies. Public goods, such as defence, would not be provided by the private sector and the fear of extreme externalities, such as nuclear power disasters, could be reduced if safety standards could be raised at lower cost under public ownership. But if most of these benefits could be realized at a lower cost by regulating private firms, the argument for privatization is stronger.

Between 1979 and 1996, 12 nationalized industries were fully privatized and 2 were partially privatized. By 1998, the Post Office was the only remaining industry in public ownership and its future in the public sector is still uncertain. In addition to the nationalized industries, 19 competitive firms were also privatized during this period. So why has the UK government followed such an intensive privatization programme? Let's look at the reasons for privatization.

Reasons for Privatization

The reasons for privatization are similar to those for public ownership. How can this be? Economists who support privatization would argue that the economic and social benefits of public ownership can be achieved in the private sector with appropriate regulation – but at lower cost to the taxpayer. Only the political reasons differ. Political reasons include reducing government expenditure, deregulating industry and widening share ownership.

Why might privatization achieve the same benefits as public ownership but at a lower cost? When firms like Unipart, Britoil and Cable and Wireless were privatized, they were exposed to the full force of competition from other private firms in the same industry. Competition reduced average total cost in these firms and privatization removed the cost of government regulation.

But the other privatized firms were examples of natural monopolies or large-scale oligopolies which had to be regulated after privatization. So privatization couldn't reduce the total cost of regulation, but it could lead to reductions in costs and more efficient production. Why?

Privatized firms will be more efficient if they have less inflated costs, as shown in Figure 19.4. Costs will be lower in the private sector if the firm is:

- Exposed to competition and merger.
- Exposed to shareholder preferences.
- More efficiently regulated.

Let's take the example of the privatizations of Jaguar and Rover cars. When privatized, the car firms entered a competitive international market. Managers had to look for ways to deflate costs to raise shareholders returns in the private sector, and cost to government of direct regulation was removed.

Privatization is less efficient when it creates private monopoly as in the case of British Gas and British Telecommunications. The threat of merger is weaker because of the sheer size and value of these firms. Competition can only be achieved by separating out the service part of the business from the ownership of physical networks. For example, the sale of gas and electricity, telecommunications and travel services are retail activities and can be highly competitive. It is only the network of pipes, lines and road or track that is a natural monopoly. More extensive and expensive regulation is needed to remove entry barriers in retailing, and to control the price of access to the network to encourage new entrants and competition. You can read about OFTEL's problems regulating BT with the growth of calls to the internet in *Reading Between the Lines* on page pp. 476–477.

Privatization and Regulatory Capture

Our model of regulatory capture suggests that private monopolies will have inflated costs under rate of return regulation. The new regulatory bodies, such as OFTEL and OFGEM, have adopted price cap regulation using the RPI minus X formula to improve efficiency. RPI is the retail price index and the X-factor is a percentage reduction to improve X-efficiency. The formula sets the price cap in real terms so that real prices in the industry fall over time, forcing managers to improve efficiency to maintain profits. It is applied only to a basket of the industry's prices. So if retail prices are rising at 6 per cent and the X-factor set by OFFER is 2 per cent, the maximum increase in overall electricity service prices is 4 per cent. The formula cuts the cost of regulation in other ways. It avoids the problem of estimating average costs, gaining access to detailed accounting information, setting individual prices or tariffs, or directly controlling profits.

Let's look at one case study of the impact of UK privatization, National Power. National Power was privatized in 1991 and Figure 19.6 shows that it has performed well since then despite regulation in the coal and electricity markets. National Power was worth £6.8 billion in 1998. It had profits of £725 million, sales at £3.2 billion, generated a dividend of 27 pence per share, and employed 4,290 people. National Power was in decline when privatized but it has increased its profits from £479 million despite falling sales. Privatization has led to dramatic cuts in cost through shedding over half its workforce and cutting overheads. It failed in its domestic strategy to become an integrated power company by buying a regional electricity company, when the Competition Commission blocked its bid to buy Southern Electric. Its new strategy for global growth is paying off, with £1.2 billion invested in Turkey, Australia, India and the USA. Foreign profits have grown from nothing to £130 million in just four years. Privatization has given National Power the scope to manage the industry's decline and look for growth elsewhere.

The benefits of privatization have been questioned by some economists. If increased efficiency arises from improved competition rather than shareholder preferences, there will be little improvement in privatized monopolies[1]. Government wealth, and therefore social welfare, may be lower after privatization if firms are sold at a discount price.

Figure 19.6 The Effect of Privatization of National Power

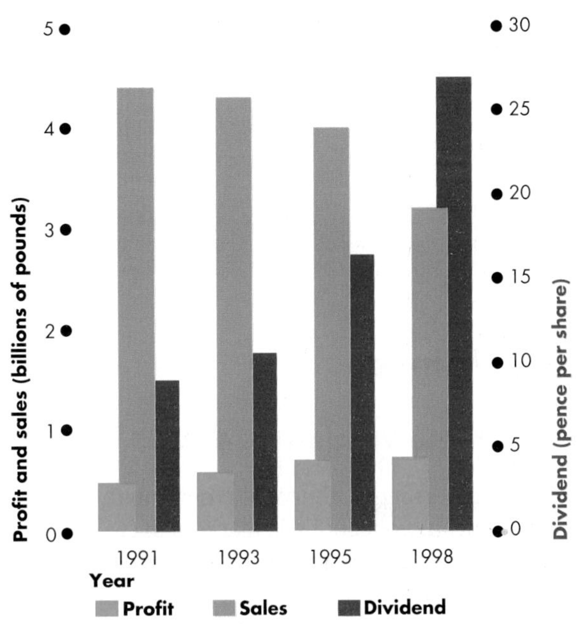

National Power has performed well since privatization in 1991, despite regulation and falling sales. Profits have increased by 50 per cent from £479 million to £725 million, and the dividend has increased by 200 per cent from 9 pence per share to 27 pence per share. Competition has forced National Power to cut domestic costs drastically and to focus on global growth.

Cost cutting will lead to a fall in quality and service provision, reducing consumer surplus. If privatization merely shifts surplus from consumers and employees to shareholders and managers, it will not have achieved its objectives. So has privatization gained the benefits of public ownership at a lower cost? The jury is still out – empirical studies of performance in the privatized industries are inconclusive[2].

In this chapter, we've seen how the government intervenes in markets to affect prices, quantities, the gains from trade and the division of these gains

1 J. Vickers and G. Yarrow, *Privatization: An Economic Analysis*, London, MIT Press, 1988.

2 M. Bishop, J. Kay and C. Mayer (eds), *Privatization and Economic Performance*, Oxford, Oxford University Press, 1995.

between consumers and producers when there is monopoly or oligopoly. We've seen that there is a conflict between the pursuit of the public interest – achieving allocative efficiency – and the pursuit of the special interests of producers – maximizing producer surplus or economic profit. The political and legal arenas are the places in which these conflicts are resolved. We've reviewed the two theories – public interest and capture – concerning the type and scope of government intervention. We've explained the shift from public ownership to privatization by comparing the benefits and costs of regulation through public ownership and regulation after privatization.

Summary

Key Points

Market Intervention (p. 454)

- The government intervenes to regulate monopolistic and oligopolistic markets in two main ways: regulation (and deregulation) and monopoly control laws.
- Regulation by various agencies is the control of prices, product standards and conditions of entry into industries.
- Monopoly laws control three activities by firms: monopoly, mergers, and restrictive practices.

Economic Theory of Regulation (pp. 454–456)

- Consumers and producers express their demand for the regulation that influences their surpluses by voting, lobbying and making campaign contributions.
- The larger the surplus that can be generated by a particular regulation and the smaller the number of people adversely affected, the larger is the demand for the regulation.
- Regulation is supplied by politicians who pursue their own best interest.
- The larger the surplus per person generated and the larger the number of persons affected by it, the larger is the supply of regulation.
- Public interest theory predicts that total surplus will be maximized; capture theory predicts that producer surplus will be maximized.

Regulation and Deregulation (pp. 456–464)

- Firms are regulated at all levels, from the decisions of the European Union, to national government regulation, local authority regulation and voluntary regulation through industrial and professional organizations.
- Regulation is conducted by regulatory agencies controlled by politically appointed bureaucrats and staffed by a permanent bureaucracy of experts.
- Two types of industries are regulated: natural monopolies and cartels.
- Although the number of regulatory agencies continues to grow with the creation of special agencies to control privatized monopolies, there has been a tendency to deregulate many areas of the economy.
- Public interest theory predicts that deregulation occurs because the balance of power has shifted to consumers who demand lower prices, but they are also likely to demand more regulation serving their interests

Monopoly and Competition Policy (pp. 464–468)

- Monopoly control law allows governments to control monopoly and monopolistic practices.
- Monopoly control laws define monopoly in terms of market power and are also used to control oligopolies and mergers.
- The focus of UK legislation is on establishing the *form* of monopoly and restrictive

practice. The focus of EU law is on impact of monopoly power and the *effect* of restrictive practices.

- While the overall thrust of monopoly control law is directed towards serving the public interest, but it may favour producers because it is administered by bureaucrats and politicians.

Public Ownership and Privatization (pp. 468–472)

- European countries have a long history of public ownership of firms, but many of these firms have now been privatized – sold to private investors.
- There are three reasons for public ownership – social, political and economic.
- Privatization will achieve the same economic and social outcomes if the costs of regulation are lower in the private sector than in the public sector.
- Regulatory costs fall where privatization of monopolies exposes firms to competition for service provision, shareholder preferences for profits and an alternative regulatory framework adopting a price cap formula.

Key Figures and Tables 

Key Terms

Review Questions

1 What are the two main ways in which the government can intervene in the marketplace?

2 What is consumer surplus? How is it calculated and how is it represented in a diagram?

3 What is producer surplus? How is it calculated and how is it represented in a diagram?

4 What is total surplus? How is it calculated and how is it represented in a diagram?

5 Why do consumers demand regulation? In what kinds of industries would their demands for regulation be greatest?

6 Why do producers demand regulation? In what kinds of industries would their demands for regulation be greatest?

7 Explain the public interest and capture theories of the supply of regulation. What does each theory imply about the behaviour of politicians?

8 How is oligopoly regulated in the United Kingdom? In whose interest is it regulated?

9 What are the main monopoly control laws in force in the United Kingdom today?

Problems

1 Cascade Springs plc is an unregulated natural monopoly that bottles water from a natural spring high in the Scottish highlands. The total fixed cost incurred by Cascade Springs is £160,000 and its marginal cost is 10 pence a bottle. The demand for bottled water from Cascade Springs is as follows:

Price (pence per bottle)	Quantity demanded (thousands of bottles per year)
100	0
90	200
80	400
70	600
60	800
50	1,000
40	1,200
30	1,400
20	1,600
10	1,800
0	2,000

a What is the price of a bottle of water?
b How many bottles does Cascade Springs sell?
c Does Cascade Springs maximize total surplus or producer surplus?

2 The government regulates Cascade Springs in Problem 1 by imposing a marginal cost pricing rule.

a What is the price of a bottle of water?
b How many bottles does Cascade Springs sell?
c What is Cascade Springs' producer surplus?
d What is consumer surplus?
e Is the regulation in the public interest or in the private interet?

3 The government regulates Cascade Springs in Problem 1 by imposing an average cost pricing rule.

a What is the price of a bottle of water?
b How many bottles does Cascade Springs sell?
c What is Cascade Springs' producer surplus?
d What is consumer surplus?
e Is the regulation in the public interest or in the private interest?

4 The value of the capital invested in Cascade Springs in Problem 1 is £2 million. The government introduces a rate of return regulation requiring the firm to sell its water for a price that gives it a rate of return of 5 per cent on its capital.

a What is the price of a bottle of water?
b How many bottles does Cascade Springs sell?
c What is Cascade Springs' producer surplus?
d What is consumer surplus?
e Is the regulation in the public interest or in the private interest?

5 Faced with the rate of return regulation of Problem 4, Cascade Springs pads its costs by paying a special bonus to its owner that it counts as a cost.

a Counting the bonus as part of the producer surplus, what is the size of the bonus that maximizes producer surplus and that makes the measured rate of return equal to 5 per cent as required by the regulation?
b How many bottles does Cascade Springs sell?
c What is Cascade Springs' producer surplus?
d What is consumer surplus?
e Is the regulation in the public interest or in the private interest?

6 Two airlines share an international route.

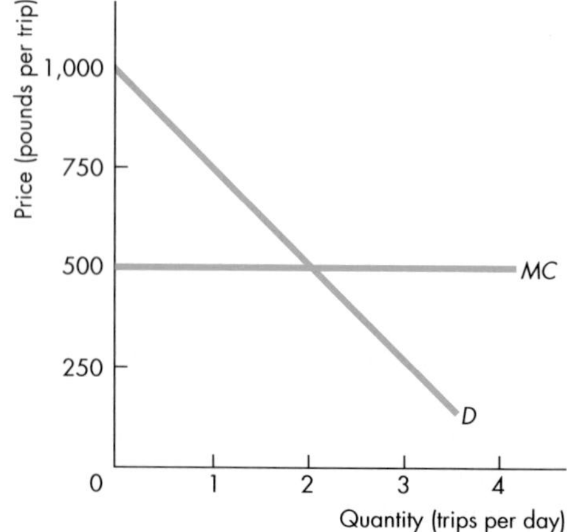

The figure shows the demand curve for trips on this route and marginal cost curve that each firm faces. This air route is regulated.

a What is the price of a trip and what is the number of trips per day if the regulation is in the public interest?
b What is the price of a trip and what is the number of trips per day if the regulation is in the producer interest?
c What is the deadweight loss if the regulation is in the producer interest?
d What do you need to know to predict whether the regulation will be in the public interest or the producer interest?

7 Two phone companies offer local calls in an area. The figure shows the demand curve for calls and the marginal cost curves of each firm. These firms are regulated.

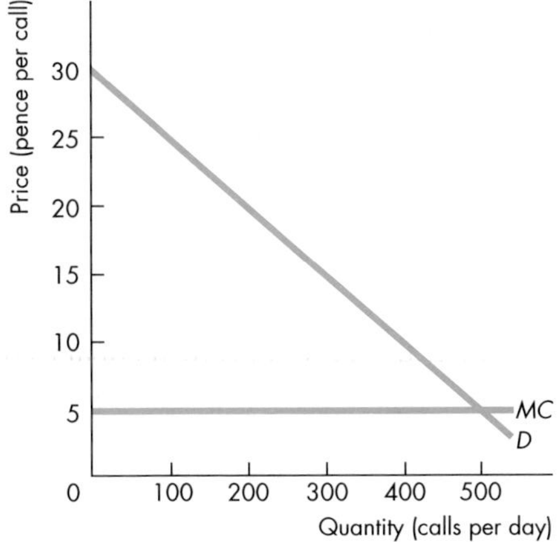

a What is the price of a call and what is the number of calls per day if the regulation is in the public interest?
b What is the price of a call and what is the number of calls per day if the regulation is in the producer interest?
c What is the deadweight loss if the regulation is in the producer interest?
d What do you need to know to predict whether the regulation will be in the public interest or the producer interest?

8 Read the story about regulating British Telecommunication's pricing of domestic calls to the internet in *Reading Between the Lines* on pp. 476–477 and then answer the following questions:

a How can BT generate economic profit from charging for calls to the internet?
b Why has BT focused on developing its dominance in domestic calls to the internet?
c What effect would 'local loop unbundling' have on competition and price for local calls.
d What effect would 'local loop unbundling' have on BT's profits?
e Is it better to regulate price for calls or open access to new entrants into line supply? Explain your answer.

9 Use the link on the Parkin, Powell and Matthews Web site to visit the Federal Trade Commission where you can obtain information about Intel, the computer chip maker.

a What was the FTC's problem with Intel?
b What did Intel agree to do?
c Explain how Intel's agreement will influence the price, quantity and consumer and producer surplus in the market for computer chips.

Regulation and Competition for Internet Calls

The Guardian, 28 May 99

Oftel eyes BT's net gains

David Teather

British Telecom could face a showdown with industry regulator Oftel over the level of profits earned by the company on the back of the explosive growth of the internet.

Oftel is about to begin its review for the next pricing formula capping the price BT charges consumers, and the watchdog is considering a tougher stance to curb the company's earnings from carrying calls to the net.

Last week BT disclosed record profits of £4.3bn against the fastest growth rates in traffic it has experienced in almost a decade. Around 18% of local calls on BT lines were to the internet, up from 8% the previous year. Because of the ubiquity of BT's network most residential internet traffic goes over its lines.

"The forthcoming review of BT's price controls will consider a wide range of issues, including the impact that growth of internet traffic has had on the level of BT's profits," said an Oftel spokesman.

"The review will also look at the level of current and future competition in the various markets that BT operates in, including internet access."

The current formula, of retail price index minus 4.5%, runs until October 2001. The objective of the formula is to control prices where there is inadequate competition to prevent BT from making "excessive" profits. The focus of price control is local and national residential calls where BT still dominates the market.

Some 4.5 million households are linked to the internet, according to some industry analysts, and a fuller understanding of how the market will grow is crucial to Oftel.

Oftel is conducting research to compare the cost of internet access across the world to establish whether the UK is unusually expensive. It hopes to have a draft by next month.

But the watchdog faces a dilemma over price caps on BT. There are concerns that if prices are brought down too far it could also prevent rivals from entering the market.

The price review may also be influenced by Oftel's current consultation into the breaking up of BT's "local loop", the wires which physically connect the home to the exchange.

One option is "local loop unbundling", which would allow rivals to buy or lease lines to domestic consumers, cutting BT out of the equation. A second consultative document will be published next month.

The Essence of the Story

- Oftel, the telecommunications industry regulator, is considering tough measures to curb British Telecommunications (BT) record profits in the light of unprecedented growth in traffic in local calls to the internet.
- Because BT has a virtual monopoly in domestic calls, it reaps the full benefit of the rise in demand as domestic internet usage grows.
- The current price cap formula runs until October 2000 and is designed to limit BT's potential to make excessive profits from its dominance in the residential call market.
- Oftel may increase the price cap but it must be careful not to set the price cap too low as it may prevent new entry into the market.
- Another possibility is to increase competition from new entry by selling or leasing the BT 'local loop' – the wire network which connects the home to the exchange – to other firms.

Economic Analysis

- BT operates an effective monopoly in domestic call supply.

- Figure 1 shows BT faces a downward sloping demand curve for domestic calls, D_0, with marginal cost MC_0, marginal revenue, MR_0 and average total cost, ATC_0. BT maximizes profit by setting $MR_0 = MC_0$, supplying Q_m calls at price P_m.

- The 8 per cent increase in traffic for local calls to the internet raises demand to D_{98} and allows BT to raise the price to P'_m and increase monopoly profit from the dark blue area to the dark blue plus light blue area.

- BT's price increases for domestic calls are currently capped at the RPI minus 4.5 per cent. BT can only raise price to P_R as shown in Figure 2. The quantity of calls increases to Q_R and economic profit is restricted to the dark blue area.

- Another method of reducing BT's monopoly profit is to open up the market to competition by breaking the 'local loop' network. The effect is shown in Figure 3.

- Demand and supply initially are D_{98} and $S_0 = MC_0$ as in Figure 1. New entrants see profit potential and enter the market by buying or leasing part of the 'local loop'. Supply shifts out to S_1 in Figure 3 and price falls to the competitive level P_C and quantity increases to Q_C.

- If Oftel tries to open up the market and maintain the price cap on BT, it has to avoid setting the price too low to put off new entrants.

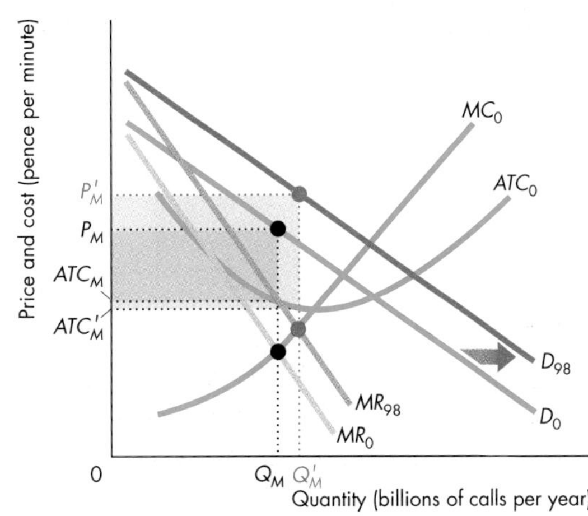

Figure 1 BT's monopoly

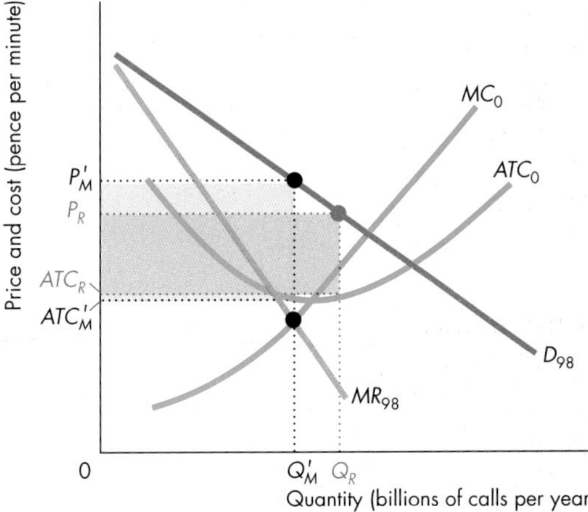

Figure 2 Oftel's price cap

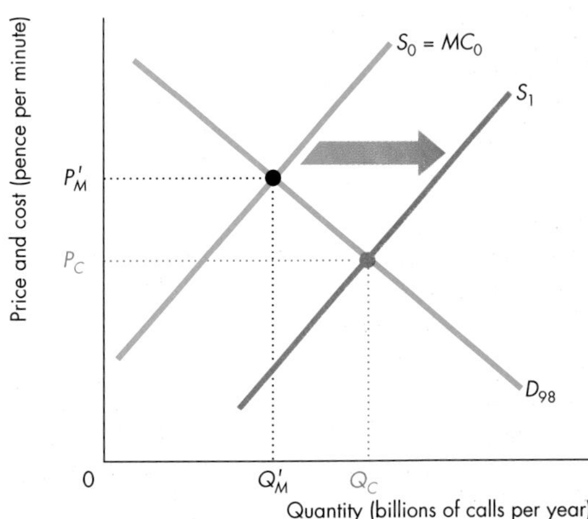

Figure 3 A competitive market

Externalities, the Environment and Knowledge

After studying this chapter you will be able to:

- Explain how property rights can overcome externalities
- Identify how emission charges, standards, marketable permits and taxes can be used to achieve efficiency in the face of external costs
- Explain the costs and benefits of a carbon-fuel tax, and explain why we do not have such a tax
- Explain how grants, subsidies and public provision can make the quantity of education, training and invention more efficient
- Explain how patents increase efficiency

Greener and Smarter

We hear a lot about our endangered planet. We burn huge quantities of fossil fuels – coal, natural gas and oil – that cause acid rain and possibly global warming. The persistent and large-scale use of chlorofluorocarbons (CFCs) may have caused irreparable damage to the earth's ozone layer. We clear acres of rain forest every day. In doing so we destroy rare trees and plants, the habitats of thousands of species of animals, and also the most important storage place for the carbon dioxide that our cars and power stations pump out. We dump toxic waste into rivers, lakes and oceans. Everyone is put at risk by the continued damage to our environment and yet no one individual can take the necessary action to protect it. What, if anything, can government do to protect our environment? How can government action help us to take account of the damage that we cause others every time we turn on our heating or drive our cars? ◆ Almost every day, we hear about a new discovery. The advance of knowledge seems boundless. And more and more people are learning more and more of what is already known. The stock of knowledge – what is known and how many people know it – is increasing apparently without bound each year. But is our stock of knowledge advancing fast enough? Are we spending enough on research and development? And do we spend enough on education? Do enough people remain in school for long enough? Would we be better off if we spent more on research and education?

◆ ◆ ◆ ◆ In this chapter we study market failure problems that arise because many of our actions affect other people, for good or ill, in ways that we do not take into account when we make our own market choices. We study two important areas – the environment and the accumulation of knowledge. But first we need to look at the underlying market failure problem of externalities.

Externalities and Government Policy

An **externality** is a cost or benefit of a production or consumption activity that spills over to affect people other than those who decide the scale of the activity. An *external cost* is the cost of producing a good or service that is not borne by its consumers or producers but by other people. Typical examples are pollution produced by factories, congestion on our roads, and the health effects of smokey atmospheres on non-smokers. An *external benefit* is the benefit of consuming a good or service that does not accrue to its consumers or producers but to other people. Externalities occur when the consumption or production of a good or service creates another good or service that does not have a market. Typical examples include the social effects of education and exercise.

The existence of external costs and external benefits is a major source of *market failure*. There is a tendency for the market economy to overproduce goods and services that have external costs and to underproduce goods and services that have external benefits. That is, externalities create inefficiency.

When market failure occurs, either we live with the inefficiency it creates or we try to achieve greater efficiency by making some *public choices* to use government policy. Governments can use several policies to achieve a more efficient allocation of resources in the face of externalities – to decrease production where there are external costs and increase it where there are external benefits – and this chapter explains these actions. Let's look first at the external costs that affect the environment.

Economics of the Environment

Popular discussions of the environment usually pay little attention to economics. They focus on physical aspects of the environment, not costs and benefits. A common assumption is that if people's actions cause *any* environmental degradation, these actions must cease. In contrast, an economic study of the environment emphasizes costs and benefits. An economist talks about the efficient amount of pollution or environmental damage. This emphasis on costs and benefits does not mean that economists, as citizens, do not share the same goals as others and do not value a healthy environment. Nor does it mean that economists have the right answers and everyone else has the wrong ones (or vice versa). Economics provides a set of tools and principles which clarify the issues. It does not provide an agreed list of solutions.

The starting point for an economic analysis of the environment is the demand for a healthy environment.

The Demand for Environmental Quality

Environmental problems are not new, nor is the desire to find solutions to environmental problems new. The demand for a clean and healthy environment has grown and is higher today than it has ever been. We express our demand for a better environment in a number of ways. We can join 'green' organizations to lobby governments for environmental regulations and policies. We can vote for political parties that reflect our views and we can buy 'green' products. Figure 20.1 gives one indicator of the growth in the demand for a better environment – the growth in the number of people who pay subscriptions to environmental organizations. Between 1981 and 1996, the demand for membership of most voluntary environmental organizations in the United Kingdom more than doubled. By 1996, there were 4.9 million members of environmental organizations.

The demand for a better environment has grown for two reasons:

1 Increased incomes.
2 Increased knowledge of the sources of environmental problems.

As our incomes increase, we demand a larger range of goods and services and one of these 'goods' is a high-quality environment. We value clean air, unspoiled natural scenery and wildlife, and we are willing to pay to protect these valuable resources.

As our knowledge of the effects of our actions on the environment grows, so we are able to take measures that improve the environment. For example, now that we know how sulphur dioxide causes acid rain and how clearing rain forests destroys natural stores of carbon dioxide, we are able, in principle, to design measures that limit these problems.

Figure 20.1 Membership of Environmental Groups

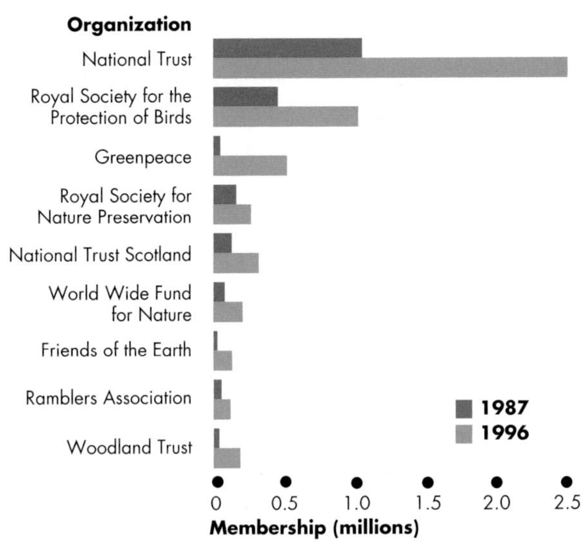

There were 4.9 million members of UK voluntary environmental organizations in 1996. The demand for membership of most organizations more than doubled between 1981 and 1996.

Source: Central Statistical Office, *Membership of Voluntary Environmental Organizations, Social Trends*, London, HMSO, 1998, Table 11.4.

Let's look at the range of environmental problems that have been identified and the actions that create these problems.

The Sources of Environment Problems

Environmental problems arise from pollution of the air, water and land and these individual sources of pollution interact through the *ecosystem*.

Air Pollution Figure 20.2(a) shows the five economic activities that create most of our air pollution. It also shows the relative contributions of each activity. More than two-thirds of air pollution comes from road transport and industrial processes. Only one-sixth arises from coal and gas-fired electric power generation.

A common belief is that air pollution is getting worse. On many fronts, as we will see later in this chapter, *global* air pollution is getting worse. But air pollution in the United Kingdom is getting less severe for some substances. Figure 20.2(b) shows projected trends in the emissions of a major pollutant – carbon dioxide. Carbon dioxide is a 'greenhouse' gas thought to create global warming and increases are mostly created by economic activity. Total emissions fell between 1970 and 1980 but increased after 1980. The projected rise to 2020 is mainly due to increasing use of cars and rising trends in fuel consumption in the production of goods and services.

While the facts about the sources and trends in air pollution are not in doubt, there is considerable disagreement in the scientific community about the *effects* of air pollution. The least controversial problem is *acid rain,* which is caused by sulphur dioxide and nitrogen oxide emissions from coal- and oil-fired power stations. Acid rain begins with air pollution and it leads to water pollution and damages vegetation.

More controversial are airborne substances (suspended particulates) such as lead from leaded petrol and diesel fuel. Some scientists believe that in sufficiently large concentrations, these substances (of which currently 189 have been identified) cause cancer, asthma and other life-threatening conditions.

Even more controversial is *global warming*, which some scientists believe results from the carbon dioxide emissions of road transport and power stations, methane created by cows and other livestock, nitrous oxide emissions from power stations and from fertilizers, and chlorofluorocarbons or CFCs from refrigeration equipment and (in the past) aerosols. The earth's average temperature has increased over the past 100 years, but most of the increase occurred *before* 1940. Determining what causes changes in the earth's temperature and separating out the effect of carbon dioxide and other factors is proving to be difficult.

Equally controversial is the problem of *ozone layer depletion.* There is no doubt that a hole in the ozone layer exists over Antarctica. There is also no doubt that the ozone layer protects us from cancer-causing ultraviolet rays from the sun. But how the ozone layer is influenced by our industrial activity is simply not understood at this time.

While air pollution from leaded petrol has almost been eliminated in developed economies, sulphur dioxide and the so-called greenhouse gases are a much tougher problem to tackle. The alternatives to road vehicles and power stations are costly or have

Figure 20.2 Air Pollution

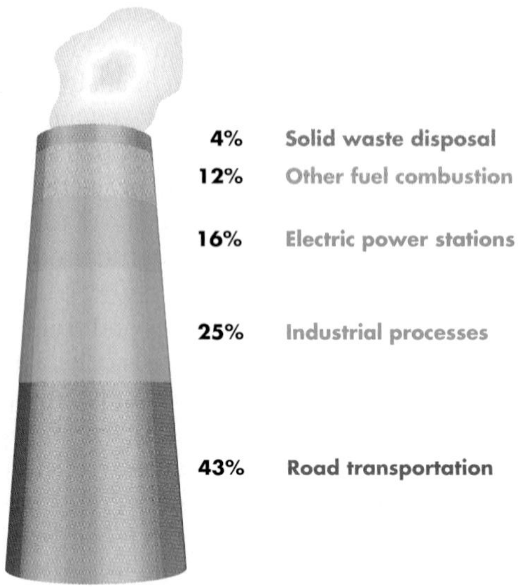

(a) Sources of emission

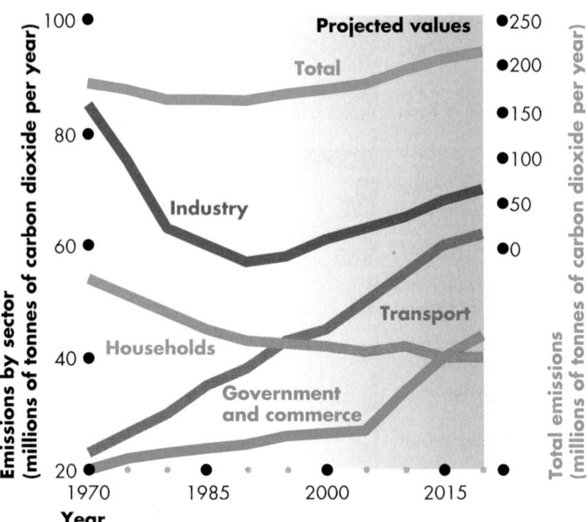

(b) UK carbon dioxide emissions

Part (a) shows that road transport is the largest source of air pollution, followed by industrial production and power stations. Part (b) shows that carbon dioxide emissions – the most important gas thought to cause global warming – fell after 1970 but have recently begun to rise. Forecasts of future emissions suggest the most important source of increase will be from transport – particularly increased use of cars.

Source: Royal Commission on Environmental Pollution, *18th Report*, London, HMSO, 1994 and UK Department of the Environment, Transport and the Regions, 1998.

environmental problems of their own. Road vehicles can be made greener in a variety of ways. One way is to use alternative fuels such as alcohol, natural gas, propane and butane, and hydrogen. Another way is to reduce exhaust emissions by fitting catalytic converters and changing the chemistry of petrol. Similarly, electric power can be generated in cleaner ways by harnessing solar power, tidal power, or geothermal power. Although technically possible, these methods are more costly than conventional carbon-fuelled generators. Another alternative is nuclear power. This method is good for air pollution but bad for land and water pollution because there is no known safe method of disposing of spent nuclear fuel.

Water Pollution The largest sources of water pollution are the dumping of industrial waste and treated sewage in lakes and rivers and the run-off from agricultural fertilizers. A more dramatic source is the accidental spilling of crude oil into the oceans, such as the Exxon Valdez spill in Alaska and an even larger spill in the Russian Arctic in 1994. The most frightening is the dumping of nuclear waste in the ocean. In 1997 there were 200 major substantiated water pollution incidents in the UK, of which the largest share, 30 per cent, were of agricultural origin.

Polluting the waterways and oceans has two main alternatives. One is the chemical processing of waste to render it inert or biodegradable. The other, in wide use for nuclear waste, is to use land sites for storage in secure containers.

Land Pollution Land pollution arises from dumping toxic waste products. Ordinary household rubbish does not pose a pollution problem unless toxic elements in the rubbish seep into the water supply. This possibility increases as less suitable landfill sites are used. It is estimated that 80 per

Figure 20.3 Externalities and the Coase Theorem

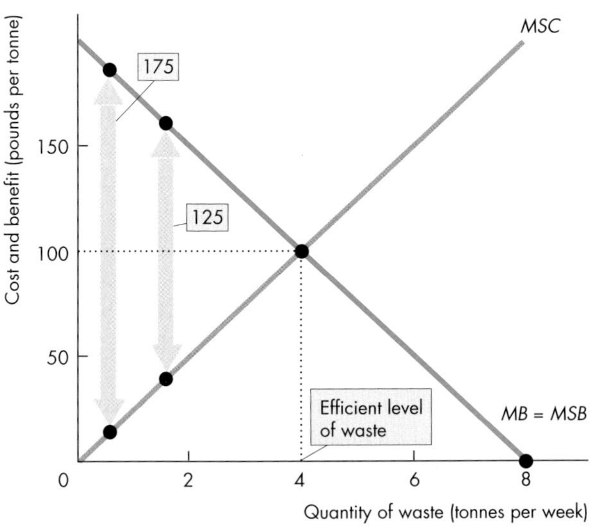

(a) Marginal cost and marginal benefit

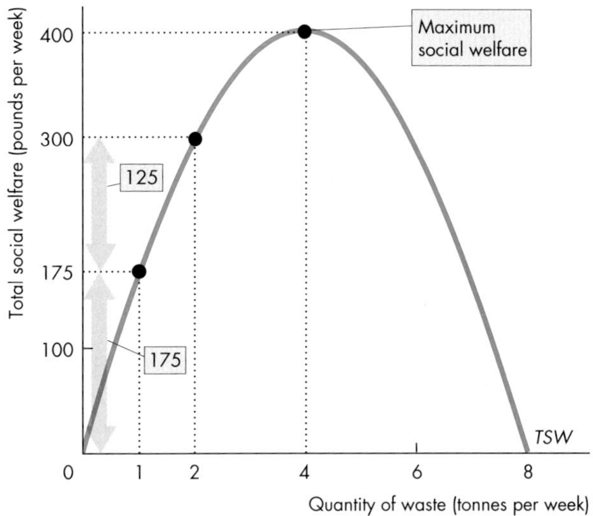

(b) Total social welfare

The *MB* curve in part (a) is the factory's marginal benefit curve which equals marginal social benefit, *MSB*. The *MSC* curve measures the marginal social cost to the fishing club of one additional tonne of waste being dumped in the river. If no one owns the river, the factory maximizes *MB* by dumping 8 tonnes a week. This is inefficient. The efficient level of dumping shown in part (b) is 4 tonnes a week – where *MSB* equals *MSC* and *TSW* is maximized. Using the Coase theorem from part (a), if the polluter owns the river, the victim will pay £400 a week (£100 a tonne × 4 tonnes a week) to the polluter for the assurance that pollution will not exceed 4 tonnes a week. If the victim owns the river, the polluter will pay £400 for pollution rights to dump 4 tonnes a week.

cent of existing landfills will be full by 2010. Some countries such as Japan and the Netherlands have run out of landfills already. The alternatives to landfill are recycling and incineration. Recycling is an apparently attractive alternative, but it requires an investment in new technologies to be effective. Incineration is a high-cost alternative to landfill and it produces air pollution.

We've seen that the demand for a quality environment has grown and we've described the range of environmental problems. Let's now look at the ways these problems can be handled. We'll begin by looking at property rights and how they relate to environmental externalities.

Property Rights and Environmental Externalities

Externalities arise when there are no markets for a good or service because of an *absence* of property rights. **Property rights** are social arrangements that govern the ownership, use and disposal of factors of production and goods and services. In modern societies, a property right is a legally established title that is enforceable in the courts.

You can see that property rights are absent when externalities arise by thinking about the examples we've already reviewed. No one owns the air, the rivers and the oceans. So it is no one's private business to ensure that these resources are used in an efficient way. In fact, there is an incentive to use them more than if there were property rights.

Figure 20.3 shows how an environmental externality arises in the absence of property rights using our earlier example of a chemicals factory which dumps toxic waste upstream from a fishing club. The *MB* curve in part (a) is the factory's marginal benefit curve. It tells us how much an additional tonne of waste dumped into the river is worth to the factory. The marginal value to the firm of dumping waste in the river falls as the quantity increases. If the factory has the property rights, the *MB* curve would also be the firm's demand curve for the use of the river, which is a factor of production. The demand for a factor of production slopes downward because of the law of diminishing returns (see Chapter 15). As there are no external benefits from dumping waste, the *MB* curve is also the marginal social benefit, *MSB*.

The *MSC* curve in part (a) of Figure 20.3 is the marginal social cost of one additional tonne of waste being dumped in the river. It rises as the quantity of waste being dumped increases. The *MSC* curve measures the marginal cost to the fishing club of reduced fish stocks and fish quality as the firm dumps an additional tonne of waste in the river. If the fishing club has the property rights, the *MSC* curve would also be the fishing club's supply curve of river use to the firm. The supply curve slopes upward because the greater the quantity of waste, the smaller is the quantity of fish and the more the club's members are willing to pay for a marginal increase in fish stock and quality.

The factory is upstream from the fishing club and the factory must decide how to dispose of its waste. If no one owns the stream, the marginal cost of waste disposal to the factory is zero. The factory maximizes total benefit – the area under *MB* – by dumping 8 tonnes of waste a week as shown in part (a) of Figure 20.3. The *MSC* curve, shows that the fishing club bears a cost of £200 a tonne when 8 tonnes of waste a week are dumped. So the factory has an incentive to dump 8 tonnes of waste a week because it can ignore the cost borne by the members of the fishing club. Dumping 8 tonnes of waste a week is inefficient and social welfare is not maximized. Let's see why.

The efficient level of dumping waste is 4 tonnes a week, where *MSB* equals *MSC*. This amount generates the maximum level of total social welfare – £400 a week – as shown in part (b) of Figure 20.3. Total social welfare is the difference between total social benefit – the area under the *MSB* curve, and total social cost – the area under the *MSC* curve. Each additional unit of waste dumped adds more to total social benefit than total social cost up to 4 tonnes of waste a week. The first tonne dumped generates £175 of total social welfare. The second tonne dumped adds £125 pounds raising total social welfare to £300 (£175 + £125). After the fourth tonne, each additional tonne of waste dumped adds more to total social cost than to total social benefit, so total social welfare falls. If property rights to the river are not clearly defined, the market will lead to an inefficient amount of dumping of waste – at 8 tonnes a week – and total social welfare will fall to zero.

Sometimes it is possible to correct an externality by establishing a market – creating property rights where they did not exist before. For example, suppose that the property right in the river was assigned by law to the chemicals factory. Because the river is now the property of the factory, the fishing club must pay the factory for the right to fish in the river. But the price that the club is willing to pay depends on the number and quality of fish, which in turn depends on how much waste the factory dumps in the river. The greater the amount of pollution, the smaller is the amount the fishing club is willing to pay for the right to fish. Similarly, the smaller the amount of pollution, the greater is the amount the fishing club is willing to pay for the right to fish. The chemicals factory is now confronted with the cost of its pollution decision. It might still decide to pollute, but if it does it faces the opportunity cost of its actions – foregone revenue from the fishing club.

Suppose that the fishing club, not the chemicals factory, owns the river. In this case, the factory must pay a fee to the fishing club for the right to dump its waste. The more waste it dumps (equivalently, the more fish it kills), the more it must pay. Again, the factory faces an opportunity cost for the pollution it creates – the fee paid to the fishing club.

The Coase Theorem

So does it matter how property rights are assigned? At first thought, the assignment seems crucial, but in 1960, Ronald Coase had a remarkable insight, now known as the Coase theorem. The **Coase theorem** states that if property rights exist and transactions costs are low, private transactions are efficient. In other words, with property rights and low transactions costs, there are no externalities. All the costs and benefits are taken into account by the transacting parties. So it doesn't matter how the property rights are assigned.

You can see the Coase theorem at work by looking again at part (a) of Figure 20.3. At the efficient level of waste – 4 tonnes a week – the fishing club bears a cost of £100 for the last tonne dumped in the river, and the factory gets a benefit of £100 a tonne dumped. If waste disposal is restricted below 4 tonnes a week, an increase in waste disposal benefits the factory more than it costs the club. The factory will bribe the club to put up with more waste disposal and both the club and the factory can gain. If waste disposal exceeds 4 tonnes a week, an increase in waste disposal costs the club more than it benefits the factory. The club will now bribe the factory to cut its waste disposal and again, both the club and the factory can gain. Only when the level of waste disposal is 4 tonnes a week – the efficient level – can neither party do any better.

The outcome is the same regardless of who owns the river. If the factory owns it, the club pays £400 for fishing rights and for an agreement that waste disposal will not exceed 4 tonnes a week. If the club owns the river, the factory pays £400 for the right to dump 4 tonnes of waste a week.

Assigning property rights works in this example because the transactions costs are low. The factory and the fishing club can easily sit down and negotiate the deal that produces the efficient outcome. When property rights are assigned in this way, external factors become *internalized*. Property rights create markets that work like Adam Smith's 'invisible hand' to achieve an efficient outcome – marginal cost equals marginal benefit – with everyone pursuing their own self-interest.

But in many situations transactions costs are high and property rights cannot be enforced. Imagine, for example, the transactions costs of 8 million people who live in Sweden trying to negotiate an agreement with the 5,000 factories in the United Kingdom that emit sulphur dioxide and cause acid rain! In a case such as this, governments resort to alternative methods of coping with externalities. They use a range of policies including:

- Emission charges.
- Emission standards.
- Marketable permits.
- Taxes.

Economics in History on pp. 500–501 reviews some examples of the use of these methods and how ideas about how to cope with externalities have changed. In the United Kingdom, the government has established the Environment Agency (EA), to coordinate and administer the country's environment policies. Let's look at the tools the EA could use and see how they work.

Emission Charges

Emission charges are a method of using the market to achieve efficiency, even in the face of externalities. The government (or the regulatory agency established by the government) sets the emission charges, which are, in effect, a price per unit of pollution. The more pollution a firm creates, the more it pays in emission charges. This method of dealing with environmental externalities is common throughout Europe. For example, in France, Germany and the Netherlands water polluters pay a waste disposal charge.

To work out the emission charge that achieves efficiency, the regulator must determine the marginal social cost and marginal social benefit of pollution. **Marginal social cost** is the marginal cost incurred by the producer of a good – marginal private cost – *plus* the marginal cost imposed on others – the external cost. **Marginal social benefit** is the marginal benefit received by the consumer of a good – marginal private benefit – *plus* the marginal benefit to others – the external benefit. To achieve efficiency, the price per unit of pollution must be set to make the marginal social cost of the pollution equal to its marginal social benefit.

Figure 20.4 illustrates an efficient emissions charge for sulphur dioxide pollution. The marginal benefit of pollution is *MB* and accrues to the polluters alone. It is also the marginal social benefit of pollution, *MSB*, as there is no external benefit. The marginal social cost of pollution is *MSC* and is entirely an external cost, falling on other firms and people who live in the affected country. The efficient level of sulphur dioxide emissions is 10 million tonnes a year – where $MSB = MSC$. This can be achieved by setting an emission charge of £10 per tonne. Polluters carry on increasing emissions until the marginal benefit just equals the charge per tonne.

In practice, it is hard to determine the marginal benefit of pollution. The people who are best informed about the marginal benefit, the polluters, have an incentive to mislead the regulators about the benefit. As a result, if a pollution charge is used, the most likely outcome is for the price to be set too low. For example, in Figure 20.4, the price might be set at £7 per tonne. At this price, polluters find it worthwhile to pay for 15 million tonnes a year. At this level of pollution, the marginal social cost is £15 a tonne and the amount of pollution exceeds the efficient level.

One way of overcoming excess pollution is to impose general emission standards, which dictate the maximum safe quantity of a pollutant in any output of waste. A more sophisticated method is to issue quantitative limits that firms can buy and sell – marketable permits. Let's look at these two methods.

Figure 20.4 Emission Charges

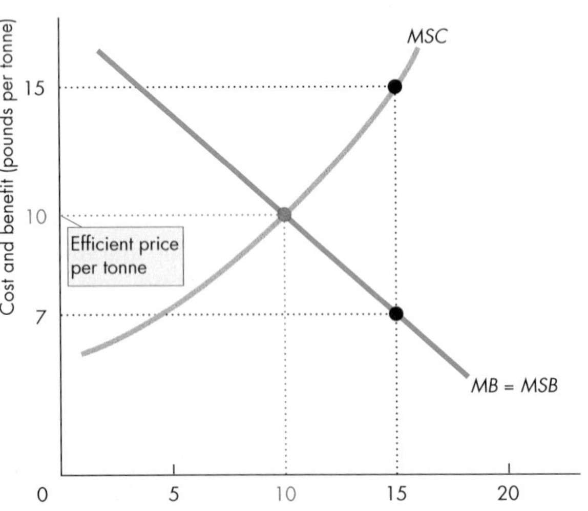

Power stations obtain marginal benefits from sulphur dioxide emissions of *MB* and everyone else bears a marginal social cost of *MSC*. The efficient level of pollution – 10 million tonnes a year in this example – is achieved by imposing an emission charge on power stations of £10 a tonne. If the emission charge is set too low, at £7 a tonne, the resulting amount of pollution is greater than the efficient amount – at 15 million tonnes a year. In this case, the marginal social cost is £15 a tonne, and it exceeds the marginal benefit of £7 a tonne.

Emission Standards

Instead of imposing emission charges on polluters, pollution agencies might set a single emission standard. An **emission standard** is a regulation which limits the quantity of the pollutant in any volume of waste and sets penalties for breaking the regulation. Emission standards for water and air are widely used in the United Kingdom and in the European Union's environmental policy. For example, since 1994, the UK government has set car exhaust emission standards, and all cars over three years old are now tested as part of the annual MOT (Ministry of Transport) certificate. The benefit of using a uniform standard is that it is simple and cheap to apply. The problem is that standards are inefficient. Let's see why.

If firm *H* has a higher marginal benefit than firm *L*, an efficiency gain can be achieved by decreasing the standard for firm *L* and increasing the standard for firm *H*. As it is virtually impossible to determine the marginal benefits of each firm in practice, quantitative restrictions cannot be allocated to each producer in an efficient way. Uniform emission standards will always be inefficient. Despite their inefficiency, standards are widely used because it is easy for producers to comply with a uniform standard. Also, it is often difficult to value the damage caused by pollutants to establish the marginal external cost. Policies that attempt to set a price for pollution cannot succeed unless the value of the marginal external cost is known.

Marketable Permits

Marketable permits are a clever way of overcoming the need for the regulator to know every firm's marginal benefit schedule. Permit trading is a key element of the US Clean Air Acts but has not been implemented in Europe. Each firm can be allocated a permit to emit a certain amount of pollution. Firms may also buy and sell such permits.

Figure 20.5 shows how such a system works and can achieve efficiency. Some firms have low marginal benefits from sulphur emissions, shown as MB_L in part (a). Others have a high marginal benefit, shown as MB_H in part (b). For the economy as a whole, the marginal benefit is MB_E in part (c). The marginal social cost of sulphur emissions is *MSC*, also shown in part (c). The efficient level of emissions is 10 million tonnes a year, the quantity at which marginal social cost equals marginal social benefit.

Suppose the EA allocates permits for a total of 10 million tonnes of sulphur emissions a year. And suppose the permits are allocated equally to the two groups of firms – 5 million tonnes each. The firms in part (a) value their last tonne of pollution permitted at £5. The firms in part (b) value their last tonne of pollution permitted at £15 a tonne. With a market in permits, the firms in part (a) sell some of their permits to those in part (b). Both types of firm gain from the trade.

If the market in permits is competitive, the price at which permits trade is £10 per tonne. At this price, low-benefit firms (part a) sell permits for 3 million tonnes of sulphur emissions to the high-benefit firms (part b). After these transactions, the low-benefit firms (part a) have S_L permits and the high-benefit firms (part b) have S_H permits and the allocation is efficient.

Figure 20.5 Marketable Pollution Permits

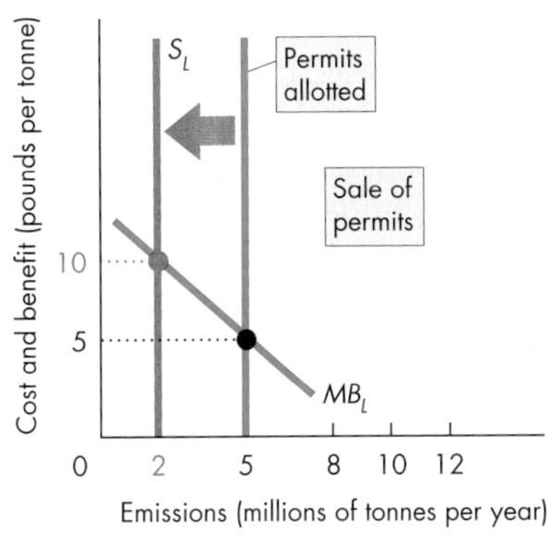

(a) Low-benefit firms

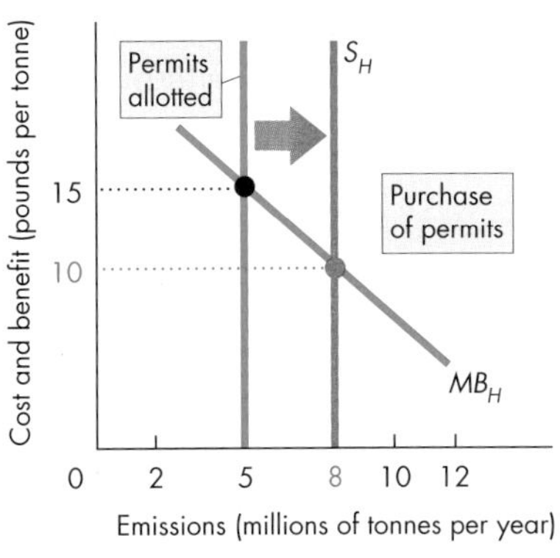

(b) High-benefit firms

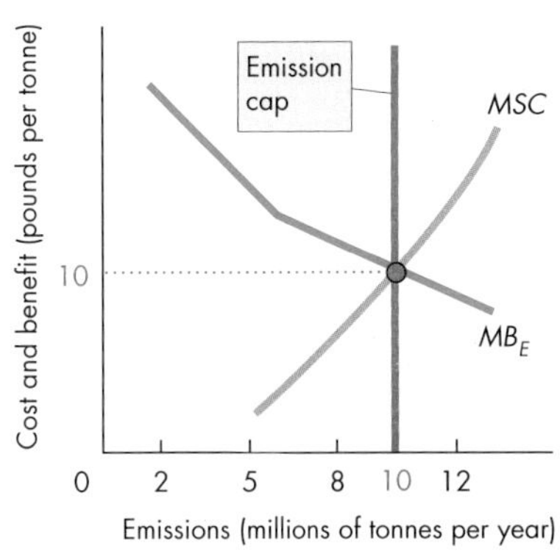

(c) Economy

Some firms obtain low marginal benefits from pollution, MB_L in part (a), and some obtain high marginal benefits, MB_H in part (b). The marginal social cost is *MSC* in part (c). Marginal benefit for the economy is MB_E in part (c). Pollution permits are issued that limit pollution to 10 million tonnes a year (the efficient level) and each type of firm gets the same limit, 5 million tonnes a year. Initially, low-benefit firms value their permits at £5 a tonne and high-benefit firms value their permits at £15 a tonne. High-benefit firms buy permits for 3 million tonnes of pollution from low-benefit firms for a market price of £10 a tonne.

Evidence from the United States suggests that permit trading can be administratively costly if there are a great many polluters. By contrast, if there are only a few polluters, these firms may buy up all available permits and refuse to trade them – leading to a barrier to entry to new firms. Also, permit trading will not lead to the efficient level of emissions in each firm unless the efficient level of total emissions is known to start with. The benefit of permit trading is that for any given level of permits allocated, trading will ensure that they are efficiently distributed between different producers.

Taxes and External Costs

Taxes can be used to provide incentives for producers or consumers to cut back on an activity that creates external costs. A tax used in this way to control pollution is called a **green tax**. The European Union wants to introduce a 'green' tax on carbon fuels in power stations and vehicles because they are a major source of pollution. To see how this type of 'green' tax works, let's look at the market for petrol shown in Figure 20.6. The demand curve for petrol, *D*, is also the marginal benefit curve, *MB*. This curve tells us how much consumers value different amounts of petrol. The curve *MC* measures the marginal *private* cost of using petrol – the costs directly incurred by the producers of these services.

The costs borne by drivers are not the only costs. External costs arise from the urban smog, air toxins and greenhouse gases caused by vehicle emissions. When all the external marginal costs are added to the marginal cost faced by the producer, we obtain the marginal *social* cost of petrol, shown by *MSC* in the figure.

If the petrol market is competitive and unregulated, drivers will balance the marginal cost of petrol, *MC*, against their own marginal benefit, *MB*, and buy Q_0 litres of petrol at a price of P_0 per litre. At this level of petrol use, the marginal social cost is SC_0. The marginal social cost minus the marginal private cost, $SC_0 - P_0$, is the marginal cost imposed on others – the marginal external cost.

Suppose the EU imposes a new 'green' tax on petrol and that it sets the tax equal to the external marginal cost. The tax makes the suppliers of petrol incur a marginal cost equal to the marginal social cost. That is, the marginal private cost plus the tax equals the marginal social cost. The market supply curve is now the same as the *MSC* curve. The price

Figure 20.6 Taxes and Pollution

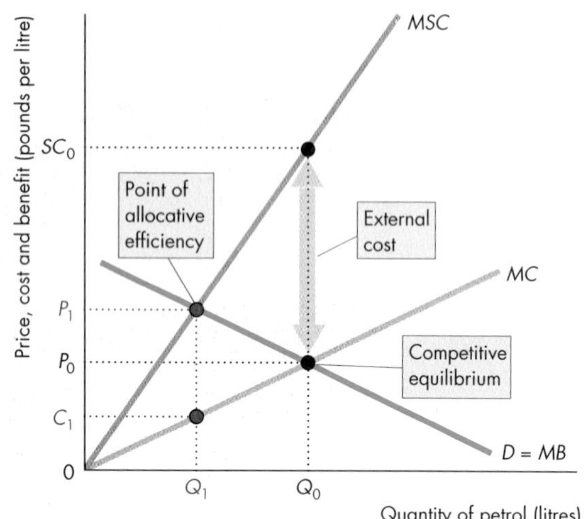

The demand curve for petrol is also the marginal benefit curve ($D = MB$). The marginal cost curve of producing petrol is MC. If the market is competitive, Q_0 litres of petrol are produced and the price is P_0 per litre. The marginal social cost of petrol is shown by the curve MSC. Because of environmental pollution, the marginal social cost of petrol, SC_0, exceeds the marginal private cost, P_0, when the quantity of petrol is Q_0. If the government imposes a tax on petrol supply equal to the external cost, producers face a marginal cost equal to the MSC curve. The price of petrol increases to P_1 per litre and the quantity decreases to Q_1 litres. Allocative efficiency is achieved.

of petrol rises to P_1 a litre and at this price, the quantity bought falls to Q_1. The marginal cost of the resources used in producing Q_1 litres of petrol is C_1, and the marginal external cost is P_1 minus C_1. That marginal external cost is paid by the consumer through the tax.

The situation at the price P_1 and the quantity Q_1 is efficient. At an output rate above Q_1, marginal social cost exceeds marginal benefit, so net benefit increases by decreasing petrol production. At an output rate below Q_1, marginal benefit exceeds marginal social cost, so net benefit increases by increasing petrol production.

A Carbon-fuel Tax? The European Union introduced the idea of a green tax on carbon emissions as part of its new sustainable environmental policy in 1992. The issue is still pressing. Today, annual carbon emissions worldwide are a staggering 6 billion tonnes. By 2050, with current policies, that annual total is predicted to be 24 billion tonnes. If the rich countries used carbon taxes to keep emissions to their 1990 level and the developing countries remove subsidies from coal and oil, total emissions in 2050 might be held at 14 billion tonnes. So why have the European Union and other rich countries worldwide failed to introduce carbon taxes in all states?

Uncertainty About Global Warming Part of the reason we do not have a high, broad-based, carbon-fuel tax is that the scientific evidence that carbon emissions produce global warming is not accepted by everyone. Climatologists are uncertain about how carbon emissions translate into atmospheric concentrations – about how the *flow* of emissions translates into a *stock* of pollution. The main uncertainty arises because carbon drains from the atmosphere into the oceans and vegetation at a rate that is not well understood. Climatologists are also uncertain about the connection between carbon concentration and temperature. Economists are uncertain about how a temperature increase translates into economic costs and benefits. Some economists believe the costs and benefits are almost zero, while others believe that a temperature increase of 3 °C by 2090 will reduce the total output of goods and services by 20 per cent.

Present Cost and Future Benefit Another factor weighing against a large change in fuel use is that the costs would be borne now while the benefits, if any, would accrue many years in the future. To compare future benefits with current costs, we must use an interest rate. If the interest rate is 5 per cent a year, a pound today becomes more than £17,000 in 200 years. So at an interest rate of 5 per cent a year, it is worth spending £1 million today only if this expenditure avoids £17 billion in environmental damage in 2195.

Because large uncertain future benefits are needed to justify small current costs, a general tax on carbon fuels is not a high priority on the political agenda.

International Factors A final factor against a large change in fuel use is the international pattern of the use of carbon fuels. At present, carbon pollution comes in even doses from the industrial

(OECD)[1] countries and the developing countries. But by 2050, three-quarters of the carbon pollution will come from the developing countries (if the trends persist). One reason for the high pollution rate in some developing countries is that their governments *subsidize* the use of coal or oil. These subsidies lower producers' marginal costs and encourage the use of fuel beyond the efficient quantity – and by a large amount.

A Global Warming Dilemma

With the high output rate of greenhouse gases in the developing world, the European Union and the other industrial countries are faced with a global warming dilemma[2]. Decreasing pollution is costly and brings benefits. But the benefits depend on all countries taking action to limit pollution. If the European Union acts alone, other countries will gain benefits, but the European Union bears the cost of limiting pollution and gets almost no benefits. So it is worthwhile taking steps to limit global pollution only if all nations act together.

The global warming dilemma faced by the European Union and the developing countries is shown in Table 20.1. The numbers are hypothetical. Each country (we'll call the developing countries a country) has two possible policies: to introduce a carbon tax or to pollute. If each country pollutes, it receives a zero net return (by assumption) shown in the top-left square in the table. If each country introduces a carbon tax, it bears the cost of using more expensive fuels and gets the benefit of less pollution. Its net return is £25 billion, as shown in the bottom-right square of the table. If the European Union alone introduces a carbon tax, the European Union pays £50 billion more than it benefits and the developing countries benefit by £50 billion more than they pay, as shown in the top-right corner of the table. Finally, if the developing countries alone introduce a carbon tax, they lose £50 billion and the European Union gains £50 billion, as shown in the bottom-left corner of the table.

Table 20.1 A Global Warming Dilemma

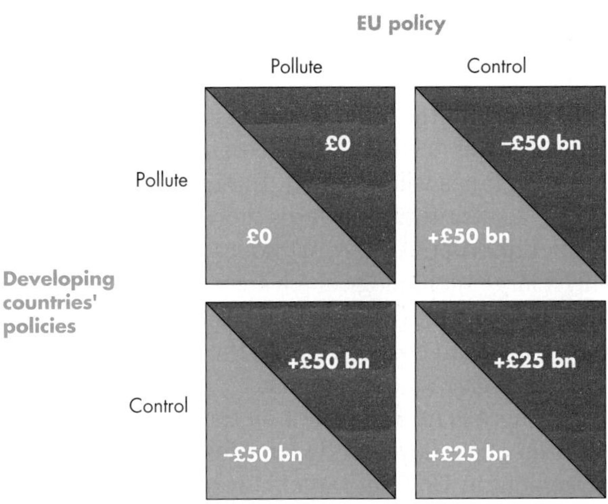

If the European Union and developing countries both pollute, their payoffs are those shown in the top-left square. If neither pollutes, their payoffs are shown in the bottom-right square. When one country pollutes and the other one does not, their payoffs are shown in the top-right and bottom-left squares. The outcome of this game is for both countries to pollute. The structure of this game is the same as that of the prisoners' dilemma (see p. 333).

Confronted with these possible payoffs, the European Union reasons as follows. If the developing countries do not introduce a carbon tax, we break even if we pollute and we lose £50 billion if we introduce a tax. Conclusion, we are better off polluting. If the developing countries introduce a tax, we gain £50 billion if we pollute and £25 billion if we introduce a tax. Again, we are better off polluting. The developing countries reach the same conclusion. So no one introduces a carbon tax and pollution continues unabated.

Treaties and International Agreements

To break the dilemma, international agreements – treaties – might be negotiated. But such treaties must have incentives for countries to comply with their agreements. Otherwise, even with a treaty, the situation remains as we've just described and illustrated in Table 20.1.

One such international agreement is the *climate convention* that came into effect on 21 March 1994.

1 The OECD is the Organization for Economic Cooperation and Development, an international agency based in Paris, the member nations of which include the United States, Canada, Japan and the industrial countries of Western Europe and Australasia.
2 This dilemma is like the 'prisoners' dilemma' that is explained in Chapter 14 on pp. 332–333.

This convention is an agreement among 60 countries to limit their output of greenhouse gases. But the convention does not have economic teeth. The poorer countries are merely asked to list their sources of greenhouse gases. The rich countries must show how, by 2000, they will return to their 1990 emission levels.

To return to the 1990 emission levels, the rich countries will need stiff increases in energy taxes, and such taxes will be costly. Energy taxes will induce a substitution towards more costly but cleaner alternative fuels. Without energy taxes, only a large technological advance in solar, wind, tidal, or nuclear power that makes these sources less costly than coal can create the incentive needed to give up carbon fuels.

But there is no agreement on the use of energy taxes amongst developed countries. The Kyoto agreement in 1997 set targets for reducing six greenhouse gases including carbon dioxide, but it was still not ratified in 1999 . Whilst the European Union is promoting the use of EU-wide energy taxes as the appropriate strategy, the US is still resistant.

Review

- When externalities are present, the market allocation is not efficient.
- If by assigning property rights an externality can be eliminated, an efficient allocation can be achieved.
- With the right information, governments can use emission charges, pollution standards, taxes or permits to induce the efficient quantity of pollution, even in the face of externalities.
- When an externality goes beyond the scope of one country, effective international cooperation is necessary to achieve an efficient outcome.

Economics of Knowledge

Knowledge is both a consumer good and a factor of production. The demand for knowledge – the willingness to pay to acquire knowledge – depends on the marginal benefit it provides to its possessor. As a consumer good, knowledge provides utility and this is one source of its marginal benefit. As a factor of production – part of the stock of capital – knowledge increases productivity and this is another source of its marginal benefit.

Knowledge creates benefits not only for its possessor, but for others as well – external benefits. External benefits arise from education and training – passing on existing knowledge to others. When children learn basic skills at school, they are better able to communicate and interact with each other. Similarly, when people are trained at work, they make better employees for other firms. But when people make decisions about how much schooling to undertake, or when firms decide about how much training to provide, they do not value the external benefits created.

External benefits also arise from research and development activities that lead to the creation of new knowledge. Once someone has worked out how to do something, others can copy the basic idea. They do have to work to copy an idea, so they face an opportunity cost. But (usually) they do not have to pay the person who made the discovery to use it. When Isaac Newton worked out the formulas for calculating the rate of response of one variable to another – calculus – everyone was free to use his method. When a spreadsheet program called VisiCalc was invented, others were free to copy the basic idea. Lotus Corporation developed its 1-2-3 and later Microsoft created Excel and both became highly successful, but they did not pay for the key idea first used in VisiCalc.

When people make decisions about the quantity of education to undertake, or when firms decide on the amount of research and development and training that they provide, they balance the *private* marginal costs against the private marginal benefits. They do not take into account the value of the external benefits. As a result, if we were to leave education, training and research and development to individual market choice we would get too little of these activities. To deliver them in efficient quantities, we make public choices through government policy to modify the market outcome.

Governments can use a range of policies to achieve an efficient allocation of resources in the presence of the external benefits from education and research and development. Three important policies are:

1 Subsidies.
2 Below-cost provision.
3 Patents.

Subsidies

A **subsidy** is a payment made by the government to producers that depends on the level of output. By subsidizing private activities, government can in principle encourage private decisions to be taken in the public interest. A government subsidy programme might alternatively enable private producers to capture resources for themselves. Although subsidies cannot be guaranteed to work successfully, we'll study an example in which they do achieve their desired objective.

Figure 20.7 shows how subsidizing education can increase the amount of education undertaken and achieve allocative efficiency. Suppose that the marginal cost of producing a student–year of college or university education is a constant £10,000. This marginal social cost is shown by the *MSC* curve. We'll assume that all these costs are borne by the colleges and there are no external costs. The maximum price that students (or parents) are willing to pay for an additional year of study determines the marginal private benefit curve and the demand curve for education. This curve is *MPB* = *D*. In this example, a competitive market in private university or college education results in 2 million students being enrolled and tuition fees of £10,000 a year.

Suppose that the external benefit – the benefit derived by people other than those who receive the education – results in external benefits. The marginal social benefit – marginal private benefit plus marginal external benefit – is the curve *MSB*. Allocative efficiency occurs when marginal social cost equals marginal social benefit. In the example in Figure 20.7, this occurs when 4 million students are enrolled. One way of getting 4 million students enrolled is to subsidize private universities or colleges. In our example, a subsidy of £8,000 per student per year paid to the colleges does the job. With a subsidy of £8,000 and marginal cost of £10,000, colleges and universities earn an economic profit on any fee above £2,000. Competition drives the tuition fee down to £2,000 and at this price, the quantity demanded is 4 million. So a subsidy can achieve an efficient outcome.

A subsidy can also be used to increase the stock of knowledge through research and development

Figure 20.7 Efficiency in Education

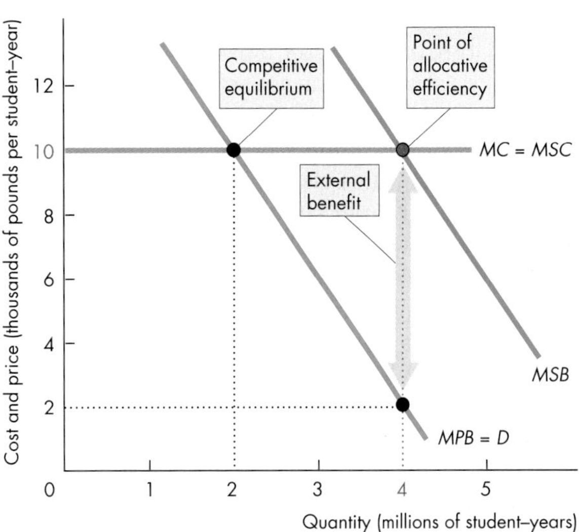

The demand curve for education measures the marginal private benefit of education (*MPB* = *D*). The curve *MSC* shows the marginal social cost of education – in this example, £10,000 per student–year. If college education is provided in a competitive market with no government intervention, tuition is £10,000 a year and 2 million students are enrolled in college. Education produces an external benefit and adding the external benefit to the marginal private benefit gives marginal social benefit, *MSB*. Allocative efficiency is achieved if the government provides education services on a scale such that marginal social cost equals marginal social benefit. This scale of provision is 4 million students a year, which is achieved if the government either subsidizes private colleges or provides education below cost in public colleges. In this example, people pay an annual tuition fee of £2,000 and the government pays £8,000.

in industry and through subsidized training. By subsidizing these activities, the government can move the allocation of resources towards a more efficient outcome. Another way to achieve an efficient amount of education and research and development is through public provision sold below cost.

Below-cost Provision

Instead of subsidizing private colleges and universities, the government can establish public sector colleges and universities that provide schooling below cost. Instead of subsidizing research and development in industry and the universities, the government can establish its own research facilities and make discoveries available to others. Let's see how this approach works by returning to the example in Figure 20.7.

By creating public sector universities with places for 4 million students, the government can supply the efficient quantity of higher education directly. To ensure that this number of places is taken up, the public universities charge a tuition fee, in this example, of £2,000 per student per year. At this price, the number of people who choose to attend college makes the marginal social benefit of education equal to its marginal cost.

In a similar way, government could set up its own research centres to develop technology and test innovations in defence and agriculture, or in health or transport. The government centres would undertake research to create new technology and sell the right to use the technology to private industry at a price below marginal cost. This would ensure that technology is widely transferred throughout industry so that the marginal social benefit of technology use is equal to its marginal cost.

We've now looked at two examples of how government action can help market participants take account of the external benefits deriving from education to achieve an outcome different from that of a private unregulated market. In reality, governments use both methods of encouraging an efficient quantity of education. They subsidize private colleges and universities and run their own institutions, selling their services at below cost. But in education, the public sector is by far the larger. In research and development, subsidies to the private sector are far larger and government provides little direct research.

Patents

Knowledge may well be the only factor of production that does not display *diminishing marginal productivity*. More knowledge (about the right things) makes people more productive. And there seems to be no tendency for the additional productivity from additional knowledge to diminish.

For example, in just 15 years, advances in knowledge about microprocessors has given us a sequence of processor chips that has made our personal computers increasingly powerful. Each advance in knowledge about how to design and manufacture a processor chip has brought apparently ever larger increments in performance and productivity. In the space of 80 years, we have moved from a simple one-seater plane to the most modern Boeing 747, which can carry 400 people halfway around the world non-stop. These examples can be repeated again and again in fields as diverse as agriculture, biogenetics, communications, engineering, entertainment, medicine and publishing.

A key reason why the stock of knowledge increases without diminishing returns is the sheer number of different techniques that can in principle be tried. Paul Romer explains this fact with an amazing example. Suppose, says Romer,

> that to make a finished good, 20 different parts have to be attached to a frame, one at a time. A worker could proceed in numerical order, attaching part one first, then part two . . . Or the worker could proceed in some other order, starting with part ten, then adding part seven . . . With 20 parts, a standard (but incredible) calculation shows that there are about 10^{18} different sequences one can use for assembling the final good. This number is larger than the total number of seconds that have elapsed since the big bang created the universe, so we can be confident that in all activities, only a very small fraction of the possible sequences have ever been tried[3].

Think about all the processes and all the products and all the different bits and pieces that go into each, and you can see that we have only begun to scratch around the edges of what is possible.

---

3 From Paul Romer 'Ideas and Things', in *The Future Surveyed*, a supplement to *The Economist*, 11 September 1993, pp. 71–72. © 1993 The Economist Newspaper Group, Inc. The 'standard calculation' that Romer refers to is the number of ways of selecting and arranging in order 20 objects from 20 objects – also called the number of permutations of 20 objects 20 at a time. This number is *factorial* 20, or $20! = 20 \times 19 \times 18 \times \ldots \times 2 \times 1 = 10^{18.4}$.

A standard theory (challenged by observations made by the Hubble space telescope in 1994) is that a big bang started the universe 15 billion years, or $10^{17.7}$ seconds, ago. Although $10^{18.4}$ and $10^{17.7}$ look similar, $10^{18.4}$ is *five* times as large as $10^{17.7}$, so if you started trying alternative sequences at the moment of the big bang and took only one second per trial you would still have tried only one fifth of the possibilities. Amazing?

Because knowledge is productive and creates external benefits, it is necessary to use government policy to ensure that markets face sufficient incentives to produce the efficient level of effort in invention and innovation. The main way of creating the right incentives is to provide the creators of knowledge with property rights in their discoveries – called **intellectual property rights**. The legal device for creating intellectual property rights is the patent or copyright. A **patent** or **copyright** is a government-sanctioned exclusive right granted to the inventor of a good, service, or productive process, to produce, use and sell the invention for a given number of years. A patent enables the developer of a new idea to prevent, for a limited number of years, others from benefiting freely from an invention. But to obtain the protection of the law, an inventor must make knowledge of the invention public.

Although patents encourage invention and innovation, they do so at an economic cost. While a patent is in place, its holder has a monopoly – generating more market failure. To maximize profit, a monopoly (patent holder) produces the quantity at which marginal cost equals marginal revenue. The monopoly sets the price above marginal cost and equal to the highest price at which the profit-maximizing quantity can be sold. In this situation, consumers value the good more highly (are willing to pay more for one more unit of it) than its marginal cost. So the quantity of the good available is less than the efficient quantity.

But without a patent, less effort is put into developing new goods, services, or processes and the flow of new inventions is slowed. So the efficient outcome is a compromise that balances the social welfare gain of more inventions against the social welfare loss of temporary monopoly power in newly invented activities.

Review

- Knowledge is a good and a factor of production that creates external benefits.
- External benefits arise from education and training – passing on existing knowledge to others; and from research and development – creating new knowledge.
- Government policy can achieve an efficient stock of education and training through subsidies, below-cost provision.
- Subsidies, below-cost provision and patents can deliver an efficient stock of knowledge.
- Knowledge does not seem to have diminishing returns, so government policy is needed to encourage the development of new ideas.
- Patents and copyrights create a temporary monopoly so the gain from more knowledge must be balanced against the loss from monopoly.

When we started looking at government regulations and policy in Chapter 18, pp. 430–451, we identified three reasons for government intervention. You might want to go back to Figure 18.2, p. 433, to remind yourself that governments intervene to reduce the inefficiency caused by market failure, to improve equity and to stabilize the macroeconomic environment. We've now completed our study of the main problems of market failure. We have looked at the inefficiency arising from the provision of public goods, the impact of monopoly and oligopoly in industry and finally, in this chapter, the problems of externalities. We've also seen that regulation and policies, and even the politicians and bureaucrats who supply them, can lead to inefficiency. So efficient intervention must balance the benefits of intervention against costs. We've now completed our study of *microeconomics*. We've learned how all economic problems arise from scarcity, that scarcity forces us to make choices and that choice imposes cost – opportunity cost. Prices (*relative prices*) are opportunity costs and are determined by the interactions of buyers and sellers in markets. People choose what goods to buy and what factors of production to sell to maximize utility. Firms choose what goods to sell and what factors to buy to maximize profit. People and firms interact in markets, but the resulting equilibrium is inefficient because of market failure and often unfair because of the resulting distribution of incomes and wealth. Government policy can raise social welfare by modifying the market outcome to provide public goods, redistribute income and wealth, curb monopoly and cope with externalities, uncertainty and limited information.

Summary

Key Points

Externalities and Government Policy (p. 480)

- External costs and external benefits create inefficiency.
- Government policy can be used to reduce the impact of external costs and benefits and raise social welfare.

Economics of the Environment (pp. 480–490)

- Popular discussion of the environment frames the debate in terms of right and wrong, but economists emphasize costs and benefits and a need to find a way to balance the two.
- The demand for environmental policies has grown because incomes have grown and awareness of the connection between actions and the environment has increased.
- Air pollution in the form of urban smog, air toxins, acid rain, global warming, and ozone layer depletion arise from road transport, power stations and industrial processes.
- Externalities (environmental and others) arise when property rights are absent. Sometimes it is possible to overcome an externality by assigning a property right.
- The Coase theorem states that private market transactions are efficient – there are no externalities. In this case, the same efficient outcome is achieved regardless of who has the property right, the polluter or the victim.
- When property rights cannot be assigned, governments might overcome environmental externalities by using emission charges, uniform standards, marketable permits, or taxes.
- Standards are inefficient but widely used because it is difficult to identify the information needed to set efficient charges, permits or taxes.
- Global externalities, such as greenhouse gases and substances that deplete the earth's ozone layer, can be overcome only by international action. Each country acting alone has insufficient incentive to act in the interest of the world as a whole. There is also a great deal of scientific uncertainty and disagreement about the effects of greenhouse gases and ozone depletion, and in the face of this uncertainty, international resolve to act is weak.
- The world is locked in a type of 'prisoners' dilemma' game in which it is in every country's self-interest to let other countries carry the costs of environmental policies.

Economics of Knowledge (pp. 490–493)

- Knowledge is both a consumer good and a factor of production that creates external benefits.
- External benefits from education – passing on existing knowledge to others – arise because the skills and training equip people to interact and communicate more effectively.
- External benefits from research – creating new knowledge – arise because once someone has worked out how to do something, others can copy the basic idea.
- Governments can use policies to encourage the efficient level of education, training and innovation to take place.
- Three devices are available to governments: subsidies, below-cost provision and patents.
- Subsidies and public provision can achieve an efficient provision of education and training.
- Patents and copyrights create intellectual property rights and increase the incentive to innovate. As patents create a temporary monopoly, the cost must be balanced against the benefit of more inventive activity.

Key Figures

Key Terms

Coase theorem, 484
Copyright, 493
Emission charges, 485
Emission standard, 486
Externality, 480
Green tax, 487
Intellectual property rights, 493
Marginal social benefit, 485
Marginal social cost, 485
Marketable permits, 486
Patent, 493
Property right, 483
Subsidy, 491

Review Questions

1 What are externalities?

2 Give two examples of negative externalities and two examples of positive externalities.

3 Why is an external cost a problem?

4 Why is an external benefit a problem?

5 What are the main air pollution problems and what are their sources?

6 What are the main economic activities that cause air pollution?

7 Why has the demand for a better environment increased?

8 What do property rights have to do with externalities?

9 State the Coase theorem. Under what conditions does the Coase theorem apply?

10 Explain why property rights assigned either to the polluter or to the victim of pollution give an efficient amount of pollution if transactions costs are low.

11 What is an emission charge and how does it work?

12 What are the pros and cons of a high, broad-based carbon tax and why don't we have such a tax?

13 What is a marketable pollution permit and how does it work?

14 How might a tax be used to overcome an external cost?

15 What is the global warming dilemma?

16 Why are emission standards inefficient and why are they widely used?

17 Is the efficient rate of pollution zero? Explain your answer.

18 What are the externalities problems posed by knowledge?

19 Why do we have free schooling?

20 Why might government want to subsidise research in universities?

21 What is a patent and how does it work?

22 Explain how a patent works.

Problems

1 A trout farmer and a pesticide maker are located next to each other on the side of a lake. The pesticide maker can dispose of waste by dumping it in the lake or by transporting it to a safe land storage place. The marginal cost of road haulage is a constant £100 a tonne. The trout farmer's profit depends on how much waste the pesticide maker dumps in the lake and is as follows:

Quantity of waste (tonnes per week)	Trout farmer's profit (pounds per week)
0	1,000
1	500
2	300
3	200
4	150
5	125
6	110
7	100

a What is the efficient amount of waste to be dumped in the lake?

b If the trout farmer owns the lake, how much waste will be dumped and how much will the pesticide maker pay to the farmer for each tonne dumped?

c If the pesticide maker owns the lake, how much waste will be dumped and how much will the farmer pay to the factory to rent space on the lake?

2 Using the information given in Problem 1, suppose that no one owns the lake, and that the government introduces a pollution charge.

a What is the price per tonne of waste dumped that will achieve an efficient outcome?

b Explain the connection between the answer to this Problem and the answer to Problem 1.

3 Using the information given in Problem 1, suppose that no one owns the lake, and that the government issues marketable pollution permits to both the farmer and the factory. They may each dump equal amounts of waste in the lake and the total that may be dumped is the efficient amount.

a What is the quantity that may be dumped in the lake?

b What is the market price of a permit? Who buys and who sells?

c What is the connection between the answer to this Problem and the answers to Problems 1 and 2?

4 A steel smelter is located at the edge of a residential area. The table shows the cost of cutting the pollution of the smelter. It also shows the property taxes that residents are willing to pay at different levels of pollution. Assume that the increase in property taxes that residents are willing to pay measures the change in total benefit of cleaner air that results from a change in the percentage cut in pollution levels.

Pollution Level Cut (percentage)	Property taxes willingly paid (£ per day)	Total Cost of Pollution Cut (£ per day)
0	0	0
10	150	10
20	285	25
30	405	45
40	510	70
50	600	100
60	675	135
70	735	175
80	780	220
90	810	270
100	825	325

a What is the efficient percentage cut in pollution?

b With no regulation of pollution, how much pollution would there be?

c If the town owns the smelter, how much pollution would there be?

d If the smelter owns the town, how much pollution would there be?

5 Using the information given in Problem 4, suppose that the town government introduces a pollution charge.

a What is the tax per percentage waste dumped that will achieve an efficient outcome?

b Explain the connection between the answer to this problem and the answer to Problem 4.

6 Using the information given in Problem 4, suppose that the town government issues marketable pollution permits to both the residents and the smelter. Each may pollute the are by the same percentage, and the total is the efficient amount.

a What is the efficient percentage of pollution?
b What is the market price of a permit? Who buys and who sells?
c What is the connection between the answer to this problem and the answers to Problems 4 and 5?

7 The marginal cost of educating a student is £5,000 a year and is constant. The marginal private benefit schedule is as follows:

Quantity of education (student–years)	Marginal private benefit (pounds per student–year)
0	10,000
1,000	5,000
2,000	3,000
3,000	2,000
4,000	1,500
5,000	1,250
6,000	1,100
7,000	1,000

a With no government involvement in education and if the colleges are competitive, how many students are enrolled in college and what is the annual tuition fee?
b Suppose the external benefit from education is £4,000 per student–year and is constant. If the government provides the efficient amount of education, how many college places does it offer and what is the annual tuition fee?

8 Use the links on the Parkin, Powell and Matthews Web site to get two viewpoints on global warming. Then answer the following questions:

a What are the benefits and costs of greenhouse gas emissions?
b Do you think the environmentalists are correct in the view that greenhouse gas emissions must be cut or do you think the costs of reducing greenhouse gas emissions exceed the benefits? Explain your answer.
c If greenhouse gas emissions are to be reduced, should reductions be achieved by assigning quotas or by using the price mechanism?

9 Use the Parkin, Powell and Matthews Web site to visit the Environment Agency and then answer the following questions:

a Describe the trend in emissions of carbon dioxide and sulphur dioxide into the atmosphere for all UK sources over the past 20 years.
b Describe the trend in nitrogen oxides and volatile organic compounds into the atmosphere for all UK sources over the past 20 years.
c Do these figures give any indication of the success of environmental policies to control emissions?

10 To decrease the amount of overfishing in their territorial waters, the governments of Iceland and New Zealand have introduced private property rights with an allocation of Individual Transferable Quotas (ITQs). To check out the effects of this system, use the link on the Parkin, Powell and Matthews Web site to visit the Fraser Institute in Vancouver. Then answer the following questions:

a Would the introduction of ITQs in the United Kingdom help to replenish UK fish stocks?
b Explain why ITQs generate an incentive not to overfish.
c Who would oppose ITQs and why?

W http://www.econ100.com

Externalities and Oil Spills

The Guardian, 16 January 1999

Port fined £4m for oil tanker spill

Geoffrey Gibbs

Milford Haven Port Authority was fined a record £4 million for the huge spill three years ago that polluted long stretches of the environmentally sensitive south-west Wales coast and caused millions of pounds of damage to the region's tourism and fishing industries.

Around 72,000 tonnes of crude oil poured into the sea after the Russian-crewed tanker ran aground at the entrance to Milford Haven on February 15, 1996, while being taken into harbour by an inexperienced pilot.

The clean-up operation cost at least £60 million.

This week the port authority pleaded guilty at Cardiff crown court to one charge under the Water Resources Act of causing polluting matter to enter controlled waters.

Ed Gallagher, chief executive of the Environment Agency, which brought the prosecution, said the penalty imposed by Mr Justice Steel made it a good day for those concerned about the environment. It would send a strong signal to those who produced and transported oil that they must take more care.

Mr Justice Steel told the authority that a substantial fine was needed "to reflect the genuine and justified public concern" about the incident.

The previous largest fine in a pollution case in Britain was £1 million paid by Shell UK in 1990 after 150 tonnes of crude oil leaked from a pipeline into the River Mersey.

The judge said the Sea Empress had run aground because of the "careless" navigation of a port authority pilot, who had never before attempted to take a vessel of similar size into the harbour close to low tide.

"The pilot was put in a position by the port authority where he could make an error of navigation," he said. It was significant that the authority had since reviewed its grading, training and examination of pilots.

The authority — a public trust whose chairman and certain other board members are appointed by the transport secretary — said that with costs and legal fees it was facing a bill of £6 million.

The Essence of the Story

- Milford Haven Port Authority was fined a record fine of £4 million for the oil spill disaster that polluted the environmentally sensitive coast of south-west Wales and damaged the local fishing and tourism industry.
- About 72,000 tonnes of crude oil was spilled into the sea when a tanker ran aground while being taken into harbour by an inexperienced pilot.
- The Environment Agency brought a case against the port authority under the Water Resources Act, following a £60 millon clean-up operation.
- The record fine sends strong signals to crude oil transporters that they must take more care and that the public is genuinely concerned.
- The accident occurred because the pilot was inexperienced. The port authority has since changed its training programmes.

Economic Analysis

■ The oil spill caused external costs in terms of damage to the environment and damage to the fishing and tourism industries. The total cost of the clean-up operation was £60 million.

■ Figure 1 shows the impact of external costs on efficiency. The marginal social benefit of transporting oil is shown as *MSB* and the marginal social cost, *MSC*, is the sum of marginal private costs, *MPC*, and marginal external costs, *MEC*.

■ Port authorities and tanker companies make decisions about how much oil to transport by equating their private (or production) costs, *MPC*, with the marginal social benefit, transporting oil, MSB, at quantity Q_1 and price P_1. The total external cost is valued at £60 million, the cost of the clean-up.

■ Figure 2 shows the inefficiency associated with external costs. The level of total social welfare associated with Q_1 is lower at point TSW_a than the level associated with point Q_3. Q_3 is the efficient point which maximizes social welfare and where *MSB* equals *MSC* in Figure 1.

■ Imposing a record fine on the port authority sends strong signals to take more care. The fine raises the marginal private cost to the port authority to *MPC* + fine as shown in Figure 1 but because the fine is less than the marginal external cost, it does not make *MPC* equal *MSC*.

■ Figure 1 shows that an increase in the *MPC* to *MPC* + fine raises the price of transporting oil and reduces the quantity of oil transported towards the efficient level.

■ A high fine also raises the perceived *MPC* to other tanker operators and port authorities if they believe the agency will take action against them for similar spills.

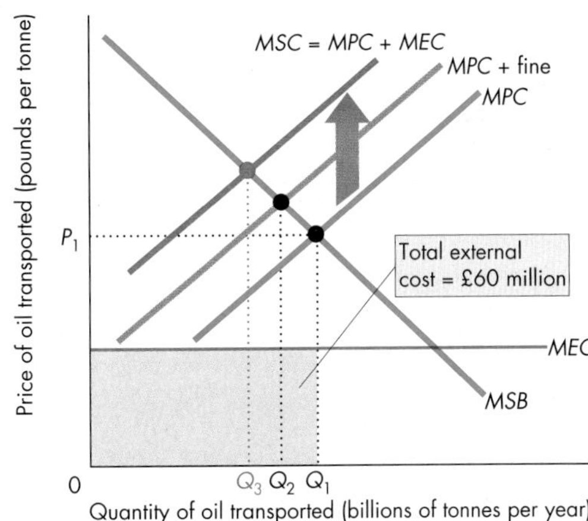

Figure 1 Externalities from oil spills

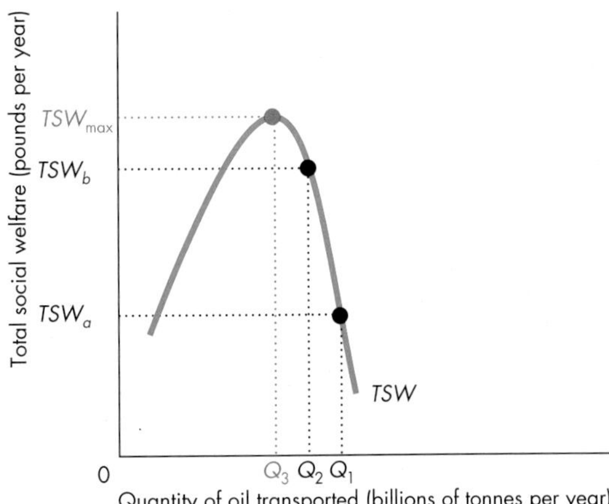

Figure 2 Maximizing social welfare

Understanding Externalities

"The question to be decided is: is the value of fish lost greater or less than the value of the product which contamination of the stream makes possible?"

Ronald H. Coase *The Problem of Social Cost*

The Economist: Ronald Coase

Ronald Coase (1910–), was born in England and educated at the London School of Economics, where he was deeply influenced by his teacher, Arnold Plant, and by the issues of his youth: Communist central planning versus free markets.

Professor Coase has lived in the United States since 1951. He first visited America as a 20-year-old on a travelling scholarship during the depths of the Great Depression. It was on this visit, and before he had completed his bachelor's degree, that he conceived the ideas that 60 years later were to earn him the 1991 Nobel Prize for Economic Science. He discovered and clarified the significance of transaction costs and property rights for the functioning of the economy. Ronald Coase has revolutionized the way we think about property rights and externalities and has opened up the growing field of law and economics.

The Issues and Ideas

As knowledge accumulates, we are becoming more sensitive to environmental externalities. We are also developing more sensitive methods of dealing with them. But all the methods involve a public choice.

Urban smog, which is both unpleasant and dangerous to breathe, forms when sunlight reacts with emissions from the exhausts of motor vehicles. Because of this external cost, we set emission standards and tax petrol. Emission standards increase the cost of a vehicle, and petrol taxes increase the cost of the marginal kilometre travelled. The higher costs decrease the quantity demanded of road transportation and so decrease the amount of pollution it creates. Is the value of cleaner urban air worth the higher cost of transportation? The public choices of voters, regulators and law-makers answer this question.

Acid rain, which imposes a cost on everyone who lives in its path, falls from sulphur-laden clouds produced by electric utility chimneys. This external cost is being tackled with a market solution. This solution is marketable permits, the price and allocation of which are determined by the forces of supply and demand. Private choices determine the demand for pollution permits, but a public choice determines the supply.

As cars stream onto a motorway at morning rush hour, the motorway clogs and becomes an expensive car park. Each rush-hour traveller imposes external costs on all the others. Today, road users bear private congestion costs but do not face a share of the external congestion costs they create. But a market solution to this problem is now technologically feasible. It is a solution that charges road users a fee similar to a toll that varies with the time of day and degree of congestion. Confronted with the social marginal cost of their actions, each road user makes a choice and the market for motorway space is efficient. Here, a public choice to use a market solution leaves the final decision about the degree of congestion to private choices.

Then . . .

The River Thames had a reputation in early Victorian times for sustaining many aspects of commercial trade, including fishing. However, as the nineteenth century progressed, the number of factories sited near the river and using it as a dumping ground for waste products increased greatly. The result was a decline in fish stocks, particularly in salmon, until the 1940s when the Thames became incapable of sustaining a viable fish stock.

. . . And Now

Today, the Thames supports a diverse fish stock including the occasional salmon just as it did many years ago. The river is no longer viewed as a conduit for rubbish, industrial waste and chemicals and the result is a burgeoning ecosystem including many nesting birds. Pollutants are recognized as having potential externalities and the Department for the Environment is enforcing much more stringent laws regarding dumping. The imposition of penalities has shown how the River Thames' externality problem has been reduced by government regulation.

Trying These Ideas Today

Using your knowledge of environmental economics from Chapter 20, and what you have read about the success of environmental policy, you should be able to answer the following questions:

- Ronald Coase was the first economist clearly to explain the underlying cause of external costs of pollution. Why did the lack of clearly defined property rights to clean water cause the River Thames to become so polluted?
- How do the pollution fines and environmental standards imposed on modern industry around the River Thames today affect property rights to clean water?
- The technology now exists to fit cars with electronic tags to charge for the use of roads. How will this technology affect the property rights to accessing roads?

Part 7

Macroeconomics and Fundamentals

Talking with **Alan Walters**

Sir Alan Arthur Walters is Vice-Chairman of AIG Trading Corporation. He was previously Professor of Economics at the Johns Hopkins University, Baltimore, Maryland, from 1976 until 1991, and Personal Economic Adviser to the Prime Minister (on secondment), 1981–84 and 1989. He was born in 1926 and educated at Alderman Newton's Secondary School, Leicester, and University College, Leicester (now the University of Leicester). He was appointed Professor of Econometrics and Head of the Department of Econometrics and Social Statistics at the University of Birmingham in 1961. Subsequently he was Sir Ernest Cassel Professor of Economics in the University of London (at the LSE), 1968–76. Since 1984, he has been a Senior Fellow at the American Enterprise Institute.

Among his numerous appointments, Professor Walters has held visiting professorships at the University of Virginia (Autumn 1966), the Massachusetts Institute of Technology (1967), and Monash University, Melbourne (1970). He was Economic Adviser to the World Bank, 1976–80, 1984–88.

He has contributed widely to professional and learned journals, and his books (as author, contributor or editor) include: *Growth without Development* (1966); *The Economics of Road User Charges* (1968); *An Introduction to Econometrics* (1969, 2nd edn 1971); *The Economics of Ocean Freight Rates* (1969); *Noise and Prices* (1974); *Microeconomic Theory* (1977); *Port Pricing and Investment Policy for Developing Countries* (1979); and *Britain's Economic Renaissance* (1986).

Who are the economists that have inspired you?

The great one, of course, is Milton Friedman. I am also a great admirer of Alfred Marshall. Going back even further the great economist was David Hume, and Adam Smith, but David Hume is my favourite.

You became well known as Chief Economics Adviser to Mrs Thatcher, the Prime Minister in the 1980s. What did you find interesting about working for Mrs Thatcher?

The most interesting thing was that she had both moral and intellectual integrity. You could depend on her. She would listen to an argument. If you won the argument with her, you won it. You won the argument on your reasoning.

As an economist, how would you describe yourself?

My main interest is in policy. In the past I have been interested in the quantification of economics such as the measurement of production functions and transport economics. Since 1957 I also worked on monetary economics and on microeconomics. I have had a lot of interests really. I was on the Roskill Commission on London's Third Airport when Cost-Benefit was in its heyday and, of course, I have done a lot of work with the World Bank on Cost-Benefit.

The economic policies initiated under Mrs Thatcher have been described as Thatcherism. Is there such a thing as Thatcherism? What is it?

Oh yes. I think it is quite marked. The first element of Thatcherism was the 1981 budget which was the opposite of a Keynesian budget. It marked a watershed because I don't think we will ever go back to a Keynesian analysis. The main task was to get the financial sector right, to get financial confidence and credibility in financial markets. We had had almost a decade of government budget deficits of 7 per cent of GDP. To get down to about 3–3.5 per cent deficit was I think the start of Thatcherism. Then we could do all sorts of things. We could do privatization. Deregulation particularly of financial markets and also the turnaround in industry where essentially we said, 'don't ask us to bail you out' as you have done in the past. You are on your own. Just as important was the deregulation of the labour market. All those things add up to a sea change in British economic policy. Of course, there were traces of it before such as Healey's budget but the trouble was that he gave up so quickly whereas Mrs Thatcher carried on.

Was there ever a Thatcher economic miracle?

Miracle is a bit exaggerated I think. But considering that there was a considerable turnaround and you can see it in the growth figures from the 1981 budget onwards, there was a continuous expansion for 9 years. Much longer than any other expansion in history. Productivity growth took off. The rate of inflation went down by the end of 1982 to less than 5 per cent. It wobbled around then for the rest of the decade. True, most of the OECD started introducing disinflationary policies during the 1980s. But if you look at the European countries outside the ERM, Sweden and so on, reduced their inflation even faster than those in the ERM.

Some economists have a theorem or a law named after them, you have a 'critique' named after you. What is the Walter's critique?

Basically, if you have a pegged exchange rate system, then you essentially give up monetary policy. In the extreme case, monetary policy is determined by the interest rate parity. Then you cannot use monetary policy to fight inflation. Even worse, you get inflationary countries adopting even more deflationary policies, and deflationary countries adopting highly restrictive monetary policies. In other words it induces perverse monetary policies. The transmission mechanism works through capital movements. Let's say Britain is inflating at 10% and Germany at zero. In a steady state of course there is devaluation each year of 10% and the 10% devaluation is consistent then with inflation. Now, let us peg sterling to the DM. If German interest rates were 2%, and British interest rates were 12% (both with real interest rates of 2%) before, then this is going to tempt portfolio holders out of deutschemarks into sterling so you get a flood of capital from Germany to the UK. Now this will not go on for ever and after a while exchange rates will have to adjust, then you get the capital flow going the other way. It is massive capital flows, we have seen with the break up of the ERM and recently in the far east. The point is, it induces perverse monetary policies. Say, if Britain has the same interest rate as Germany, say 6% she still has a negative 4% real interest rate. Germany has positive real interest rates, quite big ones too. So your monetary policy is doing the opposite of what you want.

How do you use your economics in your business today?

Generally speaking you are concerned with whether a country is running a good policy or a bad policy and where it is likely to go and whether it will lead to pressures on the exchange rate, devaluation or interest rate rises or both and how they are going to develop. So really the concentration is on macroeconomic policy – fairly short term too. I am reluctant, however, to do any forecasting, largely because I do not think I am any good at it . . . but there are those who disagree.

What advice would you give a student starting out on an economics degree today?

Firstly I would advise them to think concretely. When I say think concretely I mean apply elementary demand and supply analysis in a sophisticated way. It is difficult, but so rewarding . . .

A First Look at Macroeconomics

After studying this chapter you will be able to:

- Describe the origins of macroeconomics and the problems it deals with
- Describe the long-term trends and short-term fluctuations in economic growth, unemployment, inflation and the balance of international payments
- Explain why economic growth, unemployment, inflation and the balance of international payments are important
- Identify the macroeconomic policy challenges and describe the tools available for meeting them

Overheating?

During the past 100 years, the quantity of goods and services produced in the United Kingdom has increased by 550 per cent. In 1997, production expanded more quickly than the average. This rapid growth raised fears that the economy was overheating. How does an economy overheat? Why was rapid economic growth feared? Isn't more output always a good thing? ◆ One reason overheating was feared is because it was thought that output growth was faster than the economy's capacity to sustain that growth. Another reason was the decrease in unemployment to two million. But how can the economy be overheating when so many people are unemployed? Why can't *everyone* who wants a job find one? ◆ Prices have increased slowly in recent years. But with rapid production growth and falling unemployment, it was feared that inflation might break out again. That's what overheating means – an economy growing so quickly that inflation increases. What exactly is inflation, and why does it matter? ◆ A consequence of an overheated economy is that it sucks in goods and services from abroad on a large scale and brings a larger balance of international payments deficit. Why does it matter if we have a balance of payments deficit? ◆ To prevent the economy from overheat- ing and inflation increasing, the Bank of England or the government may take preventive action. What kinds of actions does the government or the Bank of England take? How do those actions influence production, jobs, inflation and the ability of people to compete in the global marketplace?

◆ ◆ ◆ ◆ These questions are the subject matter of macroeconomics – the branch of economics that seeks to understand economic growth, unemployment, inflation and the balance of international payments and to design policies to improve macroeconomic performance. The macroeconomic events through which we are now living are tumultuous and exciting. With what you learn in these chapters, you will be able to understand these events, the policy challenges they bring and the political debate they stir. ◆ Let's begin by looking at the origins of macroeconomics and the key issues it deals with.

Origins and Issues of Macroeconomics

Economists began to study long-term economic growth, inflation and international payments as long ago as the 1750s, and this work was the beginning of macroeconomics. But modern macroeconomics emerged much later, as a response to the **Great Depression**, a decade (1929–39) of high unemployment and stagnant production throughout the world economy. In the United Kingdom, the Great Depression came on top of an existing situation of slump and mass unemployment. In the worst year, 1931, total production fell by over 5 per cent and in the following year unemployment reached a record 15 per cent of the workforce. These were years of human misery on a scale that is hard to imagine today. A deep pessimism about the ability of the market economy to work properly was created. Many people believed that the experience of mass unemployment demonstrated that the economic system of private ownership and free markets was a failure. The perceived failure was so extreme that it raised the deeply disturbing question of whether liberal–democratic political institutions could survive.

The economic dogma of the period had no solutions. The major alternative economic system of central planning and the political system of socialism seemed increasingly attractive to many people. It was in this climate of economic depression and political and intellectual turmoil that macroeconomics emerged. Its origin was the publication in 1936 of John Maynard Keynes' *The General Theory of Employment, Interest, and Money* (see *Economics in History* on pp. 526–527).

Short-term versus Long-term Goals

Keynes' theory was that depression and high unemployment result from insufficient private spending and that to cure these problems, the government must increase its spending. Keynes' focus was primarily the *short term*. He wanted to cure an immediate and serious problem almost regardless of what the *long-term* consequences of the cure might be. 'In the long run', said Keynes, 'we're all dead'.

But Keynes believed that after his cure for depression had restored the economy to a normal condition, the long-term problems of inflation and economic growth would become the central ones. He even suspected that his cure for depression, increased government spending, might trigger inflation and also might lower the long-term growth rate of production. With a lower long-term growth rate, fewer jobs would be created. If this outcome did occur, a policy aimed at lowering unemployment might end up increasing it in the long run.

By the late 1960s and through the 1970s, these long-term concerns became a reality. Inflation increased, economic growth slowed down, and in some countries unemployment became persistently high. The causes of these developments are complex. But they point to an inescapable conclusion: the long-term issues of inflation, slow growth and persistent unemployment and the short-term issues of depression and economic fluctuations intertwine, and are most usefully studied together. So although macroeconomics was reborn during the Great Depression, it has today returned to its older tradition. Nowadays, it is a subject that tries to understand the long-term issues of economic growth and inflation as well as short-term economic fluctuations and the unemployment these fluctuations bring.

The Road Ahead

There is no unique way to study macroeconomics. Because its rebirth was a product of economic depression, it was common for many years to pay most attention to short-term output fluctuations and unemployment. But long-term issues were never completely forgotten. During the late 1960s and 1970s, when a serious inflation emerged, this topic returned to prominence. Rising inflation in this period was coupled with a slowing down in long-term growth and rising unemployment. A new word had come into being to describe this phenomenon – **stagflation**. Economists redirected their energy towards tackling this problem. In the 1990s, when information technologies have shrunk the globe, the international dimension of macroeconomics has become more prominent. The result of all these events is that modern macroeconomics is a broad subject that pays attention to all the issues we've just reviewed: long-term economic growth, unemployment, inflation and international economic activity.

Over the past 40 years, economists have developed a clearer understanding of the forces that determine macroeconomic performance and they have devised policies that, while imperfect, stand some chance of preventing the extremes of depression and inflation. Your main goal is to become familiar with the theories of macroeconomics and the policies they make possible. To set you on your path towards this goal, we're going to take a first look at the macroeconomic issues of economic growth, unemployment, inflation and the balance of international payments and learn why they are problems that merit our attention.

Economic Growth

Your parents are richer than your grandparents were when they were young. But are you going to be richer than your parents? And are your children going to be richer than you? The answers depend on the rate of economic growth.

Economic growth is the expansion of the economy's capacity to produce goods and services. It is an expansion of the economy's production possibilities and can be pictured as an outward shift of the production possibility frontier (*PPF*) (see Chapter 3, pp. 43–46).

We measure economic growth by the increase in real gross domestic product. **Real gross domestic product** (also called **real GDP**) is the value of *aggregate* or *total* production – the output of all the country's farms, factories, shops and offices – measured in the prices of a single year. At the present time, real GDP in the United Kingdom is measured in prices that prevailed in 1990 (1990 prices). We use the prices of a single year so that we can eliminate the influence of *inflation* – the increase in prices – and determine how much production has grown from one year to another. (The concept of real GDP is explained more fully in Chapter 22 on pp. 543–547.)

Real GDP is not a perfect measure of total production. For example, it does not include the things we produce for ourselves such as do-it-yourself jobs (DIY) in the home or other housework. Nor does it include things people produce that is illegal or is legal but unrecorded so as to avoid taxes – known as the underground economy. But despite its shortcomings real GDP is the broadest measure of total production available. What does it tell us about economic growth in the United Kingdom and other countries in Europe?

Economic Growth in the United Kingdom

Figure 21.1 shows real GDP in the United Kingdom since 1960 and it highlights two features of economic growth:

1 The growth of potential GDP.

2 Fluctuations of real GDP around potential GDP.

The Growth of Potential GDP

Potential GDP is the real GDP the economy would produce if all its resources – labour, capital, land and entrepreneurial ability – were fully employed. The rate of long-term economic growth is measured by the steepness of the potential GDP line.

Look closely at Figure 21.1. You can see that there are four trends in potential GDP. The potential GDP line is steeper in the 1960s than in the 1970s and steeper again in the 1980s and again in the 1990s. During the 1960s, potential GDP grew at an average annual rate of 2.9 per cent a year. Growth slowed during the 1970s as a result of a **productivity growth slowdown** – a slowdown in the growth rate of output per person. Growth in potential GDP in the 1970s was at an average of only 2.0 per cent. Faster growth in potential GDP returned during the 1980s and 1990s. Growth in potential GDP in the 1980s was 2.1 per cent and in the 1990s was 2.4 per cent.

Why did the productivity growth slowdown occur? Was the United Kingdom alone in experiencing such an event? Why was the poor productivity performance reversed in the 1980s? What are the consequences of both events?

The two 'why' questions are not easy ones to answer fully. Many factors were at work in the 1970s, but two were critical: oil price shocks and rapid inflation. The oil price shocks of 1973–74 triggered the development of new energy-saving technologies and a high level of investment in energy efficient equipment. But these innovations and investments did not increase labour productivity. The rapid inflation of the 1970s brought increased uncertainty and made it hard for people to make wise long-term investment decisions. This brief explanation of the productivity slowdown is expanded in Chapter 32. The improvement in productivity growth in the 1980s in the United Kingdom may have also been owing to the supply side policies carried out by the government and the return of low inflation.

Figure 21.1 Economic Growth in the United Kingdom: 1960–1998

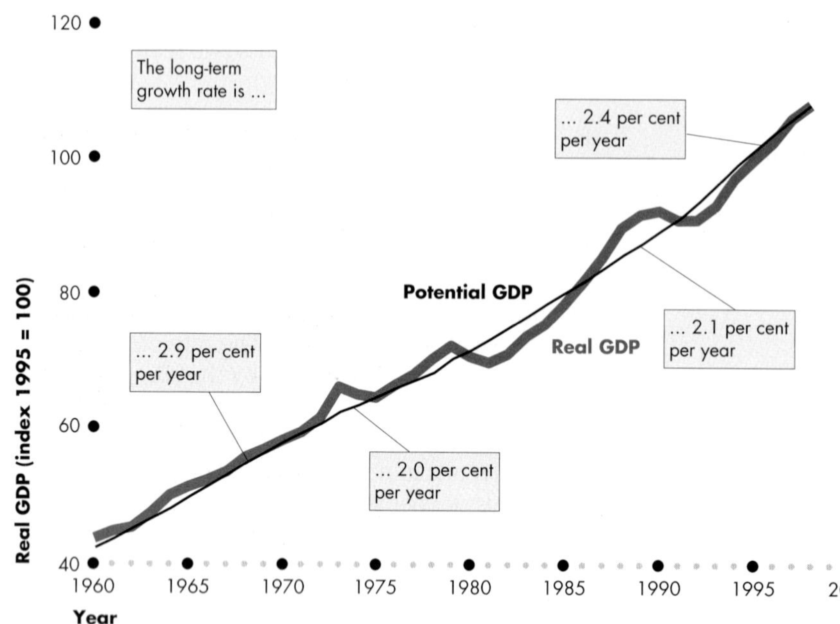

The long-term economic growth rate, measured by the growth of potential GDP, was 2.9 per cent a year during the 1960s but slowed to 2.0 per cent a year during the 1970s, 2.1 in the 1980s and 2.4 per cent in the 1990s. Real GDP fluctuates around potential GDP.

Sources: ONS, *Economic Trends Annual Supplement*, 1998; Lombard Street Research Ltd; estimates of potential GDP are obtained by applying a Hodrick–Prescott Filter.

Was the United Kingdom alone in experiencing a productivity growth slowdown? No. We'll see some other examples later in this chapter when we look at long-term growth around the world. But it was alone in experiencing a productivity growth revival in the 1980s. The consequence is that we have much smaller incomes today than we would have had if productivity growth had not slowed. But let's now look at the second feature of economic growth, namely the fluctuations around trend.

Fluctuations Around Trend Real GDP fluctuates around potential GDP in a business cycle. A **business cycle** is the periodic but irregular up and down movement in economic activity. It is measured by fluctuations in real GDP around potential GDP. When real GDP is less than potential GDP, some resources are underused. For example, some labour is unemployed and capital is underutilized. When real GDP is greater than potential GDP, some resources are being overused. For example, many people are working longer hours than they are willing to put up with in the long run and capital is being worked so intensively that there is no time to keep it in prime working order.

Business cycles are not regular, predictable, or repeating cycles like the phases of the moon. Their timing changes unpredictably. But cycles do have some things in common. Every business cycle has two turning points:

1 Peak.
2 Trough.

and two phases:

1 Recession.
2 Expansion.

Figure 21.2 shows these features of the most recent business cycle. A *peak* is the upper turning point of a business cycle where an expansion ends and a recession begins. A peak occurred in the second quarter of 1990. A *trough* is the lower turning point of a business cycle where a recession ends and a recovery begins. A trough occurred in the first quarter of 1992.

A **recession** is a period during which real GDP decreases – the growth rate of real GDP is negative – for at least two successive quarters. In Figure 21.2,

Figure 21.2 The Most Recent UK Business Cycle

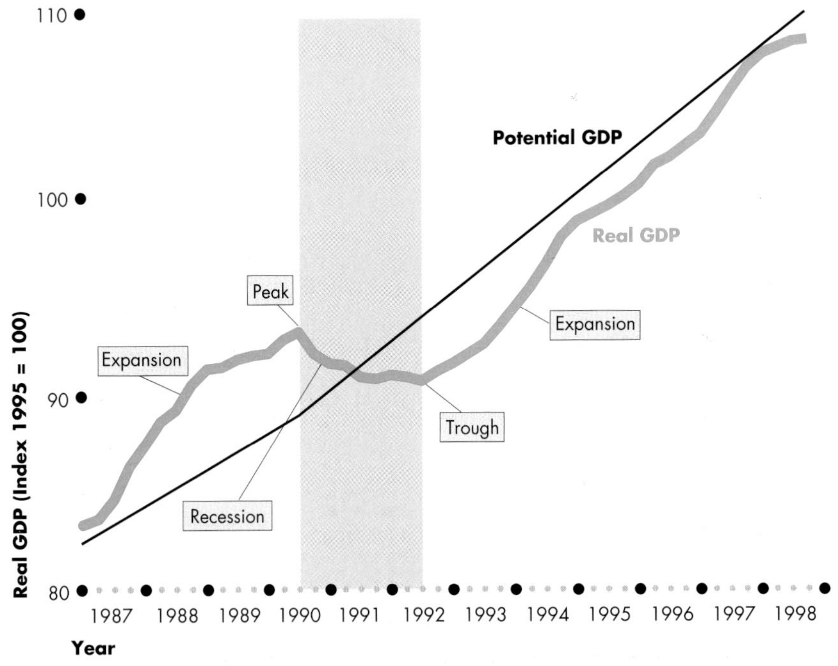

A business cycle has two turning points: a peak and a trough. In the most recent business cycle, the peak occurred in the second quarter of 1990 and the trough occurred in the first quarter of 1992. A business cycle has two phases: recession and expansion. The most recent recession ran from the peak in 1990 to the trough in 1992 as indicated by the pink area on the figure. The expansion ran from the trough in 1992 to end-1998.

Source: ONS.

a recession began in the second quarter of 1990 and ended in the first quarter of 1992.

An **expansion** is a period during which real GDP increases. It begins at a trough and ends at a peak. In Figure 21.2, an expansion ended at the 1990 peak and another expansion began at the 1992 trough.

The Recent Recession in Historical Perspective

The recession of 1990–92 that is shown in Figure 21.2 seemed pretty severe while we were passing through it, but compared with earlier recessions it was relatively mild. You can see how mild it was by looking at Figure 21.3, which shows a longer history of economic growth. The most precipitous decline in real GDP occurred immediately after World War I. A large fall in real GDP also occurred in 1931 and immediately following World War II. In more recent times, milder decreases in real GDP occurred during the mid-1970s – the time of oil price hikes by OPEC – and during the early 1980s and early 1990s.

While each of these economic downturns was considered to be severe at the time, you can see that the downturn that occurred in the interwar period was more severe than anything that followed it. This episode was so extreme that we don't call it a recession. We call it a depression. The term *depression* is used to describe a severe contraction of production that brings extreme and prolonged hardship.

The fact that the last truly great depression occurred before governments started taking policy actions to stabilize the economy (and before the birth of macroeconomics) has led to speculation that perhaps macroeconomics has made a contribution to economic stability. We'll examine this speculation on a number of occasions in this book.

We've seen that real GDP has increased over the long term. We've seen that long-term growth slowed during the 1970s and picked up in the 1980s. We've seen that recessions have interrupted the broad upward sweep of real GDP. Is the UK experience typical? Do other countries share this experience? Let's see if they do.

Economic Growth Around the World

A country might have a rapid growth rate of real GDP, but it might also have a rapid population growth rate. To compare growth rates over time

Figure 21.3 Long-term Economic Growth in the United Kingdom

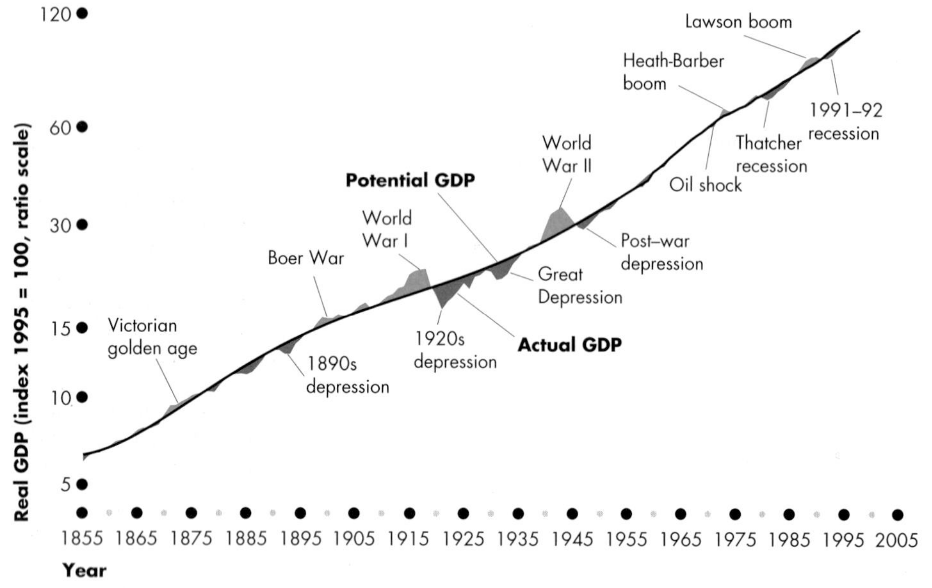

The thin black line shows potential GDP. Along this line, real GDP grew at an average rate of 1.9 per cent a year between 1856 and 1998. The blue areas show when real GDP was above potential GDP and the red areas show when it was below potential GDP. During some periods, such as World War II, real GDP expanded quickly. During other periods, such as the Great Depression and more recently in 1974–75, 1980–81 and 1990–92, real GDP declined.

Sources: GDP 1855–1947: C. H. Feinstein, *National Income Expenditure and Output of the United Kingdom, 1855–1965*, 1972, Cambridge, Cambridge University Press; GDP 1948–1998 Datastream; Potential GDP Lombard Street Research Ltd.

and across countries, we use the growth rate of real GDP *per person*. **Real GDP per person** is real GDP divided by the population.

Figure 21.4 shows the growth of real GDP per person between 1960 and 1996 for four major economies: the United States, Japan, Germany and the United Kingdom. Three features of the paths of real GDP per person stand out:

1 Similar productivity growth slowdowns.
2 Similar business cycles.
3 Different long-term trends in potential GDP.

Similar Productivity Growth Slowdowns The countries shown in Figure 21.4 have experienced similar productivity growth slowdowns. Between 1960 and 1973 UK real GDP growth per person was 2.7 per cent a year, but it slowed to 2.0 per cent in the 1970s and 1980s and 1.3 per cent in the 1990s. In the United States, growth of real GDP per person was 2.9 per cent a year during the 1960s, but it slowed to 1.5 per cent a year during the 1970s and 1980s and 0.9 per cent in the 1990s. In Germany, the growth of real GDP per person slowed from 3.5 per cent a year in the 1960s to 2.0 per cent a year during the 1970s and 1980s and 1.0 per cent in the 1990s. In Japan, the slowdown was more spectacular, from 8.2 per cent a year during the 1960s to 3.1 per cent a year during the 1970s and 1980s and 1.5 per cent in the 1990s.

The slowdown experienced by these economies was also experienced by almost every country. The exceptions were the major oil producers.

Similar Business Cycles The major economies have experienced similar business cycles. Each economy had an expansion running from the early or mid-1960s to 1973, a recession from 1973 to 1975, an expansion to 1979, another recession in the early 1980s, and a long expansion through the rest of the 1980s followed by recession and recovery in the early 1990s.

Like the common productivity growth slowdown, this common business cycle is shared by most economies around the world.

Different Long-term Trends in Potential GDP Perhaps the most striking feature of Figure 21.4 is the variation in the long-term growth rates of the big economies. In 1960, real GDP per person was

Figure 21.4 Economic Growth in Four Major OECD Economies

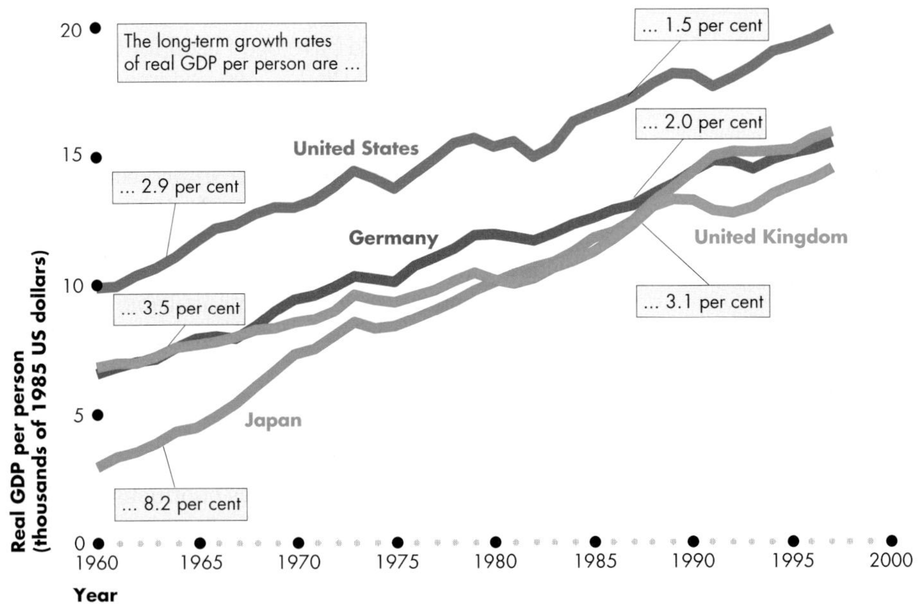

Economic growth in the four large economies, the United States, Germany, Japan and the United Kingdom has followed a similar pattern. The growth rate in all three countries slowed during the 1970s and 1980s and each country has similar business cycles. But Japan has grown fastest and Germany too has grown faster than the United States.

Sources: The data for 1960 through 1992 are from 'The Penn World Table', *Quarterly Journal of Economics*, May 1991, pp. 327–368. New computer disk supplement (Mark 5.6a). The data use comparable international relative prices converted to 1985 US dollars. The data for 1993–1996 are from *International Financial Statistics* (Washington, DC: International Monetary Fund, 1997).

$6,800 in the United Kingdom, $9,800 in the United States, $6,600 in Germany and $3,000 in Japan. So, in round numbers, in 1960, the United Kingdom produced over twice as much per person as Japan, a little more than Germany and about two thirds that of the United States.

But during the 1960s, Japan's output streaked upward like a rocket. When UK long-term growth in real GDP per person was 2.3 per cent a year, in the United States it was 2.9 per cent, Germany achieved a rate of 3.5 per cent a year, and real GDP in Japan grew at an astonishing 8.2 per cent a year. These differences in the long-term growth trend survived the productivity growth slowdown. After the slowdown, when Japan's growth rate more than halved, its growth of real GDP per person still exceeded the US rate before the slowdown.

Because it has achieved such a high growth rate, Japan has narrowed the gap between its own production level and that of the other economies. But a major banking and financial crisis in Japan has resulted in a fall in output in 1997 and 1998. The stagnation in Japan's growth rate will have major consequences for the fast growing economies of East Asia and for the world economy in geneeral. It is too early to tell whether the financial crisis will permanently lower the long-term growth rate in Japan (look at *Reading Between the Lines* on pp. 524–525 for an examination of the global impact of the financial crisis in East Asia).

Figure 21.5 compares the growth rates of the industrial countries and other economies between 1978 and 1996. Among the industrial countries (shown by the red bars) Japan has grown the fastest and the European Union has grown the slowest. The US growth rate has been toward the low end of the range for industrialized countries. The developing countries and the countries in transition to a market economy have experienced a wide range of growth rates. The most rapid growth has occurred in Asia, where the average growth rate has exceeded 7 per cent a year – over three times the European Union growth rate. The slowest growth has been in Russia and other countries of Central and Eastern Europe where production has shrunk. Africa has also grown slowly. With the exception of these regions, growth rates in the developing countries have exceeded that of the European Union.

Figure 21.5 Growth Rates Around the World

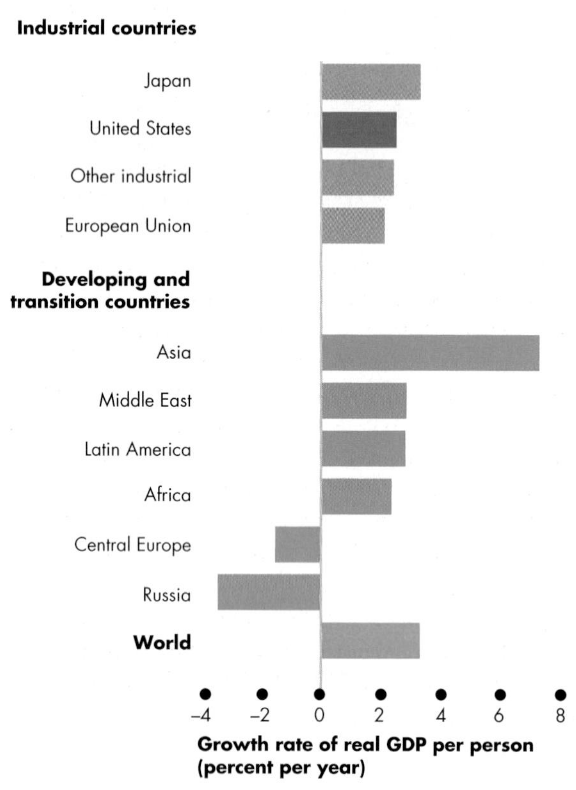

Between 1978 and 1996, the growth rate of real GDP has been lower in the United States than in some other industrial countries. The developing countries of Asia have had the most rapid growth rates and those of Africa, Central and Eastern Europe, and Russia have had the slowest growth.

Source: *World Economic Outlook* (Washington DC: International Monetary Fund, October 1996), pp. 167, 173–176.

Benefits and Costs of Economic Growth

What are the benefits and costs of economic growth? Does it matter if the long-term growth rate slows down as it did during the 1970s?

The main benefit of long-term economic growth is expanded consumption possibilities, including greater welfare and support for the poor, the elderly and the disadvantaged. Other benefits include more expenditure on education and health, better roads, and more and better housing. We can even have a cleaner environment.

When the long-term growth rate slows, the resources that would have been used for these benefits are lost and the loss can be large. However, it must be understood that the proportion of a country's resources devoted to welfare issues and the long-term rate of growth are interrelated. It is certainly the case that the lower the long-term rate of growth the fewer resources are available for welfare. But it is also true that if more resources are spent on welfare there are fewer available for the productive sectors that generate growth. Finding the balance between resources available for current consumption such as welfare spending and resources devoted to future consumption through growth is one of the big issues of macroeconomics.

While economic growth brings enormous benefits, it also has costs. The main cost of economic growth is the current consumption foregone. To sustain a high growth rate over a large number of years, resources must be devoted to advancing technology and accumulating capital rather than to producing goods and services for current consumption.

A second possible cost of faster long-term economic growth is more rapid depletion of exhaustible natural resources such as oil and natural gas. A third possible cost is environmental degradation such as increased pollution of the air, rivers and oceans. But none of these problems are inevitable. The technological advances that bring economic growth often help us to economize on natural resources and to achieve a cleaner environment. For example, more efficient internal combustion engines have decreased the amount of petrol a car uses and cut lead and carbon emissions.

A fourth possible cost of faster long-term economic growth is more frequent changes in the jobs we do and the place we live. Faster long-term growth means that the number of new businesses starting up increases and possibly existing businesses fail at a faster pace. With the birth and death of businesses, jobs are created and destroyed. Faster long-term growth increases the pace of job creation and job destruction. In a fast-growing economy, people must be ready to accept changes in the jobs they do and the places in which they live and to bear the costs of these changes.

The choices that people make, to balance the benefits and costs of economic growth, determine the actual pace of economic growth. We'll study these choices and their consequences in Chapters 26, and 27.

Review

- Economic growth is the expansion of production possibilities. The long-term trend in economic growth is measured by the growth rate of potential GDP.
- Long-term growth in Europe, the United States, Japan and other countries slowed during the 1970s, but was restored to some extent in the 1980s in the United Kingdom, the United States and Japan.
- Real GDP growth fluctuates in a business cycle. An expansion to a peak is followed by a recession, trough, recovery, and finally a new expansion.
- The main benefit of economic growth is expanded consumption possibilities. The main costs are less current consumption, possibly resource depletion and environmental pollution, and rapid changes in jobs and locations.

We've seen that real GDP grows and that it also fluctuates over the business cycle. Business cycles bring fluctuations in jobs and unemployment. Let's now examine this core macroeconomic problem.

Jobs and Unemployment

What kind of labour market will you enter when you graduate? Your decision to take a university course may have been prompted by your assessment of the chances of securing a good job after taking a degree. Whether there will be plenty of good jobs to choose from, or whether you will be forced to take a low-paying job that doesn't use your education will depend, in part, on the total number of jobs available and on the unemployment rate.

Jobs

Between 1979 and 1997 4.4 million jobs were created in the European Union. This number may appear to be impressive but let's put it in an international perspective. In the United States – a comparably sized economy – 35 million jobs were created over the same period. In the United Kingdom the number of jobs created were 1.4 million. But these figures disguise the considerable changes that have been going on in the jobs market. There has been a general switch from manufacturing jobs to services, from male to female workers and from full-time to part-time. Of course new jobs are created every month, but there are many that are also destroyed. The pace of job creation and destruction fluctuates over the business cycle. More jobs are destroyed than created during a recession, so the number of jobs decreases. But more jobs are created than destroyed during a recovery and expansion, so the number of jobs increases. For example, 1.7 million jobs were lost between 1979 and 1983. In the long recovery to 1989 3.2 million jobs were created, in the recession of 1990–1992 the number of jobs fell by nearly 1.9 million and in the recovery from 1993 to 1997 1.8 million jobs were created.

Unemployment

An internationally recognized definition of unemployment is that a person is defined as being **unemployed** if he or she does not have a job but is available for work, willing to work and has made some effort to find work within the previous four weeks. The sum of the people who are unemployed and the people who are employed is called the workforce. The **unemployment rate** is the percentage of the people in the workforce who are unemployed. (The concepts of the workforce and unemployment are explained more fully in Chapter 23 on pp. 554–564.)

The unemployment rate is not a perfect measure of the underutilization of labour for two main reasons. First, it excludes discouraged workers. A **discouraged worker** is a person who does not have a job, is available for work and willing to work, but who has given up the effort to find work. Many people switch between the unemployment and discouraged worker categories in both directions every month. Second, the unemployment rate measures unemployed persons rather than unemployed

Figure 21.6 Unemployment in the United Kingdom: 1855–1998

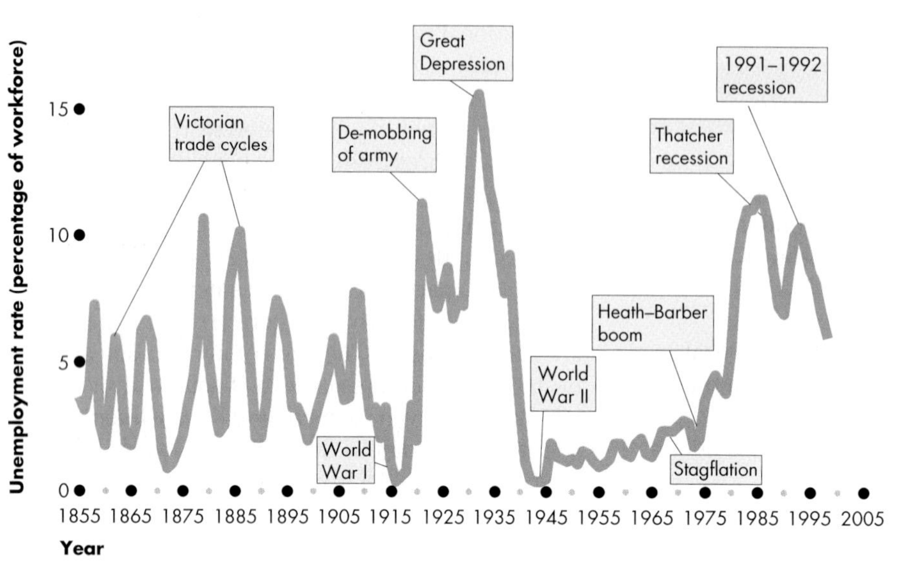

Unemployment is a persistent feature of economic life, but its rate varies. At its worst – during the Great Depression – nearly 16 per cent of the workforce was unemployed. Even in recent recessions, the unemployment rate climbed to 11 per cent. Between 1945 and the late 1960s unemployment remained stable. From the mid-1970s, there has been a general tendency for the unemployment rate to increase.

Sources: C. H. Feinstein, *National Income Expenditure and Output of the United Kingdom, 1855–1965*, 1972, Cambridge, Cambridge University Press; Eurostat.

labour hours. It excludes those people who have a part-time job but who want a full-time job.

Despite these two limitations, the unemployment rate is the best available measure of underused labour resources. Let's look at some facts about unemployment.

Unemployment in the United Kingdom

Figure 21.6 shows the unemployment rate in the United Kingdom from 1855 to 1998. Two features stand out. First, we have had high unemployment in the past. Unemployment in the depressed interwar years reached a peak of 15.6 per cent. In the period after World War II the average unemployment rate remained low until the late 1970s.

Second, although we have not recently experienced anything as high as the mass unemployment of the interwar years, we have seen high unemployment rates during recessions. The figure highlights two recent experiences – the 1980–81 recession and the 1990–1992 recession.

But how does UK unemployment compare with unemployment in other countries?

Unemployment Around the World

Figure 21.7 shows the unemployment rate in the United States, the European Union, Japan and the United Kingdom. Over the period shown in this figure, US unemployment averaged 6.7 per cent, much higher than Japanese unemployment, which averaged 2.6 per cent, but lower than unemployment in the European Union, which averaged 9.3 per cent, and in the United Kingdom, which also averaged 9.3 per cent.

The figure shows that unemployment fluctuates over the business cycle. It increases during a recession and decreases during an expansion. The cycle in the United States is out of phase with the United Kingdom and Europe. Unemployment in the UK has risen and fallen faster than the EU average. In contrast, Japanese unemployment has been remarkably stable.

We've looked at some facts about unemployment in the United Kingdom and in other countries. Let's now look at some of the consequences of unemployment that make it the serious problem that it is.

Figure 21.7 Unemployment in the Industrial Economies

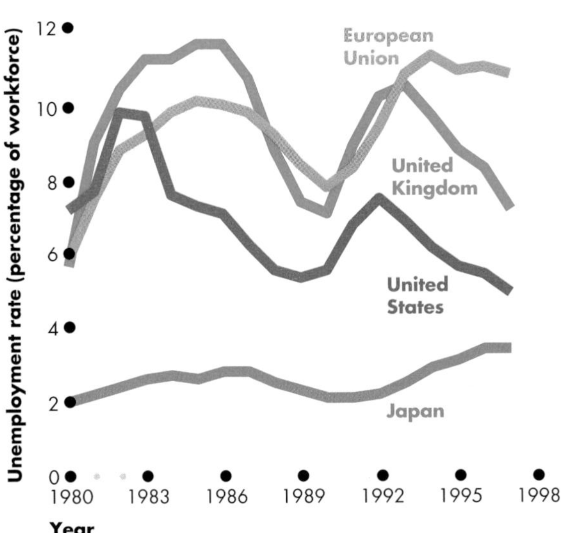

The unemployment rate in the European Union has in general been higher than that in the United States. The UK unemployment rate has increased faster than the EU average but also fallen faster. EU unemployment has a cycle that is out of phase with the United States. Japanese unemployment barely changed in the 1980s but has risen in the 1990s.

Source: Eurostat.

Why Unemployment is a Problem

Unemployment is a serious economic, social and personal problem for two main reasons:

1 Lost production and incomes.
2 Lost human capital.

Lost Production and Incomes The loss of a job brings an immediate loss of income. This loss can be devastating for the person who faces it. Jobseeker's allowance creates a short term safety net but does not always provide the same living standard as a job.

Lost Human Capital Prolonged unemployment can permanently damage a person's job prospects. For example, a middle-aged manager loses his job when his firm downsizes. Short of income, he takes a job as a taxi driver. After a year he discovers that he cannot compete with young MBA graduates. He eventually finds a job as a shop manager and at a lower wage than his previous managerial job. He has lost some of his human capital.

Review

- The total number of jobs in the United Kingdom today is about 1.4 million more than in 1979.
- The unemployment rate fluctuates but unemployment never disappears.
- Unemployment brings a loss of income and human capital.

Let's now turn to the third major issue for macroeconomics: inflation.

Inflation

Inflation is a process of rising prices. We measure the *inflation rate* as the percentage change in the *average* level of prices or **price level**. A common measure of the price level is the *Retail Prices Index* (RPI). The RPI tells us how the average price of all the goods and services bought by a typical household changes from month to month. (The RPI is explained in Chapter 22, pp. 539–543). Every month the television news and the newspapers report the rate of inflation. How is this calculated?

So that you can see in a concrete way how the inflation rate is measured, let's do a calculation. In December 1996, the RPI was 154.4, and in December 1997, it was 160.0, so the inflation rate during 1997 was:

$$\text{Inflation} = \frac{160.0 - 154.4}{154.4} \times 100$$
$$= 3.6\%$$

Inflation in the United Kingdom

Figure 21.8 shows the UK inflation rate from 1960 to 1997. You can see from this figure that during the early 1960s the inflation rate was between 2 and 3 per cent a year. Inflation began to increase in the

Figure 21.8 Inflation in the United Kingdom: 1960–1998

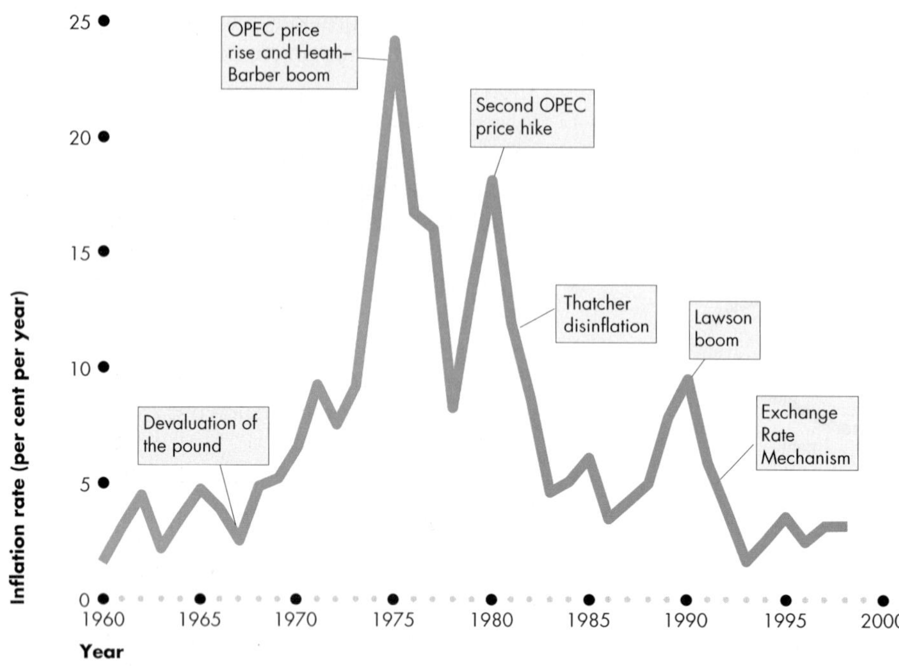

Inflation has been a persistent feature of economic life in the United Kingdom. The inflation rate was low in the first half of the 1960s, but it increased during the second half with the rise in world inflation. It increased further with the OPEC oil price hikes but declined during the Thatcher years of the 1980s as a result of policy actions. The inflation rate rose at the end of the 1980s and has fallen during the 1990s.

Source: ONS Office, *Economic Trends Annual Supplement*, 1998 and *Economic Trends*, July 1998.

late 1960s, but the largest increases occurred in 1975 and 1980. These were years in which the actions of OPEC resulted in exceptionally large increases in the price of oil, but domestic policies also contributed to the inflation process. Inflation was brought under control in the early 1980s when the government instructed, the Bank of England to push interest rates up in an effort to reduce demand. Today the Monetary Policy Committee of the Bank of England targets a measure of the Retail Price Index excluding the influence of mortgage rates – known as RPIX.

The inflation rate rises and falls over the years, but it rarely becomes negative. If the inflation rate is negative, the price *level* is falling. Since the 1930s, the price level has generally risen – the inflation rate has been positive. Thus even when the inflation rate is low, as it was in 1961 and 1993, the price level is rising.

Inflation Around the World

Figure 21.9 shows inflation in the major industrial countries since 1970. You can see in part (a) that the inflation rates in the industrial countries have had a similar pattern. You can see that all the industrial countries shared the burst of double-digit inflation during the 1970s and the fall in inflation during the 1980s. You can see in part (b) that the average inflation rate of industrial countries has been low compared with that of the developing countries. Among the developing countries, the most extreme inflation has occurred in the former Yugoslavia, where its rate has exceeded 6000 per cent per year.

Why is Inflation a Problem?

If inflation were predictable, it would not be much of a problem. But inflation is not predictable. Unpredictable inflation makes the economy behave like a giant casino in which some people gain and some lose and no one can accurately predict where the gains and losses will fall. Gains and losses occur because of unpredictable changes in the value of money. Money is used as a measuring rod of value in the transactions that we undertake. Borrowers and lenders, workers and employers all make

Figure 21.9 Inflation Around the World

(a) Inflation in industrial economies

(b) Industrial countries and developing countries

Inflation in the UK is similar to that in the other industrial countries. Its peaks have typically been above that of the EU average and higher than in the United States. Compared with the developing countries, inflation in the industrial countries is low.

Source: International Monetary Fund, *International Financial Statistics Yearbook*, 1998, Washington, DC.

contracts in terms of money. If the value of money varies unpredictably over time, then the amounts *really* paid and received – the quantity of goods that the money will buy – also fluctuate unpredictably. Measuring value with a measuring rod whose units vary is a bit like trying to measure a piece of cloth with an elastic ruler. The size of the cloth depends on how tightly the ruler is stretched.

In a rapid inflation, resources are diverted from productive activities to forecasting inflation. It becomes more profitable to forecast the inflation rate correctly than to invent a new product. Doctors, lawyers, accountants, farmers – just about everyone – can make themselves better off, not by practising the profession for which they have been trained but by becoming amateur economists and inflation forecasters. From a social perspective, this diversion of talent resulting from inflation is like throwing our scarce resources on to the rubbish heap. This waste of resources is a cost of inflation.

The most serious type of inflation is called *hyperinflation* – an inflation rate that exceeds 50 per cent a month. Hyperinflation is rare, but it occurred in Germany, Poland and Hungary during the 1920s and Hungary and China during the 1940s. At the height of these hyperinflations, workers were paid twice a day because money lost its value so quickly. As soon as they were paid, people rushed off to spend their wages before they lost too much value. But hyperinflation is not just a historical curiosity. In 1994, the African country of Zaire had a hyperinflation that peaked at a *monthly* inflation rate of 76 per cent. Also during 1994, Brazil almost reached the hyperinflation stratosphere with a monthly inflation rate of 40 per cent. A cup of coffee that cost 15 cruzeiros in 1980 cost 22 *billion* cruzeiros in 1994. With numbers this big, Brazil twice changed the name of its currency and twice lopped off three zeros to keep the magnitudes of monetary values manageable.

Inflation imposes costs, but lowering inflation is also costly. Policies that lower the inflation rate increase the unemployment rate. Most economists think that the increase in unemployment that accompanies a fall in inflation is temporary. Others say that higher unemployment is a permanent cost of low inflation. The cost of lowering inflation must be evaluated when an anti-inflation policy is followed.

Review

- Inflation is a process of rising prices and a falling value of money.
- Inflation is a serious problem because its rate is usually unpredictable.
- Unpredictable inflation brings unpredictable gains and losses to borrowers and lenders, workers and employers, and because it diverts resources from producing goods and services to predicting inflation.

We've now looked at economic growth and the business cycle, unemployment and inflation, let's turn to the fourth macroeconomic problem: the balance of international payments. What happens when a country buys more from other countries than it sells to them? Does it face the problem that you and I would face if we spent more than we earned? Does it run out of money? Let's look at these questions.

Figure 21.10 The UK Current Account Balance: 1960–1998

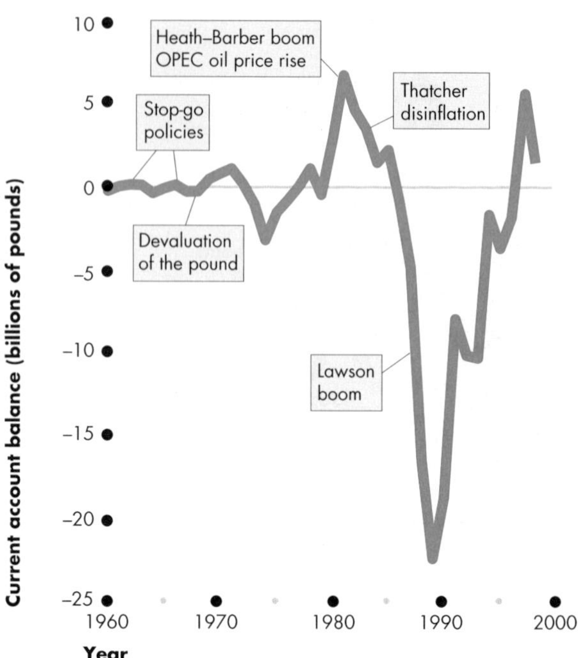

The current account records our exports and imports of goods and services. During the 1960s, our current account was generally in balance. In the mid-1970s, a deficit emerged following the expansionary policies of the Conservative Heath government. The early 1980s saw a sizeable surplus following the deflationary policies of Mrs Thatcher. During the expansion of the late 1980s, a large deficit emerged, but it has fallen since the recession of 1990–92, and reached a surplus in 1997–8.

Source: *Economic Trends Annual Supplement*, 1998 and *Pink Book*, 1998.

International Payments

When we import goods and services from the rest of the world, we make payments to foreigners. When we export goods and services to the rest of the world, we receive payments from foreigners. We keep track of the values of our imports and exports in our international current account.

The Current Account

The **current account** records the receipts from exports (sales of goods and services to other countries), the payments for imports (purchases of goods and services from other countries), income from workers employed abroad, income from investments abroad, and transfers by the government to the European Union (EU). The largest component of the current account in the UK is the trade in goods and services. The current account is made up of credit entries and debit entries. The credit entries are exports of goods and services, incomes received from workers abroad and investments abroad and receipts of transfers from the EU. The debit entries are imports of goods and services, incomes payable on foreign workers employed in the UK and investments by foreigners in the UK, and transfer payments to the EU. If our credits exceed our debits, we have a current account surplus. If our debits exceed our credits, we have a current account deficit.

The Current Account in the United Kingdom

Figure 21.10 shows the history of the UK current account since 1960. It shows that the United Kingdom has always had a problem with the balance of trade. The current account was in deficit in several years in the 1960s. It built up a surplus between 1969 and 1972 and slipped into deficit at the time of the OPEC oil crisis. Large surpluses occurred in the first half of the 1980s and deficits in the second half.

The current account balance fluctuates with the business cycle. In a recession, imports fall and the deficit decreases (or the surplus increases). During an expansion, imports rise and the current account deficit increases. For example, a large deficit emerged during the period of the major expansion of demand engineered by the Conservative Heath administration between 1973 and 1974. During the early 1980s, a huge surplus was generated following the deflationary policies of the Conservative Thatcher government. But after 1986, a persistent current account deficit emerged with the economic boom of the late 1980s. At times the deficit has been large. In 1989, for example, it was £21.4 billion. How can we have a persistent current account deficit? The answer is because we have a capital and financial account surplus.

The Capital and Financial Account

The **capital and financial account** records the receipts from foreign investments in the United Kingdom and UK investments in the rest of the world. When we have a current account deficit, we borrow from foreigners or we sell some UK assets to foreigners to pay for it. When we have a current account surplus, we loan our surplus to the rest of the world or we buy foreign assets.

So a current account surplus is always matched by a capital account deficit, and a current account deficit is always matched by a capital and financial account surplus. We do not, as a nation, run out of cash to pay our bills. But is borrowing from the rest of the world a problem? It might be, but it is not inevitably a problem.

Just as an individual can borrow to consume, so also can a country. Borrowing to consume is usually not a good idea. It builds up a debt that grows as interest is added to the debt, and at some point the debt plus the interest must be paid off. But an individual or a country can also borrow to invest in assets that earn interest. Borrowing to invest in assets that earn interest is potentially profitable. It creates an income stream that can pay off a debt and the interest on the debt. So long as the interest rate earned on the investment exceeds that on the debt, the deficit and the debt do not pose a problem.

You will learn more about the balance of international payments further on in this book.

Review

- The current account records the receipts from exports and the payments for imports.
- When imports exceed exports, we have a current account deficit.
- The current account balance is cyclical. It increases during an expansion and decreases during a recession.
- A current account deficit is matched by a capital and financial account surplus.

Let's close this chapter by looking at the macroeconomic policy challenges.

Macroeconomic Policy Challenges and Tools

From the time of Adam Smith's *The Wealth of Nations* until the establishment of macroeconomics in 1936, the general view was that the proper role of government in economic life was to provide the legal framework in which people could freely pursue their own best interests. The macroeconomics of Keynes, published in the *General Theory of Employment, Interest, and Money* in 1936, challenged this view and argued that government could (and should) take policy actions aimed at achieving and maintaining full employment.

The policy goal of full employment became the declared objective of the government following the publication of the White Paper on Employment Policy in 1944.

Policy Challenges

Today, the widely agreed challenges for macroeconomic policy in the UK and the rest of the EU are to:

1 Boost long-term growth.
2 Stabilize the business cycle.
3 Lower unemployment.
4 Keep inflation low.
5 Prevent a large current account deficit.
6 Prevent the government budget deficit from increasing above 3 per cent of GDP.

But how can we do all these things? What are the tools available to pursue the macroeconomic policy challenges?

Macroeconomic policy tools are divided into two broad categories:

1 Fiscal policy.
2 Monetary policy.

Fiscal Policy **Fiscal policy** is the government's attempt to influence the economy by setting and changing taxes, government spending, and the government's deficit and debt. This range of policy actions is under the control of the Chancellor of the Exchequer and the Treasury. Fiscal policy can be used to try to change the total amount of spending or to change incentives so that investment and productivity increase. When the economy is in a recession, the government might cut taxes or increase its spending in an attempt to lower the unemployment rate. Conversely, when the economy is expanding and real GDP is above potential, the government might increase taxes or cut its spending in an attempt to prevent the economy from overheating.

Through most of the 1970s and 1980s, the government has spent more than it has raised in taxes. When government spending exceeds tax revenues, the government has a **budget deficit**. The government has stated as a long-term objective the desirability of eliminating the budget deficit. Also the Maastricht Treaty imposes certain constraints on the fiscal deficits of member countries in the European Union as a condition of economic convergence within the European Monetary Union (EMU). The constraints include a budget deficit target of 3 per cent of GDP. While the UK government is a signatory to the treaty it has opted to remain outside the first wave which began on January 1999. The stated aim of the Blair led Labour government is to join EMU when the economic conditions are right. But the existence of a budget deficit target has limited the scope for using fiscal policy to stabilize the business cycle.

Monetary Policy **Monetary policy** consists of changes in interest rates and in the amount of money in the economy. This range of policy actions is under the control of the Bank of England. The Bank of England has been granted operational independence with the task of keeping inflation within a narrow range (currently between 1.5 and 2.5 per cent). A committee of experts (the Monetary Policy Committee – MPC) including academics and senior officials from the Bank of England determine monetary policy by setting the rate of interest. When the economy is in recession and inflation looks like falling below the lower band, the MPC might lower interest rates and inject money into the economy. When the economy is expanding too quickly, it might increase interest rates in an attempt to prevent the economy from overheating.

The European Central Bank which came into existence with the birth of the EMU in January 1999 also has the objective of price stability defined as keeping inflation within the narrow band of 0–2 per cent.

Review

- The macroeconomic policy challenges are to boost long-term growth, stabilize the business cycle, lower unemployment, maintain low inflation and prevent a large current account deficit.
- To meet these challenges, the government uses fiscal policy tools – taxes and government spending.
- The Maastricht Treaty specifies an upper limit to the budget deficit for countries within the EMU. Countries that want to join EMU in the second wave will also have to meet this limit.
- The Bank of England uses monetary policy tools – interest rates and money supply.

In your study of macroeconomics, you will find out what is currently known about the causes of long-term economic growth, business cycles, unemployment, inflation and the international balance of payments, and about the policy choices and challenges that the government faces. The next step in your pursuit of these goals is to learn more about macroeconomic measurement – about how we measure real GDP and the price level.

Summary

Key Points

Origins and Issues of Macroeconomics (pp. 506–507)

- Macroeconomics studies both the long-term trends and short-term fluctuations in economic growth, unemployment, inflation and the balance of international payments.

Economic Growth (pp. 507–513)

- Economic growth is the expansion of the economy's capacity to produce goods and services, measured by the increase in real GDP. Real GDP fluctuates around potential GDP in a business cycle. Every business cycle has an expansion, peak, recession, trough, recovery and new expansion.
- When we compare countries, we find similar productivity growth slowdowns and similar business cycles but different long-term trends in potential GDP.
- The main benefit of long-term economic growth is expanded consumption possibilities, and the main costs are reduced current consumption.

Jobs and Unemployment (pp. 513–515)

- The rate at which jobs are created and destroyed in the UK varies with the business cycle. Just over 500,000 jobs a year are created in the expansion phase of a business cycle. But just under 500,000 jobs a year are lost in the contraction phase.
- The UK unemployment rate fluctuates over the business cycle. It rises during a recession and falls during an expansion.
- The UK unemployment rate is lower than the average for the European Union but higher than in Japan or the United States.
- Unemployment is a serious economic, social and personal problem. It can permanently damage a person's job prospects.

Inflation (pp. 515–518)

- Inflation is a process of rising prices which is measured by the percentage change in a price index such as the RPI.
- Inflation is a problem because it lowers the value of money at an unpredictable rate and makes money less useful as a measuring rod of value.

International Payments (pp. 518–519)

- When imports exceed exports, a nation has a current account deficit. The current account balance is cyclical and fluctuates with the business cycle – the current account deficit decreases in a recession and increases in an expansion.
- A current account deficit is financed by borrowing from abroad or by selling UK assets to foreigners. International borrowing and lending and asset sales and purchases are recorded in the capital account.

Macroeconomic Policy Challenges and Tools (pp. 519–520)

- The challenges for macroeconomic policy are to boost long-term growth, stabilize the business cycle, lower unemployment, maintain low inflation and prevent a large current account deficit.
- The tools available for meeting these challenges are fiscal policy and monetary policy.

Key Figures

Key Terms

Budget deficit, 520
Business cycle, 508
Capital account, 519
Current account, 518
Discouraged worker, 513
Economic growth, 507
Expansion, 509
Fiscal policy, 520
Great Depression, 506
Inflation, 515
Monetary policy, 520
Potential GDP, 507
Price level, 515
Productivity growth slowdown, 507
Real gross domestic product (real GDP), 507
Recession, 508
Stagflation, 506
Unemployed, 513
Unemployment rate, 513

Review Questions

1 Distinguish between real GDP and potential GDP.

2 Is real GDP an ideal measure of total production? Explain why or why not.

3 What is economic growth?

4 How is the long-term economic growth rate measured?

5 What are the benefits of long-term economic growth?

6 What are the costs of long-term economic growth?

7 What is a business cycle? Describe its phases.

8 What is unemployment? How is it measured in the United Kingdom? Do you think it is an accurate measure?

9 What does the unemployment rate tell us about the amount of joblessness? Explain your answer.

10 What are the main costs of unemployment?

11 What is inflation?

12 What are some of the costs of inflation?

Problems

1 The figure shows real GDP in Germany from the first quarter of 1991 to the second quarter of 1994. Use the figure to answer the following questions:

a How many recessions did Germany experience during this period?
b In which quarters, if any, did Germany experience a recovery?
c In which quarters, if any, did Germany experience a business cycle peak?
d In which quarters, if any, did Germany experience a business cycle trough?
e In which quarters, if any, did Germany experience an expansion?

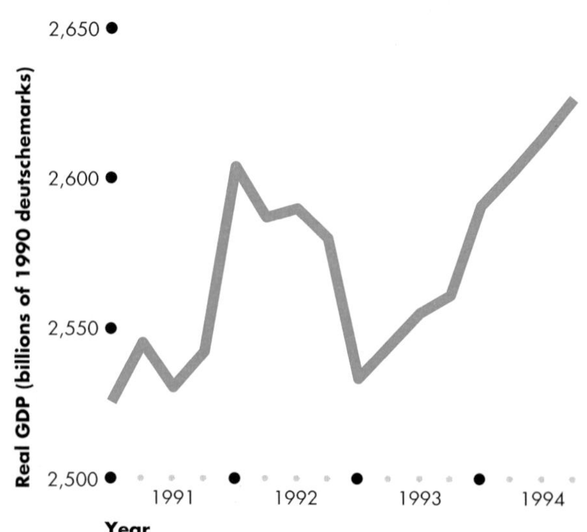

2 Obtain data on inflation in the United Kingdom, the United States, Japan and Germany since 1980. You will find these data in *International Financial Statistics* or the *European Economy* in your college library. Draw a graph of the data and answer the following questions. Which country has had:

a The highest inflation rate?
b The lowest inflation rate?
c The fastest rising inflation rate?
d The fastest falling inflation rate?

3 Study *Reading Between the Lines* on pp. 524–525 and then answer the following questions:

a What has happened to growth in the East Asian economies in 1998?
b What might prolong the recovery in East Asia?
c What danger does a prolonged recession in East Asia pose for the Western economies?

4 Use the Parkin, Powell and Matthews Web site to link on to the ONS site and obtain data on quarterly real GDP for the United Kingdom since the fourth quarter of 1998 and update Figure 21.2. Use what you have discovered to answer the following questions:

a Is the UK economy in expansion or is it slowing?
b If the economy is slowing, how long has it been slowing? If the economy is expanding, how long has the economy been in expansion?
c During the last year, has the growth rate sped up or slowed?

If you have access to the *Economics in Action* interactive software, try these problems

5 Use Variable Graphing in Chapter 21 on the *Economics in Action* CD to answer the following questions. In which country in 1996 was:

a The growth rate of real GDP highest: The United States, France, Japan, or Canada?
b The unemployment rate lowest: the United States, Sweden, the United Kingdom, or Canada?
c The inflation rate lowest: the United States, Finland, Italy, or Canada?
d The government budget deficit (as a percentage of GDP) smallest: the United States, Australia, Ireland, or Canada?
e Is it possible to say in which country consumption possibilities are growing faster? Why or why not?

6 Use Variable Graphing in Chapter 21 on the *Economics in Action* CD to answer the following questions. Which country, in 1996, had:

a The largest budget surplus: the United States, Japan, the United Kingdom, or Canada?
b The largest current account deficit: the United States, Japan, Germany, or Canada?

7 Use Variable Graphing in Chapter 21 on the *Economics in Action* CD to make a scatter diagram of inflation and unemployment in the United States.

a Describe the relationship.
b Do you think that low unemployment brings an increase in the inflation rate?

W http://www.econ100.com

The Asian Financial Crisis

Financial Times, 9 April 1998

Asia's financial crisis is forecast to have long knock-on effect

Robert Chote

Asia's financial crisis will prompt a $100bn (£60bn) turnaround in the current account positions of the victim countries, the Organisation for Economic Co-operation and Development (OECD) said yesterday.

Last year, South Korea and the four member nations of the Association of South-east Asian Nations (Asean) involved had already seen a $30bn swing into surplus, with $70bn more, likely this year and next. But the OECD believed the move into the black might be smaller if the devalued currencies bounced back or exports were constrained by a lack of trade credits.

This year and next, the Asian crisis was expected to produce current account deteriorations of $40bn in the US, $34bn in Japan and $47bn in the European Union. This 'Asia effect' was likely to be more than offset in Japan and the EU, where trade surpluses overall were forecast to widen. But in the US it would contribute to an $83bn current account deterioration in 1998–99.

The Asian crisis had had a marked effect on growth forecasts for the OECD area, comprising the main industrialised nations. Since the OECD's last Economic Outlook, the area's growth forecast has been revised down to 2.6 per cent this year and next, dominated by the weaker outlook in Japan and Korea. Japan's economy was expected to shrink 0.3 per cent this year and grow 1.3 per cent in 1999.

The US economy was still expected to grow 2.7 per cent this year, but now looked likely to expand 2.1 per cent in 1999 rather than 1.9 per cent.

Growth in the EU had been revised down fractionally to 2.7 per cent for this year but held at 2.8 per cent for 1999.

The Essence of the Story

- The Asian financial crisis will result in a turnaround in the current account positions of Korea and the countries of the South-east Asian nations (Asean).
- The Asean economies and Korea will see current account deficits swing round to large current account surpluses.
- The devaluation of the Korean and Asean currencies has contributed to a current account deficit of $83 billion in the USA.
- The Asian crisis has had a negative effect on growth prospects in the OECD.
- Except for the US, the economies of Japan and the EU are forecasted to grow at a slower rate than was originally expected.

Economic Analysis

■ The devaluation of the Korean and the Asean economies currencies has made exports from these countries cheaper, resulting in a current account surplus.

■ The recovery in exports in Korea and the Asean economies could be smaller if their currencies bounced back or if trade was constrained by a lack of trade credit from the developed world.

■ The weakness of the economies in East Asia will reduce demand for Western exports, which in turn will harm growth in the USA and Europe.

■ Figure 1 shows the growth performance in the East Asian economies in the latest quarter available for 1998. In all countries but China output has fallen. The weak performance in East Asia will moderate expectations of growth in the Western economies.

■ Figure 2 shows the performance of the Western economies in 1998 alongside what was predicted according to *The Economist* poll of forecasters made in May 1998. In the UK and Italy, actual growth was much less than predicted. Only in the USA was growth higher than predicted.

■ The continuing recession in the Far East will hit Western exports to that region and growth will slow in 1999. Figure 3 shows the forecasts made in May 1998 for growth in 1999 compared with forecasts made in March 1999. Except for the USA the general expectation is that growth in the West will be lower than originally thought.

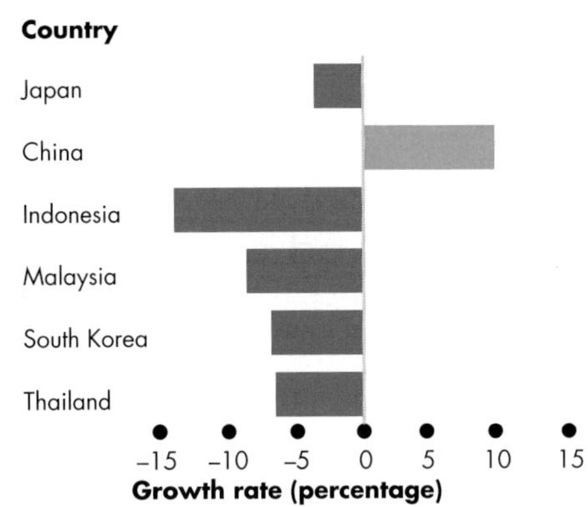

Figure 1 East Asian economies growth rate

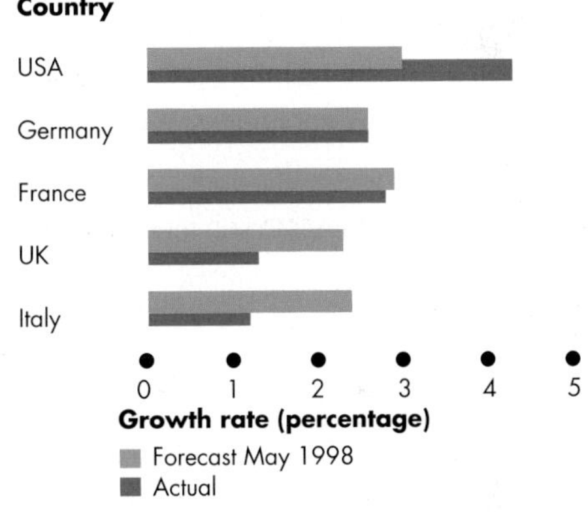

Figure 2 Western economies actual and forecast growth rates 1998

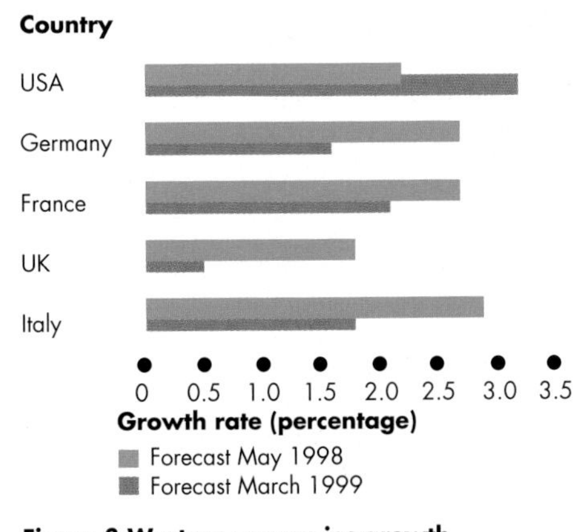

Figure 3 Western economies growth forecast 1999

Macroeconomic Revolutions

". . . The ideas of economists and political philosophers, both when they are right and when they are wrong, are more powerful than is commonly understood. Indeed the world is ruled by little else."

John Maynard Keynes *The General Theory of Employment, Interest and Money*

The Economist: John Maynard Keynes

John Maynard Keynes, born in England in 1883, was one of the outstanding minds of the twentieth century. He wrote on probability as well as economics, represented Britain at the Versailles peace conference at the end of World War I, was a master speculator on international financial markets (an activity he conducted from bed every morning and which made and lost him several fortunes), and played a prominent role in creating the International Monetary Fund. He was a member of the Bloomsbury Group, a circle of outstanding artists and writers that included E.M. Forster, Bertrand Russell and Virginia Woolf. Keynes was a controversial and quick-witted figure. A critic once complained that Keynes had changed his opinion in some matter, to which Keynes retorted, "When I discover I am wrong, I change my mind. What do you do?"

The Issues and Ideas

During the Industrial Revolution, as technological change created new jobs and destroyed old ones, people began to wonder whether the economy could create enough jobs and sufficient demand to buy all the things that the new industrial economy could produce.

Jean-Baptiste Say argued that production creates incomes that are sufficient to buy everything that is produced – supply creates its own demand – an idea that came to be called Say's Law.

Say and Keynes would have had a lot to disagree about. Jean-Baptiste Say, born in Lyon, France, in 1767 (he was 9 years old when Adam Smith's *The Wealth of Nations* was published), suffered the wrath of Napoleon for his views on government and the economy. Today, Say would be considered a 'supply sider'. Say was the most famous economist of his era on both sides of the Atlantic. His book, *Traité d'économie politique* (*A Treatise on Political Economy*), published in 1803, became a best selling university economics textbook in both Europe and America.

As the Great Depression of the 1930s became more severe and more prolonged, Say's Law looked less and less relevant. John Maynard Keynes revolutionized macroeconomic thinking by turning Say's Law on its head, arguing that production does not depend on supply. Instead, it depends on what people are willing to buy – on demand. Or as Keynes put it, production depends on *effective demand.* It is possible, argued Keynes, for people to refuse to spend all of their incomes. If businesses fail to spend on new capital the amount that people plan to save, demand might be less than supply. In this situation, resources might go unemployed and remain unemployed indefinitely.

The influence of Keynes persists even today, more than 60 years after the publication of his main work. But during the past 20 years, Nobel Laureate Robert E. Lucas, Jr, with significant contributions from a list of outstanding macroeconomists too long to name, has further revolutionized macroeconomics. Today, we know a lot about economic growth, unemployment, inflation and business cycles. And we know how to use fiscal policy and monetary policy to improve macroeconomic performance. But we don't yet have all the answers. Macroeconomics remains a field of lively controversy and exciting research.

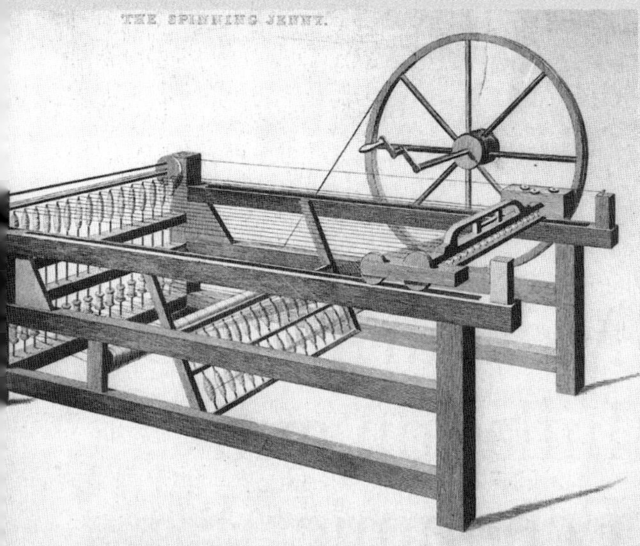

Then . . .

In 1776, James Hargreaves, an English weaver and carpenter, developed a simple hand-operated machine called a spinning jenny (pictured here). Using this machine, a person could spin 80 threads at once. Thousands of hand-wheel spinners, operators of machines that could spin only one thread, lost their jobs. They protested by wrecking spinning jennies. In the long run, the displaced hand-wheel spinners found work, often in factories that manufactured the machines that had destroyed their previous jobs. From the earliest days of the Industrial Revolution to the present day, people have lost their jobs as new technologies have automated what human effort had previously been needed to accomplish.

. . . And Now

Advances in computer technology have made it possible for us to dial our own telephone calls to any part of the world and get connected in a flash. A task that was once performed by telephone operators, who made connections along copper wires, is now performed faster and more reliably by computers along fibre-optic cables. Just as the Industrial Revolution transformed the textile industry, so today's Information Revolution is transforming the telecommunications industry. In the process, the mix of jobs is changing. There are fewer jobs for telephone operators but more jobs for telephone systems designers, builders, managers and marketers. In the long run, as people spend the income they earn in their changing jobs, supply creates its own demand, just as Say predicted. But does supply create its own demand in the short run, when displaced workers are unemployed?

CHAPTER 22

Measuring GDP, Inflation and Economic Growth

After studying this chapter you will be able to:

- Explain why aggregate income, expenditure and output are equal
- Explain how GDP is measured
- Explain how the Retail Prices Index (RPI) and the GDP deflator are measured
- Explain the shortcomings of changes in the RPI and the GDP deflator as measures of inflation
- Explain how real GDP is measured
- Explain the shortcomings of real GDP growth as a measure of improvements in living standards

Economic Barometers

When Mercedes-Benz contemplates opening a car plant in the United States, it pays close attention to long-term forecasts of US real GDP. When British Telecommunications plans to expand its fibre optics network, it uses forecasts of long-term growth in the UK economy. The outcome of many business decisions turns on the quality of forecasts of global and national macroeconomic conditions. ◆ Key inputs for making economic forecasts are the latest estimates of the gross domestic product, or GDP. The GDP data are a barometer of our country's economy. Economists pore over the latest numbers looking at past trends and seeking patterns that might give a glimpse of the future. How do economic statisticians add up all the economic activity of the country to arrive at the number called GDP? What exactly *is* GDP? ◆ Most of the time, our economy grows and sometimes it shrinks. But to reveal the rate of growth (or shrinkage), we must remove the effects of inflation on GDP and assess how *real* GDP is changing. How do we remove the inflation component of GDP to reveal real GDP? ◆ From economists to housewives, all types of people pay close attention to another economic barometer, the Retail Prices Index, or RPI. The Office for National Statistics publishes new figures each month, and analysts in newspapers and on TV quickly leap to conclusions about the causes of recent changes in prices and the prospects for future changes. How does the government determine the RPI? How well does it measure a consumer's living costs and the inflation rate? ◆ Some countries are rich while others are poor and only now are in the process of developing their industries and reaching their productive potential. How do we compare incomes in one country with incomes in another? How can we make international comparisons of GDP?

◆ ◆ ◆ ◆ In this chapter you are going to find out how economic statisticians measure real GDP and the price level. You are also going to learn how they use these measures to assess the economic growth rate and the inflation rate and to compare macroeconomic performance across countries.

Gross Domestic Product

Gross domestic product (GDP) is the value of *aggregate* or *total* production of goods and services in a country during a given time period – usually a year. The GDP of the United Kingdom, which measures the value of aggregate output in the United Kingdom during a year, was £786.6 billion in 1997. How was this number calculated? What does it mean? You are going to discover the answers to these questions in this chapter. But first, how is GDP calculated? Two fundamental concepts form the foundation on which GDP measurements are made:

1. The distinction between stocks and flows.
2. The equality of income, expenditure and the value of production.

Stocks and Flows

To keep track of our personal economic transactions and the economic transactions of a country, we distinguish between stocks and flows. A **stock** is a quantity that exists at a point in time. The water in a bath is a stock. So is the number of CDs that you own and the amount of money in your savings deposit. A **flow** is a quantity per unit of time. The water that is running from an open tap into a bath is a flow. So is the number of CDs that you buy in a month and the amount of income that you earn in a month. GDP is another flow. It is the value of production in a country *in a given time period.*

Capital and Investment The key macroeconomic stock is **capital**, the plant, equipment, buildings and stocks of raw materials and semifinished goods that are used to produce other goods and services. The amount of capital in the economy is a crucial factor that influences GDP. Two macroeconomic *flows* change the *stock* of capital: investment and depreciation. **Investment** is the purchase of new plant, equipment and buildings and the additions to stocks. Investment *increases* the stock of capital. **Depreciation** is the decrease in the stock of capital that results from wear and tear and the passage of time. Another name for depreciation is capital consumption. The total amount spent on adding to the stock of capital and on replacing depreciated capital is called **gross investment**. The amount spent on adding to the stock of capital is called **net investment**. Net investment equals gross investment minus depreciation.

Figure 22.1 Capital and Investment 

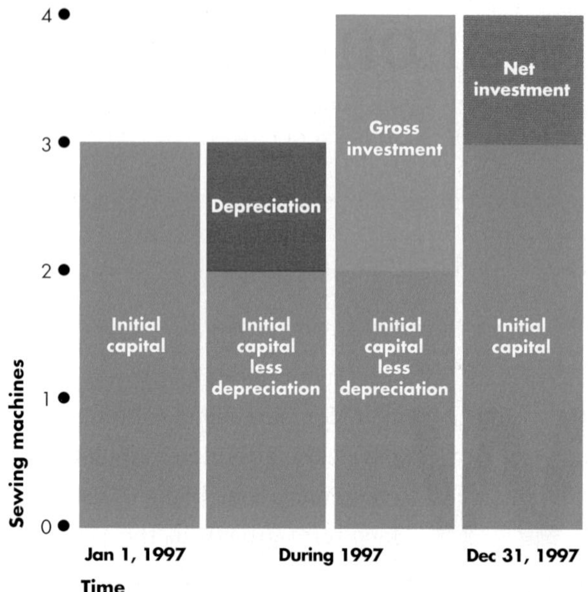

The Best Jeans denim factory's capital stock at the end of 1995 equals its capital stock at the beginning of the year plus its net investment. Net investment is equal to gross investment less depreciation. Best Jeans' gross investment is the 2 new sewing machines bought during the year, and its depreciation is the 1 sewing machine that it scrapped during the year.

Figure 22.1 illustrates these concepts. On 1 January 1997, Tom's Tapes Inc. had 3 machines. This quantity was its initial capital. During 1997, Tom's scrapped an older machine. This quantity is its depreciation. After depreciation, Tom's stock of capital was down to 2 machines. But also during 1997, Tom's bought 2 new machines. This amount is its gross investment. By 31 December 1997, Tom's Tapes had 4 machines so its capital had increased by 1 machine. This amount is Tom's net investment. Tom's net investment equals its gross investment (the purchase of 2 new machines) minus its depreciation (1 machine scrapped).

The example of Tom's Tapes factory can be applied to the economy as a whole. The nation's capital stock decreases because capital depreciates and increases because of gross investment. The change in the nation's capital stock from one year to the next equals its net investment.

Wealth and Saving Another macroeconomic stock is **wealth**, which is the value of all the things that people own. What people *own*, a stock, is related to what they *earn*, a flow. People *earn* an *income*, which is the amount they receive during a given time period from supplying the services of factors of production. Income can be either consumed or saved. **Consumption expenditure** is the amount spent on consumption goods and services. **Saving** is the amount of income left over after meeting consumption expenditures. Saving adds to wealth, and dissaving (negative saving) decreases wealth.

For example, at the end of the academic year, you have a £500 overdraft on your bank account and computer equipment worth £1,000. That's all you own. Your wealth is £500. Suppose that over the summer you earn an income of £3,000. You are extremely careful and spend only £500. When Uni starts again you have paid off your overdraft and you have £2,000 in your savings account. Your wealth is now £3,000. Your wealth has increased by £2,500 which equals your saving of £2,500. And your saving of £2,500 equals your income during the summer of £3,000 minus your consumption expenditure of £500.

National wealth and national saving work just like this personal example. The wealth of a nation at the start of a year equals its wealth at the start of the previous year plus its saving during the year. And its saving equals its income minus its consumption.

We'll make the idea of the nation's income and consumption more precise a bit later in this chapter. Before doing so, let's see what the stocks and flows that we've just learned about imply for the recurring theme of macroeconomics: short-term fluctuations and long-term trends in production.

The Short Term Meets the Long Term You saw in Chapter 21 that potential GDP grows steadily, year after year. You also saw that real GDP grows and fluctuates around potential GDP. Both the long-term growth in potential GDP *and* the short-term fluctuations in real GDP are influenced by the stocks and flows that you've just studied. One of the reasons that potential GDP grows is that the capital stock grows. And one of the reasons that real GDP fluctuates is that investment fluctuates. So capital and investment as well as wealth and saving are part of the key to understanding the growth and fluctuations of GDP.

The flows of investment and saving together with the flows of income and consumption expenditure interact in a circular flow of income and expenditure. In this circular flow, income equals expenditure, which also equals the value of production. This amazing equality is the foundation on which a nation's economic accounts are built and from which its GDP is measured.

The Equality of Income, Expenditure and the Value of Output

To see that for the economy as a whole, income equals expenditure and also equals the value of output, we study the circular flow of income and expenditure. Figure 22.2 illustrates the circular flow. In the figure, the economy consists of four sectors: households, firms, governments and the rest of the world (the purple diamonds). It has three aggregate markets: factor markets, goods and services markets and financial markets. Let's focus first on households and firms.

Households and Firms Households sell and firms buy the services of labour, capital, land and entrepreneurship in factor markets. For these factor services, firms pay income to households – wages for labour services, interest for the use of capital, rent for the use of land and profits for entrepreneurship. Firms' retained earnings – profits that are not distributed to households – are also part of the household sector's income. (You can think of retained earnings as being income that households save and lend back to firms.) Figure 22.2 shows the *aggregate income* received by all households in payment for factor services by the blue dots labelled Y.

Firms sell and households buy consumer goods and services – such as beer, and pizzas, microwave ovens and dry cleaning services – in the markets for goods and services. The aggregate payment that households make for these goods and services is *consumption expenditure*. Figure 22.2 shows consumption expenditure by the red dots labelled C.

Firms buy and sell new capital equipment in the goods market. For example, Compaq sells 1,000 PCs to Virgin or BAC sells an aircraft to British Airways. Some of what firms produce might not be sold at all and is added to stock. For example, if Ford (UK)

Figure 22.2 The Circular Flow of Income and Expenditure

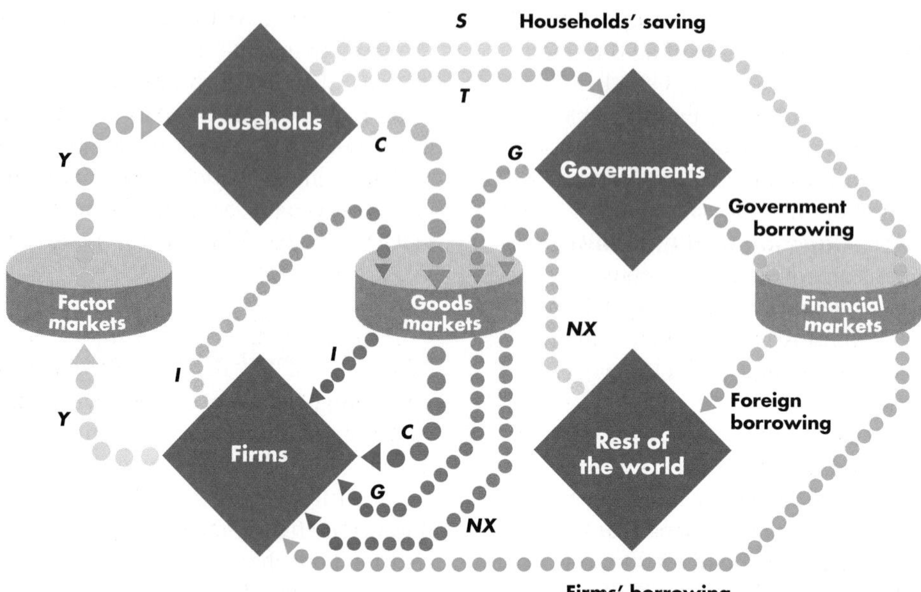

In the circular flow of income and expenditure, households receive incomes (Y) from firms (blue flow) and make consumption expenditures (C); firms make investment expenditures (I); governments purchase goods and services (G); the rest of the world purchases net exports (NX) – (red flows). Aggregate income (blue flow) equals aggregate expenditure (red flows).

Households' saving (S) and net taxes (NT) leak from the circular flow. Firms borrow to finance their investment expenditures and governments and the rest of the world borrow to finance their deficits or lend their surpluses – (green flows).

produces 1,000 cars and sells 950 of them, the other 50 cars remain unsold and Ford's stock of cars increases by 50. When a firm adds unsold output to stock, we can think of the firm as buying goods from itself. The purchase of new plant, equipment and buildings and the additions to stocks are *investment*. Figure 22.2 shows investment by the red dots labelled *I*. Notice that in the figure investment flows from firms through the goods markets and back to firms. Some firms produce capital goods and other firms buy them (and firms 'buy' stocks from themselves).

Firms finance their investment by borrowing from households in financial markets. Households place their saving and firms do their borrowing in the financial markets. Figure 22.2 shows these flows by the green dots labelled 'Households' saving' or *S* and 'Firms' borrowing'. These flows are neither income nor expenditure. Income is a payment for the services of a factor of production and expenditure is a payment for goods or services.

Governments Governments buy goods and services from firms. In Figure 22.2, these **government purchases** are shown as the red flow *G*. Governments pay for their purchases from taxes. Figure 22.2 shows taxes as net taxes by the green dots *T*. **Net taxes** are taxes paid to governments minus transfer payments received from governments and minus interest payments on government debt. *Transfer payments* are cash transfers from governments to households and firms such as social security benefits, unemployment compensation and subsidies.

When government purchases (G) exceed net taxes (T), the government sector has a budget deficit, which it finances by borrowing in financial markets. This borrowing is shown by the green dots labelled 'Government borrowing'.

Rest of World Sector Firms export goods and services to the rest of the world and import goods and services from the rest of the world. The value of exports minus the value of imports is called **net exports**. Figure 22.2 shows net exports by the red flow NX.

If net exports are positive and flow from the rest of the world to firms, the rest of the world is in deficit with us and we are in surplus. To finance its deficit the rest of the world either borrows from the domestic economy or sells domestic assets that it owns. These transactions take place in financial markets and they are shown by the green flow labelled 'Foreign borrowing'. If net exports are negative and flow from firms to the rest of the world, we are in deficit and the rest of the world is in surplus with us. We finance our deficit by either borrowing from the rest of the world or selling foreign assets that we own. Again, these transactions take place in financial markets. To illustrate this case in the figure, we would reverse the directions of the flows of net exports and foreign borrowing.

To help you keep track of the different types of flows that make up the circular flow of income and expenditure, they are colour-coded. In Figure 22.2, red flows are expenditures on goods and services, blue flows are incomes, and green flows are financial transfers. So the expenditure flows (red flows) are consumption expenditure, investment, government purchases and net exports. The income flow (blue flow) is aggregate income. The financial transfers (green flows) are saving, net taxes, government borrowing, foreign borrowing and firms' borrowing.

Gross Domestic Product Gross domestic product is the value of *aggregate output* in a country during a year. Output can be valued in two ways:

1 By what buyers pay for it.
2 By what it costs producers to make it.

To buyers, goods are worth the prices paid for them. To producers, goods are worth what it costs to make them. If these two values are equal, we'll have a unique concept of GDP regardless of which one we use.

Fortunately, the two concepts of value do give the same answer. Let's see why.

Expenditure Equals Income The total amount that buyers pay for the goods and services produced is *aggregate expenditure*. Let's focus on aggregate expenditure in Figure 22.2. The expenditures on goods and services are shown by the red flows. Firms' revenues from the sale of goods and services equal consumption expenditure (C) plus investment by firms (I) plus government purchases of goods and services including investment (G) plus net exports (NX). The sum of these four flows is equal to aggregate expenditure on goods and services.

The total amount it costs producers to make goods and services is equal to the incomes paid for factor services. This amount is shown by the blue flow in Figure 22.2.

The sum of the red flows equals the blue flow. The reason is that everything a firm receives from the sale of its output is paid out as incomes to the owners of the factors of production that it employs. That is:

$$Y = C + I + G + NX$$

or aggregate income (Y) equals aggregate expenditure ($C + I + G + NX$).

The buyers of aggregate output pay an amount equal to aggregate expenditure, and the sellers of aggregate output pay an amount equal to aggregate income. But because aggregate expenditure equals aggregate income, these two methods of valuing aggregate output give the same answer. So aggregate output, that is GDP, equals aggregate expenditure or aggregate income.

The circular flow of income and expenditure is the foundation on which the national economic accounts are built. It is used to provide the two approaches to measuring GDP and it is used to create other accounts that help us to keep track of the flows of saving and investment, the government's budget, and the balance of our exports and imports.

Let's look next at how the circular flows you've just studied enable us to keep track of how investment is financed.

How Investment is Financed

Investment, which adds to the stock of capital, is one of the determinants of the rate at which aggregate output grows. Investment is financed by national saving and by borrowing from the rest of the world.

National Saving The sum of household saving and government saving is called **national saving**. Household saving is aggregate income minus net taxes $(Y - T)$, which is called *disposable income*, less consumption expenditure. So:

$$S = (Y - T) - C$$

Government saving equals net taxes minus government purchases, $(T - G)$. If $(T - G)$ is positive, the government has a budget surplus and this surplus is added to household saving as an additional source of finance for investment. But if $(T - G)$ is negative, the government has a budget deficit. In this case, part of household saving is used to finance the government deficit. So:

$$\text{National saving} = S + (T - G)$$

Borrowing From the Rest of the World If foreigners spend more on UK goods and services than we spend on theirs, they must borrow from us to pay the difference. That is, if the value of exports (X) exceeds the value of imports (M), we must lend to the rest of the world an amount equal to $X - M$. In this situation, part of our national saving flows to the rest of the world and is not available to finance investment.

Conversely, if we spend more on foreign goods and services than the rest of the world spends on ours, we must borrow from the rest of the world to pay the difference. That is, we must borrow from the rest of the world an amount equal to $M - X$. In this case, part of the rest of the world's saving flows into the United Kingdom and becomes available to finance investment.

In 1997, investment in the United Kingdom was £136.6 billion. This investment was financed by £126.8 billion of national saving and £9.8 billion from borrowing from the rest of the world.

Review

- Output, income and expenditure are flows. Capital and wealth are stocks. The flow of investment adds to the stock of capital and the flow of saving adds to the stock of wealth.
- Aggregate expenditure, the sum of consumption expenditure, investment, government purchases and net exports, equals aggregate income.
- Aggregate expenditure equals aggregate income equals GDP.
- Investment is financed by national saving plus borrowing from the rest of the world.

Let's now see how the Office for National Statistics (ONS) use the circular flow of income and expenditure to measure GDP.

Measuring UK GDP

To measure GDP, the ONS uses three approaches:

1 Expenditure approach.
2 Factor incomes approach.
3 Output approach.

The Expenditure Approach

The *expenditure approach* measures GDP by collecting data on consumption expenditure (C), investment (I), government purchases of goods and services (G) and net exports (NX). Table 22.1 illustrates this approach. The numbers refer to 1997 and are in millions of pounds. To measure GDP using the expenditure approach, we add together the individual components in Table 22.1.

Table 22.1 GDP: The Expenditure Approach

Item	Symbol	Amount in 1997 (millions of pounds)	Percentage of GDP
Personal consumption expenditures	C	519,100	64.7
Gross domestic investment + stockbuilding	I	136,592	17.0
Government purchases of goods and services	G	147,406	18.3
Net exports	NX	−632	−0.0
Statistical discrepency		−494	−0.0
Gross domestic product	Y	801,972	100.0

The expenditure approach measures GDP by adding together personal consumption expenditures (C), gross private domestic investment plus stockbuilding (I), government purchases of goods and services (G), and net exports (NX).

Source: ONS, *UK National Accounts: The Blue Book*, 1998, London.

Personal consumption expenditures are the expenditures by households on goods and services produced in the United Kingdom. They include goods such as beer, CDs, books and magazines as well as services such as insurance, banking and legal advice. They do not include the purchase of new residential houses, which is counted as part of investment.

Gross private domestic investment is expenditure on capital equipment and buildings by firms and expenditure on new residential houses by households. It also includes the change in firms' stocks.

Government purchases of goods and services are the purchases of goods and services by all levels of government – from Westminster to the local town hall. This item of expenditure includes the cost of providing national defence, law and order, street lighting, refuse collection, and so on. It does not include *transfer payments*. Such payments do not represent a purchase of goods and services but rather a transfer of funds from government to households.

Net exports of goods and services are the value of exports minus the value of imports. When Rover sells a car to a buyer in the United States, the value of that car is part of UK exports. When your local VW dealer stocks up on the latest model, its expenditure is part of UK imports.

Table 22.1 shows the relative importance of the four items of aggregate expenditure. The largest component is personal consumption expenditure and the smallest is net exports (negative in 1997).

Expenditures Not in GDP Aggregate expenditure, which equals GDP, does not include all the things that people and businesses buy. To distinguish total expenditure on GDP from other items of spending, we call the expenditure included in GDP *final expenditure*. Items that are not part of final expenditure and not part of GDP include the purchase of:

1 Intermediate goods and services.
2 Second-hand goods.
3 Financial securities.

Intermediate goods and services are the goods and services that firms buy from each other and use as inputs in the goods and services that they eventually sell to final users. An example of an intermediate good is a computer chip that Dell buys from Intel. A Dell computer is a final good, but an Intel chip is an intermediate good. To count the expenditure on intermediate goods and services as well as the expenditure on the final good involves counting the same thing twice – known as *double counting*.

Some goods are sometimes intermediate goods and sometimes final goods. For example, the ice cream that you buy on a hot summer day is a final good, but the ice cream that a restaurant buys and uses to make a dessert is an intermediate good. Whether a good is intermediate or final depends on what it is used for, and not on what it is.

Expenditure on *second-hand* goods is not part of GDP because these goods were counted as part of GDP in the period in which they were produced and in which they were new goods. For example, a 1988 car was part of GDP in 1988. If the car is sold in the second-hand car market in 1995, the amount paid for the car is not part of GDP in 1995.

Firms often sell *financial securities* such as bonds and stocks to finance purchases of newly produced capital goods. The expenditure on newly produced capital goods is part of GDP, but the expenditure on financial securities is not. GDP includes the amount spent on new capital, not the amount spent on pieces of paper.

Let's look at the second way of measuring GDP.

The Factor Incomes Approach

The *factor incomes approach* measures GDP by summing all the incomes paid by firms to households for the services of the factors of production they hire – wages for labour, interest for capital, rent for land and profits paid for entrepreneurship. Let's see how the factor incomes approach works.

Factor incomes are divided into four categories:

1 Compensation of employees.
2 Rent.
3 Gross trading profits and surplus.
4 Income from self-employment.

Compensation of employees is the total payments by firms for labour services. This item includes the net wages and salaries (called take-home pay) that workers receive each week or month plus taxes withheld on earnings plus fringe benefits such as social security and pension fund contributions.

Rent is the payment for the use of land and other rented inputs. It includes payments for rented housing and imputed rent for owner-occupied housing. (Imputed rent is an estimate of what homeowners would pay to rent the housing they own and use themselves. By including this item in the national income accounts, we measure the total value of housing services, whether they are owned or rented.)

Gross trading profits and surplus are the total profits made by corporations and the surpluses generated by publicly owned enterprises. Some of these profits are paid to households in the form of dividends, and some are retained by corporations as undistributed profits. The surpluses from public enterprises are either retained by the enterprises or paid to the government as part of its general revenue.

Income from self employment is a mixture of the elements that we have just reviewed. The proprietor of an owner-operated business supplies labour, capital and perhaps land and buildings to the business. It is difficult to split up the income earned by an owner-operator into its component parts – compensation for labour, payment for the use of capital, rent payments for the use of land or buildings and profit – so the national income accounts lump all these separate incomes into one category – called *mixed income*.

In fact it is difficult to separate out profits from rent. Many corporations own property on which they earn rents and are declared as profits. The Office for National Statistics (ONS) identifies the profits and surpluses of each sector – private, public, financial and non-financial corporations and lumps them together and calls them *Total Operating Surplus*.

The sum of these components of factor incomes is called *domestic income at factor cost*. It is not GDP. One further adjustment is needed to get to GDP – from factor cost to market prices.

Factor Cost to Market Price When we add up all the final expenditures on goods and services, we arrive at a total called gross domestic product at *market prices*. These expenditures are valued at the market prices that people pay for the various goods and services. Another way of valuing goods and services is at factor cost. *Factor cost* is the value of a good or service measured by adding together the costs of all the factors of production used to produce it. If the only economic transactions were between households and firms – if there were no government taxes or subsidies – the market price and factor cost values would be the same. But the presence of indirect taxes and subsidies makes these two methods of valuation differ.

An *indirect tax* is a tax paid by consumers when they buy goods and services. (In contrast, a *direct tax* is a tax on income.) Value added tax (VAT) and purchase taxes on alcohol, petrol and tobacco are indirect taxes. Because of indirect taxes, consumers pay more for some goods and services than producers receive. The market price is greater than the factor cost. For example, at a VAT rate of 17.5 per cent the purchase of a CD at a cost of £10.99 means you will have paid £9.35 as the cost price and £1.64 VAT.

A *subsidy* is a payment by the government to a producer. Payments made to your local Training and Enterprise Council (TEC) are to subsidize training courses. Because of subsidies, consumers pay less for some goods and services than producers receive. The market price is less than the factor cost.

To use the factor incomes approach to measure GDP, we must add indirect taxes to total factor incomes and subtract subsidies. Making this adjustment gets us to GDP.

Table 22.2 summarizes these calculations and shows how the factor incomes approach leads to the same estimate of GDP as the expenditure approach. The ONS no longer separates out income from self employment, rental income and profits and surpluses. These are now treated as surpluses to different sectors and added together. The measures of profits and surpluses exclude the gains made from the appreciation of assets and so the factor incomes added together with taxes less subsidies should give us GDP at market prices. Table 22.2 shows the relative magnitudes of the various factor incomes. As you can see, compensation of employees make up by far the largest factor income.

The Output Approach

The third method used to measure GDP is the output method. This method measures the contribution that an industry makes to GDP. But to measure the value of production of an individual industry, we must be careful to count only the value added by that industry. **Value added** is the value of a firm's production minus the value of the *intermediate goods* bought from other firms. Equivalently, it is the sum of the incomes (including profits) paid to

Table 22.2 GDP: The Factor Incomes Approach

Item	Amount in 1997 (millions of pounds)	Percentage of GDP
Wages and salaries	432,280	53.9
Mixed income	42,623	5.3
Total Operating Surplus	218,539	27.3
Indirect taxes *less* Subsidies	107,537	13.4
Statistical discrepancy	993	0.1
Gross domestic product	801,972	100.0

The sum of all factor incomes equals domestic income at factor cost. GDP equals net domestic income plus taxes less subsidies. In 1997, GDP measured by the factor incomes approach was £801,972 million. Compensation of Employees was by far the largest part of total factor incomes.

Source: ONS, *UK National Accounts: The Blue Book*, 1998, London.

Figure 22.3 Value Added and Final Expenditure

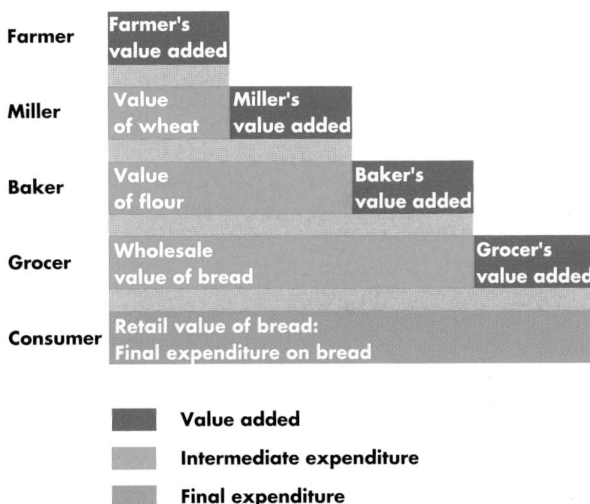

A consumer's expenditure on a loaf of bread is equal to the sum of the value added at each stage in its production. Intermediate expenditure, for example the amount paid for the purchase of flour by the baker from the miller, equals the value added by the farmer and the miller. If intermediate expenditure is included in the total, then parts of value added are counted twice.

the factors of production used by the firm to produce its output. Let's illustrate value added by looking at the production of a loaf of bread.

Figure 22.3 takes you through the brief life of a loaf of bread. It starts with the farmer, who grows the wheat. To do so, the farmer hires labour, capital equipment and land. Wages are paid to farm workers and interest and rent are paid. The farmer also earns a profit. The entire value of the wheat produced is the farmer's value added. The miller buys wheat from the farmer and turns it into flour. To do so, the miller hires labour and capital equipment. Wages are paid to mill workers, interest is paid on the capital and the miller earns a profit. The miller has now added value to the wheat bought from the farmer. The baker buys flour from the miller. The price of the flour includes the value added by the farmer and by the miller. The baker adds more value by turning the flour into bread. Wages are paid to bakery workers, interest is paid on the capital used by the baker and the baker earns a profit. The grocer buys the bread from the baker. The price paid by the grocer includes the value added by the farmer, the miller and the baker. At this stage the value of the loaf is its *wholesale* value. The grocer adds further value by making the loaf available in a convenient place at a convenient time. The consumer buys the bread for a price – its *retail price* – that includes the value added by the farmer, the miller, the baker and the grocer.

Final Goods and Intermediate Goods To value output, we count only *value added* because the sum of the value added at each stage of production equals expenditure on the *final good*. By using value added, we avoid double counting. In the above example, the only thing that has been produced and consumed is a loaf of bread – shown by the green bar in Figure 22.3. The value added at each stage is shown by the red bars, and the sum of the red bars equals the green bar. The transactions involving intermediate goods, shown by the blue bars, are not part of value added and are not counted as part of the value of output or of GDP.

Figure 22.4 shows the contribution of each sector to total output in the United Kingdom. The share of each sector is given by the value added contribution of each sector. The sum of the value of each sector gives GDP at factor cost.

Figure 22.4 Aggregate Expenditure, Output and Income

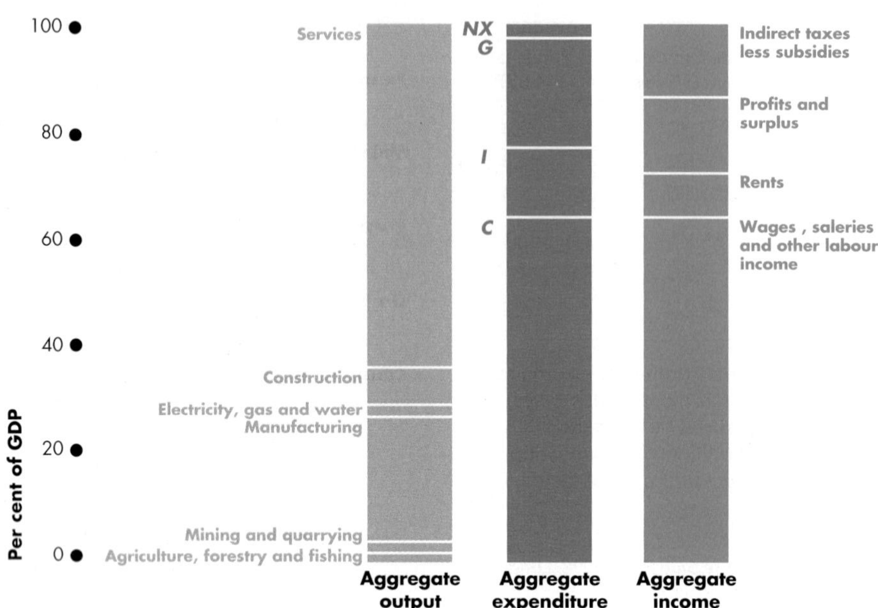

The orange bar illustrates the components of aggregate output and their relative magnitudes. It shows the share of each industrial sector's contribution to GDP. The total GDP is the value added by all activities that produce goods and services. The smallest components are agriculture, forestry and fishing, mining and quarrying, and electricity, gas and water. The largest contribution is from services.

The red bar illustrates the components of aggregate expenditure as well as their relative magnitudes. Net exports, the smallest component, can be either a positive or negative value.

The green bar illustrates the components of aggregate income and their relative magnitudes. The smallest component is rents and the largest is wages, salaries and other labour income.

The figure illustrates the equality between aggregate expenditure, aggregate output and aggregate income.

Source: ONS, *National Income Accounts*, 1998, *Blue Book*.

Aggregate Expenditure, Income and GDP Output You've seen that aggregate expenditure equals aggregate income. And you've seen that the ONS uses both aggregate expenditure and aggregate income to measure GDP. Why does it use two approaches when they are supposed to be the same? The answer is that although the two concepts of the value of aggregate output are identical, the actual measurements, which are based on samples of information, give slightly different answers. The expenditure approach uses data from *Family Expenditure Survey*, house building, business investment, the accounts of central and local government, HM Customs and Excise records and many other sources. The factor incomes approach uses data supplied by the Inland Revenue. None of these sources gives a complete coverage of all the items that make up aggregate expenditure and aggregate factor incomes. So by using the two approaches, the ONS can check one aggregate against the other. The discrepancy (known as the *Initial Residual Difference* – IRD) has at times been large and has been used as an indicator of the underground economy. The discrepancy is used to adjust both income and expenditure to make them equal.

Figure 22.4 shows this equality between the approaches to measuring GDP and gives a snapshot summary of the expenditure, income and output concepts. It also shows the relative magnitudes of the components of aggregate expenditure and aggregate income.

Review

- The expenditure approach to measuring GDP sums consumption expenditure, investment, government purchases and net exports.
- The factor incomes approach to measuring GDP sums wages, interest, rent and profits.
- To value the production of an industry, we use the value added of that industry.

So far, in our study of GDP and its measurement, we've been concerned with the nominal (or money) value of GDP and its components. But GDP can change either because prices change or because there is a change in the volume of goods and services produced – a change in real GDP. Let's now see how we measure the price level and distinguish between the nominal value and the real value of GDP.

The Price Level and Inflation

The *price level* is the average level of prices measured by a *price index*. To construct a price index, we take a basket of goods and services and calculate its value in the current period and its value in a base period. The price index is the value of the basket in the current period expressed as a percentage of the value of the same basket in the base period.

Two main price indexes are used to measure the price level in the United Kingdom today. They are:

1 The Retail Prices Index.

2 The GDP deflator.

Retail Prices Index

The **Retail Prices Index (RPI)** measures the average level of prices of the goods and services that a typical UK household consumes. The RPI is published every month by the ONS. To construct the RPI, the ONS first selects a base period. Currently, it is 13 January 1987. Then it surveys consumer spending patterns to determine the typical or average 'basket' of goods and services that people buy in the base period. Around 500 different goods and services feature in the RPI.

Every month, the ONS sends a team of observers to more than 180 geographical locations in the United Kingdom and takes some 150,000 price quotations to record the prices for the 500 items. When all the data are in, the RPI is calculated by valuing the basket of goods and services at the current month's prices. That value is expressed as a percentage of the value of the same basket in the base period.

To see more precisely how the RPI is calculated, let's work through a simplified example. Table 22.3 summarizes the calculations. Let's suppose that there are only three goods in the typical consumer's basket: apples, haircuts and bus rides. The table shows the quantities bought and the prices prevailing in the base period. It also shows total expenditure in the base period. The typical consumer buys 200 bus rides at 30 pence each and so spends £60 on bus rides. Expenditure on apples and haircuts is worked out in the same way. Total expenditure is the sum of expenditures on the three goods, which is £98.

To calculate the price index for the current period, we need only to discover the prices of the goods in the current period. We do not need to know the quantities bought. Let's suppose that the prices are those set out in Table 22.3 under 'Current period'. We can now calculate the current period's value of the (base-period) basket of goods by using the current period's prices. For example, the current price of apples is down to 24 pence a kilogram, so the current period's value of the base-period quantity (5 kilograms) is £1.20. The base-period quantities of haircuts and bus rides are valued at this period's prices in a similar way. The total value of the base-period basket in the current period is £107.80.

We can now calculate the RPI – the ratio of this period's value of the basket to the base period's value, multiplied by 100. In this example the RPI for the current period is 109. The RPI for the base period is, by definition, 100.

The ONS also publishes a price index that eliminates the mortgage interest component of typical household expenditure on the basket of goods. The main reason for the exclusion of mortgage interest is because the RPI will show a rise in prices when the rate of interest is raised to control inflation. The new price index is known as the RPIX. It is argued that RPIX is a better indicator of underlying inflation. While there is some truth in this argument, it is also true that mortgage interest payment is a valid expenditure by households.

Table 22.3 The Retail Price Index: A Simplified Calculation

Base period basket	Base period		Current period	
	Price	Expenditure	Price	Expenditure
5 kilograms of apples	£0.40/kilogram	£2.00	£0.24/kilogram	£1.20
6 haircuts	£6.00 each	£36.00	£6.10 each	£36.60
200 bus rides	£0.30 each	£60.00	£0.35 each	£70.00
Total expenditure		£98.00		£107.80
RPI	$\frac{£98.00}{£98.00} \times 100 = 100$		$\frac{£107.80}{£98.00} \times 100 = 110$	

A fixed basket of goods – 5 kilograms of apples, 6 haircuts and 200 bus rides – is valued in the base period at £98. Prices change, and that same basket is valued at £107.80 in the current period. The RPI is equal to the current-period value of the basket divided by the base-period value of the basket multiplied by 100. In the base period the RPI is 100, and in the current period the RPI is 110.

Table 22.4 Nominal GDP, Real GDP and the GDP Deflator: Simplified Calculations

Current year output	Base-period values		Current-period values	
	Price	Expenditure	Price	Expenditure
4,240 kilograms of apples	50p/kilogram	£2,120	52.5p/kilogram	£2,226
5 computers	£1,000 each	£5,000	£1,050 each	£2,226
1,060 metres of red tape	50p/metre	£530	50p/metre	£530
	Real GDP	**£7,650**	**Nominal GDP**	**£8,006**

$$\text{GDP deflator} = \frac{£8,606}{£7,650} \times 100 = 104.7$$

An imaginary economy produces only apples, computers and red tape. In the current period, nominal GDP is £8,006. If the current-period quantities are valued at the base-period prices, we obtain a measure of real GDP, which is £7,650. The GDP deflator in the current period – which is calculated by dividing nominal GDP by real GDP in that period and multiplying by 100 – is 104.7.

GDP Deflator

The **GDP deflator** measures the average level of prices of all the goods and services that are included in GDP. Currently, the base period for the GDP deflator is 1990.

We are going to learn how to calculate the GDP deflator by studying an imaginary economy that has just three final goods: a consumption good that households buy (apples), a capital good that firms buy (computers) and a good that the government buys (red tape). Net exports are zero in this example. Table 22.4 summarizes the calculations of the GDP deflator in this economy.

To calculate the GDP deflator, we use the formula;

$$\text{GDP deflator} = \frac{\text{Nominal GDP}}{\text{Real GDP}} \times 100$$

To calculate nominal GDP, we use the expenditure approach. The table shows the quantities of the final goods and their prices. To calculate nominal GDP, we work out the expenditure on each good and then total the three

Figure 22.5 The GDP Balloon

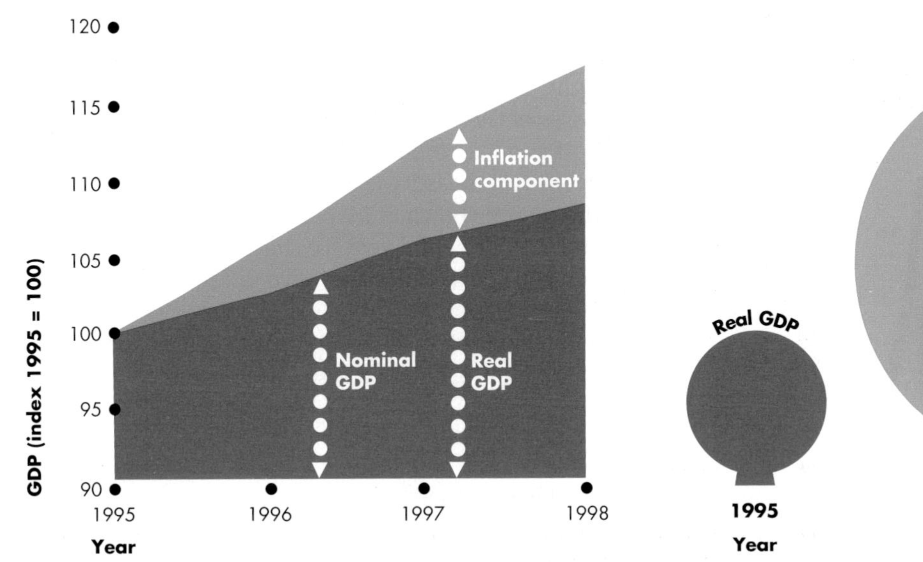

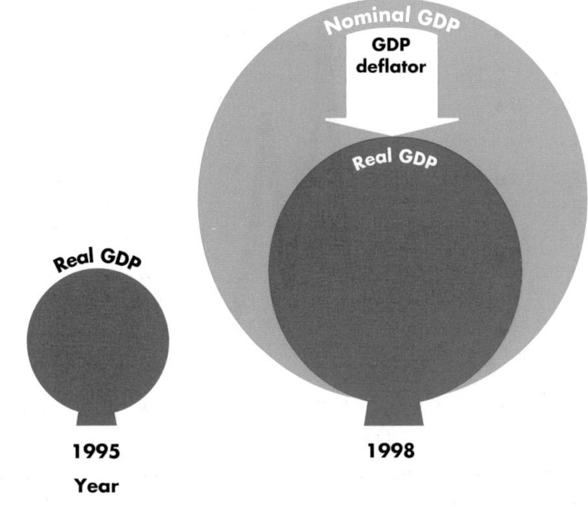

Part of the rise in GDP comes from inflation and part from increased production – an increase in real GDP (part a). The GDP deflator lets some air out of the GDP balloon (part b) so that we can see the extent to which production has grown.

Source: ONS, *Economic Trends*, April 1998.

expenditures. Consumption expenditure (apples) is £2,226, investment (computers) is £5,250 and government purchases (red tape) are £530, so nominal GDP is £8,006.

Now let's calculate real GDP, a measure of the physical volume of output. To do so, we value the current-period quantities at the base-period prices. Because the base year is 1990, we refer to the units in which real GDP is measured as '1990 prices'. The table shows the prices for the base period. Real expenditure on apples for the current period is 4,240 kilograms valued at 50 pence a kilogram, which is £2,120. If we perform the same types of calculations for computers and red tape and add up the real expenditures, we arrive at a real GDP of £7,650.

Let's put the numbers we've found into the formula for the GDP deflator. Nominal GDP is £8,006 and real GDP is £7,650, so the GDP deflator is:

$$\text{GDP deflator} = \frac{£8{,}606}{£7{,}650} \times 100 = 104.7$$

Notice that when the current period is also the base period, nominal GDP equals real GDP and the GDP deflator is 100.

You can think of nominal GDP as a balloon that is being blown up by growing production and rising prices. Figure 22.5 illustrates this idea. The GDP deflator lets the inflation air out of the nominal GDP balloon – the contribution of rising prices – so that we can see what has happened to *real* GDP. The red balloon for 1993 shows real GDP in that year. The green balloon shows *nominal* GDP in 1997. The red balloon for 1997 shows real GDP for that year. To see real GDP in 1997, we *deflate* nominal GDP using the GDP deflator.

What the Inflation Numbers Mean

A major purpose of the RPI and the GDP deflator is to measure inflation, and the measures are put to practical use. For example, the RPI is used to determine cost of living adjustments to state pensions, jobseekers' allowance, other social security payments

Figure 22.6 Measures of Inflation

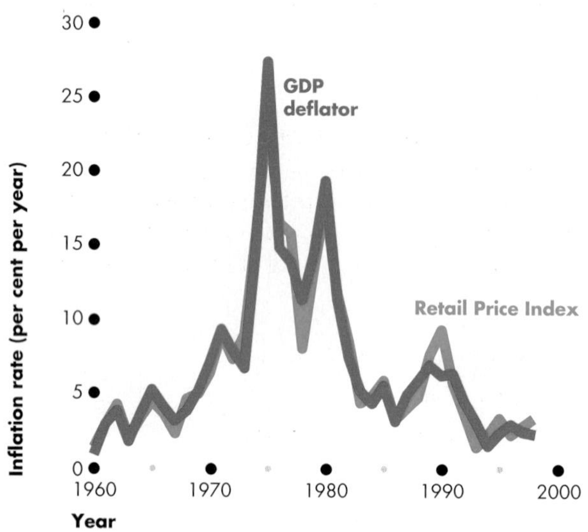

The RPI and the GDP deflator have similar averages – RPI 7.0 per cent a year and GDP deflator 7.1 per cent a year – over the period shown here. The government has put forward the RPIX as a more appropriate measure of the underlying inflation rate. The RPIX is the RPI *excluding* mortgage interest. The main reason the government prefers the RPIX is because if the rate of interest is raised to choke off a build-up in inflationary pressure, the resulting rise in mortgage interest rates raises the general RPI but not the RPIX. In general, the RPI fluctuates more than the GDP deflator but both measures probably overstate the inflation rate.

Source: ONS, *Economic Trends Annual Supplement*, 1998 and *Economic Trends*, April 1998.

and upward adjustment of tax allowances – the income ranges over which different income tax rates apply. How good a measure of inflation does the RPI or the GDP deflator give? Does a 2.7 per cent increase in the RPI mean that the cost of living has increased by 2.7 per cent? And does a 3 per cent increase in the GDP deflator mean that the prices of the goods and services that make up real GDP have increased by 3 per cent? Let's find out.

Measuring the inflation rate accurately is of crucial importance. It tells us how the value of money is changing, and it affects our assessment of changes in real GDP. A 1 per cent upward bias in the estimated inflation rate translates into a 1 per cent downward bias in the estimated growth rate of real GDP and real wage rates. And a 1 per cent a year bias sustained over 10 years throws the estimate of real GDP and real wages off by more than 10 per cent.

Despite the importance of getting the numbers right, the RPI and the GDP deflator give different views of the inflation rate, and neither index is a perfect measure. Figure 22.6 shows the difference in the two measures. The average inflation rate over the period shown is 7.0 per cent a year for the RPI and 7.1 per cent a year for the GDP deflator but as you can see at times they give different messages about inflation.

Worse, *both* measures of inflation probably overstate the inflation rate. The main sources of bias are:

- New goods bias.
- Quality change bias.
- Substitution bias.

New Goods Bias New goods keep replacing old goods. For example, CDs have replaced LP records and PCs have replaced typewriters. If you want to compare the price level in 1995 with that in 1975, you somehow have to compare the price of a CD and a computer today with that of an LP and typewriter in 1975. Because CDs and PCs are more expensive today than LPs and typewriters, the arrival of these new goods puts an upward bias into the estimate of the price level.

Quality Change Bias Most goods undergo constant quality improvement. Cars, computers, CD players and even textbooks get better year after year. Improvements in quality often mean increases in price. But such price increases are not inflation. For example, suppose that a 1995 car is 5 per cent better and costs 5 per cent more than a 1994 car. Adjusted for the quality change, the price of the car has been constant. But in calculating the RPI, the price of the car will be counted as having increased by 5 per cent.

Estimates have been made of the importance of quality change bias, especially for obvious changes such as those in cars and computers. Allowing for quality improvements changes the inflation picture by between 1 and 2 percentage points a year, on the average, according to some economists. That is, correctly measured, the inflation rate might be as much as 2 percentage points a year less than the published numbers.

Substitution Bias A change in the RPI measures the percentage change in the price of a *fixed* basket of goods and services. But changes in relative prices lead consumers to seek less costly items. For example, by shopping more frequently at discount stores and less frequently at convenience stores, consumers can cut the prices they pay. By using discount fares on airlines, they can cut the cost of travel. This kind of substitution of cheaper items for more costly items is not picked up by the RPI. Because consumers make such substitutions, a price index based on a fixed basket overstates the effects of a given price change on the inflation rate.

To reduce the bias problems, the ONS revises the basket used for calculating the RPI about every five years based on the spending patterns of households within a specified income group. Yet despite periodic updating, the RPI is of limited value for making comparisons of the cost of living over long periods of time and even has shortcomings as a measure of year-to-year inflation rates.

Review

- The Retail Prices Index measures the average prices of a fixed basket of consumption items bought by a typical urban household.
- The GDP deflator measures the average prices of the items that make up GDP.
- The RPI and GDP deflator may overstate the inflation rate by an estimated 1 per cent and 2 per cent a year.

You now know how inflation is calculated and what the inflation numbers mean. You also know that by letting the inflationary air out of the GDP balloon, we can reveal real GDP. But what does real GDP really mean? Let's find out.

What Real GDP Means

Estimates of real GDP and the real GDP growth rate are used for many purposes. But the three main uses are:

1 To assess changes in economic welfare over time.
2 To make international comparisons of GDP.
3 For business cycle assesment and forecasting.

Economic Welfare

Economic welfare is a comprehensive measure of the general state of well-being. Improvements in economic welfare depend on the growth of real GDP. But they also depend on many other factors not measured by GDP. Some of these factors are:

- Quality improvements.
- Household production.
- The underground economy.
- Health and life expectancy.
- Leisure time.
- The environment.
- Political freedom and social justice.

Quality Improvements You have seen that the price indices we use to measure inflation give a downward biased estimate of the growth rate of real GDP. When car prices rise because cars have improved (becoming safer, faster, more fuel efficient, more comfortable), the RPI and the GDP deflator count the price increase as inflation. So what is really an increase in production is counted as an increase in price rather than an increase in real GDP. It is deflated away by the wrongly measured higher price level.

Household Production An enormous amount of production takes place every day in our homes. Changing a light bulb, cutting the grass, washing the car and growing vegetables are all examples of productive activities that do not involve market transactions and are not counted as part of GDP.

Household production has become much more capital intensive over the years. As a result, less labour is used in household production than in earlier periods. For example, a microwave meal that takes just a few minutes to prepare uses a great deal of capital and almost no labour. Because we use less labour and more capital in household production, it is not easy to work out whether this type of production has increased or decreased over time. But it is likely that market production counted in GDP has increasingly replaced household production. Two trends point in this direction. One is the trend in female employment, which has increased from 46 per cent of the female population of working age in 1960 to 67 per cent in 1997. The other trend is the marketization of traditionally home-produced goods and services. For example, more and more households now buy takeaways, eat in fast food restaurants and use nursery services. This trend means that increasing proportions of food preparation and child care that used to be part of household production are now measured as part of GDP.

The Underground Economy The *underground economy* is the part of the economy purposely hidden from view by the people operating in it to avoid taxes and regulations or because the goods and services they are producing are illegal. Because underground economic activity is unreported, it is omitted from GDP.

The underground economy is easy to describe, even if it is hard to measure. It includes the production and distribution of drugs, production that uses illegal labour that is paid less than the minimum wage, and jobs done for cash to avoid paying income taxes. This last category might be quite large and includes tips earned by taxi drivers, hairdressers, and hotel and restaurant workers. Estimates of the scale of the underground economy range between 3.5 and 14.5 per cent of GDP (£28 billion to £110 billion) in the United Kingdom and much more in some countries.

Provided the underground economy is a reasonably stable proportion of the total economy, its omission from GDP does not pose a problem. The growth rate of real GDP still gives a useful estimate of the long-term growth rate and of business cycle fluctuations. But sometimes production shifts from the underground to the rest of the economy and sometimes it shifts the other way. The underground economy expands relative to the rest of the economy if taxes become especially high or if regulations become especially restricting. And the underground economy shrinks relative to the rest of the economy if the burden of taxes and regulations are eased. During the 1980s, when tax rates were cut, there was an increase in tax revenues. Some of this may have been owing to the existing workforce, particularly high-paid labour, working harder, taking greater risks and being more productive, but some of it could have been owing to a switch from what was previously underground activity to recorded activity. So some part (but probably a small part) of the expansion of real GDP during the 1980s represented a shift from the underground economy rather than an increase in production.

Health and Life Expectancy Good health and a long life – the hopes of everyone – do not show up in real GDP, at least not directly. A higher real GDP does enable us to spend more on medical research, health care, healthy food and exercise equipment. And as real GDP has increased, our life expectancy has lengthened – from 70 years at the end of World War II to approaching 80 years today. Infant deaths and death in childbirth, two fearful scourges of the nineteenth century, have almost been eliminated.

But we face new health and life expectancy problems every year. AIDS, drug abuse, suicide and murder are taking young lives at a rate that causes serious concern. And in recent years, the number of households, mostly single parent families, which are living below the official poverty level has increased. When we take these negative influences into account, we see that real GDP growth overstates the improvements in economic welfare.

Leisure Time Leisure time is an economic good that adds to our economic welfare. Other things remaining the same, the more leisure we have, the better off we are. Our time spent working is valued as part of GDP, but our leisure time is not. Yet from the point of view of economic welfare, that leisure time must be at least as valuable to us as the wage that we earn for the last hour worked. If it was not, we would work instead of taking the leisure. Over the years, leisure time has steadily increased. The working week has become shorter, and the number and length of holidays have increased.

These improvements in economic well-being are not reflected in GDP.

The Environment The environment is directly affected by economic activity. The burning of hydrocarbon fuels is the most visible activity that damages our environment. But it is not the only example. The depletion of exhaustible resources, the mass clearing of forests, and the pollution of lakes and rivers are other major environmental consequences of industrial production.

Resources used to protect the environment are valued as part of GDP. For example, the value of catalytic converters that help to protect the atmosphere from carbon emissions are part of GDP. But if we did not use such pieces of equipment and instead polluted the atmosphere, we would not count the deteriorating air that we were breathing as a negative part of GDP.

An industrial society possibly produces more atmospheric pollution than an agricultural society does. But it is not always the case that such pollution increases as we become wealthier. One of the things that wealthy people value is a clean environment, and they devote resources to protecting it. Compare the pollution that was discovered in the former East Germany and the former Soviet Union in the late 1980s with pollution in the western developed countries. East Germany, a relatively poor country, polluted its rivers, lakes and atmosphere in a way that would have been unimaginable in wealthy West Germany.

Political Freedom and Social Justice Most people value political freedoms such as those provided by the western democracies. They also value social justice or fairness – equality of opportunity and of access to social security safety nets that protect people from the extremes of misfortune.

A country might have a large real GDP per person, but have limited political freedom and equity. For example, a small elite might enjoy political liberty and extreme wealth while the vast majority are effectively enslaved and live in abject poverty. Such an economy would generally be regarded as having less economic welfare than one that had the same amount of real GDP but in which political freedoms were enjoyed by everyone. Today, China has rapid real GDP growth but limited political freedoms, while Russia has a decreasing real GDP and an emerging democratic political system. Economists have no easy way to determine which of these countries is better off.

The Bottom Line What is the bottom line? Do we get the wrong message about changes (or differences) in economic welfare by looking at changes (or differences) in real GDP? The influences omitted from real GDP are probably important and could be large. Developing countries have a larger underground economy and a larger amount of household production than do developed countries. So as an economy develops and grows, part of the apparent growth might reflect a switch from underground to recorded production and from home production to market production. This measurement error overstates the rate of economic growth and the improvement in economic welfare.

Other influences on living standards include the amount of leisure time available, the quality of the environment, the security of jobs and homes, the safety of city streets, and so on. It is possible to construct broader measures that combine the many influences that contribute to human happiness. Real GDP will be one element in these broader measures, but it will by no means be the whole of them.

The Office for National Statistics has recently rebased UK GDP in 1995 prices and has altered the accounting system to bring it into line with the 1995 European System of Accounts. Look at *Reading Between the Lines* on pp. 550–551.

International Comparisons of GDP

All the problems we've just reviewed affect the economic welfare of every country, so, in order to make international comparisons of economic welfare, factors additional to real GDP must be used. But real GDP comparisons are a major component of international welfare comparisons and two special problems arise in making these comparisons. First, the real GDP of one country must be converted into the same currency units as the real GDP of the other country. Second, the same prices must be used to value the goods and services in the countries being compared. Let's look at these two problems by using a striking example, a comparison of the United States and China.

In 1992 (the most recent year for which we can make this comparison), real GDP per person in the United States was $24,408. The official Chinese statistics published by the International Monetary Fund (IMF) say that real GDP per person in China in 1992 was 2,028 Yuan (the Yuan is the currency of China). On average, during 1992, $1 US was worth 5.762 Yuan. If we use this exchange rate to convert Chinese Yuan into US dollars, we get a value of $352.

The official comparison of China and the United States makes China look extremely poor. In 1992, real GDP per person in the United States was 69 times that in China.

Figure 22.7 shows the official story of real GDP in China between 1968 and 1992. But Figure 22.7 also shows another story. It shows an estimate of real GDP per person in China that is much larger than the official measure. Let's see how this alternative measurement is made.

GDP in the United States is measured by using prices that prevail in the United States. China's GDP

Figure 22.7 Two Views of GDP in China

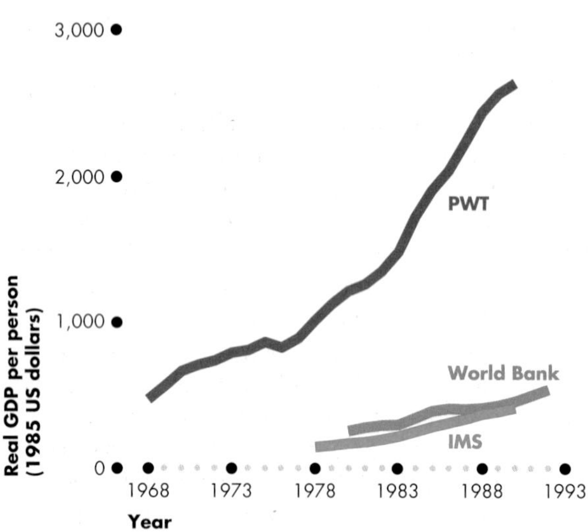

According to the official statistics of the International Monetary Fund and the World Bank, China is a poor developing country. But according to an alternative view based on purchasing power prices, China has a GDP more than six times the official view and has the world's third largest total production.

Sources: IMF, *International Financial Statistics Yearbook*, 1994, Washington, DC; World Bank, *World Development Report*, 1994, Washington, DC; Robert Summers and Alan Heston, New computer diskette (Mark 5.5), 15 June 1993, distributed by the National Bureau of Economic Research to update The Penn World Table (Mark 5): An Expanded Set of International Comparisons, 1950–1988, *Quarterly Journal Of Economics*, May 1991, 327–368; and author's calculations.

is measured by using prices that prevail in China. But the relative prices in the two countries are very different. Some goods that are expensive in the United States cost very little in China. These items get a small weight in China's real GDP. If, instead of using China's prices, all the goods and services produced in China are valued at the prices prevailing in the United States, then a more valid comparison can be made of GDP in the two countries. Such a comparison uses prices called *purchasing power parity prices*.

Robert Summers and Alan Heston, economists in the Center for International Comparisons at the University of Pennsylvania, have used purchasing power parity prices to construct real GDP data for more than one hundred countries. These data, which are published in the Penn World Table (PWT), tell a remarkable story about China. The PWT data use 1985 as the base year, so they are measured in 1985 dollars. According to the Penn World Table, in 1992, real GDP per person in the United States was 12 times that of China, not the 69 times shown in the official data.

Figure 22.7 shows the PWT view of China and compares it with the official view. The difference in the two views arises from the prices used. The official statistics use Chinese prices, while the PWT data use purchasing power parity prices.

Despite large differences in estimates of the level of China's real GDP, there is much less doubt about its growth rate. The economy of China is expanding at an extraordinary rate.

US real GDP is measured quite reliably. But China's is not. The alternative measures of China's real GDP are somewhat unreliable, and the truth about GDP in China is not known.

Business Cycle Assessment and Forecasting

Did the Bank of England need to raise interest rates and slow down the economy during 1997? On the basis of the information available the Monetary Policy Committee (the committee of the Bank of England that decides monetary policy) decided that it did indeed need to take such action. But don't the measures of inflation used to calculate real GDP overstate the inflation rate? They do, but not in a cyclical way. They are out by a similar amount every year. So while the possible mismeasurement of inflation may lead to wrong estimates of long-term real GDP growth, it probably does not cause a wrong assessment of the phase of the business cycle.

The fluctuations in economic activity measured by real GDP tell a reasonably accurate story about the phase of the business cycle the economy is in. When real GDP grows the economy is in a business cycle expansion phase and when real GDP shrinks (for two quarters) the economy is in a recession. Also, as real GDP fluctuates, so do employment and unemployment.

But real GDP fluctuations probably exaggerate or overstate the fluctuations in total production and economic welfare. The reason is that when business activity slows down in a recession, household production increases and so does leisure time. When business activity speeds up in an expansion phase, household production and leisure time decrease. Because household production and leisure time increase in a recession and decrease in an expansion, they are countercyclical. As a result, real GDP fluctuations tend to overstate the fluctuations in total production and in economic welfare. But the directions of change of real GDP, total output and economic welfare are probably the same.

Review

- Real GDP is not an accurate measure of economic welfare because it undervalues quality improvements, omits some production and ignores indicators of economic welfare such as health and life expectancy, leisure time, the environment and political freedom.
- To make international comparisons of real GDP, we must use purchasing power parity prices.
- Real GDP understates the long-term growth rate and overstates business cycle fluctuations.

In Chapter 21, pp. 507–519, we studied the macroeconomic performance of the United Kingdom in recent years – the growth and fluctuations in real GDP, unemployment, inflation and the balance of international payments. We've now studied the methods used to measure some of these indicators of macroeconomic performance. We've seen how real GDP and the price level are measured, and we've seen what these measures mean. In Chapter 24, we study aggregate demand and aggregate supply. This aggregate model parallels the demand and supply model of a single market. And it serves as an overview and backdrop against which to place your study of economic growth, unemployment, and inflation. An understanding of this model will help you find your way through what can sometimes seem like a macroeconomic maze.

Summary

Key Points

Gross Domestic Product (pp. 530–534)

- Gross domestic product (GDP) is the value of aggregate output in a country in a given time period (usually a year).
- The concept of GDP is based on the circular flow of expenditure and income.
- Aggregate expenditure on goods and services equals aggregate income.
- The value of aggregate output – GDP – is equal to aggregate expenditure or aggregate income.

Measuring UK GDP (pp. 534–539)

- Because aggregate expenditure, aggregate income and the value of aggregate output are equal, we can measure GDP by either the expenditure approach or the factor incomes approach.
- The expenditure approach adds together consumption expenditure, investment, government purchases of goods and services and net exports to arrive at an estimate of GDP.
- The factor incomes approach adds together the incomes paid to the factors of production – labour, capital, land and profit paid to entrepreneurs.
- To use the factor incomes approach, it is necessary to add capital consumption (depreciation) to arrive at GDP.

The Price Level and Inflation (pp. 539–543)

- The two main indices that measure the price level are the Retail Prices Index and the GDP deflator.
- The RPI measures the average price level of goods and services typically consumed by UK households.

- The GDP deflator measures the average price level of all the goods and services that make up GDP.
- Inflation is measured by the rate of change of the RPI or the GDP deflator.
- The RPI and the GDP deflator give an upward-biased measure of inflation because some goods disappear and new goods become available, the quality of goods and services changes over time.

What Real GDP Means (pp. 543–547)

- Real GDP is not a perfect measure of either aggregate economic activity or economic welfare.
- Real GDP excludes quality improvements, household production, underground production, environmental damage and the contribution to economic welfare of health and life expectancy, leisure time, and political freedom and equity.

Key Figures and Tables 

Key Terms

Review Questions

1 List the components of aggregate expenditure.

2 What are the components of aggregate income?

3 Why does aggregate income equal aggregate expenditure?

4 Why does the value of output (or GDP) equal aggregate income?

5 Distinguish between government purchases of goods and services and transfer payments.

6 What are injections into the circular flow of income and expenditure? What are leakages?

7 How does the ONS measure GDP?

8 What is the distinction between expenditure on final goods and expenditure on intermediate goods?

9 What is value added? How is it calculated?

10 What are the two main price indices used to measure the price level?

11 How is the Retail Prices Index (RPI) calculated? Why does the government prefer to use the RPIX as a measure of inflation?

12 How is the basket of goods and services used in constructing the RPI chosen? Is it the same basket in 1998 as it was in 1955? If not, how is it different?

Problems

1 The following transactions took place in Europaland last year:

Item	Billions of euros
Wages paid to labour	800,000
Consumption expenditure	600,000
Taxes	250,000
Government transfer payments	50,000
Firms' profits	200,000
Investment	250,000
Government purchases	200,000
Exports	300,000
Saving	300,000
Imports	250,000

a Calculate Europaland's GDP.
b Did you use the expenditure approach or the factor incomes approach to make this calculation?
c What extra information do you need in order to calculate net domestic product?

2 Anne, the owner of The Cheesecake Factory in Liverpool, spends £100 on eggs, £50 on flour, £45 on milk, £10 on gas and electricity, and £60 on wages each week to produce 200 cakes. She sells her cakes for £1.50 each. Calculate the value added per cake at The Cheesecake Factory.

3 A typical family living on Rocky Island consumes only apple juice, bananas and cloth. Prices in the base year were £4 a litre for apple juice, £3 a kilogram for bananas and £5 a metre for cloth. In the base year, the typical family spent £40 on apple juice, £45 on bananas and £25 on cloth. In the current year, apple juice costs £3 a litre, bananas cost £4 a kilogram and cloth costs £7 a metre. Calculate the Retail Prices Index on Rocky Island in the current year and the inflation rate between the base year and the current year.

4 An economy has the following real GDP and nominal GDP in 1999, 2000 and 2001. The currency units are denoted in euroMarks (EM):

Year	Real GDP	Nominal GDP
1999	€M1,000 billion	€M1,000 billion
2000	€M1,050 billion	€M1,200 billion
2001	€M1,200 billion	€M1,500 billion

a What was the GDP deflator in 1999?
b What was the GDP deflator in 2000?
c What is the inflation rate as measured by the GDP deflator between 2000 and 2001?
d What is the percentage increase in the price level between 1999 and 2000 as measured by the GDP deflator?

5 A typical family on Sandy Island consumes only juice and cloth. Last year, which was the base year, the family spent €40 (40 euros) on juice and €25 on cloth. In the base year, juice was €4 a bottle and cloth was €5 a length. In the current year, juice is €4 a bottle and cloth is €6 a length. Calculate:

a The basket used in the RPI.
b The RPI in the current year.
c The inflation rate in the current year.

6 Study *Reading Between the Lines* on pp. 550–551 and then answer the following questions:

a Which items that were previously classified as inputs in the production process have been re-classified as capital investment in the new National Accounts?
b How was output in the education sector calculated under the former system of National Accounting and how is it done in the new National Accounts?
c How does the new system of national accounts affect economic decision makers such as the Treasury or Bank of England?

7 Use the Parkin, Powell and Matthews Web site to link on to the ONS site. There you can obtain data on real GDP and nominal GDP for the United Kingdom.

a What is the GDP deflator for the most recent year available?
b What was the GDP deflator in the previous year?
c What is the inflation rate as measured by the GDP deflator between these two years?
d What is real GDP for the most recent year available?
e What was real GDP in the previous year?
f What is the real GDP growth rate between these two years?
g Check from the data you have obtained that the growth in nominal GDP is the growth in real GDP less the rate of inflation as measured by the GDP deflator.

W http://www.econ100.com

Measuring the Economy

Financial Times, 3 August 1998 

Officials set to rewrite recent economic history

This year's Blue Book will alter the way the UK national accounts are calculated, says **Robert Chote**

The Office for National Statistics will rewrite Britain's recent economic history.

The big day is September 24, when the ONS will publish its annual "Blue Book" of UK national accounts. Official estimates of the economy's size, composition and growth will all be revised.

To the extent that this alters people's assessment of the gap between actual economic output and the "potential" level thought to be consistent with stable inflation, it will alter their view of the appropriate levels for interest rates and government borrowing.

■ For the first time the accounts will be arranged according to the 1995 European System of Accounts.

This will raise cash and inflation-adjusted measures of economic activity for recent years because spending on software, mineral exploration and some military spending will be classified as capital investment rather than inputs used up in the production of other goods and services.

Measures of growth in 1989 and 1990 will be reduced because this was when domestic rates (henceforth counted as part of consumer spending) were replaced by the "community charge" (treated as a tax on income).

Estimates of gross national product will also be reduced because the treatment of value-added tax revenue paid to the European Union will change.

■ The ONS will include the activities of more companies in the national accounts by combining its own business register – based on VAT registrations – with that compiled by the employment department from companies' income tax records.

■ The output of parts of the public sector will be measured directly for the first time, rather than using inputs – such as employment or procurement – as a proxy.

■ Eurostat, the European statistical agency, is pressing its national counterparts to improve the coverage of their national accounts. As part of this exercise the ONS will review the adjustment it makes to the national accounts for tax evasion.

The Essence of the Story

■ On September 24 1998, the ONS published the revised method of calculating the national accounts conforming to the 1995 European System of Accounts.

■ Reclassifying inputs in the production process as outputs will raise estimates of real GDP.

■ Domestic rates which was part of household spending was replaced by the 'community charge' which is treated as a tax on income.

■ Output estimates will be raised by matching the records of firms kept by HM Customs for VAT registration with those kept by the Employment Department based on income tax returns.

■ Output of services will be measured by quality adjusted outputs rather than based on inputs and improved estimates of the black economy will be used to account for tax evasion.

Economic Analysis

■ The rebasing of GDP from 1990 prices to 1995 prices will reduce measures of economic activity because the weight given to parts of the economy for which prices are rising slowly is lower in the new accounts.

■ However, other components of GDP will be given higher weight and measured more accurately such as output from the public sector, output from small businesses, and output from the 'black economy'.

■ Figure 1 shows GDP at market prices using the old system of accounts and the new system of accounts. The new system of accounts shows a systematic increase in measured GDP.

■ You can see from Figure 2 that the higher measure of GDP is not because of higher measured consumer spending. Consumer spending on the new accounts is lower than in the old accounts because of the re-classification of domestic rates and the community charge as a tax on income rather than a household expenditure.

■ Figure 3 shows the evolution of real GDP obtained from both systems of accounts based on an index 1990 = 100. Relative to 1990, the new accounts show less of a fall in output in the 1990–92 recession and a faster upturn in the recovery. Real GDP in 1997 is higher on the new accounts than on the old accounts.

■ The improvement in GDP on the new accounts is due to better measurement of public sector output and output from small firms, reclassification of inputs as outputs and better estimates of the 'black economy'.

■ The problem for policy makers and economic forecasters is that the new data has re-written the history of the 1990–92 recession and could present a changed picture of real GDP relative to potential GDP as seen in Figure 21.2.

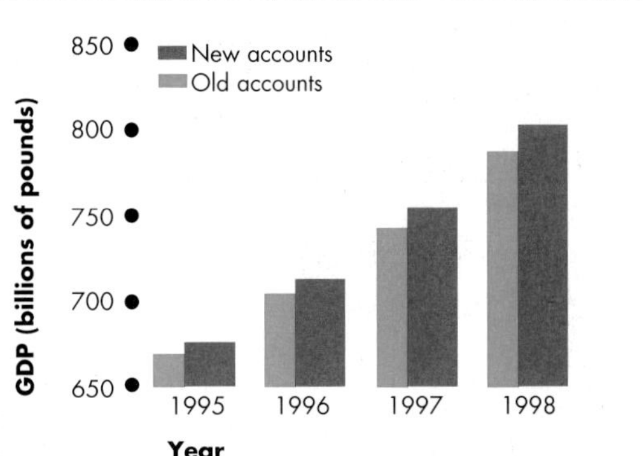

Figure 1 Old and new system of national accounts

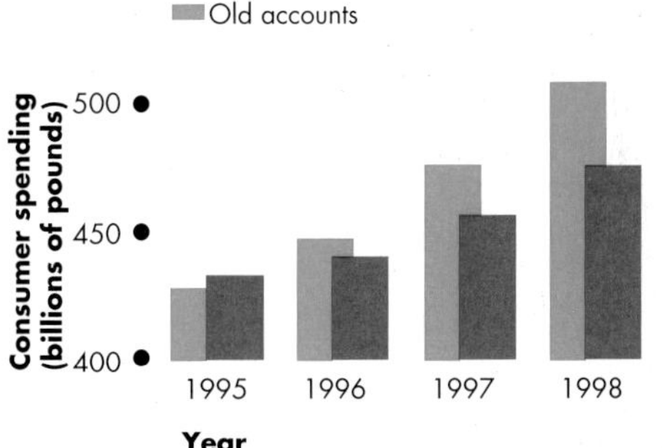

Figure 2 Consumer spending

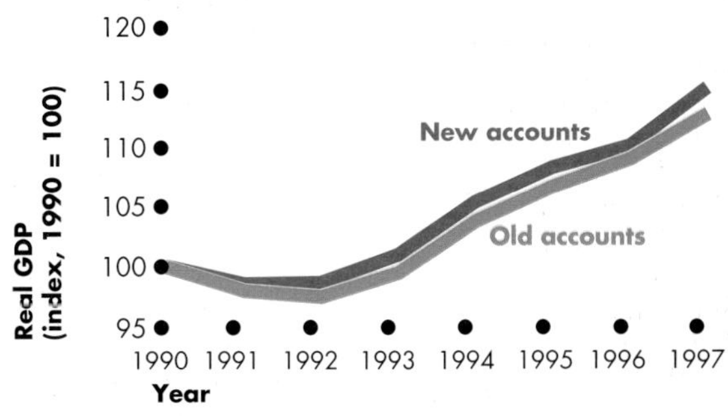

Figure 3 Real GDP

Employment and Unemployment

After studying this chapter you will be able to:

- Define the unemployment rate, the work-force economic activity rate, the economic activity rate and aggregate hours
- Describe the trends and fluctuations in the indicators of labour market performance
- Describe the sources of unemployment, its duration and the groups most affected by it
- Explain how employment and wage rates are determined by demand and supply in the labour market

Vital Signs

Each month, we chart the course of the unemployment rate as a measure of economic health. How do we measure the unemployment rate? What does it tell us? Is it a reliable vital sign for the economy? ◆ December 1992 was a month in which unemployment peaked at almost 3 million. How can this large number of people be unemployed? How do people become unemployed? Do most of them get fired or do most simply quit their jobs to look for better ones? How long do spells of unemployment last for most people? A week or two or several months? And how does the length of unemployment spell vary over the business cycle? ◆ You may know that unemployment is more common among young people than older people. It affects ethnic minorities much more severely than whites. Why isn't unemployment 'shared' more equitably by all age and racial groups? ◆ Another feature of the labour market that we regularly monitor is the number of people working. This number fluctuates as the unemployment rate fluctuates. At the start of 1998, 27 million people in the United Kingdom had a job. What does this information tell us about the health of the economy? Does the number of jobs grow quickly enough to keep pace with the increase in population? ◆ The European Union is an economy that is comparable in size with the United States, but unemployment in the EU is nearly twice as high as in the USA. Why is this? What special factors contribute to unemployment in Europe that do not exist in the USA? ◆ Yet other signs of economic health are the hours people work and the wages they receive. Are work hours growing as quickly as the number of people with jobs? Or are most of the new jobs part time? Also, are most new jobs high-wage or low-wage jobs?

◆ ◆ ◆ ◆ These are the questions we study in this chapter. You will discover that while there are things about the UK labour market that are not healthy there are other aspects that give grounds for optimism. The economy has been creating good jobs that pay good wages and benefits. But you'll also see that the economy has destroyed many jobs. While some people have seen their wages rise, others have seen no change and a few have seen their wages fall. So there have been big changes in the distribution of jobs and big changes in spread between the highest and the lowest wages. We begin by looking at the key labour market indicators and the way they are measured.

Employment and Wages

The quantity of real GDP supplied depends on the quantities of labour and capital and the state of technology. Potential GDP depends on the quantity of capital, labour and technology employed at *full employment*. In this chapter we study the forces that determine the quantity of labour employed and the concept of full employment. We begin by learning how the state of the labour market is observed and measured.

Population Survey

The Office for National Statistics (ONS), periodically publishes a measure of employment in the United Kingdom based on the Labour Force Survey (LFS), which is a survey of households. The LFS conforms to internationally recognized norms set out by the International Labour Organization and includes demographic information such as age, qualifications and ethnic origin. Because LFS surveys are conducted in all EU and OECD countries they are also useful for international comparison.

Unemployment figures are obtained in two different ways: from the LFS and from the claimant count. To be counted as *unemployed* in the LFS, people must be available for work within the two weeks following their interview and must be in one of three categories:

1. Without work, but having made specific efforts to find a job within the previous four weeks.
2. Waiting to be called back to a job from which they have been laid off.
3. Waiting to start a new job within 30 days.

The claimant count measures unemployment as the number of people who are eligible and claim unemployment-related benefits (jobseekers' allowance). This measure differs from the LFS and is sensitive to changes in the regulations for benefit entitlement. For example, a married woman who wishes to return to work after a period of absence from the labour market is not counted as being unemployed according to the claimant count but is counted in the LFS. Similarly, young people under the age of 18 are excluded from the claimant count but are included in the LFS.

The LFS defines the **working-age population** as the total number of people aged between 16 years and retirement who are not in jail, hospital, or some other form of institutional care. The working-age population is divided into two groups: those who are economically active (the **workforce**) and those who are economically inactive. The workforce is also divided into two groups: the employed and the unemployed. So the workforce is the sum of the employed and the unemployed.

To be counted as employed, a person must have either a full-time job or a part-time job. This includes students who do part-time work while at college. People in the working-age population who are neither employed nor unemployed are classified as not in the workforce.

Figure 23.1 shows the population categories used by the LFS. Total employment including part-time workers in the first quarter of 1998 was 27 million.

Figure 23.1 Population Work Force Categories

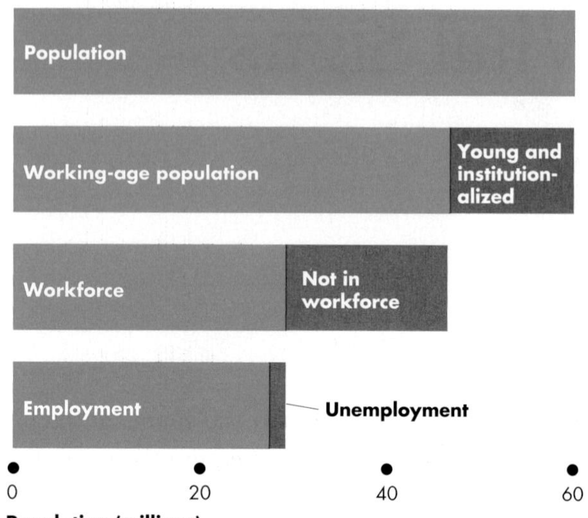

The population is divided into the working-age population and the young and institutionalized. The working-age population is divided into the workforce and those not in the workforce. The workforce is divided into the employed and the unemployed.

Source: *Labour Market Trends*, February 1999.

Figure 23.2 Employment, Unemployment and Economic Activity Rate: 1960–1998

The state of the labour market is indicated by the economic activity rate, the employment-to-population ratio and the unemployment rate. The economic activity rate has increased a little since 1960. The employment-to-population ratio has decreased slightly and fluctuates with the business cycle, but it has fluctuated more in the 1980s and 1990s.

Sources: ONS, *Annual Abstract of Statistics*, 1998.

Three Labour Market Indicators

We can use official data to calculate three indicators of the state of the labour market which are shown in Figure 23.2. They are:

1. The unemployment rate.
2. The economic activity rate.
3. The employment-to-population ratio.

The Unemployment Rate The amount of unemployment is an indicator of the extent to which people who want jobs can't find them. The **unemployment rate** is the percentage of the people in the workforce who are unemployed. That is:

$$\text{Unemployment rate} = \frac{\text{Number of people unemployed}}{\text{Workforce}} \times 100$$

and

$$\text{Workforce} = \text{Number of people employed} + \text{Number of people unemployed}$$

In March 1998, the number of people employed in the United Kingdom according to the LFS was 27 million and the number unemployed was 1.8 million. By using the above equations, you can verify that the workforce was 28.8 million, and the unemployment rate was 6.3 per cent in the UK. In contrast, the unemployment rate in Euroland (the 11 countries that make up the European Monetary Union) was 10.6 per cent and in the United States, was 4.7 per cent.

The unemployment rate in Figure 23.2 (graphed in orange and plotted on the right scale) shows how labour market conditions have changed. The average unemployment rate in the 1960s and 1970s was 2.5 per cent, but the average rate in the 1980s and 1990s is 9 per cent. Unemployment reached its most recent peak in 1993 following the recession of 1990–92, and a trough in 1990.

The Economic Activity Rate The number of people who join the workforce is an indicator of the willingness of the people of working age to take jobs. The **economic activity rate** is the percentage of the working-age population who are members of the workforce. That is:

$$\text{Activity rate} = \frac{\text{Workforce}}{\text{Working-age population}} \times 100$$

In March 1998, the workforce was 28.8 million and the working-age population was 46 million. By using the above equation, you can calculate the workforce economic activity rate. It was 62.6 per cent.

In Figure 23.2, the economic activity rate (graphed in red and plotted on the left scale) tells us about the growth of the workforce relative to the population. It has increased a little, rising from 61.2 per cent in 1960 to 62.6 per cent in 1998. It peaked in 1990. It has also had some mild fluctuations, resulting from unsuccessful job seekers becoming discouraged workers. **Discouraged workers** are people who during a recession temporarily leave the workforce and who during a recovery and expansion re-enter the workforce and become more active job seekers. The movements of discouraged workers out of and back into the workforce change the economic activity rate. Fluctuations in the workforce economic activity rate give an estimate of the number of discouraged workers.

Figure 23.3 The Changing Face of the Labour Market

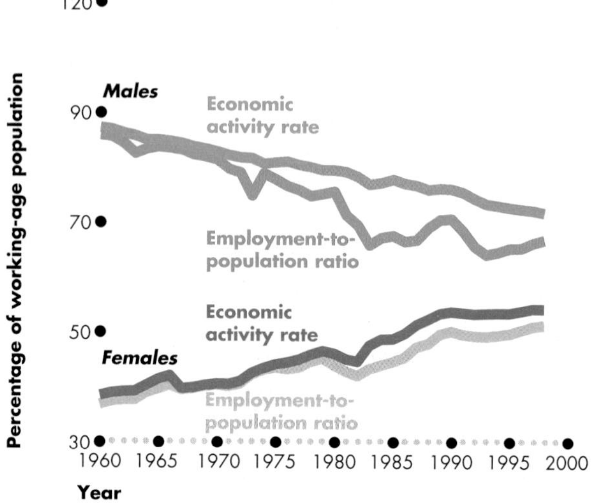

The male participation rate and the employment-to-population ratio have decreased. This is because increasing numbers of men are in higher education, some are retiring earlier and some are specializing in the household jobs that were previously done by women. The female participation rate has been rising and many new jobs are part time employing female labour.

Source: Department of Employment, *Employment Gazette Historical Supplement, Labour Market Trends*, February 1999.

The Employment-to-population Ratio The number of people of working age who have jobs is an indicator of the availability of jobs and the degree of match between people's skills and jobs. The **employment-to-population ratio** is the percentage of the people of working age who have jobs. That is:

$$\text{Employment-to-population ratio} = \frac{\text{Number of people employed}}{\text{Working-age population}} \times 100$$

In March 1998, employment in the United Kingdom was 27 million and the working-age population was 46 million. By using the above equation, you can calculate the employment-to-population ratio. It was 58.7 per cent.

The employment-to-population ratio in Figure 23.2 (graphed in blue and plotted against the left scale) tells us about the growth in the number of people employed relative to the population. This ratio has decreased slightly from 59.7 per cent in 1960 to 58.7 per cent in the 1990s. The fact that the employment-to-population ratio has decreased means that the economy has created jobs at a slower rate than the working-age population has grown. This labour market indicator also fluctuates, and its fluctuations coincide with but are opposite to those in the unemployment rate. The employment-to-population ratio falls during a recession and increases during a recovery and expansion.

Why has the economic activity rate increased and the employment-to-population ratio decreased? The main reason is an increase in the unemployment rate. Between 1960 and 1998, the rate of unemployment increased from 2.4 per cent to 6.2 per cent, reaching a peak of 12.2 per cent in 1983. In other words, the total number of jobs has not kept up with the increase in the working-age population. But this statement has to be qualified. Figure 23.3 shows that the female workforce economic activity rate has increased from 38 per cent in 1960 to 54 per cent in 1998. Other things are also changing. Shorter working hours, higher productivity and an increased emphasis on white-collar jobs have expanded the job opportunities and wages available to women. At the same time, technological advances have increased productivity in the home and freed women from some of their more traditional jobs outside the job market.

Figure 23.3 also shows another remarkable fact about the UK workforce: the economic activity rate and the employment-to-population ratio for men have *decreased*. Between 1960 and 1998, the male workforce economic activity rate decreased from 87 per cent to 72 per cent. It has decreased because increasing numbers of men are in higher education, some are retiring earlier and some are specializing in the household jobs that previously were done almost exclusively by women.

Aggregate Hours

The three labour market indicators that we've just examined are useful signs of the health of the economy and directly measure what matters to most people: jobs. But they don't tell us the quantity of labour used to produce GDP, and we can't use them to calculate the productivity of labour. The productivity of labour is significant because it influences the wages people earn.

The reason the number of people employed does not measure the quantity of labour employed is that jobs are not all the same. Some jobs are part time and involve just a few hours of work a week. Others are full time, and some of these involve regular overtime work. For example, one shop might hire six students who each work for three hours a day. Another might hire two full-time workers who each work nine hours a day. The number of people employed in these two shops is eight, but six of the eight do the same total amount of work as the other two. To determine the total amount of labour used to produce GDP, we measure labour in hours rather than in jobs. **Aggregate hours** is the total number of hours worked by all the people employed, both full time and part time, during a year.

Figure 23.4(a) shows aggregate hours in the economy from 1970 to 1998. They fluctuate around a flat trend. Between 1970 and 1998, the number of people employed in the UK economy increased by about 8 per cent. However, during that same period, aggregate hours fell by 1 per cent. Why the difference? Because average weekly hours per worker have fallen over the same period.

Figure 23.4(b) shows average weekly hours per worker. From around 36.2 hours a week in 1970, average hours per worker decreased to 33.2 hours a week in 1998. This shortening of the average workweek has arisen partly because of a decrease in the average hours worked by full-time workers but mainly because the number of part-time jobs has increased faster than the number of full-time jobs.

Figure 23.4 Aggregate Hours: 1970–1998

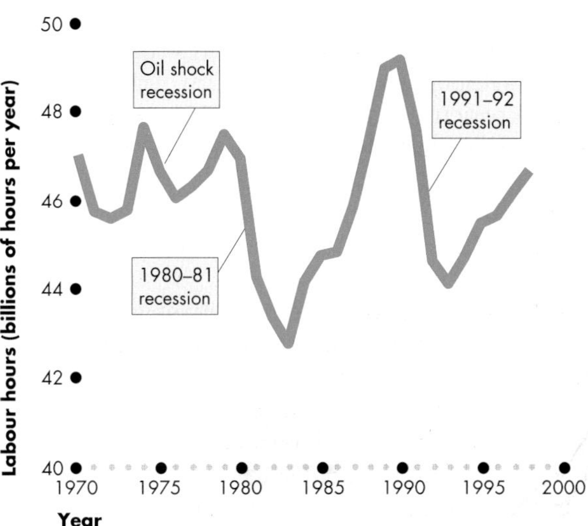

(a) Aggregate hours

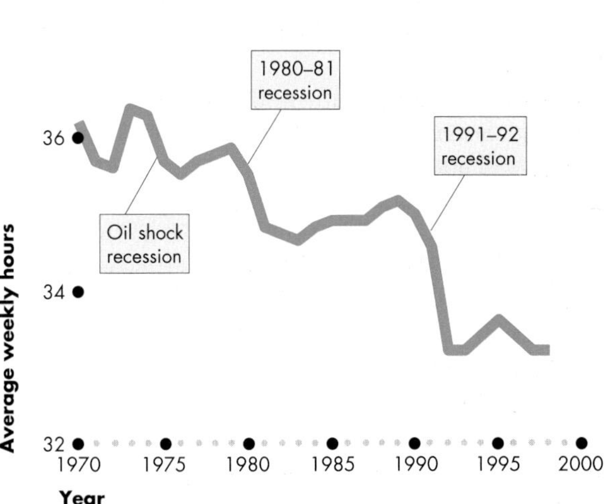

(b) Average weekly hours per person

Aggregate hours (part a) measure the total labour used to produce real GDP more accurately than does the number of people employed because an increasing proportion of jobs are part time. Between 1970 and 1998, aggregate hours fluctuated around a flat trend. Fluctuations in aggregate hours coincide with business cycle fluctuations. Aggregate hours have stayed the same while the number of jobs has increased because the average workweek has shortened (part b).

Sources: *Labour Force Survey*; Quantime Ltd; and the author's calculations.

Fluctuations in aggregate hours and average hours per worker line up with the business cycle. Figure 23.4 highlights the past three recessions during which aggregate hours decreased and average hours per worker decreased more quickly than the trend. While both measures show a fall that corresponds with the downturn of the economy in a recession, aggregate hours fall by more because people lose their jobs.

Wage Rates

The **real wage rate** is the quantity of goods and services that an hour's work can buy. It is equal to the money wage rate (pounds per hour) divided by the price level. If we use the GDP deflator as the price level, the real wage rate is expressed in 1990 pounds because the GDP deflator is 100 in 1990. The real wage rate is a significant economic variable because it measures the reward for labour.

What has happened to the real wage rate in the United Kingdom? Figure 23.5 answers this question. It shows three measures of the average hourly real wage rate in the UK economy between 1970 and 1998.

The first measure of the real wage rate is the New Earnings Survey calculation of the average hourly earnings of adult manual workers measured in 1995 pounds. This measure of the hourly wage rate reached a peak of £4.85 in 1976. It fell to £4.70 in 1977 but accelerated in the second half of the 1980s, slowed in the first half of the 1990s and accelerated in the second half.

The second measure of the hourly real wage rate is based on the national income accounts. It is calculated by dividing total wages and salaries by aggregate hours. This measure of the hourly wage rate is broader than the first and includes the incomes of all types of labour, whether their rate of pay is calculated by the hour or not. It includes managers and supervisors and all types of workers. This measure shows a sustained upward trend during the 1970s and 1980s and a flattening in the 1990s.

An increasing proportion of labour cost now takes the form of employer's add-on costs, such as employer's National Insurance contributions, and graduated pension contributions. To take this trend into account, Figure 23.5 shows a third measure of the hourly real wage rate, which equals *real labour compensation* – wages, salaries and supplements

Figure 23.5 Real Wage Rates: 1970–1998

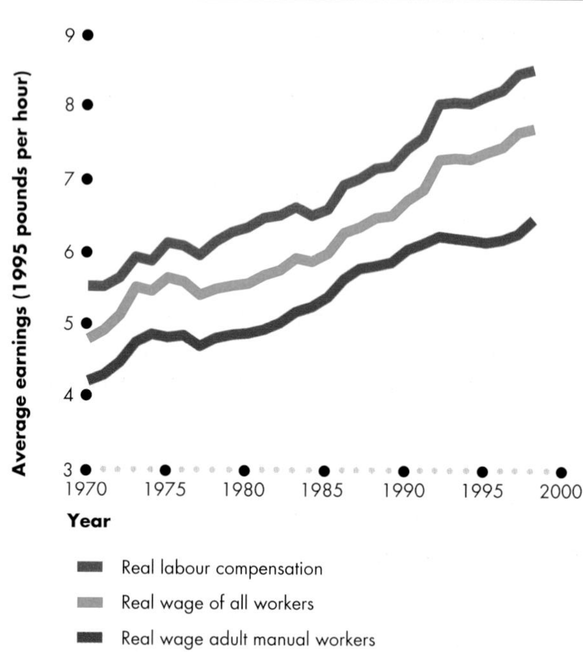

The average hourly real wage rate of manual workers kept pace with the other two measures based on national income accounts. It accelerated in the late 1980s but slowed in the 1990s. All three measures of average hourly real wage rates reflect the productivity growth slowdown of the 1970s.

Sources: *New Earnings Survey*; Liverpool Macroeconomics Research Group; and the author's calculations.

– divided by aggregate hours. This measure is the most comprehensive one available, and it shows that the average hourly wage rate has increased. All three measures show that there was a common slowdown coinciding with the productivity slowdown of the 1970s.

Review

- The workforce economic activity rate and the employment-to-population ratio have an upward trend and fluctuate with the business cycle.

- The female workforce economic activity rate has increased but the male workforce economic activity rate has decreased.
- Aggregate hours have fluctuated with total employment but have not grown as quickly because the average working week has shortened.
- Average hourly earnings have grown, but their growth rate slowed with the productivity growth slowdown of the 1970s.

We've seen that employment grows and that employment and unemployment fluctuate with the business cycle. Let's now focus more sharply on unemployment.

Unemployment and Full Employment

How do people become unemployed, how long do they remain unemployed and who is at greatest risk of becoming unemployed? Let's answer these questions by looking at the anatomy of unemployment.

The Anatomy of Unemployment

People become unemployed if they:

1 Lose their jobs.
2 Leave their jobs.
3 Enter or re-enter the workforce.

People end a spell of unemployment if they:

1 Are hired or recalled.
2 Withdraw from the workforce.

People who are laid off, either permanently or temporarily, from their jobs are called **job losers**. Some job losers become unemployed but some immediately withdraw from the workforce. People who voluntarily quit their jobs are called **job leavers**. Like job losers, some job leavers become unemployed and search for a better job, while others withdraw from the workforce temporarily or permanently retire from work. People who enter or re-enter the workforce are called **entrants** and **re-entrants**. Entrants are mainly people who have just left school. Some entrants get a job straight away and are never unemployed, but many spend time searching for their first job and during this period they are unemployed. Re-entrants are people who have previously withdrawn from the workforce. Most of these people are formerly discouraged workers or women returning to the labour market after an extended absence while raising a family. But an increasing number of unemployed people have been in this state for a period longer than a year. They are referred to as the **long-term unemployed**. Figure 23.6 shows these labour market categories.

Figure 23.6 Labour Market Flows

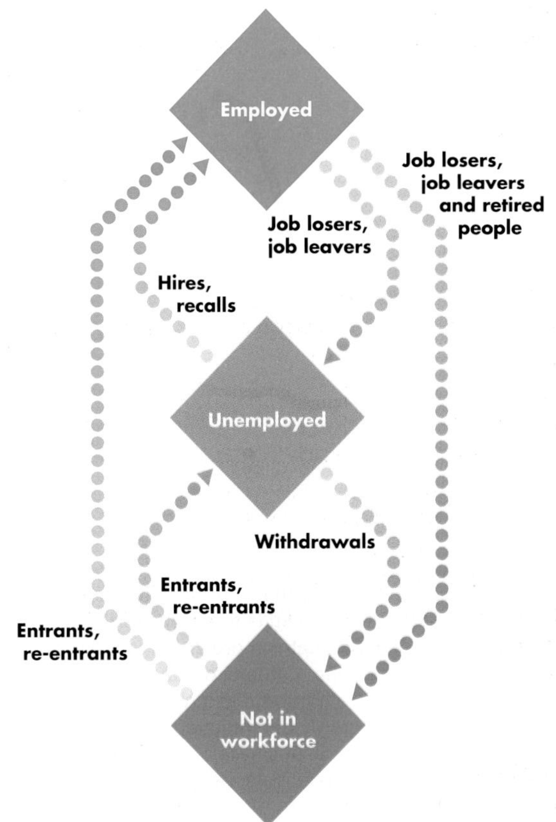

Unemployment results from employed people losing or leaving their jobs (job losers and job leavers) and from people entering the workforce (entrants and re-entrants). Unemployment ends because people get hired or recalled or because they withdraw from the workforce.

Figure 23.7 Unemployment by Reasons

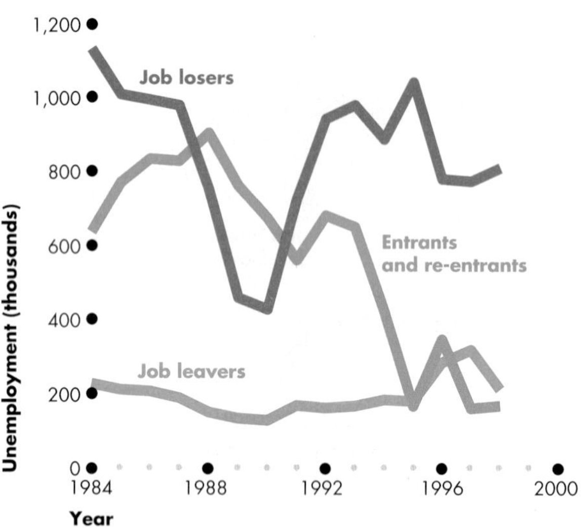

Everyone who is unemployed is a job loser, a job leaver, or an entrant/re-entrant into the workforce. Most of the unemployment that exists results from job loss. The number of job losers fluctuates more closely with the business cycle than do the numbers of job losers and entrants and re-entrants. Entrants and re-entrants are the second most commonly unemployed people. Their number fluctuates with the business cycle because of discouraged workers. Job leavers are the least common unemployed people.

Sources: *Labour Force Survey*; Quantime Ltd; and the author's calculations.

Figure 23.8 Unemployment by Duration

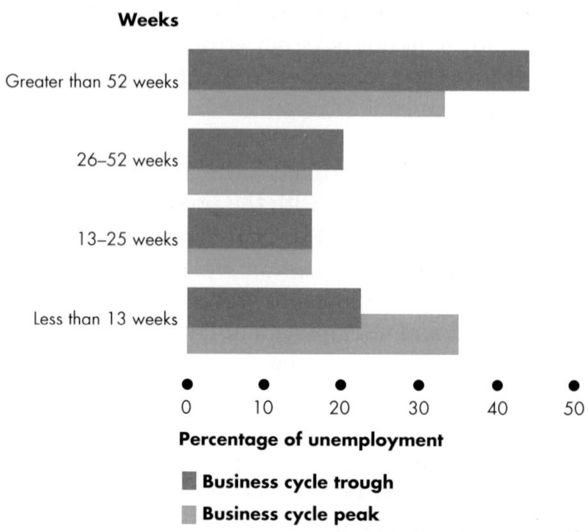

At a business cycle peak when unemployment is at its lowest level, 35 per cent of unemployment lasts for under 13 weeks, 16 per cent lasts for 13–25 weeks, 16 per cent lasts for 26–52 weeks and 33 per cent lasts for one year or more. At a business cycle trough when unemployment is at its highest level, only 20 per cent of unemployment lasts for under 13 weeks, 16 per cent lasts for 13–25 weeks, 20 per cent lasts for 26–52 weeks and 44 per cent lasts for one year or more.

Sources: *Labour Force Survey*; Quantime Ltd.

Let's see how much unemployment arises from the three different ways in which people can become unemployed.

The Sources of Unemployment Figure 23.7 shows unemployment by reason for becoming unemployed. Job losers are the biggest source of unemployment. These are the people that make up the redundancy statistics we hear so regularly on the television news and read in the newspapers. Their number fluctuates a great deal. In the recession of 1992, nearly 34 per cent of the unemployment was due to job losses. In contrast, in the business cycle peak year of 1990, fewer than 22 per cent of the unemployed were job losers.

Entrants are also a significant component of the unemployed. They are picked up in the LFS as school leavers. On any given day in 1997, over one-tenth of those recently unemployed were entrants to the labour market.

Job leavers are the smallest and most stable source of unemployment. On any given day in 1997, fewer than 316,000 people were unemployed because they were job leavers. The number of job leavers is remarkably constant.

The Duration of Unemployment Some people are unemployed for a week or two, and others are unemployed for periods of a year or more. Figure 23.8 examines the duration of unemployment at the peak and the trough of the business cycle. We can see that in the peak a higher proportion of the unemployed were jobless for under 13 weeks than in the trough, and a lower proportion of the unemployed were jobless for more than 13 weeks than in the trough. But the most noticeable feature is the proportion of people who have been unemployed for over one year. This is the definition of long-term unemployment, which is a pressing social problem both in the United Kingdom and in the rest of the European Union. In the peak of 1989, 33 per cent of the jobless population were classified as long-term unemployed; in the trough of 1992 that proportion increased to 44 per cent. While most people who are unemployed find work within a year, the proportion of the long-term unemployed has remained stubbornly in the range 35–45 per cent over the business cycle.

The Demographics of Unemployment

Figure 23.9(a) and (b) shows unemployment for different demographic groups. The figure shows that the high unemployment rates occur among young workers, especially young men, and also ethnic minority groups, especially among blacks. In the spring of 1997, the unemployment rate of all ethnic minorities was about 15 per cent; for blacks as a whole it was 20 per cent compared with whites for whom it was about 9 per cent. Figure 23.9(b) shows that the gap between white and non-white unemployment increases in the trough and decreases in the peak. Teenagers also have a higher than average unemployment rate. In spring 1997, the unemployment rate of all 16–17 year-olds was 18.2 per cent, while that of teenage men was 19.5 per cent.

Why are teenage unemployment rates so high? There are three reasons. First, young people are still in the process of discovering what they are good at and trying different lines of work. So they leave their jobs more frequently than older workers. Second, firms sometimes hire teenagers on a short-term trial basis. So the rate of job loss is higher for teenagers than for other people. Third, most teenagers are not in the workforce but are at school. This means that the percentage of the teenage population unemployed is much lower than the teenage unemployment rate. For example, in autumn 1998, 338,000 teenagers (16–19 years old) were unemployed and 1,621,000 were employed, and the teenage unemployment rate (all races) was 17.3 per cent. But 1,565,000 teenagers were in full time education. That is, 17 per cent of the teenage workforce or 11.8 per cent of the teenage population is unemployed.

Figure 23.9 Unemployment by Demographic Group

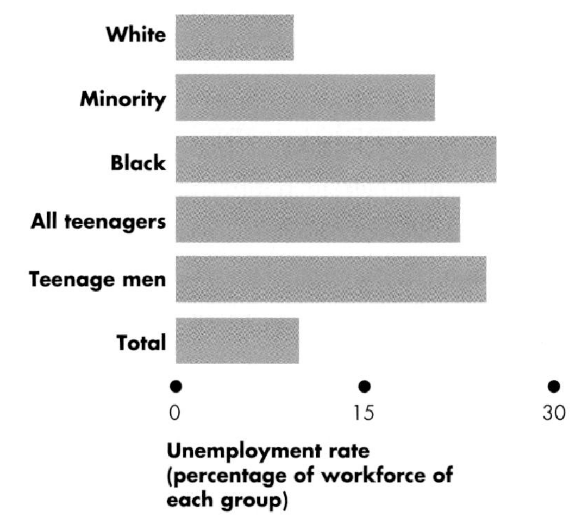

(a) Demographic groups

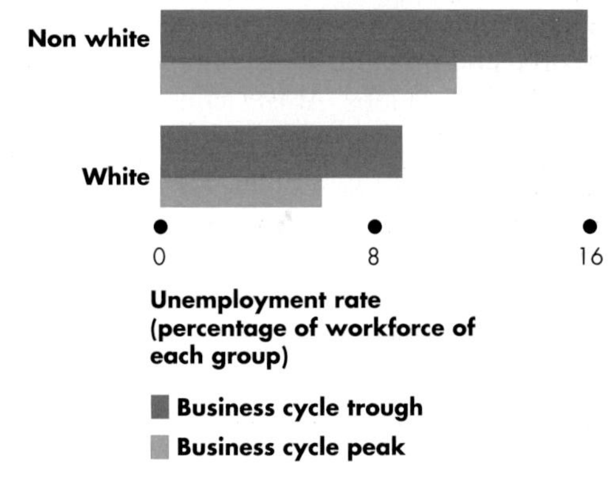

(b) Ethnic groups

Teenagers experience unemployment rates nearly two-and-a-half times higher than the average, and unemployment among blacks is over two-and-a-half times the average. Even at a business cycle trough when unemployment is at its highest rate, the ratio of non-white to white unemployment is 1.7.

Sources: *Labour Force Survey*; Spring 1997.

Ethnic minorities' unemployment rates are higher than white unemployment rates. One reason is that ethnic minorities face unequal opportunities and possible discrimination in the labour market. In the peak of the business cycle unemployment among non-whites is 1.8 times higher than unemployment among whites. Even in the trough of the business cycle when unemployment is higher all round, the ratio of non-white to white unemployment falls to only 1.7.

Types of Unemployment

Unemployment is classified into three types that are based on its causes. They are:

1 Frictional.

2 Structural.

3 Cyclical.

Frictional Unemployment

Frictional unemployment is the unemployment that arises from normal labour turnover. Frictional unemployment is not usually regarded as a problem, but it is a permanent, long-term phenomenon.

Normal labour turnover arises for two reasons. First, people are constantly entering the workforce – young people leave school, mothers return to the workforce and previously discouraged workers try once more to find jobs. At the same time, other people retire and create job vacancies for the new entrants and re-entrants to fill. This constant churning of the individuals in the workforce is the first reason for normal labour turnover.

The second reason is the constant churning of individual businesses. Some businesses fail, close down and lay off their workers. Other new businesses start up and hire workers. The people who lose their jobs in this process are frictionally unemployed and are trying to match their skills to jobs that are opening up.

The unending flow of people into and out of the workforce and of job creation and job destruction creates the need for people to search for jobs and for businesses to search for workers. Always there are businesses with unfilled jobs and people seeking jobs. Look in your local newspaper and you will see that there are always some jobs being advertised. Businesses don't usually hire the first person who applies for a job, and unemployed people don't usually take the first job that comes their way. Instead, both firms and workers spend time searching out what they believe will be the best match available. By this process of search, people can match their own skills and interests with the available jobs and find a satisfying job and income. While these unemployed people are searching, they are frictionally unemployed.

The amount of frictional unemployment depends on the rate at which people enter and re-enter the workforce and on the rate at which jobs are created and destroyed. During the 1960s, the amount of frictional unemployment increased as a consequence of the post-war baby boom that began during the 1940s. By the 1960s, the baby boom created a bulge in the number of school leavers. As these people entered the workforce, the amount of frictional unemployment increased.

The amount of frictional unemployment is also influenced by the level of unemployment benefit. The greater the number of people covered by unemployment benefit (jobseekers allowance) and the more generous the benefit, the longer is the average time taken in job search and the greater is the amount of frictional unemployment. The LFS indicates that 92 per cent of the unemployed are covered by unemployment benefit. Studies of unemployment in the European Union indicate that a strong statistical correlation exists between the length of time people are able to receive unemployment benefit and the duration of unemployment.

Structural Unemployment

Structural unemployment is the unemployment that arises when changes in technology or international competition destroy jobs that use different skills or are located in different regions from the new jobs that are created. Structural unemployment usually lasts longer than frictional unemployment because it is often necessary to retrain and possibly relocate to find a job. For example, on the day the shipyards in the Upper Clyde announced the loss of 600 jobs, a computer chip company in Gwent announced the creation of 750 new jobs. The unemployed former shipyard workers remain unemployed for several months until they move home, retrain and get one of the new jobs being created in other parts of the country.

Structural unemployment is painful, especially for older workers for whom the best available option might be to retire early, but with a lower income than they had expected. For example, a shipyard worker from Humberside who is made redundant may reluctantly accept to remain unemployed rather than retrain, accept a lower wage for another type of job, or move south where new jobs are being created. Such a person has opted to join the ranks of the long-term unemployed. The decision to accept long-term unemployment is governed by the options available to and the constraints on the structurally unemployed person. A person with different circumstances may make an entirely different decision. A younger person with family commitments may retrain, or take a job as a taxi driver in the short term until a better opportunity turns up, or relocate to take advantage of job opportunities elsewhere. One of the many factors that influence a person's decision is the level of unemployment benefit. The higher the level of benefit, the less incentive there is to accept the alternatives to long-term unemployment.

At certain times structural unemployment can become a serious long-term problem. It began to increase in the 1970s during the period of stagflation, when an increasingly competitive international environment brought a decline in the number of jobs in traditional industries.

Cyclical Unemployment **Cyclical unemployment** is the fluctuating unemployment that coincides with the business cycle. It is a repeating short-term problem. The amount of cyclical unemployment increases during a recession and decreases during a recovery and expansion. A worker in a car components factory who is laid off because the economy is in a recession and who gets rehired some months later when the recovery begins has experienced cyclical unemployment.

Figure 23.10 illustrates cyclical unemployment in the United Kingdom between 1980 and 1998. Part (a) shows the fluctuations of real GDP around potential GDP. Part (b) shows fluctuations in the unemployment rate around a line labelled 'Natural rate of unemployment'. The **natural rate of unemployment** is the unemployment rate when there is no cyclical unemployment or, equivalently, when all the unemployment is frictional and structural. The divergence of the unemployment rate from the natural rate is cyclical unemployment.

In Figure 23.10, the unemployment rate fluctuates around the natural rate of unemployment (part b) just as real GDP fluctuates around potential GDP (part a). When the unemployment rate equals the natural rate of unemployment, real GDP equals potential GDP. When the unemployment rate is less than the natural rate of unemployment, real GDP is greater than potential GDP. And when the unemployment rate is greater than the natural rate of unemployment, real GDP is less than potential GDP.

Figure 23.10 Unemployment and Real GDP

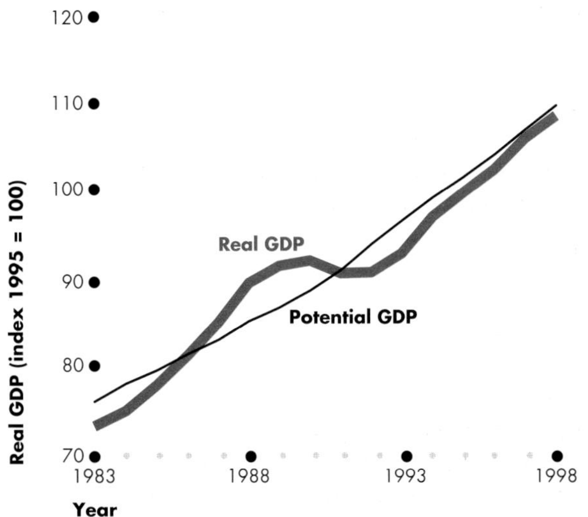

(a) Real GDP and potential GDP

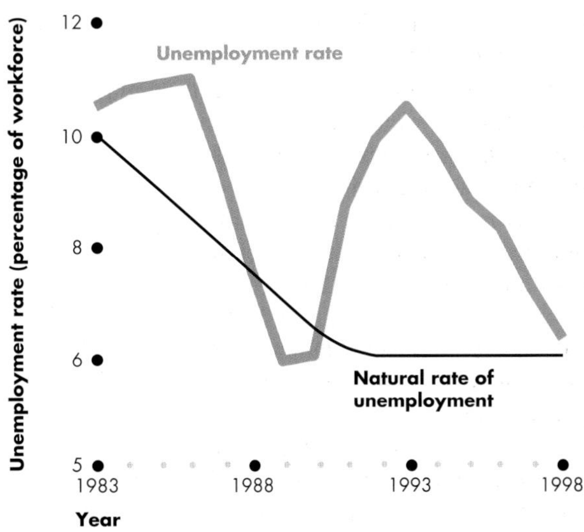

(b) Unemployment and the natural rate of unemployment

As real GDP fluctuates around potential GDP (part a), the unemployment rate fluctuates around the natural rate of unemployment (part b). In the recession of 1992–1993, the unemployment rate peaked at 10 per cent. The labour market reforms of the 1980s helped to reduce the natural rate of unemployment. We don't know how far the natural rate of unemployment has fallen.

Sources: Lombard Street Research Ltd; and author's estimates.

However, it is not always the case that when GDP equals potential GDP, unemployment equals the natural rate. While it is true to argue that when unemployment is at its natural rate GDP is at its potential, the reverse is not always the case. This is because, while production of goods and services can be increased by working the existing employed workforce more intensively through increased overtime, the process of hiring labour takes time. Hence adjustments to the unemployment rate can lag behind the movements in GDP.

Full Employment

There is always *some* unemployment – someone looking for a job or laid off and waiting to be recalled. So what do we mean by full employment? **Full employment** occurs when the unemployment rate equals the natural rate of unemployment. There can be quite a lot of unemployment at full employment, and the term 'full employment' is an example of a technical economic term that does not correspond with everyday ideas. The term 'natural rate of unemployment' is another example of a technical economic term that does not correspond with everyday language. We can think of the natural rate of unemployment as the rate of unemployment when all markets are in equilibrium. Anther way of thinking about the natural rate of unemployment is that it is the rate of unemployment that produces a stable (unchanging) rate of inflation.

For most people, there is nothing *natural* about unemployment – especially for the unemployed. These terms remind us that frictions and structural changes are unavoidable features of the economy and that they create unemployment.

In Figure 23.10(b), the natural rate of unemployment was 10.5 per cent in 1980 and it falls consistently to under 6 per cent in 1998. This view of the natural rate of unemployment in the United Kingdom is an estimate that some, but not all, economists would accept.

There is not much controversy about the existence of a natural rate of unemployment. Nor is there much controversy that it fluctuates. The natural rate of unemployment arises from the existence of frictional and structural unemployment, and it fluctuates because the frictions and the amount of structural change fluctuate. But there is controversy about the magnitude of the natural rate of unemployment and the extent to which it fluctuates. Some economists believe that the natural rate of unemployment fluctuates frequently, and that at times of rapid demographic and technological change, its rate can be high. Others argue that restrictive practices by trade unions and increases in real unemployment benefits will increase the natural rate, and that the labour market reforms of the 1980s led to a reduction in the natural rate to an even lower figure than that shown in Figure 23.10(b).

Review

- The people who become unemployed are job losers, job leavers and workforce entrants or re-entrants.
- Unemployment can be frictional (normal labour market turnover), structural (a long-lasting decline in a region or industry), or cyclical (in line with the business cycle).
- When all the unemployment is frictional and structural (when there is no cyclical unemployment), the unemployment rate is equal to the natural rate of unemployment.
- When the unemployment rate is equal to the natural rate of unemployment, there is full employment.

We've described the trends and fluctuations in employment, wage rates and unemployment. And we've described the labour market flows that bring changes in employment and unemployment. We've also described the anatomy of unemployment and classified it as frictional, structural and cyclical. It is now time to explain the trends and fluctuations. We begin by explaining the trends in employment and wage rates.

Explaining Employment and Wage Rates

We can understand the amount of employment and the wage rate by using the model of demand and supply and applying it to the labour market.

Figure 23.11 The Labour Market

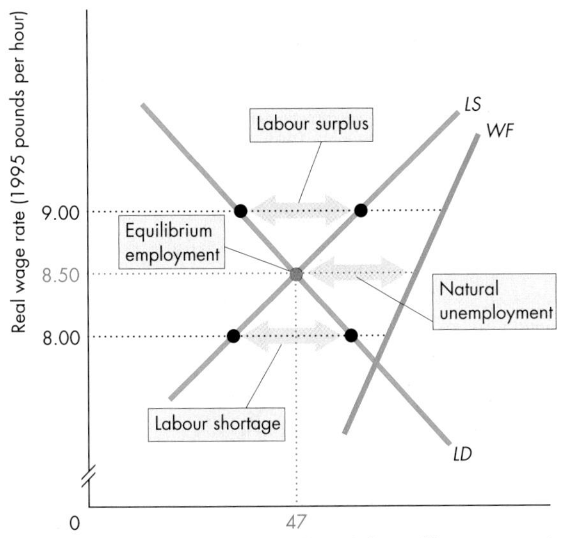

The labour demand curve, *LD*, shows the aggregate hours of labour that firms plan to hire at each real wage rate. The labour supply curve, *LS*, shows the aggregate hours that households plan to work at each wage rate. In equilibrium, the real wage rate is £8.50 an hour in 1995 prices. The *WF* curve shows the potential hours available if everyone of working age who wants to work at a particular wage rate is employed. The gap between the *LS* curve and the *WF* curve defines the natural rate of unemployment. The slope of the *WF* curve is steeper than the *LS* curve because as the real wage rises the gap between the *LS* and *WF* curves narrows.

Demand and Supply in the Labour Market

Figure 23.11 illustrates the labour market in 1998. The x-axis measures the quantity of labour employed as *aggregate hours* – billions of hours per year. The y-axis measures the real wage rate. The figure has three curves, a labour demand curve, a labour supply curve and a workforce curve. In the labour market, firms demand labour and households supply labour.

The **labour demand curve** shows the quantity of labour that firms plan to hire at each possible real wage rate. The lower the real wage rate, the greater is the quantity of labour that firms plan to hire. That is, the labour demand curve slopes downward. The reason the quantity of labour demanded depends on the *real* wage rate is that firms care only about the amount they pay for labour relative to the amount they get for their output. If money wages and prices change in the same proportion, the quantity of labour that firms plan to hire is unaffected.

The **labour supply curve** shows the quantity of available labour that households plan to supply at each possible real wage rate. The higher the real wage rate, the greater is the quantity of labour that households plan to supply. That is, the labour supply curve slopes upward. The reason the quantity of labour supplied depends on the *real* wage rate is that households care only about the amount they are paid for their labour relative to the price they must pay for the things they buy. If money wages and prices change in the same proportion, the quantity of labour that households plan to supply is unaffected. An increase in restrictive practices by trade unions will reduce the number of hours worked and will result in a leftward shift of the labour supply curve.

The **workforce curve** shows the potential quantity of labour available for employment at a particular real wage rate. The potential quantity of labour is made up of the actual supply of available labour and labour hours expended in job search and in long-term structural unemployment. The gap between the labour supply curve and the workforce curve is the natural rate of unemployment. The workforce curve is steeper than the labour supply curve because as real wages rise, the amount of labour hours expended in job search declines and even those who are in long-term structural unemployment will be willing to take on any kind of work.

The reason the quantity of labour demanded increases as the real wage rate decreases – the labour demand curve slopes downward – is that firms strive to maximize profit. If the wage rate at which they can hire labour falls relative to the price they can get for their output, they have an incentive to expand production and hire more labour. And the reason the quantity of labour supplied increases as the real wage rate increases – the labour supply curve slopes upward – is that households strive to use their scarce time in the most efficient way. If the wage rate they are offered rises relative to the prices they must pay for goods and services, they have a stronger incentive to work.

Labour demand and labour supply interact to determine the equilibrium level of employment, unemployment and the real wage rate. In Figure 23.11, at an average real wage rate below £8.50 an hour based on 1995 prices, there is a labour shortage. People find jobs easily, but businesses are short of labour. But this situation doesn't last for ever. Because there is a shortage of labour, the real wage rate rises towards the equilibrium wage rate of £8.50 an hour.

At wage rates above £8.50 an hour, there is a labour surplus. People have a hard time finding jobs and businesses can easily hire all the labour they want. Unemployment will be a mixture of the labour surplus created by the excess supply of labour and the natural rate shown by the gap between the labour supply curve and the workforce curve. In this situation, the real wage rate falls towards the equilibrium wage rate. In equilibrium the actual unemployment rate coincides with the natural rate.

The Trends in Employment and Wage Rates

We can use the model of labour demand and labour supply to understand the long-term trends in aggregate hours and real wage rates. We saw in Figure 23.4 that aggregate hours in 1998 were much the same as in 1970. We saw in Figure 23.5 that the real wage rate increased. The average real wage rate for the entire economy, including the value of pay supplements, increased from £5.50 an hour in 1970 to about £8.50 an hour in 1998. We also saw in Figure 23.2 that the unemployment rate increased from 2.4 per cent in 1970 to 6.2 per cent in 1998.

Figure 23.12 shows how these changes came about. In 1970, the labour demand curve was LD_{70} and the labour supply curve was LS_{70}. The equilibrium real wage rate was £5.50 an hour, and 47 billion hours of labour were employed.

Throughout the period since World War II, labour has become more and more productive. The reason is that capital per worker has increased and technology has advanced. We'll explore the reasons for this increased labour productivity in Chapter 32. But regardless of the reasons, the effect of an increase in labour productivity is an increase in the demand for labour. If an hour of labour can produce more output, firms are willing to pay a higher wage rate to hire that hour of labour. This would be shown by a rightward shift in the labour demand curve, resulting in a rise in the real wage and an increase in the quantity of labour employed. This increase in demand is shown by a rightward shift in the labour demand curve from LD_{70} to LD_{98}.

At the same time the population grew and so did the working-age population. With a larger working-age population, the supply of labour available for work increased. This increase is shown by the rightward shift in the workforce curve from WF_{70} to WF_{98}. Normally, we would expect the supply of labour to shift in the same direction; however, labour supply decreased, and the labour supply curve shifted leftwards from LS_{70} to LS_{98}, resulting

Figure 23.12 Explaining the Trends in Employment and Real Wage Rates 

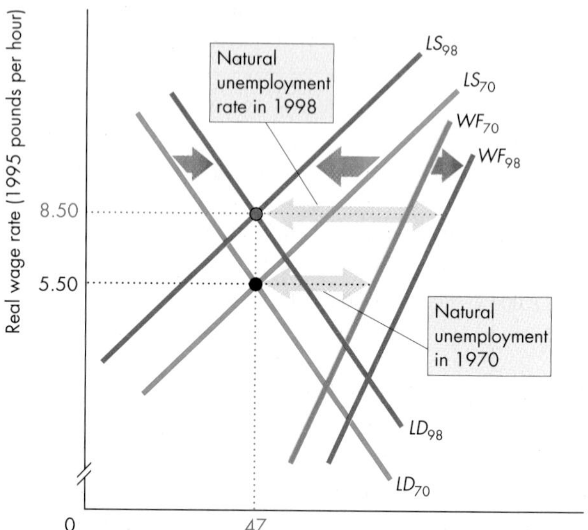

In 1970, the labour demand curve was LD_{70} and the labour supply curve was LS_{70}. The equilibrium real wage rate was £5.50 an hour in 1995 prices, and 47 billion hours of labour were employed. Over the years, labour became more and more productive. The demand curve shifted rightward to LD_{98}. At the same time, an increase in the working-age population increased the potential supply of labour, and the workforce curve shifted rightward to WF_{98}. An increase in union militancy and restrictive practices led to a leftward shift of the LS curve to LS_{98}. As a result the quantity of labour employed remained the same, the average real wage rose and unemployment increased.

in roughly the same amount of labour hours being hired in 1998 as in 1970. How could this be? There are a number of microeconomic reasons behind the leftward shift in aggregate labour supply. During the 1970s there was an increase in trade union militancy aimed at increasing the cost of labour and protecting the interest of those employed (known as *insiders* – see ahead to the next section, Explaining Unemployment). At the same time, taxes on income increased reducing incentives to work and creating a substitution for leisure, and unemployment benefits increased worsening the *benefit trap* – see Chapter 17, p. 415. This resulted in the leftward shift of the labour supply curve.

During the 1980s, trade union reform, tax cuts and other supply side policies by the government were aimed at making the labour market more flexible. This had the effect of relieving the pressures caused by structural change in the economy which resulted in more jobs but not more hours worked. The jobs that were destroyed in the 1980s were mostly in manufacturing and in the low skill sectors. These jobs were replaced by high skilled ones in high-tech industries and in services and also part-time jobs, mostly in services and assembly related work.

Technological change and international competition during the 1980s and 90s, brought a decrease in the demand for labour in manufacturing. The same technological change and international competition that destroyed jobs in manufacturing created jobs in servces and also high tech areas. There was an increase in demand for labour in these growing sectors. Those who lost their jobs in manufacturing had to look for work in services. So while the demand curve for labour in manufacturing shifted left, the supply curve for labour in the service sector shifted to the right. The overall efffect was to shift the aggregate supply of labour leftwards.

Thus the quantity of labour employed remained the same, the average real wage rate increased, and unemployment increased. But also the natural rate of unemployment increased.

Review

- The labour demand curve shows the quantity of labour that firms plan to hire at each real wage rate. The labour demand curve slopes downward because a fall in the real wage rate gives firms a stronger incentive to increase production and hire more labour.
- The labour supply curve shows the quantity of labour that households plan to supply at each real wage rate. The labour supply curve slopes upward because a rise in the real wage rate gives households a stronger incentive to work.
- Labour demand and labour supply interact to determine the level of employment and the equilibrium real wage rate.
- The workforce curve shows the potential supply of labour at a particular real wage, but separates the supply of labour to the labour market by making allowance for the natural rate of unemployment.

We've now studied the main trends in employment and wage rates, and we have seen how the demand and supply model can help us to understand these trends. Our next task is to explain unemployment.

Explaining Unemployment

We've described *how* people become unemployed – they are job losers, job leavers, or workforce entrants and re-entrants. And we have classified unemployment – it can be frictional, structural and cyclical. But this description and classification do not *explain* unemployment. Why is there always some unemployment and why does its rate fluctuate? Unemployment is always present for three reasons:

1. Job search.
2. Job rationing.
3. Sticky wages.

Job Search

Job search is the activity of people looking for acceptable vacant jobs. The labour market is in a constant state of change. Jobs are destroyed and created as businesses fail and new businesses start up and as new technologies and new markets evolve. In the process, people lose jobs. Other people enter or re-enter the labour market. Yet other people leave their jobs to look for better ones and others retire. This constant churning in the labour market means that there are always some people looking for jobs – the unemployed. Job search even takes place when the quantity of labour demanded equals the quantity supplied. In this situation, some people have not yet found a job and some jobs have not yet been filled.

Job search explains frictional, structural and cyclical unemployment. All three types of unemployment occur because job losers, job leavers, and workforce entrants and re-entrants don't know about all the jobs available to them so they must take time to *search* for an acceptable one. This search takes time, and the average amount of time varies. When there is a small amount of structural change and when the economy is close to a business cycle peak, search times are low and the unemployment rate is low. But when structural change is rapid and when the economy is in a recession, search times increase and the unemployment rate increases.

Although job search is cyclical, it also changes more slowly and brings changes in the natural rate of unemployment. The main sources of these slower changes are:

- Demographic change.
- Unemployment benefit.
- Technological change.
- Hysteresis.

Demographic Change An increase in the proportion of the working-age population brings an increase in the entry rate into the workforce and an increase in the unemployment rate. This is described by a rightward shift in the *WF* curve in Figure 25.12. A bulge in the birth rate occurred in the late 1940s and early 1950s, following World War II. This bulge increased the proportion of new entrants into the workforce during the 1970s and brought an increase in the unemployment rate. Another demographic trend is an increase in the number of households with two working adults. If unemployment hits one person with income coming in from the other, job search can take longer, increasing frictional unemployment.

Unemployment Benefit The length of time that an unemployed person spends searching for a job depends, in part, on the opportunity cost of job search. With no income during a period of unemployment, an unemployed person faces a high opportunity cost of job search. In this situation, search is likely to be short and an unattractive job is likely to be accepted as a better alternative to continuing a costly search process. With generous unemployment benefits, the opportunity cost of job search is low. In this situation, search is likely to be prolonged. An unemployed worker will hold out for the ideal job.

The opportunity cost of job search has fallen over the years as unemployment benefits have increased. In 1966, unemployment benefit included a flat-rate component and an earnings-related component. As a result of these changes, the natural rate of unemployment was on an upward trend during the 1970s. In 1982, earnings-related benefit was abolished in the United Kingdom and during the 1990s the conditions for the receipt of benefit were tightened. During the 1980s and 90s estimates of the natural rate decreased.

Technological Change Labour market flows and unemployment are influenced by the pace and direction of technological change. Sometimes technological change brings a *structural slump*, in which some industries die and regions suffer and other industries are born and regions flourish. When these events occur, labour turnover is high – the flows between employment and unemployment and the pool of unemployed people increases. The decline of traditional heavy industries such as shipbuilding, steel and coal and the rapid expansion of industries in the electronics and car components sectors are examples of the effects of technological change and sources of the increase in unemployment during the 1970s and early 1980s. While these changes were taking place, the natural rate of unemployment increased. Supply side policies that increased job market flexibility in the 1980s resulted in the labour market being able to adjust more rapidly to technoogical shocks.

Hysteresis The unemployment rate fluctuates around the natural rate of unemployment. But it is possible that the natural rate itself depends on the path of the actual unemployment rate. So where the unemployment rate ends up depends on where it has been. Such a process is called **hysteresis**.

If hysteresis is present, then an increase in the unemployment rate brings an increase in the natural rate. A possible source of hysteresis is that the human capital of unemployed workers depreciates, and people who experience long bouts of unemployment usually find it difficult to get new jobs as good as the ones they have lost. An increase in the number of long-term unemployed workers means an increase in the amount of human capital lost and possibly a permanent increase in the natural rate of unemployment. The hysteresis theory is controversial and has not yet been thoroughly tested, but it is also consistent with the view that the long-term unemployed are willing to remain on state benefits indefinitely.

Job search unemployment is present even when the quantity of labour demanded equals the quantity supplied. The other possible explanations of unemployment are based on the view that the quantity of labour demanded does not always equal the quantity supplied.

Job Rationing

Job rationing is the practice of paying employed people a wage that creates an excess supply of labour and a shortage of jobs. Three reasons why jobs might be rationed are:

1 Efficiency wages.
2 Insider interest.
3 The minimum wage.

Efficiency wages A firm can increase its labour productivity by paying wages above the competitive wage rate. The higher wage attracts a higher quality of labour, encourages greater work effort, and cuts down on the firm's labour turnover rate and recruiting costs. But the higher wage also adds to the firm's costs. So a firm offers a wage rate that balances productivity gains and additional costs. The wage rate that maximizes profit is called the **efficiency wage**.

The efficiency wage will be higher than the competitive equilibrium wage. If it was lower than the competitive wage, competition for labour would bid the wage up. With an efficiency wage above the competitive wage, some labour is unemployed and employed workers have an incentive to perform well to avoid being fired.

The payment of efficiency wages is another reason the natural rate of unemployment is not zero.

Insider Interest Why don't firms cut their wage costs by offering jobs to unemployed workers for a lower wage rate than that paid to existing workers? One explanation, called **insider–outsider theory**, is that to be productive, new workers – outsiders – must receive on-the-job training from existing workers – insiders. If insiders provide such training to outsiders who are paid a lower wage, the insiders' bargaining position is weakened. So insiders will not train outsiders unless outsiders receive the same rate of pay as insiders.

When bargaining for a pay deal, unions represent only the interests of insiders so the wage agreed exceeds the competitive wage and there are always outsiders unable to find work. Thus the pursuit of rational self-interest by insiders is another reason the natural rate of unemployment is positive. The weakening of trade union power through legislation may have reduced the insiders' bargaining position.

The Minimum Wage A minimum wage is legislated by the government at a level higher than the one the market would determine. As a result, the quantity of labour supplied exceeds the quantity demanded and jobs are rationed. The minimum wage for the UK is £3.60 an hour for workers aged 22 and over. A lower minimum wage of £3.20 exists for those on training programmes, and a lower wage of £3 for 18–21 year-olds. It is estimated that the minimum wage will only affect 4.3 per cent of employees in London, but 11.6 per cent of employees in the north east. It will also affect nearly one-third of employees in the hotel and restaurant business and a quarter of security guards and cleaners.

Minimum wages exist in a number of EU countries. The 'Social Chapter' of the Treaty of European Union gives the EU commission and the European Court powers in enforcing the minimum wage. While a minimum wage will be expected to result in job rationing, there are arguments in favour of such a policy. One argument is that if firms are forced to pay a minimum wage, they will have to use labour more efficiently and improve productivity. The improvement in productivity will result in very small effects on job rationing and therefore unemployment. One study that was published to coincide with the introduction of the minimum wage in the UK on 1 April 1999, predicted that only 80,000 jobs over 2–3 years would be lost as a result, of which a half would be in the wholesaling, hotel and catering sectors.

Job rationing is a possible reason for a high natural rate of unemployment. It is a source of persistent and possibly high frictional unemployment. The distinction between unemployment that arises from job search and that which arises from job rationing can be illustrated by musical chairs. If there are equal numbers of chairs (jobs) and players (people who want jobs), when the music stops, everyone finds a chair. If there are more players than chairs, when the music stops, some players can't find a chair. The chairs are rationed. The minumum wage has contributed to higher unemployment for the young and unskilled.

Job rationing is a source of long-term frictional unemployment. The final explanation of unemployment is one reason why unemployment is cyclical.

Sticky Wages

Wages don't change as often as prices do. So if the demand for labour decreases, the real wage rate begins to move towards its new equilibrium, but it takes some time to get there. During this process of gradual wage adjustment, there is a surplus of labour and unemployment is temporarily high.

Figure 23.13 illustrates this type of unemployment. Initially, the demand for labour is LD_0 and the supply of labour is LS. The equilibrium level of employment is L_0 billion hours and the real wage rate is W_0 an hour. The demand for labour then decreases and the demand curve shifts leftward to LD_1. But the real wage rate is temporarily sticky at W_0 an hour. At this real wage rate and in the new conditions, firms are willing to hire only L_1 billion hours of labour. So there is a surplus of $L_0 - L_1$ billion hours and extra unemployment is created.

Eventually, as prices and wages change, the real wage rate falls to its equilibrium level. In this example, when the real wage rate has fallen to W_1 an hour, the quantity of labour demanded equals the quantity supplied and the surplus of labour vanishes. The only unemployment that remains is the natural rate of unemployment consistent with the new equilibrium.

Figure 23.13 Sticky Wages and Unemployment

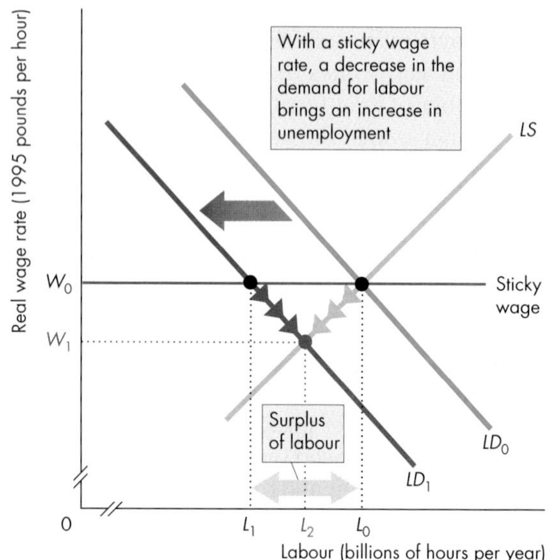

When the demand for labour is LD_0 and the supply of labour is LS, employment is L_0 billion hours and the real wage rate is W_0 an hour. The demand for labour decreases and the demand curve shifts leftward to LD_1 but the real wage rate is sticky at W_0 an hour. Employment decreases and there is a surplus of $L_0 - L_1$ billion hours. Eventually, the real wage rate falls to W_1 an hour and the quantity of labour employed increases to L_2 billion hours.

Review

- Unemployment is always present because of job search.
- The natural rate of unemployment depends on the age distribution of the population, unemployment benefit and technological change.
- Some unemployment also results from job rationing and sticky wages.

You now know how the quantity of labour employed is determined. Your next task is to study the factors that influence the quantity of capital. Capital is accumulated as a result of savings and investment decisions. These decisions are studied in Chapter 32. It explains how consumption, investment and saving decisions are made, and it sets the scene for your study of economic growth in Chapter 32.

Summary

Key Points

Employment and Wages (pp. 554–559)

- The population is divided into four labour market categories: employed, unemployed, not in the workforce, and young and institutionalized people.
- The workforce is the sum of the employed and the unemployed.
- The working-age population is the sum of the workforce and the people not in the workforce.
- The population is the sum of the working-age population and young and institutionalized people.
- These population categories are used to calculate the unemployment rate, the workforce economic activity rate and the employment-to-population ratio.
- The economic activity rate and the employment-to-population ratio fluctuate with the business cycle.
- The female economic activity rate has increased but the male economic activity rate has decreased.
- Aggregate hours, the total number of hours worked by all the people employed during a year, has remained roughly constant, but it also fluctuates in line with the business cycle. While aggregate hours have remained roughly the same in the past 25 years, average hours per worker have decreased.
- The average hourly real wage rate of adult manual workers has kept pace with other measures of real wages. It increased slightly ahead of the average in the second half of the 1980s but slowed down in the 1990s.
- Broader measures of average hourly real wage rates were slightly ahead of the average in the second half of the 1980s but slowed down in the 1990s.

Unemployment and Full Employment (pp. 559–564)

- The unemployment rate rises because people lose their jobs (*job losers*), leave their jobs (*job leavers*) and enter (or re-enter) the workforce (*entrants or re-entrants*), and it falls because people get hired or recalled or withdraw from the workforce.
- The duration of unemployment fluctuates over the business cycle but the phase of the business cycle makes little difference to the demographic patterns in unemployment.
- Unemployment can be *frictional* (arising from normal labour market turnover), *structural* (arising when there is a long-lasting decline in the number of jobs available in a region or industry) and *cyclical* (arising from the business cycle).
- When all the unemployment is frictional and structural, unemployment is at its natural rate, and there is *full employment*.
- There can be a substantial amount of unemployment at full employment, and the natural rate of unemployment fluctuates because of fluctuations in frictional and structural unemployment.

Explaining Employment and Wage Rates (pp. 564–567)

- Employment and wage rates can be understood by using the demand and supply model and applying it to the labour market.
- The *labour demand curve*, which shows the quantity of labour that firms plan to hire at each possible real wage rate, slopes downward. The quantity of labour demanded increases if the *real* wage rate falls because the cost of labour

falls relative to the price firms get for their output.

- The *labour supply curve*, which shows the quantity of labour that households plan to supply at each possible real wage rate, slopes upward. The quantity of labour supplied increases if the *real* wage rate increases because households face a stronger incentive to work. Labour demand and labour supply interact to determine the level of employment and the real wage rate.
- The *workforce curve* shows the potential amount of labour available for employment at a particular real wage rate. The gap between the labour supply curve and the workforce curve defines the *natural rate of unemployment.* As real wages rise the natural rate of unemployment declines, since more people find it easier to match their work preferences to job availability.
- Real wage rates and employment have increased over the years because both labour demand and labour supply have increased, but labour demand has increased by more than labour supply. Labour demand has increased because labour has become more productive, and labour supply has increased because the working-age population has grown and because restrictive practices have declined.

Explaining Unemployment (pp. 567–570)

- Unemployment arises from *job search*, *job rationing* and *sticky wages*.
- The amount of job search unemployment fluctuates with the business cycle, but it also changes for other reasons, which bring changes in the natural rate of unemployment. These other reasons are: demographic change, changes to unemployment benefit entitlement and technological change.
- Job search might be subject to a hysteresis effect.
- A high unemployment rate brings an increase in the natural rate of unemployment because the human capital of long-term unemployed workers depreciates and they find it hard to get new jobs.
- Job rationing, which can arise from efficiency wages, insider interest and the minimum wage, can be the source of long-term frictional unemployment.
- Sticky wages – the gradual adjustment of wage rates – can bring cyclical unemployment.

Key Figures

Key Terms

Review Questions

1 How is unemployment measured according to the Labour Force Survey?

2 Define the unemployment rate, the economic activity rate and the employment-to-population ratio.

3 Define aggregate hours. Why might aggregate hours be a more accurate measure of the total labour input than the number of people employed?

4 Name three measures of average hourly earnings and describe how each one changed between 1970 and 1996.

5 How do people become unemployed? What is the most common way and which is the one that fluctuates most?

6 How does the duration of unemployment vary over the business cycle?

7 Which groups of the population experience the highest unemployment rates?

8 Distinguish between frictional, structural and cyclical unemployment.

9 What is the natural rate of unemployment and what is full employment?

10 What is the relationship between the unemployment rate and real GDP over the business cycle?

11 Explain how demand and supply in the labour market determine the level of employment and the real wage rate.

12 What are the main changes in demand and supply in the labour market that have brought employment growth?

13 What are the main changes in demand and supply in the labour market that have brought a slowdown in the rate of increase in real wage rates?

14 What are the three main explanations of unemployment?

Problems

1 The Labour Force Survey measured the following numbers in the winter of 1998: workforce 29.1 million, employment 27.3 million, working-age population 46.1 million. Calculate:

a The unemployment rate.
b The economic activity rate.
c The employment-to-population ratio.

2 During 1998, the working-age population increased by 143,000, employment increased by 301,000, and the workforce increased by 265,000. What happened to the level of unemployment and what do you believe happened to the number of discouraged workers?

3 In January 1998, the LFS unemployment rate was 6.4 per cent. In January 1997, the unemployment rate was 7.4 per cent. What do you predict happened in 1997 to the numbers of:

a Job losers?
b Job leavers?
c Workforce entrants and re-entrants?

4 The labour market in an economy is described by the figure. Initially, demand is LD_0 but then it decreases to LD_1.

a What are the initial levels of employment hours and real wage rate?

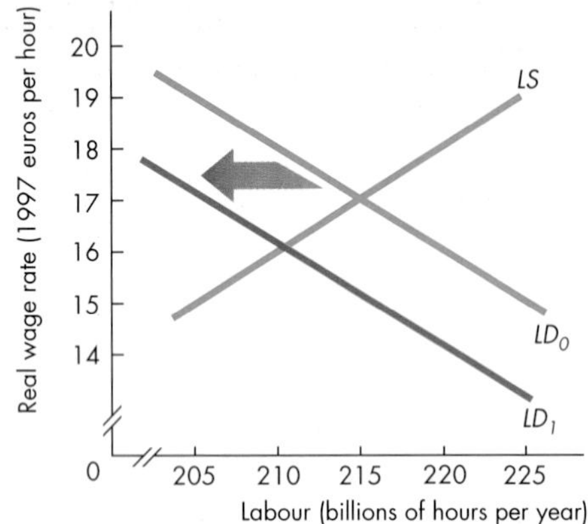

b When the demand for labour decreases, what are the new levels of employment hours and real wage rate if wages are completely flexible?

c When the demand for labour decreases and if the real wage rate is sticky and does not change:

1 What is the level of employment hours?
2 What is the quantity of employment hours supplied?
3 What is the number of hours that are unemployed?
4 During the time that the real wage rate is stuck above its equilibrium level, is the unemployment rate greater than, less than, or equal to the natural rate of unemployment?

5 You are told the following facts about the economy of Big Time: all the people work in either fishing, Big Time's traditional economic activity, or video game production, Big Time's new found bonanza industry. The working-age population is growing by 1 million people a year and the number of jobs is growing by 1.2 million a year. But jobs in fishing are disappearing at a rate of 2 million a year and jobs are being created in video game production at a rate of 3.2 million a year. What do you predict is happening to wage rates, employment, and unemployment in Big Time both in total and in its two industries? Draw two labour market figures, one for the fishing industry and one for the video games industry, and show how the demand and supply curves are shifting and how wage rates and employment levels are changing.

6 You have been given the following data on GDP and unemployment for the economy of Mainland. The data for real GDP and potential GDP is presented as an index and are measured in the same units.

Year	Real GDP (index)	Potential GDP (index)	Unemployment (per cent of the workforce)
1986	103.0	100.0	5.0
1987	105.1	103.0	5.7
1988	106.1	106.1	6.0
1989	107.2	109.3	6.6
1990	109.3	112.6	7.0
1991	112.6	116.0	7.0
1992	116.5	119.5	6.8
1993	121.2	123.1	6.5
1994	125.4	126.8	6.4
1995	129.8	130.6	6.2
1996	134.5	134.5	6.0
1997	138.8	138.5	5.9

a Plot real GDP and potential GDP on a graph against year as in Figure 23.10.

b Plot the rate of unemployment against year and compare it with your graph of real and potential GDP. What do you notice about the two graphs?

c What is approximate rate of growth of potential GDP?

d What is your estimate of the natural rate of unemployment?

e By approximately how much does the rate of unemployment rise or fall if the growth of real GDP differs from the growth of potential GDP?

f What would happen to the natural rate of unemployment if potential GDP grew by only 1 per cent in 1987 but then continued to grow at the long-term rate of growth shown by the data?

7 Study *Reading Between the Lines* on pp. 566–567 and then answer the following questions:

a Why is the Bank of England worried about the fall in unemployment?

b How does the welfare system affect the unemployment rate?

c What has been happening to the composition of employment since 1990?

d Why do you think 20.3 per cent of black men and 22.9 per cent of Pakistani and Bangladeshi men are unemployed while employer's complain of skill shortages?

8 Use the links on the Parkin, Powell and Matthews Web site to obtain data on unemployment in your region.

a Compare unemployment in your region with that in the United Kingdom as a whole.
b Why do you think your region might have a higher or a lower unemployment rate than the UK average?
c Try to identify those industries that have expanded most and those that have shrunk in your region.
d What are the problems in your region's labour market that you think local government and Development Agencies can do to solve?
e Use the demand and supply model of the labour market to aid your analysis.

9 The figures below show the rate of unemployment based on the claimant count in the United Kingdom from January to August 1999.

Month	Rate (%)
January	4.6
February	4.6
March	4.6
April	4.5
May	4.5
June	4.4
July	4.3
August	4.2

a What has been the trend in UK unemployment in 1999?
b From your knowledge of the state of the UK economy, do you think unemployment is above or below the natural rate?
c If the unemployment rate is below the natural rate, what is your prediction for the economy in 2000? Has your prediction been borne out?
d If the unemployment rate is above the natural rate, explain why the natural rate has fallen?
c Is the claimant count a good measure of the rate of unemployment in the UK?

Output and Unemployment

The Essence of the Story

- The Bank of England believes that unemployment is below the natural rate of unemployment and will have to rise to stop inflation from rising.
- The implication of the Bank of England analysis is that unemployment would have to rise by 500,000 to stabilize inflation.
- In the past 30 years the USA has created 40 million jobs compared with 2 million in the UK. Immigrants to the USA get low paid jobs in hotels and restaurants but in time they move on to better jobs.
- British employers complain of skill shortages but at the same time there are high numbers of unemployed among male workers particularly ethnic minorities.
- The welfare system in the United States does not create strong disincentives to work. The New Deal in Britain will bring excluded people back into work.

The Sunday Times, 23 August 1998

Nothing natural in rising jobless

David Smith

Having spent four of the past six weeks in closer proximity to the American economy than that of Britain, a slightly different perspective is in order. The consensus among economists, in the Treasury, the Bank, including most of the MPC's members, and outside, is that unemployment has to rise, probably quite significantly, to head off inflationary pressures.

For those concerned about the assumption that there is anything natural about joblessness, it refers to the level of unemployment consistent with a stable inflation rate. So, when unemployment is above this equilibrium rate inflation will tend to fall, when it is below, it will rise.

Unemployment on the claimant-count measure was, by the way, 1.82m at the start of 1997; now it is 1.34m. The implication of the Bank's analysis is that the jobless total needs to rise by about 500,000 before we can rest easy about inflation.

The comparison with America is instructive. America has been a formidable job-creation machine, having produced almost 40m jobs over the past 30 years, during which time Britain has added not much more than 2m and Europe as a whole no net private-sector jobs.

Closer to the ground in America, you begin to see why. There is a good chance your waiter or waitress will speak little or no English. Ask for directions in a hotel and you are met with a puzzled look. In time, however, these people will be playing a full role in the job market. Out of necessity, American employers offer work to people who would not get a look-in in Britain. Here, 20.3% of black men and 22.9% of Pakistani and Bangladeshi men are unemployed. British employers instead bleat about skill shortages.

Of course, Americans, new and old, have to work. The welfare system does not allow the luxury of the question: why work? On the supply and the demand side, the economy is phenomenally successful at stretching the available workforce — reducing the natural rate of unemployment. I heard nothing in America about unemployment there having to rise to keep inflation under control.

Gordon Brown's New Deal, if it works, will bring excluded people into the job market, while the working families tax credit will reduce the disincentives to taking up a job, lowering our natural rate.

The question for the present is whether the consensus is right and a 500,000 unemployment rise is needed. I think not.

Consider the figures for employment. The number of people in work has only just recovered to its 1990 level.

Now look at the composition of employment and unemployment. Unemployment among men — traditionally used as the measure of labour-force tightness — is significantly higher than for women, three times as high on the claimant count.

Moreover, about 1m additional men of working age have become "economically inactive" in the 1990s, though not necessarily counted as unemployed. There is a significant reserve army of unemployed men out there, some of them the so-called discouraged workers. They should be re-encouraged.

Economic Analysis

■ The economists of the Bank of England and other institutions believe that unemployment is above the natural rate and therefore real GDP is above potential GDP.

■ Figure 1 describes the analytical thinking of the Bank of England economists. In 1998 Real GDP was thought to be higher than potential GDP. The price level is expected to rise unless unemployment is increased and real GDP is brought down to match potential GDP.

■ David Smith of *The Sunday Times* believes that the unemployment statistics do not give the full information. The 1990s has seen no net gain in jobs overall. Figure 2 shows that male employment has fallen since 1990, but female employment has risen. Additionally, about 1 million males of working age have become 'discouraged workers'.

■ Supply side polices can be used to re-encourage the male economically inactive population to re-enter the workforce. The natural rate of unemployment could still be lower than most economists think it is.

■ The New Deal and the working families tax credit which allows low income families to keep more of their benefits if they take up work will reduce the disincentives to taking a job and reduce the natural level of unemployment. In Figure 3, the supply side policies will shift the labour supply curve from LS_0 to LS_1 and decrease unemployment.

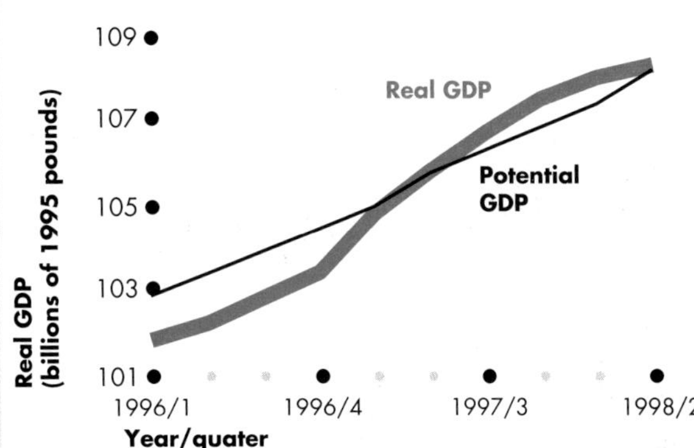

Figure 1 Real GDP and potential GDP

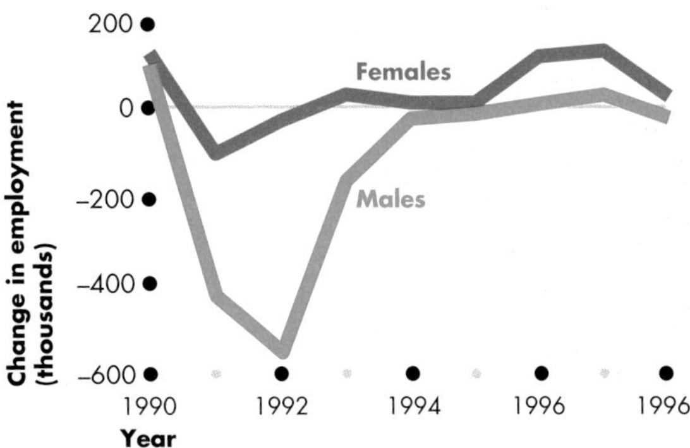

Figure 2 Increase in employment 1990–1998

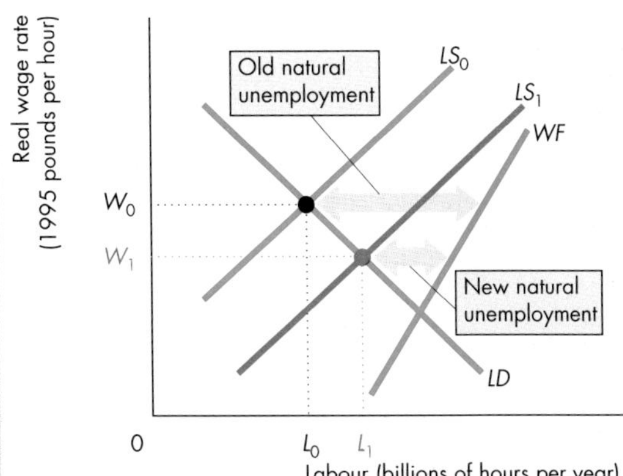

Figure 3 Decrease in natural unemployment

Aggregate Supply and Aggregate Demand

After studying this chapter you will be able to:

- Explain the purpose of the aggregate supply–aggregate demand model
- Explain what determines aggregate supply and aggregate demand
- Explain macroeconomic equilibrium
- Explain the effects of changes in aggregate demand and aggregate supply on economic growth inflation and business cycles
- Explain the recent history of economic growth inflation and business cycles in the United Kingdom

Catching the Wave

Our economy is a bit like an ocean. Like the tide, the general direction or long-term trend of the economy is predictable and is governed by fundamental forces that are reasonably well understood. And like individual waves that ebb and flow, the economy rises and falls in a sequence of cycles that seem to repeat but are never quite like anything that went before and that are hard to predict. Like champion surfers, people who study the economy sometimes learn how to catch a wave and get a good economic ride. But the economic waves are hard to read. What makes the economy ebb and flow in waves around its long-term trend? ◆ Sometimes the economic waves rise high and then crash, and sometimes they rise and roll on a high for a long period like they did during the mid-1980s. Sometimes the waves are inflationary like they were during the 1970s. And sometimes they hit a low and remain there for some time like they did during the depression years of the interwar period, and like they did during the early 1980s and early 1990s. What makes the economic waves vary so much, with real GDP growth and inflation fluctuating in unpredictable ways? ◆ The UK economy is influenced by economic and political events in other parts of the world. For example, the economic policies of our partners in the rest of the European Union, particularly the interest rate policy of the European Central Bank have implications for economic policy at home. A short-term concern is the fall-out from the financial market collapse in Asia, Russia and Latin America, which has implications for our export growth. The economy is also influenced by policy actions taken by the government and the Bank of England. How do events in the rest of the world and domestic policy actions affect production and prices?

◆ ◆ ◆ ◆ To address questions like these, we need a model of macroeconomic fluctuations – of fluctuations around the long-term trends. Our main task in this chapter is to build such a model – the *aggregate supply–aggregate demand model*. Our second task is to use the aggregate supply–aggregate demand model to answer the questions we've just posed. You'll discover that the model of aggregate supply and aggregate demand enables us to understand many important economic events which have a major impact on our lives.

Aggregate Supply

The aggregate supply–aggregate demand model enables us to understand three features of macroeconomic performance:

1 Growth of potential GDP.

2 Inflation.

3 Business cycle fluctuations.

The model uses the concepts of *aggregate* supply and *aggregate* demand to determine real GDP and the price level (the GDP deflator), other things remaining the same. We begin by looking at the fundamental limits to production that influence aggregate supply.

Aggregate Supply Fundamentals

The *quantity of real GDP supplied* (Y) depends on three factors:

1 The quantity of labour (N).

2 The quantity of capital (K).

3 The state of technology (T).

The influence of these three factors on the quantity of real GDP supplied is described by the **aggregate production function**, which is written as the equation:

$$Y = F(N, K, T)$$

Literally, the quantity of real GDP supplied is a function (F) of the factors N, K, and T. The larger any one of these factors is, the greater is Y.

At any given time, the quantity of capital and the state of technology can be viewed as fixed. They depend on decisions made in the past. The population can also be viewed as fixed but the quantity of labour is not fixed. It will depend on the total supply and demand for labour.

Firms demand labour only if it is profitable to do so. The lower the wage rate, which is the cost of labour, the greater is the quantity of labour demanded (other things being equal). Similarly, people supply labour only if doing so is the most valuable use of their time. The higher the wage rate, which is the return to labour, the greater is the quanity of labour supplied. The wage rate that makes the quantity of labour demanded equal to the quantity of labour supplied is the equilibrium wage rate. At this wage rate, there is **full employment**.

Even at full employment, there are always people who are looking for jobs and firms looking for people to employ. The reason is that there is a constant turnover in the labour market. Everyday jobs are destroyed as businesses restructure, downsize, or simply go bust. At the same time jobs are created as new businesses start up, or existing ones expand. Some workers, for a number of personal reasons, may leave to look for better positions, while others start looking for work. This continuous churning in the labour market prevents unemployment from ever dissappearing even at full employment. The unemployment rate at full employment is called the **natural rate of unemployment**.

The real GDP that is supplied when unemployment is at its natural rate is **potential GDP**. Potential GDP depends on the full employment of labour, capital and the state of technology.

To study the economy at full employment and over the business cycle we distinguish two timeframes for aggregate supply:

1 Long-run aggregate supply.

2 Short-run aggregate supply.

Long-run Aggregate Supply

The economy is constantly bombarded by events that move real GDP away from potential GDP and, equivalently, that move the unemployment rate away from equilibrium employment. Following such an event, forces operate to take real GDP back towards potential GDP and restore full employment. The **macroeconomic long run** is a time-frame that is sufficiently long for these forces to have done their work so that real GDP equals potential GDP and full employment prevails.

The **long-run aggregate supply curve** is the relationship between the quantity of real GDP supplied and the price level in the long run when real GDP equals potential GDP. Figure 24.1 illustrates long-run aggregate supply as the vertical line labelled *LAS*. Along the long-run aggregate supply curve, as the price level changes, real GDP remains at potential GDP, which in Figure 24.1 is £750 billion. The long-run aggregate supply curve is always vertical and located at potential GDP.

The long-run aggregate supply curve is vertical because potential GDP is independent of the price level. The reason for this independence is that a movement along the long-run aggregate supply curve is accompanied by changes in *two* sets of

Figure 24.1 Long-run Aggregate Supply

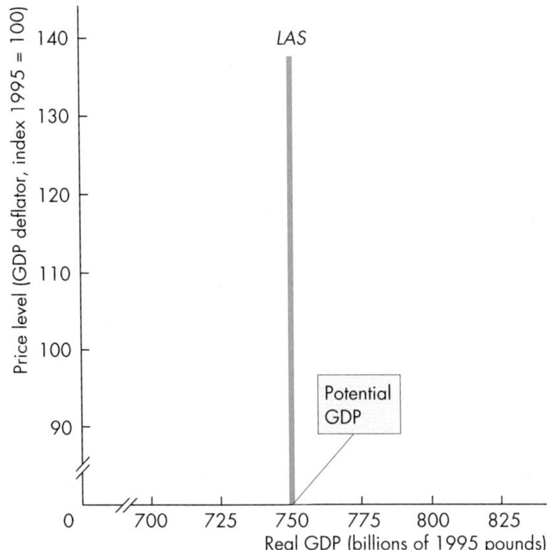

The long-run aggregate supply (*LAS*) curve shows the relationship between the quantity of real GDP supplied and the price level when real GDP equals potential GDP and there is full employment. This level of real GDP is independent of the price level so the *LAS* curve is vertical at potential GDP.

prices: the prices of goods and services (the price level) and the prices of factors of production. A 10 per cent increase in the prices of goods and services is matched by a 10 per cent increase in wage rates and in other factor prices. That is, the price level, wage rate and other factor prices all change by the same percentage and *relative prices* and the *real wage rate* remain constant. When the price level changes but relative prices and the real wage rate remain constant, real GDP also remains constant.

Production at a Pepsi Plant You can see why real GDP remains constant in these circumstances by thinking about production decisions at a Pepsi bottling plant. The plant is producing the quantity of Pepsi that maximizes profit. It could increase production further but to do so it would have to incur a higher *marginal cost* (see Chapter 11). If the price of bottled Pepsi increased and wage rates and other bottling costs did not change, the firm would have an incentive to increase its production. But if the price of bottled Pepsi increases and wage rates and other bottling costs also increase by the same percentage, the firm has no incentive to change its production.

Short-run Aggregate Supply

The **macroeconomic short run** is a period during which GDP is above or below potential GDP. At the same time unemployment is lower or higher than the natural rate.

The **short-run aggregate supply curve** is the relationship between the quantity of real GDP supplied and the price level in the short run when the money wage rate and all other influences on production plans remain constant. For the economy as a whole, with the money wage rate and other factor prices remaining the same. Figure 24.2 illustrates this short-run aggregate supply response as an aggregate supply schedule and as the upward-sloping curve labelled *SAS*. This curve is based on the short-run aggregate supply schedule and each point on the aggregate supply curve corresponds to a row of the aggregate supply schedule. For example, point *a* on the short-run aggregate supply curve and row *a* of the schedule tell us that if the price level is 100, the quantity of real GDP supplied is £550 billion.

Back at the Pepsi Plant You can see why the short-run aggregate supply curve slopes upward by going back to the Pepsi bottling plant. Recall that the plant is producing at the profit maximizing position. If the price of bottled Pepsi rises and wage rates and other bottling costs don't change, the firm has an incentive to increase its production. The higher price for Pepsi more than covers the *marginal cost* of hiring more labour, and its profit rises. So in this situation, the firm increases its production.

Again, what's true for Pepsi bottlers is true for the producers of all goods and services. So when the price level rises and the money wage rate and other factor prices remain constant, aggregate production and the quantity of real GDP supplied increase.

Movements Along *LAS* and *SAS*

Figure 24.3 summarizes what you've just learned about the *LAS* and *SAS* curves. A rise in the price level and an equal percentage rise in the money

Figure 24.2 Short-run Aggregate Supply

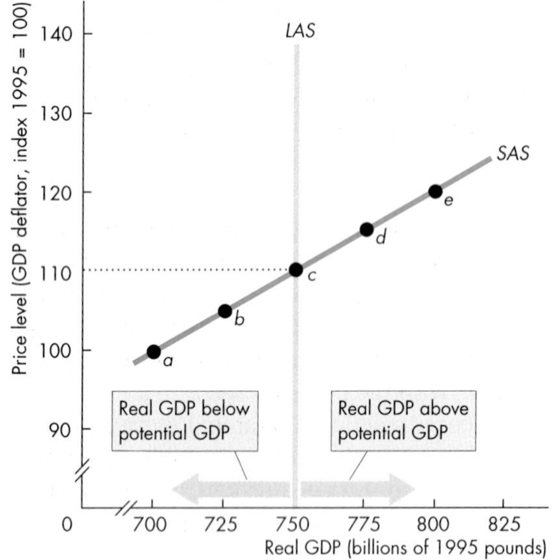

	Price Level (GDP deflator)	Real GDP (billions of 1995 pounds)
a	100	700
b	105	725
c	110	750
d	115	775
e	120	800

The short-run aggregate supply (*SAS*) curve shows the relationship between the quantity of real GDP supplied and the price level when the money wage rate, other factor prices and potential GDP are constant. The short-run aggregate supply curve *SAS* is based on the schedule in the table. The *SAS* curve is upward-sloping because firms' costs increase as the rate of output increases so a higher price is needed to bring forth an increase in the quantity produced.

Figure 24.3 Movements Along the Aggregate Supply Curves

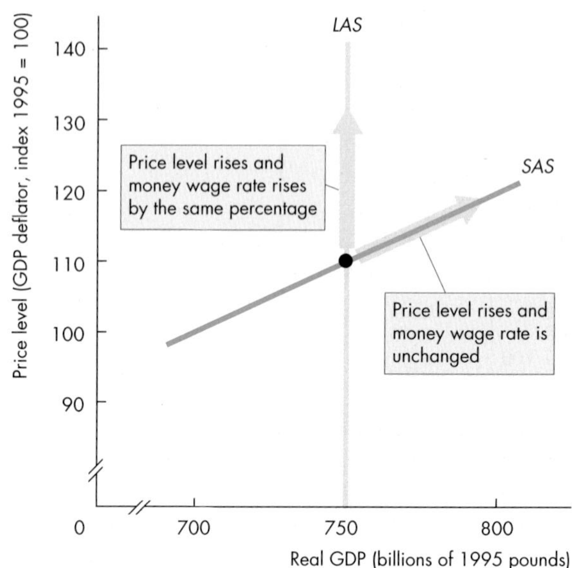

A rise in the price level with the money wage rate unchanged brings an increase in the quantity of real GDP supplied and a movement along the short-run aggregate supply curve. A rise in the price level with an equal percentage rise in the money wage rate keeps the quantity of real GDP supplied constant and brings a movement along the long-run aggregate supply curve.

wage rate brings a movement along the *LAS* curve. Real GDP remains constant at potential GDP. A rise in the price level and no change in the money wage rate bring a movement along the *SAS* curve.

You've now learned about the long-run and short-run aggregate supply curves and the factors that make the long-run aggregate supply curve vertical and the short-run aggregate supply curve slope upward. But what makes aggregate supply change? Let's find out.

Changes in Aggregate Supply

You've just seen that a change in the price level, other things remaining the same, brings a movement along the aggregate supply curves but it does not change aggregate supply. Aggregate supply changes when any other influences on production plans change. Let's study these influences beginning with those that affect potential GDP.

Changes in Poential GDP Long-run aggregate supply changes when potential GDP changes and potential GDP changes for three reasons:

1 Change in the full-employment quantity of labour hours.
2 Change in the quantity of capital.
3 Improvement in technology.

Change in the full-employment quantity of labour hours Suppose there are two identical Pepsi bottling plants except that one employs 100 hours of labour and the other employs 10 hours of labour. The plant with more labour produces more bottles of Pepsi. The same is true for the economy as a whole. The larger the number of labour hours utilized at full-employment, the greater is potential GDP.

Over time, potential GDP increases because the labour force increases. With constant capital and technology, potential GDP increases only if the the full-employment quantity of labour hours increases. Fluctuations in employment and labour hours over the business cycle bring fluctuations around potential GDP. But they are not changes in potential GDP.

Change in the quantity of capital A Pepsi plant that has two production lines has more capital and produces more output than the a Pepsi plant that has one production line. For the economy as a whole, the larger the capital stock, the more productive the workforce is, the greater is the output that it can produce. The capital-rich UK economy produces a vastly greater real GDP per hour of labour than countries that have a small amount of capital, such as the developing countries. But the fast-growing capital stock of the Asian economies is bringing faster real GDP growth than the United Kingdom and other EU countries have achieved.

Capital includes *human capital*. The manager of one Pepsi plant is an economics graduate with an MBA and its workforce has an average of 10 years' experience. The manager of another identical plant has no business training and its workforce is new to bottling. The first plant has a higher stock of human capital than the second and its output is larger. For the economy as a whole, the larger the stock of *human capital* – the skills that people have acquired at school and through on-the-job training – the greater is potential GDP.

Improvement in technology One Pepsi plant has a production line that was designed in the 1970s before the computer age. Another uses the latest robot technology. Even with a smaller workforce, the second plant produces more bottles per day than the first plant. Technological change – inventing new and better ways of doing things – enables firms to produce more from any given amount of inputs. So even with a constant workforce and constant capital stock, improvements in technology increase production and increase aggregate supply (Chapter 32, pp. 808–811). Technological advances have been by far the most important source of increased production over the past two centuries. As a result of technological advances, in the UK today, one farm worker produces enough to feed 60 people in a year, and one carworker can produce 12 cars and trucks in a year.

Changes in Short-run Aggregate Supply All the factors that influence long-run aggregate supply also influence short-run aggregate supply. That is, if potential GDP increases, more real GDP is supplied in the long run but also more real GDP is supplied at each price level in the short run. So short-run aggregate supply increases.

The only influences on short-run aggregate supply that do not also change long-run aggregate supply are the money wage rate and the money price of any other factor of production. Money wages affect short-run aggregate supply through their influence on firms' costs. The higher the money wage rate, the higher are firms' costs and the smaller is the quantity that firms are willing to supply at each price level. Thus an increase in the money wage rate decreases short-run aggregate supply.

Changes in money wages do not affect long-run aggregate supply. The reason is that along the long-run aggregate supply curve real GDP remains constant at potential GDP because when the money wage changes, the price level also changes by the same percentage. So real wages are unchanged and the labour market is back in equilibrium.

Shifts in *LAS* and *SAS* Figure 24.4 illustrates changes in long-run aggregate supply and short-run aggregate supply as shifts in the aggregate supply curves. Part (a) shows the effects of a change in potential GDP. Initially, the long-run aggregate supply is LAS_0 and short-run aggregate supply is SAS_0. An improvement in technology or increase in capital increases potential GDP to £800 billion. As a result, the long-run aggregate supply increases and the long-run aggregate supply curve shifts rightward to LAS_1. Short-run aggregate supply also increases and the short-run aggregate supply curve shifts rightward to SAS_1.

Figure 24.4(b) shows the effects of an increase in the money wage rate (or other factor price) on aggregate supply. Initially, the short-run aggregate

Figure 24.4 Changes in Aggregate Supply

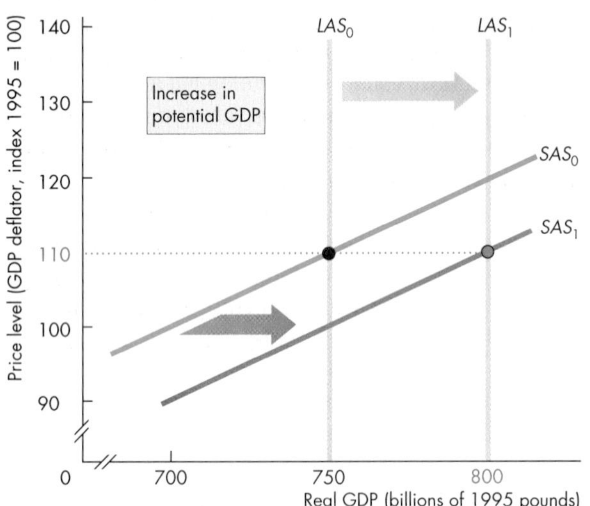

(a) Change in potential GDP shifts *LAS* and *SAS*

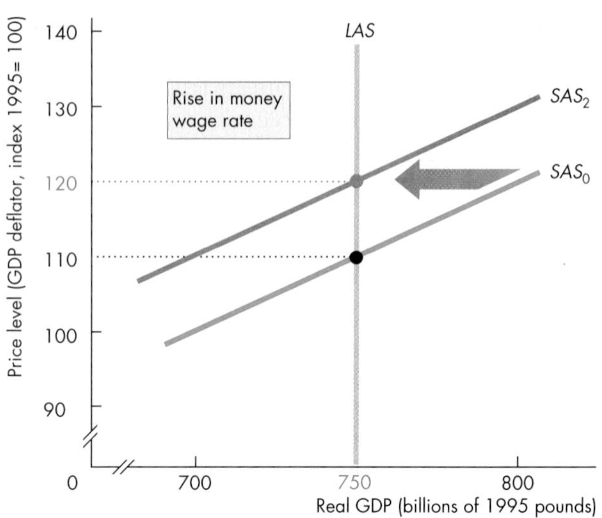

(b) Change in the money wage rate shifts *SAS*

In part (a), an increase in potential GDP increases both long-run aggregate supply and short-run aggregate supply and shifts both aggregate supply curves rightward from LAS_0 to LAS_1 and from SAS_0 to SAS_1.

In part (b), a rise in the money wage rate decreases short-run aggregate supply and shifts the short-run aggregate supply curve leftward from SAS_0 to SAS_2. A rise in the money wage rate does not change long-run aggregate supply so the *LAS* curve does not shift.

supply curve is SAS_0. A rise in the money wage rate *decreases* short-run aggregate supply and shifts the short-run aggregate supply curve leftward to SAS_2. Long-run aggregate supply does not change when the money wage rate changes, so the *LAS* curve remains at *LAS*.

Review

- A change in the price level that is accompanied by an equal percentage change in the money wage rate keeps real GDP at potential GDP and is shown as a movement along the LAS curve.
- A rise in the price level with no change in the money wage rate brings an increase in the quantity of real GDP supplied and a movement along the SAS curve.
- An increase in potential GDP increases both long-run aggregate supply and short-run aggregate supply and shifts the *LAS* curve and the *SAS* curve rightward.
- An increase in the money wage rate (or other factor price) decreases short-run aggregate supply but leaves long-run aggregate supply unchanged and shifts the *SAS* curve leftward.

Aggregate Demand

Real GDP equals aggregate expenditure which is the sum of consumption expenditure (C), investment (I), government purchases (G) and net exports (X) (see Chapter 22, pp. 543–547). *Aggregate planned expenditure* is the total amount of final goods and services produced in the UK that households, businesses, governments and foreigners plan to buy. What factors determine these spending plans? Spending plans depend on a number of factors but we first focus on the

Figure 24.5 Aggregate Demand

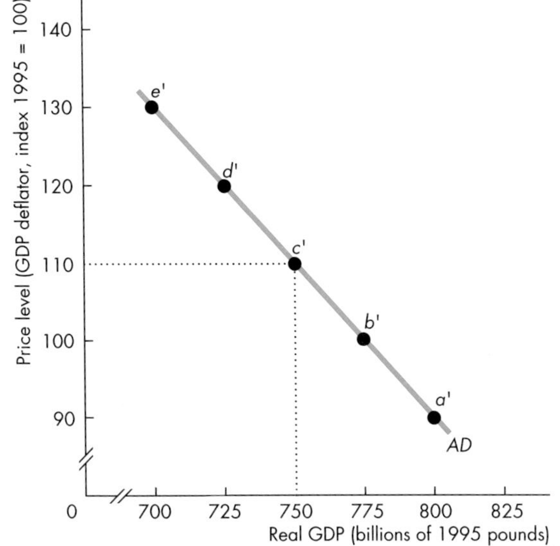

	Price Level (GDP deflator)	Real GDP (billions of 1990 pounds)
a'	90	800
b'	100	775
c'	110	750
d'	120	725
e'	130	700

The aggregate demand curve (*AD*) shows the relationship between the quantity of real GDP demanded and the price level. The aggregate demand curve is based on the schedule in the table. Each point *a'* to *e'* on the curve corresponds to the row in the table identified by the same letter. Thus when the price level is 110, the quantity of real GDP demanded is £750 billion, illustrated by point *c'* in the figure.

relationship on the quantity of real GDP demanded and the price level.

Figure 24.5 illustrates aggregate demand as an aggregate demand schedule and as the downward-sloping curve labelled *AD*. This aggregate demand curve is based on the aggregate demand schedule and each point on the aggregate demand curve corresponds to a row of the aggregate demand schedule. For example, point *c'* on the aggregate demand curve and row *c'* of the aggregate demand schedule tell us that if the price level is 110, the quantity of real GDP demanded is £750 billion.

In constructing the aggregate demand schedule and aggregate demand curve, we hold constant all the influences on the quantity of real GDP demanded other than the price level and the interest rate. As the price level changes, the interest rate also changes (for a reason that is explained below) and there is a movement along the aggregate demand curve. A change in any of the other influences on the quantity of real GDP demanded results in a new aggregate demand schedule and a shift in the aggregate demand curve. But why does the aggregate demand curve slope downwards? Let's see why.

Why the Aggregate Demand Curve Slopes Downward

The aggregate demand curve slopes downward for two reasons.

1 Real money balances effect.

2 Substitution effects.

Real Money Balances Effect **Money** in the United Kingdom is currency and bank and building society deposits – the things you use to buy goods and services and pay bills. In most other countries of the European Union, money is simply currency and bank deposits. **Real money** is the *purchasing power* of money or the quantity of goods and services that money will buy. It is measured by the quantity of money divided by the price level. The **real money balances effect** is the change in the quantity of real GDP demanded that results from a change in the quantity of real money. The greater the quantity of real money – the greater the purchasing power of money – the greater is the quantity of real GDP demanded. But the quantity of real money increases if the price level falls, so a fall in the price level brings an increase in the quantity of real GDP demanded and a movement along the aggregate demand curve.

To see how the real money balances effect works, think about your own spending plans. You have £5 to spend, and coffee costs £1 a cup. Your money can buy 5 cups of coffee. But if coffee costs 50 pence a cup, your £5 can buy 10 cups. The lower the price, the more you can buy with a given quantity of money so the greater is your purchasing power. And the greater your purchasing power, the more goods you plan to buy.

Substitution Effects The substitution effect is made up of two components; the **intertemporal substitution effect** and the **international substitution effect**. The intertemporal substitution effect involves the substitution of goods in the future for goods in the present. This comes about through a change in the rate of interest. When the price level rises, other things remaining the same, the interest rate rises. The reason is connected to the *real money balances effect* that you've just learned about. With a higher price level, people have less purchasing power, so the amount they want to lend decreases and the amount they want to borrow increases (again, other things remaining the same). A decrease in the supply of loans and an increase in the demand for loans means that interest rates rise. But the higher the interest rate, the less the expenditure by people and firms on capital and consumer durables. Also by not buying today, but by saving, you can earn interest and increase the amount available for spending in the future. The international substitution effect works through international prices. The higher the price level in the United Kingdom, other things remaining the same, the higher are the prices of UK-produced goods and services relative to foreign-produced goods and services and the fewer UK-produced goods and services people buy. So the higher the price level, other things remaining the same, the smaller is the quantity of real GDP demanded. An example of international substitution is your decision to buy a Honda car that was made in Japan instead of a Ford made in the United Kingdom. Another example is your decision to take a holiday in Spain instead of Cornwall.

For the reasons we've just reviewed, the aggregate demand curve slopes downward. The higher the price level in the United Kingdom, the smaller is the quantity demanded of UK-produced goods and services – UK real GDP. The reverse is the case for a lower price level. But how do other influences on spending plans affect aggregate demand?

Figure 24.6 Changes in the Quantity of Real GDP Demanded

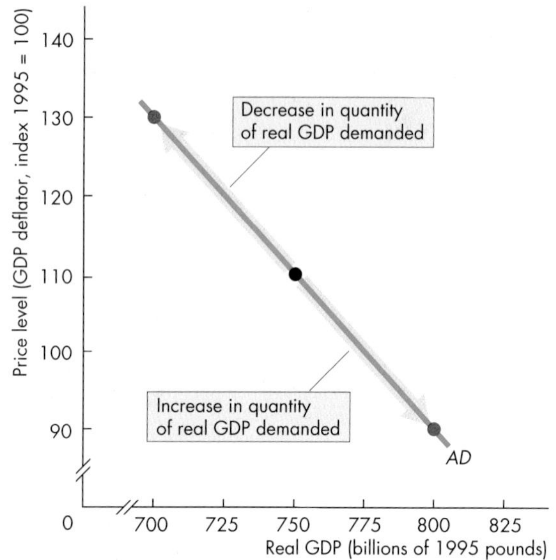

The quantity of real GDP demanded

Decreases if the price level *increases*	*Increases* if the price level *decreases*

because of the:

Real money balances effect

◆ An increase in the price level decreases the quantity of real money	◆ A decrease in the price level increases the quantity of real money

Intertemporal substitution effect

◆ An increase in the price level increases interest rates	◆ A decrease in the price level decreases interest rates

International substitution effect

◆ An increase in the price level increases the cost of domestic goods and services relative to foreign goods and services	◆ A decrease in the price level decreases the cost of domestic goods and services relative to foreign goods and services

Changes in Aggregate Demand

The aggregate demand schedule and aggregate demand curve describe aggregate demand at a point in time. But aggregate demand frequently changes. As a consequence, the aggregate demand curve frequently shifts. The main influences on aggregate demand that shift the aggregate demand curve are:

- Expectations.
- International factors.
- Fiscal policy and monetary policy.

Expectations Expectations about future incomes, inflation and profits influence people's decisions about spending today. An increase in expected future income, other things remaining the same, increases the amount that households plan to spend today on consumption goods and consumer durables and increases aggregate demand. The reverse is the case when households expect slow future income growth, or even a decline in income.

An increase in the expected future inflation rate, other things remaining the same, leads to an increase in aggregate demand because people decide to buy more goods and services today before prices rise. An increase in firms' expected future profit increases their demands for new capital equipment and increases aggregate demand.

International Factors Two main international factors that influence aggregate demand are the foreign exchange rate and foreign income. A change in the UK price level, other things remaining the same, changes the prices of domestically produced goods and services *relative* to the prices of goods and services produced in other countries. Another influence on the price of UK-produced goods and services relative to those produced abroad is the *foreign exchange rate.* The foreign exchange rate is the amount of a foreign currency that you can buy with £1. A rise (appreciation) in the foreign exchange rate decreases aggregate demand. To see how, suppose that £1 is worth 1,800 South Korean won. You can buy a Samsung portable TV (made in South Korea) that costs 180,000 won for £100. If the price of a Ferguson TV (made in the United Kingdom) is the same, you may be willing to buy the Ferguson TV. Now suppose the pound rises to 2,000 won and you now pay only £90 to buy the 180,000 won needed to buy the Samsung TV. You may substitute the Samsung for the Ferguson. The demand for UK-made TVs falls as the foreign exchange value of the pound rises. So as the foreign exchange value of the pound rises, everything else remaining the same, aggregate demand decreases.

The income of foreigners affects the aggregate demand for UK-produced goods and services. For example, an increase in income in the United States, Japan and Germany increases the demand by American, Japanese and German consumers and producers for UK-produced consumption goods and capital goods. The United Kingdom is an open economy, which means that it exports and imports a significant part of its GDP (approximately one-third). Thus these sources of change in aggregate demand have always been important in UK history.

The Asian crisis has had a strong impact on world demand and UK export demand in particular. The exports of goods grew by only 1 per cent in 1998 compared with 8 per cent in 1997. The devaluation of the South Korean won and the other currencies of East Asia has made their goods cheaper to UK importers. Imports of goods rose by 8 per cent in 1998 and 9 per cent in 1997.

Fiscal Policy and Monetary Policy **Fiscal policy** is the government's attempt to influence the economy by setting and changing taxes, government spending, and the government's deficit and debt. The scale of government purchases of goods and services has a direct effect on aggregate demand. If taxes are held constant, the more hospitals, motorways, schools, and colleges the government funds, the larger are government purchases of goods and services and so the larger is aggregate demand. A decrease in taxes increases aggregate demand. An increase in transfer payments – unemployment benefits, social security benefits and welfare payments – also increases aggregate demand. Both of these influences operate by increasing households' *disposable* income. The higher the level of disposable income, the greater is the demand for goods and services. Because lower taxes and higher transfer payments increase disposable income, they also increase aggregate demand.

Decisions about the money supply and interest rates are made by the Bank of England. These decisions influence aggregate demand. The Bank of England's attempt to influence the economy by varying the money supply and interest rates is called **monetary policy**. The money supply is determined by the Bank of England and the banks and building societies (in a process described in Chapters 27, and 28). The greater the *quantity of money* the greater is the level of aggregate demand. An easy way to see why money affects aggregate demand is to imagine what would happen if the Bank used helicopters to sprinkle millions of pounds worth of new £10 notes across the country. We would all stop whatever we were doing and rush out to pick up our share of the newly available money. But we wouldn't just put the money we picked up in the bank. We would spend some of it, so our demand for goods and services would increase. Although this story is pretty extreme, it does illustrate that an increase in the quantity of money increases aggregate demand.

Figure 24.7 Changes in Aggregate Demand

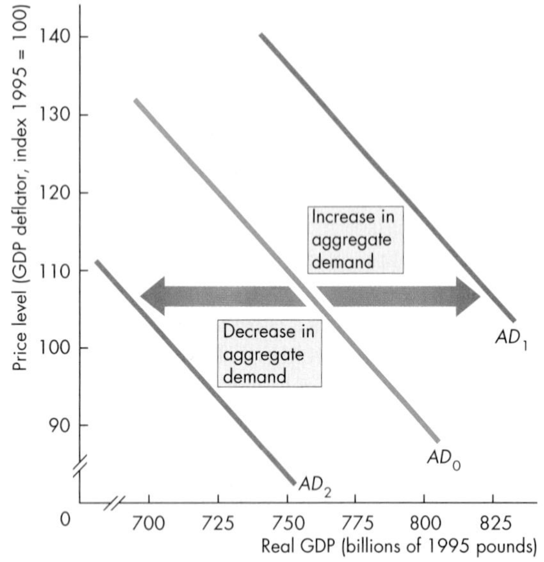

Aggregate demand

Decreases if:	**Increases if:**
◆ Expected inflation or expected profits decrease	◆ Expected inflation or expected profits increase
◆ The exchange rate increases or foreign income decreases	◆ The exchange rate decreases or foreign income increases
◆ Fiscal policy decreases government spending or increases taxes	◆ Fiscal policy increases government spending or decreases taxes
◆ Monetary policy decreases the money supply and increases interest rates	◆ Monetary policy increases the money supply and decreases interest rates

In practice, changes in the quantity of money are brought about by a change in the interest rate at which the Bank of England is willing to lend to the commercial banks (the bank rate), and so have an additional influence on aggregate demand by changing the amount of investment and the demand for consumer durables. The Bank speeds up the rate at which new money is being injected into the economy by lowering the bank rate, banks have more funds to lend and interest rates fall. The Bank slows down the pace at which it is creating money by raising the bank rate, commercial banks have less funds to lend and interest rates rise. Thus a change in the quantity of money has a second effect on aggregate demand, operating through its effects on commercial bank interest rates.

Now that we've reviewed the factors that influence aggregate demand, let's summarize their effects on the aggregate demand curve.

Shifts of the Aggregate Demand Curve

We illustrate a change in aggregate demand as a shift in the aggregate demand curve. Figure 24.7 illustrates two changes in aggregate demand, and summarizes the factors bringing about such changes. Aggregate demand is initially AD_0, the same as in Figure 24.5.

The aggregate demand curve shifts rightward, from AD_0 to AD_1 when expected future profit increases, the expected inflation rate increases, the foreign exchange rate falls, income in the rest of the world increases, government purchases of goods and services increase, taxes are cut, transfer payments increase, or the money supply increases and interest rates fall.

The aggregate demand curve shifts leftward, from AD_0 to AD_2, when expected future profit decreases, the expected inflation rate decreases, the foreign exchange rate rises, income in the rest of the world decreases, government purchases of goods and services decrease, taxes are increased, transfer payments decrease, or the money supply decreases and interest rates rise.

Review

- ◆ The aggregate demand curve shows the effect of a change in the price level on the quantity of real GDP demanded, other things remaining the same.
- ◆ An increase in the price level brings a decrease in the quantity of real GDP demanded because it decreases the quantity of real money balances, increases the rate of interest, increases the price of goods in the present relative to goods in the future, and increases the price of domestic goods relative to foreign goods.

- Other influences on aggregate spending plans (expectations, international factors, fiscal policy and monetary policy) change aggregate demand and shift the aggregate demand curve.

Macroeconomic Equilibrium

The purpose of the aggregate supply–aggregate demand model is to understand and predict changes in real GDP and the price level. To achieve this purpose, we combine aggregate supply and aggregate demand and determine macroeconomic equilibrium. There is a macroeconomic equilibrium for each of the time-frames for aggregate supply: a long-run equilibrium and a short-run equilibrium. Long-run equilibrium is the state towards which the economy is heading. Short-run equilibrium describes the state of the economy at each point in time on its path towards long-run macroeconomic equilibrium. We'll begin our study of macroeconomic equilibrium by looking at the short run.

Short-run Macroeconomic Equilibrium

The aggregate demand curve tells us the quantity of real GDP demanded at each price level, and the short-run aggregate supply curve tells us the quantity of real GDP supplied at each price level. **Short-run macroeconomic equilibrium** occurs when the quantity of real GDP demanded equals the short-run quantity of real GDP supplied at the point of intersection of the *AD* curve and the *SAS* curve. Figure 24.8 illustrates such an equilibrium at a price level of 110 and real GDP of £750 billion (point *c* and *c*').

To see why this position is an equilibrium, let's work out what happens if the price level is something other than 110. Suppose, for example, that the price level is 120 and that real GDP is £800 billion (at point *e*) on the *SAS* curve. The quantity of real GDP demanded is less than £800 billion so firms are unable to sell all their output. Unwanted stocks pile up and firms cut both production and prices. Production and prices are cut until firms can sell all their output. This situation occurs only when real GDP is £750 billion and the price level is 110.

Next consider what happens if the price level is 100 and real GDP is £700 billion (at point *a*) on the *SAS* curve. The quantity of real GDP demanded exceeds £700 billion so firms are not able to meet demand. Stocks are running out and customers are clamouring for goods. So firms increase production and raise their prices. Production and prices are increased until firms can meet demand. This situation occurs only when real GDP is £750 billion and the price level is 110.

Figure 24.8 Short-run Macroeconomic Equilibrium

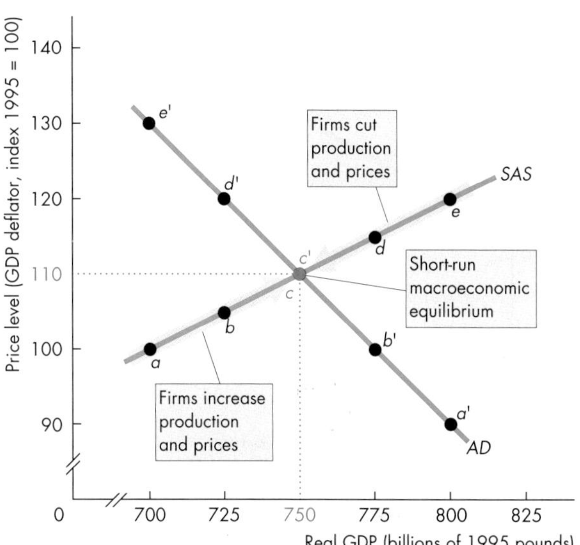

Short-run macroeconomic equilibrium occurs when real GDP demanded equals real GDP supplied at the intersection of the aggregate demand curve (*AD*) and the short-run aggregate supply curve (*SAS*). Here, such an equilibrium occurs at points *c* and *c*' where the price level is 110 and real GDP is £750 billion. If the price level was 120 and real GDP was £800 billion, point *e*, firms would not be able to sell all their output. They would decrease production and cut prices. If the price level was 100 and real GDP was £700 billion, point *a*, people would not be able to buy all the goods they demanded. Firms would increase production and raise their prices. Only when the price level is 110 and real GDP is £750 billion can firms sell all they produce and people buy all they demand. This is the short-run macroeconomic equilibrium.

Short-run Macroeconomic Equilibrium and Business Cycles

Short-run macroeconomic equilibrium does not necessarily occur at full employment. At full employment, the economy is on its *long-run*

Figure 24.9 Three Types of Macroeconomic Equilibrium

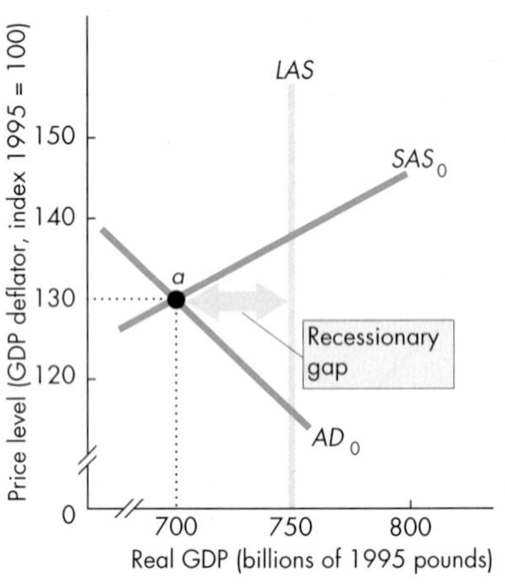

(a) Below full-employment equilibrium

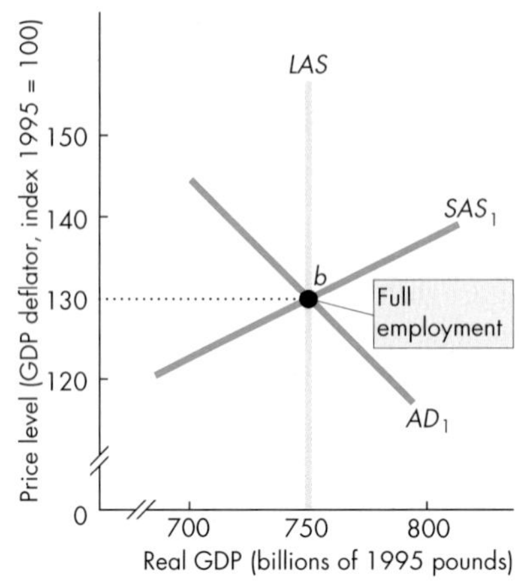

(b) Full-employment equilibrium

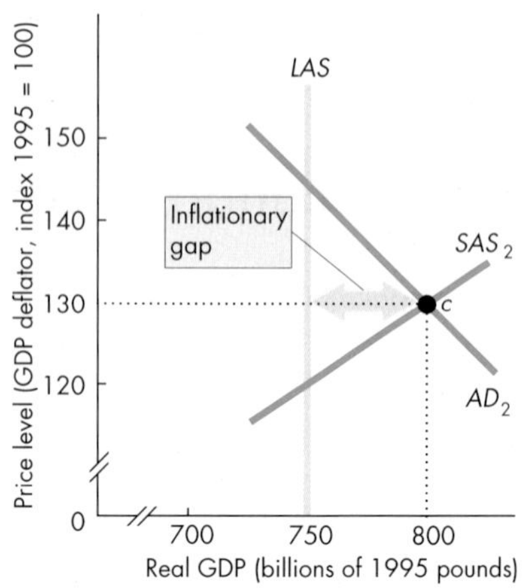

(c) Above full-employment equilibrium

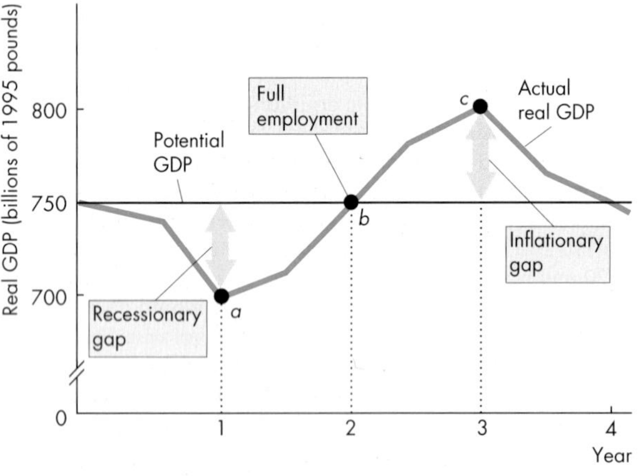

(d) Fluctuations in real GDP

Part (a) shows a below full-employment equilibrium, part (b) shows a full-employment equilibrium, part (c) shows an above full-employment equilibrium and part (d) shows how real GDP fluctuates around potential GDP in a business cycle. In year 1, there is a recessionary gap and the economy is at point *a* (in parts a and d). In year 2, there is full employment and the economy is at point *b* (in parts b and d). In year 3, there is an inflationary gap and the economy is at point *c* (in parts c and d).

aggregate supply curve. But short-run macroeconomic equilibrium occurs at the intersection of the *short-run* aggregate supply curve and the aggregate demand curve and can occur at, below, or above potential GDP. We can see this fact by considering the three possible cases shown in Figure 24.9.

In part (a) there is a below full-employment equilibrium. A **below full-employment equilibrium** is a macroeconomic equilibrium in which potential GDP exceeds real GDP. The amount by which potential GDP exceeds real GDP is called a **recessionary gap**. This name reminds us that a gap has opened up between potential GDP and real GDP either because the economy has experienced a recession or because real GDP, while growing, has grown more slowly than the long-term growth rate.

The below full-employment equilibrium illustrated in Figure 24.9(a) occurs where aggregate demand curve AD_0 intersects short-run aggregate supply curve SAS_0 at a real GDP of £700 billion and a price level of 110. The recessionary gap is £50 billion. The UK economy was in a situation similar to that shown in Figure 24.9(a) in 1980–81 and again in 1991–92. In those years, unemployment was high and real GDP was less than potential GDP.

Figure 24.9(b) is an example of full-employment equilibrium. **Full-employment equilibrium** is a macroeconomic equilibrium in which real GDP equals potential GDP. In this example, the equilibrium occurs where the aggregate demand curve AD_1 intersects the short-run aggregate supply curve SAS_1 at an actual and potential GDP of £750 billion. The economy was in a situation such as that shown in Figure 24.9(b) in 1986 and in 1998.

Figure 24.9(c) illustrates an above full-employment equilibrium. An **above full-employment equilibrium** is a macroeconomic equilibrium in which real GDP exceeds potential GDP. The amount by which real GDP exceeds potential GDP is called an **inflationary gap**. This name reminds us that a gap has opened up between real GDP and potential GDP which is placing inflationary pressure on the economy.

The above full-employment equilibrium illustrated in Figure 24.9(c) occurs where the aggregate demand curve AD_2 intersects the short-run aggregate supply curve SAS_2 at a real GDP of £800 billion and a price level of 110. There is an inflationary gap of £50 billion. The economy was in a situation similar to that depicted in part (c) in 1987–89.

The economy moves from one type of equilibrium to another as a result of fluctuations in aggregate demand and in short-run aggregate supply. These fluctuations produce fluctuations in real GDP and the price level. Figure 24.9(d) shows how real GDP fluctuates around potential GDP.

Long-term Growth and Inflation

Long-term economic growth comes about because, over time, the long-run aggregate supply curve shifts rightward. The pace at which it shifts is determined by the growth rate of potential GDP (see Chapter 32, pp. 807–811).

Inflation comes about because, over time, the aggregate demand curve shifts rightward at a faster pace than the shift in the long-run aggregate supply curve. The pace at which it shifts is determined mainly by the growth rate of the quantity of money. At times when the quantity of money is increasing rapidly, aggregate demand is increasing quickly and the inflation rate is high. When the growth rate of the quantity of money slows down, other things remaining the same, the inflation rate eventually slows down.

But the economy does not experience steady real GDP growth and steady inflation. Instead, it fluctuates around its long-term growth path and its long-term inflation rate. When we study these fluctuations, we ignore the long-term trends. We examine how GDP and the price level are determined in a model economy that has no trends. By ignoring the trends, we can see the short-term fluctuations more clearly.

Let's now look at some of the sources of fluctuations around the long-term trends.

Fluctuations in Aggregate Demand

We're going to work out how real GDP and the price level change following an increase in aggregate demand. Let's suppose that the economy starts out at full employment and, as illustrated in Figure 24.10(a), is producing £750 billion worth of goods and services at a price level of 130. The economy is on the aggregate demand curve AD_0, the short-run aggregate supply curve SAS_0 and the long-run aggregate supply curve *LAS*.

Now suppose that the world economy grows more quickly and the demand for UK-made goods increases in Japan and the United States. The increase in exports increases aggregate demand and the aggregate demand curve shifts rightward. Suppose that the aggregate demand curve shifts from AD_0 to AD_1 in Figure 24.10(a).

Faced with an increase in demand firms increase production and raise prices. For the economy as a whole, real GDP increases and the price level rises. Real GDP rises to £775 billion and the price level rises to 115. In this short-run macroeconomic equilibrium, firms are producing the quantities they want to produce, given the price level and the money wage rate. But the economy is at an above full-employment equilibrium. Real GDP exceeds potential GDP, and there is an inflationary gap.

The increase in aggregate demand has increased the prices of all goods and services. Faced with higher prices, firms have increased their output rates. At this stage, prices of goods and services have increased but wage rates have not changed. (Recall that as we move along a short-run aggregate supply curve, wage rates are constant.)

The economy cannot produce in excess of potential GDP forever. Why not? What are the forces at work that bring real GDP back to potential GDP and restore full employment?

Figure 24.10 An Increase in Aggregate Demand

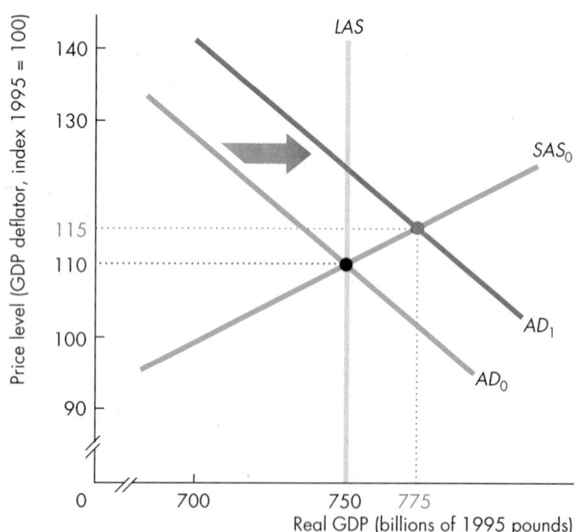

(a) Short-run effect

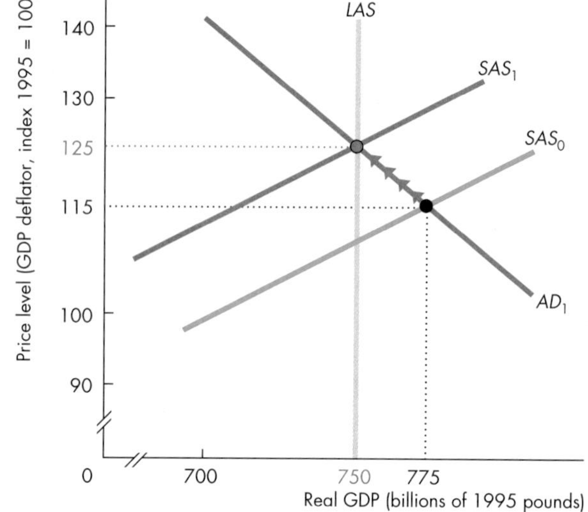

(b) Long-run effect

An increase in aggregate demand shifts the aggregate demand curve from AD_0 to AD_1. Initially (part a), with sticky prices, real GDP increases from £750 billion to £775 billion along the *SAS* curve. Firms start to raise their prices and cut back production (part b) and the *SAS* curve shifts upward. In the short-run equilibrium, real GDP is £775 billion and the price level rises to 115. In this situation, there is an inflationary gap. The money wage rate rises and the short-run aggregate supply curve shifts leftward from SAS_0 to SAS_1 in part (b). As it shifts, it intersects the aggregate demand curve AD_1 at higher price levels and lower real GDP levels. Eventually, the price level rises to 125 and real GDP falls back to £750 billion – potential GDP and full employment.

If the price level has increased and wage rates have remained constant, workers have experienced a fall in the purchasing power of their wages. Furthermore, firms have experienced an increase in revenue and no change in their costs. Firms' profits have increased. In these circumstances, workers demand higher wages, and firms, anxious to maintain their employment and output levels, meet those demands. If firms do not raise wage rates, they either lose workers or have to hire less productive ones.

As wage rates rise, the short-run aggregate supply curve begins to shift leftward. In Figure 24.10(b), the short-run aggregate supply curve moves from SAS_0 towards SAS_1. The rise in wages and the shift in the *SAS* curve produce a sequence of new equilibrium positions. Along the adjustment path, real GDP falls and the price level rises and the economy moves up along its aggregate demand curve as shown by the arrow heads in the figure. Eventually, wages will have risen by so much that the *SAS* curve is SAS_1. At this time, the aggregate demand curve AD_1 intersects SAS_1 at a full-employment equilibrium. The price level has risen to 125, and real GDP is back where it started, at potential GDP. Unemployment is again at its natural rate.

Throughout the adjustment process, higher wage rates raise firms' costs and, with rising costs, firms offer a smaller quantity of goods and services for sale at any given price level. By the time the adjustment is over, firms are producing the same amount as they initially produced, but at higher prices and higher costs.

A decrease in aggregate demand has similar but opposite effects to those that we've just studied. That is, a decrease in aggregate demand decreases real GDP to less than potential GDP and unemploy-

Figure 24.11 A Decrease in Aggregate Supply

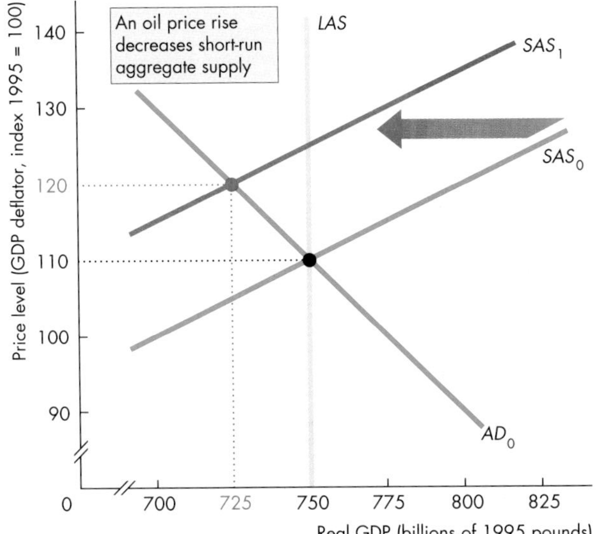

An increase in the price of oil decreases short-run aggregate supply and shifts the short-run aggregate supply curve leftward from SAS_0 to SAS_1. Real GDP falls from £750 billion to £725 billion and the price level increases from 110 to 120. The economy experiences both recession and inflation – stagflation.

ment increases above its natural rate. A recessionary gap emerges. Firms cut prices. The lower price level increases the purchasing power of wages, and increases firms' costs relative to their output prices because wages remain unchanged. Eventually, the slack economy leads to falling wage rates and the short-run aggregate supply curve shifts rightward. Real GDP gradually returns to potential GDP and full employment is restored.

Let's now work out how real GDP and the price level change when aggregate supply changes.

Fluctuations in Aggregate Supply

Fluctuations in short-run aggregate supply can bring fluctuations in real GDP around potential GDP. We'll study a decrease in aggregate supply. Suppose that initially, real GDP equals potential GDP. Then there is a large but temporary rise in the money price of raw materials. (Similar to an increase in the price of oil as in 1973–74 and again in 1979–80 when OPEC used its market muscle). What happens to real GDP and the price level?

Figure 24.11 answers this question. The aggregate demand curve is AD_0, the short-run aggregate supply curve is SAS_0 and the long-run aggregate supply curve is LAS_0. Equilibrium real GDP is £750 billion, which equals potential GDP, and the price level is 110. Then the price of oil rises. Faced with a higher price of raw materials, firms' costs rise and they decrease production. Short-run aggregate supply decreases, and the short-run aggregate supply curve shifts leftward to SAS_1.

As a result of this decrease in short-run aggregate supply, the economy moves to a new equilibrium where SAS_1 intersects the aggregate demand curve AD_0. The price level rises to 120, and real GDP decreases to £725 billion. Because real GDP falls, the economy experiences recession. Because the price level increases, the economy experiences inflation. Such a combination of recession and inflation – called *stagflation* – actually occurred in the mid-1970s.

Review

- Short-run macroeconomic equilibrium explains how real GDP and the price level change over time.
- There are three types of short-run macroeconomic equilibrium: (1) below full-employment equilibrium (a situation in which potential GDP exceeds real GDP and there is a recessionary gap); (2) full-employment equilibrium (a situation in which real GDP equals potential GDP); (3) above full-employment equilibrium (a situation in which real GDP exceeds potential GDP and there is an inflationary gap).
- The price level fluctuates and real GDP fluctuates around potential GDP because of fluctuations in aggregate demand and short-run aggregate supply.

Let's put our new knowledge to work and see how it helps us understand macroeconomic performance.

Long-term Growth, Inflation and Cycles in the UK Economy

The economy is continually changing. If you imagine the economy as a video, then an aggregate supply–aggregate demand figure such as Figure 24.11 is a freeze-frame. We're going to run the video – an instant replay – but keep our finger on the freeze-frame button, looking at some important parts of the previous action. Let's run the video from 1960.

Figure 24.12 shows the state of the economy in 1960 at the point of intersection of its aggregate demand curve AD_{60} and short-run aggregate supply curve SAS_{60}. Real GDP was £230 billion and the GDP deflator was 10 (less than one-tenth of its 1998 level).

By 1998, the economy had reached the point marked by the intersection of aggregate demand curve AD_{98} and short-run aggregate supply curve SAS_{98}. Real GDP was £773 billion and the GDP deflator was 108.4.

There are three important features of the economy's path traced by the points:

1 Long-term growth.

2 Inflation.

3 Cycles.

Long-term Growth Over the years, real GDP grows – shown in Figure 24.12 by the rightward movement of the points. The faster the growth rate of real GDP, the larger is the horizontal distance between successive dots in the figure. The force generating long-term growth is an increase in long-run aggregate supply. And long-run aggregate supply increases because of workforce growth, the accumulation of capital – both physical plant and equipment and human capital – the discovery of new resources and technological change.

Figure 24.12 Aggregate Supply and Aggregate Demand: 1960–1998

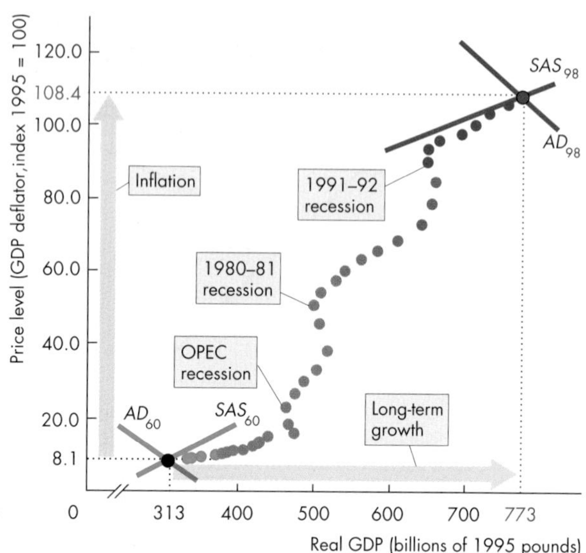

Each point indicates the value of the GDP deflator and real GDP in a given year. In 1960, these variables were determined by the intersection of the aggregate demand curve AD_{60} and the short-run aggregate supply curve SAS_{60}. Each point is generated by the gradual shifting of the *AD* and *SAS* curves. By 1998, the curves were AD_{98} and SAS_{98}. Real GDP grew and the price level increased. But growth and inflation did not proceed smoothly. Real GDP grew quickly and inflation was moderate in the 1960s; real GDP growth sagged in 1974–75 and again, more strongly, in 1980–81. The 1974–75 slowdown was caused by an unusually sharp increase in oil prices. The 1980–81 recession was caused by a sharp slowdown in the growth of aggregate demand, which resulted mainly from Mrs Thatcher's tough monetary policy. Inflation was rapid during the 1970s but slowed after the 1980–81 recession. The period from 1982 to 1989 was one of strong, persistent recovery. A recession began in 1991 and a recovery took place in 1994.

Inflation The price level rises over the years – shown in Figure 24.12 by the upward movement of the points. The more rapid the inflation rate, the larger is the vertical distance between successive dots in the figure. The main force generating the persistent increase in the price level is a tendency for aggregate demand to increase at a faster pace than the increase in long-run aggregate supply. All of the factors that increase aggregate demand and shift the aggregate demand curve influence the pace of inflation. But one factor – the growth of the quantity of money – is the most important source of *persistent* increases in aggregate demand and persistent inflation.

Source: *The Economist*, 25–31 July 1998.

Cycles Over the years, the economy grows and shrinks in cycles – shown in Figure 24.12 by the wavelike pattern made by the points, with recessions highlighted in red. The cycles arise because both the expansion of short-run aggregate supply and the growth of aggregate demand do not proceed at a fixed, steady pace. Recessions are difficult to predict, but since World War II they have not been as severe as recessions before the war or as suggested in the cartoon.

The Evolving Economy: 1960–1997

During the 1960s, real GDP growth was rapid and inflation was low. This was a period of rapid increases in aggregate supply and of moderate increases in aggregate demand.

The mid-1970s were years of rapid inflation and recession – of stagflation. The major sources of these developments were a series of massive oil price increases and domestic supply side factors that produced X-inefficiency in production that shifted the short-run aggregate supply curve leftward, and rapid increases in the quantity of money that shifted the aggregate demand curve rightward. Recession occurred because the aggregate supply curve shifted leftward at a faster pace than the aggregate demand shifted rightward.

The rest of the 1970s saw high inflation – the price level increased quickly – and only moderate growth in real GDP.

In 1979 the government introduced a policy to keep aggregate demand growth in check. In 1980–81 most people expected high inflation to persist, and wages grew at a rate consistent with those expectations. The short-run aggregate supply curve shifted leftward. Aggregate demand increased only a little, but not fast enough to make inflation as high as most people expected. As a consequence, during 1980–81 the leftward shift of the short-run aggregate supply curve was so strong relative to the weak growth of aggregate demand that the economy went into a deep recession.

The main factor in the recovery in long-term growth was the introduction of supply side policies, which weakened the power of trade unions and altered work practices, lower direct taxes and greater competition through deregulation of markets (and privatization) resulted in a sustained rightward shift of the long-run aggregate supply curve. Aggregate demand growth kept pace with the growth of aggregate supply. Sustained-but-steady growth in aggregate supply and aggregate demand kept real GDP growing and inflation steady until 1986–87. The economy moved from a recession with real GDP less than potential GDP in 1980–81 to above full-employment in 1987–90. Inflation began to rise during this period and it was in this condition when a decrease in aggregate demand led to the 1990–92 recession. The economy again embarked on a path of expansion during 1994.

The aggregate supply–aggregate demand model can be used to understand long-term growth, inflation and business cycles. The model is a useful one because it enables us to keep our eye on the big picture – on the broad trends and cycles in inflation and real GDP. But the model lacks detail. It does not tell us as much as we need to know about the components of aggregate demand – consumption, investment, government purchases of goods and services, and exports and imports. It doesn't tell us what determines interest rates or wage rates or even, directly, what determines employment and unemployment. In the following chapters, we're going to start to fill in that detail.

Summary

Key Points

Aggregate Supply (pp. 580–584)

- In the long run, real GDP equals potential GDP and there is full employment. The long-run aggregate supply curve is vertical – long-run aggregate supply is independent of the price level – at potential GDP. Long-run aggregate supply changes only when potential GDP changes.
- In the short run, real GDP deviates from potential GDP. Short-run aggregate supply is the relationship between the quantity of real GDP supplied and the price level when wage rates and other factor prices are constant. The short-run aggregate supply curve is upward-sloping – with factor prices and all other influences on supply held constant.
- A change in potential GDP changes both long-run and shrt-run aggregate supply. A change in factor prices changes short-run aggregate supply only.

Aggregate Demand (pp. 584–589)

- Other things held constant, the higher the price level, the smaller is the quantity of real GDP demanded – the aggregate demand curve slopes downward.
- The aggregate demand curve slopes downward for two reasons: money and goods are substitutes (*real money balances effect*); goods today and goods in the future or domestic goods and foreign goods are substitutes (*substitution effect*).
- The main factors that change aggregate demand – and shift the aggregate demand curve – are expectations about future inflation and profits, international factors (economic conditions in the rest of the world and the foreign exchange rate), fiscal policy (government purchases of goods and services and taxes) and monetary policy (the money supply and interest rates).

Macroeconomic Equilibrium (pp. 589–593)

- In a long-run macroeconomic equilibrium, real GDP equals potential GDP and aggregate demand determines the price level.
- In a short-run macroeconomic equilibrium, real GDP and the price level are determined simultaneously by the interaction of aggregate demand and short-run aggregate supply. Short-run macroeconomic equilibrium tells us how real GDP and the price level evolve.
- Below full-employment equilibrium occurs when equilibrium real GDP is less than potential GDP. There is a recessionary gap and unemployment exceeds its natural rate. When equilibrium real GDP exceeds potential GDP, there is an inflationary gap and unemployment is less than its natural rate.
- Long-term growth of real GDP occurs because potential GDP increases. Inflation occurs because aggregate demand grows more quickly than potential GDP.
- Fluctuations in aggregate demand and short-run aggregate supply bring fluctuations in the price level and deviations of real GDP from potential GDP.

Long-term Growth, Inflation and Cycles in the UK Economy (pp. 594–595)

- Long-term growth is the growth of potential GDP.
- Inflation persists in the economy because of steady increases in aggregate demand brought about by increases in the quantity of money.
- The economy experiences cycles because the short-run aggregate supply and aggregate demand curves shift at an uneven pace.
- Large oil price hikes in 1973 and 1974 signalled the beginning of stagflation.
- Restraint in aggregate demand growth in 1980–81 resulted in recession in those years and a lower inflation rate.
- Steady technological advance and capital accumulation resulted in a sustained expansion from 1982 to 1989.
- A slowdown in aggregate demand growth brought recession in 1991.
- Recovery in the domestic and world economies saw a small improvement in the trend rate of growth.

Key Figures

Key Terms

Review Questions

1 Name and distinguish between two macroeconomic time-frames.

2 What is long-run aggregate supply?

3 What is short-run aggregate supply?

4 Distinguish between short-run aggregate supply and long-run aggregate supply.

5 Consider the following events:

a Potential GDP increases.
b The money wage rate rises.
c The price level rises.
d The money wage rate and the price level rise by the same percentages.

Say which of these events, if any, change: (1) long-run aggregate supply but not short-run aggregate supply; (2) short-run aggregate supply but not long-run aggregate supply; (3) both short-run aggregate supply and long-run aggregate supply; and which, if any, bring a movement along (4) the long-run aggregate supply curve, (5) the short-run aggregate supply curve; and (6) both the short-run and the long-run aggregate supply curves.

6 What is aggregate demand?

7 What is the difference between aggregate demand, the quantity of real GDP demanded and aggregate planned expenditure?

8 List the main factors that affect aggregate demand. Separate them into those that increase aggregate demand and those that decrease it.

9 Which of the following do not affect aggregate demand:

a Quantity of money?
b Interest rates?
c Technological change?
d Human capital?

10 Define short-run macroeconomic equilibrium.

11 Distinguish between a below full-employment equilibrium and full-employment equilibrium.

12 Work out the initial, the short-run and the long-run effects of an increase in the quantity of money on the price level and real GDP.

13 Work out the short-run effect of an increase in the price of oil on the price level and real GDP.

14 What are the main factors generating growth of real GDP, inflation and cycles in the UK economy.

Problems

1 The following events occur that influence the economy of Toughtimes:

- A deep recession hits the world economy
- Oil prices rise sharply
- Businesses expect huge losses in the near future.

a Explain the separate effects of each of these events on real GDP and the price level in Toughtimes, starting from a position of long-run equilibrium.
b Explain the combined effects of these events on real GDP and the price level in Toughtimes, starting from a position of long-run equilibrium.
c Explain what the Toughtimes government and central bank can do to overcome the problems faced by the economy.

2 The following events occur that influence the economy of Lilliput:

- A strong expansion of the world economy.
- The government of Lilliput raise taxes.
- Businesses expect profits to fall in the near future.

a Explain the separate effects of each of these events on real GDP and the price level in Lilliput, starting from a position of long-run equilibrium.
b Explain the combined effects of these events on real GDP and the price level in Lilliput, starting from a position of long-run equilibrium.
c Explain what the government of Lilliput can do to overcome the problems faced by the economy.

3 The economy of Mainland has the following aggregate demand and supply schedules:

Price level	Real GDP demanded	Real GDP supplied in the short run
	(billions of 1995 euros)	
90	450	350
100	400	400
110	350	450
120	300	500
130	250	550
140	200	600

a In a figure, plot the aggregate demand curve and short-run aggregate supply curve.
b What are the values of real GDP and the price level in Mainland in a short-run macroeconomic equilibrium?
c Mainland's potential GDP is €500 billion. Plot the long-run aggregate supply curve in the same figure in which you answered part (a).

4 In Problem 3, aggregate demand is increased by €100 billion. How do real GDP and the price level change in the short run?

5 In Problem 3, aggregate supply decreases by €100 billion. What now is the short-run macroeconomic equilibrium?

6 You are the chief economic adviser at HM Treasury and you are trying to work out where

the economy is likely to go next year. You have the following forecasts for the *AD*, *SAS*, and *LAS* curves:

Price level	Real GDP demanded	Short-run real GDP supplied	Long-run aggregate supply
		(billions of 1990 pounds)	
115	650	350	520
120	600	450	520
125	550	550	520
130	500	650	520

This year, real GDP is £500 billion and the price level is 120.

The prime minister wants answers to the following questions:

a What is your forecast of next year's real GDP?
b What is your forecast of next year's price level?
c What is your forecast of the inflation rate?
d Will unemployment be above or below its natural rate?
e Will there be a recessionary gap or an inflationary gap? By how much?

7 The following figure shows the aggregate supply and aggregate demand curves in an economy. Initially, short-run aggregate supply is SAS_0 and aggregate demand is AD_0. Then some events change aggregate demand and the aggregate demand curve shifts rightward to AD_1. Later, some further events change aggregate supply and the short-run aggregate supply curve shifts leftward to SAS_1.

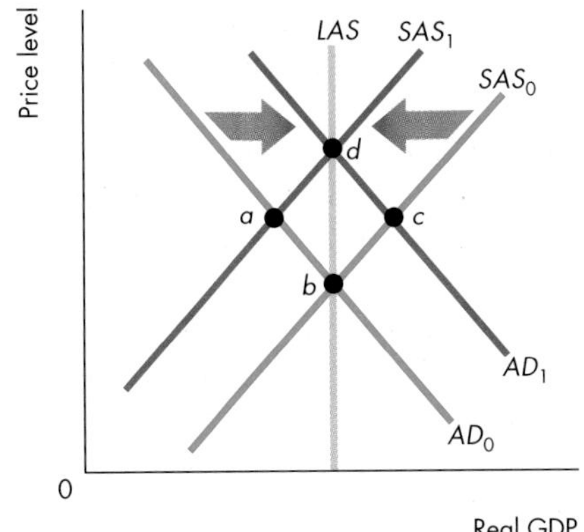

a What is the initial equilibrium point?
b What is the equilibrium point after the change in aggregate demand?
c What is the equilibrium point after the change in aggregate supply?
d What events could have changed aggregate demand from AD_0 to AD_1?
e What events could have changed aggregate supply from SAS_0 to SAS_1?
f After the increase in aggregate demand but before the increase in aggregate supply, is the real GDP greater than or less than potential GDP?

8 Carefully draw some figures similar to those in this chapter and use the information in Problem 3 to explain:

a What has to be done to aggregate demand to achieve full employment.
b What the inflation rate is if aggregate demand is manipulated to achieve full employment.

9 After you have studied *Reading Between the Lines* on pp. 600–601, answer the following questions.

a What is happening to the growth in real GDP during 1998 and 1999?
b What is happening to the rate of inflation during 1998 and 1999?
c Why has the Bank of England cut interest rates in 1999?
d What could happen to inflation and real output if interest rates are cut too fast? Too slow?

10 Use the links on the Parkin, Powell and Matthews Web site to obtain the 1999 data on real GDP and the price level for the UK. Then:

a Use the data to update Figure 24.12.
b What has happened to real GDP and the price level?
c What has happened to aggregate demand and short-run aggregate supply in 1999?

W http://www.econ100.com

Aggregate Supply and Aggregate Demand in Action

The Economist, 13 February 1999

More cuts eventually?

Asked what gave him most trouble as prime minister, Harold Macmillan famously replied: 'Events, dear boy, events.' Given the same question about setting interest rates, the nine members of the Bank of England's monetary policy committee (MPC) might give a like answer.

Witness the speed with which the MPC has been obliged to cut interest rates in the past few months. The reasons are set out in the MPC's latest *Inflation Report*, a quarterly publication in which it explains its conduct of monetary policy, published on February 10th. When the previous report came out in November, the MPC had just trimmed interest rates to 6.75%. The November report, as always, contained inflation projections for the following two years on the assumption that interest rates remain unchanged. Not surprisingly, the central forecast was that inflation (excluding mortgage-interest payments) would stay around the target of 2.5% set by the government. Any other forecast would have been, in effect, an admission that rates were either too high or too low.

Yet rates were cut by half a point four weeks later, have been cut twice more since, and are now 5.5%.

The events explaining the short shelf-life of November's inflation projections, fall into three groups.

First, the prospects for the world economy have deteriorated: growth in the eurozone looks likely to be weaker than had been expected; America's strong economic performance and growing trade deficit, are unlikely to be sustainable; and if capital flows to emerging markets fall further in the wake of the Brazilian crisis, rich countries as a whole are likely to export less. Second, domestic demand in Britain, especially consumer expenditure, has been lower than expected. Thanks to weaker demand at home and abroad, the Bank now expects GDP growth to be "close to zero" in the first half of this year before recovering in the second. And third, surveys suggest that worries about inflationary pressure in the labour market, which lay behind interest-rate increases in the second half of 1997 and the first half of 1998, are now less acute.

Once again, in this month's report, the central projection for inflation is that it will stay on target if rates are unchanged. But, just as they did in November, most commentators think that interest rates will fall again soon. Are they right?

The Essence of the Story

- The weakness of the eurozone economies, the expectation that the high growth in the United States economy is not sustainable and the fallout from the Brazilian crisis means that the developed economies are likely to export less during 1999.
- The growth in domestic demand ($C + I + G$) in the UK has turned out to be less than expected and will grow slowly in 1999 because of high interest rates in the previous year.
- The Bank of England predicted inflation of 2.5 per cent in 1999 on the basis of unchanged interest rates. But interest rates had been cut from 6.75 per cent to 5.5 per cent since the forecast had been made.
- The reason is that events have overtaken the forecast.
- Most forecasters are predicting interest rates to fall further but the Bank of England is giving nothing away, and is waiting for 'events' to help in its decision making.

Economic Analysis

- The article asks why the Bank of England Monetary Policy Committee felt the need to lower interest rates four weeks after making a forecast of inflation of 2.5 per cent on the basis of unchanged interest rates.

- The article points out that events have altered the prospects for the economy.

- The world economy has slowed down and domestic demand has weakened because of relatively high interest rates in the previous year.

- Figure 1 shows that GDP growth has slowed in the first quarter of 1999. Figure 2 shows that inflation has fallen below the Bank of England target of 2.5 per cent a year in the first four months of 1999.

- Figure 3 shows that if interest rates are not cut and domestic demand stimulated output growth will continue to weaken and inflation fall further.

- Figure 3 shows an increase in aggregate demand shifted the *AD* curve from AD_{98} to AD_{99}, but the increase in potential GDP is seen as a shift from LAS_{98} to LAS_{99}. The recessionary gap will cause the money wage rate to rise very slowly and therefore the inflationary pressure is likely to be moderate. But the recessionary gap will create a level of inflation that is much lower than the predicted 2.5 per cent and a lower growth in output. Lower interest rates will push the AD curve out further to AD'_{99} and create higher growth.

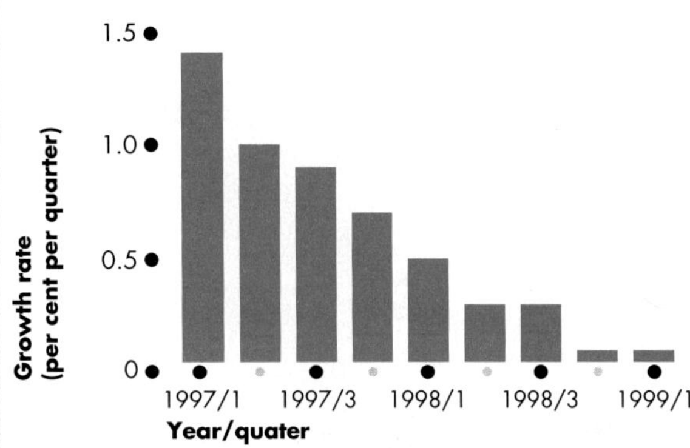

Figure 1 Growth rate of real GDP

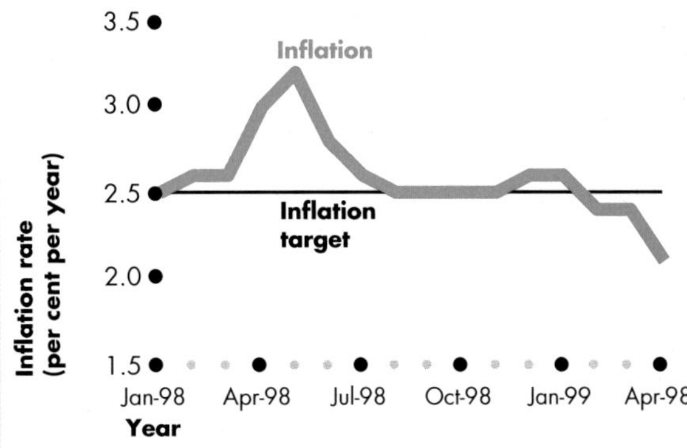

Figure 2 Inflation as a measured by Retail Price Index

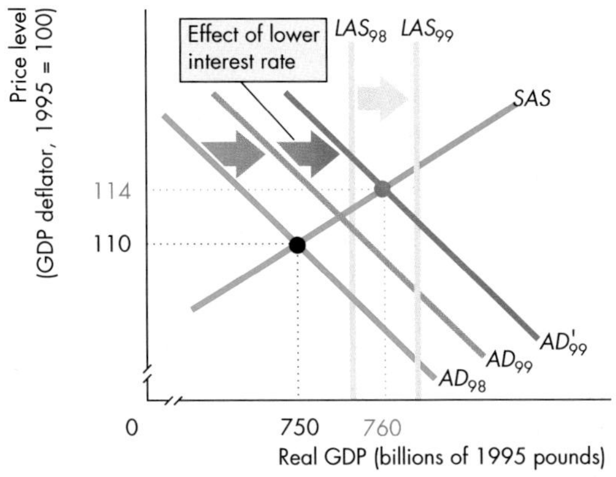

Figure 3 Growth speeds up as inflation slows

CHAPTER 25

Expenditure Multipliers

After studying this chapter you will be able to:

- Explain how expenditure plans are determined
- Explain how real GDP is determined when the price level is fixed
- Explain the expenditure multiplier
- Explain how imports and taxes influence the multiplier
- Explain how recessions and recoveries begin
- Explain the relationship between aggregate expenditure and aggregate demand
- Explain how the multiplier gets smaller as the price level changes

Economic Amplifier or Shock Absorber?

At the Baths of Caracalla in Rome, Luciano Pavarotti begins his passionate rendition of *Nessun Dorma* in the bel canto style he is famous for. Moving to a louder passage, the volume of his voice increases and, with the aid of electronic amplification, booms across the open-air concert stadium. ◆ Brian Tyrer, an Everton supporter, is driving some of his friends in his BMW to Goodison Park to see Everton play Manchester. Some of the roads around Liverpool are badly potholed. The car's wheels are bouncing and vibrating, but Brian and his friends are completely undisturbed, thanks to the car's efficient shock absorbers. ◆ Investment and exports fluctuate like the volume of Pavarotti's voice and the uneven surface of a Liverpool road. How does the economy react to those fluctuations? Does it react like Brian's BMW, absorbing the shocks and providing a smooth ride for the economy's passengers? Or does it behave like Pavarotti's amplifier, blowing up the fluctuations and spreading them out to affect the many millions of participants in an economic opera concert? Is the economic machine built to a design that we simply have to put up with, or does it change over time? Also, can the government modify the design of the economy and change its amplifying and shock-absorbing powers in a way that gives us all a smoother ride?

◆ ◆ ◆ ◆ You will explore these questions in this chapter. You will learn how a recession or a recovery begins when a change in investment or exports triggers a larger change in *aggregate* expenditure and real GDP – like the amplifier. You will also learn how, over the years, imports and income taxes have lowered the power of the amplifier. Finally, you will discover that in contrast to the initial amplification effect, the economy's imperfect shock absorbers, which are price and wage changes, pull real GDP back towards the long-term growth path of potential GDP.

To achieve these objectives, we use a model called the *aggregate expenditure model*. This model explains changes in aggregate expenditure in a very short time frame during which prices do not change.

Fixed Prices and Expenditure Plans

Most firms are like your local supermarket. They set their prices, advertise their products and services, and sell the quantities their customers are willing to buy. If they persistently sell a greater quantity than they plan to and are constantly running out of stocks, they eventually raise their prices. And if they persistently sell a smaller quantity than they plan to and have stocks piling up, they eventually cut their prices. But in the very short term their prices are fixed. They hold the prices they have set, and the quantities they sell depend on demand, not supply.

The Aggregate Implications of Fixed Prices

Fixed prices have two immediate implications for the economy as a whole:

1 Because each firm's price is fixed, the *price level* is fixed.

2 Because demand determines the quantities that each firm sells, *aggregate demand* determines the aggregate quantity of goods and services sold, which equals real GDP.

So to understand the fluctuations in real GDP when the price level is fixed, we must understand aggregate demand fluctuations. The aggregate expenditure model explains fluctuations in aggregate demand by identifying the forces that determine expenditure plans.

Expenditure Plans

The components of aggregate expenditure are:

1 Consumption expenditure.

2 Investment.

3 Government purchases of goods and services.

4 Net exports (exports *minus* imports).

These four components of aggregate expenditure sum to real GDP (see Chapter 22, pp. 543–547).

Aggregate planned expenditure is equal to *planned* consumption expenditure plus *planned* investment plus *planned* government purchases plus *planned* exports minus *planned* imports.

In the very short term, *planned* investment, *planned* government purchases and *planned* exports are fixed. But *planned* consumption expenditure and *planned* imports are not fixed. They depend on the level of real GDP itself.

A Two-way Relationship between Aggregate Expenditure and GDP Because real GDP influences consumption expenditure and imports, and because consumption expenditure and imports are components of aggregate expenditure, there is a two-way relationship between aggregate expenditure and GDP. Other things remaining the same:

1 An increase in real GDP increases aggregate planned expenditure.

2 An increase in aggregate expenditure increases real GDP.

You are going to learn how this two-way relationship between aggregate expenditure and real GDP determines real GDP when the price level is fixed. The starting point is to consider the first piece of the two-way relationship – the influence of real GDP on planned consumption expenditure and saving.

Consumption Function and Saving Function

Consumption and saving are influenced by several factors and the more important ones are:

- Real interest rate.
- Disposable income.
- Purchasing power of assets minus debts.
- Expected future income.

The ways that consumption and saving are influenced by these factors are explained in Chapter 31 (see pp. 785–787). Here we will focus on the relationship between consumption and disposable income when all other factors (the real interest rate, the purchasing power of assets minus debts and expected future income) are constant. We do this because disposable income and consumption are interrelated. Each helps to determine the other.

Consumption and Saving Plans The table in Figure 25.1 shows an example of the relationship among planned consumption expenditure, planned saving and disposable income. It lists the

Figure 25.1 Consumption and Saving Function

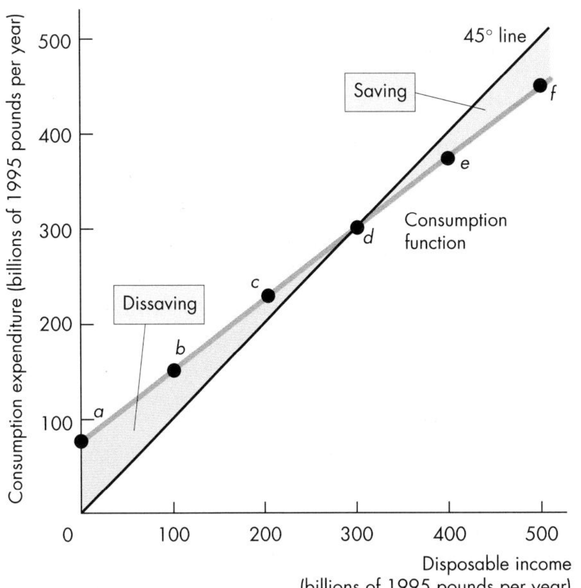

(a) Consumption function

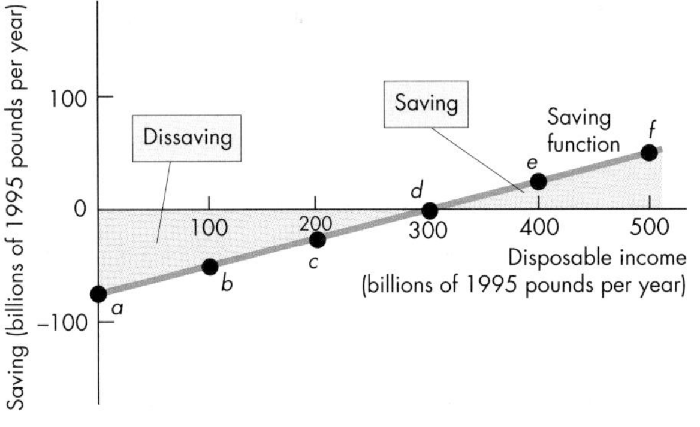

(b) Saving function

	Disposable income	Planned consumption expenditure	Planned saving
		(billions of 1995 pounds per year)	
a	0	75	–75
b	100	150	–50
c	200	225	–25
d	300	300	0
e	400	375	25
f	500	450	50

The table shows consumption expenditure and saving plans at various levels of disposable income. Part (a) of the figure shows the relationship between consumption expenditure and disposable income (the consumption function). Part (b) shows the relationship between saving and disposable income (the saving function). Points *a* to *f* on the consumption and saving functions correspond to the rows in the table.

The 45° line in part (a) is the line along which consumption expenditure equals disposable income. Consumption expenditure plus saving equals disposable income. When the consumption function is above the 45° line, saving is negative (dissaving occurs) and the saving function is below the horizontal axis. When the consumption function is below the 45° line, saving is positive and the saving function is above the horizontal axis. At the point where the consumption function intersects the 45° line, all disposable income is consumed, saving is zero and the saving function intersects the horizontal axis.

consumption expenditure and the saving that people plan to undertake at each level of disposable income. Notice that at each level of disposable income, consumption expenditure plus saving always equals disposable income. The reason is that households can only consume or save their disposable income. So planned consumption plus planned saving always equals disposable income.

The relationship between consumption expenditure and disposable income, other things remaining the same, is called the **consumption function**. The relationship between saving and disposable income, other things remaining the same, is called the **saving function**. Let's study the consumption and saving functions, beginning with the consumption function.

Consumption Function Figure 25.1(a) shows a consumption function. The y-axis measures consumption expenditure and the x-axis measures disposable income. Along the consumption function, the points labelled a to f correspond to the rows of the table. For example, point *e* shows that when disposable income is £400 billion, consumption expenditure is £375 billion. Along the consumption function, as disposable income increases, consumption expenditure also increases.

At point *a* on the consumption function, consumption expenditure is £75 billion even though disposable income is zero. This consumption expenditure is called *autonomous consumption.* It is the amount of consumption expenditure that would take place in the short run, even if people had no current income. Consumption expenditure in excess of this amount is called *induced consumption.* It is expenditure that is induced by an increase in disposable income.

45° Line Figure 25.1(a) also contains a line labelled '45° line'. At each point on this line, consumption expenditure (on the *y*-axis) equals disposable income (on the *x*-axis). In the range over which the consumption function lies above the 45° line – between *a* and *d* – consumption expenditure exceeds disposable income; in the range over which the consumption function lies below the 45° line – between *d* and *f* – consumption expenditure is less than disposable income; and at the point at which the consumption function intersects the 45° line – at point *d* – consumption expenditure equals disposable income.

Saving Function Figure 25.1(b) shows a saving function. The *x*-axis is exactly the same as that in part (a). The *y*-axis measures saving. Again, the points marked *a* to *f* correspond to the rows of the table. For example, point *e* shows that when disposable income is £400 billion, saving is £25 billion. Along the saving function, as disposable income increases, saving also increases. At disposable income levels below point *d*, saving is negative. Negative saving is called *dissaving.* At disposable income levels above point *d*, saving is positive, and at point *d*, saving is zero.

Notice the connection between the two parts of Figure 25.1. When consumption expenditure exceeds disposable income in part (a), saving is negative in part (b). When disposable income exceeds consumption expenditure in part (a), saving is positive in part (b). And when consumption expenditure equals disposable income in part (a), saving is zero in part (b).

When saving is negative (when consumption expenditure exceeds disposable income), past saving is used to pay for current consumption. Such a situation cannot last forever but it can occur if disposable income falls temporarily.

Marginal Propensities to Consume and Save

The extent to which consumption expenditure changes when disposable income changes depends on the marginal propensity to consume. The **marginal propensity to consume** (*MPC*) is the fraction of a *change* in disposable income that is consumed. It is calculated as the *change* in consumption expenditure (ΔC) divided by the *change* in disposable income (ΔYD) that brought it about. That is:

$$MPC = \frac{\Delta C}{\Delta YD}$$

In the table in Figure 25.1, when disposable income increases from £300 billion to £400 billion, consumption expenditure increases from £300 billion to £375 billion. The change in disposable income of £100 billion brings about a change in consumption expenditure of £75 billion. The *MPC* is £75 billion divided by £100 billion, which equals 0.75. In Figure 25.1, the *MPC* is a constant 0.75. For example, an increase in disposable income from £200 billion to £300 billion increases consumption expenditure from £225 billion to £300 billion, so again the *MPC* is 0.75.

The **marginal propensity to save** (*MPS*) is the fraction of a *change* in disposable income that is saved. It is calculated as the *change* in saving (ΔS) divided by the *change* in disposable income (ΔYD) that brought it about. That is:

$$MPS = \frac{\Delta S}{\Delta YD}$$

Again, using the numbers in the table in Figure 25.1, an increase in disposable income from £300 billion to £400 billion increases saving from zero to £25 billion. The change in disposable income of £100 billion brings about a change in saving of £25 billion. The *MPS* is £25 billion divided by £100 billion, which equals 0.25. In Figure 25.1, the *MPS* is a constant 0.25. For example, an increase in disposable income from £200 billion to £300 billion increases saving from –£25 billion to zero, so again the *MPS* is 0.25.

The marginal propensity to consume plus the marginal propensity to save must always equal 1.

This is because what is not consumed out of disposable income is always saved. You can see that from the equation:

$$\Delta C + \Delta S = \Delta YD$$

Divide both sides of the equation by the change in disposable income to obtain:

$$\frac{\Delta C}{\Delta YD} + \frac{\Delta S}{\Delta YD} = 1$$

$\Delta C/\Delta YD$, is the *marginal propensity to consume* (MPC) and $\Delta S/\Delta YD$ is the *marginal propensity to save* (MPS), so:

$$MPC + MPS = 1$$

Marginal Propensities and Slopes You can think of the marginal propensity to consume as the slope of the consumption function shown in Figure 25.2(a). A £100 billion increase in disposable income from £300 billion to £400 billion is the base of the red triangle. The increase in consumption expenditure that results from this increase in income is £75 billion and is the height of the triangle. The slope of the consumption function is given by the formula 'slope equals rise over run' and is £75 billion divided by £100 billion, which equals 0.75 – the *MPC*.

The marginal propensity to save is the slope of the saving function in Figure 25.2(b). A £100 billion increase in disposable income from £300 billion to £400 billion (the base of the red triangle) increases saving by £25 billion (the height of the triangle). The slope of the saving function is £25 billion divided by £100 billion, which equals 0.25 – the *MPS*.

The marginal propensity to consume plus the marginal propensity to save always equals 1.

Other Influences on Consumption Expenditure and Saving

You've seen that a change in disposable income leads to changes in consumption expenditure and saving. A change in disposable income brings movements along the consumption function and saving function. A change in other influences on consumption expenditure and saving shifts both the consumption function and the saving function. These other factors include the real interest rate, expected future income and the purchasing power of net assets (see Chapter 31, pp. 785–787).

When the real interest rate falls or when the purchasing power of net assets (assets minus debts)

Figure 25.2 Marginal Propensities to Consume and Save

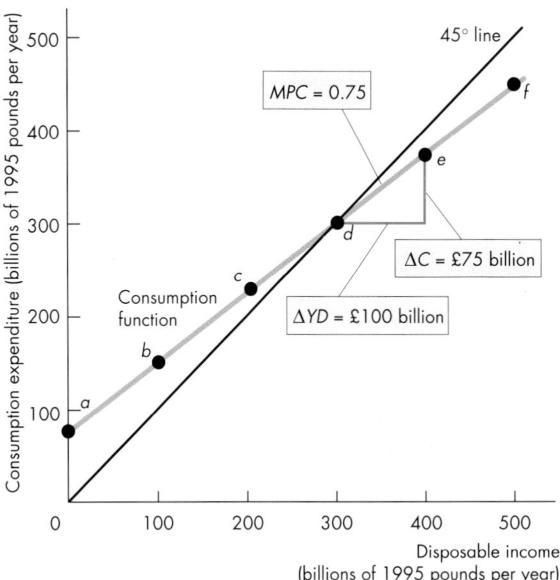

(a) Consumption function

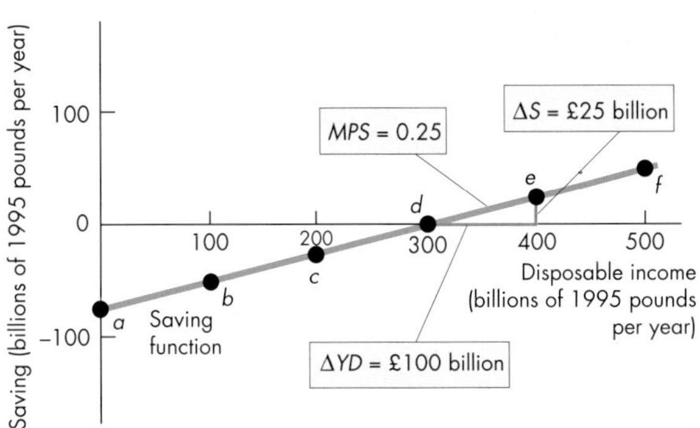

(b) Saving function

The marginal propensity to consume, *MPC*, is equal to the change in consumption expenditure divided by the change in disposable income, other things remaining the same. It is measured by the slope of the consumption function. In part (a), the *MPC* is 0.75. The marginal propensity to save, *MPS*, is equal to the change in saving divided by the change in disposable income, other things remaining the same. It is measured by the slope of the saving function. In part (b), the *MPS* is 0.25.

Figure 25.3 Shifts in the Consumption and Saving Functions

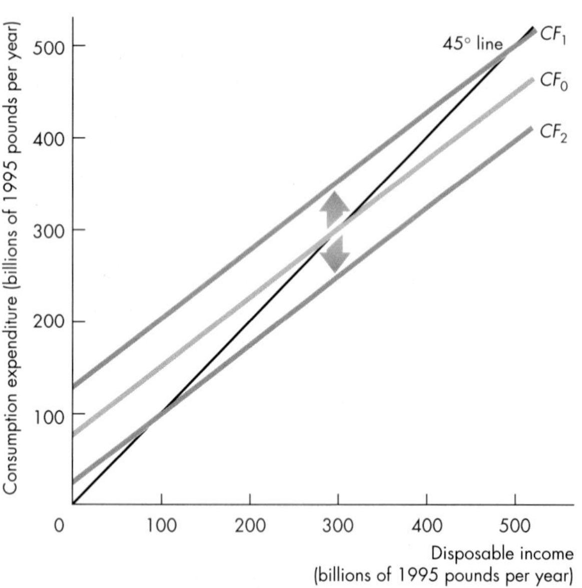

(a) Consumption function

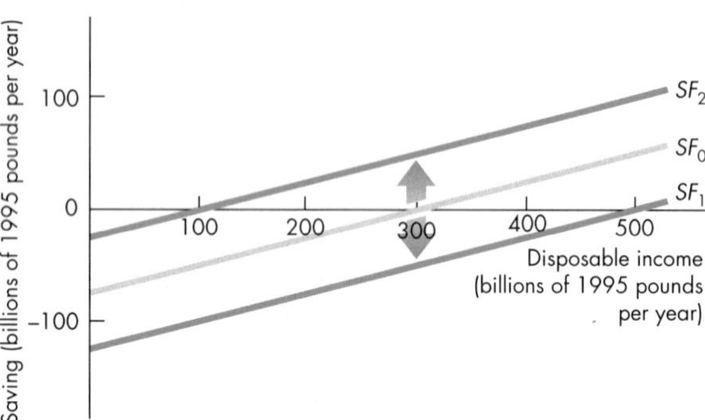

(b) Saving function

A fall in the real interest rate, an increase in the purchasing power of net assets, or an increase in expected future income increases consumption expenditure, shifts the consumption function upward from CF_0 to CF_1 and shifts the saving function downward from SF_0 to SF_1. Similarly, a rise in the real interest rate, a decrease in the purchasing power of net assets, or a decrease in expected future income shifts the consumption function downward from CF_0 to CF_2 and shifts the saving function upward from SF_0 to SF_2.

or expected future income increases, consumption expenditure increases and saving decreases. Figure 25.3 shows the effects of these changes on the consumption function and the saving function. The consumption function shifts upward from CF_0 to CF_1, and the saving function shifts downward from SF_0 to SF_1. Such shifts commonly occur during the expansion phase of the business cycle because, at such times, expected future income increases.

When the real interest rate rises or when the purchasing power of net assets or expected future income decreases, consumption decreases and saving increases. Figure 25.3 also shows the effects of these changes on the consumption function and the saving function. The consumption function shifts downward from CF_0 to CF_2, and the saving function shifts upward from SF_0 to SF_2. Such shifts often occur when a recession begins because at such a time, expected future income decreases.

We've studied the theory of the consumption function. Let's now see how that theory applies to the economy.

The Consumption Function

Figure 25.4 shows the consumption function in the United Kingdom. Each point identified by a blue dot represents consumption expenditure and disposable income for a particular year. (The dots are for the years 1970–98.) The orange line shows the average relationship between consumption expenditure and disposable income and is an estimate of the consumption function. The slope of this line is 0.9, which means that a £100 billion increase in disposable income brings a £90 billion increase in consumption expenditure. That is, on the average, over the period 1970–98, the marginal propensity to consume in the United Kingdom was about 0.9. Also, on the average, autonomous consumption is zero. That is, if disposable income were zero, consumption expenditure would also be zero.

The relationship between consumption expenditure and disposable income in any given year does not fall exactly on the orange line. The reason is that the position of the consumption function in each year depends on other factors – such as the real interest rate, expected future income and the purchasing power of net assets – which influence consumption expenditure and shift the consumption function.

Figure 25.4 The UK Consumption Function

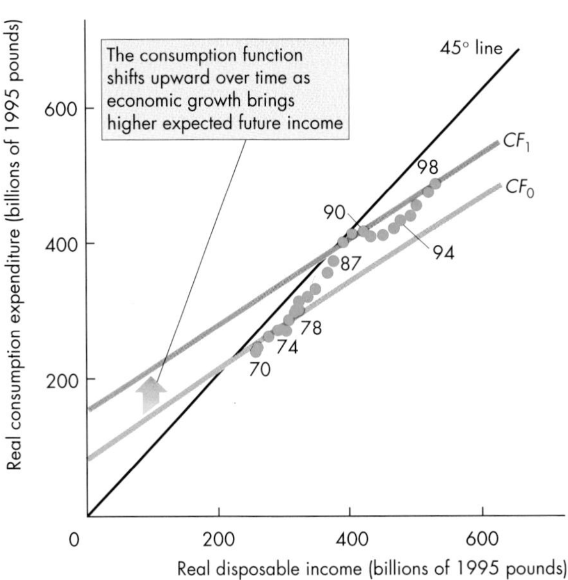

Each blue dot represents consumption expenditure and disposable income for a particular year. The orange lines are an estimate of the UK consumption function in 1970 and 1998.

Consumption as a Function of Real GDP

You've seen that consumption expenditure changes when disposable income changes. Disposable income changes when either real GDP changes or net taxes change. If tax rates don't change, real GDP is the only influence on disposable income and so when prices are fixed, consumption depends not only on disposable income but also on real GDP. We use this link between consumption and real GDP to determine equilibrium expenditure. But before we do so, we need to look at one further component of aggregate expenditure: imports. Like consumption expenditure, imports are also influenced by real GDP.

Import Function

Imports to the United Kingdom are determined by a number of factors, but in the short run with fixed prices, one factor dominates and that is UK real GDP.

Other things remaining the same, the greater the United Kingdom real GDP, the larger is the quantity of United Kingdom imports. So an increase in real GDP brings an increase in imports, and the magnitude of the increase in imports is determined by the marginal propensity to import. The **marginal propensity to import** is the fraction of an increase in real GDP that is spent on imports. It is calculated as the change in imports divided by the change in real GDP that brought it about, other things remaining the same. So, for example, if real GDP increases by £100 billion and imports increase by £30 billion, the marginal propensity to import is 0.3. The marginal propensity to import has been increasing in the UK. In 1970 it was 0.2. In 1980 it was 0.33.

Review

- Consumption expenditure and imports are influenced by real GDP.
- The marginal propensity to consume is the proportion of an increase in disposable income that is consumed.
- The influence of real GDP on consumption expenditure is determined by the marginal propensity to consume, and the influence of real GDP on imports is determined by the marginal propensity to import.

We've studied the influence of real GDP on consumption expenditure and imports. Next we will see how these components of aggregate expenditure interact with investment, government purchases and exports to determine aggregate expenditure and real GDP.

Real GDP with a Fixed Price Level

We are now going to discover how aggregate expenditure plans interact to determine real GDP when the price level is fixed. The first step in this process is to look at the relationship between aggregate planned expenditure and real GDP.

Figure 25.5 Aggregate Expenditure

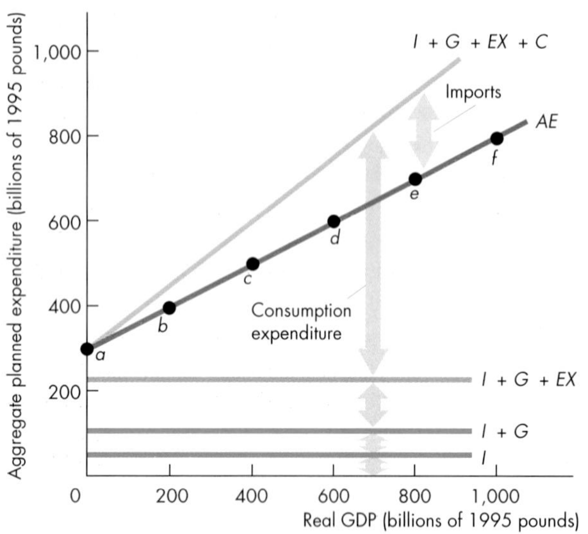

The relationship between aggregate planned expenditure and real GDP is shown by an aggregate expenditure schedule and illustrated by an aggregate expenditure curve. Aggregate planned expenditure is the sum of planned consumption expenditure, investment, government purchases of goods and services, and net exports. For example, in row *b* of the table, when real GDP is £200 billion, planned consumption expenditure is £225 billion, planned investment is £50 billion, planned government purchases of goods and services are £55 billion, planned exports are £120 billion, and planned imports are £50 billion. Thus when real GDP is £200 billion, aggregate planned expenditure is £400 billion (£225 + £50 + £55 + £120 – £50). The schedule shows that aggregate planned expenditure increases as real GDP increases. This relationship is graphed as the aggregate expenditure curve *AE*, the line *af*. The components of aggregate expenditure that increase with real GDP are consumption expenditure and imports. The other components – investment, government purchases and exports – do not vary with real GDP.

	Real GDP (Y)	Consumption expenditure (C)	Investment (I)	Government purchases (G)	Exports (EX)	Imports (IM)	Aggregate expenditure ($AE = C + I + G + NX$)
		Planned expenditure (billions of 1990 pounds)					
a	0	75	50	55	120	0	300
b	200	225	50	55	120	50	400
c	400	375	50	55	120	100	500
d	600	525	50	55	120	150	600
e	800	675	50	55	120	200	700
f	1,000	825	50	55	120	250	800

The relationship between aggregate planned expenditure and real GDP can be described by either an aggregate expenditure schedule or an aggregate expenditure curve. The *aggregate expenditure schedule* lists aggregate planned expenditure generated at each level of real GDP. The *aggregate expenditure curve* is a graph of the aggregate expenditure schedule.

Aggregate Planned Expenditure and Real GDP

The table in Figure 25.5 sets out an aggregate expenditure schedule together with the components of aggregate planned expenditure. To calculate aggregate planned expenditure at a given real GDP, we add the various components together. The first column of the table shows real GDP and the second column shows the consumption expenditure generated by each level of real GDP. When real GDP is £200 billion, consumption expenditure is £225 billion. A £200 billion increase in real GDP generates an £150 billion increase in consumption expenditure.

The next two columns show investment and government purchases of goods and services. Investment depends on the real interest rate and the expected rate of profit (see Chapter 31, p. 783). At a given point in time these factors generate a level of investment that is independent of real GDP. Suppose this amount of investment is £50 billion. Government purchases of goods and services are also independent of real GDP and their value is £55 billion.

The next two columns show exports and imports. Exports are influenced by events in the rest of the world, prices of foreign-produced goods and services relative to the prices of similar goods and services produced at home, and foreign exchange rates. But they are not directly affected by real GDP in the United Kingdom. In the table, exports appear as a constant £120 billion. In contrast, imports increase as real GDP increases. A £200 billion increase in real GDP generates a £50 billion increase in imports.

The final column of the table shows aggregate planned expenditure. This amount is the sum of planned consumption expenditure, investment, government purchases of goods and services, and exports minus imports.

Figure 25.5 plots an aggregate expenditure curve. Real GDP is shown on the x-axis and aggregate planned expenditure on the y-axis. The aggregate expenditure curve is the red line *AE*. Points a to f on this curve correspond to the rows of the table. The *AE* curve is a graph of aggregate planned expenditure (the last column) plotted against real GDP (the first column).

Figure 25.5 also shows the components of aggregate expenditure. The constant components – investment (I), government purchases of goods and services (G), and exports (EX) – are shown by the horizontal lines in the figure. Consumption expenditure (C) is the vertical gap between the lines labelled $I + G + EX + C$ and $I + G + EX$.

To construct the *AE* curve, subtract imports (IM) from the $I + G + EX + C$ line. Aggregate expenditure is expenditure on UK-produced goods and services. But the components of aggregate expenditure, C, I and G, include expenditure on imported goods and services. For example, a student's purchase of a new motorbike is part of consumption expenditure, but if that motorbike is a Honda made in Japan, expenditure on it must be subtracted from consumption expenditure to find out how much is spent on goods and services produced in the United Kingdom – on UK real GDP. Money paid to Honda for car imports from Japan does not add to aggregate expenditure in the United Kingdom.

Figure 25.5 shows that aggregate planned expenditure increases as real GDP increases. But as real GDP increases only some of the components of aggregate planned expenditure increase. These components are consumption expenditure and imports. The sum of the components of aggregate expenditure that vary with real GDP is called **induced expenditure**. The sum of the components of aggregate expenditure that are not influenced by real GDP is called **autonomous expenditure**. The components of autonomous expenditure are investment, government purchases, exports and the part of consumption expenditure that does not vary with real GDP. That is, autonomous expenditure is equal to the level of aggregate planned expenditure when real GDP is zero. In Figure 25.5, autonomous expenditure is £300 billion. As real GDP increases from zero to £200 billion, aggregate expenditure increases from £300 billion to £400 billion. Induced expenditure is £100 billion – £400 billion minus £300 billion.

The aggregate expenditure curve summarizes the relationship between aggregate planned expenditure and real GDP. But what determines the point on the aggregate expenditure curve at which the economy operates? What determines real GDP?

Actual Expenditure, Planned Expenditure and Real GDP

Actual aggregate expenditure is always equal to real GDP, as we saw in Chapter 22, pp. 534–539. But aggregate *planned* expenditure is not necessarily equal to actual aggregate expenditure and, therefore, is not necessarily equal to real GDP. How can actual expenditure and planned expenditure differ from each other? Why don't expenditure plans get implemented? The main reason is that firms might end up with more stocks than planned or with less stocks than planned. People carry out their consumption expenditure plans, the government implements its planned purchases of goods and services, and net exports are as planned. Firms carry out their plans to purchase new buildings, plant and equipment. One component of investment, however, is the increase in firms' stocks of goods. When aggregate planned expenditure differs from real GDP, firms end up with more or less stocks than they had planned. If aggregate planned expenditure is less than real GDP, stocks increase, and if aggregate planned expenditure exceeds real GDP, stocks decrease.

Equilibrium Expenditure

Equilibrium expenditure is the level of aggregate expenditure that occurs when aggregate *planned* expenditure equals real GDP. It is a level of aggregate expenditure and real GDP at which everyone's spending plans are fulfilled. When the price level is fixed, equilibrium expenditure determines real GDP.

Figure 25.6 Equilibrium Expenditure

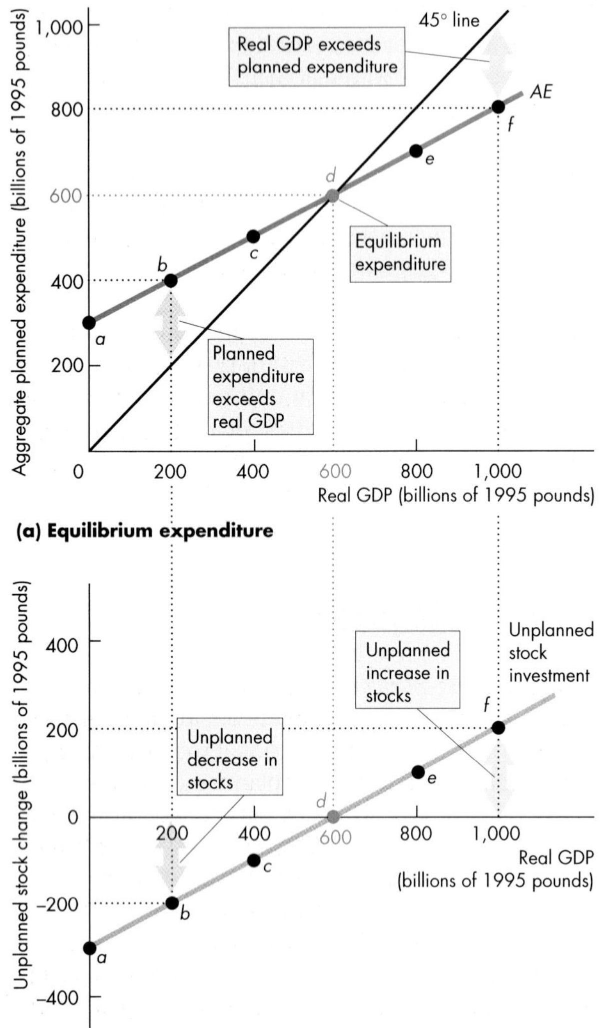

	Real GDP (*Y*)	Aggregate planned expenditure (*AE*) (billions of 1990 pounds)	Unplanned stock change (*Y* – *AE*)
a	0	300	–300
b	200	400	–200
c	400	500	–100
d	600	600	0
e	800	700	100
f	1,000	800	200

The table shows expenditure plans at different levels of real GDP. When real GDP is £600 billion, aggregate planned expenditure equals real GDP. Part (a) of the figure illustrates equilibrium expenditure, which occurs when aggregate planned expenditure equals real GDP at the intersection of the 45° line and the *AE* curve. Part (b) of the figure shows the forces that bring about equilibrium expenditure. When aggregate planned expenditure exceeds real GDP stocks decrease – for example, point *b* in both parts of the figure. Firms increase production and real GDP increases. When aggregate planned expenditure is less than real GDP stocks increase – for example, point *d* in both parts of the figure. Firms decrease production and real GDP decreases. When aggregate planned expenditure equals real GDP there are no unplanned stock changes and real GDP remains constant at equilibrium expenditure.

When aggregate planned expenditure and actual aggregate expenditure are unequal, a process of convergence towards equilibrium expenditure occurs. And throughout this convergence process real GDP adjusts. Let's examine equilibrium expenditure and the process that brings it about.

Figure 25.6(a) illustrates equilibrium expenditure. The table sets out aggregate planned expenditure at various levels of real GDP. These values are plotted as points *a* to *f* along the *AE* curve. The 45° line shows all the points at which aggregate planned expenditure equals actual aggregate expenditure (and equals real GDP). Thus where the aggregate expenditure curve intersects the 45° line, point *d*, aggregate planned expenditure equals actual aggregate expenditure. Point *d* illustrates equilibrium expenditure and determines real GDP. At this point, real GDP is £600 billion.

Convergence to Equilibrium

What are the forces that move aggregate expenditure towards its equilibrium level? To answer this question, we must look at a situation in which aggregate expenditure is away from its equilibrium level. Suppose that in Figure 25.6, real GDP is £200 billion. With real GDP at £200 billion, aggregate expenditure is also £200 billion. But aggregate *planned* expenditure is £400 billion (point *b* in Figure 25.6(a)). Aggregate planned expenditure exceeds *actual* expenditure. When people spend £400 billion, and firms produce goods and services worth £200 billion, firms' stocks fall by £200 billion (point *b* in Figure 25.7(b)). Because the change in stocks is part of investment, *actual* investment is £200 billion less than *planned* investment.

Real GDP doesn't remain at £200 billion for long. Firms have stock targets based on their sales. When the ratio of stocks to sales falls below target, firms increase production to restore stocks to the target level. To increase stocks, firms hire additional labour and increase production. Suppose that they increase production in the next period by £200 billion. Real GDP increases by £200 billion to £400 billion. But again, aggregate planned expenditure exceeds real GDP. When real GDP is £400 billion, aggregate planned expenditure is £500 billion (point *c* in Figure 25.6(a)). Again, stocks decrease but this time by less than before. With real GDP of £400 billion and aggregate planned expenditure of £500 billion, stocks decrease by £100 billion (point *c* in Figure 25.6(b)). Again, firms hire additional labour and production increases; real GDP increases yet further.

The process that we have just described – planned expenditure exceeds real GDP, stocks decrease and production increases to restore the level of stocks – ends when real GDP has reached £600 billion. At this real GDP, there is an equilibrium. There are no unplanned stock changes and firms do not change their production.

You can do a similar experiment to the one we've just done, but starting with a level of real GDP greater than equilibrium expenditure. In this case, planned expenditure is less than actual expenditure, stocks pile up and firms cut production. As before, real GDP keeps on changing (decreasing this time) until it reaches its equilibrium level of £600 billion.

Review

- Equilibrium expenditure occurs when aggregate planned expenditure equals real GDP.
- Equilibrium expenditure results from an adjustment in real GDP.
- If real GDP and aggregate expenditure are less than their equilibrium levels, an unplanned fall in stocks leads firms to increase production and real GDP increases.
- If real GDP and aggregate expenditure are greater than their equilibrium levels, an unplanned rise in stocks leads firms to decrease production and real GDP decreases.

We've learned that when the price level is fixed, real GDP is determined by equilibrium expenditure. And we have seen how unplanned changes in stocks and the production response they generate bring a convergence towards equilibrium. We're now going to study *changes* in equilibrium. And we are going to discover an economic amplifier called the multiplier.

The Multiplier

Investment and exports can change for many reasons. A fall in the real interest rate might induce firms to increase their planned investment. A major wave of innovation, such as occurred with the spread of IT in the 1980s, might increase expected future profits and lead firms to increase their planned investment. Stiff competition in the car industry from Japanese or South Korean imports might force Ford, Vauxhall and Rover to increase their investment in robotic assembly lines. An economic boom in developing countries might lead to a large increase in their expenditure on UK-produced goods and services – on UK exports. These are all examples of increases in autonomous expenditure.

When autonomous expenditure increases, aggregate expenditure increases, and so too does equilibrium expenditure. The increase in equilibrium expenditure and real GDP is larger than the change in autonomous expenditure. The **multiplier** is the amount by which a change in autonomous expenditure is magnified or multiplied to determine the change in equilibrium expenditure and real GDP.

It is easiest to get the basic idea of the multiplier if we work with an example economy in which there are no income taxes and no imports. So we'll first assume that these factors are absent. Then, when you understand the basic idea, we'll bring these factors back into play and see what difference they make to the multiplier.

The Basic Idea of the Multiplier

Suppose that investment increases. The additional expenditure by businesses means that aggregate expenditure and real GDP increases. Disposable income also increases, and with no income taxes, real GDP and disposable income increase by the same amount. The increase in disposable income brings an increase in consumption expenditure. And the increased consumption expenditure adds even more to aggregate expenditure. Real GDP and disposable income increase further, and so does consumption expenditure. The initial increase in investment brings an even bigger increase in aggregate expenditure because it induces an increase in consumption expenditure. The magnitude of the increase in aggregate expenditure that results from an increase in autonomous expenditure is determined by the *multiplier*.

The table in Figure 25.7 sets out aggregate planned expenditure. Initially, when real GDP is £500 billion, aggregate planned expenditure is £525 billion. For each £100 billion increase in real GDP, aggregate planned expenditure increases by £75 billion. This aggregate expenditure schedule is shown in the figure as the aggregate expenditure curve AE_0. Initially, equilibrium expenditure is £600 billion. You can see this equilibrium in row *b* of the table, and in the figure where the curve AE_0 intersects the 45° line at the point marked *b*.

Now suppose that autonomous expenditure increases by £50 billion. What happens to equilibrium expenditure? You can see the answer in Figure 25.7. When this increase in autonomous expenditure is added to the original aggregate planned expenditure, aggregate planned expenditure increases by £50 billion at each level of real GDP. The new aggregate expenditure curve is AE_1. The new equilibrium expenditure, highlighted in the table (row *d'*), occurs where AE_1 intersects the 45° line and is £800 billion (point *d'*). At this point, aggregate planned expenditure equals real GDP.

The Multiplier Effect

In Figure 25.7, the increase in autonomous expenditure of £50 billion increases equilibrium expenditure by £200 billion. That is, the change in autonomous expenditure leads to an amplified change in equilibrium expenditure. This amplified change is the *multiplier effect* – equilibrium expenditure increases by *more than* the increase in autonomous expenditure.

Initially, when autonomous expenditure increases, aggregate planned expenditure exceeds real GDP. As a result, stocks decrease. Firms respond by increasing production so as to restore their stocks to the target level. As production increases, so does

Figure 25.7 The Multiplier

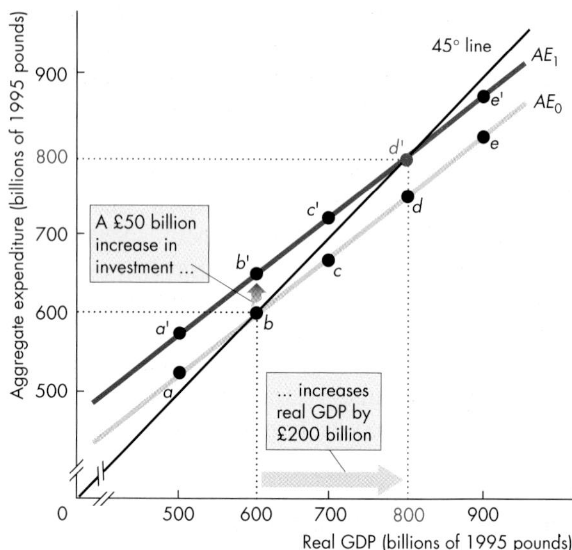

Real GDP (*Y*)		Aggregate planned expenditure Original (AE_0) (billions of 1990 pounds)		Aggregate planned expenditure New (AE_1)
500	*a*	525	*a'*	575
600	*b*	600	*b'*	650
700	*c*	675	*c'*	725
800	*d*	750	*d'*	800
900	*e*	825	*e'*	875

A £50 billion increase in autonomous expenditure shifts the *AE* curve upward by £50 billion from AE_0 to AE_1. Equilibrium expenditure increases by £200 billion from £600 billion to £800 billion. The increase in equilibrium expenditure is 4 times the increase in autonomous expenditure, so the multiplier is 4.

real GDP. With a higher level of real GDP, *induced expenditure* increases. Thus equilibrium expenditure increases by the sum of the initial increase in autonomous expenditure and the increase in induced expenditure. In this example, induced expenditure increases by £150 billion, so equilibrium expenditure increases by £200 billion.

Although we have just analysed the effects of an *increase* in autonomous expenditure, the same analysis applies to a decrease in autonomous expenditure. If initially the aggregate expenditure curve is AE_1, equilibrium expenditure and real GDP are £800 billion. A decrease in autonomous expenditure of £50 billion shifts the aggregate expenditure curve downward by £50 billion to AE_0. Equilibrium expenditure decreases from £800 billion to £600 billion. The decrease in equilibrium expenditure (£200 billion) is larger than the decrease in autonomous expenditure that brought it about. In this example, the multiplier is 4.

Why is the Multiplier Greater than 1?

We've seen that equilibrium expenditure increases by more than the increase in autonomous expenditure. This makes the multiplier greater than 1. How come? Why does equilibrium expenditure increase by more than the increase in autonomous expenditure?

The multiplier is greater than 1 because of induced expenditure – an increase in autonomous expenditure *induces* further increases in expenditure. If British Telecommunications spends £10 million on a new video communications system, aggregate expenditure and real GDP immediately increase by £10 million. But that is not the end of the story. Electrical engineers and construction workers now have more income, and they spend part of the extra income on cars, microwaves, holidays and a host of other goods and services. Real GDP now rises by the initial £10 million plus the extra consumption expenditure induced by the £10 million increase in income. The producers of cars, microwaves, holidays and other goods now have increased incomes, and they, in turn, spend part of the increase in their incomes on consumption goods and services. Additional income induces additional expenditure, which creates additional income.

We have seen that a change in autonomous expenditure has a multiplier effect on real GDP. But how big is the multiplier effect?

The Size of the Multiplier

Suppose that the economy is in a recession. Profit prospects start to look better and firms are making plans for large increases in investment. The world economy is also heading towards recovery, and exports are increasing. The question on everyone's lips is: how strong will the recovery be? This is a hard question to answer. But an important ingredient in the answer is working out the size of the multiplier.

The *multiplier* is the amount by which a change in autonomous expenditure is multiplied to determine the change in equilibrium expenditure that it generates. To calculate the multiplier, we divide the change in equilibrium expenditure by the change in autonomous expenditure. Let's calculate the multiplier for the example in Figure 25.8. Initially, equilibrium expenditure is £600 billion. Then autonomous expenditure increases by £50 billion, and equilibrium expenditure increases by £200 billion to £800 billion.

The multiplier is:

$$\text{Multiplier} = \frac{\Delta \text{ equilibrium expenditure}}{\Delta \text{ autonomous expenditure}}$$

$$= \frac{\pounds 200 \text{ billion}}{\pounds 50 \text{ billion}}$$

$$= 4$$

The Multiplier and the Marginal Propensities to Consume and Save

What determines the magnitude of the multiplier? The answer is the marginal propensity to consume. The larger the marginal propensity to consume, the larger is the multiplier. To see why, let's do a calculation.

Aggregate expenditure and real GDP (Y), change because consumption expenditure, (C), changes and investment, (I), changes. The change in GDP equals the change in consumption expenditure plus the change in investment. That is:

$$\Delta Y = \Delta C + \Delta I$$

But the change in consumption expenditure is determined by the change in real GDP and the *MPC*. It is:

$$\Delta C = MPC \times \Delta Y$$

Now combine these two facts to give:

$$\Delta Y = MPC \times \Delta Y + \Delta I$$

Figure 25.8 The Multiplier Process 

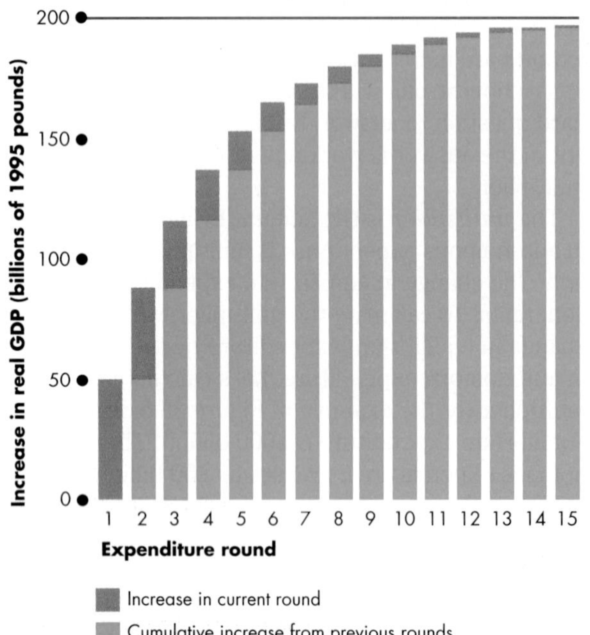

Autonomous expenditure increases in round 1 by £50 billion. As a result, real GDP increases by the same amount. With a marginal propensity to consume of 0.75, each additional pound of real GDP induces an additional 0.75 of a pound of aggregate expenditure. The round 1 increase in real GDP induces an increase in consumption expenditure of £37.5 billion in round 2. At the end of round 2, real GDP has increased by £87.5 billion. The extra £37.5 billion of real GDP in round 2 induces a further increase in consumption expenditure of £28.1 billion in round 3. Real GDP increases yet further to £115.6 billion. This process continues with real GDP increasing by ever smaller amounts. When the process comes to an end, real GDP has increased by a total of £200 billion.

Now, solve for the change in Y as:

$$(1 - MPC) \times \Delta Y = \Delta I$$

and rearranging:

$$\Delta Y = \frac{\Delta I}{(1 - MPC)}$$

The multiplier that we want to calculate is:

$$\text{Multiplier} = \frac{\Delta Y}{\Delta I}$$

So divide both sides of the previous equation by the change in I to give:

$$\text{Multiplier} = \frac{\Delta Y}{\Delta I} = \frac{\Delta I}{(1 - MPC)}$$

Using the numbers for Figure 25.8, the MPC is 0.75, so the multiplier is:

$$\text{Multiplier} = \frac{1}{(1 - 0.75)} = \frac{1}{0.25} = 4$$

There is another formula for the multiplier. Because the marginal propensity to consume (MPC) plus the marginal propensity to save (MPS) adds up to 1, the term $(1 - MPC)$ equals MPS. Therefore, another formula for the multiplier is:

$$\text{Multiplier} = \frac{1}{MPS}$$

Again using the numbers in Figure 25.8:

$$\text{Multiplier} = \frac{1}{0.25} = 4$$

Because the marginal propensity to save (MPS) is a fraction – a number lying between 0 and 1 – the multiplier is greater than 1.

Figure 25.8 illustrates the multiplier process. In round 1, autonomous expenditure increases by £50 billion. At this time, induced expenditure does not change, so aggregate expenditure and real GDP increase by £50 billion. In round 2, the larger real GDP induces more consumption expenditure. Induced expenditure increases by 0.75 times the increase in real GDP, so the increase in real GDP of £50 billion induces a further increase in expenditure of £37.5 billion. This change in induced expenditure, when added to the initial change in autonomous expenditure, increases aggregate expenditure and real GDP by £87.5 billion. The round 2 increase in real GDP induces a round 3 increase in expenditure. The process repeats through successive rounds. Each increase in real GDP is 0.75 times the previous increase. The cumulative increase in real GDP gradually approaches £200 billion.

So far, we've ignored imports and income taxes. Let's now see how these two factors influence the multiplier.

Imports and Income Taxes

The multiplier is determined, in general, not only by the marginal propensity to consume but also by the marginal propensity to import and by the marginal tax rate. Imports make the multiplier smaller than it otherwise would be. To see why, think about what happens following an increase in investment. An increase in investment increases real GDP, which in

Figure 25.9 The Multiplier and the Slope of the *AE* Curve

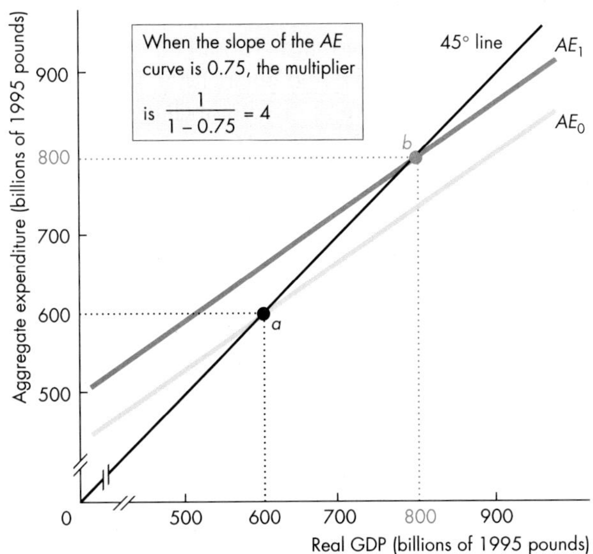

(a) Multiplier is 4

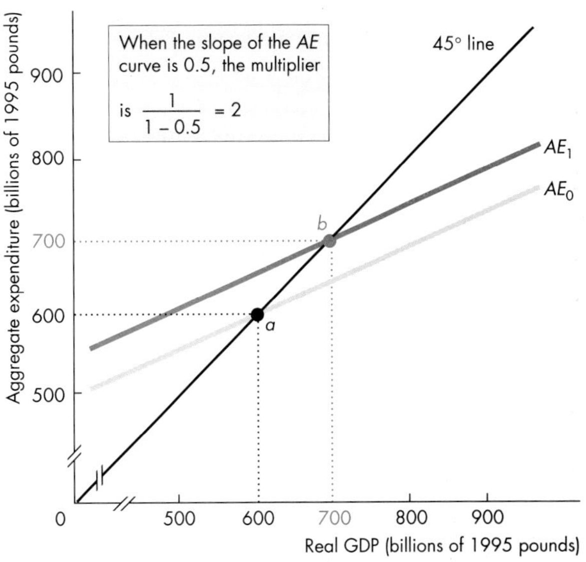

(b) Multiplier is 2

Imports and income taxes make the *AE* curve less steep and reduce the value of the multiplier. In part (a), with no imports and income taxes the slope of the *AE* curve is 0.75 (the marginal propensity to consume) and the multiplier is 4 . But with imports and income taxes, the slope of the *AE* curve is less than the marginal propensity to consume. In part (b), the slope of the *AE* curve is 0.5. In this case, the multiplier is 2.

turn increases consumption expenditure. But part of investment and part of the consumption expenditure are expenditure on imported goods and services, not UK-produced goods and services. It is the expenditure on only UK-produced goods and services that increases real GDP in the United Kingdom.

Income taxes also make the multiplier smaller than it otherwise would be. Again, think about what happens following an increase in investment. An increase in investment increases real GDP. Because income taxes increase with income, the increase in real GDP increases income taxes. And the increase in income taxes decreases disposable income. Consumption expenditure depends on disposable income, so the greater the increase in income taxes, the smaller is the increase in consumption expenditure, other things remaining the same. It is only the increase in *disposable* income that induces an increase in consumption expenditure.

The marginal propensity to import and the marginal tax rate together with the marginal propensity to consume determine the slope of the *AE* curve and the multiplier. The multiplier is equal to 1 divided by 1 minus the slope of the *AE* curve. Figure 25.9 compares two situations. In Figure 25.9(a) there are no imports and no taxes. The marginal propensity to consume, which also equals the slope of the *AE* curve, is 0.75 and the multiplier is 4. In Figure 25.9(b) imports and income taxes decrease the slope of the *AE* curve to 0.5. In this case the multiplier is 2.

Over time, the value of the multiplier changes as tax rates change and as the marginal propensity to consume and the marginal propensity to import change. These ongoing changes make the multiplier hard to predict. But they do not change the fundamental fact that an initial change in autonomous expenditure leads to a magnified change in aggregate expenditure and real GDP.

Now that we've studied the multiplier and the factors that influence its magnitude, let's use what we've learned to gain some insights into the most critical points in the life of an economy: business cycle turning points.

Business Cycle Turning Points

At a business cycle trough, the economy moves from recession into recovery and at a peak, it moves from recovery, into recession. Economists understand these turning points like seismologists understand earthquakes. They know quite a lot about the forces that produce them and the mechanisms at work when they occur, but they can't predict them. The forces that bring business cycle turning points are the swings in autonomous expenditure – in investment and exports. The mechanism that gives momentum to the new direction the economy is taking is the multiplier process that we've just studied. Let's use what we've now learned to examine these turning points.

An Expansion Begins An expansion is triggered by an increase in autonomous expenditure that increases aggregate planned expenditure. At the moment the economy turns the corner into recovery, aggregate planned expenditure exceeds real GDP. In this situation, firms see their stocks taking an unplanned dive. The recovery now begins. To meet their stock targets, firms increase production and real GDP begins to increase. This initial increase in real GDP brings higher incomes that stimulate consumption expenditure. The multiplier process kicks in and the recovery picks up speed. The expansion ends when real GDP has increased to equal aggregate planned expenditure and there are no unplanned stock changes.

A Recession Begins The process we've just described works in reverse at a business cycle peak. A recession is triggered by a decrease in autonomous expenditure that decreases aggregate planned expenditure. At the moment the economy turns the corner into recession, real GDP exceeds aggregate planned expenditure. In this situation, firms see unplanned stocks piling up. The recession now begins. To lower their stocks, firms cut production and real GDP begins to decrease. This initial decrease in real GDP brings lower incomes that cut consumption expenditure. The multiplier process reinforces the initial cut in autonomous expenditure and the recession takes hold. The recession ends when real GDP has fallen to equal aggregate planned expenditure and there are no unplanned stock changes. *Reading Between the Lines* on pp. 628–629 examines the French multiplier in action.

The Next UK Recession? During 1998 consumption began to slow and stocks increased in the United Kingdom. If these stock increases were planned, they would *not* trigger a change in production. But if they were unplanned, firms would cut production and real GDP growth could fall in 1999. However, a reduction in the rate of growth of GDP is not a reduction in the level of GDP. Many economists are predicting a growth slowdown in 1999. It is much harder to predict exactly when the next recession will occur.

Review

- A change in autonomous expenditure changes real GDP by an amount determined by the multiplier.
- The greater the marginal propensity to consume, the smaller is the marginal propensity to import, and the smaller the marginal tax rate, the larger is the multiplier.
- Fluctuations in autonomous expenditure brings business cycle turning points.

We've seen that the economy does not operate like the shock absorbers on Brian Tyrer's car. The economy's potholes and bumps are changes in autonomous expenditure – mainly brought about by changes in investment and exports. And while the price level is fixed, these economic potholes and bumps are not smoothed out. Instead they are amplified. But we've only considered the adjustments in spending that occur in the very short term when the price level is fixed. What happens when the price level changes? And what happens in the long run? Let's answer these questions.

The Multiplier, Real GDP and the Price Level

When firms are having trouble keeping up with sales and their stocks fall below target, they increase production, but at some point they raise their prices. Similarly, when firms find unwanted stocks piling up, they decrease production, but eventually they cut their prices. So far, we've studied the macroeconomic consequences of firms changing their production levels when their sales change, but we've not looked at the effects of price changes. When individual firms change their prices, the economy's price level changes.

To study the simultaneous determination of real GDP and the price level, we use the *aggregate demand–aggregate supply model*, which is explained in Chapter 27, pp. 672–678. There is a connection between the aggregate demand–aggregate supply model and the equilibrium expenditure model that we've used in this chapter. The key to the relationship between these two models is the distinction between the aggregate *expenditure* curve and the aggregate *demand* curve.

Aggregate Expenditure and Aggregate Demand

The aggregate expenditure curve is the relationship between the aggregate planned expenditure and real GDP, all other influences on aggregate planned expenditure remaining the same. The aggregate demand curve is the relationship between the aggregate quantity of goods and services demanded and the price level, all other influences on aggregate demand remaining the same. Let's explore the links between these two relationships.

Aggregate Expenditure and the Price Level

At a given price level, there is a given level of aggregate planned expenditure. But if the price level changes, so does aggregate planned expenditure. Why? There are two main reasons. We examined these reasons in more detail in Chapter 24, pp. 585–586. They are:

1 The real money balances effect.
2 The substitution effect.

Real money is the purchasing power of money, which is measured by the quantity of money divided by the price level. A rise in the price level, other things remaining the same, decreases the quantity of real money and a smaller quantity of real money decreases aggregate planned expenditure – the *real money balances effect*. A rise in the price level, other things remaining the same, makes current goods and services more costly relative to future goods and services, and results in a delay in purchases – the *intertemporal substitution effect*. A rise in the price level, other things remaining the same, makes UK-produced goods more expensive relative to foreign-produced goods and services, and increases imports and decreases exports – the *international substitution effect*.

When the price level rises, each of these effects reduces aggregate planned expenditure at each level of real GDP. As a result, when the price level rises, the aggregate expenditure curve shifts downward. A fall in the price level has the opposite effect. When the price level falls, the aggregate expenditure curve shifts upward.

Figure 25.10(a) illustrates these effects. When the price level is 130, the aggregate expenditure curve is AE_0, which intersects the 45° line at point *b*. Equilibrium expenditure and real GDP are £600 billion. If the price level increases to 170, the aggregate expenditure curve shifts downward to AE_1, which intersects the 45° line at point *a*. Equilibrium expenditure and real GDP are £400 billion. If the price level decreases to 90, the aggregate expenditure curve shifts upward to AE_2, which intersects the 45° line at point *c*. Equilibrium expenditure and real GDP are £800 billion.

We've just seen that when the price level changes, other things remaining the same, the aggregate expenditure curve shifts and equilibrium expenditure changes. And when the price level changes, other things remaining the same, there is a movement along the aggregate demand curve. Figure 25.10(b) illustrates these movements. At a price level of 130, the aggregate quantity of goods and services demanded is £600 billion – point *b* on the aggregate demand curve *AD*. If the price level increases to 170, the aggregate quantity of goods and services demanded decreases to £400 billion. There is a movement along the aggregate demand curve to point *a*. If the price level decreases to 90, the aggregate quantity of goods and services demanded increases to £800 billion. There is a movement along the aggregate demand curve to point *c*.

Each point on the aggregate demand curve corresponds to a point of equilibrium expenditure. The equilibrium expenditure points *a*, *b* and *c* in Figure 25.10(a) correspond to points *a*, *b* and *c* on the aggregate demand curve in Figure 25.10(b).

When the price level changes, other things remaining the same, the aggregate expenditure curve shifts and there is a movement along the aggregate

Figure 25.10 Aggregate Demand

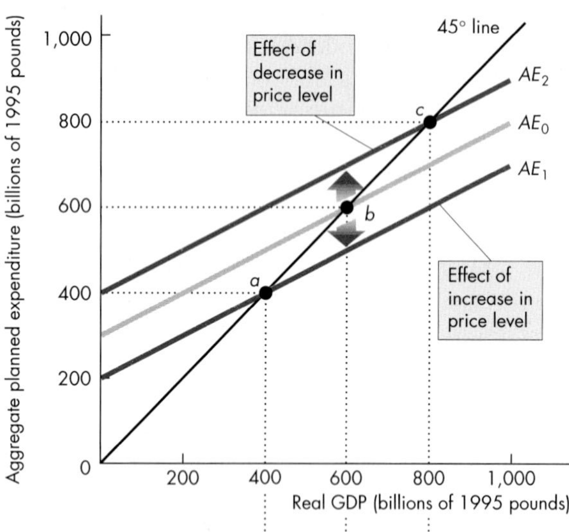

(a) Equilibrium expenditure

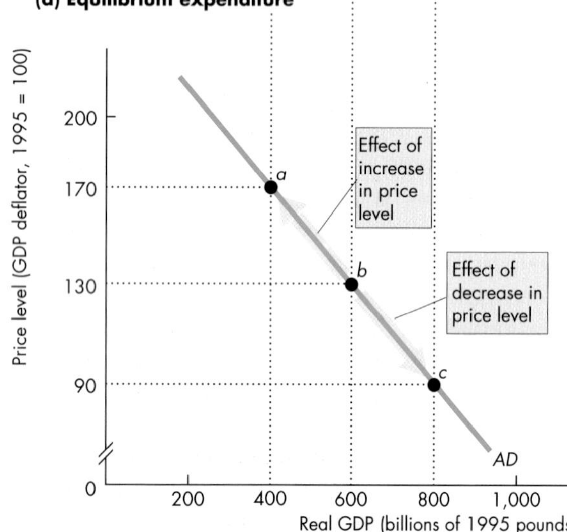

(b) Aggregate demand

The position of the *AE* curve depends on the price level. When the price level is 130, the *AE* curve is AE_0. Equilibrium expenditure is at point *b*, and real GDP demanded is £600 billion. When the price level rises to 170, the *AE* curve shifts downward to AE_1, and equilibrium expenditure is at point *a*. Real GDP demanded is £400 billion. When the price level falls to 90, the *AE* curve shifts upward to AE_2, and equilibrium expenditure is at point *c*. Real GDP demanded is £800 billion.

Part (b) shows the *AD* curve. A change in the price level shifts the *AE* curve but results in a *movement along* the *AD* curve. Points *a*, *b* and *c* on the *AD* curve correspond to the equilibrium expenditure points *a*, *b* and *c* in part (a).

demand curve. When any other influence on aggregate planned expenditure changes, both the aggregate expenditure curve and the aggregate demand curve shift. For example, an increase in investment or in exports increases both aggregate planned expenditure and aggregate demand and shifts both the *AE* curve and the *AD* curve. Figure 25.11 illustrates the effect of such an increase.

Initially, the aggregate expenditure curve is AE_0 in part (a) and the aggregate demand curve is AD_0 in part (b). The price level is 130, real GDP is £600 billion, and the economy is at point *a* in both parts of the figure. Now suppose that investment increases by £100 billion. At a constant price level of 130, the aggregate expenditure curve shifts upward to AE_1. This curve intersects the 45° line at an equilibrium expenditure of £800 billion (point *b*). This equilibrium expenditure of £800 billion is the aggregate quantity of goods and services demanded at a price level of 130, as shown by point *b* in part (b). Point *b* lies on a new aggregate demand curve. The aggregate demand curve has shifted rightward to AD_1.

But how do we know by how much the *AD* curve shifts? The answer is determined by the multiplier. The larger the multiplier, the larger is the shift in the aggregate demand curve that results from a given change in autonomous expenditure. In this example, the multiplier is 2. A £100 billion increase in investment produces a £200 billion increase in the aggregate quantity of goods and services demanded at each price level. That is, a £100 billion increase in autonomous expenditure shifts the aggregate demand curve rightward by £200 billion.

A decrease in autonomous expenditure shifts the aggregate expenditure curve downward and shifts the aggregate demand curve leftward. You can see these effects by reversing the change that we've just studied. Suppose that the economy is initially at point *b* on the aggregate expenditure curve AE_1 and the aggregate demand curve AD_1. A decrease in autonomous expenditure shifts the aggregate planned expenditure curve downward to AE_0. The aggregate quantity of goods and services demanded falls from £800 billion to £600 billion and the aggregate demand curve shifts leftward to AD_0.

We can summarize what we have just discovered in the following way. An increase in autonomous expenditure arising from some source other than a change in the price level shifts the *AE* curve upward and the *AD* curve rightward. The magnitude of the shift of the *AD* curve is determined by the change in autonomous expenditure and the multiplier.

Figure 25.11 A Change in Aggregate Demand

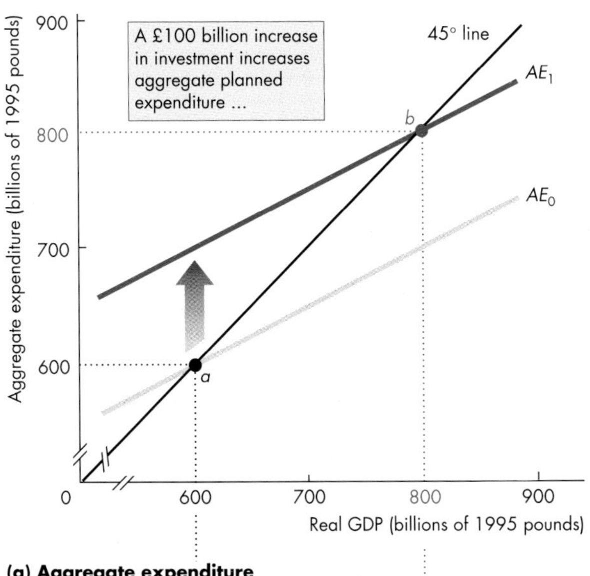

(a) Aggregate expenditure

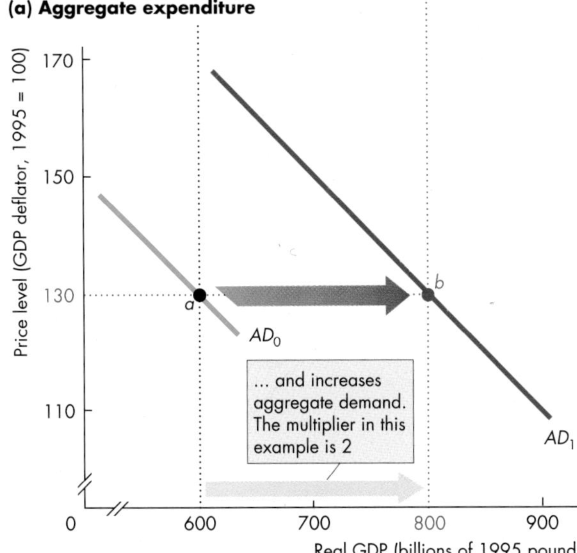

(b) Aggregate demand

The price level is 130. When the aggregate expenditure curve is AE_0 (part a), the aggregate demand curve is AD_0 (part b). An increase in autonomous expenditure shifts the aggregate expenditure curve upward to AE_1. The new equilibrium occurs where AE_1 intersects the 45° line at a real GDP of £800 billion. Because the quantity of real GDP demanded at a price level of 130 increases to £800 billion, the aggregate demand curve shifts rightward to AD_1. The magnitude of the rightward shift of the aggregate demand curve is determined by the change in autonomous expenditure and the size of the multiplier.

Equilibrium GDP and the Price Level

In Chapter 24, we learned that aggregate demand and short-run aggregate supply determine equilibrium real GDP and the price level. We've now put aggregate demand under a more powerful microscope and discovered that a change in investment (or in any component of autonomous expenditure) changes aggregate demand and shifts the aggregate demand curve. The magnitude of the shift depends on the multiplier. But whether a change in autonomous expenditure results ultimately in a change in real GDP, or a change in the price level, or some combination of the two depends on aggregate supply. There are two time-frames to consider:

1 The short run.
2 The long run.

First, we'll see what happens in the short run. Then we'll look at the long run.

An Increase in Aggregate Demand in the Short Run Figure 25.12 describes the economy. In part (a), the aggregate expenditure curve is AE_0, and equilibrium expenditure and real GDP are £600 billion – point a. In part (b), aggregate demand is AD_0 and the short-run aggregate supply curve is SAS. (Look at Chapter 24, pp. 582–589, if you need to refresh your understanding of this curve.) Equilibrium is at point a, where the aggregate demand and short-run aggregate supply curves intersect. The price level is 130 and real GDP is £600 billion.

Now suppose that investment increases by £100 billion. With the price level fixed at 130, the aggregate expenditure curve shifts upward to AE_1. Equilibrium expenditure increases to £800 billion – point b in part (a). In part (b), the aggregate demand curve shifts rightward by £200 billion, from AD_0 to AD_1. How far the aggregate demand curve shifts is determined by the multiplier when the price level is fixed. But with this new aggregate demand curve, the price level does not remain fixed. The price level rises and as it does so, the aggregate expenditure curve shifts downward. The short-run equilibrium occurs when the aggregate expenditure curve has shifted downward to AE_2 and the new aggregate demand curve, AD_1, intersects the short-run aggregate supply curve. Real GDP is £760 billion and the price level is 136 (at point c).

Figure 25.12 The Multiplier in the Short Run

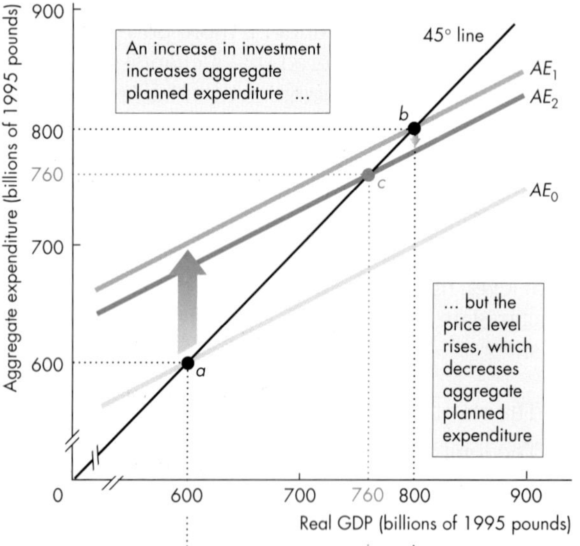

(a) Aggregate expenditure

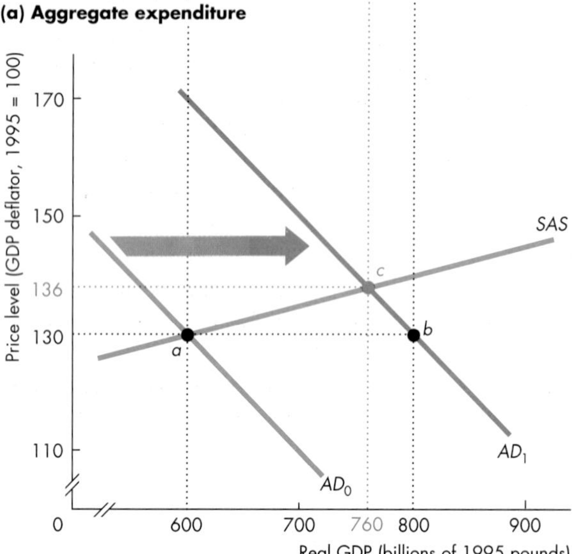

(b) Aggregate demand

An increase in investment shifts the *AE* curve upward from AE_0 to AE_1 (part a). As a result, the *AD* curve shifts from AD_0 to AD_1 (part b). The distance *ab* is determined by the multiplier when the price level is sticky. At the price level 130, there is excess demand. The price level rises, and the higher price level shifts the *AE* curve downward to AE_2. The economy moves to point *c* in both parts. With flexible prices, the multiplier is smaller than when prices are sticky. The steeper the *SAS* curve, the larger is the increase in the price level, the smaller is the increase in real GDP, and the smaller is the multiplier.

Figure 25.13 The Multiplier in the Long Run

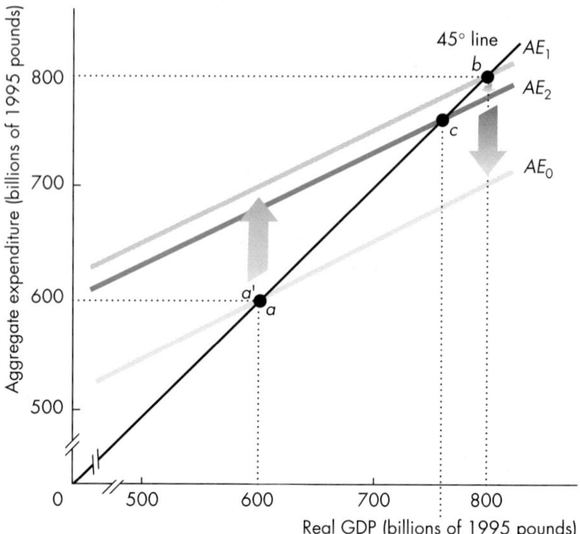

(a) Aggregate expenditure

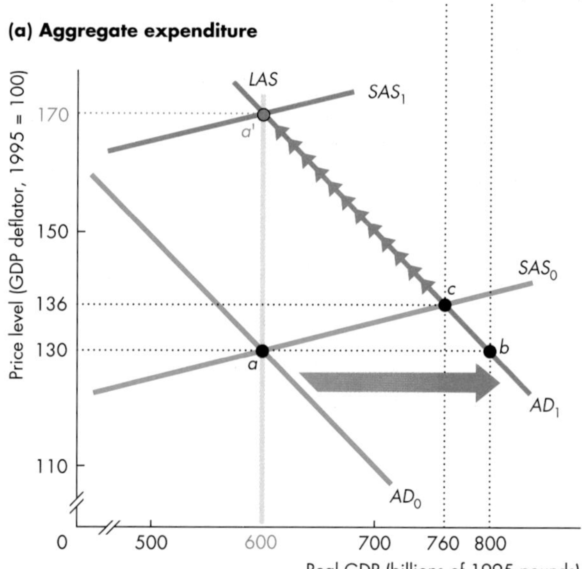

(b) Aggregate demand

Starting from point *a*, an increase in investment shifts the *AE* curve to AE_1 and shifts the *AD* curve to AD_1. In the short run, the economy moves to point *c*. In the long run, the money wage rate rises, the *SAS* curve shifts to SAS_1, the *AE* curve shifts back to AE_0, the price level rises and real GDP falls. The economy moves to point *a*' and the long-run multiplier is zero.

Taking price level effects into account, the increase in investment still has a multiplier effect on real GDP, but the effect is smaller than it would be if the price level was fixed forever. The steeper the slope of the short-run aggregate supply curve, the larger is the increase in the price level and the smaller is the multiplier effect on real GDP.

An Increase in Aggregate Demand in the Long Run In the long run, the economy is at full-employment equilibrium and on its long-run aggregate supply curve. When the economy is at full employment, an increase in aggregate demand has the same short-run effect as we've just worked out, but its long-run effect is different.

Figure 25.13 illustrates the long-run effect. Potential GDP is £600 billion so long-run aggregate supply is *LAS*. When investment increases by £100 billion, the aggregate expenditure curve shifts upward to AE_1 and the aggregate demand curve shifts rightward to AD_1. The price level rises to a short-run equilibrium with real GDP at £760 billion and the price level at 136. But this situation is an above full-employment equilibrium. The workforce is more than fully employed, and there are shortages of labour. The money wage rate begins to rise. The higher money wage rate increases costs, and short-run aggregate supply decreases. The *SAS* curve begins to shift leftward. As a result, the price level increases further. As the price level rises, aggregate planned expenditure decreases and the *AE* curve shifts downwards toward AE_0. Eventually, when the money wage rate and the price level have increased by the same percentage, real GDP is again at its full-employment level. The multiplier in the long run is zero.

Review

- A change in the price level shifts the *AE* curve and brings a movement along the *AD* curve.
- A change in autonomous expenditure not caused by a change in the price level shifts both the *AE* curve and the *AD* curve, and the multiplier determines the magnitude of the shift in the *AD* curve.
- The increase in real GDP that results from an increase in autonomous expenditure is smaller than the increase in aggregate demand.
- An increase in aggregate demand at full employment leaves real GDP unchanged but increases the price level. The long-run multiplier is zero.

We've now seen how real GDP deviates from its long-term growth path when aggregate demand fluctuates, and we've studied the multiplier effect that amplifies the disturbances to aggregate demand. In the next three chapters we're going to see how macroeconomic policy can be used to smooth economic fluctuations. In Chapter 26, we study fiscal policy and discover what the government can do (and can't do) with taxes and its own spending to smooth economic fluctuations and stimulate production, and in Chapters 27 and 28, we study money and the actions the government, the Bank of England and the European Central Bank can take to smooth fluctuations and to restrain inflation.

Summary

Key Points

Fixed Prices and Expenditure Plans (pp. 604–609)

- When the *price level* is fixed, *aggregate* expenditure determines real GDP.
- *Planned* consumption expenditure is determined by disposable income.
- The influence of disposable income on consumption expenditure is determined by the marginal propensity to consume (*MPC*), which is equal to the slope of the consumption function.
- The influence of real GDP on imports is described by the import function. An increase in real GDP brings an increase in imports, and the magnitude of the increase in imports is determined by the marginal propensity to import.

Real GDP with a Fixed Price Level (pp. 609–613)

- The aggregate expenditure curve shows the relationship between aggregate *planned* expenditure and real GDP.
- *Actual* aggregate expenditure is always equal to real GDP. But aggregate *planned* expenditure is not necessarily equal to actual aggregate expenditure and real GDP.
- Equilibrium expenditure occurs when aggregate planned expenditure equals real GDP.

The Multiplier (pp. 613–618)

- The multiplier is the magnified effect of a change in autonomous expenditure on real GDP.
- The multiplier is equal to 1 divided by the marginal propensity to save.
- The larger the marginal propensity to consume, the smaller the marginal propensity to save, the larger is the multiplier.
- The multiplier is also influenced by the marginal propensity to import and by the marginal income tax rate.

The Multiplier, Real GDP and the Price Level (pp. 618–623)

- The aggregate demand curve is the relationship between the quantity of real GDP demanded and the price level, other things remaining the same.
- The aggregate expenditure curve is the relationship between aggregate planned expenditure and real GDP, other things remaining the same.
- At a given price level, there is a given aggregate expenditure curve. A change in the price level changes aggregate planned expenditure and shifts the aggregate expenditure curve. A change in the price level also creates a movement along the aggregate demand curve. Thus a movement along the aggregate demand curve is associated with a shift in the aggregate expenditure curve.
- A change in autonomous expenditure not caused by a change in the price level shifts the aggregate expenditure curve and also shifts the aggregate demand curve.
- The size of the shift in the aggregate demand curve depends on the size of the multiplier and the change in autonomous expenditure.
- The multiplier decreases as the price level changes and in the long run the multiplier is zero.

Key Figures

Key Terms

Aggregate planned expenditure, 604
Autonomous expenditure, 611
Consumption function, 605
Equilibrium expenditure, 611
Induced expenditure, 611
Marginal propensity to consume, 606
Marginal propensity to import, 609
Marginal propensity to save, 606
Multiplier, 613
Saving function, 605

Review Questions

1 What are the main implications of fixed prices for the economy as a whole?

2 Explain the two-way relationship between real GDP and aggregate expenditure.

3 What is the main influence on consumption expenditure and saving in the short term?

4 What are the consumption function and the saving function?

5 What is the relationship between the consumption function and the saving function?

6 What is the marginal propensity to consume? Why is it less than 1?

7 Explain the relationship between the marginal propensity to consume and the marginal propensity to save.

8 What is the relationship between the marginal propensity to consume and the slope of the consumption function?

9 What is the relationship between consumption expenditure and GDP and why does the relationship arise?

10 What is the import function and the marginal propensity to import?

11 What is the aggregate expenditure schedule and aggregate expenditure curve?

12 Distinguish between induced expenditure and autonomous expenditure.

13 How is equilibrium expenditure determined?

14 Explain how a recovery gets going when aggregate planned expenditure exceeds real GDP.

15 Explain why an increase in autonomous expenditure shifts the aggregate expenditure curve upward.

16 What is the multiplier?

17 Explain the multiplier process.

18 Why is the multiplier greater than 1? What determines the size of the multiplier?

19 Explain the influence of the marginal propensity to consume, imports and taxes on the size of the multiplier.

20 Describe the relationship between the aggregate expenditure curve and the aggregate demand curve.

21 Explain why the aggregate expenditure curve shifts downward when the price level increases.

22 What happens to the aggregate expenditure curve and the aggregate demand curve when the price level changes and everything else is constant?

23 Explain why an increase in autonomous expenditure increases aggregate demand.

24 Explain why the multiplier is larger in the very short run when the price level is fixed than it is when the price level changes.

25 Explain why the multiplier is zero in the long run.

Problems

1 You are given the following information about the economy of Eurasthania:

Disposable income (millions of euros per year)	Consumption expenditure (millions of euros per year)
0	5
10	10
20	15
30	20
40	25

a Calculate Eurasthania's marginal propensity to consume.

b Calculate Eurasthania's saving at each level of disposable income.

c Calculate Eurasthania's marginal propensity to save.

d Draw a graph to illustrate the consumption function. Calculate its slope.

e Over what range of disposable income does Eurasthania dissave?

2 You are given the following information about the economy of Happy Isle. When disposable income is zero, consumption expenditure is $80 billion. The marginal propensity to consume is 0.75. Investment is $400 billion; government

purchases of goods and services are £600 billion; taxes are a constant £500 billion and do not vary as income varies.

a Calculate autonomous expenditure.
b What is the consumption function?
c What is the saving function?
d Calculate the marginal propensity to consume.
e Calculate the marginal propensity to save.
f What is the equation that describes the aggregate expenditure curve?
g Calculate equilibrium expenditure.

3 You are given the following information about the economy of Zeeland. Autonomous consumption expenditure is £100 billion and the marginal propensity to consume is 0.9. Investment is £460 billion, government purchases of goods and services are £400 billion, taxes are a constant £400 billion – they do not vary with income. Exports are £350 billion and imports are 10 per cent of GDP.

a What is the consumption function?
b What is the equation that describes the aggregate expenditure curve.
c Calculate equilibrium expenditure.
d Calculate the slope of the aggregate expenditure curve in Zeeland.
e If investment falls to £360 billion, what is the change in equilibrium expenditure and what is the size of the multiplier?

4 Suppose that the economy of Zeeland is as described in Problem 3. The price level in Zeeland is 100 and real GDP equals potential GDP.

a If investment increases by £100 billion, what happens to the quantity of real GDP demanded?
b In the short run, does equilibrium real GDP increase by more than, less than, or the same amount as the increase in the quantity of real GDP demanded?
c In the long run, does equilibrium real GDP increase by more than, less than, or the same amount as the increase in the quantity of real GDP demanded?
d In the short run, does the price level in Zeeland rise, fall, or remain unchanged?
e In the long run, does the price level in Zeeland rise, fall, or remain unchanged?

5 Study *Reading Between the Lines* on pp. 628–629 and then answer the following questions.

a What is the explanation for the improvement in French consumer spending in 1998?
b What is the explanation for the improvement in French investment spending in 1998?
c What is the explanation for the slow growth in French exports in 1998?
d Why has aggregate expenditure in France increased in 1998?

6 Visit the Penn World Table Web site (linked from the Parkin, Powell and Matthews site) and obtain data on real GDP per person and consumption as a percentage of real GDP for the United States, China, South Africa, and Mexico since 1960.

a In a spreadsheet, multiply your real GDP data by the consumption percentage and divide by 100 to obtain data on real consumption expenditure per person.
b Make graphs like Figure 25.4, which show the relationship between consumption and real GDP for these four countries.
c Based on the numbers you've obtained, in which country do you expect the multiplier to be largest (other things being equal)?
d What other data would you need in order to calculate the multipliers for these countries?
e You are an Economic Assistant at HM Treasury. You've been asked to draft a note for the Chancellor that explains the power and limitations of the multiplier. The Chancellor wants only 250 words of crisp, clear, jargon-free explanation together with a lively example by tomorrow morning.

W http://www.econ100.com

Appendix to Chapter 25

Imports, Taxes and the Multiplier

To work out the effects of imports and taxes on the multiplier, begin with the aggregate expenditure equation. Real GDP, Y, equals consumption expenditure, C, plus investment, I, plus government purchases, G, plus exports, EX, minus imports, IM. That is:

$$Y = C + I + G + EX - IM$$

Investment plus government purchases plus exports are *autonomous expenditure*, which we'll call A. So, more simply:

$$Y = C + A - IM$$

The changes in real GDP and the component of aggregate expenditure are:

$$\Delta Y = \Delta C + \Delta A - \Delta IM$$

The change in consumption expenditure is equal to the marginal propensity to consume, MPC, multiplied by the change in disposable income, YD. That is:

$$\Delta C = MPC \times \Delta YD$$

The change in disposable income, YD, equals the change in real GDP minus the change in taxes, T. That is:

$$\Delta YD = \Delta Y - \Delta T$$

The change in taxes equals the change in real GDP multiplied by the marginal tax rate, MTR. That is:

$$\Delta T = MTR \times \Delta Y$$

Combining these last three relationships gives:

$$\Delta C = MPC \times (\Delta Y - MTR \times \Delta Y)$$

Or:

$$\Delta C = MPC \times (1 - MTR) \times \Delta Y$$

The change in imports equals the marginal propensity to import, MPI, multiplied by real GDP. That is:

$$\Delta IM = MPI \times \Delta Y$$

Using the last two equations with the fact that:

$$\Delta Y = \Delta C + \Delta A - \Delta IM$$

gives:

$$\Delta Y = MPC \times (1 - MTR) \times \Delta Y + \Delta A - MPI \times \Delta Y$$

which means that:

$$(1 - MPC(1 - MTR) + MPI) \times \Delta Y = \Delta A$$

So, the multiplier is:

$$\frac{\Delta Y}{\Delta A} = \frac{1}{(1 - MPC(1 - MTR) + MPI)}$$

Paris is Breathing Easier

The Essence of the Story

Business Week, 27 July 1998

Paris is Breathing Easier

James C. Cooper and Kathleen Madigan

Fueled by slow but steady improvement in its job market, France is leading euro-area growth. A domestic-led recovery is taking root, more than offsetting the Asian drag on exports.

While France still has key structural problems, especially in its labor markets, the outlook for this year and next is quite good. Economists generally agree with the government's projection of 3% growth in 1998, up from 2.3% in 1997, and the fastest since 1989.

Consumers are leading the way, stoked by income gains and the highest confidence in three years. In June, more consumers thought it was a good time to buy, more saw their financial situations improving, and job worries eased further. Joblessness, which hit a postwar high of 12.6% last year, is down to 11.9% in May, and it will go lower. France is expected to create 300,000 jobs in 1998. With inflation projected to stay at a low 1%, those job gains are boosting buying power.

Recent reports suggest that second-quarter consumer spending rose even faster than in the first quarter. Retail sales are strong, helped by the World Cup, and car sales are up 10% in the first half. Also, with builders' confidence the highest in six years, new construction is lifting demand for building materials and home-related goods.

A capital-spending recovery is also under way and it will gain speed, fueled by higher profits, low interest rates, rising capacity use, and the need to modernize. Business investment in the first quarter posted the strongest gain in two years. The latest business-confidence survey shows that more companies expect to lift output than at any time since 1989. Also, prospects that faster growth will lift profits but not inflation have pushed the CAC 40-stock index up 44% this year.

While April's trade deficit with Asia—excluding Japan—was the highest in seven years, France sends only 10% of its exports to Asia, while 60% go to Europe and the U.S. Continued strength in those markets, plus new vibrancy in domestic demand, means solid growth in coming quarters.

- Expectations of higher income have led to an increase of consumer spending in France during 1998.
- Spending in the second quarter rose faster than the first quarter helped by the World Cup being held in France in 1998.
- A recovery in capital spending in the first quarter of 1998 has been generated by lower interest rates, higher profits and increased capacity.
- Business and consumer confidence has improved sharply during 1998. An extra 300,000 jobs are expected to be created and inflation is expected to remain at 1 per cent.
- Domestic demand growth has offset slow growth in exports caused by the Asian crisis. The April 1998 trade deficit with Asia – excluding Japan, was the highest in seven years.

Economic Analysis

■ The Asian crisis has weakened export demand in France. But domestic demand is expected to improve and generate a recovery.

■ Consumer spending has increased because expectations of future income have increased. More jobs in the economy and expectation of improved financial conditions has increased consumer confidence.

■ Investment has increased because interest rates have fallen and expected future profit has increased.

■ Exports have fallen because the Asian crisis has reduced foreign demand for French goods. Consumption and investment are components of domestic demand, while exports are part of external demand.

■ Figure 1 shows the increase in investment more than offsetting the decrease in exports so that $I_0 + G_0 + X_0$ first shifts down to $I_0 + G_0 + X_1$ where X_1 is less than X_0, and then $I_0 + G_0 + X_1$ shifts up to $I_1 + G_0 + X_1$, where I_1 is greater than I_0.

■ Figure 1 also shows aggregate planned expenditure shifting up for unchanged consumption.

■ However, the consumption function also increases because of higher expected income and Figure 2 shows the consumption function rising from CF_0 to CF_1.

■ Figure 3 shows aggregate expenditure shifting from AE_0 to AE_2 caused by an increase in domestic autonomous spending more than offsetting the decrease in exports.

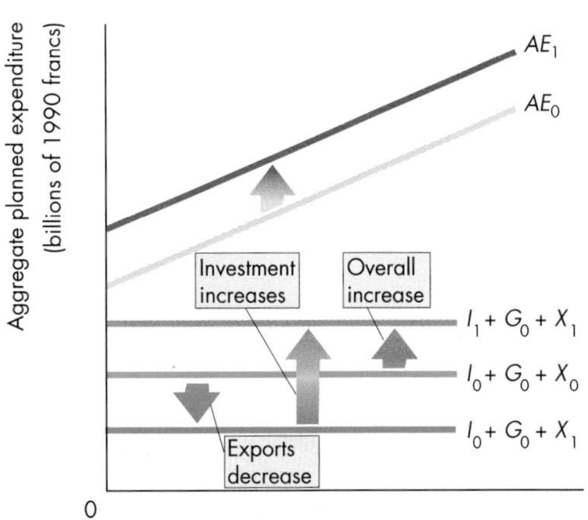

Figure 1 Aggregate expenditure

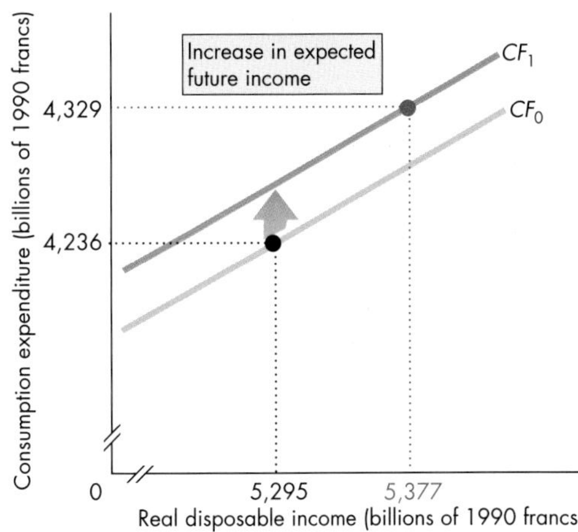

Figure 2 Increase in autonomous consumption

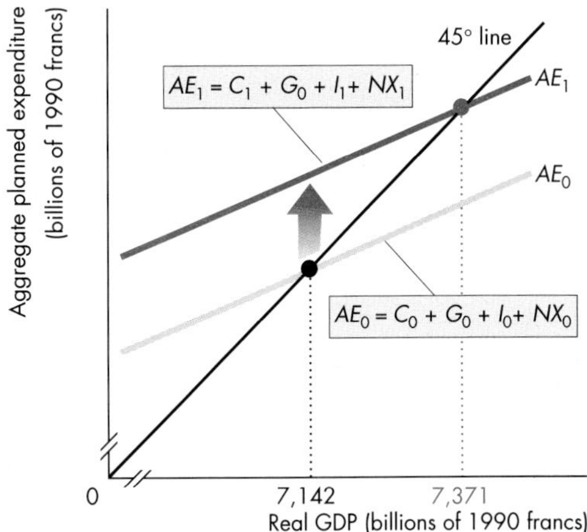

Figure 3 Equilibrium expenditure

CHAPTER 26

Fiscal Policy

After studying this chapter you will be able to:

- Describe the recent history of government expenditures, tax revenues, and the budget deficit in the UK
- Distinguish between automatic and discretionary fiscal policy
- Define and explain the fiscal policy multipliers
- Explain the effects of fiscal policy in both the short run and the long run
- Distinguish between and explain the demand side and the supply side effects of fiscal policy

Balancing Acts at Westminster

In November 1998, the government planned to spend £358 billion between 1999 and 2000. What are the effects of government spending on the economy? Does it create jobs? Or does it destroy them? Does a pound spent by the government on goods and services have the same effect as a pound spent by someone else? ◆ Although the government planned to *spend* 40 pence of every pound earned, it planned to tax us by 39 pence in every pound earned. Its plans were for tax and social security revenues of £333 billion. What are the effects of taxes on the economy? Do taxes harm employment and economic growth? ◆ The plan to have tax revenues fall short of expenditures is not uncommon in developed economies. The last time the United Kingdom had a budget surplus was in 1990, but usually the government has planned to spend more than it expected to receive. ◆ The United Kingdom is not alone in Europe in this respect. All the governments of the countries in the European Union, except for Luxembourg and Ireland, ended up spending more than they received in revenues during 1998. ◆ Government debt as a percentage of GDP rose from 34 per cent in 1991 to 50 per cent in 1998. Does it matter if the government doesn't balance its books? What are the effects of an ongoing government deficit and accumulating debt? Do they slow down economic growth? Do they impose a burden on future generations – on you and your children? Many of the countries that belong to the European Monetary Union have different levels of government deficits and government debt as a proportion of GDP. The stability pact made by countries in the EMU have specified ceilings on their budget deficits. For some countries this will mean reducing government expenditure and possibly imposing higher taxes. What will be the likely effects of such a policy on the individual countries and in Europe generally?

◆ ◆ ◆ ◆ These are the questions that you will explore in this chapter. We'll begin by describing the budget and the components that contribute to it. We'll also look at the development of the budget in the United Kingdom and other EU countries. We'll then use the multiplier analysis of Chapter 25 and the aggregate supply–aggregate demand model of Chapter 24 to study the effects of the budget on the economy.

The Government Budget

Every year the Chancellor of the Exchequer makes an annual statement to Parliament of the expenditures and tax revenues of the government. The main purpose of the statement – known as the budget – is to:

1 To state the items of expenditure of the government and to lay out the plans to finance its activities.

2 To stabilize the economy.

The first purpose of the budget – and its original purpose – is to ensure that funds are available to finance the business of the government. Until the view that government spending can play a part in generating aggregate demand became generally accepted, the budget had no other purpose. The second purpose is to pursue the government's fiscal policy. **Fiscal policy** is the use of the budget to achieve macroeconomic objectives such as full employment, sustained long-term economic growth and price-level stability. It is this second purpose that we focus on in this chapter.

Table 26.1 The Public Finances in 1997–1998 and 1998–1999

Item	1997/98	1998/99
	(billions of pounds)	
Expenditure	320.9	334.5
Expenditure on goods and services	163.9	172.6
Transfer payments	128.5	133.8
Debt interest	28.5	28.1
Total receipts	315.7	333.0
Value added taxes and other indirect taxes	120.4	127.6
Taxes on Income	110.7	116.3
Social security contributions	50.7	53.9
Other receipts and royalties	33.9	35.2
Financial deficit	5.1	1.6
Financial transactions	–2.5	–0.7
PSNCR	2.6	2.3

Source: HM Treasury, *Budget 98* No 620, London, HMSO, March 1998.

Highlights of the 1998 Budget

Table 26.1 shows the main items in the **government budget**. The numbers are projected amounts for the fiscal years April 1998 to end-March 1999. Notice first the three main parts of the table: *expenditures* are the government's outlays, *total receipts* are the government's receipts and the *deficit* is the amount by which the government's expenditures exceed its tax revenues. The next item is the public corporations' market and overseas borrowing. This represents the net borrowing of the industries that come under state control. In the United Kingdom this item is small and is expected to decline as more and more public enterprises are privatized. The final item is the Public Sector Net Cash Requirement (PSNCR) which refers to the deficit for the public sector as a whole.

Expenditures Expenditures are classified in three categories:

1 Expenditure on goods and services.

2 Transfer payments.

3 Debt interest.

The largest item of spending, is government expenditure. *Expenditure on goods and services* are expenditures on final goods and services. These expenditures include those on defence, the National Health Service, computers for schools, construction of new roads and motorways, and urban regeneration. This component of the budget is government purchases of goods and services that appears in the circular flow of expenditure and income and in the national income and product accounts (see Chapter 22, p. 532).

Transfer payments are payments to individuals, businesses, other levels of government and the rest of the world. It includes social security benefits, health care, unemployment benefits, welfare supplements, grants to local authorities and aid to developing countries.

Debt interest is the interest on the government debt minus interest received by the government on its own investments.

Total current receipts Total current receipts come from four sources:

1 Taxes on income.

2 Social security contributions.

Figure 26.1 The UK Government Spending

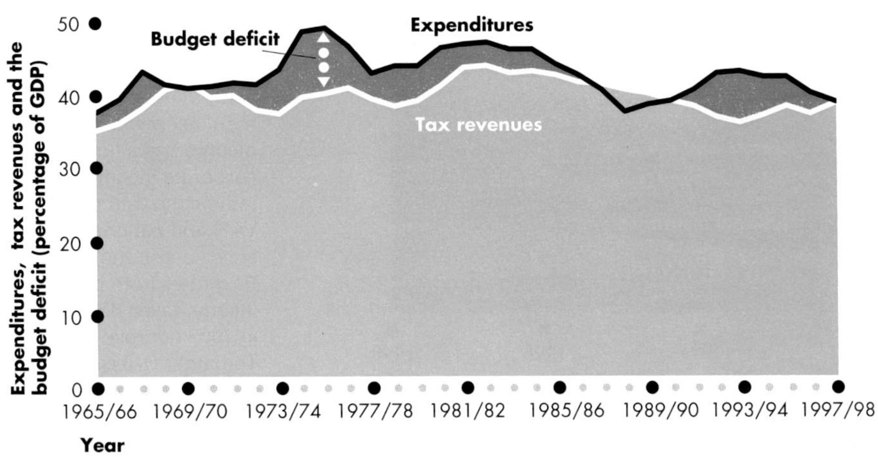

The figure records the UK government's expenditures, tax revenues and budget deficit from 1965/66 to 1997/98. In the late 1960s, the deficit was small, but during the 1970s it became large and persisted through to the 1980s. A budget surplus occurred in the late 1980s, but the budget deficit increased again in the 1990s. The increase in the 1990s came about through a combination of a decrease in tax revenues from tax cuts in the 1980s and an increase in expenditures. The budget was in balance in 1997/98.

Source: HM Treasury, *Budget Report 1988.*

3 Value added taxes (VAT) and other taxes on expenditure.
4 Other receipts and royalties.

The largest source of revenue is *taxes on expenditure*. These are the taxes paid by consumers on goods that carry VAT (currently 17.5 per cent), and special duties and taxes on gambling, alcoholic drinks, petrol and luxury items. The second largest source is taxes on *income*, which includes taxes on corporate profits. These are the taxes paid by individuals on their incomes and the taxes expected from the profits of businesses and the rates businesses pay for government services. Third in size are *social security contributions*. These are taxes paid by workers and employers to fund the welfare and health programmes. Fourth in size are *other receipts and royalties*. These are small items including oil royalties, stamp duties, car taxes, miscellaneous rents, dividends from abroad and profits from nationalized industries.

Deficit The government's budget balance is equal to its tax revenues minus its expenditures. That is:

Budget balance = Tax revenues – Expenditures

If tax revenues exceed expenditures, the government has a **budget surplus**. If expenditures exceed tax revenues, the government has a **budget deficit**. If tax revenues equal expenditures, the government has a **balanced budget**. In 1998/99, with projected expenditures of £334.5 billion and tax revenues of £333 billion, the government projected a budget deficit of £1.6 billion. After allowing for a small repayment from public corporations the projected PSNCR was £2.3 billion.

This is quite a small cash requirement, but this was not the case in previous years. To get a better sense of the magnitude of taxes, spending and the deficit we often express them as percentages of GDP. Expressing them in this way lets us see how large government is relative to the size of the economy, and it also helps us to study *changes* in the scale of government over time.

How typical is the budget of 1998? Let's look at its recent history.

The Budget in Historical Perspective

Figure 26.1 shows the government's tax revenues, expenditures and budget deficit since 1965/66. Throughout most of this period there was a budget deficit. The deficit rises in recessions and falls in recoveries. The deficit rose to a peak following the recession of the 1970s. Government receipts were actually higher than expenditures in the fiscal years 1987–89. But the deficit increased again during the 1990s and has fallen sharply in recent years.

Figure 26.2 UK Government Tax Revenues and Expenditures

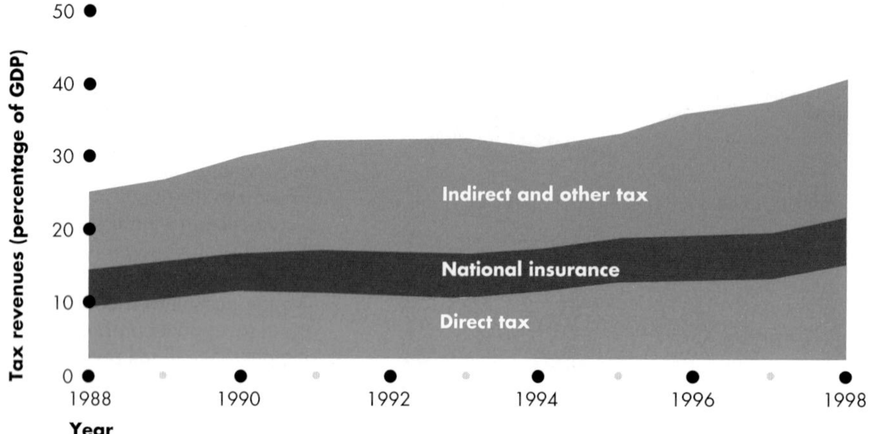

(a) Tax revenues

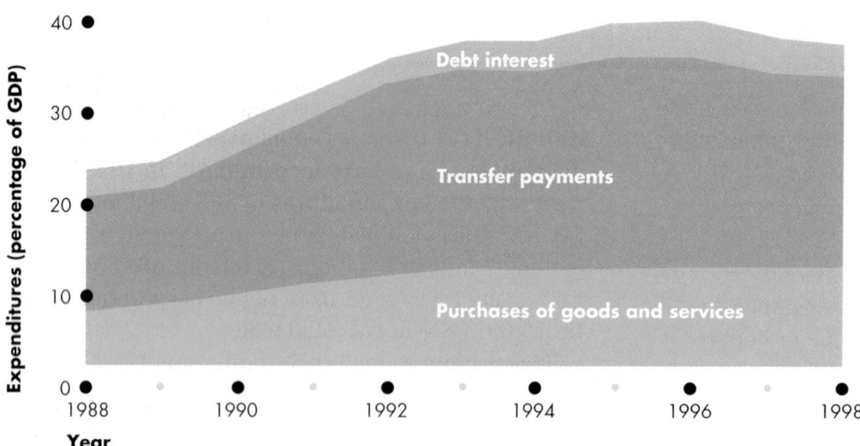

(b) Expenditures

Part (a) shows the three components of government tax revenues: direct income taxes (including corporate income taxes), indirect taxes (including VAT) and national insurance contributions. Revenues from direct income taxes declined in 1993 but rose in 1994. The other two components of tax revenues remained steady.

Part (b) shows three components of government expenditures: purchases of goods and services, debt interest and transfer payments. Purchases of goods and services has remained largely constant in the past eight years. Transfer payments have risen in the 1990s recession. Debt interest has fallen since 1996.

Source: HM Treasury, *Budget Report 1998.*

Why did the government deficit grow so sharply in the 1990s? The immediate answer is that expenditures increased and tax revenues decreased. But which components of expenditures increased and which sources of tax revenues decreased? Let's look at tax revenues and expenditures in a bit more detail.

Tax Revenues Figure 26.2(a) shows the components of tax revenues received by the government as a percentage of GDP, between 1988 and 1998. Central government receipts increased as a percentage of GDP to 1991 and then declined in the folowing three years. The reason for this is that the recession reduced the amount of tax receipts obtained from direct taxes. Firms' profits declined, reducing the take from corporate taxes, and the increase in unemployment reduced the amount of tax gained from personal taxes.

Expenditures Figure 26.2(b) shows the components of central government expenditures as percentages of GDP, between 1988 and 1998. Total expenditures increased as a proportion of GDP during the first half of the 1990s. The main reason for this is that transfer payments increased

Figure 26.3 The Government Debt of Italy and Belgium

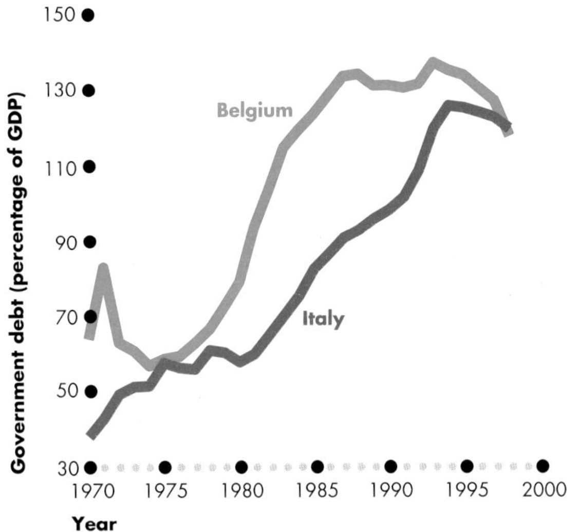

(a) The government debt of Italy and Belgium

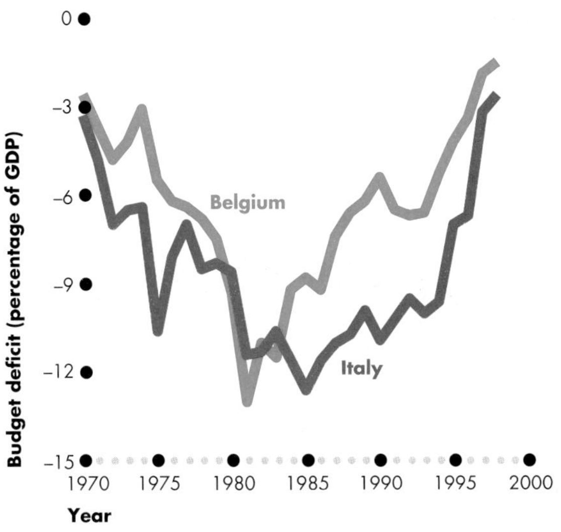

(b) The budget deficit of Italy and Belgium

In part (a) you can see the government debt (the accumulation of past budget deficits less past budget surpluses) of Italy and Belgium. Both countries had debt in excess of 100 per cent of GDP in 1998. Both countries have reduced their debt since 1994. In part (b) you can see the budget deficits of both countries. The peak in the deficit occurred in the recession of the early 1980s. Since the 1980s, both countries have been struggling to get their respective budget deficits below the 3 per cent target set as a condition for European Monetary Union.

Source: European Union, *1998*, DG II.

substantially while purchases of goods and services increased only slightly. Transfer payments increased because the unemployment and early retirements caused by the recession have led to a higher level of benefit and welfare payments.

Part of government expenditure is the payment of interest on the existing level of debt held by individuals. A high level of debt means that more interest payments have to be made. The United Kingdom does not have a high level of debt in relation to its GDP in comparison with many other countries in the European Union. However, high debt interest payments can make it difficult for a country to control its deficit. To understand why, we need to see the connection between the deficit and government debt.

Deficit and Debt **Government debt** is the total amount of borrowing by the government. It is the sum of past deficits minus the sum of past surpluses. If the government has a deficit, its debt increases, and if it has a surplus, its debt decreases. Once a persistent deficit emerges, the deficit begins to feed on itself. The deficit leads to increased borrowing; increased borrowing leads to larger interest payments; and larger interest payments lead to a larger deficit. This is one of the reasons high-debt countries like Italy and Belgium find it difficult to reduce their debt.

Figure 26.3(a) shows the history of government debt in Italy and Belgium since 1970. In the case of Italy, the level of debt as a proportion of GDP doubled in the decade of the 1980s. With Belgium, the level of debt increased sharply in the recession years of the early 1980s but has declined only moderately at the end of the decade. Figure 26.3(b) shows the budget deficits of each country as a percentage of GDP. A negative value in the chart indicates that revenues are less than expenditures. The peak in the deficit occurred in the recession of

Figure 26.4 Government Deficits and Debt in the European Union

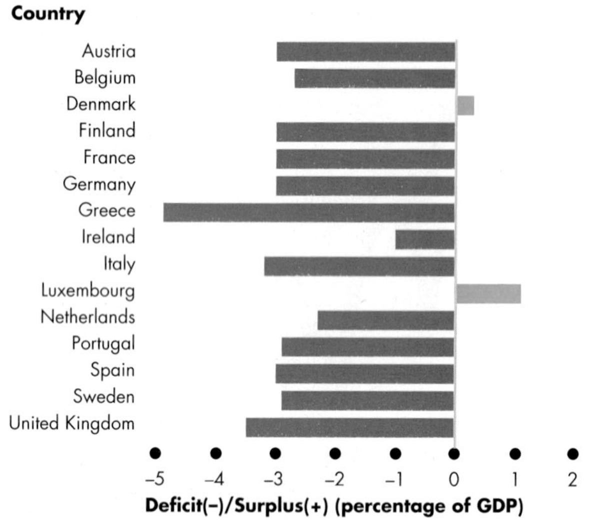

(a) Government deficits in European Union

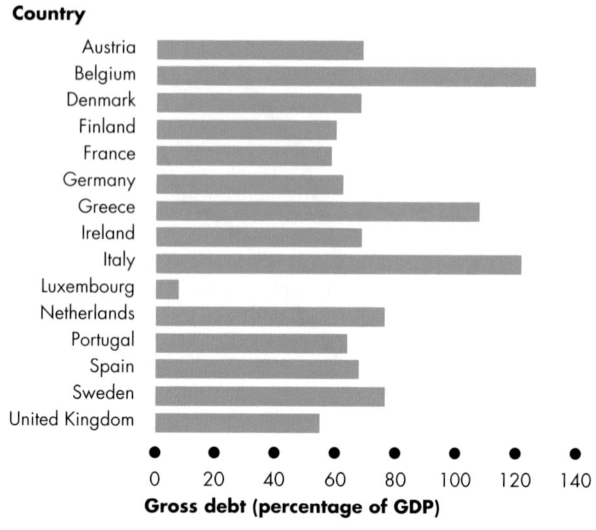

(b) General government gross debt

Part (a) shows that almost all countries in the European Union had budget deficits in 1997. The largest ones are Greece, Italy and the UK, and the smallest are Denmark, Ireland and Luxembourg, which have a budget surplus. Part (b) shows that many countries in the European Union have large levels of debt in relation to GDP. These include Belgium, Greece and Italy. Countries with low relative levels of debt include Luxembourg, Germany, France, Finland, Portugal and the United Kingdom.

Source: European Union, *European Economy Annual Report for 1998.*

the early 1980s, but both countries succeeded in controlling their deficit in 1998 to qualify for entry to the European Monetary Union.

Debt and Capital When individuals and businesses incur debts, they usually do so to buy capital – assets that yield a return. In fact, the main point of debt is to enable people to buy assets that will earn a return that exceeds the interest paid on the debt. The government is similar to individuals and businesses in this regard. Much government expenditure is on public assets that yield a return. Roads, bridges, schools and universities, public libraries and the stock of national defence capital all yield a social rate of return that probably far exceeds the interest rate the government pays on its debt.

Total government debt in the United Kingdom was around £410 billion in 1998, whereas the capital stock of the general government – that is, central government, local governments and public enterprises – was nearly £425 billion. Therefore the UK public finances are not in bad shape. But how do the deficit and debt compare with deficits and debts in the rest of the European Union?

The Budget Deficit and Debt Levels in a European Perspective

Do other countries in Europe have large budget deficits or do they have budget surpluses? Are their levels of debt comparable with that of the United Kingdom? Figure 26.4 answers these questions. Figure 26.4(a) shows the government budget deficits of all countries in the European Union as a percentage of GDP in 1997. Figure 26.4(b) shows the levels of debt as a percentage of GDP. All the members of the European Union except Luxembourg and Denmark had budget deficits in 1997. Some countries have levels of debt in excess of 100 per cent of GDP. The countries that have joined the EMU have a stabilty pact that places a ceiling of 3 per cent of GDP on their budget deficits. This can be sustained by cuts in government spending or increases in taxes. What will be the likely effects of such cuts in spending? This question will be examined in the next section.

Review

- Fiscal policy is created by the government and ratified by Parliament and is a key tool designed to influence employment and economic activity.
- Each year, the budget is proposed by the Chancellor of the Exchequer and presented to Parliament.
- For many years, the government has run a budget deficit – expenditures have exceeded tax revenues – but the United Kingdom is not unusual. Virtually all countries in the EU run budget deficits.

We have now described the government budget. Your next task is to study the effects of fiscal policy on the economy. We'll begin by learning about its effects on expenditure plans when the price level is sticky. You will see that fiscal policy has multiplier effects like the expenditure multipliers that are explained in Chapter 25. Then we'll study the influences of fiscal policy on both aggregate demand and aggregate supply and look at its short-run and long-run effects on real GDP and the price level.

Fiscal Policy Multipliers

Fiscal policy actions can be either automatic or discretionary. **Automatic fiscal policy** is a change in fiscal policy that is triggered by the state of the economy. For example, an increase in unemployment triggers an *automatic* increase in payments to unemployed workers. A fall in incomes triggers an *automatic* decrease in tax receipts. That is, fiscal policy adjusts automatically. **Discretionary fiscal policy** is a policy action that is initiated by the Chancellor of the Exchequer. It requires a change in tax laws or in some spending programme. For example, a decrease in the standard rate of income tax or an increase in defence spending are discretionary fiscal policy actions. That is, discretionary fiscal policy is a deliberate policy action.

We begin by studying the effects of *discretionary* changes in government spending and taxes. To focus on the essentials, we'll initially study a model economy that is simpler than the one in which we live. In our model economy, there is no international trade and the taxes are all lump sum. **Lump-sum taxes** are taxes that do not vary with real GDP. They are fixed by the government and they change only when the government changes them. Lump-sum taxes are rare in reality and they are generally considered to be unfair because rich people and poor people pay the same amount of tax. (It is said that the former prime minister, Margaret Thatcher, lost her job because of the unpopularity of a lump-sum tax called the 'poll tax', which was a fixed tax per person to pay for local government services.) We use lump-sum taxes in our model economy only because they make the principles we are studying easier to understand. Once we've grasped the principles, we'll explore our real economy with its international trade and income taxes – taxes that *do* vary with real GDP.

Like our real economy, the model economy we study is constantly bombarded by shocks. Exports fluctuate because incomes fluctuate in the rest of the world. Business investment fluctuates because of swings in profit expectations and interest rates. These fluctuations set up multiplier effects that begin a recession or a recovery. If a recession takes hold, unemployment increases and incomes fall. If a recovery becomes too strong, inflationary pressures build up. To minimize the effects of these swings in spending, the government might change either its purchases of goods and services or net taxes (taxes minus transfer payments, see Chapter 22, p. 532). By changing either of these items, the government can influence aggregate expenditure and real GDP. But it also changes its budget deficit or surplus. An alternative fiscal policy action is to change purchases and taxes together so budget balance does not change. We are going to study the initial effects of these discretionary fiscal policy actions in the very short run when the price level is sticky. Each of these actions creates a multiplier effect on real GDP. These multipliers are:

- The government purchases multiplier.
- The lump-sum tax multiplier.
- The balanced budget multiplier.

Table 26.2 The Government Purchases Multiplier

	Real GDP (*Y*)	Taxes (*T*)	Disposable income (*Y–T*)	Consumption expenditure (*C*)	Investment (*I*)	Initial government purchases (*G*)	Initial aggregate planned expenditure (*AE* = *C* + *I* + *G*)	New government purchases (*G'*)	New aggregate planned expenditure (*AE'* = *C* + *I* + *G'*)
					(billions of pounds)				
a	500	50	450	375	100	50	525	100	575
b	600	50	550	450	100	50	600	100	650
c	700	50	650	525	100	50	675	100	725
d	800	50	750	600	100	50	750	100	800
e	900	50	850	675	100	50	825	100	875

The Government Purchases Multiplier

The **government purchases multiplier** is the amount by which a change in government purchases of goods and services is multiplied to determine the change in equilibrium expenditure that it generates.

Government purchases are a component of aggregate expenditure. So when government purchases change, aggregate expenditure changes and so does real GDP. The change in real GDP induces a change in consumption expenditure which brings an additional change in aggregate expenditure. A multiplier process ensues. This multiplier process is like the one described in Chapter 25, pp. 613–618. Let's look at an example.

Peace Dividend Multiplier After the fall of the Berlin Wall and the ending of the cold war, the NATO countries looked forward to a reduction in expenditure on defence and a scaling back of arms spending. In the United Kingdom, this has led to a rationalization of military installations and restructuring of operations. Part of the restructuring has been the downgrading of the Rosyth naval base in Scotland, and the removal of its main operations to Portsmouth in the south of England. The downgrading of the Rosyth naval base will hit hard a region that is already blighted by high unemployment. The reduction in military expenditure will have severe effects on the region's GDP and employment in the short term. Because military personnel and workers on the base spend most of their incomes locally, consumption expenditure in the region depends on defence spending in the area. Retail shops and hotels depend on the spending power of people whose incomes are associated or linked with the base. In the long term the Rosyth area will learn to develop other types of industries but in the short term there will be negative multiplier effects for the region.

The Size of the Multiplier Table 26.2 illustrates the government purchases multiplier with a numerical example. The first column lists various possible levels of real GDP. Our task is to find equilibrium expenditure and the change in real GDP when government purchases change. The second column shows taxes. They are fixed at £50 billion, regardless of the level of real GDP. (This is an assumption that keeps your attention on the key idea and makes the calculations easier to do.) The third column calculates disposable income. Because taxes are lump sum, disposable income equals real GDP minus the £50 billion of taxes. For example, in row *b*, real GDP is £600 billion and disposable income is £550 billion. The next column shows consumption expenditure. In this example, the *marginal propensity to consume* is 0.75 or 3/4. That is, a £1 increase in disposable income brings a 75 pence increase in consumption expenditure. Check this fact by calculating the increase in consumption expenditure when disposable income increases by £100 billion from row *b* to row *c*. Consumption expenditure increases by £75 billion. The next column shows investment, which is a constant of £100 billion. And the next column shows the initial level of government purchases, which is £50 billion. Aggregate planned expenditure is the sum of consumption expenditure, investment and government purchases.

Equilibrium expenditure and real GDP occur when aggregate planned expenditure equals real GDP. In this example, equilibrium expenditure is £600 billion (highlighted in row *b* of the table.)

The final two columns of the table show what happens when government purchases increase by £50 billion to £100 billion. Aggregate planned expenditure increases by £50 billion at each level of real GDP. For example, at the initial real GDP of £600 billion, aggregate planned expenditure increases to £650 billion. Because aggregate planned expenditure exceeds real GDP, stocks decrease and firms increase production to restore their stocks. Output, incomes and expenditure continue to increase. The increased incomes bring a further increase in aggregate planned expenditure. But aggregate planned expenditure increases by less than income, and eventually a new equilibrium is reached. In this example, the new equilibrium expenditure is at a real GDP of £800 billion.

A £50 billion increase in government purchases has increased equilibrium expenditure and real GDP by £200 billion. Therefore the government purchases multiplier is 4. The size of the multiplier depends on the marginal propensity to consume, which in this example, is 3/4. The following formula shows the connection between the government purchases multiplier and the marginal propensity to consume (*MPC*):

$$\text{Government purchases multiplier} = \frac{1}{(1 - MPC)}$$

Let's check this formula by using the numbers in the above example. The marginal propensity to consume is 3/4, so the government purchases multiplier is 4.

Figure 26.5 illustrates the government purchases multiplier. Initially, aggregate planned expenditure is shown by the curve labelled AE_0. The points on this curve, labelled *a* to *e*, correspond with the rows of Table 26.2. This aggregate expenditure curve intersects the 45° line at the equilibrium level of real GDP, which is £600 billion.

When government purchases increase by £50 billion, the aggregate expenditure curve shifts upward by that amount to AE_1. With this new aggregate expenditure curve, equilibrium real GDP increases to £800 billion. The increase in real GDP is four times the increase in government purchases. The government purchases multiplier is 4.

You've seen that in the very short term, when the price level is sticky, an increase in government purchases increases real GDP. But to produce more output, more people must be employed, so in the short term an increase in government purchases can create jobs.

Changing its purchases of goods and services is one way in which the government can try to stimulate the economy. A second way in which the government might act to increase real GDP in the very short run is by decreasing lump-sum taxes. Let's see how this action works.

The Lump-sum Tax Multiplier

The **lump-sum tax multiplier** is the amount by which a change in lump-sum taxes is multiplied to determine the change in equilibrium expenditure

Figure 26.5 The Government Purchases Multiplier

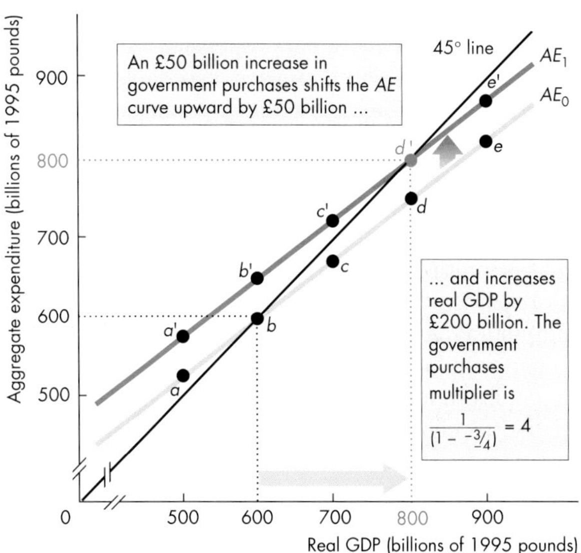

Initially, the aggregate expenditure curve is AE_0 and real GDP is £600 billion (at point *b*). An increase in government purchases of £50 billion increases aggregate planned expenditure at each level of real GDP by £50 billion. The aggregate planned expenditure curve shifts upward from AE_0 to AE_1 – a parallel shift. At the initial real GDP of £600 billion, aggregate planned expenditure is now £650 billion. Because aggregate planned expenditure is greater than real GDP, real GDP increases. The new equilibrium is reached when real GDP is £800 billion – the point at which the AE_1 curve intersects the 45° line (at *d'*). In this example, the government purchases multiplier is 4.

that it generates. An *increase* in taxes leads to a *decrease* in disposable income and a decrease in aggregate expenditure. The amount by which aggregate expenditure initially decreases is determined by the marginal propensity to consume. In our example, the marginal propensity to consume is 3/4, so a £1 tax cut increases disposable income by £1 and increases aggregate expenditure initially by 75 pence.

This initial change in aggregate expenditure has a multiplier just like the government purchases multiplier. We've seen that the government purchases multiplier is $1/(1 - MPC)$. Because a tax *increase* leads to a *decrease* in expenditure, the lump-sum tax multiplier is *negative*. And because a change in lump-sum taxes changes aggregate expenditure initially by only the *MPC* multiplied by the tax change, the lump-sum tax multiplier is equal to:

$$\text{Lump-sum tax multiplier} = \frac{-MPC}{(1 - MPC)}$$

In our example, the marginal propensity to consume is 3/4, so the lump-sum multiplier is:

$$\text{Lump-sum tax multiplier} = \frac{-3/4}{(1 - 3/4)} = -3$$

Figure 26.6 illustrates the lump-sum tax multiplier. Initially, the aggregate expenditure curve is AE_0 and equilibrium expenditure is £800 billion. Taxes increase by £100 billion and disposable income falls by that amount. With a marginal propensity to consume of 3/4, aggregate expenditure decreases initially by £75 billion and the aggregate expenditure curve shifts downward by that amount to AE_1. Equilibrium expenditure and real GDP fall by £300 billion to £500 billion. The lump-sum tax multiplier is −3.

Lump-sum Transfers The lump-sum tax multiplier also tells us the effects of a change in lump-sum transfer payments. Transfer payments are like negative taxes, so an increase in transfer payments works like a decrease in taxes. Because the tax multiplier is negative, a decrease in taxes increases expenditure. An increase in transfer payments also increases expenditure. So the lump-sum transfer payments multiplier is positive. It is:

$$\text{Lump-sum transfer payments multiplier} = \frac{MPC}{(1 - MPC)}$$

Figure 26.6 The Lump-sum Tax Multiplier

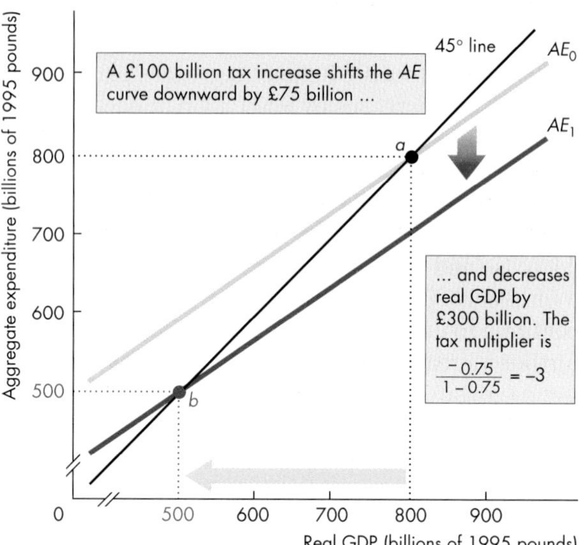

Initially, the aggregate expenditure curve is AE_0, and equilibrium expenditure is £800 billion. The marginal propensity to consume is 0.75. Lump-sum taxes increase by £100 billion, so disposable income falls by £100 billion. The decrease in aggregate expenditure is found by multiplying this change in disposable income by the marginal propensity to consume and is £100 billion × 0.75 = £75 billion. The aggregate expenditure curve shifts *downward* by this amount to AE_1. Equilibrium expenditure falls by £300 billion, and the lump-sum tax multiplier is −3.

The Balanced Budget Multiplier

A balanced budget fiscal policy action is one that changes *both* government purchases and taxes by the same amount so that the government's budget deficit or surplus remains *unchanged*. The **balanced budget multiplier** is the amount by which a simultaneous and equal change in government purchases and taxes is multiplied to determine the change in equilibrium expenditure. What is the multiplier effect of this fiscal policy action?

To find out, we must combine the government purchases multiplier and the lump-sum tax multiplier. These two multipliers are:

$$\text{Government purchases multiplier} = \frac{1}{(1 - MPC)}$$

$$\text{Lump-sum tax multiplier} = \frac{-MPC}{(1 - MPC)}$$

Adding these two multipliers gives the balanced budget multiplier, which is:

$$\text{Balanced budget multiplier} = \frac{1 - MPC}{1 - MPC} = 1$$

The balanced budget is smaller than the other multipliers but it is not zero. This fact is interesting because it means that in principle, fiscal policy can be used to increase aggregate planned expenditure if a recession is expected without increasing the government deficit. It also means that in the long run, as government grows, even if the growth of taxes keeps pace with the growth of expenditures, government adds to aggregate demand and squeezes out some private consumption expenditure or private investment, or both.

Induced Taxes and Welfare Spending

In the examples we've studied so far, taxes are lump-sum taxes. But in reality, net taxes (taxes minus transfer payments) vary with the state of the economy.

On the tax revenues side of the budget, the government passes tax laws that define the tax *rates* to be paid, not the tax *pounds* to be paid. As a consequence, tax *revenues* depend on real GDP. We call those taxes that vary as real GDP varies **induced taxes**. If the economy is in an expansion phase of the business cycle, induced taxes increase because real GDP increases. If the economy is in a recession phase of the business cycle, induced taxes decrease because real GDP decreases.

On the government expenditures side of the budget, the government pays out various benefits, principally to unemployed workers in the form of job seekers allowance. But it also subsidizes training programmes and start-up schemes, which result in transfer payments that depend on the economic state of individual citizens and businesses. For example, when the economy is in a recession, unemployment is high and government transfer payments increase. When the economy is in a boom, transfer payments decline.

The existence of induced taxes and benefits decreases the government purchases and lump-sum tax multipliers because they loosen the link between real GDP and disposable income and so dampen the effect of a change in real GDP on consumption expenditure. When real GDP increases, induced taxes increase and benefits decrease. So disposable income does not increase by as much as the increase in real GDP. As a result, consumption expenditure does not increase by as much as it otherwise would have done and the multiplier effect is reduced.

The extent to which induced taxes and benefits decrease the multiplier depends on the *marginal tax rate*. The marginal tax rate is the proportion of an additional pound of real GDP that flows to the government in net taxes (taxes minus transfer payments). The higher the marginal tax rate, the larger is the proportion of an additional pound of real GDP that is paid to the government and the smaller is the induced change in consumption expenditure. The smaller the change in consumption expenditure induced by a change in real GDP, the smaller is the multiplier effect of a change in government purchases or lump-sum taxes.

International Trade and Fiscal Policy Multipliers

Not all expenditure on final goods and services in the United Kingdom is on domestically produced goods and services. Some of it is on imports – foreign-produced goods and services. The extent to which an additional pound of real GDP is spent on imports is determined by the *marginal propensity to import*. Expenditure on imports does not generate UK real GDP and does not lead to an increase in UK consumption expenditure. The larger the marginal propensity to import, the smaller is the increase in consumption expenditure induced by an increase in real GDP and the smaller are the government purchases and lump-sum tax multipliers. (Imports affect the fiscal policy multipliers in exactly the same way that they influence the investment multiplier, as explained in Chapter 25, see p. 618).

In today's increasingly global economy in which the marginal propensity to import is much greater than it was 20 years ago, the fiscal policy multipliers are smaller than they used to be.

So far, we've studied *discretionary* fiscal policy. Let's look at automatic stabilizers.

Automatic Stabilizers

Automatic stabilizers are mechanisms that operate without the need for explicit action by the government. Their very name is borrowed from engineering and conjures up images of shock absorbers, thermostats and sophisticated devices that keep aircraft and ships steady in turbulent air and seas. Automatic fiscal stabilizers arise from the fact that income taxes and transfer payments fluctuate with real GDP. If real GDP begins to fall, tax revenues also fall and transfer payments rise. These changes in taxes and transfers affect the economy. Let's study the budget deficit over the business cycle.

Fiscal Policy over the Business Cycle Figure 26.7 shows the business cycle and fluctuations in the budget deficit since 1980. Part (a) shows the fluctuations of real GDP around potential GDP. Part (b) shows the government budget deficit (the PSNCR). Both parts highlight the most recent recession by shading this period. By comparing the two parts of the figure, you can see the relationship between the business cycle and the budget deficit. As a rule, when the economy is in the expansion phase of a business cycle, the budget deficit declines. (In the figure, a declining deficit means a deficit that is getting closer to zero.) As the expansion slows before the recession begins, the budget deficit increases. It continues to increase during the recession and for a further period after the recession is over. Then, when the expansion is well under way, the budget deficit declines again.

The budget deficit fluctuates with the business cycle because both tax revenues and expenditures fluctuate with real GDP. As real GDP increases during an expansion, tax revenues increase and transfer payments decrease, so the budget deficit automatically decreases. As real GDP decreases during a recession, tax revenues decrease and transfer payments increase, so the budget deficit automatically increases.

Fluctuations in investment or exports have a multiplier efffect on real GDP. But automatic fluctuations in tax revenues (and the budget deficit) act as an automatic stabilizer. They decrease the swings in disposable income and make the multiplier effect smaller. They dampen both the expansions and recessions.

The Cyclically Adjusted Deficit The cyclically adjusted deficit is a measure for judging whether the budget deficit is cyclical or structural. A **cyclical deficit** is a budget deficit that is present only because real GDP is less than potential GDP and taxes are temporarily low and transfer

Figure 26.7 The Business Cycle and the Budget Deficit

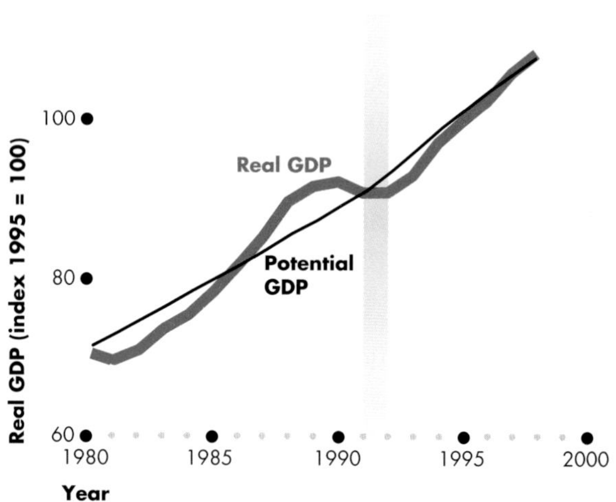

(a) Real GDP and potential GDP

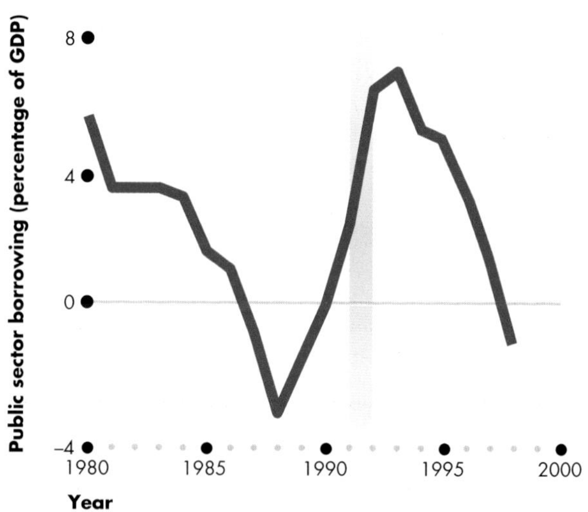

(b) The UK public sector borrowing requirement

As real GDP fluctuates around potential GDP (part a), the budget deficit fluctuates (part b). During a recession (shaded areas), tax revenues decrease, transfer payments increase and the budget deficit increases. The deficit also increases *before* a recession as the growth rate of real GDP slows and *after* a recession before the growth rate of real GDP speeds up. When the growth rate of real GDP is high during a recovery, tax revenues increase, transfer payments decrease and the deficit decreases.

Sources: ONS and Lombard Street Research Ltd.

Figure 26.8 Cyclical and Structural Deficits

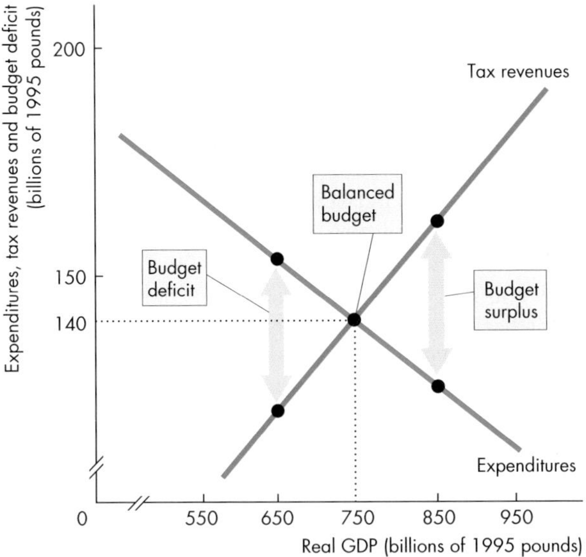

Government expenditures (blue line) decrease as real GDP increases because transfer payments decrease. Tax revenues (green line) increase as real GDP increases because most taxes are linked to income and expenditures. If real GDP is £750 billion, the government has a *balanced budget*. If real GDP is less than £750 billion, expenditures exceed tax revenues and the government has a budget deficit. If real GDP exceeds £750 billion, expenditures are less than tax revenues and the government has a budget surplus. If potential GDP is £750 billion, there is not a structural deficit – the budget deficits and surpluses are cyclical. But if potential GDP is less than £750 billion, there is a structural deficit.

Figure 26.9 Structural Budget Deficits in the European Union

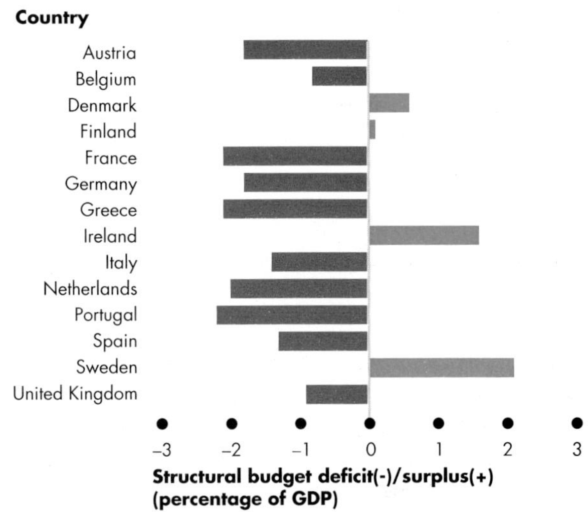

The OECD calculates that most of the countries in the European Union will have had a structural budget deficit in 1998. The United Kingdom is projected to have a structural budget deficit of 1.0 per cent of potential GDP. Portugal, France and Greece are expected to have higher structural budget deficits, while Belgium, Ireland and Sweden are expected to have structural budget surpluses.

Source: *OECD Economic Outlook*, December 1998. Reproduced by permission of the OECD.

payments are temporarily high. A **structural deficit** is a budget that is in deficit even though real GDP equals potential GDP. With a structural deficit, expenditures are too high relative to tax revenues over the entire business cycle.

Figure 26.8 illustrates the concepts of cyclical and structural deficits. The blue curve shows expenditures. When real GDP is less than potential GDP, transfer payments are temporarily high. As real GDP increases, transfer payments fall and expenditures decrease. The green curve shows tax revenues. Because most taxes increase with income, tax revenues increase as real GDP increases. In this example, if real GDP is £750 billion, the government has a *balanced budget*. Expenditures and tax revenues each equal £140 billion. If real GDP is £650 billion, expenditures exceed tax revenues and there is a budget deficit. And if real GDP is £850 billion, expenditures are less than tax revenues and there is a budget surplus.

To determine whether there is a structural deficit, we need to know potential GDP. If, in Figure 26.8, potential GDP is £750 billion, the budget has a structural deficit of zero. As the real GDP fluctuates, the budget fluctuates around zero. If, in Figure 26.8, potential GDP is £650 billion, there is a structural deficit, and if potential GDP is £850 billion, there is a structural surplus.

The OECD estimate that the United Kingdom has a structural budget deficit of only 0.9 per cent of potential GDP. The OECD calculate that there are a number of countries in the EU that have significant structural budget deficits. Figure 26.9 shows a selection of countries' structural budget deficits. Sweden, Ireland and Denmark have structural budget surpluses, but France, Greece, Portugal and Netherlands have large structural budget deficits. This means that unless public expenditure is brought under control, these countries will still have budget deficits even when real GDP equals potential GDP.

Review

- When the price level is fixed, a change in government purchases or lump-sum taxes has a multiplier effect on real GDP.
- The multiplier effect of a change in government purchases is greater than that of a change in lump-sum taxes because a pound of taxes initially changes aggregate expenditure by less than a pound.
- The presence of income taxes and international trade reduces the fiscal policy multipliers.
- Income taxes and unemployment benefits work as automatic stabilizers to dampen the business cycle.

We have now seen the immediate effects of fiscal policy when the price level is sticky. The next task is to see how, with the passage of more time and with some price level adjustments, these multiplier effects are modified.

Fiscal Policy Multipliers and the Price Level

We've seen how real GDP responds to changes in fiscal policy when the price level is fixed and all the adjustments that take place are in spending, income and production. Once production starts to change, prices also start to change. The price level and real GDP change together, and the economy moves to a new short-run equilibrium.

To study the simultaneous changes in real GDP and the price level that result from fiscal policy, we use the *AS–AD* model of Chapter 24, pp. 589–593. In the long run, the price level and the money wage rate responds to fiscal policy. As these adjustments occur the economy moves to a new long-run equilibrium.

We begin by looking at the effects of fiscal policy on aggregate demand and the *AD* curve.

Fiscal Policy and Aggregate Demand

The relationship between aggregate demand, aggregate expenditure, and equilibrium expenditure is covered in Chapter 25, pp. 609–613. You are now going to use what you learned there to work out what happens to aggregate demand, the price level, real GDP and jobs when fiscal policy changes. We'll start by looking at the effects of a change in fiscal policy on aggregate demand.

Figure 26.10 shows the effects of an increase in government purchases on aggregate demand. Initially, the aggregate expenditure curve is AE_0 in part (a), and the aggregate demand curve is AD_0 in part (b). The price level is 110, real GDP is £750 billion, and the economy is at point *a* in both parts of the figure. Now suppose that government purchases increase by £50 billion. At a constant price level of 110, the aggregate expenditure curve shifts upward to AE_1. This curve intersects the 45° line at an equilibrium expenditure of £950 billion at point *b*. This amount is the aggregate quantity of goods and services demanded at a price level of 110, as shown by point *b* in part (b). Point *b* lies on a new aggregate demand curve. The aggregate demand curve has shifted rightward to AD_1.

The distance by which the aggregate demand curve shifts rightward is determined by the government purchases multiplier. The larger the multiplier, the larger is the shift in the aggregate demand curve resulting from a given change in government purchases. In this example, a £50 billion increase in government purchases produces a £200 billion increase in the aggregate quantity of goods and services demanded at each price level. The multiplier is 4. So the £50 billion increase in government purchases shifts the aggregate demand curve rightward by £200 billion.

Figure 26.10 shows the effects of an increase in government purchases. But a similar effect occurs for *any* expansionary fiscal policy. An **expansionary fiscal policy** is an increase in government expenditures or a decrease in tax revenues.

Figure 26.10 Changes in Government Purchases and Aggregate Demand

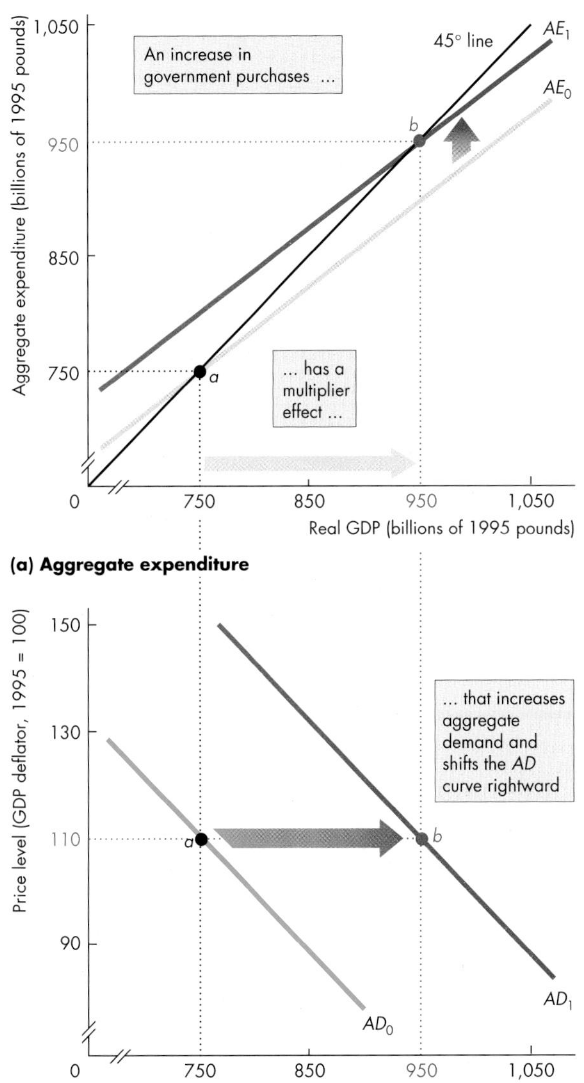

The price level is 130. When the aggregate expenditure curve is AE_0 (part a), the aggregate demand curve is AD_0 (part b). An increase in government purchases shifts the aggregate expenditure curve upward to AE_1. The new equilibrium occurs where AE_1 intersects the 45° line at a real GDP of £800 billion. Because the quantity of real GDP demanded at a price level of 130 increases to £800 billion, the aggregate demand curve shifts rightward to AD_1. The magnitude of the rightward shift of the aggregate demand curve is determined by the change in government purchases and the size of the multiplier.

Figure 26.10 can also be used to illustrate the effects of a contractionary fiscal policy. A **contractionary fiscal policy** is a decrease in government expenditures or an increase in tax revenues. In this case, start at point *b* in each part of the figure and decrease government expenditure. Aggregate demand decreases from AD_1 to AD_0.

Equilibrium GDP and the Price Level in the Short Run We've seen how an increase in government purchases increases aggregate demand. Let's now see how it changes real GDP and the price level. Figure 26.11(a) describes the economy. Aggregate demand is AD_0 and the short-run aggregate supply curve is *SAS*. (Check back to Chapter 24, if you need to refresh your understanding of the *SAS* curve.) Equilibrium is at point *a*, where the aggregate demand and short-run aggregate supply curves intersect. The price level is 110, and real GDP is £750 billion.

An increase in government purchases of £50 billion shifts the aggregate demand curve rightward from AD_0 to AD_1. While the price level is fixed at 110, the economy moves towards point *b* and real GDP increases towards £950 billion. But during the adjustment process, the price level does not remain constant. It gradually rises and the economy moves along the short-run aggregate supply curve to the point of intersection of the short-run aggregate supply curve and the new aggregate demand curve – point *c*. The price level rises to 126 and real GDP increases to £900 billion.

When we take the price-level effect into account, the increase in government purchases still has a multiplier effect on real GDP, but the effect is smaller than it would be if the price level remained constant. Also, the steeper the slope of the short-run aggregate supply curve, the larger is the increase in the price level, and the smaller is the increase in real GDP, the smaller is the government purchases multiplier. But the multiplier is not zero.

In the long run, real GDP equals potential GDP – the economy is at full-employment equilibrium. When real GDP equals potential GDP, an increase in aggregate demand has the same short-run effect as we have just worked out, but the long-run effect is different. The increasse in aggregate demand raises the price level, but in the long-run real GDP remains at potential GDP.

Let's see what happens if the government embarks on an expansionary fiscal policy when real GDP equals potential GDP.

Figure 26.11 Fiscal Policy, Real GDP and the Price Level

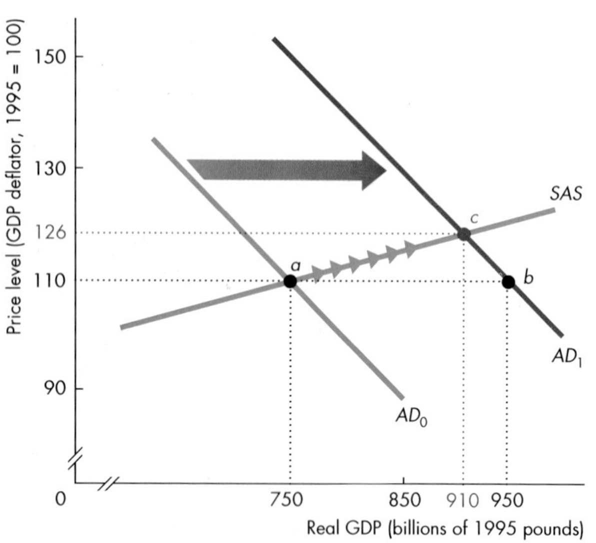

(a) Short-run effect

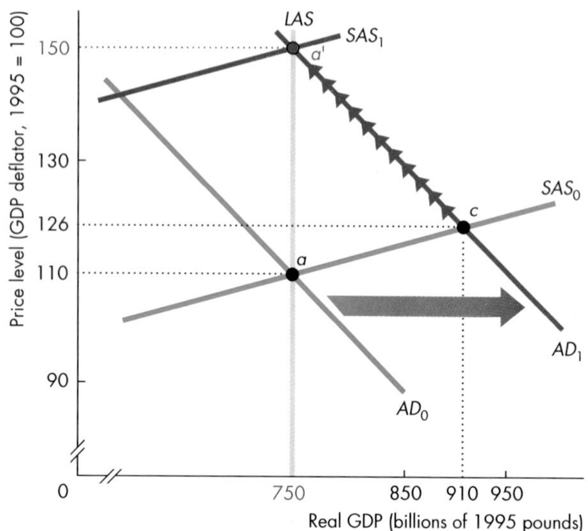

(b) Long-run effect

An increase in government purchases shifts the *AD* curve from AD_0 to AD_1. With a sticky price level, real GDP would have increased from £750 billion to £950 billion – to point *b*. But in the short run, the price level is not sticky and the economy moves along the *SAS* curve to point *c*. The price level increases to 126, and real GDP increases to £910 billion. The steeper the *SAS* curve, the larger is the increase in the price level and the smaller is the increase in real GDP.

Fiscal Expansion at Potential GDP

When real GDP equals potential GDP, unemployment is equal to the natural rate of unemployment. Suppose that the actual and natural rates of unemployment are high so that the government misakenly thinks that the unemployment rate exceeds the natural rate. The government tries to lower the unemployment rate by using an expansionary fiscal policy.

Figure 26.11(b) shows the effect of an expansionary fiscal policy when real GDP equals potential GDP. In this example, potential GDP is £750 billion. Aggregate demand increases and the aggregate demand curve shifts rightward from AD_0 to AD_1. The short-run equilibrium, point *c*, is an above full-employment equilibrium. The workforce is more than fully employed, and there are shortages of labour. Wage rates begin to increase. Higher wage rates increase costs, and short-run aggregate supply decreases. The *SAS* curve begins to shift leftward from SAS_0 to SAS_1. The economy moves up along the aggregate demand curve AD_1 toward point *a'*.

Eventually, when all adjustments to wage rates and the price level have been made, the price level is 150 and real GDP is again at potential GDP of £750 billion. The multiplier in the long run is zero. There has been a temporary decrease in the unemployment rate during the process you've just looked at but not a permanent decrease.

Review

- Changes in the price level decrease the effect of the fiscal policy multiplier on real GDP.
- When real GDP is less than potential GDP the effect of the fiscal policy multiplier on real GDP is greater than zero.
- In the long run, when real GDP equals potential GDP, fiscal policy influences only the price level. The multiplier effect on real GDP is zero.

Figure 26.12 Supply-Side Effects of Fiscal Policy

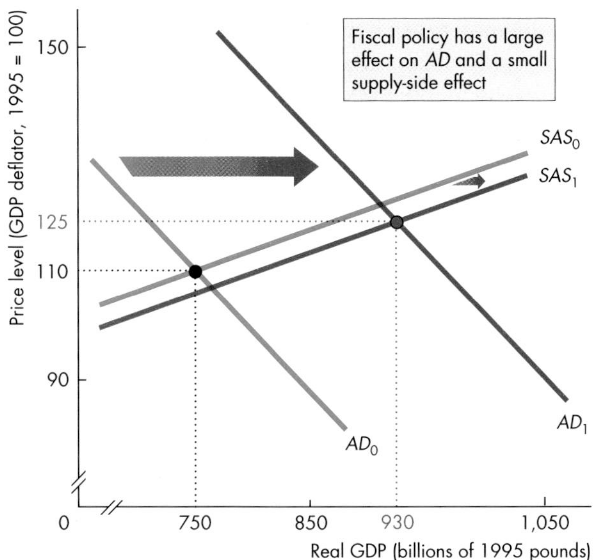

(a) The traditional view

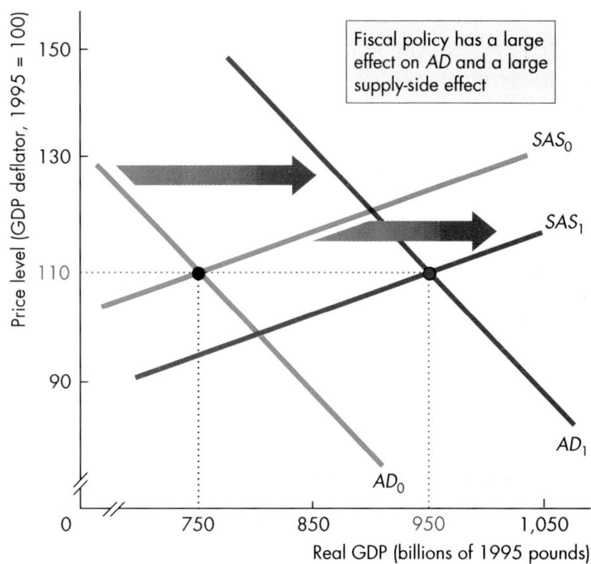

(b) The supply-side view

An expansionary fiscal policy such as a tax cut increases aggregate demand and shifts the *AD* curve rightward from AD_0 to AD_1 (both parts). Such a policy change also has a supply-side effect. If the supply-side effect is small, the *SAS* curve shifts rightward from SAS_0 to SAS_1 in part (a). In this case, the demand-side effect dominates the supply-side effect, real GDP increases and the price level rises.

If the supply-side effect of a tax cut is large, the *SAS* curve shifts rightward from SAS_0 to SAS_1 in part (b). In this case, the supply-side effect is as large as the demand-side effect. Real GDP increases and the price level remains constant. But if the supply-side effect was larger than the demand-side effect, the price level would actually fall.

Fiscal Policy and Aggregate Supply

So far we've considered only the demand-side effects of fiscal policy. But fiscal policy also has supply-side effects. On the expenditures side, the government buys capital goods, which increases the quantity of real GDP supplied. On the tax revenues side, taxes on labour income act as a disincentive to work and decrease the quantity of labour employed and the quantity of real GDP supplied. With fewer people employed, the jobless rate is higher.

Similarly, taxes on interest income weaken the incentive to save and invest and so decrease the quantity of capital and decrease the quantity of real GDP supplied. This effect is an ongoing one that affects not only the current level of real GDP but also the trend growth rate of potential GDP.

The influences of fiscal policy on the quantity of real GDP supplied mean that to assess the impact of an expansionary fiscal policy, especially a tax cut, we must take into account changes in both aggregate demand and aggregate supply.

Figure 26.12 shows the supply-side effects of an expansionary fiscal policy such as a tax cut. Part (a) shows the effects that are most likely to occur. An expansionary fiscal policy has a large effect on aggregate demand and a small effect on aggregate supply. The aggregate demand curve shifts rightward by a larger amount than the rightward shift in the short-run aggregate supply curve. The outcome is a rise in the price level and an increase in real GDP.

During the 1980s, a school of thought known as the *supply-siders* became prominent in the United States. Although their ideas did not catch on as well in the United Kingdom, they did have their supporters. Supply-siders believe that tax cuts would strengthen incentives and have a large effect on aggregate supply. Figure 26.12(b) shows the effects that supply-siders believe might occur. An expansionary fiscal policy still has a large effect on aggregate demand but it has a similarly large effect on aggregate supply. The aggregate demand curve and the short-run aggregate supply curve shift rightward by similar amounts. In this particular case, the price level remains constant and real GDP increases. A slightly larger increase in aggregate supply would have brought a fall in the price level, a possibility that some supply-siders believe could occur.

The general point that everyone agrees with is that an expansionary fiscal policy that strengthens incentives increases real GDP by more and is less inflationary than one that does not change or that weakens incentives.

Review

- Income taxes have incentive effects on the supply of labour and supply of capital, and a cut in the income tax rate increases potential GDP.
- A tax cut increases both aggregate supply and aggregate demand. There is disagreement about which effect is larger. A tax cut increases real GDP, but it can either raise or lower the price level.

You've seen how fiscal policy influences the way real GDP fluctuates around its trend and how it influences the long-term growth rate of real GDP. Your next task is to study the other main arm of macroeconomic policy, monetary policy. We begin in the next chapter by describing the monetary system of a modern economy.

Summary

Key Points

The Government Budget (pp. 632–637)

- The government budget finances the activities of the government and is used to stabilize real GDP.
- Tax revenues come from personal income and corporate taxes, social security contributions, and indirect taxes.
- Government expenditures include transfer payments, purchases of goods and services, and debt interest.
- The budget balance is equal to tax revenues minus expenditures.

Fiscal Policy Multipliers (pp. 637–644)

- Fiscal policy actions are either automatic, or discretionary.
- The government purchases multiplier equals $1/(1 - MPC)$. The lump-sum tax multiplier equals $-MPC/(1 - MPC)$.
- The balanced budget multiplier equals 1.
- Income taxes and benefits make each of the multipliers smaller than they otherwise would be. They also bring fluctuations in tax revenues and transfer payments over the business cycle and help the shock-absorbing capacities of the economy.

Fiscal Policy Multipliers and the Price Level (pp. 644–646)

- An expansionary fiscal policy increases aggregate demand and shifts the aggregate demand curve rightward. It increases real GDP and raises the price level.
- A contractionary fiscal policy has the opposite effect.
- Price level changes dampen fiscal policy multiplier effects.
- When real GDP equals potential GDP, an expansionary fiscal policy increases the price level but leaves real GDP unchanged.
- The fiscal policy multiplier in the long-run is zero.

Fiscal Policy and Aggregate Supply (pp. 647–648)

- Fiscal policy has supply-side effects because the government buys capital goods that increase aggregate supply and taxes weaken the incentives to work, save and invest.
- These supply-side influences mean that an expansionary fiscal policy increases real GDP and if the supply-side effect is stronger than the demand-side effect, an expansionary fiscal policy might lower the price level.

Key Figures

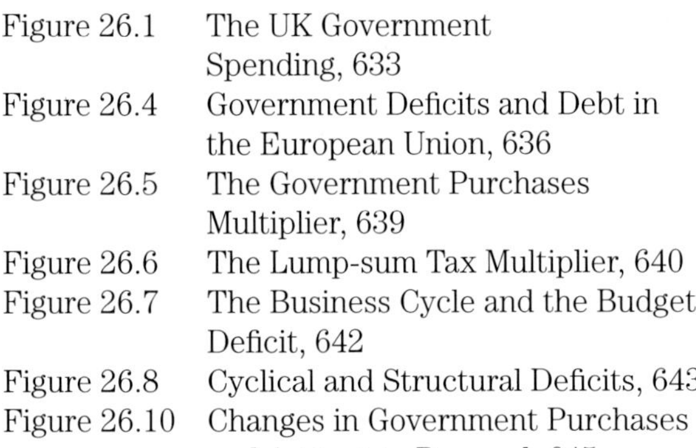

Key Terms

Automatic fiscal policy, 637
Balanced budget, 633
Balanced budget multiplier, 640
Budget deficit or PSNCR, 633
Budget surplus, 633
Contractionary fiscal policy, 645
Cyclically adjusted deficit, 642
Discretionary fiscal policy, 637
Expansionary fiscal policy, 644
Fiscal policy, 632
Government budget, 632
Government debt, 635
Government purchases multiplier, 638
Induced taxes, 641
Lump-sum taxes, 637
Lump-sum tax multiplier, 639
Structural deficit, 643

Review Questions

1. Describe the main purposes of the government budget.
2. Describe the features of the 1998 UK government budget.
3. List the main sources of tax revenues and the main components of expenditures in the UK.
4. Compare the UK government budget deficit with deficits in other EU countries.
5. Compare the UK debt–income ratio with those of other EU countries.
6. Distinguish between automatic and discretionary fiscal policy.
7. Explain why an increase in government purchases has a multiplier effect on real GDP when the price level is sticky.
8. Explain why the lump-sum tax multiplier is smaller than the government purchases multiplier.
9. Explain why there is an increase in real GDP when both taxes and expenditures increase by the same amount.
10. Explain how induced taxes and benefits influence the fiscal policy multipliers.
11. Explain how international trade influences the fiscal policy multipliers.

12 Explain how the deficit fluctuates over the business cycle and define the structural deficit.

13 Explain how the multiplier effect is modified in the short run when the price level begins to change.

14 Explain what happens following an increase in government purchases if real GDP equals potential GDP.

15 Explain why the deficit can be a burden on future generations.

Problems

1 You are given the following information about the economy of Euroland. Autonomous consumption expenditure is 10 billion euros and the marginal propensity to consume is 0.9. Investment is 50 billion euros, government purchases of goods and services are 40 billion euros, lump-sum taxes are 40 billion euros. Euroland has no exports and no imports.

- a The government cuts its purchases of goods and services to 30 billion euros. What is the change in equilibrium expenditure?
- b What is the value of the government purchases multiplier?
- c The government continues to purchase 40 billion euros worth of goods and services and cuts lump-sum taxes to 30 billion euros. What is the change in equilibrium expenditure?
- d What is the value of the tax multiplier?
- e The government simultaneously cuts both its purchases of goods and services and taxes to 30 billion euros. What is the change in equilibrium expenditure?
- f What is the value of the balanced budget multiplier?

2 Euroland becomes outward looking and starts to export. Its exports are 50 billion euros. It also begins to import and its imports are 10 per cent of GDP. Everything else is the same as in Problem 1.

- a The government cuts its purchases of goods and services to 30 billion euros. What is the change in equilibrium expenditure?
- b What is the value of the government purchases multiplier?
- c Is the new government purchases multiplier in Euroland greater or smaller than it was in Problem 1? Why?
- d The government continues to purchase 40 billion euros worth of goods and services and cuts lump-sum taxes to 30 billion euros. What is the change in equilibrium expenditure?
- e What is the value of the tax multiplier?
- f The government simultaneously cuts both its purchases of goods and services and taxes to 30 billion euros. What is the change in equilibrium expenditure?
- g What is the value of the balanced budget multiplier? Compare the balanced budget multiplier in this case with the one in Problem 1.

3 In the economy of Euroland, the marginal propensity to consume is 0.8. Investment is 60 billion euros, government purchases of goods and services are 50 billion euros, and lump-sum taxes are 60 billion euros. Euroland has no exports and no imports.

- a The government increases its purchases of goods and services to 60 billion euros. What is the change in equilibrium expenditure?
- b What is the value of the government purchases multiplier?
- c The government continues to purchase 60 billion euros worth of goods and services and increases lump-sum taxes to 70 billion euros. What is the change in equilibrium expenditure?
- d What is the value of the tax multiplier?
- e The government simultaneously increases both its purchases of goods and services and taxes by 10 billion euros. What is the change in equilibrium expenditure? Why does equilibrium expenditure increase?

4 An economy has no foreign trade and has only lump-sum taxes. Its lump-sum tax multiplier is

four-fifths the magnitude of its government purchases multiplier. What is the marginal propensity to consume in this economy?

5 Suppose that the price level in the economy of Euroland as described in Problem 1 is 100. The economy is also at full employment.

a If the government of Euroland increases its purchases of goods and services by 10 billion euros, what happens to the quantity of real GDP demanded?

b In the short run, does equilibrium real GDP increase by more than, less than, or the same amount as the increase in the quantity of real GDP demanded?

c In the long run, does equilibrium real GDP increase by more than, less than, or the same amount as the increase in the quantity of real GDP demanded?

d In the short run, does the price level in Euroland rise, fall, or remain unchanged?

e In the long run, does the price level in Euroland rise, fall, or remain unchanged?

6 Suppose that the price level in the economy of Euroland as described in Problem 1 is 100. The economy is still at full employment.

a If the government decreases its purchases of goods and services by 5 billion euros, what happens to the quantity of real GDP demanded?

b How does Euroland's aggregate demand curve change? Draw a two-part diagram that is similar to Figure 26.10 to illustrate the change in both the *AE* curve and the *AD* curve.

c In the short run, does equilibrium real GDP decrease by more than, less than, or the same amount as the increase in the quantity of real GDP demanded?

d In the short run, does the price level in Euroland rise, fall, or remain unchanged?

e Why does real GDP decrease by a smaller amount than the decrease in aggregate demand?

7 In the figure, aggregate demand is initially AD_0 and short-run aggregate supply is initially SAS_0. A tax cut increases aggregate demand to AD_1. This same tax cut influences incentives and increases aggregate supply. At first, there is no supply-side effect. Then short-run aggregate supply increases to SAS_1. Eventually, short-run aggregate supply increases to SAS_2.

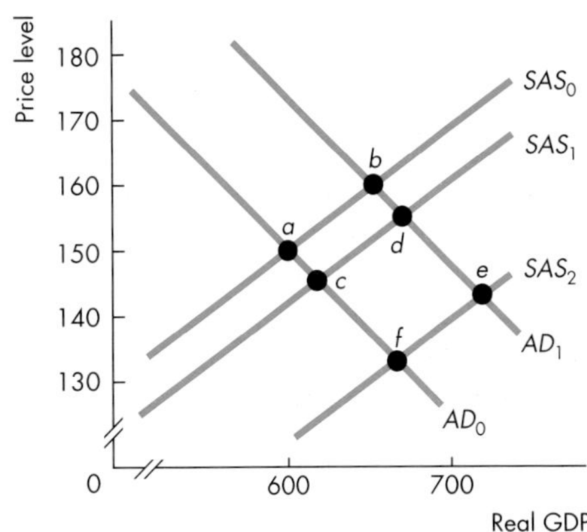

8 Study *Reading Between the Lines* on pp. 652–653, and then answer the following questions.

a Analyse the potential outcome on the Italian economy of a cut in the budget deficit.

b What are the implications for the budget deficit if the economy is in decline because of weak exports?

c How does your answer change if supply-side factors are significant?

9 Use the link on the Parkin, Powell and Matthews Web site to obtain data on the amounts of government expenditure in the main industrial countries. Then use the fiscal policy multiplier analysis that you've learned about in this chapter to predict which countries have strong automatic stabilizers and which have weak ones. Explain the reasons for your predictions.

Fiscal Policy in Italy

Business Week, 8 March 1999

Lowering the deficit, *poco a poco*

James C. Cooper and Kathleen Madigan

On Feb. 8, the European Union's Finance Ministers gave the O.K. to Italy's three-year budget and economic plan, but they cautioned that more spending cuts may be needed. Indeed, with economic growth faltering, analysts believe that the blueprint is too ambitious but that the downward deficit trend should remain in place.

The government says it will cut its deficit from an expected 2.7% of GDP in 1998, to 2% in 1999, and down to 1% by 2001. However, growth will almost certainly fall short of the budget's projection of 2.5% growth for 1999. Officials already have said that yet-to-be-reported 1998 growth was only about 1.4%, and on Feb. 15, the government sliced its 1999 forecast to only 2%, which most economists believe is still too high.

The unexpectedly sharp drop in December industrial production suggests that Italy's 1998 weakness, the worst in the euro zone, is carrying into 1999. Indeed, output through February remained weak based on the latest survey by the industry group Confindustria. The malaise in the euro zone's third-largest economy accents the region's broader frailty, recently highlighted by Germany's 0.4% drop in fourth-quarter GDP. Like Germany, Italy depends heavily on exports, more than half of which go to its European neighbors, where Italy's export growth is stagnant. Foreign shipments to Asia and other depressed markets are off sharply.

Italy, which was admitted to the euro zone with overall debt at twice the euro zone guideline of 60% of GDP, must maintain its new fiscal responsibility. But the weak, three-month-old government is also committed to reducing unemployment.

The good news is that the sharp drop in interest rates in the runup to the euro will spur growth later in 1999, and with one-year rates well below the 4.5% budget projection, significant savings on debt service will offset some of the revenues lost to slower growth. The likely result: While the 1999 deficit will not make the 2% goal without politically and economically difficult interim action, the deficit should still come in well below the 1998 level.

The Essence of the Story

- The European Union finance Ministers agreed to a three-budget plan for Italy but warned that the deficit may need to be cut further.
- The Italian government plans to cut its budget deficit from 2.7 per cent of GDP to 2 per cent in 1999 and to 1 per cent by 2000.
- The unexpected decline in Italian real GDP growth means that tax revenues are less than expected and meeting the targets will be difficult.
- The government was admitted to the European Monetary Union with an overall debt to GDP ratio in excess of twice the guideline of 60 per cent and is expected to show fiscal responsibility by cutting the budget deficit.
- The problem for the Italian government is that they are also committed to reducing unemployment.

Economic Analysis

■ What are the likely effects of the proposed cuts in the government budget deficit if they do actually occur? Any effects will depend on whether the cuts are considered to be permanent or temporary.

■ Since the target budget deficit was announced in advance, people may think that the implied cuts in government spending are permanent. Or they may think that the government has little room to manoeuvre given its committment to reduce unemployment and expect the government not to cut the deficit.

■ Figure 1 shows the possible effect of the government plan to cut the deficit. The economy is initially at point *a*. Figure 2 shows that the growth in real GDP was declining in 1998. If the cuts are temporary or if they are not believed, aggregate demand in Figure 1 will increase only moderately from AD_{98} to AD_{99}. Real GDP and inflation will rise very little.

■ The LAS curve moves from LAS_{98} to LAS_{99} creating a larger recessionary gap and higher or at least not lower unemployment.

■ If the cuts are expected to be permanent, the rate of interest on Italian bonds will decline and creating significant saving on the debt service. Italian firms borrowing in the Italian capital market will pay a lower rate of interest and invest causing aggregate supply to increase. Figure 3 shows this effect.

■ In Figure 3, potential GDP increases the long-run aggregate supply curve shifts from LAS_{98} to LAS_{99}, and the short-run aggregate supply curve shifts to SAS_{99}. The real GDP growth rate increases and the inflation rate slows even further.

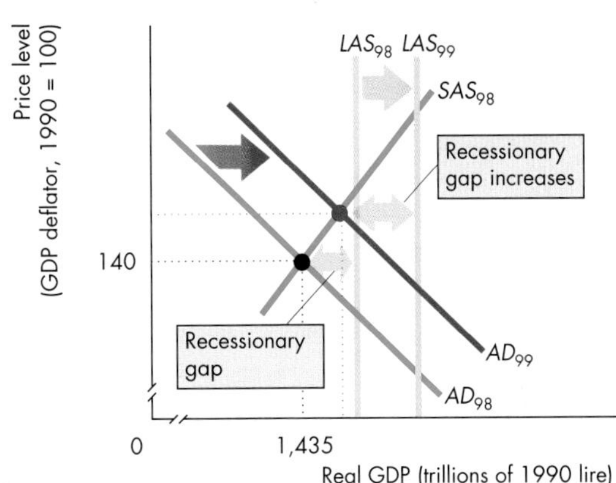

Figure 1 Planned cut in deficit

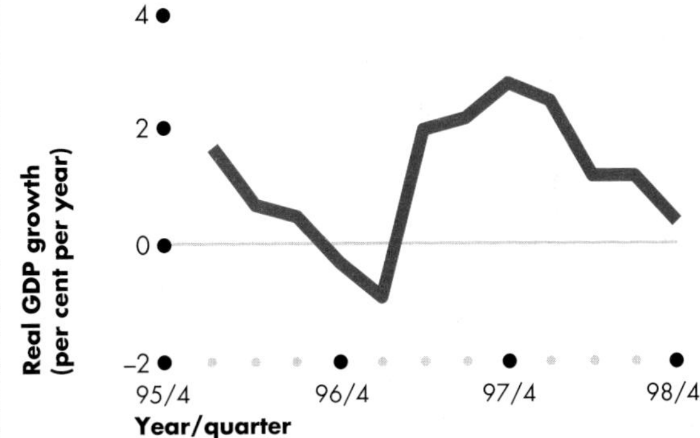

Figure 2 Real GDP growth

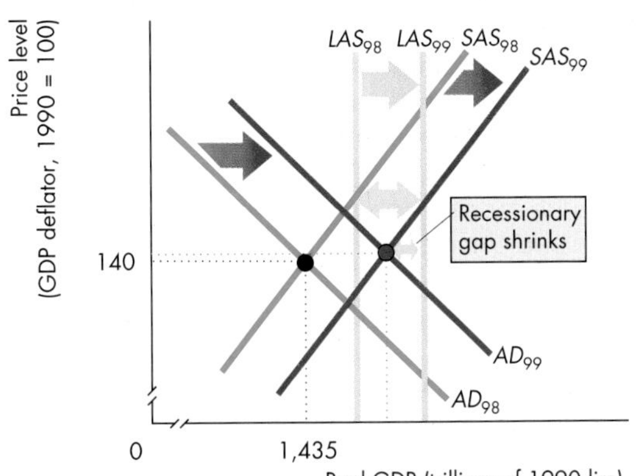

Figure 3 Permanent cut in deficit

Part 8

The Central Bank and Monetary Policy

Talking with **Charles Goodhart**

Charles Goodhart, CBE, FBA is the Norman Sosnow Professor of Banking and Finance at the London School of Economics. Before joining the LSE in 1985, he worked at the Bank of England for seventeen years as a monetary adviser, becoming a Chief Adviser in 1980. In 1997 he was appointed one of the outside independent members of the Bank of England's new Monetary Policy Committee. Earlier he had taught at Cambridge and LSE. Besides numerous articles, he has written a couple of books on monetary history, and a graduate monetary textbook, *Money, Information and Uncertainty* (2nd edn 1989); and has published two collections of papers on monetary policy, *Monetary Theory and Practice* (1984) and *The Central Bank and The Financial System* (1995); and an institutional study of *The Evolution of Central Banks*, revised and republished (MIT Press) in 1988.

How did you become interested in economics?

My father had always wanted me to become a businessman but I started off with economics in Cambridge and then found that I was fascinated by it and reasonably good at it. I also thought that I might be able to contribute.

Many economists of our generation were influenced by the debates between Keynesians and Monetarists – do these debates have any relevance for economic policy today?

I think they do. Particularly as to the relative effectiveness of fiscal and monetary policy. Although that kind of debate has been somewhat overshadowed and overtaken by the larger debate between the Neo-Classicals, who believe in very flexible wages and prices, and the older schools which implicitly believed in a degree of inertia in price wage adjustments. In many respects some of the older monetarists and older Keynesians are now hardly distinguishable but are both now quite sharply distinguishable from, real business cycle theorists and those who believe that the best paradigm to start with is a perfectly functioning market.

What is monetary targeting? Do you think it is important?

Monetary targeting depends on a stable relationship between monetary growth and the growth of nominal incomes or to put it another way, velocity is a predictable function of a small number of variables. Unfortunately the degree of predictability of velocity was never high enough to be able to use monetary targets with great conviction as a means of trying to control inflation and so consequently I have always been in favour of a degree of nominal income or inflation targeting but not strictly monetary targeting. With an inflation targeting framework one uses the single instrument of interest rates to try and directly control the rate of and growth of inflation over the appropriate horizon which because of the lags is somewhere between a one-year to a two-and-a-half-year horizon.

Not many people have an economic law named after them. Can you explain what Goodhart's Law is?

It is a kind of version of the Lucas Critique. The Lucas Critique – which is a much more serious piece of economics than Goodhart's Law – says that peoples' behaviour depends on their expectations of how the authorities are going to behave and when the authorities behave in a different way then peoples' own behaviour will adjust and you cannot assess how that is going to happen beforehand. So, for example, if there exists an apparent relationship between economic behaviour and a set of variables within the economy, then if the authorities try and use that relationship to guide the economy, they will find that the relationship changes out from under them. In some respects Goodhart's Law goes beyond the Lucas Critique and covers other aspects as well. One of the aspects is that once the government has tied itself to trying to use a variable to guide the economy, in order to show they have been successful, the government itself will have an incentive to corrupt or to adjust the variable simply to appear successful. Say you have a monetary target, there is some incentive for the Government to shift accounting practices or techniques so as to make the monetary growth come equal to the target and thereby themselves change the system. So that the relationship between money and nominal income will become weaker than it had been in the past.

You are a member of The Bank of England Monetary Policy Committee. What should the Bank of England be doing to minimize the risk of inflation and recession?

Our requirement is to try and achieve a steady rate of growth of RPIX inflation growth at a stable two-and-a-half per cent per year. Our objective is given to us by the Chancellor. Our aim is to vary interest rates so as to make the actual inflation some year to two years ahead, come into line with what the Chancellor has chosen for us. We do not have any control over the longer term trend growth of incomes. What we can do is to try and bring inflation back to our target over a sensible horizon. We don't try and vary interest rates and asset prices, for example, too dramatically in order to get back to target very quickly and thereby lead to undesirable short-term fluctuations in output. What we cannot control and have no intention of trying to, is the average rate of growth of output. What we can try and limit is unnecessary fluctuations in output around the trend that is given by real factors and nothing to do with us.

Which economists have influenced you most and why?

My favourite economists are George Shackle and James Tobin. They both seem to me to have a clearer idea about the order or the nature of uncertainties of the economy and the way that they deal with those uncertainties. Another economist who I have always been very fond of is Hyman Minsky. Of course, one is entirely influenced by Keynes, but then, of the English economists, Dennis Roberts, most but not all of the time, and John Hicks, was, of course, enormously important.

CHAPTER 27

Money

After studying this chapter you will be able to:

- Define money and describe its functions
- Explain the economic functions of banks and other financial institutions
- Describe the financial innovations of the 1980s
- Explain how banks create money
- Explain why the quantity of money is an important economic magnitude
- Explain the quantity theory of money

Money Makes the World Go Around

Money, like fire and the wheel, has been around for a very long time. An incredible array of items have served as money. Cowrie shells were used in the Pacific Islands, wampum (beads made from shells) were used by North American Indians, whales' teeth were used by Fijians and tobacco was used by early American colonists. In ancient Greece, cattle served as money, indeed the word 'pecuniary' is derived from *pecunia*, the Latin for money, which in turn is derived from *pecus*, meaning cattle. Today, when we want to buy something, we use coins or notes, write a cheque, or present a credit card. Tomorrow, we'll use a 'smart card' that keeps track of spending and that our pocket computer can read. Are all these things money? ◆ When we deposit some coins or notes into a bank or building society, is that still money? What happens when the bank or building society lends the money in our deposit to someone else? How can we get our money back if it's been lent out? Does lending by banks and building societies create money – out of thin air? ◆ In the 1970s, there were two types of account with banks. There were demand deposits that did not pay interest, and there were time deposits, or deposit accounts as they are known in the United Kingdom, that did pay interest. Today, there's a wide variety of accounts that provide the convenience of a cheque facility and the income of a savings deposit. Why were these new kinds of bank deposits introduced? ◆ During the 1970s and periods of the 1980s, the quantity of money in existence in the United Kingdom increased very quickly, but in the 1990s it increased at a much slower pace. In Russia and in some Latin American countries the quantity of money has increased at an extremely rapid pace. In Switzerland and Germany, the quantity of money has increased at a slower pace. Does the rate of increase in the quantity of money matter? What are the effects of an increasing quantity of money on our economy?

◆ ◆ ◆ ◆ In this chapter we'll study that useful invention: money. We'll look at its functions, its different forms, and the way it is defined and measured in the United Kingdom today. We'll also study banks and other financial institutions and explain how they create money. Finally, we'll examine the effects of money growth on the economy.

What Is Money?

What do cowrie shells, wampum, whales' teeth, tobacco, cattle and pennies have in common? Why are they all examples of money? To answer these questions we need a definition of money. **Money** is any commodity or token that is generally acceptable as a means of payment. A **means of payment** is a method of settling a debt. When a payment has been made there is no remaining obligation between the parties to a transaction. So what cowrie shells, wampum, whales' teeth, cattle and pennies have in common is that they have served (or still do serve) as the means of payment. But money has three other functions as:

1 A medium of exchange.
2 A unit of account.
3 A store of value.

Table 27.1 The Unit of Account Function of Money Simplifies Price Comparisons

Good	Price in money units	Price in units of another good
Cinema ticket	£4.00 each	4 pints of beer
Beer	£1.00 per pint	2 ice-cream cones
Ice cream	£0.50 per cone	1 cup of tea
Tea	£0.50 per cup	5 rolls of mints
Mints	£0.10 per roll	1 local phone call

Money as a unit of account. 1 cinema ticket costs £4 and 1 cup of tea costs 50 pence, so a film costs 8 cups of tea (£4.00/0.5 = 24).
No unit of account. You go to a cinema and learn that the price of a film is 4 pints of beer. You go to a café and learn that a cup of tea cost 5 rolls of mints. But how many rolls of mints does seeing a film cost you? To answer that question, you go to the Students' Union bar and find that a pint of beer costs 2 ice-cream cones. Now you head for the ice-cream shop, where an ice cream costs one cup of tea. Now you get out your pocket calculator: 1 film costs 4 pints of beer, or 8 ice-cream cones, or 8 cups of tea, or 40 rolls of mints!

Medium of Exchange

A *medium of exchange* is an object that is generally accepted in exchange for goods and services. Money acts as such a medium. Without money, it would be necessary to exchange goods and services directly for other goods and services – an exchange called **barter**. For example, if you want to buy a hamburger, you offer the paperback novel you've just finished reading in exchange for it. Barter requires a *double coincidence of wants*, a situation that occurs when Erika wants to buy what Kazia wants to sell, and Kazia wants to buy what Erika wants to sell. To get your hamburger, you must find someone who's selling hamburgers and who wants your paperback novel. Money guarantees that there is a double coincidence of wants because people with something to sell will always accept money in exchange for it. Money acts as a lubricant that smoothes the mechanism of exchange.

Unit of Account

A *unit of account* is an agreed measure for stating the prices of goods and services. To get the most out of your budget you have to figure out, among other things, whether seeing one more film is worth the price you have to pay, not in pounds and pence, but in terms of the number of ice creams, beers and cups of tea that you have to give up. It's easy to do such calculations when all these goods have prices in terms of pounds and pence (see Table 27.1). If a cinema ticket costs £4 and a pint of beer in the Students' Union costs £1, you know straight away that seeing one more film costs you 4 pints of beer. If a cup of tea costs 50 pence, one more cinema ticket costs 8 cups of tea. You need only one calculation to figure out the opportunity cost of any pair of goods and services.

But imagine how troublesome it would be if your local cinema posted its price as 4 pints of beer; and if the Students' Union announced that the price of a pint of beer was 2 ice-cream cones; and if the corner shop posted the price of an ice-cream cone as 1 cup of tea; and if the café priced a cup of tea as 5 rolls of mints! Now how much running around and calculating do you have to do to work out how much that film is going to cost you in terms of the beer, ice cream, tea, or mints that you must give up to see it? You get the answer for beer straight away from the sign posted at the cinema, but for all the other goods you're going to have to visit many different stores to establish the price of each commodity in terms of another and then calculate prices in units that are relevant for your own decision. Cover up the column labelled 'price in money units' in Table 27.1 and see how hard it is to figure out the number of local telephone calls it costs to see one film. It is much simpler for everyone to express their prices in terms of pounds and pence.

Store of Value

Any commodity or token that can be held and exchanged later for goods and services is called a *store of value*. Money acts as a store of value. If it did not, it would not be acceptable in exchange for goods and services. The more stable the value of a commodity or token, the better it can act as a store of value, and the more useful it is as money. There are no stores of value that are completely safe. The value of a physical object, such as a house, a car, or a work of art, fluctuates over time. The value of commodities and tokens used as money also fluctuate and, when there is inflation, they persistently fall in value.

Money must satisfy all three functions discussed above. Therefore money must be a medium of exchange, a unit of account and a store of value. But the most important function is the medium of exchange. Something can be a store of value, like a national savings account you can obtain at the post office, but it cannot be used to buy something. Similarly, a unit of account alone is not money unless it is first a medium of exchange. An example of a unit of account that is not money in the strict sense is the euro. The euro becomes money in the strict sense when it comes into general circulation in 2002.

The objects used as money have evolved over many centuries and we can identify four main forms of money:

1 Commodity money.
2 Convertible paper money.
3 Fiat money.
4 Deposit money.

Commodity Money

A physical commodity that is valued in its own right and also used as a means of payment is **commodity money**. An amazing array of items have served as commodity money at different times and places, seven of which were described at the beginning of this chapter. But the most common commodity monies have been coins made from metals such as gold, silver and copper. The first known coins were made in Lydia, a Greek city-state, at the beginning of the seventh century BC.

There are two problems with commodity money. First, there is a constant temptation to cheat on the value of the money. Two methods of cheating have been commonly used – clipping and debasement. *Clipping* is reducing the size of coins by an imperceptible amount, thereby lowering their metallic content. *Debasement* is the creation of a coin that has a lower silver or gold content (the balance being made up of some cheaper metal).

The temptation to lower the value of commodity money led to a phenomenon known as Gresham's Law, after the sixteenth-century British financial expert, Sir Thomas Gresham. **Gresham's Law** is the tendency for bad (debased) money to drive good (not debased) money out of circulation. To see why Gresham's Law works, suppose you are paid with two coins, one debased and the other not. Each coin has the same value if you use it to buy goods. But the good coin is more valuable as a commodity than it is as money. You will not, therefore, use the good coin as money. You will always pay with a debased coin (if you have one). In this way, bad money drives good money out of circulation.

The second problem with commodity money is its opportunity cost. Gold and silver used as money could be used to make jewellery or ornaments instead. This opportunity cost creates incentives to find alternatives to the commodity itself for use in the exchange process. One such alternative is a paper claim to commodity money.

Convertible Paper Money

When a paper claim to a commodity circulates as a means of payment, that claim is called **convertible paper money**. The first known example of paper money occurred in China during the Ming dynasty (1368–99 AD). This form of money was also used extensively throughout Europe in the Middle Ages.

The inventiveness of goldsmiths and their clients led to the widespread use of convertible paper money. Because gold was valuable, goldsmiths had well-guarded safes in which to keep their own gold. They also rented space to artisans and others who wanted to put their gold in safe-keeping and issued a receipt entitling them to reclaim their 'deposits' on demand. (These receipts were similar to the cloakroom ticket that you get at a theatre or museum.) Because the gold receipts entitled the holder of the receipt to reclaim gold, they were 'as good as gold' and circulated as money. When Isabella of Spain bought some land from Henry IV, she simply gave him a gold receipt for the appropriate value. The paper money is *backed* by the gold held by a goldsmith and is *convertible* into commodity money – gold.

Fractional Backing – the Origin of Banking

Once a convertible paper money system is operating and people are using paper claims to gold rather than gold itself as the means of payment, goldsmiths notice that their vaults are storing a lot of gold that is never withdrawn. This gives them a brilliant idea. Why not lend people gold receipts? The goldsmith can charge interest on the loan and the loan is created just by writing on a piece of paper. As long as the number of such receipts created is not too large in relation to the stock of gold in the goldsmith's safe, the goldsmith is in no danger of not being able to honour his promise to convert receipts into gold on demand. The gold in the goldsmith's safe is a *fraction* of the gold receipts in circulation. By this device, *fractionally backed* convertible paper money was invented.

Except for a brief period after World War I, between 1921 and 1931, the United Kingdom was on a **gold standard**. The gold standard was a monetary system with fractionally backed convertible paper in which the pound sterling could be converted into gold at a guaranteed value on demand. The gold value of the pound was fixed by the market price of gold in terms of silver and the silver content of the shilling. The old units of account had 20 shillings to the pound, which gave the convertible value of the pound to gold as the value of the silver content of 20 shillings. Until the 1880s the United Kingdom was the only country in the world that maintained a gold standard. Being on the gold standard meant that it was easy to calculate the value of one currency, such as the pound, in terms of another, such as the US dollar. The amount of gold one pound sterling could be exchanged for was just over 486 per cent of the amount of gold one US dollar could buy, and so the value of the pound was fixed at $4.86 until 1931.

Even with fractionally backed paper money, valuable commodities that could be used for other productive activities are tied up in the exchange process. There remains an incentive to find a yet more efficient way of facilitating exchange and of freeing up the commodities used to back the paper money. This alternative is fiat money.

Fiat Money

The term *fiat* means 'let it be done' or 'by order of the authority'. **Fiat money** is an intrinsically worthless (or almost worthless) commodity that serves the functions of money. Some of the earliest fiat monies were the continental currency issued during the American War of Independence and the 'greenbacks' issued during the American Civil War, which circulated until 1879. These early experiments with fiat money ended in rapid inflation because the amount of money created was allowed to increase quickly, causing the money to lose value. Provided the quantity of fiat money is not allowed to grow too rapidly, it has a reasonably steady value in terms of the goods and services that it buys.

The notes and coins that we use in the United Kingdom today – collectively known as **currency** – are examples of fiat money. They are money because the government, through the Bank of England, declares them to be so. The Bank of England, which is the UK central bank, has a virtual monopoly in issuing notes in the UK. In Scotland, various banks issue similar notes but they are fully backed by Bank of England notes. Because of the creation of fiat money, people are willing to accept a piece of paper with a special watermark, printed in special ink and worth not more than a few pence as a commodity, in exchange for £20 worth of goods and services. The small metal coin that we call 10 pence is worth almost nothing as a piece of metal, but it pays for a local phone call and many other small commodities. The replacement of commodity money by fiat money enables the commodities themselves to be used productively.

Deposit Money

In the modern world, there is a fourth type of money – deposit money. **Deposit money** consists of deposits at banks and building societies. This type of money is an accounting entry in an electronic database in the banks' and building societies' computers. It is money because it is used to settle debts. In fact, it is the main means of settling debts in modern societies. The owner of a deposit transfers ownership to another person simply by writing a cheque – an instruction to a bank – that tells the bank to change its database, debiting the account of one depositor and crediting the account of another.

We'll have more to say about deposit money shortly. But before doing so, let's look at the different forms of money and their relative magnitudes in the United Kingdom today.

The Measure of Money

In most countries, money consists of *currency* (notes and coins) and *deposits* at banks and other financial institutions. There are different types of deposits and, as a result, different measures of money. Deposits are classified as sight deposits and time deposits. A sight deposit is a chequeable deposit. A person holding such a deposit will issue cheques from their sight deposit account. A time deposit is a deposit that has a fixed term to maturity. Although this is not usually a chequeable deposit, technological advances in the banking industry have made it easy to switch funds from time deposits to sight deposits. The cost of switching funds is the bank charge and the penalty of lost interest. Because of the ease with which time deposits can be switched into sight deposits, they are included in the definition of money. The official measure of money in the United Kingdom is known as **M4**. M4 includes currency held by the public and their holdings of bank and building society deposits, but does *not* include currency held by banks and building societies. In Germany and France, the main measure of money is M3. M3 basically consists of currency in circulation plus sight and time deposits.

The many measures of money used in the United Kingdom during the 1980s have been superseded by the definition for M4. Other measures of money that have been in use include M0, non-interest bearing M1, M2, and £M3. Each definition includes various types of bank and building society deposits. For example, M1 includes only bank sight deposits and £M3 includes sterling time deposits. Figure 27.1 gives a schematic description of money in the UK.

Is M4 Really Money?

Money is the means of payment. So the test of whether an asset is money is whether it serves as a means of payment. Currency passes the test. What about deposits? Chequeing deposits are money because they can be transferred from one person to another by writing a cheque. Such a transfer of ownership is equivalent to handing over currency. Both banks and building societies issue chequeable deposits.

But what about time deposits? A few time deposits are just as much a means of payment as a sight deposit. You can use the cash dispenser (automated teller machine – ATM) to transfer funds directly from such accounts to pay for your purchase. But most time deposits are not direct means of payments. They are *liquid assets*. **Liquidity** is the property of being instantly convertible into a means of payment with little loss in value. Most time deposits have this property, but there are some deposits that do not. These are large deposits known as *Certificates of Deposits* or CDs. CDs have maturities from three months to up to two years. They are not bank and building society deposits in the normal sense as they have to be held for the period of the maturity, but they can be sold in the financial markets quickly and easily. Because time deposits are quickly and easily converted into currency or chequeing deposits, they are operationally similar to sight deposits but technically they are not money.

Currency is only a small part of our money. It accounts for only 3 per cent of M4, while bank deposits account for 62 per cent and building society deposits represent 35 per cent. Chequeing deposits at banks and building societies total more than 66 per cent.

Deposits are Money but Cheques are Not

In defining money, we included, along with currency, deposits at banks and other financial institutions. But we did not count the cheques that people write as money. Why are deposits money and cheques not?

To see why deposits are money but cheques are not, think about what happens when Colleen buys some roller blades for £100 from Rocky's Rollers. When Colleen goes to Rocky's shop she has £250 in her deposit account at the Co-op Bank. Rocky has £1,000 in his deposit account – at the same bank, as it happens. The total deposits of these two people is £1,250. On June 11, Colleen writes a cheque for £100. Rocky takes the cheque to Co-op Bank straight away and deposits it. Rocky's bank balance rises from £1,000 to £1,100. But when the bank credits Rocky's account with £100, it also debits Colleen's account £100, so that her balance falls from £250 to £150. The total deposits of Colleen and Rocky are still the same as before, £1,250. Rocky now has £100 more and Colleen £100 less

Figure 27.1 Schematic Representation of Money Supply

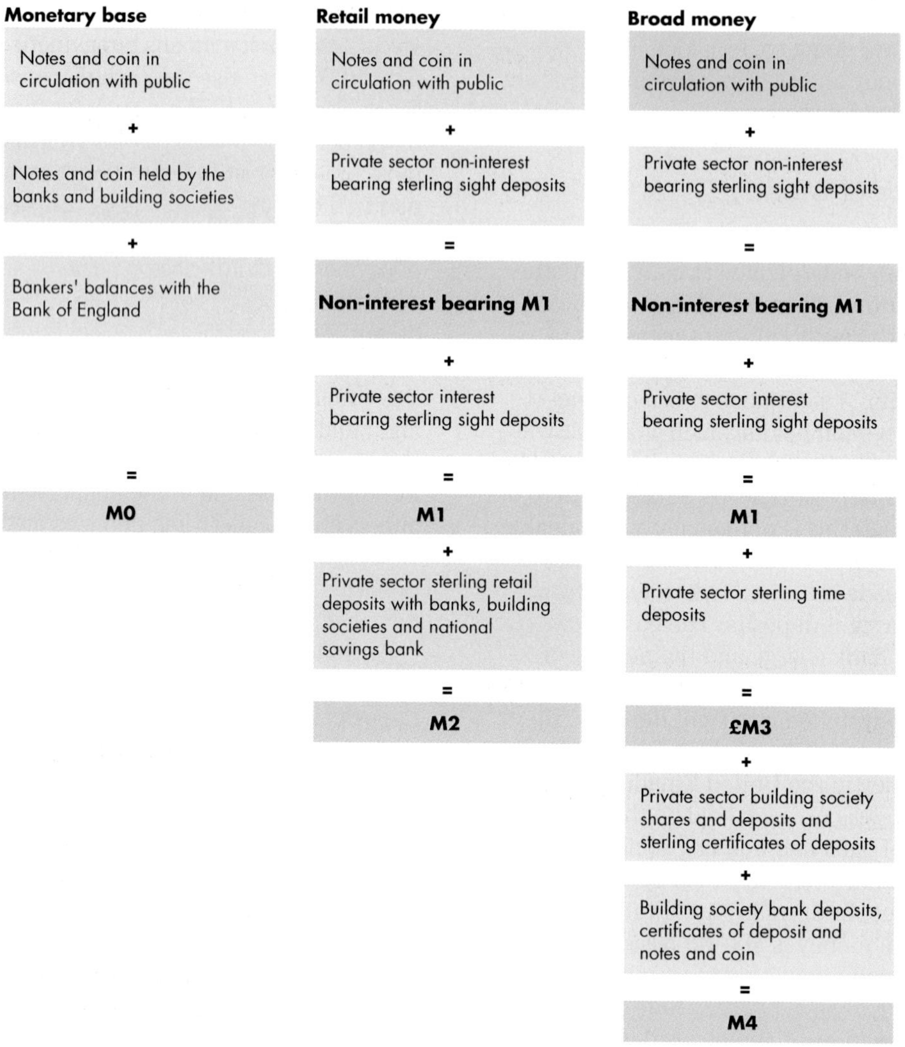

Monetary base	Retail money	Broad money
Notes and coin in circulation with public	Notes and coin in circulation with public	Notes and coin in circulation with public
+	+	+
Notes and coin held by the banks and building societies	Private sector non-interest bearing sterling sight deposits	Private sector non-interest bearing sterling sight deposits
+	=	=
Bankers' balances with the Bank of England	**Non-interest bearing M1**	**Non-interest bearing M1**
	+	+
	Private sector interest bearing sterling sight deposits	Private sector interest bearing sterling sight deposits
=	=	=
M0	**M1**	**M1**
	+	+
	Private sector sterling retail deposits with banks, building societies and national savings bank	Private sector sterling time deposits
	=	=
	M2	**£M3**
		+
		Private sector building society shares and deposits and sterling certificates of deposits
		+
		Building society bank deposits, certificates of deposit and notes and coin
		=
		M4

There are many measures of money in the United Kingdom. The narrowest measure is M0 and the broadest is M4.

than before. These transactions are summarized in Table 27.2.

This transaction has transferred money from Colleen to Rocky. The cheque itself was never money. There wasn't an extra £100 worth of money while the cheque was in circulation. The cheque was an instruction to the bank to transfer money from Colleen to Rocky.

In the example, Colleen and Rocky use the same bank. The same story, but with additional steps, describes what happens if Colleen and Rocky use different banks. Rocky's bank credits the cheque to Rocky's account and then takes the cheque to a cheque-clearing centre. Colleen's bank pays Rocky's bank £100 and then debits Colleen's account £100. This process can take a few days, but the principles are the same as when two people use the same bank.

Credit Cards are Not Money So cheques are not money. But what about credit cards? Isn't having a credit card in your wallet and presenting the card to

Figure 27.2 The Official Measure of Money

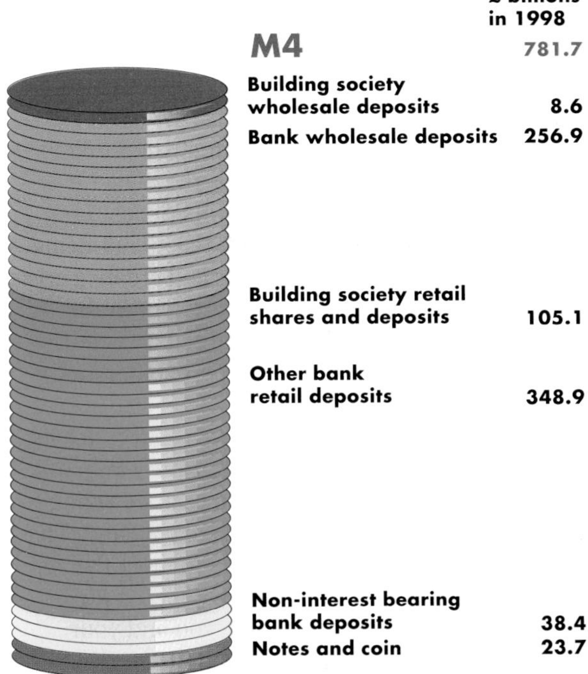

M4 is the broadest measure of money. It includes notes and coin, bank deposits and building society deposits.

Source: Bank of England.

Table 27.2 Paying by Cheque

Colleen's Chequeing Deposit Account

Date	Item	Debit	Credit	Balance
June 1	Opening balance			£250.00 CR*
June 11	Rocky's Rollers	£100.00		£150.00 CR

Rocky's Rollers Chequeing Deposit Account

Date	Item	Debit	Credit	Balance
June 1	Opening balance			£1,000.00 CR
June 11	Colleen buys roller blades		£100.00	£1,100.00 CR

*CR means 'credit': the bank owes the depositor.

pay for your roller blades the same thing as using money? Why aren't credit cards somehow valued and counted as part of the quantity of money?

When you pay by cheque you are usually asked to guarantee the cheque with a *cheque guarantee card*. It would never occur to you to think of your *cheque guarantee card* as money. It's just an ID card. But it is an ID card that enables you to guarantee your cheque up to a certain value. A credit card is also an ID card but one that lets you take a loan at the instant you buy something. When you sign a credit card sales slip, you are saying: 'I agree to pay for these goods when the credit card company bills me'. Once you get your statement from the credit card company, you must make the minimum payment due (or clear your balance). To make that payment you need money – you need to have currency or a chequeing deposit to pay the credit card company. So although you use a credit card when you buy something, the credit card is not the *means of payment* and it is not money.

Review

- Money is the means of payment and has three functions: medium of exchange, unit of account and store of value.
- A commodity can serve as money, but modern societies use fiat money and deposit money.
- The main component of money in the UK today is deposits at banks and building societies.
- Neither cheques nor credit cards are money.

We've seen that the main component of money in the United Kingdom is deposits at banks and building societies. Let's take a closer look at these institutions.

Financial Intermediaries

We are going to study the banking and financial system by first describing the variety of financial intermediaries that operate in the United Kingdom today. Then we'll examine the operations of banks and of other financial intermediaries. After describing the main features of financial intermediaries, we'll examine their economic functions, describing what they produce and how they make a profit.

A **financial intermediary** is a firm that takes deposits from households and firms and makes loans to other households and firms. There are two types of financial intermediary whose deposits are components of the nation's money:

1 Banks.
2 Building societies.

Let's begin by looking at the banks.

Banks

A **bank** is a private firm, licensed by the Bank of England under the Banking Act of 1987 to take deposits and make loans and operate in the United Kingdom. There are over 400 commercial banks in the United Kingdom today. These banks can be categorized into two main groups: retail banks and wholesale banks. The distinction between retail banks and wholesale banks is based on the size of deposit. In general, the minimum deposit accepted by a wholesale bank is £250,000 while retail banks accept deposits as small as £1. Retail banks operate extensive branch networks, while wholesale banks have few branches and operate mainly in London. Wholesale banks form a varied group, comprising UK merchant banks, other UK banks such as finance houses that specialize in lending to businesses, leasing companies that specialize in financing the leasing of equipment to businesses, other small regional banks and overseas banks.

To understand the operations of commercial banks, it is useful to study their balance sheets. The *balance sheet* of a bank (or of any other business) is a list of assets, liabilities and net worth. *Assets* are what the bank owns, *liabilities* are what the bank owes and *net worth*, which is equal to assets minus liabilities, is the value of the bank to its shareholders – its owners. A bank's balance sheet can be described by the equation:

$$\text{Liabilities} + \text{Net worth} = \text{Assets}$$

Among a bank's liabilities are the deposits that are part of the nation's money. Your deposit at the bank is a liability to your bank (and an asset to you) because the bank must repay your deposit (and sometimes the interest on it too) whenever you decide to take your money out of the bank.

Profit and Prudence: A Balancing Act The aim of a bank is to maximize its net worth – its value to its stockholders. To achieve this objective, a bank lends the money deposited with it at interest rates higher than the rates it pays for deposits. But a bank must perform a delicate balancing act. Lending is risky, and the more it ties up its deposits in high-risk, high-interest rate loans, the bigger is its chance of not being able to repay its depositors. And if depositors perceive a high risk of not being repaid, they withdraw their funds and create a crisis for the bank. So a bank must be prudent in the way it uses its deposits, balancing security for the depositors against profit for its shareholders.

Reserves and Loans To achieve security for its depositors, a bank divides its funds into two parts: reserves and loans. **Reserves** are cash in a bank's vault plus its deposits at the Bank of England. The cash in a bank's vaults is a reserve to meet the demands that its customers place on it – it keeps that ATM replenished every time you and your friends need to use it for a midnight pizza. A commercial bank's deposit at the Bank of England is similar to your deposit at your own bank. Commercial banks use these deposits in the same way that you use your bank account. A commercial bank deposits cash into or draws cash out of its account at the Bank of England and writes cheques on that account to settle debts with other banks.

If a bank kept all its assets as cash in its vault or as deposits at the Bank of England, it wouldn't make any profit. In fact it keeps only a small fraction of its funds in reserves and lends the rest. A bank makes three different types of loan, or equivalently, holds three different types of asset. They are:

1 Liquid assets.
2 Investment securities.
3 Loans.

A bank's *liquid assets* are government Treasury bills and commercial bills. These assets can be sold and instantly converted into cash with virtually no risk of loss. Because liquid assets are virtually risk free, they have a low interest rate.

A bank's *investment securities* are longer-term government bonds and other bonds. These assets can be sold quickly and converted into cash but at prices that fluctuate. Because their prices fluctuate, these assets are riskier than liquid assets but they also have a higher interest rate.

A bank's *loans* are lines of credit extended to companies to finance the purchase of capital equipment and stocks, and to households – personal loans – to finance consumer durable goods, such as cars or boats. The outstanding balances on credit card accounts are also bank loans. Loans are the riskiest assets of a bank because they cannot be converted into cash until they are due to be repaid. And some borrowers default and never repay. Because they are the riskiest of a bank's assets, they also carry the highest interest rate.

Commercial bank deposits are only one component of the nation's money. But building societies also take deposits that form part of the nation's money.

Building Societies

A **building society** is a financial intermediary that traditionally obtained its funds from savings deposits (sometimes called share accounts) and that made long-term mortgage loans to home buyers. The first building societies were founded in the late eighteenth century as *mutuals*. A mutual is an organization that belongs to its members. In the case of a building society, its mutual status means that by law it belongs to its depositors and borrowers. Up until the 1980s the societies had concentrated on their traditional function of lending to home buyers. However, the societies had begun to compete with the banks in the late 1970s by offering depositors accounts that gave them instant access to their money but paid a rate of interest for a minimum amount left in the account. The Building Societies Act of 1986 allowed for the progressive deregulation of the societies enabling them to offer financial products that brought them directly into competition with the banks. The act also enabled building societies to give up their mutual status and become banks. The Abbey National, took this route in 1989 and became a bank, similarly the merged Halifax/Leeds building society did the same in 1997. Many of the larger Building Societies have demutualized or plan to demutualize in the coming years.

The structure and balance sheets of building societies are similar to those of banks. Like banks, they have developed a branch network, and they have liabilities that are deposits and CDs. Like bank deposits, building society deposits are chequeable and are accepted in shops in exchange for goods. Building societies also offer similar services to banks, such as credit cards, personal lending and foreign currency.

The assets of building societies include cash reserves, but unlike the banks they do not have to hold deposits at the Bank of England. However, they do hold deposits and CDs at commercial banks. They also hold liquid assets such as CDs of other building societies and Treasury bills. Like banks, they also hold government bonds, but unlike banks most of building society lending is for house purchase. These assets have a much longer maturity than the normal lending of the commercial banks. Mortgage loans are typically for 25 years and are viewed as very safe assets.

The Economic Functions of Financial Intermediaries

All financial intermediaries make a profit from the spread between the interest rate they pay on deposits and the interest rate at which they lend. Why can financial intermediaries borrow at a low interest rate and lend at a higher one? What services do they perform that makes their depositors willing to put up with a low interest rate and their borrowers willing to pay a higher one?

Financial intermediaries provide four main services that people are willing to pay for:

1 Creating liquidity.
2 Minimizing the cost of obtaining funds.
3 Minimizing the cost of monitoring borrowers.
4 Pooling risk.

Creating Liquidity Financial intermediaries create liquidity. *Liquid* assets are those that are easily and with certainty convertible into money. Some of the liabilities of financial intermediaries are themselves money; others are highly liquid assets that are easily converted into money.

Financial intermediaries create liquidity by borrowing short and lending long. Borrowing short means taking deposits but standing ready to repay them at short notice (and even at no notice in the case of chequeing deposits). Lending long means making loan commitments for a prearranged, and often quite long, period of time. For example, when a person makes a deposit with a building society, that deposit can be withdrawn at any time. But the building society makes a lending commitment for perhaps up to 25 years to a home buyer.

Minimizing the Cost of Obtaining Funds Finding someone from whom to borrow can be a costly business. Imagine how troublesome it would be if there were no financial intermediaries. A firm that was looking for £1 million to buy a new production plant would probably have to hunt around for several dozen people from whom to borrow in order to acquire enough funds for its capital project. Financial intermediaries lower such costs. A firm needing £1 million can go to a single financial intermediary to obtain those funds. The financial intermediary has to borrow from a large number of people, but it's not doing that just for this one firm and the £1 million it wants to borrow. The financial intermediary can establish an organization capable of raising funds from a large number of depositors and can spread the cost of this activity over a large number of borrowers.

Borrowing a very large amount may be too much for one financial intermediary. This is because a single financial intermediary may not be willing to take the risk of exposing itself to one large borrower. In such cases a number of financial intermediaries are brought together and each intermediary will lend a proportion of the total loan. This is called a 'syndicated loan' and is typical of the way a large loan, such as the loan to build the Channel Tunnel, is raised in the international financial market.

Minimizing the Cost of Monitoring Borrowers Lending money is a risky business. There's always a danger that the borrower may not repay. Most of the money lent gets used by firms to invest in projects that they hope will return a profit. But sometimes these hopes are not fulfilled. Checking up on the activities of a borrower and ensuring that the best possible decisions are being made for making a profit and avoiding a loss is a costly and specialized activity. Imagine how costly it would be if each and every household that lent money to a firm had to incur the costs of monitoring that firm directly. By depositing funds with a financial intermediary, households avoid those costs. The financial intermediary performs the monitoring activity by using specialized resources that have a much lower cost than that which each household would incur if it had to undertake the activity individually.

Pooling Risk As we noted above, lending money is risky. There is always a chance of not being repaid – of default. The risk of default can be reduced by lending to a large number of different individuals. In such a situation, if one person defaults on a loan it is a nuisance but not a disaster. In contrast, if only one person borrows and that person defaults on the loan, the entire loan is a write-off. Financial intermediaries enable people to pool risk in an efficient way. Thousands of people lend money to any one financial intermediary and, in turn, the financial intermediary re-lends the money to hundreds, and perhaps thousands, of individual firms. If any one firm defaults on its loan, that default is spread across all the depositors with the intermediary and no individual depositor is left exposed to a high degree of risk.

Lending a large amount of money to one person or one firm is also a risky business. If that person or firm defaults on the loan, the write-off of the loan could endanger the viability of the financial intermediary.

Review

- Money consists of currency and deposits owned by people and businesses at commercial banks and building societies.
- Most of the nation's money is made up of deposits.
- The main economic functions of financial intermediaries are to create liquidity, to minimize the cost of obtaining funds and of monitoring borrowers, and to pool risk.

Financial Regulation, Deregulation and Innovation

Financial intermediaries are highly regulated institutions. But regulation is not static, and in the 1980s some important changes in their regulation as well as deregulation took place. Also, the institutions are not static. In their pursuit of profit, they constantly seek lower-cost ways of obtaining funds, monitoring borrowers, pooling risk and creating liquidity. They are also inventive in seeking ways to avoid the costs imposed on them by financial regulation. Let's take a look at regulation, deregulation and innovation in the financial sector in recent years.

Financial Regulation

Financial intermediaries face two types of regulation:

1 Deposit insurance.

2 Balance sheet rules.

Deposit Insurance The deposits of financial intermediaries are insured by the Bank of England deposit protection scheme. The scheme is financed by a flat rate contribution by banks in proportion to their deposits. The scheme covers 90 per cent of the first £20,000 per depositor. Therefore small depositors are basically covered for up to 90 per cent of the value of their deposits but large depositors have cover only up to £20,000.

The existence of deposit insurance provides protection for depositors in the event that a financial intermediary fails. But it also limits the incentive for the owner of a financial intermediary to make safe investments and loans. Some economists believe that deposit insurance can create a banking system that is prone to take excessive risks with depositors' money. This is the problem of *moral hazard*. Because depositors are sure that their deposits are insured, they do not keep an eye on what banks are doing with their money. Banks in turn, knowing that depositors are not worried about their funds, will aim to maximize profits by lending to high-risk businesses. It has been argued that this is precisely what happened with Savings & Loans associations (S&Ls) in the United States in the 1980s. Savers, knowing that their deposits were being used to make high-risk loans, did not remove their deposits from S&Ls because they knew they had the security of deposit insurance. The S&L owners making high-risk loans knew they were making a one-way bet. If their loans paid off, they made a high rate of return. If they failed and could not meet their obligations to the depositors, the insurance fund would step in. Bad loans were good business!

Because of this type of problem, all financial intermediaries face regulation of their balance sheets.

Balance Sheet Rules The most important balance sheet regulations are:

1 Capital requirements.

2 Reserve requirements.

Capital requirements are the minimum amount of an owner's own financial resources that must be put into an intermediary. This amount must be sufficiently large to discourage owners from making loans that are too risky. Banks in the EU and in the developed economies are moving away from a specified capital requirement set at 8 per cent of its assets, to voluntary ratios based on individual bank's assesment of risk. Different banks will eventually have different capital-asset ratios based on the type of assets they hold on their balance sheets. The riskier the assets, the more capital they will hold.

Reserve requirements are rules setting out the minimum percentages of deposits that must be held in currency or other safe, liquid assets. These minimum percentages vary across the different types of intermediary and deposit. The Bank of England does not specify a reserve requirement, however, banks in other EU countries have reserve requirements and countries in the EMU have a common set of reserve requirements specified by the European Central Bank.

Deregulation in the 1980s

The 1980s was a period of deregulation of the banking and financial system in the United Kingdom. In 1979 exchange controls were abolished. The abolition of these controls meant that banks could borrow and lend overseas unhindered. The most important deregulatory measure in 1980 was the abolition of the *corset*. The corset was a system of regulation that controlled the amount of deposits the banks were allowed to take. With the removal of this and other controls, banks were free to compete with building societies in the market for housing finance. A further deregulatory measure was the removal in 1983 of the arrangement whereby the building societies fixed the interest rate on mortgages. This measure injected further competition into the mortgage market, because now any individual building society could set its interest rate according to the pressures of the market and not wait for all the remaining building societies to change their interest rates together. In 1986 the Building Societies Act allowed the societies to offer similar services to those of banks.

Financial Innovation

The development of new financial products – of new ways of borrowing and lending – is called **financial innovation**. The aim of financial innovation is to lower the cost of borrowing or increase the return from lending or, more simply, to increase the profit from financial intermediation. There are three main influences on financial innovation. They are:

1 Economic environment.

2 Technology.

3 Regulation.

The pace of financial innovation was remarkable in the 1980s, and all three of these forces played a role.

Economic Environment Some of the innovations that occurred in the 1970s and 1980s were a response to high inflation and high interest rates. An important example is the development of variable interest rate loans for businesses. Traditionally, companies had borrowed long-term funds at fixed interest rates. Rising interest rates brought rising borrowing costs for banks, which led them to develop variable rate lending. Another important innovation in the 1970s was the payment of interest on sight deposits. This had the effect of making the holding of bank deposits as opposed to a savings account more attractive. In the 1980s, depositors who maintained a certain minimum amount in their sight deposit accounts had all bank charges waived, making such accounts even more attractive.

Technology Other financial innovations resulted from technological change, most notably that associated with the decreased cost of computing and long-distance communication. The use of ATMs and direct debit cards such as Switch cards, which allow stores to debit your bank or building society account directly, is an example of the advance of financial innovation caused by improved technology. The growth in the use of credit cards and the development of international financial markets – for example, the increased importance of Eurodollar[1] – are consequences of technological change. The Mondex card is another example of technological innovation. It is a 'smart card' that has an implication for the payments system. The Mondex card allows a person to carry units of money that can be used electronically as a medium of exchange. It can be credited from their bank account and debited for purchases. It is hoped that one day the Mondex card will replace cash and cheques as the medium of exchange. Experiments with the Mondex card are not conclusive. Many people still like to carry and pay using cash or cheques.

Regulation A good deal of financial innovation takes place to avoid regulation. For example, when the corset was in operation in the 1970s, banks were not allowed to expand their deposits beyond a certain point. Other financial intermediaries sprang up with different types of deposit to grab the business that banks had to turn away.

Deregulation, Innovation and Money

Deregulation and financial innovation that have led to the development of new types of deposit account have brought important changes in the composition of the nation's money. In the 1960s, M1 consisted of only currency and chequeing sight deposits at commercial banks. In the 1980s, other new types of chequeing deposits expanded while traditional chequeing sight deposits declined. Similar changes took place in the composition of money. Bank time deposits expanded and building society share accounts began to offer the same services as bank accounts. The result of these changes was that the definition of the money supply altered and a new measure – M4 – was born.

Review

- The 1980s saw a wave of financial deregulation that blurred the distinction between commercial banks and building societies.
- Financial intermediaries constantly seek new ways of making a profit and react to the changing economic environment, new technologies and regulations.

1 Eurodollars are US dollar bank accounts held in other countries, mainly in Europe. They were 'invented' during the 1960s when the former Soviet Union wanted the security and convenience of holding funds in US dollars but was unwilling to place deposits in US banks.

◆ Deregulation and innovation in the 1980s brought new types of deposit that changed the composition of the nation's money.

Because financial intermediaries are able to create liquidity and to create assets that are a means of payment – money – they occupy a unique place in our economy and exert an important influence on the quantity of money in existence. Let's see how money is created.

How Banks Create Money

Banks create money[2]. But this doesn't mean that they have smoke-filled back rooms in which counterfeiters are busily working. Remember, most money is deposits, not currency. What banks create is deposits and they do so by making loans. But the amount of deposits they can create is limited by their reserves.

Reserves: Actual and Required

We've seen that banks don't have £100 in notes for every £100 that people have deposited with them. In fact, a typical bank today has about 60 pence in currency and another 26 pence on deposit at the Bank of England, a total reserve of less than £1, for every £100 deposited in it. But there is no need for panic. Banks have learned, from experience, that these reserve levels are adequate for ordinary business needs.

The fraction of a bank's total deposits that are held in reserves is called the **reserve ratio**. The value of the reserve ratio is influenced by the actions of a bank's depositors. If a depositor withdraws currency from a bank, the reserve ratio decreases. If a depositor puts currency into a bank, the reserve ratio increases.

The **required reserve ratio** is the ratio of reserves to deposits that banks are required, by regulation, to hold. A bank's *required reserves* are equal to its deposits multiplied by the required reserve ratio. A bank's **desired reserve ratio** is the ratio of reserves to deposits that banks consider as prudent to hold in order to meet withdrawals and to carry on their business. A bank's desired reserves are equal to its deposits multiplied by the desired reserve ratio. Actual reserves minus *required* or *desired reserves* are **excess reserves**. Whenever banks have excess reserves, they are able to create money.

To see how banks create money we are going to look at two model banking systems. In the first model there is only one bank. In the second model there are many banks.

Creating Deposits by Making Loans in a One-bank Economy

In the model banking system that we'll study, there is only one bank and its required reserve ratio is 25 per cent. That is, for each £1 deposited, the bank keeps 25 pence in reserves and lends the rest. The balance sheet of One-and-Only Bank is shown in Figure 27.3(a). Its deposits are £400 million and its reserves are 25 per cent of this amount – £100 million. Its loans are equal to deposits minus reserves and are £300 million.

The story begins with Silas Marner, who has decided that it is too dangerous to keep on hiding his fortune under his mattress. Silas has been holding his fortune in currency and has a nest egg of £1 million. He decides to put his £1 million on deposit at the One-and-Only Bank. On the day that Silas makes his deposit, the One-and-Only Bank's balance sheet changes and the new situation is shown in Figure 27.3(b). The bank now has £101 million in reserves and £401 million in deposits. It still has loans of £300 million.

The bank now has *excess reserves*. With reserves of £101 million, the bank would like to have deposits of £404 million and loans of £303 million. And being the One-and-Only Bank, the manager knows the reserves will remain at £101 million. That is, she knows that when she makes a loan, the amount lent remains on deposit at the One-and-Only Bank. She knows, for example, that all the suppliers of Sky's-the-Limit Construction, her biggest borrower, are also depositors of One-and-Only. So she knows that if she makes the loan that Sky's-the-Limit has just requested, the deposit she lends will never leave One-and-Only. When Sky's-the-Limit uses part of its new loan to pay £100,000 to I-Dig-It Building Company for some excavations, the One-and-Only Bank simply moves the funds from Sky's-the-Limit's chequeing account to I-Dig-It's chequeing account.

So the manager of One-and-Only calls Sky's-the-Limit's accountant and offers to lend the maximum that she can. How much does she lend? She lends

2 In this section, we'll use the term *banks* to refer to all the depository institutions whose deposits are part of the money supply: commercial banks and building societies.

Figure 27.3 Creating Money at the One-and-Only Bank

(a) Balance sheet on January 1

Assets (millions of pounds)		**Liabilities** (millions of pounds)	
Reserves	£100	Deposits	£400
Loans	£300		
Total	£400	Total	£400

(b) Balance sheet on January 2

Assets (millions of pounds)		**Liabilities** (millions of pounds)	
Reserves	£101	Deposits	£401
Loans	£300		
Total	£401	Total	£401

(c) Balance sheet on January 3

Assets (millions of pounds)		**Liabilities** (millions of pounds)	
Reserves	£101	Deposits	£404
Loans	£303		
Total	£404	Total	£404

In part (a), the One-and-Only Bank has deposits of £400 million, loans of £300 million and reserves of £100 million. The bank's desired reserve ratio is 25 per cent. When the bank receives a deposit of £1 million (part b), it has excess reserves. It lends £3 million and creates a further £3 million of deposits. Deposits increase by £3 million and loans increase by £3 million (in part c).

£3 million. By lending £3 million, One-and-Only's balance sheet changes to the one shown in Figure 27.3(c). Loans increase by £3 million to £303 million. The loan shows up in Sky's-the-Limit's deposit initially and total deposits increase to £404 million – £400 million plus Silas Marner's deposit of £1 million plus the newly created deposit of £3 million. The bank now has no excess reserves and has reached the limit of its ability to create money.

The Deposit Multiplier

The **deposit multiplier** is the amount by which an increase in bank reserves is multiplied to calculate the increase in bank deposits. That is:

$$\text{Deposit multiplier} = \frac{\text{Change in deposits}}{\text{Change in reserves}}$$

In the example we've just worked through, the deposit multiplier is 4. The £1 million increase in reserves created a £4 million increase in deposits. The deposit multiplier is linked to the required reserve ratio by the following equation:

$$\text{Deposit multiplier} = \frac{1}{\text{Desired revenue ratio}}$$

In the example, the desired reserve ratio is 25 per cent, or 0.25. That is:

$$\text{Deposit multiplier} = 1/0.25$$
$$= 4$$

Creating Deposits by Making Loans with Many Banks

If you told the student loans officer at your own bank that she creates money, she wouldn't believe you. Bankers see themselves as lending the money they receive from others, not creating money. But in fact, even though each bank only lends what it receives, the banking *system* creates money. To see how, let's look at another example.

Figure 27.4 is going to keep track of what is happening in the process of money creation by a banking system in which each bank has a required reserve ratio of 25 per cent. The process begins when Alan decides to decrease his currency holding and put £100,000 on deposit. Now Alan's bank has £100,000 of new deposits and £100,000 of additional reserves. With a required reserve ratio of 25 per cent, the bank keeps £25,000 on reserve and lends £75,000 to Amy. Amy writes a cheque for £75,000 to buy a photocopy-shop franchise from Barbara. At this point, Alan's Bank has a new deposit of £100,000, new loans of £75,000 and new reserves of £25,000. You can see this situation in Figure 27.4 as the first row of the 'running tally'.

For Alan's bank, that is the end of the story. But it's not the end of the story for the entire banking system. Barbara deposits her cheque for £75,000 in another bank, which has an increase in deposits and reserves of £75,000. This bank puts 25 per cent of its increase in deposits, £18,750 into reserve and lends £56,250 to Bob. And Bob writes a cheque to Carl to pay off a business loan. The current state of play is seen in Figure 27.4. Now, bank reserves have increased by £43,750 (£25,000 plus £18,750), loans have increased by £131,250 (£75,000 plus £56,250)

Figure 27.4 The Multiple Creation of Bank Deposits

The sequence

Deposit £100,000

Reserve £25,000 | Loan £75,000

Deposit £75,000

Reserve £18,750 | Loan £56,250

Deposit £56,250

Reserve £14,063 | Loan £42,187

Deposit £42,187

Reserve £10,547 | Loan £31,640

and so on ...

The running tally

Reserves	Loans	Deposits
£25,000	£75,000	£100,000
£43,750	£131,250	£175,000
£57,813	£173,437	£231,250
£68,360	£205,077	£273,437
● ● ▼	● ● ▼	● ● ▼
£100,000	£300,000	£400,000

When a bank receives deposits, it keeps 25 per cent in reserves and lends 75 per cent. The amount lent becomes a new deposit at another bank. The next bank in the sequence keeps 25 per cent and lends 75 per cent, and the process continues until the banking system has created enough deposits to eliminate its excess reserves. The running tally tells us the amount of deposits and loans created at each stage. At the end of the process, an additional £100,000 of reserves creates an additional £400,000 of deposits.

and deposits have increased by £175,000 (£100,000 plus £75,000).

When Carl takes his cheque to his bank, its deposits and reserves increase by £56,250, £14,060 of which it keeps in reserve and £42,190 of which it lends. This process continues until there are no excess reserves in the banking system. But the process takes a lot of further steps. One additional step is shown in Figure 27.4. The figure also shows the final tallies – reserves increase by £100,000, loans increase by £300,000 and deposits increase by £400,000.

The sequence in Figure 27.4 is the first four stages of the entire process. To figure out the entire process, look closely at the numbers in the figure. At each stage, the loan is 75 per cent (0.75) of the previous loan and the deposit is 0.75 of the previous deposit. Call that proportion L ($L = 0.75$). The complete sequence is:

$$1 + L + L^2 + L^3 + \ldots$$

Remember, L is a fraction, so at each stage in this sequence the amount of new loans gets smaller. The total number of loans made at the end of the process is the above sum which is[3]:

$$\frac{1}{(1 - L)}$$

3 Both here and in the expenditure multiplier process in Chapter 28, the sequence of values is called a convergent geometric series. To find the sum of such a series, begin by calling the sum S. Then write out the sum as:

$$S = 1 + L + L^2 + L^3 + \ldots$$

Multiply by L to give:

$$LS = L + L^2 + L^3 + \ldots$$

and then subtract the second equation from the first to give:

$$S(1 - L) = 1$$

or:

$$S = 1 \div (1 - L)$$

Using the numbers from the example, the total increase in deposits is:

$$
\begin{aligned}
&\$100{,}000 + 75{,}000 + 56{,}250 + 42{,}190 + \ldots \\
&= \$100{,}000 \times (1 + 0.75 + 0.5625 + 0.4219 + \ldots) \\
&= \$100{,}000 \times (1 + 0.75 + 0.75^2 + 0.75^3 + \ldots) \\
&= \$100{,}000 \times (1 \div (1 - 0.75)) \\
&= \$100{,}000 \times (1 \div 0.25) \\
&= \$100{,}000 \times 4 \\
&= \$400{,}000
\end{aligned}
$$

By using the same method, you can check that the totals for reserves and loans are the ones shown in Figure 27.4.

So even though each bank only lends the money it receives, the banking system as a whole does create money by making loans. And the amount created is the same in a multibank system as in a one-bank system.

The Deposit Multiplier in the United Kingdom

The deposit multiplier in the United Kingdom works in the same way as the deposit multiplier we've just worked out for a hypothetical economy. But the actual deposit multiplier differs from the one we've just calculated for two reasons. First, there is no required reserve ratio for UK banks, and retail banks, wholesale banks and building societies have different desired reserves of highly liquid assets, which include government Treasury bills and short-term loans. The desired ratio will be smaller than the one we have used here. Second, not all the loans made by banks return to them in the form of reserves. Some of the loans remain outside the banks and are held as currency. The smaller required reserve ratio makes the UK multiplier larger than the above example. But the other two factors make the UK multiplier smaller.

Review

- Banks create deposits by making loans, and the amount they can lend is determined by their reserves and their desired reserve ratio.
- Each time a bank makes a loan, both deposits and desired reserves increase.
- When deposits are at a level that makes desired reserves equal to actual reserves, the banks have reached the limit of their ability to create money.
- A change in reserves brings about a multiple change in deposits and the deposit multiplier equals 1 divided by the desired reserve ratio.

We've now seen what money is and how banks create it. The amount of money created by the banks has a powerful influence on the economy. Our next task is to examine that influence.

Money, Real GDP and the Price Level

You now know that in a modern economy such as that of the United Kingdom today, most of the money is bank deposits. You've seen that banks actually create money by making loans. Does the quantity of money created by the banking and financial system matter? What effect does money have? Does it matter whether the quantity of money increases quickly or slowly? In particular, how does the quantity of money influence real GDP, the price level and the inflation rate?

We're going to answer these questions first by using the aggregate supply–aggregate demand model, which explains how money affects real GDP and the price level in the short run. Then we're going to study a theory called the quantity theory of money, which explains how money growth influences inflation in the long run. We'll also look at some historical and international evidence on the relationship between money growth and inflation.

The Short-run Effects of a Change in the Quantity of Money

Figure 27.5 illustrates the *AS–AD* model that explains how real GDP and the price level are determined in the short run. (For a full explanation of the *AS–AD* model, see Chapter 24, pp. 580–589) We are going to use this model to study the short-run effect of a change in the quantity of money on real GDP and the price level. Potential GDP is £750 billion and the

Figure 27.5 Short-run Effects of a Change in the Quantity of Money

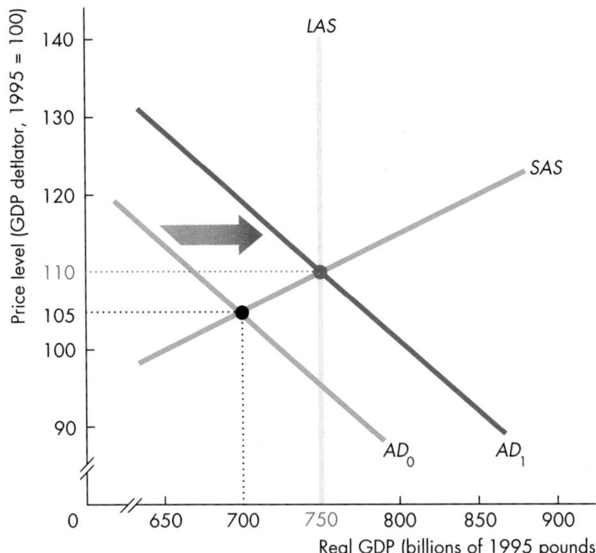

Real GDP is less than potential GDP. An increase in the quantity of money increases aggregate demand and shifts the aggregate demand curve rightward from AD_0 to AD_1. The price level rises to 110 and real GDP expands to £750 billion. The increase in the quantity of money moves real GDP to potential GDP.

long-run aggregate supply curve is *LAS*. The short-run aggregate supply curve is *SAS*. Initially, the aggregate demand curve is AD_0. Equilibrium real GDP is £700 billion and the price level is 100 at the intersection of the *AD* curve and the *SAS* curve.

Suppose there is now an increase in the quantity of money. This increase results from the process of money creation we've just studied. With more money in their bank accounts, people plan to increase their consumption expenditure and businesses plan to increase their investment. Aggregate demand increases and the aggregate demand curve shifts rightward to AD_1. A new equilibrium emerges at the intersection point of AD_1 and *SAS*. Real GDP expands to £750 billion and the price level rises to 110. Real GDP now equals potential GDP and there is full employment. This increase in the quantity of money has increased both real GDP and the price level.

Now imagine the reverse situation. Real GDP is initially £750 billion and the price level is 110 at the intersection point of AD_1 and *SAS*. The quantity of money *decreases*. With *less* money in their bank accounts, people and businesses plan to decrease their expenditures. Aggregate demand decreases and the aggregate demand curve shifts leftward to AD_0. A recession occurs as real GDP shrinks to £700 billion and the price level falls to 100.

These influences of the quantity of money on real GDP and the price level are *short-run* effects. In the long run, a change in the quantity of money, perhaps surprisingly, has no effect on real GDP. All its effects are on the price level. Let's see why this outcome occurs.

The Long-run Effects of a Change in the Quantity of Money

Figure 27.6 explains how real GDP and the price level are determined in both the short run and the long run. Again, potential GDP is £750 billion and the long-run aggregate supply curve is *LAS*. The short-run aggregate supply curve is SAS_1. Initially, the aggregate demand curve is AD_1. Equilibrium real GDP is £750 billion and the price level is 110. So real GDP equals potential GDP and there is full employment.

Now suppose the quantity of money increases. Aggregate demand increases and the aggregate demand curve shifts rightward to AD_2. The new short-run equilibrium is at the intersection point of AD_2 and SAS_1. The price level rises to 115, and real GDP expands to £800 billion. This short-run adjustment has put real GDP above potential GDP and decreased unemployment below the natural rate. A shortage of labour raises the money wage rate. As the money wage rate rises, short-run aggregate supply decreases and the *SAS* curve shifts leftward towards SAS_2. As short-run aggregate supply decreases, the price level rises to 121 and real GDP decreases back to potential GDP at £750 billion.

Thus from one full-employment equilibrium to another, an increase in the quantity of money increases the price level and has no effect on real GDP. This relationship between the quantity of money and the price level at full employment is made more precise by the quantity theory of money, which tells us about the quantitative link between money growth and inflation.

Figure 27.6 Long-run Effects of a Change in the Quantity of Money

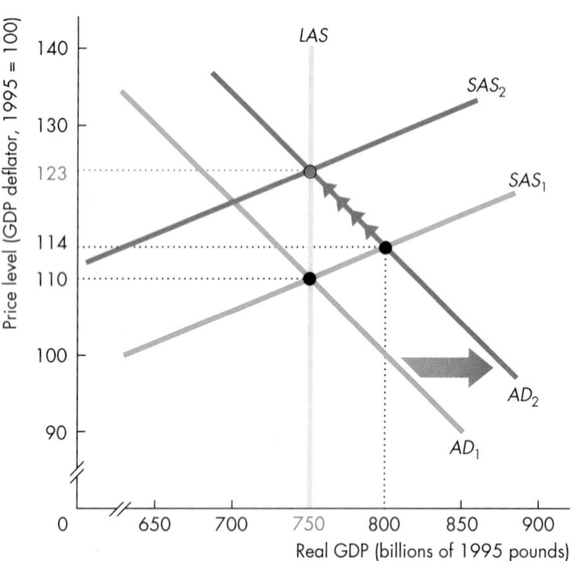

Real GDP equals potential GDP. An increase in the quantity of money shifts the aggregate demand curve from AD_1 to AD_2. The price level rises to 114 and real GDP increases to £800 billion. Real GDP exceeds potential GDP and the money wage rate rises. Short-run aggregate supply decreases and the *SAS* curve shifts leftward from SAS_1 to SAS_2. Real GDP returns to potential GDP and the price level rises to 123. In the long run, the increase in the quantity of money increases the price level and has no effect on real GDP.

The Quantity Theory of Money

The **quantity theory of money** is the proposition that in the long run, an increase in the quantity of money brings an equal percentage increase in the price level. The original basis of the quantity theory of money is a concept known as the velocity of circulation and an equation called the equation of exchange.

The **velocity of circulation** is the average number of times a unit of money is used annually to buy the goods and services that make up GDP. GDP is equal to the price level (P) multiplied by real GDP (Y). That is:

$$GDP = PY$$

Call the quantity of money M. The velocity of circulation, V, is determined by the equation:

$$V = PY/M$$

For example, if GDP is £750 billion and the quantity of money is £375 billion, the velocity of circulation is 2. On the average, each unit of money circulates twice in its use to purchase the final goods and services that make up GDP. That is, each unit of money is used twice in a year to buy GDP.

Figure 27.7 shows the history of the velocity of circulation of M4 in the United Kingdom and M3 in Germany. You can see that the velocity of circulation has been falling steadily in both countries. The reason the velocity of circulation has decreased is because deregulation and financial innovation have created new types of deposit and higher interest rates on those deposits have attracted funds that were normally held as savings. More and more people are having their salaries and wages paid directly into bank accounts and now use cheques and direct debit cards. Direct debit cards enable shops to debit sums of money electronically from your bank account. They are substitutes for cheques.

Banks also have developed better methods of cash management and need to keep fewer stocks in their vaults. Except in the 'hidden' economy where cash is the main medium of exchange, today more people use cheques and cards than use cash. You can see that velocity fell faster in the UK than in Germany during the 1980s. This is becasue the pace of deregulation and financial innovation was faster in the UK than in Germany. The flatenning out of the M4 velocity in the 1990s is a signal that the pace of deregulation and financial innovation may have come to an end.

The **equation of exchange** states that the quantity of money (M) multiplied by the velocity of circulation (V) equals GDP, or:

$$MV = PY$$

Given the definition of the velocity of circulation, this equation is always true – it is true by definition. With M equal to £375 billion and V equal to 2, MV is equal to £750 billion, the value of GDP.

The equation of exchange becomes the quantity theory of money by making two assumptions:

1 The velocity of circulation is not influenced by the quantity of money.

2 Potential real GDP is not influenced by the quantity of money.

If these two assumptions are true, the equation of exchange tells us that in the long run, a given

Figure 27.7 The Velocity of Circulation in the United Kingdom and Germany: 1969–1998

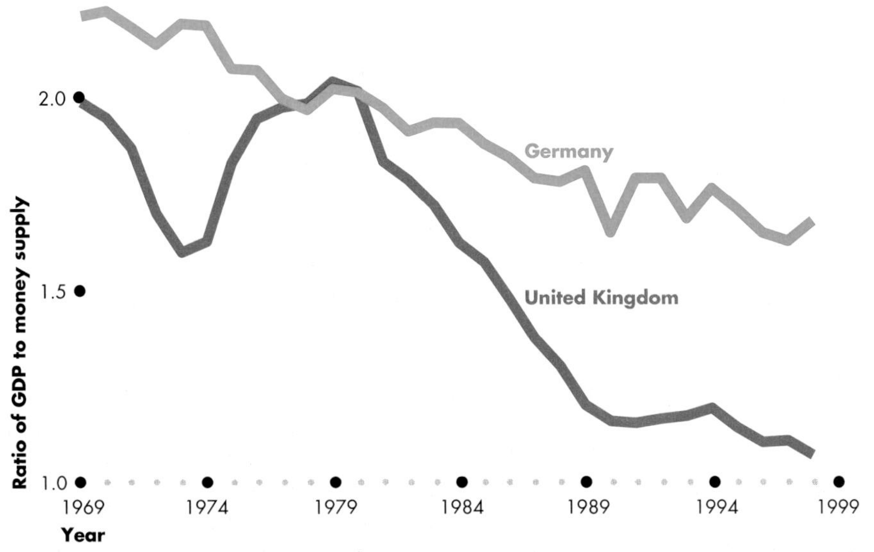

The velocity of circulation has declined steadily in both economies because the cash substitutes that have resulted from financial innovation are new types of deposit that are part of the money supply. The pace of financial innovation has been faster in the UK than Germany.

Sources: *Bank of England* and Bundesbank.

percentage change in the quantity of money brings about an equal percentage change in the price level. You can see why by solving the equation of exchange for the price level. Dividing both sides of the equation by real GDP (Y) gives:

$$P = (V/Y)M$$

In the long run, real GDP (Y) equals potential GDP, so if potential GDP and velocity are not influenced by the quantity of money, the relationship between the change in the price level (ΔP) and the change in the quantity of money (ΔM) is:

$$\Delta P = (V/Y)\ \Delta M$$

Divide this equation by the previous one ($P = (V/Y)M$) to give:

$$\Delta P/P = \Delta M/M$$

($\Delta P/P$) is the percentage increase in the price level and ($\Delta M/M$) is the percentage increase in the quantity of money. So this equation is the quantity theory of money. In the long run, the percentage increase in the price level equals the percentage increase in the quantity of money.

The Quantity Theory and the *AS–AD* Model

The quantity theory of money can be interpreted in terms of the *AS–AD* model. The aggregate demand curve is a relationship between the quantity of real GDP demanded (Y) and the price level (P), other things remaining constant. We can obtain such a relationship from the equation of exchange:

$$MV = PY$$

Dividing both sides of this equation by real GDP (Y) gives:

$$P = MV/Y$$

This equation may be interpreted as describing an aggregate demand curve. In Chapter 24 (pp. 584–587) you saw that the aggregate demand curve slopes downward – as the price level increases the quantity of real GDP demanded decreases. The above equation also shows such a relationship between the price level and the quantity of real GDP demanded. For a given quantity of money (M) and a given velocity of circulation (V), the higher

Figure 27.8 Money Growth and Inflation in the United Kingdom: 1964–1996

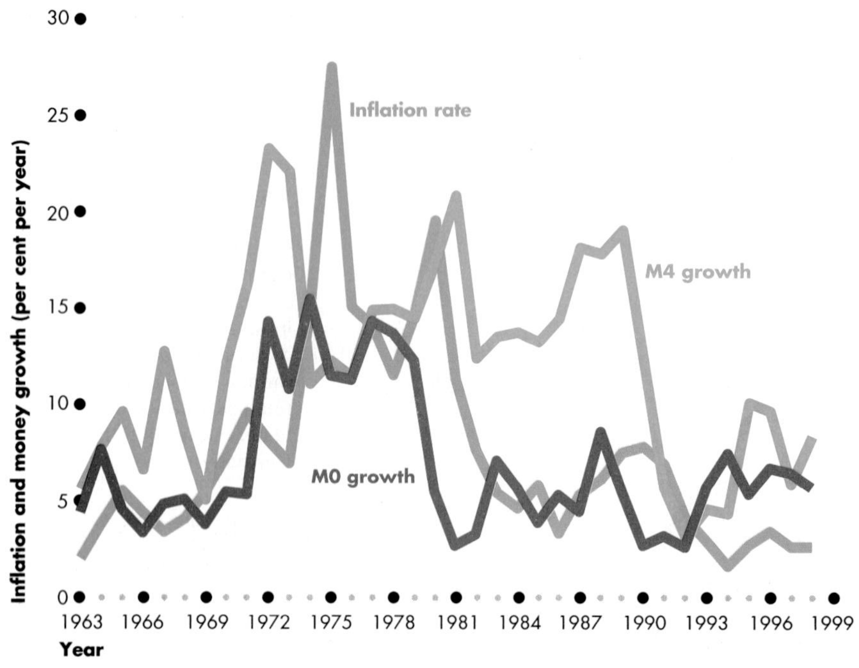

Year-to-year fluctuations in money growth and inflation are loosely correlated. The growth of M4 and inflation appeared to have a strong correlation in the 1960s and 1970s but that correlation has weakened in the 1980s. The growth of M0 and inflation have a stronger correlation in the 1980s.

Source: *Bank of England.*

the price level (P), the smaller is the quantity of real GDP demanded (Y).

In general, when the quantity of money changes, the velocity of circulation might also change. But the quantity theory asserts that velocity is not influenced by the quantity of money. If this assumption is correct, an increase in the quantity of money increases aggregate demand and shifts the aggregate demand curve upward by the same amount as the percentage change in the quantity of money.

The quantity theory of money also asserts that real GDP, which in the long run equals potential GDP, is not influenced by the quantity of money. This assertion is true in the *AS–AD* model. Figure 27.6 shows the quantity theory result in the *AS–AD* model. Initially the economy is at full employment on the long-run aggregate supply curve *LAS* and at the intersection of the aggregate demand curve AD_1 and the short-run aggregate supply curve SAS_1. A 10 per cent increase in the quantity of money shifts the aggregate demand curve from AD_1 to AD_2. This shift, measured by the vertical distance between the two demand curves, is 10 per cent.

In the long run, wages rise (also by 10 per cent) and shift the *SAS* curve leftward to SAS_2. A new full-employment (long-run) equilibrium occurs at the intersection of AD_2 and SAS_2. Real GDP remains at potential GDP of £750 billion and the price level rises to 121. The new price level is 10 per cent higher than the initial one (121 – 110 = 11, which is 10 per cent of 110).

So the *AS–AD* model predicts the same outcome as the quantity theory of money. The *AS–AD* model also predicts a less precise relationship between the quantity of money and the price level in the short run than in the long run. For example, Figure 27.5 shows that starting out with unemployment, an increase in the quantity of money increases real GDP. In this case, a 10 per cent increase in the money supply increases the price level from 110 to 115 – a 4.5 per cent increase. That is, the price level changes by a smaller percentage than the percentage change in the quantity of money.

How good a theory is the quantity theory of money? Let's answer this question by looking at the relationship between money and the price level, both historically and internationally.

Historical Evidence on the Quantity Theory of Money

The percentage increase in the price level is the inflation rate, and the percentage increase in the quantity of money is the money supply growth rate. So the quantity theory predictions can be cast in terms of money growth and inflation. The quantity theory predicts that at a given level of potential GDP and in the long run, the inflation rate will equal the money growth rate. But over time, potential GDP expands. Taking this expansion into account, the quantity theory predicts that in the long run, the inflation rate will equal the money growth rate minus the growth rate of potential GDP.

We can test the quantity theory of money by looking at the historical relationship between money growth and inflation in the United Kingdom. Figure 27.8 shows this relationship for the years between 1963 and 1998. The inflation rate is the percentage change in the GDP deflator and the two alternative money growth rates are based on M0 and M4. The chart shows year-to-year changes in money and the price level. These changes show the relationship between money growth and inflation. If the quantity theory is a reasonable guide to reality, there should be a strong correlation between inflation and money growth.

The data are broadly consistent with the quantity theory. The money growth rate and the inflation rate are correlated but the relationship is not precise. In the 1960s and 1970s, M4 growth preceded changes in inflation and M0 appeared to follow. In the 1980s, the relationship between M4 growth and inflation appears to have broken down, but a closer relationship can be observed between M0 growth and inflation. In the 1990s, the association between the rate of growth of M0 and inflation has weakened. The reason why the correlation between M4 and inflation in the 1980s was weaker is because of the deregulation and financial innovation during that period.

International Evidence on the Quantity Theory of Money

Another way to test the quantity theory of money is to look at the cross-country relationship between money growth and inflation. Figure 27.9 shows this relationship for 60 countries during the 1980s. By looking at a decade average, we again are smoothing out the short-run effects of money growth and

Figure 27.9 Money Growth and Inflation in the World Economy

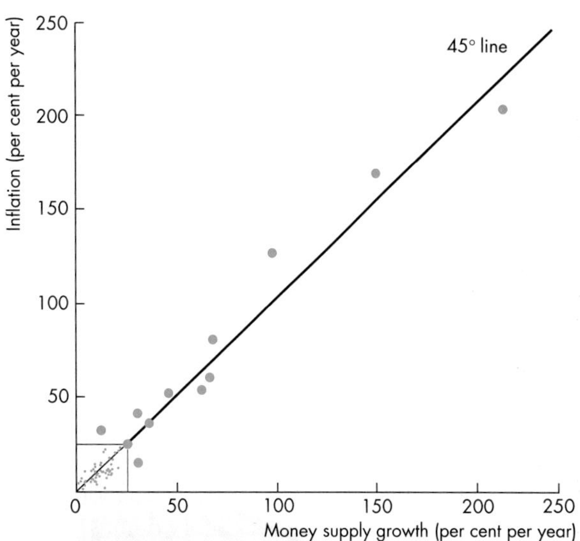

(a) All countries

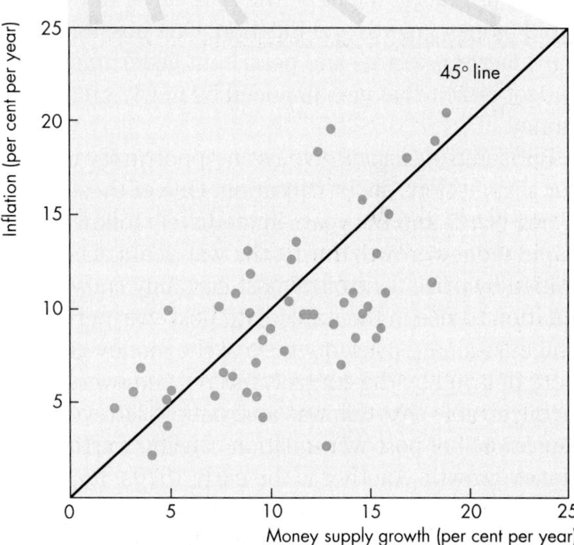

(b) Low-inflation countries

Inflation and money growth in 60 countries (in part a) and low-inflation countries (in part b) show that money growth is one influence, though not the only influence, on inflation.

Source: Federal Reserve Bank of St Louis, *Review*, May/June 1988, p. 15.

focusing on the long-run effects. There is in these data an unmistakable tendency for high money growth to be associated with high inflation. Some further evidence from the experience of Serbia during the 1990s can be seen in *Reading Between the Lines* on pp. 682–683.

Correlation, Causation and Other Influences

Both the historical evidence for the United Kingdom and the international data tell us that in the long run, money growth and inflation are correlated. But the correlation between money growth and inflation does not tell us that money growth causes inflation. Money growth might cause inflation; inflation might cause money growth; or some third variable might simultaneously cause inflation and money growth.

According to the quantity theory and according to the *AS–AD* model, causation runs from money growth to inflation. But neither theory denies the possibility that at different times and places, causation might run in the other direction, or that some third factor might be the root cause of both rapid money growth and inflation. One possible third factor is a large and persistent government budget deficit that gets financed by newly created money.

But some occasions give us an opportunity to test our assumptions about causation. One of these is World War II and the years immediately following it. Rapid money growth during the war years accompanied by price controls almost certainly caused inflation to rise in the immediate post-war period. The inflationary consequences of the money growth were delayed by the controls but not removed. It is inconceivable that this was an example of reverse causation – of post-war inflation causing wartime money growth. Another is the early 1970s. Rapid money growth that began during the early 1970s almost certainly caused the high and persistent inflation of the mid-1970s.

The combination of historical and international correlations between money growth and inflation, and independent evidence about the direction of causation, leads to the conclusion that the quantity theory is correct in the long run. It explains the long-term fundamental source of inflation. But the quantity theory is not correct in the short run. To understand the short-term fluctuations in inflation, the joint effects of a change in the quantity of money on real GDP, the velocity of circulation and the price level must be explained. The *AS–AD* model provides this explanation. It also points to the possibility of other factors that influence both aggregate supply and aggregate demand influencing the inflation rate independently of the money growth rate.

Review

- The quantity of money influences the price level and real GDP.
- In the short run, an increase in the quantity of money increases aggregate demand and increases both the price level and real GDP.
- In the long run, when real GDP equals potential GDP, an increase in the quantity of money brings an equal percentage increase in the price level (the quantity theory of money).
- The long-run historical and international evidence on the relationship between money growth and inflation supports the quantity theory.

Before you leave the subject of this chapter, look at Reading Between the Lines on pp. 682–683 and see how rapid money growth has brought inflation in Serbia. In the next chapter, we're going to study the role of the central bank and monetary policy. We'll see how the central bank's actions can change the quantity of money and influence interest rates, which in turn influence aggregate demand. Then, in Chapter 30, we'll return to the problem of inflation and explore more deeply its causes, its consequences and ways of keeping it under control.

Summary

Key Points

What is Money? (pp. 658–663)

- Money is the means of payment and it has three functions. It is a medium of exchange, a unit of account and a store of value.
- The earliest forms of money were commodities.
- In the modern world, we use a fiat money system. The biggest component of money is deposit money.
- The two main measures of money in the United Kingdom today are M0 and M4.
- M0 consists of currency held by the public, the banks, the building societies and banks' deposits at the Bank of England.
- M4 is currency held by the public and all bank and building society sight and time deposits.

Financial Intermediaries (pp. 663–666)

- The main financial intermediaries whose liabilities are money are commercial banks and building societies.
- These institutions take in deposits, hold cash and liquid assets as reserves to ensure that they can meet their depositors' demands for currency, and use the rest of their financial resources either to buy securities or to make loans.
- Financial intermediaries provide four main economic services. They create liquidity, minimize the cost of obtaining funds, minimize the cost of monitoring borrowers and pool risks.

Financial Regulation, Deregulation and Innovation (pp. 666–669)

- Financial intermediaries are regulated to protect depositors.
- Small depositors have their deposits insured by the Bank of England and owners of intermediaries are required to put a certain minimum amount of their own financial resources into the financial intermediary.
- In the 1980s, banks began to make mortgage loans and building societies began to offer bank services.
- Deregulation in the 1980s removed restrictions on bank and building society activities.
- The continual search for profitable financial opportunities leads to financial innovation – to the creation of new financial products such as new types of deposit and loan.

How Banks Create Money (pp. 669–672)

- Banks create money by making loans.
- The total quantity of deposits that can be supported by a given amount of reserves (the deposit multiplier) is equal to 1 divided by the desired reserve ratio.

Money, Real GDP and the Price Level (pp. 672–678)

- An increase in the quantity of money increases aggregate demand and, in the short run, increases both the price level and real GDP.
- In the long run an increase in the quantity of money increases the price level and leaves real GDP unchanged.
- Like the AS–AD model, the quantity theory of money predicts no long-run relationship between money and real GDP.

Key Figures

Key Terms

Bank, 664
Barter, 658
Building society, 665
Currency, 660
Deposit multiplier, 670
Equation of exchange, 674
Excess reserves, 669
Financial innovation, 668
Financial intermediary, 664
Liquidity, 661
M4, 661
Means of payment, 658
Money, 658
Quantity theory of money, 674
Required reserve ratio, 669
Reserve ratio, 669
Reserves, 664
Velocity of circulation, 674

Review Questions

1 What is money? What are its functions?

2 What are the different forms of money?

3 What are the two main measures of money in the United Kingdom today?

4 Are cheques and credit cards money? Explain your answer.

5 What is a financial intermediary?

6 What are the main items in the balance sheet of a commercial bank?

7 What are the economic functions of financial intermediaries?

8 How do banks make a profit and how do they create money?

9 Describe the main types of financial regulation that financial intermediaries face.

10 Describe the deregulation of financial intermediaries that took place in the 1980s.

11 What is financial innovation? Explain the financial innovation that took place in the 1980s.

12 Define the deposit multiplier. Explain why it equals 1 divided by the desired reserve ratio.

13 What does the aggregate supply–aggregate demand model predict about the effects of a change in the quantity of money on the price level and real GDP when the economy is initially:

a In a recession?
b At full employment?

14 What is the equation of exchange and the velocity of circulation? What assumptions are necessary to make the equation of exchange the quantity theory of money?

15 What is the evidence on the quantity theory of money?

Problems

1 Money includes which of the following items?

a Bank of England notes in the commercial bank's vaults.
b Your Visa card.
c The coins inside public phones.
d Bank of England notes in your wallet.
e The cheque you have just written to pay for your rent.
f The student loan you took last August to pay for your hall of residence fees.

2 Which of the following items are fiat money? Which are private debt money?

a Chequeing deposits at National Westminster Bank.
b IBM shares held by individuals.
c Gold bars held by banks.
d The £5 commemorative crown for the Queen's Jubilee.
e A government Treasury bill.
f A building society share account.

3 Sara withdraws £1,000 from her share account at the Burnley Building Society, keeps £50 in cash and deposits the balance in her chequeing deposit at the Midland Bank. What is the immediate change in M0 and M4?

4 The commercial banks in the kingdom of Ruritania have the following assets and liabilities:

Total reserves	250 million euros
Loans	1,000 million euros
Deposits	2,000 million euros
Total assets	2,500 million euros

a Construct the commercial banks' balance sheet. If you are missing any assets call them 'other assets', if you are missing any liabilities call them 'other liabilities'.
b Calculate the commercial banks' reserve ratio.
c If the reserve ratio in (b) is equal to the commercial banks' desired reserve ratio, calculate the deposit multiplier.

5 An immigrant arrives in Transylvania with 1,200 euros. The 1,200 euros is put into a bank deposit. All the banks in Transylvania have a required reserve ratio of 10 per cent.

a What is the initial increase in the quantity of money of Transylvania?
b What is the initial increase in the quantity of bank deposits when the immigrant arrives?
c How much does the immigrant's bank lend out?
d Use a format similar to that in Figure 27.2 to set out the transactions that take place and calculate the amount lent and the amount of deposits created, assuming that all the funds lent are returned to the banking system in the form of deposits.
e By how much has the quantity of money increased after the bank has made 20 loans?
f What is the total increase in the quantity of money, in bank loans and in bank deposits?

6 Quantecon is a country in which the quantity theory of money operates. The country has a constant population, capital stock and technology. In year 1, real GDP was £400 million, the price level was 200 and the velocity of circulation of money was 20. In year 2, the quantity of money was 20 per cent higher than in year 1.

a What was the quantity of money in Quantecon in year 1?
b What was the quantity of money in Quantecon in year 2?
c What was the price level in Quantecon in year 2?
d What was the level of real GDP in Quantecon in year 2?
e What was the velocity of circulation in Quantecon in year 2?

7 Study *Reading Between the Lines* on pp. 682–683 and then answer the following questions:

a How has Serbia coped with the problem of finding a stable unit of account?
b What has happened to the velocity of circulation of money in Serbia?
c How do people protect themselves from a falling value of money in Serbia?
d Why has Serbia's inflation rate been higher than its money supply growth rate in some years? Does this fact contradict the quantity theory of money?

8 Use the link on the Parkin, Powell and Matthews Web site to visit Mark Bernkopf's Central Banking Resource Center. Read the short article on Electronic Cash and also read 'The End of Cash' by James Gleick (first published in the *New York Times Magazine* 16 June 1996). Then answer the following questions:

a What is e-cash?
b Mark Bernkopf asks: 'Will "e-cash" enable private currencies to overturn the ability of governments to make monetary policy?' Will it? Why or why not?
c When you buy an item on the Internet and pay by using a form of e-cash, are you using money? Explain why or why not.
d In your opinion, is the concern about e-cash a real concern or hype?

 http://www.econ100.com

The Quantity Theory in Action

The New York Times, 15 December 1996

Serbia Tries to Buy Social Peace with Back Pay

Chris Hedges

Belgrade, Serbia, Dec. 14—Business is brisk on the corner of Goce Delceva and Bulever Lenjina streets. And when business here prospers, the rest of Serbia suffers.

"We can't sell German marks fast enough," said Predrag Aleksic, who stood with a cluster of nine other black market money vendors.

"People cash their pension or salary checks at the bank and come out here to get at least some of it in foreign currency. We are seeing more and more new dinar bills, which means our Government is probably printing lots of money."

Serbia's economy, in a tailspin following decades of Communism and years of mismanagement and sanctions, seems headed for a new crisis.

After a year of relative stability, the local currency, the dinar, has begun to plummet in value. The Government of President Slobodan Milosevic, in an apparent bid to mute public unrest over the government's cancellation of election results, which has triggered huge demonstrations on the streets here every day for the last three weeks, has promised to pay pensions, salaries, student grants and social welfare payments that have been in arrears.

But economists say that to carry out this program, which requires hundreds of million of dollars, the government has begun to print money without the reserves to back it.

They also worry that the infusion of cash into the shaky economy has already triggered a devaluation that may snowball into hyperinflation by next year. . . .

This morning, as tens of thousands of students and opposition politicians again marched through central Belgrade, lines of elderly pensioners, many in threadbare coats, gathered at a branch of Jugobanka in the city's New Belgrade section. Most worked for three or four decades in state-owned companies and now live on pensions of less than $100 a month.

For the first time in 12 months, these men and women received full pension checks today, although the payment covered only the month of October. The Government has promised to pay all pension payments for this year by the end of this month. . . .

Economists fear that the days of disastrous hyperinflation in 1993, which saw the value of the currency drop by 10 or 20 percent in a single day, could return. . . .

Street vendors, who clogged the sidewalks selling everything from eggs to videotapes outside the Merkator shopping mall, said sales had fallen by half over the last month.

"People aren't buying," said Nikola Suskavcevic, as he stood next to an array of cheap household goods spread out over the hood of his small car. "Everyone is scared about what will happen next." . . .

The Essence of the Story

- The government of Serbia is creating money at a rapid rate and prices are rising rapidly.
- To avoid losses, people cash their cheques at the bank and then sell their dinars for foreign currency on the black market.
- The government has promised to pay arrears of pensions, salaries, student grants and social welfare, but economists say the government will create the money to make these payments.
- People fear that injecting even more money into the economy will cause hyperinflation.

Economic Analysis

■ Current economic data for Serbia are not available. But data for Yugoslavia (of which present day Serbia is a part) are.

■ Figure 1 shows the inflation rate in Yugoslavia from 1986 through 1992 and the money supply growth rate through 1990. (Note that these growth rates are *thousands* of per cent per year!)

■ Hyperinflation is defined as an inflation rate greater than 50 per cent per month or 12,875 per cent per year. Serbia doesn't have hyperinflation, but its inflation rate is high.

■ Figure 1 shows that money growth and inflation tend to move in a similar direction.

■ The quantity theory of money can be used to explain the movements in money growth and inflation.

■ The table contains some relevant data: inflation rate, real GDP growth, money growth and the change in velocity for 1986, 1987 and 1988. (These are the last three years for which we have GDP data for this country.)

■ Velocity changes, but on the average, over a number of years, it is remarkably stable. Also, real GDP growth does not change much. But as the money supply growth rate changes, so also does the inflation rate change.

■ Between 1985 and 1988, money growth and inflation were 136 per cent a year each and real GDP and velocity barely changed. With numbers like these, it is clear that money growth generates inflation.

■ When inflation is as high and variable as it has been in Serbia, money ceases to work well as a medium of exchange, a unit of account, or a store of value.

■ So people don't want to hold Serbian dinars. They prefer to hold German marks, a currency that has stable buying power. So the velocity of circulation of dinars is high.

■ The higher the inflation rate, the more quickly people try to spend their income and the higher is the velocity of circulation. Figure 2 shows that in low-inflation Japan, the velocity is less than in Yugoslavia. And in high-inflation Brazil and hyperinflation Zaire, the velocity is greater than in Yugoslavia.

■ Serbian money growth occurs not because the government is trying to cause inflation but because it has no way of financing its deficit other than by money printing.

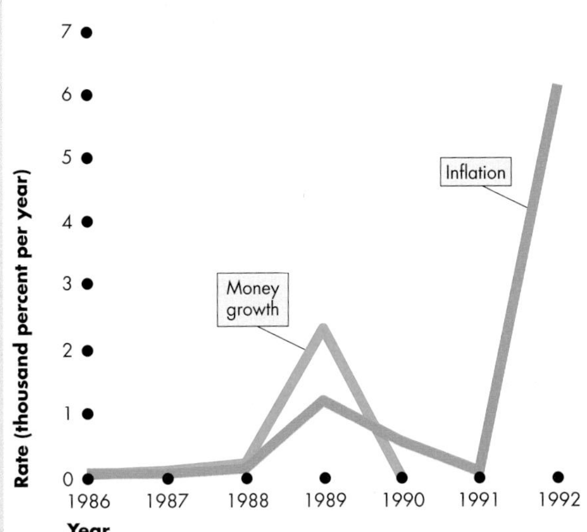

Figure 1 Inflation and money growth in Yugoslavia

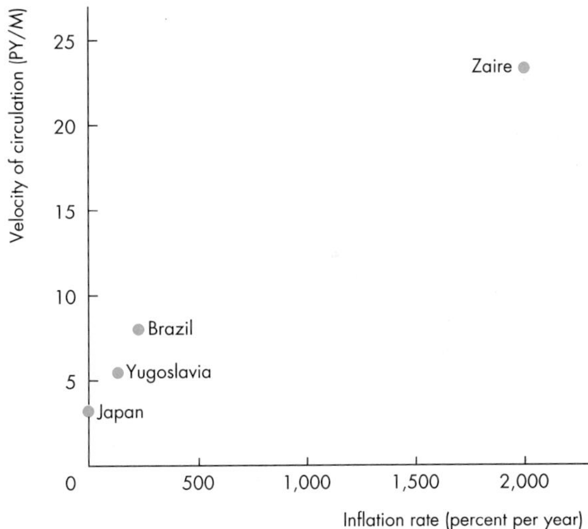

Figure 2 Inflation and velocity

	Inflation rate	Real GDP growth (per cent per year)	Money growth	Change in velocity
1986	88.4	3.5	110.4	–7.3
1987	125.0	–1.0	99.5	11.7
1988	211.8	–2.0	215.1	–3.0
Average	**136.4**	**0.1**	**136.5**	**0.1**

Source: *International Financial Statistics Yearbook, 1995,* (Washington DC: International Monetary Fund).

Money and Inflation

"Inflation is always and everywhere a monetary phenomenon."

Milton Friedman *The Counter-Revolution in Monetary Theory*

The Economist: Milton Friedman

Milton Friedman was born into a poor immigrant family in New York City in 1912. He was an undergraduate at Rutgers and graduate student at Columbia University during the Great Depression. Today, Professor Friedman is a Senior Fellow at the Hoover Institution at Stanford University. But his reputation was built between 1946 and 1983, when he was a leading member of the "Chicago School", which developed an approach to economics at the University of Chicago based on the views that free markets allocate resources efficiently and that stable and low money supply growth deliver macroeconomic stability.

Friedman has advanced our understanding of the forces that determine aggregate demand and clarified the effects of the quantity of money. For this work, he was awarded the 1977 Nobel Prize for Economic Science (much overdue in the opinion of his many admirers).

By reasoning from basic economic principles, Friedman predicted that persistent demand stimulation would *not* increase output but *would* cause inflation. When output growth slowed and inflation broke out in the 1970s, Friedman seemed like a prophet and, for a time, his policy prescription, known as "monetarism", was embraced around the world.

The Issues and Ideas

The combination of history and economics has taught us a lot about the causes of inflation. Severe inflation – hyperinflation – arises from a breakdown of the normal fiscal policy processes at times of war or political upheaval. Tax revenues fall short of government spending, and newly printed money fills the gap between them. As inflation increases, the quantity of money needed to make payments increases, and a shortage of money can even result. So the rate of money growth increases yet further, and prices rise yet faster. Eventually, the monetary system collapses. Such was the experience of Germany during the 1920s and Brazil during the 1990s.

In earlier times, when commodities were used as money, inflation resulted from the discovery of new sources of money. The most recent occurrence of this type of inflation was at the end of the nineteenth century when gold, then used as money, was discovered in Australia, the Klondike and South Africa.

In modern times, inflation has resulted from increases in the money supply that has accommodated increases in costs. The most dramatic of such inflations occurred during the 1970s when central banks around the world accommodated oil price increases.

To avoid inflation, money supply growth must be held in check. But at times of severe cost pressure, central banks feel a strong tug in the direction of avoiding recession and accommodating the cost pressure.

Yet some countries have avoided inflation more effectively than others. One source of success is central bank independence. Traditionally, in low-inflation countries such as Germany, the central bank decides how much money to create and at what level to set interest rates and does not take instructions from the government. In former high-inflation countries, such as Italy, the central bank takes direct orders from the government about interest rates and money supply growth. The architects of a new monetary system for the European Union have noticed this connection between central bank independence and inflation, and they have modelled the European Central Bank on Germany's Bundesbank.

Then . . .

When inflation is especially rapid, as it was in Germany in 1923, money becomes almost worthless. In Germany at that time, bank notes were more valuable as fire kindling than as money, and the sight of people burning Reichmarks was a common one. To avoid having to hold money for too long, wages were paid and spent twice a day. Banks took deposits and made loans, but at interest rates that compensated both depositors and the bank for the falling value of money – interest rates that could exceed 100 per cent a month. The price of a dinner might double during the course of an evening, making lingering over coffee a very expensive pastime.

. . . And Now

In 1994, Brazil had a computer-age hyperinflation, an inflation rate that was close to 50 per cent a month. Banks installed ATMs on almost every street corner and refilled them several times an hour. Brazilians tried to avoid holding currency. As soon as they were paid, they went shopping and bought enough food to get them through to the next payday. Some shoppers filled as many as six carts on a single monthly trip to the supermarket. Also, instead of using currency, Brazilians used credit cards whenever possible. But they paid their card balances off quickly because the interest rate on unpaid balances was 50 per cent a month. Only at such a high interest rate did it pay banks to lend to cardholders, because banks themselves were paying interest rates of 40 per cent a month to induce customers to keep their money in the bank.

CHAPTER 28

The Central Bank and Monetary Policy

After studying this chapter you will be able to:

- Describe the role of the Bank of England
- Describe the tools used by the Bank of England to conduct its monetary policy
- Explain what an open market operation is and how it works
- Explain how an open market operation changes the money supply
- Explain how a central bank controls the money supply
- Explain what determines the demand for money
- Explain how the Bank of England influences interest rates
- Explain how interest rates influence the economy

Inside the Old Lady

During the 1980s many young economists working in financial institutions in the City of London used a great deal of ingenuity in trying to predict the monthly money supply figures ahead of their publication. Why did they do this? The reason is that by predicting the money supply figures ahead of the Bank of England they were hoping to predict the movement of interest rates and the reaction of the financial markets so that they could take speculative positions on behalf of their institutions. ◆ During 1998, interest rates were raised to 7.5 per cent and many economic analysts working in the City of London warned of a rapidly slowing economy. Indeed, the rate of growth of the economy slowed down from 3.1 per cent in the first quarter of 1998 to 1.1 per cent in the fourth quarter. Between June 1997 and June 1998, the interest rate went up from 6.5 per cent in steps of 0.25 per cent to 7.5 per cent. From October 1998 to April 1999 interest rates fell to 5.25 per cent. ◆ Why do interest rates move up and down in this yo-yo fashion? What determines interest rates? Is there some reason for their up-and-down behaviour or is it purely random? You suspect that there is some reason. You may read in the newspapers that the Bank of England supports an interest rate rise because money supply growth is too high. Then, some months later, you may read that the Bank of England supports an interest rate cut because output growth is expected to fall. How does the Bank of England change interest rates? How do interest rates influence the economy? And how do interest rates keep inflation in check?

◆ ◆ ◆ ◆ In this chapter you will learn about the Bank of England and monetary policy. You will learn how the Bank of England and other central banks influence interest rates and how interest rates influence the economy. You'll discover that interest rates depend, in part, on the amount of money in existence. You will also discover how the Bank of England influences the quantity of money to influence interest rates as it attempts to smooth the business cycle and keep inflation in check.

The Bank of England

The **Bank of England**, affectionately known as the 'Old Lady of Threadneedle Street' and referred to as the Bank, is the central bank of the United Kingdom. A **central bank** is a bankers' bank and a public authority charged with regulating and controlling a nation's monetary and financial institutions and markets. As the bankers' bank, the Bank provides banking services to the commercial banks. But a central bank is not a citizens' bank. That is, the Bank does not provide general banking services for businesses and individual citizens.

The Bank conducts the nation's **monetary policy**, which means that it adjusts the quantity of money in circulation. The Bank's goal in its conduct of monetary policy is to keep inflation within a specified target range but its other objectives are to moderate the business cycle, and manage and sometimes defend the exchange rate. Complete success in the pursuit of these goals is impossible, and the Bank's more modest goal is to improve the performance of the economy and to get closer to the goals than a 'hands off' approach would achieve. Whether the Bank succeeds in improving economic performance is a matter on which there is a variety of opinion.

If the United Kingdom joins the European Monetary Union (EMU), the powers the Bank of England currently exercises over monetary policy will be handed over to the **European Central Bank (ECB)** in Frankfurt. The ECB, through its Governing Council which consists of ECB officials and the Governors of the currently eleven participating countries of the EMU meet regularly to set the rate of interest for the countries in the EMU. For the time being the UK remains outside the EMU which allows the Bank of England to decide monetary policy for the UK.

Our aim in this chapter is to learn about the tools available to the Bank in its conduct of monetary policy and the effects of the Bank's actions on the economy. Our starting point is to examine the origins and describe the structure of the Bank.

The Origins and Functions of the Bank of England

The Bank was formally recognized as the central bank of the United Kingdom in the 1946 Bank of England Act. It had been established in 1694 by an act of Parliament following a loan of £1.2 million by a syndicate of wealthy individuals to the government of King William and Queen Mary. The creation of the Bank formalized the process whereby the syndicate lent to the government in return for the right to issue bank notes. Between 1688 and 1815, the United Kingdom was involved in seven wars and several small conflicts which needed funding. The growing dependence on the Bank for raising funds in times of crisis created the role of the government's bank. In April 1997, the government made the Bank of England operationally independent in the determination of monetary policy.

The functions of the Bank of England as a central bank have developed over the three centuries since its creation. Today these functions can be summarized as:

- Banker to the government.
- Bankers' bank.
- Lender of last resort.
- Regulator of banks.
- Manager of monetary policy.

Let us briefly examine each of these functions.

Banker to the Government

The banker to the government means that the government's own deposits – called public deposits – are held at the Bank of England. These are the accounts of the revenue raising agencies such as the Inland Revenue and HM Customs and Excise, and the spending departments such as the Ministry of Defence. A business that needs to pay tax will pay a cheque to the Inland Revenue, which will eventually be deposited at the Bank of England. If the Ministry of Defence has to pay for a new fighting ship, it will issue a cheque based on its account at the Bank. Acting as the government's bank also means that the Bank handles the government's borrowing needs. There are two ways in which the government can borrow: directly from the Bank of England in the form of a loan or by selling bonds. Direct lending amounts to the same thing as printing money. The alternative is to manage the government's borrowing by selling government bonds to the public. The function of selling government debt gives the Bank a pivotal role in the conduct of monetary policy.

Banker's Bank

The commercial banks keep a certain amount of money as deposits at the Bank of England. This is a convenient means by which banks can settle debts they have with each other by simply transferring funds between accounts at the Bank. The Bank is also the sole effective issuer of bank notes. If the general public increase their demand for notes, this will result in a decrease in the amount of notes kept by the banks. The banks will replenish their stock of notes by cashing their deposits at the Bank of England. The Bank of England in turn will issue bank notes as it has an effective monopoly. Even though the Scottish banks issue their own bank notes they must be backed fully by Bank of England notes.

Lender of Last Resort The Bank of England acts as the lender of last resort to the banking system. It operates on two levels. On a day-to-day basis, when the commercial banks run short of cash, it is the Bank of England that restores the cash levels of the banks. Unlike in other countries, the commercial banks do not borrow directly from the Bank of England but through the *discount houses*. Discount houses exist by borrowing very short-term money from banks – called *money at call* – and buying Treasury bills, commercial bills and local authority bills. The discount houses also have a special relationship with the Bank of England, so that if the commercial banks are short of cash and they call in their short-term loans to the discount houses, the discount houses can obtain the cash to pay the banks from the Bank of England. Figure 28.1 describes the pivotal role of the discount houses in the UK financial system. The rate of interest at which the Bank is prepared to lend to the discount houses will have implications for short-term interest rates and the general level of interest rates. The Bank of England also acts as lender of last resort to any individual bank or group of banks that are experiencing liquidity problems. The aim of the Bank is to ensure the smooth working of the financial system.

Regulator of Banks As the Bank ultimately guarantees the stability of the banking and financial system, it also faces the problem of moral hazard (see Chapter 27, p. 667). Some economists argue that banks may be tempted to act imprudently if they think that the central bank is always there to provide liquidity in a crisis. To guard against this possibility, the central bank also undertakes the prudential regulation of commercial banks. In the UK, regulation is based on the supervision of individual banks by the Financial Services Authority.

Figure 28.1 The Discount Houses and the Financial System

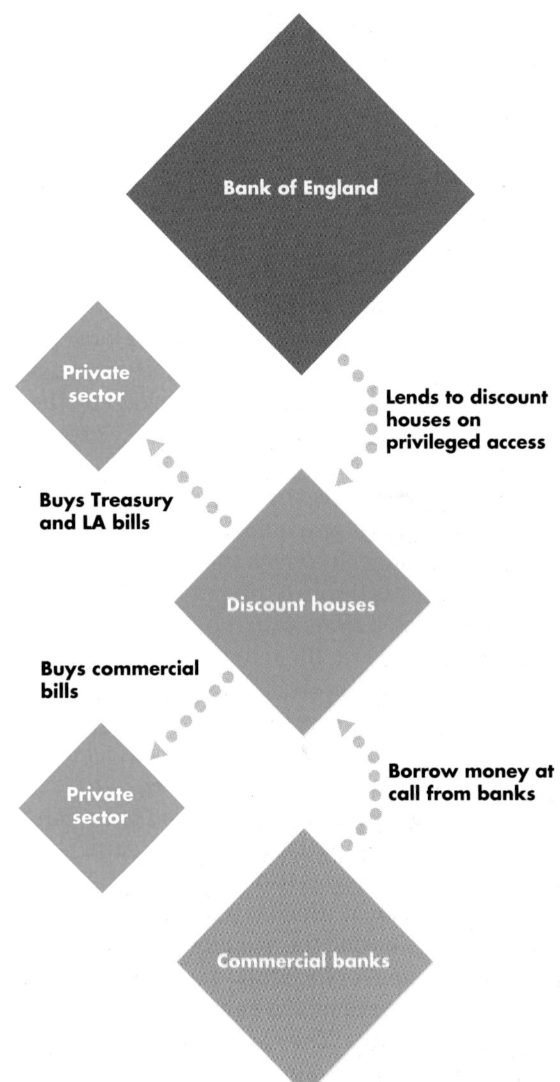

The discount houses play a pivotal role in the UK financial system. They take very short-term loans from the commercial banks, known as money at call. These loans are part of the banking system's liquid reserves and can be recalled at any time. When the discount houses are short of funds they have privileged access to lender of last resort loans from the Bank of England. They use their funds to buy Treasury bills, commercial bills and local authority bills.

There are two levels at which a central bank can monitor and regulate commercial banks. At one level, it licenses the entry and establishment of a bank. The central bank must be convinced that a new commercial bank is a fit and proper organization to conduct the business of banking, and any breach of the set criteria will result in loss of authorization to act as a bank. At the second level, the central bank or an independent agent monitors the liquidity and capital adequacy of the commercial bank. We examined such regulations in Chapter 27.

Manager of Monetary Policy The Bank of England is operationally independent in the conduct of monetary policy. This means that it is no longer the agent of the government but determines monetary policy based on a set of objectives decided by the Chancellor of the Exchequer. The primary objective of the Bank is to maintain inflation between $1\frac{1}{2}$ and $2\frac{1}{2}$ per cent but it is also concerned with output growth because that also influences inflation.

The main channel by which the Bank conducts monetary policy is through the setting of the rate of interest at which it deals with the discount houses. For 270 years to 1972, the rate of interest at which the Bank lent to the discount houses was announced and known as the *bank rate*. After 13 October, 1972, the rate at which the Bank acted as lender of last resort was referred to as the *minimum lending rate* or MLR. The MLR ceased to be continuously posted after 20 August, 1981. After this date the discount houses had to apply to the Bank to find out the rate at which it would make last resort loans. Following the abandonment of the continuous posting of the MLR, the base rates of the major banks became the indicator of the broad level of interest rates. The banks' base rates are in turn influenced by the rate at which the discount houses can obtain funds from the Bank of England. The Bank influences the commercial banks' base rate by signalling to the discount houses that it will be willing to lend at a specific rate.

The Bank's Financial Structure

For accounting purposes, the Bank of England is separated into two departments: the Issue department and the Banking department. The Issue department is treated as part of the government, whereas the Banking department is a public corporation. The separation is largely historical and is not particularly important from an analytical viewpoint. The Issue department is the bank note issuing arm of the Bank of England and the Banking department takes deposits from the commercial banks. Also, the Issue department has as its liabilities the notes in circulation including the notes held by the Banking department. Table 28.1 shows the consolidated balance sheet of the Bank of England. It is arrived at by adding the assets and liabilities of the two departments and subtracting the assets of the one department that are liabilities of the other.

The largest liability of the Bank of England is notes in circulation. The reason these are entered as a liability is because when Bank of England notes were in principle convertible into coin or gold, the note represented a liability which could be redeemed on demand. Up until 1931, it was possible in principle to redeem Bank of England notes for gold. Since 1931, the note issue has been backed by securities, most of which are government securities as seen on the asset side of the balance sheet. Bank notes are non-convertible, which means that they cannot be converted into anything. But the tradition of being able to convert Bank of England notes remains even though the reality is different. If you look at a £10 note it says on it *I promise to pay the bearer on demand the sum of Ten pounds.* This only means that the Bank of England is willing to accept one £10 note for another. While notes are the liability of the Bank of England, coin is issued by the Royal Mint and is therefore not a liability.

The other important liability of the Bank of England is the commercial banks' deposits it holds. These are the deposits that the commercial banks

Table 28.1 Balance sheet of the Bank of England, 16 December 1998

Assets (billions of pounds)		Liabilities (billions of pounds)	
Government securities	17.2	Notes in circulation	24.6
Other securities	8.8	Public deposits	0.2
Advances and other accounts	3.3	Bankers' deposits	1.4
Premises, equipment and other	2.1	Reserves and other accounts	5.2
Total	**28.4**	**Total**	**28.4**

Source: *Financial Statistics* March 1999, ONS.

keep at the Bank of England to act as a means of clearing interbank debt. At the end of the working day, if the National Westminster Bank has a deficit with Barclays Bank, funds can be transferred from the National Westminster account to the Barclays account held at the Bank of England. The banks' deposits at the Bank of England include a mandatory 0.35 per cent of the eligible deposits at commercial banks. Eligible deposits are defined as sterling deposits of up to two years' maturity.

Public deposits are the deposits of individual government departments. The final item on the liability side of the balance sheet are accounts held by foreign central banks such as the German Bundesbank or the US Federal Reserve.

The asset side of the balance sheet shows that the Bank of England holds government securities, such as Treasury bills and government bonds and lending to the government. Other securities that are held by the Issue department include commercial bills issued by businesses.

The two largest items on the liabilities side of the Bank's balance sheet make up most of the monetary base. The **monetary base** is also known as M0. In theory, a central bank can control the supply of the monetary base, and through it control the total money supply and interest rates. However, traditionally the Bank of England has not attempted to control the supply of M0. As we shall see the main instrument of control is the rate of interest.

The Bank's Policy Tools

We have seen that the Bank of England has many responsibilities, but we'll examine its most important one – regulating the amount of money. How does the Bank or indeed any central bank control the money supply? It uses three main policy tools to achieve its objectives:

1 Required reserve ratios.
2 Discount rate.
3 Open market operations.

Required Reserve Ratios As a rule central banks require that commercial banks have minimum reserve requirements in the form of cash or liquidity holdings as a percentage of deposits. This minimum percentage is known as a *required reserve ratio*. The practice of minimum required reserve ratios varies from central bank to central bank. Most central banks determine a required reserve ratio for each type of deposit. The ECB has set a minimum reseve ratio of 2 per cent for all banks in the 11 countries in the European Monetary Union.

By increasing required reserve ratios, the central bank can create a shortage of reserves for the banking system and decrease bank lending. A decrease in lending decreases the money supply by a process similar to that described in Chapter 27. We'll look at this process later in this chapter.

Although changes in required reserve ratios can be used to influence the money supply, a central bank rarely uses this policy tool. That is, the central bank does not often *change* required reserve ratios as an active tool to *change* the money supply. In the United Kingdom, the last time the Bank of England used this method was in the mid-1970s. The current requirement for United Kingdom banks is to keep 0.35 per cent of their eligible deposits with the Bank of England. The commercial banks keep a little extra at the Bank of England to cover interbank transactions. These extra deposits are called *operational deposits*.

Discount Rate The **discount rate** is the interest rate at which the central bank stands ready to lend reserves to commercial banks. In the United Kingdom this is done by altering the cost of lender of last resort facilities to the discount houses. A rise in the discount rate makes it more costly for banks to borrow reserves from the central bank and encourages them to cut their lending, which reduces the money supply. A fall in the discount rate makes it less costly for banks to borrow reserves from the central bank and stimulates bank lending, which increases the money supply. In the United Kingdom, a rise in the lender of last resort interest rate to discount houses means that if the commercial banks recall any of their loans to the discount houses – remember that these are the highly liquid assets of the commercial banks – the discount houses will have to borrow the extra funds from the Bank of England at these new rates. To avoid lending at lower rates than those imposed by the Bank of England, the discount houses will raise their lending rates, which will cause borrowers to borrow less from them and more from the commercial banks. But if the discount houses do not lend as much as they did before the rise in the interest rate, they will not borrow as much from the commercial banks. Since the commercial banks need to lend to the discount houses as part of their liquid assets, they will find that they do not have enough reserves to maintain a prudent balance between their need to lend and make money and their need to meet withdrawals of deposits by depositors. To guard against this possibility, the commercial banks will reduce their lending by raising their own lending rates. In reality, as soon as the Bank of England signals that the interest rate to the discount houses is to rise, the commercial banks respond immediately by raising their base rates.

Open Market Operations An **open market operation** is the purchase or sale of government securities – Treasury bills and bonds – by the Bank of England in the open market. The term 'open market' refers to commercial banks and the general public but not the government. Thus when the Bank of England conducts an open market operation, it does a transaction with a bank or some other business but it does not transact with the government.

Open market operations influence the money supply. We'll study the details of this influence in the next section. Briefly, when the Bank sells government securities it receives payment with bank deposits and bank reserves, which creates tighter monetary and credit conditions. With lower reserves, the banks cut their lending, and the money supply decreases. When the Bank buys government securities, it pays for them with bank deposits and bank reserves, which creates looser monetary and credit conditions. With extra reserves, the banks increase their lending, and the money supply increases.

Accountability and Control of the Central Bank

In some countries central banks decide monetary policy and in other countries the central bank is virtually an arm of government policy. Since May 1997, the Bank of England conducts monetary policy independently of the government. Monetary policy is set by a committee of experts known as the Monetary Policy Committee. The Monetary Policy Committee is made up of the Governor, the Deputy Governor and seven other members including three academic economists. The Committee meets monthly to set the discount rate. The decision to raise, lower, or keep interest rates the same is made by a vote. The minutes of the monthly meeting are published so that everyone can see the level of agreement between the members and how they voted. The purpose of publishing the minutes is to introduce a sense of openness to the deliberations. In contrast, the governing council of the ECB do not publish their minutes. The argument for secrecy is that the governors of individual country central banks would be free of political pressure if their voting behaviour was not publicly known.

Central banks all over the world face some kind of political pressure at some time. The political constraints will depend on the legal relationship between the government and the central bank, and the history and traditions that have governed this relationship. The relationship can range from total dependence to one of total independence.

Dependence Versus Independence for the Central Bank

A dependent central bank acts entirely as the agent of the government and carries out monetary policy dictated by it. The argument for dependence is that monetary policy is a political issue and therefore central banks must follow the dictates of their political masters. While, some central banks are not independent in the sense of having to follow the policy dictated by the government, it does not mean that it has no power. Few democratic governments will be willing to run the risk of the governor of the central bank resigning because of a disagreement with the government. Therefore the notion of dependence is one of degree. A low degree of dependence means a high degree of independence and vice versa.

However, economists have argued that higher inflation is usually associated with countries that have central banks with low degrees of independence. The reason for this is that governments are inclined to conduct relaxed monetary policies at election times. The evidence appears to confirm that countries with central banks that have high degrees of independence are associated with lower inflation than the average, while countries with central banks that have low degrees of independence are associated with higher inflation than the average. The notion that low inflation is the outcome of monetary policy followed by an independent central bank is not entirely convincing. Japan, for instance, has a dependent central bank but a history of relatively low inflation.

The new European Central Bank is an independent central bank modelled on the existing

Bundesbank. All countries that belong to the EMU have independent central banks and countries that hope to join the EMU at a later stage are expected to give independence to their respective central banks.

Review

- The Bank of England is the central bank of the United Kingdom.
- A central bank conducts a nation's monetary policy and supervises the financial system.
- A central bank's policy tools are the required reserve ratio, the discount rate and open market operations.
- Monetary policy in the United Kingdom is determined by the Monetary Policy Committee.
- To change the quantity of money, the Bank of England changes the rate of interest or conducts open market operations.
- Evidence supports the argument that an independent central bank follows a low inflation monetary policy.

Next, we're going to study how the Bank of England influences the quantity of money.

Controlling the Money Supply

The Bank constantly monitors and adjusts the quantity of money in the economy. To change the quantity of money, the Bank conducts an open market operation. When the Bank *buys* securities in an open market operation, the monetary base *increases*, banks *increase* their lending and the quantity of money *increases*. When the Bank *sells* securities in an open market operation, the monetary base *decreases*, banks *decrease* their lending and the quantity of money *decreases*.

Let's study these changes in the quantity of money, beginning with the effects of open market operations on the monetary base.

How an Open Market Operation Works

When the Bank of England conducts an open market operation, the reserves of the banking system, a component of the monetary base, change. To see why this outcome occurs, we'll trace the effects of an open market operation both when the Bank *buys* securities and when it *sells* securities.

The Bank Buys Securities Suppose the Bank buys £100 million of government securities in the open market. There are two cases to consider: when the Bank buys from a commercial bank and when it buys from the public (a person or business that is not a commercial bank). The outcome is essentially the same in either case, but you need to be convinced of this fact so we'll study the two cases, starting with the simplest case in which the Bank buys from a commercial bank.

Buys from Commercial Bank When the Bank buys £100 million of securities from Barclays bank, two things happen:

1 Barclays has £100 million fewer securities and the Bank of England has £100 million more securities.
2 The Bank of England pays for the securities by crediting Barclays deposit account at the Bank of England by £100 million.

Figure 28.2(a) shows the effects of these actions on the balance sheets of the Bank of England and Barclays. Ownership of the securities passes from Barclays to the Bank of England, so Barclays' assets decrease by £100 million and the Bank of England's assets increase by £100 million – shown by the blue arrow running from Barclays to the Bank of England. The Bank of England pays for the securities by crediting Barclays' deposit account – its reserves – at the Bank by £100 million – shown by the green arrow running from the Bank to Barclays. This action increases the monetary base and increases the reserves of the banking system.

The Bank of England's assets increase by £100 million and its liabilities also increase by £100 million. Barclays' total assets remain constant but their composition changes. Its deposits at the Bank increase by £100 million and its holdings of government securities decrease by £100 million. So the bank has additional reserves, which it can use to make loans.

Figure 28.2 The Bank Buys Securities in the Open Market

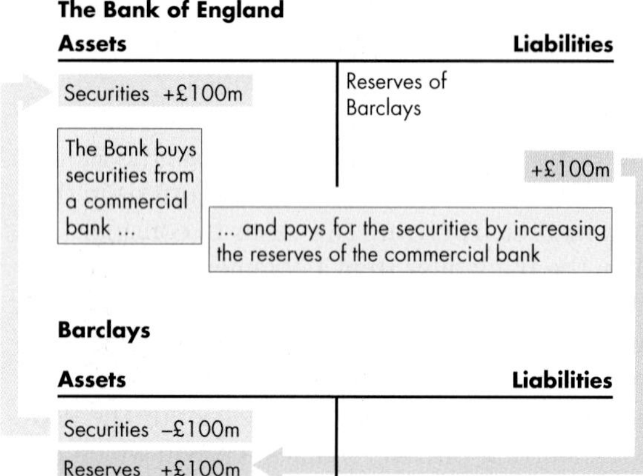

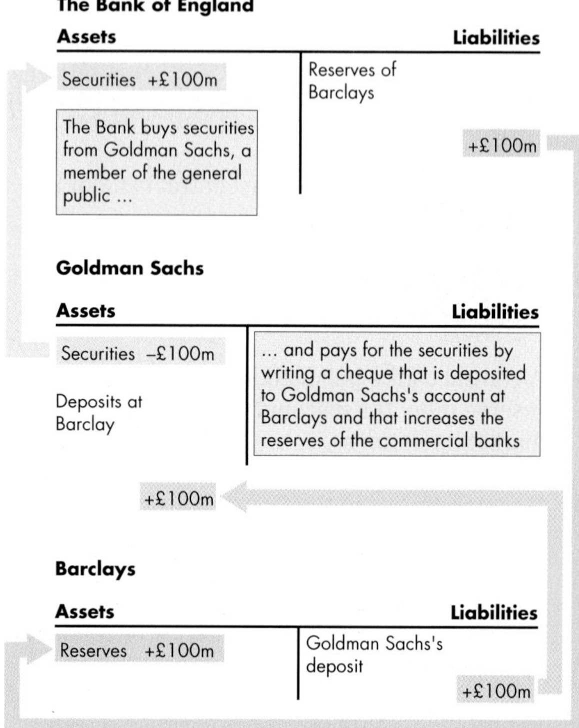

When the Bank buys securities in the open market, bank reserves increase. If the Bank buys from a commercial bank (part a), bank reserves increase when the Bank pays the bank for the securities. If the Bank buys from the public (part b), bank deposits and bank reserves increase when the seller of the securities deposits the Bank's cheque and the commercial bank collects payment from the Bank.

We've just seen that when the Bank buys government securities from a bank, the bank's reserves increase. But what happens if the Bank buys government securities from the public – say from Goldman Sachs International, a financial services company?

Buys from Public When the Bank of England buys £100 million of securities from Goldman Sachs, three things happen:

1 Goldman Sachs has £100 million fewer securities and the Bank has £100 million more securities.
2 The Bank pays for the securities with a cheque for £100 million drawn on itself, which Goldman Sachs deposits in its account at Barclays.
3 Barclays collects payment of this cheque from the Bank of England, and £100 million is deposited in Barclays' deposit account at the Bank of England.

Figure 28.2(b) shows the effects of these actions on the balance sheets of the Bank, Goldman Sachs and Barclays. Ownership of the securities passes from Goldman Sachs to the Bank, so Goldman Sachs's assets decrease by £100 million and the Bank's assets increase by £100 million – shown by the blue arrow running from Goldman Sachs to the Bank. The Bank pays for the securities with a cheque payable to Goldman Sachs. This payment increases Goldman Sachs's deposit at Barclays by £100 million and it also increases Barclays' reserves by £100 million – shown by the green arrow running from the Bank to Barclays and the red arrow running from Barclays to Goldman Sachs. Just as when the Bank of England buys from a bank, this action increases the monetary base and increases the reserves of the banking system.

Again, the Bank's assets increase by £100 million and its liabilities also increase by £100 million. Goldman Sachs has the same total assets as before, but

Figure 28.3 A Round in the Multiplier Process Following an Open Market Operation

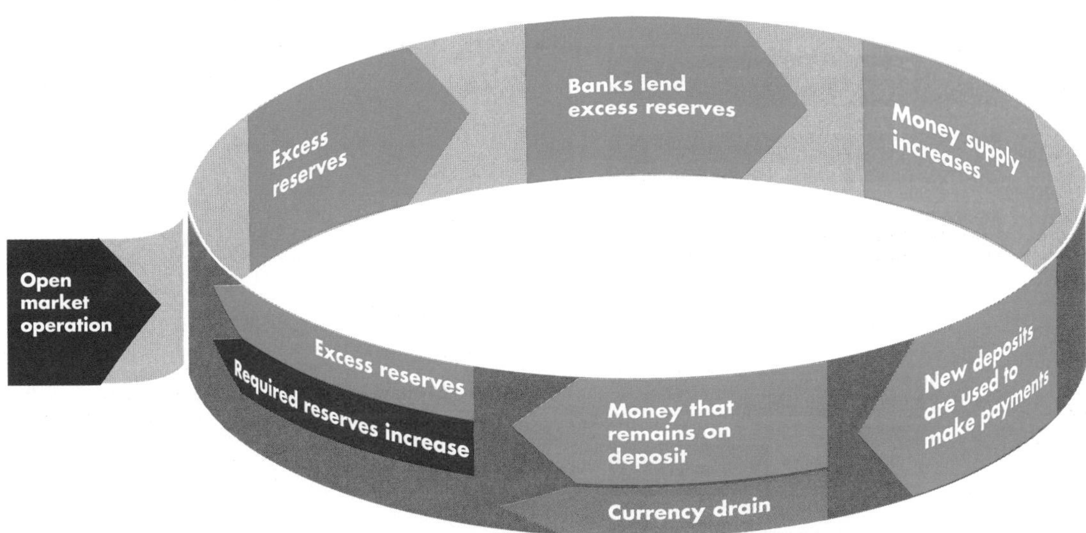

An open market purchase of government securities increases bank reserves and creates excess reserves. Banks lend the excess reserves and new loans are used to make payments. Households and firms receiving payments keep some of the receipts in the form of currency – a currency drain – and place the rest on deposit in banks. The increase in bank deposits increases banks' reserves, but also increases banks' desired reserves. Desired reserves increase by less than actual reserves, so the banks still have some excess reserves, although less than before. The process repeats until excess reserves have been eliminated. There are two components to the increase in the quantity of money: the currency drain and the increase in deposits.

their composition has changed. It now has more money and fewer securities. Barclays' total assets increase and so do its liabilities. Its deposits at the Bank of England – its reserves – increase by £100 million and its deposit liability to Goldman Sachs increases by £100 million. Because its reserves have increased by the same amount as its deposits, the bank has excess reserves, which it can use to make loans.

We've now studied what happens when the Bank of England buys government securities from either a bank or the public. If the Bank *sells* securities, all the stages that you have studied are reversed. Reserves decrease, and the commercial banks are short of reserves.

The effects of an open market operation on the balance sheets of the Bank and the commercial banks that we have just described represent only the beginning of the story. With an increase in their reserves, the commercial banks are able to make more loans, which increases the quantity of money. Conversely, with a decrease in reserves, the commercial banks must cut loans, which decreases the quantity of money.

We learned how loans create deposits in Chapter 27. Here, we build on that basic idea but instead of studying the link between bank reserves and deposits, we examine the related broader link between the quantity of money and the monetary base.

Monetary Base and Bank Reserves

The *monetary base* is the sum of notes and coins, and bankers' deposits at the Bank. It is known as M0 and is used by the Bank of England Monetary Policy Committee as an indicator of monetary conditions in the economy. The monetary base is held either by banks as *reserves* or outside the banks as currency in circulation. When the monetary base increases, both bank reserves and currency in circulation increase. Only the increase in bank

Figure 28.4 The Multiplier Effect of an Open Market Operation

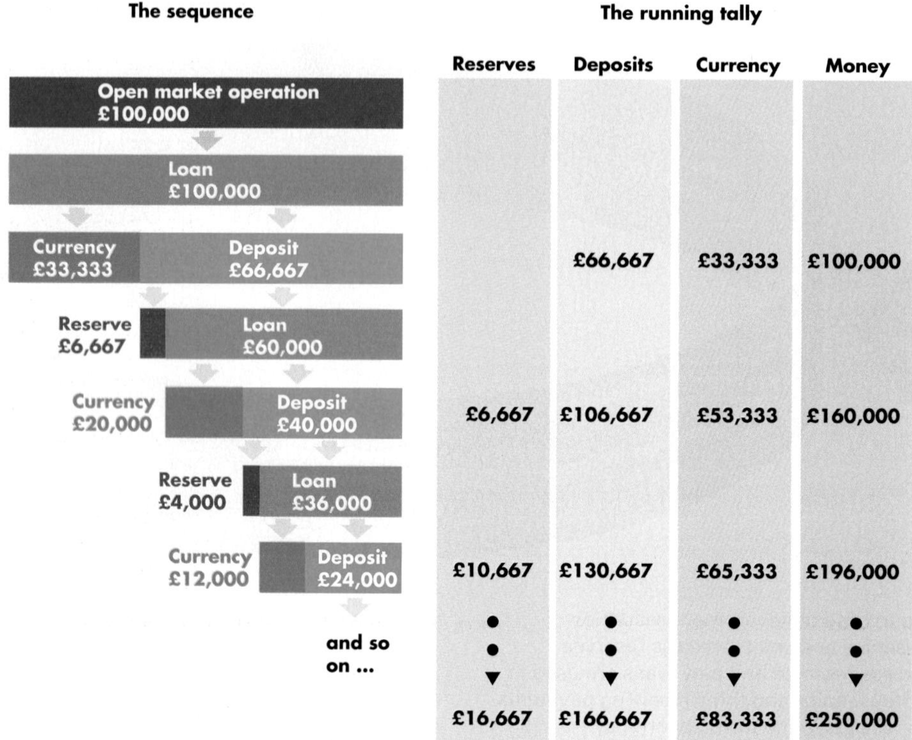

When the Bank provides the banks with £100,000 of additional reserves in an open market operation, the banks lend those reserves. Of the amount lent, £33,333 (33.33 per cent) leaves the banks in a currency drain and £66,667 remains on deposit. With additional deposits, desired reserves increase by £6,667 (10 per cent required reserves ratio) and the banks lend £60,000. Of this amount, £20,000 leaves the banks in a currency drain and £40,000 remains on deposit. The process keeps repeating until the banks have created enough deposits to eliminate their excess reserves. The running tally tells us the amounts of reserves, deposits, currency drain and money created at each stage. At the end of the process, an additional £100,000 of reserves creates an additional £250,000 of money.

reserves can be used by banks to make loans and create additional money. An increase in currency held outside the banks is called a **currency drain**. A currency drain reduces the amount of additional money that can be created from a given increase in the monetary base.

The **money multiplier** is the amount by which a change in the monetary base is multiplied to determine the resulting change in the quantity of money. It is related to but differs from the deposit multiplier that we studied in Chapter 27. The *deposit multiplier* is the amount by which a change in bank reserves is multiplied to determine the change in bank deposits.

Let's now look at the money multiplier.

The Multiplier Effect of an Open Market Operation

Let's work out the multiplier effect of an open market operation in which the Bank buys securities from the banks. In this case, although the open market operation increases the banks' reserves, it has no immediate effect on the quantity of money. The banks are holding more reserves and fewer securities and they have excess reserves. When the banks have excess reserves, the sequence of events shown in Figure 28.3 takes place. These events are:

- Banks lend excess reserves.
- Deposits are created equal in value to the new loans.

Figure 28.5 The Cumulative Effects of an Open Market Operation

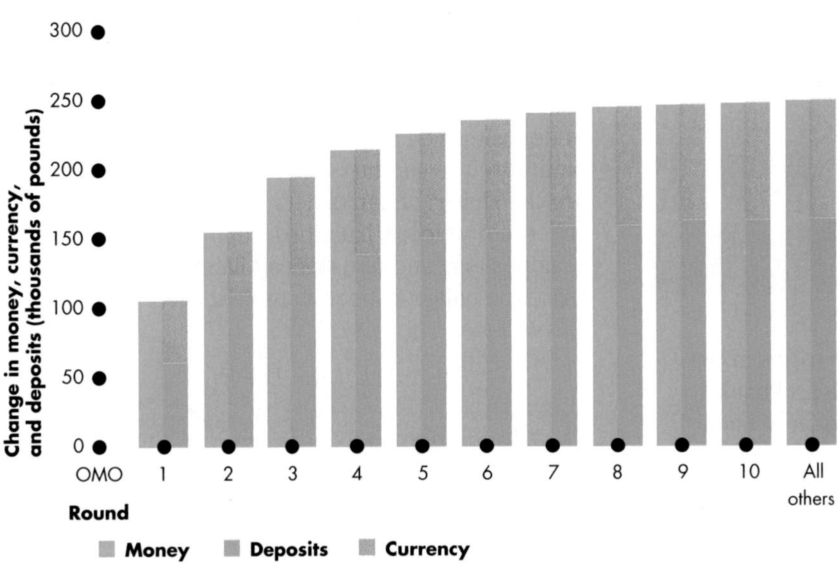

An open market operation (OMO) in which the Bank buys £100,000 government securities from the commercial banks has no immediate effect on the money supply but creates excess reserves in the banking system. When loans are made with these reserves, bank deposits and currency holdings increase. Each time new loans are made, part of the loan drains out from the banks and is held as currency, and part of the loan stays in the banking system in the form of additional deposits and additional reserves. The commercial banks continue to increase their lending until excess reserves have been eliminated. The magnitude of the ultimate increase in the money supply is determined by the money multiplier.

- The new deposits are used to make payments.
- Households and firms receive payments from the borrowers.
- Part of the receipts are held as currency – a *currency drain*.
- Part of the receipts remain as deposits in banks.
- Desired reserves increase (by a fraction – the desired reserve ratio – of the increase in deposits).
- Excess reserves decrease, but remain positive.
- Banks lend the excess reserves and the process repeats itself.

The sequence repeats in a series of rounds, but each round begins with a smaller quantity of excess reserves than did the previous one. The process continues until excess reserves have finally been eliminated.

Figure 28.4 illustrates these rounds and keeps track of the magnitudes of the increases in reserves, loans, deposits, currency and money that result from an open market operation of £100,000. In this figure, the *currency drain* is 33.33 per cent and the *desired reserve ratio* is 10 per cent.

The Bank buys £100,000 of securities from the banks. The banks' reserves increase by this amount but deposits do not change. The banks have excess reserves of £100,000, and they lend those reserves. When the banks lend £100,000 of excess reserves, £66,667 remains in the banks as deposits and £33,333 drains off and is held outside the banks as currency. The quantity of money has now increased by £100,000 – the increase in deposits plus the increase in currency holdings.

The increased bank deposits of £66,667 generate an increase in desired reserves of 10 per cent of that amount, which is £6,667. Actual reserves have increased by the same amount as the increase in deposits – £66,667. So the banks now have excess reserves of £60,000. At this stage we have gone around the circle shown in Figure 28.3 once. The process we've just described repeats but begins with excess reserves of £60,000. Figure 28.4 shows the next two rounds. At the end of the process, the quantity of money has increased by £250,000.

Figure 28.5 illustrates the accumulated increase in the quantity of money and in its components: bank deposits and currency. When the open market operation takes place (labelled OMO in the figure), there is no initial change in either the quantity of money or its components. Then, after the first round of bank lending, the quantity of money increases by £100,000 – the size of the open market operation. In successive rounds, the quantity of money and its components continue to increase but by successively smaller amounts until, after 10 rounds, the quantities of currency and deposits and their sum, the quantity of money, have almost reached the values to which they are ultimately heading.

Review

- When the central bank buys securities in the open market, the monetary base and bank reserves increase and an expansion of bank lending increases the quantity of money.
- When the central bank sells securities in the open market, the monetary base and bank reserves decrease and the resulting contraction of bank lending decreases the quantity of money.

United Kingdom Money Supply

Let us briefly review the factors that contribute to changes in the money supply from what we have learned so far. We know that increased bank lending raises the money supply. The sale of government bonds, an open market operation, decreases the money supply. An increase in monetary base decreases the money supply through the money multiplier. We also know that in principle the money supply can be increased by reducing the reserve ratio, although this method of monetary control is rarely used by central banks. Let us bring all these factors together to set out a complete statement of the determinants of the change in the money supply. The ingredients for this statement will need the balance sheets of the commercial banks and building societies, the financing requirement of government fiscal policy, M0 and M4.

We can think of the consolidated balance sheet of banks and building societies as the assets that are made up of loans (advances) to the private sector and cash reserves including bankers' deposits at the Bank of England. We are ignoring all the other types of assets such as Treasury bills, commercial bills and other securities. Let's call the level of loans issued L and cash reserves R. The largest liabilities of the banks and building societies are their deposits. These are the sight deposits and time deposits of the commercial banks, the share accounts of the building societies and certificates of deposits. The other liabilities of the commercial banks are the capital of their shareholders. These are the shares of banks held by people and are called non-deposit liabilities, calling the total level of deposits D and non-deposit liabilities E, we can write the balance sheet statement *assets = liabilities* as

$$L + R = D + E$$

The Financing of Fiscal Policy In Chapter 26, pp. 637–641, we examined the role of fiscal policy in the macroeconomy. The government deficit, which is government sector spending less revenues, is referred to as the *Public Sector Net Cash Requirement* (PSNCR). It is called the PSNCR because the deficit has to be financed by borrowing cash. The three ways the government finances its deficit are: borrowing from the public by selling bonds, borrowing from abroad by selling bonds to foreigners and borrowing from the Bank of England, issuing base money. The sale of bonds to the public is the addition to the existing stock of bonds (B) and is denoted as ΔB – the *change in bonds*. The sale of bonds to foreigners is the addition to the existing stock of bonds held by people outside the United Kingdom (F) and is denoted as ΔF – the *change in the stock of bonds held by foreigners*. The issue of base money is the addition to the existing stock of base money (M0) and is denoted as ΔM0 – the *change in* M0. Therefore the PSBR can be stated as follows. The government deficit can be financed by selling bonds to the public, selling bonds to foreigners or issuing base money or any combination of all three.

$$PSNCR = \Delta \text{M0} + \Delta B + \Delta F$$

The Measure of Money We examined the measures of money in the United Kingdom in Chapter 27, pp. 661–663. We can state M0 as being made up of currency in circulation with the public, and cash reserves of the banks and building societies including bankers' deposits at the Bank of England (R). Let us denote the amount of currency in circulation as C. The definition of M4 is currency in

Table 28.2 M4 Counterparts

Year	PSNCR	Purchases of public sector debt by UK private sector $-\Delta B$	External and foreign currency counterparts $-\Delta F$	Sterling lending to the UK private sector ΔA	Net non-deposit sterling liabilities	Change in money stock ΔM4
1991	7,661	–5,543	–2,525	36,762	–8,621	27,682
1992	28,664	–20,092	–3,721	25,757	–12,314	18,115
1993	42,503	–30,195	3,478	22,636	–41,766	23,843
1994	39,342	–22,949	–6,235	31,605	–15,021	25,292
1995	35,446	–21,860	–6,553	57,743	–8,336	56,116
1996	24,778	–19,104	5,711	59,129	–12,124	59,436
1997	11,773	–13,050	19,292	68,597	–6,240	80,455
1998	–6,654	3,433	6,034	63,459	–7,986	58,325

Source: Office for National Statistics, *Financial Statistics, March 1999*, No. 443, HMSO, London. Numbers do not add up to ΔM4 because of rounding.

circulation with the public plus all bank and building society deposits and share accounts including certificates of deposits. These two measures of money can be stated as:

$$\text{M0} = C + R$$

$$\text{M4} = C + D$$

The Change in the Money Supply We can use the above four equations to arrive at a statement about the factors that determine the money supply in the United Kingdom. We can begin by eliminating currency from the two equations for M0 and M4. This is done by equating $C = \text{M0} - R$ and $C = \text{M4} - D$. This gives us an expression for M4 as: $\text{M4} = \text{M0} - R + D$. We can now eliminate D from this expression by using the equation describing the bank and building society balance sheet. Now the equation becomes: $\text{M4} = \text{M0} - R + L + R - E$. Notice that reserves get cancelled out and we arrive at a shorter expression: $\text{M4} = \text{M0} + L - E$. Before we proceed any further, we note that the expression for M4 can also be stated in terms of changes. That is, the change in M4 is the change in M0 and the change in bank and building society loans and advances less the change in non-deposit liabilities:

$$\Delta\text{M4} = \Delta\text{M0} + \Delta L - \Delta E$$

We can now eliminate ΔM0 from this expression by using the statement describing the financing of the government deficit – the PSNCR. From the expression for the PSNCR we have: $\Delta\text{M0} = \text{PSNCR} - \Delta B - \Delta F$. Substituting this into the expression for ΔM4 above we arrive at our final statement:

$$\Delta\text{M4} = PSNCR - \Delta B - \Delta F + \Delta L - \Delta E$$

The expression for the *change in* M4 describes what is known as the M4 *counterparts*. This expression states that the money supply increases as a result of the government deficit – the PSNCR and increases in bank and building society lending. The money supply decreases if the government, through the Bank of England, increases its sales of government bonds and increases if it decreases its sales of government bonds – an open market operation. The money supply will increase if the government reduces its borrowing from foreigners, and the money supply will decrease if it increases its borrowing from abroad. Table 28.2 shows how the counterparts to M4 have evolved in recent years[1]. The columns in Table 28.2 correspond to each of the counterparts of M4. You can see that in recent years the government deficit has been contributing to the increase in the money supply,

1 In reality the external component of the counterparts will include the currency transactions of the Bank of England in carrying out policies to defend the value of the pound, and the foreign currency transactions of the commercial banks.

but that this increase has been largely offset by borrowing from the UK public – that is, the non-bank private sector. The penultimate column is the change in non-deposit liabilities, which is the increase in banks' share capital. The shareholders capital is also a liability of the bank, but it is a non-deposit liability. The major contributor to the increase in the money supply has been the increase in bank and building society lending.

Review

- The change in the total supply of money in the United Kingdom is influenced by the financing of the government budget deficit (the PSNCR), by open market operations (the sale or purchase of government bonds), and the increase in bank and building society lending.
- The M4 counterparts describe the different influences on the change in the money supply. Bank lending has the largest influence. The second largest influence is the PSNCR.

The central bank's objective in conducting open market operations, or taking other actions that influence the quantity of money in circulation are not simply to affect the money supply for its own sake. An important objective is to influence the course of the economy – especially the level of output, employment and prices – by influencing aggregate demand. But the central banks influence on aggregate demand is indirect. Its immediate objective is to move interest rates up or down. To work out the effects of the central bank's actions on interest rates, we need to work out how and why interest rates change when the quantity of money changes. We'll discover the answer to these questions by first studying the demand for money.

The Demand for Money

The amount of money we *receive* each week in payment for our labour is income – a flow. The amount of money that we hold in our wallets or in a sight deposit account at our local bank is an inventory – a stock. There is no limit to how much income – or flow – we would like to receive each week. But there is a limit to how big a stock of money each of us would like to hold, on the average.

The Influences on Money Holding

The quantity of money that people choose to hold depends on four main factors. They are:

1. The price level.
2. The interest rate.
3. Real GDP.
4. Financial innovation.

Let's look at each of them.

The Price Level The quantity of money measured in current pounds is called the quantity of *nominal money*. The quantity of nominal money demanded is proportional to the price level, other things remaining the same. That is, if the price level (GDP deflator) increases by 10 per cent, people will want to hold 10 per cent more nominal money than before, other things remaining the same. What matters is not the number of pounds that you hold but their buying power. If you hold £20 to buy your weekly groceries and beer at the Students' Union, you will increase your money holding to £22 pounds if the prices of groceries and beer – and your student grant – increase by 10 per cent.

The quantity of money measured in constant pounds (for example, in 1995 pounds) is called *real money*. Real money is equal to nominal money divided by the price level. The quantity of real money demanded is independent of the price level. In the above example, you held £20, on the average, at the original price level. When the price level increased by 10 per cent, you increased your average cash holding by 10 per cent, keeping your *real* cash holding constant. Your £22 pounds at the new price level is the same quantity of *real money* as your £20 pounds at the original price level.

The Interest Rate A fundamental principle of economics is that as the opportunity cost of something increases, people try to find substitutes for it. Money is no exception. The higher the opportunity cost of holding money, other things remaining the same, the lower is the quantity of real money demanded. But what is the opportunity cost of holding money? It is the interest rate. But which interest rate? Bank and building society deposits of a certain type earn interest. So money, if held as a time deposit, earns interest. Do we mean the interest rate on bank and building society deposits? Surely a rise in the bank and building society deposit rate makes money more attractive and a rise in this rate will increase the demand for money not lower it? The interest rate we mean is the interest paid on a financial asset that is a close substitute for money. To see why, recall that the opportunity cost of any activity is the value of the best alternative foregone. The alternative to holding money is holding an interest-earning financial asset such as a savings bond or Treasury bill. By holding money instead, you forego the additional interest that you otherwise would have received. This foregone additional interest is the opportunity cost of holding money.

Money loses value because of inflation. Why isn't the inflation rate part of the cost of holding money? It is – other things remaining the same, the higher the expected inflation rate, the higher are interest rates and the higher, therefore, is the opportunity cost of holding money.

Real GDP The quantity of money that households and firms plan to hold depends on the amount they are spending, and the quantity of money demanded in the economy as a whole depends on aggregate expenditure – real GDP.

Again, suppose that you hold an average of £20 to finance your weekly purchases of goods. Now imagine that the prices of these goods and of all other goods remain constant but that your income increases. As a consequence, you now spend more and you also keep a larger amount of money on hand to finance your higher volume of expenditure.

Financial Innovation Financial innovations have altered the quantity of money held by people. Specifically these are the introduction of:

1 Interest-bearing sight deposits.
2 Automatic transfers between sight and time deposits.
3 Automatic teller machines.
4 Credit cards.
5 Bank debit cards.

These innovations have occurred because of the development of computing power that has lowered the cost of calculations and record keeping.

Figure 28.6 The Demand for Money

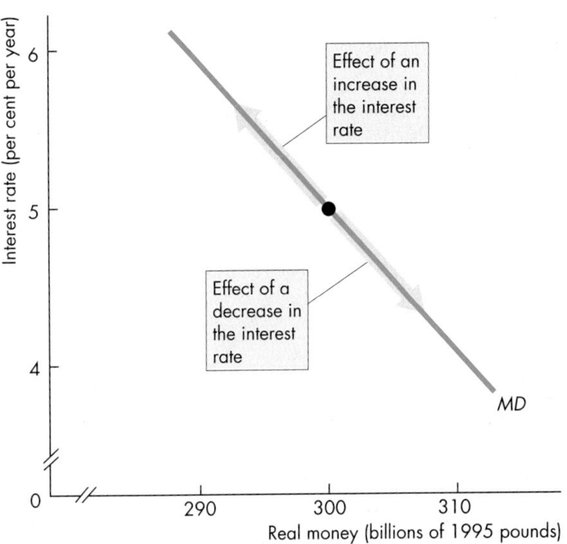

The demand for money curve, *MD*, shows that the lower the interest rate, the larger is the quantity of money that people plan to hold. The demand curve for money slopes downward because the interest rate is the opportunity cost of holding money. The higher the interest rate, the larger is the interest foregone on holding another asset. A change in the interest rate leads to a movement along the demand curve.

We can summarize the effects of the influences on money holding by using the demand for money curve.

The Demand for Money Curve

The *demand for money* is the relationship between the quantity of real money demanded and the interest rate, holding constant all other influences on the amount of money that people wish to hold. Figure 28.6 shows a demand for money curve, *MD*. When the interest rate rises, everything else remaining the same, the opportunity cost of holding money rises and the quantity of money demanded decreases – there is a movement along the demand for money curve. Similarly, when the interest rate falls, the opportunity cost of holding money falls and the quantity of money demanded increases – there is a downward movement along the demand for money curve.

Figure 28.7 Changes in the Demand for Money

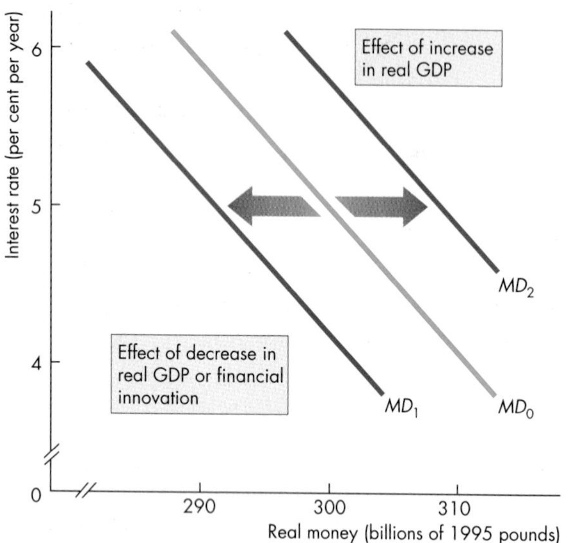

A decrease in real GDP decreases the demand for money and shifts the demand curve leftward from MD_0 to MD_1. An increase in real GDP increases the demand for money and shifts the demand curve rightward from MD_0 to MD_2. Financial innovation generally decreases the demand for money.

Figure 28.8 The Demand for Money in the United Kingdom

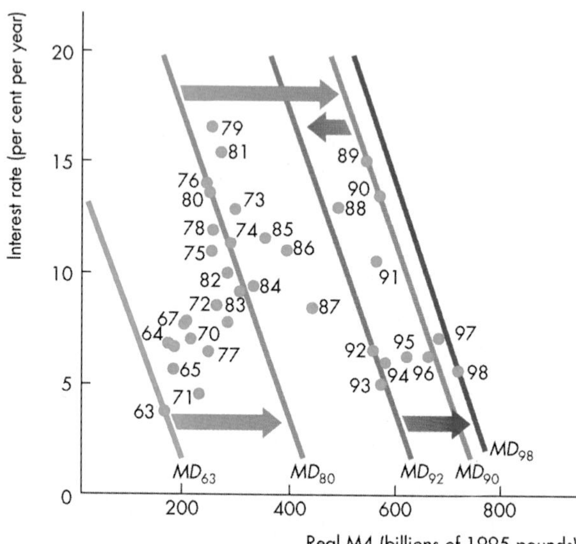

The figure shows the demand for real M4 – the quantity of M4 graphed against the interest rate. The demand for M4 has increased – its demand curve has shifted rightward – because financial innovation developed new types of deposit that are part of M4.

Source: Bank of England.

Shifts in the Demand Curve for Real Money

Figure 28.7 shows the effects of factors that change the demand for money. A decrease in real GDP decreases the demand for money and shifts the demand curve leftward from MD_0 to MD_1. An increase in real GDP has the opposite effect. It increases the demand for money and shifts the demand curve rightward from MD_0 to MD_2. The influence of financial innovation on the demand for money curve is more complicated. It might increase the demand for some types of deposit and decrease the demand for others – and decrease the demand for currency. We'll look at its effects by studying the demand for money in the United Kingdom.

The Demand for Money in the United Kingdom

Figure 28.8 shows the relationship between the interest rate and the quantity of real money demanded in the United Kingdom since 1963. Each dot shows the interest rate and the amount of real money held in a given year.

During the 1960s and 1970s, the demand for M4 increased and the demand curve shifted rightward. During the 1980s – a period of strong financial innovation and deregulation – the demand for M4 increased and the demand curve shifted further to the right. During the recession of the 1990s, the demand for M4 fell and the demand curve shifted leftward for a brief period but in the following recovery the demand for M4 increased and the demand curve continued to shift rightward.

Why did these shifts in the demand for money occur? Firstly, the increase in real income caused an increase in the demand for money at every given rate of interest, but secondly, financial innovation also played a part. The evolution of new financial products has lead to a steady decrease in the demand for bank deposits. In addition, the abolition of certain types of control on the commercial banks' ability to take deposits meant that more and more businesses and financial institutions began to deposit their money with banks, causing the demand for M4 to shift rightward.

Review

- The demand for money curve shows the relationship between the quantity of real money demanded and the interest rate with all other influences on money holding unchanged.
- An increase in the interest rate brings a decrease in the quantity of money demanded and a movement along the demand curve for real money.
- Other influences on the quantity of real money demanded are real GDP and financial innovation.
- An increase in real GDP increases the demand for money and shifts the demand curve rightward.
- Financial innovations have increased the demand for M4.

We now know what determines the demand for money. And we've seen that a key factor is the interest rate – the opportunity cost of holding money. But what determines the interest rate? Let's find out.

Interest Rate Determination

An interest rate is the percentage yield on a financial asset such as a *bond* or a *share*. The higher the the price of a financial asset, other things equal, the lower is the interest rate. An example will make things clearer. Suppose the government sells a bond to the public that promises to pay £10 a year. A bond is a promise to make a sequence of future payments. There are many different possible sequences but the most simple one, for our purposes, is the case of a bond called a perpetuity. A *perpetuity* is a bond that promises to pay a certain fixed amount of money each year forever – in our example £10. The fixed pound payment is called the *coupon*. If the price of the bond is £100, the interest rate is 10 per cent per year – £10 is 10 per cent of £100. If the price of the bond is £50, the interest rate is 20 per cent – £10 is 20 per cent of £50. And if the bond costs £200, the interest rate is 5 per cent – which gives £10 return on a £200 bond holding.

There is an inverse relationship between the price of a bond and the interest rate earned on the bond. People divide their wealth between money and bonds as well as other interest yielding assets. The amount they hold as money will depend on the interest rate earned on bonds.

Money Market Equilibrium

The interest rate is determined at each point in time by equilibrium in the markets for financial assets. The quantity of money supplied is determined by the actions of the banking system and the Bank of England. On any given day, the supply of M4 money is a fixed quantity. The *real* quantity of money supplied is equal to the nominal quantity supplied divided by the price level. At a given moment in time, there is a particular price level and so the quantity of real money supplied is also a fixed amount. The supply curve of real money is shown in Figure 28.9 as the vertical line labelled *MS*. The quantity of real money supplied is £300 billion.

The demand for real money depends on the level of real GDP and on the interest rate. When the quantity of money supplied equals the quantity of money demanded, the money market is in equilibrium. Figure 28.9 illustrates equilibrium in the money market. Equilibrium is achieved by changes in the interest rate. If the interest rate is too high, people demand a smaller quantity of money than the quantity supplied. They are holding too much money. In this situation, they try to get rid of money by buying bonds. As they do so, the price of bonds rises and the interest rate falls. Conversely, if the interest rate is too low, people demand a larger quantity of money than the quantity supplied. They are holding too little money. In this situation, they try to get more money by selling bonds. As they do so, the price of bonds falls and the interest rate rises. Only when the interest rate is at the level at which people are holding the quantity of money supplied do they willingly hold the money and take no actions to change the interest rate.

Figure 28.9 Money Market Equilibrium

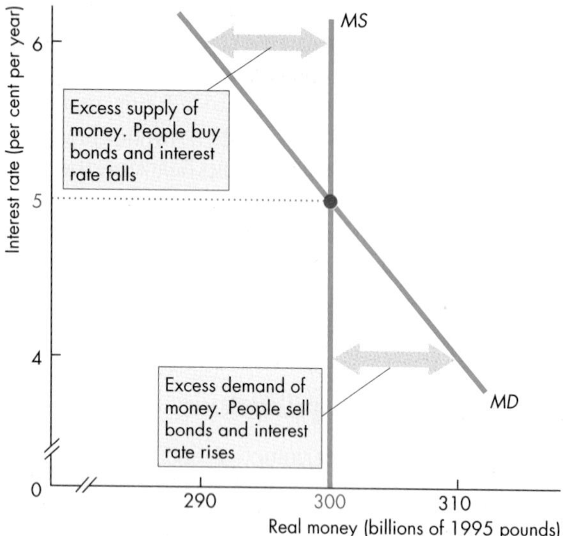

Money market equilibrium occurs when the interest rate has adjusted to make the quantity of money demanded equal to the quantity supplied. Here, equilibrium occurs at an interest rate of 5 per cent. At interest rates above 5 per cent, the quantity of money demanded is less than the quantity supplied, so people sell bonds and the interest rate falls. At interest rates below 5 per cent, the quantity of real money demanded exceeds the quantity supplied, so people buy bonds and the interest rate rises. Only at 5 per cent is the quantity of real money in existence willingly held.

Figure 28.10 Interest Rate Changes

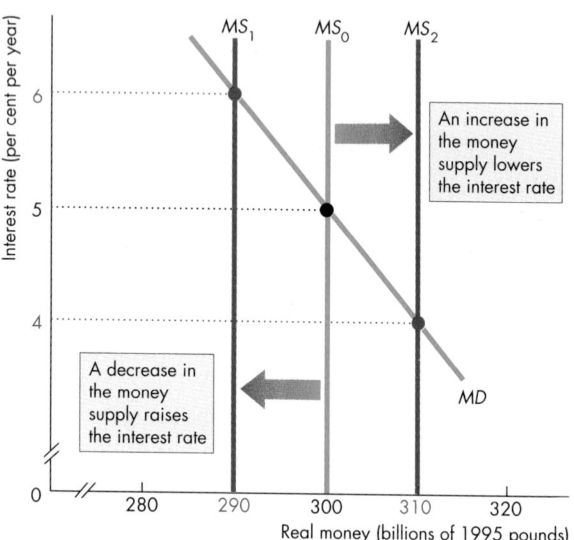

An open market sale of securities shifts the money supply curve leftward to MS_1 and the interest rate rises to 6 per cent. An open market purchase of securities shifts the money supply curve rightward to MS_2 and the interest rate falls to 4 per cent.

Changing the Interest Rate

Suppose that the economy is overheating and the central bank fears that inflation is about to rise. It decides to take action to decrease aggregate demand and spending. To do so, it wants to raise interest rates and discourage borrowing and expenditure on goods and services. What does the central bank do?

The central bank sells securities in the open market. As it does so, it mops up bank reserves and induces the banks to cut their lending. The banks make a smaller quantity of new loans each day until the stock of loans outstanding has fallen to a level consistent with the new lower level of reserves. The money supply decreases.

Suppose that the central bank undertakes open market operations on a sufficiently large scale to decrease the money supply from £300 billion to £290 billion. As a consequence, the supply curve of real money shifts leftward, as shown in Figure 28.10, from MS_0 to MS_1.

The demand for money is shown by *MD*. This curve tells us the quantity of money that households and firms plan to hold at each interest rate. With an interest rate of 5 per cent, and with £290 billion of money in the economy, firms and households are now holding less money than they wish to hold. They attempt to increase their money holding by selling financial assets. As they do so, the prices of bonds and stocks fall and the interest rate rises. When the interest rate has increased to 6 per cent, people are willing to hold the smaller £290 billion stock of money that the Bank and the banks have created.

Conversely, suppose that the economy is slowing and the central bank fears recession. It decides to take action to stimulate spending and increases the money supply. In this case, the Bank buys securities. As it does so, it increases bank reserves and induces the banks to increase their lending. The banks make new loans until the stock of loans outstanding has increased to a level consistent with the new higher level of reserves. Suppose that the Bank undertakes an open market sale of securities on a scale big enough to increase the real money supply to £310 billion. Now the supply of money curve shifts rightward, as shown in Figure 28.10, from MS_0 to MS_2. With more money available, people attempt to get rid of money by buying interest-earning assets. As they do so, asset prices rise and interest rates fall. Equilibrium occurs when the interest rate has fallen to 4 per cent, at which point the new higher money stock of £310 billion is willingly held.

The Bank of England and Control of the Money Supply

This description of how the central bank controls the money supply through open market operations is a simplification of how the Bank of England actually operates in the money market. If the Bank sells government securities through an open market purchase, the commercial banks will find that they are short of reserves and their first action is to recall the overnight loans – money at call – with the discount houses. The discount houses in turn will exercise their access to the Bank of England by taking a lender of last resort loan. The Bank will then post a higher rate of interest at which it will be prepared to lend. This will force discount houses to raise the interest rates on their lending and commercial banks will do the same, as described on pp. 696–698. The higher rate of interest will lead to a cut in bank lending and the money supply will decline, and for a given price level, the real money supply declines.

Review

- Interest rates are determined by equilibrium in asset markets.
- Short-term interest rates are determined by the demand for and supply of money. When the quantity of money demanded equals the quantity supplied, the interest rate is at its equilibrium level.
- To increase the interest rate, the Bank sells securities and decreases the money supply. (To decrease the interest rate, the Bank buys securities and increases the money supply.)

You've now seen how the interest rate is determined and how the actions of the Bank of England can influence the interest rate. We are now going to examine the influence of the interest rate on expenditure plans.

The Interest Rate and Expenditure Plans

You've seen that the interest rate affects the quantity of money that people plan to hold. The interest rate also influences people's spending decisions. The reason is the same in both cases. The interest rate is an opportunity cost. But the interest rate that is relevant for the money holding decision is not quite the same as the interest rate that is relevant for a spending decision. Let's find out why.

Nominal Interest and Real Interest

We distinguish between two interest rates: the nominal interest rate and the real interest rate. The nominal interest rate is the percentage return on an asset such as a bond expressed in terms of money. It is the interest rate that is quoted in everyday transactions and news reports. The real interest rate is the percentage return on an asset expressed in terms of what money will buy. It is the nominal interest rate adjusted for inflation and is approximately equal to the nominal interest rate minus the inflation rate[2].

Here, we'll use the approximate formula. Suppose that the nominal interest rate is 10 per cent a year

2 The exact calculation allows for the change in the purchasing power of the interest as well as the amount of the loan. To calculate the *exact* real interest rate, use the formula: *real interest rate* = *nominal interest rate* – *inflation rate* divided by (1 + *inflation rate*/100). If the nominal interest rate is 10 per cent and the inflation rate is 4 per cent, the real interest rate is (10 – 4) ÷ (1 + 0.04) = 5.77 per cent. The lower the inflation rate, the better is the approximation.

and the inflation rate is 4 per cent a year. The real interest rate is 6 per cent a year – 10 per cent minus 4 per cent.

To see why the real interest rate is 6 per cent, think about the following example. Jackie lends Joe $1,000 for one year. At the end of the year, Joe repays Jackie the $1,000 plus interest. At 10 per cent a year, the interest is $100, so Jackie receives $1,100 from Joe.

Because of inflation, the money that Joe uses to repay Jackie is worth less than the money that Jackie originally loaned to Joe. At an inflation rate of 4 per cent a year, Jackie needs an extra $40 a year to compensate her for the fall in the value of money. So when Joe repays the loan, Jackie needs $1,040 to buy the same items that she could have bought for $1,000 when she made the loan. Because Joe pays Jackie $1,100, the interest that she *really* earns is $60, which is 6 per cent of the $1,000 that she lent to Joe.

Interest Rate and Opportunity Cost

Now that you understand the distinction between the nominal interest rate and the real interest rate, let's think about the effects of interest rates on decisions.

The interest rate influences decisions because it is an opportunity cost. *The nominal interest rate is the opportunity cost of holding money.* And it is the nominal interest rate that is determined by the demand for real money and the supply of real money in the money market. To see why the nominal interest rate is the opportunity cost of holding money, think about the *real* interest rate on money compared with the real interest rate on other financial assets. Money loses value at the inflation rate. So the real interest rate on money equals *minus* the inflation rate. The real interest rate on other financial assets equals the nominal interest rate minus the inflation rate. So the difference between the real interest rate on money and the real interest rate on other financial assets is the nominal interest rate. By holding money rather than some other financial asset, we incur a *real* opportunity cost equal to the nominal interest rate.

The real interest rate is the opportunity cost of spending. Spending more today means spending less in the future. But spending one additional dollar today means cutting future spending by more than a dollar. And the real amount by which future spending must be cut is determined by the *real* interest rate.

A change in the real interest rate changes the opportunity cost of two components of aggregate expenditure:

- Consumption expenditure.
- Investment.

Consumption Expenditure

Other things remaining the same, the lower the real interest rate, the greater is the amount of consumption expenditure and the smaller is the amount of saving.

You can see why the real interest rate influences consumption expenditure and saving by thinking about the effect of the interest rate on a student loan. If the real interest rate on a student loan fell to 1 per cent a year, students would be happy to take larger loans and spend more. But if the real interest rate on a student loan jumped to 20 per cent a year, students would cut their expenditure, buying cheaper food and finding lower-rent accommodation for example, to pay off their loans as quickly as possible.

The effect of the real interest rate on consumption expenditure is probably not large. And it is certainly not as powerful as the effect of disposable income that we studied in Chapter 25 (pp. 608–609). You can think of the real interest rate as influencing *autonomous consumption expenditure*. The lower the real interest rate, the greater is autonomous consumption expenditure.

Investment

Other things remaining the same, the lower the real interest rate, the greater is the amount of investment.

The funds used to finance investment might be borrowed, or they might be the financial resources of the firm's owners (the firm's retained earnings). But regardless of the source of the funds, the opportunity cost of the funds is the real interest rate. The real interest paid on borrowed funds is an obvious cost. The real interest rate is also the cost of using retained earnings because these funds could be loaned to another firm. The real interest rate foregone is the opportunity cost of using retained earnings to finance an investment project.

To decide whether to invest in new capital, firms compare the real interest rate with the expected profit rate from the investment. For example, suppose that Ford(UK) expects to earn 20 per cent a year from a new car assembly plant. It is profitable for Ford(UK) to invest in this new plant as long as the real interest rate is less than 20 per cent a year. That is, at a real interest rate below 20 per cent a year, Ford(UK) will build this assembly line, and at a real interest rate in excess of 20 per cent a year, it will not. Some projects are profitable at a high real interest rate, but other projects are profitable only at a low real interest rate. So the higher the real interest rate, the smaller is the number of projects that are worth undertaking and the smaller is the amount of investment.

The interest rate has another effect on expenditure plans. It changes net exports. Let's find out why.

Net Exports and the Interest Rate

Net exports change when the interest rate changes because, other things remaining the same, a change in the interest rate changes the exchange rate.

Net Exports and the Exchange Rate Let's first see why the exchange rate influences exports and imports. When a Briton buys a Dell PC that is shipped from the USA, the price of the PC equals the US dollar price converted into sterling. If the PC price is US$2,000, and if the exchange rate is 1.60 $s per £, the PC price in the UK is £12,500. If the pound sterling rises to 1.65 $s per £, the PC price in the UK falls to £1212.12. When the price of a US PC falls, the UK imports more PCs.

Similarly, when a US retailer buys a consignment of Burberry raincoats from London, the price of the consignment of 100 raincoats equals the UK sterling price converted into US dollars. If the price of a Burberry is £100 each, the consignment is £10,000 and if the exchange rate is 1.60 $s per £, the price in the United States is $16,000 for the consignment. If the pound sterling rises to 1.65 $s per £, the price of the consignment in the United States *rises* to $16,500. When the price of a British rainwear rises, Americans buy fewer of them and Britain's exports decrease.

So when the pound sterlng rises, imports increase, exports decrease, and net exports decrease. Similarly, when the pound sterling falls, imports decrease, exports increase, and net exports increase.

The Interest Rate and the Exchange Rate When the interest rate in the UK rises, and other things remain the same, the pound sterling exchange rate rises. The reason is that more people move funds into the UK to take advantage of the higher interest rate. But when money flows into the UK, the demand for pounds increases, so the pound sterling exchange rate (the price) rises. And when the interest rate in the UK falls, and other things remain the same, the pound sterling exchange rate falls.

Because the interest rate influences the exchange rate, it also influences net exports. A rise in the interest rate decreases net exports and a fall in the interest rate increases net exports, other things remaining the same.

Money, Interest and Expenditure

Figure 28.11 illustrates the effects of money and the interest rate on expenditure plans. In part (a), the demand for money is *MD* and the supply of money is MS_0. Part (b) shows the relationships between the real interest rate and expenditure plans.

The *CD* curve shows the relationship between autonomous consumption expenditure and the real interest rate, other things remaining the same.

The curve labelled *CD* + *ID* shows the influence of the real interest rate on the sum of autonomous consumption expenditure and investment. And the *IE* curve in Figure 28.11(b) shows the relationship between all the components of aggregate expenditure and the real interest rate.

We'll assume that the inflation rate is zero so that the nominal interest rate (on the y-axis of part a) equals the real interest rate (on the y-axis of part b). So, when the interest rate is 5 per cent a year, interest-sensitive expenditure is £100 billion.

If the quantity of real money increases to £700 billion, the supply of money curve shifts rightward to MS_1 and the interest rate falls to 3 per cent a year. Interest-sensitive expenditure increases to £150 billion. If the quantity of real money decreases to £500 billion, the supply of money curve shifts leftward to MS_2 and the interest rate rises to 7 per cent a year. Interest-sensitive expenditure decreases to £50 billion.

You've now seen how the quantity of money influences the interest rate and how the interest rate influences expenditure plans. Next we will see how the Bank of England has used monetary policy to influence the course of the economy. Then, in the

Figure 28.11 Money, Interest and Expenditure

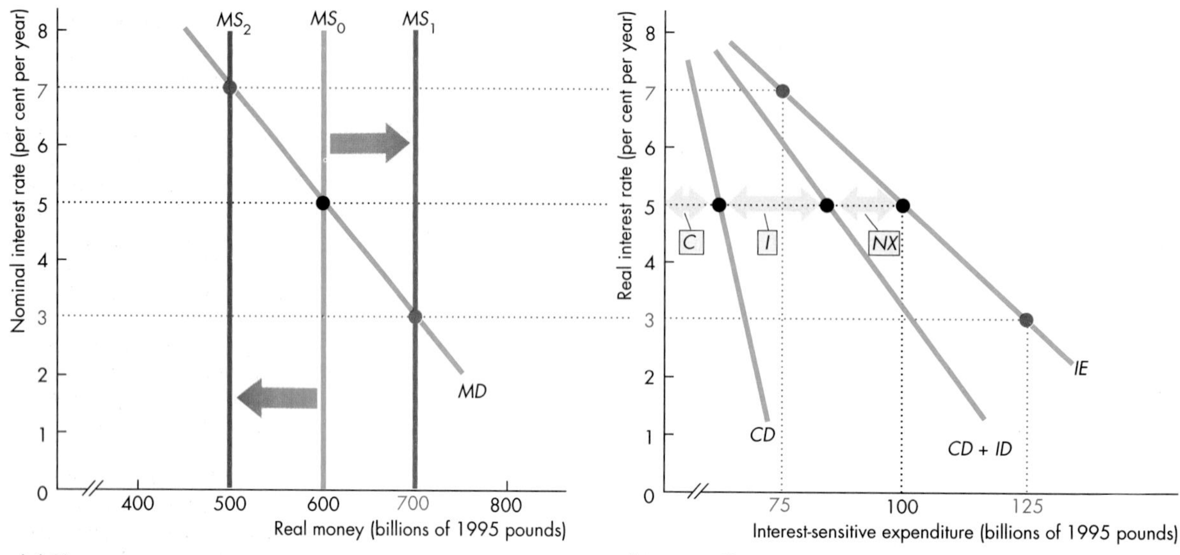

In part (a), when the money supply increases from MS_0 to MS_1, the interest rate falls from 5 per cent a year to 3 per cent a year and when the money supply decreases from MS_0 to MS_2, the interest rate rises from 5 per cent a year to 7 per cent a year. In part (b), when the real interest rate is 5 per cent a year, interest-sensitive expenditure is £100 billion a year. Other things remaining the same, when the interest rate falls to 3 per cent a year, expenditure increases to £150 billion a year and when the interest rate rises to 7 per cent a year, expenditure decreases to £50 billion a year.

next Chapter, we will see how fiscal policy and monetary policy interact to influence the course of the economy.

Review

- The real interest rate is approximately the nominal interest rate less the rate of inflation.
- The nominal interest rate influences the quantity of money people wish to hold.
- The real interest influences the amount of expenditure people undertake.
- The interest rate influence net exports by influencing the exchange rate.

Monetary Policy

You have now learned a great deal about the Bank of England, the monetary policy actions it can take and the effects of those actions on short-term interest rates. But you are possibly thinking: all this sounds nice in theory, but does it really happen? Does the Bank actually do the things we've learned about in this chapter? Indeed, it does happen, and sometimes with dramatic effect. To see the Bank in action, we'll do two things. First, we'll look at the fluctuations in short-term interest rates in the United Kingdom since 1979 and see how the Bank has influenced those fluctuations. Second, we'll focus on two episodes in the life of the Bank, one from the turbulent years of the early 1980s and the other in recent years since the United Kingdom left the Exchange Rate Mechanism of the European Monetary System.

Figure 28.12 Money and Interest Rates

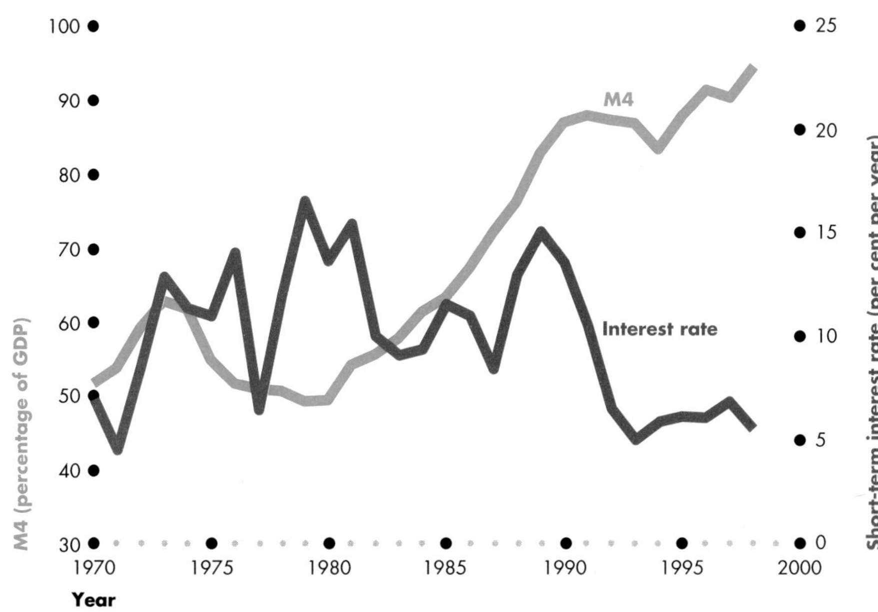

When the ratio of M4 to GDP (measured on the left scale) rises, either the supply of money increases or the demand for money decreases. The result, before 1985, is that a fall in the short-term rate of interest (measured on the right scale) is matched by a rise in M4 relative to GDP. Similarly, when the ratio of M4 to GDP falls, either the supply of money decreases or the demand for money increases and (again before 1985) this is associated with the short-term rate rising. After 1985, the relationship between M4 and interest rates broke down because of deregulation and financial innovation.

Sources: *Bank of England Statistical Abstract*, 1995, and *Economic Trends Annual Supplement*, 1996.

The Bank of England in Action

You've seen that the immediate effect of the Bank's actions is a change in the short-term interest rate. But does the short-term interest rate rise and fall in response to changes in the quantity of money, like the theory we've just studied predicts? Mostly, but not quite always, it does. Figure 28.12 illustrates this connection. It shows the Treasury bill rate at the end of the year and M4 expressed as a percentage of GDP. The reason for expressing M4 as a percentage of GDP is that we can see both the supply side and demand side effects on interest rates in a single measure. Interest rates rise if the quantity of money decreases. Interest rates also rise if the demand for money increases. But the demand for money increases if GDP increases. So the ratio of M4 to GDP rises either if the supply of money increases (M4 increases) or if the demand for money decreases (GDP decreases).

You can see by studying Figure 28.12 that between 1973 and 1980, the rise in the interest rate is matched by a decrease in the ratio of M4 to GDP. Lower interest rates between 1982 and 1987 were matched by an increase in the ratio of M4 to GDP. An increase in the supply of money relative to the demand for money brought a fall in the interest rate in the 1980s. And a decrease in the supply of money relative to the demand for money brought a rise in the interest rate between 1979 and 1981.

You can also see in Figure 28.12 that after 1985, the former relationship between money and interest rates broke down and a longer lag emerged between changes in the rate of interest and subsequent changes in the M4 to GDP ratio. When the interest rate rose in 1988, the M4 to GDP ratio did not fall but its rate of increase began to decrease a year later. The reason the demand for M4 continued to rise is that as interest rates rose so did the interest rate on time deposits, and people continued to demand M4 deposits. It was only when the differential between the time deposit rate and the rate of interest on government securities widened that the increase in M4 relative to GDP began to decline.

You've now seen that we can explain short-term interest rate fluctuations as arising from fluctuations in the supply of money relative to the demand for money. But this relationship doesn't tell us whether actions by the Bank or fluctuations in GDP

Figure 28.13 Short-term Interest Rates

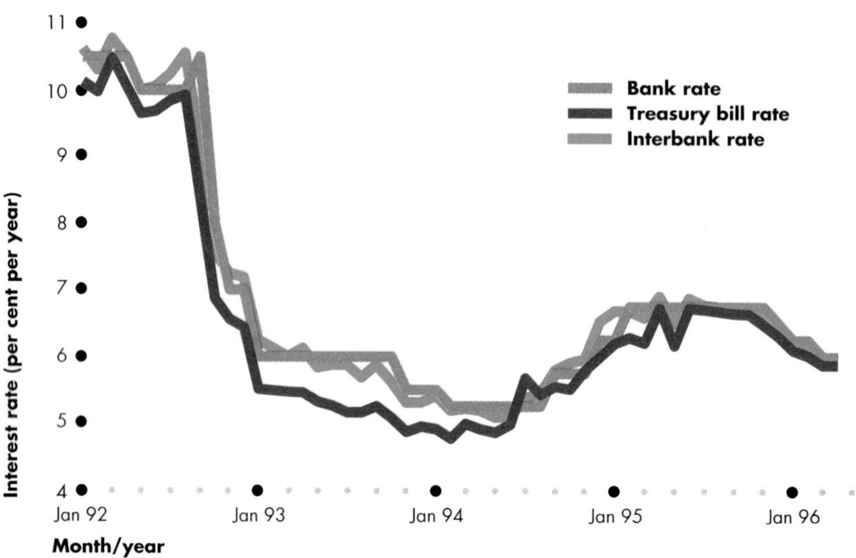

Short-term interest rates, 1992–1996

The graph shows the movement of the Bank of England base rate – referred to in the chart as the Bank rate – at which it lends to discount houses, with the rate of interest at which banks lend to each other – the interbank rate – and the Treasury bill rate between 1992 and 1996. Notice how the rates of interest move together. The Bank directly determines the base rate at which the Bank lends to the discount houses, but all short-term interest rates move up and down together so the Bank influences all short-term rates such as the three-month Treasury bill rate (the rate at which the government borrows in the short term) and the interbank rate (the rate at which banks lend to each other).

Source: ONS.

brought the fluctuations in the M4 to GDP ratio. Do the Bank's own actions move interest rates around? Let's answer this question by looking at two episodes in the life of the Bank.

The Bank in Action 1992–1996 Figure 28.13 shows the course of the Bank of England lending rate to the discount houses – the retail banks' base rate, the rate at which the commercial banks lend to each other – the interbank rate and the three – month Treasury bill rate between January 1992 and April 1996. Notice how closely the three interest rates move together. During this time the Bank was not independent of the government. Being the agent of the government of the day, the policies of the government constrain the actions of the Bank. One of the additional constraints the Bank faced was to sustain the value of the pound within the Exchange Rate Mechanism (ERM) of the European Monetary System. In 1990 the United Kingdom joined the ERM. This caused the Bank to raise the rate of interest and to keep it high to help maintain the value of the pound in the ERM. The policy of a high rate of interest was brought in to curb inflation, which had begun to rise sharply in the late 1980s. The ERM was expected to underpin the counter-inflation policy. The policy was effective in reducing aggregate demand and inflation, but the reduction in aggregate demand also resulted in a rise in unemployment and a fall in output. The pound was viewed by many people, including speculators, as being overvalued and in need of a devaluation. The pressure for a devaluation grew and on 17 September 1992 the pound left the ERM, was devalued and interest rates were allowed to fall to stimulate aggregate demand.

You can see from Figure 28.13 that the Bank was successful in reducing interest rates to increase

Figure 28.14 Monetary Policy and the Interest Rate

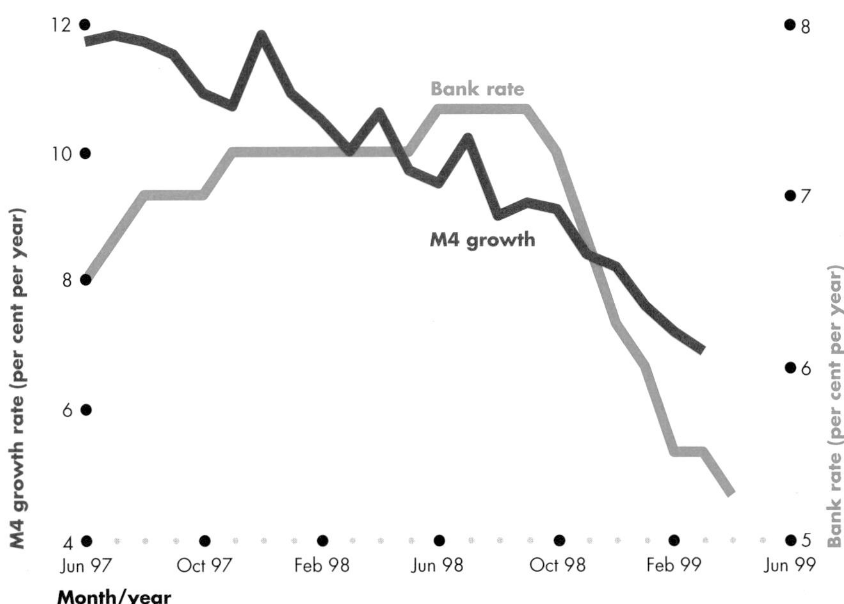

The Bank of England alters interest rates by creating a change in the supply of money relative to the demand for money. If the supply of money is growing too fast, the Bank of England engineers a rise in the rate of interest by creating a decrease in the supply of money relative to demand. Once the rate of growth of money has declined and the threat of inflation reduced, the rate of interest is lowered.

Source: Bank of England.

demand and raising them when it thought that the economy was recovering too quickly in 1994. You can also see that at times the market rates of interest preceded the movement in the Bank's rate and at other times they followed. The reason for this is that at times the markets were anticipating the Bank of England's action, and at other times they either did not anticipate it or they were waiting to see if the Bank would stick to or reverse its action.

We have seen that the Bank's actions do move interest rates around but now let us now look at a more recent episode of the Bank in action that shows the relationship between interest rates and the money supply growth. This episode explains why interest rates were raised and lowered.

The Bank in Action 1997–1999 Figure 28.14 shows the rate of growth of M4 and the Bank's base rate of interest between June 1996 and March 1999. At the begining of the period the Bank had been made operationally independent with the task of bringing inflation under control and keeping it within the narrow bands of 2.5–1.5 per cent. If the long-run rate of growth of the economy is about 2.5 per cent and inflation is to remain between 2.5 and 1.5 per cent, then long-run GDP must grow at between 4 and 5 per cent (inflation plus the rate of growth of ***real*** GDP). If the money supply is growing at above the rate of growth of long-run GDP, then the ratio of M4 to GDP will be rising. The Bank will have to raise interest rates to reduce the rate of growth of money and lower it once money supply growth has fallen and inflation is under control. In June 1996, money supply growth was 11.7 per cent per year. Such a rate of growth of money if left unchecked will eventually create higher inflation. Figure 28.14 shows that interest rates were raised from 6.5 per cent in June 1996 to 7.5 per cent in June 1997 and held there for several months. By September, the rate of growth of the money supply had fallen to 9.2 per cent. As the economy slowed and the rate of growth of money continued to fall, interest rates were lowered so as to not allow the rate of growth of money to fall too fast. By March 1999, the rate of growth of money had fallen to 6.9 per cent.

Profiting by Predicting the Bank of England

The Bank of England influences interest rates by its open market operations and as lender of last resort to loans to discount houses. By increasing the money supply, the Bank can lower interest rates; by lowering the money supply, the Bank can increase interest rates. Sometimes such actions are taken to offset other influences and keep interest rates steady. At other times the Bank moves interest rates up or down. The higher the interest rate, the lower is the price of a bond; the lower the interest rate, the higher is the price of a bond. Thus predicting interest rates is the same as predicting bond prices. Predicting that interest rates are going to fall is the same as predicting that bond prices are going to rise – a good time to buy bonds. Predicting that interest rates are going to rise is the same as predicting that bond prices are going to fall – a good time to sell bonds.

Because the Bank is the major player whose actions influence interest rates and bond prices, predicting what the Bank will do is profitable and a good deal of effort goes into this activity. But people who anticipate that the Bank is about to ease monetary policy and increase the money supply buy bonds straight away, pushing their prices upward and pushing interest rates downward, *before* the Bank acts. Similarly, people who anticipate that the Bank is about to tighten monetary policy and decrease the money supply sell bonds straight away, pushing their prices downward and pushing interest rates upward, before the Bank acts. In other words, bond prices and interest rates change as soon as the Bank's actions are foreseen. By the time the Bank actually takes its actions, if those actions are correctly foreseen, they have no effect. The effects occur in anticipation of the Bank's actions. Only changes in the money supply that are not foreseen change the interest rate at the time that those changes occur.

The Ripple Effects of Monetary Policy

You've now seen that the Bank's actions do indeed change interest rates and seek to influence the course of the economy. These monetary policy measures work by changing aggregate demand. When the Bank slows money growth and pushes interest rates up, it decreases aggregate demand, which slows both real GDP growth and inflation. When the Bank speeds up money growth and lowers interest rates, it increases aggregate demand, which speeds up real GDP growth and inflation. The mechanism through which aggregate demand changes involves several channels. Higher interest rates bring a decrease in consumption expenditure and investment. Higher interest rates bring an appreciation in the exchange rate that makes UK exports more expensive and imports less costly. So net exports decrease. Tighter bank credit brings fewer loans, which reinforces the effects of higher interest rates on consumption expenditure and investment. What we have just described is sometimes referred to as the transmission mechanism of monetary policy.

Schematically, the effects of the Bank's actions ripple through the economy in the following way:

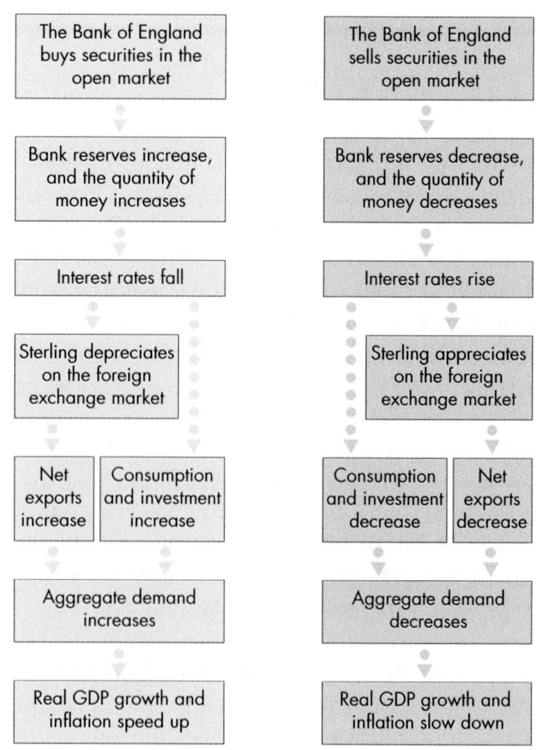

Figure 28.15 Interest Rates and Real GDP Growth

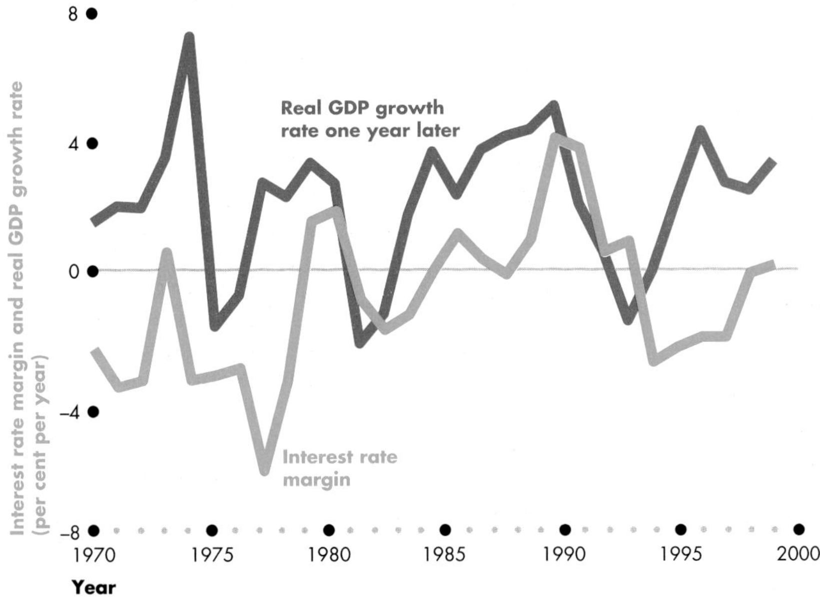

When the Bank increases short-term interest rates, the short-term rate rises above the long-term rate and later real GDP growth slows down. Similarly, when the Bank decreases short-term interest rates, the short-term rate falls below the long-term rate and later real GDP growth speeds up.

Source: ONS.

Interest Rates and the Business Cycle

You've seen the connection between the Bank's actions and interest rates in Figures 28.13 and 28.14. What about the ripple effects that we've just described? Do they really occur? Do changes in interest rates ultimately influence the real GDP growth rate? Yes they do. You can see these effects in Figure 28.15. The blue line shows the short-term interest rate minus the long-term interest rate. The short-term interest rate is influenced by the Bank in the way that you've studied earlier in this chapter. The long-term interest rate is determined by saving and investment plans (see Chapter 31, pp. 792–794) and by long-term inflation expectations (see Chapter 30, pp. 768–770). The red line in Figure 28.14 is the real GDP growth rate *one year later.* You can see that when short-term interest rates rise or long-term interest rates fall the real GDP growth rate slows down in the following year. Long-term interest rates fluctuate less than short-term rates, so when short-term rates rise above long-term rates, it is because the Bank has pushed short-term rates upward. And when short-term rates fall below long-term rates, it is because the Bank has pushed short-term rates downward. So when the Bank stimulates aggregate demand the GDP growth rate speeds up, and when the Bank lowers aggregate demand, the real GDP growth rate slows down. The inflation rate also increases and decreases in sympathy with these fluctuations in real GDP growth.

Review

- The Bank directly controls the interest rate at which lender of last resort loans are made to discount houses and ultimately the banking system.
- Most of the time fluctuations in short-term interest rates mirror fluctuations in the ratio of M4 to GDP.
- When the money supply change is unanticipated, interest rates change at the same time as the change in the money supply. When a money supply change is anticipated, interest rates change ahead of the change in the money supply.

- When the Bank lowers (raises) interest rates, aggregate demand increases (decreases) and real GDP growth and inflation speed up (slow down).

In this chapter, we've studied the determination of interest rates and discovered how the Bank can influence interest rates by open market operations that change the quantity of money. We've also seen how interest rates influence expenditure plans, which in turn influence aggregate demand. In the next chapter, we're going to explore fiscal and monetary policy interact to influence the course of the economy.

Summary

Key Points

The Bank of England (pp. 688–693)

- The Bank of England is the central bank of the United Kingdom.
- The European Central Bank is the central bank for the countries in the EMU.
- The central bank influences the economy by setting the base lending rate at which it is willing to lend to the banking system – and by open market operations.

Controlling the Money Supply (pp. 693–698)

- By buying government securities in the market (an open market purchase), the Bank is able to increase the reserves available to banks.
- As a result, there is an expansion of bank lending and the quantity of money increases.
- By selling government securities, the Bank is able to decrease the reserves of banks and other financial institutions, thereby curtailing loans and decreasing the quantity of money.

United Kingdom Money Supply (pp. 698–700)

- The process of the money supply in the United Kingdom is best understood by the method of counterparts.
- The M4 counterpart describes the different influences on the money supply.
- The change in the money supply is influenced by the government budget deficit, by the sale or purchase of government bonds, and by the increase in bank and building society lending.

The Demand for Money (pp. 700–703)

- The quantity of money demanded is the amount of money that people plan to hold on the average.
- The quantity of nominal money demanded is proportional to the price level, and the quantity of real money demanded depends on the interest rate and real GDP.
- A higher interest rate induces a smaller quantity of real money demanded – a movement along the demand curve for real money.
- A higher level of real GDP induces a larger demand for real money – a shift in the demand curve for real money.
- Technological changes in the financial sector also change the demand for money and shift the demand curve for real money.

Interest Rate Determination (pp. 703–705)

- There is an inverse relationship between the interest rate and the price of a financial asset.
- The higher the interest rate, the lower is the price of a financial asset.
- Money market equilibrium achieves an interest rate and asset price that make the quantity of

real money demanded equal to the quantity supplied.

- Changes in interest rates achieve equilibrium in the markets for money and financial assets.
- There is an inverse relationship between the interest rate and the price of a financial asset.
- The higher the interest rate, the lower is the price of a financial asset.
- Money market equilibrium achieves an interest rate and asset price that make the quantity of real money available willingly held. If the quantity of real money is increased by the actions of the Bank, the interest rate falls and the prices of financial assets rise.

Interest Rate and Expenditure Plans (pp. 705–708)

- The real interest rate approximately equals the nominal interest rate minus the inflation rate.
- The nominal interest rate is the opportunity cost of holding money.
- The real interest rate is the opportunity cost of consumption expenditure and investment.
- A fall in the interest rate increases interest sensitive expenditure.
- A fall in the interest rate leads to a fall in the pound sterling exchange rate and an improvement in net trade.
- A rise in the interest rate leads to a rise in the pound sterling exchange rate and a fall in net trade.

Monetary Policy (pp. 708–714)

- The Bank of England directly controls the discount rate, but all short-term rates fluctuate together.
- The fluctuations in short-term interest rates are usually mirrored by fluctuations in the ratio of M4 to GDP.
- Before the 1980s, rises and falls in the interest rate were matched by decreases or increases in the ratio of M4 to GDP.
- After 1980, the relationship between M4 and interest rates broke down because of financial innovation and deregulation of the banking market.
- People attempt to profit by predicting the actions of the Bank.
- To the extent that they can predict the Bank, interest rates and the prices of financial assets move in anticipation of the Bank's actions rather than in response to them.
- When the Bank lowers interest rates, it increases aggregate demand, which speeds real GDP growth and inflation.
- When the Bank raises interest rates, it decreases aggregate demand, which slows real GDP growth and inflation.

Key Figures

Key Terms

Review Questions

1 What are the main functions of the Bank of England?

2 What are the three policy tools of a central bank? Which of these is the Bank of England's most frequently used tool?

3 What is the effect of an increase in required reserves?

4 What is the effect of an increase in the discount rate?

5 What is an open market operation?

6 If the central bank of a country wants to decrease the quantity of money, does it buy or sell government securities in the open market?

7 Trace the events that follow an open market purchase of securities by a central bank from a commercial bank.

8 Trace the events that follow an open market purchase of securities by a central bank from the general public.

9 Trace the events that follow an open market sale of securities by a central bank to a commercial bank.

10 Trace the events that follow an open market sale of securities by a central bank to the general public.

11 Describe the events that take place when banks have excess reserves.

12 What is the money multiplier?

13 Distinguish between nominal money and real money.

14 What do we mean by the M4 counterpart?

15 What has traditionally been the largest element in the M4 counterparts?

16 What determines the demand for money?

17 What is the opportunity cost of holding money?

18 What happens to the interest rate on a bond if the price of the bond increases?

19 How does equilibrium come about in the money market?

20 What happens to the interest rate if the money supply increases?

21 Trace the ripple effects of the Bank's actions when it increases the interest rate.

22 Explain why it pays people to try to predict the Bank's actions.

Problems

1 You are given the following information about the economy of Nocoin. The banks have deposits of £300 billion. Their reserves are £15 billion, two-thirds of which is in deposits with the central bank. There are £30 billion notes outside the banks. There are no coins in Nocoin!

a Calculate the monetary base.
b Calculate the currency drain.
c Calculate the money supply.
d Calculate the money multiplier.

2 Suppose that the Bank of Nocoin, the central bank, undertakes an open market purchase of securities of £500,000 What happens to the money supply? Explain why the change in the money supply is not equal to the change in the monetary base.

3 You are given the following information about the economy of Miniland. For each $1 increase in real GDP, the demand for real money increases by 25 pence, other things remaining the same. Also, if the interest rate increases by 1 percentage point (for example, from 4 per cent to 5 per cent), the quantity of real money demanded falls by $50. If real GDP is $1,000 and the price level is 1:

a At what interest rate is no money held?
b How much real money is held at an interest rate of 10 per cent?
c Draw a graph of the demand for real money.

4 Given the demand for real money in Miniland, if the price level is 1, real GDP is $1,000 and the real money supply is $150, what is the equilibrium in the money market?

5 Suppose that the Bank of Miniland, the central bank, wants to lower the interest rate by 1 percentage point. By how much would it have to change the real money supply to achieve this objective?

6 You are given the following information about the economy of Miniland. For each $1 increase in real GDP, the demand for real money increases by 25 pence, other things remaining the same. Also, if the interest rate increases by 1 percentage point (for example, from 4 per cent to 5 per cent), the quantity of real money demanded falls by $50. Suppose that the Bank of Miniland, the central bank, wants to lower the interest rate by 1 percentage point. By how much would it have to change the real money supply to achieve that objective?

7 Study *Reading Between the Lines* on pp. 718–719 and then answer the following questions:

a Why is the Japanese government planning to give out ¥30,000 gift vouchers to everyone in Japan?
b What is the likely impact of this policy?
c What alternative policies are open to the Japanese government?

8 Use the links on the Parkin, Powell and Matthews Web site to link on the Bank of England Web site. Find the latest data on M0, M4 and the base interest rate as well as the latest minutes of the Monetary Policy Committee (MPC). Then answer the following questions.

a Is the Bank trying to slow economic growth or speed it up? How can you tell which?
b What has the MPC decided about interest rates in the past month?
c Skim the latest minutes of the MPC and see if you can discover which way interest rates will move at the next meeting by the voting behaviour of its members.
d In light of the Bank's recent actions, what ripple effects do you expect over the coming months?
e What do you think the effects of the Bank's recent actions will be on bond prices and stock prices?

W http://www.econ100.com

Monetary Policy in Japan

Financial Times, 6 October 1998 

Happy Mondays: Japan's antidote to depression

Paul Abrahams

Milton Friedman would be amused. The Nobel prize winning economist, who once joked that the fastest way to boost money supply was to throw dollar bills out of helicopters, may soon see a variant of this idea put to the test.

The Japanese government said yesterday it was considering plans to hand out ¥30,000 (£130) gift vouchers to every one of the country's 125m inhabitants.

The government is also considering a "Happy Monday" scheme, which would turn an increasing number of Mondays into holidays in a bid to persuade consumers to go shopping instead of going to work.

These are desperate times in Tokyo, as the government seeks to head off what some economists believe is an imminent depression.

Yesterday, the Nikkei average of 225 leading shares fell another 2 per cent to 12,948, its lowest since January 1986. Today, the government is set to cut its forecast for gross domestic product this financial year to minus 1.8 per cent. A few months ago, it was predicting 1.9 per cent growth.

The economics of the gift voucher scheme are perhaps a little more rational than those of Friedman's free dollar bills. Like more orthodox methods of stimulating an economy, such as printing money or cutting taxes, recipients of the dollar bills could choose to save the benefit rather than spend it immediately. But because the vouchers would have a limited shelf life, people would have to spend them quickly, giving a fast, if ultimately illusory, boost to the economy.

Yesterday, economists suggested the effect of the vouchers would be a boost to the economy of only ¥3,750bn, or 0.7 of a percentage point.

Robert Feldman, economist at Morgan Stanley, said: "What they need to do is more drastic; say, abolishing central government income tax, which would provide a boost of ¥19,000bn to the economy.

The Essence of the Story

- The Japanese government is considering making a gift of ¥30,000 (£130) to each of the 125 million inhabitants of the country.
- The government is also considering increasing the number of public holidays on a Monday to encourage people to go shopping.
- The Japanese economy is heading towards depression. Real GDP is expected to fall by 1.8 per cent in 1998.
- The government hopes to stimulate spending by providing free gift vouchers with a limited shelf life.
- The impact of the policy is expected to increase real GDP by 0.7 of a percentage point.
- Another policy the government could consider is a cut in income taxes to boost the economy.

Economic Analysis

■ The Japanese economy is heading towards depression and is at a point where aggregate demand intersects short-run aggregate supply at less than long-run aggregate supply as shown in Figure 1.

■ An increase in the money supply will stimulate spending through the real balance effect. However, the Japanese government is afraid that an increase in the money supply will be saved rather than spent.

■ As an alternative to increasing the money supply, they are considering issuing free gift vouchers worth £130 to everyone. The vouchers can only be used to buy goods and have a limited shelf life meaning that they become worthless if they are not spent.

■ Figure 2 shows the effect on aggregate demand of the free gift vouchers. Aggregate demand shifts from AD_0 to AD_1.

■ The effect of the policy which is only temporary, is expected to generate an extra ¥3,750 billion or 0.7 of a percentage point of real GDP.

■ Figure 3 shows that real GDP has fallen by 2.8 per cent in 1998. Real GDP growth was 0.1 per cent in the first quarter of 1999 bringing hope that the worst of the recession is over.

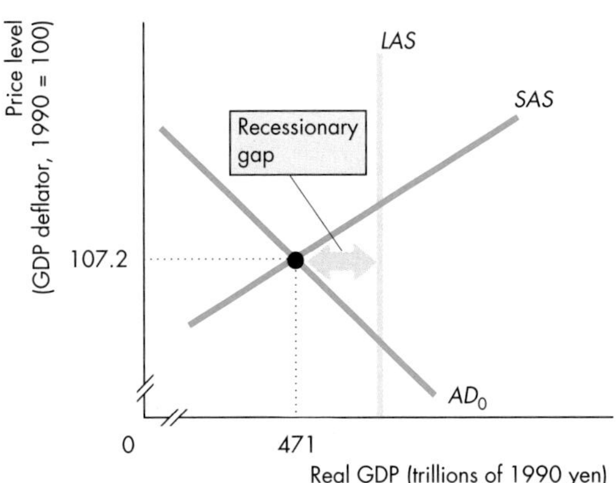

Figure 1 Japan in recession

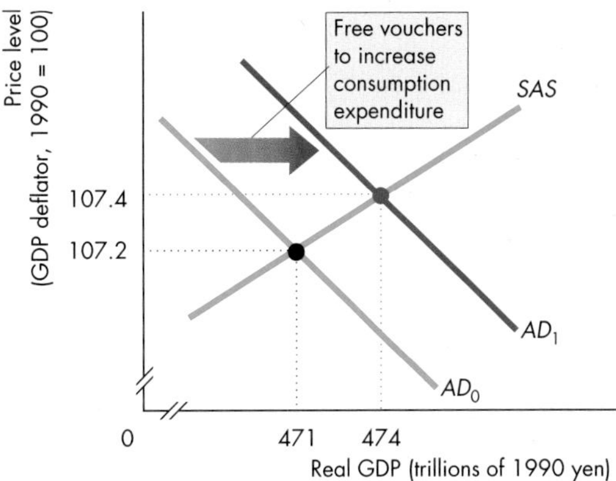

Figure 2 Aggregate demand increases

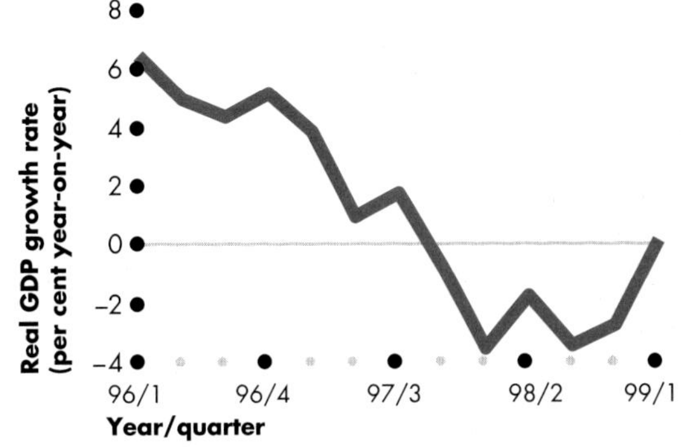

Figure 3 Real GDP growth

CHAPTER 29

Fiscal and Monetary Interactions

After studying this chapter, you will be able to:

- Explain how fiscal and monetary policy interact to influence interest rates and aggregate demand
- Explain the relative effectiveness of fiscal policy and monetary policy
- Describe the Keynesian-monetarist controversy about policy and explain how the controversy was settled
- Explain how the mix of fiscal and monetary policies influences the composition of aggregate expenditure
- Explain how fiscal and monetary policy influence real GDP and the price level

Brownian Commotion

In March 1999, the Chancellor of the Exchequer, Mr Gordon Brown, in his budget speech to Parliament, announced net tax cuts of £6 billion over the next three years. In the square mile of the City of London, the Bank of England pulls the nation's monetary policy levers that influence interest rates and the exchange rate. How does the government's fiscal policy interact with the Bank of England's monetary policy to influence interest rates, the exchange rate, and real GDP? ◆ Sometimes, fiscal policy and monetary policy are in harmony with each other. At other times, they come into conflict. Do fiscal and monetary policies need to be coordinated? Are they equivalent to each other? ◆ If a recession is looming on the horizon, is an interest rate cut by the Bank of England just as good as a tax cut by Parliament? Or is one of these actions likely to have more desirable effects than the other? ◆ If the economy is overheating, is an interest rate hike by the Bank of England just as good as a tax increase by Parliament? Or again, is one of these actions likely to have more desirable effects than the other? ◆ When the government has a large budget deficit, must interest rates rise? Can the Bank of England simply give the government some newly created money so that it can increase spending without putting stress on capital markets and raising interest rates?

◆ ◆ ◆ ◆ We are going to answer these questions in this chapter. You already know a lot about the effects of fiscal policy and monetary policy. And you know that their ultimate effects work through their influences on both aggregate demand and aggregate supply. This chapter gives you a deeper understanding of the aggregate demand side of the economy and how the combined actions of the government and the Bank of England affect aggregate demand.

Macroeconomic Equilibrium

Our goal in this chapter is to learn how changes in government expenditure and changes in the quantity of money interact to change real GDP, the price level, and the interest rate. But before we study the effects of *changes* in these policy variables, we must describe the state of the economy with a given level of government expenditure and a given quantity of money.

The Basic Idea

Aggregate demand and short-run aggregate supply determine real GDP and the price level. And the demand for and supply of real money determine the interest rate. But aggregate demand and the money market are linked together.

Other things remaining the same, the greater the level of aggregate demand the higher are real GDP and the price level. A higher real GDP means a greater demand for money; a higher price level means a smaller supply of real money; so a greater level of aggregate demand means a higher interest rate.

And aggregate demand depends on the interest rate. The reason is that consumption expenditure, investment and net exports are influenced by the interest rate (see Chapter 28, pp. 706–707). So, other things remaining the same, the lower the interest rate, the greater is aggregate demand.

Only one level of aggregate demand and one interest rate are consistent with each other in macroeconomic equilibrium. Figure 29.1 describes this unique equilibrium.

AD–AS Equilibrium

In Figure 29.1(a) the intersection of the aggregate demand curve, *AD*, and the short-run aggregate supply curve, *SAS*, determines real GDP at £750 billion and the price level at 110.

The equilibrium amounts of consumption expenditure, investment, government expenditures and net exports lie behind the *AD* curve. But some components of these expenditures are influenced by the interest rate. And the interest rate, in turn, is determined by equilibrium in the money market. Assume that interest-sensitive expenditures total £100 billion, government expenditure is £100 billion, and the rest of real GDP totals £550 billion.

Money Market Equilibrium and Interest-sensitive Expenditure

In Figure 29.1(b) the intersection of the demand for money curve, *MD*, and the supply of money curve, *MS*, determines the interest rate at 5 per cent a year.

The position of the *MD* curve depends on the level of real GDP. Suppose that the demand for money curve shown in the figure describes the demand for money when real GDP is £750 billion, which is equilibrium real GDP in Figure 29.1(a).

The position of the *MS* curve depends on the quantity of nominal money and the price level. Suppose that the supply of money curve shown in the figure describes the supply of real money when the price level is 110, which is the equilibrium price level in Figure 29.1(a).

In Figure 29.1(c), the *IE* curve determines the level of interest-sensitive expenditure at the equilibrium interest rate of 5 per cent a year. Interest-sensitive expenditure is £100 billion, which is the level of this expenditure that lies behind the aggregate demand curve *AD* in Figure 29.1(a).

Check the Equilibrium

The *AD–AS* equilibrium in Figure 29.1(a), the money market equilibrium in Figure 29.1(b), and interest-sensitive expenditure in Figure 29.1(c) are consistent with each other. And there is no other equilibrium.

To check this claim, assume that aggregate demand is less than *AD* in Figure 29.1(a) so that real GDP is less than £750 billion. If this assumption is correct, the demand for money curve lies to the left of *MD* in Figure 29.1(b) and the equilibrium interest rate is less than 5 per cent a year. With an interest rate less than 5 per cent a year, interest-sensitive expenditure exceeds the £100 billion in Figure 29.1(c). If interest-sensitive expenditure exceeds £100 billion, the *AD* curve lies to the right of the one shown in Figure 29.1(a) and equilibrium real GDP exceeds £750 billion. Thus if we assume a real GDP of less than £750 billion, equilibrium real GDP is greater than £750 billion. There is an inconsistency. The assumed equilibrium real GDP is too small.

Now assume that aggregate demand is greater than *AD* in Figure 29.1(a) so that real GDP exceeds £750 billion. If this assumption is correct, the demand for money curve lies to the right of

Figure 29.1 Equilibrium Real GDP, Price Level, Interest Rate and Expenditure

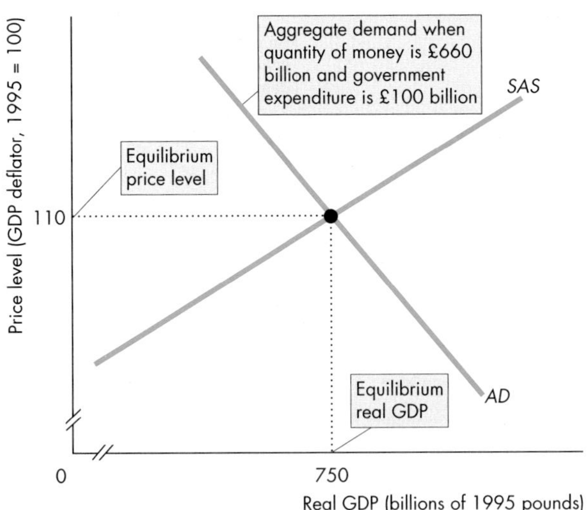

(a) Aggregate supply and aggregate demand

In part (a), the intersection of the aggregate demand curve, *AD*, and the short-run aggregate supply curve, *SAS*, determines real GDP at £750 billion and the price level at 110. Behind the *AD* curve, interest-sensitive expenditure is £100 billion, government expenditure is £100 billion and the rest of real GDP is £550 billion. In part (b), when real GDP is £750 billion, the demand for money is *MD* and when the price level is 110, the supply of (real) money is *MS*. The intersection of the demand for money curve, *MD*, and the supply of money curve, *MS*, determines the interest rate at 5 per cent a year. In part (c), on the *IE* curve, interest-sensitive expenditure is £100 billion at the equilibrium interest rate of 5 per cent a year.

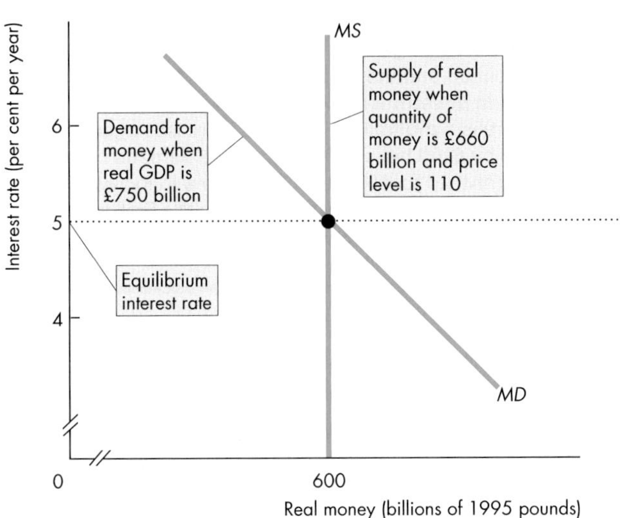

(b) Money and the interest rate

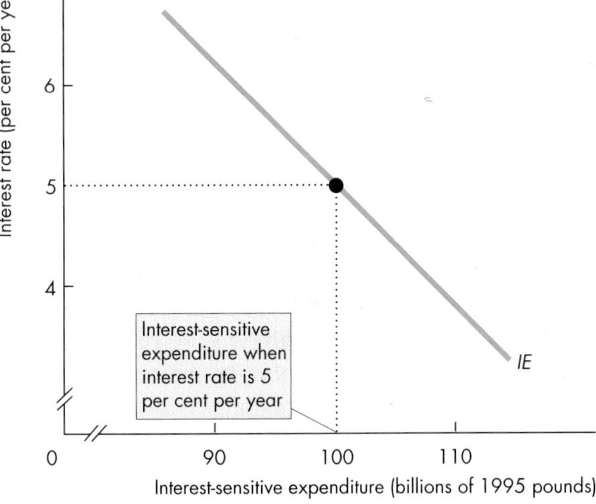

(c) Expenditure and the interest rate

MD in Figure 29.1(b) and the equilibrium interest rate exceeds 5 per cent a year. With an interest rate above 5 per cent a year, interest-sensitive expenditure is less than the £100 billion in Figure 29.1(c), in which case the *AD* curve must lie to the left of the one shown in Figure 29.1(a) and equilibrium real GDP must be smaller than £750 billion. Thus if we assume that real GDP exceeds £750 billion, equilibrium real GDP is less than £750 billion. There is another inconsistency. The assumed equilibrium real GDP is too large.

Only one level of aggregate demand delivers the same money market equilibrium and *AD–AS* equilibrium. In this example, it is the aggregate demand curve *AD* in Figure 29.1(a). Assuming this level of aggregate demand implies this level of aggregate demand. Assuming a lower level of aggregate demand implies a higher level. And assuming a higher level of aggregate demand implies a lower level.

Now that you understand how aggregate demand and the interest rate are simultaneously determined, let's study the effects of a change in government expenditures.

Fiscal Policy in the Short Run

Real GDP growth is slowing, and the Chancellor is concerned that a recession is likely. So the government decides to try to head off the recession by using fiscal policy to stimulate aggregate demand. A fiscal policy that increases aggregate demand is called an *expansionary fiscal policy*.

The effects of an expansionary fiscal policy are similar to those of throwing a pebble into a pond. There's an initial splash followed by a series of ripples that become ever smaller. The initial splash is the 'first round effect' of the fiscal policy action. The ripples are the 'second round effects'. You've already met the first round effects in Chapter 26, pp. 644–648, so here is a refresher.

First Round Effects of Fiscal Policy

The economy starts out in the position shown in Figure 29.1. Real GDP is £750 billion, the price level is 110, the interest rate is 5 per cent a year, and interest-sensitive expenditure is £100 billion. The government now increases its expenditures on goods and services by £50 billion.

Figure 29.2 shows the first round effects of this action. The increase in government expenditures has a multiplier effect because it induces an increase in consumption expenditure. (You can refresh you memory about the government expenditures multiplier on pp. 638–641.) Let's assume that the multiplier is 4, so a £50 billion increase in government expenditure increases aggregate demand at a given price level by £200 billion. The aggregate demand curve shifts rightward from AD_0 to AD_1. At a price level of 110, the quantity of real GDP demanded increases from £750 billion to £950 billion.

Real GDP now starts to increase and the price level starts to rise. These are the first round effects of expansionary fiscal policy.

Figure 29.2 First Round Effects of an Expansionary Fiscal Policy

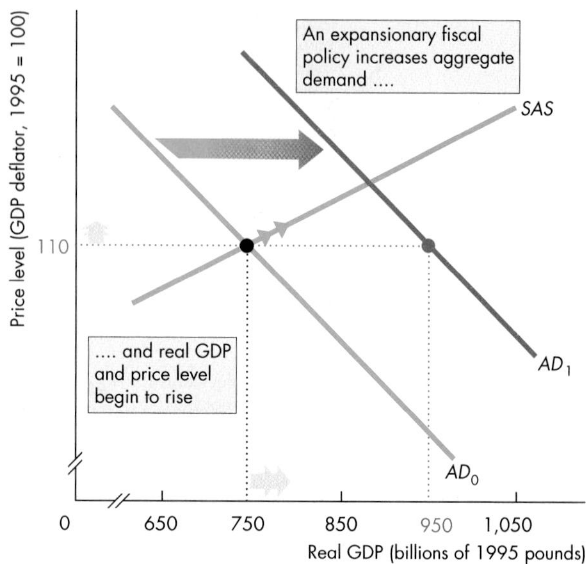

Initially, the aggregate demand curve is AD_0, real GDP is £750 billion and the price level is 110. A £50 billion increase in government expenditures on goods and services has a multiplier effect and increases aggregate demand by £200 billion. The aggregate demand curve shifts rightward to AD_1. Real GDP begins to increase and the price level begins to rise. These are the first round effects of an expansionary fiscal policy.

Second Round Effects of Fiscal Policy

Through the second round, real GDP increases and the price level rises until a new macroeconomic equilibrium is reached. But to find that equilibrium and to describe the changes that result from the initial increase in government expenditures, we must keep track of further changes in the money market and in expenditure plans.

It is easier to keep track of the second round effects if we split them into two parts, one that results from the increasing real GDP and the other that results from the rising price level. We follow these effects in Figure 29.3.

First, the increasing real GDP increases the demand for money. In Figure 29.3(a), the demand for money curve shifts rightward. Eventually, it shifts to MD_1 and the interest rate rises to 6 per cent a year. At this interest rate, interest-sensitive

Figure 29.3 Second Round Effects of an Expansionary Fiscal Policy

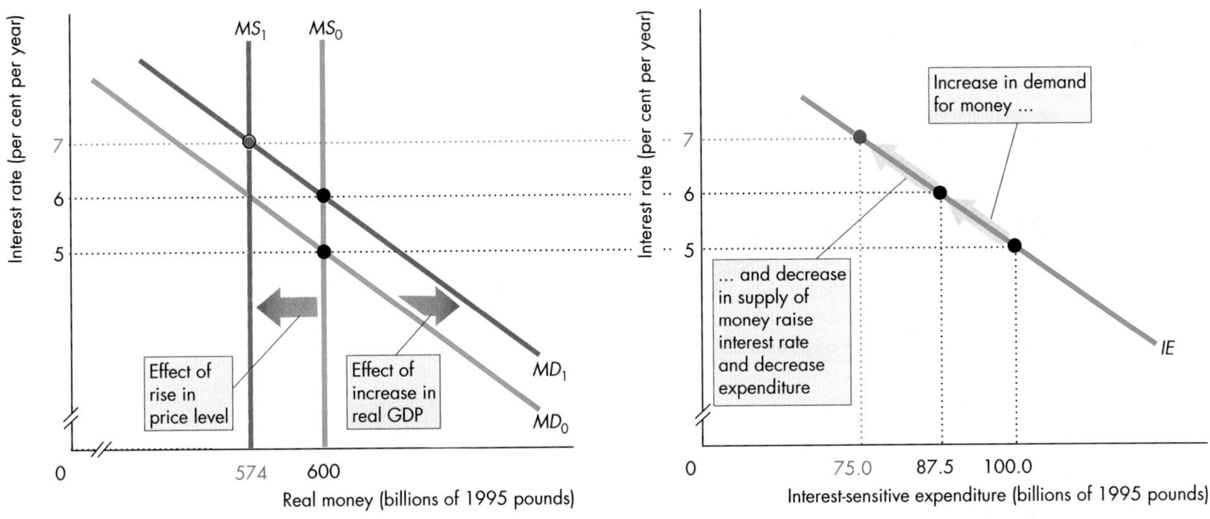

(a) Money and the interest rate

(b) Expenditure and the interest rate

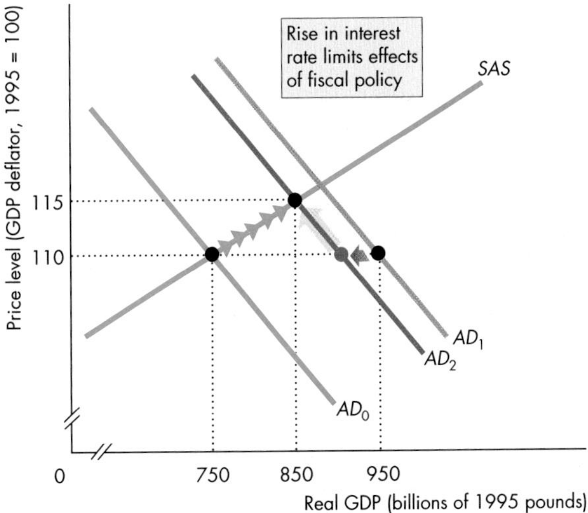

(c) Aggregate supply and aggregate demand

Initially, (part a) the demand curve for money is MD_0, the supply of real money is *MS* and the interest rate is 5 per cent a year. With an interest rate of 5 per cent a year, interest-sensitive expenditure is £100 billion on the curve *IE* (part b). With the increased level of government expenditures, the aggregate demand curve is AD_1 (part c). Real GDP is increasing, and the price level is rising. The increasing real GDP increases the demand for money and the demand for money curve shifts rightward to MD_1. The higher interest rate decreases interest-sensitive expenditure, which decreases aggregate demand to AD_2. The rising price level brings a movement along the new *AD* curve. It does so because it decreases the supply of real money to MS_1, which in turn raises the interest rate further and decreases expenditure. The new equilibrium occurs when real GDP has increased to £850 billion and the price level has risen to 115.

expenditure decreases to £87.5 billion in Figure 29.3(b). The decrease in planned expenditure decreases aggregate demand and the aggregate demand curve shifts leftward to AD_2 in Figure 29.3(c).

Second, with a given quantity of nominal money, the rising price level decreases the quantity of real money. In Figure 29.3(a), the money supply curve shifts leftward to MS_1. The decrease in the quantity of real money raises the interest rate further to 7 per cent a year. In Figure 29.3(b), the higher interest rate decreases interest-sensitive expenditure to £75 billion. Because this decrease in spending plans is induced by a rise in the price level, it decreases the quantity of real GDP demanded and is shown as a movement along the aggregate demand curve AD_2 in Figure 29.3(c).

During this second round process, real GDP is increasing and the price level is rising in a gradual movement up along the short-run aggregate supply

Figure 29.4 How the Economy Adjusts to an Expansionary Fiscal Policy

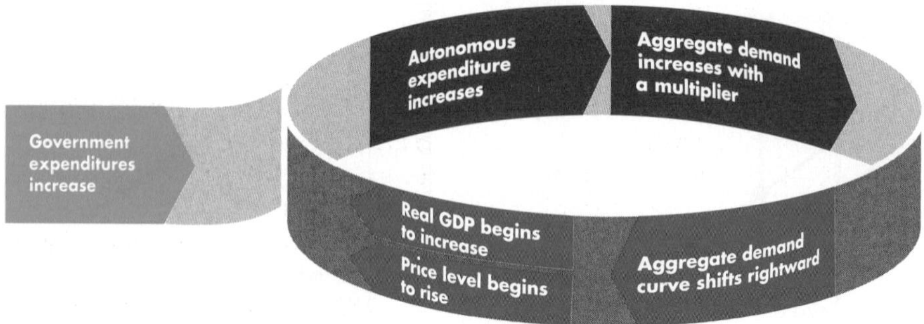

(a) First round effect of expansionary fiscal policy

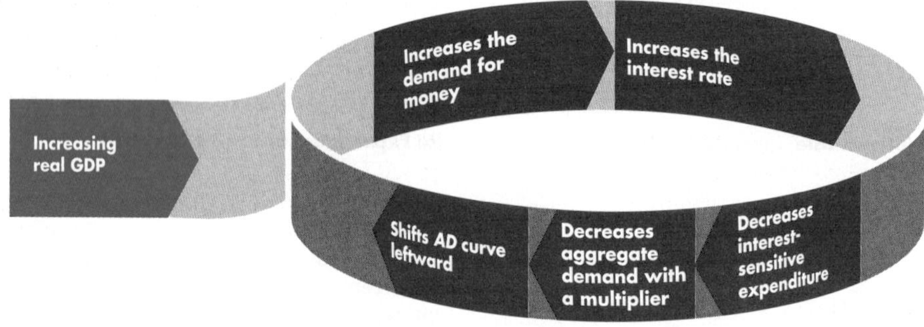

(b) Second round real GDP effect

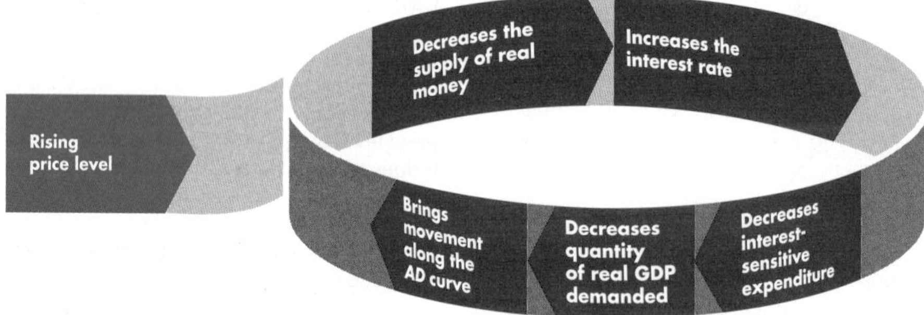

(c) Second round price level effect

curve as indicated by the arrows. In the new equilibrium, real GDP is \$850 billion, the price level is 115, the interest rate is 7 per cent a year, and interest-sensitive expenditure is \$75 billion.

Just as the initial equilibrium in Figure 29.1 was consistent, so the new equilibrium is consistent. The *AD–AS* equilibrium in Figure 29.3(a), the money market equilibrium in Figure 29.3(b), and interest-sensitive expenditure in Figure 29.3(c) are all consistent with each other. And there is no other equilibrium.

Figure 29.4 summarizes the first round and the two parts of the second round adjustments as the economy responds to an expansionary fiscal action.

Other Fiscal Policies

A change in government expenditures is only one possible fiscal policy action. Others are a change in transfer payments, such as an increase in unemployment compensation or an increase in social benefits and a change in taxes. All fiscal policy actions work by changing expenditure. But the magnitude of the initial change in expenditure differs for different fiscal actions. For example, changes in taxes and transfer payments change expenditure by smaller amounts than a change in government expenditures on goods and services. But fiscal policy actions that change autonomous expenditure by a given amount and in a given direction have similar effects on equilibrium real GDP, the price level, and the interest rate regardless of the initial fiscal action. Let's take a closer look at the effect of the rise in the interest rate.

Crowding Out and Crowding In

Because an expansionary fiscal policy increases the interest rate, it decreases all the interest-sensitive components of aggregate expenditure. One of these components is investment and the decrease in investment that results from an expansionary fiscal action is called crowding out.

Crowding out may be partial or complete. Partial crowding out occurs when the decrease in investment is less than the increase in government expenditures. This is the normal case – and the case we've just seen.

Complete crowding out occurs if the decrease in investment equals the initial increase in government expenditures. For complete crowding out to occur, a small change in the demand for real money must lead to a large change in the interest rate, and the change in the interest rate must lead to a large change in investment.

But another potential influence of government expenditures on investment works in the opposite direction to the crowding-out effect and is called 'crowding in'. Crowding in is the tendency for expansionary fiscal policy to *increase* investment. This effect works in three ways.

First, in a recession, an expansionary fiscal policy might create expectations of a more speedy recovery and bring an increase in expected profits. Higher expected profits might increase investment despite a higher interest rate.

Second, government expenditures might be productive and lead to more profitable business opportunities. For example, a new government-built highway might cut the cost of transporting a farmer's produce to a market and induce the farmer to invest in a new fleet of refrigerated trucks.

Third, if an expansionary fiscal policy takes the form of a cut in taxes on business profits, firms' after-tax profits increase and investment might increase.

The Exchange Rate and International Crowding Out

We've seen that an expansionary fiscal policy leads to higher interest rates. But a change in interest rates also affects the exchange rate. Higher interest rates make the dollar rise in value against other currencies. With interest rates higher in the UK than in the rest of the world, funds flow into Britain and people around the world demand more pounds sterling. As the pound rises in value, foreigners find UK-produced goods and services more expensive and UK residents find imports less expensive. Exports decrease and imports increase – net exports decrease. The tendency for an expansionary fiscal policy to decrease net exports is called international crowding out. The decrease in net exports offsets, to some degree, the initial increase in aggregate expenditure brought about by an expansionary fiscal policy.

Review

- In the first round following an expansionary fiscal policy, aggregate demand increases, real GDP starts to increase and the price level starts to rise.
- In the second round, the increasing real GDP increases the demand for money, which raises the interest rate, decreases interest-sensitive expenditure, and decreases aggregate demand.
- Also in the second round, the rising price level decreases the supply of money, which raises the interest rate, decreases interest-sensitive expenditure, and decreases the quantity of real GDP demanded.
- The rise in the interest rate decreases investment and there is crowding-out. If fiscal stimulation increases investment there is crowding-in.
- The rise in the interest rate makes the pound sterling rise, which decreases net exports.

Figure 29.5 First Round Effects of an Expansionary Monetary Policy

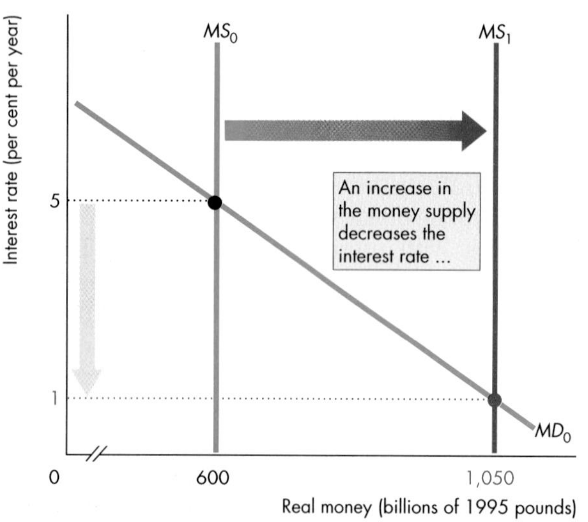

(a) Change in money supply

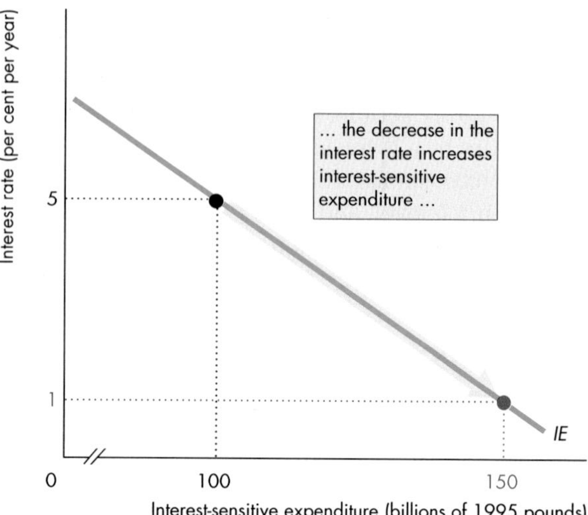

(b) Change in expenditure

(c) Change in aggregate demand

Initially, the demand curve for real money is MD_0, the real money supply is MS_0, and the interest rate is 5 per cent a year (part a). With an interest rate of 5 per cent a year, interest-sensitive expenditure is £100 billion on the *IE* curve (part b). The aggregate demand curve is AD_0 and equilibrium real GDP £750 billion and the price level is 110 (part c). An increase in the quantity of money shifts the money supply curve rightward to MS_1 (part a). The increased money supply lowers the interest rate to 1 per cent a year and interest-sensitive expenditure increases to £150 billion (part b). The increase in expenditure increases aggregate demand to AD_1 (in part c). Real GDP begins to increase and the price level begins to rise.

Monetary Policy in the Short Run

To study the effects of an expansionary monetary policy, we look at the first round effects and the second round effects, just as we did for fiscal policy. Figure 29.5 describes the economy, which is initially in the situation that we studied in Figure 29.1. The quantity of money is £600 billion, the interest rate is 5 per cent a year, interest-sensitive expenditure is £100 billion, real GDP is £750 billion and the price level is 110.

The Bank of England now increases the money supply so that the quantity of money increases to £1,155 billion. With a price level of 110, the quantity of real money increases to £1,050 billion. Figure 29.5(a) shows the immediate effect. The real money supply curve shifts rightward from MS_0 to MS_1, and the interest rate falls from 5 per cent to

Figure 29.6 Second Round Effects of an Expansionary Monetary Policy 

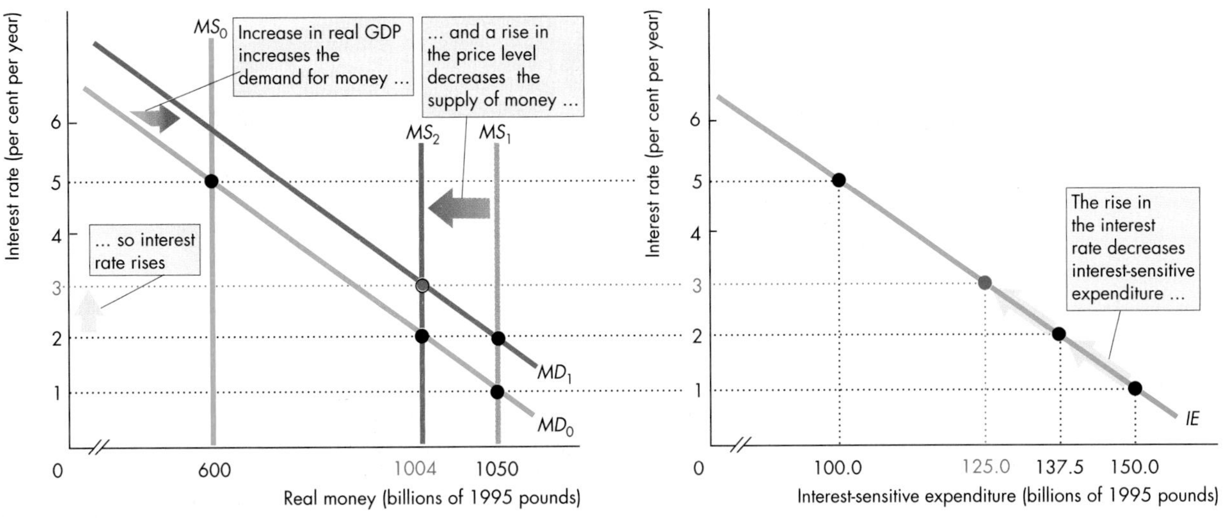

(a) Money and the interest rate

(b) Decrease in expenditure

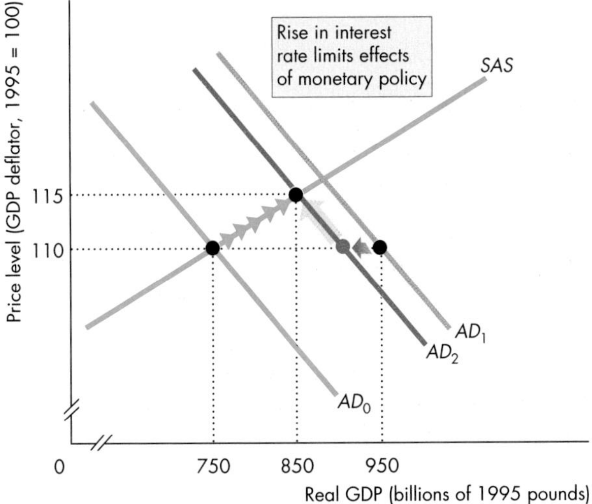

(c) Aggregate demand and aggregate supply

At the start of the second round, the demand curve for money is still MD_0 (part a), the supply of real money is MS_1, and the interest rate is 1 per cent a year. With an interest rate of 1 per cent a year, interest-sensitive expenditure is £150 billion on the curve *IE* (part b). With the increased quantity of money and expenditure level, the aggregate demand curve is AD_1 (part c). Real GDP is increasing and the price level is rising. The increasing real GDP increases the demand for money and the demand for money curve shifts rightward to MD_1. The higher interest rate decreases interest-sensitive expenditure, which decreases aggregate demand to AD_2. The rising price level brings a movement along the new *AD* curve. It does so because it decreases the supply of real money to MS_2, which in turn raises the interest rate further and decreases expenditure. The new equilibrium occurs when real GDP has increased to £850 billion and the price level has risen to 115.

1 per cent a year. The lower interest rate increases interest-sensitive expenditure to £150 billion (part c). The increase in interest-sensitive expenditure increases aggregate demand and shifts the *AD* curve rightward from AD_0 to AD_1 (part c). The increase in aggregate demand sets off a multiplier process in which real GDP and the price level begin to increase towards their equilibrium levels.

These are the first round effects of an expansionary monetary policy. An increase in the money supply lowers the interest rate and increases aggregate demand. Real GDP and the price level begin to increase.

Let's now look at the second round effects.

Second Round Effects

The increasing real GDP and rising price level set off the second round, which Figure 29.6(b) illustrates. And as in the case of fiscal policy, it is

Figure 29.7 How the Economy Adjusts to an Expansionary Monetary Policy

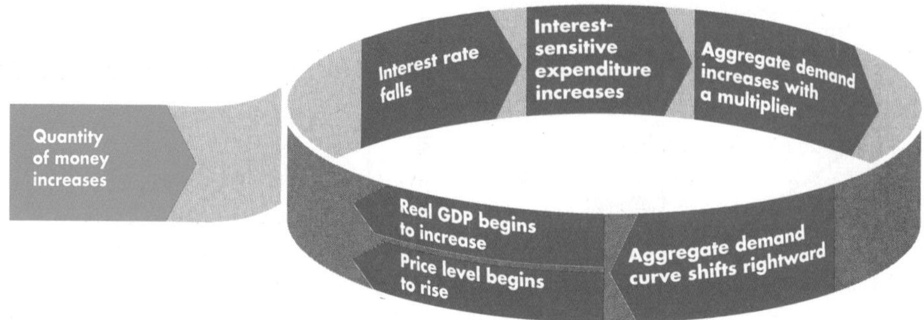

(a) First round effect of expansionary monetary policy

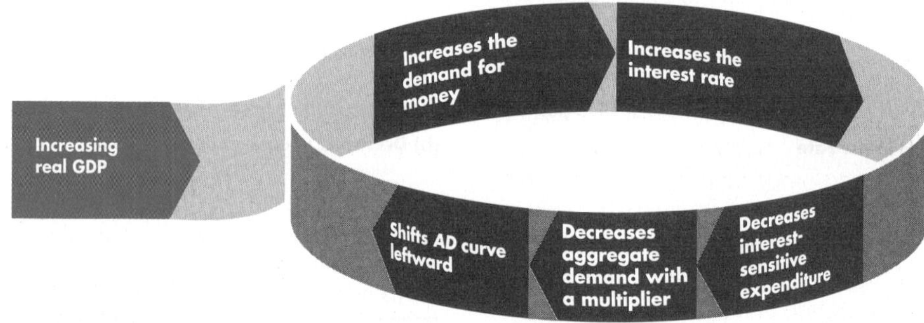

(b) Second round real GDP effect

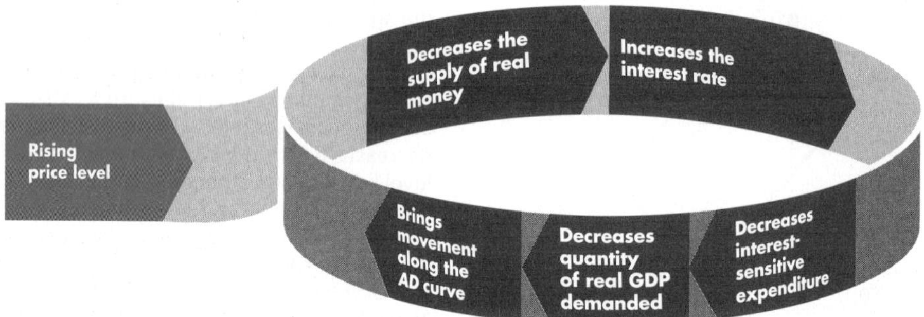

(c) Second round price level effect

best to break the second round into two parts: the consequence of increasing real GDP and the consequence of the rising price level.

The increasing real GDP increases the demand for money from MD_0 to MD_1 in Figure 29.6(a). The increased demand for money raises the interest rate to 2 per cent a year. The higher interest rate brings a decrease in interest-sensitive expenditure from \$150 billion to \$137.5 billion in Figure 29.6(b). And the lower level of expenditure decreases aggregate demand and shifts the aggregate demand curve leftward to AD_2 in Figure 29.6(c).

The rising price level brings a movement along the new aggregate demand curve in Figure 29.6(c). This movement occurs because the rising price level decreases the real money supply. As the price level rises, the real money supply decreases to \$1004 billion and the money supply curve shifts leftward to MS_2 (part a). The interest rate rises further to 3 per cent a year. And interest-sensitive expenditure decreases to \$125 billion (part b).

In the new short-run equilibrium, real GDP has increased to \$850 billion, and the price level has risen to 115, where aggregate demand curve AD_2

intersects the short-run aggregate supply curve *SAS*.

The demand for money is MD_1, the supply of (real) money is MS_2, and the interest rate is 3 per cent a year in part (a). With an interest rate of 3 per cent a year, interest-sensitive expenditure is $125 billion (part b).

The new equilibrium is the only consistent one and is like that of Figure 29.1. Figure 29.7 summarizes the adjustments that occur to bring the economy to this new equilibrium.

Money and the Exchange Rate

An increase in the money supply lowers the interest rate. If the interest rate falls but does not fall in the rest of the eurozone, the United States and Japan, international investors buy the now higher-yielding foreign assets and sell the relatively lower-yielding British assets. As they make these transactions, they sell pounds sterling. So the pound depreciates against other currencies. (This mechanism is explained in greater detail in Chapter 36, pp. 926–934.)

With a cheaper pound, foreigners face lower prices for British produced goods and services and Britons face higher prices for foreign-produced goods and services. Foreigners increase their imports from the UK, and Britons decrease their imports from the rest of the world. British net exports increase and real GDP and the price level increase further.

Review

- In the first round following an expansionary monetary policy, the interest rate falls, aggregate demand increases, real GDP starts to increase and the price level starts to rise.
- In the second round, the increasing real GDP increases the demand for money, which raises the interest rate, decreases interest-sensitive expenditure and decreases aggregate demand.
- Also, in the second round, the rising price level decreases the supply of money, which raises the interest rate, decreases interest-sensitive expenditure and decreases the quantity of real GDP demanded.
- The fall in the interest rate increases investment and makes the pound depreciate which increases net exports.

Relative Effectiveness of Policies

We've seen that aggregate demand and real GDP are influenced by both fiscal and monetary policy. But which policy is the more potent? This question was once at the centre of a controversy among macroeconomists. Later in this section we'll look at that controversy and see how it was settled. But we begin by discovering what determines the effectiveness of fiscal policy.

Effectiveness of Fiscal Policy

The effectiveness of fiscal policy is measured by the magnitude of the increase in aggregate demand that results from a given increase in government expenditures (or decrease in taxes). The effectiveness of fiscal policy depends on the strength of the crowding-out effect. Fiscal policy is most powerful if no crowding out occurs. Fiscal policy is impotent if there is complete crowding out. And the strength of the crowding-out effect depends on two things:

1. The responsiveness of expenditure to the interest rate.
2. The responsiveness of the quantity of money demanded to the interest rate.

If expenditure is not very responsive to a change in the interest rate, the crowding-out effect is small. But if expenditure is highly responsive to a change in the interest rate, the crowding-out effect is large. Other things remaining the same, the smaller the responsiveness of expenditure to the interest rate, the smaller is the crowding-out effect and the more effective is fiscal policy.

The responsiveness of the quantity of money demanded to the interest rate also affects the size of the crowding-out effect. An increase in real GDP increases the demand for money and with no change in the supply of money, the interest rate rises. But the extent to which the interest rate rises depends on the responsiveness of the quantity of money demanded to the interest rate. Other things remaining the same, the greater the responsiveness of the quantity of money demanded to the interest rate, the smaller is the rise in the interest rate, the smaller is the crowding-out effect, and the more effective is fiscal policy.

Effectiveness of Monetary Policy

The effectiveness of monetary policy is measured by the magnitude of the increase in aggregate demand that results from a given increase in the money supply. The effectiveness of monetary policy depends on the same two factors that influence the effectiveness of fiscal policy:

1 The responsiveness of the quantity of money demanded to the interest rate.

2 The responsiveness of expenditure to the interest rate.

The starting point for monetary policy is a change in the quantity of money that changes the interest rate. A given change in the quantity of money might bring a small change or a large change in the interest rate. Other things being the same, the larger the initial change in the interest rate, the more effective is monetary policy. And the initial change in the interest rate is greater, the less responsive is the quantity of money demanded to the interest rate.

But effectiveness of monetary policy also depends on how much expenditure changes. If expenditure is not very responsive to a change in the interest rate, monetary actions do not have much effect on expenditure. But if expenditure is highly responsive to a change in the interest rate, monetary actions have a large effect on aggregate expenditure. The greater the responsiveness of expenditure to the interest rate, the more effective is monetary policy.

The effectiveness of fiscal policy and monetary policy that you've just studied were once controversial. During the 1950s and 1960s, this issue lay at the heart of what was called the Keynesian-monetarist controversy. Let's look at the dispute and see how it was resolved.

The Keynesian–Monetarist Controversy

The Keynesian–monetarist controversy was an ongoing dispute in macroeconomics between two broad groups of economists. A Keynesian is a macroeconomist whose views about the functioning of the economy are based on the theories of John Maynard Keynes, published in Keynes's *General Theory* (see pp. 526–527). Keynesians regard the economy as being inherently unstable and as requiring active government intervention to achieve stability. Traditionally they assigned a low degree of importance to monetary policy and a high degree of importance to fiscal policy. Modern Keynesians assign a high degree of importance to both types of policy. A monetarist is a macroeconomist whose views about the functioning of the economy are based on theories most forcefully set forth by Milton Friedman (see pp. 684–685). Monetarists regard the economy as being inherently stable and as requiring no active government intervention. Monetarists believe that most macroeconomic fluctuations are caused by fluctuations in the quantity of money. Traditionally they assigned a low degree of importance to fiscal policy. But modern monetarists, like modern Keynesians, assign a high degree of importance to both types of policy.

The nature of the Keynesian-monetarist debate has changed over the years. During the 1950s and 1960s, it was a debate about the relative effectiveness of fiscal policy and monetary policy in changing aggregate demand. We can see the essence of that debate by making three points of view distinct:

1 Extreme Keynesianism.

2 Extreme monetarism.

3 Intermediate position.

Extreme Keynesianism The extreme Keynesian hypothesis is that a change in the money supply has no effect on aggregate demand, and a change in government expenditures on goods and services or in taxes has a large effect on aggregate demand. The two circumstances in which a change in the money supply has no effect on aggregate demand are:

1 Expenditure demand is completely insensitive to the interest rate.

2 The demand for real money is highly sensitive to the interest rate.

If expenditure is completely insensitive to the interest rate (if the *IE* curve is vertical), a change in the money supply changes interest rates, but those changes do not affect aggregate planned expenditure. Monetary policy is impotent.

If the demand for real money is highly sensitive to the interest rate (if the *MD* curve is horizontal), people are willing to hold any amount of money at a given interest rate – a situation called a *liquidity trap*. With a liquidity trap, a change in the money supply affects only the amount of money held. It does not affect interest rates. With an unchanged interest rate, expenditure remains constant. Monetary policy is impotent. Some people believe that Japan was in a liquidity trap during the late 1990s.

Extreme Monetarism The extreme monetarist hypothesis is that a change in government expenditures on goods and services or in taxes has no effect on aggregate demand and that a change in the money supply has a large effect on aggregate demand. Two circumstances give rise to these predictions:

1 Expenditure is highly sensitive to the interest rate.
2 The demand for real money is completely insensitive to the interest rate.

If an increase in government expenditures on goods and services induces an increase in interest rates that is sufficiently large to reduce expenditure by the same amount as the initial increase in government expenditures, then fiscal policy has no effect on aggregate demand. This outcome is complete crowding out. For this result to occur, either the demand for real money must be insensitive to the interest rate – a fixed amount of money is held regardless of the interest rate – or expenditure must be highly sensitive to the interest rate – any amount of expenditure will be undertaken at a given interest rate.

The Intermediate Position The intermediate position is that both fiscal and monetary policy affect aggregate demand. Crowding out is not complete, so fiscal policy does have an effect. There is no liquidity trap and expenditure responds to interest rates, so monetary policy does indeed affect aggregate demand. This position is the one that now appears to be correct and is the one that we've spent most of this chapter exploring. Let's see how economists came to this conclusion.

Sorting Out the Competing Claims

The dispute between monetarists, Keynesians and those taking an intermediate position was essentially a disagreement about the magnitudes of two economic parameters:

1 The responsiveness of expenditure to the interest rate.
2 The responsiveness of the demand for real money to the interest rate.

If expenditure is highly sensitive to the interest rate or the demand for real money is barely sensitive to the interest rate, then monetary policy is powerful and fiscal policy relatively ineffective. In this case, the world looks similar to the claims of extreme monetarists. If expenditure is very insensitive to the interest rate, or the demand for real money is highly sensitive, then fiscal policy is powerful and monetary policy is relatively ineffective. In this case, the world looks similar to the claims of the extreme Keynesians.

By using statistical methods to study the demand for real money and expenditure and by using data from a wide variety of historical and national experiences, economists were able to settle this dispute. Neither extreme position turned out to be supported by the evidence and the intermediate position won. The demand curve for real money slopes downward. And expenditure *is* interest sensitive. Neither demand curve is vertical nor horizontal, so the extreme Keynesian and extreme monetarist hypotheses are rejected.

Interest Rate and Exchange Rate Effectiveness

Although fiscal policy and monetary policy are alternative ways of changing aggregate demand, they have opposing effects on the interest rate and the exchange rate. A fiscal policy action that increases aggregate demand raises the interest rate and increases the exchange rate. A monetary policy action that increases aggregate demand lowers the interest rate and decreases the exchange rate. Because of these opposing effects on interest rates and the exchange rate, if the two policies are combined to increase aggregate demand, their separate effects on the interest rate and the exchange rate can be minimized.

Review

- The relative effectiveness of fiscal and monetary policies depends on how sensitive expenditure and the demand for money to the interest rate.

- Other things being equal, the less expenditure and the more money demand responds to a change in the interest rate, the more effective is fiscal policy and the less effective is monetary policy.
- Other things being equal, the more expenditure responds and the less money demand responds to a change in the interest rate, the less effective is fiscal policy and the more effective is monetary policy.

We're now going to look at expansionary fiscal and monetary policy at full employment.

Policy Actions at Full Employment

An expansionary fiscal policy or monetary policy can bring the economy to full employment. But it is often difficult to determine whether the economy is below full employment. So an expansionary fiscal policy or monetary policy might be undertaken when the economy is at full employment. What happens then? Let's answer this question starting with an expansionary fiscal policy.

Expansionary Fiscal Policy at Full Employment

Suppose the economy is at full employment and the government increases expenditure. All the effects that we worked out earlier in this chapter occur. Except that these effects determine only a *short-run equilibrium*. That is, the first round and second round effects of policy both occur in the short run. There is a third round, which is the long-run adjustment.

Starting out at full employment, an expansionary fiscal policy will create an above full-employment equilibrium in which there is an *inflationary gap*. The money wage rate begins to rise, short-run aggregate supply decreases, and a long-run adjustment occurs in which real GDP decreases to potential GDP and the price level rises.

Figure 29.8 illustrates the combined first and second round short-run effects and the third round long-run adjustment.

In Figure 29.8, potential GDP is £750 billion. Real GDP equals potential GDP on aggregate demand curve AD_0 and short-run aggregate supply curve SAS_0. An expansionary fiscal action increases aggregate demand. The combined first round and second round effect increases aggregate demand to AD_1. Real GDP increases to £850 billion and the price level rises to 120. There is an inflationary gap of £100 billion.

With the economy at above full-employment, a shortage of labour puts upward pressure on the money wage rate, which now begins to rise. And a third round of adjustment begins. The rising money wage rate decreases short-run aggregate supply and the SAS curve starts moving leftward towards SAS_1.

As the short-run aggregate supply decreases, real GDP decreases and the price level rises. This process continues until the inflationary gap has been eliminated at full employment. At the long-run

Figure 29.8 Fiscal Policy at Full Employment

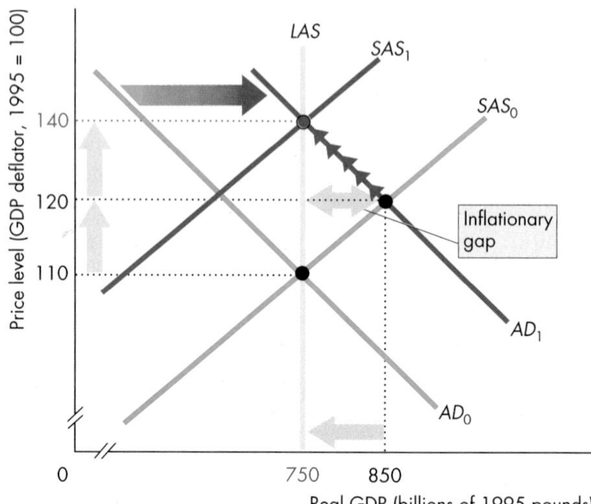

The long-run aggregate supply curve is *LAS* and initially the aggregate demand curve is AD_0 and the short-run aggregate supply curve is SAS_0. Real GDP is £750 billion and the GDP deflator is 110. Fiscal and monetary policy changes shift the aggregate demand curve to AD_1. At the new short-run equilibrium, real GDP is £850 billion and the GDP deflator is 120. Because real GDP exceeds potential GDP, the money wage rate begins to rise and the short-run aggregate supply curve begins to shift leftward to SAS_1. At the new long-run equilibrium, the GDP deflator is 140 and real GDP is back at its original level.

equilibrium is a real GDP of £750, which is potential GDP, and a price level of 140.

Crowding Out at Full Employment

You've just seen that when government expenditures increase at full employment, the long-run change in real GDP is zero. The entire effect of the increase in aggregate demand is to increase the price level. This outcome implies that at full employment, an increase in government expenditures either *completely crowds out investment*, or *creates an international (net exports) deficit*, or results in a combination of the two.

The easiest way to see why is to recall that aggregate expenditure, which equals consumption expenditure, C, plus investment, I, plus government expenditures, G, plus net exports, NX, equals real GDP. That is:

$$Y = C + I + G + NX$$

Comparing the initial situation with the outcome, real GDP has not changed. So consumption, which depends on income (GDP), has not changed. With no change in Y and C, the sum $I + G + NX$ is constant between the two situations.

But government expenditures have increased, so either investment or net exports must have decreased. If net exports have not changed, investment has decreased by the full amount of the increase in government expenditures. If investment has not changed, net exports have decreased by an amount equal to the increase in government expenditures. A decrease in net exports is an increase in our international deficit.

You've now seen that the effects of expansionary fiscal policy are extremely sensitive to the state of the economy when the policy action is taken. At less than full employment, an expansionary fiscal policy can move the economy towards full employment. At full employment, an expansionary fiscal policy raises the price level, crowds out investment and creates an international deficit.

Expansionary Monetary Policy at Full Employment

Now suppose the economy is at full employment and the Bank of England increases the money supply. Again, all the effects that we worked out earlier in this chapter occur. But again, these effects determine only a *short-run equilibrium*. That is, the first round and second round effects of monetary policy both occur in the short run. And again, there is a third round, which is the long-run adjustment.

Starting out at full employment, an expansionary monetary policy will create an above full-employment equilibrium in which there is an *inflationary gap*. The money wage rate begins to rise, short-run aggregate supply decreases, and a long-run adjustment occurs in which real GDP decreases to potential GDP and the price level rises.

Figure 29.8, which illustrates the effects of an expansionary fiscal policy at full employment also illustrates the effects of an expansionary monetary policy at full employment.

In the short run, an expansionary monetary policy increases real GDP and the price level. But in the long run, it increases only the price level and leaves real GDP unchanged at potential GDP.

Long-run Neutrality

In the long run, a change in the quantity of money changes only the price level and leaves real GDP unchanged. The independence of real GDP from the quantity of money is an example of the long-run neutrality of money.

But long-run neutrality applies not only to real GDP but also to all real variables. The so-called long-run neutrality proposition is that in the long run, a change in the quantity of money changes the price level and leaves all real variables unchanged.

You can see this outcome in the case of real GDP in Figure 29.8. Because a change in the quantity of money leaves real GDP unchanged, it also leaves consumption expenditure unchanged. With no change in real GDP, the demand for money does not change. The price level rises by the same percentage as the increase in the quantity of money, so the supply of real money does not change. With no change in the demand for money and no change in the supply of real money, the interest rate does not change. And with no change in the interest rate, expenditure remains the same. Finally, with no change in real GDP, consumption expenditure, investment, and government expenditures, net exports are unchanged.

Review

- In the short run, an expansionary fiscal policy or monetary policy increases real GDP and the price level.
- In the long run, an expansionary fiscal policy at full employment raises the price level, leaves real GDP unchanged, but crowds out investment or brings a net exports deficit.
- In the long run, an expansionary monetary policy at full employment raises the price level, leaves real GDP unchanged, and leaves the real interest rate and composition of expenditure unchanged.

Policy Coordination and Conflict

So far, we've studied fiscal policy and monetary policy in isolation from each other. We are now going to consider what happens if the two branches of policy are coordinated and if they come into conflict.

Policy coordination occurs when the government and the Bank of England work together to achieve a common set of goals. Policy conflict occurs when the government and the Bank of England pursue different goals and the actions of one make it harder (perhaps impossible) for the other to achieve its goals.

Policy Coordination

The basis for policy coordination is the fact that either fiscal policy or monetary policy can be used to increase aggregate demand. Starting from a position of *unemployment equilibrium*, an increase in aggregate demand increases real GDP and decreases unemployment. If the size of the policy action is well judged, it can restore full employment. Similarly, starting from a position of *above full-employment equilibrium*, a decrease in aggregate demand decreases real GDP and can, if the size of the policy action is well judged, eliminate an *inflationary gap*. Because either a fiscal policy or a monetary policy action can achieve these objectives, the two policies can (in principle) be combined to also achieve the same outcome.

If either or both policies can restore full employment and eliminate inflation, why does it matter which policy is used? It matters because the two policies have different side effects – different effects on other variables about which people care. These side effects work through the influence of policy on two key variables:

1 The interest rate.

2 The exchange rate.

Interest Rate Effects An expansionary fiscal policy *raises* the interest rate while an expansionary monetary policy *lowers* the interest rate. When the interest rate changes, investment changes, so an expansionary fiscal policy lowers investment (crowding out) while an expansionary monetary policy increases investment. So if an expansionary fiscal policy increases aggregate demand, consumption expenditure increases and investment decreases. But if an expansionary monetary policy increases aggregate demand, consumption expenditure and investment increase.

By coordinating fiscal policy and monetary policy and increasing aggregate demand with an appropriate combination of the two, it is possible to increase real GDP and lower unemployment with either no change in the interest rate, or with any desired change in the interest rate. A big dose of fiscal expansion and a small dose of monetary expansion raises the interest rate and lowers investment while a small dose of fiscal expansion and a big dose of monetary expansion lowers the interest rate.

The interest rate affects our long-term growth prospects because the growth rate of potential GDP depends on the level of investment. The connection between investment, capital and growth is explained in Chapters 31, pp. 780–781, and 32.

Exchange Rate Effects An expansionary fiscal policy raises not only the interest rate but also the exchange rate. In contrast, an expansionary monetary policy *lowers* the exchange rate. When the exchange rate changes, net exports change. An expansionary fiscal policy lowers net exports (international crowding out) while an expansionary monetary policy increases net exports. So if full employment is restored by expansionary policy, net exports decrease with fiscal expansion and increase with monetary expansion.

Policy Conflict

Policy conflicts are not planned. But they sometimes happen. When they arise, it is usually because of a divergence of the political priorities of the government and the objectives of the Bank of England.

The government pays a lot of attention to employment and production over a short time horizon. It looks for policies that make its re-election chances high. The Bank of England pays a lot of attention to price level stability and has a long time horizon. It doesn't have an election to worry about.

So a situation might arise in which the government wants the Bank to pursue an expansionary monetary policy but the Bank wants to keep its foot on the monetary brake. The government says that an increase in the money supply is essential to lower interest rates and the exchange rate and to boost investment and exports. The Bank says that the problem is with fiscal policy. Spending is too high and revenues too low. With fiscal policy too expansionary, interest rates and the exchange rate are high and they cannot be lowered permanently by monetary policy. To lower interest rates and give investment and exports a boost, fiscal policy must become contractionary. Only then can an expansionary monetary policy be pursued.

A further potential conflict between the government and the Bank of England concerns the financing of the government deficit. A government deficit can be financed either by borrowing from the general public or by borrowing from the Bank. If the government borrows from the general public, it must pay interest on its debt. If it borrows from the Bank, it pays interest to the Bank. But the government owns the Bank, so the interest comes back to the government. Financing a deficit by selling debt to the central bank costs the government no interest. So the temptation to sell debt to the central bank is strong.

But when the Bank of England buys government debt, it pays for the debt with newly created monetary base. The money supply increases. And such finance leads to inflation. In many countries, for example in Eastern Europe, Latin America and Africa, government deficits are financed by the central bank.

In the UK, they are not. Indeed, the independence of the Bank of England and of the central banks in the EU ensures that such a possibility cannot happen.

Review

- By coordinating fiscal policy and monetary policy, aggregate demand can be changed (in either direction) and accompanied by either a rise, fall or no change in the interest rate or the exchange rate.
- Governments usually take a shorter-term view than the central bank, so policy conflicts can arise.
- If the government pursues an expansionary policy while the Bank pursues a contractionary policy, interest rates and the exchange rate rise and there is crowding out.
- Inflation can be avoided despite a government deficit if the central bank resists financing the deficit with newly created money. The best way of avoiding this is to make the central bank independent.

You have now studied the interaction of fiscal policy and monetary policy. *Reading Between the Lines* on pages 750–751 takes a further look at the way these two sets of policies interact by studying the policy actions of 1998. You've seen that these policies are alternative ways of changing aggregate demand and real GDP. But they have different effects on interest rates and the exchange rate. You've seen what determines the relative effectiveness of fiscal and monetary policies and how the mix of these policies can influence the composition of aggregate expenditure. But you've also seen that the ultimate effects of these policies on real GDP and the price level depend not only on the behaviour of aggregate demand but also on aggregate supply and the state of the labour market.

Summary

Key Points

Macroeconomic Equilibrium (pp. 722–724)

- Equilibrium real GDP, the price level and the interest rate are determined simultaneously by equilibrium in the money market and equality of aggregate demand and aggregate supply.

Fiscal Policy in the Short Run (pp. 724–727)

- The first round effects of an expansionary fiscal policy are an increase in aggregate demand, increasing real GDP, and a rising price level.
- The second round effects are an increasing demand for money and a decreasing supply of (real) money that limit the increase in real GDP and the rise in the price level.
- Interest-sensitive expenditure, which includes investment and net exports, decreases.

Monetary Policy in the Short Run (pp. 728–731)

- The first round effects of an expansionary monetary policy are a fall in the interest rate, an increase in aggregate demand, an increasing real GDP and a rising price level.
- The second round effects are an increasing demand for money and a decreasing supply of (real) money that limit the increase in real GDP and the rise in the price level.
- Interest-sensitive expenditure, which includes investment and net exports, increases.

Relative Effectiveness of Policies (pp. 731–734)

- The relative effectiveness of fiscal and monetary policy depends on the interest-sensitivity of expenditure and the demand for money.
- The extreme Keynesian position is that only fiscal policy affects aggregate demand. The extreme monetarist position is that only monetary policy affects aggregate demand. Neither extreme is correct.
- The mix of fiscal and monetary policy influences the composition of aggregate demand.

Policy Actions at Full Employment (pp. 734–736)

- An expansionary fiscal policy at full employment increases real GDP and the price level in the short run but increases only the price level in the long run. Complete crowding of investment occurs or the international deficit increases.
- An expansionary monetary policy at full employment increases real GDP and the price level in the short run but increases only the price level in the long run. Money is neutral – has no real effects – in the long run.

Policy Coordination and Conflict (pp. 736–737)

- Policy coordination can make changes in the interest rate and the exchange rate small.
- Policy conflict can avoid inflation in the face of a government deficit.

Key Figures

Key Terms

Crowding in, 727
Crowding out, 727
International crowding out, 727
Keynesian, 732
Long-run neutrality, 735
Monetarist, 732
Policy conflict, 737
Policy coordination, 736

Review Questions

1 What is meant by macroeconomic equilibrium?

2 Trace through the first round effect of an expansionary fiscal policy.

3 Trace through the second round effect of an expansionary fiscal policy.

4 Trace through the first round effect of an expansionary monetary policy.

5 Trace through the second round effect of an expansionary monetary policy.

6 What is the effect of an increase in the discount rate?

7 What is crowding out?

8 On what two factors does the strength of crowding out depend?

9 What does the relative effectiveness of fiscal and monetary policy depend on?

10 Describe the position of the extreme Keynesian.

11 Describe the position of the extreme monetarist.

12 What is long-run neutrality?

13 What is policy coordination?

14 What is policy conflict?

Problems

1 In the economy described in Figure 29.5, suppose the government decreases its expenditures on goods and services by £50 billion.

a Work out the first round effects.
b Explain how real GDP and the interest rate change.
c Explain the second round effects that take the economy to a new equilibrium.

2 In the economy described in Figure 29.5, suppose the government increases its expenditures on goods and services by £25 billion.

a Work out the first round effects.
b Explain how real GDP and the interest rate change.
c Explain the second round effects that take the economy to a new equilibrium.
d Compare the equilibrium in this case with the one described in the chapter on pp. 724–726. In which case does real GDP change more? In which case does the interest rate change more? Why?

3 In the economy described in Figure 29.5, suppose the Bank of England decreases the money supply by £150 billion.

a Work out the first round effects.
b Explain how real GDP and the interest rate change.
c Explain the second round effects that take the economy to a new equilibrium.

4 In the economy described in Figure 29.5, suppose the Bank of England increases the money supply by £250 billion.

a Work out the first round effects.
b Explain how real GDP and the interest rate change.
c Explain the second round effects that take the economy to a new equilibrium.
d Compare the equilibrium in this case with the one described in the chapter on pp. 728–731. In which case does real GDP change more? In which case does the interest rate change more? Why?

5 The economies of two countries, Alpha and Beta, are identical in every way except the following: in Alpha, a change in the interest rate of 1 percentage point (for example, from 5 per cent to 6 per cent) results in a £1 billion change in the quantity of real money demanded. In Beta, a change in the interest rate of 1 percentage point results in a £0.1 billion change in the quantity of real money demanded.

a In which economy does an increase in government expenditures on goods and services have a larger effect on real GDP?
b In which economy is the crowding-out effect weaker?
c In which economy does a change in the money supply have a larger effect on equilibrium real GDP?
d Which economy, if either, is closer to the Keynesian extreme and which is closer to the monetarist extreme?

6 The economies of two countries, Gamma and Delta, are identical in every way except the following: in Gamma, a change in the interest rate of 1 percentage point (for example, from 5 per cent to 6 per cent) results in a £0.1 billion change in the quantity of real money demanded. In Delta, a change in the interest rate of 1 percentage point results in a £10 billion change in the quantity of real money demanded.

a In which economy does an increase in government expenditures on goods and services have a larger effect on real GDP?
b In which economy is the crowding-out effect weaker?
c In which economy does a change in the money supply have a larger effect on equilibrium real GDP?
d Which economy, if either, is closer to the Keynesian extreme and which is closer to the monetarist extreme?

7 The economy is in a recession and the government wants to increase aggregate demand, stimulate exports and increase investment. It has three policy options: increase government expenditures on goods and services, decrease taxes and increase the money supply.

a Explain the mechanisms at work under each alternative policy.
b What is the effect of each policy on the composition of aggregate demand?
c What are the short-run effects of each policy on real GDP and the price level?
d Which policy would you recommend that the government adopt? Why?

8 The economy has an inflationary gap and the government wants to decrease aggregate demand, cut exports and decrease investment. It has three policy options: decrease government expenditures on goods and services, increase taxes and decrease the money supply.

a Explain the mechanisms at work under each alternative policy.
b What is the effect of each policy on the composition of aggregate demand?
c What are the short-run effects of each policy on real GDP and the price level?
d Which policy would you recommend that the government adopt? Why?

9 The economy is at full employment, but the government is disappointed with the growth rate of real GDP. It wants to increase real GDP growth by stimulating investment. At the same time, it wants to avoid an increase in the price level.

a Suggest a combination of fiscal and monetary policies that will achieve the government's objective.

b Which policy would you recommend that the government adopt?
c Explain the mechanisms at work under your recommended policy.
d What is the effect of your recommended policy on the composition of aggregate demand?
e What are the short-run and long-run effects of your recommended policy on real GDP and the price level?

10 The economy is at full employment, and the government is worried that the growth rate of real GDP is too high because it is depleting the country's natural resources. It wants to lower real GDP growth by lowering investment. At the same time it wants to avoid a fall in the price level.

a Suggest a combination of fiscal and monetary policies that will achieve the government's objective.
b Which policy would you recommend that the government adopt?
c Explain the mechanisms at work under your recommended policy.
d What is the effect of your recommended policy on the composition of aggregate demand?
e What are the short-run and long-run effects of your recommended policy on real GDP and the price level?

11 Study *Reading Between the Lines* on pp. 750–751 and then answer the following questions:

a Why does the Chancellor of the Exchequer think the economy is in good shape?
b What are your predictions about the fiscal policy the government will pursue next year?
c What do you predict the effects of fiscal policy will be on real GDP, the price level, interest rates, investment, the exchange rate and net exports?
d What actions do you think the Bank of England needs to take to ensure that the economy expands but without an upturn in the inflation rate?
e What would happen if the Bank of England decided to raise interest rates? Explain the likely effects on real GDP, the price level, investment, the exchange rate and net exports.

12 Use the link on the Parkin, Powell and Matthews Web site to visit the Web site of Office of National Statistics and look at the current economic conditions. On the basis of the current state of the UK economy, and in the light of what you now know about fiscal and monetary policy interaction, what do you predict would happen to real GDP and the price level:

a If the Bank of England conducted an expansionary monetary policy?
b If the Bank of England conducted a contractionary monetary policy?
c If the government conducted an expansionary fiscal policy?
d If the government conducted a contractionary fiscal policy?
e If the Bank of England conducted an expansionary monetary policy and the government conducted a contractionary fiscal policy?
f If the Bank of England conducted a contractionary monetary policy and the government conducted an expansionary fiscal policy?

W http://www.econ100.com

Appendix to Chapter 29
The *IS–LM* Model of Aggregate Demand

Equilibrium Expenditure and Real GDP

Aggregate planned expenditure depends on real GDP because consumption increases as real GDP increases. Aggregate planned expenditure also depends on the interest rate because the higher the interest rate, the lower is planned investment. These two influences on aggregate planned expenditure give rise to the *IS* curve.

The *IS* Curve

The *IS* curve shows combinations of real GDP and the interest rate at which aggregate expenditure is at its equilibrium level – aggregate planned expenditure equals real GDP.

Figure A29.1 shows how the *IS* curve is derived. Part (a) is similar to Figure 25.5. The 45° line shows all the points at which aggregate planned expenditure equals real GDP. Curves AE_a AE_b, and AE_c, are aggregate planned expenditure curves. Curve AE_a represents aggregate planned expenditure when the interest rate is 6 per cent (row *a* of the table). Curve AE_b shows aggregate planned expenditure when the interest rate is 5 per cent (row *b*) and AE_c shows aggregate planned expenditure when the interest rate is 4 per cent (row *c*).

There is just one expenditure equilibrium on each of these aggregate planned expenditure curves. On curve AE_a, the expenditure equilibrium is at point *a*, where real GDP is £550 billion. The expenditure equilibrium on AE_b, occurs at point *b*, where real GDP is £750 billion. The expenditure equilibrium on AE_c, occurs at point *c*, where real GDP is £950 billion.

Figure A29.1(b) shows each expenditure equilibrium again but highlights the relationship between the interest rate and real GDP at the expenditure equilibrium. Its horizontal axis, like Figure A29.1(a), measures real GDP. Its vertical axis measures the interest rate. Point *a* in part (b) illustrates the expenditure equilibrium at point *a* in part (a) of the figure (or in row *a* of the table). It tells us that if the interest rate is 6 per cent, the expenditure equilibrium occurs at a real GDP of £550 billion. Points *b* and *c* in the figure illustrate the expenditure equilibrium at points *b* and *c* of part (a). The continuous line through these points is the *IS* curve.

Some relationships show 'cause' and 'effect'. For example, the consumption function in Chapter 25, pp. 605–606, tells us the level of consumption

Figure A29.1 Aggregate Planned Expenditure, Flow Equilibrium and the *IS* Curve

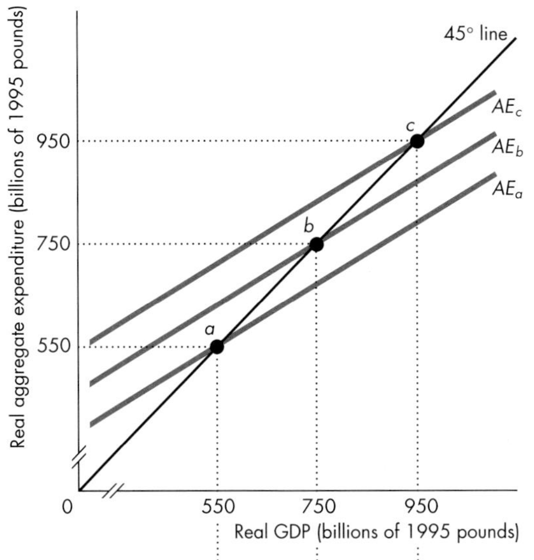

(a) Aggregate expenditure and real GDP

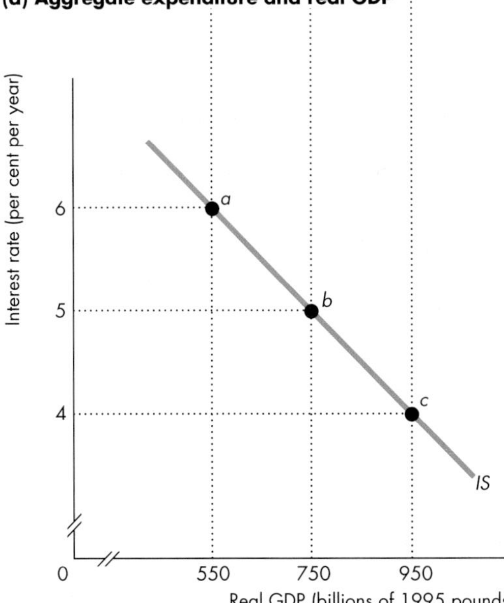

(b) The *IS* curve

The table shows aggregate planned expenditure – the sum of autonomous expenditure and induced expenditure – that occurs at different combinations of the interest rate and real GDP. For example, if the interest rate is 5 per cent and real GDP is £950 billion, aggregate planned expenditure is £790 billion (top right-hand number). Flow equilibrium (equality of aggregate planned expenditure and real GDP) is shown by the green squares. Each of rows *a*, *b* and *c* represents an aggregate expenditure schedule, plotted as the aggregate expenditure curves AE_a, AE_b and AE_c, respectively, in part (a). Expenditure equilibrium positions are shown in part (a), where these *AE* curves intersect the 45° line and are marked *a*, *b* and *c*. Part (b) shows these same equilibrium positions but highlights the combinations of the interest rate and the real GDP at which they occur. The line connecting those points is the *IS* curve.

	Interest rate (per cent per year)	Autonomous expenditure (billions of 1995 pounds)	Aggregate planned expenditure (billions of 1995 pounds)		
a	6	220	550	670	790
b	5	300	630	750	870
c	4	380	710	830	950
Induced expenditure			330	450	570
Real GDP (billions of 1995 pounds)			550	750	950

(effect) at a particular level of income. The investment demand curve tells us the level of investment (effect) at a particular interest rate (cause). The *IS* curve is *not* a 'cause and effect' relationship. It can be read in two ways. It tells us that if the interest rate is 6 per cent, then aggregate planned expenditure equals real GDP only if real GDP is £750 billion. It also tells us that if real GDP is £750 billion, then the interest rate at which aggregate planned expenditure equals real GDP is 5 per cent.

The *IS* curve shows combinations of the interest rate and real GDP at which aggregate expenditure is at its equilibrium level. To determine the interest rate and real GDP, we need an additional relationship between those two variables. That second relationship between interest rates and real GDP comes from equilibrium in the money market.

Money Market Equilibrium

We have seen that the quantity of money demanded depends on the price level, real GDP and the interest rate. The quantity of money demanded is proportional to the price level. If the price level doubles, so does the quantity of money demanded. Real money is the ratio of the quantity of money to the price level. The quantity of real money demanded increases as real GDP increases and decreases as the interest rate increases.

The supply of money is determined by the actions of the Bank of England, the commercial banks and other financial intermediaries. Given those commercial actions, and given the price level, there is a given quantity of real money in existence. Money market equilibrium occurs when the quantity of real money supplied is equal to the quantity demanded. Equilibrium in the money market is a stock equilibrium. Figure A29.2 contains a numerical example that enables us to study money market equilibrium.

Suppose that the quantity of money supplied is £800 billion. Suppose also that the GDP deflator is 100 so that the quantity of real money supplied is also £800 billion. The real money supply is shown in the bottom part of the table. Money market equilibrium occurs when the quantity of real money demanded equals the quantity supplied. The table tells us about the demand for real money. Each row tells us how much real money is demanded at a given interest rate as real GDP varies and each column tells us how much is demanded at a given real GDP as the interest rate varies. For example, at an interest rate of 6 per cent and real GDP at £550 billion, the quantity of real money demanded is £700 billion. Alternatively, at an interest rate of 5 per cent and real GDP of £750 billion, the quantity of real money demanded is £800 billion. The rest of the numbers in the table are read in a similar way.

Money market equilibrium occurs when the quantity of real money demanded equals the quantity supplied, £800 billion in this example. The green squares in the table indicate positions of money market equilibrium – combinations of interest rate and real GDP at which the quantity of money demanded is equal to the quantity supplied. For example, look at column *d*. Real GDP is £550 billion, and the quantity of real money demanded is £800 billion (equal to the quantity supplied) when the interest rate is 4 per cent. Thus at real GDP of £550 billion and an interest rate of 4 per cent, the money market is in equilibrium. At the other two green squares the interest rate is such that the quantity of real money demanded is £800 billion when real GDP is £750 billion and £950 billion respectively. That is, the green squares show combinations of the interest rate and real GDP at which the money market is in equilibrium.

The *LM* Curve

The *LM* curve shows the combinations of real GDP and the interest rate at which the quantity of real money demanded equals the quantity of real money supplied. Figure A29.2 derives the *LM* curve. Part (a) shows the demand and supply curves for real money. The quantity supplied is fixed at £800 billion, so the supply curve *MS* is vertical. Each of the columns of the table labelled *d*, *e* and *f* is a demand schedule for real money – a schedule that tells us how the quantity of real money demanded rises as the interest rate falls. There is a different schedule for each level of real GDP. These three demand schedules for real money are graphed as demand curves for real money in part (a) of the figure as MD_d, MD_e and MD_f. For example, when real GDP is £550 billion, the demand curve for real money is and MD_d. Money market equilibrium occurs at the intersection of the supply curve and the demand curves for real money at points *d*, *e* and *f* in part (a).

Figure A29.2(b) shows each money market equilibrium again but highlights the relationship between the interest rate and real GDP at which an equilibrium occurs. Points *d*, *e* and *f* in part (b) illustrate the money market equilibrium represented by the green squares in the table and by those similarly labelled points in part (a). The continuous line through these points is the *LM* curve. The *LM* curve shows the interest rate and real GDP at which money market equilibrium occurs when the real money supply is £800 billion.

Like the *IS* curve, the *LM* curve does not have a 'cause and effect' interpretation. The *LM* curve illustrated in Figure A29.2(b) tells us that if the quantity of real money supplied is £800 billion and real GDP is £550 billion, then for money market equilibrium the interest rate is 3 per cent. It also tells us that if the quantity of real money supplied is

Figure A29.2 The Money Market, Stock Equilibrium and the *LM* Curve

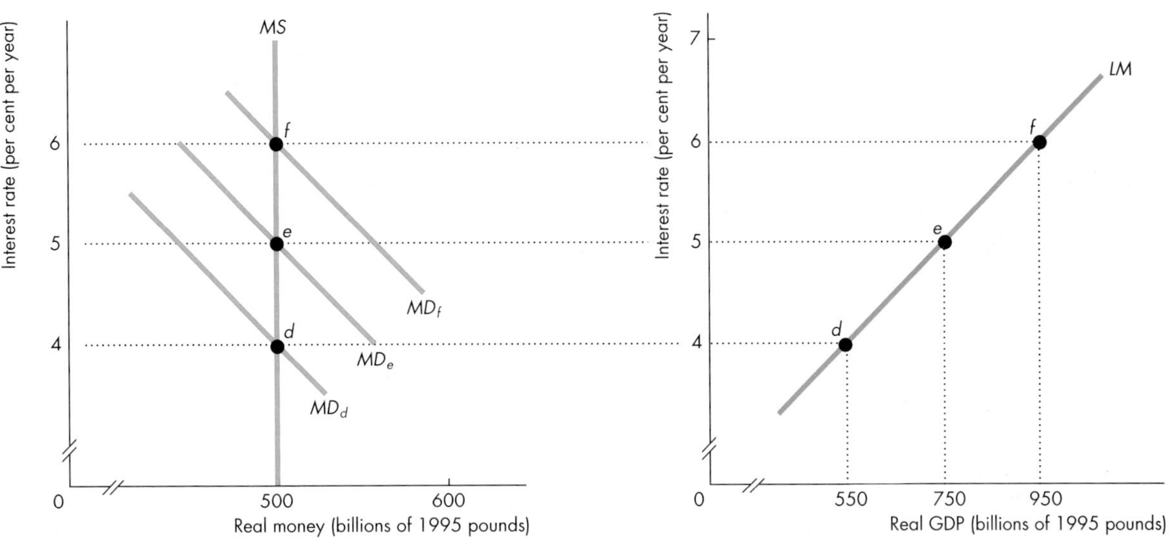

(a) Money market equilibrium

(b) The *LM* curve

Interest rate (per cent per year)	Quantity of real money demanded (billions of 1995 pounds)		
6	400	450	500
5	450	500	550
4	500	550	600
Real GDP	550	750	950
Real money supply (billions of 1995 pounds)	500 d	500 e	500 f

The table shows the quantity of real money demanded at different combinations of the interest rate and real GDP. For example, if the interest rate is 5 per cent and real GDP is £550 billion, the quantity of real money demanded is £400 billion (top-left number). Stock equilibrium – equality between the quantity of real money demanded and supplied – is shown by the green squares. Each of the columns *d*, *e* and *f* represents a demand schedule for real money, plotted as the demand curves for real money MD_d, MD_e and MD_f, respectively, in part (a). Money market equilibrium positions are shown in part (a), where these *MD* curves intersect the supply curve of real money *MS* and are marked *d*, *e* and *f*. Part (b) shows these same equilibrium positions but highlights the combinations of the interest rate and real GDP at which they occur. The line connecting those points is the *LM* curve.

£800 billion and the interest is 4 per cent, then for money market equilibrium real GDP is £550 billion. That is, the *LM* curve shows combinations of the interest rate and real GDP at which there is money market equilibrium.

We now have two relationships between the interest rate and real GDP. The *IS* curve and the *LM* curve. Together, and at a given price level, these two relationships determine the interest rate or real GDP. They also enable us to derive the *aggregate demand curve*. Let's see how.

Equilibrium and the Aggregate Demand Curve

Equilibrium real GDP and the interest rate are shown in Figure A29.3, which brings together the *IS* curve and the *LM* curve. This equilibrium is at the point of intersection of the *IS* curve and *LM* curve. Point *b* on the *IS* curve is a point of expenditure equilibrium. The interest rate and real GDP are such that aggregate real expenditure equals real GDP. Point *e* on the *LM* curve is a point of money

Figure A29.3 *IS–LM* Equilibrium

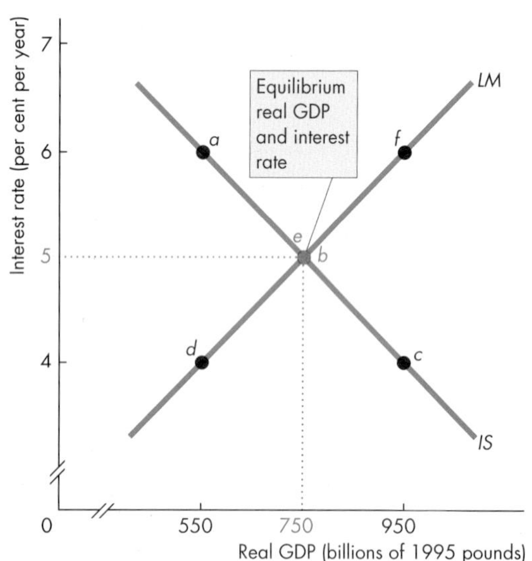

All points on the *IS* curve are points where aggregate planned expenditure equals real GDP. All points on the *LM* curve are points at which the quantity of real money demanded equals the quantity of real money supplied. The intersection of the *IS* curve on the *LM* curve determines the equilibrium interest rate and real GDP – 5 per cent and £750 billion. At this interest rate and real GDP, there is flow equilibrium in the goods market and stock equilibrium in the money market.

market equilibrium. The interest rate and real GDP are such that the quantity of real money demanded equals the quantity of real money supplied. At this intersection point, there is both flow equilibrium in the goods market and stock equilibrium in the money market. The equilibrium interest rate is 5 per cent and real GDP is £750 billion.

At all other points, there is no expenditure equilibrium or the money market is not in equilibrium or both. At a point such as *a*, the economy is on its *IS* curve but off its *LM* curve. With real GDP at £550 billion and the interest rate at 6 per cent, the interest rate is too high or real GDP is too low for money market equilibrium. Interest rates adjust quickly and would fall to 4 per cent to bring about money market equilibrium putting the economy at point *d*, a point on the *LM* curve. But point *d* is off the *IS* curve. At point *d*, with the interest rate at 4 per cent and real GDP at £550 billion, aggregate planned expenditure exceeds real GDP. By checking back to the table in Figure A29.1, you can see that aggregate planned expenditure is £790 billion, which exceeds real GDP of £550 billion. With aggregate planned expenditure larger than real GDP, real GDP will increase. But as real GDP increases, so does the demand for real money and so does the interest rate. Real GDP and the interest rate would rise, and continue to do so, until the point of intersection of the *IS* and *LM* curves is reached.

The account that we have just given of what *would* happen if the economy was at a point like *a* or *d* tells us that the economy cannot be at such points. The forces that operate in such situations would be so strong that they would always push the economy to the intersection of the *IS* and *LM* curves.

The Effects of a Change in Price Level on the *LM* Curve

The price level enters the *IS–LM* model to determine the quantity of real money supplied. The Bank of England determines the money supply as a certain number of current pounds. The higher the price level, the lower is the real value of those pounds. Because the price level affects the quantity of real money supplied, it also affects the *LM* curve. Let's see how.

Begin by asking what happens if the price level, instead of being 100, is 120 – 20 per cent higher than before. The money supply is £800 billion. With a GDP deflator of 120, the real money supply is £666.67 billion. (The real money supply is £800 billion divided by 1.2, which equals £666.67 billion.) For money market equilibrium we can see in the table of Figure A29.2 what happens to the interest rate at a real GDP of £750 billion. With a GDP deflator of 120, the interest rate rises to 6 per cent in order to decrease the quantity of real money demanded to £666.67 billion – equal to the real money supply. Thus with a GDP deflator of 120, an interest rate of 6 per cent and real GDP of £750 billion become a point on the *LM* curve – point *g* in Figure A29.4(a).

Next, suppose that the GDP deflator is lower than the original case – 86 instead of 100. Now the real money supply becomes £930.2 billion. Again for money market equilibrium we can see in the table of Figure A29.2 what happens to the interest rate at a real GDP of £750 billion. With a GDP deflator of 86, the interest rate falls to 4 per cent in order to increase the quantity of real money demanded. Thus with a GDP deflator of 86, an interest rate of

Figure A29.4 Deriving the Aggregate Demand Curve

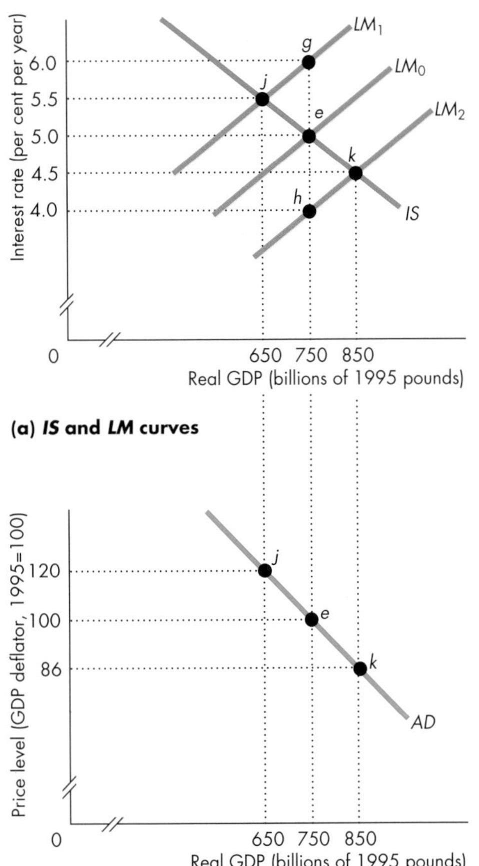

In part (a), if the GDP deflator is 100, the *LM* curve is LM_0. If the GDP deflator increases to 120, the *LM* curve shifts to the left to LM_1. A lower real money supply requires a higher interest rate at each level of real GDP for money market equilibrium. For example, if real GDP is £750 billion, the interest rate has to increase from 5 per cent to 6 per cent (point *g*). If the price level falls, the real money supply increases and the *LM* curve shifts to the right to LM_2. If real GDP is £750 billion, the interest rate falls to 4 per cent (point *h*) to maintain money market equilibrium. When the GDP deflator is 100, the *IS* and *LM* curves intersect at point *e* – real GDP of £750 billion. This equilibrium is shown in part (b) at point *e* on aggregate demand curve *AD*. This point tells us that when the GDP deflator is 100, the quantity of real GDP demanded is £750 billion. If the GDP deflator is 120, the *LM* curve is LM_1 and real GDP is £650 billion. A second point on the aggregate demand curve is found at *j*. If the GDP deflator is 86, the *LM* curve is LM_2 and real GDP is £850 billion. Another point on the aggregate demand curve is generated at point *k*. Joining points *j*, *e* and *k* gives the aggregate demand curve.

4 per cent and real GDP of £750 billion become a point on the *LM* curve – point *h* in Figure A29.4(a).

The *LM* Curve Shift The example that we have worked through tells us that there is a different *LM* curve for each price level. Figure A29.4(a) illustrates the *LM* curves for the three different price levels we have considered. The initial *LM* curve has the GDP deflator equal to 100. This curve has been relabelled as LM_0 in Figure A29.4(a). When the GDP deflator is 120 and real GDP is £750 billion, the interest rate that achieves equilibrium in the money market is 6 per cent. This equilibrium is shown as point *g* on curve LM_1 in Figure A29.4(a). The entire *LM* curve shifts left to LM_1 in order to pass through point *g*. When the GDP deflator is 86 and real GDP is £750 billion, the interest rate that achieves equilibrium in the money market is 4 per cent. This equilibrium is shown as point *h* on the curve LM_2 in Figure A29.4(a). Again, the entire *LM* curve shifts right to LM_2 in order to pass through point *h*.

Now that we have worked out the effects of a change in the price level on the position of the *LM* curve, we can derive the aggregate demand curve.

The Aggregate Demand Curve Derived

Figure A29.4 shows the derivation. Part (a) shows the *IS* curve and the three *LM* curves associated with the three different price levels (GDP deflators of 86, 100 and 120). When the GDP deflator is 100, the *LM* curve is LM_0. Equilibrium is at point *e* where real GDP is £750 billion and the equilibrium interest rate is 5 per cent. If the GDP deflator is 120, the *LM* curve is LM_1. Equilibrium is at point *j* where real GDP is £650 billion and the interest rate is 5.5 per cent. If the GDP deflator is 86, the *LM* curve is LM_2. Equilibrium is at point *k* where real GDP is £850 billion and the interest rate is 4.5 per cent. At each price level there is a different equilibrium real GDP and interest rate.

Part (b) traces the aggregate demand curve. The price level is measured on the vertical axis of part (b) and real GDP on the horizontal axis. When the GDP deflator is 100, equilibrium real GDP is £750 billion (point *e*). When the GDP deflator is 120 equilibrium real GDP is £650 billion (point *j*). And when the GDP deflator is 86, real GDP demanded is £850 billion (point *k*). Each of these points corresponds to the same point in part (a). The line joining these in part (b) is the aggregate demand curve.

Figure A29.5 Fiscal Policy and Monetary Policy (Normal Case)

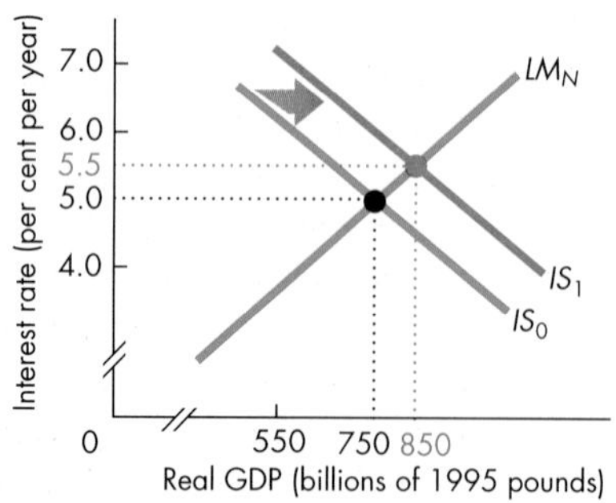

(a) Fiscal policy: normal case

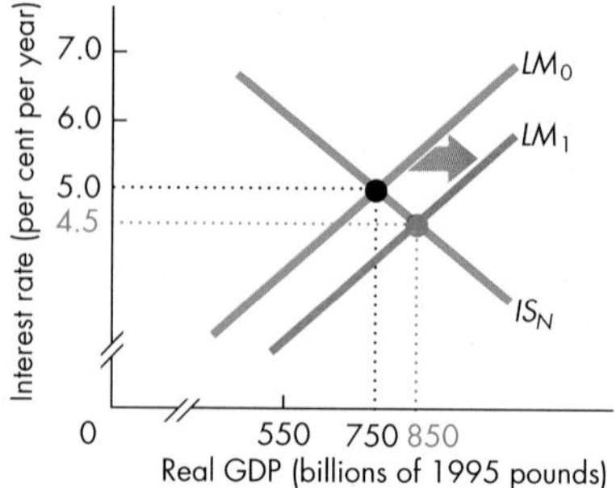

(b) Monetary policy: normal case

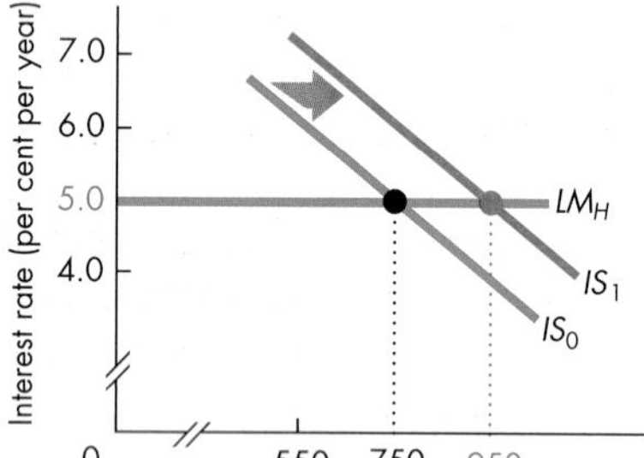

(c) Fiscal policy: maximum effect on GDP

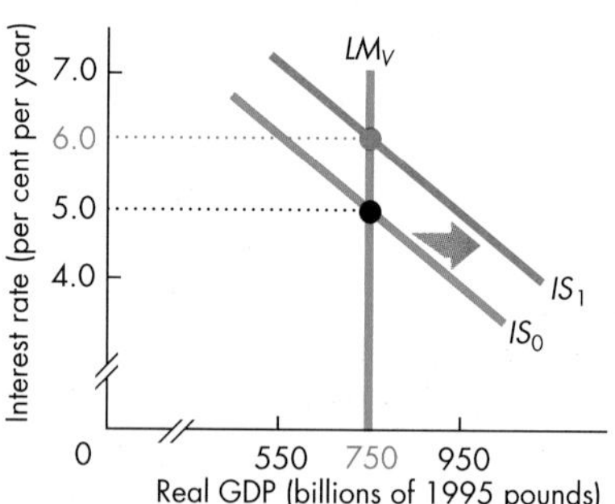

(d) Fiscal policy: no effect on GDP

An increase in government purchases or an autonomous tax cut shifts the *IS* curve to the right. The effects of fiscal policy on real GDP and the interest rate depend on the slope of the *LM* curve. In the normal case (part a), interest rates and real GDP rise. An increase in the money supply shifts the *LM* curve to the right. The effect of the monetary action on interest rates and real GDP depends on the slope of the *IS* curve. In the normal case (part b), interest rates fall and real GDP rises. The lower interest rates stimulate investment. If there is a 'liquidity trap', the *LM* curve is horizontal (part c), fiscal policy has the maximum effect on GDP, but monetary policy has no effect. If the demand for money is insensitive to the rate of interest, the *LM* curve is vertical (part d), fiscal policy has no effect on GDP. But monetary policy will shift the *LM* curve and will have minimum effect.

Now that we have derived the demand curve we can work out the effects of fiscal and monetary policy.

Fiscal and Monetary Policy

Figure A29.5(a) and (b) illustrates the effects of a change in fiscal and monetary policy. Parts (a) and (b) illustrate the normal cases and parts (c) and (d) illustrate the special cases.

In part (a) and (b), the *LM* curve is upward sloping. Fiscal policy is taken as either a rise in government purchases or a cut in autonomous taxes that shifts the *IS* curve from IS_0 to IS_1. A change in government purchases or in taxes shifts the *IS* curve and the aggregate demand curve. An expansionary fiscal policy shifts the *IS* curve up to the right and the aggregate demand curve up to the right. A contractionary fiscal policy shifts the *IS* curve and the aggregate demand curve down to the left. When the *IS* curve shifts because of an expansionary fiscal policy, the interest rate rises and so does real GDP. But the increase in real GDP is less than the magnitude of the shift in the *IS* curve. The reason is that the rise in the rate of interest leads to a decrease in investment which partially offsets the effect of the increase in expenditure caused by the expansionary fiscal policy. This is what is meant by partial 'crowding out'. Figure A29.5(a) shows the effect of fiscal policy on the rate of interest and real GDP.

Monetary policy is taken as an increase in the money supply. We saw earlier in this appendix that when the *LM* curve shifts because of a change in the price level, equilibrium GDP changes and there is a movement along the aggregate demand curve. But a change in the money supply also shifts the *LM* curve. An increase in the money supply shifts the *LM* curve down to the right and the aggregate demand curve up to the right. A decrease in the money supply shifts the *LM* curve up to the left and the aggregate demand curve down to the left. The magnitude of the shift in the aggregate demand curve caused by a shift in the *LM* curve will be due to two factors – the size of the shift of the *LM* curve and the slope of the *IS* curve. Figure 29.5(b) illustrates the effect of an expansionary monetary policy. The *LM* curve shifts from LM_0 to LM_1. You can see that the result of this is a lower interest rate and higher real GDP. The rise in real GDP occurs because the lower interest rate induced by the expansionary monetary policy creates extra investment and increases aggregate demand.

Parts (c) and (d) illustrate the two extreme cases which can be considered as extreme Keynesian and extreme monetarist. The extreme Keynesian case is when the *LM* curve is horizontal (LM_H). The *LM* curve is horizontal only if there is a 'liquidity trap' – a situation when people are willing to hold any quantity of money at a specific rate of interest. This situation may describe what has been happening in Japan in 1997–99. When the *IS* curve shifts to the right, real GDP increases by the same amount as the shift to the right of the *IS* curve. The reason is that the rate of interest does not rise and there is no partial 'crowding out'.

The extreme monetarist case is when the *LM* curve is vertical (LM_V). In this case, although the *IS* curve shifts to the right as in the extreme Keynesian case, the higher interest rate reduces investment by exactly the same as the increase in initial expenditure resulting from the expansionary fiscal policy. There is full 'crowding out'. Full 'crowding out' occurs if the demand for money is completely insensitive to the interest rate. Notice that the extreme monetarist case shows that fiscal policy is completely ineffective and the extreme Keynesian case shows that fiscal policy is fully effective.

In contrast you can see that in the extreme Keynesian case monetary policy is ineffective. This is because any increase in the money supply is willingly held because the demand for money is perfectly elastic at the specific interest rate. So an increase in the money supply will not result in a lowering of the rate of interest and investment will therefore remain unchanged. In the extreme monetarist case, an increase in the money supply causes a shift to the right of LM_V. You can try this yourself and see that the result is a lower rate of interest and higher real GDP.

Fiscal and Monetary Policy in Action

The Economist, 21 March 1998

Eddie's Choice

Growth and inflation

As expected, Gordon Brown reported that the public finances were in good health, and getting better. The government will need to borrow £5 billion ($8.4 billion) in 1997–98 and £3.9 billion next year; two years after that, the government should start repaying debt. Last July, he was forecasting a public-sector borrowing requirement of £13.3 billion this year and £5.4 billion next.

For this, Mr Brown can give thanks not just for a buoyant economy, which has pushed up tax revenues and held down social-security spending, but also for his own tight control of public spending. Even so, some City economists think that he should have tightened fiscal policy further still.

Their complaint is less that the economy is out of control than that it is out of balance. Consumer spending has been strong in recent months. But exporters are struggling, because the expectation that the Bank of England will raise interest rates again is helping to keep sterling strong. Higher taxes on the consumer, say the chancellor's critics, would have reduced the pressure on the Bank to raise rates. That would have weakened sterling, and eased exporters' pain.

Most economists expect the Bank to raise rates soon by a quarter of a percentage point, to 7.5%.

But the call on the fiscal stance was far from being the no-brainer that all this might suggest. The reason is that the economy is delicately poised.

The trouble is that no one knows quite how sharply the economy will slow. Most pundits, and the Treasury, are forecasting a "soft landing"—ie, a short period of growth slightly below the long-term trend of about 2¼%, followed by a return to trend. Meanwhile, inflation (excluding mortgage-interest payments) should rise above the Bank of England's target of 2.5% before coming back on track.

The Essence of the Story

- In the budget of 1998, the Chancellor of the Exchequer, Gordon Brown, announced that the public finances were in good shape.
- The government plans to borrow £5 billion in 1997/8 and £3.9 billion in 1998/9 but two years later plans to repay debt.
- The Chancellor's critics argue that the government should have tightened fiscal policy more.
- Consumer spending has remained strong, exporters are struggling because of a value of the pound.
- The Bank of England is expected to raise interest rates further to dampen domestic demand and the economy is expected to slow down in 1998.

Economic Analysis

■ The independence of the Bank of England means that monetary policy is independent of fiscal policy and set to achieve a specified inflation target. Fiscal policy is set by the government.

■ Rising monetary growth and high domestic demand has prompted the Monetary Policy Committee of the Bank of England to raise the rate of interest in 1997.

■ The higher rate of interest has stemmed the growth in demand during 1998 and has caused the exchange rate to appreciate making exports relatively more expensive.

■ Weak consumer demand in 1998 is being offset by moderately expansionary fiscal policy. The combination of tight monetary policy and moderately expansionary fiscal policy should ensure a 'soft landing' for the economy in 1998–1999.

■ In Figure 1 we can see that the demand for real money (M4) has increased faster than supply causing a rise in the rate of interest.

■ Figure 2 shows the effect of fiscal policy in shifting the *AD* curve from AD_0 (point *a*) to AD_2 (point *c*). If government spending had not increased, the *AD* curve would have shifted to AD_1 (point *b*). The price level would have been marginally lower and the increase in real GDP would have been less than £772 billion in 1995 prices.

■ Figure 3 shows that monetary growth has declined in 1998 as a result of the rise in the rate of interest and government expenditure has increased moderately.

■ The Chancellor's critics are correct in their argument that if fiscal policy had remained flat during 1998, aggregate demand would have risen less and the demand for real money would not have increased by as much. The rate of interest may not have had to rise.

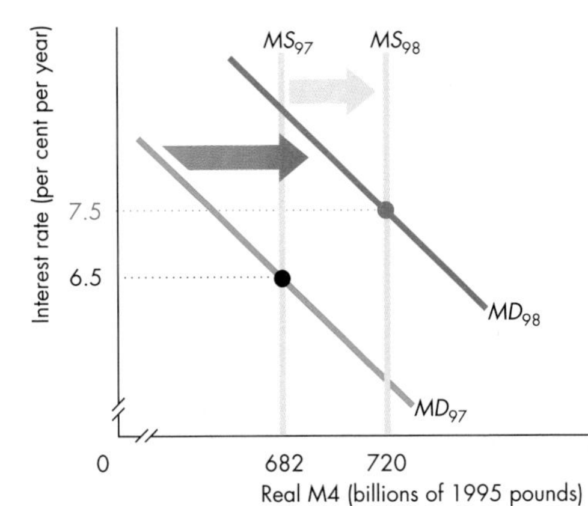

Figure 1 Money and the interest rate

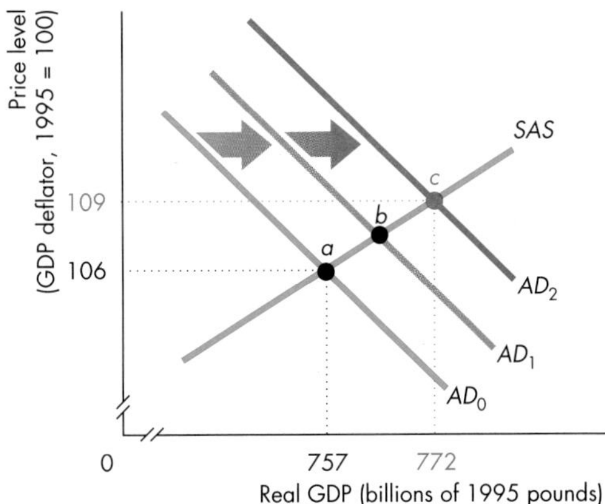

Figure 2 Real GDP and price level

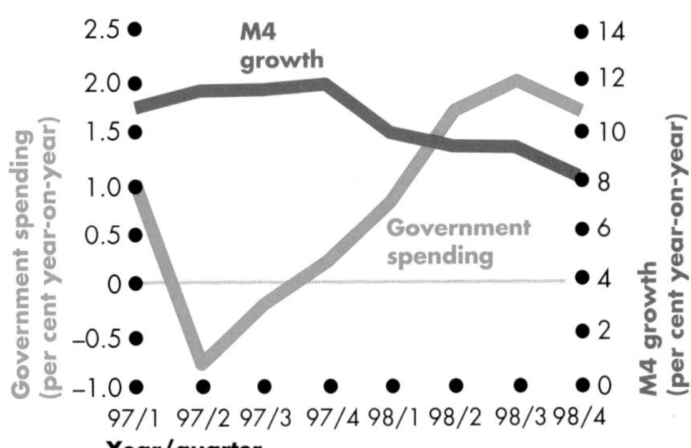

Figure 3 Fiscal and monetary indicators

CHAPTER 30

Inflation

After studying this chapter you will be able to:

- Distinguish between inflation and a one-time rise in the price level
- Explain the different ways in which inflation can be generated
- Describe how people try to forecast inflation
- Explain the short-run and long-run relationships between inflation and unemployment
- Explain the short-run and long-run relationships between inflation and interest rates
- Describe the political origins of inflation

From Rome to Russia

At the end of the third century AD, during the dying days of the Roman empire, Emperor Diocletian struggled to contain a rampant inflation. Prices increased at a rate of more than 300 per cent a year. At the end of the twentieth century, during the years of transition from a central planning system to a market economy, President Boris Yeltsin struggled to contain an even more severe inflation in Russia. At its peak, in the winter of 1993–94, prices increased in Russia at a rate of close to 1,000 per cent a year. But the most rapid inflations in today's world are in Latin America and Africa. For example, in 1994, Brazil's inflation hit 40 per cent *per month* and the tiny African country of Zaire had an inflation rate of 75 per cent *per month*. What causes rapid inflation? ◆ In comparison with the cases just described, the United Kingdom has had remarkable price stability. Nevertheless, during the 1970s, the UK price level trebled – an inflation of more than 200 per cent over the decade. Today, along with the other rich industrial countries, the United Kingdom has a low inflation rate of about 2.5 per cent a year. Why do some countries have a low inflation rate? And why did a more serious inflation break out in the United Kingdom during the 1970s? ◆ Most of life's big economic decisions – whether to buy or rent a house, whether to save more for retirement, whether to buy stocks or keep more money in the bank – turn on what is going to happen to inflation. Will inflation increase so our savings buy less? Will inflation decrease so our debts are harder to repay? To make good decisions, we need good forecasts of inflation, not just for next year but for many years into the future. How do people try to forecast inflation? And how do expectations of inflation influence the economy? ◆ As the inflation rate rises and falls, the unemployment rate and interest rates also fluctuate. What are the links between inflation and the economy that make unemployment and interest rates fluctuate when inflation fluctuates?

◆ ◆ ◆ ◆ In this chapter you will learn about the forces that generate inflation, the effects of inflation and the way that people try to forecast inflation. You will pull together several of the threads you have been following through your study of macroeconomics. In particular, you will use the *AS–AD* model of Chapter 24 and the analysis of the money market of Chapter 28 and put them to work in understanding the process of inflation. But first, let's recall what inflation is and how its rate is measured.

Inflation and the Price Level

Inflation is a process in which the *price level is rising* and *money is losing value.* Inflation is not a serious problem today but it was in the 1970s and even towards the end of the 1980s.

If the price level rises persistently, then people need more and more money to make transactions. It is the price *level* and therefore the *value of money* that is changing, not the price of some particular commodity. For example, if the price of oil rises but prices of computers fall so that the price level (an average of prices) is constant, there is no inflation.

A one-off jump in the price level is not inflation. Inflation is an ongoing *process*, not a one-shot affair. Figure 30.1 illustrates this distinction. The red line shows the price level rising continuously. That is inflation. The blue line shows a one-off rise in the price level. This is not iflation.

To measure the inflation *rate*, we calculate the annual percentage change in the price level. Call this year's price level P_1 and last year's price level P_0. Then:

$$\text{Inflation rate} = \frac{P_1 - P_0}{P_0} \times 100$$

For example, if this year's price level is 126 and last year's price level was 120, the inflation rate is 5 per cent per year. That is:

$$\text{Inflation rate} = \frac{126 - 120}{P_{120}} \times 100$$

$$= 5 \text{ per cent per year}$$

This equation shows the connection between the *inflation rate* and the *price level*. For a given price level last year, the higher the price level in the current year, the higher is the inflation rate. If the price level is *rising*, the inflation rate is *positive*. If the price level rises at a *faster* rate, the inflation rate *increases*. Also, the higher the price level, the lower is the value of money and the higher the inflation rate.

Inflation can result from an increase in aggregate demand, a decrease in aggregate supply, or both. To study the forces that generate inflation, we distinguish two types of impulse that can get inflation started. These impulses are called:

1 Demand pull.
2 Cost push.

We'll first study a demand-pull inflation.

Figure 30.1 Inflation Versus a One-time Rise in the Price Level

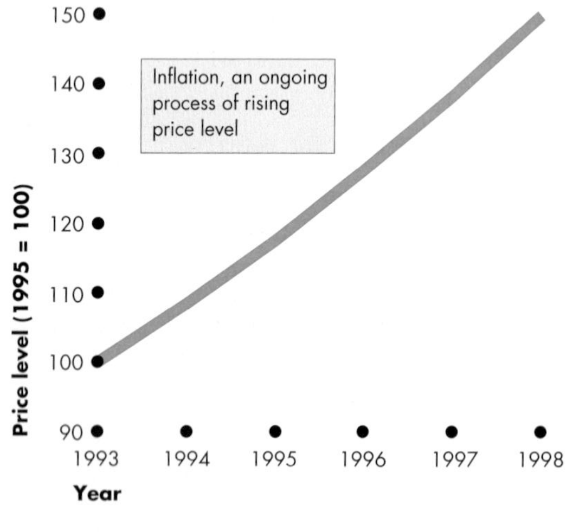

(a) Inflation

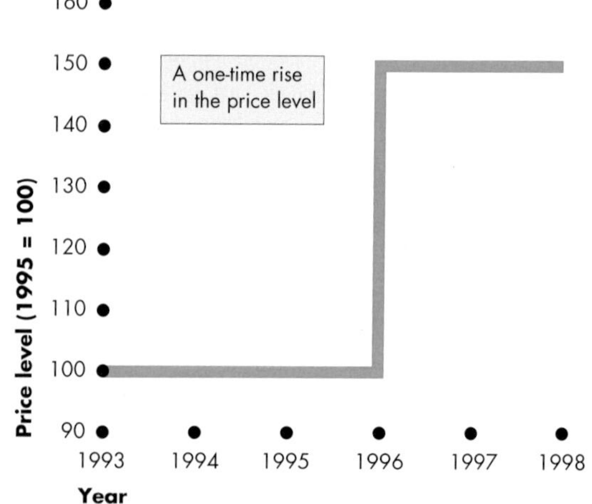

(b) One-time rise in price level

An economy experiences inflation when the price level rises persistently, as shown in part (a). An economy experiences a one-time rise in the price level if some disturbance increases the price level but does not set off an ongoing process of a rising price level, as shown in part (b).

Figure 30.2 A Demand-pull Rise in the Price Level

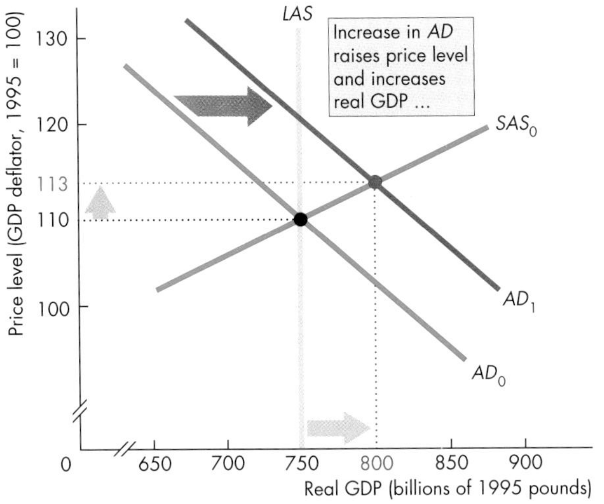

(a) Initial effect

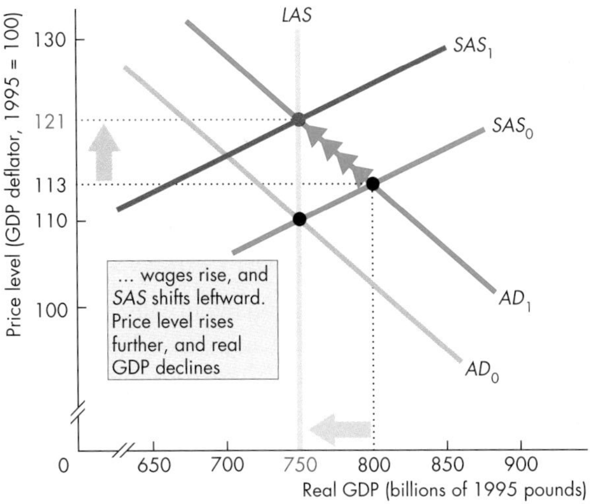

(b) Wages adjust

In part (a), the aggregate demand curve is AD_0, the short-run aggregate supply curve is SAS_0 and the long-run aggregate supply curve is *LAS*. The price level is 110 and real GDP is £750 billion, its long-run level. Aggregate demand increases to AD_1 (because the Bank increases the money supply or the government increases its purchases of goods and services). The new equilibrium occurs where AD_1 intersects SAS_0. The economy experiences inflation (the price level rises to 113) and real GDP increases to £800 billion. In part (b), starting from above full employment, wages begin to rise and the short-run aggregate supply curve shifts leftward towards SAS_1. The price level rises further, and real GDP returns to its long-run level.

Demand-pull Inflation

An inflation that results from an initial increase in aggregate demand is called **demand-pull inflation**. Such an inflation may arise from any individual factor that increases aggregate demand such as:

- An increase in the money supply.
- An increase in government purchases.
- An increase in exports.

Inflation Effect of an Increase in Aggregate Demand

Suppose that last year the price level was 110, real GDP was £750 billion and long-run real GDP was also £750 billion – shown in Figure 30.2(a). The aggregate demand curve is AD_0, the short-run aggregate supply curve is SAS_0, and the long-run aggregate supply curve is *LAS*.

In the current year, aggregate demand increases to AD_1. Such a situation arises if, for example, the government increases its purchases of goods and services or the Bank of England (the Bank) loosens its grip on the money supply. The economy moves to the point where the aggregate demand curve AD_1 intersects the short-run aggregate supply curve SAS_0. The price level rises to 115, and real GDP increases above potential GDP to £800 billion. The economy experiences 4.5 per cent inflation (a price level of 115 compared with 110 in the previous year) and a rapid expansion of real GDP. Unemployment falls below the natural rate. The next step in the unfolding story is a rise in wages.

Wage Response

Real GDP cannot remain above potential GDP for ever. With unemployment below its natural rate, there is a shortage of labour. Wages begin to increase, and the short-run aggregate supply curve starts to shift leftward. Prices rise further, and real GDP begins to fall. With no further change in aggregate demand – the aggregate demand curve remains at AD_1 – this process comes to an end when the short-run aggregate demand curve has moved to SAS_1 in Figure 30.2(b). At this time, the price level has increased to 121 and real GDP has returned to potential GDP of £750 billion, the level from which it started.

A Demand-pull Inflation Process

The process we've just studied eventually ends when, for a given increase in aggregate demand, wages have adjusted enough to restore the real wage rate to its full-employment level. We've studied a one-time rise in the price level like that described in Figure 30.1. For inflation to proceed, aggregate demand must persistently increase.

The only way in which aggregate demand can persistently increase is if the quantity of money persistently increases. The quantity of money persistently increases. Suppose the government has a large budget deficit that it finances by creating more and more money each year. In this situation, aggregate demand increases year after year. The aggregate demand curve keeps shifting rightward and puts continual upward pressure on the price level. The economy now experiences demand-pull inflation.

Figure 30.3 illustrates the process of demand-pull inflation. The starting point is the same as that shown in Figure 30.2. The aggregate demand curve is AD_0, the short-run aggregate supply curve is SAS_0, and the long-run aggregate supply curve is LAS. Real GDP is £750 billion and the price level is 110. Aggregate demand increases, shifting the aggregate demand curve to AD_1. Real GDP increases to £800 billion, and the price level rises to 115. The economy is at an above full-employment equilibrium. There is a shortage of labour and the wage rate rises, shifting the short-run aggregate supply curve to SAS_1. The price level rises to 121, and real GDP returns to its long-run level.

But the money supply increases again and aggregate demand continues to increase. The aggregate demand curve shifts rightward to AD_2. The price level rises further to 126 and real GDP again exceeds potential GDP at £800 billion. Yet again, the wage rate rises and decreases short-run aggregate supply. The SAS curve shifts to SAS_2 and the price level rises further to 133. As the money supply continues to grow, aggregate demand increases and the price level rises in an ongoing demand-pull inflation process.

The process you have just studied generates inflation – an ongoing process of a rising price level.

Demand-pull Inflation in Kalamazoo You may better understand the inflation process that we've just described by considering what is going on in an individual part of the economy, such as a Kalamazoo lemonade bottling plant. Initially, when aggregate demand increases, the demand for lemonade increases and the price of lemonade rises. Faced with a higher price, the lemonade plant works overtime and increases production. Conditions are good for workers in Kalamazoo, and the lemonade factory finds it hard to hang on to its best people.

Figure 30.3 A Demand-pull Inflation Spiral 

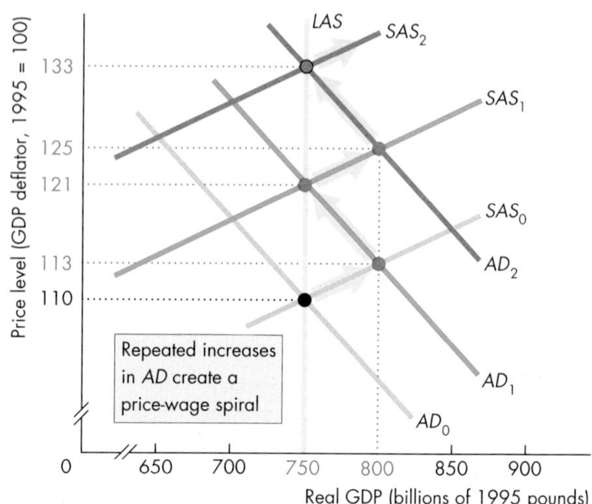

Each time the money supply increases, aggregate demand increases and the aggregate demand curve shifts rightward from AD_0 to AD_1 to AD_2, and so on. Each time real GDP goes above potential GDP and unemployment goes below the natural rate, the money wage rate rises and the short-run aggregate supply curve shifts leftward from SAS_0 to SAS_1 to SAS_2, and so on. As aggregate demand continues to increase, the price level rises from 110 through 113, 121, 125 to 133, and so on. There is a perpetual demand-pull inflation. Real GDP fluctuates between £750 billion and £800 billion.

To do so it has to offer higher wages. As wages increase, so do the costs of the lemonade factory.

What happens next depends on what happens to aggregate demand. If aggregate demand remains constant (as in Figure 30.2(b)), the firm's costs are increasing, but the price of lemonade is not increasing as quickly as its costs. Production is scaled back. Eventually, wages and costs increase by the same percentage as the price of lemonade. In real terms, the lemonade factory is in the same situation as initially – before the increase in aggregate demand. The bottling plant produces the same amount of lemonade and employs the same amount of labour as before the increase in demand.

But if aggregate demand continues to increase, so does the demand for lemonade, and the price of lemonade rises at the same rate as wages. The lemonade factory continues to operate above full employment, and there is a persistent shortage of labour. Prices and wages chase each other upward in an unending spiral.

Demand-pull Inflation in the United Kingdom

A demand-pull inflation like the one you've just studied occurred in the United Kingdom during the 1970s. In 1972–73 the government expanded the economy to reduce the level of unemployment that had been growing steadily since the late 1960s. As a consequence, the aggregate demand curve shifted rightward, the price level increased quickly and real GDP moved above its long-run or full-employment level. The money wage rate then started to rise more quickly and the short-run aggregate supply curve shifted leftward. The Bank responded with a further increase in the money supply growth rate and a demand-pull inflation spiral unfolded.

Review

- Demand-pull inflation begins when an increase in aggregate demand increases real GDP and increases the price level.
- At above full employment, the wage rate rises, short-run aggregate supply decreases, real GDP decreases and the price level rises further.
- If aggregate demand keeps increasing, wages chase prices in an unending price–wage inflation spiral.

Next, let's see how shocks to aggregate supply can create a cost-push inflation.

Cost-push Inflation

An inflation that results from an initial increase in costs is called **cost-push inflation**. The two main sources of increases in costs are:

1 An increase in money wage rates.

2 An increase in the money prices of raw materials.

At a given price level, the higher the cost of production, the smaller is the amount that firms are willing to produce. So if money wage rates rise or if the prices of raw materials (for example oil) rise, firms decrease their supply of goods and services. Aggregate supply decreases and the short-run aggregate supply curve shifts leftward[1]. Let's trace the effects of such a decrease in short-run aggregate supply on the price level and real GDP.

Initial Effect of a Decrease in Aggregate Supply

Suppose that last year the price level was 110 and real GDP was £750 billion. Long-run real GDP was also £750 billion. This situation is shown in Figure 30.4. The aggregate demand curve was AD_0, the short-run aggregate supply curve was SAS_0 and the long-run aggregate supply curve was LAS. In the current year, a sharp increase in world oil prices decreases short-run aggregate supply. The short-run aggregate supply curve shifts leftward to SAS_1. The price level rises to 117, and real GDP decreases to £700 billion. The combination of a rise in the price level and a fall in real GDP is called **stagflation**.

The events we've just studied have created a one-shot change in the price level, like that in Figure 30.1. A supply shock on its own cannot cause inflation. Something more must happen. And it often does as you will now see.

1 Some cost-push forces, such as an increase in the price of oil accompanied by a decrease in the availability of oil, can also decrease long-run aggregate supply. We'll ignore such effects here and examine cost-push factors that change only short-run aggregate supply.

Figure 30.4 A Cost-push Rise in the Price Level

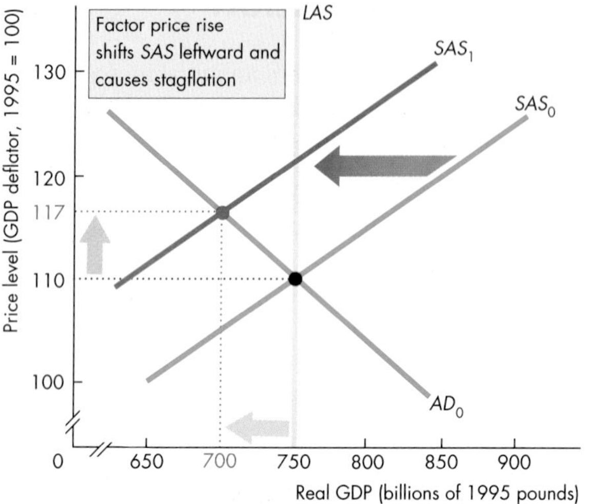

Initially, the aggregate demand curve is AD_0, the short-run aggregate supply curve is SAS_0 and the long-run aggregate supply curve is *LAS*. A decrease in aggregate supply (for example, resulting from an increase in the world price of oil) shifts the short-run aggregate supply curve to SAS_1. The economy moves to the point where the short-run aggregate supply curve SAS_1 intersects the aggregate demand curve AD_0. The price level rises to 117, and real GDP decreases to £700 billion. The economy experiences inflation and a contraction of real GDP – *stagflation*.

Figure 30.5 Aggregate Demand Response to Cost Push

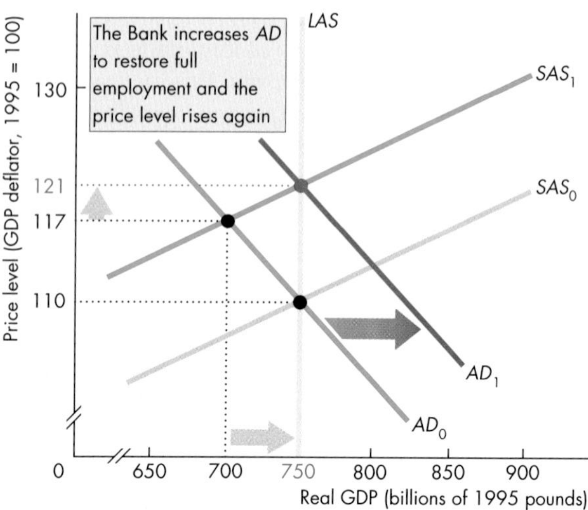

Following a cost-push increase in the price level, real GDP is below potential GDP and unemployment is above the natural rate. If the Bank responds by increasing aggregate demand to restore full employment, the aggregate demand curve shifts rightward to AD_1. The economy returns to full employment, but at the expense of higher inflation. The price level rises to 121.

Aggregate Demand Response

When real GDP falls the unemployment rate rises above the natural rate. In such a situation, there is usually an outcry of concern and a call for action to restore full employment. Suppose the Bank increases the money supply. Aggregate demand increases. In Figure 30.5, the aggregate demand curve shifts rightward to AD_1. The increase in aggregate demand has restored full employment. But the price level rises to 121, a 10 per cent rise over the original price level.

A Cost-push Inflation Process

Suppose now that the oil producers, who see the prices of everything that they buy with the dollars they receive increase by 10 per cent, decide to increase the price of oil again. Figure 30.6 continues the story. The short-run aggregate supply curve now shifts to SAS_2, and another bout of stagflation ensues. The price level rises further to 129, and real GDP falls to £700 billion. Unemployment increases above its natural rate. If the Bank responds yet again with an increase in the money supply, aggregate demand increases and the aggregate demand curve shifts to AD_2. The price level rises even higher – to 133 – and full employment is again restored. A cost-push inflation spiral results. But if the Bank does not respond, the economy remains below full employment.

You can see that the Bank has a dilemma. If it increases the money supply to restore full employment, it invites another oil price hike that will cause yet a further increase in the money supply. Inflation will rage along at a rate decided by the oil exporting countries. If the Bank keeps the lid on money supply growth, the economy operates with a high level of unemployment.

Figure 30.6 A Cost-push Inflation Spiral

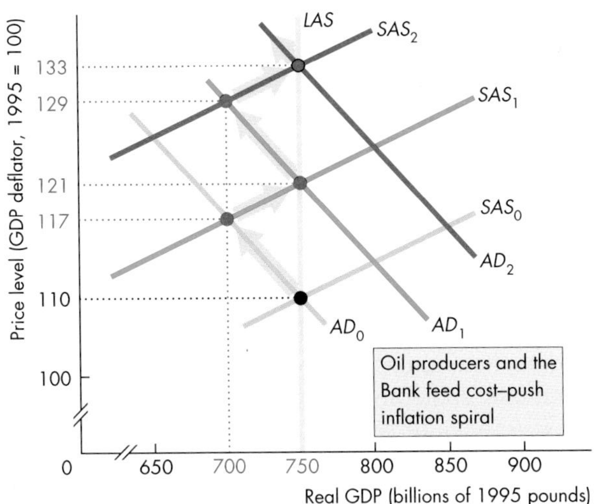

When a cost increase (for example, an increase in the world oil price) decreases short-run aggregate supply from SAS_0 to SAS_1, the price level rises to 117 and real GDP decreases to £700 billion. The Bank responds with an increase in the money supply that shifts the aggregate demand curve from AD_0 to AD_1. The price level rises again to 121 and real GDP returns to £750 billion. A further cost increase occurs, which shifts the short-run aggregate supply curve again, this time to SAS_2. Stagflation is repeated and the price level now rises to 129. The Bank responds again and the cost-push inflation spiral continues.

Cost-push Inflation in Kalamazoo What is going on in the Kalamazoo lemonade bottling plant when the economy is experiencing cost-push inflation? When the oil price increases, so do the costs of bottling lemonade. These higher costs decrease the supply of lemonade, increasing its price and decreasing the quantity produced. The lemonade plant lays off some workers. This situation will persist until either the Bank increases aggregate demand or the price of oil falls. If the Bank increases aggregate demand, as it did in the mid-1970s, the demand for lemonade increases and so does its price. The higher price of lemonade brings higher profits and the bottling plant increases its production. The lemonade factory re-hires the laid-off workers.

Cost-push Inflation in the United Kingdom A cost-push inflation like the one you've just studied occurred in the United Kingdom during the 1970s. It began in 1974 when OPEC raised the price of oil fourfold. The higher oil price decreased aggregate supply, which caused the price level to rise more quickly and real GDP to shrink. The Bank then faced a dilemma. Would it increase the quantity of money and accommodate the cost-push forces, or would it keep aggregate demand growth in check by limiting money growth? Money wages began to grow as fast as prices as the unions fought to maintain real wages. The Bank repeatedly allowed the money supply to grow fast and inflation proceeded rapidly.

Review

- Cost-push inflation starts with an increase in the money wage rate or in the money price of a raw material that decreases aggregate supply.
- Real GDP decreases and the price level rises – stagflation occurs.
- If the Bank increases aggregate demand to restore full employment, a freewheeling cost-push inflation ensues.

Effects of Inflation

Regardless of whether inflation is demand-pull or cost-push, the failure to *anticipate* it correctly results in unintended consequences. These unintended consequences impose costs on firms and workers. Let's examine these costs.

Unanticipated Inflation in the Labour Market

Unanticipated inflation has two main consequences for the operation of the labour market. They are:

1. Redistribution of income.
2. Departure from full employment.

Redistribution of Income Unanticipated inflation redistributes income between employers and workers. Sometimes employers gain at the expense of workers and sometimes they lose. If an unexpected increase in aggregate demand increases the inflation rate, then wages will not have been set high enough. Profits will be higher than expected and wages will buy fewer goods than expected. In this case, employers gain at the expense of workers. But if aggregate demand is expected to increase rapidly and it fails to do so, workers gain at the expense of employers. Anticipating a high inflation rate, wages are set too high and profits are squeezed. Redistributions between employers and workers create an incentive for both firms and workers to try to forecast inflation correctly.

Departures from Full Employment Redistribution brings gains to some and losses to others. But departures from full employment impose costs on everyone. To see why, let's return to the lemonade bottling plant in Kalamazoo. If the bottling plant and its workers do not anticipate inflation, but inflation occurs, the money wage rate does not rise to keep up with inflation. The real wage rate falls and the firm tries to hire more labour and increase production. But because the real wage rate has fallen, the firm has difficulty in attracting the labour it wants to employ. It pays overtime rates to its existing workforce and because it runs its plant at a faster pace, it incurs higher plant maintenance and parts replacement costs. Also, because the real wage rate has fallen, workers begin to quit the bottling plant to find jobs that pay a real wage rate closer to that prevailing before the outbreak of inflation. This labour turnover imposes additional costs on the firm. So even though its production increases, the firm incurs additional costs and its profit does not increase. The workers incur additional costs of job search and those who remain at the bottling plant end up feeling cheated. They've worked overtime to produce the extra output and, when they come to spend their wages, they discover that prices have increased, so their wages buy a smaller quantity of goods and services than expected.

If the bottling plant and its workers anticipate a high inflation rate that does not occur, they increase the money wage rate by too much and the real wage rate rises. At the higher real wage rate, the firm lays off some workers and the unemployment rate increases. Those workers who keep their jobs gain, but those who become unemployed lose. The bottling plant also loses because its output and profits fall.

Unanticipated Inflation in the Capital Market

Unanticipated inflation has two consequences for the operation of the capital market. They are:

1 Redistribution of income.
2 Scarcity or abundance of finance.

Redistribution of Income Unanticipated inflation redistributes income between borrowers and lenders. Sometimes borrowers gain at the expense of lenders; sometimes they lose. When inflation is unexpected, interest rates are not set high enough to compensate lenders for the falling value of money. In this case, borrowers gain and lenders lose. If inflation is expected and does not occur, interest rates will have been set too high. Then borrowers lose and lenders gain. This unintended redistribution of income between borrowers and lenders provides incentives for both parties to try and forecast inflation correctly.

Scarcity or Abundance of Finance When inflation is *higher* than expected, real interest rates are lower than expected. Borrowers wish that they had borrowed more and lenders wish that they had lent less. Both groups would have made different lending and borrowing decision if they had correctly forecasted inflation. When inflation is *lower* than expected, the real interest is higher than expected. Borrowers wish that they had borrowed less and lenders wish that they had lent more.

So unanticipated inflation imposes costs regardless of whether the inflation turns out to be higher or lower than anticipated. The presence of these costs gives everyone an incentive to forecast inflation correctly. Let's see how people go about this task.

Forecasting Inflation

People devote considerable resources to forecasting inflation. Some people specialize in economic forecasting and make a living from it. Other people buy the services of these specialists. The specialist forecasters are economists who work for public and private macroeconomic forecasting agencies and for banks, insurance companies, trade unions and large corporations. The returns these specialists make depend on the quality of their forecasts, so they have a strong incentive to forecast as accurately as possible. The most accurate forecast possible is one that is correct on the average and that has the minimum possible range of error.

Specialist forecasters use statistical models of the economy that are based on (but more detailed than) the aggregate supply–aggregate demand model that you are studying in this book. In the United Kingdom, there are publicly available forecasts of the economy produced by a range of institutions such as the National Institute of Economic and Social Research, the London Business School, Liverpool Macroeconomic Group and Oxford Economic Forecasting. Short-term forecasts are produced by HM Treasury, but City of London financial institutions also produce forecasts of the economy for their clients and there are several private forecasting agencies such as Lombard Street Research Ltd and the ITEM Group.

Forecasts that use all the relevant information available are usually the most accurate. If some information is available that can lead to a better forecast, it will be used. We call a forecast based on all the available relevant information a **rational expectation**. A rational expectation has two features:

1 It is correct on the average.
2 The range of the forecast error is as small as possible.

A forecast that is correct *on the average* is not always correct. Suppose you forecast the outcome of tossing a coin 10 times. You predict there will be 5 heads and 5 tails. On the average (repeating the experiment of coin tossing many times) you are correct. But often you will get 6 heads and 4 tails. So a rational expectation is not always the correct forecast but it is the best that anyone can do.

You've seen the effects of inflation when people fail to anticipate it. You've also seen why it pays to try and anticipate inflation. Let's now see what happens if inflation is correctly anticipated.

Anticipated Inflation

In the demand-pull and cost-push inflations that we studied earlier in this chapter, money wages are sticky. When aggregate demand increases, either to

Figure 30.7 Anticipated Inflation

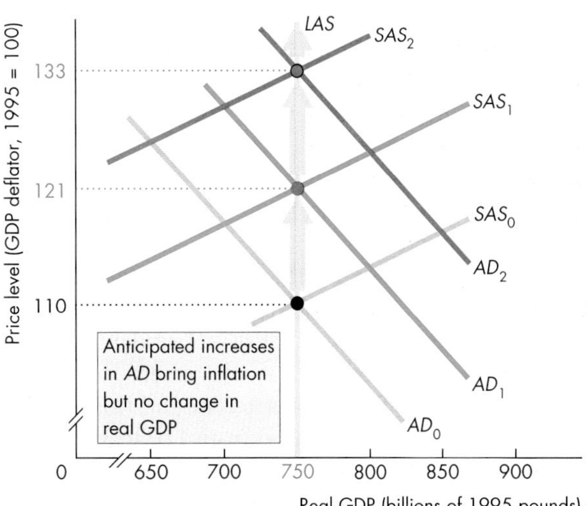

The actual and expected long-run aggregate supply curve (*LAS*) is at a real GDP of £750 billion. Last year, aggregate demand was AD_0 and the short-run aggregate supply curve was SAS_0. The actual price level was the same as the expected price level – 110. This year, aggregate demand is expected to rise to AD_1. The rational expectation of the price level changes from 110 to 121. As a result, the short-run aggregate supply curve shifts up to SAS_1. If aggregate demand actually increases as expected, the actual aggregate demand curve AD_1 is the same as the expected aggregate demand curve. Equilibrium occurs at a real GDP of £750 billion and an actual price level of 121. The inflation is correctly anticipated. Next year the process continues with aggregate demand increasing as expected to AD_2 and wages rising to shift the short-run aggregate supply curve to SAS_2. Again, real GDP remains at £600 billion and the price level rises, as anticipated, to 133.

set off a demand-pull inflation or to accommodate a cost-push inflation, the money wage does not change immediately. But if people correctly anticipate increases in aggregate demand, they will adjust money wage rates so as to keep up with anticipated inflation.

In this case, inflation proceeds with real GDP equal to potential GDP and unemployment equal to the natural rate. Figure 30.7 explains why. Suppose that last year the price level was 110 and real GDP was £750 billion, which is also potential GDP. The aggregate demand curve was AD_0, the aggregate supply curve was SAS_0 and the long-run aggregate supply curve was LAS.

Suppose that potential GDP does not change so the LAS curve does not shift. Also suppose that aggregate demand is expected to increase and that the expected aggregate demand curve for this year is AD_1. In anticipation of the increase in aggregate demand, money wage rates rise and the short-run aggregate supply curve shifts leftward. If the money wage rate rises by the same percentage as the rise in the price level, the short-run aggregate supply for next year is SAS_1.

If aggregate demand turns out to be the same as expected, the actual aggregate demand curve is AD_1. The intersection point of AD_1 and SAS_1 determines the actual price level – where the price level is 121. Between last year and this year, the price level increased from 110 to 121 and the economy experienced an inflation rate of 10 per cent, the same as the inflation rate that was anticipated. If this anticipated inflation is ongoing, in the following year aggregate demand increases further (as anticipated) and aggregate demand shifts to AD_2. Again the money wage rises to reflect anticipated inflation, and the short-run aggregate supply curve shifts to SAS_2. The price level rises by a further 10 per cent to 133.

What caused the inflation? The immediate answer is that because people expected inflation, they increased wages and increased prices. But the expectation was correct. Aggregate demand was expected to increase and it did increase. Because aggregate demand was *expected* to increase from AD_0 to AD_1, the short-run aggregate supply curve shifted upward from SAS_0 to SAS_1. Because aggregate demand actually did increase by the amount that was expected, the actual aggregate demand curve shifted from AD_0 to AD_1. The combination of the anticipated and actual shifts of the aggregate demand curve rightward produced an increase in the price level that was anticipated.

Only if aggregate demand growth is correctly forecasted does the economy follow the course described in Figure 30.7. If the expected growth rate of aggregate demand is different from its actual growth rate, the expected aggregate demand curve shifts by an amount different from the actual aggregate demand curve. The inflation rate departs from its expected level and, to some extent, there is unanticipated inflation.

Unanticipated Inflation

When aggregate demand increases by more than expected, there is some unanticipated inflation that looks just like demand-pull inflation that you examined earlier. Some inflation is expected and the money wage rate is set to reflect that expectation. The SAS curve intersects the LAS curve at the expected price level. Aggregate demand then increases, but by more than expected. The AD curve intersects the SAS curve at a level of real GDP that exceeds potential GDP. The money wage rate adjusts, aggregate demand increases again and the demand-pull spiral unwinds. So demand-pull inflation can be interpreted as being an unanticipated inflation in which aggregate demand increases by *more* than was expected.

When aggregate demand increases by less than expected, there is unanticipated inflation that looks like cost-push inflation. Again, some inflation is expected and based on this expectation, the money wage rate rises and the SAS curve shifts leftward. Aggregate demand then increases, but by *less* than expected. The AD curve intersects the SAS curve at a level of real GDP below potential GDP. Aggregate demand increases to restore full employment. But if the increase in aggregate demand is less than expected wages again rise and short-run aggregate supply again decreases and a cost-push spiral unwinds. So cost-push inflation can be interpreted as being an unanticipated inflation in which aggregate demand increases by *less* than was expected.

We've seen that only when inflation is unanticipated does real GDP depart from potential GDP. When inflation is anticipated, real GDP remains at potential GDP. Does this mean that an anticipated inflation has no costs?

The Costs of Anticipated Inflation

An anticipated inflation at a moderate rate – 2 or 3 per cent a year – probably has a small cost. But an anticipated inflation at a rapid rate is extremely costly. The costs can be summarized under four broad headings:

1 'Shoeleather costs'.
2 Efficiency costs.
3 Decrease in potential GDP.
4 Economic growth costs.

'Shoeleather Costs' The so-called 'shoeleather costs' of inflation are costs that arise from an increase in the velocity of circulation of money and an increase in the amount of running around that people do to try to avoid incurring losses from the falling value of money.

When money loses value at a rapid anticipated rate, it does not function well as a medium of exchange and people try to avoid holding money. They spend their incomes as soon as they receive them, and firms pay out incomes – wages and dividends – as soon as they receive revenue from their sales. The velocity of circulation increases. During the 1920s, when inflation in Germany reached *hyperinflation* levels (rates in excess of 50 per cent a month), wages were paid and spent twice in a single day!

The 'shoeleather costs' have been estimated to be between 1 and 2 per cent of GDP for a 10 per cent inflation. For a rapid inflation they are much higher.

Efficiency Costs At high anticipated inflation rates, people seek alternatives to money as a means of payment and use tokens and commodities or even barter, all of which are less efficient than money as a means of payment. For example, during the 1980s when inflation in Israel reached 1,000 per cent a year, the US dollar started to replace the increasingly worthless shekel. As a result, people had to keep track of the exchange rate between the shekel and the dollar hour by hour and engage in many additional and costly transactions in the foreign exchange market.

A Decrease in Potential GDP Because anticipated inflation increases transactions costs, it diverts resources from producing goods and services and it decreases potential GDP. In terms of the aggregate supply–aggregate demand model, a rapid anticipated inflation decreases potential GDP and shifts the *LAS* curve leftward. The faster the anticipated inflation rate, the further leftward the *LAS* curve shifts. By how much does potential GDP fall?

Economic Growth Costs The most serious cost of an anticipated inflation is a fall in the long-term growth rate of GDP. This cost has three sources. The first comes from the way inflation interacts with the tax system. Anticipated inflation swells the money returns on investments, but it does not change the real returns. However, money returns are taxed, so effective tax rates rise. With lower after-tax returns, businesses have less incentive to invest in new capital. A decrease in investment cuts the rate of real GDP growth. This effect becomes serious at even modest inflation rates. Let's consider an example.

Suppose the real interest rate is 4 per cent a year and the tax rate is 50 per cent. With no inflation, the nominal interest is also 4 per cent a year and 50 per cent of this rate is taxable. The real *after-tax* interest rate is 2 per cent a year (50 per cent of 4 per cent). Now suppose the inflation rate is 4 per cent a year so that the nominal rate is 8 per cent a year. The *after-tax* nominal rate is 4 per cent (50 per cent of 8 per cent). Now subtract the 4 per cent inflation rate from this amount and you see that the *after-tax real interest* rate is zero! The true tax rate on interest income is 100 per cent. If the inflation rate was greater than 4 per cent in this example, the true tax rate would exceed 100 per cent and the after-tax real interest rate would be negative.

With a low or possibly even negative after-tax real interest rate, the incentive to save is weakened and the saving rate falls. With a fall in saving, the pace of capital accumulation slows and so does the long-term growth rate of real GDP.

The second economic growth cost arises because instead of concentrating on the activities at which they have a comparative advantage, people find it more profitable to search for ways of avoiding the losses that inflation inflicts. As a result, inventive talent that might otherwise work on productive innovations works on finding ways of profiting from or avoiding losses from the inflation.

The third source of a fall in the economic growth rate arises because when the inflation rate is high, there is increased uncertainty about the long-term inflation rate. Will inflation remain high for a long time or will price stability be restored? This increased uncertainty makes long-term planning difficult and gives people a shorter-term focus. Investment falls and so the growth rate slows.

Efficiency costs and economic growth costs are estimated to be much higher than the shoeleather and other costs and range between 5 per cent and 7 per cent of GDP for a 10 per cent inflation. The productivity growth slowdown of the 1970s can be attributed partly to the inflation outburst at that time.

There are many examples of rapid anticipated inflations around the world, especially in Argentina, Bolivia and Brazil, in Russia and other East European countries, and in some of the African countries where the costs of anticipated inflation are much greater than the modest numbers given here.

Review

- Wrong inflation forecasts are costly. To minimize forecasting errors, people use all the available information and make a *rational expectation*.
- Anticipated changes in aggregate demand and aggregate supply result in anticipated inflation.
- A rapid anticipated inflation diverts resources from producing goods and services and decreases potential GDP.

We've seen that an increase in aggregate demand growth that is not fully anticipated increases both the price level and real GDP growth. It also decreases unemployment. Similarly, a decrease in aggregate demand that is not fully anticipated slows down both inflation and real GDP growth. It also increases unemployment. Do these relationships imply a trade-off between inflation and unemployment? That is, does low unemployment always bring inflation and low inflation bring high unemployment? Let's explore this question next.

Inflation and Unemployment: The Phillips Curve

The aggregate supply–aggregate demand model that we have used to obtain these results gives predictions about the level of real GDP and the price level. Given these predictions, we can work out how unemployment and inflation have changed. But the aggregate supply–aggregate demand model does not place inflation and unemployment at the centre of the stage.

Another way of studying inflation and unemployment uses a relationship called the Phillips curve. The Phillips curve approach uses the same basic ideas as the *AS–AD* model, but it focuses directly on inflation and unemployment. The Phillips curve is so named because it was popularized by a New Zealand economist, A.W. Phillips, when he was working at the London School of Economics in the 1950s. A **Phillips curve** is a curve showing the relationship between inflation and unemployment. There are two time-frames for Phillips curves:

1 The short-run Phillips curve.
2 The long-run Phillips curve.

The Short-run Phillips Curve

The **short-run Phillips curve** is a curve showing the relationship between inflation and unemployment, holding constant:

1 The expected inflation rate.
2 The natural unemployment rate.

Figure 30.8 shows a short-run Phillips curve, *SRPC*. Suppose that the expected inflation rate is 10 per cent a year and the natural unemployment rate is 6 per cent, point *a* in the figure. A short-run Phillips curve passes through this point. If inflation rises above its expected rate, the unemployment rate falls below its natural rate. This joint movement in the inflation rate and the unemployment rate is illustrated as a movement up the short-run Phillips curve from point *a* to point *b* in the figure. Similarly, if inflation falls below its expected rate, unemployment rises above the natural rate. In this case, there is movement down the short-run Phillips curve from point *a* to point *c*.

This negative relationship between inflation and unemployment along the short-run Phillips curve is explained by the aggregate supply–aggregate demand model. Figure 30.9 explains the connection between the two approaches. Suppose that, initially, inflation is anticipated to be 10 per cent a year and unemployment is at its natural rate.

In Figure 30.9 the aggregate demand curve is AD_0, the short-run aggregate supply curve is SAS_0, and the long-run aggregate supply curve is *LAS*. Real GDP is £750 billion and the price level is 100. Money growth increases aggregate demand and the aggregate demand curve shifts rightward to AD_1, and anticipating this increase in aggregate demand, the money wage rate rises, which shifts the short-run aggregate supply curve to SAS_1. The price level rises from 100 to 110 and the inflation rate is an

Figure 30.8 A Short-run Phillips Curve

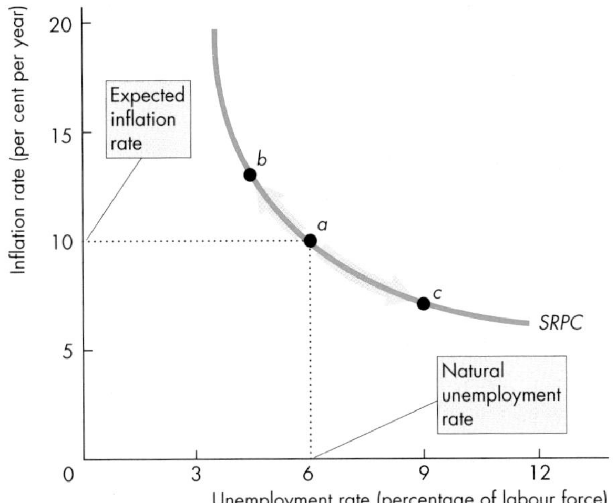

The short-run Phillips curve *SRPC* shows the relationship between inflation and unemployment at a given expected inflation rate and given natural unemployment rate. With an expected inflation rate of 10 per cent a year and a natural unemployment rate of 6 per cent, the short-run Phillips curve passes through point *a*. An unanticipated increase in aggregate demand lowers unemployment and increases inflation – a movement up the short-run Phillips curve. An unanticipated decrease in aggregate demand increases unemployment and lowers inflation – a movement down the short-run Phillips curve.

Figure 30.9 *AS–AD* and the Short-run Curve

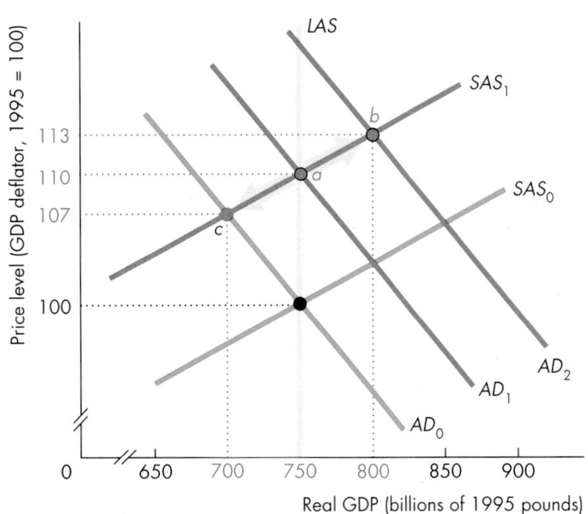

If aggregate demand is expected to increase and shift the aggregate demand curve from AD_0 to AD_1, then the money wage rate rises by an amount that shifts the short-run aggregate supply curve from SAS_0 to SAS_1. The price level rises to 110, a 10 per cent rise, and the economy is at point *a* in this figure and at point *a* on the short-run Phillips curve in Figure 30.8. If with the same expectations, aggregate demand increases and shifts the aggregate demand curve from AD_0 to AD_2, the price level rises to 113, a 13 per cent rise, and the economy is at point *b* in this figure and at point *b* on the short-run Phillips curve in Figure 30.8. If with the same expectations, aggregate demand does not change, the price level rises to 107, a 7 per cent rise, and the economy is at point *c* in this figure and at point *c* on the short-run Phillips curve in Figure 30.8.

anticipated 10 per cent a year. We can describe the economy as being at point *a* in Figure 30.9. It is also at point *a* on the short-run Phillips curve in Figure 30.8.

Now suppose that instead of increasing as expected to AD_1, aggregate demand increases to AD_2. The price level now rises to 113, a 13 per cent inflation rate and real GDP rises above potential GDP. We can now describe the economy as being at point *b* in Figure 30.9 or at point *b* on the short-run Phillips curve in Figure 30.8.

Finally, suppose that instead of increasing as expected to AD_1, aggregate demand remains constant at AD_0. The price level now rises to 107, a 7 per cent inflation rate, and real GDP falls below potential GDP. We can now describe the economy as being at point *c* in Figure 30.9 or at point *c* on the short-run Phillips curve in Figure 30.8.

The Long-run Phillips Curve

The **long-run Phillips curve** is a curve that shows the relationship between inflation and unemployment, when the actual inflation rate equals the expected inflation rate. The long-run Phillips curve is vertical at the natural unemployment rate. It is shown in Figure 30.10 as the vertical line *LRPC*. The long-run Phillips curve tells us that any anticipated inflation rate is possible at the natural unemployment rate. This proposition is the same as the one you discovered in the *AS–AD* model. When inflation is anticipated, real GDP remains at potential GDP. Real GDP being at potential

Figure 30.10 Short-run and Long-run Phillips Curves

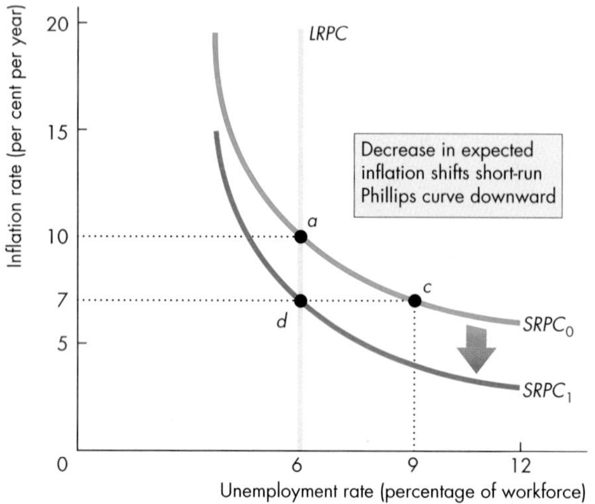

The long-run Phillips curve is *LRPC*, a vertical line at the natural unemployment rate. A fall in inflation expectations shifts the short-run Phillips curve downward by the amount of the fall in the expected inflation rate. In this figure, when the expected inflation rate falls from 10 per cent a year to 7 per cent a year, the short-run Phillips curve shifts downward from $SRPC_0$ to $SRPC_1$. The new short-run Phillips curve intersects the long-run Phillips curve at the new expected inflation rate – point *d*. With the original expected inflation rate (of 10 per cent), an inflation rate of 7 per cent a year would occur at an unemployment rate of 9 per cent, at point *c*.

Figure 30.11 A Change in the Natural Unemployment Rate

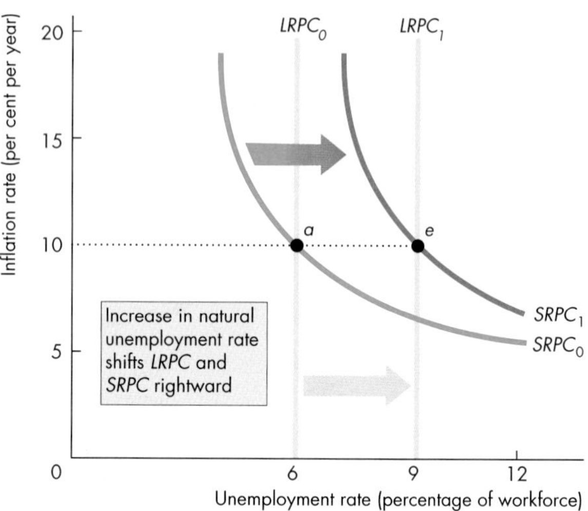

A change in the natural unemployment rate shifts both the short-run and long-run Phillips curves. Here the natural unemployment rate increases from 6 per cent to 9 per cent, and the two Phillips curves shift rightward to $SRPC_1$ and $LRPC_1$. The new long-run Phillips curve intersects the new short-run Phillips curve at the expected inflation rate – point *e*.

GDP is equivalent to unemployment being at the natural rate.

If the expected inflation rate is 10 per cent a year, the short-run Phillips curve is $SRPC_0$. If the expected inflation rate falls to 7 per cent a year, the short-run Phillips curve shifts downward to $SRPC_1$. The distance by which the short-run Phillips curve shifts downward when the expected inflation rate falls is equal to the change in the expected inflation rate.

To see why the short-run Phillips curve shifts when the expected inflation rate changes let's do a thought experiment. The economy is at full employment and a fully anticipated inflation is 10 per cent a year. The Bank now begins a permanent attack on inflation by slowing money supply growth. Aggregate demand growth slows down and the inflation rate falls to 7 per cent a year. At first, this decrease in inflation is unanticipated, so wages continue to rise at their original rate, shifting the short-run aggregate supply curve leftward at the same pace as before. Real GDP falls and unemployment increases. In Figure 30.10, the economy moves from point *a* to point *c* on the short-run Phillips curve $SRPC_0$.

If the actual inflation rate remains steady at 7 per cent a year, eventually this rate will come to be expected. As this happens, wage growth slows down and the short-run aggregate supply curve shifts leftward less quickly. Eventually it shifts leftward at the same pace at which the aggregate demand curve is shifting rightward. The actual inflation rate equals the expected inflation rate and full employment is restored. Unemployment is back at its natural rate. In Figure 30.10, the short-run Phillips curve has shifted from $SRPC_0$ to $SRPC_1$ and the economy is at point *d*.

Figure 30.12 Phillips Curves in the United Kingdom

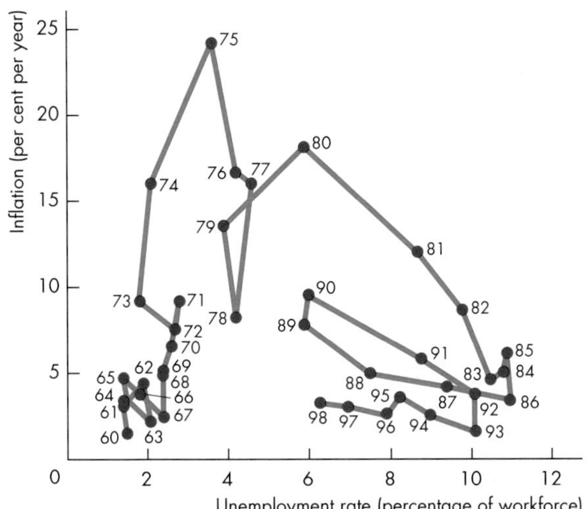

(a) Time sequence

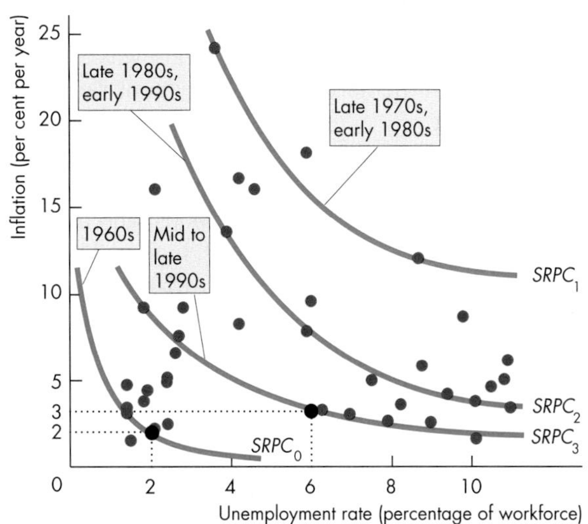

(b) Four Phillips curves

In part (a) each dot represents the combination of inflation and unemployment for a particular year in the United Kingdom. There is no clear relationship between the two variables. Part (b) interprets the data in terms of a shifting short-run Phillips curve. The short-run Phillips curve of the 1960s when the expected inflation rate was 2 per cent a year, and the natural unemployment rate was also 2 per cent is $SRPC_0$. The short-run Phillips curve of the late 1970s and early 1980s $SRPC_1$. This period has a higher natural unemployment rate and a higher expected inflation rate.

The oil price shock increased both the natural unemployment rate and the expected inflation rate in the 1970s. By the early 1980s, the effect of the oil shock and domestic supply factors had increased the natural rate of unemployment to over 10 per cent. The late 1980s and early 1990s short-run Phillips curve is $SRPC_2$. The monetary policy and supply side reforms of the Thatcher government during the 1980s caused the natural rate of unemployment to decline to 6 per cent and the expected rate of inflation to fall to 5 per cent in the mid to late 1990s as shown by $SRPC_3$.

Changes in expected inflation cause shifts in the Phillips curve. Another important source of shifts in the Phillips curve is a change in the natural rate of unemployment.

Changes in the Natural Unemployment Rate

The natural unemployment rate changes for many reasons that are explained in Chapter 23 (pp. 563–564). A change in the natural unemployment rate shifts both the short-run and the long-run Phillips curves. Such shifts are illustrated in Figure 30.11. If the natural unemployment rate increases from 6 per cent to 9 per cent, the long-run Phillips curve shifts from $LRPC_0$ to $LRPC_1$, and if expected inflation is constant at 10 per cent a year, the short-run Phillips curve shifts from $SRPC_0$ to $SRPC_1$. Because the expected inflation rate is constant, the short-run Phillips curve $SRPC_1$ intersects the long-run curve $LRPC_1$ (point e) at the same inflation rate at which the short-run Phillips curve $SRPC_0$ intersects the long-run curve $LRPC_0$ (point a).

The Phillips Curve in the United Kingdom

Figure 30.12(a) a scatter diagram between inflation and unemployment in the United Kingdom. Each dot in the figure represents the combination of inflation and unemployment for a particular year. We certainly cannot see a Phillips curve similar to that shown in Figure 30.8. But we can interpret the data in terms of a shifting short-run Phillips curve as in Figure 30.12(b).

Four short-run Phillips curves appear in the figure. The short-run Phillips curve of the 1960s is $SRPC_0$. At that time, the expected inflation rate was 2 per cent a year and the natural unemployment rate was also 2 per cent.

The short-run Phillips curve of the 1970s is $SRPC_1$. The second period has a natural unemployment rate higher than that of the 1960s, and an expected inflation rate that is much higher. The short-run Phillips curve of the late 1970s and early 1980s is $SRPC_2$. During the 1980s and 1990s the natural rate of unemployment fell and expected inflation declined. The short-run Phillips curve of the late 1980s and 1990s is $SRPC_3$.

Review

- Unanticipated changes in the inflation rate bring movements along the short-run Phillips curve.
- An unanticipated increase in the inflation rate lowers the unemployment rate, and an unanticipated decrease in the inflation rate raises the unemployment rate.
- A change in the expected inflation rate shifts the short-run Phillips curve (upward for an increase in inflation and downward for a decrease in inflation) by an amount equal to the change in the expected inflation rate.
- A change in the natural unemployment rate shifts both the short-run and the long-run Phillips curves (rightward for an increase in the natural rate and leftward for a decrease).
- The relationship between inflation and unemployment in the United Kingdom can be interpreted in terms of a shifting short-run Phillips curve.

So far, we've studied the effects of inflation on real GDP, real wages, employment and unemployment. But inflation lowers the value of money and changes the real value of the amounts borrowed and repaid. As a result, interest rates are influenced by inflation. Let's see how.

Interest Rates and Inflation

Today, good risk companies can borrow at interest rates of less than 6 per cent a year. Companies in Russia pay interest of 60 per cent, and those in Turkey pay 75 per cent a year. While companies in the UK never had to pay interest rates as high as that, they have been much higher in the 1980s. In the early 1980s, borrowing interest rates were around 14 per cent a year. Why do interest rates fluctuate so much across countries and across time? Part of the answer is explained in Chapter 31, pp. 792–794, where the forces that determine the real interest rate are explained. (The **real interest rate** is the *nominal* interest rate minus the inflation rate.) Fluctuations in the real interest rate are caused by fluctuations in saving supply and investment demand. But another part of the answer – a major part – is that the inflation rate was low during the 1960s and high during the early 1980s. With changes in the inflation rate, nominal interest rates change to make borrowers pay and to compensate lenders for the fall in the value of money. Let's see how inflation affects borrowers and lenders.

The Effects of Inflation on Borrowers and Lenders

The *nominal* interest rate is the price paid by a borrower to compensate a lender only for the amount loaned. The *real* interest rate is the price paid by a borrower to compensate a lender for the amount loaned and for the fall in the value of money that results from inflation. The forces of demand and supply determine an equilibrium real interest rate that does not depend on the inflation rate. These same forces also determine an equilibrium nominal interest rate that *does* depend on the inflation rate and that equals the equilibrium *real* interest rate plus the expected inflation rate.

To see why these outcomes occur, imagine there is no inflation and that the nominal interest rate is 4 per cent a year. The real interest rate is also 4 per cent a year. The amount that businesses and people want to borrow equals the amount that businesses and people want to lend at this real interest rate. British Petroleum (BP) is willing to pay an interest rate of 4 per cent a year to get the funds it needs to pay for its global investment in new oil exploration sites. Sue, and thousands of people like her, are willing to lend BP the amount it needs for its exploration work if they can get a *real* return of 4 per cent a year. (Sue wants to buy a new car and she plans a consumption and saving strategy to achieve this objective.)

Now suppose inflation breaks out at a steady 6 per cent a year. All prices and values, including oil exploration profits and car prices, rise by 6 per cent a year. If BP was willing to pay a 4 per cent interest rate when there was no inflation, it is now willing to pay 10 per cent interest. The reason is that its profits are rising by 6 per cent a year, owing to the 6 per cent inflation, so it is *really* paying only 4 per cent. Similarly, if Sue was willing to lend at a 4 per cent interest rate when there was no inflation, she is now willing to lend only if she gets 10 per cent interest. The price of the car Sue is planning to buy is rising by 6 per cent a year, owing to the 6 per cent inflation, so she is *really* getting only a 4 per cent interest rate.

Because borrowers are willing to pay the higher rate and lenders are willing to lend only if they receive the higher rate, when inflation is anticipated the *nominal interest rate* increases by an amount equal to the expected inflation rate. The *real interest rate* remains constant. The real interest rate might change because the supply of saving or investment demand has changed for some other reason. But a change in the expected inflation rate alone does not change the real interest rate.

Do the effects of inflation on interest rates that we have just described actually happen? Let's look at the UK experience.

Inflation and Interest Rates in the United Kingdom

Figure 30.13 shows the relationship between inflation and nominal interest rates between 1960 and 1998. The relationship between inflation and nominal interest rates in the United Kingdom is illustrated in Figure 30.13. The interest rate measured on the vertical axis is that paid by the Treasury on 3-month bills. Each point on the graph represents a year in recent UK macroeconomic history between 1960 and 1998. The blue line shows the relationship between the nominal interest rate and the inflation rate if the real interest rate is constant at 3 per cent a year, its actual average value in this period. As you can see, there is a clear relationship between the inflation rate and the interest rate, but it is not exact. When the red dot lies above the blue line, the real interest rate exceeds 3 per cent. When the red dot lies below the blue line, the real interest rate is less than 3 per cent.

During the 1960s, both inflation and nominal interest rates were low. In the early 1970s, inflation began to increase, but it was not expected to

Figure 30.13 Inflation and the Interest Rate

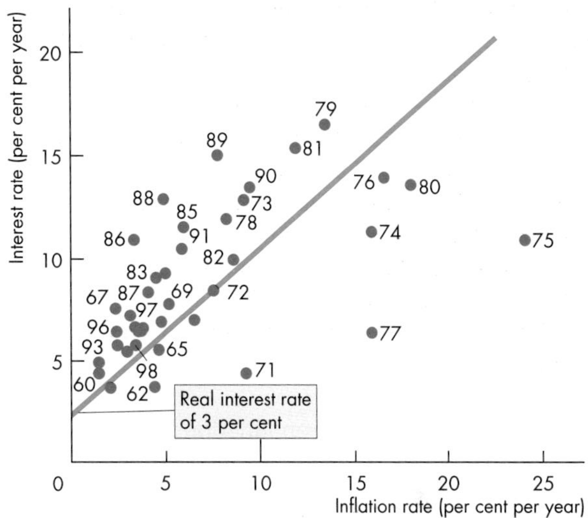

Other things remaining the same, the higher the expected inflation rate, the higher is the nominal interest rate. A graph showing the relationship between interest rates and the actual inflation rate reveals that the influence of inflation on interest rates is a powerful one. Here, the interest rate is that paid by banks on 3-month loans between each other. Each point represents a year in UK macroeconomic history between 1960 and 1998.

Source: ONS.

increase much and certainly not to persist. As a result, nominal interest rates did not rise much at that time. By the mid-1970s, there was a burst of unexpectedly high inflation. Interest rates increased somewhat but not by nearly as much as the inflation rate. During the late 1970s and early 1980s, inflation of between 15 and 20 per cent a year came to be expected as an ongoing and highly persistent phenomenon. As a result, nominal interest rates increased to around 12–14 per cent a year. Then in 1982, the inflation rate fell – at first unexpectedly. Interest rates began to fall but not nearly as quickly as the inflation rate. Short-term interest rates fell more quickly than long-term interest rates because, at that time, it was expected that inflation would be lower in the short term but not so low in the longer term.

The relationship between inflation and interest rates is even more dramatically illustrated by international experience. For example, in recent years Chile has experienced an inflation rate of around 30 per cent with nominal interest rates of about 40 per cent. Brazil has experienced inflation rates and nominal interest rates of 30 per cent a *month*. At the other extreme, such countries as Japan and Belgium have low inflation and low nominal interest rates.

Review

- The real interest rate is equal to the nominal interest rate minus the inflation rate.
- There is a strong correlation between the inflation rate and the nominal interest rate – other things remaining the same, an increase in the inflation rate brings an equal increase in the nominal interest rate.

The Politics of Inflation

We noted at the beginning of this chapter that inflation has plagued nations over many centuries, from the Roman empire to modern Russia. (There are examples of inflation from even earlier times going back to the earliest civilizations.) What are the deeper sources of inflation that are common to all these vastly different societies? The answer lies in the political situation. There are two main political sources of inflation. They are:

1 Inflation tax.
2 Poor reputation and weak credibility.

Inflation Tax

Inflation is not a tax in the usual sense. Governments don't pass inflation tax laws like income tax and sales tax laws. But inflation works just like a tax. One way in which a government can finance its expenditure is by selling bonds to the central bank. If the government sells bonds to the central bank, those bonds are paid for with new money – with an increase in the monetary base. When the government finances its expenditure in this way, the quantity of money increases. So the government gets revenues from inflation just as if it had increased taxes. And the holders of money pay this tax to the government. They do so because the real value of their money holdings decreases at a rate equal to the inflation rate.

Inflation is not used as a major source of tax revenue in the United Kingdom or in any developed economy. But in some countries it is. The closing years of the Roman empire and the transition years to a market economy in Russia and Eastern Europe are examples. In the case of the Roman empire, the empire had grown beyond its capacity to administer the collection of taxes on a scale sufficient to cover the expenditures of the government. In the case of Russia, the traditional source of government revenue was from state-owned enterprises. In the transition to a market economy, government revenue from these enterprises dried up but expenditure commitments did not decline in line with this loss of revenue. In both cases, the inflation was used to finance expenditures.

As a general rule, the inflation tax is used when conventional revenue sources are insufficient to cover expenditures and the larger the revenue shortfall, the larger is the inflation tax and the inflation rate.

Poor Reputation and Weak Credibility

One objective of fiscal and monetary policy is to stabilize aggregate demand and keep the economy close to full employment. If demand increases too quickly, the economy overheats and inflation increases. If demand increases too slowly, recession occurs and inflation declines.

One of the problems with conducting a low inflation policy is that people who need to forecast inflation and interest rates may have a different expectation of inflation from the central bank. The government, through the central bank, may conduct a policy that decreases the rate of growth of money and reduces inflation. Short-term rates of interest may decline because inflation in the short term may be lower, but long-term rates may not decline because people expect long-term inflation to remain high. This can occur if people anticipate that the policy of low monetary growth now will be reversed at some point in the future. While current inflation may be low, bond holders may anticipate higher inflation in the future and decide to sell some bonds, thus reducing the price of bonds and raising the long-term rate of interest. Why would people have such an expectation? The reason is that they do not believe that the central bank, and through it the government, will stick to its plans of keeping control of inflation. They may believe that once people adjust their expectations of inflation and anticipate low inflation, the government may be tempted to increase the money supply growth and increase aggregate demand by more than expected. In other words, people do not think that the policy has *credibility*. One reason people do not trust the government is that it may not have a *reputation* for trustworthiness. Too often governments have said one thing and done another.

A policy is credible if the cost to the government of following it is viewed as less than not following it. There is always an incentive for a government that has promised low inflation to expand the economy by increasing the growth rate of money and to temporarily reduce unemployment – particularly before an election year. The benefits of lower unemployment will be reaped immediately, but the costs of higher inflation and unemployment will be felt in the future. A government may avoid the temptation to expand demand after reducing inflation only if it values its reputation.

Some economists argue that independence for the central bank improves the credibility of a low inflation policy; others suggest that credibility is obtained by joining an exchange rate agreement such as the European Monetary System or the European Monetary Union. A good reputation for consistent macroeconomic policy can only be earned over a period of time. The German central bank, the Bundesbank, has a good reputation for low inflation. *Reading Between the Lines* on pp. 776–777 examines the credibility of recent Bank of England inflation policy.

Review

- Inflation is a source of government revenue – inflation is a tax – and when conventional revenue sources are inadequate, then an inflation tax is used.
- Inflation makes it harder for governments to establish a low inflation reputation.
- A low inflation policy is credible only if the costs of having such a policy is lower than any other, or if governments have a reputation for low inflation and trustworthiness.

You have now completed your study of inflation. This material, together with that on economic growth (Chapter 32), gives a good overview of the long-term problems that confront a modern economy. Our next task (in the following chapter) is to focus more sharply on the problems of the business cycle and unemployment. Then, with a good understanding of both the long-term trends and the business cycle fluctuations, we'll study in Chapter 33, the policy challenges that make it difficult to achieve rapid growth and avoid excessive unemployment and inflation.

Summary

Key Points

Inflation and the Price Level (p. 754)

- Inflation is a process of persistently rising prices and falling value of money.
- The price level rises when the inflation rate is positive and falls when the inflation rate is negative.

Demand-pull Inflation (pp. 755–757)

- Demand-pull inflation arises from increasing aggregate demand.
- The main factor that increases aggregate demand is an increase in the money supply or an increase in government spending.

Cost-push Inflation (pp. 757–759)

- Cost-push inflation can result from any factor that decreases aggregate supply, but the main factors are increasing wage rates and increasing prices of key raw materials.

Effects of Inflation (pp. 759–764)

- Inflation is costly when it is unanticipated because it redistributes income and wealth and creates inefficiencies in the economy.
- People try to anticipate inflation to avoid its costs. Forecasts of inflation based on all the available information are called rational expectations.
- When changes in aggregate demand are correctly anticipated, inflation is anticipated, and, if its rate is moderate, it does not affect real GDP, real wages, or employment. But a rapid anticipated inflation decreases potential GDP.

Inflation and Unemployment: The Phillips Curve (pp. 764–768)

- The short-run Phillips curve shows the trade-off between inflation and unemployment, holding constant the expected inflation rate and the natural unemployment rate.
- The long-run Phillips curve which is vertical, shows that when the actual inflation rate equals the expected inflation rate, the unemployment rate equals the natural unemployment rate.
- Unexpected changes in the inflation rate bring movements along the short-run Phillips curve.
- Changes in expected inflation shift the short-run Phillips curve.
- Changes in the natural unemployment rate shift both the short-run and long-run Phillips curves.

Interest Rates and Inflation (pp. 768–770)

- The higher the expected inflation rate, the higher is the nominal interest rate.
- As the anticipated inflation rate rises, borrowers willingly pay a higher interest rate and lenders successfully demand a higher interest rate.
- The nominal interest rate adjusts to equal the real interest rate plus the expected inflation rate.

The Politics of Inflation (pp. 770–771)

- The government can print or create new base money, so inflation is another source of revenue – it is a tax – and its rate increases when the government has financial needs that exceed the income taxes and other taxes it is able to collect.
- This source of revenue explains the extremely high inflation rates that sometimes occur and that today are present in many developing countries.
- Inflation breeds mistrust of the intentions of the government. People do not trust a government with a poor reputation when it conducts policy with the aim of reducing inflation.

Key Figures 

Key Terms

Review Questions

1 What is inflation and how is its rate measured?

2 Distinguish between the price level and the inflation rate.

3 Distinguish between demand-pull inflation and cost-push inflation.

4 Explain how a demand-pull inflation spiral occurs.

5 Explain how a cost-push inflation spiral occurs.

6 Why are wrong inflation expectations costly? Suggest some of the losses that an individual would suffer in labour markets as well as in asset markets.

7 Explain why wrong expectations do more than redistribute income.

8 Why do people devote resources to trying to forecast inflation?

9 What is a rational expectation? Explain the two features of a rational expectation.

10 Explain the rational expectations hypothesis.

11 What is the rational expectation of the price level in:

a The short run?
b The long run?

12 Explain how anticipated inflation arises.

13 What does the short-run Phillips curve show?

14 What is held constant when there is a movement along a short-run Phillips curve?

15 What does the long-run Phillips curve show?

16 What is held constant when there is a movement along a long-run Phillips curve?

17 What have been the main shifts in the UK short-run Phillips curve during the 1960s, 1970s, 1980s and 1990s?

18 What is the connection between expected inflation and nominal interest rates?

Problems

1 Work out the effects on the price level of the following unexpected events:

a An increase in the money supply.
b An increase in government purchases of goods and services.
c An increase in income taxes.
d An increase in investment demand.
e An increase in the wage rate.
f An increase in labour productivity.

2 Work out the effects on the price level of the same events listed in Problem 1 when they are correctly anticipated.

3 An economy's potential GDP is £400 billion, and it has the following expected aggregate demand and short-run aggregate supply curves:

Price level (GDP deflator)	Expected GDP demanded (billions of 1990 pounds)	Expected GDP supplied (billions of 1990 pounds)
80	500	100
100	400	300
120	300	500
140	200	700

a What is the expected price level?
b What is expected real GDP?
c Are wages expected to be fixed?

4 In the economy of Problem 3, the expected price level rises to 120.

a What is the new *SAS* curve if wages are fixed?
b What is the new *SAS* curve if wages are flexible?
c In parts (a) and (b) is real GDP expected to be above or below full employment?

5 The figure shows an economy's long-run aggregate supply curve, *LAS*, three aggregate demand curves, AD_0, AD_1, and AD_2, and three short-run aggregate supply curves, SAS_0, SAS_1, and SAS_2. The economy starts out on the curves AD_0 and SAS_0.

Some events then occur that takes the economy to the other aggregate demand curves and short-run aggregate supply curves.

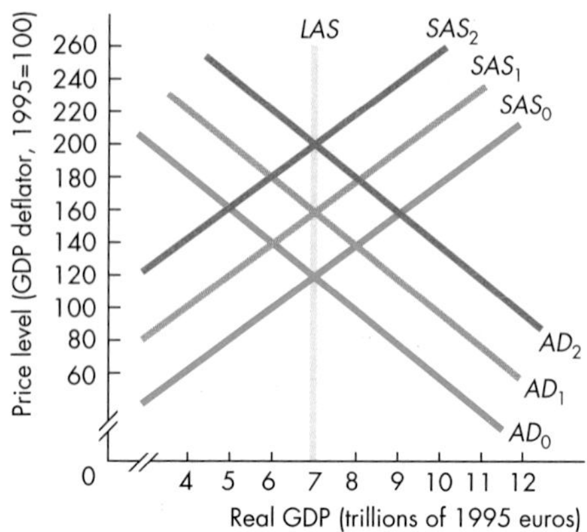

a Describe the sequence of events in the figure if there is a demand-pull inflation.
b Describe the sequence of events in the figure if there is a cost-push inflation.
c Describe the sequence of events in the figure if there is an anticipated inflation.

6 In the economy in Problem 5, aggregate demand unexpectedly increases to AD_1.

a What is the price level in the short-run?
b What is real GDP in the short-run?
c What is the price level in the long-run?
d What is real GDP in the long-run?

7 In year t, the expected aggregate demand schedule for $t + 1$ is as follows:

Price level (GDP deflator)	Expected real GDP demanded (billions of 1990 pounds)
120	400
121	390
122	380
123	370
124	360

In year t, the long-run real GDP is £380 billion and the real GDP expected for $t + 1$ is £390 billion. Calculate the period t rational expectation of the price level for period $t + 1$ if wages are:

a Fixed until $t + 1$.
b Going to be renegotiated before period $t + 1$.

8 The economy in Problem 3 has the following short-run aggregate supply schedule:

Price level (GDP deflator)	Real GDP supplied (billions of 1990 pounds)
120	320
121	350
122	380
123	410
124	440

a Under what conditions is this short-run aggregate supply schedule consistent with your answer to Problem 3?
b Calculate the actual and expected inflation rate if the aggregate demand curve is expected to shift upward by 10 per cent and if it actually does shift upward by that amount.

9 An economy has a natural unemployment rate of 4 per cent when its expected inflation is 6 per cent. Its inflation and unemployment history is as follows:

Inflation rate (per cent per year)	Unemployment rate (per cent)
10	2
8	3
6	4
4	5
2	6

a Draw a diagram of this economy's short-run and long-run Phillips curves.
b If the actual inflation rate rises from 6 per cent a year to 8 per cent a year, what is the change in the unemployment rate? Explain why it occurs.
c If the natural unemployment rate rises to 5 per cent, what is the change in the unemployment rate? Explain why it occurs.
d Go back to part (a). If the expected inflation rate falls to 4 per cent a year, what is the change in the unemployment rate? Explain why it occurs.

10 Study *Reading Between the Lines* on pp. 776–777 and then answer the following questions.

a What was the RPI inflation rate in May 1999? When was the last time inflation was this low in the UK?
b Why has the fall in inflation generated an expectation that interest rates will fall?
c What has happened to unemployment and inflation since 1997?
d How can the combination of falling inflation and falling unemployment be explained by the Phillips curve?

11 Use the link on the Parkin, Powell and Matthews Web site to obtain the latest data on inflation, unemployment, and money growth in Japan, UK, USA and Canada. Then:

a Interpret the data for each country in terms of shifting Phillips curves.
b Which country do you think has the lowest expected inflation rate? Why?

W http://www.econ100.com

The Death of Inflation?

The Times, 16 June 1999

Inflation at six-year low revives rate cut hopes

Lea Paterson and Alasdair Murray

Inflation tumbled to a six-year low in May, reviving City hopes of a fresh cut in interest rates.

The pound slipped on the foreign exchange markets following release of the better-than-expected data, which showed sharp falls in both underlying and headline inflation. The underlying rate, which excludes mortgage interest payments, dropped 0.3 points to 2.1 per cent, its lowest level since October 1994.

The headline rate also fell from 1.6 per cent in April to 1.3 per cent in May — the lowest since June 1993 — the Office for National Statistics said.

City analysts predicted that inflation is likely to fall again in the coming months, potentially pushing the headline rate below 1 per cent for the first time since the early 1960s.

Gordon Brown, Chancellor of the Exchequer, yesterday paid tribute to the Monetary Policy Committee for achieving such low and stable levels of inflation. "The general record of the MPC is that they have got it right. Inflation expectations in the economy as well as inflation itself have come down," Mr Brown told the House of Commons Treasury Select Committee.

The Chancellor added that Britain could be on the verge of a sustained period of low inflation and strong growth similar to that recently experienced by the United States.

If Britain's economic performance continues to improve, the inflation target could eventually be lowered, Mr Brown said.

However, Eddie George, Governor of the Bank of England, sounded a note of caution, admitting that there was "a degree of luck" in the MPC's record over the past year. He told the House of Lords Monetary Policy Committee that the Bank needed to remain vigilant on inflation.

Mr George said: "It would be totally misleading to say that because inflation was less than 2.5 per cent we can forget about that and focus on the problems of the economy."

Most — but not all — City analysts said the data made further rate cuts more likely.

The Essence of the Story

- The inflation rate in the UK fell to a historical low of 1.3 per cent a year in May 1999. This was the lowest rate since June 1993. The RPIX inflation rate fell to 2.1 per cent.
- The expectation in the City of London is that the rate of inflation will continue to fall in the coming months.
- The Chancellor expressed the expectation that Britain is on the point of a sustained period of high growt and low inflation like the United States.
- The lower rate of inflation will put pressure on the Bank of England to cut interest rates further but the Governor of the Bank said that there has been an element of luck in reducing inflation thus far. The Monetary Policy Committee needs to remain vigilant on inflation.

Economic Analysis

■ The fall in the rate of inflation can be attributed to the tight monetary policy followed by the Bank of England. The money supply was increased less than the increase in money demand when inflation was expected to rise so that the rate of interest was raised. When inflation was expected to fall, money supply was increased faster than the increase in money demand so that the rate of interest fell.

■ The tightness of monetary policy and the credibility of the Bank's policy has generated low inflation expectations. Figure 1 shows the path of the monthly inflation rate and the unemployment rate based on the claimant count. They have both been falling in 1998 and 1999.

■ Figure 2 shows the effect of a fall in expected inflation. The short-run Phillips curve falls from $SRPC_0$ to $SRPC_1$. Inflation falls and unemployment moves towards the natural rate given by *LRPC*.

■ The element of luck the Governor is referring to is to do with the fact that the Bank cannot know for sure what is the natural rate of unemployment. So far, falling unemployment has not generated higher inflation.

■ If the Bank mistakenly thinks that the natural rate is higher than the actual rate but in reality the natural rate is lower than the actual rate, inflation will rise as shown in Figure 3. It may therefore be too early to reduce interest rates and stimulate demand.

■ The government New Deal policy may have reduced the natural rate of unemployment so that the natural rate could be lower than the actual rate. However, the actual rate of unemployment is a lagging indicator of the state of the economy. So unemployment could still be falling even when the economy has slowed down.

■ The Governor is correct that the Bank must be vigilant in maintaining its fight against inflation. Inflation is not dead but just sleeping.

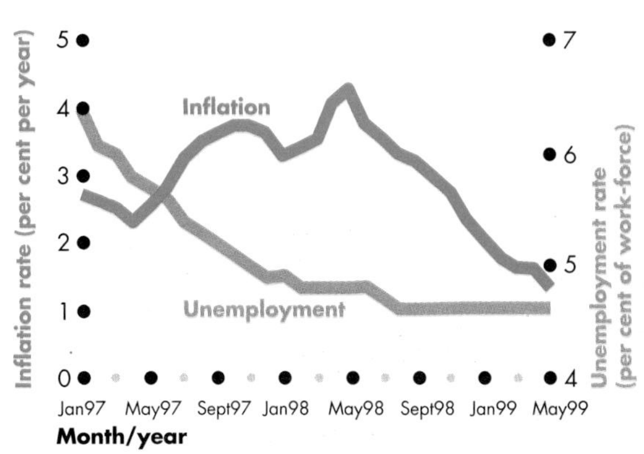

Figure 1 Inflation and unemployment

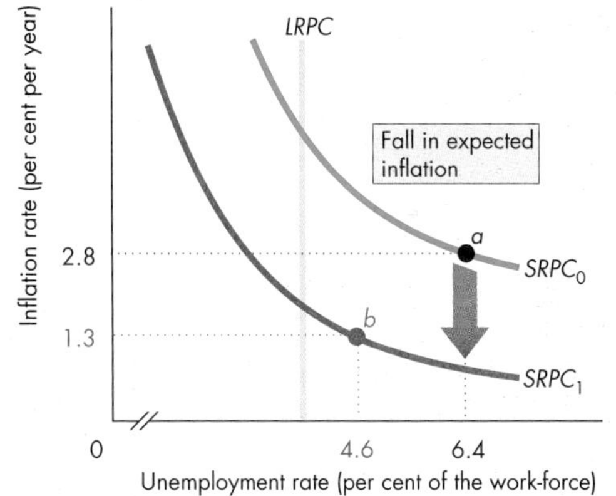

Figure 2 Natural unemployment rate below the actual rate

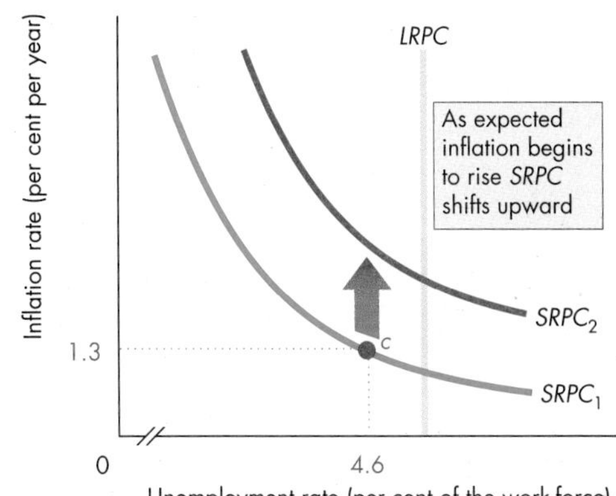

Figure 3 Actual unemployment rate below the natural rate

Capital, Investment and Saving

After studying this chapter you will be able to:

- Describe the growth and fluctuations of investment and the capital stock
- Describe the fluctuations in the real interest rate
- Explain how business investment decisions are made
- Explain how household saving and consumption decisions are made
- Explain how investment, saving and consumption interact to determine the real interest rate
- Explain how government influences the real interest rate, savings and investment

Building the Global Village

When the World Cup Final was played in Paris in 1998 more than one billion people (one-fifth of the world's population) watched the game live. This media event was made possible by an enormous investment in a global video network. An even larger investment in a vast network of computers, telecommunications equipment and databases enables a teenager in the United Kingdom to click the mouse button and surf the Internet or send an e-mail message to a 'pen-friend' in Australia. How do businesses make the investment decisions that create the amazing tools that are building a global village? ◆ Each one of us decides how much current income to save and how much to spend on consumption goods and services. Some of us spend everything we earn and can't wait for the next payday to come around. Others of us save large amounts of income. How do people make their saving and consumption decisions? ◆ Investment, saving and consumption decisions combine to determine interest rates and the long-term growth of potential GDP. How do investment, saving and consumption decisions influence the interest rate you pay on your credit card balance and the interest rate you'll pay when you take out a mortgage to buy a home? How do they influence the size of your pension when you retire?

◆ ◆ ◆ ◆ In this chapter, we study the decisions that determine the amount of capital in the economy and the return – the interest rate – that capital earns. The chapter parallels Chapter 23, which studied the decisions that determine the amount of labour in the economy and the return – the wage rate – that labour earns. When you have completed your study of these two topics, you will be able to combine them and learn about the forces that make potential GDP expand, which are explained in Chapter 32. We begin by looking at some facts about investment, capital and interest rates in the United Kingdom and around the world.

Capital and Interest

The total quantity of plant, equipment, buildings and stocks is the economy's **capital stock**. The purchase of new capital, called **gross investment**, increases the capital stock, and the wearing out and scrapping of existing capital, called **depreciation**, decreases the capital stock. The capital stock increases by the amount of **net investment** – gross investment minus depreciation. (See Chapter 22, pp. 530–531.)

Figure 31.1 shows investment and capital in the United Kingdom from 1970 to 1998. In part (a), you can see that gross investment has grown and fluctuated. In the recession years (1975, 1981–82 and 1991–92), gross investment decreased, and in the recovery and expansion years, it grew quickly. Part of gross investment replaces worn-out capital. The green line 'Replacement investment' in Figure 31.1(a) shows this amount. This component of investment has grown steadily but it has not fluctuated much.

Figure 31.1(a) also shows net investment, the addition to the capital stock. Net investment has fluctuated like gross investment. In the recession year of 1981, net investment fell to about £11.8 billion. In the business cycle peak year of 1989, it was close to £51 billion.

Figure 31.1(b) shows how the capital stock in 1995 prices has changed over the years. It grew every year and increased from around £983 billion in 1970 to £1751 billion in 1998. The growth of the capital stock slowed during the recessions, but the growth rate has been steady over the long term.

The reason the capital stock has grown every year is that net investment has been positive. The reason the fluctuations in the growth rate of the capital stock are small is that net investment is a small part of the capital stock. When net investment falls to a low during a recession, the capital stock grows at about 1.0 per cent a year. When net investment rises to a high during an expansion, the capital stock grows at about 3.7 per cent a year. On the average, the capital stock has grown at a rate of 2.1 per cent a year.

Figure 31.1 shows total investment, which includes the private and public sectors and the capital stock. Private sector investment is business investment plus investment in new homes and dwellings. Public investment is part of government purchases. The part of government purchases that is public investment creates *social infrastructure*

Figure 31.1 Investment and the Capital Stock: 1970–1998

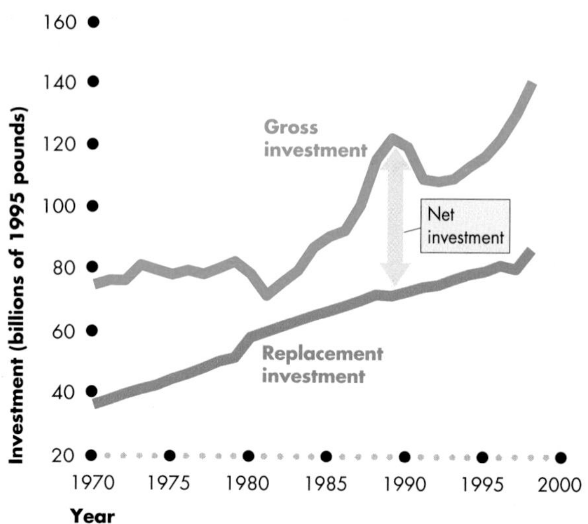

(a) Gross investment and replacement investment

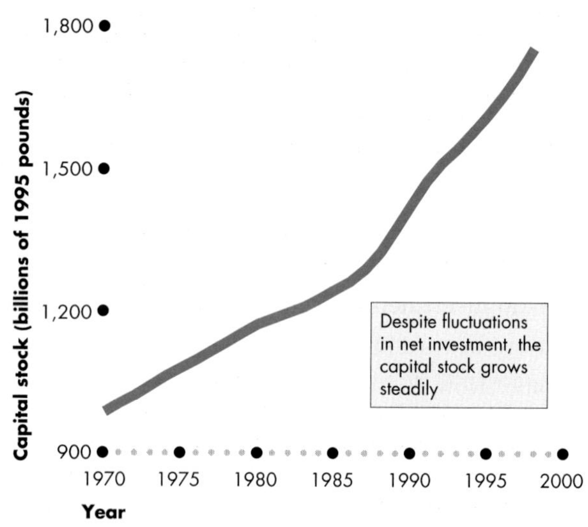

(b) Capital stock

Gross investment grows over the long term and fluctuates over the business cycle. Replacement investment grows over the long term and does not fluctuate. Net investment fluctuates between around £10 billion and £50 billion a year, but because it is a small percentage of the capital stock, the capital stock grows steadily.

Source: ONS.

Figure 31.2 Investment in the United Kingdom and World: 1970–1996

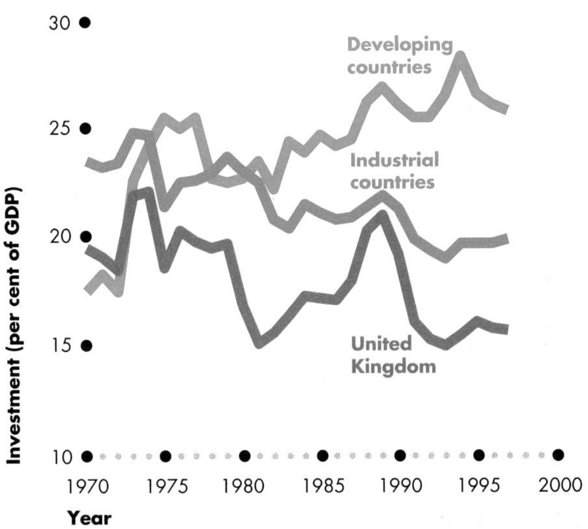

Government purchases include public investment. Total investment is business investment plus investment in new houses plus government investment. Investment in the United Kingdom is a smaller percentage of GDP than it is in many other countries. Since 1975, the developing countries have invested a larger percentage of GDP than the industrial countries.

Source: International Monetary Fund, *International Financial Statistics, Yearbook*, 1998, Washington, DC.

capital. The most basic element in the social infrastructure is the body of laws and the legal institutions that enforce them; without them our economy could not have developed. Motorways, bridges, schools and universities are other examples of social infrastructure capital that enhance productivity growth.

Investment Around the World

How does the amount of investment in the United Kingdom compare with that in other parts of the world? Figure 31.2 answers this question. So that we can make comparisons, we'll measure investment as the percentage of GDP devoted to it.

Figure 31.2 shows that investment in the United Kingdom has fluctuated between about 15 per cent and 22 per cent of GDP. This investment rate is lower than that in the other groups of countries shown in the figure – the industrial countries and the developing countries. The industrial countries are Canada, Japan, Australia, New Zealand and 18 other rich countries in Western Europe. The developing countries comprise the rest of the world. Investment in the industrial countries has fluctuated and has been on a downward trend. Investment in the developing countries has fluctuated and has followed two distinct trends: an upward trend from 1970 to 1981, and a downward trend during the 1980s.

Within the developing economies, those in Asia (such as Korea, Thailand and Malaysia) have the highest investment rates and those in Africa and Central and South America have the lowest investment rates. But most of these countries have higher investment rates than the United Kingdom.

Interest Rates

We've seen that the capital stock has grown steadily over time. But what about the return on capital? Has the return to capital grown also? Let's find out.

The return on capital is the real interest rate. The **real interest rate** is equal to the interest rate on a loan minus the inflation rate – the rate at which prices are rising. For example, if the interest rate is 10 per cent a year and the inflation rate is 4 per cent a year, then the *real* interest rate is 6 per cent a year.

Think about the following example. You borrow £1,000 to help finance a year at college. You plan to repay this loan after one year with the income from next summer's job. At the end of the year you pay out £1,100 – the £1,000 borrowed plus £100 interest. Because prices are rising by 4 per cent a year, £1,040 is needed to buy the same goods and services that £1,000 bought a year earlier. So the people who lent you £1,000 need to receive £1,040 just to replace the purchasing power that they lent. So only £60 of the interest is an addition to their purchasing power. This £60 is the *real* interest income and the real interest rate is 6 per cent a year – £60 as a percentage of the £1,000 loan.

Viewed from your perspective, the amount of summer work that earns £1,000 this year will earn £1,040 next year. So when you borrow £1,000 this year, you know that you will get £40 from the higher wages (from inflation) and will only *really* pay £60 in interest, so the real interest rate you face is 6 per cent a year.

Figure 31.3
The Real Interest Rate

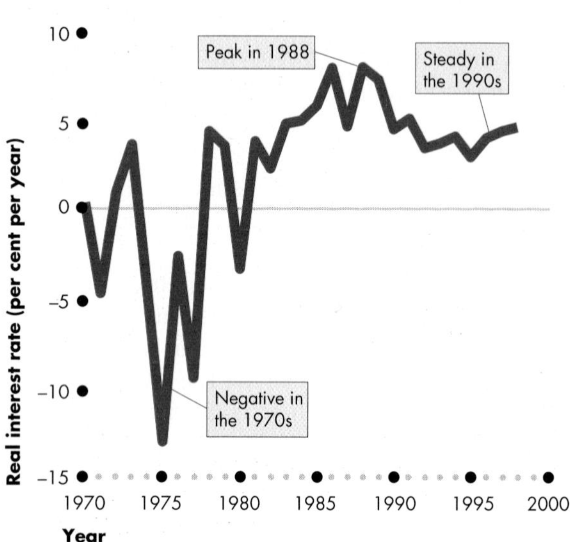

The real interest rate (here, the rate at which creditworthy UK companies can borrow) was low during the 1970s and sometimes negative. It increased strongly between 1980 and 1985 and then it decreased during 1989. It was relatively steady at about 5 per cent during the 1990s.

Source: ONS; and the author's calculations.

In the world economy, there are thousands of different interest rates. But real interest rates around the world move together. One real interest rate that fluctuates with many others is the real interest rate at which blue-chip (highly creditworthy) companies borrow in the world capital markets. In 1998, this real interest rate was about 4.7 per cent a year. The real interest rate at which house buyers and small businesses could borrow was higher, and the rate at which the government could borrow was lower. But all real interest rates tend to move up and down together.

In 1988, the real interest rate was at a peak level. In that year, big companies could borrow at an interest rate of 13 per cent a year and the inflation rate was only about 5 per cent a year, so the real interest rate was approximately 8 per cent a year. In contrast, in 1975, the real interest rate was *negative*. Big companies could borrow at about 11 per cent a year and the inflation rate was about 24 per cent a year, so the real interest rate was about –13 per cent a year.

Figure 31.3 shows the real interest rate facing big UK companies from 1970 to 1998. Three periods are striking:

1 The 1970s – mostly low and negative.
2 The 1980s – the real interest rate rose sharply reaching a peak of 8 per cent.
3 The 1990s – steady between 3 per cent and 5 per cent.

The 1970s were years of stagflation for the world economy resulting from huge oil price hikes and, in the UK particularly, trade union restrictive practice. The 1980s began with a deep recession, but then saw a near decade of expansion. The 1990s also began with a recession but expansion has not been consistent. We'll learn in this chapter how these events influenced the real interest rate.

Review

- Net investment (gross investment minus depreciation) increases the capital stock.
- Net investment fluctuates but it never becomes negative, so the capital stock grows every year. Fluctuations in the growth rate of the capital stock are small because net investment is a small fraction of the capital stock.
- Government purchases include investment in social infrastructure capital.
- The UK investment rate (the percentage of GDP invested) is lower than the rate in many other countries, especially the developing countries.
- The return on capital is the real interest rate.

We've described investment. Let's now study the business investment decisions that determine its magnitude.

Investment Decisions

How does Ford (Europe) decide how much to spend on a new car assembly plant? What determines British Telecommunication's outlays on fibre optic communications systems? The main influences on business investment decisions are:

- The expected profit rate.
- The real interest rate.

The Expected Profit Rate

Other things remaining the same, the greater the expected profit rate from new capital, the greater is the amount of investment.

Imagine that Ford (Europe) is trying to decide whether to build a new £100 million car assembly line that will produce cars for one year and then be scrapped. Ford expects a net revenue of £120 million from operating the plant. Net revenue is equal to total revenue from sales minus the cost of labour and materials. The firm's expected profit from this assembly line is £20 million, which equals £120 million (net revenue) minus £100 million (cost of the plant). The expected *profit rate* is 20 per cent a year ((£20 million ÷ £100 million) × 100).

Of the many influences on the expected profit rate, the two that stand out are:

1. The state of the business cycle.
2. Advances in technology.

During a business cycle expansion, the expected profit rate increases, and during a recession, it decreases. The business cycle influences the expected profit rate because sales and the utilization rate of capital fluctuate over the business cycle. In an expansion, an increase in sales and in the capacity utilization rate bring a higher profit rate. In a recession, a decrease in sales and in the capacity utilization rate bring a lower profit rate.

As technologies advance, profit expectations change. When a new technology first becomes available, firms expect to be on a learning curve and so expect a modest profit rate from switching to the new technology. But as firms gain experience with a new technology, they expect a higher profit rate.

The profit rate calculation does not include the firm's *opportunity cost* of the funds used to buy capital as a cost. For example, the calculation of Ford's profit rate that we've just done ignores the opportunity cost of the funds used to buy the assembly line. To decide whether to invest in a new assembly line, Ford compares the expected profit rate with the opportunity cost of the funds to be used. This opportunity cost is the real interest rate that the firm faces.

The Real Interest Rate

Other things remaining the same, the lower the real interest rate, the greater is the amount of investment. The real interest rate is the opportunity cost of the funds used to finance investment. These funds might be borrowed or might be the financial resources of the firm's owners (the firm's retained earnings). But regardless of the source of the funds, the real interest rate is the opportunity cost. The real interest paid on borrowed funds is an obvious cost. The real interest rate is the cost of using retained earnings because these funds could be lent to another firm. The real interest income foregone is the opportunity cost of using retained earnings to finance an investment project.

In the Ford example, the expected profit rate is 20 per cent a year. So it is profitable for Ford (Europe) to invest as long as the real interest rate is less than 20 per cent a year. That is, at real interest rates below 20 per cent a year, Ford (Europe) will build this assembly line, and at real interest rates in excess of 20 per cent a year, it will not. Other projects will be profitable at higher real interest rates and others will become unprofitable at lower real interest rates. Consequently, the higher the real interest rate, the smaller is the number of projects that are worth undertaking and the smaller is the amount of investment.

Investment Demand

Investment demand is the relationship between the level of investment and the real interest rate, holding all other influences on investment constant. The *investment demand schedule* lists the quantities of planned investment at each real interest rate, holding all other influences on investment constant, and the *investment demand curve* graphs this relationship.

Figure 31.4(a) shows an investment demand curve. Each point (*a* to *c*) corresponds to a row in the table. If the real interest rate is 6 per cent a year, planned investment is £100 billion. A change in the real interest rate causes a movement along the investment demand curve. If the real interest rate rises to 8 per cent a year and planned investment decreases to £80 billion, there is a movement up the investment demand curve. If the real interest rate falls to 4 per cent a year and planned investment increases to £120 billion, there is a movement down the investment demand curve.

Figure 31.4 Investment Demand

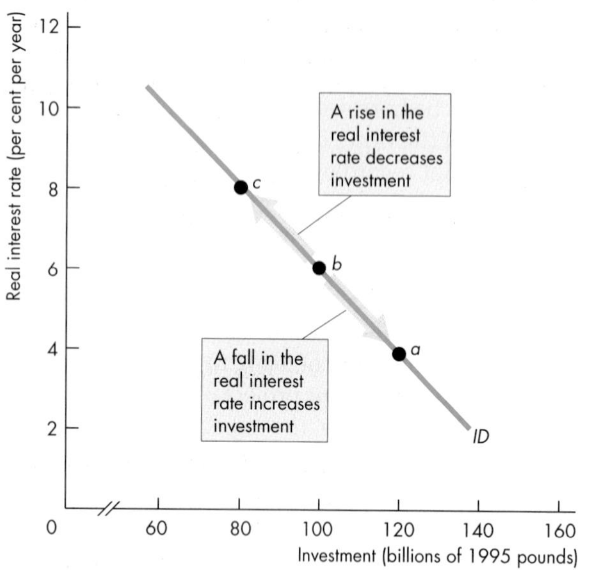

(a) The effect of a change in the real interest rate

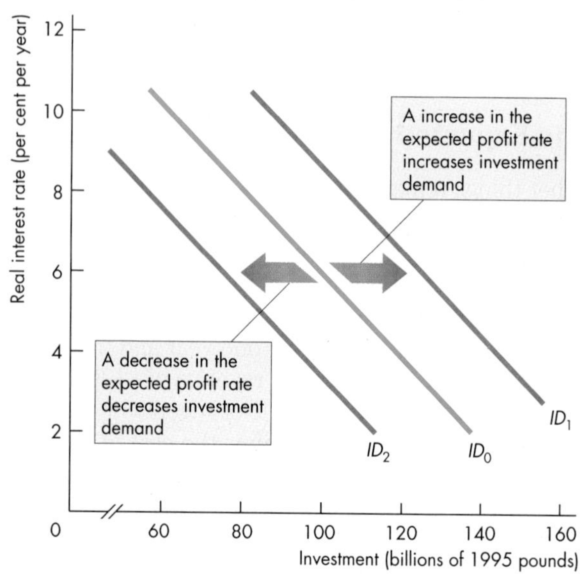

(b) The effect of a change in the expected profit rate

	Real interest rate (per cent per year)	Investment (billions of 1995 pounds) Profit rate expectations Low	Average	High
a	4	96	120	144
b	6	76	100	124
c	8	56	80	104

The table shows three investment schedules for low, average and high profit expectations. Row *b* states that when the real interest rate is 6 per cent a year, private investment is £76 billion with low profit expectations, £100 billion with average profit expectations, and £124 billion with high profit expectations. Part (a) shows the investment demand curve when firms expect the profit rate to be average. As the real interest rate rises from 6 per cent to 8 per cent, planned investment decreases – there is a movement up the investment demand curve from *b* to *c*. As the real interest rate falls from 6 per cent to 4 per cent, planned investment increases – there is a movement down the investment demand curve from *b* to *a*.

Part (b) shows how investment demand changes when the expected profit rate changes. When firms expect the profit rate to be average, the investment demand curve is ID_0 – the same curve as in part (a). When firms expect the profit rate to be high, planned investment increases at each real interest rate and the investment demand curve shifts rightward to ID_1. When firms expect the profit rate to be low, investment decreases at each real interest rate and the investment demand curve shifts leftward to ID_2.

The investment demand schedule and the position of the investment demand curve depend on the expected profit rate. Figure 31.4(b) illustrates the investment demand curve for three different states of expectations. When firms expect an average profit rate, investment demand is ID_0, the same as in part (a). But when the expected profit rate increases, investment demand increases and the investment demand curve shifts rightward to ID_1. When the expected profit rate decreases, investment demand decreases and the investment demand curve shifts leftward to ID_2. Fluctuations in the expected profit rate are the main source of fluctuations in investment demand.

We've studied the *theory* of investment demand. Let's now see how that theory helps us to understand the changes in investment in the United Kingdom.

Investment Demand in the United Kingdom

The theory of investment demand predicts that fluctuations in private sector investment result from fluctuations in the real interest rate and in future

Figure 31.5 Investment Demand in the United Kingdom

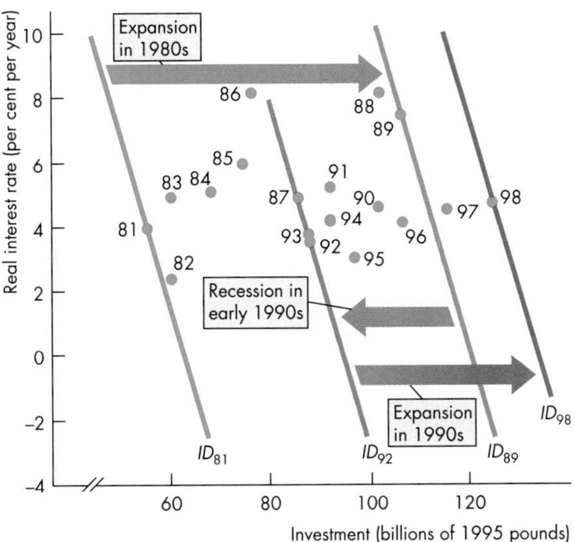

The dots show the levels of gross investment and the real interest rate in the United Kingdom for each year from 1980 to 1994. When the expected profit rate was low in the recession of the early 1980s, the investment demand curve was ID_{81}. As the expected profit rate increased during the 1980s, the investment demand curve shifted rightward. By 1988 it had shifted to ID_{89}. When the expected profit rate decreased during the recession of the 1990s, the investment demand curve shifted leftward to ID_{92}. In the recovery, investment demand increased and ID shifted right to ID_{98}.

Source: ONS; and the author's assumptions.

profit expectations. Figure 31.5 shows the relative importance of these two factors. The dots in the figure show the gross private investment and the real interest rate in the United Kingdom each year from 1981 to 1998. The figure also shows two investment demand curves – ID_{81}, and ID_{98}.

In the early 1980s, the investment demand curve was ID_{81}. The expected profit rate increased during the recovery of 1982 to the boom in 1989 and investment demand increased. This increase is shown by the rightward shift in the investment demand curve to ID_{88}. In 1990 and 1991, the expected profit rate decreased as the economy went into recession but the expected profit rate increased as the economy recovered in the upturn to 1998.

You can see in Figure 31.5 that investment fluctuates for two reasons: the real interest rate changes, which brings movements along an investment demand curve, and expectations about the profit rate change, which shift the investment demand curve. You can also see that changes in the expected profit rate (shifts of the investment demand curve) create larger fluctuations in investment than changes in the real interest rate (movements along the investment demand curve).

Review

- Investment depends on the expected profit rate and the real interest rate.
- Other things remaining the same, if the real interest rate falls, investment increases and there is a movement along the investment demand curve.
- When the expected profit rate increases, the investment demand curve shifts rightward; when the expected profit rate decreases, it shifts leftward.
- Changes in both the real interest rate and the expected profit rate play a role in creating fluctuations in investment in the United Kingdom.

Next, we study the decisions that create the funds that finance investment: saving and consumption decisions.

Saving and Consumption Decisions

Private investment is financed by domestic saving and by borrowing from the rest of the world. Domestic saving, which is the sum of private saving and government saving, is determined by decisions of households and by the government's fiscal policy. Here, we'll focus on the major source of finance for investment: the saving decisions of households.

Households must decide how to allocate their *disposable income* (earned income – wages, dividends, interest and profit – plus transfers from the government minus taxes), between saving and consumption expenditure. *Consumption expenditure* is the value of the consumption goods and services bought by households in a given time period and *saving* is defined as disposable income minus consumption expenditure. Of the many factors that influence household saving and consumption expenditure decisions, the more important ones are:

- Real interest rate.
- Disposable income.
- Purchasing power of net assets.
- Expected future income.

Real Interest Rate

Other things remaining the same, the lower the real interest rate, the greater is the amount of consumption expenditure and the smaller is the amount of saving. The real interest rate is the opportunity cost of consumption. This opportunity cost arises regardless of whether a person is a borrower or a lender. For a borrower, increasing consumption this year means paying more interest next year. For a lender, increasing consumption this year means receiving less interest next year.

The effect of the real interest rate on consumption expenditure is an example of the principle of substitution. If the opportunity cost of an action increases, people substitute other actions in its place. In this case, if the opportunity cost of current consumption increases, people cut current consumption and substitute future consumption in its place.

For example, if the real interest rate on your student loan was 12 per cent, you would probably cut your consumption expenditure (buy cheaper food, find cheaper accommodation) and borrow a smaller amount. Similarly, with a 12 per cent real interest rate, lenders try to cut back on current consumption in order to increase their lending and profit from the high real interest rate. But if the real interest rate on your student loan was 1 per cent a year, you might increase your consumption and borrow a larger amount.

Disposable Income

The higher a household's disposable income, other things remaining the same, the greater is its consumption expenditure and the greater is its saving.

For example, a student works during the summer and earns a disposable income of £2,000. She spends the entire £2,000 on consumption during the year. When she graduates as an economist, her disposable income jumps to £12,000 a year. She now spends £10,000 on consumption and saves £2,000. The increase in disposable income of £10,000 has brought an increase in consumption of £8,000 and an increase in saving of £2,000.

Purchasing Power of Net Assets

A household's assets are what it *owns* and its liabilities are what it *owes*. A household's *net assets* are its assets minus its liabilities. The purchasing power of a household's net assets, the *real* value of its net assets, are the goods and services that its net assets can buy. The higher the purchasing power of a household's net assets, other things remaining the same, the greater is its consumption expenditure. That is, if two households have the same disposable income in the current year, the household with the larger net assets will spend a larger portion of current disposable income on consumption goods and services.

For example, both Cindy and Stuart are department store executives and each earns a disposable income of £15,000 a year. Cindy has £10,000 in the bank and no debts. Stuart has no money in the bank and owes £5,000 on his car loan. Cindy spends most of her £15,000 each year, but Stuart tries to keep his consumption at £14,000 so he can pay off his car loan. (Paying off a loan is not consumption expenditure. When Stuart bought his car, that was consumption expenditure. When he pays off his loan, he is saving.)

The purchasing power of net assets is influenced by the price level. The higher the price level, other things remaining the same, the smaller is the purchasing power of net assets and the smaller is the amount of consumption expenditure. For example, if the price level rises by 10 per cent, everything else remaining the same, a household with £50,000 in a savings deposit experiences a £5,000 decrease in its purchasing power. This household will probably cut its consumption and increase its saving. (A rise in the price level decreases the real value of debts, which works in the opposite direction to the effect on the real value of assets. As the purchasing power that must be given up to repay a household's debts decreases, consumption might increase. But most households have assets that exceed their debts, so an increase in the price level brings a decrease in consumption expenditure.)

Expected Future Income

The higher a household's expected future income, other things remaining the same, the greater is its consumption expenditure. That is, if two households have the same disposable income in the current year, the household with the larger expected future income will spend a larger portion of current disposable income on consumption goods and services.

Look at Cindy and Stuart again. Cindy has just been promoted and will receive a £3,000 pay rise next year. Stuart has just been told that his contract will not be renewed at the end of the year. On receiving this news, Cindy buys a new car – increases her consumption expenditure, and Stuart cancels his summer holiday plans – decreases his consumption expenditure.

Although consumption and saving are influenced by several factors, we focus on two of them: the real interest rate and disposable income. The real interest rate, which is the opportunity cost of consumption, determines the long-run allocation of disposable income between consumption and saving. Disposable income is the key short-run influence on consumption and saving. In the rest of this chapter, our focus is the long run. In Chapters 24 and 25 we looked at the short run.

Consumption Demand and Saving Supply

If the real interest rate rises, other things remaining the same, consumption expenditure decreases and saving increases. The table in Figure 31.6 shows an example of these relationships. It lists the levels of consumption expenditure and saving that occur at three levels of the real interest rate. The relationship between consumption expenditure and the real interest rate, other things remaining the same, is called **consumption demand**, and the relationship between saving and the real interest rate, other things remaining the same, is called **saving supply**.

Consumption Demand Figure 31.6(a) shows a consumption demand curve. The x-axis measures consumption expenditure and the y-axis measures the real interest rate. Along the consumption demand curve, the points labelled a to c correspond to the rows having the same letters in the table. For example, point b indicates the real interest rate of 6 per cent a year and consumption expenditure of £350 billion. If the real interest rate rises from 6 per cent a year to 8 per cent a year, consumption expenditure decreases from £350 million to £340 billion and there is a movement along the consumption demand curve from b to c. If the real interest rate falls from 6 per cent a year to 4 per cent a year, consumption expenditure increases from £350 billion to £360 billion and there is a movement along the consumption demand curve from b to a.

Saving Supply Figure 31.6(b) shows a saving supply curve. The x-axis measures saving and the y-axis measures the real interest rate. Again, the points marked a to c correspond to the rows of the table. For example, point b indicates that when the real interest rate is 6 per cent a year, saving is £30 billion. If the real interest rate rises from 6 per cent a year to 8 per cent a year, saving increases from £30 billion to £40 billion and there is a movement along the saving supply curve from b to c. If the real interest rate falls from 6 per cent a year to 4 per cent a year, saving decreases from £30 billion to £20 billion and there is a movement along the saving supply curve from b to a.

Along the consumption demand curve and saving supply curve, all the other influences on consumption and saving are constant. One of these influences, and one of the strongest influences, is disposable income. Because disposable income is constant, consumption plus saving equals the constant level of disposable income. In the table in Figure 31.6, disposable income is a constant £380 billion. Because households can only consume or save their disposable income, consumption demand plus saving supply always equals disposable income.

Disposable Income, Consumption Expenditure and Saving

You've seen how a change in the real interest rate brings changes in consumption expenditure and saving. And you've seen how these changes bring movements along the consumption demand curve and saving supply curve.

Changes in other influences on consumption expenditure and saving *change consumption demand* and also *change saving supply*. That is, these changes alter the quantity of consumption expenditure and saving at each interest rate. They

Figure 31.6 Consumption Demand Curve and Saving Supply Curve

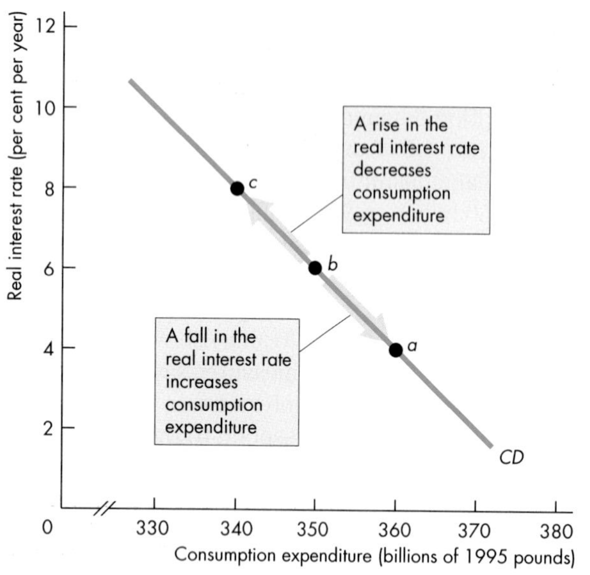

(a) Consumption demand

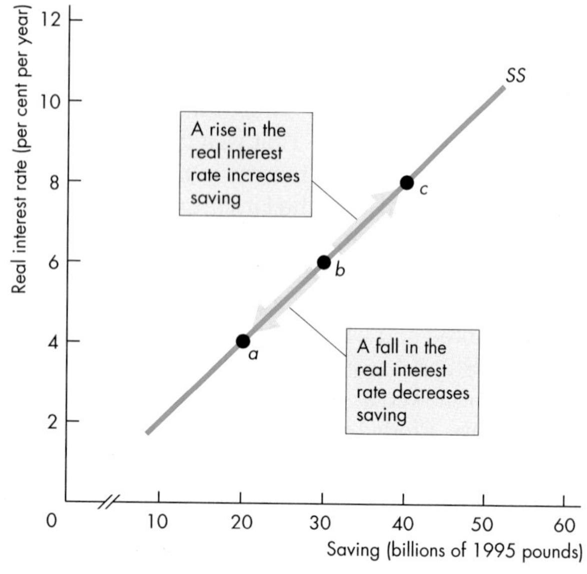

(b) Saving supply

	Real interest rate (per cent per year)	Consumption expenditure	Saving	Disposable income
		(billions of 1995 pounds)		
a	4	360	20	380
b	6	350	30	380
c	8	340	40	380

The table shows consumption expenditure and saving at various levels of the real interest rate and for a disposable income of £380 billion, all other influences on consumption and saving remaining the same. Part (a) of the figure shows the relationship between consumption expenditure and the real interest rate (the consumption demand curve, *CD*). Part (b) shows the relationship between saving and the real interest rate (the saving supply curve, *SS*). Points *a* to *c* on the consumption demand curve and saving supply curve correspond to the rows in the table. At each real interest rate, consumption expenditure plus saving equals disposable income. An increase in the real interest rate decreases consumption expenditure and increases saving. The total remains unchanged.

are illustrated as shifts in the consumption demand curve and the saving supply curve. The most important of these other factors that change consumption demand and saving supply is disposable income.

We saw in Chapter 25 (pp. 603–606) that when disposable income increases, both consumption expenditure and saving increase. The extent to which each increases is determined by the *marginal propensity to consume* and the *marginal propensity to save*.

In Figure 31.7, when disposable income increases from £380 billion to £400 billion, consumption expenditure increases from £350 billion to £366 billion. The change in disposable income is £20 billion and the change in consumption expenditure is £16 billion. The *MPC* is £16 billion divided by £20 billion, which equals 0.8.

Again, when disposable income increases from £380 billion to £400 billion, saving increases from £30 billion to £34 billion. The change in disposable income is £20 billion and the change in saving is £4 billion. The *MPS* is £4 billion divided by £20 billion, which equals 0.2.

Because an increase in disposable income increases both consumption expenditure and saving, it shifts both the consumption demand curve and the saving supply curve rightward. Figure 31.7 shows these shifts. But also, as in this example, because the

Figure 31.7 An Increase in Disposable Income

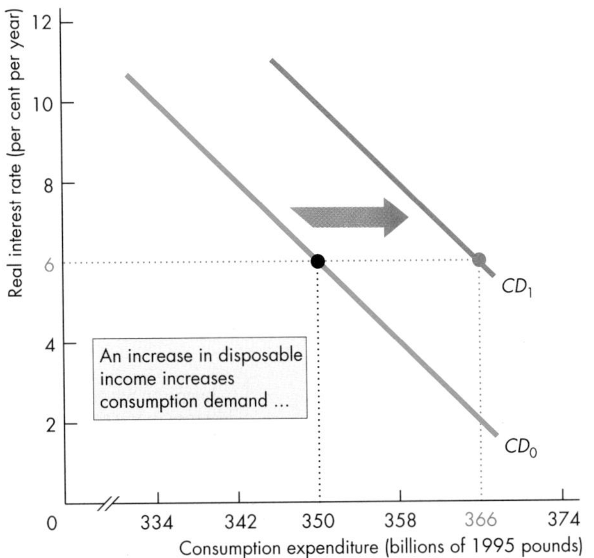

(a) Increase in consumption demand

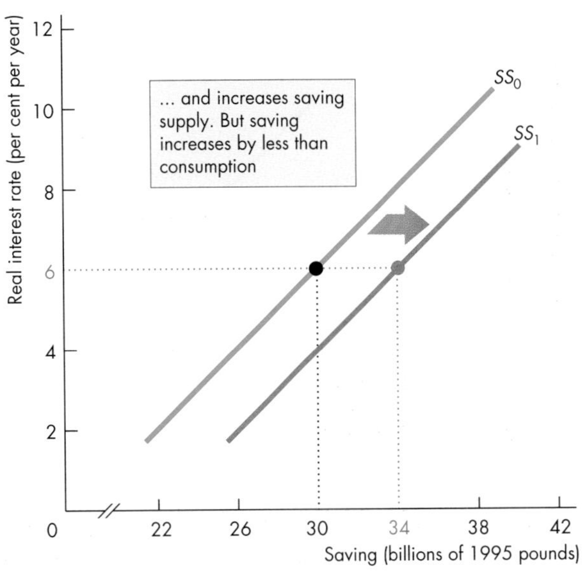

(b) Increase in saving supply

An increase in disposable income increases both consumption demand and saving supply. The marginal propensity to consume, *MPC*, determines the increase in consumption demand and the marginal propensity to save, *MPS*, determines the increase in saving supply, other things remaining the same. Here, the *MPC* is 0.8 and the *MPS* is 0.2. An increase in disposable income of £20 billion brings an increase in consumption demand of £16 billion and an increase in saving supply of £4 billion.

marginal propensity to consume is generally greater than the marginal propensity to save, an increase in disposable income increases consumption expenditure by more than it increases saving.

Other Influences on Consumption Expenditure and Saving

The other influences on consumption expenditure and saving – the purchasing power of net assets and expected future income – change consumption expenditure and saving in opposite directions, other things remaining the same. That is, any change that increases consumption expenditure, with disposable income constant, decreases saving. For example, an increase in the purchasing power of net assets increases consumption expenditure and decreases saving. The effect of such a change is shown by a rightward shift of the consumption demand curve and a leftward shift of the saving supply curve. Figure 31.8 illustrates these shifts.

We've studied the *theory* of consumption demand and saving supply and identified the key influences on these decisions. Let's now see how that theory helps us to understand the changes in consumption expenditure and saving in the United Kingdom.

Consumption Demand and Saving Supply in the United Kingdom

Figure 31.9(a) shows the UK consumption demand curve. Each point identified by a blue dot represents consumption expenditure and the real interest rate for a particular year. (The dots are for the years 1970–1998.) In 1970, the consumption demand curve was CD_{70}. This curve indicates that when the real interest rate rises, everything else remaining the same, consumption expenditure decreases. But a large change in the real interest rate brings a small change in consumption expenditure.

Figure 31.8 Other Influences on Consumption Demand and Saving Supply

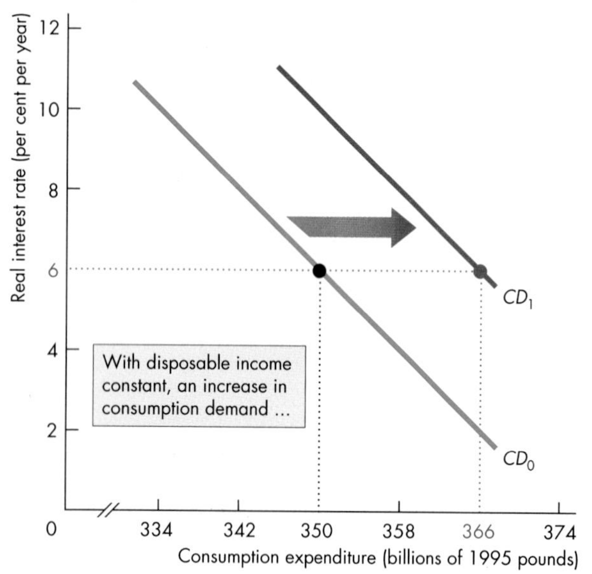

(a) Increase in consumption demand

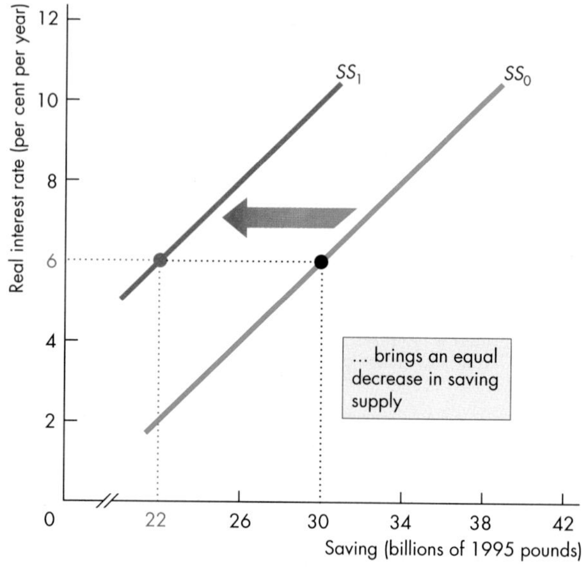

(b) Decrease in saving supply

With a given level of disposable income, an increase in the purchasing power of net assets or an increase in expected future income increases consumption demand and decreases saving supply. The consumption demand curve shifts rightward from CD_0 to CD_1 (part a) and the saving supply curve shifts leftward from SS_0 to SS_1 in part (b). The rightward shift of the *CD* curve equals the leftward shift of the *SS* curve because consumption expenditure plus saving equal a constant disposable income.

Over time, the consumption demand curve has shifted rightward, mainly because disposable income has increased. Between 1970 and 1998 disposable income increased by about £270 billion and consumption expenditure increased by £248 billion.

Figure 31.9(b) shows the UK saving supply curve. Here, each point identified by a dot represents saving and the real interest rate for a particular year. In 1970, the saving supply curve was SS_{70}. The curve indicates that when the real interest rate rises, saving increases. But as in the case of consumption, a large change in the real interest rate brings a small change in saving.

Over time, the saving supply curve has shifted rightward and for the same reason that the consumption demand has shifted rightward – because disposable income has increased. But saving supply has not increased by as much as consumption demand. Between 1970 and 1998 while disposable income increased by £270 billion, saving increased by £23 billion and the saving supply curve shifted rightward to SS_{98}.

The reason why saving supply has at times increased much less than consumption demand and even decreased at other times, is that influences other than the interest rate and disposable income have tended to increase consumption expenditure and decrease saving. During the 1980s, these influences were the purchasing power of net assets and expected future incomes. A booming stock market, rising house prices and increasing personal wealth meant that people were willing to consume more and save less. Expectations of continued rapid economic expansion, which increased expected future incomes, reinforced the effect of increasing personal wealth. The result was an increase in consumption expenditure that was in excess of the increase in disposable income. Saving increased in

Figure 31.9 Consumption Demand and Saving Supply in the United Kingdom

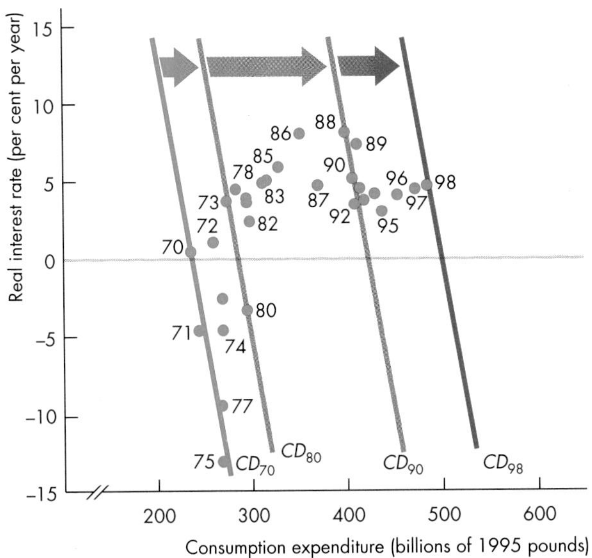

(a) Consumption demand

(b) Saving supply

Part (a) shows the consumption demand curve in the United Kingdom. Each dot represents consumption expenditure and the real interest rate for a particular year from 1970 to 1998. The blue curve CD_{70} is an estimate of the consumption demand curve for 1970. A large change in the real interest rate brings a small change in consumption expenditure. As disposable income increased, consumption demand increased and the consumption demand curve shifted rightward to CD_{80}, CD_{90}, and CD_{98}. Consumption demand increased by more during the 1980s than during the 1970s.

Part (b) shows the saving supply curve. Each dot represents saving and the real interest rate for a particular year from 1970 to 1998. The blue curve SS_{70} is an estimate of the saving supply curve for 1970. As disposable income increased, saving supply increased, and the saving supply curve shifted rightward to SS_{95}. Saving supply fell during the late 1990s.

Source: ONS; and the author's assumptions.

the first half of the 1990s as households attempted to rebuild their assets following the fall in asset values in the recesssion of 1990–91.

Review

- Consumption expenditure and saving decisions are influenced by the real interest rate, disposable income, the purchasing power of net assets and expectations of future income.
- The consumption demand curve is the relationship between consumption expenditure and the real interest rate, other things remaining the same. The consumption demand curve slopes downward.
- The saving supply curve is the relationship between saving and the real interest rate, other things remaining the same. The saving supply curve slopes upward.
- Between 1970 and 1998, the consumption demand curve in the United Kingdom shifted rightward as disposable income and net assets increased. The saving supply curve shifted rightward during most of the period between 1970 and 1998 but during the 1980s other influences on saving offset the influence of increased disposable income and saving fell.

We've now studied the decisions that determine investment, consumption expenditure and saving, and seen that both sets of decisions depend on the real interest rate.

Long-run Equilibrium in the Global Economy

We are now going to see how investment decisions together with consumption and saving decisions determine the real interest rate. To do so, we study the economy of the entire world. The reason is that there is a single world capital market. Capital is free to roam the world and seek the highest possible real rate of return, unless there are legal restrictions that hinder the movement of capital. During the 1970s, various forms of capital controls existed in the United Kingdom and in the rest of Europe. During the 1980s, these controls were gradually dismantled, allowing capital to move freely. As a result the saving of one country is not necessarily used to finance the investment of that country.

Real interest rates are not identical in every country because some countries are riskier than others and have higher real interest rates. But rates move up and down together. If a higher return is available in one country where the risk is equal to that in others, capital rushes into that country. The increase in the supply of capital lowers the interest rate and brings it into line with the countries of equal risk. If the return available in one country is lower than that in other countries of equal risk, capital leaves that country. The decrease in the supply of capital raises the real interest rate and brings it into line with countries of equal risk. The world average real interest rate and changes in the real interest rate in each country are determined by global saving and global investment. So the real interest rate is in the long run determined by global saving and global investment.

Figure 31.10 Equilibrium in the World Capital Market

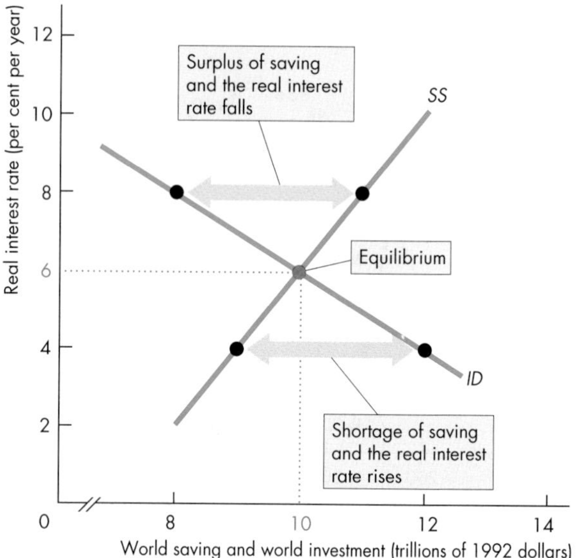

	Real interest rate (per cent per year)	Investment (trillions of 1992 dollars)	Saving
a	4	12	9
b	6	10	10
c	8	8	11

The table shows world investment and saving at three interest rates, and the figure shows the world investment demand curve, *ID*, and world saving supply curve, *SS*. If the real interest rate is 4 per cent a year, investment exceeds saving. There is a shortage of saving, and the real interest rate rises. If the real interest rate is 8 per cent a year, investment is less than saving. There is a surplus of saving, and the real interest rate falls. When the real interest rate is 6 per cent a year, investment equals saving. There is neither a shortage nor a surplus of saving, and the real interest rate is at its equilibrium level.

Determining the Real Interest Rate: *S* = *I*

Figure 31.10 shows how the real interest rate is determined. The *ID* curve is the world investment demand curve. The *SS* curve is the world saving supply curve. The higher the real interest rate, the greater is the amount of saving and the smaller is the amount of investment. In the figure, when the real interest rate exceeds 6 per cent a year, saving exceeds investment. If saving exceeds investment, borrowers have an easy time finding the loans they want, but lenders are unable to lend all the funds they have available. In this situation, the real interest rate falls. As it falls, planned investment increases and planned saving decreases. The interest rate continues to fall so long as saving exceeds investment.

When the interest rate is less than 6 per cent a year, saving is less than investment. If there is a shortage of saving, borrowers can't find the loans they want, but lenders are able to lend all the funds they have available. In this situation, the real interest

Figure 31.11 Explaining Changes in the Real Interest Rate

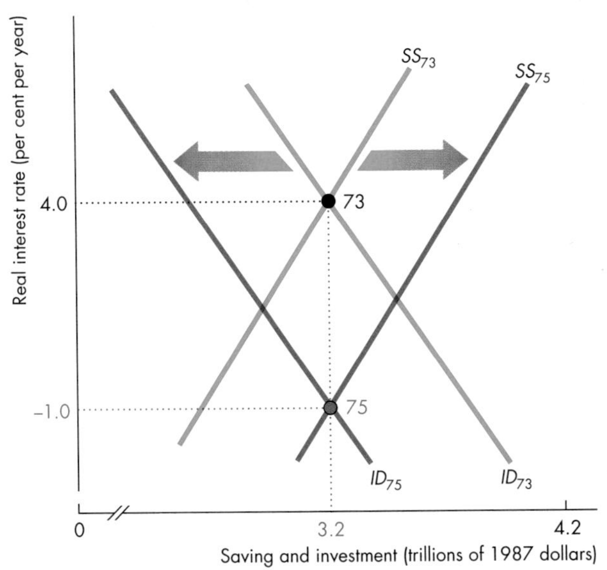

(a) Onset of growth slowdown

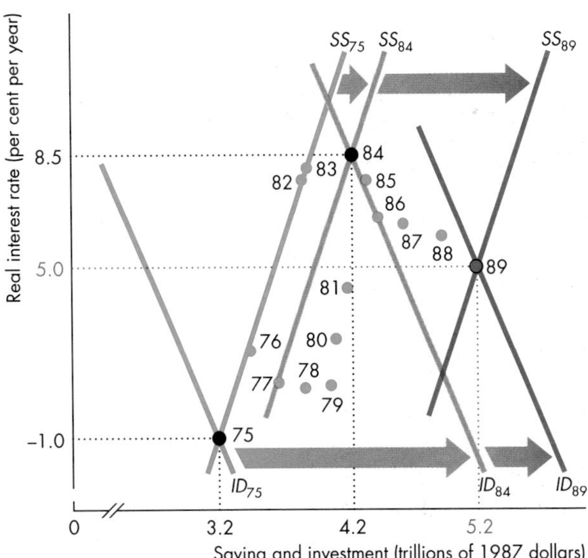

(b) 1975–1989

In 1973 (part a), world saving supply was SS_{73} and world investment demand was ID_{73}. The real interest rate was 4 per cent a year. A large increase in the world price of oil increased world saving supply and decreased world investment demand. By 1975, world saving supply was SS_{75} and world investment demand was ID_{75}, and the real interest rate was negative. By 1984 (part b), a strong economic expansion was under way and investment demand had increased to ID_{84}, but saving supply had not increased by much and was at SS_{84}. The real interest rate increased and reached a peak of 8.5 per cent in 1984. During the rest of the 1980s, saving supply increased by more than investment demand, and by 1989, the saving supply curve was at SS_{89} and the investment demand curve was at ID_{89}. The real interest rate had fallen to 5 per cent a year.

Sources: Robert Summers and Alan Heston, New computer diskette (Mark 5.5), 15 June 1993, distributed by the National Bureau of Economic Research to update The Penn World Table (Mark 5): An Expanded Set of International Comparisons, 1950–1988, *Quarterly Journal of Economics*, May 1991, 327–368; International Monetary Fund, *International Financial Statistics Yearbook*, 1994, Washington DC; *Economic Report of the President*, 1995; and the author's assumptions and calculations.

rate rises. As it rises, there is a decrease in planned investment and an increase in planned saving. The interest rate continues to rise as long as there is a shortage of saving.

Regardless of whether there is a surplus or a shortage of saving, the real interest rate changes and is pulled towards an equilibrium level. In Figure 31.10, this equilibrium is 6 per cent a year. At this interest rate there is neither a surplus nor a shortage of saving. Investors can get the funds they demand and savers can lend all the funds they have available. The plans of savers and investors are consistent with each other.

Let's use this model of global saving and investment to explain changes in the real interest rate in the world economy.

Explaining Changes in the Real Interest Rate

In 1998, the real interest rate paid by the biggest and safest companies in the world, was about 4.5 per cent a year. In the mid-1980s the real interest rate was even higher. It averaged over 8 per cent. In contrast, in the mid-1970s, the real interest rate was on average *negative*. Figure 31.11 explains why these changes in the real interest rate occurred. Each point identified by a blue dot represents world investment and world saving and the real interest rate for a particular year. In 1973, (part a) the saving supply curve was SS_{73} and the investment demand curve was ID_{73}. The real interest rate was 4 per cent, and the amount of saving and investment in the world economy was \$3.7 trillion in 1992 prices.

In 1973, the price of a barrel of oil was \$2.70. By 1975, this price was \$10.70. Oil producers and exporters experienced a huge increase in income and their saving increased. The world saving supply curve shifted rightward to SS_{75}. Oil users and importers faced steep cost increases and a collapse of profits which decreased investment demand and the world investment demand curve shifted leftward to ID_{75}. So by 1975, world saving supply was high, world investment demand was low and the real interest rate fell to −1 per cent a year.

Figure 31.11(b) takes up the story at this point. Gradually, investment demand recovered and, except for severe recession in 1982, increased each year. By 1984, the investment demand curve had shifted rightward to ID_{84}. During these same years, saving supply increased slowly. In 1984, the saving supply curve was the same as it had been in 1977. The reasons for this slow saving growth are complex. But one factor at work was the productivity growth slowdown of the 1970s. At first, the productivity growth slowdown was seen as temporary, so people still expected their future income to grow. With expected future income growth, consumption expenditure increased and saving decreased. Another factor is the emergence of large government deficits, which must be subtracted from private saving to determine total saving. The combination of a large increase in investment demand and a small increase in saving supply increased the real interest rate to 8.4 per cent in 1984, and world investment and world saving increased to \$5 trillion.

The rest of the 1980s saw a more rapid growth in the supply of saving relative to the increase in investment demand. By 1994, the investment demand curve had shifted rightward to ID_{94} and the saving supply curve had shifted to SS_{94}. As a result of these changes, the real interest rate fell to 5.6 per cent.

Review

- The real interest rate is determined by world saving supply and world investment demand.
- The world oil price explosion of 1973–74 increased oil exporters' incomes and increased saving supply and decreased investment demand. The real interest rate fell to a low point.
- The 1980s expansion increased investment demand, but saving supply grew by less and the real interest rate rose.
- During the late 1980s, investment demand increased less than saving supply and the real interest rate fell.

We've now studied the decisions that determine investment, consumption expenditure and saving, and we've seen how the real interest rate is determined. The real interest rate is determined by saving and investment in a global market. Our final task in this chapter is to return to the national economy and see how national investment, consumption and saving decisions influence a country's net exports and its net lending to or borrowing from the rest of the world.

Savings and Investment in the National Economy

Saving supply and investment demand in the world economy determine the world real rate of interest. At the equilibrium real rate of interest, world saving equals world investment.

Although world savings equals world investment, the same need not be true for the national economy. In a country investment is financed by national saving plus borrowing from the rest of the world (Chapter 22, pp. 533–534). Countries that have investment exceeding national saving, borrow from the rest of the world, and countries that that have national saving in excess of investment lend to the rest of the world. But for the world as a whole, international borrowing equals international lending.

You learned in Chapter 22, p. 534, that a country's international lending/borrowing equals its net exports. A country with a net export surplus is one that lends to the rest of the world. A country that has a net export deficit borrows from the rest of the world. Whether a country has a surplus or deficit in its international trade depends on whether its national saving exceeds or falls short of its investment.

Let's take a closer look at the role played by national saving and investment decisions and how

Figure 31.12 Saving, Investment and International Borrowing

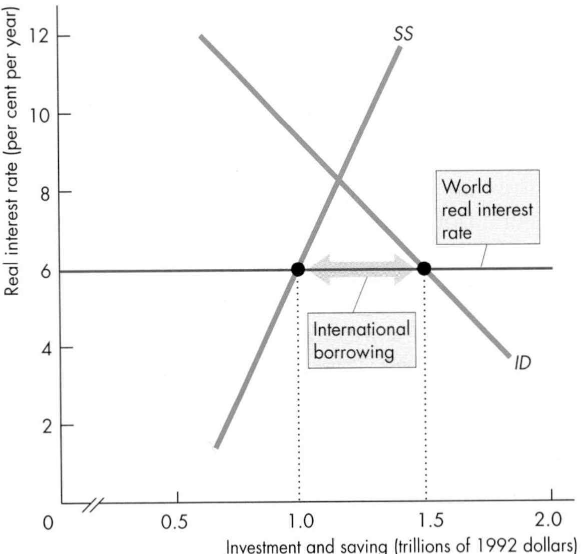

A nation's investment demand curve is *ID*, and its saving supply curve (including government saving) is *SS*. The world real interest rate is 6 per cent a year. At this interest rate, investment, which is $1.5 trillion, exceeds saving, which is $1.0 trillion. The nation borrows $0.5 trillion from the rest of the world.

they determine international borrowing. There are two channels of influence to consider.

First, each country contributes to world saving and investment and so influences the world real rate of interest. The larger the economy, the greater is that influence. For example, investment and saving decisions in the United States, the European Union and Japan have a big impact on world investment demand and world saving supply so they have a big influence on the world real interest rate. The investment and saving of other nations individually have a small impact on world investment demand and world saving supply, so they have a negligible infuence on the world real interest rate.

Second, a country's saving and investment decisions, along with the world real interest rate determine the amount a country borrows from or lends to the rest of the world. They also, equivalently, determine a country's net exports.

Figure 31.12 shows the determination of a country's international borrowing and net exports. The national investment demand curve is *ID*, and its national saving supply curve is *SS*. The world real rate is 6 per cent a year. At this real rate, national investment exceeds national saving by $0.5 trillion, so the country borrows from the rest of the world.

Government Saving and International Borrowing

We saw in Chapter 22, pp. 533–534, that the larger the amount of government saving, other things equal, the greater is national saving. The greater is national saving, the smaller is international borrowing (or the larger is international lending). So an increase in the government deficit decreases national saving and increases international borrowing.

For most of the past decade net exports by the United Kingdom have been negative. The reason is that UK national saving has been less than national investment. Government dissaving (government borrowing) during the first half of the 1990s has contributed to the shortfall. In the second half of the 1980s a low private sector saving rate was also a contributory factor.

Review

- If national investment exceeds national saving at the world real rate of interest, net exports are negative and a country borrows from the rest of the world.
- An increase in government borrowing (government deficit) increases international borrowing.

In this chapter, we've studied the factors that influence investment decisions, and consumption and saving decisions. We've also studied the way these decisions interact in global markets to determine the real interest rate. Finally, we've studied the way the real interest rate determines investment, saving and net exports in a national economy such as the United Kingdom. We've now laid the foundation on which you can study long-term economic growth. In Chapter 32, you will learn how investment, consumption and saving decisions influence the long-term growth of potential GDP.

Summary

Key Points

Capital and Interest (pp. 780–782)

- The capital stock increases by the amount of net investment. Because net investment is always positive the capital stock grows steadily.
- Investment is business investment plus investment in new houses. Some government purchases are investment in *social infrastructure capital.*
- The return on capital is the real interest rate – the interest rate on a loan minus the inflation rate. Real interest rates around the world move together.

Investment Decisions (pp. 782–785)

- Gross private investment is determined by two main factors: the real interest rate and expected profit rate.
- The higher the expected profit rate on new capital, the greater is the amount of investment, other things remaining the same. The two main influences on the expected profit rate are the phase of the business cycle and advances in technology.
- To decide whether to undertake an investment, a firm compares the expected profit rate with the opportunity cost of funds which is the real interest rate. The lower the real interest rate, the greater is the amount of investment undertaken, other things remaining the same.
- Investment demand is the relationship between the level of planned investment and the real interest rate, holding all other influences on investment constant.

Saving and Consumption Decisions (pp. 785–792)

- A household's consumption expenditure depends on its disposable income, the purchasing power of its net assets and its expected future income. The higher a household's disposable income, the purchasing power of its net assets and expected future income, the greater is its permanent income and, other things remaining the same, the greater is its consumption expenditure.
- The relationship between consumption expenditure and disposable income is called the consumption demand curve, and the relationship between saving and disposable income is called the saving supply curve.
- As disposable income increases, other things remaining the same, both consumption expenditure and saving increase.

Long-run Equilibrium in the Global Economy (pp. 792–794)

- Because capital is free to move internationally to seek the highest possible real rate of return, the real interest rate is determined in a global market.
- The equilibrium real interest rate makes global saving equal to global investment.
- In the national economy, foreign borrowing (the negative of net exports) fills the gap between domestic resources and investment, that is, net exports adjust to fill the gap between investment and national saving.

Savings and Investment in the National Economy (pp. 794–795)

- A country's investment is financed by national saving plus borrowing from the rest of the world.
- Countries that have investment exceeding national saving, borrow from the rest of the world, and countries that that have national saving in excess of investment lend to the rest of the world.

Key Figures 

Key Terms

Review Questions

1 Which component of gross investment fluctuates the most, net investment or replacement investment?

2 Why does the capital stock grow smoothly when net investment fluctuates?

3 What is the real interest rate?

4 Describe how the real interest rate has changed since 1975.

5 Explain how investment is financed.

6 What determines investment?

7 Why does a fall in the real interest rate increase investment?

8 How is investment influenced by the expected rate of profit?

9 What is the investment demand curve, what brings a movement along the investment demand curve, and what makes it shift?

10 List the main influences on consumption expenditure.

11 What is the consumption demand curve?

12 What is the saving supply curve, what brings a movement along the savings supply curve, and what makes a shift?

13 Why does a rise in the real interest rate increase saving?

14 What is the relationship between the saving supply curve and the consumption demand curve?

15 How do consumption demand and saving supply change when disposable income changes?

16 What are the marginal propensity to consume and the marginal propensity to save? Why are they less than 1 and why do they sum to 1?

17 What happens to the consumption demand curve and the saving supply curve when expected future incomes or the purchasing power of assets increases?

18 Explain how the real interest rate is determined.

19 How are net exports determined?

20 What happens to the real interest rate, investment, and private saving if government deficits around the world increase?

Problems

1 A cellular telephone assembly plant can be built for £10 million and it will have a life of one year. The firm will have to hire labour at a cost of £3 million and buy parts and fuel at a cost of a further £3 million. If the firm builds the plant, it will be able to produce cellular telephones that will sell for £17 million. Does it pay the firm to invest in this new production line at the following real interest rates:

a 5 per cent a year?
b 10 per cent a year?
c 15 per cent a year?

2 Suppose the phone producer in Problem 1 expects its total revenue to increase to £17.5 million with unchanged costs. What, in this situation, is the highest real interest rate at which it will undertake the investment? How does the firm's investment demand curve change as a result of the firm's expected profit rate increasing?

3 In 1997, the Batman family (Batman and Robin) had a disposable income of £50,000, net assets of £100,000, and an expected future income of £50,000 a year. At an interest rate of 4 per cent a year, the Batmans would save £10,000. At an interest rate of 6 per cent a year, they would save £12,500. And at an interest rate of 8 per cent a year, they would save £15,000.

a Draw a graph of the Batman family's saving supply curve for 1997.
b In 1998, everything remained the same as the year before except that the Batmans expected their future income to rise to £60,000 a year. Show the influence of this change on the Batman family's saving supply curve.
c In 1999, everything remained the same as the year before except that the Batmans disposable income increased to the £60,000 a year they expected it would the year before. The Batmans now expect their income to remain at £60,000 a year. Show the influence of this change on the Batman family's saving supply curve.
d In 2000, the stock market boomed and the Batman's assets increased by 50 per cent. Show the influence of this change on the Batman family's saving supply curve.

4 You are given the following information about a household:

Household Consumption and Saving in 1998

	Real interest rate (per cent per year)	Consumption expenditure	Saving	Disposable income
		(thousands of pounds a year)		
a	4	80	20	100
b	6	75	25	100
c	8	60	40	100

Household Consumption and Saving in 1999

	Real interest rate (per cent per year)	Consumption expenditure	Saving	Disposable income
		(thousands of pounds a year)		
a	4	88.0	22.0	110
b	6	82.5	27.5	110
c	8	66.0	44.0	110

a Draw a graph of the household's consumption demand curve and saving supply curve for 1998 and 1999.
b Calculate the household's marginal propensity to consume.
c Calculate its marginal propensity to save.

5 The year is 3050 and the economy of Alpha Centura, still isolated from all other planets, has the following consumption demand and investment demand schedules:

	Real interest rate (per cent per year)	Investment	Consumption expenditure
		(trillions of 3050 zips)	
a	4	7	28
b	5	6	24
c	6	5	20
d	7	4	16
e	8	3	12

The Alpha Centurans have a balanced government budget rule that works and government purchases are 10 trillion 3050 zips. Potential GDP on Alpha Centura is 30 trillion 3050 zips.

a What is the equilibrium real interest rate?
b What is the equilibrium level of investment?
c What is the equilibrium level of consumption expenditure?
d Find the level of saving on Alpha Centura at each interest rate shown in the table.

6 Alpha Centura and Earth discover each other and begin to pursue intergalactic economic activity. The real interest rate on Earth is 6 per cent a year. On Alpha Centura, it is the number you have calculated for Problem 5.

a Which planet borrows from the other?
b Do consumption and saving on Alpha Centura increase or decrease?
c Do consumption and saving on Earth increase or decrease?

7 Study *Reading Between the Lines* on pp. 800–801 and then answer the following questions:

a Why does interest rate policy in the US have an effect on interest rates around the world?
b Why would a recovery in the eurozone countries increase the correlation between US long-term interest rates and euro long-term interest rates?
c Why would a recovery in the eurozone countries lead to a rise in euro long-term interest rates?

8 Use the link on the Parkin, Powell and Matthews Web site to obtain data on government budget deficits from the latest *World Economic Outlook* published by the International Monetary Fund.

a What are the trends in these deficits? Are they the same as or different from those in Figure 26.4 on p. 636?
b What influence do you expect these deficits to have on the real interest rate and investment next year?

W http://www.econ100.com

World Real Interest Rates

Financial Times, 2 July 1999

US and euro-zone strengthen their bonds

Arkady Ostrovsky

Many economists were astonished in late May at the reaction of the European bond markets to the decision by the US Federal Reserve to change its interest rate "bias" towards tightening to avoid a rise in inflation.

Although US interest rates have a strong bearing on fixed income valuations elsewhere in the world, there was nothing, it seemed, in the underlying economies that could explain such strong correlation.

"Basically there is no reason for the high correlation between US and European bond yields. The cyclical position of the world's two largest economies is very different, and so is the inflation outlook," one economist insisted at the time.

This week's decision by the Fed to raise US interest rates by 25 basis points and change its bias back to neutral prompted a similar shadow movement on the part of euro-zone bond prices.

Economists say euro-zone economic growth is picking up and the correlation between US treasuries and euro-zone bonds is likely to strengthen. "If the euro-zone continues to show signs of recovery, we may move towards global synchronised growth, which will increase the correlation between US and European bond markets," says Danyelle Guyatt at Deutsche Bank.

"Demand momentum [in the euro-zone] is building at the same time that the global economy is recovering," says J.P. Morgan in a report. Analysts say the euro's weakness, cursed by politicians, is providing a strong stimulus for economic growth in Europe by stimulating exports.

As signs of economic recovery emerged, euro-zone bond prices have fallen sharply, underperforming US treasuries with the yield spread in the 10-year sector narrowing to 140 points.

The 10-year German bund, the benchmark for the euro-zone, is already yielding 4.5 per cent compared with 3.7 per cent six months ago. Observers say as inflationary expectations begin to build up, investors will demand a higher premium, and the German 10-year bund yield could be heading towards 5 per cent.

The Essence of the Story

- There is a strong correlation between US long-term interest rates and European long-term interest rates.
- European long-term interest rates reacted to the move by the Federal Reserve to raise interest rates in June 1999.
- Economic recovery in the eurozone economies would increase the correlation between US long-term interest rates and euro long-term interest rates.
- A recovery in Europe with a recovery in the global economy will put upward pressure on long-term interest rates.
- A recovery in Europe will also lead to a rise in long-term inflation expectations and long-term euro interest rates will rise reflecting a higher inflation premium.

Economic Analysis

■ The quote by an economist in the article reveals some bad economics. The cyclical position and the inflation outlook for Europe and the USA may be quite different but long-term interest rates reflect long-term concerns of inflation and growth, not short-term differences.

■ The world real rate of interest is determined by world investment demand and world supply of saving. The USA and EU are the two largest economies on the world stage. An increase in investment demand by both of these economies will result in a rise in the world real rate of interest. Figure 1 shows the world investment demand schedule ID_0 shifting to ID_1 and the long-term real rate of interest rising from r_0 to r_1.

■ The rise in the US short-term rate of interest is an attempt to forestall the potential inflation when aggregate demand is higher than potential GDP. Inflation will result and in the absence of a deflationary response by the Fed and the ECB, expectations, of long-term inflation could increase.

■ An economic recovery in the eurozone coupled with an already booming US economy could see inflation rising in the two largest economies in the world. A rise in expected long-term inflation, would also raise the long-term rate of interest. Figure 2 shows the US and German 10-year bonds. While at times the difference between them increases they basically move together.

■ The rise in long-term interest rates could be the result of either a rise in the long-term real rate of interest, a rise in the long-term expected rate of inflation or both.

■ Figure 3 shows the 10-year moving average of growth in the EU and the US and the 10-year moving average of inflation rates for both economies. What is remarkable is the convergence in the trend in inflation and how close the growth rates trends mirror each other.

■ The growth trends of both economies will reflect the trend in world investment demand. The inflation pattern will reflect world inflation expectation. In both cases, long-term interest rates in the EU will be closely correlated with long-term interest rates in the USA.

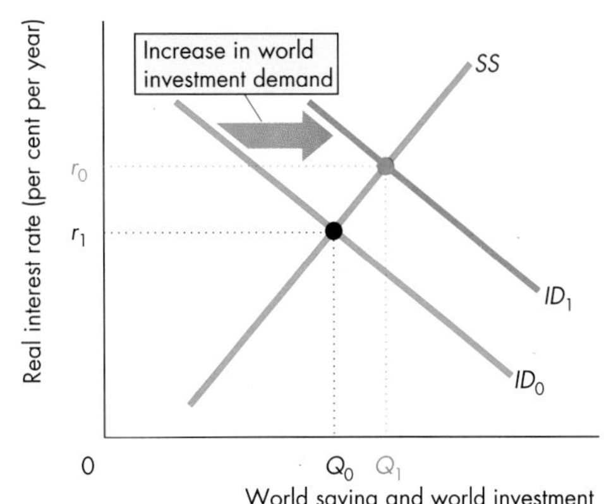

Figure 1 World capital market

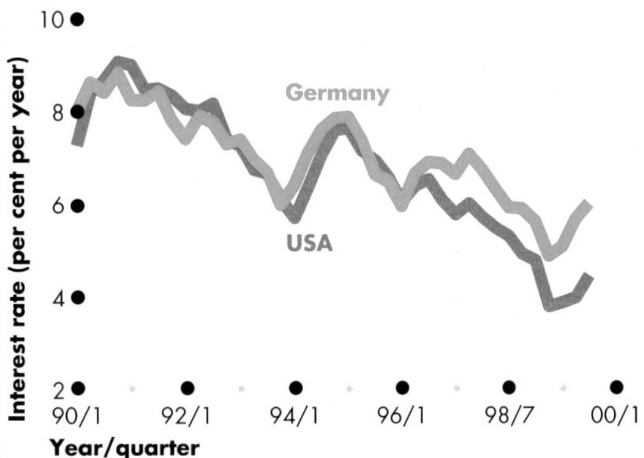

Figure 2 US and German 10-year bond rate

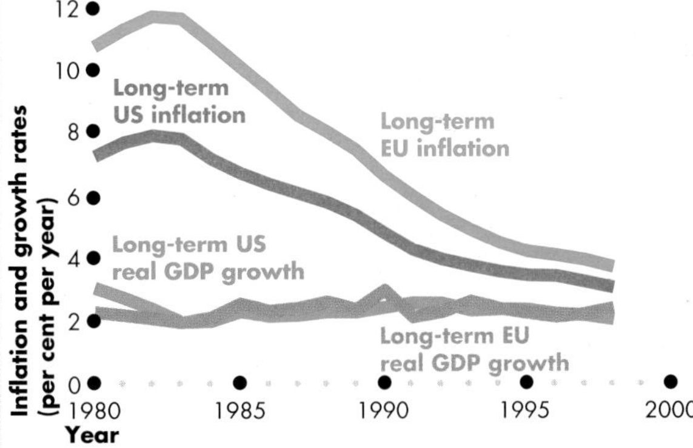

Figure 3 EU and US long-term inflation and growth rates

CHAPTER 32

Long-Term Economic Growth

After studying this chapter you will be able to:

- Describe the long-term growth trends in the United Kingdom and other countries and regions
- Identify the main sources of long-term real GDP growth
- Explain the productivity growth slowdown during the 1970s and recovery in the 1980s
- Explain the rapid economic growth rates that have been achieved in East Asia
- Explain the theories of economic growth
- Describe the policies that might be used to speed up economic growth

Economic Miracles

Real GDP per person in the United Kingdom has more than doubled between 1960 and 1997. If you stay in a university residence, the chances are that it was built during the 1960s and equipped with two power points, one for a desk lamp and one for a bedside lamp. Today, with the help of a multi-plug (or two), your room bulges with a television and VCR, CD player, electric kettle and computer – the list goes on – which were not contemplated in the 1960s when the residence was built. What has brought about this growth in productivity and incomes? ◆ Although our economy expands, its growth is uneven. In some periods, such as the 1960s, growth is rapid. In other periods, such as the 1970s and early 1980s, growth slows down. What makes our long-term growth rate vary? What can be done to prevent growth from slowing down? And what can be done to speed up economic growth? ◆ We can see even greater extremes of economic growth if we look at modern Asia. On the banks of the Li River in southern China, Songman Yang breeds cormorants, amazing birds that he trains to fish and to deliver their catch to a basket on his simple bamboo raft. Songman's work, the capital equipment and technology he uses, and the income he earns are similar to those of his ancestors going back some 2,000 years. Yet all around Songman, in China's bustling towns and cities, people are participating in an economic miracle. They are creating businesses, investing in new technologies, developing both local and global markets, and experiencing income growth of more than 6 per cent a year. Similar rapid economic growth is taking place in other economies in Asia such as Hong Kong, South Korea, Singapore and Taiwan. In all these countries, real GDP has doubled *three times* – an eightfold increase – between 1960 and 1996. Why have incomes in these Asian economies grown so rapidly? What makes an economic miracle? In recent years growth in East Asia has slowed. In some countries real GDP has fallen as a result of the financial crisis in the Far East. Is this the end of the miracle or is it a temporary fall back that will be reversed in the coming years?

◆ ◆ ◆ ◆ In this chapter we study long-term economic growth. We begin by looking more closely at the facts about long-term economic growth in the United Kingdom and other parts of the world. We then discover what makes real GDP grow, why some countries grow faster than others and why the long-term growth rate sometimes slows down. We'll also look at ways of achieving faster economic growth.

Long-term Growth Trends

The long-term growth trends that we study in this chapter are the trends in *potential GDP*. But potential GDP growth has two components, population growth and growth in potential GDP per person. It is the growth of potential GDP per person that brings rising living standards. And it is changes in the growth of potential GDP per person that are the main causes for concern about economic growth. Let's look at the growth of real GDP per person.

Growth in the UK Economy

Figure 32.1 shows real GDP per person in the United Kingdom for the 143 years from 1855 to 1998. The average growth rate over this entire period is 1.3 per cent a year. But the long-term growth rate has varied. For example, the long-term growth rate slowed during the 1970s to 1.8 per cent a year, down from 2.4 per cent a year during the 1960s. But growth picked up again in the 1980s and 90s to 2.3 per cent a year.

You can see the recent productivity growth slowdown in a longer perspective in Figure 32.1, and you can see that it is not unique. The interwar period and the early years of the 1900s had even slower growth than we have today.

In the middle of the graph are two extraordinary events: the two recessions of the interwar period and World War II in the 1940s. The recession in the interwar period and the bulge during the war obscure changes in the long-term growth trend that might have occurred within these years. But between 1919 and 1953, averaging out the depression and the war, the long-term growth rate was 1.2 per cent a year.

A major goal of this chapter is to explain why our economy grows and why the long-term growth rate varies. A related goal is to explain variations in the economic growth rate across countries. Let's look at some facts about these variations.

Real GDP Growth in the World Economy

Figure 32.2 shows real GDP growth in the largest economies in the world since 1960. The data shown in this figure are from the Penn World Tables and are measured in a common currency (1985 US

Figure 32.1 A Hundred and Forty-four Years of Economic Growth in the United Kingdom

During the 144 years from 1855 to 1998, long-run real GDP per person in the United Kingdom grew by 1.3 per cent a year, on the average. The growth rate was above average during the 1950s, 1960s, 1980s and 1990s. It was below average in the 1900s, the interwar period and 1973–1979.

Source: Charles Feinstein, *National Income Expenditure and Output of the United Kingdom 1855–1965*, Cambridge, Cambridge University Press, 1972; ONS.

Figure 32.2 Economic Growth Around the World: Catch-up or Not?

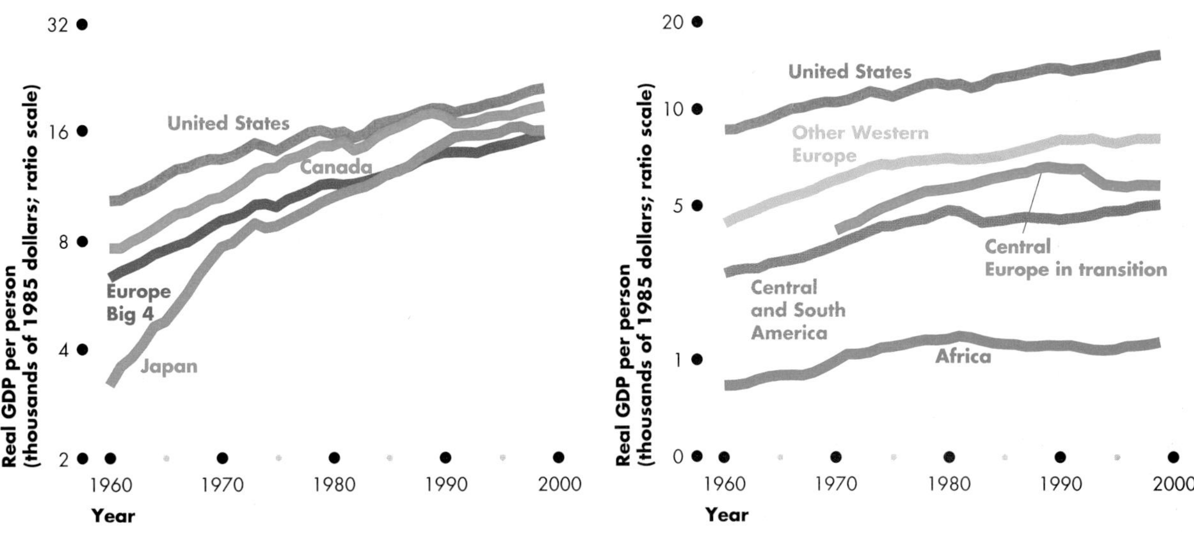

Real GDP per person has grown throughout the world economy. Among the rich industrial countries (part a), real GDP growth has been faster in low-income countries and income levels have converged. The most spectacular growth was in Japan during the 1960s. But Canada and the big four West European countries (the United Kingdom, France, Germany and Italy) have got closer to the United States income level.

Among a wider range of countries (part b), there is less sign of convergance. The gaps between the income levels of the United States, West European countries, Central and Eastern Europe, Central and South America, and Africa have remained remarkably constant.

Sources: Robert Summers and Alan Heston, http://datacentre.chass.utoronto.ca/ 'The Penn World Table (Mark 5): An Expanded Set of International Comparisons, 1950–1988', *Quarterly Journal of Economics*, May 1991, 327–368.

dollars). Part (a) looks at the richest countries. The United States has the highest real GDP per person and Canada has the second highest. But up to 1989, Canada grew faster than the United States and so was catching up.

Until 1985, the third richest countries were France, Germany, Italy and the United Kingdom. They are shown in the figure as Europe Big 4. But in 1985, the fastest growing rich country, Japan, caught up with Europe Big 4. All the countries shown in Figure 32.2(a) are catching up with the United States. Japan has caught up most, Canada has got closest and Europe Big 4 has caught up least.

Not all countries are growing faster than and catching up with the United States. Figure 32.2(b) looks at some of these. The economies of Africa and Central and South America were stagnating, not growing, during the 1980s. As a result, the gap between them and the United States widened. Western Europe other than the Big 4 grew during the 1970s and 1980s but at a rate that was roughly equal to that of the United States. So the gap remained constant. The former communist countries of Central Europe grew faster than the United States until the late 1980s and then stagnated.

The data used in Figure 32.2 are not available beyond 1992. But other data from the IMF (not shown) suggest that after 1992 real GDP per person shrank in some of the countries of Central Europe as they went through a process of traumatic political change. Also growth in Japan has stagnated as a result of its banking crisis.

Taking both parts of Figure 32.2 together, we can see that the catch-up in real GDP per person that is

Figure 32.3 Catch-up in Asia

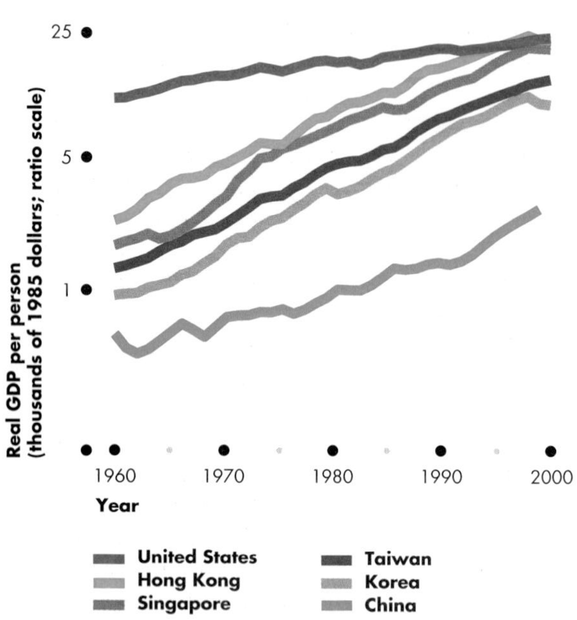

The clearest examples of catch-up have occurred in five economies in Asia. Starting out in 1960 with incomes as little as one-tenth of that in the United States, four Asian economies (Hong Kong, South Korea, Singapore and Taiwan) have substantially narrowed the gap on the United States. And from being a very poor developing country in 1960, China has caught up with the income level that Hong Kong had in 1960 and is growing at a rate that is enabling it to continue catching up with the United States.

Source: Robert Summers and Alan Heston, http://datacentre.chass.utoronto.ca/ to update The Penn World Table (Mark 5): An Expanded Set of International Comparisons, 1950–1988, *Quarterly Journal of Economics*, May 1991, 327–368.

visible in part (a) is not a global phenomenon. Some rich countries are catching up with the United States but the gaps between the United States and many poor countries are not closing.

There is another group of countries that in 1960 had low levels of real GDP per person and that are catching up with the United States and the other Western economies in a dramatic way. These are the economies of Hong Kong, South Korea, Singapore and Taiwan. Figure 32.3 shows how these economies are catching up with the United States. The figure also shows Asia's giant economy, China which is also catching up, but from a long way behind. In 1960 China's real GDP per person was 8 per cent of the United Kingdom's and 6 per cent of the United States's, but by 1992 it was 12 per cent of the United Kingdom's and 8 per cent of the United States's.

The four small Asian countries shown in Figure 32.3 are like fast trains running on the same track at similar speeds and with a roughly constant gap between them. Hong Kong is the lead train and runs about 12 years in front of Korea, which is the last train. Real GDP per person in Korea was similar to that of Hong Kong in 1978. In the 30 years between 1960 and 1990 Hong Kong transformed itself from a poor developing country into one of the world's richest countries.

The countries of East Asia have been badly affected by the financial crisis that broke out in 1997. Growth in the fastest growing economies has slowed and in 1997 output fell in a number of countries. It is difficult to predict how long the growth slowdown will last and when the countries of East Asia will revert to the fast pace of growth witnessed during the past decade.

Review

- Over the 140 years between 1855 and 1998, long-run real GDP per person in the United Kingdom grew at an average rate of 1.3 per cent a year. Slow growth occurred during the early 1900s and the interwar period, and rapid growth occurred in the 1960s and more recently in the 1980s and 1990s.
- Some countries are catching up with the developed economies, but the gaps between the rich and many poor countries are not closing.
- The economies that are catching up with the Western developed economies are Hong Kong, South Korea, Singapore, Taiwan and China. Some of these countries have seen their growth slow and in some cases their real GDP fall in recent years.

We've described some facts about economic growth in the developed economies and around the world. Our next task is to study the causes of economic growth. Economic growth is a complex process and its causes are difficult to discover. We'll study the causes of economic growth in three stages. First, we'll describe the sources of growth. Second, we'll study 'growth accounting', which is an attempt to measure the quantitative importance of the sources of growth. Third, we'll study the theories of economic growth that explain how the sources of growth interact to determine the growth rate.

The Sources of Economic Growth

Most human societies have lived for centuries and even thousands of years, with no economic growth. The key reason is that they have lacked some fundamental social institutions and arrangements that are essential preconditions for economic growth. Let's see what these preconditions are.

Preconditions for Economic Growth

The most basic precondition for economic growth is an appropriate *incentive* system. Three institutions are crucial to the creation of incentives. They are:

1 Markets.
2 Property rights.
3 Monetary exchange.

Markets enable buyers and sellers to get information and to do business with each other, and market prices send signals to buyers and sellers that create *incentives* to increase or decrease the quantities demanded and supplied. Markets enable people to specialize and trade and to save and invest. But to work well, markets need property rights and monetary exchange.

Property rights are the social arrangements that govern the ownership, use and disposal of factors of production and goods and services. They include the right to physical property (land, buildings and capital equipment), to financial property (claims by one person against another) and to intellectual property (such as inventions). Clearly established and enforced property rights give people an assurance that the income they earn and their savings will not be confiscated by a capricious government.

Monetary exchange facilitates transactions of all kinds, including the orderly transfer of private property from one person to another. Property rights and monetary exchange create incentives for people to specialize and trade, to save and invest, and to discover new technologies.

There is no unique political system that is necessary to deliver the preconditions for economic growth. Liberal democracy, founded on the fundamental principle of the rule of law, is the system that does the best job. It provides a solid base on which property rights can be established and enforced. But authoritarian political systems have sometimes provided an environment in which economic growth has occurred.

Early human societies, based on hunting and gathering, did not experience economic growth because they lacked the preconditions we've just described. Economic growth began when societies evolved these institutions. The presence of an incentive system and the institutions that create it do not guarantee that economic growth will occur. They permit it but do not make it inevitable.

The simplest way in which growth happens when the appropriate incentive system exists is that people begin to specialize in the activities at which they have a comparative advantage and trade with each other. You saw in Chapter 3, pp. 56–58, how everyone can gain from such activity. By specializing and trading, everyone can acquire goods and services at the lowest possible cost. Equivalently, everyone can obtain a greater volume of goods and services from their labour.

As an economy moves from one with little specialization to one that is highly specialized, it grows. Real GDP per person increases and the standard of living rises. But once the economy is highly specialized, this source of economic growth runs its course.

For growth to continue, people must face incentives that encourage them to pursue three activities that generate ongoing economic growth. These activities are:

1 Saving and investment in new capital.
2 Investment in human capital.
3 Discovery of new technologies.

These three sources of growth, which interact with each other, are the primary sources of the extraordinary growth in productivity during the past 200 years. Let's look at each in turn.

Saving and Investment in New Capital

Saving and investment in new capital increase the amount of capital per worker and increase human productivity. Human productivity took the most dramatic upturn when the amount of capital per worker increased during the Industrial Revolution. Production processes that use hand tools can create beautiful objects, but production methods that use large amounts of capital per worker, such as car plant assembly lines, are much more productive.

The accumulation of capital on farms, in textiles factories, in iron foundries and steel mills, in coal mines, on building sites, in chemical plants, in car plants, in banks and insurance companies, and in retail stores, have added incredibly to the productivity of our economy. From your knowledge of life 100 years ago try to imagine how productive you would be in such circumstances compared with your productivity today.

Investment in Human Capital

Human capital is fundamental to the growth process. The basic human skills of reading, writing and mathematics as well as knowledge of physical forces and chemical and biological processes are the foundation of all technological change.

But much human capital, which is extremely productive, is much more humble. It takes the form of millions of individuals learning and repetitively doing simple production tasks and becoming remarkably more productive in the task. One carefully studied example illustrates this kind of human capital. Between 1941 and 1944 (during World War II), US shipyards produced some 2,500 units of a cargo ship, called the Liberty Ship, to a standardized design. In 1941, it took 1.2 million person hours to build a ship. By 1942, it took 600,000, and by 1943, it took only 500,000. Thousands of workers and managers learned from experience and accumulated human capital that more than doubled their productivity in two years.

Discovery of New Technologies

People are many times more productive today than they were 100 years ago, not because we have more steam engines per person and more horse-drawn carriages per person, but because we have engines and transport equipment that use technologies unknown 100 years ago, which are more productive than those old technologies were. Technological change makes an enormous contribution to our increased productivity. It arises from formal research and development programmes and from informal trial and error, and it involves discovering ways of getting more out of our resources.

To reap the benefits of technological change, capital must increase. Some of the most powerful and far-reaching fundamental technologies are embodied in human capital – for example, language, writing and mathematics. But most technologies are embodied in physical capital. For example, to reap the benefits of the internal combustion engine, millions of horse-drawn carriages and horses had to be replaced by cars; and, more recently, to reap the benefits of computerized word processing, millions of typewriters had to be replaced by PCs.

Review

- Economic growth cannot occur without institutional capital that creates incentives to specialize and exchange, save and invest, and develop new technologies.
- The most significant sources of economic growth are saving and investment in new capital, the growth of human capital and the discovery of new technologies. These sources interact: human capital creates new technologies, which are embodied in both human and physical capital.

We've described the sources of economic growth. Let's now see how we can begin to quantify their contributions by studying growth accounting.

Growth Accounting

Real GDP grows because the quantities of labour and capital grow and because technology advances. The purpose of **growth accounting** is to calculate how much real GDP growth has resulted from growth of labour and capital and how much is attributable to technological change.

The first task of growth accounting is to define productivity. **Productivity** is real GDP per hour

Figure 32.4 Real GDP per Hour of Work

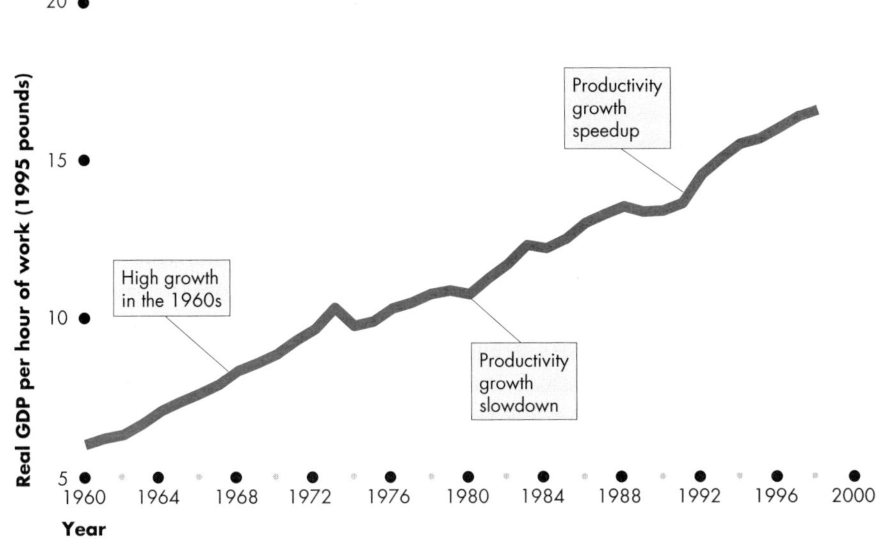

Real GDP divided by aggregate hours equals real GDP per hour of work, which is a broad measure of productivity. During the 1960s, the productivity growth rate was high. It slowed during the 1970s and speeded up again during the 1990s.

Sources: ONS, Labour Force Survey; R.C.O. Matthews, C.H. Feinstein and J.C. Odling-Smee, *British Economic Growth 1856–1953*, 1982, Oxford, Clarendon Press.

of work. It is calculated by dividing real GDP by aggregate labour hours. (Chapter 22, pp. 534–539, explains how real GDP is measured and Chapter 23, pp. 557–558, explains how aggregate hours are measured.) We are interested in productivity because it determines how much income an hour of labour can earn. Figure 32.4 shows productivity for the period 1960–98. In the 1960s productivity growth was 4.2 per cent a year. Between 1973 and 1979 it fell to 0.8 per cent per year. Productivity growth picked up again in the 1980s to 2.1 per cent and again to 2.4 per cent in the 1990s.

The second (and main) task of growth accounting is to explain the fluctuations in productivity. Growth accounting answers this question by dividing the growth in productivity into two components and then measuring the contribution of each. The components are:

1 Growth in capital per hour of work.
2 Technological change.

The technological-change includes everything that contributes to productivity growth. In particular, it includes human capital. Human capital growth and technological change are intimately interrelated. Technology advances because knowledge improves and knowledge is part of human capital.

The analytical engine of growth accounting is a relationship called the productivity function. Let's learn about this relationship and see how it is used.

The Productivity Function

The **productivity function** is the relationship that shows how real GDP per hour of work changes as the amount of capital per hour of work changes with no change in technology. Figure 32.5 illustrates the productivity function. Capital per hour of work is measured on the x-axis and real GDP per hour of work is measured on the y-axis. The figure shows two productivity functions as the curves labelled PF_0 and PF_1.

An increase in the amount of capital per hour of work results in an increase in real GDP per hour of work, which is shown by a movement along a productivity function. For example, on the curve labelled PF_0, when capital per hour of work is £20, real GDP per hour of work is £5. As capital per hour of work increases to £40, real GDP per hour of work increases to £7.

Technological change increases the amount of GDP per hour of work that can be produced by a given amount of capital per hour of work. It is shown by an upward shift of the productivity function. For example, if capital per hour of work is £20 and a

Figure 32.5 How Productivity Grows

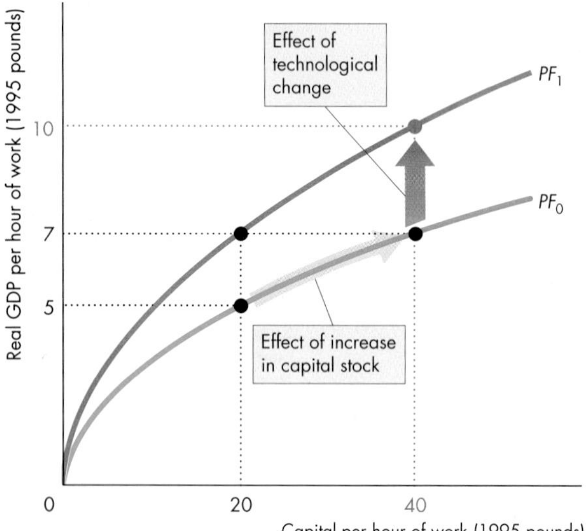

Productivity can be measured by real GDP per hour of work. Productivity can grow for two reasons: (1) capital per hour of work increases, and (2) technological advances occur. The productivity function, *PF*, shows the effects of an increase in capital per hour of work on productivity. Here, when capital per hour of work increases from £20 to £40, real GDP per hour of work increases from £5 to £7 along the productivity curve PF_0. Technological advance shifts the productivity curve upward. Here, an advance in technology shifts the productivity curve from PF_0 to PF_1. With this technological advance, real GDP per hour of work increases from £7 to £10 when there is £40 of capital per hour of work.

technological change increases real GDP per hour of work from £5 to £7, the productivity function shifts upward from PF_0 to PF_1 in Figure 32.5. Similarly, if capital per hour of work is £40, the same technological change increases real GDP per hour of work from £7 to £10 and shifts the productivity function upward from PF_0 to PF_1.

To calculate the contributions of capital growth and technological change to productivity growth, we need to know the shape and slope of the productivity function. The shape of the productivity function reflects a fundamental economic law – the law of diminishing returns. The **law of diminishing returns** states that as the quantity of one input increases with the quantities of all other inputs remaining the same, output increases but by ever smaller increments. You examined this phenomenon in Chapter 11. For example, two typists working with one computer type fewer than twice as many pages per day as one typist working with one computer.

Applied to capital, the law of diminishing returns states that if a given number of hours of work use more capital (with the same technology), the additional output that results from the additional capital gets smaller as the amount of capital increases. One typist working with two computers types fewer than twice as many pages per day as one typist working with one computer. More generally, one hour of work working with £40 of capital produces less than twice the output of one hour of work working with £20 of capital. But how much less? The answer is given by the 'one-third rule'.

The One-third Rule On the average, across all types of work, a 1 per cent increase in capital per hour of work, with no change in technology, brings a *one-third of 1 per cent* increase in output per hour of work. In the aggregate a 1 per cent increase in capital per hour of work, with no change in technology, brings a *one-third of 1 per cent* increase in real GDP per hour of work.

This one-third rule, which was first discovered by Robert Solow of the Massachusetts Institute of Technology (MIT), can be used to calculate the contributions of an increase in capital per hour of work and technological change to the growth of real GDP. Let's do such a calculation. Suppose that capital per hour of work grows by 3 per cent a year and real GDP grows by 2.5 per cent a year. The one-third rule tells us that capital growth has contributed one-third of 3 per cent, which is 1 per cent. The rest of the 2.5 per cent growth of real GDP comes from technological change. That is, technological change has contributed 1.5 per cent, which is the 2.5 per cent growth of real GDP minus the estimated 1 per cent contribution of capital growth.

Why the One-third Rule Why is the one-third rule used to separate contributions of capital growth and technological change to productivity growth? How do we know that one-third is the correct proportion? The answer is that we don't know for sure, but there is one strong piece of evidence pointing to one-third being the correct proportion. This evidence is the share of real GDP received by capital and labour.

A fundamental principle of economics is that factors of production receive incomes in proportion to their contributions to production. On the average, capital receives one-third of real GDP and labour receives two-thirds. (In 1997, for example, UK GDP was £677 billion and capital income was £250 billion[1], nearly one-third of GDP.) If the factors of production are rewarded in proportion to their contributions, then a 1 per cent increase in capital brings a one-third of 1 per cent increase in real GDP. The one-third rule is based on historical experience. It is an average and not a hard and precise fixed number.

Accounting for the Productivity Growth Slowdown and Speedup

We can use the productivity function and the one-third rule to study the reasons for the slowdown and subsequent speedup of productivity growth in the United Kingdom. Figure 32.6 shows you what has been happening.

1950 to 1973 In 1950 capital per hour of work (measured in 1995 prices) was £13.70. Real GDP per hour of work was £5.50 at the point marked 50 on PF_0 in Figure 32.6. Over the next 23 years capital per hour grew at about 2.2 per cent a year to £22.69 and GDP per hour increased at about 2.8 per cent a year to £10.32. With no change in technology, the economy would have moved to point *a* at £6.70 (one-third of the percentage increase in capital per hour) on PF_0. But rapid technological change increased productivity and shifted the productivity function upward from PF_0 to PF_1. And the economy moved to the point marked 73.

1973 to 1979 The story continues between 1973 and 1979 when capital per hour of work increased from £22.69 in 1973 to £24.22 in 1979. This is an increase of 6.7 per cent. Real GDP per hour of work increased by 54 pence to £10.86, from £10.32 in 1973, which is a 5.2 per cent increase. This increase is slightly more than two-thirds of 6.7 per cent, so technological change made a less significant contribution to real GDP growth during this period

Figure 32.6 Growth Accounting and the Productivity Growth Slowdown

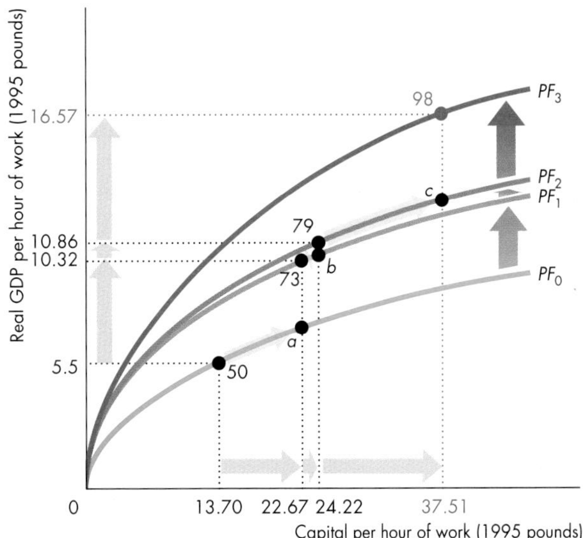

Between 1950 and 1973, which was a period of rapid growth in potential GDP, capital per hour of work increased from £13.70 to £22.69, and technological progress shifted the productivity function upward from PF_0 to PF_1. Between 1973 and 1979, when potential GDP grew slowly, capital per hour of work increased from £22.69 to £24.22 but the productivity function shifted slightly to PF_2. The technological change that occurred was absorbed by the negative effects of oil price shocks, change in the composition of output and X-inefficiency. Between 1979 and 1994, capital per hour of work increased from £24.22 to £37.51, and technological progress shifted the productivity function upward from PF_2 to PF_3. Although the growth in potential GDP was not as rapid as in the 1960s, the productivity growth rate did increase.

Sources: Figures derived from R.C.O. Matthews, C.H. Feinstein and J.C. Odling-Smee, *British Economic Growth 1856–1953*, 1982, Oxford, Clarendon Press; and A. Maddison, *Dynamic Forces in Capitalist Development*, 1991, Oxford, Oxford University Press; ONS, and the author's calculations.

and the productivity function barely shifted from PF_1 to PF_2.

The reason for the productivity growth slowdown has now been isolated. It was not the result of slower growth in capital per hour of work. Rather it occurred because the contribution of technological change to real GDP growth dried up.

1 In current accounting practices, £250 is an overestimate as it includes the income from self-employment, which cannot easily be separated into labour and capital income.

1979 to 1998 Between 1979 and 1998 technological change shifted the productivity function upward from PF_2 to PF_3. While real GDP per hour increased from £10.86 in 1979 to £16.57 in 1998 – a 52.5 per cent increase. Capital per hour of work increased from £24.22 to £37.51 – a 55 per cent increase in total. Using the one-third rule, the increase in capital per hour of work generated an extra real GDP per hour of work of roughly 18 per cent. Technological change contributed the remaining 37 per cent – roughly 1.7 per cent per year. Thus technological change resumed its contribution to productivity growth but at a slower pace than during the 1960s.

Technological Change During the Productivity Growth Slowdown

Technological change itself did not stop. On the contrary, there was a lot of it. But the technological change that occurred did not increase productivity. Instead, it offset negative shocks to productivity. We'll look at these negative factors below. We've seen that during the productivity growth slowdown of the 1970s, the contribution of technological change dried up. But why? Three factors have been identified as being responsible. They are:

1 Energy price shocks.
2 Changes in the composition of output.
3 X-inefficiency.

Energy Price Shocks The price of oil quadrupled during 1973–74 and quickly on the tail of this increase, the prices of coal and natural gas – substitutes for oil – also increased dramatically. Energy prices increased sharply again in 1979–80.

The immediate effect of higher energy prices was an increase in the rate at which fuel-intensive cars, aircraft and heating systems were scrapped. But this effect shows up in Figure 32.6 as a leftward movement along the productivity function as capital per hour of work decreased. A longer drawn out effect was the development of new energy-saving technologies. Research and development efforts concentrated on developing new types of automobile and aircraft engines, heating furnaces and industrial processes that used fuel more sparingly than their predecessors. As a result, despite a huge amount of technological change and investment in new technologies, productivity did not increase. The new technologies produced a given amount of real GDP with a much smaller amount of fuel, but not with a smaller amount of capital per hour of work. So the productivity function did not shift upward.

Changes in the Composition of Output During the 1950s and 1960s, a lot of our growth came from a movement of resources out of the farm sector into the small business sector. Farm productivity grows less quickly than small business productivity, so as resources move, average productivity grows quickly. During the 1970s and 1980s, the main movement of resources was out of manufacturing into services. Productivity growth in services is less than in manufacturing, so average productivity growth slowed. In the growth accounting exercise, this type of change shows up as a slowdown in aggregate productivity growth.

X-inefficiency During the 1970s, trade union membership as a proportion of the employed labour force increased from 45 per cent to 59 per cent. The growth in union membership brought with it an increase in restrictive practices, overmanning and an increase in strikes. The period of the 1970s is characterized as one of X-inefficiency that contributed to the increasing productivity gap between the United Kingdom and other developed economies.

Review

- Growth accounting separates out the contributions to economic growth of the growth of aggregate hours, of capital per hour and of technological change.
- The key to growth accounting is the one-third rule – the rule that a 1 per cent increase in capital per hour of work brings a one-third of 1 per cent increase in real GDP per hour of work.
- Growth accounting isolates the reason for the productivity growth slowdown. Technological change made no contribution to GDP growth between 1973 and 1979.

Growth Theory

We've seen that real GDP grows when aggregate hours of work grow, when the quantity of capital per hour of work grows and when improvements in technology (including additions to human capital) bring increases in productivity. But what is the *cause* of economic growth and what is the *effect*?

The causes of economic growth are hard to unravel because so many factors interact with each other. Population growth might create pressures on land use which result in advances in plant biology which increase crop yields, and advances in architecture and building technology which increase building heights. Here, population growth causes technological change, which in turn causes saving and investment, which in turn brings economic growth. Alternatively, a surplus of saving might lower interest rates and bring an increase in the pace of investment in human capital and physical capital which speed up the growth rate. Here, saving and investment have caused economic growth. A lucky break might bring an unlooked-for and unexpected technological advance which increases the productivity of labour and capital and causes a burst of saving and investment and rapid economic growth. Each of these possible sources of growth can operate. We must also examine the reasons why a country's long-term growth rate sometimes speeds up and sometimes slows.

We are going to look at three main theories of economic growth. All three contain some fundamental insights into the process of economic growth. But none gives a firm and sure answer to the basic question: what causes growth and makes growth rates vary? The three theories are:

1 Classical growth theory.
2 Neoclassical growth theory.
3 New growth theory.

Classical Growth Theory

Classical growth theory is a theory of economic growth based on the view that population growth is determined by the level of income per person. This theory was suggested by Adam Smith, Thomas Robert Malthus and David Ricardo, the leading economists of the late eighteenth century and early nineteenth century (see *Economics in History*, pp. 826–827).

To understand classical growth theory let's transport ourselves back to the world of 1710. Many of the 5.3 million people who lived in England at this time worked on farms or on their own land and performed their tasks using simple tools and animal power. They earned about 1 shilling and 4 pence for working a 10-hour day. Then advances in farming technology brought new types of ploughs and seeds that increased farm productivity. As farm productivity increased, farm production rose and some farm workers moved from the land to the cities, where they get work producing and selling the expanding range of farm equipment. Incomes rose and the people seemed to be prospering. But would the prosperity last? Classical growth theory says it would not.

Figure 32.7 illustrates classical growth theory and explains why it reaches a pessimistic conclusion. Before growth begins, the economy is in the situation shown in part (a). The labour demand curve is LD_0 and the labour supply curve is LS_0. There is equilibrium in the labour market: the quantity of labour demanded equals the quantity supplied at a real wage rate of 1 shilling a day and 5 million people are employed. (We will use constant 1710 prices in this example to keep it in its historical context.)

Advances in technology – in both agriculture and industry – lead to investment in new capital and labour becomes more productive. More and more businesses start up and try to hire the now more productive labour. So the demand for labour increases and the labour demand curve shifts rightward to LD_1. With this greater demand for labour, the real wage rate rises from 1 shilling a day to 2 shillings a day and this higher wage rate causes an increase in the quantity of labour supplied (a movement along the labour supply curve). In the new situation, 5.5 million people are employed.

At this stage, economic growth has occurred and everyone has benefited from it. Real GDP has increased and real wages have also increased. But the classical economists believed that this new situation could not last and would be disturbed because it would induce an increase in the population.

Classical Theory of Population Growth

The classical theory of population growth is based on the idea of a **subsistence real wage rate**. The subsistence real wage rate is the minimum real wage rate needed to maintain life. By its definition, if the actual real wage rate is less than the subsistence real wage rate, some people cannot survive

Figure 32.7 Classical Growth Theory

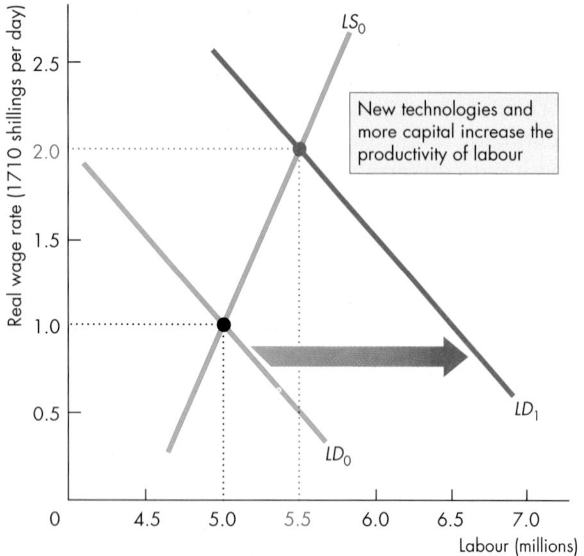

(a) Initial effect

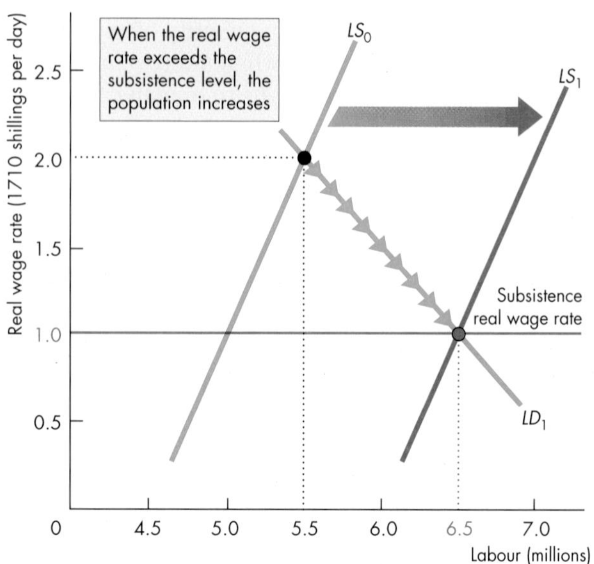

(b) Long-term effect

In classical growth theory, economic growth is temporary and the real wage rate keeps returning to the subsistence level. Initially, in part (a), the demand for labour is LD_0 and the supply of labour is LS_0. There are 5 million people employed and they earn 1 shilling a day. An advance in technology and an increase in capital increases the productivity of labour and the demand for labour increases to LD_1. The real wage rate rises to 2 shillings and the quantity of labour supplied increases to 5.5 million.

The real wage rate is now above the subsistence real wage, which in this example is 1 shilling a day. The population begins to increase. With an increase in population, the supply of labour increases and the labour supply curve shifts rightward to LS_1. As it does so, the real wage rate falls and the quantity of labour employed increases. The population stops growing when the real wage rate is back at the subsistence level.

and the population decreases. But in the classical theory, whenever the real wage rate exceeds the subsistence real wage rate, the population grows. This assumption, combined with the diminishing marginal product of labour, has a dismal implication – one that resulted in economics being called the *dismal science*. This implication is that no matter how much investment and technological change occurs, real wage rates are always pushed towards the subsistence level.

Figure 32.7(b) shows this process. Here, the subsistence real wage rate is (by assumption) 1 shilling a day. The actual real wage rate, at the intersection of LS_0 and LD_1, is 2 shillings a day. Because the actual real wage rate exceeds the subsistence real wage rate, the population grows and the labour supply increases. The labour supply curve shifts rightward to LS_1. As it does so, the real wage rate falls and the quantity of labour increases. Eventually, in the absence of further technological change, the economy comes to rest at the subsistence real wage rate of 1 shilling a day and 6.5 million people are employed.

The economy has grown, real GDP is higher and a larger population is earning the subsistence wage rate. But the benefits of economic growth have gone to the suppliers of capital and the entrepreneurs who have put the new technology to work.

The Modern Theory of Population Growth

When the classical economists were developing their ideas about population growth, a population explosion was under way. In the United Kingdom and other West European countries, advances in medicine and hygiene had lowered the death rate but the birth rate remained high. For several decades, population growth was extremely rapid. But eventually the birth rate fell and while the population continued to increase, its rate of increase was moderate.

The population growth rate is influenced by economic factors. For example, the birth rate has fallen as women's wage rates have increased and job opportunities have expanded. Also the death rate has fallen as greater investment has been made in advances in medicine. But despite the influence of economic factors, to a good approximation, the rate of population growth is independent of the rate of economic growth. To the extent that there is a connection, as incomes increase, the population growth rate eventually decreases. This inverse relation between real income growth and the population growth rate is contrary to the assumption of the classical economists and it invalidates their conclusions.

Neoclassical Growth Theory

Neoclassical growth theory is the proposition that the real GDP per person grows because technological change induces savings and investment. Technological change is the fundamental cause of growth.This theory was suggested during the 1950s by Robert Solow of MIT. In the neoclassical theory, the rate of technological change influences the rate of economic growth. But economic growth does not influence the rate of technological change. Rather, technological change is determined by chance. When we are lucky, we have rapid technological change, and when bad luck strikes, the pace of technological advance slows down. But there is nothing we can do to influence its pace.

At the heart of the neoclassical growth theory is the stock of capital and the *productivity function* – the relationship between capital per unit of labour and output per unit of labour. For simplicity, the theory assumes that people work a fixed number of hours and that everyone works. So labour equals population. The faster the capital stock per person grows, the faster real GDP and income per person grow. But what determines the growth rate of the capital stock per person? The answer is the demand for and supply of capital per person.

The Demand for and Supply of Capital per Person Figure 32.8 illustrates the neoclassical growth theory by showing how the demand for and supply of capital determine the capital stock and its growth rate. In this figure, we measure the capital stock per person on the x-axis and the real interest rate on the y-axis. The demand for capital and the supply of capital are determined by investment and saving decisions, which are described in Chapter 31, pp. 781–785. Briefly, the lower the real interest rate, the larger is the number of capital projects that are profitable and the greater is the demand for capital. On the other hand, in the short run, the lower the interest rate, the less strong is the incentive to save, rather than consume, and the smaller is the supply of capital.

In Figure 32.8, the demand for capital is shown by the downward-sloping KD_0 curve in part (a). Along this curve, as the real interest rate falls, other things remaining the same, the quantity of capital demanded increases. The supply of capital is shown by the upward-sloping KS_0 curve. Along this curve, as the real interest rate falls, other things remaining the same, the quantity of capital supplied decreases.

The real interest rate adjusts to achieve an equilibrium in which the quantity of capital demanded equals the quantity supplied. In Figure 32.8, the economy is in equilibrium at a real interest rate of 4 per cent a year and with a capital stock of £40,000 per person, shown in part (a). In the absence of technological change, capital per person converges to its equilibrium level. As a result, real GDP per person converges to a constant level and there is no economic growth.

But with technological change, real GDP per person grows. Figure 32.9 illustrates this growth process. A technological advance increases the productivity of capital and the demand for capital increases. The capital demand curve shifts rightward to KD_1. The greater demand for capital raises the real interest rate to 6 per cent a year and the higher real interest rate causes an increase in saving. The quantity of capital supplied increases to £50,000 per person.

The economy has experienced a period of economic growth. Because the capital stock per person has increased, output per person has increased. Also, labour has become more productive and the demand for labour has increased, bringing an increase in real wages and employment. But

Figure 32.8 Neoclassical Growth Theory

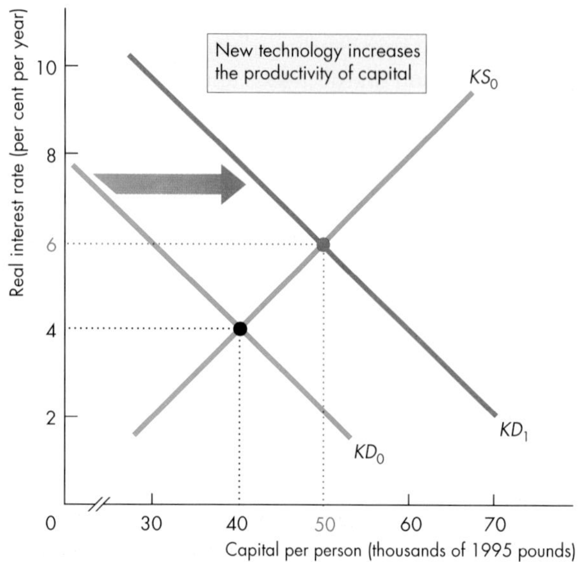

(a) Initial effect

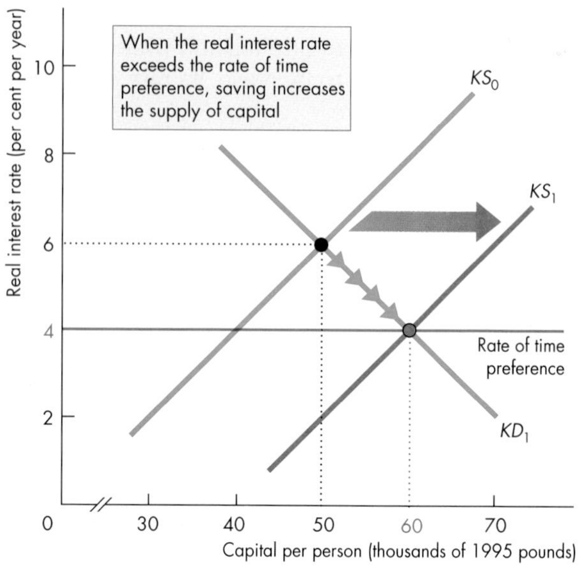

(b) Long-term effect

In neoclassical growth theory, economic growth results from technological change. In the absence of technological change, real GDP per person converges to a constant level. Initially, in part (a), the demand for capital is KD_0 and the supply of capital is KS_0. The capital stock is £40,000 per person and the real interest rate is 4 per cent a year. An advance in technology increases the productivity of capital and the demand for capital increases to KD_1. The real interest rate rises to 6 per cent a year and the quantity of capital supplied increases to £50,000.

The real interest rate is now above the rate of time preference, which in this example is 4 per cent a year (part b). Saving is positive and the supply of capital increases. The capital supply curve shifts rightward to KS_1. As it does so, the real interest rate falls and the quantity of capital per person increases. The quantity of capital per person stops growing when the real interest rate is back at the rate of time preference.

economic growth continues beyond the point shown in Figure 32.9(a). To understand why, we need to look at the neoclassical theory of saving.

Neoclassical Theory of Saving The neoclassical theory of saving is based on the idea called a constant rate of time preference. The **rate of time preference** is the target real interest rate that savers want to achieve. If the real interest rate exceeds the rate of time preference, saving is positive and the supply of capital increases. If the real interest rate is less than the rate of time preference, saving is negative and the supply of capital decreases. If the real interest rate equals the rate of time preference, people are happy with the amount of wealth they have accumulated and saving is zero.

Figure 32.8(b) illustrates the consequences of a constant rate of time preference. Here, the rate of time preference is 4 per cent a year. So when the real interest rate rises to 6 per cent a year, saving is positive and the supply of capital increases. The capital supply curve shifts rightward towards KS_1. As the supply of capital increases, the real interest rate falls and the quantity of capital demanded increases. Eventually, the economy reaches the point at which the real interest rate has fallen to equal the rate of time preference. At this point, saving is zero and the supply of capital is constant.

Throughout the process just described, real GDP per person has been increasing. The capital stock per person and real wage rates have also been increasing. The economy has experienced long-term growth.

Figure 32.9 New Growth Theory

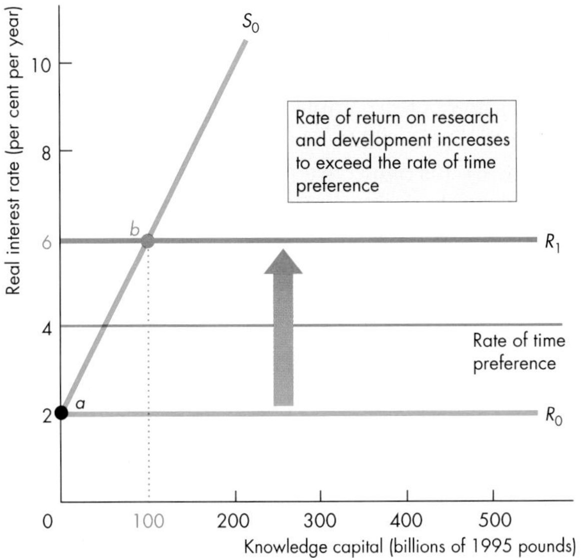

(a) Growth begins

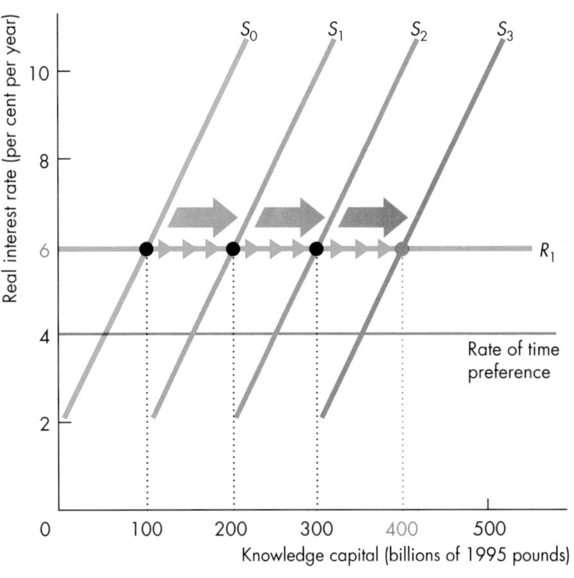

(b) Knowledge capital grows

In new growth theory, economic growth results from *endogenous* technological change. The returns to knowledge capital do not diminish and growth proceeds indefinitely. Initially, in part (a), the rate of return on knowledge capital is R_0 and the supply of knowledge capital is S_0. The stock of knowledge capital is zero. The development of the scientific method and the creation of research and development organizations increases the rate of return on knowledge capital to R_1. The real interest rate rises to 6 per cent a year and the quantity of knowledge capital supplied increases to £100 billion.

The real interest rate is now above the rate of time preference, which in this example is 4 per cent a year. Saving is positive and the supply of knowledge capital increases. The knowledge capital supply curve shifts rightward successively to S_1, S_2, S_3, and so on. As it does so, the economy grows but the real interest rate does not fall because there are no diminishing returns to knowledge capital. Growth continues as long as the rate of return on knowledge capital exceeds the rate of time preference.

Ongoing advances in technology are constantly increasing the demand for capital and raising the real interest rate above the rate of time preference. The process we've just examined repeats indefinitely to create an ongoing process of long-term economic growth.

Problems with Neoclassical Growth Theory

Neoclassical growth theory tells us how capital accumulation and saving interact to determine the economy's growth rate. But the growth rate itself depends on the *exogenous* rate of technological change. We need to go one step further and determine the rate of technological change.

Because all economies have access to the same technologies, and because capital is free to roam the world seeking the highest available rate of return, neoclassical growth theory predicts that growth rates and income levels per person will converge. While there is some sign of convergence among the rich countries (shown in Figure 32.2a), convergence does not appear to be present for all countries (as we saw in Figure 32.2b).

New growth theory attempts to overcome these two shortcomings of neoclassical growth theory.

New Growth Theory

New growth theory is a theory of economic growth based on the idea that technological change results from the choices that people make. (New growth theory is sometimes called *endogenous* *growth theory*). New growth theory starts with two facts about market economies:

1 Discoveries result from choices and actions.
2 Discoveries bring profits, and competition destroys profit.

Discoveries and Choices When someone discovers a new product or technique, they think of themselves as being lucky. They are right. But the pace at which new discoveries are made – at which technology advances – is not determined by chance. It depends on how many people are looking for a new way of doing something and how intensively they are looking.

Discoveries and Profits The spur to seeking new and better ways of producing is profit. The forces of competition are constantly squeezing profits, so to make a profit greater than the average, a person must constantly seek out either lower-cost methods of production or new and better products for which people are willing to pay a higher price. Inventors can maintain a profit for several years by taking out a patent or a copyright. But eventually, a new discovery is copied and profits disappear.

Two further facts play a key role in the new growth theory:

1 Discoveries can be used by many people at the same time.
2 Physical activities can be replicated.

Discoveries Used by All Once a profitable new discovery has been made, it is difficult to prevent others from copying it. But also, unlike inputs such as labour and capital, it can be used by everyone who knows about it without reducing its availability to others. This means that as the benefits of a new discovery are dispersed through the economy, resources are made available free to those who reap the benefit but didn't pay the price of making the discovery. But there is more.

Replicating Activities Replicas can be made of many (perhaps most) production activities. For example, there might be two, three or 53 identical firms making fibre optic cable using an identical assembly line and production technique. This means that the economy as a whole does not experience diminishing returns. (Each firm experiences diminishing returns but the economy does not).

These features of the economy can be summarized in the neat idea that knowledge – the stock of productive ideas that has been accumulated as a result of research and development efforts – is a special kind of capital that can be used by all and whose marginal product does not diminish. The implication of this simple and appealing idea is shown in Figure 32.9, which illustrates new growth theory. In this figure, we measure the knowledge capital stock on the x-axis and the real interest rate on the y-axis.

The supply of knowledge capital is shown by the upward-sloping S_0 curve. Along this curve, as the real interest rate rises, other things remaining the same, the quantity of saving and of resources devoted to accumulating knowledge capital increases.

Because the marginal product of knowledge capital does not diminish, the demand for knowledge capital does not slope downward like the demand curve for other types of capital. If knowledge capital yields a higher return than the rate of time preference, the quantity of knowledge capital demanded is unlimited. And if knowledge capital yields a lower return than the rate of time preference, then the demand for knowledge capital is zero.

Initially, before growth begins, the marginal product of knowledge capital is 2 per cent a year, shown by the horizontal line R_0 in Figure 32.9(a). At this rate of return, and given the supply of knowledge capital curve, the economy is in equilibrium at a real interest rate of 2 per cent a year and has no knowledge capital. The economy is stuck at point a.

The invention of such basic tools as language and writing (the two most basic pieces of knowledge capital), and later the development of the scientific method and the establishment of communities of scientists, inventors and research institutions. The rate of return line shifted upward to R_1. The initial effect of this increase in the return on knowledge capital was to increase the real interest rate to 6 per cent a year and to cause an increase in the quantity of knowledge capital supplied (to £100 billion in the figure). The economy moved to point b.

The economy has experienced a period of economic growth. Because the stock of knowledge capital has increased, real GDP has increased. But economic growth continues and it continues indefinitely. The reason is that the real interest rate now exceeds the rate of time preference. So saving is positive and the supply of capital (which includes knowledge capital) increases.

Figure 32.9(b) illustrates the process. The rate of time preference is 4 per cent a year and the rate of return on knowledge capital is 6 per cent a year. With positive saving, the supply curve shifts rightward and continues to do so indefinitely. The speed with which the saving supply curve shifts rightward depends on the extent to which the real interest rate exceeds the rate of time preference. The higher the marginal productivity of knowledge capital, the higher is the real interest rate and the faster the saving curve shifts rightward, so the faster the economy grows.

Unlike the neoclassical theory, with its diminishing marginal productivity of capital, which eventually lowers the real interest rate to the rate of time preference, there is no such mechanism at work in the new growth theory. Real GDP per person increases and does so indefinitely as long as people can undertake research and development that yields a higher return than the rate of time preference.

New growth theory sees the economy as a kind of perpetual motion mechanism. Economic growth is driven by our insatiable wants that lead us to pursue profit and innovate. The result of this process is new and better products. But new and better products result in firms going out of business and new firms starting up. In this process, jobs are destroyed and created. The outcome is more consumption, new and better jobs, and more leisure. All this adds up to a higher standard of living. But our insatiable wants are still there: profits, innovation, new products and higher living standards.

The economy's growth rate depends on people's ability to innovate, the rate of return to innovation and the rate of time preference, which influences the rate of saving.

Review

- Economic growth arises from improvements in human capital, increases in the capital stock and improvements in technology.
- The classical growth theory is that there is no long-term growth in the real wage rate because when the real wage rate exceeds its subsistence level, the population expands and the real wage rate falls to the subsistence level.
- The neoclassical growth theory is that growth results from technological advances that are themselves determined by chance.
- The new growth theory, the pursuit of profit brings persistent innovation and increased capital does not bring diminishing returns.

Your final task in this chapter is to examine the policy actions that might be taken to speed up the growth rate.

Achieving Faster Growth

To achieve faster economic growth, we must either increase the growth rate of capital per hour of work or increase the pace of technological advance (which includes improving human capital).

The main suggestions for achieving faster economic growth are:

- Stimulate saving.
- Stimulate research and development.
- Target high-technology industries.
- Encourage international trade.
- Improve the quality of education and training.

Stimulate Saving Saving finances investment, which brings capital accumulation and economic growth. So stimulating saving can also stimulate economic growth. Up until recent years, China, Hong Kong, Japan, South Korea, Singapore and Taiwan have experienced the highest growth rates. They also have the highest saving rates. Some countries of Africa have the lowest growth rates. They also have the lowest saving rates. The saving rates in the European Union and the other rich countries are modest.

The most obvious way in which saving could be increased is by providing tax incentives. Some incentives already exist, but more radical measures are possible. For example, instead of taxing incomes (which means taxing both consumption and saving), we could tax only consumption. Such a tax would encourage additional saving and probably increase the economy's growth rate.

Stimulate Research and Development Patents protect inventors and provide incomes that give incentives to research and development. But everyone can use the fruits of *basic* research and development efforts. For example, VisiCalc invented the basic idea of the spreadsheet, but it did not take long for Lotus Corporation to use this idea to develop the famous 1–2–3, and for Microsoft Corporation to bring out a Lotus 1–2–3 lookalike, Excel. Because basic inventions can be copied, the inventor's profit is limited. For this reason, the free market allocates too few resources to basic research.

This situation is one in which government subsidies might help. By using public funds to finance basic research and development that bring social benefits, it might be possible to encourage an efficient level of research. But the solution is not foolproof. The main problem is that some mechanism must be designed for allocating the public funds. The universities and research councils are the main channels through which public funds in the United Kingdom are used to finance research.

Target High-technology Industries It is argued by some people that by providing public funds to high-technology firms and industries, a country can become the first to exploit a new techology and can earn above average profits for a period while others are busy catching up. But this strategy can be risky and can just as likely to use resources inefficiently as to speed up growth.

Encourage International Trade Free international trade stimulates growth by extracting all the available gains from specialization and exchange. It is no accident that the fastest growing countries today are those with the fastest growing international trade – both exports and imports.

Improve the Quality of Education and Training Education and training, like basic research, brings benefits to people other than those who have received the education. By its nature, education is a good the value of which is fully appreciated only after receiving it. Like basic research the free market underprovides education and training. By funding basic education and training in skills such as language, mathematics, science and technology, the government can contribute to a nation's growth potential.

In this chapter, we've studied the sources of economic growth, learned how we can measure the contributions of hours, capital and technological change, and we've studied the theories of economic growth. Finally, we've seen some policy actions that might speed up growth rates. Economic growth is the single most decisive factor in influencing a country's living standard, but it is not the only one. Another is the extent to which the country fully employs its scarce resources, especially its labour. In recent years, unemployment has become a severe problem for many countries. In Chapters 23, 24 and 33, we study the fluctuations of real GDP and unemployment around their long-term trend.

Summary

Key Points

Long-term Growth Trends (pp. 804–807)

- Between 1855 and 1998, real GDP per person in the United Kingdom grew at an average rate of 1.3 per cent a year.
- The early 1900s, the interwar years, and 1973–1979 were the periods of slowest growth and the 1950s, 1960s, 1980s and 1990s were periods of rapid growth.
- Catch-up in real GDP per person occurs sometimes but it is not a global phenomenon. The United States is still the richest country. Some rich countries are catching up with the United States, but the gaps between the United States and many poor countries are not closing.
- Canada, France, Germany, Italy, the United Kingdom and Japan have grown faster than the United States and have been catching up.
- The gap between the United States and Africa and Central and South America has widened, and the gap has remained constant with the

former communist countries of Central and Eastern Europe.

- Hong Kong, South Korea, Singapore, Taiwan and China are catching up the fastest but their catch-up has been interrupted by the Asian crisis of 1997.

The Sources of Economic Growth (pp. 807–808)

- Economic growth occurs when an *incentive* system, which is created by markets, property rights and monetary exchange, encourages saving and investment in new capital, the growth of human capital and the discovery of new technologies.
- Saving and investment in new capital, human capital accumulation and technological advances interact to increase production and raise living standards and they are the main sources of economic growth.

Growth Accounting (pp. 808–812)

- Growth accounting measures the contributions of capital accumulation and technological change to productivity growth.
- The analytical engine of growth accounting is the productivity function, which is the relationship between real GDP per hour of work and capital per hour of work, holding technology constant.
- The contributions of capital growth and technological change to productivity growth are estimated by using the *one-third rule* – a 1 per cent increase in capital per hour of work brings a one-third of 1 per cent increase in real GDP per hour of work.
- Growth accounting isolates the reason for the productivity growth slowdown of the 1970s. Technological change made hardly any contribution to real GDP growth.

Growth Theory (pp. 813–819)

- The three main theories of economic growth are the classical theory, the neoclassical theory, and new growth theory.
- The classical theory is that the population grows whenever incomes rise above the *subsistence* level and declines whenever incomes fall below the subsistence level. This assumption, combined with the diminishing marginal product of labour, implies that incomes are always pushed towards the subsistence level.
- The neoclassical growth theory is that the long-term growth rate is determined by the rate of technological change, which in turn is determined by chance.
- New growth theory is that the growth rate depends on the costs and benefits of developing new technologies.

Achieving Faster Growth (pp. 819–820)

- To achieve faster economic growth, we must increase the growth of capital per hour of work or increase the pace of technological advance.
- It might be possible to achieve faster growth by stimulating saving, subsidizing research and development, targeting (and possibly subsidizing) high-technology industries, encouraging more international trade and encouraging more education and training.

Key Figures

Key Terms

Review Questions

1 What was the average growth rate of real GDP per person in the United Kingdom between 1855 and 1998?

2 Which countries have grown fastest since 1960 and which have grown slowest?

3 Have levels of real GDP per person across countries caught up with each other?

4 What are the three necessary preconditions for economic growth to occur?

5 What three activities can create ongoing economic growth?

6 Explain how economic growth can occur even in the absence of investment and new technologies.

7 What is growth accounting?

8 What is the main concept used in growth accounting?

9 How are the effects of capital accumulation and technological change separated by growth accounting techniques?

10 What is the one-third rule and how is it used?

11 Explain the main sources of the productivity slowdown in the United Kingdom during the 1970s.

12 Why did technological advances stop increasing productivity during the 1970s?

13 What are the main theories of economic growth?

14 What are the key assumptions of classical growth theory?

15 What are the key assumptions of neoclassical growth theory?

16 What are the key assumptions of new growth theory?

17 Contrast the neoclassical growth theory and the new growth theory.

18 Describe the main reasons why the miracle economies of Asia have been so successful.

19 What are the main policy actions that governments might take to increase the growth rate?

Problems

1 The following information has been discovered about the economy of Europa. The economy's productivity function is:

Capital per hour of work (1997 euros per hour)	Real GDP per hour of work (1997 euros per hour)
10	3.80
20	5.40
30	6.80
40	8.00
50	9.00
60	9.80
70	10.40
80	10.80

Does this economy conform to the one-third rule? If so, explain why. If not, explain why not and also explain what rule, if any, it does conform to.

2 The figure illustrates the productivity function of Macaroonia in 1995 and 1997. In 1995, capital per hour of work was E10 and in 1997 it was E25.

a Does Macaroonia experience diminishing returns? Explain your answer.
b Use growth accounting to find the contribution of the change in capital between 1995

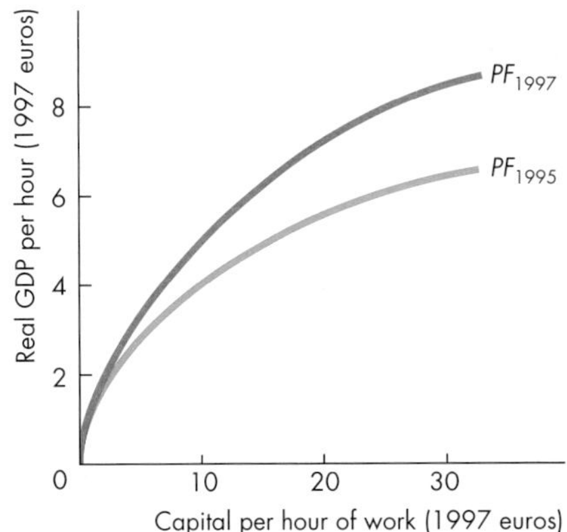

and 1997 to the growth of productivity in Macaroonia.

c Use growth accounting to find the contribution of technological change between 1995 and 1997 to the growth of productivity in Macaroonia.

3 Solovia is an economy that behaves according to the neoclassical growth model. The rate of time preference is 3 per cent a year. A technological advance increases the demand for capital and raises the interest rate to 5 per cent a year. Describe what happens in Solovia.

4 The figure illustrates the economy of New Labouria, a country that behaves according to the predictions of new growth theory. Initially, the rate of return on capital is 2 per cent a year. It then rises to 6 per cent a year.

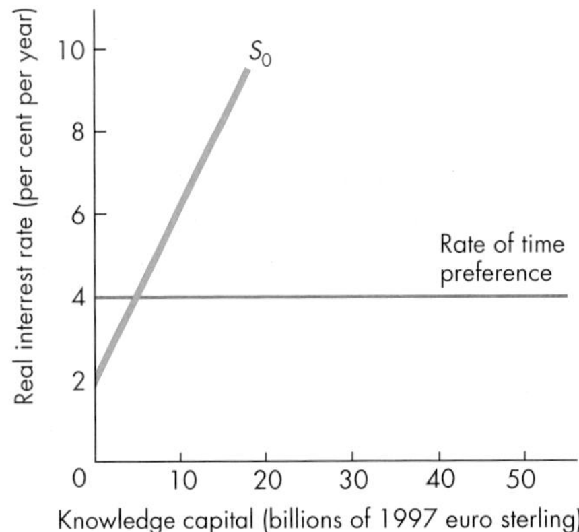

a What initially is the real interest rate and quantity of knowledge capital in New Labouria?

b What is the immediate effect of the increase in the rate of return on knowledge capital to 6 per cent a year on the real interest rate and the quantity of knowledge capital?

c If the rate of return on knowledge capital remains at 6 per cent a year, what happens in New Labouria to the real interest rate, the quantity of knowledge capital and real income per person?

5 After studying *Reading Between the Lines* on pp. 824–825, answer the following questions:

a How much extra growth per year can the UK achieve if planning laws and management practices were changed to conform with the policy prescriptions of the McKinsey report?

b Real GDP in 1990 was £658.5 billion pounds in 1995 prices and in 1998 real GDP was £772.3 billion pounds. What would real GDP have been if we had earned an extra 1.5 per cent of output a year?

c UK labour markets are more flexible than those of France and Germany, but their labour productivity is higher. How can this be explained?

6 Visit the Penn World Table Web site (linked from the Parkin, Powell and Matthews Web site) and obtain data on real GDP per person for the United States, China, South Africa and Mexico since 1960.

a Draw a graph of the data.

b Which country has the lowest real GDP per person and which has the highest?

c Which country has experienced the fastest growth rate since 1960 and which the slowest?

d Explain why the growth rates in these four countries are ranked in the order you have discovered?

e Return to the Penn World Table Web site and obtain data for any four other countries that interest you. Describe and explain the patterns that you find for these countries.

W http://www.econ100.com

Productivity and Growth

The Essence of the Story

■ A study by McKinsey, the management consultancy firm, claims that the UK could raise its economic growth by 1.5 per cent a year if it relaxed planning regulations and made it easier for companies to adopt world-class business practices.

■ The study says that economic growth averaging 3.5 per cent a year instead of 2 per cent would allow the UK to reach existing levels of US real GDP per person within 10 years.

■ Average disposable income would rise by about £2,500 a year, government revenues would grow by an extra £45 billion and there would be an increase in high paid employment.

■ The study argues that low capital investment and poor labour skills are often the consequence of market restrictions rather than primary causes.

Financial Times, 30 October 1998

Tight planning regulations 'curbing growth'

Kevin Brown and Robert Chote

The UK could raise its economic growth rate by 1.5 percentage points a year if it relaxed planning regulations and made it easier for companies to adopt world-class business practices, a productivity study by McKinsey, the management consultants, claims today.

McKinsey says economic growth averaging 3.5 per cent a year instead of 2 per cent would allow the UK to reach existing levels of US gross domestic product per capita within 10 years.

Average disposable income would rise about £2,500 a year at current prices, government tax revenues would grow by about £45bn, and there would be a surge in employment creation, including at least 75,000 highly paid jobs in information technology.

However, the report says low capital investment and poor skills are often the consequence of market restrictions rather than primary causes.

Bill Lewis, the institute's Washington-based director, said the UK had "very large" potential for rapid economic expansion because labour productivity was lower than in other big industrialised economies, in spite of the deregulation of labour and capital markets.

The report says UK labour productivity is 37 per cent lower than in the US, and 26 per cent lower than in France and western Germany. Capital productivity is higher in the UK than in both European rivals, but 10 per cent lower than in the US. In spite of the UK's higher level of capital productivity, total factor productivity, which reflects capital and labour productivity and the efficiency with which both are used, is 26 per cent lower than in the US, and 14 per cent lower than in western Germany.

It identifies the main causes of the productivity gap as:

◆ Tight planning regulations that prevent businesses such as food retailers expanding.

◆ Regulations and agreements affecting specific product markets, such as building controls on hotels; voluntary restraints on Japanese car imports, pharmacy licensing and complex life assurance tax rules.

Driving Productivity and Growth in the UK Economy, McKinsey Global Institute, Free. Tel: 0171 873 6796

Economic Analysis

■ An important element in the growth process is the development of an appropriate incentive system. Planning regulations can increase the cost of capital projects and reduce risk taking by individuals.

■ Investment increases the capital stock, which brings higher productivity. The UK has a record of low investment, as seen in Figure 31.2, p.781, compared with other industrialized economies.

■ Figure 1 shows the position of UK labour productivity compared with France, Germany and USA which may be the result of low capital investment and poor skills.

■ The improvement in labour and management skills that follow from a less regulated system is an investment in human capital which is shown in Figure 2 as an improvement in technological change. In Figure 2, the effect of technological change is to shift the productivity function up from PF_0 to PF_1.

■ The article is correct when it says that low investment is a causal factor in low growth and low productivity. But the article does not draw the link between the deregulation of the labour market, low productivity and employment.

■ Figure 3 compares the relative performance of the UK on hours worked per person. The chart shows that hours worked per person is the same as in Germany and more than in France. But unlike these two countries the UK has higher employment and lower unemployment. The higher productivity in Germany and France is the result of high labour costs resulting in the employment of high productive workers but unemployment for low productive workers.

■ The comparison with the USA is harder to explain. Both economies have deregulated labour markets but the US has even more labour deregulation. The difference in productivity performance could be due to less regulation and better management skills in the USA as McKinsey suggest.

Figure 1 Labour productivity

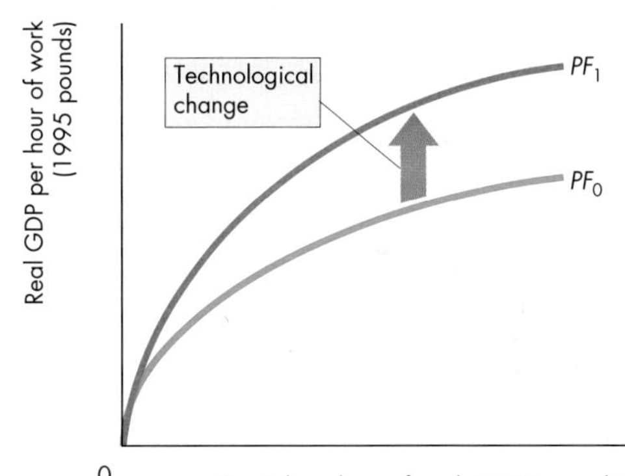

Figure 2 Productivity growth

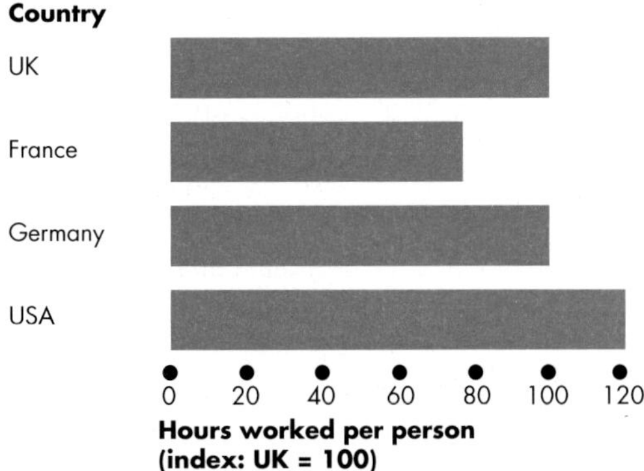

Figure 3 Average hours per person

Economic Growth

"Economic progress, in capitalist society, means turmoil."

Joseph Schumpeter
Capitalism, Socialism and Democracy

The Economist: Joseph Schumpeter

Joseph Schumpeter, the son of a textile factory owner, was born in Austria in 1883. He moved from Austria to Germany during the tumultuous 1920s when those two countries experienced hyperinflation. And in 1932, in the depths of the Great Depression, he came to the United States and became a professor of economics at Harvard University.

This creative economic thinker wrote on economic growth and development, business cycles, political systems and economic biography. He was a person of strong opinions who expressed them strongly and delighted in verbal battles.

Schumpeter has become the unwitting founder of modern growth theory. He saw the development and diffusion of new technologies by profit-seeking entrepreneurs as the source of economic progress. But he saw economic progress as a process of creative destruction – the creation of new profit opportunities and the destruction of currently profitable businesses. For Schumpeter, economic growth and the business cycle were a single phenomenon.

When Schumpeter died in 1950, he had achieved his self-expressed life's ambition: he was regarded as the world's greatest economist.

The Issues and Ideas

Technological change, capital accumulation and population growth all interact to produce economic growth. But what is cause and what is effect, and can we expect productivity and income per person to keep growing?

The classical economists of the eighteenth and nineteenth centuries believed that technological advances and capital accumulation were the engines of growth. But they also believed that no matter how successful people were at inventing more productive technologies and investing in new capital, they were destined to live at the subsistence level. These economists based their conclusion on the belief that productivity growth causes population growth, which in turn causes productivity to decline. These classical economists believed that whenever economic growth raises incomes above the subsistence level, the population will increase. And they went on to reason that the increase in population brings diminishing returns that lower productivity. As a result, incomes must always return to the subsistence level. Only when incomes are at the subsistence level is population growth held in check.

A new approach, called neoclassical growth theory, was developed by Robert Solow of MIT during the 1950s. Solow, who was one of Schumpeter's students, received the Nobel Prize for Economic Science for this work.

Solow challenged the conclusions of the classical economists. But the new theories of economic growth developed during the 1980s and 1990s went further. They stand the classical belief on its head. Today's theory of population growth is that rising income slows the population growth rate because it increases the opportunity cost of having children and lowers the opportunity cost of investing in children and equipping them with more human capital, which makes them more productive. Productivity and income grow because technology advances and the scope for further productivity growth, which is stimulated by the search for profit, is practically unlimited.

Then . . .

McCormick's Reaper. By Burgess & Key.

In 1830, a strong and experienced farm worker could harvest three acres of wheat in a day. The only capital employed was a scythe to cut the wheat, which had been used since Roman times, and a cradle on which the stalks were laid, which had been invented by Flemish farmers in the fifteenth century. With newly developed horse-drawn ploughs, harrows and planters, farmers could plant more wheat than they could harvest. But despite big efforts, no one had been able to make a machine that could replicate the swing of a scythe. Then in 1831, 22-year-old Cyrus McCormick built a machine that worked. It scared the horse that pulled it, but it did in a matter of hours what three men could accomplish in a day. Technological change has increased productivity on farms and brought economic growth. Do the facts about productivity growth mean that the classical economists, who believed that diminishing returns would push us relentlessly back to a subsistence living standard, were wrong?

. . . And Now

Today's technologies are expanding our horizons beyond the confines of our planet and are expanding our minds. Geosynchronous satellites bring us global television, voice and data communication, and more accurate weather forecasts, which incidentally increase agricultural productivity. In the foreseeable future, we might have superconductors that revolutionize the use of electric power, virtual reality theme parks and training facilities, pollution-free hydrogen cars, wristwatch telephones, and optical computers that we can talk to. With these new technologies, our ability to create yet more dazzling technologies increases. Technological change begets technological change in an (apparently) unending process and makes us ever more productive and brings ever higher incomes.

The Business Cycle

After studying this chapter you will be able to:

- Distinguish between different theories of the business cycle
- Explain the Keynesian and monetarist theories of the business cycle
- Explain the new classical and new Keynesian theories of the business cycle
- Explain real business cycle theory
- Describe the origins and mechanisms at work during a recent recession and expansion
- Describe the origins and mechanisms at work during the Great Depression

Must What Goes Up Always Come Down?

The period between the two world wars was a time of mixed fortunes for many of the people in the United Kingdom who survived the horrors of World War I (1914–18). The end of the war saw a severe recession; returning soldiers were de-mobbed and the economy was thrown back into peacetime production. After a shaky start, the economic machine was slowly getting back to work. Then, almost without warning, in October 1929, came the Wall Street crash. Share prices in the United States fell by 30 per cent and a wave of deflation was sent around the whole world. By 1933, real GDP in the United States had fallen by 30 per cent and unemployment had increased to 25 per cent of the workforce. This major downturn in the world's largest economy had severe effects on the economies of Europe. In Germany unemployment rose to 5.6 million or 30 per cent of the workforce in 1932 and in the United Kingdom it reached nearly 16 per cent. In 1931 the United Kingdom left the gold standard and joined the rest of the world in the Great Depression. ◆ By the standard of the interwar years, recent recessions have been mild. But recessions have not gone away. Our economy has experienced five recessions since World War II ended in 1945. In 1974, real GDP decreased by 1.7 per cent; in 1980, it decreased by 2.1 per cent; in 1981 it decreased again in a back-to-back recession by 1.2 per cent, and most recently, in 1991–92, it decreased by 2.6 per cent over the two years. Between these recessions, expansions took real GDP to new heights. Since the 1990s recession, real GDP has recovered. In 1994, GDP grew by 4.4 per cent, and by the end of 1998 it stood some 10 per cent higher than at the bottom of the recession. What causes a repeating sequence of recessions and expansions in our economy? Must what goes up always come down? Will we have another recession in the early years of the new millennium?

◆ ◆ ◆ ◆ In this chapter we are going to explore these questions. You will see how all the strands of macroeconomics that you've been following come together and weave a complete picture of the forces and mechanisms that generate economic growth and fluctuations in production, employment and unemployment, and inflation. You will draw on your study of the labour market, consumption, saving and investment, economic growth, aggregate supply and aggregate demand, expenditure multipliers and the money market.

Cycle Patterns, Impulses and Mechanisms

We'll begin by summarizing the key business cycle facts that we want to understand and then examine the complex patterns it makes. The business cycle is an irregular and non-repeating up-and-down movement of business activity that takes place around a generally rising trend and that shows great diversity. Figure 33.1 shows some of this diversity by comparing business cycles since the turn of the century. You can see that there are basically nine business cycle turning points we can identify since 1990. On the average, recessions have lasted about two years and real GDP has fallen from peak to trough by nearly 10 per cent. Expansions have, on the average, lasted for just over six years and real GDP has risen from trough to peak at an average of nearly 10 per cent. But these averages mask huge variations from one cycle to another. Each cycle has a different story to tell. The onset of World War I near the beginning of the century led to a boom followed by a sharp slump at the end of the war. The interwar period witnessed two cycles with a severe recession occurring in the 1930s, earning it the title of the 'Hungry Thirties'. The next big expansion occurred during World War II. But there have been five cycles since World War II with major expansions occurring during the 1960s and 1980s.

You can see by examining Figure 33.1 that although the average of peak to trough decline and trough to peak boom is almost the same, most of the downturns are not as severe as the upturns. This is because the post-World War I recession was so severe that it pulled the average down. If we exclude the years up to 1918, the average trough to peak is 10.4 per cent and the average peak to trough is 8.8 per cent. Another interesting observation is the *amplitude* – the slump–boom–slump movement of the business cycle. You can see that the slump–boom–slump cycle was greater before World War II than after. Also the *frequency* of the cycle was greater before World War II than after. The 1960s heralded a long expansion period which looks unusual compared with other expansion phases of the cycle. There is no correlation between the length of an expansion and the length of the preceding recession.

With this enormous diversity of experience, there is no simple explanation of the business cycle. Also there is no (currently available) way of forecasting when the next turning point will come. But there is a body of theory about the business cycle that helps

Figure 33.1 Some Business Cycle Patterns

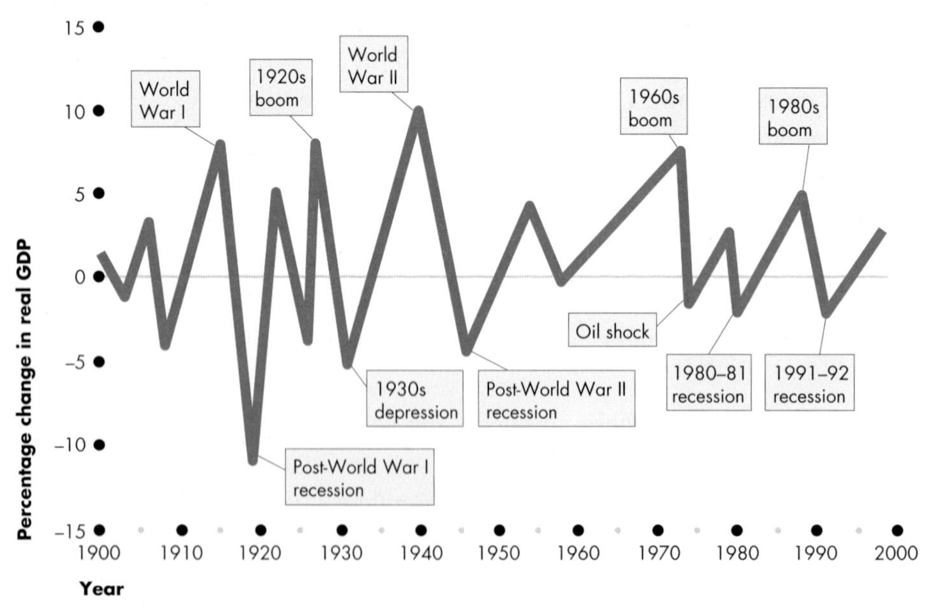

There have been nine business cycle turning points since the turn of the century. Recessions have lasted on average two years. Real GDP has fallen from peak to trough by nearly 9 per cent. Expansions have, on the average, lasted for about six years and real GDP has risen from trough to peak at an average of 10 per cent.

us to understand its causes. A good place to begin studying this theory is to distinguish the possible ways in which cycles can be created.

Cycle Impulses and Mechanisms

The business cycle can occur either because the economy is hit by a succession of impulses that alternate between the up-and-down directions or because the economy has a built-in cycle mechanism that causes it to move up and down regardless of how it is hit. Some analogies might help you to see the distinction between cycle impulses and cycle mechanisms. In a tennis match, the ball cycles from one side of the court to the other and back again in a way that is determined entirely by the impulses that hit the ball. The tide is a cycle that is determined purely by a mechanism and has no impulses. The rotation of the earth and the gravitational pull of the moon interact to bring the ebb and flow of the tide with no outside forces intervening. A child's rocking horse is an example of a cycle mechanism that needs an external force to create the cycle. If the horse is pushed, it rocks to-and-fro in a cycle. The cycle will eventually die out unless the horse is pushed again, and each time the horse is pushed the cycle temporarily becomes more severe.

The economy seems to be a bit like all three of these examples. It can be hit like a tennis ball by shocks that send it in one direction or another; it can cycle indefinitely like the ebb and flow of the tide; and it can cycle like a rocking horse in swings that get milder until another shock sets off a new burst of bigger swings. But no one is sure which of these analogies is correct because there is no fully developed theory that explains all business cycles equally well. While none of the analogies we use is perfect, they all contain some insights into the business cycle. Different theories of the cycle emphasize different outside forces (different tennis racquets) and different cycle mechanisms (rocking horse designs).

Although there are several different theories of the business cycle, they all agree about one aspect of the cycle: the central role played by investment and the accumulation of capital.

The Central Role of Investment and Capital

Whatever the shocks are that hit the economy, they hit one crucial variable: investment. Recessions begin when investment in new capital slows down and they turn into expansions when investment speeds up. Investment and capital also create a cycle propagation mechanism. They interact like the spinning earth and the sun to create an ongoing cycle.

In an expansion investment proceeds at a rapid rate and the capital stock grows quickly. Capital per hour of labour grows and labour becomes more productive. But the *law of diminishing returns* begins to operate and this brings a fall in the rate of return on capital as the gain in productivity from the additional units of capital declines. With a lower rate of return, the incentive to invest weakens and investment eventually falls. When it falls by a large amount, recession begins. If in a recession investment proceeds at a modest rate, the capital stock grows slowly and diminishing returns work in reverse.

The *AS–AD* Model

Investment and capital are just part of the business cycle mechanism. To study the broader business mechanism, we need a broader framework. That framework is the *AS–AD* model. All the theories of the business cycle can be described in terms of the *AS–AD* model of Chapter 24. Theories differ in what they identify as the impulse and the propagation mechanism. But all theories can be thought of as making assumptions about the factors that make either aggregate supply or aggregate demand fluctuate and assumptions about their interaction with each other to create a business cycle. Business cycle impulses can hit either the supply side or the demand side of the economy or both. But there are no pure supply side theories. We can classify all theories of the business cycle as:

- Aggregate demand theories, or
- Real business cycle theory.

We'll study the aggregate demand theories first. Then we'll study real business cycle theory, a more recent approach which isolates a shock that has both aggregate supply and aggregate demand effects.

Aggregate Demand Theories of the Business Cycle

Three types of aggregate demand theories of the business cycle have been proposed. They are:

1 Keynesian theory.
2 Monetarist theory.
3 Rational expectations theory.

Keynesian Theory of the Cycle

The **Keynesian theory of the business cycle** regards volatile expectations as the main source of economic fluctuations. This theory is distilled from Keynes' *General Theory of Employment, Interest and Money*. We'll explore the Keynesian theory by looking at its main impulse and the mechanism that converts this impulse into a real GDP cycle.

Keynesian Impulse The *impulse* in the Keynesian theory of the business cycle is expected future sales and profits. A change in expected future sales and profits changes the demand for new capital and changes the level of investment.

Keynes had an interesting and sophisticated view about *how* expectations of sales and profits are determined. He reasoned that these expectations would be volatile because most of the events that shape the future are unknown and impossible to forecast. So, he reasoned, news or even rumours about future tax rate changes, interest rate changes, advances in technology, global economic and political events, or any of thousands of other relevant factors that influence sales and profits, change expectations in ways that can't be quantified but that have large effects.

To emphasize the volatility and diversity of sources of changes in expected sales and profits, one of Keynes' followers, Joan Robinson, described these expectations as *animal spirits*. In using this term, Keynesians are not saying that expectations are irrational. Rather, they mean that because future sales and profits are impossible to forecast, it is rational to take a view about them based on rumours, guesses, intuition and instinct. Further, it might be rational to *change* one's view of the future, perhaps radically, in the light of scraps of new information.

Keynesian Cycle Mechanism In the Keynesian theory, once a change in animal spirits has changed investment, a cycle mechanism begins to operate that has two key elements. First, the initial change in investment has a multiplier effect. The change in investment changes *aggregate* expenditure, real GDP and disposable income. The change in disposable income changes consumption expenditure and aggregate demand changes by a multiple of the initial change in investment. (This mechanism is described in detail in Chapter 25, pp. 613–616.) The aggregate demand curve shifts rightward in an expansion and leftward in a recession.

The second element of the Keynesian cycle mechanism is the response of real GDP to a change in aggregate demand. The short-run aggregate supply curve is horizontal (or nearly so). With a horizontal *SAS* curve, swings in aggregate demand translate into swings in real GDP with no changes in the price level. But the short-run aggregate supply curve depends on the money wage rate. If the money wage rate is fixed (sticky), the *SAS* curve does not move. And if the money wage rate changes, the *SAS* curve shifts. In the Keynesian theory, the response of the money wage rate to changes in aggregate demand are *asymmetric*.

On the downside, when aggregate demand decreases and unemployment rises, the money wage rate does not change. It is completely rigid in the down direction. With a decrease in aggregate demand and no change in the money wage rate, the economy gets stuck in an unemployment equilibrium. There are no natural forces operating to restore full employment. The economy remains in that situation until animal spirits are lifted and investment increases again.

On the upside, when aggregate demand increases and unemployment falls below the natural rate, the money wage rate rises quickly. It is completely flexible in the up direction. Above full employment, the horizontal *SAS* curve plays no role and only the vertical *LAS* curve is relevant. With an increase in aggregate demand and an accompanying rise in the money wage rate, the price level rises quickly to eliminate the shortages and bring the economy back to full employment. The economy remains in that situation until animal spirits fall and investment and aggregate demand decrease.

Figures 33.2 and 33.3 illustrate the Keynesian theory of the business cycle by using the aggregate demand–aggregate supply model. In Figure 33.2, the economy is initially at full employment (point *a*) on the long-run aggregate supply curve, *LAS*, the aggregate demand curve, AD_0, and the short-run aggregate supply curve, SAS_0. A fall in animal spirits decreases investment, and aggregate demand decreases. The aggregate demand curve shifts leftward to AD_1. Real GDP falls to \$500 billion and the economy moves to point *b*. Unemployment has increased and there is a surplus of labour, but the

Figure 33.2 A Keynesian Recession

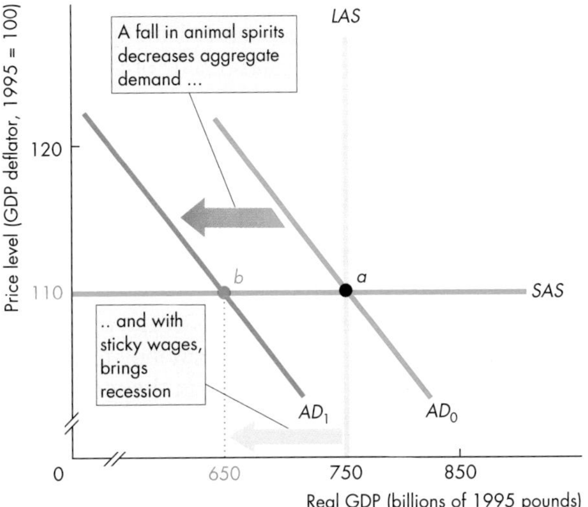

The economy is operating at point *a* at the intersection of the aggregate demand curve, AD_0, the short-run aggregate supply curve, SAS_0, and the long-run aggregate supply curve, *LAS*. A Keynesian recession begins when a fall in animal spirits causes investment demand to decrease. Aggregate demand decreases and the *AD* curve shifts leftward to AD_1. With sticky money wages and sticky price level, real GDP falls to £650 billion and the economy moves to point *b*.

Figure 33.3 A Keynesian Expansion

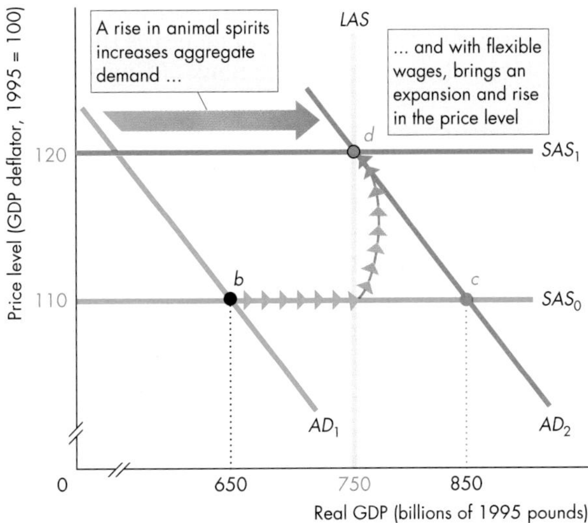

Starting at point *b*, a Keynesian expansion begins when a rise in animal spirits causes investment demand to increase. Aggregate demand increases and the *AD* curve shifts rightward to AD_2. With sticky money wages, real GDP increases to £750 billion. But the economy does not go all the way to point *c*. When full employment is reached, the money wage rate rises and the *SAS* curve shifts toward SAS_1. The price level rises as the economy heads towards point *d*.

money wage rate does not fall and the economy remains at point *b* until some force moves it away.

That force is shown in Figure 33.3. Here, starting out at point *b*, a rise in animal spirits increases aggregate demand and shifts the *AD* curve to AD_2. The multiplier process comes in to play and real GDP begins to increase. An expansion is under way. As long as real GDP remains below potential GDP (£750 billion in this example), the money wage rate and the price level remain constant. But real GDP never gets to point *c*, the point of intersection of SAS_0 and AD_2. The reason is that once real GDP exceeds potential GDP and unemployment falls below the natural rate, the money wage rate begins to rise and the *SAS* curve starts to shift upward towards SAS_1. As the money wage rate rises, the price level also rises and real GDP growth slows down. The economy follows a path like the one shown by the arrows connecting point *b*, the initial equilibrium, with point *d*, the final equilibrium.

The Keynesian business cycle is mainly like a tennis match. It is caused by outside forces – animal spirits – that change direction and set off a process that ends at an equilibrium that must be hit again by the outside forces to disturb it.

Monetarist Theory

The **monetarist theory of the business cycle** regards fluctuations in the money stock as the main source of economic fluctuations. This theory is distilled from the writings of Milton Friedman and several other economists. We'll explore the monetarist theory as we did the Keynesian theory, by looking first at its main impulse and second at the mechanism that creates a cycle in real GDP.

Monetarist Impulse The *impulse* in the monetarist theory of the business cycle is the *growth rate of the quantity of money.* A speedup in money growth brings expansion, and a slowdown in money growth brings recession. The source of the change in the growth rate of quantity of money is the monetary policy actions of the Bank of England.

Monetarist Cycle Mechanism In the monetarist theory, once the Bank has changed the money growth rate, a cycle mechanism begins to operate which, like the Keynesian mechanism, first affects aggregate demand. When the money growth rate increases, the quantity of real money in the economy increases. Interest rates fall and real money balances increase. The foreign exchange rate also falls – the pound loses value on the foreign exchange market. These initial financial market effects begin to spill over into other markets. Investment demand and exports increase, and consumers spend more on durable goods. These initial changes in expenditure have a multiplier effect, just as investment has in the Keynesian theory. Through these mechanisms, a speedup in money growth shifts the aggregate demand curve rightward and brings an expansion. Similarly, a slowdown in money growth shifts the aggregate demand curve leftward and brings a recession.

The second element of the monetarist cycle mechanism is the response of aggregate supply to a change in aggregate demand. The short-run aggregate supply curve is upward-sloping. With an upward-sloping *SAS* curve, swings in aggregate demand translate into swings in both real GDP and the price level. But monetarists think that real GDP deviations from full employment are temporary in both directions.

In monetarist theory, the money wage rate is only *temporarily sticky.* When aggregate demand decreases and unemployment rises, the money wage rate eventually begins to fall. As the money wage rate falls, so does the price level and after a period of adjustment, full employment is restored. When aggregate demand increases and unemployment falls below the natural rate, the money wage rate begins to rise. As the money wage rate rises so does the price level, and after a period of adjustment, real GDP returns to potential GDP and the unemployment rate returns to the natural rate.

Figure 33.4 illustrates the monetarist theory. In part (a), the economy is initially at full employment (point *a*) on the long-run aggregate supply curve, *LAS*, the aggregate demand curve, AD_0, and the short-run aggregate supply curve, SAS_0. A slowdown in the money growth rate decreases aggregate demand and the aggregate demand curve shifts leftward to AD_1. Real GDP falls to £700 billion and the economy moves to point *b.* Unemployment increases, and there is a surplus of labour. The money wage rate begins to fall. As the money wage rate falls, the short-run aggregate supply curve shifts from SAS_0 to SAS_1. The price level falls and real GDP begins to expand as the economy moves to point *c*, its new full-employment equilibrium, and GDP is back at its full-employment level.

Figure 33.4(b) shows the effects of the opposite initial money shock – a speedup in money growth. Here, starting out at point *c*, a rise in the money growth rate increases aggregate demand and shifts the *AD* curve to AD_2. Both real GDP and the price level rise as the economy moves to point *d*, the point of intersection of SAS_1 and AD_2. With real GDP above potential GDP and unemployment below the natural rate, the money wage rate begins to rise and the *SAS* curve starts to shift leftward towards SAS_2. As the money wage rate rises, the price level also rises and real GDP decreases. The economy moves from point *d* to point *e*, its new full-employment equilibrium.

The monetarist business cycle is like a rocking horse. It needs an outside force to get it going but once going, it rocks to-and-fro (but just once). It doesn't matter how the economy is hit. If it is hit with a money growth slowdown, the economy cycles with a recession followed by recovery. If it is hit by a money growth speedup, the economy cycles with a recovery followed by recession.

Rational Expectations Theories

A **rational expectation** is a forecast that is based on all the available relevant information. Rational expectations theories of the business cycle are theories based on the view that money wages are determined by a rational expectation of the price level. Two distinctly different rational expectations theories of the cycle have been proposed. A **new classical theory of the business cycle** regards *unanticipated* fluctuations in aggregate demand as the main source of economic fluctuations. This theory is based on the work of Robert E. Lucas Jr. A different **new Keynesian theory of the business cycle** regards *both anticipated and unanticipated*

Figure 33.4 A Monetarist Business Cycle

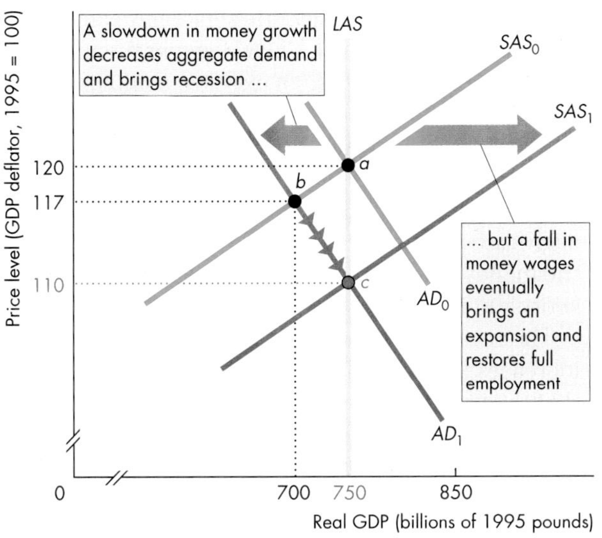

(a) Recession

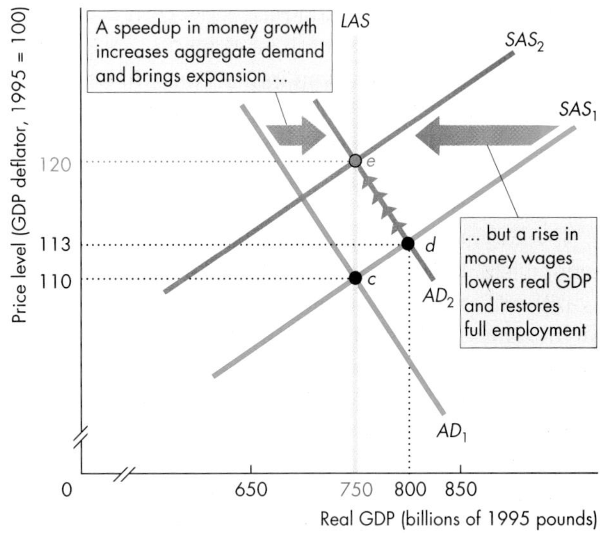

(b) Expansion

A monetarist recession begins when a slowdown in money growth decreases aggregate demand. The *AD* curve shifts leftward from AD_0 to AD_1 (part a). With sticky money wages, real GDP decreases to £700 billion and the price level falls to 110 as the economy moves from point *a* to point *b*. With a surplus of labour, the money wage rate falls and the *SAS* curve shifts rightward to SAS_1. The price level falls further, and real GDP returns to potential GDP at point *c*.

Starting at point *c* (part b), a monetarist expansion begins when an increase in money growth increases aggregate demand and shifts the *AD* curve rightward to AD_2. With sticky money wages, real GDP rises to £800 billion, the price level rises to 113, and the economy moves to point *d*. With a shortage of labour, the money wage rate rises and the *SAS* curve shifts towards SAS_2. The price level rises and real GDP decreases to potential GDP as the economy heads towards point *e*.

fluctuations in aggregate demand as sources of economic fluctuations. We'll explore these theories as we did the Keynesian and monetarist theories, by looking first at the main impulse and second at the cycle mechanism.

Rational Expectations Impulse The *impulse* that distinguishes the rational expectations theories from the other aggregate demand theories of the business cycle is the *unanticipated change in aggregate demand.* A larger than anticipated increase in aggregate demand brings an expansion and a smaller than anticipated increase in aggregate demand brings a recession. Any factor that influences aggregate demand – for example, fiscal policy, monetary policy, or developments in the world economy that influence exports – whose change is not anticipated, can bring a change in real GDP.

Rational Expectations Cycle Mechanisms

To describe the rational expectations cycle mechanisms, we'll deal first with the new classical version. When aggregate demand decreases, if the money wage rate doesn't change, real GDP and the price level both decrease. The fall in the price level increases the *real* wage rate, and employment decreases and unemployment rises. In the new classical theory, the events you've just reviewed occur only if the decrease in aggregate demand is not anticipated. If the decrease in aggregate demand *is* anticipated, both firms and workers will agree to a lower money wage rate. By doing so, they can prevent the real wage from rising and avoid a rise in the unemployment rate.

Similarly, if firms and workers anticipate an increase in aggregate demand, they expect the price level to rise and will agree to a higher money wage rate. By doing so, they can prevent the real wage from falling and avoid a fall in the unemployment rate below the natural rate.

Only fluctuations in aggregate demand that are unanticipated and not taken into account in wage contracts bring changes in real GDP. *Anticipated* changes in aggregate demand change the price level, but they leave real GDP and unemployment unchanged and do not create a business cycle.

New Keynesian economists, like new classical economists, think that money wages are influenced by rational expectations of the price level. But new Keynesians emphasize the long-term nature of most wage contracts. They say that *today's* money wages are influenced by *yesterday's* rational expectations. These expectations, which were formed in the past, are based on old information that might now be known to be incorrect. After they have made a long-term wage agreement, both firms and workers might anticipate a change in aggregate demand, which they expect will change the price level. But because they are locked into their agreement, they are unable to change money wages. So money wages are sticky in the new Keynesian theory and with sticky money wages, even an *anticipated* change in aggregate demand changes real GDP.

New classical economists say that long-term contracts are renegotiated when conditions change to make them outdated. So they do not regard long-term contracts as an obstacle to money wage flexibility, provided both parties to an agreement recognize the changed conditions. If both firms and workers expect the price level to change, they will change the agreed money wage rate to reflect that shared expectation. In this situation, anticipated changes in aggregate demand change the money wage rate and the price level and leave real GDP unchanged.

The distinctive feature of both versions of the rational expectations theory of the business cycle is the role of unanticipated changes in aggregate demand, and Figure 33.5 illustrates its effect on real GDP and the price level. Potential GDP is $750 billion and the long-run aggregate supply curve is *LAS*. Aggregate demand is expected to be *EAD*. Given potential GDP and *EAD*, the money wage rate is set at the level that is expected to bring full employment. At this money wage rate, the short-run aggregate supply curve is *SAS*. Imagine that, initially, aggregate demand equals expected aggregate demand, so there is full employment. Real GDP is $750 billion and the price level is 110. Then, unexpectedly, aggregate demand turns out to be less than expected and the aggregate demand curve shifts leftward to AD_0 (in Figure 33.5(a)). Many different aggregate demand shocks, such as a slowdown in the money growth rate or a collapse of exports, could have caused this shock. A recession begins. Real GDP falls to $700 billion and the price level falls to 107. The economy moves to point *b*. Unemployment increases and there is surplus of labour. But aggregate demand is expected to be at *EAD* so the money wage rate doesn't change and the short-run aggregate supply curve remains at *SAS*.

The recession ends when aggregate demand increases again to its expected level. A larger shock that takes aggregate demand to a level that exceeds *EAD* brings an expansion. In Figure 33.5(b), the aggregate demand curve shifts rightward to AD_1. Such an increase in aggregate demand might be caused by a speedup in the money growth rate or an export boom. Real GDP now increases to $800 billion and the price level rises to 113. The economy moves to point *c*. Unemployment is now below the natural rate. But aggregate demand is expected to be at *EAD* so the money wage rate doesn't change and the short-run aggregate supply curve remains at *SAS*.

Fluctuations in aggregate demand between AD_0 and AD_1 around expected aggregate demand *EAD* bring fluctuations in real GDP and the price level between points *b* and *c*.

The two versions of the rational expectations theory differ in their predictions about the effects of a change in expected aggregate demand. The new classical theory predicts that as soon as expected aggregate demand changes, the money wage rate also changes so the *SAS* curve shifts. The new Keynesian theory predicts that the money wage rate changes gradually when new contracts are made so that the *SAS* curve moves slowly. This difference between the two theories is crucial for policy. According to the new classical theory, anticipated policy actions change only the price level and have no effect on real GDP and unemployment. The reason is that when policy is expected to change, the money wage rate changes so the *SAS* curve shifts and offsets the effects of the policy action on real GDP. In contrast, in the new Keynesian theory, because money wages change only when new contracts are made, even anticipated policy actions change real GDP and can be used in an attempt to stabilize the cycle.

Figure 33.5 A Rational Expectations Business Cycle

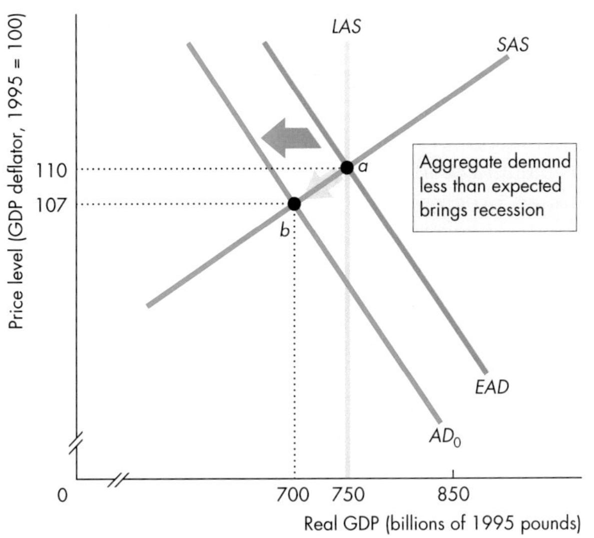

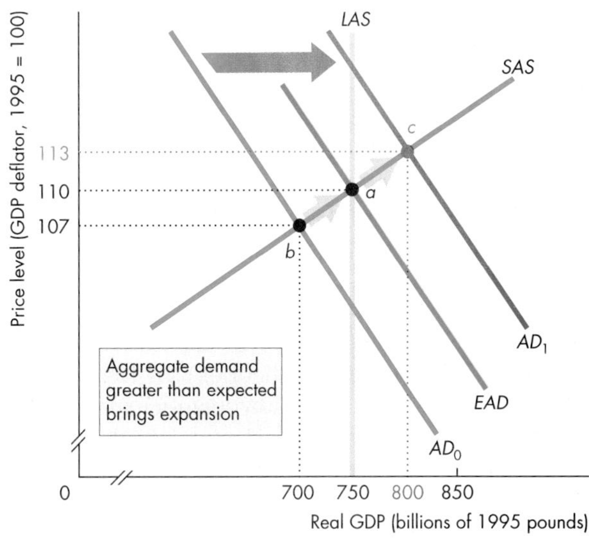

(a) Recession

(b) Expansion

The economy is expected to be at point *a* at the intersection of the *expected* aggregate demand curve, *EAD,* the short-run aggregate supply curve, *SAS,* and the long-run aggregate supply curve, *LAS.* A rational expectations recession begins when an unanticipated decrease in aggregate demand shifts the *AD* curve leftward to AD_0. With money wage rates based on the expectation that aggregate demand will be *EAD,* real GDP decreases to £700 billion and the price level falls to 107 as the economy moves to point *b.* As long as aggregate demand is *expected* to be *EAD* there is no change in the money wage rate.

A rational expectations expansion begins when an unanticipated increase in aggregate demand shifts the *AD* curve rightward from AD_0 to AD_1. With money wage rates based on the expectation that aggregate demand will be *EAD,* real GDP increases to £800 billion and the price level rises to 113 as the economy moves to point *c.* Again, as long as aggregate demand is *expected* to be *EAD,* there is no change in the money wage rate.

Like the monetarist business cycle, these rational expectations cycles are similar to rocking horses. They need an outside force to get going, but once going the economy rocks around its full-employment point. The new classical horse rocks faster and comes to rest more quickly than the new Keynesian horse.

AD–AS General Theory

All the theories of the business cycle that we've considered can be viewed as particular cases of a more general *AD–AS* theory. In this more general theory, the impulses of both the Keynesian and monetarist theories can change aggregate demand. A multiplier effect makes aggregate demand change by more than any initial change in one of the components of expenditure. The money wage rate can be viewed as responding to changes in the rational expectation of the future price level. Even if the money wage is flexible, it will change only to the extent that price level expectations change. As a result, the money wage will adjust gradually.

Although in all three types of business cycle theory that we've considered the cycle is caused by fluctuations in aggregate demand, the possibility that an occasional aggregate supply shock might occur is not ruled out. A recession could occur because aggregate supply falls. For example, a widespread drought that cuts agricultural production could cause a recession in an economy that has a large agricultural sector. But these demand theories of the cycle regard supply shocks as rare rather than normal events. Aggregate demand fluctuations are the normal ongoing sources of fluctuations.

Review

- Keynesian theory says the business cycle is caused by volatile expectations about future sales and profits – *animal spirits* – a multiplier effect and sticky money wages.
- Monetarist theory says the business cycle is caused by the Bank of England speeding up and slowing down the growth rate of money, which changes spending plans.
- New classical and new Keynesian theories (rational expectations theories) say the business cycle is caused by unanticipated fluctuations in aggregate demand. In the new classical theory, the money wage rate responds to price level expectations, and in the new Keynesian theory, the money wage rate is set by long-term contracts.

A new theory of the business cycle challenges the mainstream and traditional demand theories that you've just studied. It is called the real business cycle theory. Let's take a look at this new theory.

Real Business Cycle Theory

The newest theory of the business cycle, known as **real business cycle theory** (or RBC theory), regards random fluctuations in productivity as the main source of economic fluctuations. These productivity fluctuations are assumed to result mainly from fluctuations in the pace of technological change, but they might also have other sources such as international disturbances, climate fluctuations, or natural disasters. The origins of real business cycle theory can be traced to the rational expectations revolution set off by Robert E. Lucas Jr, but the first demonstration of the power of this theory was given by Edward Prescott and Finn Kydland, and by John Long and Charles Plosser. Today, real business cycle theory is part of a broad research agenda called *dynamic general equilibrium*, and hundreds of young macroeconomists do research on this topic.

Like our study of the demand theories, we'll explore the RBC theory by looking first at its impulse and second at the mechanism that converts that impulse into a cycle in real GDP.

The RBC Impulse

The *impulse* in the RBC theory is the *growth rate of productivity that results from technological change*. RBC theorists think this impulse is generated mainly by the process of research and development that leads to the creation and use of new technologies. Sometimes technological progress is rapid and productivity grows quickly; and at other times, progress is slow and productivity grows moderately. Occasionally, technological change is so far reaching that it makes a large amount of existing capital, especially human capital, obsolete. It also, initially, destroys jobs and shuts down businesses. These initial effects of far-reaching technological change *decrease* productivity and can create recession. Other supply shocks, such as the world oil embargo of the mid-1970s, can temporarily decrease productivity.

To isolate the RBC theory impulse – the growth rate of productivity that results from technological change – economists use the tool of growth accounting, which is explained in Chapter 32, pp. 808–812.

Figure 33.6 shows the RBC impulse for the United Kingdom from 1971 to 1998. This figure also shows that fluctuations in productivity growth are correlated with GDP fluctuations. This RBC productivity variable is a catch-all variable. Economists are not sure what it actually measures or what causes it to fluctuate.

The RBC Mechanism

The mechanism that creates the business cycle according to the RBC theory is more complex and intricate than the demand theory mechanisms. Two immediate effects follow from a change in productivity that get an expansion or a contraction going:

1 Investment demand changes.
2 Demand for labour changes.

We'll study these effects and their consequences during a recession. In an expansion, they work in the opposite direction to what is described here.

A wave of technological change makes some existing capital obsolete and temporarily lowers productivity. Firms expect the future profit rate to fall and see their labour productivity falling. With lower profit expectations, they cut back their purchases of new capital, and with lower labour

Figure 33.6 The Real Business Cycle Impulse

The real business cycle is caused by changes in technology that bring fluctuations in productivity. The fluctuations in productivity shown here are calculated by using growth accounting (the one-third rule) to remove the contribution of capital accumulation to productivity growth. Productivity fluctuations are correlated with real GDP fluctuations. Economists are not sure what the productivity variable actually measures or what causes it to fluctuate.

Sources: ONS; and the authors' calculations.

productivity they plan to lay off some workers. So the initial effect of a decrease in productivity is a decrease in investment demand and a decrease in the demand for labour.

Figure 33.7 illustrates these two initial effects of a decrease in productivity. Part (a) shows investment demand, *ID*, and saving supply, *SS*. Initially, investment demand is ID_0, and the equilibrium level of investment and saving is £100 billion at a real interest rate of 6 per cent a year. A decrease in productivity lowers the expected profit rate and decreases investment demand. The *ID* curve shifts leftward to ID_1. The real interest rate falls to 4 per cent a year, and investment and saving decrease to £100 billion.

Part (b) shows the demand for labour, *LD*, and the supply of labour, *LS*. Initially, the demand for labour is LD_0, and the equilibrium level of employment is 45 billion hours a year at a real wage rate of £7.50 an hour. The decrease in productivity decreases the demand for labour and the *LD* curve shifts leftward to LD_1.

Before we can determine the new level of employment and the real wage rate, we need to take a ripple effect into account – the key ripple effect in RBC theory.

The Key Decision: When to Work? According to the RBC theory, people decide *when* to work by doing a cost–benefit calculation. They compare the return from working in the current period with the *expected* return from working in a later period. You make such a comparison every day at college. Suppose your goal in this course is to get a first. To achieve this goal, you work pretty hard most of the time. But during the few days before the mid-term and final exams, you work especially hard. Why? Because you think the return from studying close to the exam is greater than the return from studying when the exam is a long time away. So during the term you hang around the Students' Union bar, go to parties, play squash and enjoy other leisure pursuits, but at exam time you work every evening and weekend.

Real business cycle theory says that workers behave like you. They work fewer hours, and sometimes zero hours, when the real wage rate is temporarily low and they work more hours when the real wage rate is temporarily high. But to compare properly the current wage rate with the expected future wage rate, workers must use the real interest rate. If the real interest rate is 6 per cent a year, a real wage rate of £1 an hour earned

Figure 33.7 Factor Markets in a Real Business Cycle

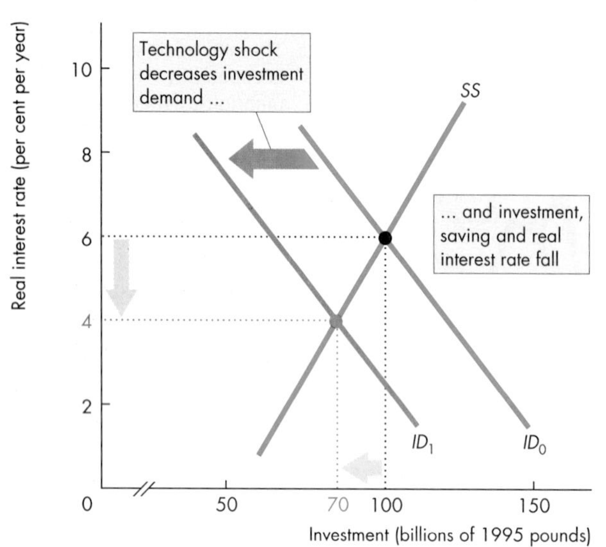

(a) Investment, saving, and interest rate

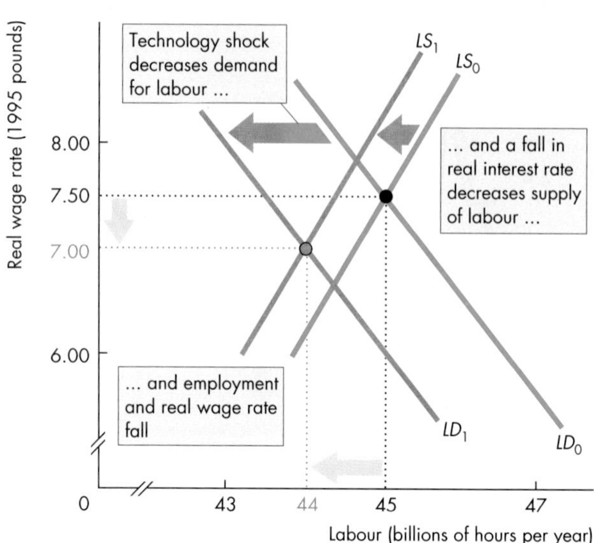

(b) Labour and wage rate

Saving supply is *SS* (part a) and, initially, investment demand is ID_0. The real interest rate is 6 per cent a year and saving and investment are £100 billion. In the labour market (part b), the demand for labour is LD_0 and the supply of labour is LS_0. The real wage rate is £7.50 an hour and employment is 45 billion hours. A technological change decreases productivity, and both investment demand and the demand for labour decrease. The two demand curves shift leftward to ID_1 and LD_1. In part (a), the real interest rate falls to 4 per cent a year, and investment and saving fall. In part (b), the fall in the real interest rate decreases the supply of labour (the when-to-work decision) and the supply curve shifts leftward to LS_1. Employment decreases to 44 billion hours and the real wage rate falls to £7.00 an hour. A recession is under way.

this week will become £1.06 a year from now. If the real wage rate is expected to be £1.05 an hour next year, today's wage of £1 looks good. By working longer hours now and shorter hours a year from now, a person can get a 1 per cent higher real wage. But suppose the real interest rate is 4 per cent a year. In this case, £1 earned now is worth £1.04 next year. Working fewer hours now and more next year is the way to get a 1 per cent higher real wage.

So the when-to-work decision depends on the real interest rate. The lower the real interest rate, other things remaining the same, the smaller is the supply of labour. Many economists think this *intertemporal substitution effect* to be of negligible size. RBC theorists say the effect is large, and it is the key element in the RBC mechanism.

You've seen in Figure 33.7(a) that the decrease in investment demand lowers the real interest rate. This fall in the real interest rate lowers the return to current work and decreases the supply of labour. In Figure 33.7(b), the labour supply curve shifts leftward to LS_1. The effect of a productivity shock on demand is larger than the effect of the fall in the real interest rate on the supply of labour. That is, the *LD* curve shifts farther leftward than does the *LS* curve. As a result, the real wage rate falls to £7 an hour and employment falls to 44 billion hours. A recession has begun and is intensifying.

Real GDP and the Price Level The next part of the RBC story traces the consequences of the changes you've just seen for real GDP and the price level. With a decrease in employment, aggregate supply decreases; and with a decrease in investment demand, aggregate demand decreases. Figure 33.8 illustrates these effects, using the *AD–AS*

Figure 33.8 *AD–AS* in a Real Business Cycle

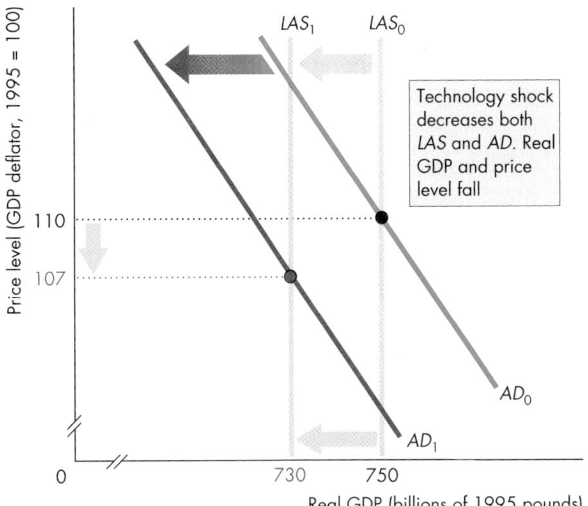

Initially, the aggregate demand curve is AD_0 and the long-run aggregate supply curve is LAS_0. Real GDP is £750 billion (which equals potential GDP) and the price level is 110. There is no *SAS* curve in the real business cycle theory because the money wage rate is flexible. The technological change described in Figure 33.6 decreases potential GDP and the *LAS* curve shifts leftward to LAS_1. The decrease in investment demand decreases aggregate demand, and the *AD* curve shifts leftward to AD_1. Real GDP decreases to £730 billion and the price level falls to 107. The economy goes into recession.

framework. Initially, the aggregate demand curve is AD_0 and the long-run aggregate supply curve is LAS_0. The price level is 110 and real GDP is £750 billion. There is no short-run aggregate supply curve in this figure because in the RBC theory, the *SAS* curve has no meaning. The labour market moves relentlessly toward its equilibrium, and the money wage rate adjusts freely (either upward or downward) to ensure that the real wage rate keeps the quantity of labour demanded equal to the quantity supplied. In the RBC theory, unemployment is always at the natural rate, and the natural rate fluctuates over the business cycle because the amount of job search fluctuates.

The decrease in employment lowers total production, and aggregate supply decreases. The *LAS* curve shifts leftward to LAS_1. The decrease in investment demand decreases aggregate demand, and the *AD* curve shifts leftward to AD_1. The price level falls to 107, and real GDP decreases to £730 billion. The economy has gone through a recession.

What Happened to Money? The name *real* business cycle theory is no accident. It reflects the central prediction of the theory: that the business cycle is caused by real things and not by nominal or monetary things. If the quantity of money changes, aggregate demand changes. But with no real change – with no change in the use of the factors of production and no change in potential GDP – the change in money changes only the price level. In real business cycle theory, this outcome occurs because the aggregate supply curve is the *LAS* curve, which pins real GDP down at potential GDP, so that when the *AD* curve changes only the price level changes.

Cycles and Growth The shock that drives the business cycle of the RBC theory is the same as the force that generates economic growth: technological change. On the average, as technology advances, productivity grows. But it grows at an uneven pace. You saw this fact when you studied growth accounting in Chapter 32. There, we focused on slow-changing trends in productivity growth. Real business cycle theory uses the same idea but says there are frequent shocks to productivity that are mostly positive but that are occasionally negative.

Criticisms of RBC Theory

RBC theory is controversial, and when economists discuss it they often generate more heat than light. Its detractors claim that its basic assumptions are just too incredible. Money wages *are* sticky, they claim, so to assume otherwise is at odds with a clear fact. Intertemporal substitution is too weak, they say, to account for large fluctuations in labour supply and employment with small changes in the real wage rate.

But what really kills the RBC story, say most economists, is an implausible impulse. Technology shocks are not capable of creating the swings in productivity that growth accounting reveals. These shocks are caused by something, they concede, but they are as likely to be caused by *changes in aggregate demand* as by technology. If they are caused by demand fluctuations, then the traditional demand theories are needed to explain these shocks.

Fluctuations in productivity do not cause the cycle but are caused by it!

Building on this theme, the critics point out that the so-called productivity fluctuations that growth accounting measures are correlated with changes in the growth rate of money and other indicators of changes in aggregate demand.

Defence of RBC Theory

The defenders of RBC theory claim that the theory works. It explains the macroeconomic facts about the business cycle and is consistent with the facts about economic growth. In effect, a single theory explains *both growth and cycles*. The growth accounting exercise that explains slowly changing trends also explains the more frequent business cycle swings. Its defenders also claim that RBC theory is consistent with a wide range of *micro-economic* evidence about labour supply decisions, labour demand and investment demand decisions, and information on the distribution of income between labour and capital.

RBC theorists acknowledge that money and the business cycle are correlated. That is, rapid money growth and expansion go together, and slow money growth and recession go together. But, they argue, causation does not run from money to real GDP as the traditional aggregate demand theories state. Instead, they view causation as running from real GDP to money – so-called reverse causation. In a recession, the initial fall in investment demand that lowers the interest rate decreases the demand for bank loans and lowers the profitability of banking. So banks increase their reserves and decrease their loans. The quantity of bank deposits and hence the quantity of money decreases. This reverse causation is responsible for the correlation between money growth and real GDP according to real business cycle theory.

Its defenders also argue that the RBC view is significant because it at least raises the possibility that the business cycle is efficient. The business cycle does not signal an economy that is misbehaving; it is business as usual. If this view is correct, it means that policy to smooth the cycle is misguided. Smoothing the troughs can be done only by taking out the peaks. But peaks are bursts of investment to take advantage of new technologies in a timely way. So smoothing the business cycle means delaying the benefits of new technologies.

Review

- The real business cycle (RBC) theory says that economic fluctuations are caused by technological change that makes productivity growth fluctuate.
- A fall in productivity decreases both investment demand and the demand for labour and lowers the real interest rate. The lower real interest rate decreases the supply of labour and employment and the real wage rate falls.
- A fall in productivity decreases both long-run aggregate supply and aggregate demand and decreases both real GDP and the price level.

You've now reviewed the main theories of the business cycle. Your next task is to examine some actual business cycles. In pursuing this task, we will focus on the recession phase of the cycle. We'll do this mainly because it is the recessions that cause most trouble. We begin by looking at the 1991–92 recession.

The 1991–92 Recession

In the theories of the business cycle that you've studied, recessions can be triggered by a variety of forces, some on the aggregate demand side and some on the aggregate supply side. Let's identify the shocks that triggered the most recent recession in the United Kingdom – the 1991–92 recession.

The Origins of the 1991–92 Recession

Two forces were at work in United Kingdom during 1990 that appear to have contributed to the recession and subsequent sluggish growth. They were:

1 Monetary policy.

2 A slowdown in the world economy.

Monetary Policy Three factors made monetary policy deflationary during 1990. First, the United Kingdom joined the Exchange Rate Mechanism (ERM) of the European Monetary System (EMS). Second, the Bank of England slowed the growth rate of the money supply. Third, German reunification

The promised green shoots of recovery showed no signs of sprouting.

Drawing by Austin. *The Guardian.*

put upward pressure on interest rates which, through the ERM, were transmitted quickly to the United Kingdom.

Inflation had reached a peak of 10 per cent by the time the United Kingdom was taken into the ERM in October 1990. Keen to restore its anti-inflation credentials, the government decided that the best way to restore low inflation was through the discipline of the ERM. The ERM is a pegged exchange rate system with a central rate and a wide or narrow band of fluctuations with other currencies in the system. The central rate was set at DM2.95 to the £1 with a band of ±6 per cent around its central rate.

When the United Kingdom entered the ERM, inflation was above that of the EU average. With the exchange rate fixed around a band of ±6 per cent this meant that UK goods became increasingly expensive in European markets. The high real interest rates that were needed to take the economy into the ERM and the loss of competitiveness had a strong negative influence on aggregate demand. The economy went into recession. Currency speculators anticipated that the UK economy could not carry on at the existing central rate of DM2.95 and expected a devaluation, causing a continuous downward pressure on the pound.

Bank of England Response To convince currency speculators that the government did not intend to devalue, the Bank of England kept interest rates higher than in the rest of Europe. However, the more the Bank resisted currency speculators by keeping interest rates high, the wider was the belief that the economy could not continue in recession with high real interest rates and that a devaluation must occur[1]. This is like a game of 'chicken' between two cars, except that it is between the Bank and speculators. Like a game of chicken, someone has to give way and be the chicken. In September 1992 the government of the United Kingdom became the chicken and left the ERM.

The extent to which the Bank slowed the economy can be seen from the slowdown in the growth rate of the money supply between 1990 and 1992 shown in Figure 33.9. The growth rate of the broad definition of money, M4, slowed from 19 per cent in the first quarter of 1990 to 3 per cent in the fourth quarter of 1992.

German Reunification In November 1989 the Berlin Wall came down, and in October 1990 East Germany was reunited with West Germany. The cost of the reunification was enormous. Fiscal transfers to the eastern states pushed the government budget into deficit. From being a net lender in the world capital market, the new Germany began its life as a net borrower. The German central bank, the Bundesbank, raised interest rates to forestall the inflationary implications of the unification. As the Deutschemark was the anchor currency for the ERM, the rise in German interest rates meant that the rest of the members of the ERM had to raise their interest rates if they were to remain within the specified bands of their respective central rates. Figure 33.10 shows the influence German interest rates had on the interest rates of the United Kingdom and France. Because France remained committed to the ERM, the Bank of France raised and lowered its short-term rate of interest in line with the German short-term interest rate. The initial aim of the Bank of England was to try and stay within the bands of the ERM by keeping interest rates high. After September 1992, the

1 This process is known as the 'Walters critique' after Professor Sir Alan Walters, who suggested that the ERM would create such destabilizing forces, p. 503

Figure 33.9 Money Supply Growth: 1990–1992

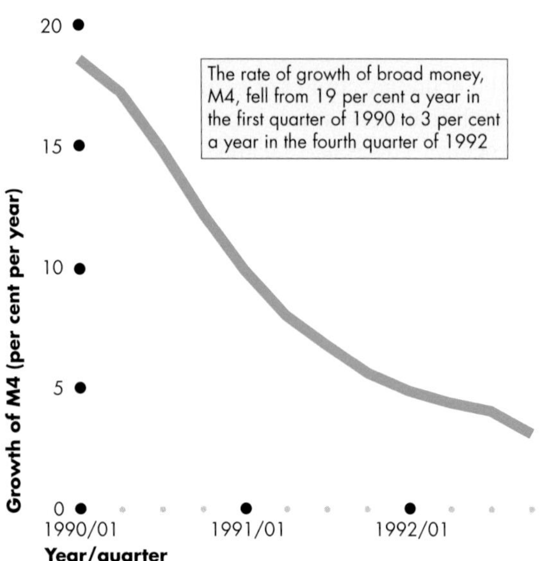

The entry of the United Kingdom into the ERM meant that the Bank of England had to pursue a tight monetary policy. The money supply growth rate began to slow during 1989. It slowed even further during 1990.

Source: *Bank of England.*

Figure 33.10 European Business Rates, 1989–1993

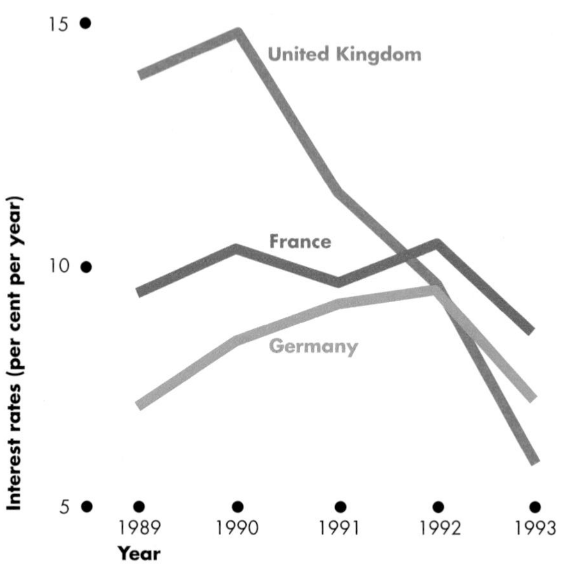

The French interest rate moved up and down with the German interest rate during this period. The UK interest rate moved up with German interest rate when the United Kingdom joined the ERM. It slipped down in 1991 as German interest rates rose. The narrowing gap between UK and German interest rates raised speculation of a withdrawal from the ERM. In September 1992, the United Kingdom left the ERM following a concerted speculative attack on the currency. UK interest rates were able to fall below German interest rates in 1993.

Source: European Union, DG–II.

short-term rate of interest in the United Kingdom was allowed to fall below that of Germany.

A Slowdown in Economic Expansion in the World Economy After its longest ever period of peacetime expansion, US real GDP growth began to slow in 1989 and 1990 and the United States went into recession in mid-1990. The slowdown of the US economy brought slower growth in demand for the rest of the world's exports and resulted in lower export volumes and a decline in world economic activity.

Let's see how the events we've just described influenced the UK economy in 1990.

Aggregate Demand and Aggregate Supply in the 1991–92 Recession

Figure 33.11 describes the effects of the various events that triggered the recession of 1991–92. The aggregate demand curve was AD_{90} and the short-run aggregate supply curve was SAS_{90}. Real GDP was £658 billion and the price level was 84.

The 1991–92 recession was caused by a decrease in both aggregate demand and aggregate supply. Aggregate demand decreased, initially, because of the high real interest rate, the overvalued exchange rate and the slowdown in the growth rate of the quantity of money. These factors were soon reinforced by the slowdown in the world economy that brought a decline in the growth of exports. The combination of these factors triggered a massive decline in investment. The resulting decrease in aggregate demand is shown by the shift of the aggregate demand curve leftward to AD_{91}. Aggregate supply decreased because money wages continued to increase throughout 1990 at a rate similar

Figure 33.11 The 1991–1992 Recession

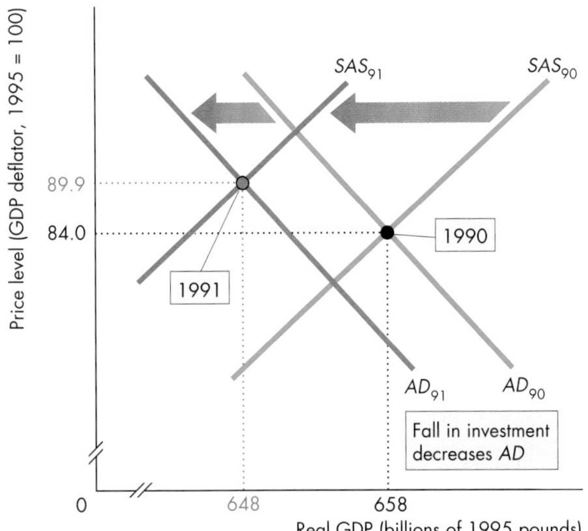

At the end of 1990, the economy was on its aggregate demand curve, AD_{90}, and its short-run aggregate supply curve, SAS_{90}, with real GDP at £658 billion and a GDP deflator of 84. The combination of a decrease in both aggregate supply and aggregate demand put the economy into recession. Real GDP decreased to £648 billion and the price level increased to 89.9.

Figure 33.12 The Labour Market in the 1990s

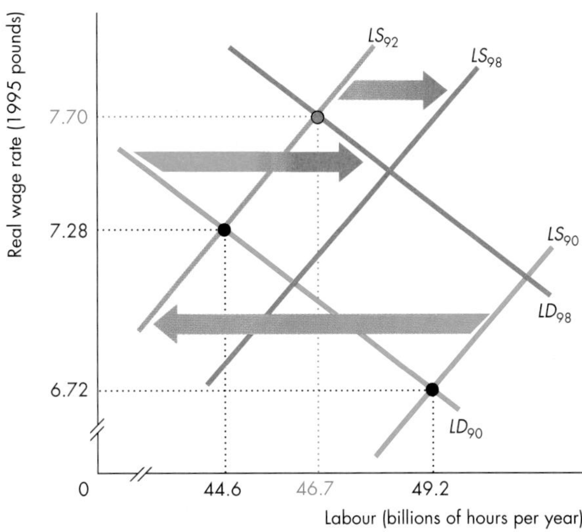

In 1990, the demand for labour was LD_{90} and the supply of labour was LS_{90}. If the quantity of labour supplied equalled the quantity of labour demanded, the real wage was £6.72 an hour and employment was 49.2 billion of hours. Money wages continued to rise because people did not anticipate the fall in inflation in 1991 and 1992, and *LS* shifted leftward to LS_{92}. Real wages increased to £7.70 and employment fell to 46.7 billion hours. In the rest of the 1990s, money wages grew less than inflation, *LS* shifted rightward to LS_{98}, and as real wages fell employment increased.

to that in 1989. This decrease in aggregate supply is shown in Figure 33.11 as the shift in the short-run aggregate supply curve leftward to SAS_{91}. (The figure does not show the long-run aggregate supply curve.)

The combined effect of the decreases in aggregate supply and aggregate demand was a decrease in real GDP to £648 billion – a 1.5 per cent decrease, and an increase in the price level to 89.9 – a 6.8 per cent increase.

You've seen how aggregate demand and aggregate supply changed during the 1991–92 recession. What happened in the labour market during this recession?

The Labour Market in the 1990s

The unemployment rate increased persistently from the beginning of 1990 to the end of 1993. Figure 33.12 shows two other facts about the labour market during this period – facts about employment and the real wage rate. As employment decreased through 1990, 1991 and 1992, the real wage rate increased. Later, during the recovery in mid-1993, employment increased and the real wage rate decreased. These movements in employment and the real wage rate suggest that the forces of supply and demand do not operate smoothly in the labour market. Money wages continued to rise because people did not anticipate the slowdown in inflation. When inflation did slow down, the real wage rate increased and the quantity of labour demanded decreased. The loss of employment meant that when inflation fell money wages fell faster. The recovery in mid-1993 also led to a rise in labour demand in the rest of the 1990s to 1998.

Review

- The 1991–92 recession was triggered by the government's decision to take the United Kingdom into the ERM at an overvalued exchange rate. The situation was aggravated by two further factors: first, the costs of German reunification raised interest rates within the ERM, and second, the world economy slowed down.
- Money wages continued to rise and the fall in inflation increased the real wage rate and lowered employment and real GDP.

You've now seen what caused the 1991–92 recession. Let's look next at the greatest of recessions – the Great Depression.

Figure 33.13 The Great Depression

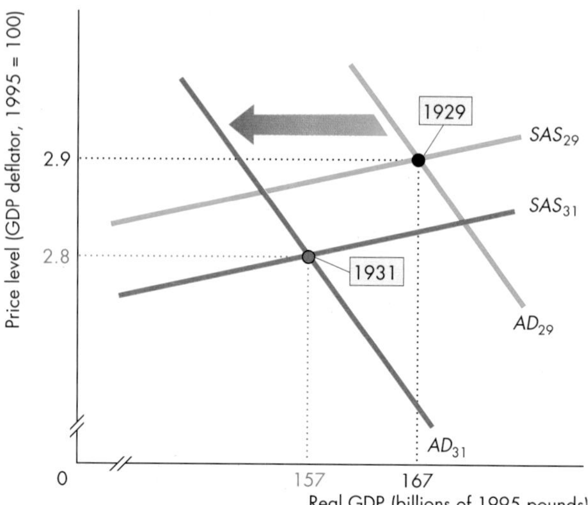

In 1929, real GDP was £167 billion and the GDP deflator was 2.9 – at the intersection of AD_{29} and SAS_{29}. Increased pessimism from a fall in world trade resulted in a drop in investment, resulting in a decrease in aggregate demand to AD_{31}. To some degree, this decrease was reflected in the labour market and wages fell, so the short-run aggregate supply curve shifted to SAS_{31}. Real GDP and the price level fell. By 1931, real GDP had fallen to £157 billion (94 per cent of its 1929 level) and the GDP deflator had fallen to 2.8 (97 per cent of its 1929 level).

The Great Depression

The late 1920s were years of economic revival in some parts of the UK economy. While the traditional industries like coal and shipbuilding stagnated, others like motor manufacturing were booming. New firms were created, and the capital stock of the nation expanded. At the beginning of 1929, UK real GDP nearly equalled potential GDP. But as that eventful year unfolded, increasing signs of economic weakness began to appear. The most dramatic events occurred in October when the US stock market collapsed, losing more than one-third of its value in two weeks. The four years that followed were years of monstrous economic depression all over the world.

Figure 33.13 shows the dimensions of the Great Depression. On the eve of the Great Depression in 1929, the economy was on aggregate demand curve AD_{29} and short-run aggregate supply curve SAS_{29}. Real GDP was £167 billion (1995 pounds) and the GDP deflator was 2.9 (1995 = 100).

In 1931, there was a widespread expectation that the price level would fall, and the money wage rate fell. With a lower money wage rate, the short-run aggregate supply curve shifted from SAS_{29} to SAS_{31}. But increased pessimism and lower trade decreased investment, and aggregate demand decreased to AD_{31}. In 1931, real GDP fell to £157 billion and the price level fell by 2.8.

Although the Great Depression brought enormous hardship, the distribution of that hardship was uneven. At its worst point, 16 per cent of the workforce had no jobs at all. Although there was unemployment benefit and other forms of poor relief, there was a considerable level of poverty for those on the dole. But the wallets of those who kept their jobs barely noticed the Great Depression. It is true that wages fell. But at the same time, the price level fell by more, so real wages actually rose. Thus those who had jobs were paid a wage rate that had an increasing buying power during the Great Depression.

You can begin to appreciate the magnitude of the Great Depression if you compare it with the 1991–92 recession. In 1991, real GDP fell by 1.5 per cent. In comparison, in 1931, it fell by 5.3 per cent.

Why the Great Depression Happened

The late 1920s were years of economic recovery in the world economy, but they were also years of increasing uncertainty. The main source of increased uncertainty was international. The world economy was going through tumultuous times. The patterns of world trade were changing as the United Kingdom began its period of relative economic decline and new economic powers such as Japan began to emerge. International currency fluctuations and the introduction of restrictive trade policies by many countries (see Chapter 35) further increased the uncertainty faced by firms. There was also domestic uncertainty arising from the restrictive monetary and fiscal policy followed by the government to ensure that the pound remained on the gold standard. Because prices in the United States fell, prices in the United Kingdom had to fall to maintain an exchange rate of $4.86 per pound sterling, and remain on the gold standard. This meant that the recovery in the United Kingdom was good but not booming like in the United States.

This environment of uncertainty was fuelled by the slowdown in the world economy following the stock market crash of 1929. It was this slowdown in the world economy which led to a drop in exports, which led to a fall in income, consumer spending and investment, which led to the initial leftward shift of the aggregate demand curve from AD_{29} to AD_{31} in Figure 33.13.

Output fell for two years after 1929, but what stopped the Great Depression in the United Kingdom developing into the disaster that hit the United States was the fact that the United Kingdom left the gold standard. Leaving the gold standard meant that the pound was no longer convertible into gold, and interest rates that were kept high to make the pound attractive relative to the price of gold in US dollars could now be lower. Indeed, interest rates fell dramatically in the 1930s. Money was cheap, and lower interest rates fuelled a consumer revival and a housebuilding boom.

What really distinguishes the Great Depression was not what happened in the United Kingdom but what happened to the world's largest economy – the United States. Between 1929 and 1933 in the United States real GDP fell by nearly 30 per cent. But economists, even to this day, have not reached an agreement on how to explain those events. One view, argued by Peter Temin[2], is that spending continued to fall for a wide variety of reasons – including a continuation of increasing pessimism and uncertainty. According to Temin's view, the continued contraction resulted from a collapse of expenditure that was independent of the decrease in the quantity of money. The investment demand curve shifted leftward. Milton Friedman and Anna J. Schwartz have argued that the continuation of the contraction was almost exclusively the result of the subsequent worsening of financial and monetary conditions[3]. According to Friedman and Schwartz, it was a severe cut in the money supply that lowered aggregate demand, prolonging the contraction and deepening the depression.

Although there is disagreement about the causes of the contraction phase of the Great Depression in the United States, the disagreement is not about the elements at work but the degree of importance attached to each. Everyone agrees that increased pessimism and uncertainty lowered investment demand, and everyone agrees that there was a massive contraction of the real money supply. Temin and his supporters assign primary importance to the fall in autonomous expenditure and secondary importance to the fall in the money supply. Friedman and Schwartz and their supporters assign primary responsibility to the money supply and regard the other factors as being of limited importance.

Let's look at the contraction of aggregate demand a bit more closely. Between 1930 and 1933, the nominal money supply in the United States decreased by 20 per cent. This decrease in the money supply was not directly induced by the Federal Reserve's actions. The *monetary base* (currency in circulation and bank reserves) hardly fell at all. But the bank deposits component of the money supply suffered an enormous collapse. It did so primarily because a large number of banks failed. Before the Great Depression, fuelled by increasing share prices and booming business conditions, bank loans expanded. But after the stock market crash and the downturn, many borrowers found themselves in hard economic times. They could not pay the interest on their loans, and they could not meet the agreed repayment schedules. Banks had deposits

2 Peter Temin, *Did Monetary Forces Cause the Great Depression*? 1976 (New York, W.W. Norton).

3 This explanation was developed by Milton Friedman and Anna J. Schwartz in *A Monetary History of the United States 1867–1960*, 1963 (Princeton, Princeton University Press), Chapter 7.

that exceeded the realistic value of the loans that they had made. When depositors withdrew funds from the banks, the banks lost reserves and many of them simply couldn't meet their depositors' demands to be repaid.

Bank failures feed on themselves and create additional failures. Seeing banks fail, people become anxious to protect themselves and so take their money out of the banks. This happened in the United States in 1930. The quantity of notes and coins in circulation increased and the volume of bank deposits declined. But the very action of people who took money out of the bank to protect their wealth accentuated the process of banking failure. Banks were increasingly short of cash and unable to meet their obligations.

Monetary contraction also occurred in the United Kingdom, although on a less serious scale than in the United States. The broad money supply fell in 1931 by 1 per cent and did not decline in any other year, in contrast to the whopping 20 per cent in the United States. Also, the United Kingdom had no serious problems with bank failure in contrast to the United States. This was because lower interest rates meant that money was cheap and also banks always had access to the Bank of England. Another reason was the development of branch banking in the United Kingdom, which meant that if a particular sector that was concentrated in a geographical region was to collapse, the commercial bank would not go down with it. The main bank office in London could shore up any loss-making branches in a region.

What role did the stock market crash of 1929 play in producing the Great Depression in the United States? It certainly created an atmosphere of fear and panic, and probably contributed to the overall air of uncertainty that dampened investment spending. It also reduced the wealth of shareholders, encouraging them to cut their consumption spending. But the direct effect of the stock market crash on consumption, although a contributory factor to the Great Depression, was not the major source of the drop in aggregate demand. It was the collapse in investment arising from increased uncertainty that brought the 1930 decline in aggregate demand.

The stock market crash was, however, a predictor of severe recession. It reflected the expectations of shareholders concerning future profit prospects. As those expectations became pessimistic, people sold their shares. There were more sellers than buyers and the prices of shares were bid lower and lower. That is, the behaviour of the stock market was a consequence of expectations about future profitability and those expectations were lowered as a result of increased uncertainty.

Can It Happen Again?

Because we have an incomplete understanding of the causes of the Great Depression, we are not able to predict such an event or to be sure that it cannot occur again. The stock market crash of 1987 did not translate into a world slowdown or a contraction anything like that of 1929. But there are some significant differences between the economy of the 1990s and that of the 1930s that make a severe depression much less likely today than it was 60 years ago. The most significant features of the economy that make severe depression less likely today are:

- Bank deposit protection.
- The Bank of England's role as lender of last resort.
- Taxes and government spending.
- Multi-income families.

Let's examine these in turn.

Bank Deposit Protection The Bank of England deposit protection scheme covers 90 per cent of the first £20,000 per depositor of the banks that come under the scheme. So small depositors are virtually fully covered. With some form of deposit insurance, depositors have little to lose if a bank fails and so have no incentive to cause a panic by withdrawing their deposits, and thereby precipitating a bank crisis.

Although bank failure was not a severe problem in the United Kingdom during the Great Depression, it clearly was an important factor in intensifying the depression in the United States. And the severity of the US recession certainly had an impact on the United Kingdom and the rest of the world. World trade fell dramatically from 1930 to 1933 with the fall in aggregate demand in the United States.

Lender of Last Resort The Bank of England is the lender of last resort in the UK economy and the individual central banks in the European Monetary Union continue to act as the lender of last resort for their country banks. If a single bank is short of reserves, it can borrow reserves from other banks. If the entire banking system is short of reserves, banks in the UK can borrow from the Bank of England. By making reserves available (at a suitable interest rate), the Bank of England is able to make the quantity of reserves in the banking system respond flexibly to the demand for those reserves. Bank failure can be prevented, or at least contained, to cases where bad management practices are the source of the problem. Widespread failures of the type that occurred in the Great Depression can be prevented.

Taxes and Government Spending The government sector was a much smaller part of the economy in 1929 than it has become today. On the eve of that earlier recession, government purchases of goods and services were less than 25 per cent of GDP. Today, government purchases exceed 40 per cent of GDP. Government transfer payments were about 6 per cent of GDP in 1929. Today, they are 18 per cent of GDP.

A higher level of government purchases of goods and services means that when recession hits, a large component of aggregate demand does not decline. But government transfer payments are the most sensitive economic stabilizer. When the economy goes into recession and depression, more people qualify for unemployment insurance and social assistance. As a consequence, although disposable income decreases, the extent of the decrease is moderated by the existence of such programmes. Consumption expenditure, in turn, does not decline by as much as it would in the absence of such government programmes. The limited decline in consumption spending further limits the overall decrease in aggregate expenditure, thereby limiting the magnitude of an economic downturn.

Multi-income Families At the time of the Great Depression, families with more than one wage earner were much less common than they are today. The workforce participation rate in 1929 was around 45 per cent. Today, it is 75 per cent. Thus even if the unemployment rate increased to around 20 per cent today, 60 per cent of the adult population would actually have jobs. During the Great Depression, only 40 per cent of the adult population had work. Multi-income families have greater security than single-income families. The chance of both (or all) income earners in a family losing their jobs simultaneously is much lower than the chance of a single earner losing work. With greater family income security, family consumption is likely to be less sensitive to fluctuations in family income that are seen as temporary. Thus when aggregate income falls, it does not induce an equivalent cut in consumption. For example, during the 1980–81 recession real GDP fell but personal consumption expenditure did not.

For the four reasons we have just reviewed, it appears the economy has better shock-absorbing characteristics today than it had in the 1920s and 1930s. Even if there is a collapse of confidence leading to a decrease in investment, the recession mechanism that is now in place will not translate that initial shock into the large and prolonged decrease in real GDP and increase in unemployment that occurred more than 60 years ago.

Because the economy is now more immune to severe recession than it was in the 1930s, even a stock market crash of the magnitude that occurred in 1987 had barely noticeable effects on spending. A crash of a similar magnitude in 1929 resulted in the collapse of investment and consumer durable purchases in the United Kingdom. In the period following the 1987 stock market crash, investment and spending on durable goods continued to grow.

None of this is to say that there might not be a deep recession or even a Great Depression in the early years of the new millennium (or beyond). But it would take a very severe shock to trigger one.

Review

- The Great Depression was brought on by the collapse in demand in the world's largest economy – the United States. The fall in demand in the United States led to a sharp downturn in world trade.
- What stopped the Great Depression in the United Kingdom developing into the scale of the collapse in the United States was that, in September 1931, the United Kingdom left the gold standard.

We have now completed our study of the business cycle. Economic analysts use theories of the business cycle to forecast recessions and booms. You can see an example of this in *Reading Between the Lines* on pp. 854–855. We have also completed our study of the science of macroeconomics and learned about the influences on long-term economic growth and inflation as well as the business cycle. We have discovered that these issues pose huge policy challenges. How can we speed up the rate of economic growth while at the same time keeping inflation low and avoiding big swings of the business cycle? Our task in the next chapter is to study these macroeconomic policy challenges.

Summary

Key Points

Cycle Patterns, Impulses and Mechanisms (pp. 830–831)

- Since the turn of the century, there have been nine business cycle turning points.
- Recessions have on the average lasted about two years, while expansions have lasted on the average about six years.
- The Great Depression was the most severe contraction of real GDP.
- Postwar recessions have been milder than prewar recessions.

Aggregate Demand Theories of the Business Cycle (pp. 831–838)

- Aggregate demand theories of the cycle are based on the aggregate supply–aggregate demand model.
- Keynesian theory is based on volatile expectations about future sales and profits.
- Monetarist theory regards fluctuations in the money stock as the main source of economic fluctuations.
- Rational expectations theories identify unanticipated fluctuations in aggregate demand as the main source of economic fluctuations.

Real Business Cycle Theory (pp. 838–842)

- In real business cycle (RBC) theory, economic fluctuations are caused by fluctuations in the influence of technological change on productivity growth.
- A temporary slowdown in the pace of technological change decreases investment demand and both the demand for labour and the supply of labour.

The 1991–92 Recession (pp. 842–846)

- Three forces contributed to the weak performance of the UK economy in the early 1990s: the ERM, the reunification of Germany and a slowdown in economic expansion in the world economy.

The Great Depression (pp. 846–850)

- The Great Depression started with increased uncertainty and pessimism that brought a fall in investment and spending.
- Increased uncertainty and pessimism also brought on the stock market crash. The crash added to the pessimistic outlook and further spending cuts occurred.
- In the United States, banks failed and the money supply decreased, resulting in a continued decrease in aggregate demand. The chaos in the United States influenced economic activity throughout the world.
- A repeat of such a depression is much less likely today. The Bank of England's willingness to act as lender of last resort and the introduction of the deposit protection scheme both reduce the risk of bank failure and financial collapse.
- Higher taxes and government spending have given the economy greater resistance against depression, and an increased workforce participation rate provides a greater measure of security, especially for families with more than one wage earner.

Key Figures ◇

Key Terms

Review Questions

1 Distinguish between a cycle impulse and a cycle mechanism and identify the impulse and mechanism in three analogies given in this chapter.

2 What is the Keynesian theory of the business cycle? Carefully distinguish its impulse and its mechanism.

3 What is the monetarist theory of the business cycle? Carefully distinguish its impulse and its mechanism.

4 What are the rational expectations theories of the business cycle? Carefully distinguish their impulses and their mechanisms.

5 What is the key difference between the new classical theory and new Keynesian theory of the business cycle?

6 What is the impulse that causes economic fluctuations according to real business cycle theory?

7 What happens to investment demand and the demand for labour if a technological change brings a large increase in productivity?

8 How is the labour supply decision influenced by the real interest rate?

9 Why is there no *SAS* curve in real business cycle theory?

10 List the main arguments against and in favour of real business cycle theory.

11 What triggered the 1991–92 recession?

12 When did the Great Depression occur? Why did it affect the United States more than the United Kingdom?

13 Describe the changes in employment and real wages in the 1991–92 recession. What is the sticky wage theory of these changes? What is the flexible wage theory of these changes?

14 What were the main causes of the onset of the Great Depression in the United States in 1929?

15 What four features of today's economy make it less likely now than in 1929 that a Great Depression will occur? Why do they make it less likely?

Problems

1 Here is a news report about the past year in Gloomland:

> 'Business confidence is low. Firms have cut back on investment and laid off tens of thousands of workers. Productivity has collapsed. Real GDP has decreased and the price level, the real wage rate, the real interest rate and the money supply have all fallen.'

Try to explain these events by using the alternative theories of the business cycle. Are the facts as reported inconsistent with any of the theories? Use diagrams to illustrate your reasoning.

2 Here is a news report about the past year in Coolland:

> 'Business confidence is high. Business investment is booming. Jobs are easy to find and firms have a hard time hiring. Productivity is growing rapidly. Real GDP has increased and the price level is stable.'

Try to explain these events by using the alternative theories of the business cycle. Are the facts as reported inconsistent with any of the theories? Use diagrams to illustrate your reasoning.

3 Use carefully drawn figures to illustrate the evolution of the economy during the recession of 1980–81 and the expansion through the rest of the 1980s according to:

a Keynesian theory.

b Monetarist theory.

c Rational expectations theories.

d Real business cycle theory.

4 The table illustrates the economy of Virtualreality. When the economy is in a long-run equilibrium, it is at row *b*. When a recession occurs in Virtualreality, the economy moves away from this position to another identified by rows *a*, *c* and *d* in the three separate markets.

	Labour market		***AS–AD***		Investment	
	Real Wage	**Employment**	**Price level**	**Real GDP**	**Real interest rate**	**Investment**
a	5	100	150	5	5	1
b	4	200	100	10	4	2
c	4	100	100	5	4	1
d	3	100	50	5	3	1

a If the Keynesian theory is the correct explanation for the recession, to which positions does the economy move?

b If the monetarist theory is the correct explanation for the recession, to which positions does the economy move?

c If the new classical rational expectations theory is the correct explanation for the recession, to which positions does the economy move?

d If the new Keynesian rational expectations theory is the correct explanation for the recession, to which positions does the economy move?

e If real business cycle theory is the correct explanation for the recession, to which positions does the economy move?

5 Suppose that when the recession occurs in Virtualreality shown in the table accompanying Problem 4, the economy moves to *a* in the labour market, *d* in *AS–AD* and *d* in investment. Which, if any, theory of the business cycle could explain this outcome?

6 Suppose that when the recession occurs in Virtualreality shown in the table accompanying Problem 4, the economy moves to row *d* in these markets. Which, if any, theory of the business cycle could explain this outcome?

7 Suppose that when the recession occurs in Virtualreality shown in the table accompanying Problem 4, the economy moves to *a* in the labour market, *a* in *AS–AD* and *d* in investment. Which, if any, theory of the business cycle could explain this outcome?

8 Suppose that when the recession occurs in Virtualreality shown in the table accompanying

Problem 4, the economy moves to c in the labour market, a in *AS–AD* and d in investment. Which, if any, theory of the business cycle could explain this outcome?

9 Suppose that when the recession occurs in Virtualreality shown in the table accompanying Problem 4, the economy moves to a in the labour market, d in *AS–AD* and a in investment. Which, if any, theory of the business cycle could explain this outcome?

10 During the 1991–92 recession, real wages increased from £7.42 (1995 pounds) an hour in 1990 to £8.04 in 1992 and employment decreased from 49.2 billion hours in 1990 to 44.6 billion hours in 1992. How can these changes be explained by the sticky and flexible wage theories?

11 Study *Reading Between the Lines* on pp. 854–855 and then answer the following questions:

a What reasons do the article give for the common business cycle between the UK and the USA?
b Examine Figure 1 in *Reading Between the Lines* and decide if the UK business cycle always matches that of the US?
c What does the article suggest is the link between share prices and spending in the UK and the USA?
d Why did the unification of Germany exaggerate the difference between the cycle of the Eurozone against that of the UK and USA?

12 Use the links on the Parkin, Powell and Matthews Web site to obtain information about the current state of the US economy. Then:

a List all of the features of the US economy during the current year that you think are consistent with a pessimistic outlook for the next two years.
b List all of the features of the US economy during the current year that you think are consistent with an optimistic outlook for the next two years.
c Describe how you think the US economy is going to evolve over the next year or two. Explain your predictions, drawing on the pessimistic and optimistic factors that you listed in parts (a) and (b) and on your knowledge of macroeconomic theory.

W http://www.econ100.com

The Convergence of the Business Cycle

The Times, 28 May 1999

Euro ties will not stop Britain dancing to the American tune

Lea Patterson

The British business cycle has far more in common with that of America than it does with its European neighbours. When the US sank into recession in 1991, the UK followed. A year or two later, when the slowdown was beginning on the Continent, both America and Britain were enjoying healthy levels of growth.

In the financial markets, too, it still holds that where the US leads, the UK follows. In these days of close cooperation with our European trading partners, why does the UK economy still move in step with America?

There are essentially three sets of reasons for the remarkable similarity between the US and UK business cycles in the recent economic past: market expectations, structural factors and one-off shocks.

Take one-off shocks first. As the accompanying chart shows, since the early 1990s, the business cycle of the 11 eurozone economies has been lagging that of America and the UK by around a year to 18 months. However, at the beginning of this decade, reunification forced Germany, Europe's largest economy, through a period of radical structural change. The knockon effects from reunification had a big impact on Germany's business cycle, and many economists believe these have yet to work themselves out of the German economic system.

Although the recent divergence between the UK and European economic cycles may have been exaggerated by reunification, this type of one-off shock is only a part of the story. UK business cycles have not only been out of line with those in major European countries, but they have also been, on average, deeper and more volatile than elsewhere.

Self-fulfilling market expectations have played an important role in keeping the UK business cycle from moving too much into line with those of its European neighbours.

When US share prices rise, so do those in the UK; and when the dollar strengthens, so does the pound. Because there is a large body of analysts that believe these US-UK relationships are robust, their beliefs become self-fulfilling. This all means that when US share prices rise — fuelling US consumption — then UK share prices rise, which fuels UK consumption. When the dollar strengthens — harming US exporters — then the pound strengthens, which harms UK exporters.

For many economists, however, structural differences are the key reason why the UK business cycle has stubbornly refused to move in line with those of the larger eurozone nations. Structurally, the UK is much more like the US than it is like large European economies such as Germany.

Both the UK and the US have oil, for example, and so are affected by sharp movements in crude prices. Large numbers of individuals in both countries have exposure to the stock market, meaning that swings in share prices will tend to have substantial knockon effects on wealth, and hence consumer spending. Both economies — especially when compared with those in the eurozone — have relatively flexible labour markets. And in both the US and the UK, the manufacturing sector is overshadowed by a large, and buoyant, services sector.

The Essence of the Story

- The British business cycle has more in common with the US business cycle than it does with the eurozone (countries of the EMU).
- Financial markets in the UK and the USA are closely linked and mirror each others movements.
- The article suggests three reasons for the UK business cycle's failure to converge with the eurozone countries.
- The first argument is that there has always been a close association between the US and UK business cycles with the US acting as leader and the UK as follower.
- The second argument is that the structure of the two economies are similar.
- The third argument is that the unification of Germany was a one-off shock. The effects of this shock continue to exert an influence on the whole eurozone economy.

Economic Analysis

■ Figure 1 shows that the UK cycle has roughly the same frequency as the US cycle but it has a stronger amplitude. Whereas the Eurozone business cycle is out of phase with the US and UK.

■ Traditionally, the US was the UK's largest export market. This link has remained solid over the past 20 years. But exports to the EU economies have grown even more. Figure 2 shows that in 1979 exports to the US by the UK were 10 per cent of total exports and to the rest of the EU were 50 per cent. In 1998, exports to the US were 14 per cent of total exports but exports to the EU had grown to 57 per cent.

■ The rational expectations theory says that a business cycle is created only if an increase in aggregate demand is unanticipated. Asserting a causal link between the US and UK economies cannot explain the common cycle. But an unexpected increase in aggregate demand could create an unexpected increase in demand for UK goods by US consumers.

■ Figure 3(a) shows an initial equilibrium for the US economy at point *a* where aggregate demand is AD_0 which is also expected aggregate demand. Aggregate demand in the US increases unexpectedly to AD_1 because of an unexpected increase in the money supply, and real GDP rises above potential GDP. US consumers increase their demand for British goods and there is an increase in aggregate demand in the UK shown in 3(b).

■ The similar structure of the two economies suggests that common technology shocks could produce similar cycle patterns as in the real business cycle theory. A technological improvement in both countries could result in an increase in labour demand and an increase in real GDP through an increase in potential GDP. But while the UK has a more flexible labour market than the eurozone countries, it is not as flexible as the US.

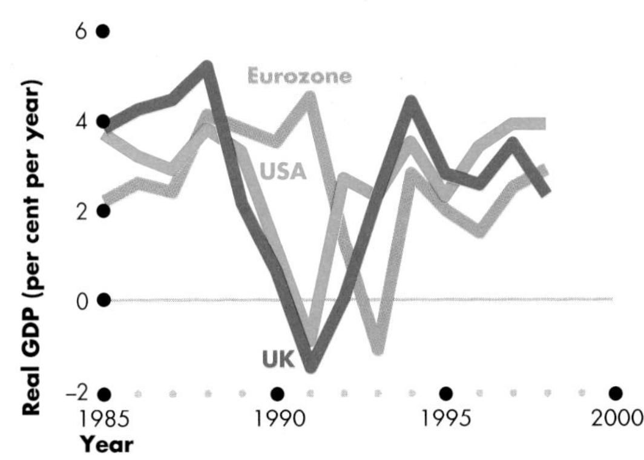

Figure 1 Business cycle

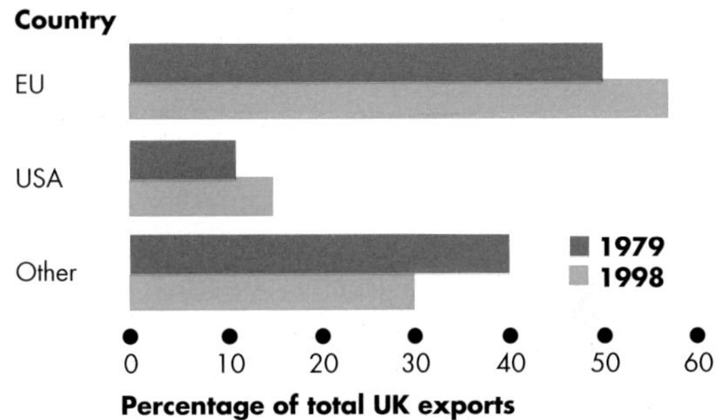

Figure 2 Destination of UK exports

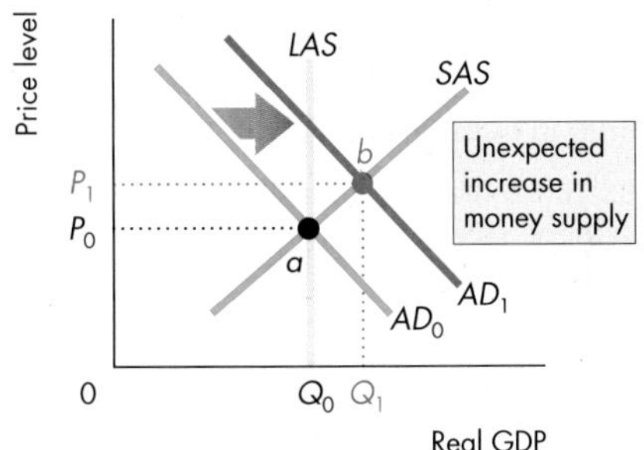

(a) The US economy

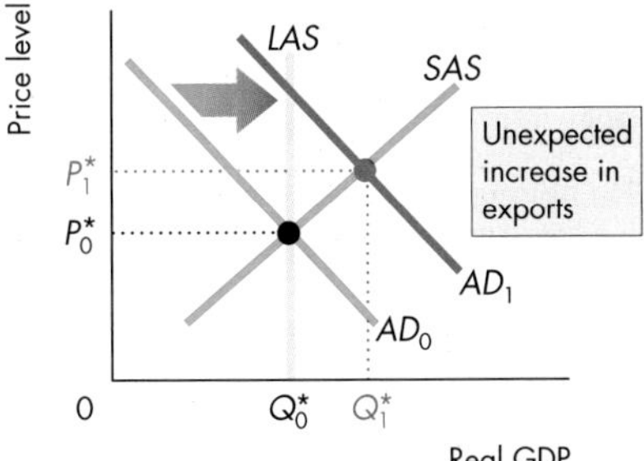

(b) The UK economy

Figure 3 UK expansion linked to US expansion

Business Cycles

"... in the great booms and depressions, ... the two big bad actors are debt disturbances and price level disturbances."

Irving Fisher
"The Debt Deflation Theory of Depressions" Econometrica, *1933*

The Economist: Irving Fisher

Irving Fisher (1867–1947) is the greatest American-born economist. The son of a Congregational minister who died as Irving was finishing high school, he paid his way through Yale and earned enough money to support his mother and younger brother by tutoring his fellow students.

Irving Fisher came to economics by way of mathematics. He was Yale's first PhD candidate in pure economics, but was a student in the mathematics department!

The contributions that Fisher made to economics cover the entire subject. He is best known for his work on the quantity theory of money (Chapter 27, pp. 674–675) and the relation between interest rates and inflation (Chapter 30, pp. 768–769). But he also wrote on the business cycle. He believed that the Great Depression was caused because the fall in the price level increased the real burden of debts. He wrote from experience: he had borrowed heavily to buy stocks in the rising market of the late 1920s and lost a fortune of perhaps 10 million dollars in the crash of 1929.

The Issues and Ideas

Economic activity has fluctuated between boom and bust for as long as we've had records. And understanding the sources of economic fluctuations has turned out to be difficult. One reason is that there are no simple patterns. Every new episode of the business cycle is different from its predecessor in some way. Some cycles are long and some short, some are mild and some severe, some begin in the Europe and some abroad. We never know with any certainty when the next turning point (down or up) is coming or what will cause it. A second reason is that the apparent waste of resources during a recession or depression seems to contradict the very foundation of economics: resources are limited and people have unlimited wants – there is scarcity. A satisfactory theory of the business cycle must explain why scarce resources don't *always* get fully employed.

One theory is that recessions result from insufficient aggregate demand. The solution is to increase government spending, cut taxes and cut interest rates. But demand stimulation must not be overdone. Countries that stimulate aggregate demand too much, such as Brazil, find their economic growth rates sagging, unemployment rising and inflation accelerating.

Today's new theory, real business cycle theory, predicts that fluctuations in aggregate demand have no effect on output and employment and change only the price level and inflation rate. But this theory ignores the real effects of financial collapse of the type that occurred in the 1930s. If banks fail on a large scale and people lose their wealth, other firms also begin to fail and jobs are destroyed. Unemployed people cut their spending, and output falls further. Demand stimulation may not be called for, but action to ensure that sound banks survive certainly is.

While economists are trying to understand the sources of the business cycle, the government and the Bank of England are doing the best they can to moderate the cycle. In the years since World War II, there appears to have been some success. Although the business cycle has not disappeared, it has become much less severe.

Then . . .

What happens to the economy when people lose confidence in banks? They withdraw their funds. These withdrawals feed on themselves, creating a snowball of withdrawals and, eventually, panic. Short of funds with which to repay depositors, banks call in loans and previously sound businesses are faced with financial distress. They close down and lay off workers. And recession deepens and turns into depression. Bank failures and the resulting decline in the nation's supply of money and credit were a significant factor in deepening and prolonging the Great Depression. But they taught us the importance of stable financial institutions and gave rise to the establishment of a bank deposit protection scheme to prevent such financial collapse.

. . . And Now

How can a building designed as a shop have no better use than to be boarded up and left empty? Not enough aggregate demand, say the Keynesians. Not so, say the real business cycle theorists. Technological change has reduced the building's current productivity as a shop to zero. But its expected future productivity is sufficiently high that it is not efficient to refit the building for some other purpose.

All unemployment, whether of buildings or people, can be explained in a similar way. For example, how can it be that during a recession, a person trained as a shop assistant is without work? Not enough aggregate demand is one answer. Another is that the current productivity of shop assistants is low, but their expected future productivity is sufficiently high that it does not pay an unemployed assistant to retrain for a job that is currently available.

CHAPTER 34

Macroeconomic Policy Challenges

After studying this chapter you will be able to:

- Describe the goals of macroeconomic policy
- Describe the main features of recent fiscal and monetary policy in the United Kingdom and the European Union
- Explain how fiscal policy and monetary policy influence long-term economic growth
- Distinguish between and evaluate fixed-rule and feedback-rule policies to stabilize the business cycle
- Explain how fiscal policy influences the natural unemployment rate
- Evaluate fixed-rule and feedback-rule policies to contain inflation and explain why lowering inflation usually brings recession

What Can Policy Do?

A widely predicted slowdown in the economy in 1998 did not stop the UK from turning in a respectable 2.1 per cent growth overall. Unemployment fell to 6.5 per cent and inflation remained low with only a 3.5 per cent rise in the retail price index. The United Kingdom was not alone in achieving a respectable macroeconomic performance in 1998 despite a slowdown in the rest of the European Union. Real GDP growth in Germany was 2.6 per cent in 1998, and in France growth was 3.2 per cent. Italy had a more pronounced slowdown with real GDP growth of 1.4 per cent. At the other end of the spectrum, the USA grew by 3.9 per cent – the same rate as in 1997, whereas in Japan real GDP fell by 2.9 per cent in 1998 ◆ There were clouds, even in the United Kingdom's economic sky. No one believed that UK real GDP growth would not slow even further in 1999. In the first quarter of 1999, real GDP grew by 0.4 per cent. Interest rates had been raised in the first half of 1998 but had been reduced in the second half when it was clear that the economy was slowing down. The danger for the UK is the possibility of the economy sliding into another recession. ◆ The wide variety of macroeconomic performance raises questions about macroeconomic policy. How do fiscal and monetary policy influence the economy? What can policy do to improve macroeconomic performance? Can the government use its fiscal policy to speed up long-term growth, keep inflation in check and maintain a low unemployment rate? Can the central bank use its monetary policy to achieve any of these ends? Are some policy goals better achieved by fiscal policy and some by monetary policy? And what specific policy actions do the best job? Are some ways of conducting policy better than others?

◆ ◆ ◆ ◆ In this chapter we're going to study the challenges of using policy to influence the economy and achieve the highest sustainable long-term growth rate and low unemployment while avoiding high inflation. At the end of the chapter, you will have a clearer and deeper understanding of the macroeconomic policy problems facing the United Kingdom and other EU countries today and of the debates that surround us concerning those problems.

Policy Goals

The goals of macroeconomic policy are to:

- Achieve the highest sustainable rate of long-term real GDP growth.
- Smooth out avoidable business cycle fluctuations.
- Maintain low unemployment.
- Maintain low inflation.

Long-term Real GDP Growth

We examined growth briefly in Chapter 21 (Figure 21.3, p. 510). Rapid sustained real GDP growth can make a profound contribution to economic well-being. With a growth rate of 2.5 per cent a year, it takes 28 years for production to double. With a growth rate of 5 per cent a year, production doubles in just over 14 years. The limits to *sustainable* growth are determined by the availability of natural resources, by environmental considerations, and by the willingness of people to save and invest in new capital and new technologies rather than consume everything they produce.

How fast can the economy grow over the long term? Between 1987 and 1998, through one complete business cycle, potential GDP grew at a rate of 2.5 per cent a year. Because the UK population grows at about 0.5 per cent a year, a real GDP growth rate of 2.5 per cent a year translates into a growth rate of real GDP per person of 2.0 per cent a year, which means that output per person doubles every 35 years. So increasing the long-term growth rate is of critical importance.

The Business Cycle

Potential GDP probably does not grow at a constant rate. Fluctuations in the pace of technological advance and in the pace of investment in new capital bring fluctuations in potential GDP. So some fluctuations in real GDP represent fluctuations in potential GDP. But when real GDP grows less quickly than potential GDP, output is lost, and when real GDP grows more quickly than potential GDP, bottlenecks arise that create inefficiencies and inflationary pressures. Keeping real GDP growth steady and equal to long-run aggregate supply growth avoids these problems.

It is not known how smooth real GDP can be made. Real business cycle theory regards all the fluctuations in real GDP as arising from fluctuations in potential GDP. The aggregate demand theories of the business cycle regard most of the fluctuations in real GDP as being avoidable deviations from potential GDP.

Unemployment

When real GDP growth slows, unemployment increases and rises above the natural rate of unemployment. The higher the unemployment rate, the longer is the time taken by unemployed people to find jobs. Productive labour is wasted and there is a slowdown in the accumulation of human capital. If high unemployment persists, serious psychological and social problems arise for the unemployed workers and their families.

When real GDP growth speeds up, unemployment decreases and falls below the natural rate of unemployment. The lower the unemployment rate, the harder it becomes for expanding industries to get the labour they need to keep growing. If extremely low unemployment persists, serious bottlenecks and production dislocations occur, sucking in imports and creating inflationary pressure.

Keeping unemployment at the natural rate avoids both of these problems. But just what is the natural rate of unemployment? Assessments vary. The actual average unemployment rate over the most recent business cycle – 1987 to 1998 – was 8.6 per cent. Most economists would put the natural rate at about 6 per cent. A few economists believe the natural rate is much lower than this, perhaps as low as 3 per cent. At the other extreme, real business cycle theorists believe the natural rate fluctuates and equals the actual unemployment rate.

If the natural unemployment rate becomes high, then a goal of policy is to lower the natural rate itself. This goal is independent of smoothing the business cycle.

Inflation

When inflation fluctuates unpredictably, money becomes less useful as a measuring rod for conducting transactions. Borrowers and lenders and employers and workers must take on extra risks. Keeping the inflation rate steady and predictable avoids these problems.

Keeping inflation steady also helps keep the value of the pound abroad steady. Other things remaining the same, if the inflation rate goes up by 1 percentage point, the pound loses 1 percent of its value against the currencies of other countries. Large and unpredictable fluctuations in the foreign exchange rate – the value of the pound against other currencies – make international trade and international borrowing and lending less profitable and limit the gains from international specialization and exchange. Keeping inflation low and predictable helps avoid such fluctuations in the exchange rate and enables international transactions to be undertaken at minimum risk and on the desired scale.

What is the most desirable inflation rate? Some economists say that the *rate* of inflation doesn't matter much as long as the rate is *predictable*. So, say these economists, any predictable inflation rate will serve well as a target for policy. But most economists believe that price stability, which they translate at an inflation rate of between 0 and 2 per cent, is desirable. The reason zero is not the target is that some price increases are due to quality improvements – a measurement bias in the price index – so a positive average *measured* inflation rate is equivalent to price stability. It has been suggested that a good definition of price stability is a situation in which no one considers inflation to be a factor in the decisions they make.

Three Core Policy Indicators: Unemployment, Inflation and Growth

Although macroeconomic policy pursues the four goals we've just considered, the goals are not independent. Three of these goals – increasing real GDP growth, smoothing the business cycle and maintaining low unemployment – are interlinked and they lie at the core of policy analysis in Europe. The level of unemployment tells us about the state of the business cycle and the structural problems

Figure 34.1 Macroeconomic Performance: EU Inflation and Unemployment, 1998

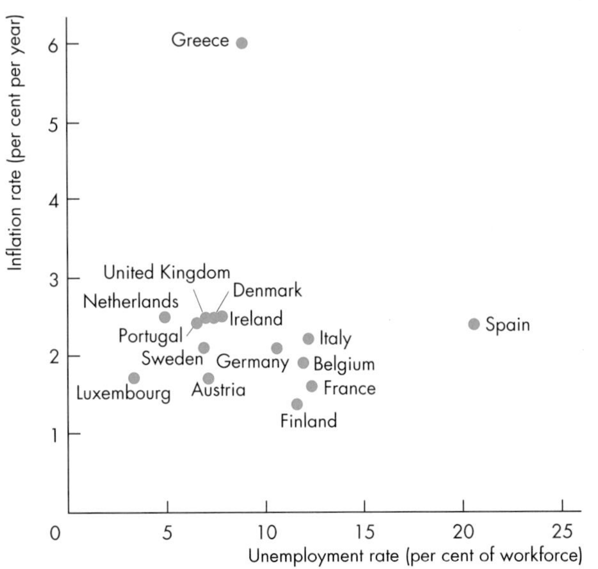

(a) Inflation and unemployment

Inflation rate (per cent per year)
Real GDP growth rate (per cent per year)
Greece
United Kingdom
Netherlands
Denmark
Portugal
Ireland
Spain
Italy
Sweden
Germany
Belgium
Austria
Luxembourg
France
Finland
0 2 4 6 8 10

(b) Inflation and real GDP growth

Unemployment, inflation and growth are important objectives of the EU states. Part (a) shows that most countries in the EU have low inflation but high unemployment. Spain has low inflation but the highest unemployment in the EU. Greece had the highest inflation in 1998. Part (b) highlights the difference in economic performance between the core countries of the EU and the periphery. The core countries of Italy, Germany and France have low inflation but low growth. The periphery of the EU, Spain, Portugal, Finland and Ireland have high growth rates. Greece has both moderate growth and high inflation.

Source: OECD, ECB.

of the economy. The goal of reducing the number of long-term unemployed people – a particularly pressing problem in the European Union – is linked to the goal of high and sustainable long-term growth. If unemployment falls below the natural rate, then growth may be too rapid. If unemployment rises above the natural rate, then growth may be too slow. So monitoring unemployment at its natural rate is equivalent to avoiding business fluctuations and keeping real GDP growing steadily at its maximum sustainable rate.

Policy performance, judged by the three core policy targets – inflation, unemployment and growth – is shown in Figure 34.1. In Figure 34.1(a), the blue dot is the coordinate of inflation and unemployment for each of the European Union countries in 1998. You can see that except for Greece, there is a strong convergence of low inflation. But unemployment remains a huge problem for some countries. Unemployment has fallen in Austria, Sweden, Portugal, Netherlands, Ireland and the UK, but remains stubbornly high in Spain and in the core area of the EU – Germany, France and Italy. Figure 34.1(b) shows the coordinates of infltion and real GDP growth in 1998. The figure shows the problem the EU has in balancing growth between the different countries in the Union. It is a particular problem for countries in the EMU. The core economies Germany and Italy has experienced low growth in 1998. France has had good growth performance but has slowed down in the last quarter of 1998 and in the first quarter of 1999. In contrast the peripheral areas of the EMU exhibit strong growth. Ireland, Spain, Portugal and Finland have experienced fast growth during 1998. The stated objectives of the European Commission are to raise the sustainable rate of growth of GDP in the European Union to 3 per cent a year, to aid the process of unemployment reduction, and to carry out microeconomic reforms to reduce the natural rate of unemployment.

Review

- The goals of macroeconomic policy are: the highest sustainable rate of long-term real GDP growth, small business fluctuations, low unemployment and low inflation.
- Keeping unemployment at the natural rate is equivalent to avoiding business fluctuations and keeping real GDP growing steadily at its highest sustainable rate.

We've examined the policy goals. Let's now look at the policy tools and the way they have been used.

Policy Tools and Performance

The tools used to try to achieve macroeconomic performance objectives are fiscal policy and monetary policy. **Fiscal policy**, which is described in Chapter 26 (pp. 632–637), is the use of the government budget to achieve macroeconomic objectives. The detailed fiscal policy tools are tax rates and government purchases of goods and services. **Monetary policy**, which is described in Chapter 26, is the adjustment of the quantity of money in circulation and interest rates by the central bank (the Bank of England) to achieve macroeconomic objectives. How fiscal and monetary policy is used together is examined in Chapter 29. How have the tools actually been used in the United Kingdom and other parts of the European Union? Let's answer this question by summarizing the main directions of fiscal and monetary policy in recent years.

Recent Fiscal Policy in the European Union

Figure 34.2 gives a broad summary of fiscal policy since 1995 for the countries of the European Union. It shows general government spending as a percentage of GDP in part (a) and the general government deficit as a percentage of GDP in part (b). Fiscal policy has been tightened considerably in most countries. The high average level of unemployment in the EU for 1997 – 10.7 per cent has made it difficult for the member states to tighten fiscal policy. Automatic fiscal policy rises when unemployment increases. But discretionary fiscal policy was tight. Most governments reduced government spending as a proportion of GDP between 1995 and 1997. The movement of the budget deficit also supported a general fiscal tightening. Economists

Figure 34.2 The Fiscal Policy Record

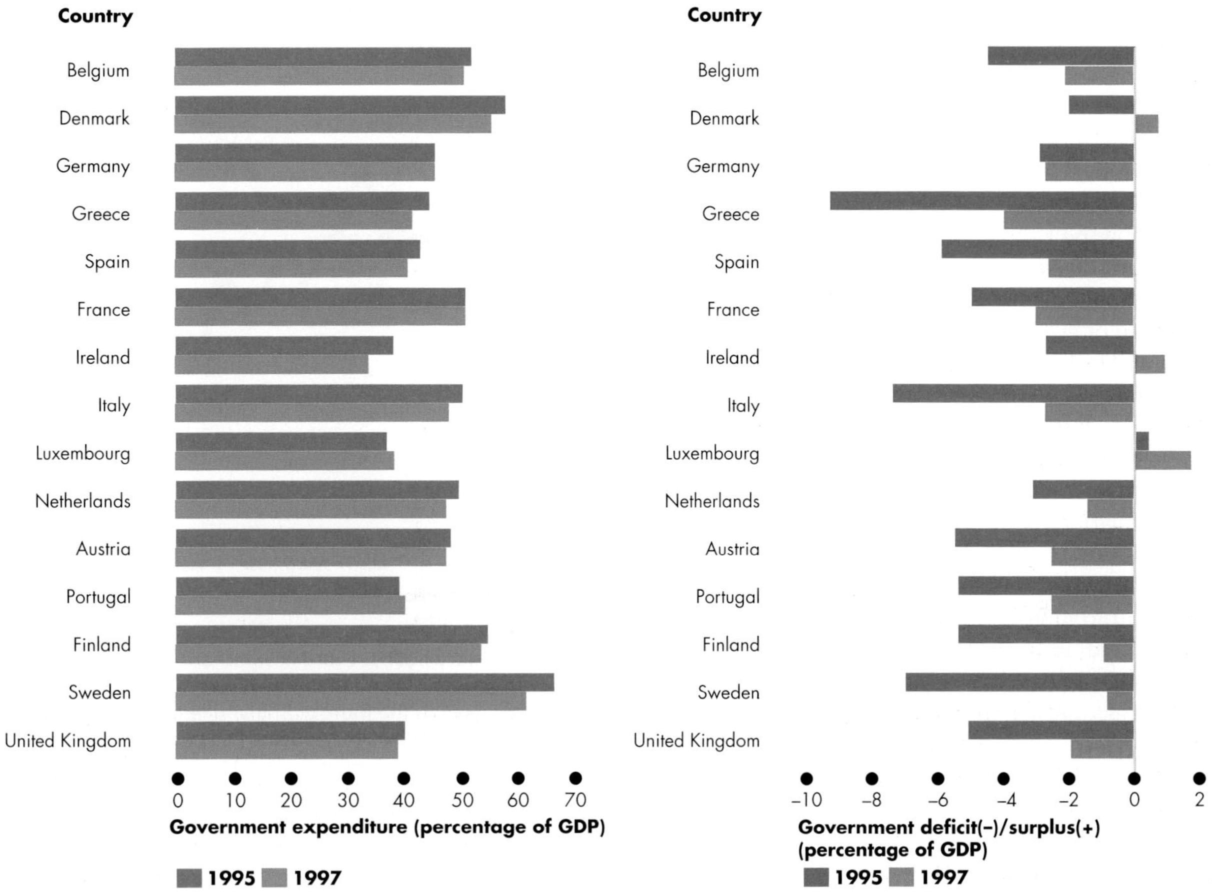

Country

Belgium
Denmark
Germany
Greece
Spain
France
Ireland
Italy
Luxembourg
Netherlands
Austria
Portugal
Finland
Sweden
United Kingdom

0 10 20 30 40 50 60 70

Government expenditure (percentage of GDP)

1995 1997

(a) General government expenditure of EU member states, 1995 and 1997

Country

Belgium
Denmark
Germany
Greece
Spain
France
Ireland
Italy
Luxembourg
Netherlands
Austria
Portugal
Finland
Sweden
United Kingdom

–10 –8 –6 –4 –2 0 2

Government deficit(–)/surplus(+) (percentage of GDP)

1995 1997

(b) General government budget deficit of EU member states, 1995 and 1997

Fiscal policy is summarized here by the performance of general government spending (part a) and the deficit (part b) between 1995 and 1997 for the EU member states. The general trend was for a tightening in fiscal policy.

Most countries reduced government expenditure and the budget deficit as a proportion of GDP, between 1995 and 1997. Denmark, Ireland and Luxembourg had budget surpluses.

Source: *European Commission Report on Convergence*, 1998.

of the Keynesian school argue that the general fiscal tightening in Europe has made it difficult to reduce the additional unemployment caused by the recession of 1990–92. But, countries in the EMU have agreed to a Stability Pact that aims to reduce budget deficits even further in 1999 and 2000. The purpose of the stability pact is to coordinate Euroland-wide fiscal policy to have a low budget deficit which would allow the European Central Bank to allow low interest rates. The low interest rate is expected to produce a favourable growth in private investment.

The stability pact has hindered governments from using fiscal policy to stabilize the economy according to Keynesian theory.

Let's now look at monetary policy.

Recent Monetary Policy in the United Kingdom and the European Union

Monetary policy in the European Union in recent years has been geared towards fulfilling stage 2 of EMU – namely coordination of monetary policy among member states' central banks with the aim of ensuring price stability. Since 1 January 1999, the monetary policy of the Euro-11 that comprise the single currency area of Euroland has been conducted by the European Central Bank (ECB) in Frankfurt. The objective of the ECB is to maintain price stability and to support the Commission's objective of non-inflationary growth. Up until the EMU, the policies of the individual country central banks have been to raise short-term interest rates to abate inflationary pressures, and to lower them when inflationary pressure has subsided.

The task of monetary policy has been to keep a lid on inflationary pressure, defined as an inflation rate of below 2 per cent a year. There has been concern as to whether one monetary policy can suit so many different countries in the EMU. In 1998, real GDP growth in Ireland was 9.1 per cent. In Spain and Netherlands real GDP growth was 3.8 per cent. In contrast, growth in the core area of the EMU, France, Germany and Italy was 3.2, 2.6 and 1.4 per cent and falling. In 1999 the ECB cut interest rates further. While this was good news for the slowing economies of the core area, it created stronger demand pressure in countries like Ireland and Spain.

Like the ECB, the Bank of England is independent in the conduct of monetary policy. The Bank of England follows an inflation target of 1.5–2.5 per cent. Figure 34.3 shows how monetary policy has been used in the United Kingdom since the Monetary Policy Committee (MPC) began to set interest rates in the UK. The red line shows the annual rate of growth of money between June 1997 and March 1999. The blue line shows the Banks' base rate of interest. The MPC inherited a situation of rapidly growing money supply. Interest rates were raised in stages from 6.5 per cent to 7.5 per cent. The rate of growth of money fell during this period to 6.9 per cent in March 1999. Inflation fell inside the target range of 2.5 per cent in the second half of 1998.

The independence of central banks in the EU with specific price stability objectives has raised concerns that monetary policy can no longer be coordinated with fiscal policy. The policy of the ECB in aiming for price stability has reduced the ability of the individual countries in Euroland to conduct stabilization policies.

Figure 34.3 The Monetary Policy Record: UK Monetary Policy, 1997–1999

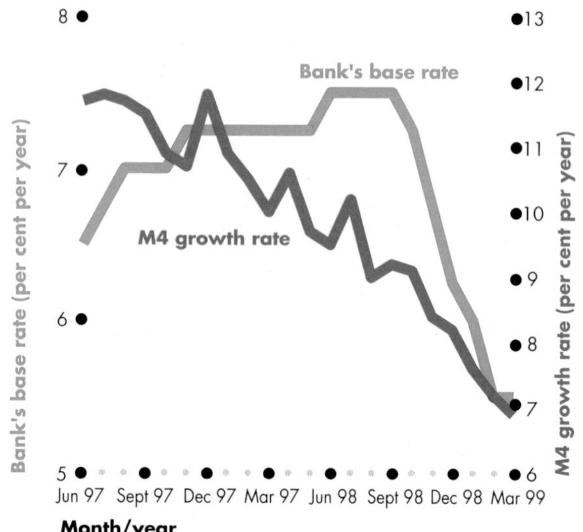

The monetary policy record is summarized here by the growth rate of M4 and the retail banks' base rate, which is closely linked to the Bank of England lender of last resort loan rate to the discount houses. The bank rate was raised during 1997 after a high growth rate of money in the first half of 1997. In 1998 the Bank hiked interest rates up to 7.5 per cent. The rate of growth of money declined during 1998 and 1999. The base rate was lowered during late 1998 and in 1999.

Sources: Bank of England.

Review

- The macroeconomic policy tools are fiscal policy and monetary policy.
- Automatic fiscal policy was expansionary during the 1990s because of high unemployment but discretionary fiscal policy was

contractionary in most EU countries in recent years, including the United Kingdom.

- Monetary policy in EU countries was tightened in the run up to EMU but has loosened in 1999.
- Monetary policy in the United Kingdom was tightened in 1998 but loosened as soon as monetary growth was brought under control.

You've now studied the goals of policy and seen the broad trends in fiscal and monetary policy in recent years for the United Kingdom and the European Union. Let's now study the ways in which policy might be better used to achieve its goals. We'll begin by looking at long-term growth policy.

Long-term Growth Policy

The sources of the long-term growth of potential GDP, which are explained in Chapter 32 (pp. 807–808), are the accumulation of physical and human capital and the advance of technology. Here, we probe more deeply into the problem of boosting the long-term growth rate.

The factors that determine long-term growth result from millions of individual decisions; the role of government in influencing growth is limited. The European Commission believes that any role that government can play should be coordinated with other members of the European Union. Policy can influence the private decisions on which long-term growth depends in three areas. Such policies would increase:

1 National saving.
2 Investment in human capital.
3 Investment in new technologies.

National Saving Policies

National saving within the EU countries equals private saving plus government saving. Figure 34.4 shows the scale of national saving within the European Union since 1960 and its private and government components. The government component is obtained by subtracting private saving from government saving. From 1960 to 1975, national saving fluctuated around an average of 25 per cent of GDP. There then began a steady slide that saw national saving fall to 21 per cent in 1975 and fluctuate between 21 and 19 per cent of GDP between 1982 and 1992. Private saving has remained remarkably stable over a long period. It actually increased a little as a percentage of GDP between 1960 and 1979, when it peaked at 22 per cent of GDP, but over the whole period it has remained between 20 and 22 per cent of EU GDP. Government saving became increasingly negative during the 1980s and 1990s.

EU investment, one of the engines of growth, is not limited by saving in the European Union. The reason is that foreign saving can be harnessed to finance EU investment. But the European Union is a mature economy with the demographic problem of an ageing population. It needs to have sufficient

Figure 34.4 National Savings Rates in the European Union: 1960–1997

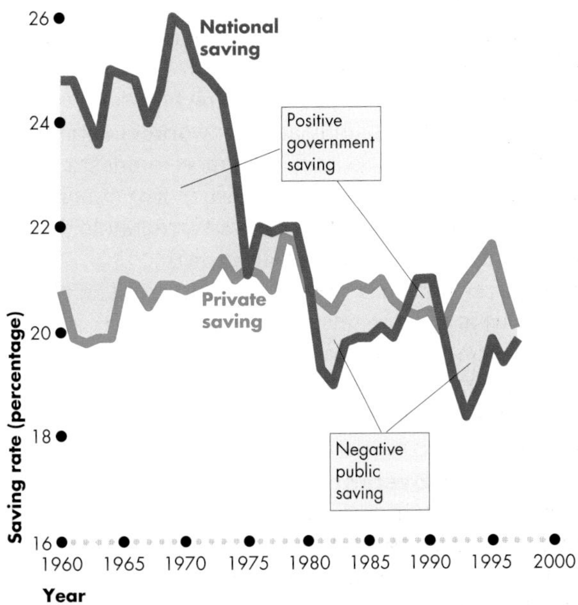

The EU gross saving rate peaked in 1970 at 25.8 per cent of EU GDP. Gross saving has fallen since that year and government saving has been the highest contributor to the fall. Private savings have remained remarkably constant since 1960, ranging between 19 and 22 per cent.

Source: European Commission.

saving to lend to the developing world and the emerging economies to meet the consumption needs of its population. Boosting the EU saving rate can help to bring faster real GDP growth for two reasons. First, the European Union represents a significant proportion of the world economy, so an increase in EU saving would increase world saving and bring lower real interest rates around the world. With lower real interest rates, investment would be boosted everywhere. The EU economy and the world economy could grow faster. Second, with more domestic saving, there might be an increase in investment in domestic high-risk, high-return new technologies that could boost long-term EU growth.

How can national saving be increased? The two points of attack are:

1 Increasing government saving.
2 Increasing private saving.

Increasing Government Saving Government saving was negative during most of the 1980s, and has been an average of –1.3 per cent of GDP during the 1990s. The decline in the national savings of the EU economy is due to the public sector deficits in many European countries. Increasing government saving means eliminating the public sector deficit of the EU countries. They are one and the same action. Achieving a substantial cut in the deficit is part of the stability pact the Euro-11 countries have accepted by Treaty as a condition of the EMU. A reduction in the deficit in the EMU countries will be difficult and will only be achieved by cuts in such sensitive areas as welfare spending.

Increasing Private Saving Private saving in the European Union as a whole has remained remarkably stable over the four decades since 1960. The only way that government actions can boost private saving is by increasing the after-tax rate of return on saving.

The most effective way of stimulating private saving is to cut taxes on interest income. But such a tax cut would be costly and could only be financed either by a further decrease in government expenditures or by increases in taxes on labour incomes or in Value Added Tax (VAT). This would be difficult politically and cannot be carried out at the EU level on existing political arrangements. So governments are limited to making minor changes to the taxation of interest income, which will have negligible effects on the saving rate.

Private Saving and Inflation Inflation erodes the value of saving, and uncertainty about future inflation is bad for saving. One further policy, therefore, that increases the saving rate is a monetary policy that preserves stable prices and minimizes uncertainty about the future value of money. Chapter 30, pp. 761–764, spells out the broader connection between inflation and real GDP and explains why low inflation may bring greater output and faster growth.

Human Capital Policies

The accumulation of human capital plays a crucial role in economic growth and two areas are relevant: schooling and on-the-job experience. Economic research shows that schooling and training pay. That is, on the average, the greater the number of years a person remains at school or in training, the higher are that person's earnings. Schooling and higher education training in Europe are fairly good by international standards. The UK government has made it a policy issue to increase the number of university places to allow one-third of all school leavers to enter higher education.

If education and on-the-job training yield higher earnings, why does the government or the European Commission need a policy towards investment in human capital? Why can't people simply be left to get on with making their own decisions about how much human capital to acquire? The answer is that the *social* returns to human capital possibly exceed the *private* returns. The extra productivity that comes from the interactions of well-educated and experienced people exceeds what each individual can achieve alone. So left to ourselves we would probably accumulate too little human capital.

Economic research has also shown that on-the-job training pays. This type of training can be formal, such as a school at work, or informal, such as learning-by-doing. The scope for government involvement in these areas is limited, but it can set an example as an employer and it can encourage best-practice training programmes for workers.

Investment in New Technologies

As Chapter 32, explains, investment in new technologies is special for two reasons. First, it appears not to run into the problem of diminishing returns that plague all other factors of production. Second, the benefits of new technologies spill over to influence all parts of the economy, not just the firms undertaking the investment. For these reasons, a particularly promising way of boosting growth is to stimulate investment in the research and development efforts that create new technologies.

Governments can fund and provide tax incentives for research and development activities. Through the various research councils, the universities and research institutes, the governments of the European Union already fund a large amount of basic research. The European Commission estimates that about 2 per cent of EU GDP, 2.8 per cent of US GDP and 3 per cent of Japanese GDP is spent on research and technological development (RTD).

Review

- Long-term growth policies focus on increasing saving and increasing investment in human capital and new technologies.
- To increase the national saving rate of the EU economies, government saving and the after-tax return on private saving must be increased and inflation must be kept in check.
- Human capital investment might be increased with improved education and on-the-job training programmes.
- Investment in new technologies can be encouraged by tax incentives.

We've seen how government might use its fiscal and monetary policies to influence long-term growth. How can it influence the business cycle and unemployment? Let's now address this question.

Business Cycle and Unemployment Policies

Many different fiscal and monetary policies can be pursued to stabilize the business cycle and prevent swings in real GDP growth and the inflation rate. But all these polices fall into three broad categories:

1. Fixed-rule policies.
2. Feedback-rule policies.
3. Discretionary policies.

Fixed-rule Policies

A **fixed-rule policy** specifies an action to be pursued independently of the state of the economy. An everyday example of a fixed rule is a stop sign. It says 'stop regardless of the state of the road ahead – even if no other vehicle is trying to use the road'. Several fixed-rule policies have been proposed for the economy. One, proposed by Milton Friedman, is to keep the quantity of money growing at a constant rate year in and year out, regardless of the state of the economy, to make the *average* inflation rate zero. Another fixed-rule policy is to balance the government budget. Fixed rules are rarely followed in practice, but they have some merits in principle; later in this chapter we'll study the way they would work if they were pursued.

Feedback-rule Policies

A **feedback-rule policy** specifies how policy actions respond to changes in the state of the economy. A give way sign is an everyday feedback rule. It says 'stop if another vehicle is attempting to use the road ahead but otherwise, proceed'. A macroeconomic feedback-rule policy is one that changes the money supply, or interest rates, or even tax rates, in response to the state of the economy. Some feedback rules guide the actions of policy-makers. For example, the Monetary Policy Committee of the Bank of England uses a feedback rule that raises interest rates when inflation is above its target. Other feedback-rule policies are automatic. For example, the automatic rise in taxes during an expansion and the automatic fall in taxes during a recession are feedback-rule policies.

Discretionary Policies

A **discretionary policy** responds to the state of the economy in a possibly unique way that uses all the information available, including perceived lessons from past 'mistakes'. An everyday discretionary policy occurs at an unmarked junction. Each driver uses discretion in deciding whether to stop and how slowly to approach the junction. Most macroeconomic policy actions have an element of discretion because every situation is to some degree unique. For example, before the Bank of England was made independent, between 1994 and 1995, interest rates were raised three times but by half percentage points in each case to forestall an expansion in the economy. The then Chancellor, Kenneth Clarke, used discretion based on lessons learned from earlier expansions. The granting of independence to the Bank of England was in part to remove government discretion. But despite the fact that all policy actions have an element of discretion, they can be regarded as modifications to a basic feedback-rule policy. Discretionary policy is sophisticated feedback policy, where the rules gradually evolve to reflect new knowledge about the way the economy works.

We'll study the effects of business cycle policy by comparing the performance of real GDP and the price level with a fixed rule and a feedback rule. Because the business cycle can result from demand shocks or supply shocks, we need to consider these two cases. We'll begin by studying demand shocks.

Stabilizing Aggregate Demand Shocks

We'll study an economy that starts out at full employment and has no inflation. Figure 34.5 illustrates this situation. The economy is on aggregate demand curve AD_0 and short-run aggregate supply curve *SAS*. These curves intersect at a point on the long-run aggregate supply curve, *LAS*. The GDP deflator is 110 and real GDP is £750 billion. Now suppose that there is an unexpected and temporary fall in aggregate demand. Let's see what happens.

Perhaps investment falls because of a wave of pessimism about the future, or perhaps exports fall because of a recession in the rest of the world. Regardless of the origin of the fall in aggregate demand, the aggregate demand curve shifts leftward, to AD_1 in the figure. The aggregate demand curve AD_1 intersects the short-run aggregate supply curve *SAS* at a GDP deflator of 105 and a real GDP of £700 billion. The economy is in a depressed state. Real GDP is below its long-run level and unemployment is above its natural rate.

Assume that the fall in aggregate demand from AD_0 to AD_1 is temporary. As confidence in the future improves, firms' investment picks up, or as economic recovery proceeds in the rest of the world, exports gradually rise. As a result, the aggregate demand curve gradually returns to AD_0, but it takes some time to do so.

Figure 34.5 A Decrease in Aggregate Demand

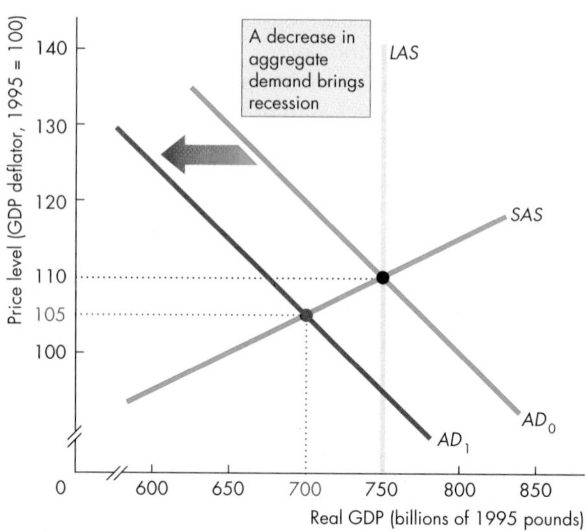

The economy starts out at full employment on aggregate demand curve AD_0 and short-run aggregate supply curve *SAS*, with the two curves intersecting on the long-run aggregate supply curve *LAS*. Real GDP is £750 billion and the GDP deflator is 110. A fall in aggregate demand (owing to pessimism about future profits, for example) unexpectedly shifts the aggregate demand curve to AD_1. Real GDP falls to £700 billion, and the GDP deflator falls to 105. The economy is in a recession.

We are going to work out how the economy responds under two alternative monetary policies during the period in which aggregate demand gradually increases to its original level: a fixed rule and a feedback rule.

Fixed Rule: Monetarism The fixed rule that we'll study here is one in which the levels of government purchases of goods and services, taxes and the deficit remain constant and the money supply remains constant. Neither fiscal policy nor monetary policy responds to the depressed economy. This is the rule advocated by *monetarists*.

The response of the economy under this fixed-rule policy is shown in Figure 34.6(a). When aggregate demand falls to AD_1, no policy measures are taken to bring the economy back to full employment. But the fall in aggregate demand is only *temporary*. As aggregate demand returns to its original level, the

Figure 34.6 Two Stabilization Policies: Aggregate Demand Shock

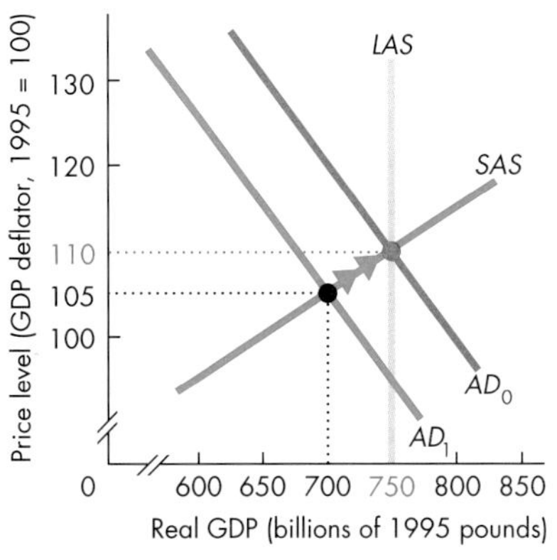

(a) Fixed rule: temporary demand shock

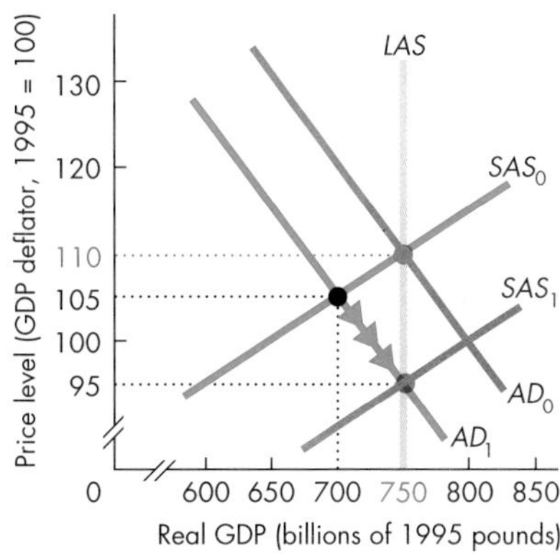

(b) Fixed rule: permanent demand shock

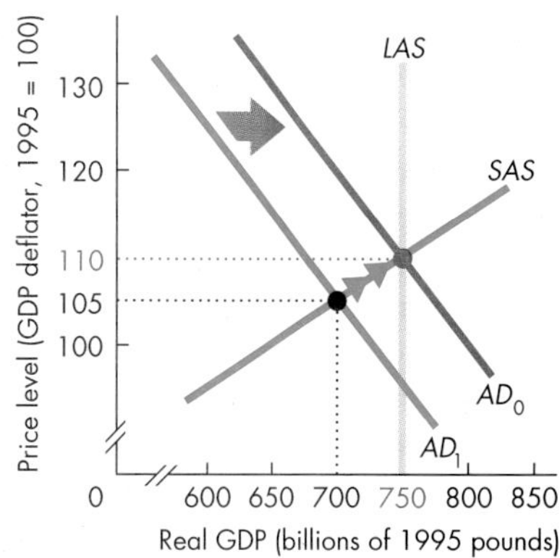

(c) Feedback rule

The economy is in a depressed state with a GDP deflator of 105 and real GDP of £700 billion. The short-run aggregate supply curve is *SAS*. If the depressed state of the economy is temporary, fixed-rule stabilization policy (part a) leaves aggregate demand initially at AD_1, so the GDP deflator remains at 105 and real GDP at £700 billion. As other influences on aggregate demand gradually increase, the aggregate demand curve shifts back to AD_0. As it does, real GDP gradually rises back to £750 billion and the GDP deflator increases to 110. When the decrease in demand is permanent, the money wage rate falls and the short-run aggregate supply curve shifts rightward to SAS_1, shown in part (b). Part (c) shows a feedback-rule stabilization policy. Expansionary fiscal and monetary policy increase aggregate demand and shift the aggregate demand curve from AD_1 to AD_0. Real GDP returns to £750 billion and the GDP deflator returns to 110. Fiscal and monetary policy becomes contractionary as the other influences on aggregate demand increase its level. As a result, the aggregate demand curve is kept steady at AD_0, real GDP remains at £750 billion and the deflator remains at 110.

aggregate demand curve shifts rightward gradually back to AD_0. As it does so, real GDP and the GDP deflator gradually increase. The GDP deflator gradually returns to 110 and real GDP to its long-run level of £750 billion, as shown in Figure 34.6(a). Throughout this process, the economy experiences more rapid growth than usual but beginning from a state of excess capacity. Unemployment remains high until the aggregate demand curve has returned to AD_0.

Figure 34.6(b) illustrates the response of the economy under a fixed rule when the decrease in aggregate demand to AD_1 is *permanent*. Gradually, with unemployment above the natural rate, the money wage rate falls and the short-run aggregate supply curve shifts rightward to SAS_1. As it does so, real GDP gradually increases and the GDP deflator falls. Real GDP gradually returns to potential GDP of £750 billion and the GDP deflator falls to 95, as shown in Figure 34.6(b). Again, throughout the adjustment, real GDP is less than potential GDP and unemployment exceeds the natural rate.

Let's contrast this adjustment with what occurs under a feedback-rule policy.

Feedback Rule: Keynesian Activism The feedback rule that we'll study is one in which government purchases of goods and services increase, taxes decrease, the deficit increases and the money supply increases when real GDP falls below its long-run level. In other words, both fiscal and monetary policy become expansionary when real GDP falls below long-run real GDP. When real GDP rises above its long-run level, both policies operate in reverse, becoming contractionary. This rule is advocated by *Keynesian activists*.

The response of the economy under this feedback rule policy is shown in Figure 34.6(c). When aggregate demand falls to AD_1, the expansionary fiscal and monetary policy increases aggregate demand, which shifts the aggregate demand curve immediately to AD_0. As other influences begin to increase aggregate demand, fiscal and monetary policy become contractionary and hold the aggregate demand curve steady at AD_0. Real GDP is held steady at £750 billion and the GDP deflator remains at 110.

The Two Rules Compared Under a fixed-rule policy, the economy goes into a recession and stays there for as long as it takes for aggregate demand to increase again under its own steam. Only gradually does the recession come to an end and the aggregate demand curve return to its original position.

Under a feedback-rule policy, the economy is pulled out of its recession by the policy action. Once back at its long-run level, real GDP is held there by a gradual, policy-induced decrease in aggregate demand that exactly offsets the increase in aggregate demand coming from private spending decisions.

The price level and real GDP fall and rise by exactly the same amounts under the two policies, but real GDP stays below capacity GDP for longer with a fixed rule than it does with a feedback rule.

So Feedback Rules are Better? Isn't it obvious that a feedback rule is better than a fixed rule? Can't the government and the Bank use feedback rules to keep the economy close to full employment with a stable price level? Of course, unforecasted events – such as a collapse in business confidence – will hit the economy from time to time. But by responding with a change in tax rates, spending, interest rates and money supply, can't the government and the Bank minimize the damage from such a shock? It appears to be so from our analysis.

Despite the apparent superiority of a feedback rule, many economists remain convinced that a fixed rule stabilizes aggregate demand more effectively than a feedback rule. These economists argue that fixed rules are better than feedback rules because:

- Full-employment real GDP is not known.
- Policy lags are longer than the forecast horizon.
- Feedback-rule policies are less predictable than fixed-rule policies.

Let's look at these arguments.

Knowledge of Full-employment Real GDP
To decide whether a feedback policy needs to stimulate aggregate demand or retard it, it is necessary to determine whether real GDP is currently above or below its full-employment level. But full-employment real GDP is not known with certainty. It depends on a large number of factors, one of which is the level of employment when unemployment is at its natural rate. But there is uncertainty and disagreement about how the labour market works, so we can only estimate the natural rate of unemployment. As a result, there is uncertainty about the *direction* in which a feedback policy should be pushing the level of aggregate demand.

Policy Lags and the Forecast Horizon
The effects of policy actions taken today are spread out over the following two years or even more. But no one is able to forecast that far ahead. The forecast horizon of the policy makers is less than one year. Furthermore, it is not possible to predict the precise timing and magnitude of the effects of policy itself. Thus feedback policies that react to today's economy may be inappropriate for the state of the economy at that uncertain future date when the policy's effects are felt.

For example, suppose that today the economy is in a recession and prices are falling. The Monetary Policy Committee reacts with an increase in the money supply growth rate. When the Bank puts on the monetary accelerator, the first reaction is a fall in interest rates. Some time later, lower interest rates produce an increase in investment and the purchases of consumer durable goods. Some time still later, this rise in expenditure increases income which in turn induces higher consumption expenditure. Later still, the higher expenditure increases the demand for labour and eventually wages and prices rise. The sectors in which the spending increases occur vary and so does the impact on employment. It can take from nine months to two years for an initial action by the Bank to cause a change in real GDP, employment and the inflation rate.

By the time the Bank's actions are having their maximum effect, the economy has moved on to a new situation. Perhaps a world economic slowdown has added a new negative effect on aggregate demand that is offsetting the government's expansionary actions. Or perhaps a boost in business confidence has increased aggregate demand yet further, adding to the government's own expansionary policy. Whatever the situation, the Bank can only take the appropriate actions today if it can forecast those future shocks to aggregate demand.

Thus to smooth the fluctuations in aggregate demand, the Bank needs to take actions today, based on a forecast of what will be happening over a period stretching two or more years into the future. It is no use taking actions a year from today to influence the situation that then prevails. It will be too late.

If the Bank economics team, is good at economic forecasting and bases its policy actions on its forecasts, then it can deliver the type of aggregate demand-smoothing performance that we assumed in the model economy we studied earlier in this chapter. But if the Bank takes policy actions that are based on today's economy rather than on the forecasted economy a year into the future, then those actions will often be inappropriate ones.

When unemployment is high and the Bank puts its foot on the accelerator, it speeds the economy back to full employment. But the Bank cannot see far enough ahead to know when to ease off the accelerator and gently tap the brake, holding the economy at its full-employment point. Usually it keeps its foot on the accelerator for too long and, after the Bank has taken its foot off the accelerator pedal, the economy races through the full-employment point and starts to experience shortages and inflationary pressures. Eventually, when inflation increases and unemployment falls below its natural rate, the Bank steps on the brake, pushing the economy back below full employment.

The Bank's own reaction to the current state of the economy has become one of the major sources of fluctuations in aggregate demand and the major factor that people have to forecast in order to make their own economic choices.

The problems for fiscal policy feedback rules are similar to those for monetary policy, but they are more severe because of the lags in the implementation of fiscal policy. The government can take actions fairly quickly. But before a fiscal policy action can be taken, the entire legislative process must be completed. Thus even before a fiscal policy action is implemented, the economy may have moved on to a new situation that calls for a different feedback from the one that is in the legislative pipeline.

Predictability of Policies To make decisions about long-term contracts for employment (wage contracts) and for borrowing and lending, people have to anticipate the future course of prices – the future inflation rate. To forecast the inflation rate, it is necessary to forecast aggregate demand. And to forecast aggregate demand, it is necessary to forecast the policy actions of the government and the Bank.

If the government and the Bank stick to rock-steady, fixed rules for tax rates, spending programmes, and money supply growth, then policy itself cannot be a contributor to unexpected fluctuations in aggregate demand.

In contrast, when a feedback rule is being pursued there is more scope for the policy actions to be unpredictable. The main reason is that feedback rules are not written down for all to see. Rather, they have to be inferred from the behaviour of the government and the Bank. The deliberations of the Bank Monetary Policy Committee are published and the decision to change or keep interest the same is explained in the Minutes. This means that over time it will be possible to predict the Bank's action by knowing what factors guided its policy in the past.

Thus with a feedback policy it is necessary to predict the variables to which the government and Bank react and the extent to which they react. Consequently, a feedback rule for fiscal and monetary policy can create more unpredictable fluctuations in aggregate demand than a fixed rule.

Economists disagree about whether these bigger fluctuations offset the potential stabilizing influence of the predictable changes the government and the Bank make. No agreed measurements have been made to settle this dispute. Nevertheless, the unpredictability of the government in its pursuit of feedback policies is an important fact of economic life, and the government does not always go out of its way to make its reactions clear. This is one of the reasons for taking monetary policy out of the hands of the government.

To the extent that the government's actions are discretionary and unpredictable, they lead to unpredictable fluctuations in aggregate demand. These fluctuations, in turn, produce fluctuations in real GDP, employment and unemployment.

It is difficult for the government to pursue a predictable feedback stabilization policy. Such policies are formulated in terms of spending programmes and tax laws announced at the time of the Budget. Because these programmes and tax laws are the outcome of a political process of negotiation between the Treasury and the spending departments of government, there can be no effective way in which a predictable feedback fiscal policy can be adhered to.

We reviewed three reasons why feedback policies may not be more effective than fixed rules in controlling aggregate demand. But there is a fourth reason why fixed rules are preferred by some economists: not all shocks to the economy are on the demand side. Advocates of feedback rules believe that most fluctuations do come from aggregate demand. Advocates of fixed rules believe that aggregate supply fluctuations are the dominant ones. Let's now see how aggregate supply fluctuations affect the economy under a fixed rule and a feedback rule. We will also see why those economists who believe that aggregate supply fluctuations are the dominant ones also favour a fixed rather than a feedback rule.

Stabilizing Aggregate Supply Shocks

Real business cycle (RBC) theorists believe that fluctuations in real GDP (and in employment and unemployment) are caused not by fluctuations in aggregate demand but by fluctuations in productivity growth. According to RBC theory, there is no useful distinction between long-run aggregate supply and short-run aggregate supply. Because wages are flexible, the labour market is always in equilibrium and unemployment is always at its natural rate. The vertical long-run aggregate supply curve is also the short-run aggregate supply curve. Fluctuations occur because of shifts in the long-run aggregate supply curve. Normally, the long-run aggregate supply curve shifts to the right – the economy expands. But the pace at which the long-run aggregate supply curve shifts to the right varies. Also, on occasion, the long-run aggregate supply curve shifts leftward, bringing a decrease in aggregate supply and a fall in real GDP.

Economic policy that influences the aggregate demand curve has no effect on real GDP. But it does affect the price level. If a feedback policy is used to increase aggregate demand every time real GDP falls, and if the RBC theory is correct, the feedback policy will make price level fluctuations more severe than they otherwise would be. To see why, consider Figure 34.7.

Figure 34.7 Responding to a Productivity Growth Slowdown

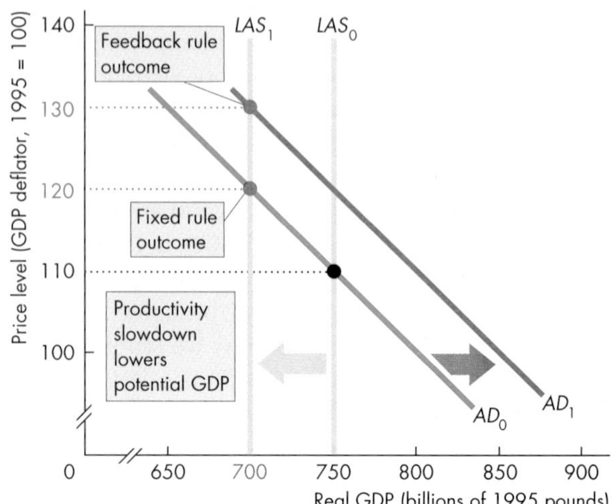

A productivity slowdown shifts the long-run aggregate supply curve from LAS_0 to LAS_1. Real GDP falls to £700 billion and the GDP deflator rises to 120. With a fixed rule, there is no change in the money supply, taxes or government spending, aggregate demand stays at AD_0, and that is the end of the matter. With a feedback rule, the Bank increases the money supply and/or the government cuts taxes or increases spending, intending to increase real GDP. Aggregate demand moves to AD_1, but the long-run result is an increase in the price level – the GDP deflator rises to 130 – with no change in real GDP.

Imagine that the economy starts out on aggregate demand curve AD_0 and long-run aggregate supply curve LAS_0 at a GDP deflator of 110 and with real GDP equal to £750 billion. Now suppose that the long-run aggregate supply curve shifts to LAS_1. An actual decrease in long-run aggregate supply can occur as a result of a severe drought or other natural catastrophe, or perhaps as the result of a disruption of international trade such as the OPEC embargo of the 1970s.

Fixed Rule With a fixed rule, the fall in the long-run aggregate supply has no effect on the Bank or the government and no effect on aggregate demand. The aggregate demand curve remains AD_0. Real GDP falls to £700 billion and the GDP deflator increases to 120.

Feedback Rule Now suppose that the Bank and the government use feedback rules. In particular, suppose that when real GDP falls, the Bank increases the money supply and Parliament approves a tax cut to increase aggregate demand. In this example, the money supply increase and the tax cut shift the aggregate demand curve to AD_1. The policy goal is to bring real GDP back to £750 billion. But the long-run aggregate supply curve has shifted so long-run real GDP has decreased to £700 billion. The increase in aggregate demand cannot cause an increase in output if the economy does not have the capacity to produce that output. So real GDP stays at £700 billion but the price level rises still further – the GDP deflator goes to 130. You can see that in this case the attempt to stabilize real GDP using a feedback policy has no effect on real GDP, but it generates a substantial price level increase.

We've now seen some of the shortcomings of using feedback rules for stabilization policy. Some economists believe that these shortcomings are serious and would like to see simple fixed rules. A popular view among some economists is to have an exchange rate rule, as in the ERM. Others, regarding the potential advantages of feedback rules as greater than their costs, advocate the continued use of such policies but with an important modification that we'll now look at.

Nominal GDP Targeting Attempting to keep the growth rate of nominal GDP steady is called **nominal GDP targeting**. This policy target was first proposed by a leading Keynesian activist economist, James Tobin of Yale University. It is a policy that recognizes the strengths of a fixed rule but that regards the monetarist fixed rule as inappropriate. Instead, nominal GDP targeting uses feedback rules for fiscal and monetary policy to hit a fixed nominal GDP growth target.

Nominal GDP growth equals the real GDP growth rate plus the inflation rate. When nominal GDP grows quickly, it is usually because the inflation rate is high. When nominal GDP grows slowly, it is usually because real GDP growth is negative – the economy is in recession. Thus if nominal GDP growth is held steady, excessive inflation and deep recession might be avoided.

Nominal GDP targeting uses feedback rules. Expansionary fiscal and/or monetary actions increase aggregate demand when nominal GDP is below target and contractionary fiscal and/or monetary actions decrease aggregate demand when nominal GDP is above target. The main problem with nominal GDP targeting is that there are long and variable time lags between the identification of a need to change aggregate demand and the effects of the policy actions taken.

Natural-Rate Policies All the business cycle stabilization policies we've considered have been directed at smoothing the cycle and keeping unemployment close to the natural rate. It is also possible to pursue policies directed towards lowering the natural rate of unemployment. But there are no simple costless ways of lowering the natural rate of unemployment.

The main policy tools that influence the natural rate of unemployment are supply side factors dealing with tax rates, employers' additional costs of hiring labour, unemployment benefits, union regulation and minimum wages. But to use these tools the government faces tough trade-offs. To lower the natural rate of unemployment, the government could lower the tax rate on income or employers' social security contributions, or lower unemployment benefits or even shorten the period for which benefits are paid. These policy actions might create hardships and have costs that exceed the cost of a high natural rate of unemployment.

Some economists have argued that the supply side policies of the 1980s in the UK had the effect of reducing the natural rate of unemployment. Taxes on income were reduced, trade union activity was regulated, employers' social security contributions were reduced and the eligibility for unemployment benefits was reduced. The outcome of all these policies has been to make the labour market more flexible and labour less costly to employ.

Review

- Fixed-rule policies keep fiscal and monetary policy steady and independent of the state of the economy.
- Feedback policies cut taxes, increase spending and speed up money supply growth when the economy is in recession and reverse these measures when the economy is overheating.

Figure 34.8 Responding to an OPEC Oil Price Increase 

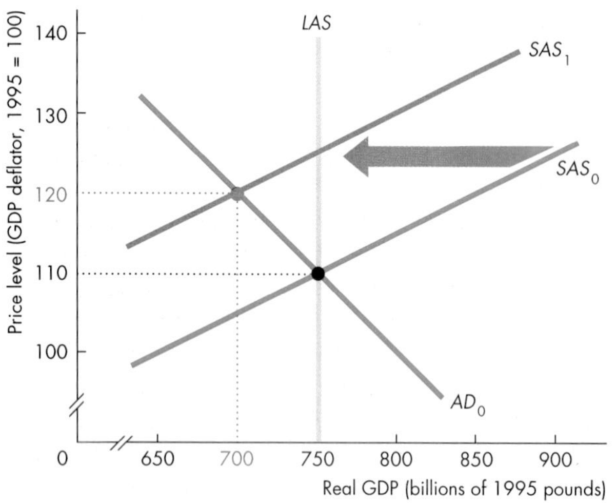

(a) Fixed rule

Price level (GDP deflator, 1995 = 100)
140
130
125
120
110
100
0
LAS
SAS1
SAS0
AD0
AD1
700
750
800
850
900
950
Real GDP (billions of 1995 pounds)

(b) Feedback rule

The economy starts out on AD_0 and SAS_0, with a GDP deflator of 110 and real GDP of £750 billion. OPEC forces up the price of oil and the short-run aggregate supply curve shifts to SAS_1. Real GDP decreases to £700 billion and the GDP deflator increases to 120. With a fixed money supply rule (part a), the Bank makes no change to aggregate demand. The economy stays depressed until the price of oil falls again, and the economy returns to its original position. With a feedback rule (part b), the Bank injects additional money and aggregate demand increases to AD_1. Real GDP returns to £750 billion (full employment) but the GDP deflator increases to 125. The economy is set for another round of cost-push inflation.

- Feedback rules apparently do a better job but we are not sure this is the case. Their successful use requires a good knowledge of the current state of the economy, an ability to forecast as far ahead as the policy actions have effects, and clarity about the feedback rules being used.

We've studied growth policy and business cycle and unemployment policy. Let's now study inflation policy.

Inflation Policy

There are two inflation policy problems. In times of price level stability, the problem is to prevent inflation from breaking out. In times of inflation, the problem is to reduce its rate and restore price stability. Avoiding demand inflation is just the opposite of avoiding demand-driven recession. So keeping aggregate demand steady is an anti-inflation policy as well as an anti-recession policy. But avoiding cost-push inflation raises some special issues that we need to consider. So we will look at two issues for inflation policy:

1 Avoiding cost-push inflation.
2 Slowing inflation.

Avoiding Cost-push Inflation

Cost-push inflation is inflation that has its origins in cost increases. In 1973–74, the world oil price exploded. Cost shocks such as these become inflationary if they are accommodated by an increase in the quantity of money. Such an increase in the quantity of money can occur if a monetary policy feedback rule is used. A fixed-rule policy for the money stock makes cost-push inflation impossible. Let's see why.

Figure 34.8 shows the economy at full employment. Aggregate demand is AD_0, short-run aggregate supply is SAS_0 and long-run aggregate supply is *LAS*. Real GDP is £750 billion and the GDP deflator is 110. Now suppose that OPEC tries to gain a temporary advantage by increasing the price of oil. The short-run aggregate supply curve shifts leftward from SAS_0 to SAS_1.

Monetarist Fixed Rule Figure 34.8(a) shows what happens if a fixed rule for monetary policy is followed and the government follows a fixed rule for fiscal policy. Suppose that the fixed rule is for zero money growth and no change in taxes or government purchases of goods and services. With these fixed rules, the government pays no attention to the fact that there has been an increase in the price of oil. No policy actions are taken. The short-run aggregate supply curve has shifted to SAS_1 but the aggregate demand curve remains at AD_0. The GDP deflator rises to 120, and real GDP falls to £700 billion. The economy has experienced *stagflation*. Unless the price of oil falls, the economy will remain depressed. But eventually, the low level of real GDP and low sales will probably bring a fall in the price of oil. When this happens, the short-run aggregate supply curve will shift back to SAS_0. The GDP deflator will fall to 110 and real GDP will increase to £750 billion.

Keynesian Feedback Rule Figure 34.8(b) shows what happens if the Bank and the government operate a feedback rule. The starting point is the same as before – the economy is on SAS_0 and AD_0 with a GDP deflator of 110 and real GDP of £750 billion. OPEC raises the price of oil and the short-run aggregate supply curve shifts to SAS_1. Real GDP falls to £700 billion and the price level rises to 120.

A monetary feedback rule is followed. That rule is to increase the quantity of money when real GDP is below potential GDP. With potential GDP perceived to be £750 billion and with actual real GDP at £700 billion, the Bank pumps money into the economy. Aggregate demand increases and the aggregate demand curve shifts rightward to AD_1. The price level rises to 125 and real GDP returns to £750 billion. The economy moves back to full employment but at a higher price level.

What if the government and Bank reacted in a different way? Let's run through the example again. OPEC engineers a new rise in the price of oil which decreases aggregate supply, and the short-run aggregate supply curve shifts leftward once more. The Bank, realizing this danger, does *not* respond to the OPEC price increase. Instead, it holds firm and even slows down the growth of aggregate demand to dampen further the inflationary consequences of OPEC's actions.

Incentives to Push Up Costs You can see that there are no checks on the incentives to push up costs if the government accommodates price rises. If some groups see a temporary gain from pushing up the price at which they are selling their resources, and if the Bank always accommodates to prevent unemployment and slack business conditions from emerging, then cost-push elements will have a free rein. But when the Bank pursues a fixed-rule policy, the incentive to attempt to steal a temporary advantage from a price increase is severely weakened. The cost of higher unemployment and lower output is a consequence that each group will have to face and recognize.

Thus a fixed rule is capable of delivering a steady inflation rate (and even zero inflation), while a feedback rule, in the face of cost-push pressures, leaves the inflation rate free to rise and fall at the whim of whichever group believes a temporary advantage to be available from pushing up its price.

Slowing Inflation

So far, we've concentrated on *avoiding* inflation. But often the problem is not to avoid inflation but to tame it. How can inflation, once it has set in, be cured? We'll look at two cases:

1 A surprise inflation reduction.
2 A credible, announced inflation reduction.

A Surprise Inflation Reduction We'll use two equivalent approaches to study the problem of lowering inflation: the aggregate supply–aggregate demand model and the Phillips curve. The *AS–AD* model tells us about real GDP and the price level, while the Phillips curve, which is explained in Chapter 30, pp. 764–768, lets us keep track of inflation and unemployment.

Figure 34.9 illustrates the economy at full employment with inflation raging at 10 per cent a year. In part (a), the economy is on aggregate demand curve AD_0 and short-run aggregate supply curve SAS_0. Real GDP is £750 billion and, at a moment in

Figure 34.9 Lowering Inflation

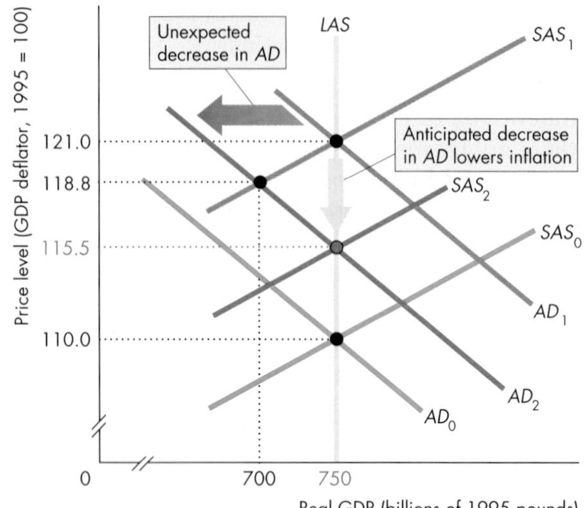

(a) Aggregate demand and aggregate supply

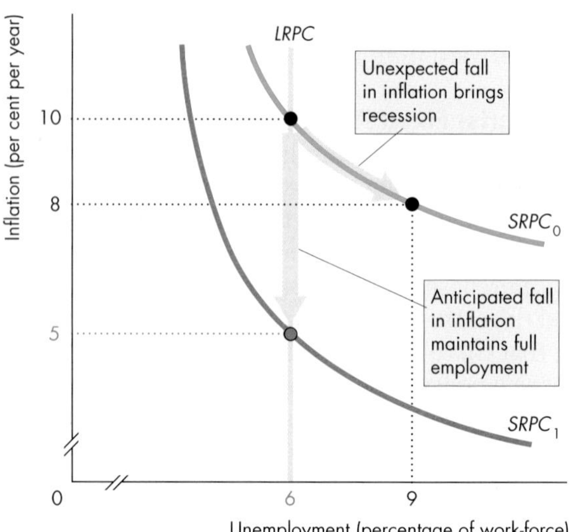

(b) Phillips curves

Initially, aggregate demand is AD_0 and short-run aggregate supply is SAS_0. Real GDP is £750 billion (its full-employment level on the long-run aggregate supply curve *LAS*). Inflation is proceeding at 10 per cent a year. If it continues to do so, the aggregate demand curve shifts to AD_1 and the short-run aggregate supply curve shifts to SAS_1. The GDP deflator rises to 121. This same situation is shown in part (b) with the economy on the short-run Phillips curve $SRPC_0$.

With an unexpected slowdown in aggregate demand growth, the aggregate demand curve (part a) shifts to AD_2, real GDP falls to £700 billion and inflation slows to 8 per cent (a GDP deflator of 118.8). In part (b), unemployment rises to 9 per cent as the economy slides down $SRPC_0$.

If a credible, announced slowdown in aggregate demand growth occurs, the short-run aggregate supply curve (part a) shifts to SAS_2, the short-run Phillips curve (part b) shifts to $SRPC_1$, inflation slows to 5 per cent, real GDP remains at £750 billion and unemployment remains at its natural rate of 6 per cent.

time, the GDP deflator is 110. With real GDP equal to potential GDP on the *LAS* curve, there is full employment. Equivalently, in part (b), the economy is on its long-run Phillips curve, *LRPC*, and short-run Phillips curve, $SRPC_0$. The inflation rate of 10 per cent a year is anticipated so unemployment is at its natural rate.

Next year, aggregate demand is *expected* to increase and the aggregate demand curve in Figure 34.9(a) is expected to shift rightward to AD_1. Expecting this increase in aggregate demand, wages increase to shift the short-run aggregate supply curve to SAS_1. If expectations are fulfilled, the GDP deflator rises to 121 – a 10 per cent inflation – and real GDP remains at its long-run level. In part (b), the economy remains at its original position – unemployment is at the natural rate and the inflation rate is 10 per cent a year.

Suppose, when no one is expecting the action, the Bank tries to slow inflation. It increases interest rates and slows money growth. Aggregate demand growth slows and the aggregate demand curve (in part a) shifts to AD_2. With no change in the expected inflation rate, wages rise by the same amount as before and the short-run aggregate supply curve shifts leftward to SAS_1. Real GDP decreases to £700 billion and the GDP deflator rises to 118.8 – an inflation rate of 8 per cent a year. In Figure 34.9(b), there is a movement along the short-run Phillips curve $SRPC_0$ as unemployment rises to 9 per cent and inflation falls to 8 per cent a year. The policy has succeeded in slowing inflation, but at the cost of recession. Real GDP is below potential GDP and unemployment is above its natural rate.

A Credible Announced Inflation Reduction

Suppose that instead of simply slowing down the growth of aggregate demand, the government announces its intention ahead of its action in a credible and convincing way, so that its announcement is believed. The lower level of aggregate demand is expected so wages increase at a pace consistent with the lower level of aggregate demand. The short-run aggregate supply curve (in Figure 34.9a) shifts leftward but only to SAS_2. Aggregate demand increases by the amount expected and the aggregate demand curve shifts to AD_2. The GDP deflator rises to 115.5 – an inflation rate of 5 per cent a year – and real GDP remains at its full-employment level.

In Figure 34.9(b), the lower expected inflation rate shifts the short-run Phillips curve downward to $SRPC_1$, and inflation falls to 5 per cent a year while unemployment remains at its natural rate.

Inflation Reduction in Practice

When the UK government slowed down inflation in 1980, the economy paid a high price. The government's monetary policy action was unexpected. As a result, it occurred in the face of wages that had been set at too high a level to be consistent with the growth of aggregate demand that the government subsequently allowed. The consequence was recession – a decrease in real GDP and a rise in unemployment. Couldn't the government have lowered inflation without causing recession by telling people far enough ahead of time that it did indeed plan to slow down the growth rate of aggregate demand?

The answer appears to be no. The main reason is that people form their expectation of the government's action (as they form expectations about anyone's actions) on the basis of actual behaviour, not on the basis of stated intentions. How many times have you told yourself that it is your firm intention to reduce weight, or to keep within a budget and put a few pounds away for a rainy day, only to discover that, despite your best intentions, your old habits win out in the end?

Forming expectations about the government's behaviour is no different except, of course, it is more complex than forecasting your own behaviour. To form expectations of the government's actions, people look at its past *actions*, not its stated intentions. On the basis of such observations they try to work out what the government's policy is, to forecast its future actions, and to forecast the effects of those actions on aggregate demand and inflation. When Mrs Thatcher came to power in June 1979, the forecast for her policy was to do the same as all previous governments had done – that is, to say one thing and do another. In other words, the Thatcher government had no reputation for an anti-inflation policy. Its credibility was low.

Over a period of time, the government won credibility for its anti-inflation policies by earning a reputation for being tough with monetary policy. But this reputation was lost after allowing inflation to rise by the end of the 1980s.

An Independent Central Bank

Recent research on central bank performance has strenthened the view that a more independent central bank can deliver a lower average inflation rate without creating either a higher unemployment rate or lower real GDP growth rate. The Treaty on European Union – the Maastricht Treaty – provides for independence for all national central banks that wish to join the EMU. The independent ECB is assigned the task of maintaining price stability (inflation below 2 per cent a year) and takes a growth rate of M3 for the Euro area of 4.5 per cent a year as its reference value for price stability over the medium term. The Bank of England do not admit to a monetary target but target inflation directly. The independence of central banks is getting to be conventional thinking. The central banks of the EU, Switzerland, and New Zealand are fully independent. Other central banks that have explicit inflation targets are: Canada, Australia and Sweden.

Review

- A fixed rule gives more effective protection against a cost-push inflation than a feedback rule.

- When inflation is tamed, a recession usually results because people form policy expectations based on past policy actions.

- An independent central bank pursuing only price stability could possibly achieve price stability with greater credibility and at lower cost in terms of unemployment and lost production.

You've examined the main issues of macroeconomic policy. You've looked at the goals of policy and the fiscal and monetary policies pursued. You've examined policies for achieving faster long-term real GDP growth and you've seen how fixed and feedback rules operate to stabilize the business cycle and contain inflation. You've also seen why lowering inflation is usually accompanied by recession and higher unemployment. You have now completed your study of macroeconomics and of the problems and challenges of improving macroeconomic performance. In this study, your main focus has been the UK and EU economies. Occasionally, we have taken into account linkages between the United Kingdom and the rest of the world. In Chapter 35, we turn our attention to the problems of the economies of the developing world and of former communist countries and see how they are moving towards industrial market economies like our own.

Summary

Key Points

Policy Goals (pp. 860–862)

- The goals of macroeconomic policy are to achieve the highest sustainable rate of long-term real GDP growth, smooth out avoidable business fluctuations, and maintain low unemployment and low inflation.

Policy Tools and Performance (pp. 862–865)

- The macroeconomic policy tools are fiscal policy and monetary policy.
- Fiscal and monetary policy within the EMU is dictated by the targets and stability pact set by the Maastricht Treaty.

Long-term Growth Policy (pp. 865–867)

- The sources of the long-term growth of potential GDP are the accumulation of physical and human capital and the advance of technology.
- Policies to increase the long-term growth rate focus on increasing saving and investment in human capital and new technologies.
- The EU national saving rate has been on a generally falling path since 1970.
- To increase the saving rate, government saving, which was negative in much of the 1980s, must be increased and incentives for private saving must be strengthened.
- Human capital investment might be increased with improved education and by improving on-the-job training programmes.
- Investment in new technologies can be encouraged by tax incentives and EU sponsored research programmes.

Business Cycle and Unemployment Policies (pp. 867–874)

- In the face of an aggregate demand shock, a fixed-rule policy takes no action to counter the shock. It permits aggregate demand to fluctuate as a result of all the independent forces that influence it.
- A feedback-rule policy adjusts taxes, government purchases, or the money supply to offset the effects of other influences on aggregate demand. An ideal feedback rule

keeps the economy at full employment, with stable prices.

- Some economists argue that feedback rules make the economy less stable because they require greater knowledge of the state of the economy than we have, they operate with time lags that extend beyond the forecast horizon, and they introduce unpredictability about policy reactions.
- By using feedback policies aimed at keeping nominal GDP growth steady – nominal GDP targeting – it is possible that the extremes of inflation and recession might be avoided.

Inflation Policy (pp. 874–878)

- A fixed rule minimizes the threat of cost-push inflation.
- A feedback rule validates cost-push inflation and leaves the price level and inflation rate free to move to wherever they are pushed.
- Inflation can be tamed, and at little or no cost in terms of lost output or excessive unemployment, by slowing the growth of aggregate demand in a credible and predictable way. But usually, when inflation is slowed down, a recession occurs.
- Published inflation targets aid the process of building up a good inflation reputation.

Key Figures 

Key Terms

Review Questions

1 What are the goals of macroeconomic policy?

2 Describe the main features of recent fiscal policy in EU countries.

3 Describe the main features of recent monetary policy in the United Kingdom since June 1997.

4 Explain the main ways in which policy can try to speed up long-term real GDP growth.

5 Explain the distinction between a fixed-rule policy and a feedback-rule policy.

6 Analyse the effects of a temporary decrease in aggregate demand if a fixed money supply rule is employed.

7 Analyse the behaviour of real GDP and the price level in the face of a permanent decrease in aggregate demand under:

a A fixed monetary rule.
b A feedback monetary rule.

8 Explain the main problems in using fiscal policy for stabilizing the economy.

9 Why do economists disagree with each other on the appropriateness of fixed and feedback rules?

10 Analyse the effects of a rise in the price of oil on real GDP and the price level if the central bank employs:

a A fixed monetary rule.
b A feedback monetary rule.

11 Explain nominal GDP targeting and why it reduces real GDP fluctuations and inflation.

12 Explain why the government's credibility affects the cost of lowering inflation.

Problems

1 A productivity growth slowdown has occurred. Explain its possible origins and describe a policy package that is designed to speed up growth again.

2 The economy is experiencing 10 per cent inflation and 7 per cent unemployment. Set out policies for the central bank and parliament to pursue which will lower both inflation and unemployment. Explain how and why your proposed policies will work.

3 The economy shown in the figure is initially on aggregate demand curve AD_0 and short-run aggregate supply curve SAS_0. Then aggregate demand decreases and the aggregate demand curve shifts leftward to AD_1.

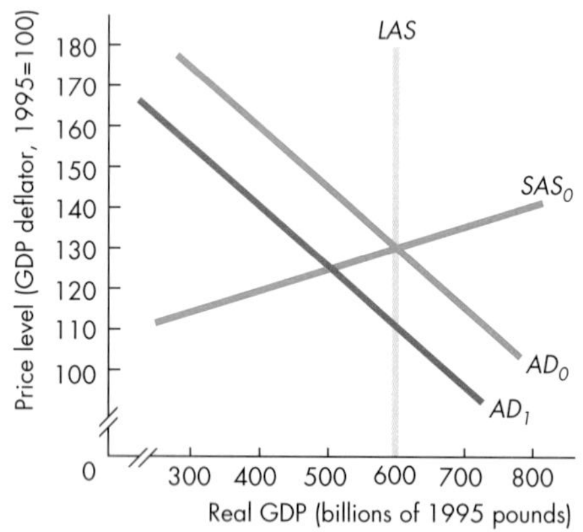

a What is the initial equilibrium real GDP and price level?
b If the decrease in aggregate demand is temporary and the government follows a fixed-rule fiscal policy, what happens to real GDP and the price level? Trace the immediate effects and the adjustment as aggregate demand returns to its original level.
c If the decrease in aggregate demand is temporary and the government follows a feedback-rule policy, what happens to real GDP and the price level? Trace the immediate effects and the adjustment as aggregate demand returns to its original level.
d If the decrease in aggregate demand is temporary and the government follows a fixed-rule fiscal policy, what happens to real GDP and the price level?

4 The economy shown in the figure is initially on aggregate demand curve AD and short-run aggregate supply curve SAS_0. Then short-run aggregate supply decreases, and the short-run aggregate supply curve shifts leftward to SAS_1.

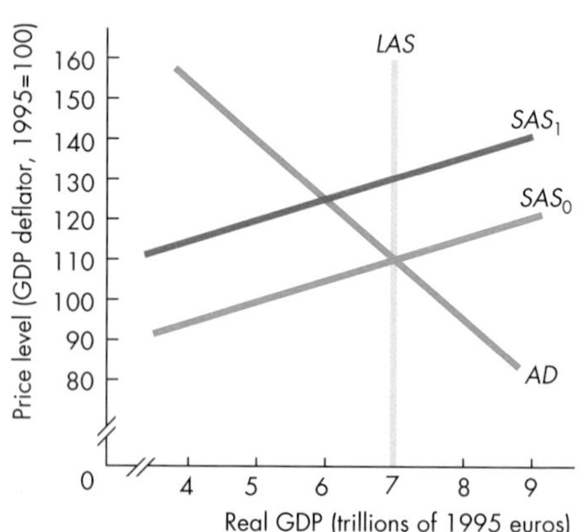

a What are the initial equilibrium real GDP and price level?
b What type of event could have caused the decrease in short-run aggregate supply?

c If the government follows a fixed-rule monetary policy, what happens to real GDP and the price level? Trace the immediate effects and the adjustment as the short-run aggregate supply returns to its original level.
d If the government follows a feedback-rule monetary policy, what happens to real GDP and the price level? Trace the immediate effects and the adjustment as aggregate demand and short-run aggregate supply respond to the policy action.

5 The economy is booming and inflation is beginning to rise, but it is widely agreed that a massive recession is just around the corner. Weigh the advantages and disadvantages of the government pursuing a fixed-rule and a feedback-rule fiscal policy.

6 The economy is in a recession and inflation is falling. It is widely agreed that a strong recovery is just around the corner. Weigh the advantages and disadvantages of the central bank pursuing a fixed-rule and a feedback-rule monetary policy.

7 You have been hired as the chief economic adviser by the Chancellor to draw up an economic plan that will maximize the chance of the government being re-elected.

a What are the macroeconomic stabilization policy elements in that plan?
b What do you have to make the economy do in an election year?
c What policy actions would help the government achieve its objectives?

(In dealing with this problem, be careful to take into account the effects of your proposed policy on expectations and the effects of those expectations on actual economic performance.)

8 The European Monetary Union is experiencing inflation of 1.5 per cent and unemployment of 10.5 per cent. Set out policies that the European Central Bank and the individual governments can follow that will maintain low inflation but reduce unemployment. Explain how and why your proposed policies will work.

9 Study *Reading Between the Lines* on pp. 882–883 and then answer the following questions.

a Why is inflation a potential problem in Spain?
b What is the prediction for real GDP growth in 1999 for Spain?
c What policy does Mr Rodrigo Rato say the government is pursuing to tackle inflation?
d What other policies is the Spanish government pursuing and what effect do you think it will it have on the economy?
e How will an expected budget surplus by 2002 help Spain in reducing its high unemployment?

Stabilization Policy Dilemma

Financial Times, 2 July 1999 

Spain expects inflation to 'drop a bit'

William Dawkins and David White

Spain is counting on increased business competition to prevent its inflation rate from getting further out of line with the rest of the euro-zone as its economy continues to surge ahead, said Rodrigo Rato, finance and economy minister.

Mr Rato told the Financial Times in an interview he expected inflation to "drop a bit" in the next few months from the recent rate of more than 2 per cent – double the level for the euro-zone.

He argued growth, expected to continue well above the euro-zone average, did not inevitably imply a divergence in price trends, and said the centre-right government would try to tackle inflation by reducing its deficit and pursuing measures to liberalise the economy.

He said the government could "in a very few years" have a budget surplus, reaffirming its target of achieving a balance in its public sector accounts in 2002, compared with this year's target deficit of 1.6 per cent of gross domestic product.

"We will at least fulfil our target for the public deficit and we will certainly take any chance to reduce it more," he said. The government would be strict in limiting the number of civil servants and keeping increases in pensions and public sector wages to the inflation rate. It would also tackle fraud in sickness benefits and seek to cut the cost of drugs paid for by the health service.

Spanish growth should stay at about 3.5 per cent this year, based on strong domestic demand, which was expanding at an annual rate of about 5.5 per cent, he said. This would mean less of a slowdown from last year's growth peak of 3.8 per cent than many private-sector economists have been predicting.

Spain had suffered "not too much damage" from recent international financial turmoil and its exports had suffered less than some other countries.

The Essence of the Story

- Strong growth of real GDP in Spain is raising fears of inflation diverging from the eurozone average.
- The Spanish government hopes that increased competition will stop inflation from rising.
- The government could have a budget surplus by 2002 compared with a target deficit of 1.6 per cent of GDP in 1999.
- The government hopes to carry out a number of other policies. These are: controlling the growth of the public sector, limiting the growth of pensions and public sector wages and tackling fraud in sickness benefits.
- The minister for finance and the economy admits that living with a euro monetary policy in which Spanish concerns have little weight is difficult but that the costs are worth the benefits.

Economic Analysis

■ Real GDP growth of 3.8 per cent in 1998 and an expected growth rate of 3.5 per cent in 1999 has raised fears that demand is growing faster than supply in Spain. Figure 1 shows aggregate demand initially at AD_0 and the economy at point *a*. Aggregate demand increases to AD_1 and the economy moves to point *b* which is in excess of potential GDP.

■ Inflation has been falling in Spain but high growth in real GDP has led to the possibility of inflation rising. Figure 2 shows the inflation and real GDP growth performance of Spain in recent years.

■ Spain is a member of the European Monetary Union and cannot conduct its own monetary policy to tackle potential inflationary problems. The reduction in the benchmark interest rate to 2.5 per cent by the ECB was the right policy for low growth in the euro core countries like Germany but the wrong policy for high growth countries like Spain.

■ The Spanish government plans to use tight fiscal policy to contain inflation. In Figure 1, it hopes to reduce demand by reducing the growth in public spending and shift AD_1 back towards potential GDP. However, in case it fails to do this fully, it is hoped that a wage policy on the public sector will stop the short-run aggregate supply curve, *SAS*, from shifting to the left and increasing inflation.

■ The main problem for Spain is its high rate of unemployment. Figure 3 shows the pattern of unemployment and inflation. Inflation has stabilized and unemployment has fallen but remains stubbornly high. The natural rate has fallen but Spain needs to have policies that increase potential GDP and reduce the natural rate of unemployment even further. The government plans to announce tax incentives for firms to conduct more research and development. Such tax policies are credible if people do not expect them to be reversed in the future. A projected budget surplus makes a reversal less likely.

■ The Spanish situation shows the difficulty of coordinating fiscal and monetary policy for countries in EMU, when monetary policy is conducted by an independent ECB that concerns itself with euro-wide inflation problems.

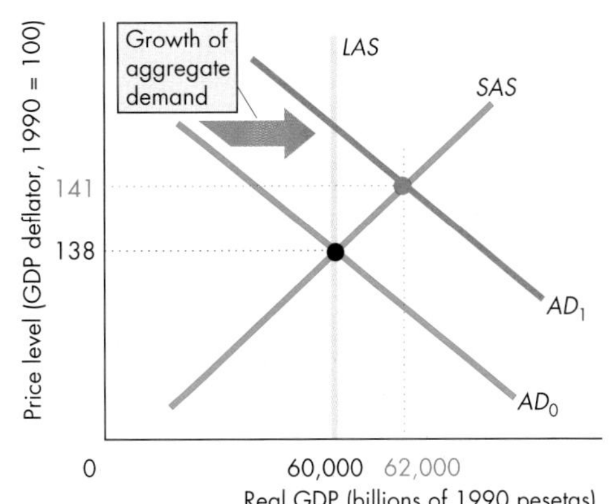

Figure 1 Strong growth and inflation fears

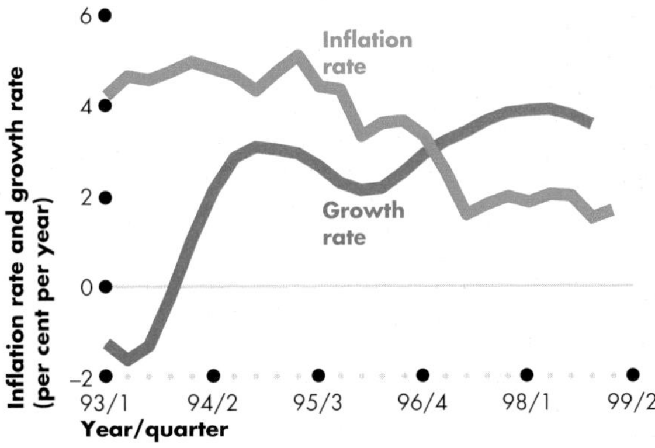

Figure 2 Real GDP growth and inflation

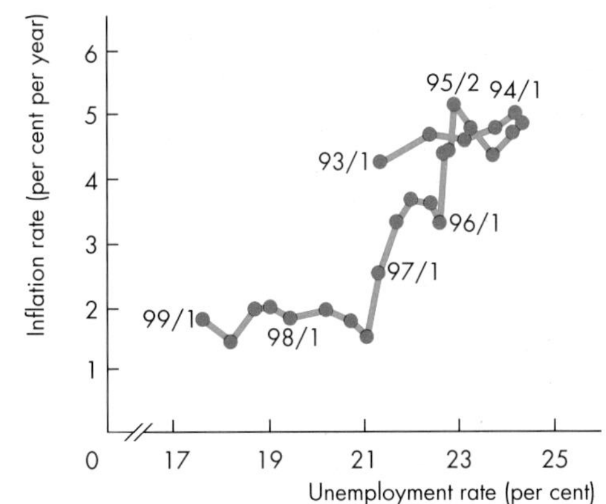

Figure 3 Inflation and unemployment

Part 9

The Euro and the Global Economy

Talking with **Otmar Issing**

Professor Otmar Issing, born in 1936, has been a member of the Executive Board of the European Central Bank since 1 June 1998. The business area for which he is responsible includes the Directorates General Economics and Research. Until May 1998 he was a Member of the Board of the Deutsche Bundesbank with a seat in the Central Bank Council. Prior to that he held Chairs of Economics at the Universities of Würzburg and Erlangen-Nürnberg. In 1991 he was awarded an honorary professorship at the University of Würzburg. From 1988 to 1990 he was a member of the Council of Experts for the Assessment of Overall Economic Developments. He is an active member of Akademie der Wissenschaften und der Literatur (Academy of Sciences and Literature), Mainz, and of the Academia Scientiarum et Artium Europaea (European Academy of Sciences and Arts). In addition to publishing numerous articles in scientific journals and periodicals, he is the author of, inter alia, two textbooks, namely *Einführung in die Geldtheorie* (Introduction to monetary theory), 11th edition, 1998, and *Einführung in die Geldpolitik* (Introduction to monetary policy), 6th edition, 1996.

What made you study economics?

My first choice was to study Latin and Greek. But soon I discovered that my youthful enthusiasm, created by excellent teachers at school, was not a sustainable basis for study. Somewhat disappointed I was looking for a totally different discipline. Attending lectures in economics I was fascinated from the very beginning by the subject as well as by the professor to whom I became assistant later.

Which economists have influenced you most?

At the beginning the professor I already mentioned. Later, and with lasting influence, a number of great economists in the tradition of Anglo-Scottish liberalism: from Adam Smith to F.A. Hayek. Also, not to forget the Germans: Walter Eucken, Gottfried Haberler and Milton Friedman.

The EMU began on 1 January 1999. Currently it is a 'unit of account'. When will it become a 'medium of exchange'?

It is not entirely correct to consider the euro, for the time being, just a unit of account. The euro is already the currency with legal tender in the euro area. European currency units, such as the Deutsche Marks, the French franc etc., legally represent national denominations of the euro.

If you are asking when we will use new euro-denominated cash in the euro area, the answer is that we have to wait until 1 January 2002. At that point in time, the new notes and coins will possibly be used together with old national ones for a period of up to 6 months. Thereafter, national currencies will cease to have legal tender in the euro area.

Can you explain the functions of the European Central Bank (ECB) and how it implements its policy?

The ECB is at the centre of the Eurosystem that also includes the national central banks of the European countries that adopted the single currency on 1 January 1999. The functions of the Eurosystem, which is governed by the decision-making bodies of the ECB, have been carefully designed and agreed upon in the international Treaty of Maastricht.

The most important task to be carried out by the Eurosystem is to define and implement the single monetary policy of the euro area. The Eurosystem, moreover, participates in the definition of the foreign exchange policy of the euro and is directly responsible for the conduct of foreign exchange operations and for the holding and management of official foreign reserves. Finally, the Eurosystem is required to promote the smooth operations of payment systems throughout the EMU, in order to ensure the uniform monetary conditions prevail across the euro area.

In pursuing these tasks, the primary objective of the Eurosystem must be to maintain price stability, i.e. a low-inflation environment for the euro area economy. In order to fulfil its mandate, the ECB has announced – even before the start of the EMU – the strategy and the operational framework which apply, respectively, in the formulation and in the implementation of the single monetary policy.

The strategy announced by the ECB is based on three main elements. The first is a quantitative definition of price stability, i.e. a numerical specification of the inflation rate that will be considered compatible with the definition of price stability mentioned in the Treaty. In order to pursue this objective, two sorts of indicators, or 'pillars', are used. The first is the rate of growth of a broad monetary aggregate, which provides information on inflation prospects through the well-known equilibrium relationship between money and prices. The second pillar encompasses other indicators, developing over time, that are believed to convey relevant information on future price developments. Overall, the two pillars are designed to jointly take into account all the available information useful for the conduct of monetary policy in the euro area.

As to the implementation of the single monetary policy, the operational framework (i.e. the set of instruments with which the Eurosystem intervenes in the market) is based on three main groups of instruments: open market operations, standing facilities and minimum reserve requirements.

Convergence has been an important factor in the setting up of the EMU, but there is as yet no common business cycle in Euroland. Does this cause a problem for monetary policy?

The process of convergence before the launch of the single currency has been remarkable. The dramatic fall of the inflation rates in many countries during the 1990s, in spite of the ERM crisis and of the relatively unfavourable cyclical conditions, is probably the clearest evidence of such convergence. Nevertheless, differences in inflation still exist and we should probably expect them to persist after the inception of the single currency. Similar considerations apply for cyclical developments.

Are these reasons for concern? If we take a closer look at the different aspects of any national economy, we find a situation in all respects similar to that of the euro area. In the case of the inflation rate, and even of the price levels, the existence of differences, for example between main cities and rural areas, is well known to everyone. Similar degrees of regional heterogeneity are apparent if one looks at the statistics on regional production. It becomes clear that divergences in the rates of growth and employment are the norm, not the exception, in any developed economy.

The single monetary policy in the euro area, therefore, faces no special difficulty in this respect. Likewise in any national economy, monetary policy will maintain an area-wide operation, letting the single currency continue to act as a stimulus for real convergence and the forces of competition reduce price differences.

The theory of currency unions appeals to the Optimum Currency Area (OCA) literature. Can you explain what an OCA is and whether you think Euroland is an OCA?

An optimum currency area is an economic region that can benefit from the adoption of a common money. Since political and monetary borders traditionally coincide, the question of whether to form a monetary union typically arises between national states. From an economic point of view, however, we can question the optimality of single currency areas at any regional level.

A single currency carries obvious advantages, such as reduced transaction costs from currency conversion, disappearance of exchange rate uncertainty for firms doing business across the area and insulation from exchange rate bubbles. Moreover, it can trigger positive externalities in financial markets and in the productive sectors of the economy, significantly improving long-run growth prospects. A common currency, however, also implies that individual regions forego the possibility of using monetary policy and/or exchange rates changes to respond to region-specific macroeconomic shocks. Consequently, the OCA literature concludes that a common currency is only optimal when the incidence of region-specific shocks is limited or when high factor mobility and wage flexibility can help to absorb their asymmetric effects.

It is not simple to assess when these conditions are satisfied in practice. The main difficulty we face is the lack of an agreed-upon system of weights to measure the intertemporal welfare implication of a monetary union. The cases for or against a currency union are therefore often constructed on the basis of international comparisons.

Altogether, it appears that a common currency can suit the euro area quite well. However, structural reforms in European labour markets need to be carried out. Besides making the European economy less vulnerable in the face of region-specific shocks, these reforms also represent the means to seriously attack the unemployment problem, and thereby to foster steadier and sustainable growth in the area.

How are fiscal and monetary policies coordinated in Euroland?

The Treaty very carefully designs the institutional setting of the Eurosystem. Its institutional independence is accompanied by substantial accountability obligations, to the European Parliament and to the public at large. The Eurosystem, moreover, has full responsibility in maintaining price stability and is expected to support the general economic policies of the community only to the extent that this is 'without prejudice' to it.

This institutional arrangement entails a clear separation of responsibilities and avoids the risk of myopic policies being forced on the Eurosystem through political pressure, possibly under the heading of policy coordination.

The Treaty, however, leaves ample room for information sharing between policy-makers. Communications can easily take place on an informal basis in a number of institutional settings, through meetings with European and national officials.

What is the 'stability pact' and why do you think it is necessary?

The Stability of Growth Pact (SGP) is firstly an important instrument for fiscal discipline at the national level. It contains a commitment to achieve medium-term balanced budgets, or a surplus, in order to avoid the risk of high structural deficits and continuation or even increase in the high level of public debt. In this respect, the SGP contributes to create the conditions for sustainable growth in the euro area.

Moreover, the SGP prescribes sanctions for breaches of the 3 per cent limit of the deficit-to-GDP ratio. This represents an important device for policy coordination, necessary to limit adverse spillover effects from undisciplined fiscal policies. Such effects could easily arise through an increase of the common interest rate, if persistent fiscal deficits in one country were interpreted as a signal of general fiscal laxity. The single monetary policy could itself be endangered by an ever-growing amount of liabilities denominated in the common currency.

The Pact is also designed to increase the flexibility of fiscal policies which was reduced in many European countries by excessively high deficits and debts. If applied rigorously, the SGP leaves sufficient room for automatic fiscal stabilizers to operate effectively without the 3 per cent constraint binding. The process of fiscal consolidation does not need to penalize excessively economic activity and growth, since, as documented by both theory and empirical results, the expectations of economic agents are likely to be positively affected by the process itself.

Finally, what advice would you give to a student of economics today?

Start at a university where a profound, solid and broadly-based education in economics is guaranteed. On this basis, complete your knowledge and view of the world abroad. If possible, try also to gain some experience in an international organization and/or worldwide operating companies.

Trading with the World

After studying this chapter you will be able to:

- Describe the trends and patterns in international trade
- Explain comparative advantage and why all countries can gain from international trade
- Explain how economies of scale and diversity of taste lead to gains from international trade
- Explain why trade restrictions reduce the volume of imports and exports and reduce our consumption possibilities
- Explain the arguments used to justify trade restrictions and show how they are flawed
- Explain why we have trade restrictions

Silk Routes and Containers

Since ancient times, people have striven to expand their trading as far as technology allowed. Marco Polo opened up the silk route between Europe and China in the thirteenth century. Today, container ships laden with cars and machines and Boeing 747s stuffed with farm-fresh foods ply sea and air routes, carrying billions of pounds worth of goods. Why do people go to such great lengths to trade with those in other countries? ◆ Low-wage Mexico has entered into a free trade agreement with high-wage Canada and the United States – the North American Free Trade Agreement or NAFTA. Within the European Union it has been estimated by the US Bureau of Labor Statistics that a German manufacturing worker is paid twice that of an equivalent British one, but a worker in Hong Kong costs one-third of his or her British equivalent. How can any country compete with another that pays its workers a fraction of European wages? Are there any industries in which Europe has an advantage? After World War II, a process of trade liberalization around the world brought about the creation of the General Agreement on Tariffs and Trade (GATT) and a gradual reduction of tariffs. What are the effects of tariffs on international trade? Why don't we have completely unrestricted international trade?

◆ ◆ ◆ ◆ In this chapter we're going to learn about international trade. We'll discover how *all* nations can gain by specializing in producing the goods and services in which they have a comparative advantage and trading with other countries. We'll discover that all countries can compete, no matter how high their wages. We'll also explain why, despite the fact that international trade brings benefits to all, countries restrict trade.

Patterns and Trends in International Trade

The goods and services that we buy from people in other countries are called **imports**. The goods and services that we sell to people in other countries are called **exports**. What are the most important things that we import and export? Most people would probably guess that a relatively rich country such as the United Kingdom imports raw materials and exports manufactured goods. While that is one feature of UK international trade, it is not its most important feature. The vast bulk of our merchandise exports *and* imports are manufactured goods. We sell foreigners Land Rovers, aircraft, machines and scientific equipment, and we buy televisions, video recorders, blue jeans and T-shirts from them. Also, we are a major exporter of primary materials, particularly North Sea oil, and we export chemical goods. We import and export a huge volume of services. Let's look at the international trade of the United Kingdom in a recent year.

UK International Trade

The **balance of trade** is the value of exports minus the value of imports. If the balance is positive, then the value of exports exceeds the value of imports and the United Kingdom is a **net exporter**. But if the balance is negative, the value of imports exceeds the value of exports and the United Kingdom is a **net importer**.

Trade in Goods About 75 per cent of UK international trade is trade in goods and 25 per cent is trade in services. Of the categories of goods traded, by far the most important is manufactured goods. The total value of exports of manufactured goods is less than the total value of imports – the United Kingdom is a net importer of manufactured goods. The United Kingdom is also a net importer of primary materials and fuels and of agricultural products. It is a net exporter of chemical goods and services. Figure 35.1 highlights some of the major items of UK imports and exports of goods. The largest items of both imports and exports are machinery and transport equipment (including motor vehicles). Our imports of machinery and transport equipment (shown by the red bars) are greater than the value of exports of these items (shown by the blue bars).

Trade in Services A quarter of UK international trade is not of goods but of services. You may be wondering how a country can 'export' and 'import' services. Let's look at some examples.

Suppose that you decided to take a holiday in Spain, travelling there from Manchester on Iberian Airways. What you buy from Iberian Airways is not a good but a transport service. Although the concept

Figure 35.1 UK Exports and Imports: 1998

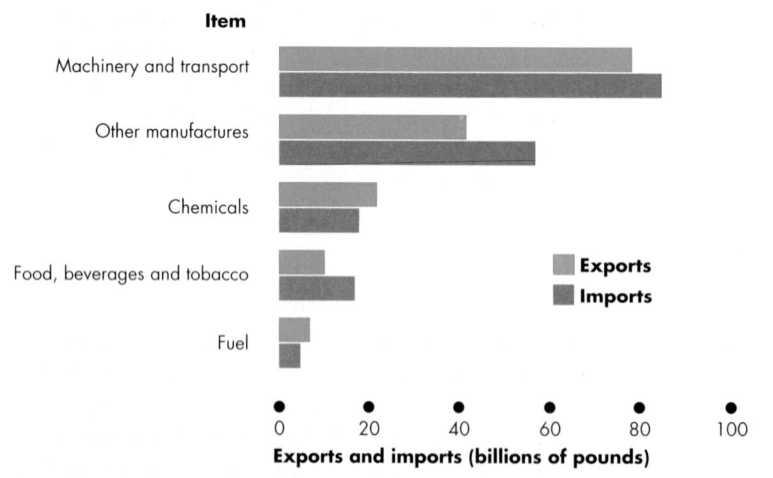

We export large quantities of capital goods such as machinery and transport equipment. We also export large quantities of manufactured goods and cars. But we import even larger quantities of some of these items. We also export and import fuel.

Source: ONS.

may sound odd at first, in economic terms you are importing that service from Spain. The money you spend in Spain on hotel bills, restaurant meals and other things is also classified as the import of services. Similarly, the holiday taken by a Spanish student in the United Kingdom counts as an export of services to Spain.

When we import TV sets from South Korea, the owner of the ship that carries these TV sets might be Greek and the company that insures the cargo might be with Lloyds in London. The payment that we make for the transport to the Greek company is a payment for the import of services, and the payment the Greek shipowner makes to the London insurance company is a payment for the export of a service. Similarly, when a UK shipping company transports Scotch whisky to Tokyo, the transport cost is an export of a service to Japan.

Figure 35.2 The Geographical Pattern of UK International Trade: 1998

In 1998, our largest trading partner was the rest of the European Union. Within the Union our largest trading partner was Germany. Traditionally our largest trading partner was the United States, but in recent years our trade with Germany has overtaken our trade with the United States.

Source: ONS.

Geographical Patterns

The United Kingdom has trading links with almost every part of the world. Figure 35.2 shows the scale of these links in 1998. Our trade with the rest of the European Union is the largest. Within Europe, the largest market for our exports is Germany. In 1998 the United Kingdom exported as much to Germany as to the United States – traditionally the United Kingdom's largest market. North America, which includes the United States, Canada and Mexico, takes a significant share of UK trade at 15 per cent of exports and 15 per cent of imports. However, our largest international trade deficit was with the rest of the European Union. The next largest deficit was with the other OECD countries, not including the United States and Canada.

Trends in Trade

International trade has always been an important part of our economic life. In 1960, we exported 14 per cent of GDP and imported 15 per cent of GDP. In 1998 exports from the UK were 34 per cent and imports were 37 per cent of GDP.

On the export side, all the major commodity categories have shared in the increased volume of international trade. Mechanical and electrical machinery and semi-manufactured goods have remained the largest components of exports and have roughly maintained their share in total exports. The one major change has been the export of fuel, which has increased from 4 per cent of exports in 1963 to 7 per cent in 1998.

But there have been dramatic changes in the composition of imports. Food and raw materials imports have declined steadily, imports of fuel have decreased as North Sea oil came on stream in the 1970s and imports of machinery of all kinds and semi-manufactured goods have increased dramatically, from 33 per cent of imports in 1963 to 85 per cent in 1998. In 1998, the balance of trade (goods and services) was a deficit of £7.9 billion.

Balance of Trade and International Borrowing

When people buy more than they sell, they have to finance the difference by borrowing. When they sell more than they buy, they can use the surplus to make loans to others. This simple principle that governs the income and expenditure and borrowing and lending of individuals and firms is also a feature of our balance of trade. If we import more than we export, we have to finance the difference by borrowing from foreigners. When we export more than we import, we make loans to foreigners to enable them to buy goods in excess of the value of the goods they have sold to us.

This chapter does *not* cover the factors that determine the *balance* of trade and the scale of international borrowing and lending that finance that balance. Our goal is to understand the factors that influence the *volume* and *directions* of international trade rather than its balance. The keys to understanding these factors are the concepts of opportunity cost and comparative advantage.

Figure 35.3 Opportunity Cost in Farmland

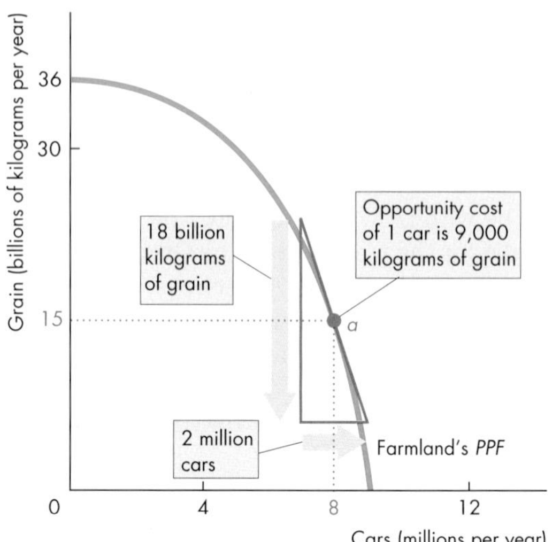

Farmland produces and consumes 15 billion kilograms of grain and 8 million cars a year. That is, it produces and consumes at point *a* on its production possibility frontier. Opportunity cost is equal to the magnitude of the slope of the production possibility frontier. The red triangle tells us that at point *a*, 18 billion kilograms of grain must be foregone to get 2 million cars. That is, at point *a*, 2 million cars cost 18 billion kilograms of grain. Equivalently, 1 car costs 9,000 kilograms of grain or 9,000 kilograms of grain cost 1 car.

Opportunity Cost and Comparative Advantage

Let's apply the lessons that we learned in Chapter 3, pp. 000–000, about the gains from trade to the trade between countries. We'll begin by recalling how we can use the production possibility frontier to measure opportunity cost.

Opportunity Cost in Farmland

Farmland (a fictitious country) can produce grain and cars at any point inside or along the production possibility frontier shown in Figure 35.3. (We're holding constant the output of all the other goods that Farmland produces.) The Farmers (the people of Farmland) are consuming all the grain and cars that they produce and they are operating at point *a* in the figure. That is, Farmland is producing and consuming 15 billion kilograms of grain and 8 million cars each year. What is the opportunity cost of a car in Farmland?

We can answer this question by calculating the slope of the production possibility frontier (*PPF*) at point *a*. The magnitude of the slope of the *PPF* measures the opportunity cost of one good in terms of the other. To measure the slope of the frontier at point *a*, place a straight line tangential to the frontier at point *a* and calculate the slope of that straight line. Recall that the formula for the slope of a line is the change in the value of the variable measured on the y-axis divided by the change in the value of the variable measured on the x-axis as we move along the line. Here, the variable measured on the y-axis is billions of kilograms of grain and the variable measured on the x-axis is millions of cars. So the slope is the change in the number of kilograms of grain divided by the change in the number of cars. As you can see from the red triangle at point a in the figure, if the number of cars produced increases by 2 million, grain production decreases by 18 billion kilograms. Therefore the magnitude of the slope is 18 billion divided by 2 million, which equals 9,000. To get one more car, the people of Farmland must give up 9,000 kilograms of grain. Thus the opportunity cost of 1 car is 9,000 kilograms of grain. Equivalently, 9,000 kilograms of grain cost 1 car. For the people of Farmland, these opportunity costs are the prices they face. The price of a car is 9,000 kilograms of grain and the price of 9,000 kilograms of grain is 1 car.

Figure 35.4 Opportunity Cost in Mobilia

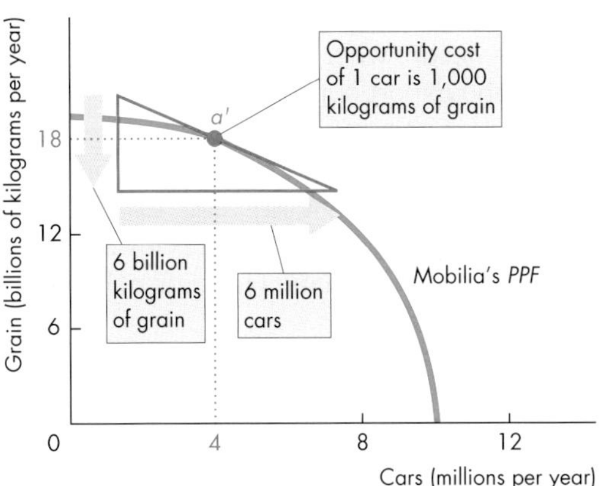

Mobilia produces and consumes 18 billion kilograms of grain and 4 million cars a year. That is, it produces and consumes at point *a*' on its production possibility frontier. Opportunity cost is equal to the magnitude of the slope of the production possibility frontier. The red triangle tells us that at point *a*', 6 billion kilograms of grain must be foregone to get 6 million cars. That is, at point *a*', 6 million cars cost 6 billion kilograms of grain. Equivalently, 1 car costs 1,000 kilograms of grain or 1,000 kilograms of grain cost 1 car.

Opportunity Cost in Mobilia

Now consider the production possibility frontier in Mobilia (another fictitious country and the only other country in our model world). Figure 35.4 illustrates its *PPF*. Like the Farmers, the Mobilians (the people in Mobilia) consume all the grain and cars that they produce. Mobilia consumes 18 billion kilograms of grain a year and 4 million cars, at point a'.

At point a', the magnitude of the slope of Mobilia's *PPF* is 6 billion kilograms of grain divided by 6 million cars, which equals 1,000 kilograms of grain per car. To get one more car, the people of Mobilia must give up 1,000 kilograms of grain. Thus the opportunity cost of 1 car is 1,000 kilograms of grain, or, equivalently, the opportunity cost of 1,000 kilograms of grain is 1 car. These are the prices faced in Mobilia.

Comparative Advantage

Cars are cheaper in Mobilia than in Farmland. One car costs 9,000 kilograms of grain in Farmland but only 1,000 kilograms of grain in Mobilia. But grain is cheaper in Farmland than in Mobilia – 9,000 kilograms of grain costs only 1 car in Farmland while that same amount of grain costs 9 cars in Mobilia.

Mobilia has a comparative advantage in car production. Farmland has a comparative advantage in grain production. A country has a **comparative advantage** in producing a good if it can produce that good at a lower opportunity cost than any other country. Let's see how opportunity cost differences and comparative advantage generate gains from international trade.

Gains from Trade

If Mobilia bought grain for what it costs Farmland to produce it, then Mobilia could buy 9,000 kilograms of grain for 1 car. That is much lower than the cost of growing grain in Mobilia, for there it costs 9 cars to produce 9,000 kilograms of grain. If the Mobilians can buy grain at the low Farmland price, they will reap some gains.

If the Farmers can buy cars for what it costs Mobilia to produce them, they will be able to obtain a car for 1,000 kilograms of grain. Because it costs 9,000 kilograms of grain to produce a car in Farmland, the Farmers would gain from such an opportunity.

In this situation, it makes sense for Mobilia to buy their grain from Farmers and for Farmers to buy their cars from Mobilia. Let's see how such profitable international trade comes about.

Reaping the Gains from Trade

We've seen that the Farmers would like to buy their cars from the Mobilians and that the Mobilians would like to buy their grain from the Farmers. Let's see how the two groups do business with each other, concentrating attention on the international market for cars.

Figure 35.5 illustrates such a market. The quantity of cars *traded internationally* is measured on the x-axis. On the y-axis we measure the price of a car. This price is expressed as the number of kilograms of grain that a car costs – the opportunity

Figure 35.5 International Trade in Cars

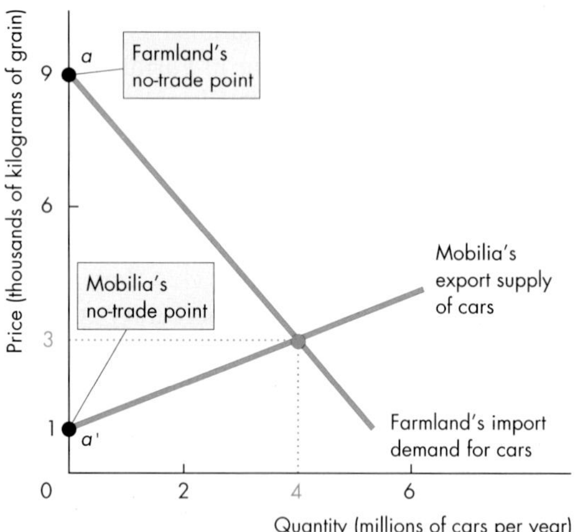

As the price of a car decreases, the quantity of imports demanded by Farmland increases – Farmland's import demand curve for cars is downward-sloping. As the price of a car increases, the quantity of cars supplied by Mobilia for export increases – Mobilia's export supply curve of cars is upward-sloping. Without international trade, the price of a car is 9,000 kilograms of grain in Farmland (point *a*) and 1,000 kilograms of grain in Mobilia (point *a'*). With free international trade, the price of a car is determined where the export supply curve intersects the import demand curve – a price of 3,000 kilograms of grain. At that price, 4 million cars a year are imported by Farmland and exported by Mobilia. The value of grain exported by Farmland and imported by Mobilia is 12 billion kilograms a year, the quantity required to pay for the cars imported.

cost of a car. If no international trade takes place, the price of a car in Farmland is 9,000 kilograms of grain, indicated by point *a* in the figure. Again, if no trade takes place, the price of a car in Mobilia is 1,000 kilograms of grain, indicated by point *a'* in the figure. The no-trade points *a* and *a'* in Figure 35.5 correspond to the points identified by those same letters in Figures 35.3 and 35.4. The lower the price of a car (in terms of grain), the greater is the quantity of cars that the Farmers are willing to import from the Mobilians. This fact is illustrated in the downward-sloping curve, which shows Farmland's import demand for cars.

The Mobilians respond in the opposite direction. The higher the price of cars (in terms of kilograms of grain), the greater is the quantity of cars that Mobilia are willing to export to Farmers. This fact is reflected in Mobilia's export supply of cars – the upward-sloping line in Figure 35.5.

The international market in cars determines the equilibrium price and quantity traded. This equilibrium occurs where the import demand curve intersects the export supply curve. In this case, the equilibrium price of a car is 3,000 kilograms of grain. Four million cars a year are exported by Mobilia and imported by Farmland. Notice that the price at which cars are traded is lower than the initial price in Farmland but higher than the initial price in Mobilia.

Balanced Trade

The number of cars exported by Mobilia – 4 million a year – is exactly equal to the number of cars imported by Farmland. How does Farmland pay for its cars? By exporting grain. How much grain does Farmland export? You can find the answer by noticing that for 1 car Farmland has to pay 3,000 kilograms of grain. Hence for 4 million cars it has to pay 12 billion kilograms of grain. Thus Farmland's exports of grain are 12 billion kilograms a year. Mobilia imports this same quantity of grain.

Mobilia is exchanging 4 million cars for 12 billion kilograms of grain each year and Farmland is doing the opposite, exchanging 12 billion kilograms of grain for 4 million cars. Trade is balanced between these two countries. The value received from exports equals the value paid out for imports.

Changes in Production and Consumption

We've seen that international trade makes it possible for Farmers to buy cars at a lower price than they can produce them for themselves. Equivalently, Farmers can sell their grain for a higher price. International trade also enables Mobilia to sell their cars for a higher price. Equivalently, Mobilia can buy grain for a lower price. Thus everybody gains. How is it possible for *everyone* to gain? What are the changes in production and consumption that accompany these gains?

An economy that does not trade with other economies has identical production and consumption possibilities. Without trade, the economy can only consume what it produces. But with international trade an economy can consume different quantities of goods from those that it produces. The production

Figure 35.6 Expanding Consumption Possibilities

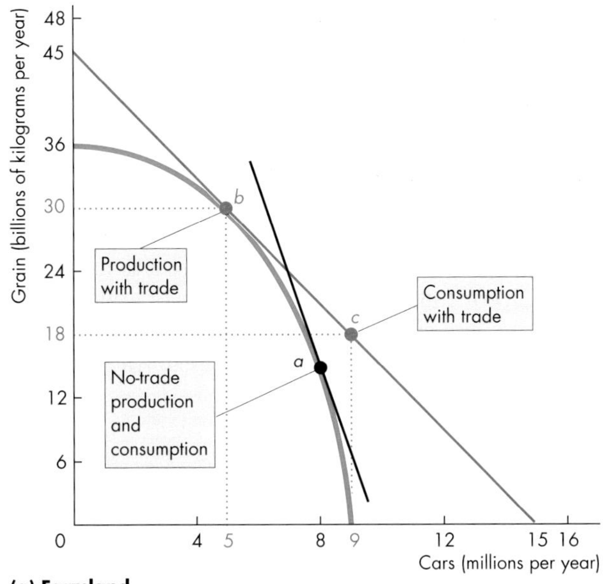

(a) Farmland

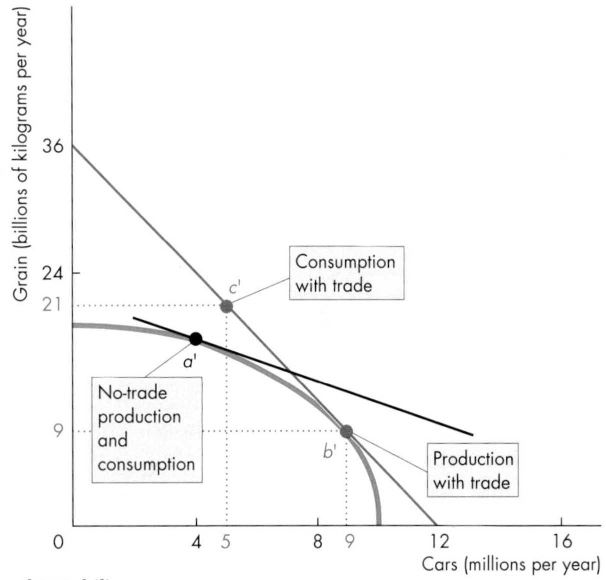

(b) Mobilia

With no international trade, the Farmers produce and consume at point *a* and the opportunity cost of a car is 9,000 kilograms of grain (the slope of the black line in part a). Also, with no international trade, the Mobilians produce and consume at point *a*' and the opportunity cost of 1,000 kilograms of grain is 1 car (the slope of the black line in part b).

Goods can be exchanged internationally at a price of 3,000 kilograms of grain for 1 car along the red line in each part of the figure. In part (a), Farmland decreases its production of cars and increases its production of grain, moving from *a* to *b*. It exports grain and imports cars, and it consumes at point *c*. The Farmers have more of both cars and grain than they would if they produced all their own consumption goods – at point *a*. In part (b), Mobilia increases car production and decreases grain production, moving from *a*' to *b*'. Mobilia exports cars and imports grain, and it consumes at point *c*'. The Movers have more of both cars and grain than they would if they produced all their own consumption goods – at point *a*'.

possibility frontier describes the limit of what a country can produce, but it does not describe the limits to what it can consume. Figure 35.6 will help you to see the distinction between production possibilities and consumption possibilities when a country trades with other countries.

First, notice that the figure has two parts, part (a) for Farmland and part (b) for Mobilia. The production possibility frontiers that you saw in Figures 35.3 and 35.4 are reproduced here. The slopes of the two black lines in the figure represent the opportunity costs in the two countries when there is no international trade. Farmland produces and consumes at point *a* and Mobilia produces and consumes at *a*'. Cars cost 9,000 kilograms of grain in Farmland and 1,000 kilograms of grain in Mobilia.

Consumption Possibilities The red line in each part of Figure 35.6 shows the country's consumption possibilities with international trade. These two red lines have the same slope and the magnitude of that slope is the opportunity cost of a car in terms of grain on the world market – 3,000 kilograms per car. The *slope* of the consumption possibilities line is common to both countries because its magnitude equals the *world* price. But the position of a country's consumption possibilities line depends on the country's production possibilities. A country cannot produce outside its production possibility curve so its consumption possibility curve touches its production possibility curve. Thus Farmland could choose to consume at point *b* with no international trade or, with international trade, at any point on its red consumption possibilities line.

Free Trade Equilibrium With international trade, the producers of cars in Mobilia can get a higher price for their output. As a result, they increase the quantity of car production. At the same time, grain producers in Mobilia are getting a lower price for their grain and so they reduce production. Producers in Mobilia adjust their output by moving along their production possibility frontier until the opportunity cost in Mobilia equals the world price (the opportunity cost in the world market). This situation arises when Mobilia is producing at point *b'* in Figure 35.6(b).

But the Mobilians do not consume at point *b'*. That is, they do not increase their consumption of cars and decrease their consumption of grain. Instead, they sell some of their car production to Farmland in exchange for some of Farmland's grain. They trade internationally. But to see how that works out, we first need to check in with Farmland to see what's happening there.

In Farmland, producers of cars now get a lower price and producers of grain get a higher price. As a consequence, producers in Farmland decrease car production and increase grain production. They adjust their outputs by moving along the production possibility frontier until the opportunity cost of a car in terms of grain equals the world price (the opportunity cost on the world market). They move to point *b* in part (a). But the Farmers do not consume at point *b*. Instead, they exchange some of their additional grain production for the now cheaper cars from Mobilia.

The figure shows us the quantities consumed in the two countries. We saw in Figure 35.5 that Mobilia exports 4 million cars a year and Farmland imports those cars. We also saw that Farmland exports 12 billion kilograms of grain a year and Mobilia imports that grain. Thus Farmland's consumption of grain is 12 billion kilograms a year less than it produces and its consumption of cars is 4 million a year more than it produces. Farmland consumes at point *c* in Figure 35.6(a).

Similarly, we know that Mobilia consumes 12 billion kilograms of grain more than it produces and 4 million cars fewer than it produces. Thus Mobilia consumes at *c'* in Figure 35.6(b).

Calculating the Gains from Trade You can now literally see the gains from trade in Figure 35.6. Without trade, Farmers produce and consume at *a* (part a) – a point on Farmland's production possibility frontier. With international trade, Farmers consume at point *c* in part (a) – a point *outside* the production possibility frontier. At point *c*, Farmers are consuming 3 billion kilograms of grain a year and 1 million cars a year more than before. These increases in consumption of both cars and grain, beyond the limits of the production possibility frontier, are the gains from international trade.

Mobilians also gain. Without trade, they consume at point *a'* in part (b) – a point on Mobilia's production possibility frontier. With international trade, they consume at point *c'* – a point outside the production possibility frontier. With international trade, Mobilia consumes 3 billion kilograms of grain a year and 1 million cars a year more than without trade. These are the gains from international trade for Mobilia.

Gains for All

In popular discussions about international trade, we hear about the need for a 'level playing field' and other measures to protect people from foreign competition. International trade seems like a type of contest in which there are winners and losers. But the trade between the Farmers and the Mobilia that you've just studied does not create winners and losers. Everyone wins.

Sellers add the net demand of foreigners to their domestic demand, and so their market expands. Buyers are faced with domestic supply plus net foreign supply and so have a larger total supply available to them.

Review

- When countries have divergent opportunity costs, they can gain from international trade.
- Each country can buy some goods and services from another country at a lower opportunity cost than it can produce them for itself.
- Gains arise when each country increases its production of those goods and services in which it has a comparative advantage (goods and services that it can produce at an opportunity cost that is lower than that of other countries) and exchanges some of its production for that of other countries.

- All countries gain from international trade. Everyone has a comparative advantage in something.

Gains from Trade in Reality

The gains from trade that we have just studied between Farmland and Mobilia in grain and cars occur in a model economy – in a world economy that we have imagined. But these same phenomena occur every day in the real global economy.

Comparative Advantage in the Global Economy

We buy cars made in Japan and Europe and we sell chemicals, pharmaceuticals and financial services to those countries in return. We buy shirts and fashion goods from the people of Sri Lanka and sell them machinery in return. We buy TV sets and video recorders from South Korea and Taiwan and sell them financial and other services as well as manufactured goods in return. We make some kinds of machines, and Europeans and Japanese make other kinds, and we exchange one type of manufactured good for another.

These are all examples of international trade generated by comparative advantage, just like the international trade between Farmland and Mobilia in our model economy. All international trade arises from comparative advantage, even when it is trade in similar goods such as tools and machines. At first, it seems puzzling that countries exchange manufactured goods. Why doesn't each developed country produce all the manufactured goods its citizens want to buy? Let's look a bit more closely at this question.

Trade in Similar Goods

Why does it make sense for the United Kingdom to produce cars for export and at the same time to import large quantities of them from Japan, Germany, Italy and Sweden? Wouldn't it make more sense to produce all the cars that we buy here in the United Kingdom? After all, we have access to the best technology available for producing cars. Car workers in the United Kingdom are surely as productive as their fellow workers in Germany and Japan. Capital equipment, production lines, robots and so on used in the manufacture of cars are as available to UK car producers as they are to any others. This line of reasoning leaves a puzzle concerning the sources of international exchange of similar commodities produced by similar people using similar equipment. Why does it happen? Why does the United Kingdom have a comparative advantage in some types of cars and Japan and Europe in others?

Diversity of Taste and Economies of Scale

The first part of the answer to the puzzle is that people have a tremendous diversity of taste. Let's stick with the example of cars. Some people prefer sports cars, some prefer estates, some prefer hatchbacks and some prefer the urban jeep look. In addition to size and type of car, there are many other ways in which cars vary. Some have low fuel consumption, some have high performance, some are spacious and comfortable, some have a large boot, some have four-wheel drive, some have front-wheel drive, some have manual gears, some are durable, some are flashy, some have a radiator grill that looks like a Greek temple, others look like a wedge. People's preferences across these many variables differ. The tremendous diversity in tastes for cars means that people would be dissatisfied if they were forced to consume from a limited range of standardized cars. People value variety and are willing to pay for it in the marketplace.

The second part of the answer to the puzzle is *economies of scale* – the tendency for the average cost of production to be lower, the larger is the scale of production. In such situations, larger and larger production runs lead to ever lower average production costs. Many manufactured goods, including cars, experience economies of scale. For example, if a car producer makes only a few hundred (or perhaps a few thousand) cars of a particular type and design, the producer must use production techniques that are much more labour-intensive and much less automated than those employed to make hundreds of thousands of cars in a particular model. With low production runs and labour-intensive production techniques, costs are high. With very large production runs and automated assembly lines, production costs are much lower. But to obtain lower costs, the automated assembly lines have to produce a large number of cars.

It is the combination of diversity of taste and economies of scale that produces comparative advantages and generates such a large amount of international trade in similar commodities. With international trade, each manufacturer of cars has the whole world market to serve. Each producer can specialize in a limited range of products and then sell its output to the world market. This arrangement enables large production runs on the most popular cars and feasible production runs even on the most customized cars demanded by only a handful of people in each country.

The situation in the market for cars is also present in many other industries, especially those producing specialized equipment and parts. For example, the United Kingdom exports machines but imports machine tools, and it exports mainframe computers but imports PCs. Thus international exchange of similar but slightly differentiated manufactured products is a highly profitable activity.

Let's see what happens when governments restrict international trade. We'll see that free trade brings the greatest possible benefits. We'll also see why, in spite of the benefits of free trade, governments sometimes restrict trade.

Trade Restrictions

Governments restrict international trade in order to protect domestic industries from foreign competition. The restriction of international trade is called **protectionism**. There are two main protectionist methods employed by governments:

1 Tariffs.
2 Non-tariff barriers.

A **tariff** is a tax that is imposed by the importing country when an imported good crosses its international boundary. A **non-tariff barrier** is any action other than a tariff that restricts international trade. Examples of non-tariff barriers are quantitative restrictions and licensing regulations which limit imports. We'll consider non-tariff barriers in more detail below. First, let's look at tariffs.

The History of Tariffs

UK tariffs today are modest compared with their historical levels. Total customs duties on imports as a percentage of imports was about 1 per cent in 1998. Countries in the European Union have no tariffs on trade with each other. In the United States, the average tariff rate is only 4 per cent. It was not always like this. In the 1930s many countries including the United Kingdom and the United States hid behind tariff barriers, but these barriers were slowly dismantled after World War II.

The reduction in tariffs since World War II followed the establishment of the General Agreement on Tariffs and Trade (GATT). The **General Agreement on Tariffs and Trade** is an international agreement designed to limit government intervention to restrict international trade. It was negotiated immediately following World War II and was signed in October 1947. Its goal is to liberalize trading activity and to provide an organization to administer more liberal trading arrangements. The GATT has a small bureaucracy located in Geneva, Switzerland.

Since the formation of the GATT, several rounds of negotiations have taken place that have resulted in general tariff reductions. One of these, the Kennedy Round that began in the early 1960s, resulted in large tariff cuts starting in 1967. Another, the Tokyo Round, resulted in further tariff cuts in 1979.

The most recent, the Uruguay Round, which started in 1986 and was completed in 1994, was the most ambitious and comprehensive of the rounds. It was an agreement among 115 countries to lower tariffs and to prevent protection through subsidies or favourable treatment from government purchases. The Uruguay Round also led to the creation of a new **World Trade Organization** (WTO). Membership of the WTO imposes greater obligations on countries to observe the GATT rules and makes subsidies much harder to use as an alternative to tariffs and other forms of protection.

In other parts of the world, trade barriers have virtually been eliminated. The *Single European Market* (SEM) in the European Union has created the largest unified tariff-free market in the world. The SEM programme has simplified border formalities for the movement of trade; capital and labour have complete freedom of movement within the European Union, other forms of protection such as non-tariff barriers are to be eliminated; and public procurement is to be made open to all EU firms. In the longer term, the SEM programme provides for all indirect taxes within the European Union to be harmonized so that no individual country can tax a good differently from another country in the Union. In 1994, discussions among the Asia-Pacific Economic group (APEC) led to an agreement in principle to work towards a free-trade area that embraces China, all the economies of East Asia and the South Pacific, and the United Kingdom and Canada. These

Figure 35.7 OECD Estimates of Average Implied Tariffs on EU Agricultural Products 1979–1997

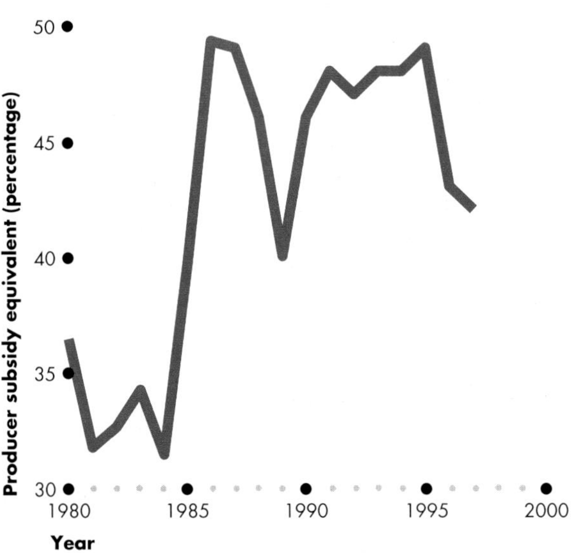

The OECD estimates the average percentage subsidy paid to EU farmers that would give them the same additional income as the actual CAP intervention price, which artificially holds agricultural prices above world prices. The graph is an estimate of the percentage by which EU prices are raised above world prices.

Sources: OECD, *Agricultural Policies in OECD Countries, Monitoring and Outlook*, 1988 and 1998.

Figure 35.8 The Effects of a Tariff

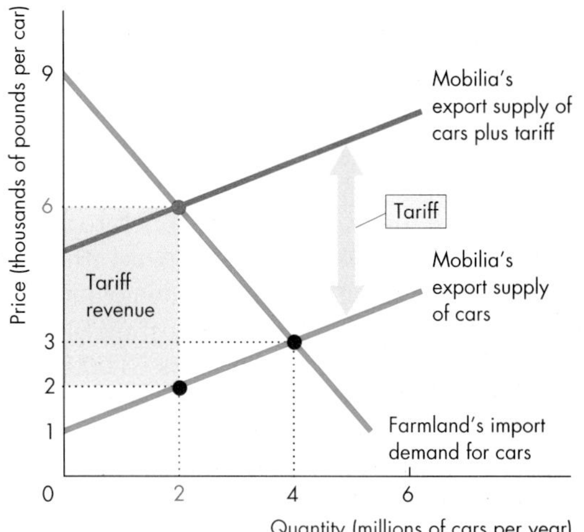

Farmland imposes a tariff on car imports from Mobilia. The tariff increases the price that Farmers have to pay for cars. It shifts the supply curve of cars in Farmland upward. The distance between the original supply curve and the new one is the amount of the tariff, £4,000 per car. The price of cars in Farmland increases and the quantity of cars imported decreases. The government of Farmland collects a tariff revenue of £4,000 per car – total of £8 billion on the 2 million cars imported. Farmland's exports of grain decrease because Mobilia now has a lower income from its exports of cars.

countries include the fastest growing economies and hold the promise of heralding a global free-trade area.

The effort to achieve freer trade underlines the fact that trade in some goods is still subject to extremely high tariffs. In the European Union, buyers of agricultural products face prices that are on average 40 per cent above world prices as part of the **Common Agricultural Policy** (CAP). The CAP is a price support programme for farmers in the European Union and acts as a tariff on non-EU agricultural products. The meat, cheese and sugar that you consume cost significantly more because of protection than they would with free international trade. Figure 35.7 shows the average protective tariff the CAP imposes on world agricultural goods. The implied average tariff varies because the world price of agricultural goods varies from year to year. You can see from Figure 35.7 that the implied average tariff has been declining in recent years.

The temptation for governments to impose tariffs is a strong one. They do, of course, provide revenue to the government, but this is not particularly large compared with other sources. Their most important attribute is that they enable the government to satisfy special interest groups in import-competing industries. But, as we'll see, free international trade brings enormous benefits that are reduced when tariffs are imposed. Let's see how.

How Tariffs Work

To analyse how tariffs work, let's return to the example of trade between Farmland and Mobilia. Figure 35.8 shows the international market for cars in which these two countries are the only traders.

The volume of trade and the price of a car are determined at the point of intersection of Mobilia's export supply curve of cars and Farmland's import demand curve for cars.

In Figure 35.8, these two countries are trading cars and grain in exactly the same way that we analysed before in Figure 35.5. Mobilia exports cars and Farmland exports grain. The volume of car imports into Farmland is 4 million a year and the world market price of a car is 3,000 kilograms of grain. To make the example more concrete and real, Figure 35.8 expresses prices in pounds rather than in units of grain and is based on a money price of grain of £1 a kilogram. With grain costing £1 a kilogram, the money price of a car is £3,000.

Now suppose that the government of Farmland, perhaps under pressure from car producers, decides to impose a tariff on imported cars. In particular, suppose that a tariff of £4,000 per car is imposed. (This is a huge tariff, but the car producers of Farmland are pretty fed up with competition from Mobilia.) What happens?

- The supply of cars in Farmland decreases.
- The price of a car in Farmland rises.
- The quantity of cars imported by Farmland decreases.
- The government of Farmland collects the tariff revenue.
- Resource use is inefficient.
- The value of exports changes by the same amount as the value of imports and trade remains balanced.

Change in the Supply of Cars Cars are no longer going to be available at the Mobilia export supply price. The tariff of £4,000 must be added to that price – the amount paid to the government of Farmland on each car imported. So the supply curve in Farmland shifts upward by the amount of the tariff as shown in Figure 35.8. The new supply curve becomes that labelled 'Mobilia's export supply of cars plus tariff'. The vertical distance between Mobilia's export supply curve and the new supply curve is the tariff imposed by the government of Farmland – £4,000 a car.

Rise in Price of Cars A new equilibrium occurs where the new supply curve intersects Farmland's import demand curve for cars. That equilibrium is at a price of £6,000 a car up from £3000 with free trade.

Fall in Imports Car imports fall from 4 million to 2 million cars a year. At the higher price of £6,000 a car, domestic car producers increase their production. Domestic grain production decreases as resources are moved into the expanding car industry.

Tariff Revenue Total expenditure on imported cars by the Farmers is £6,000 a car multiplied by the 2 million cars imported (£12 billion). But not all of that money goes to Mobilia. They receive £2,000 a car or £4 billion for the 2 million cars. The difference – £4,000 a car or a total of £8 billion for the 2 million cars – is collected by the government of Farmland as tariff revenue.

Inefficiency The people of Farmland are willing to pay £6,000 for the marginal car imported. Obviously, the government of Farmland is happy with this situation. It is now collecting £8 billion that it didn't have before. But the opportunity cost of that car is £2,000. So there is a gain from trading an extra car. In fact, there are gains – willingness to pay exceeds opportunity cost – all the way up to 4 million cars a year. Only when 4 million cars are being traded is the maximum price that a Farmer is willing to pay equal to the minimum price that is acceptable to a Mobilian. Thus restricting international trade reduces the gains from international trade.

Trade remains balanced With free trade, Farmland was paying £3,000 a car and buying 4 million cars a year from Mobilia. Thus the total amount paid to Mobilia for imports was £12 billion a year. With a tariff, Farmland's imports have been cut to 2 million cars a year and the price paid to Mobilia has also been cut to only £2,000 a car. Thus the total amount paid to Mobilia for imports has been cut to £4 billion a year. Doesn't this fact mean that Farmland is now importing less than it is exporting and has a balance of trade surplus?

It does not! The price of cars in Mobilia has fallen from £3,000 to £2,000 a car. But the price of grain remains at £1 a kilogram. So the relative price of cars has fallen and the relative price of grain has increased. With free trade, Mobilia could buy 3,000 kilograms of grain for 1 car. Now they can buy only 2,000 kilograms for 1 car. With a higher relative price of grain, the quantity demanded by Mobilia decreases and Mobilia imports less grain. But because Mobilia imports less grain, Farmland exports less grain. In fact, Farmland's grain industry suffers from two sources. First, there is a decrease in the quantity of grain sold to Mobilia. Second, there is increased competition for inputs from the now expanded car industry. Thus the tariff leads to a contraction in the scale of the grain industry in Farmland.

It seems paradoxical at first that a country imposing a tariff on cars would hurt its own export industry, lowering its exports of grain. It may help to think of it this way: Mobilians buy grain with the money they make from exporting cars to Farmland. If they export fewer cars, they cannot afford to buy as much grain. In fact, in the absence of any international borrowing and lending, Mobilia has to cut its imports of grain by exactly the same amount as the loss in revenue from its export of cars. Grain imports into Mobilia will be cut back to a value of ₤4 billion, the amount that can be paid for by the new lower revenue from Mobilia's car exports. Thus trade is still balanced in this post-tariff situation. Although the tariff has cut imports, it has also cut exports, and the cut in the value of exports is exactly equal to the cut in the value of imports. The tariff, therefore, has no effect on the *balance* of trade – it reduces the *volume* of trade.

The result that we have just derived is perhaps one of the most misunderstood aspects of international economics. On countless occasions, politicians and others have called for tariffs in order to remove a balance of trade deficit or have argued that lowering tariffs would produce a balance of trade deficit. They reach this conclusion by failing to work out all the implications of a tariff.

Let's now turn our attention to the other range of protectionist weapons – non-tariff barriers.

Non-tariff Barriers

There are two important forms of non-tariff barriers:

1 Quotas.
2 Voluntary export restraints.

A **quota** is a quantitative restriction on the import of a particular good. It specifies the maximum amount of the good that may be imported in a given period of time. A **voluntary export restraint** is an agreement between two governments in which the government of the exporting country agrees to restrain the volume of its own exports. Voluntary export restraints are often called VERs.

Non-tariff barriers have become important features of international trading arrangements in the period since World War II, and there is general agreement that non-tariff barriers are now a more severe impediment to international trade than tariffs.

Quotas are especially important in the textile industries, where there exists an international agreement called the Multi-Fibre Arrangement, which establishes quotas on a wide range of textile products. Agriculture is also subject to extensive quotas. Voluntary export restraints are particularly important in regulating the international trade in cars between Japan and the United States.

How Quotas and VERs Work

To see how a quota works, suppose that Farmland imposes a quota on car imports that restricts imports to not more than 2 million cars a year. Figure 35.9 shows the effects of this action. The

Figure 35.9 The Effects of a Quota

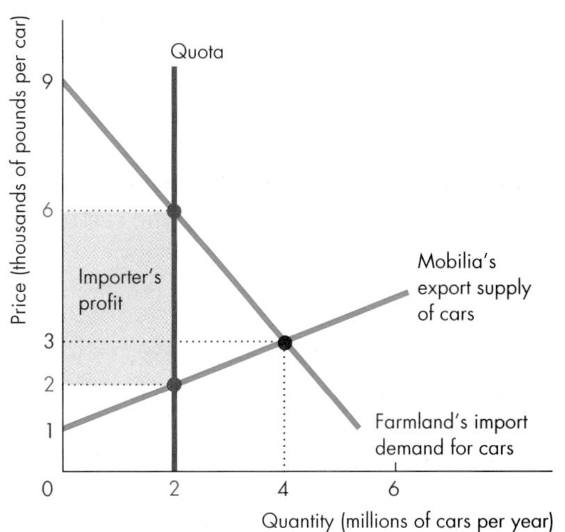

Farmland imposes a quota of 2 million cars a year on car imports from Mobilia. That quantity appears as the vertical line labelled 'Quota'. Because the quantity of cars supplied by Mobilia is restricted to 2 million, the price at which those cars will be traded increases to £6,000. Importing cars is profitable because Mobilia is willing to supply cars at £2,000 each. There is competition for import quotas – rent seeking.

quota is shown by the vertical red line at 2 million cars a year. Because it is illegal to import more than that number of cars, car importers buy only that quantity from Mobilia producers. They pay £2,000 a car to the Mobilia producers. But what do they sell their cars for? The answer is £6,000 each. Because the import supply of cars is restricted to 2 million cars a year, people with cars for sale will be able to get £6,000 each for them. The quantity of cars imported equals the quantity determined by the quota.

The value of imports – the amount paid to Mobilia – declines to £4 billion, exactly the same as in the case of the tariff. Thus with lower incomes from car exports and with a higher relative price of grain, Mobilia cut their imports of grain in exactly the same way as they did under a tariff.

The key difference between a quota and a tariff lies in who gets the profit represented by the difference between the import supply price and the domestic selling price. In the case of a tariff, that difference goes to the government of the importing country. In the case of a quota, that difference goes to the person who has the right to import under the import-quota regulations.

A voluntary export restraint is like a quota arrangement where quotas are allocated to each exporting country. The effects of voluntary export restraints are similar to those of quotas but differ from them in that the gap between the domestic price and the export price is captured not by domestic importers but by the foreign exporter. The government of the exporting country has to establish procedures for allocating the restricted volume of exports among its producers.

'Invisible' Non-tariff Barriers

In addition to quotas and VERs, there are thousands of non-tariff barriers that are virtually impossible to detect – that are almost invisible. They arise from domestic laws that are not (necessarily) aimed at restricting foreign competition but have that effect. For example, for a long time German purity laws on brewing meant that beer brewed in other countries of Europe that did not meet the specifications set out by the ancient laws could not be sold as beer in Germany. This apparently harmless law effectively restricted competition from foreign beer makers. In 1990 German citizens were allowed access to foreign beer.

Review

- When a country opens itself up to international trade and trades freely at world market prices, it expands its consumption possibilities.
- When trade is restricted, some of the gains from trade are lost.
- A country might be better off with restricted trade than with no trade but not as well off as it could be if it engaged in free trade.
- A tariff reduces the volume of imports, but it also reduces the volume of exports.
- Under both free trade and restricted trade (and without international borrowing and lending), the value of imports equals the value of exports. With restricted trade, both the total value of exports and the total value of imports are lower than under free trade, but trade is still balanced.

Let's now look at some commonly heard arguments for restricting international trade.

The Case Against Protection

For as long as countries and international trade have existed, people have debated whether a country is better off with free international trade or with protection from foreign competition. The debate continues, but for most economists a verdict has been delivered and it is the one you have just explored. Free trade is the arrangement most conducive to prosperity, and protection creates more problems than it solves. We've seen the most powerful case for free trade in the example of how Farmland and Mobilia both benefit from their comparative advantage. But there is a broader range of issues in the free-trade versus protection debate. Let's review these issues.

Three arguments for restricting international trade are:

1 National security.
2 Infant Industry.
3 Dumping.

Let's examine each in turn.

National Security

The national security argument for protection is that a country is better off if it protects its strategic industries – industries that produce defence equipment and armaments, and the industries on which the defence industries rely for their raw materials such as coal and steel and other intermediate inputs. This argument does not stand up to close scrutiny.

First, it is an argument for international isolation, for in time of war, there is no industry that does not contribute to national defence. Second, even if the case is made for maintaining or increasing the output of a strategic industry, there is always a more efficient way of doing so than by protecting the industry from international competition. A direct subsidy to the firms in a strategic industry, financed out of taxes on all sectors of the economy, would keep the industry operating at the scale judged appropriate. Such a subsidy would keep the industry operating at the scale judged appropriate, and free international trade would keep the prices faced by consumers at their world market levels.

Infant Industry

The second argument that is used to justify protection is the **infant-industry argument** – the proposition that protection is necessary to enable an infant industry to grow into a mature industry that can compete in world markets. The argument is based on the idea of *dynamic comparative advantage* which can arise from *learning-by-doing* (see Chapter 3, p. 55).

There is no doubt that learning-by-doing is a powerful engine of productivity growth and that comparative advantage evolves and changes because of on-the-job experience. But these facts do not justify protection.

First, the infant-industry argument is valid only if the benefits of learning-by-doing not only accrue to the owners and workers of the firms in the infant industry but also spill over to other industries and parts of the economy. For example, there are huge productivity gains from learning-by-doing in the manufacture of aircraft. But almost all of these gains benefit the shareholders and workers of BAe, Westland and other aircraft producers. Because the people making the decisions, bearing the risk and doing the work are the ones who benefit, they take the dynamic gains into account when they decide on the scale of their activities. In this case, almost no benefits spill over to other parts of the economy, so there is no need for government assistance to achieve an efficient outcome.

Second, even if the case is made for protecting an infant industry, it is more efficient to do so by a direct subsidy to the firms in the infant industry, with the subsidy financed out of taxes.

Dumping

Dumping occurs when a foreign firm sells its exports at a lower price than its cost of production. Dumping might be used by a firm that wants to gain a global monopoly. In this case, the firm sells at a price below its cost in order to drive domestic firms out of business. When the domestic firms have gone, the foreign firm takes advantage of its monopoly position and charges a higher price for its product. Dumping is usually regarded as a justification for temporary – countervailing – tariffs.

But there are powerful reasons to resist the dumping argument for protection. First, it is virtually impossible to detect dumping because it is hard to determine a firm's costs. As a result, the test for dumping is whether a firm's export price is below its domestic price. But this test is a weak one because it can be rational for a firm to charge a low price in markets in which the quantity demanded is highly sensitive to price and a higher price in markets in which demand is less price-sensitive.

Second, there are virtually no goods that are natural global monopolies. So even if all the domestic firms did get driven out of business in some industry, it would always be possible to find several and usually many alternative foreign sources of supply and to buy at prices determined in competitive markets.

Third, if a good or service was a truly global natural monopoly, the best way of dealing with it would be by regulation, just as in the case of domestic monopolies. Such regulation would require international cooperation.

The three arguments for protection we've just examined have an element of credibility. The counter-arguments are in general stronger so these arguments do not make the case for protection. But they are not the only arguments that you might encounter. The many other arguments commonly heard are quite simply wrong. They are fatally flawed. The most common of them are:

- Protection saves jobs.
- Because foreign labour is cheap, we need a tariff to compete.
- Protection brings diversity and stability.
- Protection penalizes lax environmental standards.
- Protection safeguards national culture.
- Protection prevents rich countries from exploiting developing countries.

Protection Saves Jobs

The argument is that when we buy shoes from Brazil or shirts from Taiwan, workers in Lancashire lose their jobs. With no earnings and poor prospects, these workers become a drain on the welfare state and they spend less, causing a ripple effect of further job losses. The proposed solution to this problem is to ban imports of cheap foreign goods and protect jobs at home. The proposal is flawed for the following reasons.

First, free trade does cost some jobs, but it also creates other jobs. It brings about a global rationalization of labour and allocates labour resources to their highest-value activities. Because of international trade in textiles, tens of thousands of workers in the United Kingdom have lost jobs because textile mills and other factories have closed. But tens of thousands of workers in other countries have got jobs because textile mills have opened there. And tens of thousands of workers in the United Kingdom have got better-paying jobs than textile workers because other industries have expanded and created more jobs than have been destroyed.

Second, imports create jobs. They create jobs for retailers which sell imported goods and for firms which service these goods. They also create jobs by creating incomes in the rest of the world, some of which are spent on UK-made goods and services.

Although protection does not save jobs, it changes the mix of jobs. But it does so at inordinate cost. For example, in the United States jobs in the textile industry are protected by quotas imposed under an international agreement called the Multi-Fibre Arrangement. It has been estimated by the US International Trade Commission (ITC) that because of quotas 72,000 jobs exist in textiles that would otherwise disappear, and that annual clothing expenditure in the United States is $15.9 billion or $700 per family higher than it would be with free trade. Equivalently, the ITC estimates that each textile job saved costs $221,000 a year.

Because Foreign Labour is Cheap, We Need a Tariff to Compete

The late Sir James Goldsmith, multimillionaire and Euro MP, argued that if Europe does not build protective tariffs against cheap imports from the newly industrializing economies of East Asia, there will be a loss of jobs that will threaten the way of life in Europe. The loss of jobs will occur as firms relocate in the Far East to take advantage of cheap labour. Let's see what's wrong with this view.

The labour cost of a unit of output equals the wage rate divided by labour productivity. For example, if a UK production assembly worker earns $30 an hour and produces 10 units of output an hour, the average labour cost of a unit of output is $3. (We will use dollars to measure the outputs of workers from different countries.) If a Chinese production assembly worker earns $3 an hour and produces 1 unit of output an hour, the average labour cost of a unit of output is $3. Other things remaining the same, the higher a worker's productivity, the higher is the worker's wage rate. High-wage workers have high productivity. Low-wage workers have low productivity.

Although high-wage UK workers are more productive, on the average, than low-wage Chinese workers, there are differences across industries. UK labour is relatively more productive at some activities than others. For example, the productivity of UK workers in producing chemical products, luxury cars and high-quality engineering is relatively higher than in the production of metals and some standardized machine parts. The activities in which UK workers are relatively more productive than their Chinese counterparts are those in which the United Kingdom has a *comparative advantage*. By engaging in free trade, increasing our production and exports of the goods at which we have a comparative advantage and decreasing our production and imports of the goods at which our trading partners have a comparative advantage, we can make ourselves and the citizens of other countries better off.

Protection Brings Diversity and Stability

A diversified investment portfolio is less risky than one that has all its eggs in one basket. The same is true for an economy's production. A diversified economy fluctuates less than an economy that produces only one or two goods.

But big, rich, diversified economies like the United States, Japan and the European Union do not have this type of stability problem. Even a country like Saudi Arabia, which produces almost only one good (oil), can benefit from specializing in the activity at which it has a comparative advantage and then investing in a wide range of other countries to bring greater stability to its income and consumption.

Protection Penalizes Lax Environmental Standards

A new argument for protection that was used extensively in the Uruguay Round of the GATT negotiations is that many poorer countries, such as Mexico, do not have the same environmental policies we have and, because they are willing to pollute and we are not, we cannot compete with them without tariffs. So if they want free trade with the richer and 'greener' countries, they must clean up their environments to our standards.

The environment argument for trade restrictions is weak. First, it is not true that all poorer countries have significantly lower environmental protection standards than the United Kingdom has. Many poor countries, and the former communist countries of Eastern Europe, do have a bad record on the environment. But some countries, one of which is Mexico, have strict laws and they enforce them. Second, a poor country cannot afford to be as concerned about its environment as a rich country can. The best hope for a better environment in Mexico and in other developing countries is rapid income growth through free trade. As their incomes grow, developing countries such as Mexico will have the *means* to match their desires to improve their environment.

Protection Safeguards National Culture

A national culture argument for protection is one that is frequently heard in Europe. The expressed fear is that free trade in books, magazines, film and television programmes means the erosion of local culture and the domination of US culture. The argument continues, that it is necessary to protect domestic culture industries to ensure the survival of national cultural identity. This is an argument that is often used in connection with the European film industry.

Protection of these industries usually takes the form of non-tarrif barriers. For example, local content regulations on radio and television broadcasting and in magazines is often required.

The cultural identity argument for protection has no merit, and it is one more example of rent seeking (see Chapter 00, pp. 000–000). Writers, publishers and broadcasters want to limit foreign competition so that they can earn larger economic profits. There is no actual danger to national culture. In fact, many of the creators of so-called American cultural products are not Americans, but the talented citizens of other countries, ensuring the survival of their national culture in Hollywood! Also, if national culture is in danger, there is no surer way of helping it on its way down than by impoverishing the nation whose culture it is. Protection is an effective way of doing just that.

Protection Prevents Rich Countries from Exploiting Developing Countries

Another new argument for protection is that international trade must be restricted to prevent the people of the rich industrial world from exploiting the poorer people of the developing countries, forcing them to work for slave wages.

Wage rates in some developing countries are, indeed, very low. But by trading with developing countries, we increase the demand for the goods that these countries produce, and, more significantly, we increase the demand for their labour. When the demand for labour in developing countries increases, the wage rate also increases. So, far from exploiting people in developing countries, trade improves their opportunities and increases their incomes.

We have reviewed the arguments commonly heard in favour of protection and the counter-arguments against them. There is one counter-argument to protection that is general and quite overwhelming. Protection invites retaliation and can trigger a trade war. The best example of a trade war occurred during the Great Depression of the 1930s when the Smoot-Hawley Tariff was introduced in the United States.

Country after country retaliated with its own tariff and in a short time, world trade had almost disappeared. The costs to all countries were large and led to a renewed international resolve to avoid such self-defeating moves in future. They also led to the creation of the GATT and are the impetus behind NAFTA, APEC and the European Union.

Review

- Trade restrictions aimed at national security goals, stimulating the growth of new industries and restraining foreign monopoly have little merit.
- Trade restrictions to save jobs, compensate for low foreign wages, make the economy more diversified and compensate for costly environmental policies are misguided.
- The main arguments against trade restrictions are that subsidies and anti-monopoly policies can achieve domestic goals more efficiently than protection and that protection can trigger a trade war in which all countries lose.

Why is International Trade Restricted?

Why, despite all the arguments against protection, is trade restricted? There are two key reasons:

1 Tariff revenue.

2 Rent seeking.

Tariff Revenue

Government revenue is costly to collect. In the developed economies, income taxes, VAT, and excise taxes are the major sources of revenue. A tariff plays a very small role if at all. But governments in developing countries have a difficult time in collecting taxes from their citizens. Much economic activity takes place in the informal sector, with few financial records. So only a small amount of revenue is collected from income taxes and indirect taxes from these countries. The one area in which economic transactions are well recorded and audited is in international trade. So this activity is an attractive base for tax collection in these countries and is used more extensively than in the developed countries.

Rent Seeking

The major reason why international trade is restricted is because of rent seeking. Free trade increases consumption possibilities *on the average* but not everyone shares in the gain and some people even lose. Free trade brings benefits to some and costs to others, with total benefits exceeding total costs. The uneven distribution of costs and benefits is the principal impediment to achieving more liberal international trade.

Returning to our example of international trade in cars and grain between Farmland and Mobilia, the benefits from free trade accrue to all the producers of grain and those producers of cars who would not have to bear the costs of adjusting to a smaller car industry. These costs are transition costs, not permanent costs. The costs of moving to free trade are borne by those car producers and their employees who have to become grain producers. The number of people who gain will, in general, be enormous compared with the number who lose. The gain per person will, therefore, be rather small. The loss per person to those who bear the loss will be large. Because the loss that falls on those who bear it is large, it will pay those people to incur considerable expense in order to lobby against free trade. On the other hand, it will not pay those who gain to organize to achieve free trade. The gain from trade for any one individual is too small for that individual to spend much time or money on a political organization to achieve free trade. The loss from free trade will be seen as being so great by those bearing that loss that they *will* find it profitable to join a political organization to prevent free trade. Each group is optimizing – weighing benefits against costs and choosing the best action for themselves. The anti-free trade group will, therefore, undertake a larger quantity of political lobbying than the pro-free trade group.

Compensating Losers

If, in total, the gains from free international trade exceed the losses, why don't those who gain compensate those who lose so that everyone is in favour of free trade? To some degree, such compensation does take place.

The losers from freer or marginal improvements in international trade are compensated indirectly through the normal unemployment benefit payments. But only limited attempts are made to compensate those who lose from total free international trade. The main reason full compensation is not attempted is that the costs of identifying all the losers and estimating the value of their losses would be enormous. Also, it would never be clear whether or not a person who has fallen on hard times is suffering because of free trade or for other reasons, perhaps reasons largely under the control of the individual. Furthermore, some people who look like losers at one point in time may, in fact, end up gaining. The young coal worker in the Rhondda who loses his job and becomes a computer assembly worker in Newport resents the loss of work and the need to move. But a year or two later, looking back on events, he counts himself fortunate. He's made a move that has increased his income and given him greater job security.

It is because we do not, in general, compensate the losers from free international trade that protectionism is such a popular and permanent feature of our national economic and political life.

Political Outcome

The political outcome that emerges from this activity is one in which a modest amount of restriction on international trade occurs and is maintained. Politicians react to constituencies pressing for protection and find it necessary, in order to get re-elected, to support legislative programmes that protect those constituencies. The producers of protected goods are far more vocal and much more sensitive swing-voters than the consumers of such goods. The political outcome, therefore, often leans in the direction of maintaining protection.

Review

- International Trade is restricted because tariffs raise revenue for governments and because tariffs create gains (economic rents) for some and losses for others.
- The revenue from tariffs is important for developing countries but not for developed countries such as those in the EU.
- Gains from trade are spread thinly, and gains from protection accrue to a few people. It pays the few to form a lobby group to ensure that their interests are protected.

You've now seen how free international trade enables all countries to gain from increased specialization and exchange. By producing goods at which we have a comparative advantage and exchanging some of our own production for that of others, we expand our consumption possibilities. Placing impediments on that exchange when it crosses national borders restricts the extent to which we can gain from specialization and exchange. *Reading Between the Lines* on pp. 912–913 examines a specific case of a trade restriction that has been taken to the WTO for a judgement. The restriction means that consumers pay a higher price than they would in its absence. By opening our country up to free international trade, the market for the things which we sell expands and the relative price rises. The market for the things that we buy also expands and the relative price falls. All countries gain from free international trade. As a consequence of price adjustments, and in the absence of international borrowing and lending, the value of imports adjusts to equal the value of exports.

In the next chapter, we're going to study the ways in which international trade is financed, and also learn why international borrowing and lending, which permit unbalanced international trade, arise. We'll discover the forces that determine the balance of payments and the value of the pound in terms of foreign currency.

Summary

Key Points

Patterns and Trends in International Trade (pp. 890–892)

- Large flows of trade take place between rich and poor countries.
- Resource-rich countries exchange natural resources for manufactured goods, and resource-poor countries import resources in exchange for their own manufactured goods. However, by far the biggest volume of trade is in manufactured goods exchanged among the rich industrialized countries.
- Finished manufactured goods constitute the largest group of export items by the United Kingdom.
- Trade in services has grown in recent years.
- Total trade has also grown over the years.

Opportunity Cost and Comparative Advantage (pp. 892–893)

- When opportunity costs differ among countries, the country with the lowest opportunity cost of producing a good is said to have a comparative advantage in that good.
- Comparative advantage is the source of the gains from international trade.
- A country can have an absolute advantage, but not a comparative advantage, in the production of all goods.
- Every country has a comparative advantage in something.

Gains from Trade (pp. 893–897)

- Trading allows consumption to exceed production. By specializing in producing the good in which it has a comparative advantage and then trading some of that good for imports, a country can consume at points outside its production possibility frontier.
- Each country can consume at such a point.
- In the absence of international borrowing and lending, trade is balanced as prices adjust to reflect the international supply and demand for goods.
- The world price balances the production and consumption plans of the trading parties.
- At the equilibrium price, trade is balanced.

Gains from Trade in Reality (pp. 897–898)

- Comparative advantage explains the enormous volume and diversity of international trade that takes place in the world.
- Much trade, however, takes the form of exchanging similar goods for each other – one type of car for another. Such trade arises because of economies of scale in the face of diversified tastes.

Trade Restrictions (pp. 898–902)

- A country can restrict international trade by imposing tariffs or non-tariff barriers – quotas and voluntary export restraints.
- All trade restrictions raise the domestic price of imported goods, lower the volume of imports and reduce the total value of imports.
- They also reduce the total value of exports by the same amount as the reduction in the value of imports.

The Case Against Protection (pp. 902–906)

- Three arguments for trade restrictions – the national security argument, the infant-industry argument and the dumping argument – are weak.
- Other arguments for protection – that it saves jobs, is necessary because foreign labour is cheap, makes the economy diversified and stable, protects national culture, and is needed to offset the costs of environmental policies that poorer countries do not incur – are fatally flawed.

Why is International Trade Restricted? (pp. 906–907)

- Trade is often restricted because, although it increases consumption possibilities *on the average*, a small number of losers bear a large loss per person and a large number of gainers enjoy a small gain per person.
- Those who lose from free trade undertake a larger quantity of political lobbying than those who gain from it.

Key Figures

Key Terms

Review Questions

1 What are the main exports and imports of the United Kingdom?

2 How does the United Kingdom trade services internationally?

3 Which items of international trade have been growing the most quickly in recent years?

4 What is comparative advantage? Why does it lead to gains from international trade?

5 Explain why international trade brings gains to all countries.

6 Distinguish between comparative advantage and absolute advantage.

7 Explain why all countries have a comparative advantage in something.

8 Explain why we import and export such large quantities of certain similar goods – such as cars, for example.

9 What are the main ways in which we restrict international trade?

10 What are the effects of a tariff?

11 What are the effects of a quota?

12 What are the effects of a voluntary export restraint?

13 Describe the main trends in tariffs and non-tariff barriers.

14 Why do countries restrict international trade?

Problems

1 Figures 35.3 and 35.4 illustrate Farmland's and Mobilia's production possibilities.

a Calculate the opportunity cost of cars in Farmland at the point on the production possibility frontier at which 4 million cars are produced.
b Calculate the opportunity cost of a car in Mobilia when it produces 8 million cars.
c With no trade, Farmland produces 4 million cars and Mobilia produces 8 million cars. Which country has a comparative advantage in the production of cars?
d If there is no trade between Farmland and Mobilia, how much grain is consumed and how many cars are bought in each country?

2 Suppose that the two countries in Problem 1 trade freely.

a Which country exports grain?
b What adjustments will be made to the amount of each good produced by each country?
c What adjustment will be made to the amount of each good consumed by each country?
d What can you say about the price of a car under free trade?

3 Compare the total production of each good produced in Problems 1 and 2.

4 Compare the situation in Problems 1 and 2 with that analysed in this chapter. Why does Mobilia export cars in the chapter but import them in Problem 2?

5 The following figure depicts the international market for soybeans.

a What is the world price of soybeans if there is free trade between these countries?
b If the country that imports soybeans imposes a tariff of £2 per kilogram, what is the world price of soybeans and what quantity of soybeans is traded internationally? What is the price of soybeans in the importing country? Calculate the tariff revenue.

6 If the importing country in Problem 5(a) imposes a quota of 300 million kilograms, what is the price of soybeans in the importing country? What is the revenue from the quota and who gets this revenue?

7 If the exporting country in Problem 5(a) imposes a VER of 300 million kilograms of soybeans, what is the world price of soybeans? What is the revenue of soybean growers in the exporting country? Which country gains from the VER?

8 Suppose that the exporting country in Problem 5(a) subsidizes production by paying its farmers £1 a kilogram for soybeans harvested.

a What is the price of soybeans in the importing country?
b What action might soybean growers in the importing country take? Why?

9 Suppose that the exporting country in Problem 5 subsidizes production by paying its farmers £1 a tonne for soybeans harvested.

a What is the price of soybeans in the importing country?
b What action might soybean growers in the importing country take? Why?

10 Countries Atlantis and Magic Kingdom produce only food and balloon rides and have the following production possibility frontiers as shown in the figure:

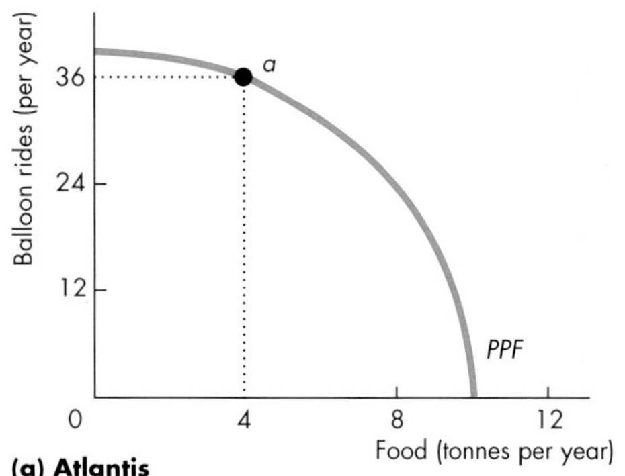

(a) Atlantis

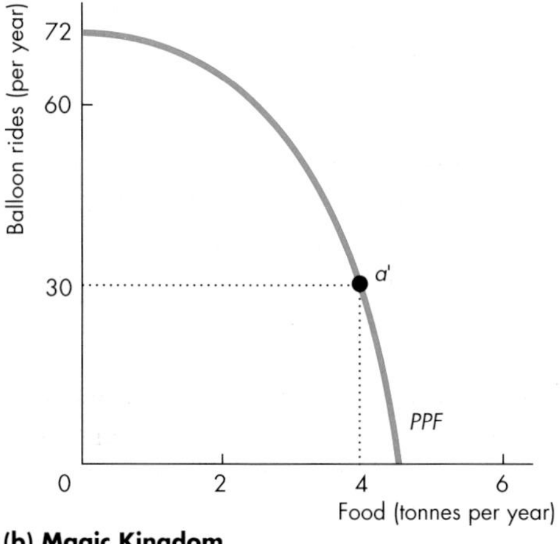

(b) Magic Kingdom

a If Atlantis produces at point *a*, what is its opportunity cost of a balloon ride?

b What are the consumption possibilities of Atlantis?

c If Magic Kingdom produces at point *a*, what is its opportunity cost of a balloon ride?

d What are the consumption possibilities of Magic Kingdom?

e Which country has a comparative advantage in producing food?

11 Study *Reading Between the Lines* on pp. 912–913 and then answer the following questions.

a Why is there an effective quota on US distributed bananas from Central America?

b Why is the US threatening a trade war with the EU over the import agreements for bananas?

c What is the likely effect of allowing free trade in bananas on the price and consumption of bananas in the EU?

d What is the likely effect of allowing free trade in bananas on the income of African, Carribean and Pacific banana exporting countries?

e How can protectionist measures worsen competitiveness and export performance in the ACP countries?

Going Bananas about Trade

Financial Times, 11 November 1998 

Bananas battle goes to the brink

Guy de Jonquières

Why is the US, which grows almost no bananas, threatening a trade war with the European Union over its arrangements for importing the fruit? And why is the EU, normally so keen to accuse the US of seeking to "manage" trade with other countries, determined to defend its own right to do so in this case?

The explanation dates back to July 1993, when the European Union sought to complete its internal market by introducing a single banana import regime. This limited its total imports and segregated volumes between fruit from African, Caribbean and Pacific (ACP) countries and "dollar" bananas from central America.

The regime aimed to unify a patchwork of national policies. Until then, Britain and France had given preferential access to imports from their former colonies in the ACP region. Other countries, including Germany, the Netherlands and Sweden, where consumers prefer "dollar" fruit, allowed unrestricted trade.

The new policy, agreed after much internal EU dissent, enraged leading US distributors of "dollar" bananas, such as Chiquita Brands and Dole. Its introduction coincided with a slump in their profits, caused partly by their decision to step up production in the apparent belief that Europe was about to open its market completely.

The US twice complained to the old General Agreement on Tariffs and Trade that the regime violated world trade rules. The EU was able to use the Gatt's elastic procedures to deflect the complaint. But a third US challenge, under the stricter procedures of the World Trade Organisation, the Gatt's successor, was more successful.

The WTO's appellate body, its final tribunal in trade disputes, found against the banana regime last year. The EU was given until next January to comply with the decision, or face the threat of legal trade retaliation by the US and central American banana producers.

The EU is in the process of amending the regime. However, the US says its revised policy does not comply with the WTO ruling. US banana distributors, led by Chiquita, say the new arrangement will give them no better access to the EU market than the old one.

The EU says that opening its market further, as the US wants, would undermine the purpose of the regime. It would enable competition from "dollar" bananas to drive out much more expensive fruit from the ACP countries, which the EU's import arrangements are intended to protect.

The Essence of the Story

- The USA is threatening the EU with a trade war over its import policy on bananas.
- The EU is accused of imposing a quota on US distributed 'Chiquita' and 'Dole' brand bananas from Central America, in preference to bananas exported by the African, Caribbean and Pacific (ACP) countries.
- This is the third time the US have complained about the EU policy. The first two times the complaint was made to GATT but the EU could use the GATT's rules to deflect the complaint. The third appeal to the WTO, which has stricter rules, was upheld.
- The EU was given till January 1999 to comply or face legal trade retaliation by the US and Central American banana producers.
- The EU says that opening the market for bananas would mean that cheaper 'dollar' bananas would drive out the more expensive variety from the ACP countries.

Economic Analysis

■ The article says that US distributors have stepped up production of bananas on the assumption that the EU would open the banana market for trade. The EU accepts that 'dollar' bananas are cheaper than ACP bananas.

■ The article gives the impression that 'dollar' bananas are just the same as ACP bananas and that the supply curve for 'dollar' bananas would lie below the supply curve for ACP bananas. In reality the ACP bananas are thinner and sweeter and the bananas from Central America are bigger and fatter. They are also used extensively in canned fruit, preserves and juice.

■ While they are not the same type of banana (they are not perfect substitutes), they are highly substitutable. Figure 1 shows the effect of the operation of the quota on the 'dollar' bananas. P_1^* is the price paid by the consumer and P_0^* is the price paid to the supplier. The gap represents the rent accrued to the importer.

Figure 2 shows the market for ACP bananas. The market is in equilibrium at price P_0.

■ The effect of the removal of the quota can be seen in Figure 1. The price of 'dollar' bananas falls to P_0^* (in red) and the quantity consumed increases from Q_0^* to Q_1^*. The effect of a lower price for 'dollar' bananas means that people substitute and consume less ACP bananas. In Figure 2, the demand for ACP bananas shifts left from D_0 to D_1, the price and quantity consumed decline to P_1 and Q_1.

■ The article is wrong to suggest that opening the market will mean that cheap 'dollar' bananas will drive out the more expensive ACP bananas.

■ Figure 3 shows the value of banana imports into the UK by country. In 1998 the UK imported bananas worth £78.6 million from Central America and imported £117.3 million from the ACP countries. Jamaica, St Lucia and Costa Rica are the largest exporters of bananas to the UK.

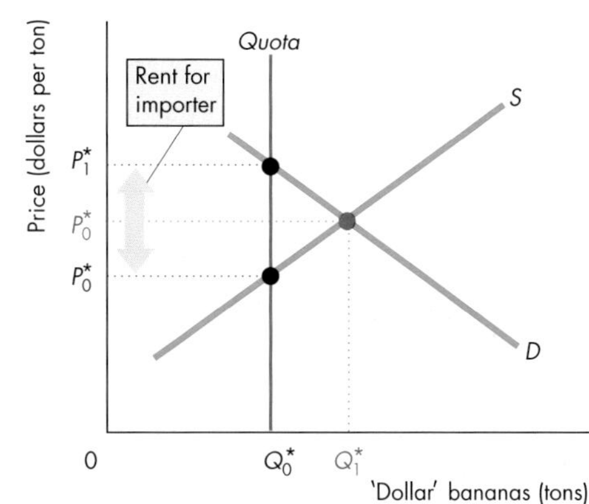

Figure 1 Market for 'Dollar' bananas

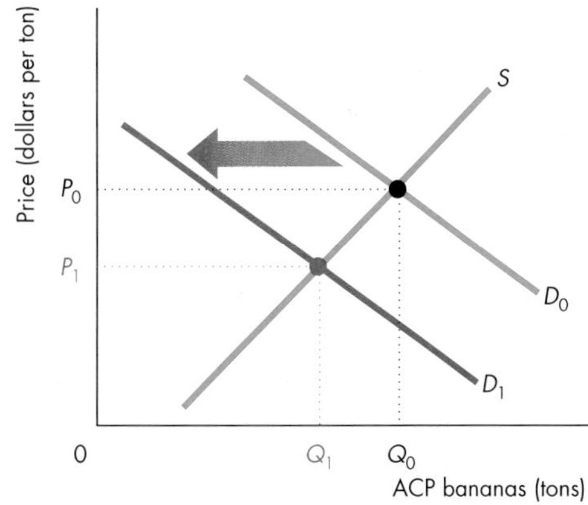

Figure 2 Market for ACP bananas

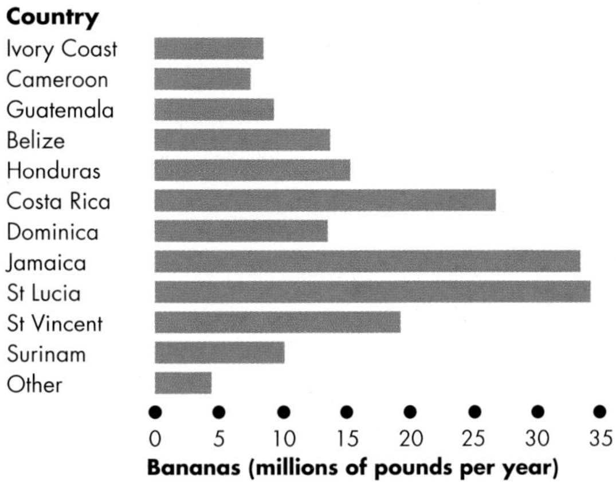

Figure 3 Value of UK imports

Understanding the Gains from International Trade

"Under a system of perfectly free commerce, each country naturally devotes its capital and labour to such employments as are most beneficial to each."

David Ricardo
The Principles of Political Economy and Taxation, 1817

The Economist: David Ricardo

David Ricardo (1772–1832) was a highly successful 27-year-old stockbroker when he stumbled on a copy of Adam Smith's *The Wealth of Nations* (see p. 24) on a weekend visit to the country. He was immediately hooked and went on to become the most celebrated economist of his age and one of the all-time great economists. One of his many contributions was to develop the principle of comparative advantage, the foundation on which the modern theory of international trade is built. The example he used to illustrate this principle was the trade between England and Portugal in cloth and wine.

The General Agreement on Tariffs and Trade (GATT) was established as a reaction against the devastation wrought by beggar-my-neighbour tariffs imposed during the 1930s. But it is also a triumph for the logic first worked out by Smith and Ricardo.

The Issues and Ideas

Until the mid-eighteenth century, it was generally believed that the purpose of international trade was to keep exports greater than imports and to pile up gold. If gold was accumulated, it was believed, the nation would prosper; and if gold was lost through an international deficit, the nation would be drained of money and impoverished. These beliefs are called *mercantilism*, and the *mercantilists* were pamphleteers who advocated with missionary fervour the pursuit of an international surplus. If exports did not exceed imports, the mercantilists wanted imports restricted.

In the 1740s, David Hume explained that as the quantity of money (gold) changes, so does the price level, and the nation's *real* wealth is unaffected. In the 1770s, Adam Smith argued that import restrictions would lower the gains from specialization and make a nation poorer, and 30 years later, David Ricardo proved the law of comparative advantage and demonstrated the superiority of free trade. Mercantilism was intellectually bankrupt but remained politically powerful.

Gradually, through the nineteenth century, the mercantilist influence waned and North America and Western Europe prospered in an environment of increasingly free international trade. But despite remarkable advances in economic understanding, mercantilism never quite died. It had a brief and devastating revival in the 1920s and 1930s when tariff hikes brought about the collapse of international trade and accentuated the Great Depression. It subsided again after World War II with the establishment of the General Agreement on Tariffs and Trade (GATT).

But mercantilism lingers on. The often expressed view that the United States should restrict Japanese imports and reduce its deficit with Japan and fears that the NAFTA will bring economic ruin to the United States are modern manifestations of mercantilism. It would be interesting to have David Hume, Adam Smith and David Ricardo commenting on these views. But we know what they would say – the same things that they said to the eighteenth century mercantilists. And they would still be right today.

Then . . .

In the eighteenth century, when mercantilists and economists were debating the pros and cons of free international exchange, the available transportation technology limited the gains from international trade. Sailing ships with tiny cargo holds took nearly a month to cross the Atlantic Ocean. But the potential gains were large, and so was the incentive to cut shipping costs. By the 1850s, the clipper ship had been developed, cutting the journey from Boston to Liverpool to only $12\frac{1}{4}$ days. Half a century later, 10,000-ton steamships were sailing between America and England in just four days. As sailing times and costs declined, so the gains from international trade increased and the volume of trade expanded.

. . . And Now

The container ship has revolutionized international trade and contributed to its continued expansion. Today, most goods cross the oceans in containers – metal boxes – packed into and piled on top of ships like the one opposite. Container technology has cut the cost of ocean shipping by economizing on handling and by making cargoes harder to steal, lowering insurance costs. It is unlikely that there would be much international trade in goods such as television sets and VCRs without this technology. High-value and perishable cargoes such as flowers and fresh foods, as well as urgent courier packages, travel by air. Every day, dozens of cargo-laden 747s fly between all major European cities and destinations across the Atlantic and Pacific Oceans.

The Balance of Payments, the Pound and the Euro

After studying this chapter you will be able to:

- Explain how international trade is financed
- Describe a country's balance of payments accounts
- Explain what determines the amount of international borrowing and lending
- Explain how the foreign exchange value of the pound is determined
- Explain why the foreign exchange value of the pound fluctuates
- Understand the implications of European Monetary Union

A Mounting Debt and a Sinking Pound

In 1986, the United Kingdom owned £721.2 billion in assets abroad and foreigners owned £622.9 billion of assets in the United Kingdom. Foreign assets exceeded foreigners' assets in the United Kingdom so that net foreign assets – the difference between what people in the United Kingdom hold of foreign assets and what foreigners hold of UK assets – were £98.3 billion. In 1998 the balance had tipped the other way. Net foreign assets were –£58 billion. What caused this turnaround? Part of the reason is that the United Kingdom is a good place to invest and foreign companies have been buying UK firms or setting up companies. Think of BMW's acquisition of Rover, Nestlés purchase of Rowntree, or the Hongkong & Shanghai Bank's purchase of Midland Bank. Why have foreigners been buying more businesses in the United Kingdom than British people have been buying abroad? ◆ In 1971, one pound sterling was enough to buy 8.5 Deutschemarks, and 2.44 US dollars. In mid-1999, that same pound bought only DM3 and $1.60. But the slide in the value of the pound from DM8.5 to DM3 or from $2.44 to $1.60 was not a smooth one. At some times the pound rose in value against all currencies, as it did, for example, in 1980. In 1999, the pound rose against the euro – the new currency of the European Monetary Union (EMU). But at other times the pound's slide was precipitous, as in September 1992 when the pound left the Exchange Rate Mechanism (ERM). What makes the pound fluctuate in value against other currencies? Why have the fluctuations been particularly extreme, as in the 1980s and in 1992? Is there anything we can do to stabilize the value of the pound? Can an exchange rate agreement help to stabilize the pound?

◆ ◆ ◆ ◆ International economics has always been an important issue for an economy such as the United Kingdom. In this chapter we're going to study the questions that we've just raised. We're going to discover why the United Kingdom has become such an attractive target for foreign investors; why the value of the pound fluctuates against the values of other currencies; and why interest rates vary from country to country.

Financing International Trade

When Currys, an electrical goods retail chain, imports Sony CD players, it does not pay for them with pounds – it uses Japanese yen. When Harrods imports Armani suits, it pays for them with Italian lire. And when a Japanese retail company buys a consignment of Scotch malt whisky, it uses pounds sterling. Whenever we buy things from another country, we use the currency of that country in order to make the transaction. It doesn't make any difference what the item being traded is; it might be a consumer good or a capital good, a building, or even a firm.

We're going to study the markets in which money – in different types of currencies – is bought and sold. But first we're going to look at the scale of international trading and borrowing and lending and at the way in which we keep our records of these transactions. Such records are called the balance of payments accounts.

Table 36.1 UK Balance of Payments Accounts in 1997

Current account	**(billions of pounds)**
Net trade in goods	−11.8
Net trade in services	+11.1
Net income	+12.2
Net transfers	−3.5
Current account balance	+8.0
Capital and financial account	
Capital account	+0.3
Foreign investment in the UK	−258.6
UK investment abroad	+248.1
Capital account balance	−10.2
Change in reserve assets	
Decrease (+) in official UK reserves	+2.4
Balancing item	0.2

Source: UK Balance of Payments: The Pink Book, 1998, ONS, London.

Balance of Payments Accounts

A country's **balance of payments accounts** record its international trading and its borrowing and lending. There are three balance of payments accounts:

1 Current account.

2 Capital and financial account.

3 Change in reserve assets.

The **current account** records the receipts from the sale of goods and services to foreigners, the payments for goods and services bought from foreigners, and gifts and other transfers (such as foreign aid payments) received from and paid to foreigners. By far the largest items in the current account are the receipts from the sale of goods and services to foreigners (the value of exports) and the payments made for goods and services bought from foreigners (the value of imports). Net income is the earnings from foreign financial assets such as bonds and shares, and net earnings of UK workers abroad and foreign workers in the UK. Net transfers – gifts to foreigners minus gifts from foreigners – are relatively small items. The **capital and financial account** records all the international borrowing and lending transactions. Whereas the earnings from investments abroad are recorded in the current account, the financial account balance records the actual investments abroad and foreigners investments in the UK. It is the difference between the amount that a country lends to and borrows from the rest of the world. The **change in reserve assets** shows the net increase or decrease in a country's holdings of foreign currency reserves that comes about from the official financing of the difference between the current account and the capital and financial accounts. In practice, the change in reserve assets is an item in the capital and financial accounts. It is itemized seperately here so that you can see how the financing of the gap between current and capital and financial accounts adds to or subtracts from reserve assets.

Table 36.1 shows the UK balance of payments accounts in 1997. Items in the current account and financial account that provide foreign currency to the United Kingdom have a plus sign and items that cost the United Kingdom foreign currency have a minus sign. The table shows that in 1997, UK imports of goods exceeded UK exports of goods and the net trade in goods had a deficit of £11.8 billion. But exports of services exceeded imports so that net trade in services was in surplus by £11.2 billion. How do we pay for imports that exceed the value of our exports? That is, how do we pay for our current account deficit? We pay by borrowing from abroad. The financial

Figure 36.1 The Balance of Payments: 1975–1997

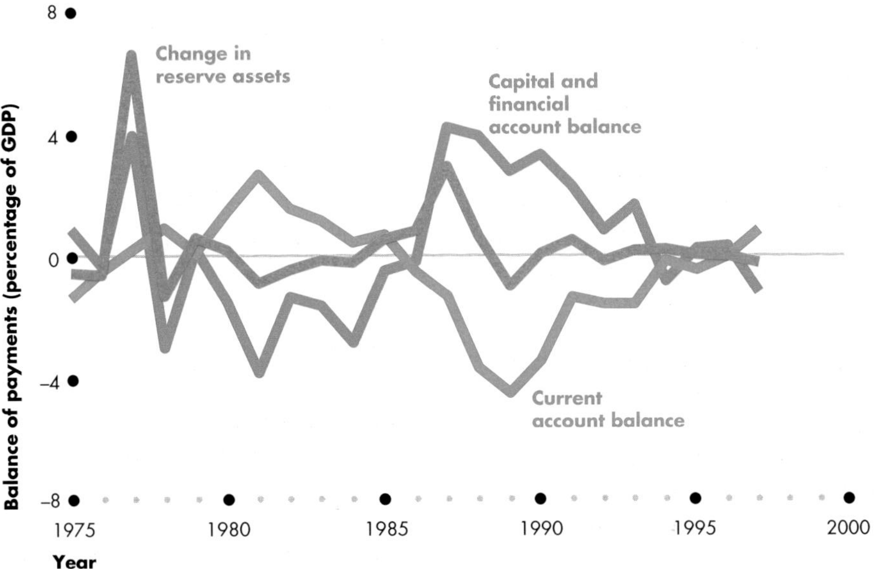

The balance of payments fluctuated during the 1970s, but during the early 1980s, a large current account surplus arose. The increase in the price of oil in 1979 helped to produce a current account surplus. The capital and financial account balance mirrors the current account balance. When the current account balance is positive, the capital and financial account balance is negative – we lend to the rest of the world – and when the current account balance is negative, the capital and financial account balance is positive – we borrow from the rest of the world. Fluctuations in the change in reserve assets are usually small compared with fluctuations in the current account balance and the capital and financial account balance. A special case was the large inflow of reserves in 1977 which was the result of IMF-initiated policies in December 1976.

Source: ONS.

account tells us by how much. We borrowed £35.8 billion but made loans of £38.4 billion. Thus our identified net foreign lending was £2.6 billion.

In theory our net borrowing or lending from abroad minus our current account deficit represents the balance that is financed from official UK reserves. Official UK reserves are the government's holdings of foreign currency. In 1997, those reserves decreased by £2.4 billion, but this did not close the gap between the current account deficit and the capital and financial account balance. The remainder is made up by a statistical discrepancy known as the balancing item. This discrepancy represents a combination of capital and current account transactions such as unidentified borrowing from abroad, illegal international trade – for example, the import of illegal drugs – and transactions not reported in order to evade tariffs or taxes.

The numbers in Table 36.1 give a snapshot of the balance of payments accounts in 1997. Figure 36.1 puts that snapshot into perspective by showing the balance of payments between 1987 and 1997. Because the economy grows and the price level rises, changes in the sterling value of the balance of payments do not convey much information. To remove the influences of growth and inflation, Figure 36.1 shows the balance of payments as a percentage of nominal GDP.

As you can see, the current account balance is almost a mirror image of the capital and financial account balance. The change in reserve assets is small compared with the balances on these other two accounts. A large current account deficit (and capital and financial account surplus) occured during the late 1980s, but declined after 1990.

You will perhaps obtain a better understanding of the balance of payments accounts and the way in which they are linked together if you consider the income and expenditure, borrowing and lending, and the bank account of an individual.

Individual Analogy An individual's current account records the income from supplying the services of factors of production and the expenditure on goods and services. Consider, for example, Joanne. She earned an income in 1995 of £25,000. Joanne has £10,000 worth of investments that earned her an income of £1,000. Joanne's current account shows an income of £26,000. Joanne spent £18,000 buying goods and services for consumption. She also bought a new house, which cost her £60,000. So Joanne's total expenditure was £78,000. The difference between her expenditure and income is £52,000 (£78,000 minus £26,000). This amount is Joanne's current account deficit.

To pay for expenditure of £52,000 in excess of her income, Joanne has either to use the money that she has in the bank or to take out a loan. In fact Joanne took a mortgage of £50,000 to help buy her house. This mortgage was the only borrowing that Joanne did, so her capital and financial account surplus was £50,000. With a current account deficit of £52,000 and a capital and financial account surplus of £50,000, Joanne is still £2,000 short. She got that £2,000 from her own bank account. Her cash holdings decreased by £2,000.

Joanne's income from her work and investments is analogous to a country's income from its exports. Her purchases of goods and services, including her purchase of a house, are analogous to a country's imports. Joanne's mortgage – borrowing from someone else – is analogous to a country's foreign borrowing. The change in her own bank account is analogous to the change in the country's reserve assets.

Borrowers and Lenders, Debtors and Creditors

A country that is borrowing more from the rest of the world than it is lending to it is called a **net borrower**. Similarly, a **net lender** is a country that is lending more to the rest of the world than it is borrowing from it. A net borrower might be going deeper into debt or might simply be reducing its net assets held in the rest of the world. The total stock of foreign investment determines whether a country is a debtor or a creditor. A **debtor nation** is a country that during its entire history has borrowed more from the rest of the world than it has lent to it. It has a stock of outstanding debt to the rest of the world that exceeds the stock of its own claims on the rest of the world. The United Kingdom briefly became a debtor nation in 1990 and has been a debtor since 1996. A **creditor nation** is a country that has invested more in the rest of the world than other countries have invested in it. The largest creditor nation today is Japan.

At the heart of the distinction between a net borrower/net lender and a debtor/creditor nation is the distinction between flows and stocks, which you have encountered many times in your study of macroeconomics. Borrowing and lending are flows – amounts borrowed or lent per unit of time. Debts are stocks – amounts owed at a point in time. The flow of borrowing and lending changes the stock of debt. But the outstanding stock of debt depends mainly on past flows of borrowing and lending, not on the current period's flows. The current period's flows determine the *change* in the stock of debt outstanding.

During the 1960s and the 1970s, the United Kingdom would periodically swing from surplus to deficit on its current account. When it was in current account surplus it had a deficit on its capital account. On the whole the United Kingdom was a net lender to the rest of the world. It was not until the late 1980s that it became a significant net borrower. Between 1987 and 1993, borrowing continued each year. In 1994 and 1997 it became a net lender.

Most countries are net borrowers. But a small number of countries, which includes oil-rich Saudi Arabia and Venezuela, and Japan, are huge net lenders.

The United Kingdom today is a small net lender, but it is not yet back to being a creditor nation. There are many countries that are debtor nations. The United States is one. But the largest debtor nations are the capital-hungry developing countries. The international debt of these countries grew from less than a third to more than a half of their gross domestic product during the 1980s and created what was called the 'Third World debt crisis'.

Does it matter if a country is a net borrower rather than a net lender? The answer to this question depends mainly on what the net borrower is doing with the borrowed money. If borrowing is

Table 36.2 The Current Account Balance, Net Foreign Borrowing and the Financing of Investment

	Symbols and equations	UK in 1997 (billions of pounds)
(a) VARIABLES		
Gross domestic product (GDP)	Y	802.0
Consumption expenditure	C	519.1
Investment	I	136.6
Government purchases of goods and services	G	147.4
Exports of goods and services	X	228.7
Imports of goods and services	M	229.8
Saving	S	144.7
Taxes, net of transfer payments	T	138.2
(b) DOMESTIC INCOME AND EXPENDITURE		
Aggregate expenditure	(1) $Y = C + I + G + X - M$	
Uses of income	(2) $Y = C + S + T$	
Subtracting (1) from (2)	(3) $0 = I - S + G - T + X - M$	
(c) SURPLUSES AND DEFICITS		
Current account	(4) $X - M = (T - G) + (S - I)$ $= 228.7 - 229.8 = -1.1$	
Government budget	(5) $T - G = 138.2 - 147.4 = -9.2$	
Private sector	(6) $S - I = 144.7 - 136.6 = 8.1$	
(d) FINANCING INVESTMENT		
Investment is financed by the sum of:		
private saving,	$S = 144.7$	
net government saving and	$T - G = -9.2$	
net foreign saving	$M - X = 1.1$	
That is:	(7) $I = S + (T - G) + (M - X) = 136.6$	

Source: ONS, *Economic Trends Annual Supplement*, 1998, London.

financing investment that in turn is generating economic growth and higher income, borrowing is not a problem. If the borrowed money is being used to finance consumption, then higher interest payments are being incurred and, as a consequence, consumption will eventually have to be reduced. In this case, the more the borrowing and the longer it goes on, the greater is the reduction in consumption that will eventually be necessary. We'll see below whether the United Kingdom has been borrowing for investment or for consumption.

Current Account Balance

What determines the current account balance and the scale of a country's net foreign borrowing or lending?

To answer this question, we need to recall and use some of the things that we learned about the national income accounts. Table 36.2 will refresh your memory and summarize the necessary calculations for you. Part (a) lists the national income variables that are needed, with their symbols. Their values in the United Kingdom in 1997 are also shown.

Part (b) presents two key national income equations. First, equation (1) reminds us that GDP, Y, equals aggregate expenditure, which is the sum of consumption expenditure, C, investment, I, government purchases of goods and services, G, and net exports (exports, X, minus imports, M). Equation (2) reminds us that aggregate income is used in three different ways. It can be consumed, saved or paid to the government in the form of taxes (net of transfer payments). Equation (1) tells us how our expenditure generates our income. Equation (2) tells us how we dispose of that income.

Part (c) of the table takes you into some new territory. It examines surpluses and deficits. We'll look at three surpluses/deficits – those of the current account, the government's budget and the private sector. To get at these surpluses and deficits, first subtract equation (2) from equation (1) in Table 36.2. The result is equation (3). By rearranging equation (3), we obtain a relationship for the current account – exports minus imports – that appears as equation (4) in the table[1].

The current account, in equation (4), is made up of two components. The first is taxes minus government spending and the second is saving minus investment. These items are the surpluses/deficits of the government and private sectors. Taxes (net of transfer payments) minus government purchases of goods and services is the budget surplus or deficit. If that number is positive, the government's budget is a surplus and if the number

1 *Net exports*, which is exports minus imports, in the national income accounts, are approximately equal to the current account balance. There are some small differences in the definitions used in the national income accounts and the balance of payments accounts but, for most purposes, you can regard net exports and the current account balance as being equal. The statistical discrepancy in the 1997 national accounts is added to imports to complete the adding up procedure of Table 36.2.

Figure 36.2 Sector Balances

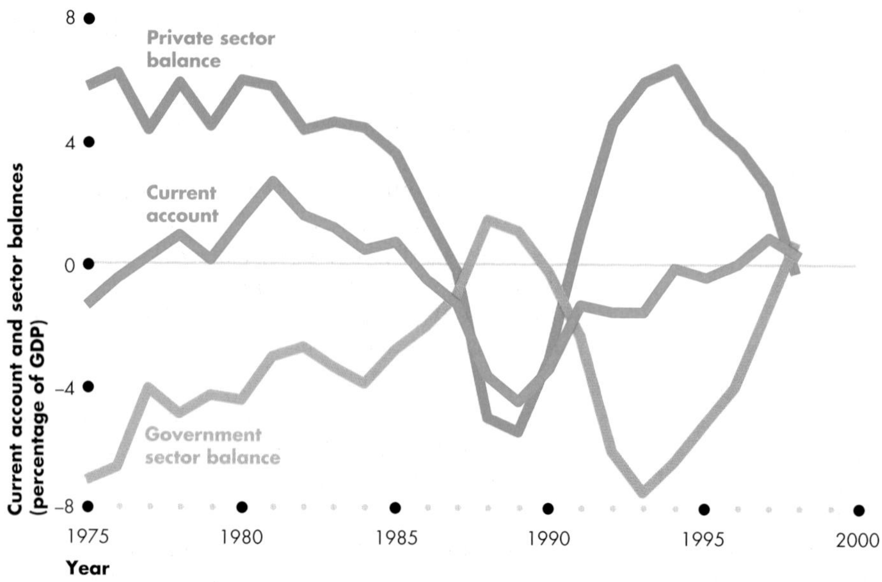

The private sector balance tends to mirror the government deficit. The private sector surplus as a proportion of GDP was stable between 1975 and 1982. It began to decline in the mid-1980s. In the late 1980s the private sector was in deficit while the government sector was in surplus. During the 1990s the private sector surplus increased as consumption fell and savings rose during the recession, but the government sector was in deficit while the current account was also in deficit. The twin deficits of the government and external sectors also occurred in the 1970s. By 1998 each sector had reached balance.

Source: ONS.

is negative, it is a deficit. The **private sector surplus or deficit** is the difference between saving and investment. If saving exceeds investment, the private sector has a surplus to lend to other sectors. If investment exceeds saving, the private sector has a deficit that has to be financed by borrowing from other sectors. As you can see from our calculations, the current account deficit is equal to the sum of the other two deficits – the government's budget deficit and the private sector surplus. In the UK in 1997, the private sector had a surplus of £8.1 billion and the government sector had a deficit of £9.2 billion. The government sector deficit minus the private sector surplus equalled the current account deficit of £1.1 billion.

Part (d) of Table 36.2 shows you how investment is financed. To increase investment, either private saving, the government surplus, or the current account deficit, must increase.

The calculations that we've just performed are really nothing more than book keeping. We've manipulated the national income accounts and discovered that the current account deficit is just the sum of the deficits of the government and private sectors. But these calculations do reveal a fundamental fact: our international balance of payments can change only if either our government budget balance changes or our private sector financial balance changes.

We've seen that our international deficit is equal to the sum of the government deficit and the private sector surplus. Is the private sector surplus equal to the government's budget deficit so that the external account deficit is zero? Does an increase in the government budget deficit bring an increase in the current account deficit?

You can see the answer to this question by looking at Figure 36.2. In this figure, the general government sector budget balance is plotted alongside the current account balance and the private sector balance. To remove the effects of growth and inflation, all three balances are measured as percentages of nominal GDP. Over the whole period (1972–94), the private sector balance tends to mirror the government deficit. Between 1975 and 1982, the private sector surplus was roughly a stable proportion of GDP. The current account was in deficit between 1973 and 1975 but was roughly in balance for the rest of the 1970s. The private sector surplus began to decline in the mid-1980s and the declining government sector deficit meant that the current account was in surplus. In the late 1980s the private sector was in deficit while the government sector was in surplus. During the 1990s the private sector surplus increased during the recession. Also the government deficit was matched by a current account deficit. Notice that at the end of the 1980s the government sector was in surplus while the current account was in deficit. When the paths of the government deficit and the current account deficit diverge, their divergence is accommodated by changes in the private sector surplus.

Is the UK Borrowing for Consumption or Investment?

We noted above that whether international borrowing is a problem or not depends on what that borrowing is used for. Since 1987, the United Kingdom has borrowed nearly £8 billion a year, on the average. Over these same years, the government sector has had an average deficit of £19 billion a year, and the private sector has had an average surplus (saving minus investment has been positive) of £11 billion a year. So private sector saving has been more than sufficient to pay for investment in plant and equipment. Does the fact that foreign borrowing has financed a government deficit mean that we are borrowing to consume?

Our foreign borrowing probably has been financing public consumption to some degree. But not all government purchases are consumption purchases. Over 10 per cent of government purchases are of investment goods. But there is no sure way to divide government purchases into a consumption component and an investment component. Some items, such as the expenditure on improved roads and bridges, are clearly investment. But what about expenditure on education and health care? Are these expenditures consumption or investment? A case can be made that they are investment – investment in human capital – and that they earn a rate of return at least equal to the interest rate that we pay on our foreign debt.

However, most of the foreign investment in the United Kingdom is in the private sector and is undertaken in the pursuit of the highest available profit. Foreigners diversify their lending to spread their risk. We do the same. Some of our saving is used to finance investment in firms in the United Kingdom, some is lent to the government and some is used to finance investment in other countries.

Review

- When we buy goods from or invest in the rest of the world, we use foreign currency; and when foreigners buy goods from or invest in the United Kingdom, they use sterling.
- We record international transactions in the balance of payments accounts: current account (exports and imports of goods and services); capital and financial account (net foreign borrowing or lending); and official settlements account (change in official UK reserves).
- The current account deficit is equal to the sum of the government budget deficit and the private sector surplus.
- Changes in the government deficit can change both the private sector surplus and the current account deficit.

Sterling in the Global Market

When we buy foreign goods or invest in another country, we have to obtain some of that country's currency to make the transaction. When foreigners buy UK-produced goods or invest in the United Kingdom, they have to obtain sterling. We get foreign currency and foreigners get pounds sterling in the foreign exchange market. The **foreign exchange market** is the market in which the currency of one country is exchanged for the currency of another. The foreign exchange market is made up of thousands of people: importers and exporters, banks and specialists in the buying and selling of foreign exchange called foreign exchange brokers. The foreign exchange market opens on Monday morning in Hong Kong. As the day advances, markets open in Singapore, Tokyo, Bahrain, Frankfurt, London, New York, Chicago and San Francisco. As the West Coast markets in the United States close, Hong Kong is only an hour away from opening for the next day of business. The sun barely sets on the foreign exchange market. Dealers around the world are continually in contact by telephone and on any given day, billions of dollars, yen, Deutschemarks and pounds change hands.

The price at which one currency exchanges for another is called a **foreign exchange rate**. For example, on 27 May 1999, one pound sterling bought 2.98 Deutschemarks, 194.4 Japanese yen, 1.59 US dollars and 1.53 euros. The exchange rate between the US dollar and the pound sterling was £0.63 per $1, and the rate between euros and the pound was £0.65 per euro. Exchange rates can be expressed either way.

The actions of the foreign exchange brokers make the foreign exchange market highly efficient. Exchange rates are almost identical no matter where in the world the transaction is taking place. If euros were cheap in London and expensive in Tokyo, within a flash someone would have placed a buy order in London and a sell order in Tokyo, thereby increasing demand in one place and increasing supply in another, moving the prices to equality.

Foreign Exchange Systems

Foreign exchange rates are of critical importance for millions of people. They affect the costs of things as diverse as foreign holidays and imported cars. They affect the number of pounds that we get for the lamb we sell to France and the luxury cars we sell to the United States. Because of their importance, governments pay a great deal of attention to what is happening in the foreign exchange market and, more than that, take actions designed to achieve what they regard as desirable movements in exchange rates. In deciding how to act in the foreign exchange market, a government must choose among three alternative strategies that give rise to three foreign exchange systems. They are:

1 Fixed exchange rate.
2 Flexible exchange rate.
3 Managed exchange rate.

A **fixed exchange rate** is a system in which the value of a country's currency is pegged by the country's central bank. Under a fixed exchange rate system the Bank of England would declare the pound sterling to be worth a certain number of units of some other currency and would take actions on the foreign exchange market to try to maintain the pound's declared value. Below we'll study what those foreign exchange market actions would be.

A **flexible exchange rate** is a system in which the value of a country's currency is determined by market forces in the absence of central bank intervention. Under a flexible exchange rate, the Bank of England would take no actions on the foreign exchange market.

A **managed exchange rate** is a system in which the value of a country's currency is not fixed at some pre-announced level but is influenced by central bank intervention in the foreign exchange market. This intervention is in the form of using the official reserves to buy or sell the currency to stabilize its value.

Like many currencies the pound has experienced all three exchange rate systems at some time in its history. So before we learn how the foreign exchange market operates in these three systems, let's look at the recent history of the foreign exchange market.

Recent Exchange Rate History

At the end of World War II, the major countries of the world set up the International Monetary Fund (IMF). The **International Monetary Fund** is an international organization that monitors balance of payments and exchange rate activities. The IMF is based in Washington, DC. It came into being as a result of negotiations between the United States and the United Kingdom during World War II. In July 1944, at Bretton Woods, New Hampshire, 44 countries signed the Articles of Agreement of the IMF. At the centre of these agreements was the establishment of a worldwide system of fixed exchange rates among currencies. The anchor for this fixed exchange rate system was gold. One ounce of gold was defined to be worth 35 US dollars. All other currencies were pegged to the US dollar at a fixed exchange rate. For example, the pound sterling was set to be worth $4.80 and the Japanese yen was set at 360 yen per dollar. The rules of the Bretton Woods system allowed for countries to alter the exchange rates subject to agreement. The pound was devalued in September 1949 and November 1967, to $2.80 and $2.40 respectively. Although the fixed exchange rate system established in 1944 served the world well during the 1950s and early 1960s, it came under increasing strain in the late 1960s and, by 1971, the order had almost collapsed. In the period since 1971, the world has operated with different countries adopting a variety of flexible and managed exchange rate arrangements as well as fixed exchange rates. Some currencies have increased in

Figure 36.3 Exchange Rates

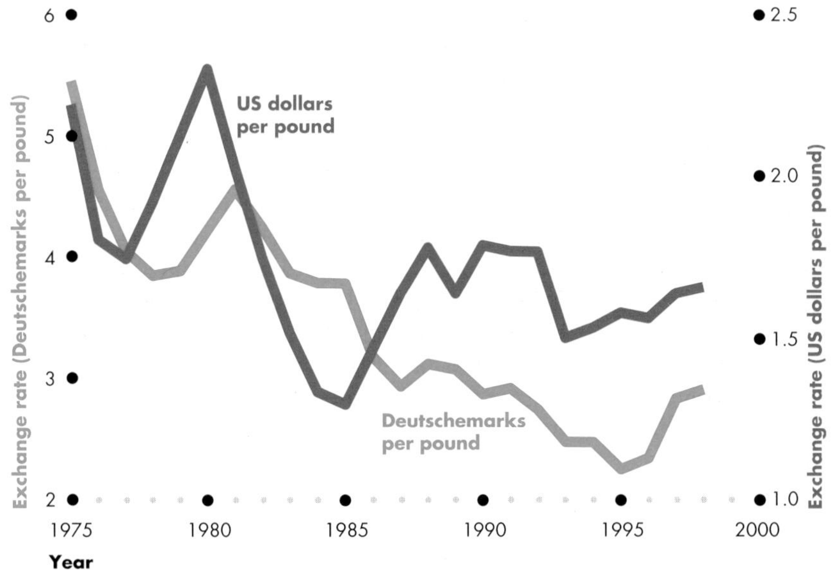

The exchange rate is the price at which two currencies can be traded. The Deutschemark–sterling exchange rate, expressed as Deutschemarks per pound, shows that the pound has fallen in value – depreciated – against the Deutschemark. The dollar exchange rate is expressed as US dollars per pound. The pound depreciated against the US dollar between 1980 and 1985 and appreciated against the dollar between 1985 and 1988, and remained stable since then.

Source: ONS.

value, and others have declined. The pound sterling and the US dollar are among the currencies that have declined, while the Japanese yen is the currency that has had the most spectacular increase in value. In 1972, the pound's link with the dollar was broken and the pound began to float. At times between 1972 and 1990, the Bank of England intervened to influence the value of the pound, but there were also times when it was allowed to float freely.

Figure 36.3 shows what happened to the exchange rate between 1975 and 1998. The blue line shows the value of the pound against the German Deutschemark. The value of the pound has fallen against the Deutschemark – the pound has depreciated. **Currency depreciation** is the fall in the value of one currency in terms of another currency. For example, in 1975, the pound was worth DM5.447 and in 1998 it was worth DM2.914. So the pound has depreciated by DM2.533 or 46 per cent of its 1975 value.

Although the pound has depreciated in terms of the Deutschemark, it has not depreciated at the same rate against all other currencies. The red line of Figure 36.3 shows the value of the pound against the US dollar. During the mid-1980s the pound depreciated more against the US dollar than against the Deutschemark. As you can see, the value of the pound depreciated strongly against the US dollar from 1980 to 1985; and after 1985 it appreciated against the dollar and stabilized around $1.55 but continued to depreciate against the Deutschemark until 1996 when it began to appreciate.

Review

- There are three possible foreign exchange market systems: fixed, flexible and managed.
- Between the end of World War II and 1971, the world economy had a fixed exchange rate system. Since 1971, it has had a mixture of flexible and managed systems.
- The pound has fluctuated against the dollar but has fallen against the Deutschemark up until 1996.

Why did the pound fluctuate so much in the early 1980s? Why did it climb in value against the dollar during 1980 and then decline steadily again a few years after? To answer questions like these, we need to know what determines the foreign exchange rate. What determines the foreign currency value of the pound?

Exchange Rate Determination

The exchange rate is the price of the pound sterling in terms of other currencies. Just like any other price, the exchange rate is determined by demand and supply – the demand for pounds and the supply of pounds. But what exactly do we mean by the demand for and supply of pounds? And what is the quantity of sterling?

The quantity of sterling demanded in the foreign exchange market is the amount that people would buy on a given day at a particular exchange rate (price) if they found a willing seller. The quantity of sterling supplied in the foreign exchange market is the amount that people would sell on a given day at a particular exchange rate (price) if they found a willing buyer. What determines the quantities of sterling demanded and supplied in the foreign exchange market?

To answer this question, we need to think about the alternative to demanding and supplying pounds sterling. For a demander of sterling, the alternative is to hang on to foreign currency. For a supplier, the alternative is to hang on to sterling. The decision to buy or sell is also the decision to hold sterling or foreign currency.

To understand the forces that determine demand and supply in the foreign exchange market, we need to study people's decisions about the quantities of pounds sterling and foreign currencies to hold. Let's see what we mean by the quantity of sterling held.

The Quantity of Pounds

The **quantity of sterling assets** (which we'll call the quantity of pounds sterling) is the *net stock* of financial assets denominated in pounds sterling held outside the Bank of England and the public sector. Three things about the quantity of sterling need to be emphasized.

First, the quantity of sterling is a *stock*, not a *flow*. People make decisions about the quantity of sterling to hold (a stock) and about the quantities to buy and sell (flows) in the foreign exchange market. But it is the decision about how much sterling to hold that determines whether people plan to buy or sell sterling.

Second, the quantity of sterling is a stock *denominated in pounds sterling*. The denomination of an asset defines the units in which a debt must be repaid. It is possible to make a loan using currency of any denomination. The UK government could borrow in US dollars. If it did borrow in dollars, it would issue a bond denominated in dollars. Such a bond would be a promise to pay an agreed number of dollars at an agreed date. It would not be a sterling debt and, even though issued by the government, it would not be part of the supply of sterling. Many governments actually do issue bonds in currencies other than their own. The Canadian government, for example, issues bonds denominated in US dollars.

Third, the supply of sterling is a *net* supply – the quantity of assets *minus* the quantity of liabilities. This means that the quantity of sterling supplied does not include sterling assets created by private households, firms, financial institutions, or foreigners. The reason is that when a private debt is created, there is both an asset (for the holder) and a liability (for the issuer), so the *net* financial asset is zero. For example, if Pat loans Matt £1,000, then Pat's asset of £1,000 cancels out Matt's £1,000 liability. The quantity of sterling includes only the sterling liabilities of the government *plus* those of the Bank of England. This quantity is equal to the government debt held outside the Bank of England, plus the sterling liabilities of the Bank of England – the monetary base. In the United Kingdom, the monetary base is also known as M0. We first came across the monetary base in Chapter 00, pp. 000–000. The quantity of pounds sterling is:

$$\text{Quantity of pounds sterling} = \begin{array}{c}\text{Government debt}\\ \text{held outside the}\\ \text{Bank of England}\end{array} + \begin{array}{c}\text{Monetary}\\ \text{base}\end{array}$$

We've seen what sterling assets are. Let's now study the demand for and the supply of these assets and see what makes the demand and supply change.

The Demand for Sterling Assets

The law of demand applies to sterling assets just as it does to anything else that people value. The quantity of sterling demanded increases when the price of sterling in terms of foreign currency falls and decreases when the price of sterling in terms of foreign currency rises. Suppose, for example, that the pound is trading at DM2.90. If the pound rises to DM3.00, with everything else remaining the same, the quantity of sterling demanded decreases and if the pound falls to DM2.80, with everything else remaining the same, the quantity of sterling demanded increases. There are two separate reasons why the law of demand applies to sterling:

1 Transactions effect.
2 Expected capital gains effect.

Transactions Effect A transactions cost is incurred whenever a foreign currency is converted into pounds. This transactions cost can be avoided by holding a stock of sterling. With such a stock, it is not necessary to convert foreign currency into sterling on the foreign exchange market each time a sterling payment must be made. The larger the value of sterling payments, the larger is the inventory of stock that people hold. But the value of sterling payments depends on the exchange rate. The lower the value of the pound, with everything else remaining the same, the larger is the demand for UK exports and the lower is UK demand for imports. Hence the lower the value of the pound, the larger is the value of sterling payments and the greater is the demand for sterling. Foreigners demand more pounds to buy US exports and we demand fewer units of foreign currency and more pounds as we switch from importing to buying UK-produced goods.

Expected Capital Gains Effect Suppose you think the pound will be worth $1.50 by the end of the month. If today, it is trading at $1.55 per pound, and if your prediction about the future value of the pound is correct, you can make a quick capital gain. Suppose you buy £1,000-worth of dollars today. You get $1,550 for your £1,000. If the exchange rate at the end of the month is $1.5 per pound, as you predict it will be, you can sell your $1,550 for £1,033.33 (1,550 divided by 1.5 equals 1,033.33). (If your bank charges you £8 in fees, you've made a profit of £25.33 on these transactions.) If you are pretty confident about your prediction, you will not hold sterling during the current month. You will hold dollars instead.

If today the pound is trading not at $1.55 but at $1.45 per pound, and if your prediction about the future value of the pound – $1.50 – is correct, you will incur a capital loss if you undertake the transactions we've just looked at. If you buy £1,000-worth of dollars today, you now get only $1,450 for your £1,000. If the exchange rate at the end of the month is $1.50 per pound, as you predict it will be, you will sell your $1,450 for £966.67 (1,450 divided by 1.5 equals 966.67). (If your bank charges you £8 in fees, you've incurred a loss of £41.33 on these transactions.) You will hang on to your pounds during the current month. You will *not* hold dollars instead.

For a given expected future value of the pound, the lower the current value of sterling, the greater is the expected capital gain from holding sterling and the greater is the quantity of sterling demanded.

Figure 36.4 shows the relationship between the foreign currency price of the pound sterling in terms of US dollars and the quantity of sterling assets demanded – the demand curve for sterling assets.

Figure 36.4 The Demand for Sterling Assets

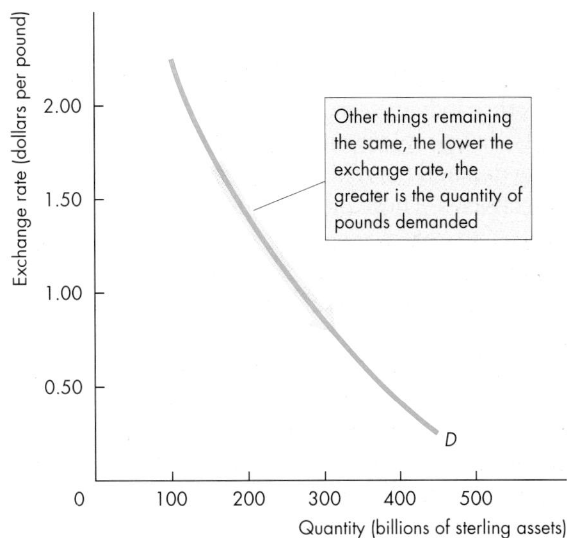

The quantity of sterling assets that people demand, other things remaining the same, depends on the exchange rate. The lower the exchange rate (the smaller the amount of foreign currency per pound sterling), the larger is the quantity of sterling assets demanded. The increased quantity demanded arises from an increase in the volume of sterling trade (foreigners buy more UK goods and we buy fewer foreign goods) and an increase in the expected appreciation (or decrease in the expected depreciation) of sterling assets.

When the foreign exchange rate changes, other things remaining the same, there is a movement along the demand curve.

Changes in the Demand for Sterling Assets

Any other influence on the quantity of sterling assets that people want to hold results in a shift in the demand curve. Demand either increases or decreases. These other influences are:

- UK GDP.
- The expected future value of the pound.
- The UK interest rate differential.

UK GDP You've seen that a transactions cost can be avoided by holding a stock of sterling and that the larger the value of sterling payments, the larger is the stock of sterling that people hold. A major influence on the value of sterling payments is UK GDP. An increase in UK GDP brings an increase in the value of sterling payments, which increases the demand for sterling. When the demand for sterling increases, the demand curve for sterling shifts rightward.

The Expected Future Value of Sterling You've seen that for a given expected future value of the pound, the lower the current value of the pound, the greater is the expected capital gain from holding pounds and the greater is the quantity of sterling demanded. But what happens if the expected future value of the pound changes while the current exchange rate is unchanged?

You can answer this question by returning to the capital gain example. Suppose the pound is trading at \$1.55 and you think it is going to fall to \$1.50 by the end of the month. You are confident in your view and you buy \$1,550 with your £1,000. At the end of the month, the dollar falls to \$1.50 as you predicted it would. You now sell your \$1,550 and buy pounds. At \$1.5 per pound, you collect £1,025.33 after paying bank charges. You have made a capital gain. In this circumstance, you hold dollars rather than pounds during this month. But suppose the pound is trading at \$1.55 and you think it is going to rise to \$1.60 by the end of the month. If in this situation you do the transactions we've just considered, you will incur a capital loss. Your £1,000 still buys \$1,550 but, when you sell these dollars at the end of the month at \$1.60 per pound, you collect only £960.75 after deduction of £8 for bank charges. In this circumstance, you hold pounds rather than dollars during this month.

The lower the expected future value of the pound, other things remaining the same, the smaller is the demand for sterling (and the greater is the demand for other currencies). Similarly, the higher the expected future value of the pound, other things remaining the same, the greater is the demand for sterling (and the smaller is the demand for other currencies).

The UK Interest Rate Differential People and businesses buy financial assets to make a return that has two components: a capital gain and an interest rate. You've just seen how the expected capital gain is determined by the current exchange rate and the expected future exchange rate. Let's now look at the interest component of the return on financial assets.

People can hold sterling assets or foreign currency assets. To choose the currencies in which to hold their wealth, people look at the interest rate on sterling assets and compare it with the interest rate on a foreign currency asset. The interest rate on a sterling asset minus the interest rate on a foreign currency asset is called the UK interest rate differential. If the interest rate on sterling assets increases and the interest rate on a foreign currency asset remains constant, the **UK interest rate differential** increases. The larger the UK interest rate differential, the greater is the demand for sterling assets.

Table 36.3 summarizes the above discussion of the influences on the demand for sterling.

The Supply of Sterling Assets

Remember that the *flows* of pounds and other currencies through the foreign exchange market are determined by decisions about *stocks*. A decrease in the demand for sterling brings a flow of pounds sterling on to the foreign exchange market. But this flow of sterling on to the market is *not* what we mean when we talk about the *supply of sterling*. The supply of sterling is the quantity of sterling assets available for people to hold.

The quantity of sterling supplied is determined by the actions of the Bank of England. We've seen that the quantity of sterling is equal to government debt plus the monetary base. Of these two items, the monetary base is by far the smallest. But it

Table 36.3 The Demand for Sterling Assets 

THE LAW OF DEMAND

The quantity of sterling assets demanded

Increases if:	*Decreases if:*
◆ The foreign exchange rate falls	◆ The foreign exchange rate rises

CHANGES IN DEMAND

The demand for sterling assets

Increases if:	*Decreases if:*
◆ UK GDP increases	◆ UK GDP decreases
◆ The expected future value of the pound sterling rises	◆ The expected future value of the pound sterling falls
◆ The UK interest rate differential increases	◆ The UK interest rate differential decreases

Table 36.4 The Supply of Sterling Assets 

SUPPLY

Fixed exchange rate system

The supply curve of sterling assets is horizontal at the fixed exchange rate.

Managed exchange rate

In order to smooth fluctuations in the price of the pound sterling, the quantity of sterling assets supplied by the Bank of England increases if the foreign currency price of the pound rises and decreases if the foreign currency price of the pound falls. The supply curve of sterling assets is upward-sloping.

Flexible exchange rate

The supply curve of sterling assets is vertical.

CHANGES IN SUPPLY

The supply of sterling assets

Increases if:	*Decreases if:*
◆ The UK government has a deficit	◆ The UK government has a surplus
◆ The Bank of England buys foreign currency	◆ The Bank of England sells foreign currency

plays a crucial role in determining the supply of sterling. The behaviour of the monetary base depends crucially on the foreign exchange rate system.

In a fixed exchange rate system, the supply curve of sterling assets is horizontal at the chosen exchange rate. The Bank of England stands ready to supply whatever quantity of sterling assets is demanded in exchange for foreign currency assets at the fixed exchange rate. In a managed exchange rate system, the Bank of England wants to smooth fluctuations in the exchange rate, and the supply curve of sterling assets is upward-sloping. The higher the foreign exchange rate, the larger is the quantity of sterling assets supplied by the Bank of England in exchange for foreign currency assets. In a flexible exchange rate system, a fixed quantity of sterling assets is supplied, regardless of their price. As a consequence, in a flexible exchange rate system, the supply curve of sterling assets is vertical.

Changes in the Supply of Sterling Assets

There are two ways in which the quantity of sterling supplied can change:

1 The government has a budget deficit or surplus.

2 The Bank of England buys or sells foreign currency assets.

The government influences the quantity of sterling assets supplied through its budget. If the government has a budget deficit, it borrows by issuing bonds, which are denominated in pounds sterling. The sale of new government bonds to finance a deficit increases the supply of sterling assets. Similarly, if the government has a budget surplus, it buys back previously issued bonds and the supply of sterling assets decreases.

The Bank of England influences the quantity of sterling supplied through its transactions in the foreign exchange market. If the Bank buys foreign currency, it increases the quantity of sterling assets supplied. If the Bank sells foreign currency, it decreases the quantity of sterling assets supplied.

An open market operation in which the Bank buys or sells government securities changes the monetary base but it does not change the quantity of sterling assets supplied. It changes the composition of sterling assets supplied. For example, if the Bank buys government bonds, the quantity of sterling denominated bonds decreases and the monetary base increases. But the increase in the monetary base equals the decrease in sterling bonds so the total quantity of sterling assets remains unchanged.

Table 36.4 summarizes the above discussion of the influences on the supply of sterling assets.

Figure 36.5 Three Exchange Rate Systems

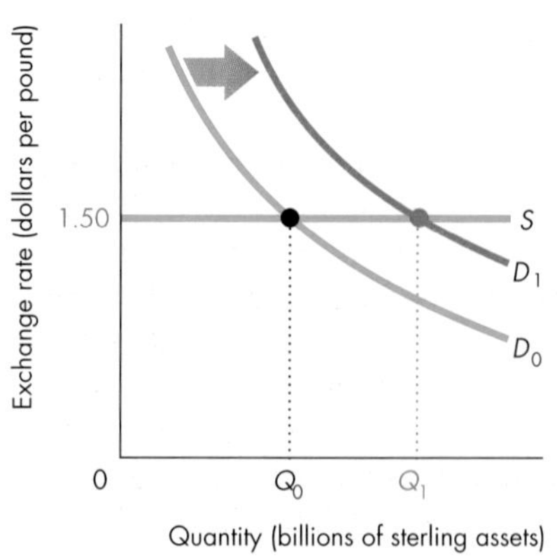

(a) Fixed exchange rate

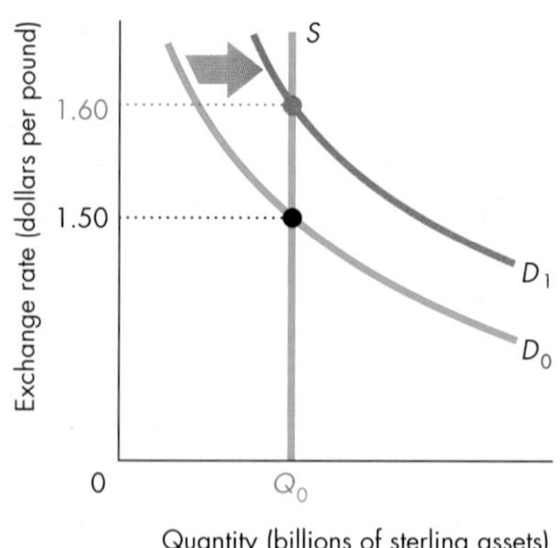

(b) Flexible exchange rate

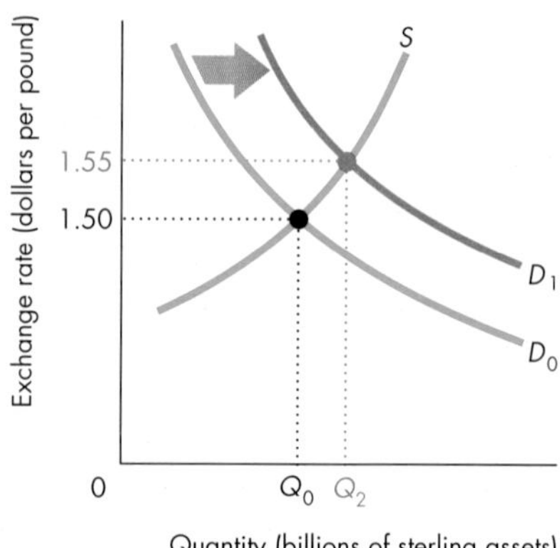

(c) Managed exchange rate

In a fixed exchange rate system (part a), the Bank of England stands ready to supply sterling assets or to take sterling assets off the market (supplying foreign currency in exchange) at a fixed exchange rate. The supply curve for sterling assets is horizontal. Fluctuations in demand lead to fluctuations in the quantity of sterling assets outstanding and to fluctuations in the nation's official holdings of foreign exchange. If demand increases from D_0 to D_1, the quantity of sterling assets increases from Q_0 to Q_1 and the exchange rate does not change. In a flexible exchange rate system (part b), the quantity of sterling assets is fixed so that the supply curve is vertical. An increase in the demand for sterling assets from D_0 to D_1 results only in an increase in the value of the pound – the exchange rate rises from $1.50 to $1.60. The quantity of sterling assets remains constant at Q_0. In a managed exchange rate system (part c), the Bank of England has an upward-sloping supply curve of sterling assets, so that if demand increases from D_0 to D_1, the pound sterling appreciates but the quantity of sterling assets supplied also increases – from Q_0 to Q_2. The increase in the quantity of sterling assets supplied moderates the rise in the value of the pound sterling but does not completely prevent it as in the case of fixed exchange rates.

The Market for Sterling

Let's now bring the demand and supply sides of the market for sterling assets together and determine the exchange rate. Figure 36.5 shows how the exchange rate is determined in the three systems for fixed, flexible and managed exchange rates. The demand side of the market is the same in the three cases but the supply side differs. First, let's look at a fixed exchange rate system such as that from the end of World War II to 1971.

Fixed Exchange Rate This case is illustrated in Figure 36.5(a). The supply curve of sterling is horizontal at the fixed exchange rate of $1.50 per pound. If the demand curve is D_0, the quantity of sterling assets is Q_0. An increase in demand to D_1 results in an increase in the quantity of sterling assets from Q_0 to Q_1 but no change in the exchange rate.

Flexible Exchange Rate Next look at Figure 36.5(b), which shows what happens in a flexible exchange rate system. In this case, the quantity of sterling assets supplied is fixed at Q_0, so the supply curve of sterling assets is vertical. If the demand curve for sterling is D_0, the exchange rate is $1.50 per pound. If the demand for sterling increases from D_0 to D_1, the exchange rate increases to $1.60 per pound.

Managed Exchange Rate Finally, consider a managed exchange rate system, which appears in Figure 36.5(c). Here, the supply curve is upward-sloping. When the demand curve is D_0, the exchange rate is $1.50 per pound. If demand increases to D_1, the dollar value of the pound rises but only to $1.55 per pound. Compared with the flexible exchange rate case, the same increase in demand results in a smaller increase in the exchange rate when it is managed. The reason for this is that the quantity supplied increases in the managed exchange rate case.

Exchange Rate System and Official Reserves The behaviour of the official financing balance (change in reserves) depends on the foreign exchange rate system. The official financing account of the balance of payments records the change in the country's official holdings (by the government and the Bank of England) of foreign currency. In a fixed exchange rate system (as shown in Figure 36.5(a)), every time the demand for sterling assets changes, the Bank must change the quantity of sterling assets supplied to match it. When the Bank has to increase the quantity of sterling assets supplied, it does so by offering sterling assets in exchange for foreign currency assets. In this case, the official holdings of foreign exchange reserves increase. If the demand for sterling assets decreases, the Bank must decrease the quantity of sterling assets supplied. To decrease the quantity of sterling supplied, the Bank buys pounds and pays for them with its foreign exchange reserves. In this case, official foreign exchange reserves decrease. Thus with a fixed exchange rate, fluctuations in the demand for sterling assets result in fluctuations in official reserves.

In a flexible exchange rate system, there is no central bank intervention in the foreign exchange market. Regardless of what happens to the demand for sterling, no action is taken to change the quantity of sterling supplied. Therefore there are no changes in the country's official reserves. In this case, the official financing balance is zero and there is no change in official foreign currency reserves.

With a managed exchange rate, official holdings of foreign exchange are adjusted to meet fluctuations in demand but in a less extreme manner than in a fixed exchange rate system. As a consequence, fluctuations in the official financing balance are smaller in a managed floating system than in a fixed exchange rate system.

The Exchange Rate in the Long Run We have seen how changes in the expected future exchange rate can influence the demand for sterling assets. If the exchange rate regime is floating or managed, we know that an expectation that the future exchange rate will rise results in a rightward shift of the demand for sterling assets and an appreciation of the exchange rate. So an expectation of a rise in the future exchange rate will result in a rise in the current exchange rate if the exchange rate is not fixed. But we have not said why the future exchange rate is expected to be different from the current exchange rate. However, before we discuss this we need to understand two important arguments.

First, we must recognize that the argument that the current exchange rate is influenced by the expected exchange rate in one month's time means that in turn the exchange rate in one month's time is influenced by the expectation of the exchange rate in two months' time. This argument can be extended to any future value of the exchange rate.

Second, we can appeal to rational expectations (we looked at this in Chapter 33, pp. 834–837). The expected exchange rate in one month's time will, on the average, be the actual exchange rate in one month's time. So the current exchange rate will depend partly on the expected exchange rate in one month's time. The expected future exchange rate will, on the average, be correct, and the expected future exchange rate will depend partly on the expected exchange rate further in the future. We can extend this argument to the point where the current exchange rate will depend partly on the expected exchange rate somewhere in the distant future. Another way of looking at it is that the current exchange rate is influenced by the expected exchange rate in the long-run.

Purchasing Power Parity Purchasing power parity (PPP) is a condition that holds when the prices of goods in different countries are equalized once adjustment is made for the exchange rate. For example, suppose the price of Levi jeans in the UK is £20. Suppose the same pair of jeans costs $30 in the United States, and the exchange rate is $1.50 per pound. Then we have PPP in Levi jeans. This means that the jeans can be bought for the same price in both countries once we take into account the exchange rate (£20 = $30 divided by 1.50).

PPP is a condition that results from the application of *the law of one price* and *arbitrage* in international trade. The law of one price simply states that two identical goods must sell for the same price. How do we know that the law of one price holds? Imagine what would happen if it did not. Suppose for some reason that Doc Marten boots can be bought for £5 less in Glasgow than in London. An enterprising person could buy Doc Marten boots in Glasgow and sell them at a higher price in London. The process of buying or selling something to exploit a price differential to make a riskless profit is known as arbitrage. What would be the effect of this arbitrage process on Doc Marten boots? The retailers of Doc Martens in Glasgow will face a run down of their stocks and will have to order more from the suppliers. The suppliers will face additional costs of diverting resources to meet the extra demand in Glasgow and will demand a higher price. In the meantime, shoe retailers in London will find that they are building up stocks as they will no longer be selling the same volume as in the past. In an attempt to move the stock they will lower the prices of Doc Martens in London. The result will be that the prices of Doc Martens in Glasgow and London will converge until it will no longer be profitable to ship the boots from one area to another. This occurs when the prices are the same. In reality small differences will exist to allow for the costs of transportation.

International Arbitrage The same process of arbitrage can be applied to trade across countries. Let's go back to the example of the Levi jeans. Suppose Levis are selling for £30 in the United Kingdom and $30 in the United States and the exchange rate is $1.50 per pound. It will pay to import Levis into the United Kingdom from the United States and to sell them for a profit. In the long run, this process will cause prices of Levis to change in the United Kingdom and in the United States. But imagine what happens when we apply this logic to many goods, not just Levis. Identical goods in the United States will be selling at a lower price than in the United Kingdom after allowing for the exchange rate. Firms in the United Kingdom will import more US goods and pay for them in dollars. At the same time, UK exporters will export fewer goods to the United States. The demand for dollar assets will rise and the demand for sterling assets will fall. Hence the price of sterling in terms of the dollar will decline. To go back to our example of the Levi jeans, PPP in Levis will be restored when the exchange rate falls to $1 per pound (£30 = $30 divided by $1 per pound). In other words, we can state that the price of goods in the United Kingdom measured in sterling $P(£)$ is equal to the price of goods in the United States measured in dollars $P(\$)$ divided by the exchange rate (S – dollars per pound):

$$P(£) = \frac{P(\$)}{S}$$

We can rearrange this equation to arrive at an expression for the exchange rate in the long-run:

$$S = \frac{P(\$)}{P(£)}$$

We now have a theory that explains what determines the exchange rate in the long run. The exchange rate will adjust so as to bring about PPP in the long run. So if the price of goods in the UK were higher than in the United States, the exchange rate with the dollar would decline in the long run. In reality there are many difficulties with the theory of PPP. There are difficulties in constructing comparable price indices between countries. The theory of PPP holds only for identical goods, but not all goods are identical – Levi jeans are an exception, not the rule. Similarly, not all goods are traded. Some goods are sold only in the United Kingdom and there is no international competition or arbitrage process that brings about a PPP in them. These goods are known as *non-traded goods*. A haircut is an often used as an example of a non-traded good. It is not possible to buy a cheap haircut in Spain and sell it at a profit in Sweden. Transport costs, taxes and tariffs are other factors that also reduce the convergence to PPP. However, the evidence that PPP holds on a long-run basis is strong.

Why is the Exchange Rate So Volatile?

There have been times during the 1970s, the early 1980s and early 1990s when the pound has moved dramatically. On some of these occasions sterling has depreciated spectacularly, but on other occasions it has appreciated strongly.

The main reason the exchange rate fluctuates so remarkably is that fluctuations in supply and demand are not always independent of each other. Sometimes a change in supply will trigger a change in demand that reinforces the effect of the change in supply. Let's see how these effects work by looking at two episodes, one in which sterling rose in value and one in which it fell.

An Appreciating Pound: 1979–81 Between 1979 and 1981, the value of sterling against the Deutschemark appreciated by over 17 per cent. Figure 36.6(a) explains why this happened. In 1979, the demand and supply curves were those labelled D_{79} and S_{79}. The Deutschemark rate was 3.89 – where the supply and demand curves intersect. The period between 1980 and 1981 was one of severe recession. This recession was brought about in part by the

Figure 36.6 Why the Exchange Rate is so Volatile

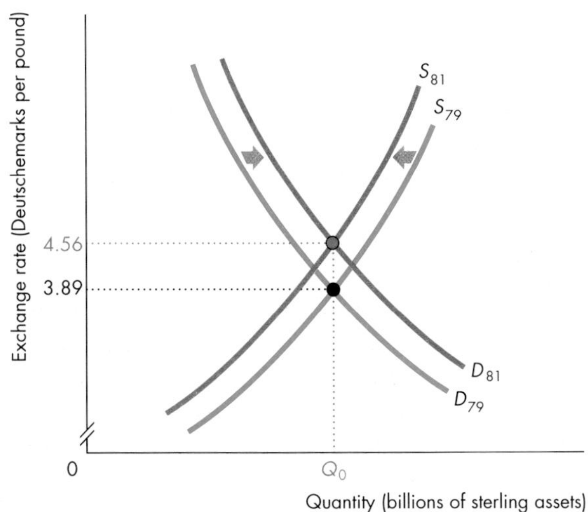

(a) 1979 to 1981

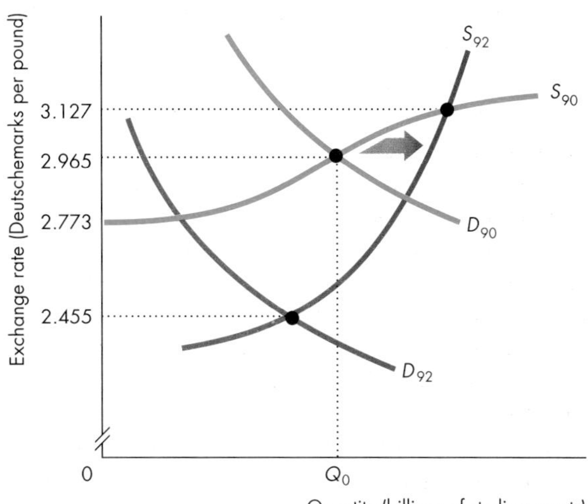

(b) 1990 to 1992

The exchange rate is volatile because shifts in the demand and supply curves for sterling assets are not independent of each other. Between 1979 and 1981 (part a), the DM–sterling exchange rate appreciated from 3.89 to 4.56. The supply curve of sterling assets shifted leftward and higher interest rates and expectations of a rise in the exchange rate induced an increase in demand for sterling assets, shifting the demand curve rightward. The result was a large appreciation of the pound. The rise in the price of oil also added to the expectation of a rise in the value of the pound sterling. Between October 1990 and October 1992 (in part b), the quantity of sterling assets increased and the supply curve of sterling shifted rightward. As the pound started to fall in value, further falls were expected so the demand for pounds sterling decreased and the demand curve shifted leftward. The result was a steep fall in the exchange rate, from DM2.965 in October 1990 to DM2.455 in October 1992.

tight monetary policy pursued by the new conservative government. The Bank of England raised interest rates sharply in November 1979, cutting back the supply of sterling assets. The direct effect was a shift in the supply curve from S_{79} to S_{81} – a decrease in the supply of sterling. But higher UK interest rates induced an increase in the demand for sterling assets. Furthermore, the tight monetary policy created expectations that inflation would fall in the future and that the fall in inflation would make UK inflation lower than inflation in the rest of the world. This means that people expected the UK price level to fall relative to the world price level. The implication of PPP is that the exchange rate was expected to rise in the long run. We know from our discussion of exchange rate expectations that the implication of an expected appreciation of the exchange rate in the long run is an expectation of a rise in the exchange rate in the near future, which causes the demand for sterling assets to rise even further. As a result the demand curve shifted from D_{79} to D_{81}. These two shifts reinforced each other, increasing the exchange rate to 4.56. But there were other factors that also contributed to the rise in the exchange rate. The oil shock of 1979 meant that UK exports of North Sea oil would result in higher dollar receipts, and a stronger current account added to the expectation of a rise in the value of sterling.

A Depreciating Pound: 1990–1992 There was a spectacular depreciation of the pound in terms of the Deutschemark from DM2.965 in October 1990 to DM2.455 in October 1992 – a fall of over 17 per cent. This fall came about in the following way. First, in October 1990, the United Kingdom was taken into the Exchange Rate Mechanism (ERM) of the European Monetary System (EMS) at a central parity of DM2.95. The ERM is like a fixed exchange rate system but with a band around the central parity in which the value of the currency is allowed to fluctuate. The United Kingdom entered the ERM with a band of ±6 per cent around the central parity of DM2.95. The demand and supply curves were those labelled D_{90} and S_{90} in Figure 36.6(b). The supply curve is shaped in this elongated reverse 'S' because it is meant to show the upper and lower bounds at which the Bank of England will support the currency around its central parity. The Deutschemark price of the pound – the price at which these two curves intersect – was DM2.965 per pound. In retrospect this was an unsustainable rate of exchange given the large current account deficit in 1989–90. To keep sterling at its central parity, the Bank had to raise interest rates and tighten monetary policy. The economy moved sharply into recession, raising expectations that interest rates would have to fall. The expectation of lower interest rates fuelled expectations of lower exchange rates in the future, causing the demand for sterling assets to fall and pushing the exchange rate to the bottom of the band. A large government budget deficit increased the supply of sterling assets and the supply of sterling assets curve shifted rightward from S_{90} to S_{92}. Because the expected future value of the pound fell, the demand for sterling assets decreased from D_{90} to D_{92}. The result of this combined increase in supply and decrease in demand was a dramatic fall in the value of the pound to DM2.455 on 16 September 1992.

Before completing this chapter let's look at two recent events that mark turning points in the international financial economy. The first is the Asian financial crisis. The Asian financial crisis saw sharp movements in far Eastern exchange rates, collapsing asset prices and a deflation that threatened the stability of the world economy. The second is the European Monetary Union. On 1 January 1999 eleven countries of the the Eurpean Union joined a single currency union. The creation of a new currency for Europe – the euro, is the realization of the dream of stronger economic and political union, and challenges the dominance of the US dollar as an international currency.

Review

- The exchange rate is determined by the demand for and supply of sterling.
- In a fixed exchange rate system, a change in the demand for sterling is matched by a change in the quantity of sterling supplied by the Bank of England and the exchange rate does not change.
- In a flexible exchange rate system, fluctuations in the exchange rate can be large because changes in supply change the expected future exchange rate and induce a change in demand that reinforces the effect of the change in supply.
- In a managed exchange rate system, the Bank of England tries to smooth fluctuations in the exchange rate by changing the quantity of sterling supplied when the demand for sterling changes but by less than in a fixed exchange rate system.

The Asian Crisis

We saw in Chapter 32, p. 806, that some economies in Asia have been catching up rapidly with the United States and Western Europe. In 1997 the economies of the far east suffered a strong financial shock that sent their economies into a severe recession. Real GDP in Korea, Thailand and Indonesia fell by 6.8 per cent, 15.5 per cent and 7 per cent respectively over 1998. What was the cause of this catastrophic collapse in the Tiger economies of the far east? There are three interconnected contributory factors. These are:

1 Financial fragility.
2 Overinvestment and excess capacity.
3 A pegged exchange rate.

Financial Fragility Financial fragility is the susceptibility of the financial system to collapse following a shock to the economy. Fragility occurs when the deregulation of a non-mature financial system leads to a rapid growth in bank credit and imprudent lending by banks and other financial intermediaries. Real estate values increased sharply feeding on the rapid growth of bank credit which in turn generated higher bank lending. Liberalization of the banking system was not followed through with other reforms. In particular, weak and inefficient financial intermediaries that existed under the former regime of tight regulation did not leave

Figure 36.7 The Movement of the Thai Baht, Korean Won and Indonesian Rupiah against the US Dollar

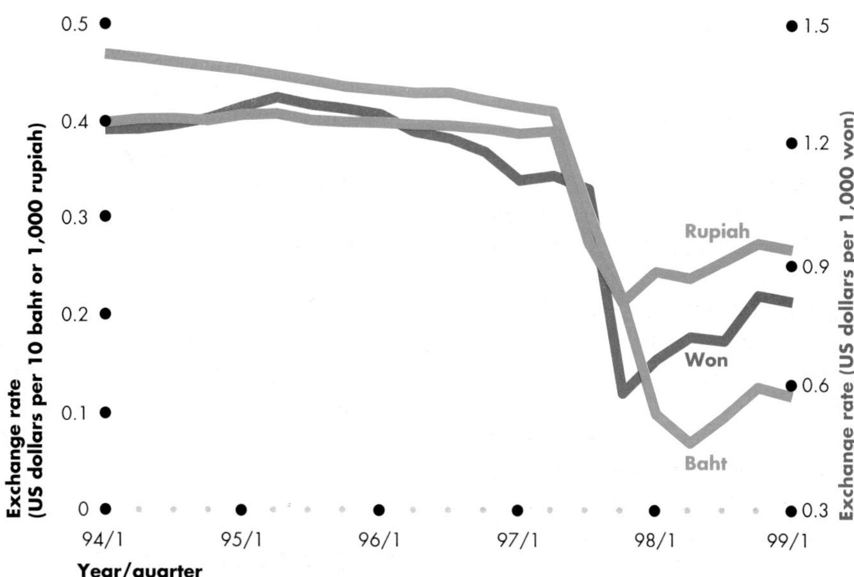

Before 1997, the Thai baht, Korean won and Indonesian rupiah were either pegged to the US dollar or managed within a narrow band. The elimination of exchange rate risk and the good opportunities for investment in the fast growing far eastern economies led to a strong inflow of capital from the developed economies. Once it was realized that the investments would not yield the returns expected by the investors, there was a strong capital outflow which represented a sharp fall in the demand for far eastern economies financial assets. The baht and rupiah were the first currencies to depreciate against the dollar. The won and several other currencies followed soon after.

Source: IMF.

the industry. Implicit or explicit government guarantees allowed inefficient banks to continue to operate and meet the growing demand for bank credit.

Overinvestment and Excess Capacity The rapid growth of the Asian economies in the 1980s and 1990s led investors to underestimate the risks of overinvestment and the resultant decline in its marginal rate of return. Expectations of high returns fuelled the demand for bank credit. The realization that overinvestment was leading to excess capacity, falling prices and declining returns caused investors to withdraw their funds as banks faced defaults and problems of solvency.

A Pegged Exchange Rate A pegged exchange rate to the US dollar reduced exchange rate risk and encouraged a rapid inflow of private capital. Much of this was short-term bank borrowing from the banks of the developed economies. Private capital inflows to the Asian economies excluding China[2] was \$77 billion in 1996. Once investors realized that the expected returns on investment were unlikely to materialize, the capital inflows swiftly became capital outflows. In the first half of 1997 capital flows were \$62 billion. In the second half, capital flows were –\$108 billion. The capital outflows represented a decrease in the demand for the Asian currencies and an increase in demand for US dollars. Figure 36.7 shows the movement of the Thai baht, Korean won and Indonesian rupiah against the US dollar. The fall in demand for the Asian currencies was caused by the expectation of a

2 India, Indonesia, Korea, Malaysia, Phillipines, Singapore, Taiwan and Thailand.

Table 36.5 Determination of the Euro Conversion Rates

Country	Currency unit	Units per euro
Belgium	franc	40.3399
Germany	deutschemark	1.95583
Spain	peseta	166.386
France	franc	6.55957
Ireland	pound	0.787564
Italy	lira	1936.27
Luxembourg	franc	40.3399
Netherland	guilder	2.20371
Austria	schilling	13.7603
Portugal	escudo	200.482
Finland	markka	5.94573

Source: ECB Press Release, 31 December 1998.

depreciation caused by Western investors divesting themselves of their Asian investments. An attempt by the governments of the Asian economies to defend the peg only exacerbated the outflow by increasing the expectation of a depreciation. In the second half of 1997, the capital outflows got so large, the central banks of the affected economies stopped intervening in the foreign exchange markets and allowed their currencies to float.

The collapse of the financial system led to a sharp fall in real estate values and a decrease in people's wealth which in turn resulted in a downward shift in aggregate demand. The fall in demand also reduced the demand for Western imports which would have had adverse effects on world economic activity if not for the Federal Reserve lowering interest rates and maintaining the domestic demand of the United States economy.

The European Monetary Union

On 1 January 1999 some 11 countries of the European Union formed a monetary union (euroland) whereby the value of the currency of each participating economy was irrevocably fixed against the euro. Table 36.5 shows the exchange rates for the 11 participating countries.

Monetary policy for the 11 countries would be conducted by the European Central Bank. The amendment to the Treaty of Rome in 1991 at Maastricht in the Netherlands laid the foundations for Economic and Monetary Union in Europe (**EMU**). A single currency is the natural outcome of closer economic integration and the development of the *Single European Market*. There are good arguments in favour of a single currency. Since the purpose of a single European market is to remove all barriers to trade and to promote competition, a single currency has the advantage of ensuring that all prices in the European Union will be denominated in a common unit and the process of arbitrage will enforce the law of one price, just like our example of the Doc Marten boots in Glasgow and London. Countries will not be able to exploit a competitive advantage by artificially lowering the price of their exports through devaluation.

Other arguments are that a single currency will remove foreign exchange transactions costs – the costs associated with exchanging pesetas for francs at a bank or travel agent, such as commission charges or the margin between buy and sell exchange rates we see posted in banks and currency exchanges. The removal of these costs will benefit the consumer, who will know that a eurofranc in France will buy the same as a euromark in Germany. A single currency will also remove foreign exchange risk associated with exports and imports. For example, Alpine Gardens, an Austrian garden company, has ordered a consignment of garden gnomes to be supplied by a UK company, Britannia Gnomes Ltd, in three months' time. The contract and the price are set today, but payment will take place in three months' time. Alpine Gardens has to pay £50,000 in three months' time. To protect itself against an adverse change in the exchange rate, it pays a small premium to insure against an exchange rate change[3]. It is argued that the reduction in exchange rate risk could improve trade between EU countries. The total benefit of the removal of transactions costs associated with currency exchange has been

3 Alpine Gardens buys sterling in the forward market, paying a commission to the foreign currency operator which ensures the delivery of £50,000 in three months' time at an exchange rate specified today irrespective of what the exchange rate will be in three months' time.

estimated as 0.4 per cent of EU GDP[4]. The removal of exchange risk will mean that many large companies would no longer need to diversify their operations across boundaries but consolidate them on one location. This will cause a significant redistribution of wealth and jobs in euroland.

While the arguments in favour of a single currency are largely microeconomic, the arguments against are largely macroeconomic. There is the criticism of the 'one size fits all' approach to monetary policy. The main cost of EMU is the loss of an independent monetary policy and the adoption of strict fiscal controls in acccordance with the stability pact. But how important is the loss of an independent monetary policy and what difference will the stability pact make? It depends on the frequency of the shocks that hit one country that do not hit other euroland countries. For example, if Italy were in recession but the other countries in euroland were not, it would not be possible for interest rates to be lowered, the exchange rate to be devalued or fiscal policy to be expansionary in Italy to stimulate the economy. So how could the economy recover? The Delors Report[5] states that an EMU will consist not only of a common market with free mobility of capital and labour, but also of a common competition policy and a common regional policy. A common regional policy implies that fiscal transfers can be made to Italy from the other countries of the European Union. However, before fiscal transfers can be made from some countries in euroland to others, there has to be a political consensus on the part of the donor countries and the receiver countries, which in turn can only occur if there is a political union. This is perhaps the greatest objection to EMU for some people. A single currency implies a political union. A loss of monetary sovereignty implies a loss of political sovereignty.

Review

- The Asian financial crisis was precipitated by an over expansion of credit and overinvestment resulting in excess capacity and declining expected returns on investment.
- The exchange rate peg that the Asian countries followed made it easier for capital flow in and flow out with a change in investor sentiment.
- The Stability Pact specifies a target for the participating countries budget deficits in Euroland. The EMU implies a loss of monetary sovereignty.

You've now discovered what determines a country's current account balance and the value of its currency. You have used what you have learned to examine the sterling exchange rate movements of 1979–81, the collapse of the ERM and the Asian financial crisis. You've examined the implications of EMU. *Reading Between the Lines* on pp. 942–943 examines the value of the euro against the pound sterling and its short-term determinants.

4 Commission of the European Communities, 'One Market, One Money: An Evaluation of the Potential Benefits and Costs of Forming an Economic and Monetary Union', 1990, *European Economy*, 44, Brussels.
5 Committee for the Study of Economic and Monetary Union, 'Report on Economic and Monetary Union in the European Community', 1989, Luxembourg.

Summary

Key Points

Financing International Trade (pp. 918–923)

- International trade, borrowing and lending are financed using foreign currency.
- A country's international transactions are recorded in its balance of payments accounts.
- The current account records receipts and expenditures connected with the sale and purchase of goods and services, as well as investment income and net transfers to and from the rest of the world; the capital and financial account records international borrowing and lending transactions.

Sterling in the Global Market (pp. 923–926)

- Foreign currency is obtained in exchange for domestic currency in the foreign exchange market.
- The exchange rate can be fixed, flexible or managed. A fixed exchange rate is one that is pegged by a central bank.
- A flexible exchange rate is one that adjusts freely with no central bank intervention in the foreign exchange market.
- A managed exchange rate is one in which the central bank smoothes out fluctuations but does not peg the rate at a fixed value.

Exchange Rate Determination (pp. 926–934)

- The exchange rate is determined by the demand for and supply of sterling assets. The quantity of sterling assets demanded, a stock, is greater the lower the exchange rate. A change in the exchange rate brings a movement along the demand curve for sterling.
- Changes in UK GDP, the expected future exchange rate and the UK interest rate differential change the demand for sterling and bring a shift in the demand curve.
- The supply of sterling assets depends on the exchange rate system.
- In a fixed exchange rate system, the supply curve is horizontal; in a flexible exchange rate system, the supply curve is vertical; in a managed exchange rate system, the supply curve is upward-sloping. The position of the supply curve depends on the government's budget and the Bank of England's monetary policy.
- The larger the budget deficit or the greater the purchases of foreign currency by the Bank of England, the greater is the supply of sterling.

The Asian Crisis (pp. 934–936)

- Three interconnected factors caused the Asian Crisis of 1997/1998: financial fragility, overinvestment and excess capacity and a pegged exchange rate.

The European Monetary Union (pp. 936–937)

- The EMU came into being on 1 January 1999 with 11 countries of the EU joining the first wave of the currency union.
- The arguments in favour of a single currency are mostly microeconomic.
- The arguments against are mostly macroeconomic and political.

Key Figures and Tables 

Key Terms

Balance of payments accounts, 918
Capital and Financial account, 918
Change in reserve assets, 918
Creditor nation, 920
Currency depreciation, 925
Current account, 918
Debtor nation, 920
European Monetary Union (EMU), 936
Fixed exchange rate, 924
Flexible exchange rate, 924
Foreign exchange market, 923
Foreign exchange rate, 924
Managed exchange rate, 924
Net borrower, 920
Net lender, 920
Private sector surplus or deficit, 922
Quantity of sterling assets, 926

Review Questions

1 What are the three accounts that make up the balance of payments accounts?

2 What are the transactions recorded in a country's current account, capital and financial account and change in reserve assets?

3 What is the relationship between the balance on the current account, the capital and financial account, and the change in reserve assets?

4 Distinguish between a country that is a net borrower and one that is a creditor. Are net borrowers always creditors? Are creditors always net borrowers?

5 What is the connection between a country's current account balance, the government's budget deficit and the private sector surplus?

6 Why do fluctuations in the government budget balance lead to fluctuations in the current account balance?

7 What is a currency appreciation? What is a currency depreciation?

8 Explain why the quantity of sterling demanded in the foreign exchange market depends on the exchange rate.

9 Explain why the quantity of sterling supplied in the foreign exchange market depends on the exchange rate.

10 Distinguish among the three exchange rate systems: fixed, flexible and managed.

11 Review the main influences on the quantity of sterling assets that people demand.

12 Review the influences on the supply of sterling assets.

13 How does the supply curve of sterling differ in the three exchange rate systems?

14 Why does the foreign exchange value of sterling fluctuate so much?

15 What is purchasing power parity? Give an example of purchasing power parity.

16 How can the Bank of England limit the fluctuations in the pound sterling?

Problems

1 The citizens of Silecon, whose currency is the grain, conduct the following transactions in 1999:

Item	Billions of grains
Imports of goods and services	350
Exports of goods and services	500
Borrowing from the rest of the world	60
Lending to the rest of the world	200
Increase in official holdings of foreign currency	10

a Set out the three balance of payments accounts for Silecon.
b Does Silecon have a flexible exchange rate?

2 The figure at the bottom of the next page shows the flows of income and expenditure in Dream Land in 1999. The amounts are in billions of euros. GDP in Dream Land is €60 billion.

a Calculate Dream Land's net exports.
b Calculate saving in Dream Land.
c Calculate the private sector deficit.
d Calculate the government sector deficit.
e Show the relationship between your answers to a, c and d.

3 You are told the following about Ecflex, a country with a flexible exchange rate whose currency is the band:

Item	Billion bands
GDP	100
Consumption expenditure	60
Government purchases of goods and services	24
Investment	22
Exports of goods and services	20
Government budget deficit	4

Calculate the following for Ecflex:

a Imports of goods and services.
b Current account balance.
c Capital account balance.
d Taxes (net of transfer payments).
e Private sector deficit/surplus.

4 A country's currency appreciates and its holdings of foreign currency reserves increase. What can you say about the following:

a The exchange rate system being pursued by the country.
b The country's current account.
c The change in the country's reserve assets.

5 The foreign exchange market is shown in the figure. The demand for pounds sterling decreases from D_0 to D_1.

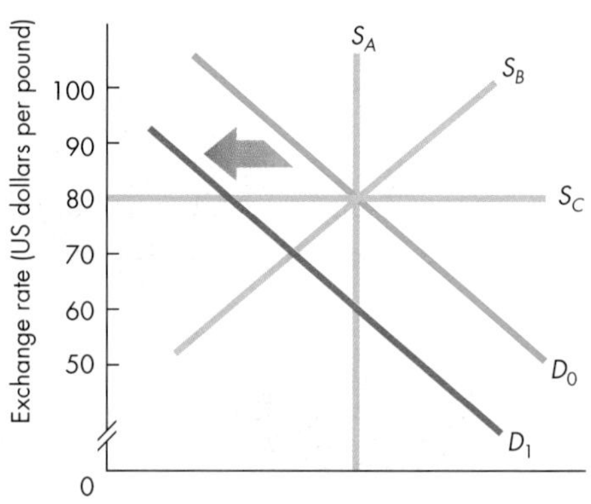

a Explain the influences on the market that might have caused this fall in the demand for pounds sterling.
b Which curve is the supply of pounds sterling if the exchange rate is fixed? Explain what happens to the exchange rate and the balance for official financing account in this case when the demand for pounds sterling decreases from D_0 to D_1.
c Which curve is the supply of pounds sterling if the exchange rate is flexible? Explain what happens to the exchange rate and the balance for official financing account in this case when the demand for pounds sterling decreases from D_0 to D_1.
d Which curve is the supply of pounds sterling if the exchange rate is managed? Explain what happens to the exchange rate and the balance for official financing account in this case when the demand for pounds sterling decreases from D_0 to D_1.

6 Study *Reading Between the Lines* on pp. 942–943 and then answer the following questions.

a What events in the foreign exchange market does the news article describe?
b What are the fundamental reasons for the weakness of the euro?
c What other explanations does the article give for the fall in the value of the euro?
d How can the ECB influence the value of the euro?

7 Use the link on the Parkin, Powell and Matthews Web site to get recent data on the exchange rate of the US dollar against the pound sterling and the Japanese yen. Then:

a Use the demand and supply model of the foreign exchange market to explain the changes (or absence of changes) in the exchange rates.
b What specific events might have changed exchange rate expectations?
c What forces might have prevented the exchange rates from changing?
d What information would you need to be able to determine whether central bank intervention has prevented either exchange rate from changing by as much as it otherwise would have?

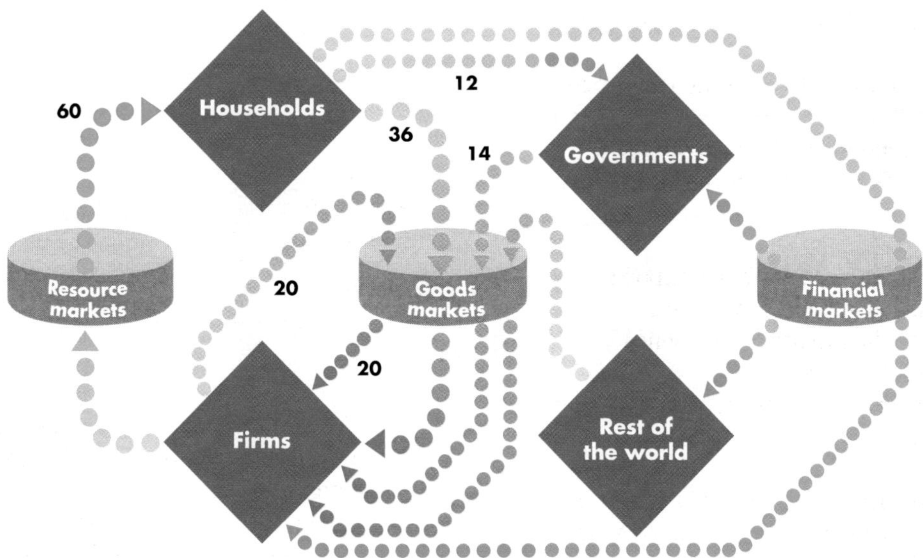

W http://www.econ100.com

Foreign Exchange Markets in Action

Evening Standard, 27 May 1999

Parity with dollar edges closer as euro agony goes on

Jane Padgham

The battered euro plunged to yet another record low against the dollar today, with the market now setting its sights on driving it to parity.

Overnight trade in New York had sent the currency beyond yesterday's lows, before selling continued in Asia. As European markets opened, a fresh wave of selling propelled the euro to $1.0407, more than 12% below the highs at its launch.

Experts blamed a slew of negative factors. The slowdown in the eurozone economies, fears of an escalation of the war in Kosovo and the authorities' apparent indifference about the euro's slide, were all exerting downward pressure.

Today it emerged that even the relatively buoyant French economy is slowing, with output up only 0.3% in the first quarter compared with 0.7% at the end of last year.

Against this fundamental back-drop, the near-term outlook for the euro remains bleak.

A host of European officials again said they were not concerned about the euro's slump, insisting it had the potential to recover.

Bank of England chief Eddie George told MPs that last year's global economic turmoil was contributing to imbalances in the eurozone. "Now is not necessarily a typical representation of the kind of tensions that are likely to occur. The severity of the slowdown is pretty unusual," he said.

The Essence of the Story

- The value of the euro has fallen 12 per cent against the dollar since 1 January 1999.
- The fundamental reason for the weakness of the euro is the slowdown in the eurozone economy. Even the relatively buoyant French economy has slowed in the first quarter of 1999.
- Other factors that have contributed to the weakness of the euro is the Kosovo crisis. The crisis on Europe's doorstep has been the source of added of political risk.
- The apparent indifference of the ECB to the slide in the euro has also added to the weakness of the euro.
- Eddie George, the Governor of the Bank of England, said that the economic turmoil of the previous year has contributed to the economic imbalance in the eurozone.

Economic Analysis

■ The value of the euro had fallen to \$1.041 by the end of May 1999. Compared with a value of \$1.185 on 1 January 1999, when the euro came into existence, this represented a 12 per cent drop in its value.

■ First, it is important to check that the weakness of the euro against the \$ is not just the mirror effect of the strength of the \$ against all currencies. Figure 1 shows the movement of the euro against the US \$, the pound sterling and the Japanese yen.

■ The euro has fallen against all three currencies although not by the same amount. It has fallen more against the US \$ than the Japanese yen or UK £. The strength of the US \$ is partly the reason for the fall in the value of the euro against the \$.

■ The fundamental factor in the fall in the euro is the slowdown in the eurozone countries. Figure 2 shows the rate of growth of real GDP in the four quarters to 1999 Q1 for the USA and the eurozone economies. The demand for dollars has risen but the demand for euros has fallen.

■ Figure 3 shows the demand for euros relative to the US dollar falls from D_{Jan} to D_{May}.

■ But a second factor that has contributed to the fall in the demand for euros has been the increase in political risk caused by the Kosovo crisis. The war in the Balkans has put political pressure on the German and Italian governments who both need the support of smaller parties to remain in power.

■ A third factor is the apparent indifference of the ECB to the slide in the euro which means that the financial market does not expect the euro to stabilize in the near future. The expectation of a continued fall in the euro also adds to the fall in demand.

■ A fourth factor which is not mentioned in the article is that the ECB lowered the rate of interest in late April in response to the slowdown in the eurozone. The fall in the rate of interest below that of the US has also contributed to the fall in demand.

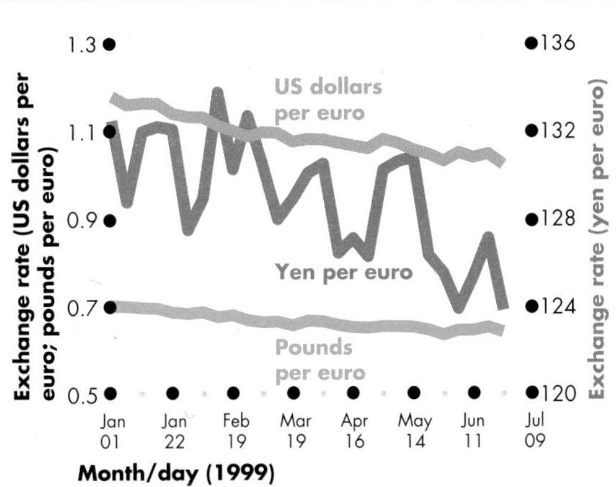

Figure 1 Foreign exchange value of the euro

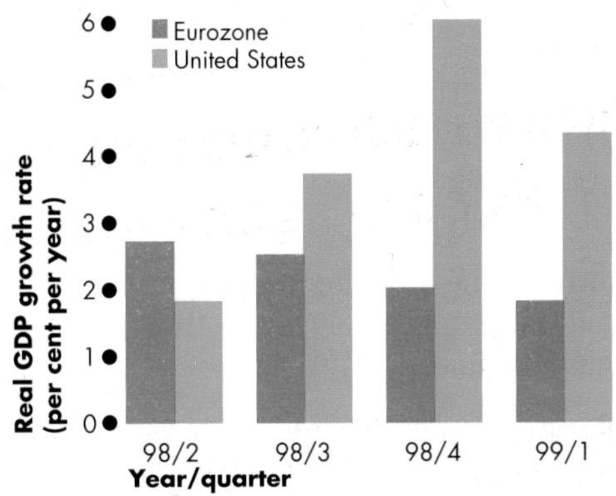

Figure 2 Eurozone and US real GDP growth

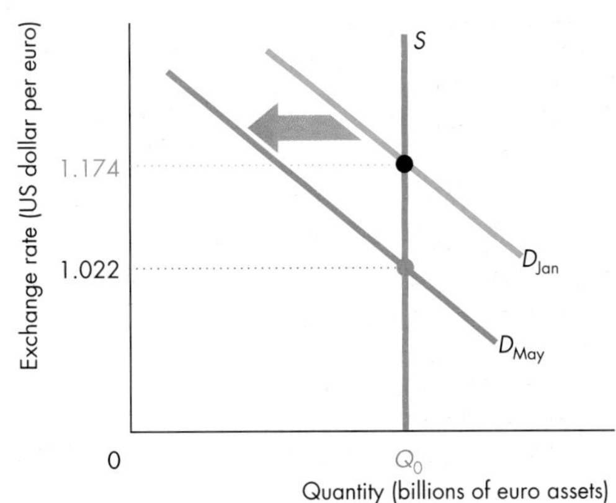

Figure 3 Foreign exchange market

GLOSSARY

Above full-employment equilibrium A situation in which macroeconomic equilibrium occurs at a level of real GDP above long-run real GDP.

Absolute advantage A person has an absolute advantage in the production of two goods if by using the same quantities of inputs, that person can produce more of both goods than another person. A country has an absolute advantage if its output per unit of inputs of all goods is larger than that of another country.

Aggregate demand The relationship between the aggregate quantity of goods and services demanded (real GDP demanded) and the price level (the GDP deflator).

Aggregate hours The total number of hours worked by all the people employed, both full-time and part-time, during a year.

Aggregate planned expenditure The expenditure that economic agents (households, firms, governments and foreigners) plan to undertake in given circumstances.

Aggregate production function The relationship that shows how the maximum real GDP attainable varies as quantities of factors of production vary.

Allocative efficiency A situation that occurs when no resources are wasted – when no one can be made better off without someone else being made worse off. Allocative efficiency is also called Pareto efficiency.

Arc elasticity of demand The value of elasticity of demand between two points calculated by the average price method.

Automatic fiscal policy A change in fiscal policy that is triggered by the state of the economy.

Autonomous expenditure The sum of those components of aggregate planned expenditure that are not influenced by real GDP.

Average cost pricing rule A rule that sets price equal to average total cost.

Average fixed cost Total fixed cost per unit of output – total fixed cost divided by output.

Average product The average productivity of a factor of production – total product divided by the quantity of the factor employed.

Average revenue The revenue per unit of output sold – total revenue divided by the quantity sold. Average revenue also equals price.

Average total cost Total cost per unit of output.

Average variable cost Total variable cost per unit of output.

Balance of payments accounts A country's record of international trading, borrowing and lending.

Balance of trade The value of exports minus the value of imports.

Balanced budget A government budget in which tax revenues and expenditures are equal.

Balanced budget multiplier The amount by which a simultaneous and equal change in goverment purchases and taxes is multiplied to determine the change in equilibrium expenditure.

Bank A private firm licensed by the Bank of England under the Banking Act of 1987 to take deposits and make loans and operate in the United Kingdom.

Bank of England The central bank of the United Kingdom.

Barriers to entry Legal or natural impediments protecting a firm from competition from potential new entrants.

Barter The direct exchange of one good or service for other goods and services.

Below full-employment equilibrium A macroeconomic equilibrium in which potential GDP exceeds real GDP.

Bilateral monopoly A situation in which there is a single seller (a monopoly) and a single buyer (a monopsony).

Black market An illegal trading arrangement in which buyers and sellers do business at a price higher than the legally imposed price ceiling.

Bond A legally enforceable debt obligation to pay specified amounts of money at specified future dates.

Bond market A market in which the bonds of corporations and governments are traded.

Budget deficit A government's budget balance that is negative – expenditures exceed tax revenues.

Budget line The limits to a household's consumption choices.

Budget surplus A government's budget balance that is positive – tax revenues exceed expenditures.

Building society A financial intermediary that traditionally obtained its funds from savings deposits (sometimes called share accounts) and that made long-term mortgage loans to home buyers.

Business cycle The periodic but irregular up-and-down movement in economic activity, measured by fluctuations in real GDP and other macroeconomic variables.

Capital The equipment, buildings, tools and manufactured goods that are used in the production of goods and services.

Capital and financial account A record of a country's international borrowing and lending transactions.

Capital accumulation The growth of capital resources.

Capital stock The stock of plant, equipment, buildings (including residential housing) and unsold finished goods.

Capture theory A theory of regulation that states that the regulations are supplied to satisfy the demand of producers to maximize producer surplus – to maximize economic profit.

Cartel A group of firms that has entered into a collusive agreement to restrict output so as to increase prices and profits.

Central bank A public authority charged with regulating and controlling a country's monetary policy and financial institutions and markets.

Central plan A detailed economic blueprint that sets out *what* will be produced, *how*, *when* and *where* it will be produced, and *who* will get what is produced, and that establishes a set of sanctions and rewards designed to ensure that the plan is fulfilled as fully as possible.

Ceteris paribus Other things being equal – all other relevant things remaining the same.

Change in demand A change in buyers' plans that occurs when some influence on those plans other than the price of the good changes. It is illustrated by a shift of the demand curve.

Change in supply A change in sellers' plans that occurs when some influence on those plans other than the price of the good changes. It is illustrated by a shift of the supply curve.

Change in the quantity demanded A change in buyers' plans that occurs when the price of a good changes but all other influences on buyers' plans remain unchanged. It is illustrated by a movement along the demand curve.

Change in the quantity supplied A change in sellers' plans that occurs when the price of a good changes but all other influences on sellers' plans remain unchanged. It is illustrated by a movement along the supply curve.

Classical growth theory A theory of economic growth based on the view that population growth is determined by the level of income per person.

Coase theorem The proposition that if property rights exist and transactions costs are low, private transactions are efficient – equivalently, there are no externalities.

Collective bargaining A process of negotiation between representatives of employers and unions.

Collusive agreement An agreement between two (or more) producers to restrict output so as to increase prices and profits.

Commodity money A physical commodity that is valued in its own right and is also used as a means of payment.

Common Agricultural Policy (CAP) The agricultural policy implemented by the European Union in member countries.

Company A firm owned by two or more shareholders.

Comparative advantage A person or country has a comparative advantage in an activity if that person or country can perform the activity at a lower opportunity cost than anyone else or any other country.

Competition A situation where individuals and firms are forced into a contest for the command of scarce resources because of scarcity.

Complement A good that is used in conjunction with another good.

Constant returns to scale Technological conditions under which a given percentage increase in all the firm's inputs results in the firm's output increasing by the same percentage.

Consumer efficiency A situation that occurs when consumers cannot make themselves better off by reallocating their budgets.

Consumer equilibrium A situation in which a consumer has allocated his or her income in the way that maximizes his or her utility.

Consumer surplus The value that the consumer places on a good minus the price paid for it.

Consumption demand The relationship between consumption expenditure and the real interest rate, other things remaining the same.

Consumption expenditure The total payment made by households for consumption goods and services.

Consumption function The relationship between consumption expenditure and disposable income, other things remaining the same.

Contestable market A market structure in which there is one firm (or a small number of firms) and because of freedom of entry and exit, the firm (or firms) faces competition from potential entrants and so operates like a perfectly competitive firm.

Contractionary fiscal policy A decrease in government expenditures or an increase in tax revenues.

Convertible paper money A paper claim to a commodity (such as gold) that circulates as a means of payment.

Copyright A government-sanctioned exclusive right granted to the inventor of a good, service, or productive process to produce, use, and sell the invention for a given number of years.

Corporation A large-scale firm owned by shareholders whose liability is legally limited to the value of their initial investment.

Cost-push inflation Inflation that results from an initial increase in costs.

Creditor nation A country that has invested more in the rest of the world than other countries have invested in it.

Cross elasticity of demand The responsiveness of the demand for a good to the price of a substitute or complement, other things remaining the same. It is calculated as the percentage change in the quantity demanded of the good divided by the percentage change in the price of the substitute or complement.

Cross-section graph A graph that shows the values of an economic variable for different groups in a population at a point in time.

Crowding out The tendency for an increase in government purchases of goods and services to bring a decrease in investment.

Currency The notes and coins that we use today.

Currency depreciation The fall in the value of one currency in terms of another currency.

Currency drain An increase in currency held outside banks.

Current account A record of receipts from the sale of goods and services to foreigners, the payments for goods and services bought from foreigners, the interest income received from and paid to foreigners, and gifts and other transfers (such as foreign aid payments) received from and paid to foreigners.

Cyclical deficit A budget deficit that is present only because real GDP is less than potential GDP and taxes are temporarily low and transfer payments are temporarily high.

Cyclical unemployment The unemployment arising from the slowdown in the pace of economic expansion.

Cyclically adjusted deficit The budget deficit that would occur if the economy were at full employment.

Deadweight loss A measure of allocative inefficiency. It is equal to the loss in total surplus (consumer surplus plus producer surplus) that results from producing less than the efficient level of output.

Debtor nation A country that during its entire history has borrowed more from the rest of the world than it has lent to it.

Decentralized planning An economic system that combines state ownership of capital and land with incentives based on a mixture of market prices and laws and regulations.

Decreasing returns to scale Technological conditions under which a given percentage increase in all the firm's inputs results in the firm's output increasing by a smaller percentage.

Demand The relationship between the quantity of a good that consumers plan to buy and the price of the good, with all other influences on buyers' plans remaining the same. It is described by a demand schedule and illustrated by a demand curve.

Demand curve A curve that shows the relationship between the quantity demanded of a good and its price, all other influences on consumers' planned purchases remaining the same.

Demand-pull inflation Inflation that results from an initial increase in aggregate demand.

Deposit money Deposits at banks and other financial institutions; an accounting entry in an electronic database in the banks' and other financial institutions' computers.

Deposit multiplier The amount by which an increase in bank reserves is multiplied to calculate the increase in bank deposits.

Depreciation The decrease in the value of capital stock or the value of a durable input that results from wear and tear and the passage of time.

Deregulation The removal of regulatory rules to restrict or control economic activity in price setting, product standards, trading standards and the conditions under which firms can enter an industry.

Derived demand Demand for an item not for its own sake but for use in the production of goods and services.

Desired reserve ratio Ratio of reserves to deposits that banks consider as prudent to hold in order to meet withdrawals and to carry on their business.

Diminishing marginal rate of substitution The general tendency for the marginal rate of substitution of one good for another to diminish as a consumer increases consumption of the first good.

Diminishing marginal returns The tendency for the marginal product of a variable factor eventually to diminish as additional units of the variable factor are employed.

Diminishing marginal utility The marginal utility that a consumer gets from a good decreases as more of the good is consumed.

Direct relationship A relationship between two variables that move in the same direction.

Discount rate The interest rate at which the central bank stands ready to lend reserves to commercial banks.

Discounting The conversion of a future amount of money to its present value.

Discouraged workers People who do not have jobs and would like to work but have stopped seeking work.

Discretionary fiscal policy A policy action that is initiated by the Chancellor of the Exchequer.

Discretionary policy A policy that responds to the state of the economy in a possibly unique way that uses all the information available, including perceived lessons from past 'mistakes'.

Discrimination Occurs in the labour market when employment decisions are taken on the basis of ethnic origin or gender rather than ability.

Diseconomies of scale Technological conditions under which long-run average cost increases as output increases.

Dominant strategy equilibrium The outcome of a game in which there is a single best strategy (a dominant strategy) for each player, regardless of the strategy of the other players.

Dumping The sale of a good in a foreign market for a lower price than in the domestic market or for a lower price than its cost of production.

Duopoly A market structure in which two producers of a good or service compete.

Dynamic comparative advantage A comparative advantage that a person or country possesses as a result of having specialized in a particular activity and then, as a result of learning-by-doing, becoming the producer with the lowest opportunity cost.

Economic activity rate The state of the labour market is indicated by this, the employment-to-population ratio and the unemployment rate.

Economic depreciation The decrease in the market price of a piece of capital over a given period.

Economic efficiency A situation that occurs when the cost of producing a given output is as low as possible.

Economic growth The expansion of production possibilities that results from capital accumulation and technological change.

Economic information Data on prices, quantities and qualities of goods and services and factors of production.

Economic model A description of some aspect of the economic world that includes only those features of the world that are needed for the purpose at hand.

Economic profit A firm's total revenue minus its opportunity cost.

Economic rent The income received by the owner of a factor of production in excess of the amount required to induce that owner to offer the factor for use.

Economic stability The absence of wide fluctuations in the economic growth rate, the level of employment and average prices.

Economic theory A generalization that summarizes what we think we understand about the economic choices that people make and the performance of industries and entire economies.

Economics The study of the choices people make to cope with scarcity.

Economies of scale Technological conditions under which long-run average cost decreases as output increases.

Economies of scope Decreases in average total cost made possible by increasing the range of goods produced.

Economy A mechanism that allocates scarce resources among competing uses.

Efficiency A point in production where it is not possible to produce more of one good without producing less of some other good.

Efficiency wage The wage rate that maximizes profit.

Efficient choice Choice which leads to the production of the most highly valued goods and services and the efficient use of resources.

Efficient market A market in which the actual price embodies all currently available relevant information.

Elastic Where a small percentage change in price results in a proportionately larger change in the quantity demanded.

Elasticity of supply The responsiveness of the quantity supplied of a good to a change in its price, other things remaining the same.

Emission charges Any form of pollution control that uses the market to create incentives for producers to cut pollution emissions.

Emission standards Pollution control in the form of regulations limiting the quantity of pollution emissions.

Employment-to-population ratio The percentage of people of working age who have jobs.

Entrants People who enter the workforce.

Entrepreneurial ability A special type of human resource that organizes the other three factors of production – labour, land and capital – and makes business decisions, innovates and bears business risk.

Environment capital Includes elements of land which are lost forever when used in the production process as well as the degree of biodiversity among species and the ability of the environment to absorb waste from production.

Equal pay for equal worth Where employees are paid the same wage for different jobs considered to be of comparable worth.

Equation of exchange An equation that states that the quantity of money multiplied by the velocity of circulation equals GDP.

Equilibrium expenditure The level of aggregate planned expenditure that equals real GDP.

Equilibrium price The price at which the quantity demanded equals the quantity supplied.

Equilibrium quantity The quantity bought and sold at the equilibrium price.

Equity In economics, equity has two meanings: economic justice or fairness and the owner's stake in a business.

Equity withdrawal Borrowing by owner–occupiers from the mortgage issuer against the value of their home without actually moving house.

European Currency Unit (ECU) A composite currency unit made up of the currencies of the member countries of the European Union.

European Monetary System (EMS) The system by which members of the European Union cooperate on monetary matters to achieve exchange rate stability.

European Monetary Union (EMU) A currency union of all participating member countries of the European Union, where a single currency, the Euro, will replace individual country currencies.

Excess reserves A bank's actual reserves minus its required reserves.

Exchange efficiency A situation in which a good or service is exchanged at a price that equals both the marginal social benefit and the marginal social cost of the good or service.

Exchange Rate Mechanism (ERM) A system of pegged exchange rates among participating currencies. It is a parity grid system where each currency has a set of bilateral central parities and a band by which it is allowed to float.

Excise tax A tax on the sale of a good or service. The tax is paid when the good or service is bought.

Exhaustible natural resources Natural resources that can be used only once and that cannot be replaced once they have been used.

Expansion A business cycle phase in which there is a speedup in the pace of economic activity.

Expansionary fiscal policy An increase in government expenditure or a decrease in tax revenues.

Expected utility The average utility arising from all possible outcomes.

Exports The goods and services that we sell to people in other countries.

External benefits Benefits that accrue to members of the society other than the buyer of the good.

External costs Costs that are borne by members of society other than the producer of the good.

External diseconomies Factors outside the control of a firm that raise the firm's costs as the industry produces a larger output.

External economies Factors beyond the control of a firm that lower the firm's costs as the industry produces a larger output.

Externality A cost or a benefit arising from an economic activity that affects people other than those who decide the scale of the activity.

Factors of production The economy's productive resources – land, labour, capital and entrepreneurial ability.

Feedback-rule policy A rule that specifies how policy actions respond to changes in the state of the economy.

Fiat money An intrinsically worthless (or almost worthless) commodity that serves the functions of money.

Financial capital The supply of funds by households to firms for the purchase of capital, either directly through share ownership or indirectly through the financial and banking system.

Financial innovation The development of new financial products – new ways of borrowing and lending.

Financial intermediary An institution that receives deposits and makes loans.

Firm An institution that hires factors of production and that organizes those factors to produce and sell goods and services.

Fiscal policy The government's attempt to influence the economy by varying its purchases of goods and services and taxes to smooth the fluctuations in aggregate expenditure; use of the government budget to achieve macroeconomic objectives such as full employment, sustained long-term economic growth and price level stability.

Five-firm concentration ratio The percentage of the value of sales accounted for by the largest five firms in one industry.

Fixed cost The cost of a fixed input; a cost that is independent of the output level.

Fixed exchange rate A system in which the value of a country's currency is pegged by the country's central bank.

Fixed-rule policy A rule that specifies an action to be pursued independently of the state of the economy.

Flexible exchange rate A system in which the value of a country's currency is determined by market forces in the absence of central bank intervention.

Flow A quantity per unit of time.

Foreign exchange market The market in which the currency of one country is exchanged for the currency of another.

Foreign exchange rate The price at which one currency exchanges for another.

Free rider A person who consumes a good without paying for it.

Frictional unemployment Unemployment arising from normal labour turnover – new entrants are constantly coming into the labour market, and firms are constantly laying off workers and hiring new workers.

Full employment A situation which occurs when the unemployment rate equals the natural rate of unemployment – when all unemployment is frictional and structural and there is no cyclical unemployment.

Full employment equilibrium Macroeconomic equilibrium in which real GDP equals potential GDP.

Futures market An organized market operated on a futures exchange in which large-scale contracts for the future delivery of goods can be exchanged.

Fundamental economic problem How to use limited resources to produce and consume the most highly valued goods and services.

Game theory A method of analysing strategic behaviour.

GDP deflator A price index that measures the average level of the prices of all goods and services that make up GDP.

General Agreement on Tariffs and Trade An international agreement that limits government intervention to restrict international trade.

Gold standard A monetary system with fractionally backed convertible paper in which a currency could be converted into gold at a guaranteed value on demand.

Government budget Finances the activities of the government.

Government debt The total amount of borrowing that the government has undertaken and the total amount that it owes to households, firms and foreigners.

Government purchases Goods and services bought by the government.

Government purchases multiplier The amount by which a change in government purchases of goods and services is multiplied to determine the change in equilibrium expenditure that it generates.

Great Depression A decade (1929–39) of high unemployment and stagnant production throughout the world economy.

Green tax A form of pollution control where a tax equal to the marginal external cost of pollution is charged on output.

Gresham's Law The tendency for bad (debased) money to drive good (not debased) money out of circulation.

Gross domestic product (GDP) The value of all final goods and services produced in the economy in a year.

Gross investment The amount spent on replacing depreciated capital and on net additions to the capital stock.

Growth accounting A method of calculating how much real GDP growth has resulted from growth of labour and capital and how much is attributable to technological change.

Hotelling Principle The proposition that the market for the stock of a natural resource is in equilibrium when the price of the resource is expected to rise at a rate equal to the interest rate on similarly risky assets.

Human capital The skill and knowledge of people, arising from their education and on-the-job training.

Hysteresis The idea that the natural rate of unemployment depends on the path of the actual unemployment rate; where the unemployment rate ends up depends on where it has been.

Implicit rental rate The rent that a firm pays to itself for the use of the assets that it owns.

Import function The relationship between imports and real GDP.

Imports The goods and services that we buy from people in other countries.

Incentive An inducement to take a particular action.

Incentive regulation scheme A regulation that gives a firm an incentive to operate efficiently and keep costs under control.

Income effect The change in consumption that results from a change in the consumer's income, other things remaining the same.

Income elasticity of demand The responsiveness of demand to a change in income, other things remaining the same. It is calculated as the percentage change in the quantity demanded divided by the percentage change in income.

Increasing marginal returns The tendency for the marginal product of a variable factor initially to increase as additional units of the variable factor are employed.

Increasing returns to scale Technological conditions under which a given percentage increase in all the firm's inputs results in the firm's output increasing by a larger percentage.

Indifference curve A line that shows combinations of goods among which a consumer is indifferent.

Individual demand The relationship between the quantity of a good or service demanded by a single individual and the price of a good or service.

Induced expenditure The part of aggregate planned expenditure on UK-produced goods and services that varies as real GDP varies.

Induced taxes Taxes that vary as real GDP varies.

Industrial union A group of workers who have a variety of skills and job types but who work for the same firm or industry.

Inelastic Where a small percentage change in price results in a proportionately smaller change in the quantity demanded.

Infant-industry argument The proposition that protection is necessary to enable an infant industry to grow into a mature industry that can compete in world markets.

Inferior good A good for which demand decreases as income increases.

Inflation An upward movement in the average level of prices; a process in which the price level is rising and money is losing value.

Inflationary gap Actual real GDP minus potential GDP when actual real GDP exceeds potential GDP.

Information cost The cost of acquiring information on prices, quantities and qualities of goods and services and factors of production – the opportunity cost of economic information.

Insider–outsider theory A theory of job rationing that says that to be productive, new workers – outsiders – must receive on-the-job training from existing workers – insiders.

Intellectual property rights Property rights for discoveries owned by the creators of knowledge.

Interest rate The amount received by a lender and paid by a borrower expressed as a percentage of the amount of the loan.

Intermediate goods and services Goods and services that are used as inputs into the production process of another good or service.

International Monetary Fund (IMF) An international organization that monitors balance of payments and exchange rate activities.

International substitution effect The substitution of domestic goods and services for foreign goods and services or of foreign goods and services for domestic goods and services.

Intertemporal substitution effect The substitution of goods and services now for goods and services later or of goods and services later for goods and services now.

Inverse relationship A relationship between variables that move in opposite directions.

Investment The purchase of new plant, equipment and buildings and additions to stock.

Investment demand The relationship between the level of planned investment and the real interest rate, all other influences on investment remaining the same.

Isocost line A line showing all possible combinations of two inputs that can be bought for a given total cost.

Isocost map A map of all possible isocost lines, holding the price of inputs constant.

Isoquant A curve showing the possible combinations of two inputs required to produce a given quantity of output.

Isoquant map A map of all possible isoquants.

Job leavers People who voluntarily quit their jobs.

Job losers People who are laid off, either permanently or temporarily, from their jobs.

Job rationing The practice of paying employed people a wage that creates an excess supply of labour and a shortage of jobs, and increases the natural rate of unemployment.

Job search The activity of people looking for acceptable vacant jobs.

Keynesian theory of the business cycle A theory that regards volatile expectations as the main source of economic fluctuations.

Labour The time and effort that people allocate to producing goods and services.

Labour demand curve A curve that shows the quantity of labour that firms plan to hire at each possible real wage rate.

Labour supply curve A curve that shows the quantity of labour that households plan to supply at each possible real wage rate.

Land All the natural resources used to produce goods and services.

Law of diminishing returns A law stating that as the quantity of one input increases with the quantities of all other inputs remaining the same, output increases but by ever smaller increments.

Learning-by-doing People become more productive in an activity (learn) just by repeatedly producing a particular good or service (doing).

Least-cost technique The combination of inputs to produce a given output that minimizes total cost.

Legal monopoly A market structure in which there is one firm and entry is restricted by the granting of a public franchise, licence, patent or copyright, or the firm has acquired ownership of a significant portion of a key resource.

Limit pricing The practice of charging a price below the monopoly profit-maximizing price and producing a quantity greater than that at which marginal revenue equals marginal cost so as to deter entry.

Limited information and uncertainty A form of market failure caused when the assumption of full information and full knowledge of all future outcomes fails to hold.

Limited resources The land, labour, capital and entrepreneurship used to produce goods and services.

Linear relationship A relationship between two variables that is illustrated by a straight line.

Liquidity The property of being instantly convertible into a means of payment with little loss in value.

Loan market A market in which households and firms make and receive loans.

Long run A period of time in which a firm can vary the quantities of all its inputs.

Long-run aggregate supply curve The relationship between the aggregate quantity of final goods and services (GDP) supplied and the price level (GDP deflator), other things remaining the same and there is full employment.

Long-run cost The cost of production when a firm uses the economically efficient plant size.

Long-run Phillips curve A curve that shows the relationship between inflation and unemployment when the actual inflation rate equals the expected inflation rate.

Long-term unemployed People who have remained unemployed for over 12 months.

Lorenz curve A curve that plots the cumulative percentage of income against the cumulative percentage of population.

Lump-sum tax multiplier The amount by which a change in lump-sum taxes is multiplied to determine the change in equilibrium expenditure that it generates.

Lump-sum taxes Taxes that are fixed by the government and do not vary with real GDP.

M0 Consists of currency held by the public, the banks, the building societies and banks' deposits at the Bank of England. See also Monetary base.

M4 Currency held by the public and all bank and building society sight and time deposits.

Macroeconomic long run A period that is sufficiently long for the prices of all the factors of production to have adjusted to any disturbance.

Macroeconomic short run A period during which the prices of goods and services change in response to changes in demand and supply but the prices of factors of production do not change.

Macroeconomics The study of the national economy and the global economy, the way that economic aggregates grow and fluctuate, and the effects of government actions on them.

Managed exchange rate A system in which the value of a country's currency is not fixed at some pre-announced level but is influenced by central bank intervention in the foreign exchange market.

Marginal benefit The extra benefit received from a small increase in the consumption of a good or service. It is calculated as the increase in total benefit divided by the increase in consumption.

Marginal cost The change in total cost that results from a unit increase in output. It is calculated as the increase in total cost divided by the increase in output.

Marginal cost pricing rule A rule that sets the price of a good or service equal to the marginal cost of producing it.

Marginal product The extra output produced as a result of a small increase in the variable factor. It is calculated as the increase in total product divided by the increase in the variable factor employed, when the quantities of all other factors are constant.

Marginal propensity to consume The fraction of the last pound of disposable income that is spent on consumption goods and services.

Marginal propensity to import The fraction of the last pound of real GDP spent on imports.

Marginal propensity to save The fraction of the last pound of disposable income that is saved.

Marginal rate of substitution The slope of an isoquant showing how much one input must increase for a given decrease in another input to keep output constant. (The rate at which a person will give up one good or service in order to get more of another good or service and at the same time remain indifferent.)

Marginal revenue The extra total revenue received from selling one additional unit of the good or service. It is calculated as the change in total revenue divided by the change in quantity sold.

Marginal revenue product The extra total revenue received from employing one more unit of a factor of production while the quantity of all other factors remains the same. It is calculated as the increase in total revenue divided by the increase in the quantity of the factor.

Marginal social benefit The marginal benefit received by the producer of a good (marginal private benefit) plus the marginal benefit received by other members of society (external benefit).

Marginal social cost The marginal cost incurred by the producer of a good (marginal private cost) plus the marginal cost imposed on other members of society (external cost).

Marginal utility The change in total utility resulting from a one-unit increase in the quantity of a good consumed.

Marginal utility per pound spent The marginal utility obtained from the last unit of a good consumed divided by the price of the good.

Market Any arrangement that enables buyers and sellers to get information and to do business with each other.

Market activity People undertake market activity when they buy goods and services in goods (or services) markets or sell the services of the factors of production that they own in factor markets.

Market demand The total demand for a good or service by everyone in the population. It is illustrated by the market demand curve.

Market failure The failure of an unregulated market to achieve an efficient allocation of resources.

Market socialism An economic system that combines state ownership of capital and land with incentives based on a mixture of market prices and laws and regulations.

Maximize total utility A major assumption of marginal utility theory which implies that individuals choose as if they made the marginal utility per pound spent on each good equal.

Means of payment A method of settling a debt.

Median voter theorem The proposition that political parties will pursue policies that appeal most to the median voter.

Merger The combining of the assets of two firms to form a single, new firm.

Microeconomics The study of the decisions of people and businesses, the interactions of those decisions in markets, and the effects of government regulation and taxes on the prices and quantities of goods and services.

Minimum wage The wage below which it is illegal to employ someone under minimum wage law.

Minimum wage law A regulation that prohibits labour services being paid at less than a specified wage rate.

Monetarist theory of the business cycle A theory that regards fluctuations in the money stock as the main source of economic fluctuations.

Monetary base The sum of the notes and coins in circulation and banks' deposits at the Central Bank. See also M0.

Monetary policy The government's attempt to achieve macroeconomic objectives by adjusting the quantity of money in circulation and interest rates.

Money Any commodity or token that is generally acceptable as a means of payment for goods and services.

Money multiplier The amount by which a change in the monetary base is multiplied to determine the resulting change in the quantity of money.

Monopolistic competition A market structure in which a large number of firms compete with each other by making similar but slightly different products.

Monopoly An industry that produces a good or service for which no close substitute exists and in which there is one supplier that is protected from competition by a barrier preventing the entry of new firms.

Monopoly control law A law that defines and regulates practices which lead to the monopoly structure and monopoly power in industry.

Monopoly power The ability to exercise the power of a monopoly to raise price by restricting output.

Monopsony A market structure in which there is just a single buyer.

Moral hazard A situation in which one of the parties to an agreement has an incentive, after the agreement is made, to act in a manner that brings additional benefits to himself or herself at the expense of the other party.

Multiplier The change in equilibrium real GDP divided by the change in autonomous expenditure.

Nash equilibrium The outcome of a game that occurs when player A takes the best possible action given the action of player B, and player B takes the best possible action given the action of player A.

National saving Private saving plus government saving; also equals GDP minus consumption expenditure minus government purchases.

Natural monopoly A monopoly that occurs when one firm can supply the entire market at a lower price than two or more firms can.

Natural rate of unemployment The unemployment rate when the economy is at full employment.

Natural resources The non-produced factors of production, which can be exhaustible or non-exhaustible.

Negative income tax A redistribution scheme that gives every family a *guaranteed annual income* and decreases the family's benefit at a specified *benefit-loss rate* as its market income increases.

Negative relationship A relationship between variables that move in opposite directions.

Neo-classical growth theory A theory of economic growth that explains how saving, investment and economic growth respond to population growth and technological change.

Net borrower A country that is borrowing more from the rest of the world than it is lending to it.

Net exporter A country whose value of exports exceeds its value of imports – its balance of trade is positive.

Net exports The expenditure by foreigners on UK-produced goods minus the expenditure by UK residents on foreign-produced goods – exports minus imports.

Net importer A country whose value of imports exceeds its value of exports – its balance of trade is negative.

Net investment Net additions to the capital stock – gross investment minus depreciation.

Net lender A country that is lending more to the rest of the world than it is borrowing from it.

Net present value The present value of the future flow of marginal revenue product generated by capital minus the cost of the capital.

Net taxes Taxes paid to governments minus transfer payments received from governments.

New classical theory of the business cycle A rational expectations theory of the business cycle that regards unanticipated fluctuations in aggregate demand as the main source of economic fluctuations.

New growth theory A theory of economic growth based on the idea that technological change results from the choices that people make in the pursuit of ever greater profit.

New Keynesian theory of the business cycle A rational expectations theory of the business cycle that regards unanticipated fluctuations in aggregate demand as the main source of economic fluctuations.

Nominal GDP targeting An attempt to keep the growth rate of nominal GDP steady.

Nominal interest rate The interest rate actually paid and received in the marketplace.

Non-excludable A property of market failure in the form of public goods where non-payers cannot be excluded from receiving the benefits of the public good or service.

Non-exhaustible natural resources Natural resources that can be used repeatedly without depleting what is available for future use.

Non-market activity Leisure and non-market production activities, including education and training, shopping, cooking and other activities in the home.

Non-rival A property of market failure in the form of public goods where one person's consumption of the good or service does not affect the consumption possibilities of anyone else.

Non-tariff barrier An action other than a tariff that restricts international trade.

Normal good A good for which demand increases as income increases.

Normal profit The expected return for supplying entrepreneurial ability.

Oligopoly A market structure in which a small number of producers compete with each other.

Open market operation The purchase or sale of government securities by the Bank of England designed to influence the money supply.

Opportunity cost The opportunity cost of an action is the best forgone alternative.

Pareto efficiency Another term for allocative efficiency where the market could not reallocate resources through trade, production or consumption to make at least one person better off without making anybody else worse off.

Patent A government-sanctioned exclusive right granted to the inventor of a good, service, or productive process to produce, use and sell the invention for a given number of years.

Payment system The generally accepted method of payment for trade in an economy.

Payoff matrix A table that shows the payoffs for every possible action by each player for every possible action by each other player.

Perfect competition A market structure in which there are many firms; each firm sells an identical product; there are many buyers; there are no restrictions on entry into the industry; firms in the industry have no advantage over potential new entrants; and firms and buyers are completely informed about the price of each firm's product.

Perfectly elastic demand Demand with an infinite price elasticity; the quantity demanded is infinitely responsive to a change in price.

Perfectly inelastic demand Demand with a price elasticity of zero; the quantity demanded remains constant when the price changes.

Phillips curve A curve that shows a relationship between inflation and unemployment.

Political equilibrium A situation in which the choices of voters, politicians and bureaucrats are all compatible and in which no one group can improve its position by making a different choice.

Poor definition of property rights A form of market failure where the legal rights to property are not clearly defined.

Positive relationship A relationship between two variables that move in the same direction.

Potential GDP A situation in which all the economy's labour, capital, land and entrepreneurial ability are fully employed.

Poverty A state in which a family's income is too low to be able to buy the quantities of food, shelter and clothing that are deemed necessary.

Preferences A person's likes and dislikes for goods and services which are described by the economist's measure of utility.

Present value The amount of money that, if invested today, will grow to be as large as a given future amount when the interest that it will earn is taken into account.

Price ceiling A regulation that makes it illegal to charge a price higher than a specified level.

Price discrimination The practice of charging some customers a lower price than others for an identical good or of charging an individual customer a lower price per unit on a large purchase than on a small one, even though the cost of servicing all customers is the same.

Price effect The change in consumption that results from a change in the price of a good or service, other things remaining the same.

Price elasticity of demand The responsiveness of the quantity demanded of a good to a change in the price of a good or service, other things remaining the same.

Price level The average level of prices as measured by a price index.

Price taker A firm that cannot influence the price of the good or service it produces.

Principal–agent problem A form of market failure arising in a contractual relationship when one party, the principal, cannot fully monitor the activities of the other party, the agent.

Private information Information that is available to one person but is too costly for anyone else to obtain.

Private sector surplus or deficit The difference between saving and investment.

Privatization The process of selling a public company or public sector assets to private shareholders.

Producer efficiency A situation in which it is not possible to produce more of one good without producing less of some other good.

Producer surplus The price a producer gets for a good or service minus the opportunity cost of producing it.

Product differentiation Making a good or service slightly different from that of a competing firm.

Production efficiency The level of production when no more of one good can be produced without producing less of some other good.

Production function The relationship that shows how the maximum output attainable varies as quantities of all inputs vary.

Production possibility frontier The boundary between those combinations of goods and services that can be produced and those that cannot.

Productivity The amount of output produced per unit of inputs used to produce it.

Productivity function A relationship that shows how real GDP per hour of labour changes as the amount of capital per hour of labour changes with no change in technology.

Productivity growth slowdown A slowdown in the growth rate of output per person.

Progressive income tax A tax on income at a marginal rate that increases with the level of income.

Property rights Social arrangements that govern the ownership, use and disposal of factors of production and goods and services.

Proportional income tax A tax on income that remains at a constant rate, regardless of the level of income.

Protectionism The restriction of international trade.

Public choice theory A theory predicting the behaviour of the government sector of the economy as the outcome of the individual choices made by voters, politicians and bureaucrats interacting in a political marketplace.

Public good A good or service that can be consumed simultaneously by everyone and from which no one can be excluded.

Public interest theory A theory of regulation that states that regulations are supplied to satisfy the demand of consumers and producers to maximize total surplus – that is, to attain allocative efficiency.

Public ownership Ownership of corporations by government rather than private shareholders.

Public Sector Borrowing Requirement (PSBR) The budget deficit of the government and public corporations.

Public Sector Debt Repayment (PDSR) The budget surplus of the government and public corporations.

Quantity demanded The amount of a good or service that consumers plan to buy during a given time period at a particular price.

Quantity of sterling assets The net stock of financial assets denominated in pounds sterling held outside the Bank of England and the government.

Quantity supplied The amount of a good or service that producers plan to sell during a given time period at a particular price.

Quantity theory of money The proposition that in the long run, an increase in the quantity of money brings an equal percentage increase in the price level.

Quota A restriction on the quantity of a good that a firm is permitted to produce or that a country is permitted to import.

Rate of return regulation A regulation that determines a regulated price by setting the price at a level that enables the regulated firm to earn a specified target percentage return on its capital.

Rate of time preference The target real interest rate that savers want to achieve.

Rational expectation A forecast based on all available relevant information.

Rational ignorance The decision not to acquire information because the cost of doing so exceeds the expected benefit.

Real business cycle theory A theory that regards random fluctuations in productivity that result from technological change as the main source of economic fluctuations.

Real exchange rate An index number that gives the opportunity cost of foreign-produced goods and services in terms of UK-produced goods and services.

Real GDP per person Real GDP divided by the population.

Real gross domestic product (real GDP) The output of final goods and services valued at prices prevailing in the base period.

Real income The quantity of a good that a consumer's income will buy. It is the consumer's income expressed in units of a good and is calculated as income divided by the price of the good.

Real interest rate The interest rate paid by a borrower and received by a lender after taking into account the change in the value of money resulting from inflation; the nominal interest rate minus the inflation rate.

Real money A measure of money based on the quantity of goods and services it will buy.

Real money balances effect

Real price A relative price where the money price of a good is divided by the price of a representative basket of goods.

Real wage rate The wage rate per hour expressed in constant pounds.

Recession A downturn in the level of economic activity in which real GDP falls in two successive quarters.

Recessionary gap Potential GDP minus actual real GDP when actual real GDP is less than potential GDP.

Re-entrants People who re-enter the workforce.

Regressive income tax A tax on income at a marginal rate that decreases with the level of income.

Regulation Rules enforced by a government agency to restrict or control economic activity in price setting, product standards, trading standards and the conditions under which firms can enter an industry.

Relative price The ratio of the price of one good or service to the price of another good or service. A relative price is an opportunity cost.

Rent ceiling A regulation that makes it illegal to charge a rent higher than a specified level.

Rent seeking The activity of searching out or creating a monopoly from which an economic profit can be made.

Required reserve ratio The ratio of reserves to deposits that banks are required, by regulation, to hold.

Reservation price The highest price that a buyer is willing to pay for a good.

Reservation wage The lowest wage rate for which a person will supply labour to the market. Below that wage, the person will not supply labour.

Reserve ratio The fraction of a bank's total deposits that are held in reserves.

Reserves Cash in a bank's vault plus the bank's deposits at the Bank of England.

Restrictive practice An agreement between two firms not to compete in some respect such as price, output levels or quality.

Retail Prices Index (RPI) An index of the prices of a basket of goods purchased by a typical UK family.

Returns to scale The increase in output that results when a firm increases all its inputs by the same percentage.

Risk A situation in which more than one outcome might occur and the probability of each possible outcome can be estimated.

Saving Income minus consumption. Saving is measured in the national income accounts as disposable income (income less taxes) minus consumption expenditure.

Saving function The relationship between saving and disposable income, other things remaining the same.

Saving supply The relationship between saving and the real interest rate, other things remaining the same.

Savings bank A financial intermediary owned by its depositors that accepts deposits and makes loans, mostly for consumer mortgages.

Scarcity The universal state in which wants exceed resources.

Scatter diagram A diagram that plots the value of one economic variable against the value of another.

Search activity The time spent in looking for someone with whom to do business.

Shares Long-term assets issued by firms which can be traded in stock markets.

Short run The short run in microeconomics has two meanings. For the firm, it is the period of time in which the quantity of at least one of its inputs is fixed and the quantities of the other inputs can be varied. The fixed input is usually capital – that is, the firm has a given plant size. For the industry, the short run is the period of time in which each firm has a given plant size and the number of firms in the industry is fixed.

Short-run aggregate supply curve A curve showing the relationship between the quantity of real GDP supplied and the price level, other things remaining the same.

Short-run industry supply curve A curve that shows how the quantity supplied by the industry varies as the market price varies when the plant size of each firm and the number of firms in the industry remain the same.

Short-run macroeconomic equilibrium A situation that occurs when the quantity of real GDP demanded equals the short-run quantity of real GDP supplied at the point of intersection of the *AD* curve and the *SAS* curve.

Short-run Phillips curve A curve showing the relationship between inflation and unemployment, when the expected inflation rate and the natural rate of unemployment remain the same.

Shutdown point The price and output level at which the firm just covers its total variable cost. In the short run, the firm is indifferent between producing the profit-maximizing output and shutting down temporarily. If it produces, it makes a loss equal to its total fixed cost.

Signal An action taken outside a market that conveys information that can be used by that market.

Slope The change in the value of the variable measured on the y-axis divided by the change in the value of the variable measured on the x-axis.

Socialism An economic system with state ownership of capital and land and incentives based on laws and regulations.

Stagflation The combination of a rise in the price level and a fall in real GDP.

Stock A quantity measured at a point in time.

Stock market A market in which the shares of corporations are traded.

Strategies All the possible actions of each player in a game.

Structural deficit A budget that is in deficit even though real GDP equals potential GDP; expenditures are high relative to tax revenues over the entire business cycle.

Structural unemployment The unemployment that arises when there is a decline in the number of jobs available in a particular region or industry.

Subsidy A payment made by the government to producers that depends on the level of output.

Subsistence real wage rate The minimum real wage rate needed to maintain life.

Substitute A good that can be used in place of another good.

Substitution effect The effect of a change in price of one good or service on a consumer's consumption of goods and services when the consumer remains indifferent between the original and the new consumption bundles – that is, the consumer remains on the same indifference curve.

Sunk cost The past economic depreciation of a firm's capital (buildings, plant and equipment).

Supply The relationship between the quantity of a good that producers plan to sell and the price of the good, with all other influences on sellers' plans remaining the same. It is described by a supply schedule and illustrated by a supply curve.

Supply curve A curve that shows the relationship between the quantity supplied and the price of a good, all other influences on producers' planned sales remaining the same.

Takeover The purchase of the stock of one firm by another firm.

Tariff A tax on an import by the government of the importing country.

Technological efficiency A situation that occurs when it is not possible to increase output without increasing inputs.

Technological progress The development of new and better ways of producing goods and services and the development of new goods.

Time series graph A line graph of one or more economic variables plotted over time.

Total cost The sum of the costs of all the inputs a firm uses in production.

Total fixed cost The total cost of the fixed inputs.

Total product The total output produced by a firm in a given period of time.

Total revenue The value of a firm's sales. It is calculated as the price of the good multiplied by the quantity sold.

Total surplus The sum of consumer surplus and producer surplus.

Total utility The total benefit or satisfaction that a person gets from the consumption of goods and services.

Total variable cost The total cost of the variable inputs.

Trade-off A constraint that entails giving up one thing to get something else.

Trade union A group of workers organized principally for the purpose of increasing wages and improving conditions.

Trade-weighted index The value of a basket of currencies in which the weight placed on each currency is related to its importance in UK international trade.

Transactions costs The costs incurred in searching for someone with whom to do business, in reaching an agreement about the price and other aspects of the exchange, and in ensuring that the terms of the agreement are fulfilled.

Transfer earnings The income that an owner of a factor of production requires to induce the owner to supply the factor.

Trend A general direction (rising or falling) in which a variable is moving over the long term.

UK interest rate differential The interest rate on a UK sterling asset minus the interest rate on a foreign currency asset.

Uncertainty A situation in which more than one event might occur but it is not known which will occur.

Unemployed A person who does not have a job but is available for work, willing to work and has made some effort to find work within the previous four weeks.

Unemployment rate The number of people unemployed expressed as a percentage of the workforce.

Unit elastic demand Demand with a price elasticity of 1; the percentage change in the quantity demanded equals the percentage change in price.

Utility The benefit or satisfaction that a person gets from the consumption of a good or service.

Utility of wealth The amount of utility that a person attaches to a given amount of wealth.

Utility maximization The attainment of the greatest possible utility.

Value The maximum amount that a person is willing to pay for a good.

Value added The value of a firm's output minus the value of the intermediate goods bought from other firms.

Variable cost A cost that varies with the output level. It is the cost of a variable input.

Velocity of circulation The average number of times a pound is used annually to buy the goods and services that make up GDP.

Voluntary export restraint (VER) A self-imposed restriction by an exporting country on the volume of its exports of a particular good.

Wealth The value of all the things that people own.

Welfare state capitalism An economic system that combines the private ownership of capital and land with state interventions in markets that modify the price signals to which people respond.

Workforce curve This shows the potential quantity of labour available for employment at a particular real wage rate.

Workforce The sum of employed and unemployed people.

Working-age population The total number of people aged 16 and over who are not in jail, hospital, or some other form of institutional care.

INDEX

Note: Entries and page numbers in **bold** refer to key terms; those in *italics* refer to Figures